M000012438

LET'S GO:

SOUTHEAST ASIA

is the best book for anyone traveling on a budget. Here's why:

■ **No other guidebook has as many budget listings.**

In Southeast Asia we list over 7,500 budget travel bargains. We tell you the cheapest way to get around, and where to get an inexpensive and satisfying meal once you've arrived. We give hundreds of money-saving tips that anyone can use, plus invaluable advice on discounts and deals for students, children, families, and senior travelers.

■ **Let's Go researchers have to make it on their own.**

Our Harvard-Radcliffe researcher-writers travel on budgets as tight as your own—no expense accounts, no free hotel rooms.

■ **Let's Go is completely revised each year.**

We don't just update the prices, we go back to the place. If a charming guest house has become an overpriced tourist trap, we'll replace the listing with a new and better one.

■ **No other guidebook includes all this:**

Honest, engaging coverage of both the cities and the countryside; up-to-the-minute prices, directions, addresses, phone numbers, and opening hours; in-depth essays on local culture, history, and politics; comprehensive listings on transportation between and within regions and cities; straight advice on work and study, budget accommodations, sights, nightlife, and food; detailed city and regional maps; and much more.

■ **Let's Go is for anyone who wants to see Southeast Asia on a budget.**

LET'S GO PUBLICATIONS

Let's Go: Alaska & The Pacific Northwest
Let's Go: Britain & Ireland
Let's Go: California
Let's Go: Central America
Let's Go: Eastern Europe
Let's Go: Europe
Let's Go: France
Let's Go: Germany
Let's Go: Greece & Turkey
Let's Go: Ireland
Let's Go: Israel & Egypt
Let's Go: Italy
Let's Go: London
Let's Go: Mexico
Let's Go: New York City
Let's Go: Paris
Let's Go: Rome
Let's Go: Southeast Asia
Let's Go: Spain & Portugal
Let's Go: Switzerland & Austria
Let's Go: USA
Let's Go: Washington, D.C.

Map Guides (coming March 1996)

Let's Go: Boston
Let's Go: London
Let's Go: New York City
Let's Go: Paris
Let's Go: San Francisco
Let's Go: Washington, D.C.

LET'S GO

The Budget Guide to

SOUTHEAST ASIA 1996

Jesse Grayman
Editor

Andrew Williams
Associate Editor

Pai C. Yang
Associate Editor

Amy E. Yeager
Assistant Editor

St. Martin's Press New York

HELPING LET'S GO

If you want to share your discoveries, suggestions, or corrections, please drop us a line. We read every piece of correspondence, whether a postcard, a 10-page e-mail, or a coconut. All suggestions are passed along to our researcher-writers. Please note that mail received after May 1996 may be too late for the 1997 book, but will be retained for the following edition. Address mail to:

Let's Go: Southeast Asia
One Story Street
Cambridge, MA 02138
USA

Visit Let's Go at **http://www.letsgo.com/,** or send e-mail to:

fanmail@letsgo.com
Subject: "Let's Go: Southeast Asia"

In addition to the invaluable travel advice our readers share with us, many are kind enough to offer their services as researchers or editors. Unfortunately, the charter of Let's Go, Inc. enables us to employ only currently enrolled Harvard-Radcliffe students.

Maps by David Lindroth copyright © 1996, 1995, 1994 by St. Martin's Press, Inc.

Map revisions pp. 169, 184-185, 281, 299, 360, 377, 405, 437, 484, 494-495 by Let's Go, Inc.

Distributed outside the USA and Canada by Macmillan.

Let's Go: Southeast Asia. Copyright © 1996 by Let's Go, Inc. All rights reserved. Printed in the United States of America. No part of this book may be used or reproduced in any manner whatsoever without written permission except in the case of brief quotations embodied in critical articles or reviews. For information, address St. Martin's Press, 175 Fifth Avenue, New York, NY 10010, USA.

ISBN: 0-312-13554-8

First edition
10 9 8 7 6 5 4 3 2 1

Let's Go: Southeast Asia is written by Let's Go Publications, One Story Street, Cambridge, MA 02138, USA.

Let's Go® and the thumb logo are trademarks of Let's Go, Inc.
Printed in the USA on recycled paper with biodegradable soy ink.

Contents

Maps

About Let's Go

THIRTY-SIX YEARS OF WISDOM

Back in 1960, a few students at Harvard University banded together to produce a 20-page pamphlet offering a collection of tips on budget travel in Europe. This modest, mimeographed packet was offered to passengers as an extra on their student charter flights to Europe. The following year, students traveling to Europe researched the first full-fledged edition of *Let's Go: Europe*, a pocket-sized book featuring irreverent write-ups of sights and a decidedly youthful slant. Throughout the 60s, our guides reflected the times; one section of the 1968 *Let's Go: Europe* discussed "Street Singing in Europe on No Dollars a Day," which we said "has very little to do with music." The 1969 guide to America led off with sound advice on San Francisco's Haight-Ashbury ("dig the scene"). During the 70s and 80s, we gradually added regional and city guides, and expanded coverage into the Middle East, Central America, and Asia.

We've seen a lot in 36 years. *Let's Go: Europe* is now the world's best-selling international guide, translated into seven languages. And our guides are still researched, written, and produced entirely by students who know first-hand how to see the world on the cheap. As the budget travel world expands, so does Let's Go. The first editions of *Let's Go: Central America* and *Let's Go: Southeast Asia* hit the shelves this year, and *Let's Go: India & Nepal* is right on their heels. Our useful new series of map guides combine concise city coverage with vivid fold-out maps. Our new guides bring our total number of titles, with their spirit of adventure and their honesty, accuracy, and editorial integrity, to 28.

HOW WE DO IT

Each guide is completely revised and updated every year by a well-traveled set of 200 students, who work on all aspects of each guide's development. Every winter, we recruit over 110 researchers and 50 editors to write our books anew. After several months of training, Researcher-Writers hit the road for seven weeks of exploration, from Anchorage to Ankara, Estonia to El Salvador, Iceland to Indonesia. Those hired possess a rare combination of budget travel sense, writing ability, stamina, and courage. Train strikes, stolen luggage, food poisoning, and irate tourist officials are all part of a day's work. Editors work from spring to fall, massaging copy written on Himalayan bus rides into witty yet informative prose. A student staff of typesetters, cartographers, publicists, and managers keeps our lively and sophisticated team together. In September, the collected efforts of the summer are delivered to our printer, who turns them into books in record time. And even as you read this, work on next year's editions is well underway.

WHY WE DO IT

At Let's Go, our goal is to give you a great vacation. We don't think of budget travel as the last recourse of the destitute; we believe that it's the only way to travel. Living cheaply and simply brings you closer to the real people and places you've been saving up to visit. Our book will ease your anxieties and answer your questions about the basics—to help you get off the beaten track and explore. Once you learn the ropes, we encourage you to put Let's Go away now and then to strike out on your own. As any seasoned traveler will tell you, the best discoveries are often those you make yourself. When you find something worth sharing, drop us a line. We're Let's Go Publications, One Story Street, Cambridge, MA 02138, USA (e-mail: LetsGo@delphi.com).

HAPPY TRAVELS!

Acknowledgments

Top thanks to Amy Yeager for joining us, wrapping up the Essentials, taming Indonesia, & for enthusiastically taking on what we couldn't stomach. Celeste for giving Vietnam a good morning. Haneen, for constructive understanding. Our interns, Dave Tannenbaum and Joy Somberg, for map relief. Derek M. for the *Ramayana* graybox. Sean D. & Timur for adopting us. Ingrid, typist *extraordinaire,* & Montira, *our* proofer. Alexis A., Pete K., & Eleni "Melaka" G. for last minute MEs. Amanda & Sam for fighting for our revisions. Eunice & Mike for our typesetting demands. Tim for being pro-SEA. Maia, Glenn, Nadim, Jay, Cindy, Kate, & Liz for helping us wrap it all up. And of course, the FrameMaker Thesaurus for filling our days with delectation, and Sean F. for giving us the technology.**—Team Southeast Asia**

Enormously dedicated beyond expectation, thanks Andy & Pai for bringing this project to completion. See you at the Alamo in Malang! Thanks to: Amy for playing all our "games"; Haneen for brunch & fest; Celeste for chats in P-town; Sean "J. Cuervo" D.; Debby, GWW, & Derek for Dudley support; Soekarno & his people. Love to: Wahju, Sara, Raph, Jen T., Amina & my family: Mom, Dad, Stan, Allyson, Chris, Kate, Matt, Ethan, Sammy, Grammy, Grandad, Grandma & Grandpa. Dedicated to Bapak & Ibu Sutono and family. Bapak, I wish you could see this.**—JG**

Thanks so much to Mom & Pop, my big brothers, K-Rabb, Martin, Taz, Brady, Jason, FUP!, UUSC, friends in Pforz & Adams, Full Circle, home-friends, English teachers, Stevie Wonder, Taj Mahal, Dr. John, A&P, Sam, Nadim, Tim, Nat, Derek, Celeste, & Tom. Especially, Jesse, Pai, Amy and our RWs, cause it worked. Glory to God.**—AW**

Mille grazie: Jesse, Andy, Amy...*Merdeka!* Celeste=the best! Cindy, Chia, Mikey, Tors, CC, Munnie...what'd I do without you? Lydia...to UGH reviews! Krzys, *dzięki kanapa.* Nora & MayCha for being there. Ron & Joyce for their support. My dear family, Mom & Dad, I love you. And JAS, who will always be remembered.**—PCY**

Editor	Jesse Grayman
Associate Editor	Andrew Williams
Associate Editor	Pai C. Yang
Assistant Editor	Amy E. Yeager
Managing Editor	Haneen M. Rabie
Publishing Director	Sean Fitzpatrick
Production Manager	Michael L. Cisneros
Associate Production Manager	Eunice C. Park
Cartography Manager	Samuel P. Trumbull
Associate Cartography Manager	Amanda K. Bean
Editorial Manager	Timothy S. Perlstein
Financial Manager	Katarzyna Drozd
Personnel Manager	Sean K. Desmond
Publicity Manager	Timur Okay Harry Hiçyılmaz
Associate Publicity Manager	Eleni N. Gage
General Manager	Richard Olken
Assistant General Manager	Anne E. Chisholm
Office Coordinator	Jennifer L. Schuberth
Director of Advertising and Sales	Jean C. Anderson
Sales Assistant Manager	Sammy Lai
Sales Representatives	Matthew S. Abramson
	Delphine Gabbay, Godffrey Williams

Researcher-Writers

Jonathan Barnes *West Coast Peninsular Malaysia, Singapore, Hong Kong*
Jon impressed us with his wide-eyed enthusiasm for all things Malaysian at every turn. After falling in love with Langkawi, Jon proceeded onward to give us a kinder, gentler KL and a big thumbs-up for Melaka. His charisma and good looks won the favor of tourist agencies, fellow travelers, locals, and editors alike!

Suzanne Brown *West Java, South Sumatra, West Sumatra*
Surfing and skinny-dipping her way through Java and Sumatra, Susie admirably held her own through the fair *and* the seedy parts of her itinerary. A flawless hunter of safe and clean budget traveler haunts, Susie went that extra kilometer to give us the West Sumatra coverage we needed. Nice job, Susie!

Robert Hopper *South Thailand, East Coast Peninsular Malaysia, Pulau Bintan*
Snaking his way south from the Kra Isthmus to the Riau Archipelago, this R-W veteran bypassed Phuket for the amorous Perhentian Islands, smiling serenely in the face of any *Let's Go* challenge. Astute and informed, Robert's excellent copy came back replete with surreal musings that kept us entertained all summer.

holly Kretschmar *Central Java, East Java, Bali*
Armed with Bahasa Indonesia and a keen anthropologist's eye, holly captured Java and Bali in well-researched prose that is sensitive to the locals *and* the needs of the *Let's Go* reader. Forever lost in markets and local hangouts, holly's copy reveals an Indonesia you won't see on Club-Med brochures. *Let's Go* joins holly in thanking Wahju Laksana and his family for facilitating her research in Central Java.

Diep Nguyen *South Vietnam*
Diep kept us paralyzed with anticipation all summer for her copybatches. From the steamy nightclubs of Ho Chi Minh City to the steamy nightclubs of Saigon, Diep shimmied her way into R-W history. Pooh Bear and pulchritudinous platypus thank her, and Celeste too.

Hoang B. Nguyen *North and South Vietnam*
What's that I see? It's Henry racing through his north Vietnam itinerary, sampling every local brew on the way! With time left to spare, Henry gave Diep a hand in the south and discovered his roots in Nha Trang, knocking us out cold with *Let's Go* prose sent by fax that would even make his unruly grandmother proud. *Sweeet!*

Sophia Scott *North, Central, and Northeast Thailand*
Surmounting frustration, Sophia just kept on going...even after a monkey stole her clothes and an ATM ate her credit card; even after her pack fell in a puddle of oil and her motorbike was stolen; even after getting lost on a jungle trek, Sophia found a moment each day to complete her itinerary thoroughly, send us news clippings, write grayboxes, do the daily *Bangkok Post* crossword, and still keep on going...

John Schoellerman *Central, East Coat, and South Thailand*
After suffering Bangkok, John was rewarded with beaches and islands galore! After scavenging bitchin' markets, wading through aquamarine bays with pack in tow, and admiring the Buddhist path, John helped us rethink our philosophy toward this book. Despite the distance, we heard him loud and clear.

Benjamin Wilkinson *Cambodia, Northeast Thailand, Laos, North Sumatra*
Upon arrival in Phnom Penh, Ben's itinerary was quickly revised due to an unforseen visit by the Khmer Rouge in Kampot. *Whoops!* Not to be thwarted, the *lingga* king of Team Southeast Asia gave us supernatural coverage of Cambodia and Laos, covering Isaan in between. *Let's Go* also thanks Ben for covering North Sumatra. Let there be no doubt about it, Ben is the Sir Stamford Raffles of the entire series.

How To Use This Book

Welcome to the inaugural text of *Let's Go: Southeast Asia.* This book gives you the tools to excavate the budget offerings of Cambodia, Hong Kong, Laos, Peninsular Malaysia, Singapore, Thailand, Vietnam, and Western Indonesia. This is a travel guide, not a color-by-numbers blueprint of the region, culture, or your vacation.

The book begins with a general **Essentials** section which discusses preparations you should make before a journey to Southeast Asia as well as general information that will be useful once you are there. Countries are arranged alphabetically and at the beginning of each country, there is an **Essentials** and a **Life and Times** section which provide a practical and cultural background to the nation. City write-ups begin with the capital city of the country, and continue in a logical path as much as local geography and political borders permit. Within city listings, **Orientation** and **Practical Information** sections lay out the town and compile crucial data. **Accommodations, Food,** and **Entertainment** sections are generally listed in preferential order: best values and funkiest options rank at the top. **Sights, Near** and **Around** sections of towns are arranged in an orderly geographical pattern.

Our R-Ws' favorite comment this summer was to exclaim that "Europe is for wimps!" Indeed, travel in Southeast Asia requires more stamina and patience, and it's not always safe. By all means let your adventurous spirit guide you, but pay attention to our **boldfaced warnings** and warnings in **white boxes** which alert you to the special precautions one should take while travelling through a specific region.

On a lighter note, *Let's Go* is pleased to introduce the addition of **gray boxes** to the series. Gray boxes tell you about things that don't ordinarily fit into standard *Let's Go* format, but which we think are points of interest worthy of inclusion. Subjects run the gamut from local legends to explanations of hot political issues. Be sure to check out our box of this year's recommended sights and activities on page 59.

Another new feature, still in its infancy and unique to this *Let's Go* guide, is the issue of **responsible tourism** (see page 52). During our two years of producing a *Let's Go: Thailand* guide, we have received a pile of opinionated reader mail whose size alone testifies to the importance of this issue in Southeast Asia.

As editors of a guide to Southeast Asia, we've made a conscious effort to not only bring you to the greatest sights of the region, but also to include the perspectives of the people we write about and to present a picture of everyday life in Southeast Asia. Our goal has been to tap into a point of view that may run counter to commonly held perceptions of the "exotic Far East." With that said, we hope you find this book to be useful, informative, and hilarious; have a blast (but not literally), and send us lots of reader mail!

A NOTE TO OUR READERS

The information for this book is gathered by Let's Go researchers during the summer months. Each listing is derived from the assigned researcher's opinion based upon his or her visit at a particular time. The opinions are expressed in a candid and forthright manner. Other travelers might disagree. Those traveling at a different time may have different experiences since prices, dates, hours, and conditions are always subject to change. You are urged to check beforehand to avoid inconvenience and surprises. Travel always involves a certain degree of risk, especially in low-cost areas. When traveling, especially on a budget, you should always take particular care to ensure your safety.

SOUTHEAST ASIA

Stretching from the hypothermic highlands of Laos and Vietnam to the equatorial islands of Indonesia, the vast and diverse region of Southeast Asia incorporates a patchwork of complex influences. It is the continuing project of thousands of years of sea trade, religious dissemination, colonial influence, expanding empires, political strategies, and ethnic identifications. For every country and people these factors have played differing roles in forming unique identities. The origins of the various ethnicities are the subjects of legend and speculation: the Tai-Kadai people who came from southern China and formed the Thai and Lao kingdoms, the Malays from Indonesia who intermarried with Indian traders and princes to become the Khmer people, and a few dashes of Chinese migration thrown in for good measure. Indian influence is perhaps the one factor that provides a semblance of unity to Southeast Asia, where Hinduism, Buddhism, the *Ramayana,* and Indic philosophies continue to comingle with local custom and subtly define the region. The great kingdoms of Siam and Angkor to the north, and of Srivijaya and Majapahit to the south, all borrowed from the Indian subcontinent to build their own empires. From these shared beginnings, however, the countries of Southeast Asia have taken on their own identities. Islam swept through the island trade routes of Southeast Asia from the 7th to 13th centuries, Vietnam came under increasing Chinese influence, while Thailand remained impervious to foreign penetration. Kingdoms have mixed, matched, and migrated; European powers have divided, conquered, and colonized; and in the wake of colonialism, nation-states have formed, collapsed, and rebuilt themselves. As one visits the region, it becomes clear that although nationalism is alive and well in Southeast Asia, the modern boundaries are but the current face of a captivating jigsaw puzzle that has been worked for millennia.

Essentials

PLANNING YOUR TRIP

WHEN TO GO

The weather in Southeast Asia is hot and humid, with temperatures fluctuating around 27°C (80°F) all year, anywhere south of highland Vietnam. Most countries have a "rainy" season, which ranges from May to September in the north countries, and runs later in the year the farther you travel south; by the time you get to Bali the rainy season lasts from November to May. The closer to the equator the more consistently hot the weather will be, and the less difference seasonal changes will make. Malaysia takes great pride in having no seasons and claims to live in summer all year long. Many countries have a high season and a low season for tourism. These may depend upon the rainy season, a local monsoon season, or school vacations. What low season means for you is reduced services and reduced traffic at reduced prices; certain beaches and islands may close down all together. High seasons will bring floods of people to every popular beach or resort. The definitive answer on when to go? Whenever is best for you. Southeast Asia offers such diverse options that something will always be available for the budget traveler.

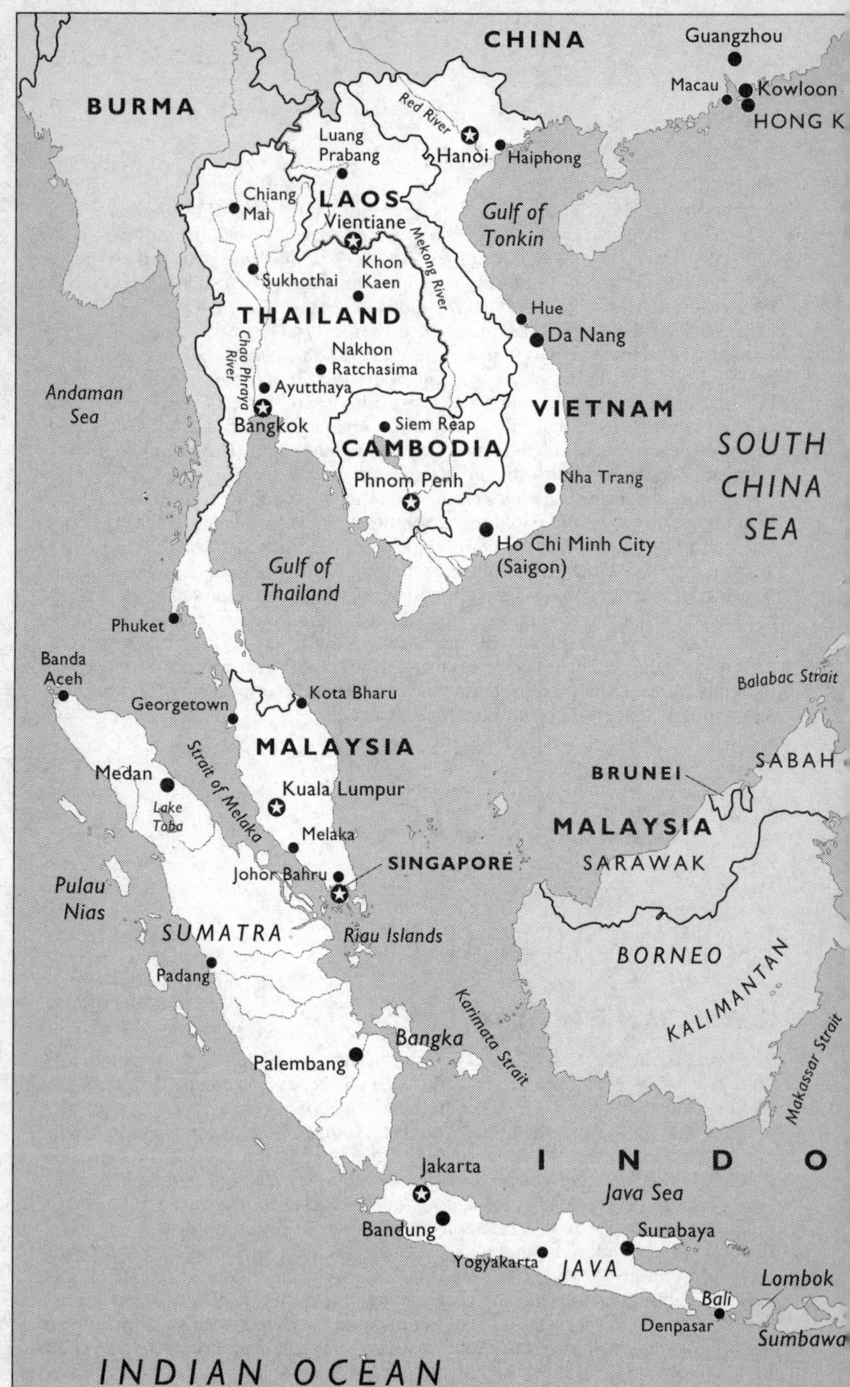
CHINA
Guangzhou
Macau
Kowloon
HONG K
BURMA
Red River
Hanoi
Haiphong
Luang
Prabang
LAOS
Chiang
Mai
Vientiane
Gulf of
Tonkin
Mekong River
Khon
Kaen
Sukhothai
THAILAND
Hue
Da Nang
Chao Phraya
River
Nakhon
Ratchasima
Ayutthaya
Andaman
Sea
Bangkok
VIETNAM
Siem Reap
CAMBODIA
SOUTH
CHINA
SEA
Phnom Penh
Nha Trang
Ho Chi Minh City
(Saigon)
Gulf of
Thailand
Phuket
Banda
Aceh
Balabac Strait
Kota Bharu
Georgetown
MALAYSIA
SABAH
BRUNEI
Medan
Strait of Melaka
Kuala Lumpur
Lake
Toba
MALAYSIA
Melaka
SINGAPORE
SARAWAK
Johor Bahru
Pulau
Nias
SUMATRA
Riau Islands
BORNEO
Padang
KALIMANTAN
Karimata Strait
Bangka
Makassar Strait
Palembang
I N D O
Jakarta
Java Sea
Bandung
Surabaya
Yogyakarta
JAVA
Lombok
Bali
Denpasar
Sumbawa
INDIAN OCEAN

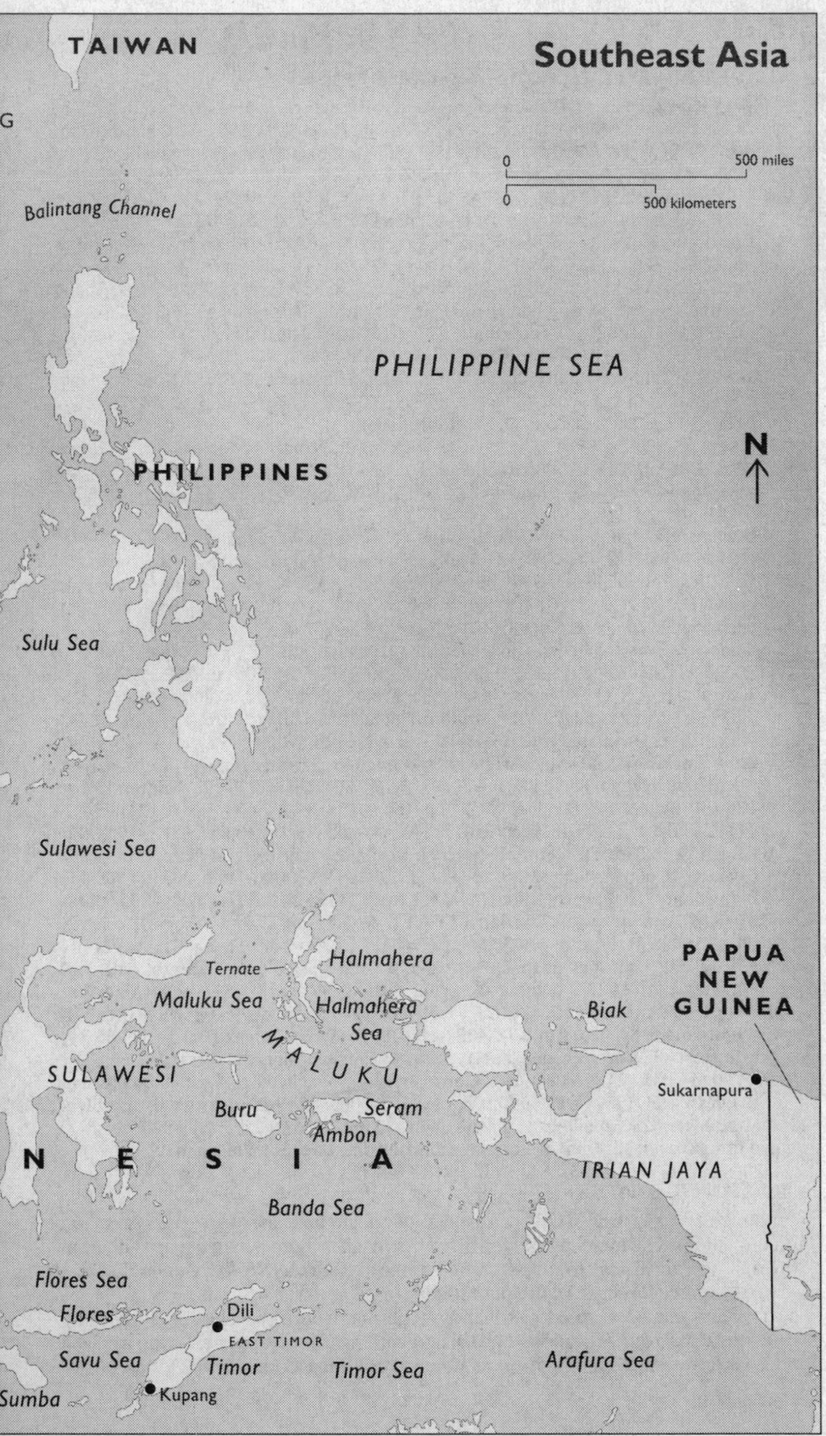
Southeast Asia
TAIWAN
G
0
500 miles
0
500 kilometers
Balintang Channel
PHILIPPINE SEA
N
PHILIPPINES
Sulu Sea
Sulawesi Sea
Ternate
Halmahera
Maluku Sea
Halmahera Sea
MALUKU
PAPUA NEW GUINEA
Biak
Sukarnapura
SULAWESI
Buru
Seram
Ambon
N E S I A
IRIAN JAYA
Banda Sea
Flores Sea
Flores
Dili
EAST TIMOR
Savu Sea
Timor
Timor Sea
Arafura Sea
Sumba
Kupang

■■■ EDUCATE YOUR MIND

GOVERNMENT INFORMATION OFFICES

Hong Kong Tourist Association: Australia: Level 5, 55 Harrington St., The Rocks, Sydney, NSW 2000 (tel. (02) 251 28 55; fax (02) 247 56 20). **Canada:** Suite 909, 347 Bay St., Toronto, Ont. M5H 2R7 (tel. (416) 366-2389; fax (416) 366-1098). **Europe, Africa, and the Middle East:** 4th/5th Fl., 125 Pall Mall, London SW1Y 5EA (tel. (0171) 930 47 75; fax (0171) 930 47 77). **New Zealand:** P.O. Box 2120, Auckland (tel. (09) 575 27 07; fax (09) 575 26 20). **South Africa:** c/o Development Promotions Ltd. 7th Fl., Everite House, 20 De Korte St., Braamfontein 2001 (tel. (011) 339 49 63; fax (011) 339 24 74). **US: East:** 5th Fl., 590 Fifth Ave., New York, NY 10036-4706 (tel. (212) 869-5008/9; fax (212) 730-2605). **Central:** Suite 200, 610 Enterprise Dr., Oak Brook, IL 60521 (tel. (708) 575-2828; fax (708) 575-2829). **West:** Suite 1220, 10940 Wilshire Blvd., Los Angeles, CA 90024-3915 (tel. (310) 208-4583; fax (310) 208-1869).

Indonesia Tourist Promotion Office: Australia and the South Pacific: Level 10, 5 Elizabeth St., Sydney, NSW 2000 (tel. (02) 233 36 30; fax (02) 233 36 29 or (02) 357 34 78). **Europe:** Wießenhuttenstraße 17 D.6000 Frankfurt/Main 1 Germany (tel. (069) 233 677/78; fax (069) 230 840). **North America:** 3457 Wilshire Blvd., Los Angeles, CA 90010-2203 (tel. (213) 387-2078; fax (213) 380-4876). **UK and Scandinavia:** 3-4 Hanover St., London W1R 9HH (tel. (0171) 493 00 30 or (0171) 493 03 34).

Tourism Malaysia: Australia: Ground Fl., 65 York St., Sydney, NSW 2000 (tel. (02) 299 44 41/2; fax (02) 321 14 21). **Canada:** 830 Burrard St., Vancouver, BC V6Z 2K4 (tel. (604) 689-8899; fax (604) 689-8804). **UK:** 57 Trafalgar Square, London WC2N 5DU (tel. (0171) 930 79 32; fax (0171) 930 90 15). **US:** 818 W. Seventh St., Los Angeles, CA 90017 (tel. (213) 689-9702; fax (213) 689-1530).

Singapore Tourist Promotion Board: Australia: 8th Fl., St. Georges Court, 16 St. Georges Terrace, Perth, WA 6000 (tel. (09) 325 85 78; fax (09) 221 38 64); Suite 1202, Level 12 Westpac Plaza, Margaret St., Sydney NSW 2000 (tel. (02) 241 77 71/2; fax (02) 252 35 86). **Canada:** The Standard Life Centre, 121 King St. W., Suite 1000, Toronto, Ont. M5H 3T9 (tel. (416) 363-8898; fax (416) 363-5752). **New Zealand:** c/o General Travel Marketing Ltd., Dataset House, 143 Nelson St., Auckland (tel. (09) 358 11 91; fax (09) 358 11 96). **UK:** 1st Fl., Carrington House, 126-130 Regent St., London W1R 5FE (tel. (0171) 437 00 33; fax (0171) 734 21 91). **US: East:** 590 Fifth Ave., 12th Fl., New York, NY 10036 (tel. (212) 302-4861; fax (212) 302-4801). **Central:** 180N Stetson Ave., 2 Prudential Plaza, Suite 1450, Chicago, IL 60601 (tel. (312) 938-1888; fax (312) 938-0086). **West:** 8484 Wilshire Blvd., Suite 510, Beverly Hills, CA 90211 (tel. (21) 852-1901; fax (213) 852-0129).

Tourism Authority of Thailand (TAT): Australia: 12th fl., Royal Exchange Bldg., 56 Pitt St., Sydney NWS 2000 (tel. (02) 247 75 49 or (02) 247 75 40; fax (02) 251 24 65). **Canada: East:** 250 St. Clair Ave. W., Suite 306, Toronto, Ont. M4V 1R6 (tel. (416) 925-9329; fax (416) 925-2868). **West:** 10551 Shellbridge Way, Suite 157, Richmond, BC V6X 2W9 (tel. (604) 231-9030; fax (604) 231-9031). **UK:** 49 Albemarle St., London WIX 3FE (tel. (0171) 499 76 79; fax (0171) 629 55 19). **US: East:** 5 World Trade Center, Suite 3443, New York, NY 10048 (tel. (212) 432-0433; fax (212) 912-0920). **Central**: 303 E. Wacker Dr., Suite 400, Chicago, IL 60601 (tel. (312) 819-3990; fax (312) 565-0359). **West:** 3440 Wilshire Blvd., Suite 1100, Los Angeles, CA 90010 (tel. (213) 382-2353; fax (213) 389-7544).

No official overseas tourist offices for **Cambodia, Laos,** or **Vietnam.**

TALKING BOOKS

Although *Let's Go* tries to cover all aspects of budget travel, we can't put *everything* in our guides. The travel publishers listed below offer more detailed maps and information on everything from restaurants to music festivals. Most of the books listed can be ordered direct from the publisher.

Travelers can pick up etiquette and plumb the national psyches of Hong Kong, Indonesia, Malaysia, Singapore, or Thailand with the *Culture Shock!* series, available at bookstores, or from Graphic Arts Center Publishing Company, P.O. Box 10306,

Portland, OR 97210, USA. A helpful, regionally specific publication, *Tips for Travelers,* is available for US$1, as well as *Your Trip Abroad* (US$1.25), *Health Information for International Travel* (US$7), and "Background Notes" on all countries ($1 each), from the Superintendent of Documents, U.S. Government Printing Office, P.O. Box 371954, Pittsburgh, PA 15250-7954 (tel. (202) 512-1800; fax (202) 512-2250; open Mon.-Fri. 8am-4pm).

Forsyth Travel Library, P.O. Box 2975, Shawnee Mission, KS 66201 (tel. (800) 367-7984; fax (913) 384-3553). Catalog of maps, guidebooks, railpasses, timetables, travel gear, and HI youth hostel memberships. Write for free catalog and newsletter. MC, Visa, Discover.

Hippocrene Books, Inc., 171 Madison Ave., New York, NY 10016 (tel. (212) 685-4371; orders (718) 454-2366; fax (718) 454-1391). Free catalog. Publishes travel reference books, travel guides, maps, foreign-language dictionaries, and language learning guides which cover over 100 languages.

Hunter Publishing, 300 Raritan Center Pkwy., Edison, NJ 08818 (tel. (908) 225-1900; fax (908) 417-0482). Has extensive travel books, guides, language learning tapes, and quality maps, including *Thailand, Malaysia and Singapore by Rail.*

Specialty Travel Index, 305 San Anselmo Ave., Suite 313, San Anselmo, CA 94960 (tel. (415) 459-4900; fax (415) 459-4974). Publishes a bi-yearly listing of "off the

The Ramayana

The most obvious Indian influence on Southeast Asia that travelers encounter are the representations of characters, stories, and morals from the *Ramayana,* a Hindu epic that has inspired thousands of dances, paintings, and shadow puppet performances across the region. It is believed that the *Ramayana* was written about 500 BC by the sage Valmiki, and is probably based on actual events which took place between 1000 and 700 BC. Here is a brief synopsis:

The *Ramayana* tells the story of Lord Rama, crown prince of the kingdom of Kosala, in northern India. Rama was loved by all the people for his skills and wisdom, and his blue skin seemed a mark of divine grace. He won the hand of Sita, the princess of a neighboring kingdom and the most beautiful woman in the world, by snapping in two an unbendable bow that the god Siva had presented to Sita's father. Rama was all set to inherit the throne from his father, Dasaratha, when one of Dasaratha's 300 wives tricked him into promising to make her son, Bharatha, king in Rama's place. Rama, Sita, and Rama's brother Lakshmana left for the forest, where they were to live in exile for 14 years.

While Rama and Lakshmana hunted wild beasts and protected forest ascetics, Ravana, the ten-headed king of the demons, began to eye Sita. One morning a servant of Ravana's appeared before Sita in the form of a golden stag. Sita urged Rama to go capture the beautiful creature, and, while Rama was gone, Ravana abducted Sita and swept her off to his island kingdom of Lanka. Rama was at a loss while Ravana kept Sita in his palace and lavished gifts on her, hoping to win her over as a wife. Rama and Lakshmana soon met the clever monkey-god, Hanuman, however, and they won the favor of Hanuman's brother, the monkey king. Huge armies of men and beasts went to battle Ravana for Sita's return; Hanuman, whose father was the wind god, led the charge across the strait to Lanka, throwing down rocks for the others to use as stepping stones. After a long and terrifying celestial battle Ravana was slain by one of Rama's arrows.

By this time, the 14 years of exile had elapsed and it was time for Rama to assume his throne, which Bharatha deferentially handed over to him. The whole capital erupted in celebration. His mission complete, Rama finally learned that he was in fact an *avatara,* or incarnation, of the god Vishnu. There was one matter left to settle, however: Sita had been living in Ravana's household for months, and her chastity was now being questioned. Rama made Sita submit to a fire-ordeal (one of his least popular decisions), yet she emerged untouched by the flames, a virtuous wife to reign with Rama for thousands of years to come.

beaten track" and specialty tour operators ($6 for one copy; $10 for a one-year subscription).

Travel Books & Language Center, 4931 Cordell Ave., Bethesda, MD 20814 (tel. (800) 220-2665; fax (301) 951-8546). Sells over 70,000 items, including books, cassettes, atlases, dictionaries, and a wide range of specialty travel maps.

Wide World Books and Maps, 1911 N. 45th St., Seattle, WA 98103 (tel. (206) 634-3453; fax (206) 634-0558; email travelbk@nwlink.com). Knowledgeable staff. A good selection of travel guides, travel accessories, and hard-to-find maps.

LET'S GET IT ON-LINE

There is a vast amount of information available through the international computer network known as the **Internet.** Some commercial providers, such as America Online, CompuServe, and Prodigy, offer sophisticated services like **on-line airline reservations.** Even the most basic mode of access, though, can provide an over-abundance of information. Most universities and many businesses offer students and employees access to the Internet. Commercial gateways provide Internet access to the general public for a monthly fee (usually US$20-30).

That's News to Me

One primary means of transmission and discussion of information across the Internet are forums known collectively as Usenet, and individually as **newsgroups.** There are thousands of newsgroups accessible by users all over the world; sometimes, they're your best source for up-to-the-minute information. New groups are always sprouting up; unfortunately, not all groups are available from all systems, although your system administrator can usually add new groups on request. A basic news-reading program can be accessed on most UNIX systems by typing "rn" for "read news." A caveat: **most newsgroups are unmoderated,** so the quality of conversation and the reliability of information posted within them is not always certain. Before posting messages yourself, you should familiarize yourself with the standards of "netiquette" that keep discussion polite and coordinated (in theory).

There are several "hierarchies" of newsgroups. One, the "soc" groups, primarily addresses social issues and socializing; subscribe to **soc.culture.thai, soc.culture.malaysia, soc.culture.vietnamese,** or the country of your choice. Another good choice is **soc.culture.asean,** which discusses the member nations of ASEAN. The "alt" groups are a less formalized collection of newsgroups; good examples are **alt.culture.indonesia** and **alt.current-events.singapore.** "Rec" groups, such as **rec.travel.air** are oriented toward the arts, hobbies, or recreation. Some systems also provide access to the "ClariNet" newsgroups, read-only (copyrighted) groups that compile the latest wire service news; **clari.news.asia** are representative examples of such groups.

Wait a Minute Mr. Postman

There are a variety of **mailing lists** that provide anywhere from 5 to 50 messages per day related to travel, either generally or to a specific area. A good list to start from is the "Travel-L" list. Subscribe by e-mailing "listserv@mv3090.ege.edu.tr". Leave the subject blank; in the body of the message, type "subscribe travel-l <firstname> <lastname>".

Let's Give Them Something to Talk About

Internet Relay Chat, or **"IRC,"** allows real-time (typed) conservation with users around the world. The number and nature of the "channels" available is more variable than for newsgroups, but you're quite likely to find discussions on travel and/or your destination, or you can start one of your own. Like newsgroups, IRC is virtually unsupervised. From most systems, type "irc" and then type "/help newuser".

Get Caught in the Web

Three of the other services available on the Internet are **FTP** (file transfer protocol), **gopher,** and **World Wide Web;** each can be used to obtain files and other information stored in areas of other computer systems accessible to the public. Thousands of such archives exist, including many with information on travel and Southeast Asia. A particularly useful archive is **rec-travel** at ftp.cc.umanitoba.ca; it includes travelogues, U.S. State Department Advisories, and a plethora of other useful info. Use your WWW browser to check out the handy CIA World Factbook; point to "http://www.odci.gov/94fact/fb94toc/fb94toc.html". Browsing on the web can also bring you invaluable information by searching for your country specifically. Many countries have their own home pages which allow you to access general information as well as read newspapers from each day that week, week by week summaries, or month by month summaries. Private companies or individuals often set up similar services to serve Southeast Asian communites in the U.S. or Europe. Some selections may be in the language of the country you are researching, but a little perseverance can yield highly useful results.

Many Internet resources are available through more than one method. The "Student and Budget Travel Resource Guide" lists a wide variety of online travel information. It is available through the WWW at "http://asa.ugl.lib.umich.edu/chdocs/travel/travel-guide.html"; or, send e-mail to "travel-guide@umich.edu".

Learning to Fly

Learning how to navigate the Internet to these sites is not extraordinarily complex, but somewhat beyond the scope of this book; ask a system manager or computer-using friend, or check out any one of the many comprehensive guides to the Internet now available in most bookstores.

■■■ THIS FORM, AND THIS ONE...

Apply for travel documents early—processing may take several weeks or even months. Don't let your trip fall victim to the inevitable delays and bureaucratic snarls of passport agencies. You may snag speedier service in the winter off-season (between August and December). U.S. travelers for 1996 are especially encouraged to apply as early as 1986 was a boom year for passports, and they only last 10 years.

Before you depart, **photocopy all important documents and credit cards;** leave these with someone you can contact easily. **Never carry your passport, travel ticket, identification documents, money, traveler's checks, insurance, and credit cards all together,** or you'll be left high and dry in case of theft or loss.

When you travel, **always carry on your person two or more forms of identification,** including at least one photo ID (for example: a passport and a driver's license, or a passport and birth certificate). Many establishments, especially banks, require several IDs before cashing traveler's checks. Carry extra passport-size photos that you can attach to the sundry IDs you will eventually acquire.

Students should bring proof of their status to get discounts on sights and transportation. For students of U.S. universities, a current college ID will do; others should see **Youth and Student Identification** below.

For information about documents and formalities and prudent travel abroad, get the booklet *Your Trip Abroad* (US$1.25) from the Superintendent of Documents, U.S. Government Printing Office, Washington, DC 20402 (tel. (202) 783-3238).

PASSPORTS

Travelers in Southeast Asia must have a valid passport. For more information, the U.S. Department of State publishes two helpful booklets: *Passports: Applying For Them the Easy Way* (item 356A, 50¢), and *Foreign Entry Requirements* (item 354A, 50¢). Send a check to R. Woods, Consumer Information Center, Pueblo, CO 81009. **Photocopy the page of your passport that contains your photograph and**

identifying information. Your passport number is especially important. Carry this photocopy in a safe place apart from your passport, perhaps with a traveling companion, and leave another copy at home. These measures will help prove your citizenship and facilitate the issuing of a new passport. Consulates also recommend that you carry an expired passport or an official copy of your birth certificate in a part of your baggage separate from other documents.

Losing your passport can be a nightmare. It may take weeks to process a replacement, and your new passport may be valid only for a limited time. Any visas stamped in your old passport will be irretrievably lost. If it is lost or stolen, immediately notify the local police and the nearest embassy or consulate of your home government. To expedite the replacement of your passport, you will need to know all the information that you had previously recorded and photocopied, and to show identification and proof of citizenship. Some consulates can issue new passports within two days if you give them proof of citizenship. In an emergency, ask for immediate temporary traveling papers that permit you to return to your country.

Your passport is a public document belonging to your nation's government. You may have to surrender it to a foreign government official; if you don't get it back in a reasonable time, inform the nearest diplomatic mission of your home country.

Australia: Offices in Adelaide, Brisbane, Canberra, Darwin, Hobart, Melbourne, Newcastle, Perth, and Sydney. Must apply in person at a post office, Passport Office, or Australian diplomatic mission overseas. Fees are adjusted frequently. For more information, call toll free (in Australia) 131 232.

Canada: 28 regional offices across Canada. Head Office, Foreign Affairs, Ottawa, Ontario, K1A OG3 (tel. (613) 996-8885). Applications available in English and French at all passport offices, post offices, and most travel agencies (CDN$35). Valid 5 years, non-renewable. Takes 3 weeks, or 5 days if in person. For additional information, call the 24-hr. number (tel. (800) 567-6868 in Canada; in Toronto 973-3251; in Montréal 283-2152), or refer to *Bon Voyage, But...* with a list of embassies and consulates abroad. Free from any passport office or Info-Export (BPTE), External Affairs, Ottawa, Ont., K1A OG2.

Ireland: Apply by mail to either the Department of Foreign Affairs, Passport Office, Setanta Centre, Molesworth St., Dublin 2 (tel. (1) 671 16 33), or the Passport Office, 1A South Mall, Cork (tel. (21) 627 25 25). The new Passport Express service offers a 2-week turn-around, available through post offices for an extra IR£3. Applications at local Garda stations or from a passport office. Passports are valid for 10 years (IR£45). Citizens under 18 or over 65 can request a 3-year passport IR£10.

New Zealand: Contact local Link Centre, travel agent, or Representative for an application form. Return to the New Zealand Passport Office, Documents of National Identity Division, Department of Internal Affairs, Box 10-526, Wellington (tel. (04) 474 81 00). The fee is NZ$80 for an application submitted in New Zealand and varies greatly overseas. Standard processing is 10 working days.

South Africa: Applications available at any Department of Home Affairs Office.

UK: Offices in London, Liverpool, Newport, Peterborough, Glasgow, and Belfast. Application forms also available in post offices. Passports valid 10 years (£18). Takes 4-6 weeks. London office offers same-day, walk-in service; arrive early.

US: Locations in Boston, Chicago, Honolulu, Houston, Los Angeles, Miami, New Orleans, New York, Philadelphia, San Francisco, Seattle, Stamford, and Washington, D.C. Contact the U.S. Passport Information's 24-hr. recording (tel. (202) 647-0518), which offers general information, agency locations, etc. Issues and renews passports ($65 and $55 respectively). Valid 10 years. Processing may take 4 weeks. Rush service $30. For first passports, or renewing passports over 12 years old, you must apply in person. Abroad, a U.S. embassy or consulate can also issue new passports, given proof of citizenship. If your passport is lost or stolen in the U.S., report it to Passport Services, U.S. Department of State, 1111 19th St., NW, Washington, DC, 20522-1705.

EMBASSIES AND CONSULATES

Cambodia

Royal Kingdom of Cambodia Embassy: US: 4500 16th St. NW, Washington, DC 20011 (tel. (202) 726-7742; fax (202) 726-8381).

Hong Kong

Served by the **British embassies and consulates. US: Embassy:** 3100 Massachusetts Ave. NW, Washington, DC 20008 (tel. (202) 462-1340); **East:** 845 Third Ave., New York, NY 10022 (tel. (212) 745-0200); **Central:** 33 North Dearborn St., Chicago, IL 60602 (tel. (312) 346-1810); **South:** First Interstate Bank Plaza, Suite 1990, 1000 Louisiana, Houston, TX 77002 (tel. (713) 659-6270); **West:** 11766 Wilshire Blvd., Suite 400, Los Angeles, CA 90025-6536 (tel. (310) 477-3322). Call the embassy for additional addresses. **British High Commission: Australia:** Commonwealth Ave., Yarralumla, Canberra ACT 2500 (tel. (616) 270 66 66). **Canada:** 80 Elgin St., Ottawa Ont. KIP 5K7 (tel. (613) 237-1530). **New Zealand,** 44 Hill St., Wellington 1 (tel. (644) 472-6049).

Indonesia

Indonesian Consulate General: Australia: South: Beulah Park, 44 Gawler Place S.A. 5067, Adelaide (tel. (08) 430 87 42); **Southeast:** 236-238 Maroubra Rd., Maroubra, Sydney, NSW 2035 (tel. (02) 344 99 33, -96 33, -95 33, -93 33; fax (02) 349 68 54 or 349 75 96). **Canada:** 425 University Ave., 9th fl., Toronto, Ontario M5G 1T6 (tel. (416) 591-6461/2; fax (416) 591-6613). **US: East:** 5 E. 68th St., New York, NY 10021 (tel. (212) 879-0600, -0615; fax (212) 570-6206); **Central:** 2 Illinois Center, Suite 1422, 233 N. Michigan Ave., Chicago, IL 60601 (tel. (312) 938-0101, -04 and 938-0311, -12; fax (312) 938-3148); **West:** 3457 Wilshire Blvd., Los Angeles, CA 90010 (tel. (213) 383-5126; fax (213) 487-3971).

Consulate of the Republic of Indonesia: Australia: North: 20 Harry Chan Ave., Darwin Northern Territory (tel. (08) 941 00 48, -04 51; fax (08) 941 27 09); **West:** 134 Adelaide Terrace, East Perth, WA 6004, P.O. Box 6683 (tel. (09) 221 58 58; fax (09) 221 56 88). **Southeast:** 72 Queen Rd., Melbourne, VIC 3004 (tel. (03) 525 27 55; fax (03) 525 15 88). **Canada:** 15124-42 Ave., Edmonton, Alberta TGH 5LG (tel. (403) 430-8742; fax (403) 988-9768). **US: Central:** 10900 Richmond Ave., Houston, TX 77042 (tel. (713) 785-1691; fax (713) 780-9644). **West:** 111 Columbus Ave., San Francisco, CA 94133 (tel. (415) 474-9571; fax (415) 441-4320); **Very West:** Pri Tower, 733 Bishop St., P.O. Box 3379, Honolulu, HI (tel. (808) 524-4300).

Embassy of the Republic of Indonesia: Australia: 8 Darwin Ave., Yarralumla, Canberra, ACT 2600; P.O. Box 616, Kingston 2604 (tel. (06) 250 86 00; fax 250 86 66). **Canada:** 287 Maclaren St., Ottawa, Ont. K2P OL9 (tel. (613) 236-7403, -05; fax (613) 563-2858 or (613) 230-7361). **New Zealand:** 70 Glen Rd., Kelburn Wellington, P.O. Box 3543 (tel. (04) 475 86 97, -99; fax (04) 475 93 74). **UK:** 38 Grosvenor Square, London WIX 9AD (tel. (0171) 499 76 61; fax (0171) 491 49 93); **US:** United Nations, 325 E. 38th St., New York, NY 10016 (tel. (212) 972-8333; fax (212) 972-9780); 2020 Massachusetts Ave. NW, Washington, DC 20036 (tel. (202) 775-5200 to (202) 775-5207; fax (202) 775-5365).

Laos

Embassy of the Lao PDR: Australia: 1 Dalman Crescent, O'Malley, Canberra, ACT 2606 (tel. (06) 286 45 95, -69 33; fax (06) 290 19 10); **US:** 2222 S St. NW, Washington, DC 20008 (tel. (202) 332-6416; fax (202) 332-4923).

Permanent Mission of the Lao PDR to the UN: 317 E. 51st St., New York, NY 10022 (tel. (212) 832-2734; fax (212) 750-0039).

Malaysia

Embassies of Malaysia: South Africa: Carlton Hotel, Main St., Johannesburg, 2000 South Africa (tel. 330 19 11; fax 880 48 94). **US:** 2401 Massachusetts Ave. NW, Washington, DC 20008 (tel. (202) 328-2700; fax (202) 483-7661); World Trade Center Building, 350 S. Figueroa St., Suite 400, Los Angeles, CA 90071 (tel.

(213) 621-2661, -2689; fax (213) 620-8659). **Consulate General of Malaysia: US:** 630 Third Ave., 11th fl., New York, NY 10017 (tel. (212) 687-2491; fax (212) 490-8450).

High Commission of Malaysia: Australia: 7 Perth Ave., Yaralumla, Canberra, ACT 2600 (tel. (06) 273 15 43). **Canada:** 60 Boteler St., Ottowa, Ont. KIN 8Y7 (tel. (613) 237-5183/4; fax (613) 237-4852). **New Zealand:** 10 Washington Ave., Brooklyn, Wellington (tel. (03) 85 24 93, -20 19; fax (03) 85 69 73). **UK:** 45 Belgrave Square, London SWIX 8QT (tel. (0171) 235 80 33; fax (0171) 235 51 61).

Singapore

Embassy of the Republic of Singapore: US: 3501, International Place NW, Washington, DC 20008. (tel. (202) 537-3100).

Consulate General of the Republic of Singapore: Canada: Suite 1305, 999 West Hastings St., Vancouver, BC V6C 2W2. **US: West:** 2424 SE Bristol #320, Newport Beach, CA 92660 (tel. (714) 476-2330). **Central:** c/o Personnel Decisions Inc., 2000 Plaza VII, 45 S. Seventh St., Minneapolis, MN 55402 (tel. (612) 337-3643).

Singapore High Commission: Australia: 17 Forster Crescent, Yarralumla, Canberra, ACT 2600 (tel. (06) 273 39 44). **New Zealand:** 17 Kabul St., Khandallah, Wellington, P.O. Box 13-140 (tel. (04) 479 20 76). **South Africa:** 3rd Fl. Village Walk Offices, Maude Street, Sandown 2146 (tel. (011) 883 14 22). **UK:** 9 Wilton Crescent, London SW1X 8SA (tel. (0171) 235 83 15, -17).

Thailand

Royal Thai Consulate General: Australia: 75-77 Pitt St., 2nd fl., Sydney, NSW 2000 (tel. (02) 241 25 42/3). **Canada** (consulates): **Quebec:** 1155 René-Lévesque Ouest, Suite 2500, Montréal, Qué. H3B 2K4 (tel. (514) 871-9941; fax (514) 875-8967); **East:** 44th fl., Scotia Plaza, 40 King St. W., 4th fl., Toronto, Ont., M5H 3Y4 (tel. (416) 367-6750 or (416) 361-7074); **Central:** 8625 112 St., Edmonton, Alberta T6G 1K8 (tel. (403) 439-3576; fax (403) 432-1387); **West:** 736 Granville St., Suite 106, Vancouver, BC V6Z 1G3 (tel. (604) 687-1143; fax (604) 687-4434). **UK: England:** 35 Lord St., Liverpool 2 (tel. (051) 225 05 04); **Scotland:** Pacific House, 70 Wellington St., Glasgow G2 6SB (tel. (041) 248 66 77). **US: East:** 351 E. 52nd St., New York, NY 10022 (tel. (212) 754-1770, (212) 754-1893, or (212) 754-1896; fax (212) 754-1907); **Central:** 35 E. Wacker Dr., Suite 1834, Chicago, IL 60601 (tel. (312) 236-2447/8); **West:** 801 N. La Brea Ave., Los Angeles, CA 90038 (tel. (213) 937-1894).

Royal Thai Embassy: Australia, 111 Empire Circuit, Yarralumla, Canberra, ACT 2600 (tel. (06) 273 11 49, -29 37). **Canada,** 180 Island Park Dr., Ottawa, Ont., K1Y OA2 (tel. (613) 722-4444). **UK,** 29-30 Queen's Gate, London SW7 5JB (tel. (0171) 589 01 73). **New Zealand,** 2 Cook St., P.O. Box 17-226, Karori, Wellington (tel. (4) 76 86 18/9). **US,** 1024 Wisconsin Ave. NW, Washington, DC 20007 (tel. (202) 994-3608).

Vietnam

Embassy of Vietnam: Australia, 6 Tim Berra Crescent, Valley, Canberra, ACT 2600 (tel. (06) 286 60 58; fax (06) 286 45 34). **UK,** Victoria 12-14, W. 8, London (tel. (0171) 937 19 12; fax (0171) 937 61 08). **US,** 1233 20th St., NW, Suite 501, Washington, DC 20036 (tel. (202) 861-0737; fax (202) 861-0917).

VISAS

Cambodia

The easiest way to obtain a visa is upon arrival at Pochentong Airport in Phnom Penh. One-month visas are issued immediately for US$20. Those traveling overland from Vietnam can apply for visas in Ho Chi Minh City for US$20, which will take two days to process. As the hub city in Southeast Asia, Bangkok has numerous travel agencies that will grant visas in one day for an average US$25. **Visa extensions** can be made by the Immigration Office in Phnom Penh for up to six months. (See "Practical Information" on page 76 for more details.)

Hong Kong

Without a visa, British citizens may stay in Hong Kong for up to 12 months, Canadian, Australian, and New Zealand citizens may stay three months, and U.S. and South African citizens may stay one month (with round-trip tickets or proof of onward passage).

Indonesia

Visitors from any country must carry a passport valid for at least six months from their date of entry and proof of onward passage. Residents of South Africa need a visa to enter the country. No visas are necessary for residents of Australia, Canada, Ireland, New Zealand, the U.K., the U.S., and numerous other countries if they enter through one of the 'gateway' cities (see "Getting Around" on page 53); if entering through another city, obtain a visa from the Indonesian Embassy or Consulate (valid for 1 month, but extendable). No visitors may stay longer than two months.

Laos

Visa regulations change constantly, and no one, least of all the National Tourism Authority, seems able to give a definitive answer. Officially, every tourist enters the country on a 15-day tourist visa and is still assigned to one of Vientiane's 20-odd travel agencies. It is best to order a visa from an embassy in Bangkok, Hanoi, or Phnom Penh. Citizens of countries that have an embassy in Vientiane can get valid visas which must be stamped in Bangkok. For all others, it is possible to obtain quasi-legal visas in Nong Khai, Thailand, but problems can often arise once in Laos.

Visa extensions can be made through the travel agency listed on your visa for US$3-5. Ask someone who reads Lao to translate your visa. Apply at least five days before the expiration date.

Malaysia

Travelers to Malaysia from the U.S., the U.K., Australia and New Zealand can travel in Malaysia for up to 3 months without a visa. South African citizens can travel without a visa for up to 1 month. For longer stays contact the Malaysian Embassy or consulate. Travelers who wish to travel around Malaysia and return must apply for a **reentry permits** US$5.

Singapore

Travelers holding passports from Australia, Bangladesh, Brunei, Canada, Hong Kong, Malaysia, the Netherlands, New Zealand, Sri Lanka, Switzerland, U.K., and U.S. can enter and remain in Singapore for less than 14 days without an entry visa. Those planning to stay longer should apply for an extension at the Immigration Office at least two days before the grace period ends.

Thailand

Citizens from certain countries, including the U.S., Canada, Australia, and European countries, need not obtain visas if they plan to be in Thailand for less than 1 month and if they have a confirmed ticket as proof of departure. For travelers who wish to spend more time in the country, Thailand issues two main types of visas: **tourist visas** (up to 60 days, US$15) and **non-immigrant visas** for business or employment (up to 90 days, US$20). These visas may be obtained at a Thai consulate in your home nation. To apply for one, send your passport (valid for at least another 6 months from the time of the visa's issue), two passport-sized photographs, the fee (cash or money order), and the visa application form, mailed in a self-addressed stamped envelope. Every visa is valid for entry up to 90 days from its date of issue. To stay in Thailand for a longer period than specified by your visa, you will need to apply for an extension. The fee to apply for an extension is about US$25. Thirty-day transit visas may not be extended.

For those who wish to take sojourns to nearby countries, a **re-entry permit** is required to return. Applications should be made at the main Immigration Office well before departure. No **exit visa** is required to leave the country.

Vietnam

Many travelers to Vietnam go to Bangkok for fast service to obtain a **visa** to Vietnam. Keep at least two passport-sized photos handy (you may need six at some places). Visas specify where travelers can enter and leave the country. For any changes of entry/exit points, go to the Foreign Ministry in Hanoi or Ho Chi Minh City.

It is not unheard of for tourists to have a 30-day visa, only to have officials validate it for a week. Check immediately to see how many days you've been granted. If the validation stamp does not match your visa, you may be able to get it changed at the border checkpoint; if not, apply for an extension with the Ministry of Foreign Affairs. Overstaying your visa, no matter how short, is a serious violation.

Bangkok travel agencies issue visas in four days, costing US$60. "Express" visas take half the time, but are not as reliable. Visa and round-trip air ticket package deals for US$365-400 are readily available. In Bangkok, see travel agencies on Khao San Road for the best options. In Thailand, visas must be obtained from travel agencies rather than the embassy. **Visa extensions** can be granted up to 15 days at a time, for up to three months. Extensions can only be made in Hanoi and Ho Chi Minh City.

CUSTOMS: ENTERING

Cambodia

All international customs laws apply in Cambodia: 200 cigarettes, 1L of alcohol, and unlimited amounts of currency are allowed in the country. Weapons and drugs are banned from the country. The government takes drug trafficking very seriously. As one embassy official said, those who are caught with drugs "will not come out of Cambodia alive," and while marijuana is readily available in the country, users of hard drugs, like opium and cocaine "will be shot." Keep that in mind.

Hong Kong

Travelers can import up to 200 cigarettes, 50 cigars, or 250g of tobacco, and 1L of wine or spirits. Arms may be taken into custody, and must be declared. You must obtain a permit to bring ivory into or out of Hong Kong.

Indonesia

Visitors to Indonesia can carry a maximum of 2L of alcoholic beverage, 50 cigars or 200 cigarettes or 100g of tobacco, and perfume for personal use only. No radios, TV sets, narcotics, arms or ammunition, Chinese medicine, or text in Chinese characters may be imported. Upon entry, visitors must declare any cars, photographic equipment, typewriters, and tape recorders, and these must be re-exported. Although any amount of foreign currency may be taken in or out of the country, the import or export of more than Rp50,000 is prohibited. Quarantine permits are required for fresh fruit, plants, and animals, and advance approval is required for transceivers; movies or video cassettes must be cleared by the Film Censor Board.

Laos

Travelers to Laos may bring in up to 200 cigarettes, 1L of alcohol, and perfume (for personal use only), as well as any foreign currency. Lao laws prohibit weapons, drugs, and pornography.

Malaysia

Travelers can bring in 1L of alcohol, 200 cigarettes, food preparations not exceeding RM75 in value and gifts not exceeding RM200 in value. There is no restriction on the import or export of currency. Prohibited from import are pornography, prejudicial publications, knives, most broadcast receivers, all goods originating from Israel, and, of course, Rank Xerox 6500 Color Copiers. **The punishment for importing or exporting illegal drugs is the death penalty,** including "opium, 'ganja', heroin, morphine, etc.". A permit is necessary to import precious stones (apart from reasonable amounts of jewelry), gold (except coins issued by the Central Bank of Malaysia and personal jewelry), toy or real arms, CBs, animals, plants, and soil.

Singapore

Travelers can bring in, duty free, 1L of spirits, wine, or beer, but no tobacco products, and up to S$400 in gifts, food preparations, etc. Prohibited from importation are chewing gum, chewing tobacco or imitation tobacco, cigarette lighters, obscenity, "seditious and treasonable material," and toy currency. "Death for drug traffickers under Singapore law." There are no currency restrictions.

Thailand

Travelers can bring in 227g tobacco, 200 cigarettes, 50 cigars, and one bottle of liquor duty-free, as well as one still camera with five rolls of film, or one movie camera with three rolls of film. Narcotics, including opium, heroin, cocaine, marijuana, and morphine, are prohibited. The penalty for possession can range from a very long jail term to death, depending on the drug and whether or not the prosecutor can prove that you were trying to sell it. (For more on drugs, see Safety below.) Also, nix the firearms and pornography. Tourists entering the country must bring in a minimum of US$400 per person or US$800 per family.

Vietnam

Customs declaration forms ask visitors to declare quantities and makes of cameras, video and camcorders, tape recorders, and all other electric equipment being taken into the country. Foreign currency in excess of US$10,000 must be declared. Drug trafficking, weapons, and explosives are banned in Vietnam. The government is not hesitant about doling out harsh penalties, including capital punishment. As recently as 1993, a man was sentenced to death for smuggling heroin. In addition, objects deemed subversive and impure to Vietnamese society, such as pornography, will be confiscated.

CUSTOMS: HOMEWARD BOUND

Cambodia

Upon leaving Cambodia, there is an US$8 airport tax. Duty free allowances include 200 cigarettes, 1L of alcohol, and perfume (for personal use only).

Laos

There is a US$5 airport tax for all international flights. Duty free allowances include 2 bottles of liquor and 500 cigarettes. In addition, no antiques or **Buddha images** can leave the country without the authorization of the Lao government. Remember, this is a communist country that takes theft of its national heritage very seriously—you may wind up in some re-education camp if you do so.

Thailand

There is little regulation of what you can take out of the country. Where there is regulation, however, the Thai government is adamant about enforcing the law. **No Buddha images** may be taken out of the country unless you are a worshipping Buddhist or you are using them for cultural exchanges or academic purposes. A license must be obtained from the Fine Arts Department if you want to take any Buddha images or objects of art out of Thailand. To apply for a license, you must take two front view, postcard-sized pictures of the objects, a photocopy of your passport, and the objects, to one of the following locations: The National Museums Division,

Bangkok; The Chiang Mai National Museum, Chiang Mai; or the Songkhla National Museum, Songkhla. This rule regarding art does not apply to souvenirs or other objects bought in department stores. For any art purchased in the country you should keep receipts handy for presentation to customs officials.

Vietnam

Duty free allowances include 200 cigarettes, 1L of alcohol, perfume (for personal use), foreign currency, and unlimited jewelry. Antiques will not be allowed out of the country without approval from the Ministry of Culture and Information. No dong allowed out of the country. Upon leaving from Ho Chi Minh City, there is an airport tax of US$8; from Hanoi US$6. You need to show both your customs form and immigration card when leaving the country, otherwise you could be fined for losing them.

Home Countries

Australia: Citizens may import AUS$400 of goods duty free; travelers over 18 may also bring 250 cigarettes, 250g tobacco, and 1L alcohol. Amounts of AUS$5000 or more, or equivalent in foreign currency, must be reported. For information, contact the Australian Customs Service, 5 Constitution Ave., Canberra, ACT 2601 (tel. (06) 275 62 55; fax (06) 275 69 89).

Canada: Citizens may bring back up to CDN$300 worth of goods duty free once every calendar year; this amount can not be combined from various trips. This may include up to 200 cigarettes, 50 cigars, 400g loose tobacco or tobacco sticks, 1.14L wine or alcohol, and 24 355mL cans/bottles beer. For more information, write to Canadian Customs, 2265 St. Laurent Blvd., Ottawa, Ontario, K1G 4K3 (tel. (613) 993-0534). Or, from within Canada, call (800) 461-9999.

Ireland: Citizens must declare everything in excess of 200 cigarettes, 1L of alcohol, 2L still wine, 50g of perfume, 0.25L toilet water, IR£34 of other goods per adult. Travelers must be 17 or older for tobacco or alcohol products. For more info, contact The Revenue Commissioners, Dublin Castle (tel. (01) 679 27 77; fax (01) 671 20 21) or The Collector of Customs and Excise, The Custom House, Dublin 1.

New Zealand: Citizens may bring home up to NZ$700 worth of goods duty free, including 200 cigarettes, 250g tobacco, or 50 cigars. You may also bring in 4.5L of beer or wine, 1.125L of liquor. Only travelers over 17 may import tobacco or alcohol. For more information, consult the *New Zealand Customs Guide for Travelers,* available from customs offices, or contact New Zealand Customs, 50 Anzac Ave., Box 29, Auckland (tel. (09) 377 35 20; fax (09) 309 29 78).

South Africa: Citizens may import duty free: 400 cigarettes, 50 cigars, 250g tobacco, 2L wine, 1L of spirits, 250mL toilet water, 50mL perfume, and other items up to a value of SAR500. Amounts exceeding this limit but not SAR10,000 are dutiable at 20%. Goods acquired abroad and sent to the Republic as unaccompanied baggage do not qualify for any allowances. You may not export or import South African bank notes in excess of SAR500. For specific information concerning customs and excise duties, write: The Commissioner for Customs and Excise, Private Bag X47, Pretoria, 0001. This agency distributes the pamphlet, *South African Customs Information,* for visitors and residents who travel abroad. South Africans in the U.S. should contact: South African Mission to the IMF/World Bank, 3201 New Mexico Ave. #380, NW, Washington, DC 20016 (tel. (202) 364-8320/1; fax (202) 364-6008).

UK: Citizens or visitors arriving in the U.K. from outside the EC must declare any goods in excess of the following allowances: 200 cigarettes, or 100 cigarillos, or 50 cigars, or 250 g tobacco; 2L still table wine; strong liquors over 22% volume (1L); or fortified or sparkling wine, other liquors (2L); Perfume (60 cc/mL); toilet water (250 cc/mL); and £136 worth of all other goods including gifts and souvenirs. These also apply to duty free purchases within the EC, except for other goods, which has an allowance of £71. Goods obtained duty and tax paid for personal use within the EC do not require further duty. For more information, contact Her Majesty's Customs and Excise, Custom House, Nettleton Rd., Heathrow

Airport, Hounslow, Middlesex, TW6 2LA (tel. (0181) 910 37 44; fax (0181) 910 37 65).

US: Residents must declare all merchandise acquired abroad, including gifts, purchases, articles bought duty free, and purchases for others. The first US$400 worth of merchandise may be entered duty free. You may include in your personal exemption: 100 cigars, 200 cigarettes, and one liter (33.8 fl. oz.) of alcoholic beverages. The next US$1000 of merchandise is subject to a flat 10% duty rate; beyond that different duty rates apply depending upon the commodity. It's wise to keep sales slips handy, in case inspectors wish to verify your declarations.

For more information, get a copy of the booklet *Know Before You Go.* Somewhat different regulations apply to foreign nationals living in the U.S. These individuals should get a copy of *Customs Hints for Visitors (Nonresidents)* from U.S. Customs Service, Box 7407, Washington, D.C. 20044, or call (202) 927-6724.

HOW DO I KNOW YOU ARE WHO YOU SAY YOU ARE?

In the world of budget travel, youth has its privileges. The **International Student Identity Card (ISIC)** is the most widely accepted form of student identification. In many countries, this card can get you discounts on sights, theaters, museums, accommodations, train, ferry, and airplane travel, and other services. In Southeast Asia, the attitude seems to be that products and services are cheap enough for foreigners anyway that they do not need to be given extra discounts. It can't hurt to try, though. In some cases, establishments will also honor an ordinary student ID from your college or university for student discounts.

The card is useful however; it provides accident insurance of up to US$3000 as well as US$100 per day of in-hospital care for up to 60 days and repatriation (of remains) insurance. Cardholders also have access to a toll-free Traveler's Assistance hotline whose multilingual staff can provide help in medical, legal, and financial emergencies overseas. Many student travel offices issue ISICs, including Council Travel, Let's Go Travel, and STA Travel in the U.S.; Travel CUTS in Canada; and any of the organizations under the auspices of the International Student Travel Confederation (ISTC) around the world. When you apply for the card, request a copy of the International Student Identity Card Handbook, which lists by country some of the available discounts. You can also write to Council for a copy. The fee is US$15. Applicants must be a degree-seeking student of a secondary or post-secondary school. Because of the proliferation of phony ISICs, many airlines and some other services require other proof of student identity: have a signed letter from the registrar attesting to your student status and stamped with the school seal, and carry your school ID card. To obtain a card by using a credit card, please call (800) 255-1000, ext. 425. The new, US$16 **International Teacher Identity Card (ITIC)** offers similar but limited discounts, as well as medical insurance coverage. The application process is the same as for an ISIC, except teachers need to present an official document from their department chair or another school official.

Federation of International Youth Travel Organizations (FIYTO) issues a discount card to travelers who are not students but are under 26. Also known as the **International Youth Discount Travel Card,** or the **GO 25 Card,** this one-year card offers many of the same benefits as the ISIC, and most organizations that sell the ISIC also sell the GO 25 Card. A brochure that lists discounts is free when you purchase the card. To apply, bring: (1) proof of birthdate (copy of birth certificate, passport, or valid driver's license) and (2) a passport-sized photo (with your name printed on the back). The fee is US$10, US$16 (with insurance), CDN$15, or UK£5. Prices subject to change. For information, contact Council Travel in the U.S. or FIYTO in Denmark (see "Budget Travel Agencies" on page 45 for addresses).

HOSTELLING ORGANIZATIONS

The most extensive group of hostels is organized by Hostelling International (HI), the new and universal trademark name adopted by the International Youth Hostel

TOP 5 Ways to Save Money While Traveling

5. Ship yourself in a crate marked "Livestock." Remember to poke holes in the crate.

4. Board a train dressed as Elvis and sneer and say "The King rides for free."

3. Ask if you can walk through the Channel Tunnel.

2. Board the plane dressed as an airline pilot, nod to the flight attendants, and hide in the rest room until the plane lands.

1. Bring a balloon to the airline ticket counter, kneel, breathe in the helium, and ask for the kiddie fare.

But if you're serious about saving money while you're traveling abroad, just get an ISIC--the International Student Identity Card. Discounts for students on international airfares, hotels and motels, car rentals, international phone calls, financial services, and more.

The International Student Identity Card

For more information call:

1-800-GET-AN-ID

Available at Council Travel offices (see ad in this book) and universities nationwide.

CIEE: Council on International Educational Exchange
205 East 42nd Street, New York, NY 10017-5706

Federation (IYHF). Hong Kong has seven HI hostels, including those in the New Territories. Thailand has them in Ayutthaya, Bangkok, Chiang Mai, Phitsanulok, Prachuap Khiri Khan, and Rayong. Malaysia has two in Melaka and Kuala Lumpur, and one in Penang and Kota Bharu. Indonesia and Singapore have hostels that are associated with HI, but are not actually members. Indonesia has 21, across the country.

Hostelling International (HI) headquarters, 9 Guessens Rd., Welwyn Garden City, Herts, AL8 6QW, England (tel. (0707) 33 24 87). Worldwide federation of youth hostels and individual national hostelling associations. Offers an International Booking Network, which allows you to make confirmed reservations at any of almost 200 HI hostels in the US and abroad for only US$2 (in addition to the regular overnight fee). Reservations can be made for up to three consecutive nights and for groups of up to nine people, and changes can be made up to three or more days before the date of the reservation. Credit card (MC or Visa) guarantee required. To make reservations, call or visit the HI-American Youth Hostels (HI-AYH) headquarters at 733 15th St. NW, Suite 840, Washington, DC 20005 (tel. (202) 783-6161), or the travel stores of their Golden Gate, Potomac Area, and Greater Boston Councils.

The following are national HI affiliates in English-speaking countries. Membership is usually acquired through the HI affiliate in one's own country, not abroad.

Hostelling International—American Youth Hostels (HI-AYH), 733 15th St., NW, Suite 840, Washington, DC 20005 (tel. (202) 783-6161; fax (202) 783-6171). Comprised of 38 regional offices across the US which, in addition to licensing hostels (150 in 36 states and the District of Columbia), provide local members and visitors with special programs, events, trips, and activities. HI-AYH membership cards cost US$25, under 18 US$10, over 54 US$15. Membership valid for one year from date of issue. Contact AYH for ISIC, student and charter flights, travel equipment, literature on budget travel, and information on summer positions as a group leader for domestic outings.

Hostelling International—Canada (HI-C), 400-205 Catherine St., Ottawa, Ont. K2P 1C3 (tel. (613) 237-7884; fax (613) 237-7868). One-year membership fee CDN$26.75, under 18 CDN$12.84, 2-year CDN$37.45. Life membership available.

Youth Hostels Association of England and Wales (YHA), VHA Adventure Shop, 14 Southampton St., Covent Garden, London WC2E 7HY (tel. (0171) 836 10 36; fax (0171) 836 63 72). Enrollment fees are £9, under 18 £3; children aged 5-18 enrolled free when a parent joins.

An Óige, 61Mountjoy St., Dublin 7, Ireland (tel. (01) 830 45 55; fax (01) 830 58 08). 1-yr. membership £7.50; under 18 £4; family £7.50, children under 16 free.

Youth Hostel Association of Northern Ireland (YHANI), 22-32 Donegall Rd., Belfast BT12 5JN, Northern Ireland (tel. (0232) 315 435 or 32 47 33; fax (0232) 439 699). Annual membership UK£7; under 18 UK£3; family UK£14, for up to 6 children).

Scottish Youth Hostels Association (SYHA), 7 Glebe Crescent, Sterling FK8 2JA, Scotland (tel. (0786) 451 181; (0786) fax 450 198). Annual memberhsip UK£6, under 18 UK£2.50.

Australian Youth Hostels Association (AYHA), Level 3, 10 Mallett St., Camperdown, NSW, 2050 (tel. (02) 565 16 99; fax (02) 565 12 35). Fee AUS$40 when purchased by Australians for use overseas, renewal AUS$24. Under 18 AUS$12. Non YHA members traveling to Australia can join AYHA for AUS$24 and will receive a Hostelling International card.

Youth Hostels Association of New Zealand (YHANZ), P.O. Box 436, 173 Gloucester St., Christchurch 1 (tel. (03) 379 99 70; fax (03) 365 44 76). Annual membership NZ$24.

Hostel Association of South Africa, P.O. Box 4402, Capetown 8000 (tel. (21) 419 18 53). Annual membership SAR35. Good 1 year from the month of issue.

Don't forget your shades.

Presents

In the Wanderlust section of the American Express student Web site, the ultimate online resource for college students.

http://www.americanexpress.com/student

INTERNATIONAL DRIVING PERMITS

For an **International Driving Permit** you must be over 18. Submit an application, two recent passport-size photos, and a US driver's license. The one-year permit (US$10) is available from any local office of the **American Automobile Association (AAA),** or at the main office, American Automobile Association, 1000 AAA Drive, Heathrow, FL 32746-5080 (tel. (407) 444-4245; fax (407) 444-7823). For further information, contact a local AAA office. You can also get an IDP from the **American Automobile Touring Alliance,** Bayside Plaza, 188 The Embarcadero, San Francisco, CA 94105 (tel. (415) 777-4000; (415) fax 882-2141). Canadian license holders can obtain an IDP (CDN$10) through any **Canadian Automobile Association (CAA)** office, or by writing to CAA Ottawa, 2525 Carling Ave., Lincoln Hts., Ottawa, Ont. K2B 7Z2 (tel. (613) 820 1890; (613) fax 771-3046). Complete an application form and provide two passport-size photos and a valid driver's license.

■■■ MONEY MATTERS

Many budget travelers find themselves obsessed with budgeting their trip. They feel a compulsive need to spend as little money as possible: to stay in the cheapest lodgings no matter how miserable; to eat grim, tasteless gruel; and make each day's goal to spend fewer baht (or dong, rupiah, kip, ringgit, riel, Singapore dollars or Hong Kong dollars), than yesterday. When you hit the travel doldrums, use some of your money to cushion the shocks. Force yourself to go for a nice meal—in most parts of Thailand outside the major cities, this will mean spending only a little more. Spend the night in a higher-quality hotel or guest house; use your money for air conditioning and a private bathroom. Never sacrifice your health or safety for a cheaper tab.

Acquire some foreign currency before leaving home. Airport exchange rates are abominable, and purchasing a small amount of the local currency before you go will allow you to breeze through the airport while others languish in exchange counter lines. This is also a good practice in case you find yourself stuck with no money after banking hours or on a holiday, or if your flight arrives late in the evening. Bring at least enough foreign money to last for the first 24-72 hours of a trip, depending on when you arrive. Exchanging money over a weekend may be tricky, so travelers arriving on a Friday flight should bring plenty of foreign currency.

Avoid exchanging money at luxury hotels and restaurants, which will likely gouge you on both exchange rates and commission rates; the best deal is usually found at major banks. In rural areas, look for branches of banks you recognize from larger cities. In major cities, currency exchange booths controlled by major banks are everywhere. Although commission rates at the booths may be slightly higher, they are convenient and keep longer hours than the banks. It may be wise to keep some French francs, German marks, or especially the U.S. dollar on hand in case exchange booths refuse to accept other currencies. The U.S. dollar is the most readily accepted foreign currency in Southeast Asia, and in many situations it may be accepted even more than the local currency. See currency info for each country.

Remember that unless a commission rate is charged, service charges will eat up a chunk of your money each time you convert. To minimize your losses, exchange large sums of money at once, but never more than you can safely carry. It helps to plan ahead; if caught without local currency in an area with no convenient currency exchange center, you may be forced into a particularly disadvantageous deal.

TRAVELER'S CHECKS

No part of your trip is likely to cause you more headaches than money—even when you have it. Carrying large amounts of cash, even in a money belt, is unwise. Traveler's checks, which can be replaced if lost or stolen, are far safer—would Karl Malden lie to you? Although not all establishments, especially small, rural, or family-run shops, accept traveler's checks, your peace of mind will far outweigh any occasional inconvenience.

Companies don't supply traveler's checks in baht, rupiah, dong, or other regional currencies, so buy checks in your home currency—changing cash from one foreign currency to another will cost you dearly. Buy traveler's checks mostly in large denominations but also buy a little supply in small. Large notes will spare you long waits at the bank; small notes will minimize your losses if you just need a little cash to tide you through the train ride from one big city to the next.

Banks usually sell traveler's checks for a 1-2% commission. The American Automobile Association (AAA) offers its members commission-free American Express traveler's checks. Be prepared to buy at least US$100 in traveler's checks; many places will not sell less than that.

Expect red tape and delay in the event of theft or loss of traveler's checks. To expedite the refund process, keep check receipts separate from the checks and store them in a safe place or with a traveling companion; leave a list of check numbers with someone at home and the numbers of those you cash; and ask for a list of refund centers when you buy your checks. American Express and Bank of America have over 40,000 centers worldwide. Keep a separate supply of cash or traveler's checks for emergencies. Never countersign checks until you're prepared to cash them. And always bring your passport with you when you plan to use the checks.

American Express: US and **Canada** (tel. (800) 221-7282); **UK** (tel. (0800) 521 313); **New Zealand** (tel. (0800) 441 068); **Australia** (tel. (008) 251 902). Elsewhere, call US collect (tel (801) 964-6665). American Express traveler's checks are now available in 11 currencies: Australian, British, Canadian, Dutch, French, German, Japanese, Saudi Arabian, Spanish, Swiss, and US. They are the most widely recognized worldwide and the easiest to replace if lost or stolen. Checks can be purchased for a small fee at American Express Travel Service Offices, banks, and American Automobile Association offices (AAA members can buy the checks commission-free). Cardmembers can also purchase checks at American Express Dispensers at Travel Service Offices at airports and by ordering them via phone (tel. (800) ORDER-TC (673-3782)). American Express offices cash their checks commission-free (except where prohibited by national governments), although they often offer slightly worse rates than banks. You can also buy Cheques for Two which can be signed by either of two people traveling together. Request the American Express booklet "Traveler's Companion," listing travel office addresses and stolen check hotlines for each European country. Soon, traveler's checks will be available over America OnLine. Call (800) 673-3782 to find out more about this service, or check ExpressNet on America OnLine.

Citicorp: US and **Canada** (tel. (800) 645-6556); **UK** (tel. (0171) 982 40 40); from elsewhere call US collect (tel. (813) 623-1709). Sells both Citicorp and Citicorp Visa traveler's checks in US and Canadian dollars, British pounds, German marks, Swiss francs, and Japanese yen. Commission is 1-2% on check purchases. Citicorp's World Courier Service guarantees hand-delivery of traveler's checks anywhere in the world. Call 24 hrs. a day, seven days a week.

Thomas Cook MasterCard: US and **Canada** (tel. (800) 223-9920); elsewhere call US collect (tel. (609) 987-7300); **UK** (tel. (0800) 622 101; collect (1733) 502 995). Offers checks in US, Canadian, and Australian dollars, British and Cypriot pounds, French and Swiss francs, German marks, Japanese yen, Dutch guilders, Spanish pesetas, and ECUs. Commission 1-2% for purchases. Try buying checks at a Thomas Cook office for potentially lower commissions.

Visa: US (tel. (800) 227-6811); **UK** (tel. (0171) 937 8091); from anywhere else in the world call the US collect (tel. (212) 858-8500). Sells its traveler's checks by mail; call (800) 235-7366 to order them. Any kind of Visa traveler's check can be reported lost at the Visa number.

CREDIT CARDS

Credit cards are of limited use to the penniless pilgrim because low-cost budget establishments, particularly outside the more-traveled sections of the most traveled cities, rarely honor them. In some circumstances, however, a card can prove invaluable. For example, you can charge expenses incurred at most hospitals, and many foreign banks will allow you to withdraw money from ATM machines with a credit card. The past few years have brought an increasing acceptance of credit cards in Southeast Asia. However, there is stil. a great deal of variation in credit card acceptance. Sometimes a high-class restaurant may refuse all credit cards while some small shop accepts all cards under the sun. Generally, plastic is accepted at major hotels, department stores, expensive boutiques, and fine restaurants. Credit cards are not as well received at guest houses, shops frequented by locals, sidewalk merchants and food vendors, and bus and train ticket vendors. **Visa** and **MasterCard** are the most commonly accepted, followed by **American Express** and **Diner's Club.**

You can often reduce conversion fees by charging a purchase instead of changing traveler's checks. With credit cards such as American Express, Visa, and MasterCard, associated banks will give you an instant cash advance in the local currency as large as your remaining credit line. In most cases you will pay mortifying rates of interest for such an advance.

American Express (tel. (800) CASH-NOW (528-4800)) has a hefty annual fee (US$55) but offers a number of services. AmEx cardholders can cash personal checks at AmEx offices abroad. **Global Assist,** a 24-hr. hotline offering info and legal assistance in emergencies, is also available (tel. (800) 554-2639) in U.S. and Canada; from abroad call US collect (tel. (301) 214-8228). Cardholders can take advantage of the American Express Travel Service; benefits include assistance in changing airline, hotel, and car rental reservations, sending mailgrams and international cables, and holding your mail at one of the more than 1700 AmEx offices around the world.

MasterCard (tel. (800) 999-0454) and **Visa** (tel. (800) 336-8472) credit cards are sold by individual banks. Benefits depend on the type of card. If obtaining a MasterCard or Visa for travel purposes, ask bankers about specific travel services.

If your income is low, you may have difficulty acquiring an internationally recognized credit card. If a family member already has a card, it's easy to get an extra one.

Credit cards require extra vigilance. Report lost or stolen cards immediately, or you may be held responsible for forged charges. Write down the card-cancellation phone numbers for your bank and keep them separate from your cards, in a safe place. Be sure that carbons have been torn to pieces, and ask to watch your card be imprinted; an imprint onto a blank slip can be used later to charge merchandise in your name, eventually resulting in a pitched battle with your credit card company.

CASH CARDS

Automatic Teller Machines (ATMs) offer 24-hour service. ATMs are not as prevalent in Southeast Asia as in North America, but some banks in the larger cities are connected to an international money network, often PLUS (tel. (800) THE-PLUS (843-7587)) or CIRRUS (tel. (800) 4-CIRRUS (424-7787)). All major banks in Thailand now offer this service to customers, and even foreign travelers may make use of this convenience at nearly every bank branch in Bangkok. Similarly, Singapore provides ATMs at almost every turn. In contrast, Indonesia just began CIRRUS service in 1994 and Jakarta lags far behind, as do the major cities in Malaysia; service in Laos and Cambodia is virtually non-existent; in Vietnam, credit card use is gradually increasing and more widespread, but still limited to more expensive establishments. Many ATMs outside major cities will only accept cards from banks within the country, so don't count on a town's ATM to save your neck. CIRRUS service is often associated with a specific bank. Look for the following: Hong Kong, Citicard; Indonesia, Bank Bali or Citibank; Malaysia, Southern Bank Berhad; Thailand, Siam Commercial Bank.

Most ATM machines can be accessed by travelers via their Visa or MasterCard, or their bank-account card, with a hefty transaction fee for the service determined by the home bank or credit agency. Still, ATM machines do get the wholesale exchange rate, which is generally 5% better than the retail rate most banks use. Four-digit PINs (Personal Identification Numbers) are standard in most countries; memorize yours numerically, since ATM keypads don't always have letters. If your PIN is longer than four digits, ask your bank whether the first four digits will work, or whether you need a new number. Many ATMs are outdoors; don't let anyone distract you while at the machine and use discretion as you leave the machine.

MONEY FROM HOME

Sending money abroad is complicated, expensive, and extremely frustrating. Avoid wiring money by carrying a credit card, personal checks, or a separate stash of emergency traveler's checks. An **American Express card** offers the easiest way to obtain money from home; AmEx allows cardholders to draw cash from their checking accounts at any of its offices—up to US$1000 every 21 days. With someone feeding money into your account at home, you'll be set. Call **American Express** (tel. (800) 543-4080; in Canada (800) 933-3278). AmEx also offers Express Cash, with over 100,000 ATMs located in airports, hotels, banks, office complexes, and shopping areas around the world. Express Cash withdrawals are automatically debited from the Cardmember's specified bank account or line of credit. Green card holders may withdraw up to $1000 in a seven-day period. There is a 2% transaction fee for each cash withdrawal with a $2.50 minimum. To enroll in Express Cash, Cardmembers may call 1-800-CASH NOW. Outside the U.S. call collect (904) 565-7875. Unless using the AmEx service, avoid cashing checks in foreign currencies; they usually take weeks and a US$30 fee to clear.

The next best approach is to wire money through the instant international money transfer services operated by **Western Union** (tel. (800) 325-6000 in the US; 448 174 136 39 in Mexico; or (0800) 833-833 in Canada). The sender visits one of their offices or calls and either pays cash or charges the transfer to a credit card; the receiver can pick up the cash at any overseas office abroad (fee about US$29 to send $250, $70 for $1000). Does not service Laos or Cambodia. American Express is slightly cheaper and serves more countries than Western Union.

Thai post offices also offer an **International Money Order Service,** with reciprocal service between Thailand and 27 countries, including the U.S., the U.K., and Australia. It takes one day for the money to be received in the city post office, up to three days for the money to reach up-country.

If you are an American in a life-or-death situation, you can have money sent to you via the State Department's **Citizens Emergency Center,** Department of State, 2201 C St. NW, Washington, DC 20520 (tel. (202) 647-5225; (202) 647-4000 after business hours). For a fee the State Department will forward money within hours to the nearest consular office, which will disburse it according to the sender's instructions. The quickest way to get money to the State Department is through Western Union.

■■■ SAFETY

Whenever possible, *Let's Go* lists emergency, police, and consulate numbers in every large city; consult them if you encounter difficulties. Safety levels and security issues in Southeast Asia differ widely from country to country, and region to region within each country. Moreover, some of the safety concerns within these countries are very serious. It is not difficult to keep yourself out of a bad situation, but if you are not aware of what those situations are the consequences can be pretty bad. **Consult the Safety sections of each country** to remain a happy, healthy traveler.

Don't ever, ever accept free drinks, food, candy, medicine, or cigarettes from seemingly friendly strangers. What you are offered may be drugged, in which case you will at best wake up to find all of your belongings gone, or at worst, in a hospital connected to a respirator (if you wake up at all). It is a peculiarly acute problem; exercise caution.

To avoid unwanted attention, the best tactic is to **blend in** as much as possible: the gawking camera-toter is much easier prey than the casual local look-alike. Unfortunately, chances are you will not be able to fully hide the fact that you're a tourist, especially if you are not of Southeast or East Asian descent. Dress modestly. In general, the less you flaunt your income or foreign status, the less vulnerable you'll be to sticky fingers or large, blunt objects. If you do feel nervous, walking purposefully into a café or shop and checking your map there is better than doing so on a street corner. Muggings are more often impromptu than planned; anxious glances can be a sign that you have something valuable to protect. Don't ever appear apprehensive; like scabby, worm-eaten dogs, thieves can smell fear.

When you explore a new **city,** extra vigilance may be wise, but no city should force you to turn precautions into panic. When you get to a place where you'll be spending some time, find out about unsafe areas from tourist info, from the manager of your hotel or hostel, or from a local whom you trust. In particular, be aware of potential dangers in nearby border areas (see "Border Crossings" on page 50). Especially if you are traveling alone, be sure that someone at home knows your itinerary. Never say that you're traveling alone. Both men and women may want to carry small **whistles** to scare off attackers or attract attention, and it's not a bad idea to jot down the number of the police. When walking at night, turn day-time precautions into mandates. In particular, stay near crowded, well-lit areas and do not cross through parks, parking lots, or any other large, deserted areas.

There is no sure-fire set of precautions that will protect you from all situations you might encounter when you travel. A good self-defense course will give you more concrete ways to react to different types of aggression, but it might cost you more money than your trip. **Model Mugging** (East Coast (617) 232-7900; Midwest (312) 338-4545; West Coast (415) 592-7300), a national organization with offices in several major cities, teaches a very effective, comprehensive course on self-defense. (Course prices range $400-500. Women's and men's courses offered.) Community colleges frequently offer self-defense courses at more affordable prices.

Travel Assistance International by Worldwide Assistance Services, Inc., 1133 15th St. NW, Suite 400, Washington, DC 20005-2710 (tel. (800) 821-2828 or (202) 828-5894; fax (202) 331-1530), provides its members with a 24-hr. hotline for emergencies and referrals. Their year-long frequent traveler package ($226) includes medical and travel insurance, financial assistance, and help in replacing lost documents. The U.S. Department of State's pamphlet *A Safe Trip Abroad* ($1) summarizes safety information for travelers. It is available by phone (tel. (202) 783-3238) or by writing the Superintendent of Documents, U.S. Government Printing Office, Washington, DC 20402. For an official Dept. of State travel advisory on specific countries, call the 24-hr. hotline at (202) 647-5225. They offer travel warnings on crime statistics, security recommendations, and miscellaneous tips on health precautions. American citizens traveling abroad can call this number in an emergency. Pamphlets on traveling to specific areas also available. More complete info on safety while traveling may be found in *Travel Safety: Security and Safeguards at Home and Abroad,* from Hippocrene Books, Inc., 171 Madison Ave., New York, NY 10016 (tel. (212) 685-4371; orders (718) 454-2366; fax (718) 454-1391).

DRUGS

In general, stay away from drugs in Southeast Asia. Laws and even regimes can change almost overnight, and you never know what the rules and regulations are. **Some countries even carry the death penalty** for use or possession. More specific regulations can be found in each country's Essentials section.

Never agree to carry packages for strangers, especially across borders. And beware of dealers; drug enforcement agents have been known to work undercover to entrap the unsuspecting. If you are arrested, your home country's consulate can visit you, provide a list of attorneys, inform family and friends, and lend you a shoulder to cry on, but they cannot get you out of jail. As a U.S. State Department bulletin dourly states, you're virtually on your own if you become involved, however innocently, in illegal drugs. Write the Bureau of Consular Affairs, PA Room #5807, Department of State, Washington, DC 20520 (tel. (202) 647-1488) for more information and the pamphlet *Travel Warning on Drugs Abroad.*

■■■ SECURITY

Ignore all touts, including those offering taxi services from the airport, those at bus or train stations, those on the street offering personal tours, or those in front of bars promising a night of fun. They are all bound to be out for either personal gain or to lure the traveler into some trap.

Don't put money in a wallet in your back pocket. Never count your money in public and carry as little as possible. If you carry a purse, buy a sturdy one with a secure clasp, and carry it crosswise on the side, away from the street with the clasp against you. As far as packs are concerned, buy some small combination padlocks which slip through the two zippers, securing the pack shut. (Even these precautions do not always suffice: moped riders who snatch purses and backpacks sometimes tote knives to cut the straps). A **money belt** is the best way to carry cash; you can buy one at most camping supply stores or through the Forsyth Travel Library (see "Talking Books" on page 4). The best combination of convenience and invulnerability is the nylon, zippered pouch with belt that should sit inside the waist of your pants or skirt. A **neck pouch,** although less accessible, is equally safe. Avoid keeping anything precious in a fanny-pack (even if it's worn on your stomach): your valuables will be highly visible and easy to steal. In city crowds and especially on public transportation, pick-pockets are amazingly deft. Hold your bags tightly.

Making **photocopies of important documents** will allow you to replace them in case they are lost or stolen. Carry one copy separate from the documents and leave another copy at home. Safes are fine in higher-quality, more-expensive hotels where international reputation matters, but in guest houses, beware of leaving your valuables with the owner. While most are honest, it only takes one bad experience to ruin your trip. It is generally safer to carry your credit cards with you.

On **buses,** try to sit or stand in the front of the bus near the door. Keep a sharp eye out for fast-fingered pick-pockets, dastardly con artists, and conniving packs of hustlers masquerading as angel-faced children. Stay super-vigilant at bus and train stations, money-changing establishments, and other tourist-infested areas. Also, be wary in public telephone booths, and whisper your calling-card number.

Trains are notoriously easy spots for thieving. Professionals wait for tourists to fall asleep and then cart off everything they can. Steer clear of empty compartments and use caution when sizing up potential berth-mates. Try to reserve the top bunk when buying your ticket; the awkward height may deter thieves. When traveling in pairs, sleep in shifts or check on each other often. Snoozing outside can be dangerous—camping is recommended only in official, supervised campsites.

Wherever you stow your belongings, **keep your valuables on your person.** Consider this an iron-clad rule in the dorm-style rooms of some hostels. A trip to the shower can cost you a wallet or a camera. Sleep with your important worldly goods under your pillow, and put the straps of your bag around the leg of your bed. Lockers at bus and train stations are safe. You may need to bring your own padlock. Label all your belongings with your name, address, and home phone number.

■■■ HEALTH

PREPARATION H-EALTH

A hectic vacation can take its toll on your health, especially in an equatorial climate. Keeping your body strong will help ward off serious maladies; eat properly (protein and carbohydrates), drink lots of fluids, get plenty of sleep, and don't overexert yourself. To minimize the effects of jet lag, adjust to the region's schedule as soon as possible. During the hot season, take precautions against heatstroke and sunburn: drink lots of liquids, wear a hat and sunscreen, and stay inside during midday. Although shots have not been a prerequisite for visiting most of Southeast Asia for over a decade, bring an updated copy of your immunization records. You only need to get shots if you are coming from contaminated areas of the world. On the safe side, shots for typhoid, hepatitis A and B, Japanese encephalitis, rabies, and cholera are available. Undergoing an extensive innoculation regimen before your trip is necessary only if you will be doing extensive trekking in rural or heavily forested areas.

You may wish to assemble a **first-aid kit,** including: antiseptic soap, aspirin, decongestant, antihistamine, acetaminophen (Tylenol) to lower fever, diarrhea medicine (for the most common medical complaint of travelers in Southeast Asia), motion sickness medicine, Pepto-Bismol, anti-bacterial ointment, a thermometer, bandages, insect repellent, and a Swiss Army knife with tweezers and scissors.

Bring an up-to-date, detailed copy of any **medical prescriptions** you require (in legible form, stating the medication's trade name, manufacturer, chemical name, and dosage), and carry an ample supply of all medication—matching your prescription with a foreign equivalent is not always economical, easy, or safe. Distribute medication between carry-on and checked baggage in case one goes astray. Travelers with a chronic medical condition requiring regular treatment should consult their doctors before leaving. People with diabetes, for example, may need advice on adapting insulin levels for flights across multiple time zones. Bring a statement describing any pre-existing medical conditions, especially if you will be bringing insulin, syringes, or any narcotics.

Travelers with **corrective lenses** should bring an extra pair, or at least a copy of their prescription. If you wear contacts, carry a pair of glasses in case your eyes are tired or you lose a lens. Bring extra solutions, enzyme tablets, and eyedrops, as prices can be sky-high. For heat disinfection, you'll need outlet and low-voltage adapters; you may want to switch to chemical cleansers. Traveling does not always provide the most sanitary conditions for inserting and removing contact lenses—think ahead to avoid doing so on a lurching, crowded bemo.

In your passport, write the names of any people to be contacted in case of a medical emergency, and list any allergies or medical conditions to alert foreign doctors. Travelers with medical conditions that cannot be easily recognized (diabetes, epilepsy, heart conditions, etc.) may want to obtain a **Medic Alert Identification Tag.** This internationally recognized tag bracelet indicates the nature of the bearer's problem and provides the number of Medic Alert's 24-hour hotline. Attending medical personnel can call this number for information about the member's medical history. Lifetime membership (Medic Alert ID tag, annually updated wallet card) begins at US$35. Contact Medic Alert Foundation, P.O. Box 1009, Turlock, CA 95381-1009 or call the 24-hr. hotline (800) 432-5378. The **American Diabetes Association,** 1660 Duke St., Alexandria, VA 22314 (tel. (800) 232-3472) provides copies of an article "Travel and Diabetes" and diabetic ID cards—messages in 18 languages explaining the carrier's diabetic status. Contact your local ADA office for info.

Global Emergency Medical Services (GEMS) provides international medical assistance to travelers. Subscribers have immediate access 24 hours, 7 days a week, to an emergency room registered nurse who has on-line access to medical information that you provide, your primary physician, and a worldwide network of 6,000 English-speaking medical providers in 1,800 locations in 180 countries. Subscribers also receive a pocket-sized, personal, portable medical record that contains important medical information. For more info call (800) 860-1111, or write to them at 2001 Westside Drive, Suite 120, Alpharetta, GA 30201.

Let's Go should not be your only information source on common health problems while traveling, hiking, or camping. Consult your local bookstore for books on staying healthy at home or on the road, or send for the **American Red Cross' First-Aid and Safety Handbook** ($US14.95), purchasable by calling or writing to the American Red Cross, 61 Medford St., Somerville, MA 02143 (tel. (800) 564-1234). In the U.S., the American Red Cross offers many first-aid and CPR courses; these are well-taught and relatively inexpensive, so consider taking one before you go (contact your local American Red Cross office). Health info for American travelers can be obtained by calling the **U.S. Public Health Service Quarantine Station:** Chicago: (312) 894-2961 or (312) 894-2968; Honolulu: (808) 861-8531; Los Angeles: (310) 215-2365/6; Miami: (305) 526-2910; New York: (718) 553-1685; San Francisco:

(415) 876-2872; or Seattle: (206) 553-4519; or try the fax service in Atlanta (404) 332-4565.

The **International Association for Medical Assistance to Travelers (IAMAT)** provides ID cards, brochures, charts detailing tropical diseases and immunization requirements, tropical diseases, and climate and sanitation, and a worldwide directory of English-speaking physicians who will treat members for a set fee. Free membership. Contact chapters in the **U.S.,** 417 Center St., Lewiston, NY 14092 (tel. (716) 754-4883); **Canada,** 40 Regal Rd., Guelph, Ont., N1K 1B5 (tel. (519) 836-0102) or 1287 St. Clair Ave. West, Toronto, M6E 1B8 (tel. (416) 652-0137; fax (519) 836-3412); **New Zealand,** P.O. Box 5049, Christchurch 5; and **Switzerland,** 57 Voirets, 1212 Grand-Lancy-Geneva.

The **United States Centers for Disease Control** (based in Atlanta, Georgia) is an excellent source of general info on health for travelers around the world, and maintains an international travelers' hotline (tel. (404) 332-4559). If you have access to a fax, you can request printed information from the CDC fax info service; call the hotline from a phone and follow the prompts. (You will need the document code for the "disease directory," which provides the codes for info on a variety of diseases (including HIV/AIDS) and on travelers' health; it is 000004.) Or write directly to the Centers for Disease Control and Prevention (CDC), 1600 Clifton Rd. NE, Atlanta, GA 30333. To talk to a person, call (404) 639-3311, the public inquiry number. The CDC publishes the booklet Health Information for International Travelers (publication # HHS-CDC 90-8280, US$6), an annual global rundown on disease, immunization, and general health advice, including risks in particular countries. Request the booklet by calling the CDC's hotline or writing the **Superintendent of Documents,** U.S. Government Printing Office, Washington, DC 20402. (tel. (202) 783-3238).

WHAT AILS YOU?

Pay attention to the warning signals that your body may send you. You may feel fatigue and discomfort, not because of any specific illness, but simply because your body is adapting to a new climate, food, water quality, or pace when you arrive. Once you get going, some of the milder symptoms that you may safely ignore at home may be signs of something more serious; your increased exertion may wear you out and make you more susceptible to illness. The following paragraphs list some health problems you may encounter.

Water and Food

Purify any suspicious water by boiling it or treating it with iodine. Southeast Asia's tap water is not safe for drinking or teeth-brushing, even in the finest resort hotels. Except in Singapore, make it a rule not to drink the water. Bottled purified water is available virtually throughout the region. In restaurants, be sure that your bottled beverage has been opened in front of your eyes. Also, ask the waiter if the ice has been made from purified water. If you're not sure, insist on having your drink without ice. If there is no purified water, order a soft drink. Presumably, coffee and tea are all right to drink because the water has been boiled. With minor exceptions, food is safe to eat. Peel your own fruit and never eat raw food, especially shellfish or other seafood. Be sure that the cooked food you eat is still hot. Other than that, the only thing to worry about is getting acquainted with the spiciness of the food and the style of the cooking. Slowly adjusting yourself to the region's cooking will help ease the transition for your stomach. Have quick-energy, non-sugary foods with you to keep your strength up; you'll need plenty of protein and carbohydrates.

The Heat

Overwhelming heat can stop even the most ambitious adventurers dead in their tracks. It is very important to avoid heat exhaustion and heat stroke. The symptoms of **heat exhaustion** include fatigue, dizziness, headaches, and a feeling of lightness. The cause of heat exhaustion is, not surprisingly, dehydration. If you think you are suffering from heat exhaustion, get out of the sun and sit down in a cool area. Drink cool fluids and avoid physical exertion.

Heat stroke, which is very serious and sometimes fatal, takes heat exhaustion to a more dangerous level: high temperature, little or no sweating, flushed skin, unbearable headaches, delirium, convulsions, and unconsciousness. It is vital to get the victim of heat stroke to a hospital, but in the meantime, make sure to place wet towels on the victim and place him or her in a cool area; if that is absolutely impossible, at least be sure to continually fan the victim.

To prevent yourself from getting heat exhaustion or heat stroke, drink plenty of fluids; drinking the recommended eight glasses of water per day (minimum) should become second nature. Stay away from diuretics such as alcohol, coffee, and tea.

Other Maladies

Less debilitating than heatstroke, but still dangerous, is **sunburn.** Many outdoor wanderers are shocked to find themselves toasted to a crisp even though there is a thick cloud cover in their area. If you're prone to burning, carry sunscreen with you, and apply it liberally and often. Be wary of sunscreens of SPF (sun protection factor) higher than 15 or 20; higher ratings won't be of extra help, but will cost more. Wear a hat and sunglasses and a lightweight long-sleeved shirt. If you do get burned, drink lots of liquids; it'll cool you down and help your skin recover faster.

For some travelers, their visit to Southeast Asia will mean an introduction to **prickly heat,** a rash that develops when sweat is trapped under the skin. Particularly in men, the groin area is very susceptible to this rash. To alleviate itchiness, bathe often in cool water and sprinkle talcum powder over the affected area. Prickly heat is the reason why so many babies in the region are literally snow white from being covered in talcum powder.

Southeast Asia's moist, hot weather can irritate the skin in other ways as well. Various **fungal infections** (athlete's foot, jock itch, etc.) should be prevented by washing often and drying thoroughly. Wear loose-fitting clothes made of natural, absorbent fibers like cotton.

The most common problem for travelers is **diarrhea.** It has many causes, including food poisoning, bacteria, viruses, and simply adjusting to the new food. To prevent it from happening to you, wash your hands before eating, protect food from swarming flies, and stay away from scummy-looking restaurants. Drink and brush your teeth with safe water. For regular diarrhea without other symptoms, fluid loss and dehydration are the biggest concerns; lots of non-diuretic liquids are needed to combat the effects. Try a rehydration drink: a glass of safe water, ½ teaspoon of sugar, and a pinch of salt. Down several of these mixtures daily, rest, and wait for the illness to run its course. Give yourself time, but if you develop a fever or your symptoms don't go away after four or five days, you may have picked up a food- or water-borne disease. For severe cases, consult a doctor to see if antibiotics are necessary. A remedy like Immodium AD can help to relieve symptoms, but such remedies can also complicate serious infections; avoid anti-diarrheals if you suspect you have been exposed to contaminated food or water, which puts you at risk for cholera, typhoid fever, and other diseases.

Travelers to **higher altitudes** in north Laos or Vietnam must allow their bodies a couple of days to adjust to lower oxygen levels in the air before exerting themselves. If you're planning long alpine hikes, give yourself an adjustment period before you start out. Also be careful about alcohol, especially if you're used to U.S. standards for beer—many foreign brews and liquors pack more punch, and at high altitudes where there's less oxygen, any alcohol will do you in quickly.

Learn of regional hazards for forests and always be aware of snakes and other dangerous animals in the wild, even in well-traveled areas such as Angkor Wat. A more common problem is insects. **Insect bites,** particularly from mosquitoes, will plague your visit to Southeast Asia. Many (notably mosquitoes) are most active at night, and carry dangerous diseases (malaria, Lyme, and others—see below). Be sure to wear repellent, long sleeves, long pants, and socks. The most you can do for prevention is use an insect repellent containing **DEET** and wear pants and long-sleeved shirts, especially in wet or forested areas or while hiking and camping. The **CDC (Centers for Disease Control)** recommends using flying-insect-killing spray in sleeping quarters at night, and, for greater protection, spraying clothing and bedding with **permethrin,** an insect repellent licensed for use on clothing. Apply calamine lotion to insect bites to soothe the itching. More soothing, but harder to get on the road, is a bath with baking soda or oatmeal (Aveeno packages several oatmeal mixtures; just dump a half-cup or so of baking soda into a lukewarm bath). **Tiger balm** is a favorite Chinese method, and is readily available in pharmacies or from street vendors.

A fairly uncommon but irksome affliction are **parasites** (tapeworms, etc.). They can enter your body through your feet, so don't walk around barefoot outside. They can also find their way into your stomach through undercooked meat or dirty vegetables. **Giardia** is a serious parasitic disease contracted by ingesting untreated water from lakes or streams. A stool test from a doctor will uncover these critters, which can be flushed away with the help of medicine. Symptoms of general parasitic infections include swollen glands or lymph nodes, fever, rashes, itchiness, digestive complications, eye problems, and anemia. Don't let these nasty creatures shrivel you from the inside out—wear shoes, drink purified water, and avoid uncooked food.

Serious Infectious Diseases

Malaria is the most serious disease that travelers to Southeast Asia (minus Singapore) are likely to contract. It is caused by a parasite carried by the female *Anopheles* mosquito. The disease is prevalent in most tropical areas of the world, particularly in Southeast Asia. Because the incubation period for the disease varies, it could take up to weeks or months for an infected person to show any symptoms. When the disease does hit, the first symptoms include headaches, chills, general achiness, and fatigue. Next comes a very high fever and sweating. In some cases, vomiting and diarrhea also show up. If you think you may have malaria, go to the nearest hospital immediately and have a blood test. No precautions can fully protect you from contracting malaria. While traveling and for up to a year later, seek medical attention to treat any flu-like symptoms. Malaria can be fatal. Anemia, kidney failure, coma, and death can result if it goes untreated.

Malaria is generally found in heavily forested areas, which seldom see visitors from abroad. It is virtually but not entirely impossible to get malaria in urban cities, towns, and most villages. In Cambodia and Laos, however, the only "urban" areas are the capitals. The least danger exists in Thailand, Java, and Bali, where visitors are unlikely to be at risk, except near the dense forests around border areas. The CDC says that preventative medication against malaria is not necessary if you only visit relatively urban areas; however, as mentioned above, precautions should be taken to avoid being bitten by mosquitoes and to treat flu-like symptoms.

If you do decide to visit rural areas of the jungle, there are various forms of medication (no shots are available) that you can take to prevent you from catching malaria. Some doctors may prescribe mefloquine (sold under the name Lariam), taken in a 250mg tablet once a week, one week before leaving until four weeks after leaving. Mefloquine is a drug approved by the Centers for Disease Control and recommended for travel in most of Southeast Asia. The CDC warns that mefloquine should not be taken by pregnant women, children under 30 pounds, or people with a history of epilepsy, psychiatric disorder, or a known hypersensitivity to mefloquine. Carrying the drug Fansidar is often recommended, but it should only be used in the case of serious illness and when medical care is not readily available. For travelers in Thailand, the CDC recommends the drug doxycycline, taken in a 100mg dose every day including the day before entering the malarial area and continuing four weeks after leaving. Possible side effects include increased skin sensitivity to the sun; take precautions to combat this risk while using the drug. Women who take the drug for long periods may develop vaginal yeast infections. Pregnant women, children under 8, and those with a history of sensitivity to doxycycline should not take the drug. The best way to combat malaria is to listen to your physician, carry lots of insect repellent, and stay away from uninhabited jungle areas.

Mosquitoes also carry a virus that causes **dengue fever.** Dengue fever, found in most of the region, tends to be an urban malady. It exhibits symptoms similar to malaria, but certain characteristics differentiate it from its more famous cousin. Dengue fever has two stages and is characterized by its sudden onset. Stage one lasts from two to four days, and its symptoms include chills, high fever, severe headaches, swollen lymph nodes, muscle aches, and in some instances, a pink rash on the face. Then the fever quickly disappears, and profuse sweating follows. For 24 hours there is no fever, but then it suddenly appears with a rash all over the body. If you think you have contracted dengue fever, see a doctor, drink plenty of liquids, and remain in bed. It is also very important that you take acetaminophen (Tylenol) for dengue fever; do not take aspirin. Unfortunately, the only prevention for dengue fever is avoiding mosquitoes. Dengue mosquitoes bite during the day, unlike their nocturnal blood-sucking colleagues.

Rounding out the list of communicable diseases carried by mosquitoes is **Japanese encephalitis,** a disease just recently introduced into Southeast Asia. The Culex mosquito carries the virus for Japanese encephalitis, which is most prevalent in rural areas near rice fields and livestock pens, during the rainy season. Symptoms include flu-like symptoms—chills, headache, fever, vomiting, muscle fatigue—and delirium. Its symptoms rival those of malaria, but the fatality rate of Japanese encephalitis is much higher, so it is vital to admit yourself into a hospital as soon as any symptoms arise. A vaccine, JE-VAX, is available; you can be vaccinated against this disease with a three-shot series given a week apart or on a longer, safer schedule. The vaccine is effective for about a year. Serious side-effects have been associated with the vaccine, and so travelers should seriously consider whether it is necessary. The CDC claims that there is a very low chance that a traveler will be infected if proper precautions—using mosquito repellents containing DEET, sleeping under bednets, etc.—are taken.

Every year, a **cholera** epidemic makes its way east from India and Bangladesh, landing around the end of the cool season, just in time for summer. Except for Hong Kong and Singapore, most of Southeast Asia is vulnerable to outbreaks (Thailand is perhaps the least susceptible). Cholera is an acute intestinal bacteria-borne infection that works quickly and with murderous intent. The symptoms—explosive and interminable diarrhea, unstoppable vomiting, dehydration, muscle cramps, and lethargy—come suddenly, and unless quickly treated, prove fatal in a short time. It is vital for the cholera-infected to immediately find a hospital. In the meantime, the patient should guzzle liquids to battle dehydration. Cholera is passed from person to person like wildfire through contaminated food or water, human waste, and unsanitary cooking methods. The CDC recommends that travelers near infected areas peel their own fruit and eat only thoroughly cooked food.

Vaccinations are available for cholera (and typhoid fever in one shot), but they are only 50% effective in preventing illness for the first three to six months after vaccination. The CDC recommends vaccination for people with stomach ulcers, those who use anti-acid therapy, and those who will be living in unsanitary conditions in epidemic areas.

Typhoid fever, caused by a bacterium, is spread through contaminated food, water, and human waste, and through contact with an infected person. Symptoms of the disease gradually creep up on the victim. For the first week or so, a fever slowly rises, sometimes accompanied by vomiting and diarrhea. Next, a rash may appear, and delirium and dehydration seize the victim. Headaches, fatigue, loss of appetite, and constipation are also associated symptoms. Untreated, the patient may develop life-threatening pneumonia. As with other dangerous, communicable diseases, it is imperative to find quick medical care for someone with typhoid fever.

Typhoid fever is treatable with antibiotics, and a vaccine is available, although it is only 70% effective. The CDC recommends vaccination for those traveling off the beaten tourism paths, that is, those going to small cities or towns, or those staying longer than six weeks. Typhoid fever is a danger for travelers—drink only bottled or boiled water and eat only thoroughly cooked food to lower the risk of infection.

Prevalent in areas with poor sanitation, **hepatitis A** and **hepatitis B** are both caused by viruses attacking the liver. Hepatitis A, like typhoid fever, is spread through the contamination of water and food with viruses present in human feces. It is therefore important to be wary of uncooked foods that may have been contaminated during handling, such as fresh fruits and vegetables. It can also be transmitted from direct person-to-person contact. Fatigue, vomiting, nausea, fever, loss of appetite, dark urine, jaundice, light stools, and aches and pains are among the symptoms. At particular risk are travelers, especially those visiting rural areas, coming into close contact with local people, or eating in settings with poor sanitation. Hepatitis B, in contrast, is spread through the transfer of bodily fluids, such as blood, semen, and saliva, from one person to another. Its incubation period varies and can be much longer than the 30-day incubation period of hepatitis A. Thus, a person may not begin having symptoms until many years after infection.

Hepatitis has no known cure, but vaccinations are available to protect travelers against both types of hepatitis. Protection from hepatitis A requires a shot of immune globulin, which is given about a week before departure and after all other immunizations have been completed. For protection against hepatitis B, a three-shot series given in six months is required. The CDC recommends the hepatitis B vaccinations for health-care workers, sexually active travelers, long-term visitors who will have extensive contact with the local population, and anyone planning on seeking any medical treatment while in Southeast Asia, as there is a high risk for hepatitis B in the region.

Visitors should keep in mind that **rabies** is a common but little-publicized disease in Southeast Asia. Transmitted through the saliva of infected animals, it is fatal if not treated. Avoid close contact with other animals, especially strays. If you are bitten by an animal, washing the wound thoroughly with soap and water may reduce the chance of infection. If you suspect the animal is rabid, see a doctor. Once you begin having symptoms of rabies (thirst, muscle spasms), the disease is in its terminal stage, so it is absolutely necessary to act quickly if you think that you have been bitten by a rabid animal. First, the animal should be found, if possible, so that tests can ascertain whether the animal does indeed have rabies. Second, you should be admitted to a hospital, where doctors can begin giving you the six shots that will protect you from getting the disease. If you plan on traveling to an area that may have a heavy concentration of rabid animals (such as bats or wild dogs), there are three shots you should get; it takes one year to receive them in series.

Schistosomiasis is an extremely common infection caused when the larvae of the flatworm penetrate the skin. The larvae are found in fresh water, and can penetrate unbroken skin. Swimming in fresh water, especially in rural areas, should be avoided. If your skin is exposed to untreated water, the CDC recommends immediate and vigorous rubbing with a towel and/or the application of rubbing alcohol to reduce the risk of infection. If infected, you may notice an itchy localized rash; later symptoms include fever, fatigue, painful urination, diarrhea, loss of appetite, night sweats, and a hive-like rash on the body. Known foci for Schistosomiasis are east of Kuala Lumpur in Malaysia, east Cambodia and the border with Laos, as well as the Mekong River in both, the Thai border with Laos, and a few villages in Nakhon Si Thammarat province in Thailand. Schistosomiasis can be treated with drugs.

Women's Health

Women traveling in unsanitary conditions are vulnerable to **urinary tract** and **bladder infections** (cystitis), common and severely uncomfortable bacterial diseases that cause a burning sensation and painful (sometimes frequent) urination. A strong antibiotic usually gets rid of the symptoms within a couple of days. Other recommendations are to drink enormous amounts of vitamin C-rich juice and plenty of water, and to urinate frequently. Untreated bladder infections can become very serious, leading to kidney infections or pelvic inflammatory disease. Treat an infection the best you can while on the road; if it persists, see a doctor and definitely check with one when you get home. If you are prone to vaginal **yeast infections** or thrush, take an over-the-counter medication along with you, as treatments may not be readily available elsewhere.

Sanitary napkins and tampons are sometimes hard to find overseas; your preferred brands may not be available, so it is advisable to bring your own. O.B. brand tampons have minimal packaging and occupy less space in baggage. Refer to *The Handbook for Women Travellers* by Maggie and Gemma Moss or see the women's health guide *Our Bodies, Our Selves,* published by the Boston Women's Health Collective, for more extensive information specific to women's health on the road.

THE ABC'S OF STDS

While most travelers venture to Southeast Asia to see the sights, some go to the region seeking pleasure of a different sort. These travelers, particularly foreign males, may never get to see the temples of Luang Prabang or the steps of Borobudur. Instead, they see the crusty streets of Patpong and the bowels of quasi-legal bars, massage parlors, and discotheques. Above and beyond the fact that prostitution is exploitative and illegal, individuals emerging from their night have very likely contracted one of the venereal diseases that infect the prostitutes they visit. Every year, VD clinics make a killing on visitors who need medical help during their stay.

Hepatitis B is discussed above. **Syphilis** is a common STD spread through the exchange of infected bodily fluids during sexual intercourse. If left untreated, syphilis travels through three stages. In the first stage, which generally appears around three weeks after infection, soft cankers appear on the genitals, accompanied by enlarged lymph nodes in the region. Three weeks later, the second stage appears, bringing fever, rashes, painful joints, and more cankers and enlarged lymph nodes. If the sufferer still does not seek medical help, the disease enters its third stage, which lasts indefinitely—a very long period of apparent remission. Many years later, a sudden onset of inflammation in the heart and central nervous system occurs and normally leads to death. Syphilis can be treated and cured with penicillin.

Gonorrhea is another widespread and pestilent STD. It is transmitted from person to person like syphilis, but its incubation period is shorter, lasting anywhere from three to seven days. Symptoms include a discharge of pus and infection of the urethra. If left untreated, gonorrhea causes considerable discomfort. The disease can be treated with penicillin. Another STD, **chlamydia,** has symptoms identical to those of gonorrhea, but is resistant to penicillin treatment.

Herpes, caused by a virus, is a terribly discomforting STD for which there is no known cure. At the end of the 2-10-day incubation period, lesions begin to form at the site of the infection, whether it be the genital area, the mouth, or the hand. Protected sex does not necessarily keep contact with infected areas from occurring. The only way to be sure is to check for sores before touching the other individual and to pick sexual partners carefully. Lesions can eventually go away, but often recur throughout one's lifetime.

For more information call the **U.S. Center for Disease Control's STDs Hotline,** (800) 227-8922. Open Mon.-Fri. 8am-11pm, Eastern Time.

HIV and AIDS

AIDS is a growing problem in Southeast Asia. Some estimates put the proportion of HIV-positive prostitutes still working the bars and massage parlors of Bangkok at 50%. Tragically, most infected prostitutes and their customers are not aware that they carry the HIV virus. Most information on AIDS in Southeast Asia is on Thailand, for two reasons: Thailand's prostitution problem is internationally realized, and the Thai government acknowledges and is making efforts to combat the disease. In other areas, the relevant information about the population is minimal or non-existent. AIDS is found throughout Southeast Asia, and the CDC claims that heterosexual contact is the primary mode of transmission there. The World Health

Organization estimates that in Southeast Asia there are 2.5 million HIV-infected persons and 250,000 AIDS cases; only 13,000 of those are in Thailand.

Regardless of travel destination, all travelers should know the facts about HIV, the human immunodeficiency virus that causes AIDS. One of the leading causes of death world-wide, Acquired Immune Deficiency Syndrome (AIDS) is a term used to describe people who are HIV positive and whose immune systems are severely impaired. People with AIDS have difficulty fighting off even minor illnesses (like the common cold), and frequently catch opportunistic infections, diseases from which people with normally functioning immune systems are protected. **While not everyone who is HIV positive has AIDS, any person who is HIV positive can transmit this virus,** which impairs the immune system and ultimately leads to death.

The World Health Organization (WHO) estimates that 4.5 million people worldwide are living with AIDS, and about 13 million people are infected with HIV. Well over 90% of adults newly infected with HIV acquired their infection through heterosexual sex. While relatively few women were HIV positive 10 years ago, women now represent 50% of all new HIV infections. By the year 2000, the WHO estimates, the number of AIDS cases worldwide will increase to 20 million, with between 30 and 40 million people infected with HIV. HIV spreads through sexual contact, needle-sharing, and blood transfusions. The most common mode of transmission is unprotected anal or vaginal intercourse. If infected blood, semen, vaginal secretions, or breast milk come into contact with the blood of a noninfected person, transmission may occur.

The best advice is to follow all the precautions you should follow at home (always use a condom with spermicide, avoid sex with strangers or with people who engage in high-risk behavior such as IV drug use or promiscuous or unprotected sex), and stay away from prostitutes. There is no guarantee that prostitutes in need of money will not risk infecting the unwitting foreigner who is just passing through the area. Keep in mind that there is no assurance that any given person is not infected with HIV. Often an infected person exhibits no symptoms for up to 10 years. It is not until the final stage of the disease that the patient has lost a considerable amount of the immunity to diseases normally found in healthy human beings. The final stage of AIDS is terminal, and there is no cure in sight. When having sex, always assume that the other person is HIV positive.

Condoms help prevent the transmission of the virus, but only abstinence is 100% effective. Unprotected (without a condom) anal intercourse is believed to be the most risky form of sexual contact; vaginal intercourse follows, and then oral sex. Safe sex is sex in which none of your partner's potentially infected blood or sexual fluids come into contact with any of your blood or mucous membranes. Safe means using a latex condom and water-based lubricant every time you have intercourse. Condoms made of natural materials, like lambskin, *do not protect against transmission of HIV* because they are more porous than latex. Even if semen can't get through these pores, HIV can. Oil-based lubricants (like Vaseline) destroy the integrity of latex, opening the pores wider and rendering them useless in the prevention of HIV or even causing them to tear. It may not always be easy to buy condoms, and when it is, they may not be of a very high-quality. For this reason, it's a good idea to take a supply of good-quality western-made condoms with you before you depart. Condoms treated with spermicide are thought to provide extra protection. They should be stored in a cool, dark place. Heat deteriorates condoms; never carry them in a wallet or pants' pocket. A new condom should be used for each and every act of sexual intercourse in which semen, vaginal fluids or blood may be transmitted.

Never share intravenous drug, tattooing, or other needles because this is an easy way to transmit the virus blood to blood. Needles should be thoroughly flushed three times with soapy water, three times with bleach, and three more times with soapy water. If bleach is unavailable, washing needles with soapy water alone is the next best thing.

If you think you might have been exposed to HIV, you might want to get an HIV Antibody Test. This test detects only the presence of HIV antibodies, not the virus itself. Once infection has occurred, there is a window period of 3 to 6 months during which the body reacts to the virus and begins to make the antibodies that the test detects. For this reason, it makes no sense to get tested until at least 3 to 6 months after the suspect incident.

For more information on AIDS, call the **U.S. Center for Disease Control's 24-hour Hotline** at (800) 342-2437. (TTY (800) 243-7889, Mon-Fri 10am-10pm; Spanish (800) 344-7332, daily 8am-2am.)

The **World Health Organization** (tel. (202) 861-3200) provides statistics on AIDS internationally. Call the U.S. State Department (tel. (202) 647-1488; fax 647-3000); modem lovers may consult the 24-hr. electronic bulletin board at (202) 647-9225) for country-specific restrictions for HIV-positive travelers. Or write to the Bureau of Consular Affairs, #6831, Dept. of State, Washington, D.C. 20520. In Europe, call 41 22 791 46 73 (Switzerland) or the World Health Organization, Attn.: Global Program on AIDS, 20 Avenue Appia, 1211 Geneva 27, Switzerland.

For more info of the status of AIDS in Thailand, see Thailand Essentials: "Prostitution and AIDS" on page 283.

GETTING HELP

Tourist centers are full of pharmacies and drugstores selling everything from cough drops to condoms, and many pharmacists are competent enough in English to understand what you need. The majority of pharmacies will fill a prescription with a note from a doctor. Few pharmacies are open 24 hours. In an emergency, head to the nearest major hospital, which is almost certainly open all night and has an in-house pharmacy.

Outside the major tourist centers, the going is a bit rougher, although every provincial capital should have at least one small drug store. Serious problems most typically arise for those who are deep in the jungle or at a small village outpost, as the pharmacy is likely to be replaced by an herbal medicine store.

In those remote "get-away-from-it-all" towns and other un-touristed areas, try to get someone who speaks the local language to call for you if you need help, since the language barrier may otherwise be insurmountable. You might try dialing the police emergency number or arrange other transportation to the hospital. Direct phone lines are often unavailable in guest houses. High-end hotels often have English-speaking staff, direct phone lines, and transportation. Those seeking referrals should contact their embassy; these diplomatic missions often have lists of (high-priced) English-speaking doctors for the major tourist areas.

■■■ INSURANCE

Insurance is like contraception: you only really want it when it's too late. Standard **medical insurance** (especially university policies) often covers costs incurred abroad; beware of unnecessary coverage. **Medicare's** foreign travel coverage is limited and is valid only in Canada and Mexico. Canadians are protected by their home province's health insurance plan up to 90 days after leaving the country: check with the provincial Ministry of Health or Health Plan Headquarters. Australia has Reciprocal Health Care Agreements (RHCAs) with several countries; when traveling in these nations Australians are entitled to many of the services they would receive at home. The Commonwealth Department of Human Services and Health can provide more information. **Homeowners' insurance** often covers theft during travel. Homeowners are generally covered against loss of travel documents (passport, plane ticket, railpass, etc.) up to $500.

Buying an **International Student or Teacher ID Card** in the U.S. provides US$3000 worth of accident and illness insurance and US$100 per day up to 60 days of hospitalization while the card is valid, up to US$10,000 for emergency medical evacuation, as well as access to a toll-free Traveler's Assistance hotline whose multilingual staff provides help in medical, legal, and financial emergencies abroad (tel. (800) 626-2427 in the U.S.; from abroad call collect (713) 267-2525). **Council** offers an inexpensive Trip-Safe plan, with options covering medical treatment and hospitalization, accidents, baggage loss, and even charter flights missed due to illness. **STA** offers a more expensive, more comprehensive plan. (See "Budget Travel Agencies" on page 45.) Some **credit card** companies, including American Express, provide automatic car-rental and flight insurance on purchases made with the card.

Insurance companies usually require a copy of the police report for thefts, or evidence of having paid medical expenses (doctor's statements, receipts) before they will honor a claim, and may have time limits for reimbursement. Have all documents written in English to avoid possible translating fees. Always carry policy numbers and proof of insurance. If your coverage does not include on-the-spot payments or cash transferrals, budget for emergencies. Most of the carriers listed below have 24-hr. hotlines.

Access America, 6600 West Broad St., PO Box 11188, Richmond VA, 23230 (tel. (800) 284-8300; fax (804) 673-1491). Covers trip cancellation/interruption, on-the-spot hospital admittance costs, emergency medical evacuation, sickness, and baggage loss. 24-hr. hotline.

ARM Coverage, Inc./Carefree Travel Insurance, 100 Garden City Plaza, P.O. Box 9366, Garden City, NY, 11530-9366 (tel. (800) 323-3149 or (516) 294-0220; fax (516) 294-1821). Offers two comprehensive packages including coverage for trip delay, accidents, sickness, baggage loss, bag delay, accidental death and dismemberment, and travel supplier insolvency. Trip cancellation/interruption may be purchased separately for US$5.50 per US$100 of coverage. 24-hr. hotline.

Globalcare Travel Insurance, 220 Broadway, Lynnfield MA, 01940 (tel. (800) 821-2488; fax (617) 592-7720). Complete medical, legal, emergency, and travel-related services. On-the-spot payments and special student programs, including benefits for trip cancellation and interruption.

Travel Assistance International, by Worldwide Assistance Services, Inc., 1133 15th St., NW, Suite 400, Washington, DC 20005-2710 (tel. (800) 821-2828 or

Speak the Language When You Get There!

You *can*...with Audio-Forum's famous self-study audio-cassette courses. Choose your own time, pace, and place to learn the language, and save hundreds of dollars compared with the cost of a private language school.

You'll learn naturally by listening to the cassettes (while driving, jogging, or whatever) and repeating during the pauses on the tape. By the end of the course, you'll be learning and speaking comfortably in your new language.

We are pleased to offer these comprehensive courses. All feature native speakers.

- ☐ **Khmer:** 19 cassettes and 453-page text, $225.
- ☐ **Survival Indonesian:** 3 cassettes and 56-page text, $55.
- ☐ **Lao:** 16 cassettes and 242-page text, $225.
- ☐ **Survival Malay:** 3 cassettes and 56-page text, $55.
- ☐ **Basic Thai:** 12 cassettes and 427-page text, $195.
- ☐ **Basic Vietnamese:** 18 cassettes and 328-page text, $225.

There is no risk. We offer a full 3-week money-back guarantee. Our free 60-page *Whole World Language Catalog* offers courses in 92 languages. Call toll-free **1-800-243-1234**, Fax (203) 453-9774, e-mail: 74537.550@compuserve.com, or write:

Audio-Forum
Room F103, 96 Broad Street,
Guilford, CT 06437 U.S.A. • (203) 453-9794

(202) 828-5894; fax (202) 331-1530). TAI provides its members with a 24-hr. hotline for emergencies and referrals. Their year-long frequent traveler package ($226) includes medical and travel insurance, financial assistance, and help in replacing lost documents.

Travel Guard International, 1145 Clark St., Stevens Point, WI 54481 (tel. (800) 826-1300 or (715) 345-0505; fax (715) 345-0525). Comprehensive insurance programs starting at $44. Programs cover trip cancellation and interruption, bankruptcy and financial default, lost luggage, medical coverage abroad, emergency assistance, and accidental death. 24-hr. hotline.

Travel Insured International, Inc., 52-S Oakland Ave., P.O. Box 280568, East Hartford, CT 06128-0568 (tel. (800) 243-3174; fax (203) 528-8005). Insurance against accident, baggage loss, sickness, trip cancellation/interruption, travel delay, and default. Covers emergency medical evacuation and automatic flight insurance.

Wallach and Company, Inc., 107 West Federal St., P.O. Box 480, Middleburg, VA 22117-0480 (tel. (800) 237-6615; fax (703) 687-3172). Comprehensive medical insurance including evacuation and repatriation of remains and direct payment of claims to providers of services. Other optional coverages available. 24-hr. toll-free international assistance.

■■■ ALTERNATIVES TO TOURISM

Call organizations and get information before ordering their expensive books. Most places specialize in study and work in Europe, and Southeast Asia is only a small portion of their catalogue. Make sure that sufficient opportunities are available before spending your money. If you are traveling to Thailand or Indonesia, there may be excellent organizations and structured programs that provide what you are looking for; for other countries in the region you may need a bit more personal initiative.

WORK

Consider **teaching English.** Post a sign in markets or learning centers stating that you are a native speaker, and scan the classifieds of local newspapers, where residents often advertise for language instruction. Various organizations in the U.S. will place you in a (low-paying) teaching job, but securing a position will require patience and legwork, since teaching English abroad has become enormously popular in recent years. Professional English-teaching positions are harder to get; most schools require at least a bachelor's degree and training in teaching English as a foreign language.

Addison-Wesley, Jacob Way, Reading, MA 01867 (tel. (800) 322-1377 for college, (800) 552-2259 for high school). Publishes *International Jobs: Where They Are, How to Get Them* (US$14.95).

Council publishes *Work, Study, Travel Abroad: The Whole World Handbook,* which covers all continents and includes summer and long-term work abroad. Includes a list of specific programs. Published by St. Martin's Press (US$13.95). Write to CIEE-Pubs. Dept., 205 E. 42nd St., New York, NY 10017-5706.

Office of Overseas Schools, A/OS Room 245, SA-29, Dept. of State, Washington, DC 20522-2902 (tel. (703) 875-7800). Teaching jobs abroad.

Transitions Abroad Publishing, Inc., 18 Hulst Rd., P.O. Box 1300, Amherst, MA 01004 (tel./fax (800) 293-0373); publishes a bi-monthly magazine listing all kinds of opportunities and printed resources for those seeking to study, work, or travel abroad. Study fin and sperm whales in the Ligurian Sea! Be an Au Pair! The possibilities are almost endless. They also publish an *Alternative Travel Planner,* a truly exhaustive listing of information for the "active international traveler." For subscriptions (USA US$19.95 for 6 issues, Canada US$26, other countries US$38), contact them at *Transitions Abroad,* Dept. TRA, Box 3000, Denville, NJ 07834.

World Trade Academy Press, Suite 509, 50 E. 42nd St., New York, NY 10017-5480 (tel. (212) 697-4999). Publishes *Looking for Employment in Foreign Countries* (US$16.50) which gives information on federal, commercial, and volunteer jobs abroad and advice on resumes and interviews. Last updated in 1992. Thailand, Indonesia, Hong Kong, Malaysia, and Singapore.

STUDY

Foreign study seems a fail-proof good time. Programs vary tremendously in expense, academic quality, living conditions, degree of contact with local students, and exposure to the local culture and language. Most American undergraduates enroll in programs sponsored by domestic universities, and many colleges staff offices give advice and information on study abroad. Take advantage of these counselors and put in some hours in their libraries.

American Field Service (AFS), 3rd Fl., 220 E. 42nd St., New York, NY 10017 (tel. (212) 949-4242; in Springfield (800) 876-2377). Summer, semester, and year-long homestay exchange programs for high school students. Hong Kong, Indonesia, or Thailand.

American Institute for Foreign Study, College Division, 102 Greenwich Ave., Greenwich, CT 06830 (tel. (800) 727-2437; for high school students (800) 888-2247). Organizes year, semester, quarter, and summer programs for high school and college study in foreign universities. Open to adults. Minority and merit scholarships available. Programs in Hong Kong.

Institute of International Education Books (IIE Books), 809 United Nations Plaza, New York, NY 10017-3580 (tel. (212) 984-5413; fax (212) 984-5358). Puts out several reference books on study abroad. *Academic Year Abroad* (US$42 plus US$4 shipping) and *Vacation Study Abroad* (US$37 plus US$4) detail over 3800 programs offered by US colleges and universities overseas. Also offers the free pamphlet *Basic Facts on Foreign Study* and operates the International Education Information Center at the UN Plaza address, open Tues.-Fri. 11am-3:45pm. Distributes several books published by the **Central Bureau for Educational**

TRAVEL AND TEACH ENGLISH

- The Boston TEFL Teaching Certificate Course
- No Second Language Necessary
- No Teaching Experience Required
- One-month Intensive or Three-month Part-Time
- Internship with Foreign Students
- Global Placement Assistance

WORLDWIDE TEACHERS
DEVELOPMENT INSTITUTE
266 Beacon Street • Boston, MA 02116
1-800-875-5564

Visits and Exchanges in the UK, including *Study Holidays, Working Holidays,* and *Home from Home* (all CB books are US$23).

School for International Training, College Semester Abroad Admissions, Kipling Rd., P.O. Box 676, Battleboro, VT 05302 (tel. (800) 336-1616 or (802) 258-3279). Runs semester-long programs featuring cultural orientation, intensive language study, homestay, and field and independent study. Programs cost US$8200-10,300, all expenses included. Financial aid available and US financial aid is transferable. Most US colleges will transfer credit for semester work done abroad. Indonesia, Thailand, and Vietnam.

U.S. Servas Committee, 11 John Street, Suite #407, New York, NY 10038-4009 (tel. (212) 267-0252; fax (212) 267-0292; contact Nori Jaffer-Touré), is an international cooperative system devoted to promoting peace and understanding by providing opportunities for more personal contacts among people of diverse cultures. Travelers are invited to share life in hosts' homes in over 100 countries. Guests should contact hosts in advance and be prepared to follow the household routine. Homestays are two nights. Prospective travelers must submit an application with references, have an interview, and pay a membership fee of US$55, plus a US$25 deposit for up to five host lists which provide a short description of each host member. Servas is a non-profit organization and no money passes between traveler and host.

World Learning, Inc., Summer Abroad, P.O. Box 676, Battleboro, VT 05302 (tel. (800) 345-2929 or (802) 257-7751). Founded in 1932 as The U.S. Experiment in International Living, it offers high school programs in Thailand and language-training programs with elective homestays. Programs are 4-6 weeks long. Positions as group leaders are available worldwide if you are over 24, have previous in-country experience, and are fluent in the language. Indonesia, Thailand, and Vietnam.

VOLUNTEERING

Volunteering is a great opportunity to meet new people, learn a new language and culture, and help people who are less fortunate than yourself. In some instances,

From the corporate offices of Tokyo to the beaches of Bali...

TEACH ENGLISH IN FOREIGN COUNTRIES

No Second Language Necessary

- TEFL Teaching Certificate Course
- One-month Intensive or Three-month Part-Time
- Practical Training with Foreign Students
- European Direct Method
- Lifetime Job Assistance
- Student Housing Available Transworld Guest House

SUE E. MACKARNESS
Founder/Trainer
23 years in EFL/ESL
14 Years Training Teachers
Taught in 15 Countries

TRANSWORLD TEACHERS
683 Sutter Street, San Francisco, CA 94102

1-800-241-8071

America's Leading TEFL Training School

Hotline: 415-995-2554
E-mail: Trnsworld@aol.com

San Francisco
Prague

you may even receive room and board for your work. *Volunteer! The Comprehensive Guide to Voluntary Service in the U.S. and Abroad* ($8.95), offers advice and listings and is available from Council.

Archaeological Institute of America, 675 Commonwealth Ave., Boston, MA 02215 (tel. (617) 353-9361), puts out the Archaeological Fieldwork Opportunities Bulletin (US$11 plus $4), which lists over 200 field sites throughout the world. In the past, there have been opportunities for volunteer work at sites in Thailand. For a copy of the 1996 guide, contact Kendal Hunt Pub. (tel. (800) 228-0810).

Peace Corps, 1990 K St., NW, Washington, DC 20526 (tel. (800) 424-8580), has been in Thailand for over 30 years. Currently, there are about 200 volunteers in Thailand, with at least one in each province. Peace Corps offers volunteering opportunities in education, health, and agriculture. Joining means fulfilling a two-year commitment. The Thai government provides housing over that time, and volunteers receive pay comparable to that of Thai co-workers.

Volunteers for Peace, 43 Tiffany Rd., Belmont, VT 05730 (tel. (802) 259-2759; fax 259-2922). A non-profit organization that arranges for speedy placement in over 800 locations (10- to 15-people workcamps) in over 60 countries, including Thailand and Indonesia. Gives the most complete and up-to-date listings in the annual *International Workcamp Directory* (US$12). Registration fee US$150. Some workcamps are open to 16 and 17 year olds for US$175. Free newsletter.

WorldTeach, Harvard Institute for International Development, 1 Eliot St., Cambridge, MA 02138, U.S.A. (tel. (617) 495-5527). A non-profit social service program that has placed volunteers as teachers in Thailand since 1989. WorldTeach Thailand works with three departments of the Ministry of Education and places volunteers at the invitation of individual school directors and English departments. Volunteering opportunities are available in Bangkok and elsewhere. Charges a participation fee of about US$3900 that covers travel costs, health insurance, and lodging. Volunteers are required to have a bachelor's degree.

■■■ TRAVELING ALONE

Whenever possible, *Let's Go* lists emergency, police, and consulate numbers in every large city; consult them if you encounter difficulties. The biggest threats to those traveling alone are robbery and theft. However, with some common sense and extra precautions, this danger can be greatly reduced. People traveling alone should take public transportation, if possible, and never hitch rides. Lone travelers should also inspect all hotel rooms, moving elsewhere if the locks of a particular hotel seem suspect. Be very careful about hooking up with strangers. Pay special attention to the information in the Safety section above.

The lone traveler should not travel to any highly rural areas without the assistance of a guide. Every year, news stories emerge of the solo foreign traveler found robbed and killed in some remote jungle area or simply never being found. If you wish to trek, make sure that you sign up for a tour with a reputable trekking agency.

■■■ WOMEN TRAVELERS

Women exploring any area on their own inevitably face additional safety concerns. In all situations it is best to trust your instincts: if you'd feel better somewhere else, don't hesitate to move on. Avoid late-night walks; in Muslim countries the law prohibits Muslim women from walking alone at night. Although this law does not technically apply to westerners, expect strange looks and even comments or severe harassment. Remember that hitching is never safe for lone women, or even for two women traveling together. Choose train compartments occupied by other women or couples. In some parts of the region, women (foreign or local) are frequently beset by unwanted and tenacious followers. Exercise caution without feeling that you must avoid all local men.

Don't hesitate to seek out a police officer or a passerby if you are being harassed. Memorize the emergency numbers in the countries you visit, and always carry change for the phone and enough extra money for a bus or taxi. Carry a whistle or an airhorn on your keychain, and don't hesitate to use it in an emergency. A Model Mugging course (see "Safety" on page 22) will not only prepare you for a potential mugging, but also raise your confidence and your awareness of your surroundings. All of these warnings and suggestions should not discourage women from traveling alone. Don't take unnecessary risks, but don't lose your spirit of adventure either.

Invest in secure accommodations, particularly family-run guest houses with rooms that lock from the inside. Dress modestly to avoid potential problems. Though you may dress more liberally in Bangkok and other major cities, stay away from revealing tank tops and short shorts once out of town. In Muslim countries, you should dress fairly modestly even in the city, although locals do not expect to see westerners completely covered; shawls or veils would probably be overdoing it. To avoid offending the locals, particularly in smaller villages, you may wish to cover your knees with a long skirt and be sure to wear a bra. You may be harassed no matter how you're dressed. Wearing a wedding ring may discourage unwelcome suitors. Look as if you know where you're going (even when you don't) and ask women or couples for directions if you're lost or feel uncomfortable. Your best answer to verbal harassment is no answer at all (a reaction is what the harasser wants).

It has been reported that small-town police are sometimes not terribly enlightened about women. They, as well as some other men, may assume that a women traveling alone is looking for sex. Don't hesitate to call the police in an emergency, but don't place all your trust in them, particularly in un-touristed areas.

Some of the following organizations and publications may be useful.

Women Going Places, a women's travel and resource guide emphasizing women-owned enterprises. Geared toward lesbians, but offers advice appropriate for all women. US$14. Available from Inland Book Company, P.O. Box 120261, East Haven, CT 06512 (tel. (203) 467-4257) or order from a bookstore.

The Handbook for Women Travelers (£8.99), by Maggie and Gemma Moss. Encyclopedic and well-written. Contact Piaktus Books, 5 Windmill St., London, W1P 1HF, England (tel. (171) 631-0710).

A Journey of One's Own: Uncommon Advice for the Independent Woman Traveler by Thalia Zepatos (Eighth Mountain Press, US$14.95). Interesting and full of good advice, plus a specific and manageable bibliography of books and resources.

Wander Women, 136 N. Grand Ave #237, West Covina, CA 91791 (tel. (818) 966-8857). A travel and adventure networking organization for women over 40. Publishes the quarterly newsletter *Journal 'n Footnotes*. Membership fee is US$29 per year.

Women Travel: Adventures, Advice & Experience, by Miranda Davies and Natania Jansz (Penguin US$12.95). Has info on specific foreign countries plus a decent bibliography and resource index.

■■■ SENIOR TRAVELERS

AARP (American Association of Retired Persons), 601 E St., NW, Washington, DC 20049 (tel. (202) 434-2277). Members 50 and over receive benefits and services including the AARP Motoring Plan from Amoco (tel. (800) 334-3300) as well as discounts on lodging, car rental, and sight-seeing. Annual fee: US$8 per couple; US$75/lifetime membership.

Gateway Books, 2023 Clemens Road, Oakland, CA 94602, (tel. (510) 530-0299; fax (510) 530-0497). Publishes *Get Up and Go: A Guide for the Mature Traveler* (US$10.95) and *Adventures Abroad* (US$12.95), which offer general hints for the budget-conscious senior considering a long stay or even retiring abroad. For credit card orders call (800)-669-0773.

Pilot Books, 103 Cooper St., Babylon, NY 11702 (tel. (516) 422-2225). Publishes *The International Health Guide for Senior Citizens* (US$4.95, postage $1).

Unbelievably Good Deals and Great Adventures That You Absolutely Can't Get Unless You're Over 50, by Joan Rattner Heilman. After you finish reading the title page, check inside for some great tips on senior discounts and the like. Contemporary Books, US$7.95.

■■■ BISEXUAL, GAY, AND LESBIAN TRAVELERS

Attitudes regarding sexual orientation vary substantially across Southeast Asia. See the Essentials sections of each country for more detailed descriptions. Information for Vietnam, Laos, and Cambodia is practically non-existent. Travelers to these three countries should keep in mind that the people here are very conservative and religious, and often disapprove public displays of affection, heterosexuals included. The following publications are also useful sources.

Ferrari Publications, Inc., P.O. Box 37887, Phoenix, AZ 85069, (tel. (602) 863-2408). Publishers of Ferrari's *Places of Interest* (US$16), *Ferrari's Places for Men* (US$15), *Ferrari's Places for Women* (US$13), and *Inn Places: US and Worldwide Gay Accommodations* (US$16). Available in bookstores or by mail order (postage US$4.50 for the first item, $1 for each additional item).

Gay's the Word, 66 Marchmont St., London WC1N 1AB, England (tel. (0171) 278 76 54). The largest gay and lesbian bookshop in the UK; also sells videos, jewelry, and postcards. Mail order service available. No catalogue of listings, but it provides you with a list of titles germane to a given subject. Open Mon-Sat 10am-6pm, Thurs. 10am-7pm, Sun 2-6pm. The nearest tube stop is at Russell Square.

Giovanni's Room, 345 S. 12th St. Philadelphia, PA 19107 (tel. (215) 923-2960; fax (215) 923-0813). An international feminist, lesbian, and gay bookstore with mail-order service. Carries many of the publications listed here. Call or write for a free mail-order catalogue.

Inland Book Company, P.O. Box 120261, East Haven, CT. 06512 (tel. (203) 467-4257). Publishers of *Women Going Places* (US$14), an international women's travel and resource guide emphasizing women-owned enterprises, geared toward lesbians, but offering advice appropriate for all women. Available in bookstores. Inland Book Company sells directly only to distributors.

International Gay Travel Association (IGTA), P.O. Box 4974, Key West, FL 33041-4974 (tel. (305) 292-0217; fax (305) 296-6633). Services include travel agents, tour operators, aid in finding accommodations, and lists of publications for gay and lesbian travelers. Members receive a quarterly newsletter with general and specific travel advice, including info on traveling with HIV/AIDS.

Spartacus International Gay Guides, published by Bruno Demander, Postfach 110729, D-10837 Berlin, Germany (tel. (30) 615 00 30). Lists of bars, restaurants, hotels, and bookstores around the world catering to gay men. Also lists hotlines for gay men in various countries. Most importantly, Spartacus provides homosexuality laws for each country it covers. However, laws sometimes change faster than the book. Available in the US by mail order from Giovanni's Room and from Renaissance House as well as in bookstores (US$29.95).

■■■ DISABLED TRAVELERS

Most of Southeast Asia, with the notable exceptions of Singapore and Hong Kong, is not well adapted to handling travelers with disabilities. Hospitals are ill-equipped to replace broken braces or prostheses; their orthopedic materials, even in Bangkok and Jakarta, are faulty at best. Facilities for disabled travelers are, in general, poor. Public transportation (trains, buses, songthaews, tuk-tuks, etc.) is completely inaccessible. Getting on and off boats is near impossible for travelers with motor disabilities; it involves either wading out into the water and hoisting yourself into the boat or hopping from a pier a few feet down into a boat. While the classier hotels often have elevators (which may not be wheelchair accessible), most budget accommodations don't. Rural areas have no sidewalks, let alone ramps, and larger cities are packed with curbs and steps. Many sights require climbing long staircases or hiking considerable distances.

Attitudes toward people with disabilities vary across the region. In Laos and Cambodia, where an uncommonly high percentage of the population are amputees (from old land-mines and cluster-bombs), disabilities are not uncommon. However, Thai people with disabilities rarely come out in public; in Thai culture, a person with a disability is a poor reflection on his or her family. Still, travelers who aren't shy will find many people eager to aid them.

Call or write to the **World Institute on Disability** at 510 16th St., Suite 100, Oakland, CA 94612 (tel. (510) 763-4100; fax (510) 763 4109) for information on disability rights advocates around the world. In Thailand, Mr. Narong Patibatsarakich is the **Chairperson of the Council of Disabled People of Thailand** (tel. (02) 583 3031; fax (02) 583 6518), and can help provide info on Thailand's resources for the disabled. The amount of information for travelers with disabilities is still small; if you find additional publications or other information, please let us know for next year's edition.

American Foundation for the Blind, 11 Penn Plaza, New York, NY 10011 (tel. (212) 502-7600). Provides information and services for the visually impaired. Open Mon.-Fri. 8:30am-4:30pm. For a catalogue of products, contact Lighthouse Low-Vision Products at (800) 829-0500. ID cards US$10.

Facts on File, 460 Park Ave. S., New York, NY 10016 (tel. (212) 683-2244) in AK and HI. Publishers of Access to the World (US$16.95), a guide to handicap-accessible accommodations and sights. Available in bookstores or by mail order.

Mobility International, USA (MIUSA), P.O. Box 10767, Eugene, OR 97440 (tel. (503) 343-1284 voice and TDD; fax (503) 343-6812). International headquarters in Britain, 228 Borough High St., London SE1 1JX, England (tel. (0171) 403 56 88). Contacts in 30 countries. Information on travel programs, international work camps, accommodations, access guides, and organized tours for those with physical disabilities. Annual membership costs US$20, newsletter US$10. Sells updated and expanded *A World of Options: A Guide to International Educational Exchange, Community Service, and Travel for Persons with Disabilities* (US$14 for members, US$16 for non-members, postpaid).

Moss Rehab Hospital Travel Information Service, 1200 W. Tabor Rd., Philadelphia, PA 19141 (tel. (215) 456-9603). A telephone information resource center on international travel accessibility and other travel-related concerns for those with disabilities. Will refer callers to other agencies if they cannot provide information.

Society for the Advancement of Travel for the Handicapped, 347 Fifth Ave., Suite 610, New York, NY 10016 (tel. (212) 447-7284; fax (212) 725-8253). Publishes quarterly travel newsletter SATH news, as well as information sheets and booklets (free for members, US$3 each for non-members), which contain advice on trip planning for people with disabilities. Annual membership is US$45, students and seniors US$25, agents and corporations $100.

Twin Peaks Press, P.O. Box 129, Vancouver, WA 98666-0129 (tel. (360) 694-2462; MC and Visa orders (800) 637-2256; fax (360) 696-3210). Publishers of Travel for the Disabled, which provides tips and lists of accessible tourist attractions, in addition to advice on other resources for disabled travelers (US$19.95). Also publishes *Directory for Travel Agencies of the Disabled* (US$19.95), *Wheelchair Vagabond* (US$14.95), and *Directory of Accessible Van Rentals* (US$9.95). Postage US$3 for first book, US$1.50 for each additional book.

Directions Unlimited, 720 North Bedford Rd., Bedford Hills, NY 10507 (tel. (800) 533-5343 or (914) 241-1700; fax (914) 241-0243). Specializes in arranging individual and group vacations, tours, and cruises for those with physical disabilities.

Flying Wheels Travel Service, P.O. Box 382, 143 W. Bridge St., Owatonna, MN 55060 (tel. (800) 535-6790; fax (507) 451-1685). Arranges international trips for groups or individuals in wheelchairs or with other sorts of limited mobility.

The Guided Tour Inc., Elkins Park House, Suite 114B, 7900 Old York Rd., Elkins Park, PA 19027-2339 (tel. (215) 782-1370 or (800) 783-5841; fax (215) 635-2637). This organization, founded in 1972, organizes year-round travel and vacation programs, domestic and international, for persons with developmental and physical challenges—as well as those geared to the needs of persons requiring renal dialysis. Call, fax, or write for a free brochure.

■■■ TRAVELERS WITH CHILDREN

Children under two can generally fly for 10% of the adult fare on international flights (not necessarily including a seat). Ages 2 to 12 usually fly half price. Call your airline with specific questions. Traveling with a child in Southeast Asia can be a difficult adventure, as even seasoned adults have difficulty adjusting to the transportation and amenities.

Lonely Planet Publications, Embarcadero West, 155 Filbert St., Suite 251, Oakland, CA 94607 (tel. (510) 893-8555 or (800) 275-8555; fax (510) 893-8563); also P.O. Box 617, Hawthorn, Victoria 3122, Australia. Published *Travel with Children* by M. Wheeler (US$10.95, postage US$1.50 in the US).

Wilderness Press, 2440 Bancroft Way, Berkeley, CA 94704 (tel. (800) 443-7227 or (510) 843-8080; fax (510) 548-1355). Publishes *Backpacking with Babies and Small Children* (US$9.95).

■■■ TRAVELERS WITH SPECIAL DIETS

Although much Southeast Asian food contains meat or uses meat bases, *Let's Go* lists many **vegetarian** eating options. Vegetarian dishes abound throughout the region, making Southeast Asia a vegi-friendly destination. While **kosher** meals are next to nonexistent, the Muslim presence in Southeast Asia makes **halal** food a large part of the cuisine (especially in the Malay-speaking world).

Ballantine-Mitchell Publishers, Newbury House 890-900, Eastern Ave., Newbury Park, Ilford, Essex IG2 7HH (tel. (181) 599 88 66; fax (181) 599 09 84). Publishers of *The Jewish Travel Guide,* which lists synagogues, kosher restaurants, and Jewish institutions in over 80 countries. Available in the UK from Ballantine-Mitchell.

Jewish Chronicle Publications, 25 Furnival St., London EC4A 1JT, England (tel. (0171) 831 51 88). Publishes the *Jewish Travel Guide,* listing synagogues, kosher restaurants and Jewish institutions in more than 80 countries. Available in the US from Sepher-Hermon Press, 1265 46th St., Brooklyn, NY 11219 (tel. (718) 972-9010) for US$11.95, postage US$1.75.

Vegetarian Society of the U.K., Parkdale, Dunham Rd., Altringham, Cheshire WA14 4QG (tel. 44 (061) 928 07 93). Publishes the *International Vegetarian Travel Guide* (£2); it was last published in 1991, but copies are still available.

Vegetarian Times (tel. (201) 783-1129). Orders only. Publishes the *Times.*

■■■ PACKING

Pack light. This means you. Your backpack or suitcase may be feather-light when you buy it or drag it out of storage and as buoyant as your enthusiasm all the way to the airport, but as soon as the plane lands it will become a ponderous, hot, uncomfortable nuisance. Before you leave, pack your bag and take it for a walk. Try to convince yourself that you're in Southeast Asia already, sweltering in the high heat and humidity. You're hiking up mountains steeper than your college tuition bill, with flora denser than the 1995 Republican Congress. You're diving to catch an elderly monk about to fall off the bus. You're sprinting down hostel hallways, trying desperately to escape from roving bands of curious cockroaches and leaping lizards. At the slightest sign of heaviness, curb your vanity and unpack something. As a general rule, pack only what you absolutely need, then take half the clothes and twice the money. A *New York Times* correspondent recommends that you take "no more than you can carry for half a mile at a dead run." This may be extreme—and in fact, it's held in some circles that many *Times* correspondents can't run half a mile, period—but you get the idea.

LUGGAGE

Backpack: If you plan to cover most of your itinerary by foot or will be riding on a great deal of buses (and you probably will), the unbeatable baggage is a sturdy backpack with several external compartments. Some convert into a more normal-looking suitcase. This applies particularly to travelers who wish to take hill-tribe treks in north Thailand or hike through national parks and preserves. In general, **internal-frame** packs are easier to carry and more efficient for general traveling purposes. If you'll be doing extensive camping or hiking, you may want to consider an **external-frame** pack, which offers added support, distributes weight better, and allows for a sleeping bag to be strapped on. External-frame packs have been known to get caught and mangled in baggage conveyors; tie down loose parts to minimize risk. In any case, get a pack with a strong, padded hip belt to transfer weight from your shoulders to your legs. Whichever style you choose, avoid excessively low-end prices—you get what you pay for. Quality packs cost anywhere from US$125 to US$300. Packs with several compartments are best, but beware of ones with many outside zippers or flaps that could make a pick-pocket's dream come true. If checking a backpack on a flight, tape down loose straps that can catch in the conveyer belt and rip your bag apart. An empty **light-weight duffel bag** packed inside your luggage will be useful: once abroad you can fill your luggage with purchases and keep your dirty clothes in the duffel.

Light suitcase/large duffel bag: These are OK if you are going to do your exploring in a large and relatively luxurious city such as Bangkok, Singapore, Jakarta, or Ho Chi Minh City. Those striving for a more casual, unobtrusive look should take a large shoulder bag that closes securely.

Daypack or courier bag: A smaller bag, in addition to your pack, is indispensable for plane flights, sight-seeing, a picnic on the Mekong, and keeping some of your valuables on you. Make sure it's big enough to hold lunch, a camera, a water bottle, and *Let's Go*. Get one with secure zippers and closures.

Moneybelt or neck pouch: Guard your money, passport, railpass, and other important articles in either one of these, and keep it with you *at all times*. The best combination of convenience and invulnerability is the nylon, zippered pouch with belt that should sit *inside* the waist of your pants or skirt (though not too inconveniently). Neck pouches should be worn under at least one layer of clothing. Money belts and neck pouches are available at any good camping store. **Avoid the oh-so-popular "fanny pack":** it's an invitation to thieves, even worn in front. See Safety for more info on protecting you and your valuables.

CLOTHING

To get a good sense of the weather in Southeast Asia, imagine being in a steaming sauna for three weeks. You should only take clothes that will help you deal with the high average temperature and the near 100% humidity. Dark colors hide wear, tear, and stains, but lighter fabrics and colors will be cooler. Generally, natural fibers or cotton blends will prove most comfortable. The clothing you bring should be more loose than tight, or you will have to deal with the uncomfortable task of peeling an absolutely drenched shirt off your body.

Picking out what to bring on your voyage, consider the time of year you are going as well as your regional destination. For example, if you are going to Chiang Mai during the cool season, you may need to bring a light cotton sweater, as temperatures can dip to around 13°C (55°F) at night or early in the morning.

Casual clothing is generally recommended and, in most cases, appropriate. Light cotton shirts, t-shirts, trousers, jeans, shorts (not too tight or short, especially for women), skirts, and blouses should form the nucleus of your wardrobe. However, proper clothing is required for entrance to mosques, temples, certain museums, and palaces, and recommended for travel in Malaysia and Indonesia. For men, this means a dress shirt and slacks; for women, a summer dress that covers the knees and shoulders or a blouse and skirt or pants that do the same. Excessively formal attire (such as suits) is not needed.

Comfortable **walking shoes** are essential. This is not the place to cut corners, for blisters, corns, and sharp, shooting pains in your feet will provide obvious obstacles to your enjoyment of the trip. For those seeking the ultimate in comfort, **sandals** are recommended. If you take a quick survey of footwear among those living in Southeast Asia, you will learn that almost everyone wears sandals all the time. They are especially useful because your shoes will be coming off every time you enter homes, many guest houses, or rooms off the beaches. If you aren't in the mood to shell out US$50 for expensive designer brands, don't despair. Sandals are sold everywhere in the region, and even those sold in department stores and in malls are cheaper than those sold in other countries. Try to break them in before you leave, however. (Those of copious foot should beware: larger sizes are often unavailable in Southeast Asia.) For heavy-duty trekking, a pair of sturdy lace-up **hiking boots** will help out. A double pair of socks—light, absorbent cotton inside and thick wool outside—will cushion feet and keep them dry. Break in your shoes before you go, but if you do get plagued by blisters, moleskin (sold at camping/sporting goods stores) helps protect the tender area. If you only want one pair of shoes, that evolutionary cross-breed the "sneaker-hiking boot" can serve as well as a hardcore boot for most trekking and may be more comfortable for the rest of your trip's activities. Bring a pair of flip-flops for protection against the foliage and fungi that lurk in some hostel showers.

Don't forget—rain gear is essential. A waterproof jacket and a backpack cover will take care of you and your stuff at a moment's notice, which is often all you'll get. A little more cumbersome, a lightweight poncho will cover your back and pack well and serve as a ground cloth. Gore-Tex, that miracle fabric that's both waterproof and breathable, is all but mandatory if you plan on hiking.

MISCELLANEOUS

The following is not an exhaustive list, but you'll find the following miscellaneous items valuable.

small umbrella
petite alarm clock
sun hat
needle and thread
sunglasses
pocketknife
plastic water bottle
small flashlight
towel
whistle
small notebook
cold-water soap
insect repellent
tweezers
bungee cord
pens or pencils
sunscreen
toilet paper
compass
Ziploc bags (for damp clothes, soap, food, pens)
waterproof matches
moleskin (for blisters)
safety pins
a personal stereo (Walkman) with headphones
notebook and pens
pocket phrasebook
string (makeshift clothesline and lashing material)
padlock
rubber bands
flashlight
earplugs
electrical tape (for patching tears)
maps and phrasebooks
squash ball (to use as a sink plug)
garbage bags
a length of cord
clothespins
a disposable hedgehog (for fun and games)

Some items are not always available on the road:

deodorant	tampons
condoms	dancing clogs
cold-water soap	razors

Most toiletries are available in cities, so don't panic if you happen to forget your toothbrush. Don't forget deodorant, though, since something comparable may be hard to come by. Keep in mind, however, that fragrant deodorants, shampoos, and soaps attract insects and other (unwelcome) forest creatures with reckless abandon. Finding a non-scented shampoo, etc., is your best bet. For cold-water soap, all-natural **Dr. Bronner's Castile Soap,** sold at camping and health food stores, is usable for anything from washing clothes, bathing, and shampooing to brushing your teeth, (although it tastes disgusting). Rare, expensive, or of questionable quality when found in Southeast Asia are contraceptives, contact-lens fluid, prescription drugs, and tampons. If you are straight and sexually active, you will need to worry about contraception. Women on the Pill should bring enough to allow for possible loss or extended stays, and should bring a prescription, since forms of the Pill vary a good deal. The sponge is probably too bulky to be worthwhile on the road; if you use a diaphragm, be sure that you have a supply of contraceptive jelly as well. Though condoms are available, bring your favorite brand before you go; availability and quality vary (usually between poor and non-existent). It might be wise to carry a towel, soap, and toilet paper for those out-of-the-way places or very cheap hotels. To be on the safe side, buy anything you forgot to bring as soon as you arrive, so you don't find yourself in a small village at a loss for dental floss. (See "Camping and the Outdoors" on page 57.)

Electricity

In Southeast Asia electricity is 220V AC, enough to fry any 110V North American appliance. In rural areas, however, especially in Indonesia, Vietnam, and Laos, 110V may be common. In Cambodia, most areas outside of Phnom Penh are 110V. Be sure to check before using your appliances. Visit hardware stores for a converter (which changes the voltage) and an adapter (which changes the shape of the plug). To order a converter by mail (about US$20) or to receive their free and enlightening pamphlet, *Foreign Electricity is No Deep Dark Secret,* write to Franzus, Murtha Industrial Park, Railroad Ave., Beacon Falls, CT 06403 (tel. (203) 723-6664; fax (203) 723-6666). Or simply leave the hair dryer and electric razor at home.

TRAVEL IN SOUTHEAST ASIA

■■■ GETTING THERE

BUDGET TRAVEL AGENCIES

The best way to reach points in Asia with the fewest restrictions and the most peace of mind is to directly use a **commercial airline.** But you'll pay for the ease. Fortunately, you can take advantage of the numerous **discount travel agencies.** These agencies sell regular airline tickets at wholesale prices. Even though the prices are low, your seat is guaranteed (with the usual confirmation) and you can usually cancel your ticket and still receive a fairly sizeable refund. Student-oriented travel agencies such as Council Travel, STA Travel, and Travel CUTS sometimes have special deals that regular travel agents can't offer. Even if they don't, though, their ticket prices are usually among the lowest to be found.

Council Travel, the travel division of Council, is a full-service travel agency specializing in student, youth, and budget travel with over 50 offices worldwide.

Discounted Student Airfares
Eurail passes
International Student, Teacher & Youth ID Cards
Best-Selling Let's Go Travel Guides
Hostelling Essentials
Extensive Line of Travel Gear

FOR RESERVATIONS OR MORE INFORMATION, CALL
1-800-5-LETSGO
OR WRITE TO US FOR A CATALOG OF OUR SERVICES:
53A Church Street • Cambridge, MA 02138 • USA

Council offers railpasses, hostelling cards, discount airfares on scheduled airlines, low-cost accommodations, budget tours, travel gear, and international student (ISIC), youth (GO 25), and teacher (ITIC) identity cards. Forty-one offices in the US include: Emory Village, 1561 N. Decatur Rd., **Atlanta,** GA 30307 (tel. (404) 377-9997); 2000 Guadalupe, **Austin,** TX 78705 (tel. (512) 472-4931); 729 Boylston St., **Boston,** MA 02116 (tel. (617) 266-1926); 1138 13th St., **Boulder,** CO 80302 (tel. (303) 447-8101); 1153 N. Dearborn, **Chicago,** IL 60610 (tel. (312) 951-0585); 10904 Lindbrook Dr., **Los Angeles,** CA 90024 (tel. (310) 208-3551); One Datran Ctr., 9100 S. Dadeland Blvd., **Miami,** FL 33156 (tel. (305) 670-9261); 1501 University Ave. SE, **Minneapolis,** MN 55414, (tel. (612) 379-2323); 205 E. 42nd St., **New York,** NY 10017 (tel. (212) 661-1450); 3606A Chestnut St., **Philadelphia,** PA 19104 (tel. (215) 382-0343); 953 Garnet Ave., **San Diego,** CA 92109 (tel. (619) 270-6401); 530 Bush St., **San Francisco,** CA 94108 (tel. (415) 421-3473); 1314 NE 43rd St., **Seattle,** WA 98105 (tel. (206) 632-2448); 3300 M St., NW, **Washington, DC** 20007 (tel. (202) 337-6464). Also in Amherst, Ann Arbor, Bekeley, Bloomington, Cambridge (2), Chapel Hill, Columbus, Dallas, Davis, Denver, Evanston, La Jolla, Long Beach, New Haven, New Orleans, Palo Alto, Pittsburgh, Portland, Providence, Salt Lake City, Santa Barbara, and Tempe. For US cities not listed, call 800-2-COUNCIL ((800) 226-8624). Overseas offices include: 28A Poland St. (Oxford Circus), **London,** W1V 3DB (tel. (0171) 437 77 67); 22 rue des Pyramides, 75001 **Paris,** (tel. (1) 44 55 55 65); **Munich** (tel. (089) 39 50 22); **Singapore** (tel. (65) 738 70 66); and **Bangkok** (tel. (66) 228 277 05).

International Student Exchange Flights (ISE), 5010 East Shea Blvd., #A104, Scottsdale, AZ 85254 (tel. (602) 951-1177). Offers budget student flights to Europe and Asia, Eurail, HI-AYH memberships, the International Student Exchange Identity Card, and travel guides. Free catalog.

Let's Go Travel, Harvard Student Agencies, 53A Church St., Cambridge, MA 02138 (800-5-LETS GO ((800) 553-8746), or (617) 495-9649). Let's Go offers railpasses, HI-AYH memberships, ISICs, International Teacher ID cards, GO 25 cards, guidebooks (including all *Let's Go* titles), maps, bargain flights, and a complete line of budget travel gear. All items available by mail; call or write for a catalog (or see catalog in center of this publication).

STA Travel, 6560 North Scottsdale Rd. #F100, Scottsdale, AZ 85253 (tel. (800) 777-0112 nationwide). A student and youth travel organization with over 100 offices around the world and 14 US locations offering discount airfares (for travelers under 26 and full-time students under 32), railpasses, accommodations, tours, insurance, and ISICs. In the US: 429 S. Dearborn St., **Chicago,** IL 60605 (tel. (312) 786-9050); 4341 University Way NE, **Seattle,** WA 98105 (tel. (206) 633-5000); 10 Downing St., **New York,** NY 10014 (tel. (212) 477-7166); 297 Newbury St., **Boston,** MA 02115 (tel. (617) 266-6014); 3730 Walnut St. **Philadelphia,** PA 19104 (tel. (215) 382-2928); 2401 Pennsylvania Ave., Suite G, **Washington, DC** 20037 (tel. (202) 887-0912); 7202 Melrose Ave., **Los Angeles,** CA 90046 (tel. (213) 934-8722); 51 Grant Ave., **San Francisco,** CA 94108 (tel. (415) 391-8407). In the UK: Priory House, 6 Wrights Ln., **London** W8 6TA (tel. (0171) 938 47 11). In New Zealand: 10 High St., **Auckland** (tel. (09) 309 97 23). In Australia: 224 Faraday St., Carlton, **Melbourne** VIC 3050 (tel. (03) 347 69 11).

Travel Management International (TMI), Grand Ave., Minneapolis, MN 55409 (tel. (800) 245-3672). Travel service specializing in customized international trip planning; offers student fares and railpasses.

Travel CUTS (Canadian University Travel Services, Ltd.), 187 College St., Toronto, Ont. M5T 1P7 (tel. (416) 798-CUTS (798-2887); fax (416) 979-8167). Offices across Canada. Also, in the UK, 295-A Regent St., London W1R 7YA (tel. (0171) 637 31 61). Discounted European, South Pacific, and domestic flights; ISIC, GO 25, and HI hostel cards; and discount travel passes. Special fares with valid ISIC or FIYTO cards. Offers free *Student Traveller* magazine, and info on Student Work Abroad Program (SWAP).

Unitravel, 1177 North Warson Rd., St. Louis, MO 63132 (tel. (800) 325-2222; fax (314) 569-2503). Offers discounted airfares on major scheduled airlines from the North America to Europe, Africa, and Asia.

STUDENT TRAVEL.

Two ways to spend $1000:

A. 10 CDs, trendy boots, two surfwear T-shirts, wild haircut, navel ring, a new tattoo, party all week, one bottle of aspirin.

B. Air ticket to somewhere exciting, rail pass, backpack, meet people, experience new cultures, learn about the world.

Education is expensive. Spend wisely.

STA Travel: 800-777-0112 • http://www.sta-travel.com

New York: 212-627-3111
Boston: 617-266-6014
Philadelphia: 215-382-2928
Washington DC: 202-887-0912
Chicago: 312-786-9050
San Francisco: 415-391-8407
Los Angeles: 213-934-8722
Seattle: 206-633-5000

Campus Travel, 52 Grosvenor Gardens, London SW1W OAG. Campus is a large supplier of student travel products in the UK, with 37 branches throughout the country. Arranges for student cards, flights, trains, boats, and a range of related products and services. In London, telesales and bookings for Europe (tel. (0171) 730 34 02); for North America (tel. (0171) 730 21 01); worldwide (tel. (0171) 730 81 11). In Manchester (tel. (0161) 273 17 21). In Scotland (tel. (0131) 668 33 03).

CTS Travel, 220 Kensington High St., W8 London (tel. (0171) 937 33 66 for travel in Europe; (0171) 937 33 88 for travel worldwide). Specializes in student/youth travel and discount flights. Tube: High St. Kensington. Open Mon.-Fri. 9:30am-6pm, Sat. 10am-5pm. Also at 44 Goodge St., W1. Tube: Goodge St.

For more information on discount travel agencies, scan the weekend travel section of major newspapers (especially *The New York Times*). If you're looking to bypass travel agents altogether, consult the *Official Airline Guide,* 2000 Clearwater Dr., Oakbrook, IL 60521 (tel. (800) 323-3537; available in many libraries), which publishes both North American and worldwide editions. The OAG is published bi-weekly and lists every flight and connection on nearly every carrier.

■ BY PLANE

COMMERCIAL AIRLINES

Even if you pay an airline's lowest published fare, you may waste hundreds of dollars. The commercial airlines' lowest regular offer is the APEX (Advance Purchase Excursion Fare); specials advertised in newspapers may be cheaper, but have more restrictions and fewer available seats. APEX fares provide you with confirmed reservations and allow "open-jaw" tickets (landing in and returning from different cities). Generally, reservations must be made 7to 21 days in advance, with 7to 14-day minimum and up to 90-day maximum stay limits, and hefty cancellation and change penalties. For summer travel, book APEX fares early; by May you will have a hard time getting the departure date you want.

In the past, it has always paid to travel the trans-Pacific route to Southeast Asia because Asian air carriers, such as Korean Airlines or China Airlines, always offered lower fares than their European competitors, even on flights from the East Coast (opposite Southeast Asia on the globe). However, with the recent influx of American carriers into Asia and the relative weakness of the dollar, American carriers have advertised lower prices for the past few years.

CONSOLIDATORS AND CHARTERS

Ticket consolidators, also known as "bucket shops," resell unsold tickets on commercial and charter airlines. Look for their tiny ads in weekend papers (in the U.S., the *Sunday New York Times* is best), and start calling them all. In London, the real "bucket shop" center, the Air Travel Advisory Bureau (tel. (0171) 636 50 00) provides a list of consolidators. There is rarely a maximum age or stay limit; tickets are also heavily discounted, and may offer extra flexibility or bypass advance purchase requirements, since you aren't tangled in airline bureaucracy. But unlike with tickets bought through an airline, you won't be able to use your tickets on another flight if you miss yours; moreover, to get a refund you will have to go back to the consolidator, rather than the airline. Phone around and pay with a credit card so you can stop payment if you never receive your tickets. Don't be tempted solely by the low prices; find out everything you can about the agency you're considering, and get a copy of their refund policy in writing. Ask also about accommodations and car rental discounts; some consolidators have fingers in many pies. Insist on a **receipt** that gives full details about the tickets, refunds, and restrictions, and if they don't want to give you one or just generally seem clueless or shady, use a different company. Consult Kelly Monaghan's *Consolidators: Air Travel's Bargain Basement* (US$5 plus US$3.50 shipping) from the Intrepid Traveler, P.O. Box 438, New York, NY 10034, for more information and a list of consolidators.

The theory behind a **charter** is that a tour operator contracts with an airline to fly extra loads of passengers to peak-season destinations. Charter flights fly less frequently than major airlines and have more restrictions, particularly on refunds. They are also almost always fully booked, and schedules may change or be cancelled at the last moment (as late as 48 hours before the trip, without a full refund); you'll be much better off purchasing a ticket on a regularly scheduled airline. Pay with a credit card if you can; consider purchasing traveler's insurance. Study contracts closely; you don't want to end up with an unwanted overnight layover.

COURIER FLIGHTS

Anyone who can travel light should consider flying as a courier. The company hiring you will use your checked luggage space for freight; you're only allowed to bring carry-ons. Restrictions to watch for: you must be over 18 and have a valid passport; most flights are round-trip only with short fixed-length stays (usually one week); you may not be able to travel with a companion (single tickets only); and most flights are from New York. **NOW Voyager,** 74 Varick St. #307, New York, NY 10013 (tel. (213) 431-1616), acts as an agent for many courier flights from New York; it has regular flights to Bangkok, Singapore, and Tokyo, all at very low prices compared to regular discount airline tickets. Other agents to try are **Halbart Express,** 147-05 176th St., Jamaica, NY 11434 (tel. (718) 656-5000) and **Discount Travel International** (tel. (212) 362-3636).

You can also go directly through courier companies in New York, or check your bookstore or library for handbooks such as *Air Courier Bargains* (US$15 plus $3.50 shipping from the Intrepid Traveler, P.O. Box 438, New York, NY 10034). *The Courier Air Travel Handbook* (US$10 plus US$3.50 shipping) explains how to travel as an air courier and contains names, phone numbers, and contact points of courier companies. It can be ordered directly from Bookmasters, Inc., P.O. Box 2039, Mansfield, OH 44905 (tel. (800) 507-2665). A final caveat for the budget conscious: don't get so caught up in seemingly great deals. Always read the fine print; check for restrictions and hidden fees. There are amazingly cheap fares waiting to be unearthed, but you can't get something for nothing.

■■■ BORDER CROSSINGS

Thailand - Malaysia: Of the four border crossings with Thailand, the border with Malaysia is the safest. Problems in this border region largely involve internal struggles between the government and insurgents of each respective country. For Malaysia, the problem is the Communist Party of Malaya (CPM), which runs its operations in the border area with Thailand. Thailand's problems lie in the Muslim separatist movement, which is struggling to secede to Malaysia. On the whole, though, this border is safe, and travelers cross it continuously.

Thailand - Burma: Anyone traveling to this border should understand the risks involved in such an unstable place. The Mon and Karen tribespeople are locked in a war to see who will control smuggling between Burma and Thailand. In addition, the Burmese government and the secessionist Karen have been in conflict along the border, mostly in the northwest. News of foreign mercenaries fighting for the Karen has recently begun to appear in the press, although the governments of the citizens involved have denied this. It is no surprise that foreign travelers are often regarded as security risks by the Burmese (and the Karen). The area near the Golden Triangle, is much safer than the area along the western border, and it may soon be possible for travelers to take short daytrips into Burma across the north border. Travelers to Burma should be aware that they are actively supporting the State Law and Order Restoration Council (SLORC). (For more info see page 51.)

Thailand - Laos: Thanks to greatly improved Thai-Lao relations in recent years (resulting in the historic "Friendship Bridge" at Nong Khai) entering Laos has never been easier. Currently there are frequent flights from Bangkok to Vientiane and weekly flights from Chiang Mai to Vientiane as well (Lao Aviation plans to begin service from Chiang Mai to Luang Prabang sometime in 1996). Ferries link Mukdahan, Nakhon Phanom, and Chiang Khong in northeast Thailand with Savannahket, Thakhek, and Hueixai, respectively, in Laos. The only place where travelers can enter Laos on foot is at tiny Chong Mek in Ubon Ratchathani Province, 40km west of Pakxe in Champassak Province. Keep in mind that visas specifying your intended point of entry must be obtained in advance from the Lao embassy in Bangkok.

Let's Not Go: Burma 1996

Although Burma has been ruled by the army since the first military takeover in 1962, the **State Law and Order Restoration Council (SLORC)** was not born until September 8, 1988. **General Khin Nyunt's** infamous military junta of Myanmar came into power after the bloody crackdown on student anti-government demonstrations that swept the country in late 1987 and 1988, killing thousands. The SLORC promoted itself as a new entity to provide order in a chaotic nation, and initially, the SLORC seemed to make considerable progress, dismantling the socialist system and liberalizing trade, Increasing international pressure led to general elections in May 1990, but when the opposition party—the **National League for Democracy (NLD)**—won 82% of the government seats, the SLORC refused to accept the results. Instead, they placed the NLD leader, **Aung San Suu Kyi** (daughter of the murdered Burmese independence leader Aung San), under house arrest. The NLD continued to fight for democracy, under her guidance, facing arrest and torture for public speaking and distributing pamplets. Since then, the SLORC has crushed all opposition in Burma, banning gatherings of more than 5 people, establishing 4pm curfews, sentencing citizens to seven years in prison for hosting unregistered overnight guests, forcibly relocating hundreds of thousands of Burmese and ethnic minorities to desolate locales, as well as implementing forced labor for touristic development and highway construction. Documented acts of torture include hanging people from electrical fans, electrocuting a pregnant woman during interrogation, and tying naked individuals to blocks of ice.

The leaders of the democracy movement have since allied with the many ethnic minorities fighting for autonomy. One of the most powerful is the **Karen National Union (KNU).** Until it was taken in January 1995 by the SLORC and a breakaway faction, the Democratic Karen Buddhist Organization, the KNU base of Manerplaw (across from Thailand's Mae Sam Leap) was home to the All Burma Student's Democratic Front and the National Coalition Government of the Union Of Burma, led by NDL leader and cousin of Suu Kyi, Dr. Sein Win.

In 1995 the SLORC began attempts to clean up its international reputation. Most significantly, they released Suu Kyi and initiated steps to join the **Association of Southeast Asian Nations (ASEAN).** They have also scheduled a 1996 "Tourism Year" campaign. Nevertheless, the SLORC is still being criticized by the U.S., UN, and various international NGOs for human rights abuses. Furthermore, many ethnic minority groups have vowed to continue fighting for independence, even if the SLORC were to hand power over to a democratically elected congress. Ironically, the name of the country was (in theory) changed to the Union of Myanmar in 1990, so as not to exclude the non-Burmese minorities who have proved to be one of the SLORC's strongest forces of opposition.

Disputes between the SLORC and dissident groups have forced over 100,000 Karen, Shan, Mon, and Burmese political activists across the border to Thailand's northwest districts, as their villages have been burned and the populations used as slave labor by the military. The Thai government, semi-sympathetic to their causes, allows the refugees to remain in isolated village-like camps along the border. Prohibited from owning land or farming (not being Thai citizens), they subsist on wages from day labor in nearby Thai towns and grants from the government, international relief organizations, and tourism.

Thailand - Cambodia: There is no legal way to cross this border by land. The political situation is still unstable and the border is still mined and patrolled by the Khmer Rouge. Most of the mines are laid on the Cambodian side of the border, but this does not reduce the danger, and the only foreigners you'll find are volunteers working in Thailand to help refugees. There has recently (summer 1993) been fighting on the Cambodian border, but no one seems to know who is involved. The Thai military is known to have relations with the Khmer Rouge; it has been reported that they shield Pol Pot.

Laos - Cambodia: Currently entering Cambodia by any means other than air (arriving in Phnom Penh) is not possible. Theoretically, however, it is possible to enter Cambodia by boat via the southern province of Champassak along the Mekong River, the first important Cambodian city is Stung Treng. Don't expect this crossing to open until the unrest in Cambodia is resolved, however.

Laos - Vietnam: The primary overland entry point from Laos to Vietnam is at Lao Bao, on National Route 9, 300km east of Savannakhet near the central Vietnamese cities of Hue and Da Nang. Daily buses link Savannakhet with the Lao/Vietnamese frontier. Visas to enter Vietnam at Lao Bao are easily obtained from the Vietnamese embassy in Vientiane or the consulate in Savannakhet. Entering Vietnam from the northern provinces requires special permission from Hanoi, due to safety concerns this permission is frequently denied. In a perfect world it would be possible to cross from Xam Neua Province along National Route 6 (ending in Hanoi). There is also an on again off again border crossing at Deo Tay Chang Pass near Dien Bien Phu. Check with the Vietnamese embassy in Vientiane before making any plans.

Laos - Burma: As of this writing the Lao-Burmese border is closed. Attempting to cross can mean serious penalties by whichever government you are unlucky enough to be discovered by.

Vietnam - Cambodia: You can cross over by car, but visa must specify point of entry and exit. Buses run directly from Ho Chi Minh City to Phnom Penh.

Indonesia - Singapore: Wasting time is probably illegal in Singapore, and crossing the border goes something like: Walk off the pier into Indonesia. Show your passport. Tell them how long you're staying. Move on. All told, one minute. For crossing into Singapore add these steps: Customs officials fax a copy of your passport to a mysterious destination. Spit out your gum.

Indonesia - Malaysia: Travelers can enter Malaysia by boat and plane. The chief ferry route links Medan (specifically Belawan) in northern Sumatra and Georgetown in Malaysia. There are regular flights from Jakarta, Denpassar, and Medan to Kuala Lampur, as well as flights from Medan to Georgetown.

Malaysia - Singapore: The border between Johor Bahru, Malaysia and Singapore is probably the safest crossing within Southeast Asia, consisting of a quick bus ride or even a stroll across the 1056m Causeway bridge. The last time this entry point saw any real danger was during World War II when the British bombed it to keep the Japanese out of Singapore. For travelers the greatest danger is being hassled by customs officials if they see you importing gum.

Borders with China: Travelers can enter Laos from Yunnan Province in southern China through the town of Boten. Another entry point along the Chinese border is at Lao Cai, in Vietnam. Visa entry/exit points must be specified or you will be turned away.

ONCE THERE

■■■ RESPONSIBLE TOURISM

Responsible tourism has been interpreted in a number of ways by authors, travellers, and organizations. There is not a list somewhere of activities which do or do not make you a responsible tourist, and no objective criteria exists that can be used to judge your fellow traveler's guilt or innocence. Being responsible does not mean never going on a trek or never getting a glass of water from a resort development. Rather, responsible tourism means understanding the short- and long-term effects of your actions, seriously considering these effects, and realizing you are responsible for them. Only looking at part of the picture does not lead to a responsible decision. This is especially true with spending your money. When purchasing a good or service, the baht, ringgit, or riel does much more than simply provide for you—it influences the growth of industries and the lives of those who work in them. Responsible tourism means being aware of these factors and weighing them in order to make a responsible decision.

Examples of the issues one has to consider abound in this guide: supporting prostitution (directly or indirectly), supporting environment-friendly organizations, using drugs in another country, crossing the border into Burma, selecting a trekking company, trekking behavior, deciding where to buy souvenirs, or staying at a resort that is developing a peaceful patch of beach and forest. Illegal activities are usually illegal for a reason, although perhaps not what you would consider the right reason; even if you don't understand the logic behind the law, there may be issues that you are not aware of. Other questions are not so easily resolved. After researching and dealing with many of these issues over time, we as editors often come down on one side or the other, and present them in a way that we feel is responsible. The ultimate choices, however, are yours.

■■■ GETTING AROUND

BY PLANE

Often the most expensive option, planes are nonetheless important for travel to certain countries, such as Cambodia, where the only overland border crossing is a bus from Ho Chi Minh City. For greater flexiblity and cheaper prices many travelers choose to purchase plane tickets for trips across the region once they are in Southeast Asia. Check specific countries and their major cities for the major carriers and budget travel offices.

BY TRAIN

Trains are often the best way to travel long distances in Southeast Asia, especially for overnight rides, when you may need a sleeper car. However, train service is really only a viable option in Java, Thailand, Malaysia, and Singapore. Rail systems are not very extensive in much of Indonesia, are expensive and uncomfortable in Vietnam, are unsafe in Cambodia, and simply don't exist in Laos. Beware of travel agencies that claim to sell train tickets; while some are licensed to do so, many also sell fake train tickets and run away with a good deal of money. The safest thing to do is to buy a ticket directly from a train station.

BY BUS

Next to traveling by train, bus travel is the most popular way for budget travelers to get around Southeast Asia (except in Cambodia). Riding in a regular bus is often a suffocating, mind-numbing experience; taking an air-conditioned bus is only mind-numbing. Despite the awful traffic in and around large cities, most people expect their bus drivers to get from point A to point B as fast as possible—and the driver usually tries to accommodate. Expect to hear much grinding of gears and blaring of horns. Bus travel is cheap and can be more convenient, since buses can go where tracks cannot. Also, those with air-conditioning (when it works) provide a degree of climate control not found on most trains.

Government buses are often crowded, so buy **tickets** early at the bus station. As with train tickets, it is generally unwise to buy bus tickets from random travel agencies; often they are selling nothing more than useless slips of paper.

Many **private companies** offer their own bus services. Compared to government buses, private ones tend to have faster, more reckless drivers and charge a tiny bit more. Some private bus companies offer excellent service, while others should not hold an operating license; there are so many private operators in the country that it is difficult to know the quality of an operation until you're already on a bus and screaming down the highway.

BY BOAT

Travel by boat—be it by luxury inter-island ferry or motorized dugout canoe—is an exciting alternative to those oh-so-comfortable Southeast Asian buses and trains. Indeed, travelers intending to explore more remote regions of the north (specifically Laos and Cambodia), where planes, trains and even automobiles are scarce, may find boats the only option. As with other modes of transportation, the degree of comfort and safety varies widely; PELNI, the Indonesian national ferry line, operates cruise ship quality service linking major cities within the archipelago, while in Laos travelers must make their own arrangements with individual boat captains and may find themselves sharing their seat with a pig, chicken, or other barnyard friend (provided there is a "seat" at all of course). Be aware that the extent of travel possible along rivers can vary according to the season and water levels. In Cambodia travel along the country's river system is often the safest way to reach the major cities north and northeast of Phnom Penh.

BY MINIVAN OR PICK-UP TRUCK

The consistent favorite for local transportation, it consists of squeezing thousands of people into a large vehicle and zooming across town. Virtually every town has an organized (or not so organized) system, best accessed by waving down a driver, yelling out your destination, and waiting to see if he stops. They often run like buses, with fixed routes within a town or between towns, and fares fixed according to distance. In Thailand the vehicles are called songthaews, literally "two rows." The name describes the way songthaew passengers sit: along two rows of seats in the covered bed of a small pick-up. In Indonesia and Malaysia, bemos, colts, Daihatsus, angkutan kotas, sudako, or angkots, as they are randomly called, are more like small buses or vans, but the same principles apply. The people-movers typically seat 10 to 40 people, depending on the size of the vehicle and its passengers. Often, those who can't be bothered to wait for a seat simply hang on the back.

Some songthaews or angkots have a button on the roof that passengers press to signal the driver where they want to get off. If the one you're on doesn't have a button, it's customary to tap on a metal railing a few times with a coin until the driver figures out that you want off. In other towns, songthaews can be rented like taxis, with fares hammered out by driver and passenger.

BY MOTO-TRISHAW

To some, the "roving buzzsaw" is convenient boon and a symbol of the Southeast Asian experience; to others, a diesel fume-belching beast. Fans of the tuk-tuk (in Thailand) and bajajs (in Indonesia's large cities) argue that these small covered three-wheeled motorcycles are cheap compared to taxis, more convenient than buses and songthaews or angkots, small enough to dart through heavy traffic, and a tad safer than motorcycle taxis. Much of this, of course, depends upon the driver. Sometimes they flip over, providing excitement to our researchers' lives. Detractors criticize the spunky tuk-tuk for the damage it does to the environment and human ears. A bajaj can seat one to three, depending upon the size of the passengers. Low ceilings, minimal legroom, and narrow seats (not to mention a vibrating action that threatens to dismantle the vehicle's slipshod frame) could make a six-foot person forgo an auto-trishaw ride forever.

BY TRISHAW

Trishaws, not to be confused with tuk-tuks or bajajs, are tricycle rickshaws powered by the legs of drivers, many of whom have been driving them for years, ignoring the allure of their more glamorous motorized cousins. Found all across Southeast Asia, they are known as *samlors* in Thailand, *becaks* (prounounced BEY-cha) in Malaysia and Indonesia, and cyclos in Cambodia and Vietnam. Trishaws are not always found in metropolitan areas, such as Bangkok, but are elsewhere in the countries. The benefit of riding in a trishaw comes from having the vehicle all to yourself; negatives include the longer traveling time, the potential of inhaling vicious amounts of air pollution, and the sorrow of seeing an old man labor away.

BY CAR

Driving a car in Southeast Asia is not for the faint of heart. Besides swerving to avoid cars and motorcycles, travelers have to remember to drive on the left and learn to dodge people, dogs, and water buffalo. In addition, there is a general disrespect for the lines on the road. When this spills over into a contempt for the center divider and passing rules (passing while going up a hill is not uncommon), society has a recipe for disaster. On many stretches of highway, there are only two lanes—leading to loads of passing fun. The unwritten rule is that the larger the vehicle, the greater amount of respect it should be accorded.

A car is totally unnecessary in a large city; efficient transportation abounds, and taxis are ubiquitous. Also, some rental companies do not offer insurance; a serious accident may mean spending some time in jail or the hospital, shelling out a large sum of money to cover damages, or both. If you just gotta have a car, have your international driver's permit handy, as well as a substantial amount of money. The cost of renting a compact four-door sedan is typically ten times the cost of a night's stay at a guest house.

BY MOTORCYCLE, MOPED, AND SCOOTER

Motorcycles, mopeds, and scooters are probably more useful for travelers than cars. If you don't want to drive your own they can also be hired as taxis, especially in Cambodia and Vietnam. In Indonesia, keep an eye out for the *ojeks* in most major cities. Generally, motorized two-wheelers can weave in and out of congested traffic, and come in handy when touring island or jungle roads. Unfortunately, riding these puppies is worthy of a Surgeon General's warning (almost all our researchers have consistent track records of moped misfortune). The greatest number of traffic fatalities fall under the "motorcyclist" heading. In many areas, and all of Thailand, a helmet is required by law, but you will not always be provided one. As with a car, you will find yourself dodging new and exciting obstacles. A meter-long iguana provides more problems for a motorcycle, however. Remember that the larger vehicle has the right of way. Motorcycle rental shops are abundant near major tourist stops.

BY BICYCLE

If driving a car or riding a motorcycle is that hairy, and the largest vehicle can crush all smaller ones in its path, is it any surprise that few travelers ride bicycles in big cities? Rural towns with countryside or archaeological sights within biking distance are the places where bicycles really become worth the small change they're rented for.

BY THUMB

Hitchhiking is uncommon in Southeast Asia since transportation tends to be inexpensive. Hitchhiking is also dangerous, especially along highways, since most cars and trucks do not travel at speeds that make it possible to stop and pick up hitchers. Even if a ride can be flagged down, the language barrier can easily create problems for the hitcher, who might find him/herself traveling to the wrong destination (and perhaps being asked for an unexpected fee upon arrival). As always, women should take extra precautions, and in general probably should not hitchhike at all.

Let's Go urges you to use common sense and consider all the risks involved before hitchhiking. We do not recommend hitchhiking to anyone.

■■■ ACCOMMODATIONS

Southeast Asia has a variety of inexpensive alternatives to hotels and motels. Before you set out, try to locate guest houses and hostels along your route and make reservations, especially if you plan to travel during peak tourist seasons. Even if you find yourself in dire straits, don't spend the night under the stars; it's often uncomfortable and unsafe, and sometimes illegal, even in national parks and forest areas.

YOUTH HOSTELS

As a rule, hostels are dorm-style accommodations where the sexes sleep apart, often in large rooms with bunk beds. (Some hostels allow families and couples to have private rooms.) You must bring or rent your own sleep sack (two sheets sewn together); sleeping bags are often not allowed. Hostels often have kitchens and utensils for your use, and some have storage areas and laundry facilities. Many also require you to perform a communal chore, usually lasting no more than 15min.

A few hostels in Southeast Asia are members of or are affiliated with **Hostelling International (HI),** formerly the International Youth Hostel Federation, and require membership to stay there or for discounted rates (see "Hostelling Organizations" on page 15).

GUEST HOUSES

The guest house (known as a homestay in Indonesia) is the single-handed savior of the budget traveler's wallet. Surprisingly enough, the large availability of guest houses is a relatively new phenomenon and is gaining momentum in some countries faster than others. The typical guest house single is a small cubicle (roughly 3m x 3m or smaller), with faded, bare walls. Usually, no amenities are provided, meaning that travelers must provide their own soap, towels, and toilet paper. The bed is a thin twin or double bed, covered with a clean but old sheet and adorned with a squishy, flaccid pillow and perhaps a large, thin beach towel to be used as a blanket in case that once-in-a-lifetime deep freeze hits. Expect shared baths with showers and a squatting toilet that you flush by manually pouring water through its drain. Many guest houses also operate a small restaurant to cater to their guests. Make sure that you see the room you are about to rent and accept its condition. Feel free to check the lock, the lights, the fan, and the bathroom.

Keep in mind that you are ultimately responsible for all personal belongings; guest houses are notorious dens of thievery—don't think your fellow travelers are immune. Keep valuables and important documents on your person. Many guest houses offer luggage storage and safe deposit boxes; you must determine whether or not these are actually safe. While most guest houses run honest operations, it only takes one exception to ruin a fine trip. Be aware of a guest house's specific policies and obey them; meet payments as requested, observe rules regarding eating, drinking, or smoking in a room. In addition, many guest houses do not allow outside guests (read: prostitutes, but this applies to fellow travelers). This measure is implemented to protect the guest house, which may be accused of robbery when a guest's "friend" runs off with the guest's valuables.

HOTELS

In general, hotels offer more comfort than guest houses, but a price must be paid for this luxury. The cheapest hotels are akin to cheap motels, but this term is seldom used in Southeast Asia, in Indonesia the term is *losmen*. The typical inexpensive hotel provides basic amenities (soap, towel, toilet paper) in a sizable room that is sometimes carpeted and decorated with wallpaper. A private bathroom, hot water, and a bathtub are common. Rooms usually have air-conditioning and some basic furnishings, even a television and refrigerator. For the single traveler, beds tend to be of the larger double-sized variety, with sheets, a blanket, and a bed cover.

While hotels tend to be less strict regarding policies on "outside guests," most require that visitors be registered on the hotel's log book. Be as careful with your valuables as you would elsewhere.

CAMPING AND THE OUTDOORS

National parks are the most common places to camp. Some offer tents, established camp sites, and even bungalows and a cafeteria. Prospective campers need to invest in good camping equipment. Refer to "Packing" on page 42 for info on **backpacks.** Most of the better **sleeping bags,** down (lightweight and warm), or synthetic (cheaper, heavier, more durable, and warmer when wet), have ratings for specific minimum temperatures. The lower the mercury, the higher the price. Expect to pay at least US$65 for a synthetic bag and up to US$270 for real feathers. **Sleeping bag pads** range US$13-25, while air mattresses go for about US$25-50. The best **tents** are free-standing with frames and suspension systems, set up quickly, and require no staking. Good two-person tents start at about US$135, for four US$200. Other camping basics include a battery-operated **lantern** (never gas), a plastic **groundcloth,** and collapsible **water sacks. Campstoves** come in all sizes, weights, and fuel types, but none is truly cheap (US$30-120) or light. In general, **cooking equipment** can prove more of an albatross than a convenience—consider your eating requirements and preferences carefully. A **canteen, Swiss army knife, waterproof matches,** and **insect repellent** are essential items to throw in with your gear.

■■■ KEEPING IN TOUCH

MAIL

For letters sent to Southeast Asia, print the mailing address in legible English, and underline the name of the country. Write the addressee's legal name on the envelope to ensure that he or she will be able to receive and accept the mail, especially if it is being sent Poste Restante.

Mail can be sent internationally **Poste Restante** (the international phrase for General Delivery) in any city or town; it's well worth using and much more reliable than you might think. Mark the envelope "HOLD" and address it, for example, "Steveland MORRIS, Boy Wonder, Poste Restante, City, Country." Capitalize and underline the last name. The mail goes to a special desk in the central post office, unless you specify a post office by street address or postal code. Use the largest post office in the area; when possible, it is safer, quicker, and more reliable to send mail express or registered. When picking up mail, bring your passport or other ID. If the clerk insists that there is nothing for you, try checking under your first name as well.

Let's Go lists post offices in the Practical Information section for each city and most towns.

Sending mail c/o certain **American Express** offices is quite reliable; they will hold your mail for free if you have AmEx traveler's checks or a card. Mail will automatically be held 30 days; to have it held longer, write "Hold for x days" on the envelope. Again, the sender should capitalize and underline your last name, marking the envelope "Client Letter Service." A complete list of AmEx offices is available for free from AmEx (tel. (800) 528-4800) in the booklet *Traveler's Companion.*

If you need to get something to its destination with haste and want to use a commercial courier service, use Federal Express or DHL; both operate throughout Southeast Asia. **Federal Express** (all prices for pick-up, under 300 sheets of 8½ x11 paper): US$32.50 to Jakarta and Kuala Lumpur (3 business days), Bangkok, Ho Chi Minh City, Kuala Lumpur (4 business days). US$28.50 to Hong Kong and Singapore (3 business days). US$44.00 to Phnom Penh. No service to Laos. **DHL** (prices for under 30 pages and 8oz of documents) US$27 to Singapore and Hong Kong (3 business days); US$35 to Jakarta, Bangkok, and Kuala Lumpur; US$71 (documents, under 16oz.) to Vientiane, Phnom Penh, and Ho Chi Minh City. Shipping anything but documents usually involves filling out a commercial invoice. For documents to Ho Chi Minh City, use the official name—do not label it as Saigon.

Phone numbers for **Federal Express:** In the US and Canada (tel. (800) 238-5355); in London (tel. (0800) 123 800); in Sydney (tel. (02) 317 66 66); in Auckland (tel. (09) 256 83 00); in Dublin (tel. (1) 800 535 800 (Secure Corps)); in Johannesburg (11) 899 88 88). For **DHL:** In the US and Canada (tel. (800) 225-5345); in London (tel. (181) 607 40 00); in Sydney (tel. (02) 317 83 00); in Auckland (tel. (09) 636 50 00); in Dublin (tel. (1) 844 41 11); in Johannesburg (tel. (11) 482 16 66).

TELEPHONE

International Subscriber Dialing (ISD) and **International Operator Direct Connection (Home Direct)** provide international telephone service. ISD calls can be made with or without the help of an operator. Without operator assistance, an ISD call may be made from any phone with international service by dialing 001 plus the country code plus the area code plus the phone number. Prices are lowest for calls within Asia, North America, and Europe, and higher for calls to the rest of the world. If you call between 9pm and midnight or 5am and 7am, you receive a 20% discount. Calls made from midnight until 5am receive a 30% discount. There is a 10-20% surcharge for calls made from hotels. For **operator assistance,** dial 100. An operator will be standing by to assist you with either a personal call, station-to-station call, collect call, or calling card call. ISD telephones are often available at post offices.

In **IODC Home Direct** calls, special phones are pre-connected to operators within the country whose name appears on the phone. These calls are charged to the called party like collect calls. Access codes are listed in the specific countries.

TELEGRAM

To send a **telegram** overseas from the U.S., Western Union (tel. (800) 325-6000) charges US$14.32, plus US$9 outside the U.S., plus about 76¢ per word, including name and address. They have no telegram service to Laos or Cambodia.

Team Southeast Asia '96 Recommends...

Every traveler to Southeast Asia goes places that stand out for a lifetime. While *Let's Go* cannot decide what places you, dear reader, will like the most, our team of 9 researcher-writers and 3 editors has spent an entire season extensively researching places that you just might like to see. The following unranked list of "Greatest Hits" has been compiled collectively by this year's research team.

Cambodia

Angkor
Phnom Penh
Siem Reap

Hong Kong

Aberdeen Harbor
Stanley Market
Victoria Peak Gardens

Laos

Luang Prabang
Nam Ngum Lake
Pakxe and Southern Laos

Peninsular Malaysia

Jungle and tea plantation treks, Cameron Highlands
Cultural show hosted by Roselan at the Gelanggang Seni, Kota Bharu
Motorbiking through Teluk Datai and Pantai Kok, Pulau Langkawi
Melaka
Perhentian Islands
Night walks in Taman Negara
Teluk Bahang

Singapore

Chewing gum
Eating with the animals at the zoo

Thailand

Grand Palace and Wat Pho, Bangkok
Doi Pukha National Park
Erawan National Park
Kamphaeng Phet Historical Park
Ko Tao
Sea canoeing in the Andaman Sea, Krabi
The entire Mekong River route, Northeast Thailand
Pai
Sangkhlaburi
Sangkhom
Songthaew rides with lipless chickens and toothless women
Tee Lor Su Waterfall
Trat
Wat Phu Thawk

Vietnam

Dalat
Cruising on Halong Bay
Ho Chi Minh in formaldyhyde, Hanoi
Hoi An
Hue
Marble Mountains
Swimming at Nha Trang
Clubbing in Saigon
Sapa

Western Indonesia

Bengkulu
Brastagi
The orangutans at Bukit Lawang
Bukittinggi
Gedong Songo
Malang
Mt. Bromo
A night at Parangtritis
The Puncak
Picking up handfuls of Ming Dynasty porcelain at Pulau Penyeget
The *batik* market in Solo
Exploratory bike rides from Ubud
Ujung Kulon National Park
Ulu Watu
Walking blindfolded across the Alun-alun Kidul, Yogyakarta

CAMBODIA

Like the majestic temple towers of Angkor breaking through the dense jungles that vie to smother the ancient city, Cambodia, too, is transcending its own crippling history. Once the brilliant gem and artistic leader of Southeast Asia, Cambodia is now trying to resurrect its cultural traditions in an effort to heal the pain of the country's recent tragedy. During the Khmer Rouge's brief but interminable four-year reign, more than one million Cambodians were murdered. Today, these atrocities are still evident in the "Killing Fields," where the bones and ragged clothes of innocent victims can be seen, half-buried in the bleeding soil.

The Cambodian people have endured far more than their share of sorrow, and their legacy too has wrought an inescapable, if not indelible, stain on the urban fabric. Crippled soldiers loll on the sidewalks, and far too many children have grown up parentless as a result of the Khmer Rouge genocide. Unlike most other people in Southeast Asia, Cambodians are wary of foreigners. This and the continuing struggle between the new government and the insurgent Khmer Rouge make traveling through Cambodia difficult, but not impossible.

The diligent traveler who can breach the barriers into Cambodia will find a country in the process of rebirth, with the exuberant laughter of children and the beaming smiles of people proudly displaying an ancient heritage nearly eradicated less than 20 years ago.

ESSENTIALS

■■■ GEOGRAPHY

Cambodia sits near the southern tip of the Indochinese peninsula, covering 181,035sq km, roughly the size of England and Wales. The country is enclosed but mountains, while its lowland interior is one of savannas, dense forests, and rich, fertile alluvial plains. In the northeast, the Eastern Highlands rise to form a natural border with Laos. The Dangkrek Mountains run the length of the northern border with Thailand, while the Cardamom and Elephant Mountains can be found in the west and southwest of the country. Phnom Aural, Cambodia's highest peak, ascends 1813m from the Cardamom range. The Mekong River flows 500km through the east and curves by Phnom Penh, where it divides into the Lower Mekong and Bassac Rivers. Also running by the capital is the Tonle Sap River, which flows 100km downriver from the Tonle Sap, or literally "Great Lake," the largest fresh-water pond in Southeast Asia at 3000sq km. During the rainy season, between June and October, the Mekong usually floods, overflowing into the Tonle Sap River which then reverses its course and deposits the excess water into the Tonle Sap, doubling the lake's size.

■■■ WHEN TO GO

The best time to visit Cambodia is between November and April, when the temperature is cooler and the rainfall is low. From October to April, the northwest monsoon blows through the country, bringing in the dry season. Heavy rains fall with the coming of the southwest monsoon between May and October, usually accounting for more than three-fourths of Cambodia's annual rainfall. The Cardamom Mountains generally receive the heaviest rains. Rain ordinarily falls in the afternoon, when it is the most humid.

■■■ GETTING AROUND

Most tourists choose to travel in Cambodia **by plane.** Buses and trains, while they exist, are not recommended as long as the Khmer Rouge continue to menace the people. **They have been known to kill tourists. Stay away from any land travel.** Thus, inexpensive daily flights exist connecting Phnom Penh to Siem Reap (near Angkor temples, the most popular destination in Cambodia), as well as other cities, including Sihanoukville, Battambang, Kratie, Kompong Cham, and Stung Treng. (See "Practical Information" on page 76 for more details.) There is a US$4 airport tax on all domestic flights.

The only other safe option to getting around, riding the waves is a safe and enjoyable mode of transportation within Cambodia. **Boat excursions** to Siem Reap and eastern Cambodia can be easily arranged in Phnom Penh.

Travelers also have the option to move around **by car,** either by renting one or by hiring a taxi. If you choose this option, be aware that most roads are unpaved and have fallen into bad conditions, making them virtually impassable at some points. **Because of roving Khmer Rouge rebels, avoid road travel at night.**

■■■ MONEY

US$1=2300.44riel	**100riel=US$0.043**
CDN$=1692.20riel	**100riel=CDN$0.059**
UK£1=3574.88riel	**100riel=UK£0.023**
IR£1=3643.89riel	**100riel=IR£0.027**
AUS$1=1695.88riel	**100riel=AUS$0.059**
NZ$1=1508.63riel	**100riel=NZ$0.066**
SARand=629.17riel	**100riel=SARand0.159**

The Cambodian monetary unit is the **riel (r).** The riel is divided into 50, 100, 200, and 500 riel notes. The exchange rate fluctuates frequently, anywhere from 2000-2500r for US$1. In Cambodia, the US$ acts as a second currency and is widely accepted at many hotels, guest houses, and restaurants; in fact, some places will only take US$. *Let's Go* lists prices in both riel and US$. It is wise to keep small US$ notes handy.

Prices in Cambodia are still quite cheap in comparison to western countries. Hard-core budget travelers can get by on 23,000r (US$10) per day. Many nice accommodations can be had for 6900r (US$3) and meals for less than 4600r (US$2). Go crazy. **Tipping** is not necessary, but much appreciated since the average Cambodian makes about $5 per month.

■■■ KEEPING IN TOUCH

The **postal service** in Cambodia is not quite as efficient as that in the west, but it exists. Mail can take as long as two weeks to and from Cambodia. Poste Restante service is available in Phnom Penh. **Postal codes** are not used in Cambodia. **Telephones** in Phnom Penh are still scarce but gradually making its presence known. The rest of the country and many locations in the capital use cellular phones. These numbers begin with 015, 017, 018, or 023, and are followed by 6 digits. **Long-distance calls** placed from Cambodia can be costly. **Collect call** rates sometimes go as high as US$8 per minute to North America and Europe. Some places do accept incoming calls for a small charge; whenever possible, *Let's Go* has listed these places. IDD calls can be placed from Telstra phone booths found around Phnom Penh. **Country code:** 855. **Home Country Direct numbers:** Telecom Australia, 1800-881-061. U.S.: AT&T, 1800-881-001.

■■■ STAYING SAFE

Cambodians have seen a lifetime's worth of crime and violence in a few short years, so it is without surprise that crime rates here are at a minimum. What little crime there is in Cambodia is often found on the poorly lit streets at night and in raucous bars frequented by locals. Play it safe and avoid these places. **Petty thievery** is a serious problem in Phnom Penh. Keep your valuables close to you. Of course, crime is not the biggest threat to your safety in this country; the 8 to 10 million **anti-personnel mines** littering the land and roving **Khmer Rouge rebels** should be your biggest concern. Check with your embassy or find out from expatriates about travel conditions outside of Phnom Penh before venturing out yourself. The situation changes so frequently that you should not base your opinions on a single guidebook. What we have reported is the situation as of summer 1995. While drug policies in Southeast Asia tend to be harsh, Cambodia has legalized **marijuana** (for sale, possession, and consumption), which is readily available in the markets for roughly $1 per kilo.

> When traveling through the countryside or exploring ancient ruins, stay on well-trodden paths. Tourists have been killed by landmines.

■■■ HOURS AND HOLIDAYS

Many government offices, businesses, and banks open early in the morning and close around noon for a mid-day break, opening again for the afternoon. Most offices, excluding some banks, are open on Saturdays also.

Festivals and holidays in Cambodia commemorate important facets in the history of the country: the king, the land, the water, and the religion. Many businesses close during official holidays but not necessarily during long, lengthy festivals. Keep these dates in mind when planning your trip:

January: Vietnamese and Chinese New Year (varies with lunar year).
January 7: National Day celebrates the defeat of the Khmer Rouge in 1979.
April-May: The Royal Ploughing ceremony (*Bonn Chroat Preah Nongkal*) is the first of many agrarian festivals taking place throughout these two months.
April: New Year's (*Bonn Chaul Chhnam*), a 3-day affair at the end of the harvest.
May 1: Labor Day.
May 9: Genocide Day, remembering Khmer Rouge atrocities.
September: Spirits Commemoration Festival commemorates the spirits of the dead by offering food to the monks for 15 days.
October: Bonn Kathen is a month-long religious festival in which Cambodians march in procession to wats where monks change their saffron robes.
October 31: King Norodom Sihanouk's Birthday. Your only chance to see the Royal Palace which opens to the public for grand festivities.
November 9: Independence Day.
November: Bonn Om Tuk, a 3-day Water Festival (varies with lunar year).

CAMBODIA

■■■ POTPOURRI FOR $100, ALEX!

Most streets in Cambodia are narrow, unpaved affairs called either *vithei* or *phlavu.* But in Phnom Penh, French influence is evident in the wide boulevards, called *moha vithei* (or M.V.), avenues, called *rukhak vithei* (or R.V.), and traffic circles. Be aware that the names of many the streets, especially in the capital, have been changed at least three times in the past two decades by three separate governments. The ones *Let's Go* uses in this book are the official names, but locals may continue to refer to previous names. Numbered routes denote national highways, however narrow and tiny they may be.

Cambodia is seven hours ahead of Greenwich Mean Time (GMT).

LIFE AND TIMES

■■■ HISTORY

The fertile plains of Cambodia were once the foundation of powerful empires, including civilizations as early as 3000 years ago. The country itself, lying on the trade routes between China and India, is a patchwork of traditions absorbed by the people and blended into a distinct Khmer culture that, at its height, influenced the entire region of Southeast Asia.

EARLY KINGDOMS AND INDIANIZATION

The first recorded civilization arose in the 1st century AD. Called **Funan** by the Chinese—a mispronunciation of *kurung bnam,* which means "King of the Mountain"—this kingdom dominated Southeast Asia for the next five centuries. Situated on the lower reaches of the **Tonle Sap** and the **Mekong** rivers, Funan developed into a prosperous fishing, rice cultivation and trade center. Indeed, Roman, Greek, Persian, and Indian artifacts have been found in the area near Oc Eo, Vietnam, which is believed to have been Funan's main port. With increasing prosperity, Funan was able to subjugate its neighbors, extending its boundaries south to the Malay peninsula and east across most of present-day Vietnam.

Contact with foreigners through merchants, diplomats, and Brahmins fostered the spread of **Hindu** culture to Southeast Asia, profoundly forging the history, art, culture, and politics of the region. The arrival of Indian immigrants in the 4th and 5th centuries hastened this process of Indianization, so that by the end of the 5th century, Indian culture was thoroughly integrated into Funan life. The people adopted the use of a Sanskrit-based script, the worship of Hindu gods, and art styles influenced by the Gupta period in India.

In the 6th century, internal conflicts plagued the empire, rendering it vulnerable to aggression from hostile neighbors. Eventually, Funan was slowly displaced by the rising powers of **Chenla,** an Indianized dynasty originally centered in the Lao southern province of Champassak. By the end of the 7th century, Funan had become a mere vassal state to Chenla, but marriages between the two royal families managed to retain the political, social, and religious culture of the former empire.

Chenla's rulers sought to expand their kingdom by annexing present-day Laos and Thailand. However, in the 8th century, dynastic upheaval split the empire into two rival kingdoms. **Land Chenla,** centered north of the Tonle Sap, had an agrarian-based economy and was able to maintain a relatively stable existence, while **Water Chenla,** situated on the lower Mekong, was vanquished by the Javanese empire of **Sailendra** after a period of constant internal conflict.

Sun, Moon, and Star

According to Khmer legends, the people of Cambodia were born from the union of the heavens. One Kaundinya, an Indian Brahman priest, followed a most exciting dream which came to him, and eventually came to the edge of a vast great lake. There he married the beautiful Soma, daughter of the Naga king. From their union sprang forth the "lunar" dynasty (Funan). The Naga drank the waters of the lake, uncovering a fertile delta for the people to cultivate.

Some time later, in a land not too far away from Funan, an ascetic named Kambu married the beautiful and celestial Mera. They gave birth to a powerful kingdom, the "solar" dynasty (Chenla), and their descendants were known as Kambuja, the "sons of Kambu." It didn't take long for both houses to realize that a match made in heaven would unite the two kingdoms. The moon prince married the sun princess; but he betrayed his own people and aligned himself with Chenla, which subsumed Funan without difficulty.

The solar dynasty was soon eclipsed by that star of all dynasties—Angkor.

THE GOLDEN AGE OF ANGKOR

As the final step to the complete subjugation of the kingdom, Chenla's royal family was taken to the Javanese court. It was not until 800 AD, when **Jayavarman II** (802-50) returned to his family's Khmer state, that the former Chenla was freed from the suzerainty of Java. In 802 he founded the empire of **Kambuja** (from which Cambodia, or Kampuchea, took its name), beginning the history of a unified Cambodia. This empire, however, is better known as **Angkor,** named for the temple complex built near Jayavarman II's capital city as a lasting tribute to his descendents. Jayavarman II revived the Hindu cult of **devaraja,** or god-king, granting him divine status, through which he was able to rule unchallenged as the absolute monarch. Kambuja marked the beginning of Cambodia's golden age which brought the kingdom unprecedented power and brilliant achievements in art and architecture.

From the 9th to the 14th century, Angkor thrived under the rule of strong and capable monarchs. **Indravarman I** (AD 877-89) began construction of an elaborate system of canals and reservoirs that are believed to be the cornerstone of Kambuja's prosperity, freeing the kingdom from dependence on the monsoons and providing large surpluses of rice. Under **Suryavarman II** (AD 1113-50), Kambuja stretched to the Irrawady River in Burma to the west, Vietnam to the east, China to the north, and the Malay peninsula to the south. Despite such strong military victories, Suryavarman II's greatest achievement lies in the construction of **Angkor Wat,** the largest religious edifice in the world. Unfortunately, his reign was followed by 30 years of insurrection and incursion by the neighboring **Champa** kingdom in southern Vietnam which eventually captured and sacked Angkor in 1177.

The rise of **Jayavarman VII** (1181-1218), the last great king of Angkor, to the throne ended Champa's hold on the struggling empire. This king, whose reign marked the pinnacle of Kambuja's power, drove out and conquered the Chams, bringing them under Khmer rule. Unlike his predecessors, Jayavarman VII was an avid believer in **Mahayana Buddhism,** rather than the cult of *devaraja.* He sponsored the construction of numerous temples, including the building of Angkor Thom and the Bayon temple complexes, as well as rest houses, hospitals, and roads throughout the kingdom. Although a distinguished king, Jayavarman VII's religion undermined his legitimacy while his extravagant projects drained income from Kambuja's irrigation system. The wars and the public works, however long-lasting they may be, severely sapped the financial and human capital of the empire.

After Jayavarman VII's death, Kambuja entered a long period of decline, from which it never emerged. Furthermore, the spread of **Theravada Buddhism,** which came to Kambuja from Sri Lanka by way of the neighboring Thai state of Sukhothai, challenged the royal Hindu and Mahayana Buddhist cults. The humanitarian and egalitarian teachings of this religion were in direct opposition to the lavish life-style of the royal court which kept the peasants at the mercy of the whims of the throne. At this time, increased southward migration of the Tai-Kadai peoples from Mongol China began to displace the Khmers. The rising Lao kingdom of Lan Xang seized Kambuja's northern territories while the Thais waged perpetual war on the weakened kingdom. The capture of Angkor Thom by Ayutthaya (Sukhothai's successor) hailed the final defeat of the Angkor Empire in 1431.

COLONIAL RULE AND INDEPENDENCE

For the next five centuries, the remnants of Angkor struggled to maintain its existence, marked by economic, political, and cultural stagnation, known as Cambodia's "dark ages." By the mid-19th century, Cambodia had become hopelessly trapped in the territorial struggle between Thailand and Vietnam until France intervened by claiming the kingdom for itself.

France was already heavily involved with Vietnam, and sought to expand its influence in the region to ultimately gain control of the Mekong against the threat of the British in Burma and the Thais next door. In 1863, the French annexed Cambodia as a protectorate to thwart its rivals, dismissing the appeals of Khmer **King Norodom** (1860-1904) and cruelly suppressing insurrections. For the next two decades, the French colonialists exploited Cambodia's people and natural resources to the utmost, turning the country into a vast rubber plantation and rice market. When King Norodom blatantly refused to accept anymore mistreatment from their oppressors in 1884, he was forced at gun point to surrender Cambodia completely to France as a colony.

In order to gain royal support and a biddable ally, the French interfered with the succession, passing over the crown prince, in favor of Norodom's brother Sisowath, for whom they provided an extravagant life-style. The new king's collaboration with French rule essentially halted any nationalist movements similar to those of its neighbors. The French, in their development strategies for economic profit, disregarded the most basic needs of the population, such as health and education. The peasants lived in virtual enslavement to the colonial power, as their ancestors had before them to the god-kings.

When the **Japanese** seized Indochina during **World War II,** they allowed the French to remain in nominal control, while the Axis power continued on its military rampage through Southeast Asia. In 1941, the French crowned 18-year-old **Prince Norodom Sihanouk,** the grandson of Norodom, king of Cambodia. In their efforts to install a puppet government, the French underestimated Sihanouk to be weak, inexperienced, and pliable to their needs. Japan's calls for "Asia for the Asiatics" kindled anti-European feelings and galvanized nationalist struggles throughout Indochina. In Cambodia, the **Khmer Issarak** (Freedom Front) arose as the foremost nationalist movement. With persuasion from Japan, Sihanouk declared independence for his country and dissolved all treaties with the French. Nevertheless, the new Democrat-controlled government represented the interests of a pro-French elite, intent on retaining its privileges.

When the French returned in late 1945, they were compelled to keep promises made by the Free French during the war. Thus, Cambodia's colonial status was nullified and the absolute monarchy abolished. Sihanouk, however, remained a figurative head of state, trying to negotiate with the French for full independence while attempting to placate supporters of the pro-communist Khmer Issarak and the Viet Minh who were suspicious of his relations with France.

As the war between the French and the Viet Minh intensified during the late 1940s, the turmoil spilled into Cambodia. Even though the Viet Minh had stirred anti-French sentiment, the French successfully managed to divide the Cambodians. Two factions of the Issarak emerged: the dominant was strongly pro-Viet Minh while the other was largely anti-communist and wary of the Vietnamese. Under the auspices of the Viet Minh, the pro-communist Issarak formed Cambodia's first communist party, the **Khmer People's Revolutionary Party (KPRP).** Meanwhile, in Paris, Cambodian students such as **Saloth Sar (Pol Pot), Khieu Samphan**, and **Ieng Sary**—known as the **"Paris Circle"**—were introduced to Marxism and eventually joined the French Communist Party, the most disciplined and Stalinist in Western Europe. This group would come to play an important role in the development of communism in Cambodia, profoundly altering the course of its modern history.

With increased anti-French communist activities in Vietnam and Laos, as well as the insurgent guerilla war waged by the Khmer Issarak, France eventually granted complete independence to Cambodia on **November 9, 1953,** less than two weeks before their devastating defeat at Dien Bien Phu. The **Geneva Accords** of 1954 recognized Sihanouk's Royal government as the sole legitimate authority in Cambodia. The Khmer Issarak, who were instrumental in the nationalist movement, were not invited to take part in the conference. This proved to be a gross mistake on the part of the Western nations and Sihanouk, because the majority of the Issarak withdrew from Cambodia to the refuge of communist North Vietnam in order to strengthen their position. However, the Paris Circle remained to shape the destiny of the communist movement in Cambodia.

CIVIL WAR

For the people of Cambodia, independence also meant freedom from an absolute monarchy. Therefore Sihanouk abdicated in 1955, although he remained a popular political leader. Using his influence, Sihanouk played a neutrality card that kept his country out of the war raging in Vietnam and Laos in the 1960s. However, when civil war broke out in South Vietnam, Sihanouk gave his support to the Vietnamese rebels allied to Hanoi. In an effort to thwart American involvement in Cambodia, Sihanouk broke all diplomatic relations with the U.S. in 1965. Much to the indignation of the U.S., Sihanouk also allowed the Viet Minh to run the **Ho Chi Minh Trail** through Cambodia. His ambiguity and constant shifting between right and left incurred much resentment from the political elite in Cambodia. This and his refusal to cooperate with the U.S. prompted the American-backed coup of 1970 by army Commander-in-Chief **Lon Nol,** who immediately abolished the monarchy and declared the **Khmer Republic.**

Sihanouk fled into exile and his revolutionary troops joined forces with the communist **Khmer Rouge** (a term Sihanouk used for all leftist groups, but later signified Pol Pot and his supporters who gained control of the KPRP in 1960) to incite revolts throughout the country while the North Vietnamese burrowed further into Cambodia in its clandestine activities. In April 1970, B-52 and fighter bombers dropped hundreds of tons of bombs on eastern Cambodia as a prelude to invasion by American and South Vietnamese troops. Lon Nol, caught by surprise, felt angry and betrayed; Sihanouk set up a government-in-exile, immediately recognized by the communist regimes of Beijing and Hanoi and attracting the support of Khmer Rouge leaders. Civil war broke out between the two governments soon after.

During the next two years, revolutionary forces were successful in their guerilla attacks, isolating Phnom Penh from the rest of the country. At times, it was believed that they held 80% of Cambodia's territory so that by 1973, they were ready to launch an immediate, and probably successful coup on the capital. However, the US increased bombings that year, pushing revolutionary forces back and killing most of Sihanouk's supporters. As a result, the Khmer Rouge emerged as the dominant faction of the rebel insurgents.

REIGN OF TERROR

In 1975, the Khmer Rouge increased their offensive to gain control of Cambodia, finally seizing Phnom Penh on April 17, and renamed the country **Democratic Kampuchea.** Thus began one of the world's most brutal reigns of terror. The leaders of the Khmer Rouge, the so-called Paris Circle, were not incognizant or uneducated, as popularly believed; rather, they were perhaps the most intellectually elite of Asia's communist leaders. They took such drastic actions in state building because of strong communist convictions. In their doctorate theses, many of these men blamed western oppression for impeding development in their country and contended that modernization can be achieved without industrialization.

As a means to an agrarian society, Pol Pot and his Khmer Rouge exterminated their opposition and forced the Cambodian people to the countryside where they were pressed into slave labor. Cities were destroyed, modern facilities were sabotaged, and currency use was terminated. For the Khmer Rouge, it was no longer 1975, but "Year Zero." People who wore glasses or spoke foreign languages were executed without remorse. During their reign, the Khmer Rouge massacred an estimated 1.4 million people (other estimates reach as high as 2.3 million) in a horrific holocaust unknown since Adolf Hitler's gas chambers. There was no room in the new society for personal expression of any sort. People were forced to work diligently, accept poor living conditions and food rations, refrain from lavish displays of wealth, swallow their grief over the loss of loved ones, and reject their religion. Violation of these rules meant imminent execution. To avoid such a fate, about two million people fled their homeland, many of whom died along the way. For a moving and realistic look into the horror of the Khmer Rouge regime, watch the movie *The Killing Fields*.

THE VIETNAMESE INTERVENTION

For nearly four years, the world sat back and watched the death of the Cambodian people. Finally, on December 25, 1978, Vietnamese forces invaded the country, successfully driving out the Khmer Rouge within two weeks. Nevertheless, the United Nations condemned Vietnam's occupation of Kampuchea; yet, nobody else was willing to intervene. A new government was set up for the **People's Republic of Kampuchea (PRK)** under **President Heng Samrin** and **Prime Minister Hun Sen.** Many different factions resisted Vietnamese rule, including Thailand, China, and Democratic Kampuchea, represented by Sihanouk (he had previously distanced himself from the Khmer Rouge) before the UN Security Council. In an unbelievable move in September 1979, the UN General Assembly passed over the PRK, instead, recognizing the Khmer Rouge as the representative government of the Cambodian people in the United Nations. By the next year, 25 countries (mostly communist regimes) had recognized the PRK as the new legitimate government, but more than 80 countries continued to regard the Khmer Rouge as the sole authority. The Heng Samrin government, despite its unpopularity among the Cambodian people and the rest of the world, tried to restore the social and economic order of Kampuchea in the face of daunting odds.

THE NEW KINGDOM OF CAMBODIA

After more than 10 years of keeping the Khmer Rouge at bay, Vietnam withdrew its forces from Cambodia in September 1989 under harsh criticism and embargo. The Paris peace agreement in October 1991 allowed the UN to deploy the **United Nations Transit Authority in Cambodia (UNTAC),** by far their largest peacekeeping force, to monitor the ongoing civil war and resettle refugees back into the country. They oversaw the elections for a coalition government in May 1993, ensuring for the first time that all Cambodians had a chance to vote. In September, Sihanouk returned to his country and was crowned king of Cambodia again. That same year, the PRK was renamed Cambodia in an attempt to erase the horror and pain of the Khmer Rouge era from the memories of the people.

■■■ CAMBODIA TODAY

The annihilation and flight of the educated elite has posed a challenge to rebuilding the internal structures of the country. Left without a skilled workforce, Cambodia is struggling to keep up with a changing global market. Since the 1993 elections, the new government, led by co-prime ministers **Prince Ranariddh** and Hun Sen, have continued to battle the Khmer Rouge, who attempted a coup in 1994. With all the corruption and unrest, the government is moving towards authoritarianism. While fears of human rights violations abound, the Cambodian government wants to open trade with the rest of the world. When U.S. Secretary of State Warren Christopher visited the country in August 1995, the first visit of an American government official in 40 years, the prime ministers asked him to help them obtain most-favored-nation trading status from U.S. Congress. They fear that with the establishing of diplomatic relations with Vietnam, foreign investment will pour into Hanoi and Saigon, leaving Phnom Penh once again trailing in the dust. Whether Cambodia can overcome the economic and social upheavals it is experiencing and eventually become a full-fledged exporter remains to be seen.

■■■ THE PEOPLE OF CAMBODIA

In 1971, estimations placed the Cambodian population at eight million, but after the Khmer Rouge holocaust, that number had decreased dramatically to five million. However, high birth rates and the repatriation of refugees from Thailand have brought the population back to 8.8 million again; nearly half are under the age of 15. The number of Cambodians who were killed or who have fled is indeterminable, but it is estimated that two million refugees have emigrated.

The people of Cambodia tend to be more homogenous than other countries in the region, the dominant group being Khmer. Unfortunately, this is not a barrier to ethnic hostility. Rather, a high percentage of homogeneity creates a strong national identity and those not belonging to the majority are often persecuted.

It is believed that the Khmers, who make up 85% of Cambodia's population today, have inhabited the country since 2000 BC. Theories claim that the Khmer followed the Mekong River south into Cambodia from either southwest China or the Khasi Hills of northeast India. Once here, they mixed with the Malays who had been filtering into the area for several centuries. Still others contend that the Khmers come from Indonesia. Regardless of where they originated, the Khmers intermarried with other ethnic groups of Thai, Indian, Chinese and Vietnamese who migrated into the region after them, but continue to remain predominant.

The **Khmer Loeu,** or Upland Khmer, lived in forested mountains of northeastern Cambodia until the Vietnam War pushed them down to the lowlands. Like most hill tribes in Southeast Asia, the Khmer Loeu are animists and practice slash-and-burn agriculture. There are four subdivisions to this group. The **Brao** still live in the northeast along the Lao border, the **Kuy** in the northwest, the **Pear** in the Cardamon

Mountains to the west, and the **Saoch** in the Elephant Mountains to the southwest. The Khmer Loeu are slowly assimilating into mainstream Khmer culture.

Today, the **Chinese** constitute only 3% of the population, but prior to Pol Pot's time, their numbers were far greater and they dominated Cambodian politics and commerce. Large groups of Chinese began to migrate to Cambodia in the 18th and 19th centuries, settling down, intermarrying, and trading. They eventually took over the national economy and controlled banking and commerce. Like their counterparts in Thailand, the Chinese were able to successfully integrate in Cambodian society without repercussions; nor did they sacrifice their distinctiveness even after intermarriage with Khmers. When civil war erupted, many Chinese fled; of those who remained, few survived the Khmer Rouge holocaust.

Unlike the Chinese, the **Vietnamese** (or the pejorative *yuon*, as the Khmers call them) have had a difficult struggle to assimilate into Cambodian society. Driven by centuries of animosity towards Vietnamese invaders, the Khmers have in the past and continue to persecute this ethnic minority. Pogroms as recently as 1970 sanctioned the murder of innocent Vietnamese victims whose bodies were then cast into the Tonle Sap. The rise of the Khmer Rouge saw a mass exodus of the Vietnamese who feared for their lives. However, following the Vietnamese invasion in 1979, many of these people returned to Cambodia, feeling safer with the presence of the military. Today, the Vietnamese comprise only a scant 5% of the population, but the Khmer Rouge continue their animosity for the them.

Most **Chams** are descendents of the former Champa kingdom in southern Vietnam who were forced out of their homeland by the Vietnamese between the 15th and 18th centuries. The **Malays,** on the other hand, were invited to settle in Cambodia after Khmer King Chan converted to Islam in the mid-17th century. Nowadays, most Chams and Malays, who make up 3% of the population, live along the Mekong River north of Phnom Penh and regard Chur-Changvra, near Phnom Penh, as their spiritual Mecca. During their four-year reign, the Khmer Rouge ruthlessly persecuted this minority group, wiping out half the Cham-Malay population and destroying the majority of their mosques. These Muslim groups are slowly recovering from this devastation and make their living as cattle traders, silk weavers, and butchers.

■■■ CUSTOMS AND CULTURE

GETTING ALONG IN CAMBODIA

Nothing characterizes Cambodian society more than politeness. For these people, indirectness is the way of being and confrontations are avoided as much as possible. Westerners often mistake this quality to be one of timidity and meekness.

When Cambodians pass each other on the street, they are expected to bow slightly from the waist as an acknowledgment and a show of respect. However, when they salute each other, Cambodians will hold up their hands near their faces in a prayer-like clasp with fingers and palms pressed together. This greeting attests to the esteem between the two people. In a family, the husband is always greeted first, then the wife, and finally the children, in order of their age.

Furthermore, refrain from touching a Cambodian's head—an extremely offensive insult. The spirit is believed to abide in the head, making it the most sacred part of the body. It is equally insulting to point a foot at someone because that body part is considered to be the lowest in value.

RELIGION

Today, **Theravada Buddhism** (or "teaching of the elders") is the official religion in Cambodia and is followed by 85% of the population. During the Angkorian period, however, the Hindu cult of *devaraja* dominated. Even then, this religion was practiced only by the court and the upper classes. Cambodian peasants may have regarded their king as a divine being, but they continued to practice a mixture of animism, ancestor worship, and Buddhism. For more on this, see "Cosmology and the Role of Religion in Angkor" on page 97.

Buddhism, which began as a reaction to Hindu canons and an effort to reform them, influences every aspect of Cambodian life. It is a tolerant, atheist religion based on the concepts of *dharma* (Buddha's guide to right actions and belief), *karma* (the belief that one is fully responsible for one's own actions in past, present, and future lives), and *sangha* (the ascetic community within which man can improve his karma). Its compatibility with other religious beliefs makes Buddhism popular with the common people.

The wat, or temple, is the spiritual center of the Cambodian community. Despite the destruction of many of Cambodia's temples at the hands of the Khmer Rouge, many have been reconsecrated since the Vietnamese invasion. Today, there are as many wats as there were before the Cambodian civil war.

Mahayana Buddhism (or "Great Vehicle") arose to challenge the monastic emphasis of Theravada Buddhism and to appeal to a much wider audience. Eventually, Mahayana Buddhism found a foothold in Central Asia, China, Japan, and Vietnam. So it is without surprise that this sect is the religion of the majority of Chinese and Vietnamese in Cambodia. Like the Khmers, Chinese and Vietnamese Buddhists blend elements of other religious practices, such as ancestral worship, Taoism, and Confucianism with their own.

Islam is the religion of the Cham and Malay ethnic groups; however, they are divided in their beliefs. Traditional Chams, on the one hand, deem Allah to be the all-powerful God, but they also believe in other non-Islamic deities and supernatural powers. They celebrate many Muslim festivals and rituals, but often do not make the pilgrimage to Mecca. The orthodox Chams, on the other hand, bear more similarity to the Malays than their own ethnic group because of close ties and intermarriages. They have also adopted Malay customs and many speak the Malay language. Along with the Malay, orthodox Chams participate in worldwide Islamic celebrations and conferences, including the pilgrimage. There is often tension between these two sects, but Islam continues to bind them together.

What is Wat Etiquette?

Wats are sacred to Buddhists, so travelers should be respectful when visiting these structures:

1. Dress appropriately—no shorts or tank tops.
2. Hats should not be worn upon entering the grounds of the wat.
3. Ask permission to enter the main sanctuary (*wiharn*) and take off your shoes before entering.
4. Do not sit cross-legged in front of the Buddha—that would be pointing your toe at the Holy One. Instead, sit down and bend your legs to the side, keeping toes and soles away from the Buddha.
5. Do not point fingers at sacred images.
6. When talking to a monk, keep your head lower than his.
7. Bring a small offering or donation.

WOMEN IN CAMBODIA

Unlike women in most Asian societies, women in Cambodia have greater autonomy and authority. Descent and inheritance is bilateral and legal children inherit equally from their parents. The wife has considerable authority in family economics and she serves as the major ethical and religious model for the children, especially the daughters. Although women are still more or less confined to the home today, Cambodian women work as equal partners with their husbands.

■■■ THE ARTS

ARCHITECTURE

The Cambodian people have inherited one of the most remarkable artistic legacies the world has ever known—the **Angkor temples.** Although Khmer art in all its forms was inspired by Indian culture, it was the genius of the native peoples that gave expression and content to their greatest achievement.

Jayavarman II, greatly inspired by the artistic traditions of Sailendra, dreamt of establishing a powerful empire that would be supported by a strong religious cult expressed through the medium of art. Sailendra monarchs claimed the title of "Mountain Kings," and Jayavarman II too wanted to enshrine himself and his descendants in a heavenly mountain. Consequently, Khmer temples were modeled on **Mount Meru,** the sacred mountain dwelling of the gods, which houses the king's divinity and source of power—his **lingga.** The first few structures were based on the old Chenla style—usually brick pyramids that are sometimes tiered—until Jayavarman II brought in architects from Java and Champa to help design temples at Kulen and the Roluos.

However, it was not until the 10th century when Kambuja finally consolidated its power that Cambodian art flourished. Built of pinkish sandstone and laterite, early temples were simple representations of Mount Meru, consisting of a tiered pyramid topped with a sanctuary. Later temples built in the 12th century, most notably Angkor Wat, evolved into ornate and grandiose affairs. Angkor Wat, with its walls, moat, and gates, served as a temple consecrated to Vishnu as well as a heavenly palace for the *devaraja.* The walls enclosing temple complexes signify the earth, while the moats, canals, and *barays* (reservoirs) symbolize the oceans. Khmer buildings are usually oriented east to west, with the main gates to the east. The galleries and walls of the temples are covered with exquisite bas-relief carvings of high quality that depict scenes from Hindu epics and Khmer history, intertwining gods and demons with Khmer kings and *apsarases.* Typical Angkorian architecture also includes ornate lintels, false windows and doors, and long pathways to the main entrance flanked by serpentine *nagas.*

The advent of Buddhism into Khmer society did little to change the art of the kingdom, rather, this new religion thrived side by side with the Hindu cult. The only difference was that god-kings were no longer incarnations of the Hindu gods, but of Buddha himself. The reign of Jayavarman VII, a staunch Buddhist, marked a period of colossal architecture. Much of the temples still standing were constructed during this time and houses statues of the Buddha. The Bayon, the greatest of Jayavarman VII's sanctuaries, has rising towers decorated with the giant smiling faces of Lokesvara and houses one of the most impressive collections of Buddha iconography to be found anywhere in the Buddhist realm. (See "Angkor" on page 94.)

DRAMA AND DANCE

Aside from its famous temples, Angkor civilization also saw the birth of **classical dance,** a highly stylized dance form that has influenced both Thailand and Laos. In ancient times, the dance was a religious tradition, done in honor of the temple gods to bring divine blessing to the king and his people. Today, classical dance is being revived in a broad artistic movement sweeping through the country.

Based on the sacred dances of the *apsarases,* the mythological celestial nymphs of ancient Cambodia, classical dance retells the great Indian epics, particularly the *Ramayana*. When the Thai kingdom of Ayutthaya plundered Angkor, they took the Khmer dancers back with them. With the dancers, the Thais also took the art of classical dance away from the Khmer, and, as a result, dance in Cambodia died out. However, in their efforts to assert themselves over the Khmer people, the Thais reintroduced classical dance to the Cambodian people. The dance remained Khmer in style, with the exception of the use of elaborate masks and ornate costumes adopted by the Thais.

The national dance of Cambodia is the **lamthon,** which is a dance with slow graceful gestures of the hands and arm, done in a precise and highly ritualistic manner. As in classical dance, *lamthon* dancers are women who perform barefoot in order to execute their movements with ease and elegance. The **National Dance Group,** once famous throughout Southeast Asia, perished under the Khmer Rouge because of the troupe's association with the royal family. Today, thanks to the School of Fine Arts which opened in 1981, the art of dancing has been preserved through the training of new recruits.

In the country, folk plays and **shadow plays** are highly loved by the people. Shadow plays, brought to Cambodia from Java by the first *devaraja,* are based on stories from the *Ramayana,* and are often interwoven with Khmer legends. These performances consist of characters made of leather which are then painted. Troupes of shadow puppeteers often wander from festival to festival enacting their favorite legends.

LITERATURE

Literature in Cambodia never developed as fully as some of the other arts. Most early literature has been lost save for some errant Sanskrit inscriptions on monuments from the 6th century. Like its Theravada Buddhist neighbors, Cambodia's literature is, for the most part, from the Pali scriptures of the **Tripitaka,** the Buddhist canon. Several modern adaptations have been recreated from the well-known **jataka** tales. Only two Khmer epics still exist—the poem of Angkor Wat and the *Ramakerti,* which is based on the Hindu *Ramayana.* Straying from the religious realm, folk stories, such as the prosaic **lpaen** are popular with the Cambodian people. In addition, due to the colonial period, it is no surprise that French literature has played a large part in the development of modern Cambodian literature. Unfortunately, what writers there were prior to Pol Pot's reign either fled the country or perished.

MUSIC

Used to purify the heart and elevate the mind, music is an essential part of Khmer life. From funerals to weddings, live music accompanies every event. Cambodian music is a rhythmic fusion of simple Indian, Indonesian, and Thai melodies. A traditional orchestra, called **phleng pinpeat,** is a combination of **khom thom** (xylophones), violins, flutes, flageolets, bagpipe-like instruments, and drums. Tunes are learned aurally, as Cambodia does not have a system of notation for music. The most popular musical form which has shown the greatest endurance is the classical Khmer music known as **Mahori.**

In addition, Cambodians enjoy singing, and their performances are laced with much nostalgia, gusto, and comedy. The epic form, called **chrieng chapei,** is sung by men to the accompaniment of a chapei (guitar). The **ayai,** a favorite of the people, is a lively and amusing verbal joust between lovers. The last type of song, the **chrieng tar,** is a ballad full of joyful and spiritual sentiments and is often improvised and sung by groups of men and women.

OTHER ART FORMS

Cambodia's artistic tradition of **hand-weaving** has persisted for centuries. The production of the lovely material used for **sarong** and **krama** scarves remains a vibrant art form. Using crude hand-looms, village girls turn out beautiful silk and cotton in simple linear and plaid patterns, as well as more complicated designs using tie-dyed thread. The best pieces are made from vegetable dyes specially mixed for each **sampot** (traditional women's sarong), and, as a result, no two lengths of material are exactly the same.

Cambodian craftsmen once excelled in gold and silver work, producing exquisite **jewelry** and charming silver boxes. The craft was mostly stimulated by a royal and social elite demand for luxuries, and has languished in the present century, despite its temporary impetus under the French. Silver work can be found, although modern examples lack the quality of old pieces.

■■■ FOOD AND DRINK

Much like the rest of Southeast Asia, Cambodian food is an aromatic blend of hot peppers, lemon grass, mint, ginger, and sugar that add exquisite flavor to even the most bland of meat or vegetables. The basic food eaten is rice and it is present at every meal. Fish, noodles, and vegetables, especially *trakuon* (water convolvulus) round out the basic food groups. Fermented fish in sauce or paste are important protein supplements to the diet. Cambodians also consume abundant fruits like bananas, mangoes, papayas, and palm fruit.

Cambodians usually eat light breakfasts consisting of a light soup with noodles, steamed meat, or dumplings. Lunch and dinner usually feature rice, vegetables, meat, and sauce. This meal is often followed by cool, refreshing desserts or fresh fruits. Hot drinks are usually served in the morning and cool drinks during the rest of the day. Iced tea with lemon and other fresh fruit juices are common.

CRUISIN' CAMBODIA

■■■ PHNOM PENH

In Cambodia, all roads lead to Phnom Penh. Founded as a religious shrine in 1433, the capital remains the center of Cambodian Buddhism; and distances along the national highways are measured from the tall, crumbling spire of Wat Phnom's stupa. It is here that the Tonle Sap, Bassac, and Mekong Rivers converge, rivers which brought prosperity and preeminence to the Angkor court in the 12th century and eventually figures of a far less glorious variety in 1863: the first French explorers. Bewitched by her tranquil backwater charm, they promptly incorporated Cambodia into their *Union Indochinoise*. In the 1920s they boasted of "their" city as the "Paris of the East." Today the *colons* are long gone, but French influence has left an indelible stamp on Phnom Penh's physical and culinary landscape: yellow colonial mansions stud the broad palm-lined boulevards of the city's northern sector while vendors still peddle warm *baguettes* each morning.

Nearly destroyed by Pol Pot's marauders, the graceful, upturned arches of Phnom Penh's many wats still dominate the skyline of a capital city which has yet to see a skyscraper. Temples which traditionally provided shelter for the destitute and disabled now play also host to some of the countless English schools spreading like wildfire through Phnom Penh. "Hello, how are you?" competes with the *sutras* as the most popular mantra.

Perhaps it is the recent memory of genocide that explains why Phnom Penh has yet to wholeheartedly throw itself into the capitalist rat race, as Saigon and Bangkok have with orgiastic abandon. Unlike in her sister capitals, a 15-minute drive down Phnom Penh's Preah Monivong Boulevard will leave you standing amongst rice paddies, where the only pedestrians are grinning, half-naked children.

For the moment, Phnom Penh remains in limbo—full of the influences of a rich and varied past, but as yet uncertain as to where tomorrow's road may lead. For all of these reasons, while the stupendous grandeur of Angkor may be Cambodia's soul, Phnom Penh is her heart.

GETTING THERE AND AWAY

By Air

Flights into Phnom Penh arrive at **Pochentong International Airport,** 3km outside the city. Customs, immigration, and baggage claim cost $20. A taxi company inside the terminal charges $10 to go anywhere downtown. Motorcycle taxis orbiting outside charge about $3. Travelers leaving Cambodia by plane should arrive at the airport at least 2 hours in advance.

Royal Air Cambodge (formerly Air Kampuchea) offers flights from the capital to a number of provincial cities, including **Siem Reap, Sihanoukville** (Kampong Som), and **Ratanakiri.** Flights to Siem Reap leave daily at 6:45am and 3:45pm ($45 one way). Flights to Sihanoukville occur four times a week ($60 one way).

By Bus

Buses to **Saigon,** clearly marked in English, leave daily at 5am, arriving in Saigon at 3pm. Tickets should be purchased a day in advance ($5, $12 with A/C). The station is located on P. 182. To get there from the Central Market, head down M.V. Charles de Gaulle and take a right at the first traffic rotary with a crocodile and an *apsaras* in the middle. Bus station is past P. 211 on the left. Ticket office is across the street.

By Taxi

Taxis to the **Vietnamese border** can be hired across Monivong Bridge at the taxi stand opposite the Chbam Pao Market. The 3-hour ride costs $25 for the vehicle (fit as many ways as bodies can squeeze into the tiny Toyota). Most travelers find they are expected to slip a Cambodian policeman a 5-spot or so as a "gift." **Note:** Visas must indicate arrival by car and specify point of entry or you will be turned back.

ORIENTATION

Despite the city's small size, many travelers in Phnom Penh are overwhelmed by the complex web of poorly marked and unpaved side streets. The capital's byzantine naming system only adds to the confusion. Each of the three governments that have held power since 1975 renamed the major streets at least once; and many addresses on buildings and business cards have yet to catch up. Picturing the city as roughly triangular in shape makes navigation easier. The three main north-south boulevards start off quite close together—the point of the pyramid. Beginning at the **Tonle Sap River, Preah Sisowath Quay,** Phnom Penh's own Sunset Boulevard, traces the river bank to form the eastern leg of the triangle. **Moha Vithei Preah Norodom** (*moha vithei*, abbreviated M.V., is Khmer for "boulevard") begins at Wat Phnom in the north and runs past the Victory Monument. **M.V. Preah Monivong,** a commercial, financial, and residential street rolled into one, runs in a roughly straight line between two traffic rotaries—one near the **Friendship Bridge** in the north and the other just before **Monivong Bridge** in the south. Most of the sights, accommodations, and restaurants are located between M.V. Preah Monivong and the Tonle Sap River. **M.V. Charles de Gaulle** runs diagonally southwest from the Central Market, forming the western leg of the triangle. Running east-west, **Rukhak Vithei Samdech Preah Sihanouk** (*rukhak vithei,* abbreviated R.V., is Khmer for "avenue") and **M.V. Mao Tse Toung** link the north-south thoroughfares. South of R.V. Samdech Preah Sihanouk, the triangle widens out into the **Khmer district,** while M.V. Mao Tse Toung forms the base of the triangle. The numbered *phlavus* (small street, abbr. P) and *vitheis* (larger streets, abbr. V) tend to run east-west if they are even-numbered, and north-south if they are odd.

GETTING AROUND

Although traffic grows more chaotic as Phnom Penh scrambles for a larger piece of the capitalist pie, the city's oft-mentioned traffic jams are generally harmless affairs, mostly because Cambodian drivers are good-natured and polite, and lack the homicidal abandon of motorists in other Southeast Asian cities. Navigating the city on foot would be quite feasible if it weren't so damn hot by 10am. Walking expeditions are best conducted during the early morning hours, when the city's markets are at their height of activity. Phnom Penh has yet to develop a bona fide public transportation system, although a few buses dating from the Angkor period occasionally hobble down the main thoroughfares. Until this situation changes, motorcycle and cyclo are the best options, short of renting your own set of wheels.

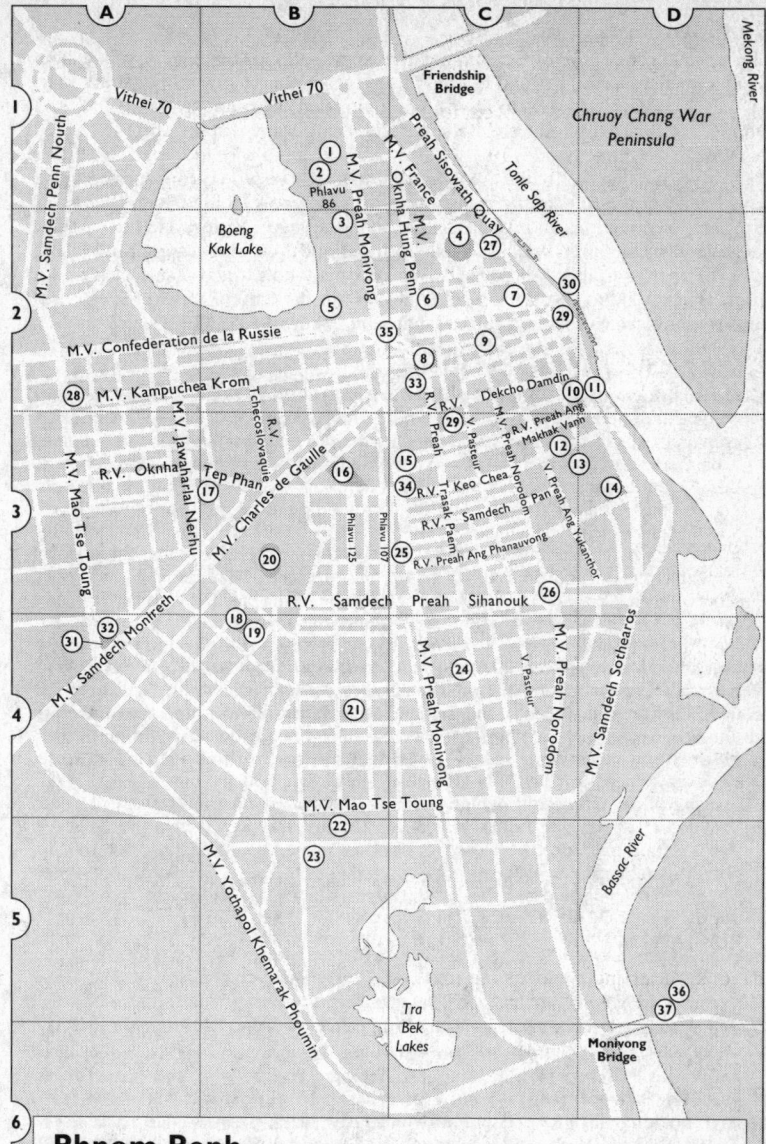

Phnom Penh

Access Medical Services, **24**
Bangkok Bank, **9**
Boengkak Amusement Park, **2**
Bus Station, **32**
Bus Station, **37**
Bus to Ho Chi Minh City, **17**
Calmette Hospital, **1**
Cambodian Commercial Bank, **35**
Central Market, **8**
Chba Ampao Market, **36**
Inter-City Bus Station, **18**
Local Bus Station, **33**
Ministry of Culture, **34**
Ministry of Information, **3**
Ministry of Tourism, **25**
Municipal Theater, **31**
National Museum of Art, **12**
Old Market, **7**
Olympic Market, **19**
Olympic Stadium, **20**
O Russei Market, **16**
Phnom Penh Tourism, **11**
Police, **29**
Post Office, **27**
Railway Station, **5**
Royal Palace, **13**
Silver Pagoda, **14**
Small Boat Rental, **30**
S.O.S. International Medical Center, **28**
Thai Farmers Bank, **6**
Tuol Sleng Genocide Museum, **21**
Tuol Tum Pong Market, **23**
Wat Koh, **15**
Wat Ounalom, **10**
Wat Phnom, **4**
Wat Tuol Tum Pong, **22**
Victory Monument, **26**

By Motorcycle and Cyclo

There are hordes of **cyclo** (three-wheeled trishaws) and **motorcycle** drivers willing to go anywhere in the city and its environs for scandalously low fares. "Moto" drivers will also take passengers to sites out of town such as Chœng Ek, Tonle Bati, and Odong. Local fares are entirely the passenger's call. Many drivers won't even suggest prices; for intracity rides 1000-2000r is average. It is a wise idea to make certain your driver understands where it is you want to go; those who do not speak English have been known to take their customers on wild goose chases, with the driver stopping for directions and the passenger trying to leave. Motorcycle drivers who speak English are often willing to tell stories about their lives during the Pol Pot period. For trips to the "Killing Fields," the drivers who gather outside the Capitol Guest House tend to speak the most English. Both the Capitol and Sun Seng guest houses rent bicycles and motorbikes for around 2300r and 11,200r respectively.

PRACTICAL INFORMATION

Tourist Information: Phnom Penh Tourism, 313 Preah Sisowath Quay (tel. 253 49 or 240 59; fax 260 43). Situated where Sisowath and M.V. Samdech Sothearos converge. Across the street from Wat Ounalom in a large white colonial building. A painted board lists the names and telephone numbers of Phnom Penh's hotels, but few budget accommodations. Look here for up-to-date safety information concerning travel outside the city. Arranges sight-seeing tours and trips to Siem Reap. Some English-speaking staff can also book visitors on private tours. No maps here, but don't worry, the Central Market carries good, inexpensive maps. Open Mon.-Fri. 7am-11:30am and 2-5:30pm, Sat. 7-noon. **Ministry of Tourism,** 3 M.V. Preah Monivong (tel. 261 07; fax 263 64). Located one block past the German Embassy on the corner of Monivong and P. 232. Telephone on sidewalk in front of building. A large staff under the burden of trying to develop the country's fledgling tourism industry; as a result travelers are overlooked. Provides lists of travel agencies and accommodations, as well as a large, glossy magazine (in English) and a few brochures (in French); but demand far outstrips supply, and the Ministry's limited budget prevents them from being given out for free. **Any information given here regarding safety outside Phnom Penh should be double checked.** Open Mon.-Fri. 7:30-11am and 2-5pm, Sat. 7:30am-noon.

Tourist Police: Office of Foreign Affairs (*Bureau des Etrangers*), on P. 154 off V. Pasteur just past the **Police Nationale Commissariat Central** (tel. 015 913 914). Office oversees the many foreign aid projects and NGOs operating in Phnom Penh. Some English spoken. Open Mon.-Sat. 7:30-11:30am and 2-3:30pm. Any emergency should be reported to the relevant embassy immediately.

Budget Travel Office: The Capitol Guest House, 14 P. 182 (tel. 641 04), near O Russei Market, is the easiest place to arrange trips to Siem Reap. By express boat, $25. Leaves at 7am, arrives around 3pm. By car and boat, $16. Leaves at 6:30am. Arrange one day in advance. **Guest House No. 50,** as well as most other guest houses, will make similar arrangements.

Embassies and Consulates: Australia, Villa 11, P. 254 (tel. 260 00/1). Consular services 8am-noon and 1-4:30pm. Also handles concerns of **Canadian citizens. Lao PDR,** 15-17 M.V. Mao Tse Toung (tel. 264 41). Visa office open Mon.-Fri. 8am-noon and 2-5pm. Transit visa $15, tourist visa $20. Visas take two working days to process and you must leave passport with embassy. **Thailand,** 75 M.V. Preah Monivong (tel. 261 82). Visa applications available Mon.-Fri. 8:30am-noon. Visa pickup, 2-5pm. 2-mo. tourist visa (1 entry $15, 2 entry $30). Officially takes 3 business days to process. Can do same-day processing in event of an emergency. **UK,** 27-29 P. 75 (tel. 271 24). Consular services Mon.-Tues., Thurs.-Fri. 8am-noon and 1:30-5pm, Wed. 8am-1pm. Also handles concerns of **New Zealand citizens. US,** 16-18 P. 228 (tel. 264 36 or 264 38). Consular services Mon.-Fri. 1:30-4:30pm. Provides up-to-date safety information for travelers. Requests that Americans planning to leave Phnom Penh, particularly for western provinces, check with the embassy first. **Vietnam,** 436 M.V. Preah Monivong (tel. 625 31). Visa applications available Mon.-Fri. 7:30am-11am and 2:30-4pm, Sat. 7:30-noon. Single entry, 1-mo. visa

$25, extension $10. Travelers must make sure to check that the visa is stamped according to the means of entry into Vietnam, i.e., by plane, land, etc. to save the frustration of being turned away at the border.

Immigration Office, P. 200, off M.V. Preah Norodom. Sign reads *"Direction des Etrangers."* 1-week visa extensions $20, 1-month $30, 3-month $60, 6-month $100. Takes 3-4 days to process. Open Mon.-Fri. 7:30-10:30am and 2-4pm, Sat. 7:30am-noon.

Currency Exchange: Foreign Trade Bank of Cambodia, 24 M.V. Preah Norodom (tel. 244 66, 238 66 or 224 66). A sprawling, pink stucco eyesore with a high fence near the Central Market next to Bangkok Bank. Exchanges dollars and traveler's checks for riel at no commission. Open Mon.-Fri. 7:30am-3:30pm. **Bangkok Bank,** 26 M.V. Preah Norodom (tel. 265 93 or 249 98). On the corner of Norodom and P. 130 near the Central Market. Visa cash advance ($10 commission for withdrawals $1-150, $30 for more up to $8000). Currently the only bank which accepts American Express, but with an exorbitant flat rate commission of $30, plus 3.5% of the amount. **Cambodian Commercial Bank,** 26 M.V. Preah Monivong (tel. 239 64). Head toward the train station, past Monorom Hotel, on the right. Will exchange dollars for riel at no commission. Visa and MC cash advances, minimum $100 ($20 commission for withdrawals $100-1000, $30 for more up to $2000). Open Mon.-Fri. 8am-3:30pm. **Thai Farmers Bank,** 114 R.V. Kramuen Sar (tel. 240 35). North of the Central Market at the corner of P. 53. Will not exchange dollars for riel. 2% commission on transactions. Visa and MC cash advances ($10 flat commission, limit of $800 per day). Open Mon.-Fri. 8am-3:30pm. The scads of money changers lining the sidewalks around the Central Market offer rates of 100r or so higher than the banks.

American Express Office: Located at **Diethelm Travel,** 8 P. 3 (tel. 266 48). No surcharge on AmEx purchases and can issue traveler's checks. Also accepts Visa and MC. Open Mon.-Fri. 7:30-11:30am and 1:30-5:30pm, Sat. 7:30-11:30am.

General Post Office: (tel. 260 11) on P. 13, past the Old Market in a large, yellow colonial building. A tall, easily visible radio tower is next door. Pick up Poste Restante letters at information counter. Mail should be addressed "Ben WILKINSON, Phallic Wonder (or name of addressee), Poste Restante, General Post Office, Phnom Penh, Cambodia." Overseas calls, fax, and telegram service available. Phone cards for local phone booths sold here. Open daily 7am-6pm.

Telephones: IDD calls can be made from all Telstra phone booths, located at the GPO, the Ministry of Tourism, and outside many of the hotels on M.V. Preah Monivong. Pay phones do not use coins, but paper phone cards which are sold at the GPO and many hotels. **City code:** 23.

Trains: The station and headquarters of the national railway system (tel. 231 15) is located in a large, yellow Art Deco building set back from M.V. Preah Monivong past Monorom Hotel. Two railway lines, one running northwest to Battambang and the other southwest to Sihanoukville. Trains for **Battambang** leave every other day, stopping at **Romeas, Pursat,** and **Moung.** Trains for **Sihanoukville** also leave every other day, stopping at **Takeo** and **Kampot.** All tickets 3000r. **Warning:** For westerners, train travel is considered highly dangerous and should be avoided as long as the current unrest persists.

Buses: Buses to **Battambang, Sihanoukville,** and other points leave from the Central Market. Minibuses to **Takeo** (500r) also depart from the Central Market. All signs are in Khmer only. Ask someone who speaks Khmer to demystify the mind-boggling system and ensure that you don't end up somewhere no one wants to be. **Warning**: Buses are a viable way of travel, but not recommended outside of Phnom Penh because of roving Khmer Rouge rebels.

Taxis: The most popular way for tourists to reach coastal destinations like Kep, Kampot, and Sihanoukville. To **Kampot** or **Sihanoukville,** $30 (4hr. each). Taxis congregate at the Central Market; negotiate for best price. Taxis will hold as many smelly backpackers as possible. Newer and cleaner taxis also leave from the Hotel Sofitel Cambodiana, but charge outrageously high prices. **Warning:** When traveling beyond Phnom Penh by car, always leave early in the day so as to be off the roads well before nightfall.

Boats: A fast, fun way to reach cities along the major rivers. **The Golden Sea Shipping Co.** (tel. 015 911 603), located about 1km beyond the Friendship Bridge along National Route 5, offers daily service to **Siem Reap** ($25 one way, 6hr.), **Kampong Cham** ($7 one way, 2hr.), and **Kratie** ($15 one way, 4hr.) Most guest houses arrange express boat service to Siem Reap.

Travel Agencies: Eurasie Travel and Tours, 204 M.V. Preah Monivong (tel. 262 68). Opposite the Pailin Hotel just south of the Central Market. Licensed representative for Air France, THAI Airways, Singapore Airlines, Silk Air, Dragon Air, and Royal Air Cambodge. One way tickets to: **Bangkok** $100, **Saigon** $50, and **Siem Reap** $45. Tickets can be bought up to 1 day in advance. Cash and travelers checks only. Open daily 7-11:30am and 2-5:30pm. **Diethelm Travel,** 8 P. 3 (tel. 266 48). Heading north, on the right between the Royal Palace and Wat Ounalom. Phnom Penh branch of Bangkok-based travel giant. Licensed representative for Swiss Air and locally-based carriers. Phnom Penh to **Bangkok** $110 one way. Open Mon.-Fri. 7:30-11:30am and 1:30-5:30pm, Sat. 7:30-11:30am.

English Language Media: Phnom Penh boasts several English papers. The **Cambodia Daily** (1000r) is the country's only English-language daily. Primarily local news, with some international coverage. An invaluable source for news on the mercurial political situation and the latest on Pol Pot's deadly antics. The bi-weekly **Phnom Penh Post** (1200r) has more detailed coverage of local news and includes a helpful map pullout section.

English Language Bookstore: Bert's Books, 69 P. 178. Near the corner of V. Pasteur and P. 178. Run by Bert, an American from Buffalo, NY, and his Khmer wife. Sells an eclectic range of paperbacks from 2300r. Carries guides to Angkor and Khmer-English phonetic dictionaries. Up-to-date safety information. Bert entertains customers with tales from his UN work during the UNTAC days. Open Mon.-Fri. 7:30am-9pm.

Cultural Organizations: Alliance Française (tel. 620 03), located on P. 184, just off M.V. Preah Monivong, sponsors weekly movies at the Centre Culturel Français across the street. Free. A schedule is posted in front.

Religious Centers: The **International Christian Assembly** (tel. 620 48) holds interdenominational services every Sunday at 5:30pm in the auditorium of the International School of Phnom Penh, 158 M.V. Preah Norodom.

Swimming Pools: The International Youth Club (tel. 272 28), east of Wat Phnom at the corner of P. 51 and 96. Charges $10 for use of the pool and gym. Open daily 7am-8:30pm. The **Hotel Sofitel Cambodiana,** 313 Preah Sisowath Quay (tel. 262 88), Phnom Penh's priciest digs, is cheaper: adults $4 and children $2 weekdays; double the price Sat.-Sun. Well-known to moto-drivers.

Pharmacies and Drug Stores: Hundreds of small drug stores sporting signs with green crosses dot the streets of Phnom Penh, but travelers should be aware that a high percentage of drugs sold in these shops are either out of date or flat-out fakes. Bring plenty of whatever prescription drugs you need. **Pharmacie de la Gare,** 124 M.V. Preah Monivong (tel. 268 55), just before the train station, carries aspirin, anti-diarrhea medicine, and anti-malaria pills. Cleaner than most. French and some English spoken. Open daily 6:30-11:30am and 1:30-7pm.

Hospitals: Health care and hygiene standards in Cambodia are well below those in Thailand and the West. In event of a serious medical emergency, the best option is to fly immediately to Bangkok. **Hospital Calmette,** 3 M.V. Preah Monivong (tel. 269 48; 24-hr. emergency: 231 73), will arrange ambulance service. French and some English spoken. **S.O.S. International Medical Center,** 83 M.V. Mao Tse Toung (tel. 015 912 765). A French doctor on call 24 hrs. Specializes in emergency care, stabilization, and evacuation to Bangkok. Examinations performed during business hours for $50. English and French spoken. Open Mon.-Fri. 8:30am-8:30pm, Sat. 8:30am-noon. **Access Medical Services,** 203 P. 63. Another western-style clinic with a British doctor and an Australian nurse.

Emergency: (tel. 117). Free at phone booths.

ACCOMMODATIONS

Although hard-core budget travelers and backpackers make up the majority of the tourists in Cambodia, Phnom Penh is still something of a one-horse town when it comes to guest houses. While there is no shortage of rooms, many are rather uninspiring affairs that lack the originality and pizazz of their budget brethren in Thailand. Happily, there are some winners here, and as the tourist industry expands, so will the number of first-class establishments. A few pointers when room-hunting: always insist on fans and mosquito netting; as there is little worse than being sweaty and insect-harassed. Ask if the guest house will provide drinking water (ideally free); this is a good indicator of how attentive the owner will be. Phnom Penh also boasts a large selection of low-end hotels which sprang up during the UNTAC boom but whose owners have since been forced to slash their rates in order to keep afloat; cheap, well-kept, A/C-equipped rooms are plentiful.

Guest House No. 9, 9 P. 93. Take P. 86 off M.V. Preah Monivong just past the Ministry of Information. Hang a left at the mosque and follow the spray-painted signs. Mercifully free from Monivong's din and grime, the enchanting location exerts a hypnotic control over road-weary travelers. Many stay for days to lie on hammocks under the thatched-roof porch built on stilts over Bœng Kak Lake. Tiny restaurant prepares cheap Khmer, Chinese, Indian, or Malaysian food. Beds in the 6-person "dormitory" 4600r. Singles 6900r. Doubles 13,800r. All with fans, shared bathrooms with Asian-style toilet, and shower. Check-out noon.

Narin Guest House No. 50, 50 P.125. Heading down M.V. Preah Monivong away from the Central Market, take a left immediately after the Ministry of Tourism. Guest House No. 50 is located on the 4th street after the Polo Club on the left. More than the good food (2300-3500r), clean rooms, and charming Khmer neighborhood, it is the family who runs the guest house that makes it one of Phnom Penh's best. Narin and his siblings bend over backwards for their guests. Meals taken family-style. Perks include free reign of the fridge, drinking water, and stereo. Singles 4600r, doubles 11,500r. Two communal bathrooms with western toilets. Laundry service. Bicycle and motorcycle rentals available. Narin arranges transport via boat to Siem Reap. No check-out time.

Sun Seng Guest House, 2214 M.V. Preah Monivong. Past the Thai Embassy opposite a small soccer stadium. Simple, clean rooms. Singles with shared showers 6900r. Doubles with bathrooms 11,500r. Only the rooms closest to the street have windows. Request the 3rd floor—it's the farthest from the noisy restaurant on the ground level. Bike and motorcycle rental. Excursions arranged through the Capitol Guest House, which is owned by the proprietor's uncle. Check-out noon.

City Lotus Restaurant and Guest House, 76 P. 172 (tel. 624 09). Located behind Monivong Hospital between P. 63 and 51. Cool and quiet, City Lotus offers hotel-quality rooms at guest house prices. All rooms have A/C and baths with flush toilets $10 (includes free breakfast). Kun, the bubbly manager, will add beds to singles upon request. The small restaurant on the ground floor serves cheap Malaysian, French, and Indian food (6000r). Good vegetarian dishes. A paperback rack at the door provides light reading. Laundry service available.

Amara Hotel, 176 P. 63 (272 60), on the corner of P. 282. Coming down R.V. Samdech Preah Sihanouk from the Victory Monument, P. 63 is just before Lucky Supermarket. This small colonial-style hotel has spacious, tiled, open-air hallways and rooms that are large enough to masquerade as squash courts. All rooms have bathroom, A/C, and fridge. Still not satisfied? Try $10 for singles and doubles alike. Some of the rooms have fabulous views of Wat Lang Ka. A "business center" in the lobby has fax and IDD telephone service. Check-out noon.

Capitol Guest House and Restaurant, 14 P. 182 (tel. 641 04). One block off Monivong just before O Russei Market. Very well-known, it's one of the older budget guest houses in Phnom Penh. Upstairs rooms are clean, if a bit shabby. Singles $3, with bathroom $4. Doubles and triples, all with bathroom $6 and $7 respectively. Neighborhood can be loud. The owner, a veritable guest house tycoon, speaks good English. Trips to Tonle Bati, Chœng Ek, and Siem Reap can be arranged here. Motorcycle and bike rental. Check-out noon.

The Happy Guest House, 197 P. 107. Adjacent to the Capitol Guest House. Clean, if monastic, rooms in the tradition of its more popular big brother. Singles $3, with bathroom $4. Doubles $4, with bathroom $6. Although only a few feet farther from the main drag than Capitol, it is mercifully more quiet here. Laundry service. Check-out noon.

Seng Sokhom's Guest House, 22 P. 111. Off P. 102 and ½ block past the Capitol II, Seng Sokhom's place is a peaceful, no-frills guest house with a very loyal following. Travelers tired of the impersonal, dormitory-esque rooms at the Capitol conglomerate occasionally find their way here. Some of the rooms have been constructed out of rather flimsy plywood partitions. Small, even by Phnom Penh's standards—8 rooms share 2 aging but clean bathrooms with western toilets. One double has its own bath. Singles $3, doubles $4. No check-out time.

The Beauty Inn, 537 M.V. Preah Monivong (tel. 645 05). Beyond the intersection with M.V. Preah Sihanouk just past the corner of P. 288 on the right. Billed as a "mini hotel," this place has refrigerator, A/C, and CNN-equipped television sets in every room, along with sandals for aching feet. The Beauty Inn is cleaner and in better condition than many of the more expensive hotels on Monivong near the Central Market. Location a bit inconvenient, but at $12 for singles, $15 for doubles, it's worth it. After 9pm all rooms are $10. Laundry service. Check-out noon.

More Expensive Accommodations

Renakse Hotel, 44 M.V. Samdech Sothearos (tel. 224 57). Opposite the grounds of the Royal Palace. This rambling, yellow, stucco building is nestled back from the road amidst a lush tropical garden. Relax in a creaking wicker chair in the open-air lobby and play out your *Indochine* fantasies. Rooms with dark wood paneling, bathrooms, and A/C. Writing desks to catch up on *Let's Go* research-writing. Singles $20, doubles $25. Check-out noon-2pm. Laundry service. Staff can arrange excursions to Siem Reap. *Bon voyage*.

La Paillote, 234 P. 53 (tel./fax 265 13). Across the street from the Central Market. Many come to La Paillote for the excellent French restaurant on the ground floor. Those travelers itching for a chance to dust off the credit card or use a pile of riel, La Paillote offers somewhat worn rooms at $20 for a single and $30 for a double. Some of the rooms have nice views and the location is unparalleled. Includes TV, fully-stocked 'fridge (goodies are extra, of course), A/C, and free breakfast—*c'est magnifique!* Reservations are advised. Visa and MC. Check-out time negotiable.

FOOD

For many a globe-trotting *gastronome*, Phnom Penh's graceful pagodas and tree-lined boulevards are merely pleasant interludes between meals. And why not? From piping-hot *baguettes* at sunrise to bowls of succulent soup at noontime to fruit shakes fit for a god-king at night, the city presents a panoply of culinary options that titillate the most discerning taste buds and assuage the tightest wallets. For "authentic" Khmer cooking, do as the locals do and make tracks for one of the city's many **markets,** most of which feature extensive food sections (see Shopping page). At about 5:30pm, **food stalls** begin to materialize along the main streets, particularly along M.V. Preah Monivong near Wat Koh and along R.V. Samdech Preah Sihanouk near the Victory Monument. A second congregation of food stalls, including some celestial fruit vendors, can be found along M.V. Preah Monivong just south of the intersection with R.V. Samdech Preah Sihanouk. Look for the fluorescent lights each stall uses to illuminate its wares. Die-hard vegetarians might have difficulty explaining to a street vendor that they cannot eat things cooked in stock. The City Lotus Restaurant serves highly praised veggie nosh. See "Accommodations" on page 78.

Raksmey Bœng Kak Restaurant, (tel. 681 04), off P. 86 on the shores of Bœng Kak Lake. Take P. 86 just past the Ministry of Information; at the mosque take a right and the restaurant is about 250m down the dirt access road. Combines delicious seafood and a great location. Built out over the lake. Popular with well-heeled locals and therefore feeds few tourists. Menu has Khmer, Chinese, and French sections. The English-speaking *maître d'* will be happy to recommend local dishes, such as sauteed shrimp with lemon grass (7000r). Most dishes 7000-12,000r. Open daily 10am-10pm.

Phnom Khieu, 138 R.V. Samdech Preah Sihanouk. On the corner of Sihanouk and P. 63. Heading west from the Victory Monument, it's on the left one block before the Lucky Supermarket. The family that operates Phnom Khieu owned a restaurant in France for years before returning to Cambodia. The small, intimate interior with A/C and a patio shaded by a willow tree might be found on any quiet *rue* in Paris. The excellent food, however, is strictly Cambodian. Generous portions and inexpensive prices ($2.50-5) heighten its appeal. Pound per pound (and every customer is bound to gain a few), one of the finest Khmer restaurants in the city. Open daily 6am-10pm.

Kim Ly Restaurant, 336 M.V. Preah Monivong. Just south of the intersection with R.V. Samdech Preah Sihanouk on the corner of Monivong and P. 282. Hidden beneath a broad awning and tinted glass doors, Kim Ly serves fabulous food in an unassuming locale. Each booth has its own fan, keeping the temperature down. If *War and Peace* were a menu, it would probably look like Kim Ly's: 14 soups, 8 vegetable dishes, 10 desserts, 36 western entrees, and a whopping 65 Chinese and Khmer dishes to drool over—all priced $1.50-14. Specialties include Szechuan soup ($3), king prawns with garlic ($14), and stuffed mushrooms ($3). The *crêpe flambée* is slathered in enough whiskey to end the meal on a high note. Open daily 10am-2pm and 5pm-2am.

The Asian International Restaurant, 96 P. 118. South of the Old Market between P. 19 and 13, this cool, quiet hideaway offers an escape from the sensory overload of the many markets nearby. Even more refreshing is the price: excellent Malaysian cooking (100% *halal*) for $1.50-2. Authentic satay chicken and noodle dishes. For dessert, the banana fritters with chocolate sauce ($1.20) are irresistible. All-you-can-eat Malaysian buffet ($5 with 1 drink) on weekends. Daily specials $2. Owner speaks near-fluent English. Open daily 7am-2pm and 6-10pm.

Restaurant Favour, (tel. 283 36) on corner of M.V. Preah Monivong and P. 208. One of the best meal deals around. Don't worry about there being no English menu—this place only serves one dish: soup known elsewhere as *sukiyaki*. Waiters bring charcoal burners to the table with a pot of bubbling stock. From there it's up to customers to concoct their own masterpiece. Ingredients to choose from include greens, mushrooms, beef, tripe, Asian meatballs, egg noodles, flat rice noodles, and rice flour chips. Just dump them in, let 'em cook, and dig in. Small (feeds 1-2) 3000r, large (feeds 4-5) 5000r. Open daily 3-9pm.

Déjà Vu Café and Restaurant, 22 P. 240 (tel. 018 813 103). Heading south down M.V. Sothearos, P. 240 is on the right at the end of the Silver Pagoda/Royal Palace compound. Déjà Vu is in a white colonial building about 200m up the road. Strains of swingin' big-band jazz infuse this place with a Casablanca-esque 1940s atmosphere. Rather expensive ($4.50-10) and small-portioned Khmer and Mediterranean fare but excellent fettuccine, lasagne, *linguini salamane,* and "Tonle Snapper." Weekend brunch ($4.50-8) and Sunday roast (lamb or pork $7.50) are popular. Open daily 11:30am-2:30pm and 6-10pm. A very hip café upstairs where patrons can munch sun-dried tomato pizza ($6). Open daily 7am-10pm.

Ponlok, 319-323 Preah Sisowath Quay (tel. 260 501). Located next to the Rock Café, this large 3-story eatery is one of the most popular in town. Its balconies overlook the Tonle Sap River. At night the restaurant is ablaze with lights and expatriates. The Chinese and Khmer fare is excellent, especially the shrimp and noodle dishes. Traditional goodies like fried sparrow also available. Menus in French and English; has pictures if words fail. Most dishes 1400-2000r. Open daily 11am-10pm.

Kirirom Restaurant, corner of P. 106 and Preah Sisowath Quay, opposite the Old Market. Kirirom is the first of several seafood joints off Sisowath along the Tonle Sap River. Come here for traditional Khmer food and a spectacular heat lightning show visible from Kirirom's porch. French and English menu offers French dishes and the usual Khmer specialties in various incarnations. Try the classic smoked fish with mango (7000r). Most dishes 7000r for a regular portion and 24,000r for big boys and girls. Vegetarian dishes 3000r. Noodle soup served for breakfast. Boats can be chartered here for $10 an hour. Open daily 7am-9pm.

Indian Restaurant, 81 M.V. Preah Monivong. Heading north on Monivong, it's on the right just before the railroad station. The Indian owner of this aptly named eatery migrated to Phnom Penh 3 years ago and has enjoyed quiet success. Get down to the kicking sitar music. Menu is as simple and straightforward as the name, but cheap (2300-5000r) and filling. Specials include *tandoor* chicken and curries. Vegetarian dishes abundant. The rich, sweet *lassi* is the antidote for beating the scorching Cambodian sun. Open daily 7am-10pm.

California Restaurant, 55 R.V. Samdech Preah Sihanouk (tel. 256 45). Coming from the Victory Monument, it's on the right 1 block before the Lucky Supermarket. Icy A/C seals in the aroma of sizzling hamburgers and good ol' American grease. Diner-type atmosphere right down to the French's mustard and Log Cabin maple syrup. The short-order cook slings flapjacks for breakfast and an assortment of western and Khmer fare for lunch and dinner. Most dishes $2-10. Popular with the expat community. Open daily 7am-9pm.

Happy Herb's Bistro, 345 Preah Sisowath Quay (tel. 623 49). Located along the riverside strip near Ponlok. An amusingly accurate reproduction of a hip American eatery, Happy Herb's has the best pizza in Phnom Penh—the chef was, after all, trained by an Italian from Chicago. Specialties include vegetarian "Hawaiian" and "Every Thing" pies. Be prepared to fork over Chicago-level prices, however: $4 for a small to $14 for a large. Steaks and chops round out the menu. English-speaking staff. Sunday brunch (9-11am) features bagels and cream cheese ($1.50).

Restaurant Neak Samot (Sea Dragon), on National Route 6A about 4-½km past the Friendship Bridge on the right. Look for a sign advertising jet-ski rentals. Operated by Ros Sothy, a Cambodian-American from Stockton, CA, Neak Samot perches above the bank of the river. The owner has done his best to create a tropical, idyllic setting, hence the carefully manicured palm trees and rather temperamental monkey. The menu offers a hodgepodge of Khmer, Chinese, and French dishes (most $6-10). Don't miss out on the mango salad and American-style river lobster. Sothy rents jet skis for $18 per hour at the dock below the restaurant. Open daily 9am-11pm.

SIGHTS

Despite its colonial reputation as "Paris of the East" gung-ho sightseers and museum-goers will find a dearth of options in Phnom Penh. Indeed, all of the "sights" can easily be covered in a single day, with plenty of time for a mid-day siesta (which travelers cannot avoid since many businesses, and especially government offices, shut down during the mid-day hours anyway). One convenient way to cover the cultural bases here is to hire a motorcycle driver for a morning. Most guest houses will arrange this, or simply flag one down on the street. This should cost around $5, and perhaps a few thousand riel more for a trip out to the Chœng Ek "Killing Fields." While many government-operated tourist attractions claim to be closed on Mondays, do not despair; money talks in Phnom Penh and, as it turns out, can also open the doors of the National Museum for an extra dollar. Ahh, the joys of capitalism.

Wat Phnom, the most sacred sight in Phnom Penh, is located on M.V. Preah Norodom, north of the Old Market. It was here that, according to legend, one Madame Penh founded a monastery atop an artificial hill to house several statues of the Buddha that she discovered hidden inside a log. During the past 300 years, Wat Phnom has been rebuilt four times. The current *wiharn,* or sanctuary, houses a number of Buddha relics and is quite beautiful: frescoes in rich crimson and gold decorate the walls and ceiling. For a look at the *grande dame* herself, view the statue of her in the small pagoda between the *wiharn* and a large stupa which houses the ashes of a 15th-century Khmer king. The small park at the base of Wat Phnom is popular with families and school children, while vendors peddle coconuts, soda, and mouth-watering glasses of sugar cane juice. Festivals and ceremonies are frequently conducted at the large pavilion just south of the hill.

Along M.V. Sothearos south of Wat Ounalom lies the **Royal Palace** and **Silver Pagoda** complex. The tall, yellow walls that enclose this mammoth compound prevents prying eyes from getting a good look at the magnificent architecture behind them. Unfortunately for would-be visitors, now that King Norodom Sihanouk has returned to the country, the grandeur of the palace is no longer accessible to the public. Thankfully, the Silver Pagoda, which is south of the Royal Palace, still is. The entrance to the pagoda's compound is across the street from the Ministry of Justice. Open Tues.-Sun. 8-10:45am and 2:15-4:45pm. Ticket $2, cameras permitted for an extra $2, and video cameras for $5 (ticket booth tel. 255 69). English or French guides can be hired for about $3; there is no set rate. Dress respectfully; no shorts or short skirts permitted. During the brief walk from the main gate to the entrance of the pagoda, a glimpse of the Royal Palace can be had. Starting at the entrance and walking clockwise (toward the river), a series of fading frescoes portraying scenes from the *Ramayana* decorate the entire length of the wall. A large stupa holds the ashes of King Ang Duong (1845-59). The pavilion beyond it shelters a statue of King Norodom. The statue, which originally depicted Napoleon III of France, was decapitated and the head replaced with a likeness of the Cambodian king. A pavilion along the south wall contains a large golden **footprint of the Buddha.**

Occupying the center of the compound is the Silver Pagoda itself, which derives its name from the 5000 silver blocks covering the floor (most of which is now safely protected by rugs). An exquisite **emerald Buddha** dating from the 1600s surveys the room, hence the pagoda is sometimes referred to as the Temple of the Emerald Buddha or Wat Phra Kaew. Other treasures include a Buddha statue made in the likeness of King Norodom inlaid with thousands of sparkling diamonds, a Burmese Buddha made from marble, and armies of smaller gold and silver Buddhas. The glass cases along the walls contain an eclectic collection of gifts presented to the royal family by foreign rulers.

North of the Royal Palace along P. 13 is the **National Museum of Arts.** Although designed by a French architect, the museum is a beautiful example of Khmer-style architecture, and more than makes up for the somewhat meager collection inside, all of which can be seen in about an hour. The first two rooms contain smaller statues and fragments dating mostly from the pre-Angkor period, including an oddly gruesome assortment of statuary appendages, hands, fingers, and feet. Moving clockwise from the southern section of the pavilion, the collection begins with the early kingdoms of Funan and Chenla (which get shortchanged compared with the much more encompassing Angkor period section), where an eight-armed statue of Vishnu from Angkor Borei towers an imposing nine feet above the ground. Other highlights include several wooden statues from Angkor Wat and a stone representation of Laksmi, Vishnu's significant other. Several ornate Bayon-style lintels provide an opportunity to closely examine the mind-boggling detail achieved by Angkor court sculptures. A central garden, framed by four symmetrical pools, contains the statue of the "Leper King" taken from the Terrace of the Leper King in Angkor Thom. (See "Terrace of the Leper King" on page 100.) The last section of the museum deals with 18th and 20th century art, and also contains some fine pottery. Unfortunately, little here is labeled in English.

For a powerful glimpse into the horror of the Khmer Rouge reign, go to **Tuol Sleng Genocide Museum** on P. 103. Look for the large "Museum of Genocidal Crimes" sign on P. 350. Open daily 8-11am and 2-5pm. Admission $2. Photography permitted. At this former high school-turned-detention center, some 20,000 people were imprisoned and tortured; only seven are known to have survived. The rest—men, women, and children, including priests, doctors, teachers, peasants, and several foreigners—met their deaths at the "Killing Fields" of Chœng Ek. Tuol Sleng has been left largely as it was in 1979; visitors are free to wander through the buildings, some of which contain gruesome torture chambers complete with gory black and white photos of the victims. Most moving is the series of rooms containing nothing but pictures of the prisoners, evidence of the cold-blooded efficiency of Pol Pot's butchers. Not for the squeamish, for some of the photos were taken after death. The museum culminates with a map of Cambodia made entirely of skulls.

Revisit the legacy of Pol Pot's atrocities at the **Chœng Ek "Killing Fields,"** some 17km south of the city. Open daily 8-11am and 2-5pm. Admission $2. This was the end of the line for more than 40,000 victims of "Brother Number One's" brutal reign of terror, prisoners from Tuol Sleng Detention Center were taken here for "liquidation." A plaque erected on the site says that the Khmer Rouge executioners, many of whom were mere children, take human form, but they have the hearts of demons. A stupa was erected in 1988; encased in glass are the skulls of some of the exhumed bodies, arranged by sex and age. Peace has returned to the surrounding villages, and behind the stupa, cows now graze amongst the mass grave, while bits of bone and clothing still litter the ground. (See "Reign of Terror" on page 67.)

Phnom Penh also has a number of wats, or Buddhist temples, many of which, tragically, were partly or wholly destroyed by the Khmer Rouge in the late 1970s. Unlike the originals, new, restored wats reflect communist architecture's penchant for concrete, and are subsequently of little artistic value. They remain, however, important fixtures in the urban community, serving as schools and shelters for the poor and disabled. **Wat Ounalom,** located on the corner of P. 154 and Preah Sisowath Quay, is the headquarters of Cambodian Buddhism. Its library, destroyed by the Khmer Rouge, once housed the complete works of the Cambodian Buddhist Institute. The first temple was built in 1443 to contain a religious relic—one of the Buddha's hairs. Some of the young monks who study here speak English and are eager to speak with visitors. **Wat Tuol Tum Pong,** on the corner of M.V. Mao Tse Toung and P. 155, just before the market named for it, is worth a visit for those passing nearby. Students recite their lessons at the school located on the temple grounds, and budding linguists greet visitors with enthusiastic hellos. South of the Central Market on M.V. Preah Monivong lies **Wat Koh,** which is home to some of the many English schools cropping up all over the city. Monks, cyclo drivers, officials, and school children alike gather to learn the tongue many hope will be the ticket to prosperity. Native English speakers are welcomed; visitors can expect to be squired around by enthusiastic teachers (many of them university students) and asked to give some cameo appearances in class. The rust-colored **Victory Monument** at the juncture of R.V. Samdech Preah Sihanouk and M.V. Preah Norodom is a tall Angkor-inspired structure signifying independence from the colonial yoke. It was built in 1954 following the end of French colonial rule. (See "Colonial Rule and Independence" on page 65.)

ENTERTAINMENT

For some (gasp!) culture beyond the usual museums and pagodas, there is little regularly scheduled entertainment.

Dance, Drama, and Music

Finding traditional Khmer dancing here can be as difficult as finding traditional Khmer dancing in say, Mobile, Alabama. Several of the pricier package tour companies arrange for private performances, but for budget travelers, the best bet is to inquire at the Ministry of Tourism and the Phnom Penh tourist office. The Ministry occasionally sponsors traditional music and dance performances at the **Chaktomuk Conference Hall** on Preah Sisowath Quay just north of the Cambodiana Hotel. As a last resort, the kitschy **"Mekong Island" Park,** intended as an "authentic showcase" of traditional Cambodian culture and sponsored in part by Tiger Beer, performs Khmer music and theater. The boat leaves from the Cambodiana Hotel daily at 9:45am, returning at 4pm. Tickets, including lunch and the shows, cost $28. For information, call the Cambodiana at tel. 262 88.

Another option can be found at the **Magic Circus Cafe and Theater** at 111 P. 360. Coming from M.V. Preah Monivong, it's on the left past the Sydney International Hotel, before the Tuol Sleng Genocide Museum. When Delphine, a theater buff, first arrived in Phnom Penh four years ago, she noticed there was a shortage of venues for Cambodia's artists. Her solution was the Magic Circus—dinner theater Phnom Penh-style, with a different act each weekend. Musicians, dancers, and shadow puppeteers, to name a few, perform at the small outdoor stage. The artists are all professional, and the Circus is the only place in town with Khmer performing arts every week. The decor is artsy; most of the light is provided by trick candles. The menu is simple and limited—couscous, chili con carne, and cheese fondue ($5). Beer

($1.50) and whiskey ($2) are also available. Performances Fri. and Sat. at 8:30pm, admission $1. A Khmer circus, complete with clowns, jugglers, and acrobats, takes place every Sunday at 5pm. The *Cambodia Daily* publishes a list of performances in its weekend edition. (See "Drama and Dance" on page 71.)

A less expensive way to "observe" Cambodian culture is to take an evening stroll along the **Tonle Sap River.** Every evening at around 6pm many families, rich and poor alike, gather to relax and picnic. Food stalls sell snacks, including Khmer yummies like roasted locust, near the pavilion opposite the Royal Palace. Buy a handful and win the giggling admiration of pint-size gourmets. Devotees flock to two small shrines flanking the pagoda, and street musicians often entertain the orderly crowds with traditional Khmer music (played on instruments vaguely similar to the xylophone). Benches facing the river fill up quickly with young lovebirds. This area, roughly from the pavilion to Kirirom Restaurant, is well-lit by Phnom Penh standards (meaning there actually are functioning street lamps), and children cavort on the lawn until 8 or 9pm.

Nightlife

Beyond a preponderance of seedy fly-by-night "discos" catering to sins of the flesh, Phnom Penh's night scene is fairly meager. There are several very mellow, rather expensive bars and a few late-running restaurants. Many visitors tire of the bar scene after one or two nights and choose to spend their evenings at a guest house, chatting and doing little of anything.

For night scene aficionados, the following is a list of some of the more popular watering holes. Most of the bars are quite clearly either Cambodian or foreign, with relatively little overlap. Residents report that Khmer bars can get quite rowdy; what little crime there is usually takes place in these establishments.

The Heart of Darkness Café, 26 P. 51. Near the corner of P. 51 and 173. The name says it all. This rather run-down bar features a wonderfully hokey demonic decor, complete with black "hearts of darkness" covering the lamps, and a stone head of Jayavarman VII bathed in red light. The stereo blasts sweet American and British rock music, and a bald pool table stands in the back room. Beer (Tiger and Heineken, $1.25), mixed drinks ($1.50-3). No cover or minimum. The management is laid-back, and even allows regulars to fix their own drinks. The preeminent backpacker/English teacher hangout. Open daily 7pm-2am.

The Rock Café, 315 Preah Sisowath Quay (tel. 223 88). On the river north of the Royal Palace near Ponlok and Happy Herb's Bistro. Much more mellow than Heart of Darkness, the Rock Café is a great place to quaff a beer or two with friends. Sit on the patio overlooking the river or at the bona fide satellite-TV equipped bar inside. Good music, also a pool table in a room decorated with the flags of all the UNTAC nations. During happy hour (6-7pm) all drinks $1, after that $1.50. Margarita pitcher $8. The western food is cheaper than most. Hamburgers $3; chips and salsa $1.50. Open daily 9:30am-2am.

The Cactus, 94 R.V. Samdech Preah Sihanouk. West of the Victory Monument, near Lucky Supermarket. Look for the illuminated green cactus out front. Owned by Luc, a Frenchman from Tahiti, Cactus is one of the primary Francophone bars in this former French possession. The decor is quaint *faux* Taco Bell, and very popular on the weekends. Cocktails $3-5, *apéritifs* from $2.50. The beer list includes Guiness, Kronenberg, and Miller, in addition to the usual local brews ($2.50). Also a full-service restaurant with an all-you-can-eat couscous fest every Tuesday night ($9). The salad bar ($2) is also stuff-your-face and includes French bread. Open daily 9:30am-2am.

The Foreign Correspondent's Club of Cambodia (FCC), 363 Preah Sisowath Quay (tel. 277 57). North of the Royal Palace on the river. A fixture of the expat community since it opened, the FCC is the preeminent journalist/NGO-type haunt. High, airy ceilings keep things, including the atmosphere, very cool. Commands a gorgeous view of the river and the National Museum. Boisterous. More booze than a Kennedy family reunion. Buffalo wings, burgers, and Mexican food are available for $4-6. Mixed drinks $3.20-3.80. Serves Tiger, Guinness, Heineken, and Angkor beer. English-language films shown every Sunday 5:30 and 8pm, $2. IDD and fax services available. Open daily 7am-until the last customers straggle home.

SHOPPING

While perhaps not yet a shopper's paradise (alas, no Gucci or Ralph Lauren) Phnom Penh is by no means purgatory either. Exploring the city's chaotic, pungent market places, in which each stall is piled high with goods of every size and description, is often far more fun and rewarding than the purchase itself. While bargaining is certainly the name of the game, keep in mind that a few thousand riel to a foreigner is serious income for the average shopkeeper, many of whom have yet to acquire the hard-nosed-rip-off-the-*farang*-at-every-turn style of the Thai traders.

Phnom Penh supports more than seven markets, all of which serve food. The market scene is an excellent way to mingle with the Khmer people, many of whom cannot afford to eat at restaurants but readily take their day-time victuals here. Most vendors set up shop at about 6:30am, and markets run at a frenetic pace until 5pm. For shopping, markets are best visited during the early morning hours. Not only is this when the Khmer do their own shopping, but it is also before the sun has risen high enough to make circulation beneath the corrugated steel roofs unbearably stifling (and "aromatic").

The **Central Market** is the hub of Phnom Penh. Most of the major streets originate here or pass near it. The market is a large Art Deco style structure built in the 1930s that now barely houses half of the countless merchants who peddle their goods here. This is the place to purchase up-to-date maps of the city, regional maps, Angkor guides, and Khmer-English phrasebooks. The requisite trinkets: Angkor statuettes, oil paintings of the temples, and nubile *apsarases* are here in force. The ever-popular "Danger! Mines!" t-shirts can be purchased for around $4.

North and east of the Central Market, along P. 108 and 15 near the river, is **Psar Char,** or the **Old Market.** If you want silk by the yard, this is the place. A large number of silk dealers ply their beautiful bolts of cloth, beginning at $4 per skirt length and rising. The atmosphere here is less touristy, and the vendors less pushy.

The **O Russei Market** sprawls along the corner of M.V. Charles de Gaulle and P. 182 near the Olympic Stadium (this should not be confused with the Olympic Market located south of the stadium along P. 199 off R.V. Samdech Preah Sihanouk). The food market is one of the largest and most pungent, since a large number of the city's garlic vendors congregate here. (Incidentally, connoisseurs of another, more potent herb, readily available for $1 per kilo, claim that O Russei offers the highest quality. *Let's Go*, of course, can neither confirm nor deny these rumors.) Beyond the food, the byzantine corridors of this market proffer the usual range of goods: everything from hardware to casting nets to wedding dresses.

Between the O Russei and Tuol Tom Pong Markets, along P. 199 south of the Olympic Stadium and R.V. Samdech Preah Sihanouk, is the mammoth **Olympic Market.** Just recently constructed, this cement phenomenon is cool, clean, and orderly—in short, not much fun. While there are a few silk vendors and Chinese merchants hawking fake gold jewelry, it is the Wal-Mart of Phnom Penh's market scene, and of little interest to most travelers.

Tuol Tom Pong Market, located along P. 155 past the wat of the same name, is home to many fruit vendors. In addition to boasting a large number of food stalls, the market wins high marks for its beautiful silk and cotton print sarongs and *kramas* (the combination scarf, headdress, and bathing suit that is de riguer here). The obligatory wooden *apsaras* carvings, soapstone Angkor miniatures, and sundry other fake antiques are also available in abundance. Tuol Tom Pong Market is located in the heart of the Khmer district and affords a glimpse of Phnom Penh that is largely sensitized in the more heavily touristed quarters north off R.V. Samdech Preah Sihanouk.

Wat Than Handicrafts, heading south on the M.V. Preah Norodom, located on the left just before the Royal Air Cambodge office. Part of an effort to aid some of the more than 35,000 men and women disabled by land mines in Cambodia. Participants are trained in a certain skill, such as tailoring, weaving, or carpentry, and their products are sold at the Wat Than showroom. Items include silk and other clothing, pillows, and pocketbooks (prices start at around $3). Tailor-made outfits are also available upon special order. For those with large backpacks, fine furniture can also be ordered. Open Mon.-Sat. 7:30am-5:30pm.

Khmera Handicrafts, on P. 360, 2 blocks off M.V. Preah Monivong. Look for the white NGO Land Rovers. The small shop sells wicker baskets, carved figurines, and clothing. All of the products are made by women and the proceeds benefit women's rights programs. Colorful silk-screened "Cambodia's Women's Association" t-shirts $4. Open Mon.-Fri. 8am-noon and 2-5pm, Sat. 8am-noon.

Sambath Neary Khmer (tel. 018 813 583), located on the corner of P. 136 and 63, facing the south side of the Central Market. For shoppers seeking some serious silk, this small outfit sells raw Cambodian and Thai silk in a plethora of patterns. Material is sold in skirt lengths, beginning at $15. The helpful proprietors will recommend tailors to have the silk made into stunning outfits. Open daily 6am-6pm.

■ AROUND PHNOM PENH

Many travelers tend to slight the ruins outside of Phnom Penh in favor of the much more impressive temple complex of Angkor. Nonetheless, there are several worthwhile sights, each of which can be easily visited in half a day. The easiest way to reach them is by motorcycle; most drivers will take tourists for about $10 depending on the distance from the capital. It is possible to rent personal transportation; but this is not advised, as the ruins tend to be located a bit off the beaten track, and can be difficult to find. Expeditions are best mounted early, so as to minimize the number of hours spent on the back of an uncomfortable bike along dusty roads in searing heat.

Ta Phrom and **Yeah Peau Temple**, located 32km south of Phnom Penh along National Road 2. The turn-off is on the right; look for the gate with three large Angkor-inspired towers. The first Phrom temple was constructed in the 7th century. The current one is believed to have been erected during the rule of Jayavarman VII (1191-1218 AD). Built of laterite and sandstone in the Bayon style, the workmanship, which is at times shoddy, contrasts markedly with both Phnom Chissor temple and Angkor Wat. Originally constructed as a Brahmanic temple, it was later reconsecrated as a Buddhist one. The lintel above the north gate depicts the mythical stirring of the sea. The false windows carved in the main, cross-shaped sanctuary are unique in Khmer architecture as they have half-drawn curtains. *Apsarases* adorn the walls.

The nearby lake of **Tonle Bati** is a popular weekend retreat for urbanites. For a few thousand riel, small, thatched-roof, elevated shacks can be rented along the water's edge. Vendors offer beer, fried chicken, and sundry other tasty treats.

The Foxy Madame

According to legend, an Angkor king, passing through the hamlet of Tonle Bati, spied the foxy young Madame Peau. As it was his prerogative as god-king, he lay down with her and then continued on his royal way. The resulting child, a boy named Phrom, went to live at the Angkor court. When he returned years later, he too spotted the lovely Peau, who had not aged. Blissfully ignorant of her true identity, he proposed. Peau, horrified, suggested that the men and women of the village have a race to see who could build a temple fastest. Phrom readily agreed, but his team of young studs was bested by the cunning maidens. Phrom's temple has better withstood the test of time, however, for Peau's temple is now nothing but a pile of rubble.

Twenty-two km down the road, **Phnom Chissor** temple rises high above the pancake-flat plains of Takeo Province. The turn-off is on the left just beyond a district high school. From there, a dusty dirt track winds 6km through a small village and past lush rice fields to the foot of the *phnom*. The kings had elephants, but now visitors must walk up the 500-plus steps. The view more than compensates for the schlep, though, as Takeo Province spreads out beneath it. Built in 1150 of laterite and sandstone, the temple was a regular on the god-king pilgrimage circuit. The central sanctuary houses the original reclining Buddha statue. In order to protect it from thieves however, the monks have hidden it behind a cluster of new images. The original can only be viewed by clambering back into the tiny sanctuary with a candle, which is cheerfully provided for a 500r tip.

Facing east, forming a direct line with Phnom Chissor, are two laterite gates, **Sen Thomol** and **Sen Ravang.** On their way to Phnom Chissor, the Brahman priests would bathe in Tonle Oun, the sacred lake in front of the first gate. The original steps are still visible leading down to the gates. Tragically, this lovely temple was nearly destroyed in 1973 when U.S. aircraft from South Vietnam bombed the surrounding region in search of the Viet Minh. The modern pagoda next to the ruins houses a very valuable statue of the Buddha. The resourceful monks, to guard against art thieves, spray painted the stone statue silver. It is the fat one in the center, surrounded by other more modern images.

ODONG

Forty km north of Phnom Penh along National Rte. 5 is the historic capital of **Odong.** Here Cambodia's monarchs ruled between 1618 and 1866. A small Buddhist community of six monks lives at the back of **Phnom Preah Reach Throap** (the tall ridge running roughly north-south) and tends the ruins. The main attraction is the ruins of **Phnom Chet Ath Roeus,** a large *wiharn* built in 1911 during the reign of King Sisowath. Originally, the brick and stone structure housed a large statue of the Buddha, which was demolished along with the sanctuary by the Khmer Rouge in 1977. Today it is a popular weekend getaway and families from the city picnic in the stand of trees at the base of the hill, visiting the temple to take in the spectacular view and carve their initials into the rubble.

Farther down the ridge are three tall stupas, the first of which houses the ashes of King Monivong (1927-41). Several smaller, crumbling stupas are visible below the main ridge at its northernmost extremity. Locals believe that a large, vicious tiger and probably several deadly cobras (for good measure) inhabit these structures. At the base of the ridge is a pavilion housing the bones of some of the victims of Khmer Rouge atrocities. Travelers should be aware that Odong was the site of pitched fighting between Khmer Rouge and Vietnamese forces in the late 70s. Although authorities report the area has been completely de-mined, care should be taken to stay on well-trodden paths. The dirt access road to Odong is opposite a Cambodian People's Party office on the left.

The road to Odong passes several small mosques, a testament to the large Cham minority that remains in Cambodia, despite ruthless Khmer Rouge persecution. Most of them merit little more than a glance, but **Nur Ul-Ihsam Mosque,** located about 38km from Phnom Penh near Odong, should be explored, if only briefly. Built more than 50 years ago, the mosque was trashed by Pol Pot's marauders. Since restored, it is now holds prayer five times per day. The local population is quite open, and visitors are welcome to observe the noontime prayers.

Be aware that bands of soldiers frequently supplement their $12 per month salaries by setting up impromptu road blocks on the way to Odong. Often they choose not to harass foreigners, but if they do, simply fork over 500r and let the driver do the talking.

■■■ SIEM REAP

Siem Reap is to Angkor what Kathmandu is to the Himalayas, a gateway city to one of the world's greatest attractions. The city marks an important victory for the Khmers over their neighboring enemies in a long, constant war during the 14th century; the name Siem Reap means "Siamese Defeated." During the 1950s the khaki-clad set braved the heat and mosquitoes for a glimpse of the magnificent ruins (before scurrying back to the Grand Hotel for a few icy mint juleps, of course). Cambodia's searing 20-year tragedy, during which Siem Reap was nearly destroyed, proved just a nightmarish interlude; the ink was scarcely dry on the 1991 peace accords before hotels and guest houses began to sprout up at a rate even the god-king's builders would have admired. Being a one-hit wonder doesn't bother Siem Reap, not when its single hit happens to be a stupendous world attraction. For travelers who struggle through Phnom Penh's chaotic, dusty streets, suffer eight-hour "express" boat trips, and vertebrae-crunching truck rides, reaching Siem Reap can be a little like arriving at the Emerald City.

Despite its position as the gateway to Angkor, Siem Reap remains to a large extent a small provincial seat: only a few of the streets have names; fewer still are paved. Perhaps most refreshing about the town is the warmth of its people. Despite years of oppression and hardship, locals have retained a real pride in their town and its magnificent heritage. They know that the sweaty flat-footed foreigners are here only to experience and share in that treasure, not to take advantage of their children. A compliment, no matter how rudimentary or simple, never fails to evoke a smile of pride and understanding in return. Angkor may be the cherished jewel, but Siem Reap is the loving keeper.

GETTING THERE AND AWAY

Presently there are only two routes to Siem Reap: by boat up the Tonle Sap River and across the lake, or by plane. If arriving by boat, travelers must register with the police, who will ask for passport numbers and tentative departure dates, when they disembark at the wharf. A bone-crunching drive to Siem Reap by Russian truck and songthaew completes the journey ($2). Trucks will deposit visitors at their preferred guest house. If arriving by air, collect bags and proceed out of the terminal to catch a taxi ($3 per person) or a motorcycle ($1) into town. Because plane tickets are relatively cheap, many travelers choose to take the boat up to Siem Reap and then fly out, which gives them more time to explore Angkor's glories. Be prepared to pay a $5 airport tax upon arrival and departure.

ORIENTATION

Fresh from the maze-like side streets of Phnom Penh, travelers to Siem Reap should have about as much trouble finding their way around town as Christopher Columbus would have sailing to the other side of his jacuzzi. The only tricky thing is that almost none of the streets are named or numbered. But with only four main streets, who needs names? Heading north from the **Tonle Sap,** the road forks at the **old bus station** (a rickety pavilion with a few taxis and motorcycle drivers) into **Vithei Sivutha** on the left, and the **west bank river road** on the right. Most guest houses listed stretch out along the southern section of V. Sivutha. About 2km later, Sivutha intersects **Rte. 6,** which runs west to the **airport** and east to the **Central Market.** The very peaceful west bank river road passes the **post office** before also intersecting with Rte. 6. This road runs past the traffic circle, the Grand Hotel, and on to Angkor Wat 7km down. Another road follows the east bank of the **Siem Reap River.** The dirt road one block east of the river road is **Vithei Wat Bo,** an important road for backpackers to know, as several of the most popular guest houses and the Bayon Restaurant are located here. V. Wat Bo intersects Rte. 6 just east of the east bank river road intersection.

PRACTICAL INFORMATION

Tourist Office: Opposite the Grand Hotel on the road to Angkor Wat but scheduled to move soon. Short on printed information and maps, but many of the employees here speak good English and are eager to please. Tickets to the temples can be purchased here (1-day $20, 2-days $40, 1-week $60). Motorcycle with driver $7-10 per day. Car and driver $25 per day also available. Guides licensed with the "Guide Association of Khmer Angkor" (English, French, and Chinese spoken) can be hired for $20 per day. Bicycles rented for $2 per day. Open Mon.-Fri. 7:30-11:30am and 2-5pm, Sat. 7:30-11:30am.

Tourist Police: The **Bureau des Etrangers (Foreigner Office),** who took your name at the boat or airport, is on V. Sivutha about 100m south of the intersection with Rte. 6 at an army barracks. No telephone number (where would you call from anyway?) but staffed 24 hrs. Some officials speak French and English.

Currency Exchange: Foreign Trade Bank of Cambodia (tel. 015 914 009) just off V. Sivutha beyond Bakheng Hotel. Will cash traveler's checks at 2% commission. No commission on dollars to riel exchange. Open Mon.-Fri. 8am-4pm, Sat. 8-11am. **Cambodian Commercial Bank** (tel. 015 914 442), south of Hotel de la Paix along V. Sivutha, opposite Vimean Akas night club. Performs Visa and MC cash advances; $20 flat fee for transactions $1-1000. 2% commission on traveler's checks exchange; no commission for dollars to riel. Open Mon.-Fri. 8am-3:30pm.

General Post Office: Along the west bank of the Siem Reap River just north of the Cambodian People's Party office and about 200m south of the intersection with Rte. 6. Look for the tall radio aerial. Postcards overseas 1200r. Poste Restante is a shot in the dark (address letters to Siem Reap Post Office, but don't hold your breath). Open daily 7am-5pm. The provincial headquarters of the **Samart** cellular phone company (tel. 015 910 020) is located in the same building. Domestic calls/fax ($1.30 per minute to Phnom Penh). No international service, but this could change soon. Open Mon.-Fri. 8am-6pm, Sat.-Sun. 8am-noon.

Telephones: International calls expensive. **Ta Prohm Hotel** (tel. 015 911 783), on the west bank of the river opposite a small park on the south end of V. Sivutha, charges $8 per minute to Europe and North America. Open daily 6am-10pm. A **"business center"** (overseas tel. 015 914 750; domestic 574 55), next to the Royal Air Cambodge office on V. Sivutha charges $6 per minute to Europe and North America. Domestic calls $1.30 per minute. Incoming calls are accepted for a $3 fee per 15 min. Open daily 7-11:30am and 2-9pm.

Travel Agencies: Diethelm Travel, 4 Rte. 6 (tel. 575 24; fax 235 7694). Located about 2km west of the river on the left, opposite Angkor Tourism. Tickets to **Phnom Penh** can be purchased 1 day in advance. Tickets to **Bangkok** should be purchased 1 week in advance. Organizes pricey package tours. Open Mon.-Fri. 7am-noon and 2-5:30pm, Sat. 7am-noon. **Royal Air Cambodge,** 005 V. Sivutha (tel. 015 914 832), north of the Hotel de la Paix on the left. Tickets to Phnom Penh ($45 one way) can be purchased up to 1 day in advance. Daily flights at around 8am and 2:30pm. Open daily 7-11am and 2-5pm.

Bike/Motorbike Rental: Bicycle and motorbike rentals are available at most guest houses for about $2 and $5-7 per day respectively.

Pharmacy: (tel. 574 67), on Rte. 6, just east of the bridge to the market. Look for a vertical Kodak sign. Carries anti-malaria medicine, anti-diarrheals, and pain-killers. Little English spoken. Open daily 6am-8pm.

Hospital: Siem Reap Provincial Hospital, located along a side street off V. Sivutha. Heading north, take a right at Cambodian Commercial Bank. Hospital is opposite the Apsara Tours branch office. Cambodian doctors are on call Mon.-Fri. 6-11am and 2-5pm, Sat. 6am-noon. Some French, little English spoken. Travelers requiring serious medical treatment should return to Phnom Penh immediately.

ACCOMMODATIONS

Just three years ago, Siem Reap boasted only four guest houses. Today there are over 20, with more on the way. Guest houses run the gamut from sumptuous mahogany and teak affairs to dirty, unkempt Attica-style boarding houses. What follows are the best of the lot; countless more line V. Sivutha north of the Hotel de la Paix.

Three new "guest houses" with slightly higher rates congregate on V. Sivutha near Monorom Restaurant. More like small hotels, they have nicer rooms than many of the low-end hotels, which tend to be dingy and bland.

The Mahogany Guest House, 0593 V. Wat Bo, about 30m south of the intersection with Rte. 6. Arguably the most popular guest house in Siem Reap. The setting, in a large mahogany house with the finest veranda in town, is its biggest advantage. Two mahogany buffalo heads with blinking red eyes add a touch of the bizarre. Small rooms, but neat as a pin, and the rich wood walls more than make up for size. Rooms share 3 bathrooms, 2 with western showers, one Asian. Singles upstairs $5, doubles $6. Less desirable ground floor rooms $4 and $5 respectively. Beer, water, and soda in the 'fridge. Laundry service.

Sun Rise Guest House No. 592, 592 V. Wat Bo, between Mom's Guest House and Mahogany Guest House. The vivacious manager photographs every guest, and maintains a very interesting guest book with their pictures and addresses. The 10 rooms are picture-perfect: high ceilings, funky red and green floor paper, and a few pictures of everyone's favorite Khmer pop divas. Guests share 5 bathrooms with western toilets (1 Asian-style downstairs) and baths with mounted shower heads. Singles $4, doubles $5. Laundry service and drinking water.

Apsaras Angkor Guest House No. 279, 279 Rte. 6. About 50m west of the bridge past the Grand Hotel, opposite an old wat near Chenla Guest House, Apsaras is set back from the main road. The Apsaras' plentiful rooms and excellent services have made it a favorite. Two buildings: rooms in the original house are small and dark but homey, while rooms in the new building are larger, lighter, and airier but more institutional. The 9 bathrooms are clean and pleasing to the olfactory glands. All 18 rooms have monster ceiling fan and portable closet. Singles $3, doubles $5, triples $6. A small restaurant serves good, cheap food (800-4000r). Laundry service.

Chenla Guest House No. 260, 260 Rte. 6. Opposite the aging wat just before Apsaras Angkor Guest House, about 50m west of the bridge past the Grand Hotel on the left. Owned by the sister of Narin (of Guest House No. 50 fame in Phnom Penh), Chenla continues the family tradition of cheap, clean rooms in an intimate, friendly environment. Those in the front building are slightly cramped, with only ¾-high walls. Rooms in the back building are larger, lighter, and painted a smurfy robin's egg blue. Shared bathrooms, with western toilets and showers, are spotless. Singles $3. Doubles $5, with bath $6. All rooms have fans, though not all are on the ceiling. Look for a third building in the near future which will house four palatial doubles outfitted with private baths and A/C ($15). Laundry service.

Mom's Guest House, 0099 V. Wat Bo, adjacent to Sun Rise Guest House, closer to Rte. 6. "Mom" may have a large family (pictures of whom decorate the walls) but there's room in her heart for you too! The owner keeps the chocolate mahogany floor spotless. Beds sport garish Barbie-skirt pink covers, with mosquito netting to match. Large ceiling fans are loud but keep the small rooms cool. Singles $4 and doubles $5 share 5 clean bathrooms. Two doubles with bath are located in Mom's sister's house. While more pricey, they are brand new, with tiled floors, double windows, and bathrooms even Howard Hughes wouldn't complain about. Drinking water is on Mom. Laundry service.

Garden House, 0129 V. Wat Bo, opposite Bayon Restaurant just south of the intersection with Rte. 6 near Mahogany, Sun Rise, and Mom's guest houses. Set back from the road a few meters amidst a lush tropical garden, this small guest house has a wonderful Swiss Family Robinson-type atmosphere in a traditional Khmer-style house. Intimate and friendly. Ideal for travelers who shun the beer-drinking socializing of larger establishments. All rooms have windows, doubles have ceiling fans. Singles $5. Doubles $6. Guests share one large western and two smaller Asian bathrooms. Tea is on the house. Laundry service.

Green Garden Home, 051 V. Sivutha, located about 200m south of the intersection with Rte. 6. Look for the blue sign. Owned by a friendly older couple, both of whom are devout francophiles. They maintain 4 airy double rooms with private bathrooms, full-length mirrors, and towels with French cartoons. All doubles $6, with A/C $12. The garden, with fruit trees and flowers, is the real jewel. The owners photograph their guests and keep them on display in the living room. Good meals for less than $2. Free drinking water and laundry are the *coup de grace*.

Villa Royal, 013 V. Sivutha (tel. 574 97), just north of Bakhong Hotel on the left opposite Monorom Restaurant. One of 3 moderately-priced, A/C-equipped mini-hotels in the area, the grandly titled Villa Royal is surrounded by tropical greenery. Completed just a year ago, Villa has rooms with writing desks and hand-held showers. Hot pink and yellow bed spreads may induce fits of nausea, and frilly pillows add a touch of the risque! Rooms are cozy with carpeting and refrigerators. Only 1 single ($10 with fan). Double with A/C $13, and hot water $15. Free drinking water. Laundry service.

FOOD

Siem Reap is ripe with excellent, inexpensive restaurants. Don't expect too much variety, but count on filling, eminently satisfying meals for under $3. Menus typically boast mostly Khmer and Chinese dishes with a sprinkling of Thai dishes tossed in for good measure. Many of the places here cater primarily to visitors; those who wish to mix with the friendly locals can head to the small **night market** on V. Sivutha opposite the old bus station and the Foreign Trade Bank. Here delicious Khmer meals of noodles, soup, BBQ pigeons, or frogs on skewers can be had for around 3000r. A small **fruit market** is next to the market. Lazy people can ask a motorcycle driver to go to the *psar rea treay* (although a stroll down the river bank when the bridges are lit up is beautiful). **Food vendors** also line the east bank of the river south of Rte. 6.

Arun Restaurant, along the east bank of the river about 50m north of the intersection with Rte. 6 on the right. An exemplary small town open-air restaurant. Arun has gained a large following amongst the backpacker crowd for its good Cambodian and Chinese food at rock-bottom prices (average $2) and Bayon-size portions. Try the fried chicken in coconut cream—a Khmer Khlassic. Offers numerous vegetarian dishes. Open daily 6am-9pm.

Chhouk Rath Restaurant, on the corner of V. Sivutha and Rte. 6. The owners and their children run the show, and the kids will be happy to arrange a duel between some of their pet Siamese fighting fish. But the main event is the excellent Khmer, Thai, and western food at knock-out prices (less than $2). Mouth-watering Thai-style fried noodles, steamed vegetables, *loc lac,* and fruit shakes (papaya, banana, and pineapple) compete favorably with food stall prices. Breakfast also served. Open daily 6am-10pm.

The Green House Restaurant, located on Rte. 6 about 20m west of the intersection with V. Sivutha on the left. Perhaps the nicest setting in Siem Reap. The entrance leads through a scruffy tropical garden, and guests are seated under a high-ceilinged open-sided wooden pavilion. The emphasis here is on Thai-Cambodian dishes. *Tom yam* with veggies, or meat and fried shrimp with curry are excellent. Other "international" foods include Chinese, Italian, and Indian. Order ahead for the large shrimp pizza ($6). Open daily 7am-10pm.

Monorom Restaurant, located on V. Sivutha opposite Vimeanthmei Guest House, about 100m north of the old bus station. This Chinese dive serves some of the best food in town. While the large interior opening onto the street may be pretty mundane, the food is anything but. Most dishes $1.50-8 depending on the size of the serving. Don't miss the roast duck ($3; grown men have been known to cry and stomp their feet when the restaurant runs out) or the mixed fried vegetables ($1.20). Chicken with curry ($2). Open daily 7am-9pm.

Bayon Restaurant, on V. Wat Bo, 30m south of the intersection with Rte. 6. Bayon's proximity to popular guest houses, coupled with its reasonably priced food and pleasant setting, have made it the pre-eminent traveler hangout. The menu ($2-4) is a smorgasbord of Thai, Khmer, and western cooking. Sautéed chicken or pork in basil leaves is scrumptious ($2), and the mixed vegetables with rice is a value at $1. Proving once more that it ain't easy bein' green in Cambodia, fried frog is available in garlic, ginger, or chili paste varieties ($2). Excellent breakfast deals for less than $2. Good place to meet fellow road warriors. Open daily 5am-9:30pm.

Restaurant Samaki, located along the road to Angkor Wat. On the right about 1km north of the Grand Hotel. Run by an elderly Chinese francophile, this cool, spotless restaurant is a popular hangout for the NGO/expat set, who come for steak and cold beer, garnished with wild tales from the UNTAC days. A mix of Khmer, Chinese, and western food (2300-7000r). Sautéed veggies (4500r). Steak cooked to order (4000r). Little English spoken. Open daily for breakfast, lunch, and dinner.

SIGHTS

With what might well be the world's most stunning architectural sights just 7km up the road, most travelers don't spend much time exploring Siem Reap itself. Apart from the market and souvenir shops, the few interesting places to visit can be seen in a couple of hours.

The **Siem Reap Crocodile Farm** is on V. Sivutha south of the old bus station on the way to the Tonle Sap. Come see these massive reptiles, that have remained largely unchanged since the dinosaur days (incidentally, that was about the last time their cages were cleaned out too). Watch little boys herd the brutes with shovels and marvel at why they don't become Khmer tartar. Open daily 6am-6pm. Admission 1000r.

A **memorial** to Khmer Rouge atrocities is located on the road to Angkor. Take the dirt road turn-off located at the "Welcome" sign 0.5km past the Grand Hotel. Follow the road to a small wat. A ramshackle wooden pavilion filled waist deep with human skulls and bones and scraps of paper is a stark, grisly reminder of the massacres that took place just 20 years ago.

For those who can't get enough Angkor architecture, **Wat Leah,** located along the east bank of the river north of Arun Restaurant, has two well-preserved Angkor-period brick sanctuaries behind the modern pagoda. One of the lintels, in fine condition, depicts the *Churning of the Sea of Milk.* (See "Angkor Wat" on page 98.)

ENTERTAINMENT

It's not that Siem Reap goes to bed early, it's that the town has never woken up. Nightlife options for foreigners are about as plentiful as the fish in the Dead Sea. (See *Let's Go Israel and Egypt 1996.*) After a hard day marveling at the wonders of Angkor Wat and environs, most travelers prefer to retire to their guest houses and share a cold beer or maybe some other mind-altering intoxicant. Want nightlife? Try a stroll down the river in the early evening—the bridge and hotels are ablaze with Christmas lights. Grab a fruit shake (1200r) at a riverside stall. Still not satisfied? There are three "night clubs" in Siem Reap—all of them catering almost exclusively to the local set. For the dyed-in-the-wool parties, check out **Vimean Akas (Sky Palace) Nightclub,** located on V. Sivutha opposite the Cambodian Commercial Bank. This place rocks to the music of a live Khmer band with a lead singer who looks like the accordion player at a bar mitzvah, except that he wears skin-tight jeans and displays a penchant for gyrating his backside. The locals get down like teenie-boppers at a sock-hop. One drink minimum. Open daily 7pm-midnight.

SHOPPING

They say 1500 *apsarases* now grace the inner walls of Angkor Wat—the rest have left and opened up souvenir stalls in Siem Reap. To find a trinket shop in this town, close your eyes, walk 25 paces in any direction, and open your eyes. A number of shops line Rte. 6 just east of the river near the V. Wat Bo intersection. They are a riel a dozen and do not merit individual description—most sell soapstone Bayons, wooden carvings, Angkor Wat relief paintings, silver baubles, and, of course, *apsarases* in every size and medium.

The **Central Market,** located about 1km down Rte. 6, east of the river, is open daily from sunrise to sunset (6:30am-5:30pm). During this period it is a beehive of activity and well worth the 15-minute walk; witness the intoxicating mix of noise, heat, and pungent aromas that make markets so fun. Maps of the Angkor complex (but not, unfortunately, of Siem Reap) can be purchased here for around $2, as can a vast array of pirated guides and picture books. Silk and cotton sarongs and *kramas* can be purchased in abundance, as well as traditional Khmer handicrafts The produce section is located in the back, where fruit-ophiles can gorge on mangos, papayas, bananas, and durians. (Not to mention enough dope to keep a stadium-full of Dead-Heads toasty for a week.)

Half of Siem Reap will try to sell you Angkor t-shirts, most of which are of poor quality. For higher quality shirts try the **Mine Field Studio,** located on the road to Angkor Wat past the Grand Hotel on the right, where the New Zealander owner of the infamous Mine Field Bar has abandoned pubs in favor of t-shirts, wall hangings, and masks. Beautiful silk-screened and hand-painted shirts ($10-15) depict the temples and scenes from the bas-reliefs that decorate them; and the ever-popular "Danger! Mines!" shirt is also sold here. Worth a trip to hear colorful stories from the owner, an experienced Southeast Asia hand. Open daily 7am-7pm.

■■■ ANGKOR

The yearning fingers of anticipation grip your chest ever-tighter as the motorcycle slips through the pre-dawn darkness. Any last vestiges of sleep have been swept away by the warm, invigorating air. As first one checkpoint, then another, are left behind, the anticipation becomes stronger until, as if on cue from some invisible sorcerer, the object of your longing materializes.

As sunlight spills over majestic stone towers and turns the placid moat into a dazzling band of liquid silver, you feel intuitively that what you are witnessing is something so awesome, so noble, and so humbling that it could only occur once. Yet this miracle has repeated itself daily for nearly a thousand years. As the haunting strains of monks reciting their morning prayers drift across the water, your heart rate returns to normal. The ancient inhabitants of this celestial city believed that the causeway before you linked the world of man to the world of gods. Their rhythm is a part of you now. This is why you came to Cambodia. This is Angkor.

GETTING THERE AND AWAY

The most common way for travelers not affiliated with pricey package tours to see the temples is simply to hire a motorcycle and driver at a cost of around $6 per day. Drivers can be arranged through your guest house in Siem Reap (most have a crew of "regulars" loosely affiliated with one guest house or another), at the tourism office opposite the Grand Hotel, or on the street.

More adventurous souls can rent their own motorbikes (or bicycles, if you're a world class cyclist or masochist) at guest houses for $6 or $7 per day. While this is considered legal by the tourist office, they and the many guards frown upon it, especially after an accident involving a local and a tourist in which a Cambodian was killed. Travelers planning to explore the temples on their own should limit their excursions to the main sights of Angkor Wat and Angkor Thom. Beyond the well-established access roads, navigation can be tricky; and at the time of this writing, some of the more isolated sites were considered highly dangerous due to the presence of heavily armed "bandits" such as those who murdered an American tourist on the road to Banteay Srei in February 1995.

Another option for those who do not relish trotting around in the heat on foot is to rent a car for $20 per day with a driver and slowly bake a la gremlin in a microwave. Cars can be hired from guest houses or from the tourist office. (See "Practical Information" on page 90.)

Angkor

TO SISOPHON
Prasat Kok Po
Banteay Thom
Banteay Prei
Krol Ko
Wat Phnom Bok
Ta Som
Neak Pean
Preah Khan
Krol Romeas
ANGKOR
Prasat Phnom Rung
West Baray
West Mebon
ANGKOR THOM
Ta Nei
Thommanom
Takeo
Chau Say Tevoda
Ta Prohm
East Mebon
East Baray
Prasat To
Banteay Samre
Prey Rup
Leak Neang
Prei Prasat
Prasat Komnap
Roluos River
Banteay Kdei
Sra Sang
Top
Bat Chum
Prasat Kravan
Baksei Chamkrong
Phnom Bakheng
Angkor Wat
Ak Yom
Prasat Kas Ho
Prasat Ta Noreay
Airport
Prasat Prei
Kuk Bangro
Siem Reap River
Killing Field Memorial
Prasat Patri
Wat Preah Einkosei
Kuk Taleh
Tram Neak
Prasat Pou Teng
Post Office
Police Station
SIEM REAP
Town Market
Lolei
TO PHNOM PENH
6
Prasat O Kaek
Preah Ko
Prasat Daunso
ROLUOS GROUP
Bakong
Prasat Rsei
Wat Chedei
Wat Athvea
Prasat Prei Monti
Prasat Kok Thlok
Svay Pream
TO PHNOM KROM
Prasat Kuk O Chrung
Prasat He Phka
Prasat Totoeng O Thngai
Prasat Trapeang Phong

Inside Angkor Thom

Baphuon, 3
Bayon, 2
Beng Thom, 1
East Gate, 12
North Gate, 15
North Khleang, 8
Phimeanakas, 4
Preah Palilay, 5
Preah Pithu, 9
South Gate, 13
South Khleang, 10
Terrace of the Elephants, 6
Terrace of the Leper King, 7
Victory Gate, 11
West Gate, 14

PRACTICAL INFORMATION

General Concerns

The government claims all of the area around Angkor has been de-mined, but take this with a large grain of salt and **stay on well trodden paths.** While looking out for landmines, keep in mind that the jungles are home to **poisonous snakes.** Potentially most dangerous are the small bright green **kraits** which, while innocuous-looking, can be deadly. King cobras with enough venom to bring down a bull elephant are rare, but not unheard of. Many have left to take staff positions in the Republican Congress, but be wary of isolated, pitch-dark chambers just the same. Bring a flashlight. A final warning: do not remove any stone fragments from the temples, no matter how "worthless" they may seem. The Cambodian government takes theft of their national heritage very seriously, and all bags are searched at the airport upon departure.

The current admission prices for a ticket into Angkor is $20 for a one-day pass, $40 for a three-day pass, and $60 for a one-week pass. Tickets can be purchased directly from the tourist office or on-site from roving ticket salesmen.

Touring Tips

Angkor's magnificent ruins hold enough secrets for several lifetimes worth of exploration. Most of us, unfortunately, have slightly less than that amount of time to spend here. Try and cover as much ground as possible on your first day, including the major sites, and then spend your remaining time either returning to those monuments that were particularly intriguing or venturing farther afield. However you choose to attack the temples, try to get an early start. By 11am temperatures will rise to over 100°F, and the genius of the Khmer architects is difficult to appreciate when sweat stings your eyes. Motorcycle drivers are more than willing to take tourists early to see the "sunrise." Daytrippers to the ruins should bring a map of the temple complex, a flashlight, drinking water, a guidebook to the monuments, and extra film.

Food at Angkor

Several small restaurants located beneath the trees opposite Angkor Wat offer reasonably priced food and a place to escape the merciless sun. Another eating option is to pick up a *baguette* and munch it in the cool shadows of the world's most spectacular outdoor restaurant!

HISTORY

According to the cult of *devaraja* adopted by Jayavarman II, the first king of Angkor, the king was the earth-bound incarnation of the gods. During the early Angkor period when Hinduism still dominated at the Khmer court, the king was believed to be a direct descendant of Siva, the "destroyer," one of the trinity of Hindu deities which includes Vishnu and Brahma. The locus of the god-king's power was his lingga, a phallic symbol that was enshrined in the tall towers of the temple complex to represent Mount Meru, home of the gods. Unfortunately many of the *linggum* at Angkor have been lost, "Bobbitt-ed," or looted, but there are some excellent examples of these phallic wonders in the National Museum in Phnom Penh. Jayavarman II (802-850 AD) himself did not live at Angkor; rather he moved his capital to several locations, one of which, **Hariharalaya,** is now a part of the **Roluos** group of monuments 10km southeast of Siem Reap.

The fourth Khmer king, **Yasovarman II** (889-900 AD) shifted the capital 30km northwest to Angkor. From this site, 7km north of modern-day Siem Reap, Jayavarman II's successors presided over a vast empire that, at its zenith dominated all of mainland Southeast Asia. The people of Angkor still remain a mystery, and archaeologists are frustrated by the limited number of written records and inscriptions scattered about the god-king's former realm. Most historians believe that the Khmer civilization's strength lay in its vast, technologically ingenious irrigation system, of which the mammoth **barays,** artificial lakes that frame the Angkor ruins, were taken to be evidence. But even this theory is questionable. Regardless of the source of their power, the Angkor kings, their coffers overflowing with booty from military escapades, had the resources to carry out vast construction projects that put even Southern California condo developers to shame. Two kings in particular are noted for their prolific building. Suryavarman II (1113-1150) is best known as the creator of Angkor Wat, widely regarded as the *magnum opus* of Khmer architecture.

Yet it was Jayavarman VII who has bequeathed to humankind this rich trove of architectural treasure. Under his supervision many of the sights that now make up the **"Grand Circuit"**—Angkor Wat, Angkor Thom, the Bayon, Preah Khan, and Ta Prohm, to name a few—were erected. Unfortunately for the Khmer, Jayavarman VII's orgy of construction proved to be their civilization's swan song. The court, its resources exhausted, gradually lost influence, and other regional powers, most notably the Thai empire of Ayutthaya, rose to take its place. In 1431, after more than 500 years of pre-eminence, Thai armies sacked Angkor Thom, marking the end of a brilliant civilization. (See "The Golden Age of Angkor" on page 64.)

COSMOLOGY AND THE ROLE OF RELIGION IN ANGKOR

The frequently asked question, just what religion were the Angkor Khmer, elicits a complicated answer. The Angkor kings practiced a faith that became an amalgamation of Brahmanism, Hinduism, and Buddhism, in which the relative influence of one over the other two varied depending upon the beliefs of a particular ruler. All were manipulated to fit the cult of *devaraja*. Thus, Jayavarman II and his immediate successors in the first period of the Angkor era, during which Hinduism predominated, were seen as the earthly incarnation of Siva, a powerful Hindu deity believed to have the power of ultimate destruction. Three hundred years later, following the adoption of Mahayana Buddhism under Jayavarman VII, the god-kings were no longer seen as Hindu deities like Siva or Vishnu but as the earth-bound incarnations of the Buddha, and life went on. The line between Hinduism and Buddhism in Angkorian Cambodia was always a fuzzy one. Buddhism, for instance, atheistic in most practices, recognized Hindu deities. The Bayon, Jayavarman VII's many-faced masterpiece, was consecrated to Buddhism, yet some of the bas-reliefs which adorn its walls depict scenes from the Hindu epics.

Throughout the Angkor period, Hindu cosmology dictated the layout of the temple complexes. A basic understanding of this belief system heightens one's respect for the vision and skill of the god-kings' architects. Each temple complex was intended to symbolize the Hindu-Buddhist universe. Angkor Wat, the mother of all Angkor temples, is an excellent example of this cosmology due to its high state of preservation. Picture yourself standing on the third level of the central sanctuary, facing west. The grounds of the complex spread out before you. Beginning at the western extreme is the moat, representing the oceans. Similarly, the thick laterite walls which enclose the temple symbolize the earth. At the center of the monument, the five towers, the arrangement of which is known as a **quincux,** represent Mount Meru, the Hindu deities' Himalayan retreat and center of creation. Many early Khmer temples were built on mountaintops for this reason. Later on, the Angkor builders simulated mountains by erecting their temples atop mounds of dirt—multi-tiered, laterite structures stacked like a wedding-cake. Classic examples of these "temple mountains" can be seen at Prey Rup and Bakong.

Although the name Angkor Wat implies a place of worship as in modern Buddhist wats, many of the tower sanctuaries you will see were used solely to house religious objects. They were rarely visited except by the king himself and high-ranking clergymen. This explains the preponderance of fake windows and doors in the architecture of the period—adequate light simply was not necessary.

For a more in depth look at the complex and the engrossing world of Angkor monuments, pick up a copy of Dawn Rooney's *A Guide to Angkor*, published by Asia Books, at a bookstore.

Angkor: A Cast of Characters

A number of deities and mythical creatures adorn the Angkor monuments:

Apsarases: These celestial waifs, which sprang forth during the *Churning of the Sea of Milk* (see "Angkor Wat" on page 98) have become virtually synonymous with Khmer architecture. Typically they are depicted facing outward with only their faces in profile. They appear differently depending on the temple. Angkor Wat *apsarases*, widely regarded as the most beautiful nymphs of the temples, appear individually. The Bayon creatures, by contrast, appear in groups of three.

Ganesha: The Hindu god of wisdom, this charming fellow has the head of an elephant. As the son of Siva, he frequently appears near his father as in the Angkor Wat bas-reliefs.

Garuda: A late addition to Angkor's characters, this half-man, half-bird enemy of the *nagas* can often be found with its chum, Vishnu.

Makara: This demonic brute is actually a sea monster, possessing a fantastic, horrible mug, vaguely reminiscent of Chinese dragon-dance costume, is often represented on lintels. Lolei, one of the Roluos temples near Angkor, contains a particularly fine representation. This beast is often portrayed with ugly, hideous creatures coming out of his mouth, such as *nagas*.

Nagas: These mythical, multi-headed serpents, so named after the Sanskrit word for snake, are legion at Angkor and guard the causeway leading to Angkor Wat. Possibly the most typical motif in Southeast Asia, *nagas* play an important role in Khmer legends, in particular the birth of Funan (see "Sun, Moon, and Star" on page 64). According to Hindu myths, the *naga* swallowed the waters of life and was either ruptured by Indra or squeezed by Vishnu's entourage to set these waters free.

Vishnu: An important Hindu deity, Vishnu was widely worshipped during the height of the Angkor period. Married to Laksmi, he is frequently portrayed with four arms, although he has the ability to assume other forms when necessary. He can be seen in the bas-reliefs of Angkor Wat both in his human form and as a tortoise during the *Churning of the Sea of Milk.* He is often depicted with a *garuda*, his sidekick.

■ THE GRAND CIRCUIT

The following summaries are arranged in the order many travelers choose to see the monuments. Beginning at Angkor Wat this "Grand Circuit" proceeds clockwise on a roughly rectangular track. All of the sights can be seen in a single day if one leaves early and does not dawdle. Remember, there are some 300 ruins in the region. Plan on spending at least three days uncovering their myriad wonders.

ANGKOR WAT

Located approximately 6km north of Siem Reap just south of Angkor Thom, this magnificent laterite and sandstone complex was constructed during the reign of Suryavarman II (1113-1150). Thirty years in the making, the massive temple was consecrated to Vishnu and is believed to be a funereal temple, which would explain why it faces west, the direction associated with death in Hindu cosmology. With its distinctive five tower quincux, symbolizing the peaks of Mount Meru, it is a classic example of the "temple mountains" designed to represent the Hindu universe in microcosm.

Flawless in every respect, Angkor Wat is widely regarded as the crowning achievement in classical Khmer art and architecture and it is also the best preserved of the major sights. You could easily spend an entire day marveling at its beauty and grandeur. Don't miss an inch, but be sure to pay particular attention to the bas-reliefs which line the walls of the first-level gallery. The reliefs, the longest in the world, progress counter-clockwise beginning on the western side. The first panel depicts the battle of Kuruksetra, from the Hindu epic *Mahabharata.* A very disheartening vision of the 32 hells in Hindu mythology lines the second half of the south wall. Large demons make *piñatas* out of the heads of the damned. Perhaps the most famous relief in all of Angkor, the *Churning of the Sea of Milk,* adorns the eastern face of the gallery. In this scene the gods and the demons have put aside their differences in order to attain *amita,* the source of immortality. Vasuki, the serpent, has offered to act as the egg-beater, and Vishnu kindly assumes the shape of a turtle to support the effort. Hanuman, a monkey, stands on his shell, directing the operation. From this divine example of conflict resolution, the enchanting *apsarases,* or celestial waifs with dimensions that would shame Kate Moss, were created. The north wall depicts Vishnu's defeat of Bana the Demon King, a curious-looking hellion mounted on a rhino. Also portrayed on the second half of the gallery is an epic battle between the gods and the demons. All of the heavyweights, including Vishnu, Siva, and Brahma, are represented. Completing the circuit, the northern panel of the west gallery depicts the battle of Lanka from the Hindu epic the *Ramayana,* which pitted the mild-mannered hero Rama against the demon Ravana, readily recognizable with his 10 heads and 20 arms.

Mounting the steps to the second level, the Gallery of 1000 Buddhas (of which only a few fragments remain) is on the right, and the Hall of Echoes is on the left. Stand in one corner of the Hall of Echoes, pound your chest like Tarzan, and feel the room reverberate (this trick can be repeated at numerous temples). Be sure to climb to the third level, which commands a stunning view of the perfectly symmetrical complex. Angkor Wat has by no means lost its spiritual value in favor of backpacking pilgrims; monks from the adjacent pagodas frequently conduct ceremonies here (indeed, the monks are credited with the temple's excellent state of preservation, as they have lived nearby for centuries and tended the site). Angkor Wat is best seen at sunrise or sunset.

PHNOM BAKHENG

Just north of Angkor Wat and slightly to the west, Phnom Bakheng was built by Yasovarman I (889-900 AD) in the late 9th century. Many travelers struggle up the very steep, rocky slope of this bona fide "temple mountain" at the end of a hard day's thrash through Angkor to enjoy a spectacular sunset and stunning view of Angkor Wat just below Phnom Bakheng to the southeast. The temple itself is built on five laterite tiers. Originally, 109 towers graced the *phnom,* corresponding to the animal zodiac cycle. The central tower is open on all four sides; come first and foremost for the view (5pm is ideal). The five towers of Angkor Wat present a perennial Kodak moment. To the south Phnom Krom, the mountain on the other side of Siem Reap, can be seen, as well as the West Baray sparkling amidst a field of green to the west.

ANGKOR THOM

Lying roughly 1.5km north of Angkor Wat is the large temple complex of Angkor Thom, constructed by Jayavarman VII (1181-1219 AD) on the site of earlier structures. The last and greatest of the Angkor Empire's capitals, it shares a cosmological layout similar to Angkor Wat's: a moat symbolizes the oceans, walls the land, and towers the peaks of Mount Meru. Within this vast former city (laid out in a 3km by 3km square) are some of the most impressive ruins, including the Bayon, Baphuon, Phimeanakas, the Terrace of Elephants, and the Terrace of the Leper King. When entering the Angkor Thom (literally "great city") from the south, you will cross a causeway lined with 54 statues of gods and demons. (The Angkor Conservancy has removed many of the remaining original heads to prevent their theft and replaced them with replicas.) The entry tower is topped by a *bayon* whose enigmatic grin has captivated artists, archaeologists, and travelers alike for 150 years.

The Bayon

Sprawling in the exact center of Angkor Thom, this temple was erected by Jayavarman VII and dedicated to Buddhism. Built about 100 years after Angkor Wat, the Bayon is unique in several respects: first, it has no surrounding laterite wall, and second, its outstanding reliefs depict, in addition to the usual epic stories, scenes of everyday life in Angkorian Cambodia that provide archaeologists with one of their only windows into this mysterious world. Visit the Bayon early. Surrounded by trees which also shade a modern pagoda, the experience of watching a new day begin amongst the 200 mysterious faces that have come to symbolize Angkor is truly sublime. Before the motorcycles and drink vendors appear in force, the only sounds are of the jungle and perhaps a few aging nuns silently padding through the temple's labyrinthine passageways, lighting fresh sticks of incense.

The faces are believed to represent the Bodhisattva Avalokitesvara, the king's divine benefactor. The Bayon contains two sets of bas-reliefs that are viewed clockwise, unlike Angkor Wat. The lower gallery adorns the outer wall and depicts everyday life in the capital. The southern gallery is widely regarded to be the finest of Bayon's bas-reliefs. The panels begin with a depiction of a battle between the Khmer and the Cham (of southern Vietnam). Khmer soldiers can be identified by their lack of headgear. The lower tier of reliefs presents a more peaceful view of Angkor life. Citizens observe cockfights, play board games, and pick lice from each other's hair. The northern gallery, only some of which was completed, contains a depiction of an Angkor circus complete with acrobats, jugglers, and Gunther Gable-Williams. The upper gallery of bas-reliefs contains stories from the Hindu epics.

Baphuon

A few hundred meters northwest of the Bayon stands the Hindu temple of Baphuon built during the second half of the 11th century by Udayadityavarman II (1050-1066 AD). Intended to symbolize Mount Meru, the central sanctuary is located on top of a massive sandstone base. A reclining Buddha, built from the rubble of a collapsed gallery, can be seen lying along the length of the western wall. Access to the temple is gained by crossing a long elevated sandstone causeway, beginning near the Terrace of the Elephants. Presently, a team of French and Cambodian archaeologists is in the process of restoring Baphuon.

Phimeanakas

Situated just north of Baphuon, this Hindu monument was erected by three successive kings, Rajendravarman (944-968 AD), Jayavarman V (968-1001 AD), and Udayadityavarman I (1001-1002 AD). It is worth a visit primarily for the view from the top of the central sanctuary. The scramble up a very steep set of laterite "stairs" can be challenging and is best attempted early in the day.

Terrace of the Elephants

First laid out by Suryavarman I (1002-1050 AD), the Terrace of the Elephants (also called the Royal Terrace) stretches for 300m from the Baphuon to the beginning of the Terrace of the Leper King, past Phimeanakas. While gazing east from the Terrace, imagine a bustling city sprawled out before your eyes in what used to be the Grand Plaza, Angkor Thom's main square. The bas-relief elephants plodding in profile along the wall are remarkable for their realism. Along the wall near the Terrace of the Leper King is a carving of a five-headed horse, perhaps the mythical Balaha.

Terrace of the Leper King

Also another legacy of Jayavarman VII, this monument, north of the Terrace of the Elephants, was dedicated to Buddhism. Two galleries of bas-reliefs line this terrace. Mythological creatures and stunning half-naked *apsarases* decorate the outer wall. The well-preserved inner wall was discovered only recently by archaeologists.

The statue of the Leper King himself is a copy; the National Museum in Phnom Penh now houses the original. The mystery of the rotund little man remains an enigma. Historians suspect that Jayavarman VII may have suffered from leprosy. Others believe the statue portrays either Yama, the god of death, or Kubera, the god of wealth. A third theory holds that the figure represents David Leper-man, god-king of late night television.

PREAH KHAN

Located northwest of the Bayon outside of Angkor Thom, Preah Khan was built by Jayavarman VII in the late 12th century as a Buddhist temple in memory of his father. An official World Heritage Site, it features a small pavilion just beyond the gate on the left, which contains an interesting series of diagrams and photographs explaining the restoration process. Other displays illustrate local flora and fauna. Grab your fedora and bullwhip; this largely unrestored temple hidden away in lush emerald jungle is straight out of an Indiana Jones adventure. The light that filters through the leafy canopy of towering banyan trees plays off the gray sandstone such that you'd swear that the *apsarases* in the corner of your eye just moved. Literally, Preah Khan means "sacred sword," and some archaeologists believe that the small two-story building located in the northeast corner of the compound, a rarity in Khmer architecture, might once have housed this Asian Excalibur. Visitors enter the temple from the west, but the original entry point, as usual in Hindu and Buddhist architecture, faces east. For an excellent view of the cross-shaped layout of the main sanctuary (and a hallmark of Angkor architecture) it is possible to scramble up the rubble onto the top of the gallery just east of the sanctuary. Continuing along the west-east axis will eventually bring you to the east gate. Here is a fine photo opportunity. The roots of several large ponro trees now envelope the laterite wall like the tentacles of a giant squid. **Warning:** This site is mined between 6pm and 6am in order to prevent further ransacking of the temple.

NEAK PEAN

Neak Pean, a Buddhist temple situated east of Preah Khan along the Grand Circuit access road was built by The Man (yes, Jayavarman VII) during the last decades of the 12th century. This small yet engrossing temple is made up of five ponds. A temple stands in the exact center of the large, central pond. Neak Pean is said to represent Lake Anauatapa, a sacred body of water in the Himalaya. The four symmetrical ponds, one at each cardinal point, represent the earth's four main rivers. A stone horse, believed to be the sacred steed, Balaha, drags several marooned sailors toward the island sanctuary in the middle of Neak Pean.

TA SOM

Lying east along the access road from Neak Pean, Ta Som, built by Jayavarman VII, is a contemporary of Neak Pean and was dedicated to Buddhism, in memory of Jesse Grayman. A small temple with one sanctuary, it is unrestored and largely in ruins. A four-faced *bayon* casts its inscrutable smile over you as you enter from the west. Note the half-drawn "curtains" on the false windows of the main sanctuary. Continue through to the east gate, whose *bayon* is now almost entirely in the clutches of fig tree roots. Damage caused by creeping vegetation such as this has been a principle threat to the preservation of the Angkor monuments.

EAST MEBON

Built by Rajendravarman II in the 10th century as a Hindu monument in memory of his parents, East Mebon stands in the middle of the East Baray southwest of Ta Som. As your motorcycle speeds south to Mebon across pancake-flat rice paddies, picture the setting as it was during the Angkor period, when the East Baray (meaning "lake") was filled with water which may or may not have been used to irrigate the fields necessary to feed the great capital city. At that time, Mebon was accessible only by boat. The five main towers, a new architectural innovation, here and at Prey Rup are precursors to Angkor Wat's towers. This classic "temple mountain" representing Mount Meru sits atop a three-tiered artificial hill constructed of laterite blocks. Entry is through the east gate—notice the *singhas,* or lions, which guard the steps to the second level. Eight brick tiers, each supported by eight-sided sandstone columns, face the four cardinal points. Note also the elephants at the corners of the first two levels. The holes on the central brick towers of the third tier were used for the application of stucco.

PREY RUP

Half a km due south of Mebon lies Prey Rup, a Hindu temple built by Rajendravarman II in the second half of the 10th century. A contemporary of East Mebon, but much more impressive, this multi-tiered structure affords a panoramic view of the East Baray to the north. (Mebon should be visible through the trees from the main sanctuary.) The two halls (or what is left of them) running parallel to the laterite wall as you enter from the east are believed to have housed pilgrims, who had made the long journey to worship Siva, the Hindu deity to which Rup was consecrated. The stone sarcophagus-like structure just past the rest halls may have been a crematorium. The five central towers atop a sandstone tier are typical of Khmer architecture during this period: all have false doors and open to the east.

On the short jaunt between Mebon and Prey Rup, lies the road leading to the enchanting pink sandstone Banteay Srei temple some 30km to the north. Alas, as of this writing Banteay Srei remained off-limits following the death of an American woman there. Check with the tourist office to see if this unfortunate situation has changed.

BANTEAY KDEI

Banteay Kdei is a Buddhist temple built by Jayavarman VII, southeast of Prey Rup near the Sra Sang reservoir. A beautiful *bayon* oversees the entrance to this unrestored temple. Take care while exploring Banteay Kdei, as many of the enclosed buildings are off-limits. Nothing would spoil a visit to Angkor quicker than a five-ton sandstone block on the noggin. The statue of the Buddha in the central sanctuary was vandalized by the Khmer Rouge, who cut off its original head (probably sitting in a private collection in Paris or New York now). Look carefully at the walls of this sanctuary and you will see very faint images of the Buddha etched in the sandstone. Before heading on to the Ta Phrom, be sure to walk over to the Sra Sang reservoir. A stone platform lined with *nagas* leads down to the water, and Sra Sang village is visible to the north.

TA PROHM

Located west of the Prey Rup, bordering Banteay Kdei, Ta Prohm was built at the end of the 12th century by Jayavarman VII as a Buddhist temple in memory of his fair mother Pai Yang. Set deep in the jungle, the noises of which provide an eerie soundtrack to your exploration, this vast crumbling temple competes with the Bayon and Angkor Wat as the most impressive of Angkor's treasures. Standing alone in a ruined sanctuary, creepers and fig trees all around you, it is not difficult to imagine how Henri Mouhot, who "re-discovered" Angkor in 1860, must have felt, for the site has changed little since then, save for pint-sized capitalists selling refreshments. Inscriptions found by archaeologists reveal that 79,365 people were employed in the upkeep of Ta Prohm during its hey-day. It is certainly huge, and a map is helpful to ensure you don't miss anything. Ten-year-old "guides" will lead you around whether you request it or not. Be careful while squirming through tiny "doors" the kids can wriggle through with ease. Marvel at the massive banyan trees that now hold a death-grip on many of the ruined galleries. A number of carvings and inscriptions decorate the walls of the galleries surrounding the central sanctuary. Many visitors make special early morning trips to Ta Prohm because of its stunning beauty in the morning light.

■ AROUND ANGKOR

WEST BARAY

West of Angkor Thom, a superb view of the half-filled lake can be had from the top of Phnom Bakheng. Believed to date from the 11th century, the West Baray was perhaps built during the reign of Udayadityavarman II. Though the debate over its function rages on, the *baray,* of which approximately half is still full of water, makes an interesting side trip for those with the time. Teenagers from Siem Reap often come here to swim and King Sihanouk, who maintained a royal residence in Siem Reap, used to take his guests water-skiing here. A small, largely destroyed temple, **West Mebon,** stands in the center of the *baray*; it is reachable by boat.

ROLUOS GROUP

About 10km southeast of Siem Reap, this collection of three temples represents the very earliest part of the Angkor period. It is believed that Jayavarman II, the man who started it all, made his capital of Harihavalaya here in the middle of the 9th century. All three temples were originally consecrated to Hinduism. Two of the three monuments, Lolei (north of the other two off Rte. 6) and Preah Ko (south off Rte. 6 and north of Bakong) are quite small. They can be seen easily in an hour. **Lolei,** which is the site of a modern Buddhist wat, boasts a few beautiful lintels on the four brick towers of the main sanctuary. The doorframes were each hewn from a single sandstone block, a characteristic of early Angkor architecture. **Preah Ko,** or "Sacred Ox," consists of a central sanctuary with six brick towers. Note the ornate sandstone false doors and particularly the eight-sided sandstone columns. Several of the towers have traces of the stucco that used to cover the brick. **Bakong,** the largest and most impressive of the Roluos Group, was once the ancient capital of Hariharalaya. It is a classic temple mountain, and its single central tower sits atop a five-tiered laterite base. The temple is entered from the east by crossing a causeway lined with *nagas* over a now dry moat. A large modern pagoda is situated at the base of the temple. The remains of a thick application of stucco can be seen on many of the buildings. Stone elephants stand at every corner of the tiers, growing smaller at each level. The four central towers afford an excellent view of the surrounding countryside and of the remarkable symmetry of the Bakong temple.

HONG KONG

For many tourists, hyper-kinetic Hong Kong stirs up well-worn stereotypes of the Far East: gliding junks, incense-clouded temples, kittenish *cheongsam*-clad Suzie Wongs, and Fu Manchu tycoons presiding over *hong* cartels. The junks and temples are still here, albeit somewhat obscured by McDonald's dazzling golden arches, shelves upon shelves of Gap khakis, and pitched battles waged in the streets between Janet Jackson and Chinese opera divas for audio supremacy. Change has come and here are the signs o' the times. Suzie has been promoted to bar hostess, while other working girls claw their way to the top as corporate-level lady bosses. The *tai-pans* of Hong Kong's mythical past have stepped off the pages of James Clavell's novels and into Armani suits, carrying cellular phones as eager business moguls. This capitalist ant colony proudly claims the world's highest per capita use of fax machines and other high-tech gadgets. And indeed, Mr. Rolex, Mrs. Rolls-Royce, and little Rémy Martin lead a peaceful, cheek-by-jowl co-existence with rhinoceros-horn aphrodisiac, rickshaws, and roast duck banquets.

ESSENTIALS

■■■ GETTING THERE AND AWAY

BY AIR

The **Hong Kong International Airport** is in Kowloon, the peninsula just north of Hong Kong Island. For flight info, call 2769 7531. The extensive and inexpensive **airbus system** is the best way to dart to major districts within Hong Kong such as Central, Wan Chai, Causeway Bay, Taikoo, North Point, and Tsim Sha Tsui. To get from the airport to Tsim Sha Tsui, take the A1 bus (HK$11). A2 runs to Central and Wan Chai; A3 to Causeway Bay; and A5 to Taikoo and North Point; each costs HK$16. Carry exact fare. Buses run daily 7am-midnight, except A5, which runs 8am-11pm. If you arrive after midnight, or simply don't wish to crowd onto a bus with bulky luggage, take one of the **taxi cabs** waiting outside the airport teminal. A ride from the airport to Tsim Sha Tsui runs about HK$40; from the airport to Causeway Bay, around HK$75. There is a HK$20 surcharge for crossing the harbor, plus HK$5 for each piece of luggage. Cab jockeys will often understand English street names, but it's helpful to have addresses written in Chinese characters.

■■■ ORIENTATION

At the tip of the **Kowloon** peninsula, sandwiched between the airport and the Hong Kong Island, is **Tsim Sha Tsui,** the country's tourist center, glistening with upscale boutiques, bars, and restaurants. **Hong Kong Island** lies across Victoria Harbor and is accessible by the MTR's island line. To the west, **Sheung Wan** is a honeycomb of cluttered streets and alleys. Eastward, **Central** and **Admiralty** sprout vertigo-inducing skyscrapers. Infamous **Wan Chai** is one stop east of Admiralty on the MTR. **Causeway Bay,** with its 13-story colossus of malls, is the next stop on the MTR. The southern part of Hong Kong Island is predominantly rural. Farther to the west is **Aberdeen,** moored to the grandiose floating Christmas tree of an eatery, the Jumbo Floating Restaurant, widely touted on posters of Hong Kong.

■■■ GETTING AROUND

MASS TRANSIT RAILWAY (MTR)

There's no subway station near the airport, but Hong Kong's super-efficient MTR is the most stress-free means of transport (HK$3.50-HK$10). Vending machines spit out tickets which are scanned at the entry gate and must be returned at the exit gate. It's good for only 90 minutes after it's scanned the first time. The three MTR lines link major areas in southern Kowloon and northern Hong Kong Island; two of the lines also run under the harbor. Each station has multiple exits. To get out at the point nearest your destination, look for the red signs to guide you to well-known sights and landmarks. Rush hour is 7:30-9:30am and 5:30-7:30pm. The system runs 6am-1am. Buy Stored Value Tickets at Hang Seng Bank branches in the stations. **Mass Transit Railway Information** (tel. 2750 0170).

BUSES AND TAXIS

Hong Kong's star-quality **bus system** generally runs around HK$2-5 payable in exact change as you board. Snag a schedule from any HKTA office. On Hong Kong Island, **China Motor Bus** runs cream-and-blue buses (tel. 2565 8556); **Citybus** operates orange buses (tel. 2873 0818). On Kowloon, cream-and-red caravans are run by **Kowloon Motor Bus** (tel. 2745 4466). **Taxis** are abundant and reasonably priced. Look for red 'For Hire' signs in windows. At night, look for the lit-up "Taxi" on the roof. Meters start at HK$11.50, then it's HK$1 per 200 meters. Round up the fare to the nearest dollar for tip. Many major thoroughfares have taxi stands.

KOWLOON-CANTON RAILWAY (KCR) AND TRAM

The **KCR** (tel. 2602 7799) runs from Kowloon Station in south Kowloon to the Chinese border (one way HK$7.50). The **tram system** links points along north Hong Kong Island. Any destination HK$1.20, 6am-1am. The tram's last stop is on the front of the vehicle in English. **Hong Kong Tramways** (tel. 2559 8918).

BOATS

The scenic way to scamper across the harbor. **Star Ferry** (tel. 2366 2576) links Central and Tsim Sha Tsui (6:30am-11:30pm, 8min., one way: HK$1.20 lower deck; HK$1.50 upper deck). Ferries connect Hong Kong Island with Macau and outlying islands from piers west of the Star Ferry concourse. The HKTA has schedules. For inquiries call **Hong Kong Ferry Co.** (tel. 2542 3082). **Boats** also run between Central and Hung Hom (daily 7am-7:20pm, lower deck HK$1.50, upper deck HK$1.80) and between Tsim Sha Tsui and Wan Chai (HK$1.50, daily 7:30am-11pm).

■■■ PRACTICAL INFORMATION

Tourist Information: Multilingual Telephone Information Service (tel. 2801 7177) answers questions about life…and tourism. Open Mon.-Fri. 8am-6pm, Sat.-Sun. and public holidays 9am-5pm. **Hong Kong Tourist Association (HKTA) Offices: HK International Airport,** near Exit 3; another one is near Exit 6 next to a money changer. Indispensable bus and ferry schedules and maps. *Official Hong Kong Guide's* "Month in Focus" gives a rundown of current sports, festivals, and performing arts. Free info packets in baggage-claim. English spoken. Open daily 8am-10:30pm. **Central Hong Kong,** Jardine House, 1 Connaught Place, Shop 8, Basement. Leave the Central MTR station (Jardine House exit), turn right, and onto the pedestrian overpass. Follow the signs. English-speaking staff. Open Mon.-Fri. 9am-6pm, Sat. 9am-1pm. Closed public holidays. **Star Ferry Concourse (Kowloon).** Left of the lower deck entrance. Open Mon.-Fri. 8am-6pm, Sat.-Sun. and holidays 9am-5pm.

Budget Travel Offices: Hong Kong Youth Hostels Association, Shek Kip Mei Estate, Block 19, Room 225, Shamshuipo, Kowloon (tel. 2788 1638; fax 2788 3105). Open Mon., Wed., and Fri. 9:30am-5:30pm, Tues. and Thurs. 9:30am-7pm,

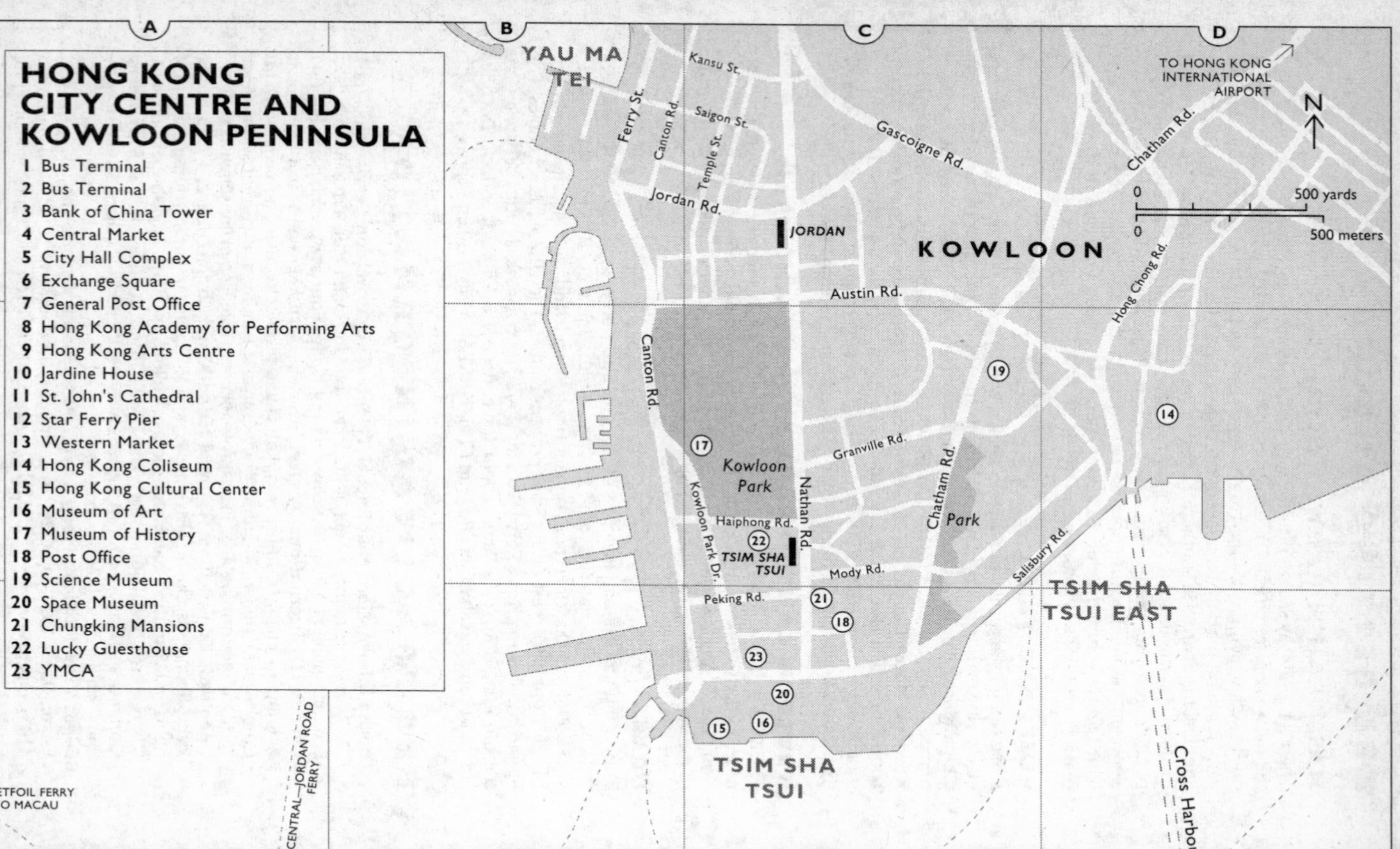

HONG KONG CITY CENTRE AND KOWLOON PENINSULA
1 Bus Terminal
2 Bus Terminal
3 Bank of China Tower
4 Central Market
5 City Hall Complex
6 Exchange Square
7 General Post Office
8 Hong Kong Academy for Performing Arts
9 Hong Kong Arts Centre
10 Jardine House
11 St. John's Cathedral
12 Star Ferry Pier
13 Western Market
14 Hong Kong Coliseum
15 Hong Kong Cultural Center
16 Museum of Art
17 Museum of History
18 Post Office
19 Science Museum
20 Space Museum
21 Chungking Mansions
22 Lucky Guesthouse
23 YMCA
A
B
C
D
1
2
3
YAU MA TEI
Kansu St.
Saigon St.
Ferry St.
Canton Rd.
Temple St.
Jordan Rd.
JORDAN
Gascoigne Rd.
Chatham Rd.
TO HONG KONG INTERNATIONAL AIRPORT
N
0
500 yards
0
500 meters
KOWLOON
Austin Rd.
Hong Chong Rd.
Canton Rd.
Kowloon Park
Granville Rd.
Chatham Rd.
Park
Nathan Rd.
Haiphong Rd.
Kowloon Park Dr.
TSIM SHA TSUI
Mody Rd.
Peking Rd.
Salisbury Rd.
TSIM SHA TSUI EAST
TSIM SHA TSUI
Cross Harbou
CENTRAL—JORDAN ROAD FERRY
JETFOIL FERRY TO MACAU

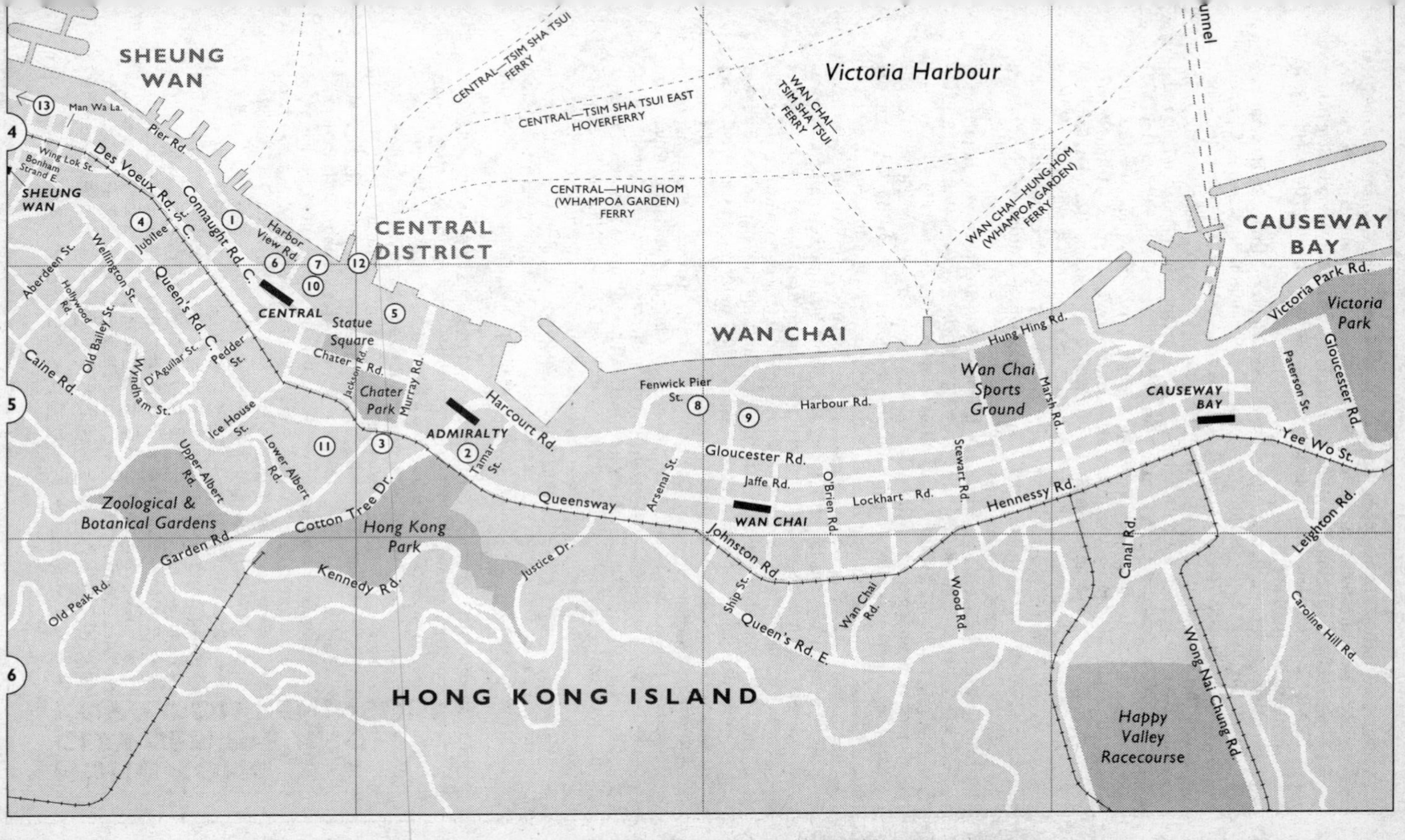
SHEUNG WAN
Victoria Harbour
unnel
CENTRAL—TSIM SHA TSUI FERRY
CENTRAL—TSIM SHA TSUI EAST HOVERFERRY
WAN CHAI—TSIM SHA TSUI FERRY
CENTRAL—HUNG HOM (WHAMPOA GARDEN) FERRY
WAN CHAI—HUNG HOM (WHAMPOA GARDEN) FERRY
CAUSEWAY BAY
Man Wa La.
Pier Rd.
Wing Lok St.
Bonham Strand E.
SHEUNG WAN
Des Voeux Rd. C.
Connaught Rd. C.
Harbor View Rd.
Jubilee St.
CENTRAL DISTRICT
Aberdeen St.
Hollywood Rd.
Wellington St.
Queen's Rd. C.
CENTRAL
Statue Square
Victoria Park Rd.
Victoria Park
Old Bailey St.
Caine Rd.
D'Aguilar St.
Pedder St.
Wyndham St.
Chater Rd.
Jackson Rd.
Chater Park
Murray Rd.
WAN CHAI
Hung Hing Rd.
Wan Chai Sports Ground
Marsh Rd.
Paterson St.
Gloucester Rd.
CAUSEWAY BAY
Fenwick Pier St.
Harbour Rd.
Harcourt Rd.
ADMIRALTY
Ice House St.
Lower Albert Rd.
Upper Albert Rd.
Tamar St.
Gloucester Rd.
Yee Wo St.
Jaffe Rd.
O'Brien Rd.
Stewart Rd.
Lockhart Rd.
Hennessy Rd.
Zoological & Botanical Gardens
Cotton Tree Dr.
Queensway
Arsenal St.
WAN CHAI
Hong Kong Park
Garden Rd.
Justice Dr.
Johnston Rd.
Canal Rd.
Leighton Rd.
Kennedy Rd.
Old Peak Rd.
Ship St.
Wan Chai Rd.
Wood Rd.
Queen's Rd. E.
Caroline Hill Rd.
Wong Nai Chung Rd.
HONG KONG ISLAND
Happy Valley Racecourse
1
2
3
4
5
6
7
8
9
10
11
12
13
4
5
6

Sat. 9:30am-1pm. **Hong Kong Student Travel Ltd.,** Trade Square, Room 501-509, 681 Cheung Sha Wan Rd., Cheung Sha Wan, Kowloon (tel. 2725 3983; fax 2725 3847). Open Mon.-Fri. 10am-6:30pm. **Tsim Sha Tsui Branch,** Star House, 10th fl., Tsim Sha Tsui (tel. 2730 3269). Open Mon.-Fri. 10am-7:30pm, Sat. 10am-6:30pm, Sun. noon-5pm.

Embassies and Consulates: Australia, Harbour Center, 24th fl., 25 Harbour Rd., Wan Chai (tel. 2827 8881). Open Mon.-Fri. 9am-noon and 2-4pm. **Canada,** Exchange Square Tower 1, 12th fl., Central (tel. 2810 4321). Open Mon.-Tues. and Thurs.-Fri. 8:30am-4pm, Wed. 8:30am-noon. **Malaysia,** Malaysia Bldg., 23rd fl., 50 Gloucester Rd., Wan Chai (tel. 2527 0921). Open Mon.-Fri. 9am-1pm and 3-5pm. **New Zealand,** 2705 Jardine House, 1 Connaught Rd., Central (tel. 2877 4488). Open Mon. and Wed.-Fri. 9am-12:30pm and 2-4pm, Tues. 10am-12:30pm and 2-4pm. **Singapore,** 901 Admiralty Center, Tower 1, 9th fl., Admiralty (tel. 2527 2212). Open Mon.-Fri. 10am-12:30pm and 2:30-5:30pm. **Thailand,** Fairmont House, 8th fl., 8 Cotton Tree Dr., Central (tel. 2521 6481-5). Open Mon.-Fri. 9am-noon and 2-5pm. **UK,** Bank of America Tower, 9th fl., 12 Harcourt Rd., Admiralty (tel. 2523 0176). Open Mon.-Fri. 8:30am-5:15pm. **US,** 26 Garden Rd., Central (tel. 2523 9011). Open Mon.-Fri. 8:30am-5:30pm.

Immigration and Visas: Hong Kong Immigration Department, Immigration Tower, 7 Gloucester Rd., Wan Chai (tel. 2829 3000). Open Mon.-Fri. 8:45am-4:30pm, Sat. 9am-11:30am. **Immigration Hotline** (tel. 2824 6111).

Currency Exchange: Hang Seng Bank, a staple of every subway station. Changes money and basic services. Open Mon.-Fri. 9am-5pm., Sat. 9am-1pm. To get to the headquarters of the major banks, from the Star Ferry Pier in Central, take the pedestrian underpass to Statue Square, turn right and cut through the square (half of which is across Chater Rd.). **Hong Kong and Shanghai Banking Corporation** is in front. **Bank of China,** to the left. Turn right on Des Voeux Rd. Central for the **Bank of East Asia** on the left, after the intersection with Ice House St. Most are open Mon.-Fri. 9am-4:30pm, Sat. 9am-12:30pm. **American Express** cardholders can use Jetco **ATMs. Visa** and **MC** holders can use Hong Kong Bank's 'Electronic Money' ATMs.

American Express Offices: Central, New World Tower, ground fl., 16-18 Queen's Road Central, Central (tel. 2844 8668). Central MTR station (China Bldg. exit). Exit opposite the Landmark Bldg. Turn right, take a left onto Queen's Road Central after the China Bldg. branch of the Hong Kong Bank. AmEx office is about ½block down, in the black-and-brown New World Tower. Mail held for 30 days free for card members and those with AmEx traveler's checks. No charge for changing traveler's checks. Open Mon.-Fri. 9am-5pm, Sat. 9am-12:30pm. **Admiralty,** 1 Pacific Place, Shop 221-222, 88 Queen's Way, Admiralty (tel. 2844 0211). Exit next to the United Center, and Pacific Place is across the street. No client mail. Open Mon.-Fri. 9am-5pm, Sat. 9am-12:30pm.

Post Offices: GPO, 2 Connaught Place, Central (tel. 92 212 333). Immediately to the right of the Star Ferry. Via MTR (Jardine House exit), take a right and get onto the pedestrian overpass, and follow signs for Jardine House, which is in front of the post office. Poste Restante held for 2 months; address to: Sir Jon BARNES, R-W stud (or name of addressee), Poste Restante, GPO, Hong Kong. Open Mon.-Fri. 8am-6pm, Sat. 8am-2pm. **Tsim Sha Tsui,** Hermes House, ground fl., 10 Middle Rd., Tsim Sha Tsui (tel. 2366 4111). Tsim Sha Tsui MTR station (Nathan Rd. exit). Pass Chungking Mansions and turn left onto Middle Rd. Hermes House is at the end of the street on the left. Address Poste Restante: Mac REBENNACK, (or name of addressee), Poste Restante, Tsim Sha Tsui Post Office, Kowloon. Mail held for 2 months. Open Mon.-Fri. 8am-6pm, Sat. 8am-2pm.

Telephones: Change phones, credit card-change phones, and phone card-change phones. Pick up phone-cards at Hong Kong Telecom Service centers, HKTA offices, or 7-Eleven and Circle K stores. Local calls cost HK$1 regardless of the call's length. For **International phone calls,** dial: 001+country code+area code+phone number. **International code:** 852. For home country operators, call the **Home Direct number** for your country: British Telecom, 800-0044. Canada Direct, 800-1100. New Zealand Telecom, 852-146-644-1108. Telecom Australia,

800-0061. Telecom Eireann, 800-0353. Telekom South Africa, 800-0027. US: AT&T, 800-1111; MCI, 800-1121; Sprint, 800-1877.

Luggage Storage: Hong Kong International Airport (tel. 769 7895), in the departure hall and in the arrival hall. HK$30 per piece for 1 day; HK$70 per piece for 2. prices go up from there.

Newspapers and Magazines: The *South China Morning Post,* the *Hong Kong Standard,* the *Asian Wall Street Journal, USA Today International,* and the *International Herald Tribune* are widely available, as are international editions of *Newsweek* and *Business Week.*

English Bookstores: Bookazine Ltd., Shop No. 102-103, Alexandra House, 1st fl., Central (tel. 2521 1649). Central MTR (Alexandra House exit). Wide selection of magazines. English spoken. Open Mon.-Sat. 9am-7pm, Sun. and holidays 10am-6pm. **Swindon Book Co., Ltd.,** 13 Lock Rd., Tsim Sha Tsui (tel. 2366 8001). Tsim Sha Tsui MTR (C1 exit), turn right at next intersection. Turn right onto Lock Rd. The store is a few shops down the street from the Hyatt; look for a big red sign overhead. *Business Week, Newsweek, The Economist..* Open Mon.-Sat. 9am-6:30pm, holidays 1-5pm. **YMCA Bookshop,** YMCA Bldg., 41 Salisbury Rd., Tsim Sha Tsui (tel. 2369 2211). Walk down Salisbury Rd. from Star Ferry; it's on the left after the pedestrian underpass. Travel guides and picture books. Foreign-language phrasebooks and newspapers, popular fiction. Open daily 8am-8pm.

Cultural Organizations: Alliance Française (tel. 2527 7825). **British Council** (tel. 2879 5138). **AFS International,** Hong Kong Arts Centre (tel. 2802 0383). **Hong Kong Arts Centre,** Pao art galleries, foreign films, and language classes. From Immigration Tower exit, take the pedestrian overpass to Central Plaza. Turn right down Gloucester Rd. past Hong Kong Telecom, then right onto Harbor Rd. It's at the end of the street in black. Galleries open daily 10am-6pm.

Pharmacy: Yau Ma Tei Jockey Club Clinic, 145 Battery St., Yau Ma Tei (tel. 388 5858). Open Mon.-Fri. 8:45am-12:30pm and 1:45-4:30pm, Sat. 8:45am-12:30pm. **Sai Ying Poon Jockey Club Clinic,** 134 Queen's Rd., Central (tel. 2859 8234). Open Mon.-Fri. 8:45am-12:30pm and 1:45-4:30pm, Sat. 8:45am-12:30pm.

Hospitals: Queen Mary Hospital, Pok Fu Lam Rd., Hong Kong Island (tel. 2819 2111). **Queen Elizabeth Hospital,** Wylie Rd., Kowloon (tel. 2710 2111). **Ambulance:** Hong Kong Island (tel. 2576 655). Kowloon (tel. 2713 5555).

Crisis Lines: AIDS Hotline: tel. 2833 0180, in English. **Hong Kong Red Cross:** tel. 2802 0021. **Marriage and Personal Counseling Service:** tel. 2523 8979.

Emergency: (Police, fire, and ambulance) tel. 999.

■■■ MONEY

US$1=HK$5.206	**HK$1=US$0.192**
CDN$1=HK$3.829	**HK$1=CDN$0.261**
UK£1=HK$8.090	**HK$1=UK£0.124**
IR£1=HK$8.246	**HK$1=IR£0.121**
AUS$1=HK$3.838	**HK$1=AUS$0.261**
NZ$1=HK$3.414	**HK$1=NZ$0.293**
SARand1=HK$1.424	**HK$1=SARand0.702**

Legal tender is the Hong Kong dollar (HK$), which has 100 cents. Government-issued coins are bronze-colored for 10 cents, 20 cents, and 50 cents; silver-colored for $1, $2, and $5. Private banks issue notes in denominations of $10, $20, $50, $500, and $1000 for those wild mornings of *dim sum* bacchanalia.

■■■ LANGUAGE

Chinese and English are both official languages, so knowledge of either will make the city accessible. Don't be surprised, however, if you resort to the "point to order" strategy in some restaurants. A variety of Chinese dialects can be heard, and China-supported Mandarin is gaining popularity as 1997 approaches. Nonetheless, the dominant Cantonese is spoken by most of Hong Kong's inhabitants.

■■■ HOURS AND HOLIDAYS

Business hours are 9am to 5pm on weekdays and 9am to noon on Saturday, but many offices close from 1 to 2pm. Most shops open every day at 10am, except during Lunar New Year, when most everything shuts down for a few days.

Public holidays and festivals for 1996 are as follows:

January 1: New Year's Day.
February 19: Lunar New Year, a 15-day festival.
April 4: Ching Ming Festival. Families visit graves and make offerings to ancestors.
April 8: Easter Holiday.
May 10: Tin Hau Festival, celebrated at temples to Tin Hau, Goddess of the Sea.
June 20: Dragon Boat (Tuen Ng) Festival. "Dragon boats" race to drums.
June 17: the Queen's birthday (the following Monday is also a holiday).
August 26: Liberation Day (the previous Saturday is also a holiday).
August-September: Festival of the Hungry Ghosts. Offerings are burned in the streets, and various locations stage Chinese opera.
September 28: Mid-Autumn Festival. Paper lanterns are lit in public places.
October 21: Chung Yeung Festival. People visit ancestral graves to make offerings.
December 25: Christmas Day.
December 26: Boxing Day.

LIFE AND TIMES

■■■ HISTORY

Hong Kong, from Heung Gong or "fragrant harbor," was largely ignored by the Chinese imperial government before the mid-1800s, although it has been inhabited for thousands of years. The original inhabitants were probably the **Yueh**, a tribe of "boat-people" and fishermen, whose descendents, the Tanka, still live in the Hong Kong area. At the beginning of what they call the first millenia out west, the region of modern Hong Kong came under Chinese control. Little mention is made of it until 1000 years later, when it served as a garrison town, and center of Pearl harvesting by Tanka divers. Around this time, discord within China brought the **"Five Great Clans,"** south. These northern Cantonese families settled on the southern tip, and established the the province of **Canton**.

In the 17th century the **Qing** dynasty evacuated the area to control piracy. This experiment was short -lived, and the sparsely populated region became a haven for Northern farmers, known as **Hakka**, or "guests." With this new economic base, the Cantonese families began to consolidate control over the market. British merchants began trading in Canton in the late 17th century, along with other Europeans who were vying for trade, and began converting this handful of small fishing villages into a thriving commercial base, exchanging **opium** for Chinese silks, spices, and silver. As the Chinese government saw capital leaving the country in exchange for a population of addicts, they restricted British trade. The drug smugglers persevered, and at the beginning of the 19th century the opium trade had more than doubled. In 1821 the British established themselves in Hong Kong, gaining a strategic economic position. When threatened with a full-scale, enforced ban on drug trafficking, the British attempted negotiations, and then struck with their naval hardware, claiming Hong Kong Island as a British territory in 1841 and then invading the mainland. Beginning with the **Treaty of Nanking,** the British and their western allies forced China to cede the area collectively known as "Hong Kong." Hong Kong Island and its surrounding waters were taken in the First Opium War (1842), Kowloon in the second (1860), and the New Territories were acquired in a 99-year lease in 1898.

The Japanese invasion of China, the establishment of the People's Republic of China, and the Korean War drove millions of Cantonese and others with their wallets to Hong Kong, bringing many professionals to the tiny island. During the late sixties, China's Cultural Revolution kept Hong Kong on edge, as its citizens realized that it would take little effort for China to subsume the tiny island. Instead, China became Hong Kong's largest trade partner.

The British and Chinese eventually questioned how useful a split colony would be to either power, once the New Territories and much of Kowloon reverted to China. To simplify things Britain signed the **Sino-British Joint Declaration** in 1984 so that all of Hong Kong will return to China at **the stroke of midnight on June 30, 1997.**

■■■ HONG KONG TODAY

Despite China's guarantee to maintain the current economy and life-style of Hong Kong until at least 2047, the impending turnover broadcasts financial and philosophical shock waves through the community, and has sent scores scurrying to the U.S., Canada, and Australia. Pro-democracy movements shirk as well, under the steady realization that the colonial Governor and Executive Council, will soon be replaced by similar figures from Beijing, leaving Hong Kong perpetually subservient. Those living on borrowed time seem to take it in stride: Mandarin language schools are making big bucks, and the growing number of Cantonese who speak the Northern dialect casually remark that they are rehearsing for 1997.

Meanwhile, the furious pace of life rumbles recklessly on for its six million inhabitants. Yuppies cruise the Lan Kwai Fong district, shuttling among transplanted pubs and trendy clubs with names like "Post-1997." Wizened sooth-sayers predict destinies; fruit-vendors hack up watermelons with Zen-like calm; and old men still lounge around temples, hunched over backgammon. The night markets groan under the weight of noodles and Nikons and are packed with sweaty backpackers and laid-back locals looking for a bargain. Yet nobody can divine how far off-kilter the city will be thrown when Beijing comes to collect the rent. Many feel the future is up for grabs, but that there are more ways things can go wrong than right. Beyond it all, Taiwan looks on as well, believing that China's handling of Hong Kong will be an omen, good or bad, regarding the likelihood of the two countries ever reuniting. For now, however, the Fragrant Harbor is reassuringly redolent with the intoxicating smell of free-enterprise.

■■■ THE PEOPLE OF HONG KONG

An incredible 98% of Hong Kong is **Chinese**, the majority of whom are of Cantonese descent and colony born and bred. The entire population is just under 6 million people, however, so there's plenty of room within that 2%, for Filipinos, Indians, Americans, Britains, and others. The fishing population of long-time islanders, the **Tanka,** make up a small percentage as well.

■■■ CUSTOMS AND CULTURE

Fortune telling, luck, astrology, superstition— these are followed in Hong Kong as probably nowhere else. Signs and omens are taken seriously, so don't make light of them; don't write in red ink; do handle paper with two hands. One of the more important customs is **feng shui** (geomancy), the correct interaction with environmental spirits. If bad luck occurs it is possible that a building was built without consulting the earth or the trees. If bad luck continues Taoist priests may have to come and reorient things.

On a more mundane level, pride and prestige are important aspects of Hong Kong culture as well; acting indecently or blowing-off someone is considered a serious affront. Prestige is plussed through quality material achievement; expensive and imported gifts often carries more weight and worth than their costs.

RELIGION

For all of the city's futuristic feel, **superstition** and **ancestor worship** co-mingle quite happily with Buddhist and Taoist deities as well as Christianity. Regardless of religion, citizens continue to appease ancestral spirits in order to succeed in the future. As in many major cities the gods of practicality, efficiency, and cold, hard cash have a strong influence. This makes **joss**, or luck, an important part of daily life, and religious practice is often focused upon increasing the good and diminishing the bad.

■■■ ARTS AND RECREATION

Hong Kong's roots in Sino-British traditions have created a city where there are at least two ways of doing everything. **Chinese Opera,** or *Wayung,* can be found in the intricate but campy Cantonese style, with its extraordinary and sometimes incomprehensible costumes and movements, as well as in the older and more classical Beijing style. Hong Kong has popular modern orchestras, one which specializes in western fare and one which plays only Chinese classics. Hong Kong's Chinese dance troupes are supplemented by a relatively young professional ballet, and avenues exist for both English and Cantonese dramatic productions.

Less cosmopolitan, but no less fun, **puppet plays** abound. Even operas are acted out by these *faux* people. Telling the stories of China's dynasties through shadow plays is a popular form of puppetry, as are rod puppets. The lion dances, with their martial arts-like movements, are very important for festivals and city life. For some bubble-gum fun Hong Kong's **Canto-Pop,** has a light rock sound, but northwestern folk music is beefing up musical output, creating a new, indigenous rock.

For a peaceful recreational pursuit, try your hand at **Mah jong,** the classic Chinese game of memory and strategy. Martial arts are popular exercise in the frantic city. **Shadow Boxing** and its hyper cousin **Kung Fu** are excellent ways to calm the system and maintain your abs of steel. For relaxation by the waves, the beaches south of the island offer good places to swim and absorb those UV rays.

■■■ FOOD AND DRINK

Hong Kong takes its food very seriously. Unfortunately, much of the excellent victuals are priced in the *haute cuisine* range, rather than the "cheap eats" range we all know and love. Chinese restaurants may have menus in Chinese only. Once you navigate your way through these difficulties, however, the end result is well worth it; 98% of all Hong Kongians agree—the Chinese food here is the best in the world!

The most popular regional cooking style is **Cantonese.** This simple semi-tropical style uses a lot of fruit, vegetables, pork, and chicken, but much less spice than that of other regions. The famous 1000-year-old eggs (no, they're not really that old) are a specialty. Steamed and stir-fry dishes are popular, and be sure to try *dim sum.* This "loveable" tradition of sampling and sharing is done best in Hong Kong.

Spicy **Szechuan** food is extremely popular among westerners in Hong Kong, characterized by its hot, spicy peppers and noodles. For seafood many try **Shanghai** food, which is spicier and oilier than Cantonese, or **Hakka,** which uses Cantonese and Shanghai styles, but is also known for using the entire animal in its dishes. With **Chiu Chow** food one often encounters the exotic and expensive—shark-fin, digested bird nests, and other aphrodisiacs and delicacies.

The classic drink is tea, which will probably come with all your meals. Green tea, *oolang,* and Black tea (*bolay*) are the three umbrella tea categories which correspond to varying levels of fermentation. Herbal and floral teas abound as well.

ON THE MAINLAND

■■■ KOWLOON

The nine legendary dragons *(kow lung)* comprising this 11sq km peninsula seem to have released Kowloon to the powers of **Tsim Sha Tsui** ("Sharp Sandy Point"), the disembarking point on the peninsula, and Hong Kong's Yellow Brick Road for disoriented shoppers hoping to dodge the Wicked Witch of Retail and return home with a bargain-priced bauble or too-cheap-to-be-true electronic gizmo. Thousands of foreigners mill around Nathan Rd., eyeballing the labyrinthine restaurants, bars, boutiques and shopping arcades. Touts accost tourists with glossy ads; hawkers pull visitors aside and show them photos of fake Rolexes, all 'high quality, low price.'

ORIENTATION

From the ferry concourse, **Salisbury Rd.** extends east-west past the Hong Kong Cultural Centre and the New World Center into Tsim Sha Tsui East. Once tagged "Nathan's Folly" after the imprudence of the British governor who designed it, **Nathan Rd.,** the main avenue of Tsim Sha Tsui, runs north-south, intersecting Salisbury Rd. near the Space Museum. The luxurious Peninsula Hotel reposes at the intersection. To the west of Nathan Rd. lies **Kowloon Park.** The Tsim Sha Tsui MTR station has exits all along Nathan Rd. Smaller streets running perpendicular off Nathan Rd. houses many of Tsim Sha Tsui's renowned shops and restaurants.

ACCOMMODATIONS

The huge, ramshackle warren of bargain-priced guest houses, **Chunking Mansions,** sits unabashedly on 36-44 Nathan Rd. between the Holiday Inn Golden Mile and the Imperial Hotel, across the street on the left. A1 airbus stops nearby. Watch your step; you can pick up a dynamite, budget hotel, or step on a lodging land mine. Marble and gold façade belies the tattered interior. Wander inside and find A, B, and C elevators on the left. D and E entryways are on the far right. The various proprietors are fast and fearless. Stand around with your luggage, and someone is bound to exhort you to have dinner in their restaurant or stay in their 'very clean, very quiet, very cheap' quarters. Dorms and guest houses a few blocks down the street await white-gloved inspection. Residents of easy street can slide into deluxe barracks studding the **Yau Ma Tei-Mongkok area.**

Peking Guest House, A2, 12th fl. (tel. 2723 8320). Funky patterned bed linens boost spirits in this clean and jovial spot. Singles HK$160, with bath HK$200. Doubles HK$220, with bath HK$260-350. Prices negotiable. Laundry service.

Welcome Guest House, A5, 7th fl. (tel. 2721 7793). The name captures management's congeniality, but not the smallness of rooms. Also has 8th-floor accommodations with cheery, pastel sheets. Singles HK$140, with bath HK$160. Doubles HK$180, with bath HK$220-240. Laundry service. Visas for China arranged.

Far East Guest House, E Block, 14th fl. (tel. 2721 2397). Rooms are the best of the lot in E block. Singles HK$140. Doubles HK$150, with bath HK$200. Rates negotiable for longer stays.

Beyond the Mansions

Victoria Hostel, 3rd fl., 33 Hankow Rd., Tsim Sha Tsui (tel. 2376 0621). A right off Peking Rd. Blue and white signs overhead. Cut through Cheung Kee Watch Co. to the stairs in the back. Budget rates make dim, chambers tolerable. Dorm HK$100. 4-bed dormitory HK$150. 6-bed dormitory HK$120. Discounts for longer stays. Lockers HK$50. Laundry service. Lunch or dinner HK$20.

Star Guest House, Flat B, 6th fl., 21 Cameron Rd. (tel. 2723 8951). Tsim Sha Tsui MTR station (Cameron Rd. exit). ½block after Carnarvon Rd., across from the Crocodile Shop. Cut through Perfect Jewellery Co. to the elevator. Phone, A/C, lockable drawers, and carpeted walls. Arranges visas for China and tours to China and Macau. Singles HK$210-270, with bath $300. Doubles with bath HK$350-380. Laundry service. 24-hr. reception.

FOOD

Prices here are somewhat higher than in other parts of the territory, but don't let a little inflation burst your gastronomic bubble—console yourself with the United Nations range of cuisines: Indian, Pakistani, Thai, Malaysian-Singaporean, Szechuan, and Cantonese. The small streets west of Nathan Rd. (Lock Rd., Hankow Rd., and Ashley Rd.) are fruitful places to look for South Asian food; the streets between Nathan Rd. and Chatham Rd., particularly Granville Rd., Cameron Rd., Carnavon Rd. and Prat Ave., are chock full of fine epicurean experiences.

Bodhi Vegetarian Restaurant, 32-34 Lock Rd., ground fl. (tel. 2366 8283 or 2739 2222). Tsim Sha Tsui station (C1 exit). Turn right and take another right at the 1st intersection. Look for the green sign near the end of the street. The largest vegetarian chain in Hong Kong, Bodhi cranks out good food in a cheerful, if institutionalized atmosphere. Entrees HK$45-50. Breakfast buffet (HK$32), lunch buffet (HK$68). *Congee* (HK$14-18). AmEx, DC, MC, Visa. Open daily 11am-11:30pm.

The Sweet Dynasty, 88 Canton Rd., ground fl. (tel. 2375 9119). From the Star Ferry, take a left off Salisbury Rd. Right before the large Fotomax sign. Charming café with traditional tables and low round stools. Chinese menu. Hot and cold drinks (HK$13-19), *congee* (HK$25-110). Open Sun.-Thurs. 11:30am-midnight, Fri.-Sat. and public holidays 11:30am-1am.

Nanjing Kitchen, ground fl., 98 Canton Rd. (tel. 2317 6201 or 2317 6212). From the Star Ferry, take a left onto Canton Rd., and keep walking. In the Friendship Stores complex (look for the red and white sign) across from Harbor City Shopping Arcade. Selection of appetizers that blows you away: noodles mixed with anything—spiced tendons, chicken (HK$20-25, up to HK$35 for seafood). Save room for other traditional classics like shredded peppery pig's ear (HK$15). 4 set dinner menus (HK$168-268) available. Open daily 11am-midnight.

SIGHTS

Tsim Sha Tsui breaks from the temple-and-street market rut with ultra-modern museums. The **Clock Tower,** a lonely remnant of the old railway station, is to the right as you step off the ferry. Next door is the **Hong Kong Cultural Centre** (tel. 2734 2009), a huge, beige complex. This HK$600 Grand Theater offers a variety of shows, from *The Phantom of the Opera* to members of the Texas Girls' Choir. Upcoming events posted in the middle of the hall (9am-9pm). The adjacent **Space Museum,** 10 Salisbury Rd. (tel. 2734 2722), a bisected golf ball, features hands-on exhibits; spend an afternoon designing an alien, dropping meteorites on the moon, or spinning in an astronaut's multi-axis chair. The Planetarium screens four Omnimax films each weekday (except Tues.) and five on Sat.-Sun. and public holidays. Open Mon.-Fri. 1-9pm, Sat.-Sun. and public holidays 10am-9pm. Admission HK$10; students and senior citizens HK$5. The Space Theater has one sky show in English, daily. Admission HK$26; students and senior citizens HK$13. Behind the Science Museum, the **Hong Kong Museum of Art** (tel. 2734 2167) guards Chinese antiquities, as well as contemporary Hong Kong art. Open Mon.-Sat. 10am-6pm, Sun. and public holidays 1-6pm. Admission HK$10; students and senior citizens HK$5.

Kowloon Park lies west of Nathan Rd. (Tsim Sha Tsui MTR station, A1 exit). The entrance is behind you. Weary road warriors can chill among fountains, pink flamingos, swimming pools resembling island lagoons, sculptures, and those dogged *tai chi* enthusiasts. Open daily 6am-midnight. Games hall open 7am-11pm. Admission free. Pools open daily 6:30am-9pm. Admission HK$16; children and seniors HK$8. The **Museum of History** (tel. 2367 1124), on the west side of the park, contains historical photographs and artifacts. Open Mon.-Thurs. and Sat. 10am-6pm, Sun. and public holidays 1-6pm. Admission HK$10; students, and senior citizens HK$5.

If the Space Museum whetted your appetite for ultra-modern gadgetry, gorge yourself at the **Hong Kong Science Museum,** 2 Science Museum Rd. (tel. 2732

3232), Tsim Sha Tsui MTR station (Cameron Rd. exit). Go right to Granville Rd., then turn right. Get on the pedestrian overpass near the Chatham Rd. intersection, and follow the red and white signs. Look for the incredible cream, pink and green hulk with a glass pyramid spouting water in front of it. A delight for budding Einsteins and their parents, the museum tweaks the cerebellum with interactive media. Open Tues.-Fri. 1-9pm, Sat.-Sun. and public holidays 10am-9pm. Admission HK$25; children, students, and senior citizens HK$15.

Bars and pubs bum around as well, particularly in the oddly shaped polygram formed by Carnarvon Rd., Cameron Rd., Chatham Rd., and Mody Rd. Tsam Tsui Shi is packed with bars, pubs, and dance clubs, including **Ned Kelly's Last Stand** and the **Old Hero Pub and Café.**

■ AROUND KOWLOON

Wong Tai Sin Temple, named after a legendary healer, is dedicated to Taoist and Buddhist deities, as well as to Confucius. Disembark at the Wong Tai Sin MTR station exit. You'll be accosted by old women offering incense and paper money; others will stuff red slips of *joss* paper into your hand in return for a few coins. Built in 1973, the structures are awash with gaudy, vibrant colors. The faithful gather at the main hall to pray and light *joss* sticks which are often removed by temple workers minutes later to make room for other worshippers. Modern-day mystics, with cellular phones and air-conditioned offices in the Fortune-telling and Oblation Arcade, stare into your future. They also find ways to change bad destiny into good. Negotiate first or you're fated for an unpleasantly large bill. Open daily 7am-5pm.

Moving north into **Yau Ma Tei,** two MTR stations away or a 20-minute walk up Nathan Rd., entertain yourself among street markets, cafés, and shops. **Jade Market,** a chief attraction, is at the intersection of Kansu St., Reclamation St., and Battery St. Leave the Jordan MTR station (Jordan Rd. exit) and walk down Nathan Rd. past the Eaton Hotel; Kansu St. is the first street on the left. Reclamation St. is the fourth; the bazaar is under the overpass, behind an outdoor fruit market. Pale green, and sometimes white, jade carved into a smorgasbord of images. Jade bracelets ward off evil spirits and protect the wearer's health. The cheapest dainties will set you back about HK$5. Open daily 10am-3:30pm.

Behind the Jade Market, on Market St. is **Tin Hau Temple.** The yard in front is frequented by the homeless and older men absorbed in card games; at the main altar, a statue of Tin Hau smiles obliviously. Open daily 7am-5:30pm. At night the area is transformed into the **Temple St. Night Market.** Fortune-tellers crowd the alley just outside the temple, hoping for a chance to feel the bumps on your cranium, or to coax their oracular parakeets into picking out an appropriate fortune. The damage for a basic palm reading is about HK$200, but you can bargain it down if you plead poverty or grave and unjust misfortune. Open daily, around 8-11pm.

Lined with songbirds in delicate teak cages, the **Bird Market** on Hong Lok Rd. is fascinating and grotesque. Stall owners sell live grasshoppers, popping them into plastic bags for you. From the Mongkok MTR station (exit C) take a left, pass a large Chinese movie theater, and take the first right. The Bird Market is about a block farther—just follow the chirps.

HONG KONG ISLAND

■■■ CENTRAL DISTRICT

The Central district hails visitors arriving on the Star Ferry. During the day, the financial and government center crawls with Filofaxed businessmen scrambling from one high-rise to another through the merging of endless crowds, cars, and trams into a stream of fearless traffic that defies the narrowness of the streets. Older, upscale tourists flex Platinum Cards in the infinite number of boutiques selling Yves St. Laurent, solid gold bars, jewelry, and 24-carat emblems of conspicuous consumption. By 7pm the streets are deserted. Only the back-alley, expat-barfly-haven of Lan Kwai Fong, and the Star Ferry concourse, where noodle vendors, set up to intercept folks rushing home, scrimmage with action-packed intensity well into the night.

ORIENTATION

Let the Star Ferry concourse be your guiding light. Stationed at the northern edge of the neighborhood, this complex shares the district's chief thoroughfare, **Connaught Rd. Central,** with the low-rising general post office and Jardine House, a white round-windowed office tower. **Des Voeux Rd. Central** and **Queen's Rd. Central,** the area's two other main streets, run south of and parallel to Connaught Rd.; **Pedder St.** and **Ice House Rd.** connect all three roads.

Central is a veritable Valhalla of epic landmarks. The Hong Kong and Shanghai Banking Corporation Headquarters Building, a steel and glass amazon, stands in an island, along with Security Pacific and the Bank of China, bordered by Des Voeux Rd. to the north, Queen's Rd. to the south and Ice House Rd. to the west. One block to the west is the well-named Landmark Building, neighboring the Edinburgh Tower. Alexandra House looms over Des Voeux Rd. across from the Landmark. Stanley St. and Wellington St. run south of and parallel to Queen's Rd. The few alleys at the southern end of D'Aguilar St. cutting across Queen's Rd. constitute the expat haunt known as **Lan Kwai Fong.**

FOOD

Hong Kong's business district favors fast-food and full-service over colorful eateries and vendors. Feast frugally in the basements of major office buildings. **Maxim's** and **Café de Coral** are options for those seeking cheap, Chinese fast food. Wander **Wellington St.** and **Stanley St.** for more authentic Indian, Pakistani, and Chinese fare. You'll find nectar and ambrosia in markets and stalls along the smaller streets west of **Pedder St. Central Market,** three floors of meat, fish, and vegetable stalls in the belly of a concrete monster on the corner of Queen's Rd. Central and Queen Victoria St. The smell is fierce, and you may have to step over puddles of pig's blood, but prices are low and the food undeniably fresh.

SIGHTS

Some of Hong Kong's most tranquil gardens provide an herbal oasis in the midst of Central's parched urban desert. On a warm day, **Statue Square** is a popular spot for a quick working lunch with a can of chrysanthemum tea. From Star Ferry, enter the pedestrian underpass; a blue sign for Statue Square will be on the left. Part of the square lies across Chater Rd., where the statue of Sir Thomas Jackson, one of Hong Kong's beloved capitalists and chief manager of the Hong Kong and Shanghai Banking Corporation, happily surveys the landscape of lucre.

Across Des Voeux Rd. Central from Statue Square is the futuristic flagship of the **Hong Kong and Shanghai Banking Corporation,** the fourth headquarters to be located on this site. The "Robot Building," completed in 1985, states in crystal-clear terms that Hong Kong won't yield its iron grip on capitalism without a fight. The interior workings of the escalators and elevators are completely exposed, as are the offices, which are open on the atrium side and glass-walled on the street side.

Hong Kong Park, a 10-hectare modern landscaping marvel on the east edge of the Central district, is a requisite stop for any visit. Follow the sidewalk from the Hong Kong Hilton as it turns onto Garden Rd. Watch for Peak Tram signs; the park's main entrance is up a staircase across the street from the tram souvenir shop. The lakes and waterfalls are popular for wedding portraits. An aviary, conservatory, and visual arts center also roost in the park. Park open daily 7am-11pm. Aviary 9am-4:30pm (with seasonal variations). Conservatory open Mon.-Fri. 9am-5pm, Sat.-Sun. and holidays 9am-6pm. Visual arts center (tel. 2521 3008) open Wed.-Mon. 10am-6pm. Mostly modern art exhibits

The **Zoological and Botanical Gardens** are just off Garden Rd. and a 10-minute walk from the Hong Kong Hilton, past St. John's Cathedral and the U.S. Consulate on the right. The main entrance is at the intersection of Garden Rd. and Upper Albert Rd. An arch commemorates the Chinese who died fighting for the Allied cause. The garden's winding paths and uphill climbs are good places to burn off those dumplings. Squawk along with the early birds and break the zombie-like concentration of folks doing *tai chi.* Open daily 6am-7pm.

ENTERTAINMENT

Central nightlife is slightly classier, some say more pretentious, than in the rest of town; many trendy pubs and clubs are in Lan Kwai Fong, an L-shaped lane off D'Aguilar St. The city-slicker-material-girl-disco-demimonde regulars often provide enough entertainment to justify the upwardly mobile cover charges and bar tabs. **Graffitti** packs in the twenty-something crowd every night, offering reasonable prices, dancing on two levels, and a moderate cover charge on Sat. night. **Club 97** draws a slightly hipper and more beautiful clientele, discouraging style-lacking budgeteers with its hefty cover and no-nonsense pair of supermodel "bouncers" at the door. Popular bars along Lan Kwai Fong are recognizable by their tendency to spill out onto the street. Prices remain fairly constant (a bit pricey) and all establishments are within walking distance of each other. You can't go wrong.

■■■ SHEUNG WAN

Just west of Central Market is Sheung Wan, where the Royal Navy dropped anchor for Britannia in 1841. Once inspiring enthusiastic comparisons to old Shanghai, the now-anemic district is surrendering to the bulldozers. Sheung Wan is still noted however for its web of streets tangled with bazaars, *dai pai dong* food stalls, and traditional shops dealing in embroidery, *objets d'art,* and ritual paper luxuries for ancestor spirits. Hot 'n spicy **street markets** pepper the alleys between Des Voeux Rd. Central and Bonham Strand. The **Macau Ferry Terminal** and the Victoria Hotel reign over the north edge of the district. **Western Market,** an Edwardian building converted into a tourist mall, slouches on New Market St. Farther south, at the corner of Ladder St. and Hollywood Rd., looms **Man Mo Temple,** where the lovelorn shake fortune-telling sticks to check on the state of their star-crossed destinies. Dedicated to the Taoist gods of literature and war, Man and Mo, the temple also houses a number of shrines to the city god and the 10 Divine Judges. Open daily 7am-5pm.

■■■ WAN CHAI

Wan Chai will probably never shake off its infamy as the setting for Richard Mason's novel, *The World of Suzie Wong*. Although the film was actually shot in Sheung Wan, Wan Chai remains linked in the imagination with brothels, bars, and furloughed sailors. In reality, much of northern Wan Chai has been transformed into a business district, where white-shirted executives close deals on their cel-phones during lunch. The south part of the district retains some of the old red-light district seediness, hosting topless bars with names like Club Gas Light and Club Hot Lips interspersed among tattoo parlors and smoky hole-in-the-wall pubs.

ORIENTATION

Between the harbor and **Gloucester Rd.** to the south is reclaimed land which is over-run with elephantine office skyscrapers. Three streets, **Jaffe Rd., Lockhart Rd.,** and **Hennessy Rd.,** run parallel to each other south of Gloucester Rd. farther inland and comprise "old" Wan Chai. They are cut perpendicularly by **Penwick St., Luard Rd., O'Brien Rd.,** and **Fleming Rd.,** which in turn meet **Johnston Rd.** where the tram tracks run. Forage for Wan Chai chow south of Gloucester Rd.; small cafés and restaurants, including some fast food shops, slink about Hennessy Rd. South of

Johnston Rd., Spring Garden Lane gurgles with tropical fish and flowers, while nearby Lee Tung St. and Tai Yuen St. host **street markets** and **food stalls.**

FOOD

Quality Herb Tea House, 84 Hennessy Rd. Wan Chai MTR station (Alliance Française exit). Corner of Luard Rd. and Hennessy Rd., across from Broadway Seafood Restaurant. Potent potables from golden teapots with dragon's head spouts in the open-air pavilion. Chinese herbal brews HK$5-9 a bowl. Little blue stickers explain each tea's special properties. Sink your sweet tooth into herbal grass jelly and red bean soup. Open daily 10am-11pm.

Vegetarian Garden, 128 Johnston Rd. (tel. 2833 9128). At the intersection of Johnston and O'Brien Rd. From the Wan Chai MTR station, turn right and walk to the end of the street; it's across the way, slightly off to the left. No English signs, only heavy gold Chinese characters. Ground floor is take-out; the restaurant is downstairs. Local clientele. *Dim sum* is ordered from a list. Superb vegetarian *shumai* (open-faced ravioli). Chili sauce blazes a fiery trail through your digestive tract. *Dim sum* (HK$10 per basket). No English menu. MC, Visa. Take-out counter open daily 7:30am-11pm. Restaurant open daily 11am-11pm.

New Maharani, ground floor, 64 Lockhart Rd. (tel. 2865 7513). Wan Chai MTR station (Immigration Tower exit). Turn left past a 7-Eleven on the right; continue past Luard Rd., on the right, opposite the Wharney hotel, a few stores down on the left. Ignore "Members Only" signs. Romantic and sophisticated, but prices stay within the rigid confines of a backpacker's budget. Chicken and mutton (HK$39-45). Vegetarian dishes (HK$28-32). Breads (HK$8-12). Mon.-Fri., HK$75 set lunch. Open daily 11am-11pm.

Kublai's, 151 Lockhart Rd. (2511 2287). Also 55 Kimberly Rd., Tsim Sha Tsui (2722 0733); and 1 Keswick St., Causeway Bay (2882 3282). Kublai and Ghengis never had it so good; nor have most who flock to this Mongolian eatery. For HK$118, fill your bowl as many times as you'd like. Select from an amazing array of veggies, meats, and fish; top it off with sauces and garnishes, and hand it to the army of cooks, who will have it ready in 10min. Incredibly tasty, a fantastic bargain, and fun for groups. AmEx, Visa, MC. Open daily 12:30-3:30pm and 6:30-11:30pm.

ENTERTAINMENT

The Wanch, 54 Jaffe Rd. (tel. 2861 1621). Wan Chai MTR station (Lockhart Rd. exit). Turn left past 7-Eleven, then right just before Brett's Seafood, and left on Jaffe Rd. The Wanch is on the left, with a Japanese flag sign. An intimate ode to Hong Kong pop culture, designed like a Star Ferry. Part of the outside is a tram and tram seats serve as booths; posters from *The World of Suzie Wong* plaster the interior. Open Sun.-Thurs. 11am-1am, Fri.-Sat. 11am-4am. Live music every night.

Carnegie's, 53-5 Lockhart Rd. (2866 6289). The "Spirit of Rock" heats up at night and goes wild on weekend. A tower of alcohol behind the bar spells disaster for the overzealous, who've been photographed stripping on the bar after a few too many. Cocktails HK$40-150. Happy hour 11am-7pm daily. Beware the "Love Muscle." Mon.-Thurs. 11am-2am, Fri.-Sat. 11am-4am, Sun. 5am-noon, 4pm-midnight.

Joe Bananas, 23 Luard Rd. (tel. 2529 18 11), at the corner with Jaffe Rd. "International" club with road signs, Beatles posters, and a portrait of Martin Luther King, Jr. No t-shirts, hats, or shorts after 6pm. Fri. and Sat. after 9pm, HK$110 cover, includes 2 drinks. 2 for 1 drinks on Wed. night. Happy hour, 11:30am-9pm. No dress code on Sun. Open Mon.-Sat. 11am-5am, Sun. 11am-4am.

■■■ CAUSEWAY BAY

The glare of neon-lit camera shops and hip western bars is subdued by dozens of funky clothing shops and old-style open-air night markets. Residential as well as commercial; innumerable "mansions" and apartment units are squeezed between Japanese department stores. *Tai chi* dominates the crack-of-dawn in Victoria Park; early risers drop into Maxim's for *dim sum* breakfast and good conversation.

ORIENTATION

Causeway Bay is divided roughly into north and south by the broad swath of **Hennessy Road,** which becomes **Yee Woo Street** as it runs east. **Gloucester Road** runs parallel to and north of Hennessy until it hits Victoria Park and makes a sharp right-angle turn, crossing Hennessy Rd./Yee Woo St. Before that intersection, **Paterson Street** connects the two. **Kingston Street** runs parallel to Gloucester Rd. South of Yee Woo St. is a beehive of small streets full of clothing stores, herbal medication, dried-food shops, and inexpensive restaurants. The Causeway Bay MTR station has six exits. The easternmost emerges onto **Great George Street** near Daimaru department store. Another comes out next to Sogo department store. Two more appear farther west at Causweay Bay Plaza on Yee Woo St., and another pops up near the mouth of Jardine's Crescent. A final exit is in the giant Times Square shopping complex, east of Jardine's Bazaar and Jardine's Crescent.

ACCOMMODATIONS

Cheap guest houses take root at Lee Garden Hill Rd. (around #68-70); similar lodgings germinate at Leishun Court, at 116 Leighton Rd. and cluster along Leighton Rd. from #30-60.

FOOD

Asakusa Shabu Beef, Shop 35-36, PJ Plaza, 22-36 Paterson St. (tel. 2882 2983). PJ Plaza is at the intersection with Great George St. Bright signs advertise the Asakusa and its neighbor, the International House of Curries. Do-it-yourselfers slam-dunk meat, vegetables, and tofu in boiling stock. 4 complete *shabu* dinners HK$140-HK$200. Or order *à la carte:* a plate of beef (HK$60), and vegetables (HK$20). Standard Japanese fare, including *donburi* (HK$45), *rāmen,* and *udon* (HK$40). AmEx, DC, MC, Visa. English spoken. Open daily 11:30am-midnight.

Maxim's Chinese Restaurant, Hong Kong Mansion, Yee Woo St. (tel. 2894 9933). Across from the Causeway Bay MTR station (Daimaru exit). Ditch your beauty sleep for *dim sum;* show up at 7:45am and savor tasty dumplings, *congee*, soup, and free, hot jasmine tea. Good-sized breakfast under HK$45. Maxim's also serves standard Chinese at reasonable prices. Open daily 7:30am-midnight. *Dim sum* 7:30am-5pm. English menu, but not for *dim sum;* just peruse and point.

SIGHTS

Escape the mundane realm of the Causeway Bay MTR (Times Square exit) and you'll find yourself at the pearly gates of shopping. A 13-level mall organized around themes such as "Suit and Dress," "Home Sweet Home," and "Dante and Virgil," **Times Square** showcases upscale designers and trendy specialties with otherworldly prices. Open daily 10am-10pm.

Opposite Times Square on Russell St. a heated **outdoor market** throbs from 8:30am-8pm selling fresh meat (chickens in wicker cages arrive hourly) along with inexpensive trinkets and juicy mangos, papayas, and star fruit.

The booming **outdoor market** at **Jardine's Bazaar** and **Jardine's Crescent** testifies to the presence of a market economy. As you emerge from the Causeway Bay MTR station (Jardine's Crescent exit), the Crescent is the small tunnel of clothing stalls to the right of the Giordano store. The Bazaar is the next street on the left, with cheap eateries, whose tables spill out onto the sidewalk with inexpensive noodles, spring rolls, dumplings, and other snacks. Peddlers offer traditional herbal medicines, preserved bean curd, tea, and clothing up and down the street. The alleyway under the red sign for the Yat Pun Henn Restaurant connects the Bazaar with the Crescent; duck in for popular outdoor dining, cold juices, and grilled squid. The show runs from around 9am, into the evening for nocturnal feeding.

The **Noon-Day Gun** squats near the harbor, across from the Excelsior Hotel. Catapulted to fame in Noel Coward's 1924 song *Mad Dogs and Englishmen* ("In Hong Kong they strike a gong and fire a noon-day gun"), the 3-lb. gun is still fired daily.

Victoria Park lends lushness to the gold and silver of the shopping district. Enter on Gloucester Rd., opposite the Park Lane Radisson. A roller-skating rink, bowling green, and swimming pool for a fee, but free jogging trails are surrounded by spacious lawn an aviary and a topiary garden. *Tai chi* zealots continue life in slow-motion; on weekends they are joined by Chinese wrestlers and martial artists. The park is home to a large flower fair during Chinese New Year and hosts local families who come to eat lotus-seed cakes and gaze at the moon during the Mid-Autumn Festival. Open daily 7am-11pm. A footbridge in the northwest corner of Victoria Park, along the path from the Model Boat Pool, leads to **Causeway Bay Typhoon Shelter,** countless floating homes. Small sampans ferry residents and deliver groceries. Look for a sign that says "passenger carrying sampan" in English (about 30min., HK$150). Visit during the Chinese New Year, when vessels swarm to the harbor.

■■■ AROUND HONG KONG

Ma Wui Hall Youth Hostel, Mount Davis Path, (tel. 2817 5715), is the closest hostel, but still a trek. Take A2 airbus to Macau Ferry Bus Terminal and then a cab (HK$50). Or catch bus #5B from Des Voeux Rd. Central next to King Fook Jewelry between Pedder St. and Queen Victoria St. From the last stop (Felix Villas), backtrack about 100m and head up the mountain path to the top of Mt. Davis, a 30-minute hike. Superb view of the harbor (but you have to earn it) and quiet cubicles. Kitchen available. Dorms for HI members HK$18, overseas non-members HK$33. Limit of 3 consecutive nights, but finagle. Reception open 7am-midnight. Locker storage. No visitors. Gate locked at midnight. Lights out 11pm. Check-out 11am.

Compared to the city below, **Victoria Peak,** the former home of the British governors, is 10°F cooler and a century back in time. The tram is the fast and scenic way to the top (daily every 10-15min., 7am-midnight; one way HK$10, round-trip HK$16). From the Hong Kong Hilton, follow the sidewalk left as it curves into Garden Rd. past St. John's Cathedral on the right. Follow the signs. The faint-hearted can take bus #15 from the Exchange Square Bus Terminal in Central (HK$5.20). Despite the Peak Tower shopping complex, the view from the top will take your breath away as surely as the tram ride. Once part of the governor's lodge, the **Peak Gardens** are a great place to view the serene outlying islands and the frenetic skyline below. Follow Mt. Austin Rd. up the mountain from the Peak Tower near the tram station for about 25 minutes. Above the gardens are viewing terraces, from which the lush green hills rise before your eyes.

One of Hong Kong's top draws, **Aberdeen** is a curious hybrid of run-down sampans and floating restaurants. Take bus #70 from Exchange Square, Central (HK$3.60) or bus #72 from Causeway Bay (HK$3.10). Trawler operators ambush tourists for harbor tours (about HK$40). Or hop on a floating restaurant's ferry to the eatery and back. A thrilling sight at night, when the restaurants wink brazenly at customers in the darkness.

Ocean Park and **Water World** playfully romp just west of Aberdeen. Ocean Park (tel. 2552 0291), which modestly declares itself "the largest and most spectacular theme park in Southeast Asia" (well, it *does* have the world's longest escalator), promotes the usual nerve-wracking, stomach-dropping roller coasters plus a goldfish pagoda, a shark aquarium, and a dolphin university. The Middle Kingdom, a theme park-within-a-theme park showcasing 17 Chinese dynasties, is near the back of the park. Open daily 10am-6pm. Admission HK$130, children 3-11 HK$65. Water World (tel. 2555 3554), however, doesn't make any attempt at intellectual pretensions. Who needs high-brow when there's a giant aquatic playpen full of slides, pools, and tanned teenagers? Open June-July 1, daily 10am-6pm; July 2-Aug. 31, daily 9am-9pm; Sept.1-mid-Sept., 10am-6pm; mid-Sept.-mid.-Oct. weekends and holidays only, 10am-6pm. Day admission HK$60; evening HK$40. Take bus #70 from Exchange Square, Central (HK$3.60) or bus #72 from Causeway Bay (HK$3.10). Get off at the first stop after the Aberdeen Tunnel and walk up the hill. Cross the street and turn left; there will be blue arrows pointing to Ocean Park.

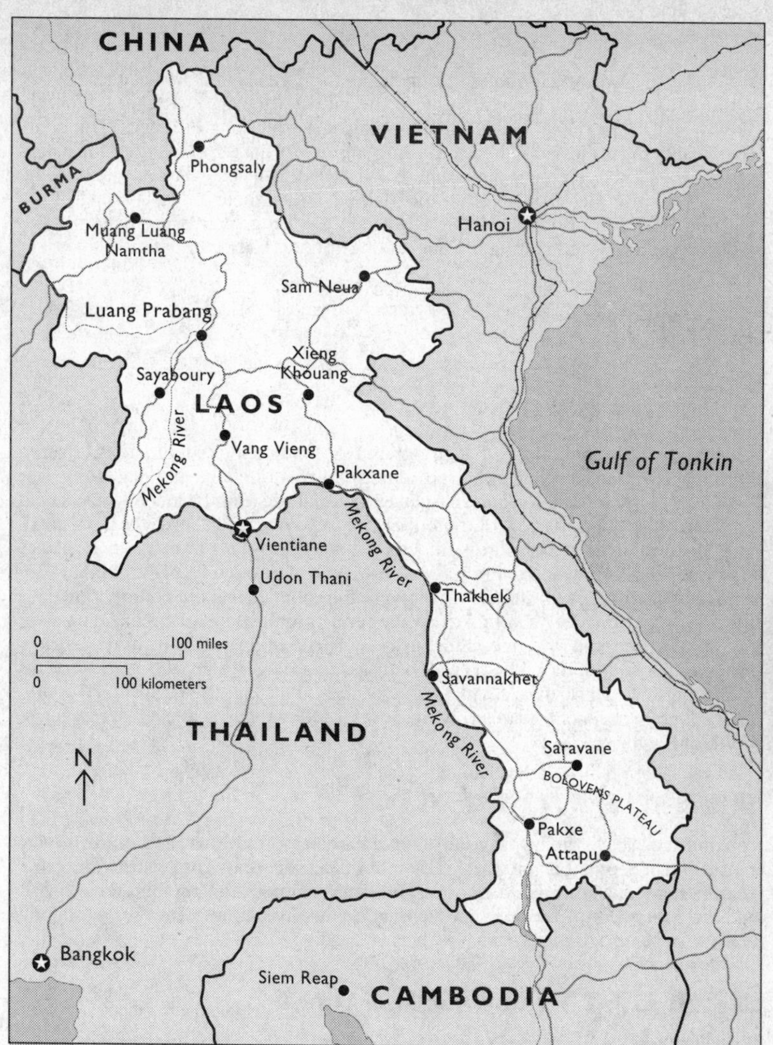

LAOS

Stepping into Laos is like traveling in time: the roads are unpaved, skyscrapers are non-existent, and bicycles outnumber cars. This mountainous, undeveloped nation seems desolate and lost among its neighboring countries, each vying for a piece of the capitalist pie. Sparsely populated with 4.5 million people, Laos is an open, wilderness country perched on the edge of the Southeast Asian frontier. The land remains relatively untouched, although it bears the scars from two million tons of bombs dropped by U.S. fighters during the Vietnam War.

Certainly, Laos, whose people are among the poorest in the world, has seen more prosperous days, but with a government dedicated to economic growth, the country is already attracting a number of investors from Thailand, Taiwan, and the U.S. Although Laos's doors are widening to the world, they are swinging open very slowly, with a good deal of starting, stopping, and squeaking of hinges. The country's leadership is anxious to avoid tumbling down the slippery slope of naked greed, drug abuse, rampant prostitution, and AIDS that it sees as by-products of the uncontrolled capitalist orgy across the Mekong. Nevertheless, the opening of the gigantic Friendship Bridge in 1993 was a step toward greater participation in the world community and visiting the enchanting country has never been easier.

ESSENTIALS

■■■ GEOGRAPHY

Laos is a landlocked country that stretches 1000km north to south and is covered with a spiderweb of rivers and high, sloping hills. Mountains and plateaus cover over 70% of the terrain, making Laos an agricultural wasteland. Only 8% of the land is arable, yet it supports 85% of the population who engage in subsistence farming. The Mekong River, which forms the country's borders with Burma and Thailand, starts in China's Qinghai Province and flows 1800km through Laos, Cambodia, Vietnam, and into the South China Sea. All rivers and tributaries in the country flow into the Mekong River. The Mekong River Valley and its fertile flood plains make up all of the agricultural and wet-rice lands in Laos. The northern half of the country is topped almost entirely with steep-slope mountain ranges, with the highest peaks found in Xieng Khouang Province, among them Phu Bia, the highest at 3000m. Laos's largest mountain plateau, which rises 1200m above sea level, sprawls just north of Phu Bia.

■■■ WHEN TO GO

As all of Laos lies in the tropic zone, it has a rainy season from the beginning of May to the end of September and a dry season from October until April. During the rainy season, road travel through the country is virtually impossible. The best time to visit to Laos is between November and February, when the temperature drops slightly and the rains turn to mist.

■■■ GETTING AROUND

Traveling beyond Vientiane Province is, in a word, hellish. Most of the roads in the country are unpaved, which means that during the dry season they are dusty and pot-holed, yet passable (albeit at a snail's pace), but during the rainy season they become rivers of mud. Road travel woes to the north in particular are compounded by the fact that many of the highways in more remote regions have yet to be repaired since the Vietnam War, when the U.S. Air Force pounded Laos mercilessly.

While travel permits between provinces are no longer necessary, authorities require travelers entering a new province to register immediately with the immigration police. This policy too appears to be on its way out, though in northern provinces, such as Luang Prabang, it is still enforced and travelers will be fined US$5 for every day they fail to check in. In the south of Laos, no one seems to care, or is even aware of this policy; travelers report never having to pay fines. Wherever possible, *Let's Go* lists the immigration office for those who wish to be on the safe side.

BY BUS

The state bus company operates a fairly comprehensive bus system within Vientiane Province (see "Practical Information" on page 135 for listings) but beyond the province, buses only run to Savannakhet and as far north as Kasi, mid-way along Rte. 13 to Luang Prabang.

BY BOAT

For centuries boat travel was the chief means of transportation within Laos (besides elephants, of course). A jaunt down the Mekong remains an intriguing option for those who have both the time and patience. Most boats are commercial vessels hauling cargo from the capital to more isolated areas, but will take on passengers. There are no set fees; just agree to one with the captain before leaving. Don't expect a luxury cruise line; bring a sleeping bag and stock up on bottled water and dry provisions. During the dry season the water level drops considerably and boats may get stuck. The exact travel time is dependent upon a number of variables, including the river current, amount of cargo, and number of stops made along the way.

BY PLANE

During the rainy season, air travel is often the only way to reach more remote areas of the country. **Lao Aviation** has a comprehensive network of domestic flights linking the capital with every region of the country from Luang Namtha along the Chinese border to Attapu in the south's "Emerald Triangle.". Flights to more obscure points only go when enough people have purchased tickets. Fares are relatively inexpensive (see "Practical Information" on page 135 for listings). Confirm your flight at least one day in advance. Arrive at the airport at least two hours early no matter what the Lao Aviation desk clerk says. Some travelers have reportedly showed up at the airport terminal at the appointed time only to find that the seat had been unceremoniously re-sold to someone else. There is a 300kip tax on all domestic flights.

■■■ MONEY

US$1=780.03kip	**10kip=US$0.013**
CDN$=573.79kip	**10kip=CDN$0.017**
UK£1=1212.17kip	**10kip=UK£0.082**
IR£1=1235.57kip	**10kip=IR£0.081**
AUS$1=575.04kip	**10kip=AUS$0.017**
NZ$1=511.54kip	**10kip=NZ$0.020**
SARand=213.34kip	**10kip=SARand0.047**

The monetary currency of Laos is the **kip.** Notes are divided into 1, 10, 20, 50, 100, and 500 denominations. *Let's Go* lists prices in both kip and US$ because the latter acts as a second currency here. The kip fluctuates often, anywhere from 700-800kip for US$1, thus the listings in kip are more accurate than those listed in US$. Along the border with Thailand, baht is widely used as well. Be advised that while baht and US$ are readily accepted as payment in Vientiane, only kip is considered legal tender, so it is technically illegal to pay in anything else. **Tipping** in restaurants and hotels is not a common occurrence, and may even be returned, but you decide. It is customary, however, to tip guides.

■■■ KEEPING IN TOUCH

Mail from Laos is somewhat reliable, although it takes a while to get where it's going. Postage is quite cheap, but many travelers prefer to send overseas packages from Thailand. Receiving mail in Laos is possible through Poste Restante. Postal officers will inspect anything that's obviously not just a letter. Address Poste Restante mail as follows: Name of addressee, Poste Restante, PTT, Vientiane, Lao People's Democratic Party (or Lao PDR).

It is hard to come by **telephones** in Laos, especially in remote areas. Phone numbers in the "urban" areas have six digits and those in the rural areas have three or six digits. For **international phone calls,** your best bet is in Vientiane (see "Practical Information" on page 135), since the country's telecommunications network is nearly non-existent. No collect or incoming calls. Most telephone services take only cash payments. Some hotels do accept credit card calls. **Telephone code:** 856.

■■■ STAYING SAFE

Laos has a low crime rate; nonetheless, travelers should always take precautions. Hold tightly onto your possessions and don't wander the streets after dark. When traveling beyond Vientiane, always keep your safety the number one priority. The road between Nam Ngum and Luang Prabang is often attacked by **rebels;** if at all possible, stay away from road travel in this area. Be careful in the Golden Triangle area near the Thai-Burmese-Laotian border known for its opium production. Locals are wary of foreigners and may give travelers a hard time. In Xieng Khouang Province and the Bolovens Plateau and along the Ho Chi Minh Trail, watch out for **cluster bombs.** The process of clearing mines is expensive and several non-governmental organizations (NGO) have taken up that task. An average of 10 people, usually children, are killed or injured every month by these bombs.

> Do not touch any unexploded bombs; even if they are old, they still work. The limbless locals should be a testament to that.

■■■ HOURS AND HOLIDAYS

Businesses in Laos open Monday through Saturday from 8am to noon and 2 to 5pm. Sundays and official holidays (indicated below) are rest days. Holidays and festivals in Laos revolve around religion and the Mekong River, the country's two lifelines. Festival dates may vary by one day each year in accordance to the lunar calendar.

January 1: International New Year (official).
January 6: Pathet Lao Day (official).
February 6: *Boun Maka Bucha* (rice roasting ceremony).
March 8: Women's Day (official).
March 22: People's Party Day (official).
April 13-16: Lao New Year (official).
May 1: International Labor Day (official).
May 5: *Boun Visaka Bucha* (rocket festival).
June 1: Children's Day (official).
August 2: *Boun Kao Padabdin* (boat racing in Luang Prabang).
August 13: Lao Issara Day (official).
August 23: Liberation Day (official).
September 2: *Boun Kao Salac* (special food offering).
October 12: Freedom from the French Day (official).
October 30, 31: *Boun Ok Phansa* (end of Buddhist Lent).
November 26-28: That Luang Festival.
December 2: Independence Day (official).
December: Hmong New Year (around harvest time).

■■■ POTPOURRI FOR $100, ALEX!

The Lao government follows the Gregorian calendar but the people still use the **lunar calendar,** based on the movement of the sun and the moon. Local time in Laos is seven hours ahead of Greenwich Mean Time (GMT).

Even though cities in Laos are not very large, they aren't so easy to navigate; many roads and side streets are often unnamed. Whenever possible, *Let's Go* has tried to list street names to help orient tourists. In Laos, there is no need to mess around with avenues, lanes, roads, terraces, places, or streets; everything is a **thanon.** The numbered national "highways" are basically provincial roads.

LIFE AND TIMES

■■■ HISTORY

Laos has never known peace. This tiny, landlocked country took a backseat in every turmoil in Southeast Asia. Trapped between expanding warring states, it was a volatile battleground whose history is one of constant invasion, foreign domination, and more invasion.

The region comprising present-day Laos belonged to the kingdom of **Funan,** founded in the 1st century AD. Centered in northern Cambodia, Funan accepted the **Hindu** culture brought into the region by Indian merchants and theologians. In the 7th century, the kingdom of **Chenla,** also a Hindu dynasty, surfaced in southern Laos to displace Funan and dominated the area for two hundred years. Chenla extended its jurisdiction throughout the Mekong Delta until internal disputes divided the kingdom. In their weakened states the two kingdoms eventually became vassals to the expanding **Sailendra Empire** on Java.

Early in the 8th century, **Tai-Kadai** groups began to migrate from southern China toward the Mekong River basin where they established independent principalities ruled by hereditary chieftains. The Lao, who belong to this ethno-linguistic family, settled in the Mekong River Valley of modern-day Laos. For the most part, migration had trickled down by the 10th century; three centuries later, however, the Mongol ascension to power in China drove another wave of Tai-Kadai peoples south.

The history of Laos as a unified nation began in 1353 with the founding of **Lane Xang,** the "Kingdom of a Million Elephants." Prior to that, Laos had been a mere vassal state to feuding empires like **Lanna Thai, Angkor,** and **Sukhothai.** With Khmer assistance, **Fa Ngum,** a Lao prince raised in the courts of Angkor and married to a Khmer princess, returned to his homeland and conquered the small states that make up Laos today. His father-in-law gave him a statue of a golden Buddha, called the **Pha Bang,** for which the royal capital of **Luang Prabang** was named after. For the next 20 years, Fa Ngum consolidated power by conquering Laos and the Khorat Plateau of northeastern Thailand. He brought missionaries from the weakening Khmer empire to introduce **Theravada Buddhism** as the state religion. Even though he was the founder of Lao nationhood, Fa Ngum was exiled by his own ministers in 1373 because of his excesses and his ruthless military commanders.

For the next 300 years, Lane Xang prospered, so that, at its zenith, it stretched all across the north of the Indochinese peninsula. **Samsenthai** (1373-1416), Fa Ngum's son, aligned the empire with the Siamese, importing from them the construction method of wats (temple-monasteries), which sprung up all over the kingdom. He divided Lane Xang into administrative districts which lasted until 1975 when the monarchy was abolished. **Phothisarat** (1520-48) moved the royal seat from Luang Prabang to **Vientiane,** which became a religious and commercial center. The king's marriage to a Lannathai princess brought that kingdom under the rule of Lane Xang. **Setthathirat** (1548-71), Phothisarat's son, ruled over both kingdoms until 1570 when Lannathai was seized by the Burmese. However, he managed to successfully defend Lane Xang against its encroaching neighbor. Today, Laotians venerate Setthathirat for bringing the **Emerald Buddha,** the most revered Buddha image in Thailand, from Lanna to Vientiane before Lanna's fall to the Burmese invaders. Under the reign of **Souligna Vongsa** (1633-94), Lane Xang saw its golden age. He was an enlightened leader who strengthened the kingdom and expanded the boundaries of Lane Xang to Yunnan to the north, Shan Burma to the west, Cambodia to the south, and Vietnam to the east. After the king's death in 1694, the kingdom erupted into chaos, while Vietnamese warlords, once allied with Lane Xang under Souligna Vongsa, menaced the land.

In 1713, three kingdoms emerged with divided loyalties to Laos's neighbors: the kingdom of Luang Prabang, ruled by Souligna's grandsons, was under the influence of China; Vientiane, under the rule of Souligna's nephew, sided with the Vietnamese empire of Hue; and **Champassak** aligned itself with Siam. The Siamese eventually overpowered all the kingdoms, annexing Vientiane in 1826, Champassak in 1846, and Luang Prabang in 1885.

At this time, the French, who had already established Vietnam as a prized protectorate, were seeking for a way to stop the British forces in Burma from expanding eastward into France's jewel colony. The solution to that dilemma thrust Laos into the territorial struggle between the British and the French, who quickly moved to establish relations with Vientiane in 1886. Less than a decade later, Siam had officially recognized Laos as a French protectorate. **Annexation** was completed by the turn of the century; however, France paid little attention to this backwater country, whose mountains and rough land were not suitable to France's plans for colonial development. Thus the French continued to invest in Vietnam and kept Laos as a buffer against the British.

The invasion of Indochina in 1941 by the Japanese marked the beginning of Laos's struggle for autonomy and independence. **King Sisavangvong,** at first reluctant to break with France, was pressured to declare independence for his country in 1945, with the support of the Japanese. But France refused to accept Lao independence. As a result, several anti-French movements arose to counter French imperialism, including the **Lao Issara** (Free Lao) under the leadership of **Prince Phetsarath** and the **Pathet Lao** (Lao Nation), the communist movement founded by Phetsarath's half-brother **Prince Souphanouvong** in the 1950s.

The Lao Issara led the movement for formal independence from France, but when the time came for negotiations, dissension divided the organization. Phetsarath's faction refused to negotiate and insisted on complete independence. The second faction, headed by another half-brother **Prince Souvanna Phouma**, believed that negotiations with the French were necessary for the creation of an independent Laos. The third was under the leadership of Souphanouvong (known as the "Red Prince") who pushed for an alliance with Ho Chi Minh's **Viet Minh** to rid the region of all western influence. All three factions came to an uneasy agreement and formal independence was finally granted in 1953. The **Geneva Accords** in July 1954 established Laos as a neutral state.

The U.S. believed that Laos, as a neutral zone, was a buffer between the communists in Vietnam and the rest of Southeast Asia—**the first "domino,"** according to Dwight Eisenhower. With the French no longer exerting control in the region, the U.S. increasingly involved itself in the conflict and sent special forces into Laos. In 1961 the Geneva talks reaffirmed Laos's neutrality and asked all foreign troops to withdraw, but both the U.S. and North Vietnam denied their presence, instead dragging the neighboring war into the isolated country.

The air war in Laos has left the country pockmarked with barren craters and unexploded bombs even to this day. From their bases in northeastern Thailand, American fighters launched a **"secret war"** in Laos for nine years. They dropped more than two million tons of bombs on Pathet Lao strongholds in the north and the **Ho Chi Minh Trail** supply line that snaked through the eastern mountains, earning the country the distinction of being the most heavily bombed country in war history. So covert was the American operation that soldiers were dressed in civilian clothes and "Laos" was erased from all military records. The country became known as the "other theater."

In the end, after the American withdrawal from Southeast Asia, Laos finally fell to the Pathet Lao on August 23, 1975. In order to consolidate their power, the communists rid themselves of their opposition by abolishing the 600-year-old monarchy and sending many political prisoners and pro-Americans to their death in "re-education camps." Souphanouvong became president and appointed **Kaysone Phomvihane,** another hard-line communist, premier of the **Lao People's Democratic Republic (LPDR).**

After years of internal conflict, corruption, and foreign dominance, many Laotians welcomed the Pathet Lao, for in this group they saw the unity of the Lao people once again. However, a third of the people fled the country and poured into Thailand, overflowing the refugee camps. Countless numbers, unfortunately, were ambushed and killed by Pathet Lao and Vietnamese soldiers who guarded the Mekong River, the Iron—or rather, Bamboo—Curtain of Southeast Asia.

■■■ LAOS TODAY

After two decades of isolation, Laos is slowly opening itself to the rest of the world. The hard-line stances of the Lao government are gradually giving way to democratic policies: in March 1991, the party voted for pro-market reforms and appointed new leaders dedicated to **"New Thinking,"** and by August 1991, Kaysone had urged the government to move toward a free-market economy, symbolized by the removal of the hammer-and-sickle from all state emblems. Later that year, the government ratified a national constitution and the U.S. agreed to repair relations with the country by sending an ambassador to Vientiane for the first time in over 15 years. **Nouhak Phoumsavan** succeeded Kaysone after his death in November 1991. A hard-line communist dedicated to carrying out his predecessor's visions, Nouhak earnestly supports free-market reforms and is working to re-establish Laos's relations with other countries, particularly Thailand, who is now its major investor.

In the last five years, over 500 foreign-investment projects have started up in Laos, whose total value is $1.1 billion. In its efforts to attract foreign interest, the Lao government is more than generous with potential investors who find that start-up costs are cheap. Furthermore, Laos is rife with natural resources; it has thus far produced only 1% of its hydroelectric power potential, while its mineral deposits remain untapped. Logging is now under strict regulation to keep the forests from depleting so rapidly, but it is still the country's largest export industry. Increased exports, new businesses, and a growing tourism industry are paying off; despite harsh criticisms for the nation's one-party government and issues of human rights violations, Laos has managed to develop a stable economy with an annual GDP growth rate of 6%.

■■■ THE PEOPLE OF LAOS

More than the wars and foreign domination, it is the people of Laos that have kept the country divided. When the borders of the country were drawn, the 68 minority ethnic groups in Laos were not accounted for. Unfortunately, that has proven to be the divisive issue hampering the unification of the country. Although they are within the boundaries of an official state, many of the ethnic groups continue to live under self-rule, thereby bringing harsh reprisals from a government dominated by the Lao ethnic majority. The Lao further exacerbate ethnic tensions by excluding hill-tribes from educational, social, and economic opportunities. In addition, Laos has suffered terribly from the loss of nearly a third of its former population since the end of the Vietnam War. Although repatriated refugees have returned to Laos, the bulk of the elite has resettled overseas.

The people in Laos are usually classified into three groups according to the altitude at which they live:

LAO LOUM

The **Lao Loum** make their homes in the verdant and rich Mekong River Valley. The ethnic Lao people began migrating into the region from southern China in the 8th century, driving out the *Lao Theung* already occupying the area. Today, this group constitutes about half the population of Laos. They can be sub-divided into several tribal groups, such as the Red Thai, the White Thai, and the Black Thai. In northern regions, some of these tribes live in the hills, but shouldn't be confused with *Lao Theung* since they are ethnically Tai-Kadai.

LAO THEUNG

Considered the highland Lao, the **Lao Theung,** consisting of 45 different tribes, are descended from the Mon-Khmers who have inhabited the region since as early as 2000 BC. The arrival of the Tai-Kadai peoples in the 8th century forced the *Lao Theung* to seek shelter in the hills where the newcomers would not venture. Called the *Kha* (a derogatory term meaning "slave") by the lowland Lao, the semi-nomadic *Lao Theung* live on the slopes of the Annamite Mountains and Bolovens Plateau. They practice slash-and-burn agriculture and thus shift their villages every few years. Most of the people are strictly animist and believe in spirits, although a number have converted to the state religion of Theravada Buddhism.

LAO SOUNG

The newest of the migrants in Southeast Asia, the Lao Soung began their southward movement into the region in the early 18th century. In Laos, they settled in the high mountains in the north which were uninhabited and similar to their former mountain homes in southern China:

The Hmong

The origins of the **Hmong,** perhaps the best known and most hated of Laos's hill-tribes, has been an enigma for many scholars. Placing high value on independence, the Hmong preferred to move constantly, rather than give up their autonomy (in fact, Hmong means "free men"). From southern China to Southeast Asia, they have always settled in remote mountains, isolating themselves from neighboring tribes. After the fall of Laos, a mass exodus to Thailand ensued following public Pathet Lao announcements ordering the annihilation of the Hmong, many of whom had been recruited by the CIA to battle Lao and Vietnamese communist forces during the war. Today, the Hmong live predominantly in Xieng Khouang and Luang Prabang provinces, and remain relatively removed from mainstream Lao society. Many Hmong charge the Lao government with human rights violations, but attempts to confirm this situation have been thwarted by the government. A group of rebels continue to wage a war against the government by sabotaging roads, and recently killed some

Free Men

The Hmong pass on history and legends through their rich, oral tradition. Over time, fact intertmingled with fiction, leaving historians to separate the two. According to early Chinese records, the Hmong (called *Miao,* meaning "barbarian") had once lived in the Yangtze River Valley before being pushed out by the Chinese. Recorded as the "first enemies" of the Chinese, the Hmong resisted Sinicization and Chinese rule and, instead, retreated to the mountains of southern China (where 5 million still live today). Even China's most brilliant generals could not overpower the Hmong in their mountain fortresses. Ultimate defeat came when the Chinese emperor falsely extended a peace treaty of a royal marriage to unite the two kingdoms. The Hmong King Sonom accepted, but he and his family were promptly executed. Other historians add that the Hmong are descendants of migrants from central Europe. Evidence of this is taken from the facial features of the people, many of whom bear striking Caucasoid characteristics, blue eyes and blond hair included. While those bearing Asiatic features were able to blend in, the Chinese proceeded to kill the Hmong who stuck out. Many others chose instead to migrate south into the high mountains of Laos, Vietnam, and Thailand to live as free men. The Vietnam War dispersed Hmong refugees all over the world, from Great Britain and France to the U.S. and Canada to French Guyana and Australia.

Australians. The majority of the Hmong are uninvolved in this unfortunate situation, but they bear the suspicion of foreigners and the brunt of government crackdowns.

The Yao

Culturally and ethnically similar to the Hmong, the **Yao** are easily distinguished by their beautifully and elaborately embroidered dresses, black turbans, and red-ruffed tunics. A unique group in Laos, the Yao have a writing system based on Chinese characters. Like other hill tribes, the Yao recognize spirits and worship their ancestors; however, they also follow Taoism as it was practiced in 13th-century China. All of these indicators point to their origins in China, but traditional Yao legends say they came from "across the sea." They are skilled craftsmen, most notable for their intricate silversmithing. Most of the Yao today live in Luang Namtha Province

■■■ CUSTOMS AND CULTURE

GETTING ALONG IN LAOS

In this country, the backwater sister of the Land of Smiles, people are known for their politeness and hospitality. Many of the religious taboos in Thailand apply here. Do not touch a person's head because it brings bad luck. Pointing the feet at any Buddha image is beyond sacrilegious and should not be done. A very stoic sort of people, the Lao try not to display emotion in public; those who do are considered to be without self-control. Although simple handshakes are more commonly used as a greeting now, people still greet each other with the *wai* or *phanom*—palms placed together in front of the face and a slight bow of the head.

RELIGION

The early inhabitants of Laos were **animists,** but today, **Theravada Buddhism** (teaching of the elders), which has existed in Laos for approximately 200 years, is the state religion. Buddhism's compatibility with other religions has made it popular with the majority of the Laotian people who also follow the cult of **phi** (spirit worship), although it has been officially banned by the government. Most of the *Lao Theung* and *Lao Soung* hill-tribes continue to practice an amalgam of ancestor worship, animism, and *phi* cult.

Theravada Buddhism originated in Sri Lanka and spread to Laos through Cambodia when Fa Ngum, the first king of Lane Xang, invited Buddhist monks to teach his people about the religion (see Cambodia "Religion" on page 69). This sect of Buddhism brought with it a scriptural and literary language called Pali, which is of northern Indian origin and related to Sanskrit. Pali, still used in Theravada Buddhism liturgy, gave its name to the schools that train monks beyond the novice stage.

For proper conduct when checking out wats, please see "What is Wat Etiquette?" on page 70.

WOMEN IN LAOS

Women have never figured prominently in the history of Laos; therefore it should be no surprise that few women do anything outside of the home. Lao society has a definitive division of labor in which men work the rice fields and hunt while women stay at home to cook and raise children. As a result, men and women share tasks and rewards equally. For the moment, the Lao PDR is pushing young people to take control of their lives and make their own decisions, but the doors to leadership roles have yet to open for women.

■■■ THE ARTS

Lao art, though influenced by Thai, Burmese, and Khmer styles, is unique and expressive. However, little is documented because the country's artistic heritage has been lost or destroyed. Well known for its extensive ornamentation, art in Laos is mostly inspired by the life of the Buddha and the *Ramayana,* which has become a vital force in Lao culture.

ARCHITECTURE

Due to a long history of constant war and foreign domination, Lao architecture never fully developed. Since many of the early structures were built of wood, little has survived time, plundering by Laos' neighbors, and saturation bombing by Americans. The best examples of original Lao architecture exist in the wats that still stand. While not as ornate as those in Thailand, Lao wats, especially in Luang Prabang, are stunning.

The **Vientiane style** of architecture found in the capital city resembles the temples of southern Thailand, with high, pointed, and layered roofs. Main sanctuaries tend to be rectangular and some have a veranda around the temple, similar to those in Bangkok. Wats in Vientiane have higher roofs, taller buildings, and more prominent entrances than those of the other two Laotian architectural styles. *Nagas* (serpents) watch over the steps leading to the main entrance of the wat, while pillars with intricate porticoes flank the doorway.

Luang Prabang takes its architectural style from that of northern Thailand. Wats in this classic style have multi-layered roofs and gracefully sweeping eaves that nearly touch the ground, giving the impression that the temple is a part of the natural environment. The pillars narrow toward the top—an imitation of the tree trunks that had originally been used as columns. A veranda at the back and the front of the wat complete this architectural form.

A third temple style is **Xieng Khouang,** which has unfortunately been irrevocably lost. During the war, Americans leveled the provincial capital city of Xieng Khouang, razing every building in sight and taking the city's architectural style with it. A few temples in a style similar to Xieng Khouang remain in Luang Prabang; they can be distinguished by their wide sloping roofs, much like the Luang Prabang style, although without the characteristic layers.

DANCE AND DRAMA

Classical dance and drama came to Laos from India via Angkor in the 14th century. But it was not until the 16th and 17th centuries that **classical theater** fully developed. Marked by the creation of a ballet, dance and drama were organized at the Royal Court and a grand orchestra consisting of xylophones, gongs, trumpets, tambourines, violins, mandolins, and wind instruments accompanied the dance. **Mimic dancers** wore rich and vibrant costumes with masks and diadems. Gestures and movements similar to that of Indian choreography depicted episodes from the *Ramayana.* Later in the development of classical theater, chanters accompanied the dancers, and ultimately, actors themselves began to talk and sing as they gesticulate and dance.

LITERATURE

Laotian literature, from its beginnings in the 16th century, has always been inspired by religion, drawn from epic songs and incantations of healers and monks. The Laotian **classical period,** which lasted until the end of the 18th century, was strongly infused with Buddhism and sought the subjects and themes of its poetry in the literature of India. The Buddhist canon, **Tripitaka,** composed of the three collections of speeches, *Discipline and Dogmatics*, is the quintessential source of religious literature in Laos. The **Jatakum,** a collection of accounts of the former lives of the Buddha Gautama, forms the most sacred of all Buddhist literature in Laos.

The sermon-chants of monks also gave birth to a great many popular **novels** in verse and prose form which attained their height at the beginning of the 19th century. An important literary genre in Laos, the novel serves a double purpose—to amuse and to instruct. Novels are usually derived from Buddhist texts and were originally written in prose in the *Tham* script until Laotian characters became popular.

Although religious novels were widespread, the Laotian people themselves cherish the later novels about love and romance.

It is poetry, however, which truly gives expression to the experiences of the Laotian people. Lyrical and epic poetry conveyed the beauty and charm of nature and, of course, the eternal theme of love. The songs of this period reflect the people's sense of humor and to their high-spirited originality.

Unfortunately, much of Lao literature is not in circulation; rather, these books are collecting dust and rotting away in some of the oldest wats in the country. A project funded by the German government is in the process of preserving these aging volumes and putting their contents on microfilm for future use.

MUSIC

Laotians possess a veritable passion for music. Songs and music are indispensable accompaniments to all celebrations and feature heavily in everyday life. In this still-sleepy country, tradition has not yet been displaced by capitalist inventions, but the strains of western culture have been transmitted here via Thailand. It is not uncommon to hear cheesy western melodies mixed with sugar-coated lyrics, making for an overpowering combination that grates on the nerves. But cheer up. Traditional music in its "pure" form still exists.

Live **mor lam** performances, involving singing jousts of intricate Lao epic poems, can be seen at the markets or temple fairs. Listen for the haunting, hollow sound of the **khene,** which is at the center of Lao traditional music. A bamboo reed instrument much like Pan's flute, only bigger, the *khene* is played at celebrations and funerals. The hill-tribes have their own versions of the *khene.* The Hmong are renowned for their *khene* players who usually display elaborate moves, steps, and jumps to the rhythm of the music at new year festivals (Dec.). A Laotian orchestra consists of the *khene,* the **so** (a two-stringed cello), the **khouy** (a bamboo flute without keys which gives a very clear sound), and the **nang-hat** (a xylophone made of wood).

In addition, vocal music is well cultivated. Since most *khene* players are men, it is not uncommon to walk through the country and hear female voices singing ballads. There are two kinds of Laotian songs. One is constituted of poems celebrating the exploits of legendary heroes. These poems, transmitted orally from generation to generation, are often improvised and changed according to the desires of the singer. The other main genre of Laotian songs deals with (what else?) love and they are often sung to the accompaniment of the *khene.*

WEAVING

Once a common household craft, weaving has emerged as an art form in its own right. Because of Laos's isolation from the rest of the world, Lao weaving has remained free of outside influences, therefore retaining its traditional patterns. Still exclusively performed by women, young girls are expected to learn the art of weaving cotton and silk with shimmering gold and silver threads (called **tdinjok**) into scarves, skirts, and other clothing. A girl is taught how to weave from an early age, and her ability to weave can only be an asset when she is courted. Popular Lao products made from these cloths include the **pha sin** (Lao sarong), the **pha baeng** (Lao shawl), and the **sin,** a bridal skirt with an elaborately embroidered hem.

HILL-TRIBE ART FORMS

Although not the dominant culture in Laos, the hill tribes have their own artistic contributions to the country. The Yao and Hmong ethnic groups are renowned for their beautiful craftsmanship in **silversmithing.** Both these groups value silver greatly and assess their wealth in terms of family silver. They make heavy neckpieces etched with intricate designs, lock-shaped pendants, earrings, chains, rings, and bracelets which are worn with their traditional dress. The Hmong are the only people in Laos who make **batik,** where cloth is covered with wax or a resin-like paste so that it becomes resistant to dyes used to decorate it. The result is a mixture of vibrant colors and brilliant patterns. Indigo-dyed *batiks* make up the main panel of Hmong skirts, with appliqué and embroidery added to them. **Appliqué** is a craft form in which cloth is cut, layered, and turned inside out for a rich collage of contrasting colors and geometric shapes. Most other hill tribes, such as the Akha, also make beautiful appliqué.

■■■ FOOD AND DRINK

The gastronomic landscape of Laos is similar to that of its neighbors, but also unique in some of its national dishes. Meals in Laos are usually taken family style with members sitting on the floor around a low rattan or bamboo dining table. The people in this country eat a lot of sweet rice (*khao niaw*), eaten by hand and usually dipped in the sauces of main dishes. Pork, chicken, and duck are the most commonly eaten meats, while game, such as wild chicken, quail, small birds, and deer, serves as a supplement. These meats are often cooked in a hodge-podge manner with eggplant, spinach, water spinach (or swamp cabbage), shallots, beans, bamboo shoots, or mushrooms. For flavoring, aromatic condiments such as tamarind, citronella, ginger, lemon grass, and hot peppers are added. Coconut and fish sauce (*nam paa*) are often used in cooking.

One must-try dish is *laap,* finely chopped meat, either raw or cooked, with spices and roasted rice grains ground to a fine powder. For something a little more filling, try *khaopoon,* thin rice noodles in a meat-and-bamboo curry sauce that are tangy and hot. The markets are a good place to get a taste of *tum som*, a spicy and pungent salad of unripe papaya mashed with garlic, tamarind, fish sauce, lime, and shrimp paste. In addition, the traveler to Laos should not miss the ubiquitous catfish (*paa beuk*) cooked in several savory ways and often eaten with fish sauce.

GET LOOSE IN LAOS

■■■ VIENTIANE

To travelers and adventure-seekers from a bygone era, the name Vientiane conjured romantic images of an exotic, beguiling, and slumbering colonial backwater, where days melted into years and the pace of life remained as sluggish as the Mekong River's current. It was said that only Saigon and Phnom Penh could rival her in beauty or enchantment. Today, while hardly a cultural backwater, the "City of Sandalwood" retains a touch of that old mystique which so entranced visitors in years past. Time seems lethargic here, and travelers fresh from the reeling chaos of Thailand or Vietnam will welcome the slow and easy pace of life in this riverine capital.

Vientiane has been the product of a vibrant mix of cultural influences since King Phothisarat first established his capital here in 1526, when Laos was known as Lane Xang, or Kingdom of a Million Elephants. During the heyday of this period, Vientiane grew rich off trade with her neighbors up and down the Mekong. Since then, Chinese, French, Vietnamese, Russian, and most noticeably these days, Thai influences have all contributed to a cultural landscape that is at times quirky and always unique. Vientiane's individuality shows in things architectural, such as the Anousavari Monument, a rather incongruous Lao/Buddhist interpretation of the Arc de Triomphe in Paris, and culinary, with dishes like *khao jii pâté,* a breakfast sandwich of sliced cucumber, pâté, and chili sauce on fresh-baked French bread.

Vientiane is a city in transition, and some fear that the opening of the Friendship Bridge in April 1994 may unleash a torrent of western, consumerist influence that will force this "jewel of the Mekong" to go the way of other Southeast Asian metropoli. Rest assured, however, that while her sister cities to the south rush head-

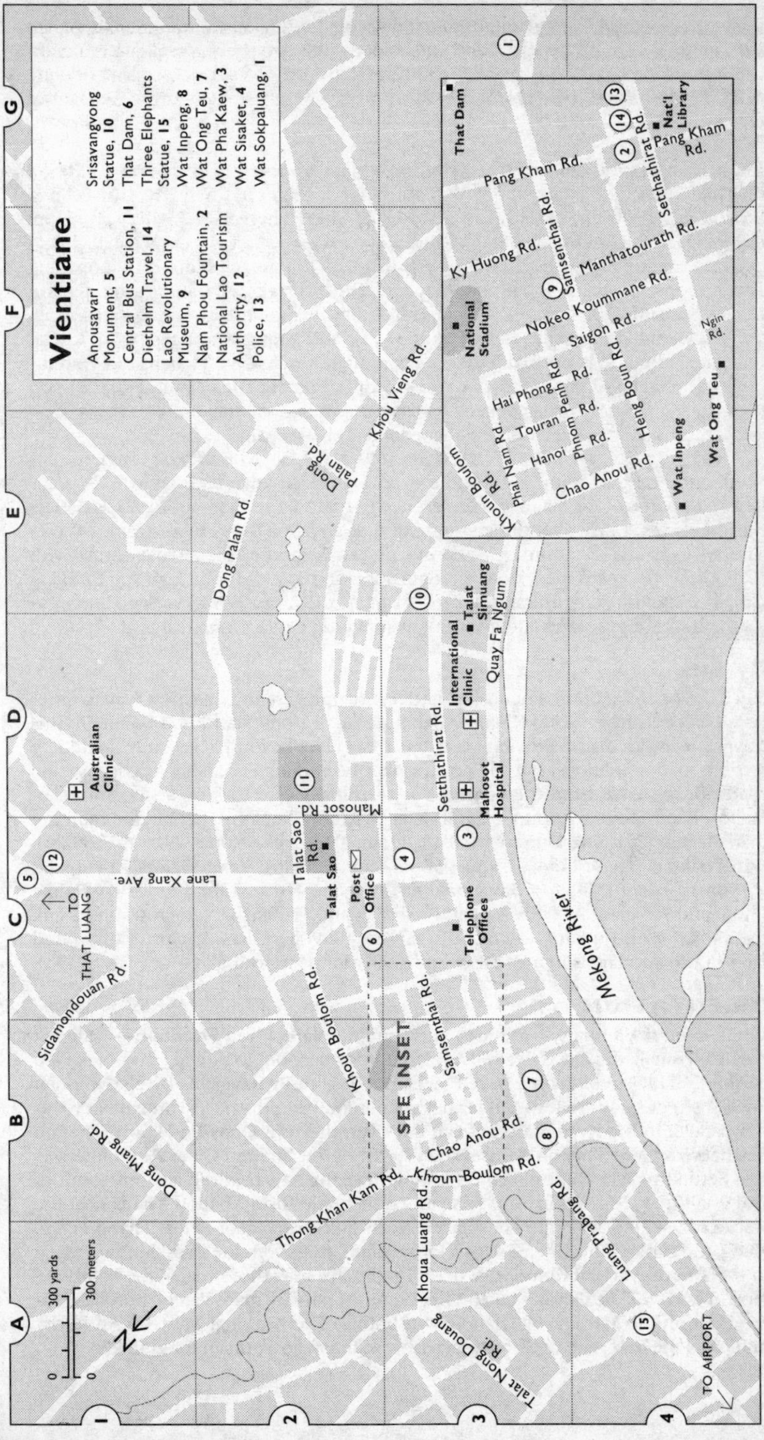

Vientiane

Anousavari Monument, **5**	Srisavangvong Statue, **10**
Central Bus Station, **11**	That Dam, **6**
Diethelm Travel, **14**	Three Elephants Statue, **15**
Lao Revolutionary Museum, **9**	Wat Inpeng, **8**
Nam Phou Fountain, **2**	Wat Ong Teu, **7**
National Lao Tourism Authority, **12**	Wat Pha Kaew, **3**
Police, **13**	Wat Sisaket, **4**
	Wat Sokpaluang, **1**

A B C D E F G
1 2 3 4
0 300 yards
0 300 meters
N
TO THAT LUANG
Sidamondouan Rd.
Dong Miang Rd.
Lane Xang Ave.
Australian Clinic
Dong Palan Rd.
Thong Khan Kam Rd.
Khoun Boulom Rd.
Talat Sao Rd.
Talat Sao
Mahosot Rd.
Post Office
Dong Palan Rd.
Khou Vieng Rd.
SEE INSET
Khoua Luang Rd.
Chao Anou Rd.
Samsenthai Rd.
Setthathirat Rd.
Talat Nong Douang Rd.
Telephone Offices
Mahosot Hospital
International Clinic
Talat Simuang
Quay Fa Ngum
Khoun Boulom Rd.
Luang Prabang Rd.
Mekong River
TO AIRPORT

Khoun Boulom Rd.
National Stadium
That Dam
Phai Nam Rd.
Hanoi Rd.
Touran Rd.
Hai Phong Rd.
Phnom Penh Rd.
Nokeo Koummane Rd.
Ky Huong Rd.
Pang Kham Rd.
Chao Anou Rd.
Saigon Rd.
Samsenthai Rd.
Heng Boun Rd.
Manthatourath Rd.
Setthathirat Rd.
Nat'l Library
Pang Kham Rd.
Wat Inpeng
Wat Ong Teu
Ngin Rd.

LAOS

long into the neon sunset of the "modern" world, change will come to Vientiane at the city's own pace—slowly.

GETTING THERE AND AWAY

By Plane

International flights land at **Wattay International Airport** (flight info tel. 212 066), on Thanon Luang Prabang about 3km north of the center of town. Tuk-tuks cost no more than 1000kip; taxis no more than 500kip. There is a $5 departure tax (3900kip) for all international flights and a 400kip service fee for domestic flights.

For **domestic** flights in and out of Vientiane, go to **Lao Aviation,** 2 Thanon Pang Kham (domestic tel. 212 058, international 212 051; fax 212 056). Cash only. To: **Luang Prabang** (10:30am, 12:30, and 3pm—may be only 1 daily during low season, $46), **Savannakhet** (daily, $61), **Pakxe** ($95), and **Xieng Khouang** ($37). Check first; the schedule is not really fixed. Some flights will leave "when they're full." **International** to: **Bangkok** (5 per week, $100), **Hanoi** (Tues., 9am, $70), **Saigon** (Fri., 7am, $125). Purchase tickets 2-3 days in advance. All major credit cards; cash only at the airport. Open Mon.-Sat. 8am-noon and 2-4:30pm.

THAI Airways, 2 Thanon Pang Kham (tel. 216 143), to **Bangkok** (daily except Wed. and Fri., 12:55pm, $100). Purchase 1 week in advance; confirm 2-3 days before departure. All major credit cards. Open Mon.-Sat. 8am-noon, 2-5pm. **Vietnam Airlines,** 62/5 Thanon Saylom (tel./fax 217 562), to **Hanoi** (Mon., Wed., Thurs., and Sun., 12:50pm, $75; connecting to **Saigon** $155). 30-day tourist **visa** $70. Allow 1 week. Open Mon.-Sat. 8am-noon and 1:30-4:30pm. **Lao Air Booking Co.,** 431 Thanon Setthathirat (tel. 216 761 or 213 197; fax 216 535). Same prices as Vietnam Airlines for fares and **visas**. All major credit cards. Open daily 8am-5pm.

LAOS

By Bus

Since the opening of the Friendship Bridge, the quickest and cheapest way to enter Laos has been from Nong Khai, a 30-minute drive from Nam Phou Fountain. Bus travel within Vientiane Province is extensive. Travel beyond is severely limited by terrible road conditions, but the government is working feverishly to improve the roads. Buses leave from the **central bus terminal** (tel. 216 507) at the corner of Mahosot and Thanon Khou Vieng (also called Khoun Boulom), behind the morning market. Buses to: **Tha Dua** (6:30, 8:45, 11am, 1:15, and 3:30pm, 50min., 200kip); **Ban Thalat** (7:10, 9, 11am, 3, and 3:30pm, 2hr., 500kip); **Vang Vieng** (7:15am and 1:30pm, 4-½hr., 1300kip); **Savannakhet** (7:30 and 10am, 12hr., 7000kip); **Pakxe** (Mon. and Fri. 4am, 11,000kip); and **Kasi** (7:30am, 1700kip). Numerous buses link the capital with outlying towns. A byzantine flowchart lists departure times and fares in Lao and English; most buses leave early in the morning.

ORIENTATION

While central Vientiane—the area surrounding **Nam Phou Fountain**—is almost comically small, the city is deceptively large, spreading out for km in a complex web of quiet, shady streets, some paved, most not. It is easily navigable by bike, though English street signs are few and far between in outlying districts. Three main roads run parallel to the river. Starting from the river, they are **Quay Fa Ngum, Thanon Setthathirat,** and **Thanon Samsenthai.** North of the **Thanon Chao Anou** intersection Setthathirat becomes **Thanon Luang Prabang** and past the airport, south of Wat Pha Kaew, Samsenthai and Setthathirat merge to form **Thanon Tha Dua** at the **statue of the king.** A number of smaller streets link these major roads. **Thanon Lane Xang,** the capital's major east-west thoroughfare, runs from the **Presidential Palace** to the **Anousavari Monument,** where it branches into three roads; the southernmost, **Thanon That Luang** runs to That Luang Stupa. City maps can be purchased at the Phimphone Market on Thanon Samsenthai. The National Tourism Authority publishes the best map of the city, available at Inter-Lao Tourism for 2000kip.

PRACTICAL INFORMATION

Tourist Office: National Tourism Authority of Lao PDR (tel. 212 248 or 212 251; fax 212 769), on Thanon Lane Xang. Heading east on Lane Xang, it's on the right just before the Anousavari gate. Polite English-speaking staff distributes a few brochures and a booklet with as much propaganda as info. Mouths the party line when it comes to individual travelers and travel outside Vientiane. **Inter-Lao Tourism** and **Diethelm Travel** (see Budget Travel below) are excellent sources of info on transportation, road conditions, and safety in the provinces. Open Mon.-Fri. 8am-5pm, Sat. 8am-noon. **Tourism Authority of Thailand (TAT),** 79/9 Thanon Lane Xang (tel. 217 157/8), next to Joint Development Bank, opposite the morning market. Maps of Isaan and other general info about tourist highlights across the river. Open Mon.-Fri. 8:30-11:30am and 2-5pm, Sat. 8:30am-noon.

Tours/Travel Agencies: In the NTA's perfect world, every tourist would enter Laos as part of a pricey package tour group, thereby pumping large sums of hard currency into the country's economy. Signing with a tour company may be the best way to visit remote areas of the country, if you can afford it. Most tour agencies will happily arrange private, custom-designed itineraries. The only international travel agency is **Diethelm Travel** (tel. 213 833; fax 216 294) on Thanon Setthathirat, in Nam Phou Square. Open Mon.-Sat. 8am-noon and 2-5pm. **Inter-Lao Tourism** (tel. 214 832 or 214 232; fax 216 306 or 214 232) on Thanon Setthathirat, opposite Nam Phou, operates a very helpful info desk. **Lao National Tourism Co. (LANA Tour),** 08/02 Thanon Lane Xang (tel. 216 671 or 212 013; fax 212 013), on the 3rd floor of the National Tourism Authority building, will help extend **visas** for about $3 per day. **Lane Xang Travel Co.** (tel. 215 804 or 212 469; fax 215 804), on Thanon Pang Kham near Nam Phou, is one of the largest agencies in the city. Open Mon.-Sat. 8am-5pm.

Embassies and Consulates: Australia (tel. 413 610, 413 805, or 413 602), on the corner of Thanon Nehru and Phone Xay. Consular hours Mon.-Thurs. 8am-noon and 1:30-5pm, Fri. 8am-12:45pm. Also handles the concerns of **Canadians. Cambodia** (tel. 314 952; fax 312 584), on Thanon Tha Dua. Open Mon.-Fri. 7:30-11:30am and 2-5pm, Sat. 7:30-11:30am. **China** (tel. 315 103 or 315 100; fax 315 101), on Thanon Wat Nak near the corner with Thanon Sokpaluang. **Thailand** (tel. 214 582-3) on Thanon Phone Kheng 1-½ blocks past the Anousavari Monument on the left. Open Mon.-Fri. 8:30am-noon and 2-3:30pm. Non-immigration visa (500฿); allow 2-3 days to process. **US** (tel. 212 581; fax 212 584), on Thanon Bartholonie, next to That Dam. Consular hours Mon.-Fri. 8am-noon and 1-5pm. **Vietnam,** 60 Thanon That Luang (tel. 413 400 or 413 403). Open Mon.-Sat. 8-11am and 2-5pm. Does not issue tourist visas. Vietnam Airlines and Lao Air Booking Co. will do.

Currency Exchange: Banque Pour le Commerce Exterieur Lao, 1 Thanon Pang Kham (tel. 213 200/1; fax 213 202). Open Mon-Fri. 8:30am-4pm, Sat. 8:30-10am. Visa and MC cash advance. **Thipphachanch Vongxay Exchange,** 108/3 Thanon Samsenthai (tel. 217 504). Open daily 8am-7pm. A number of banks also have exchange booths in the **morning market,** where exchange rates tend to be a little better. Black marketeers offer the best rates, but there is no protection against fraud.

American Express: Diethelm Travel (tel. 213 833; fax 216 294), on Thanon Setthathirat in Nam Phou Square, is the Laos representative for AmEx and issues traveler's checks. Open Mon.-Sat. 8am-noon and 2-5pm.

Post Office: GPO (tel. 216 425), on the corner of Thanon Khou Vieng and Lane Xang opposite the morning market. EMS shipping service. Poste Restante mail. **Overseas** and **telegram** service during business hours. **Postal code:** 0100.

Telephones: Central Telephone Office (tel. 214 470; fax 215 628), on Thanon Setthathirat 1 block south of Nam Phou, next to the police station. No credit card or collect calls; cash only. **Fax** and **telex** services. Open daily 7:30am-10pm. For credit card calls go to **Lane Xang Hotel** (tel. 214 102 or 214 106; fax 214 108), on Quay Fa Ngum. 1 block west of Nam Phou. **Telephone code:** 21

Local Transportation: There is no metro bus system. **Tuk-tuks** are omnipresent; Nam Phou to the Kao Liaew docks should cost no more than 1000kip. The most efficient means of transport remains the trusty **bicycle.**

Boats: A viable and scenic mode of travel. Boats heading north leave from the Kao Liaew pier, about 7km north of the city. Go there early and ask around for vessels heading to your desired destination. Boats do not leave every day so you may have to wait a few days. To **Luang Prabang** (5 days, 10,000kip). Boats to **Savannakhet** and the south leave from the commercial wharf.

Taxis: Gather at the morning market. A day around the city is 23,400kip. Also run to: **Tha Dua** (3300kip) and **Vang Vieng** (round-trip, 49,500kip). Newer, more expensive taxis can be hired from **Lang Xang Hotel** (tel. 214 102), on Quay Fa Ngum, for 24,960kip per day. Round-trip to: **Tha Dua** (15,600kip), **Ban Thalat** (50,700kip), and **Vang Vieng** (101,400kip).

Car/Motorbike Rental: Vientiane Motor, 35/1-3 Thanon Setthathirat (tel. 215 390; fax 213 970) rents four-wheel drive vehicles for ($80) per day. Motorbikes 7800kip per day. Open daily 8am-5pm.

Bicycle Rentals: Kanchana Lao Handicrafts, 102 Thanon Samsenthai (tel. 213 467), opposite the Ekalath Metropole Hotel, 1500kip per day. **Hua Guo Guest House,** and many others, around 1000kip per day.

English Bookstore: Raintree Bookshop, 25 Thanon Dang Kham (tel. 212 031). Maps of Laos and Vientiane (2500kip) and a large collection of bodice-ripper romances and horror paperbacks (2500-4500kip). Open Mon.-Sat. 9am-5:30pm.

Library: National Library (tel. 212 452) on Thanon Setthathirat, near Nam Phou, next to the back of Lane Xang Hotel. Small English and French reading room, stuffed with a broad range of periodicals, from the *Economist* to *British Library* to *Redbook*. Open Mon.-Sat. 8:30-11:30am and 2-4:30pm.

English Language Films: The Australian Embassy Recreation Club (AERC) (tel. 314 921), on Thanon Tha Dua, Km3 on the right. Shows cartoons Sat. afternoons at 4:30pm and movies Sun. nights at 7pm. Admission 1500kip. The **US Embassy** occasionally screens films as well. Inquire during consular hours.

Markets: Talat Sao, on the corner of Thanon Lane Xang and Samsenthai opposite the GPO. Open 8am-5pm. Behind the bus station on Thanon Khou Vieng is the old market, **Talat Khuadin,** a much more nitty-gritty, in-you-face affair with a lot of produce. Until recently Vientiane had a curfew, thus the night market scene remains pretty scarce; **Talat Simuang** on Quay Fa Ngum, 1 block past Mahosot Hospital, is open until around 9pm. Some prepared food is sold, but there are no places to eat it. Bring your own utensils.

Convenience Stores: Phimphone Market, 110/11 Thanon Samsenthai (tel. 216 963). From tampons to vodka. Quite possibly the only source for chips and salsa in Laos. Open daily 8am-9:30pm. **Manignom Supermarket,** 121/7 Thanon Khoun Boulom (tel. 216 050). A full-service grocery store with western toiletries and dried goods. Open daily 8am-8pm.

Swimming Pool/Sports: Lane Xang Hotel, on Quay Fa Ngum. Pool open daily 8am-8pm; 1600kip per person. **Australian Embassy Recreation Club** (tel. 314 921), on Thanon Tha Dua, Km3. Guests can use the pool, squash courts, and exercise room for 7800kip per day. Pool open daily 8am-10pm.

Pharmacy: Seng Thong Pharmacy (tel. 213 732 or 213 199), across the street and about a ½-block from the back of the morning market on the right. Friendly staff. English spoken. Recommended by Australian Embassy Clinic.

Contact Lens Supplies: Top Charoen Optical Shop, 109/1 Thanon Samsenthai (tel. 213 784). Stocks Bausch & Lomb lens cleaner. Open daily 8am-7:30pm.

Hospitals: Australian Embassy Clinic (tel. 413 603), on Thanon Nehru. Consultation Mon., Tues., Thurs., and Fri. 8:45am-12:30pm and 2-5pm, Wed. 8:30am-12:30pm. Initial consultation $20 (US$ only). Excellent staff with Australian doctor. **International Clinic, Mahosot Hospital** (tel. 214 022), on Quay Fa Ngum 1 block past the Presidential Palace and Wat Pha Kaew. Doctors speak French and English. Cash only. Open 24 hrs.

Emergency: tel. 190 or 212 707. Don't expect English-speaking dispatchers.

Police: (tel. 212 706), on Thanon Setthathirat, just south of the fountain, opposite Lane Xang Hotel. No English. You may have to interrupt their naps.

ACCOMMODATIONS

Not surprisingly in a city where just a few years ago travelers could only visit as part of pricey package tours, true budget digs are hard to come by in Vientiane. Even the cheapest rooms are still about three times as expensive as accommodations across the river in Nong Khai. Hotels tend to be grossly overpriced, especially for what you get—a dingy room with more plastic than a Tupperware factory, and a noisy Soviet-made air conditioner that will keep your body awash in sticky, luke-warm air. The best option for travelers willing to shell out a bit more kip are the upscale guest houses such as the divine Lani I, where spacious rooms in lovely colonial-style buildings complete with all the conveniences of a hotel can be yours for the same price as a night in a middle-range Eastern-bloc style monstrosity.

Hua Guo Guest House, 359 Thanon Samsenthai (tel. 216 612). A ½-block south of the Thanon Pang Kham intersection on the left. Look for the wood and glass façade. As John Wayne Bobbitt said, "It's a lot bigger than it looks." Indeed, don't let the cramped lobby fool you. This fine set-up—one of the few true guest houses in town—boasts 13 spotless rooms. Thoughtfully installed foam padding on the stairwell ceiling beams shields lanky foreign noggins. All rooms have A/C and western and Asian bathrooms. Singles $6. Doubles $10, with satellite TV $18. Triples $15. Laundry service.

Phanthavong Guest House, 69/5 Thanon Manthatourath (tel. 214 738). Heading south on Setthathirat, take a left just before Nam Phou; the guest house is on the right, a few shops past the MIC. Friendly, multilingual staff is eager to please. 2-bed rooms start at 3900kip with shared bathroom, with A/C 7800kip. Larger room 4680kip, with private western-style bath 6240kip, with A/C 11,700kip.

Ministry of Information and Culture (MIC) Guest House, 11 Thanon Manthatourath (tel. 212 362). A few doors up on the right from Setthathirat Rd., around the corner from the fountain. A basic, no-frills backpacker's crash pad (one of the frills you do without is cleanliness) but no matter, the place is wildly popular as one of the few budget accommodations in Vientiane—it fills up quickly, so come early. Dingy triples with private bath (shower, Asian toilet) 4680kip and 5680kip (slightly bigger). Laundry service. Breakfast at the cafe (200-300kip).

Phorn Thip Guest House, 72 Thanon Inpeng (tel. 217 239). Heading west on Thanon Chao Anou toward the river, pass through the intersection with Setthathirat; take a right immediately after Saysana Hotel and a left on the narrow, unpaved Inpeng. The guest house is on the left, near the end. An excellent deal relative to other up-scale Vientiane "guest houses," and a realistic budget option. A rambling, old, colonial-style house with towering ceilings, wood floors, and attractive oil paintings in the lobby and hall depicting the Laotian landscape and people. Get here early; rooms fill up fast. Small single with fan and shared bath 5600kip, with A/C 9750kip; large room with private bath 7410kip. Double 9750kip, with A/C 12,870kip. Laundry service. Entrance is locked at 11:30pm.

Samsenthai Hotel, 15 Thanon Manthatourath (tel. 216 287 or 212 116; fax 212 116), west of Setthathirat Rd., opposite the Lao Women's Union. This geriatric establishment won't win any beauty contests, but rooms are cheap and clean and the manager gets a gold medal for friendliness and patience. Ideal rooms for agoraphobes. Singles 4680kip, with A/C 7800kip. Doubles are decked with A/C and hot water 9360kip, with phone 10,920kip. Deluxe with fridge and TV 15,600kip. Laundry. Small restaurant downstairs. AmEx, Visa, MC for tabs over $100.

Senasouk Guest House, 100 Thanon Luang Prabang (tel./fax 215 567). Heading north toward the airport, it's behind the large, white Belvedere Hotel, past the elephant statue. Senasouk is a 5-min. tuk-tuk ride or 10-min. bike ride from the center of town. Large (25 rooms) and popular with foreign businessmen. Friendly, English-speaking staff. Singles with fan 6800kip, with A/C and private bathroom with hot water 10,200kip. Doubles with fan 6800kip. Deluxe with TV, fridge, and A/C 16,250kip. Laundry. Small restaurant.

Syri Guest House (tel. 212 682; fax 217 251), on Thanon Chao Anou. From the Lao Revolutionary Museum, head east on Thanon Nokeo Koummane past the tennis club; the guest house is on the right about 20m past the curve. Located in a spacious, colonial mansion that oozes old-world elegance: towering ceilings, rattan furniture, lovely 2nd floor sitting room, and patio. If you treat yourself to slightly finer digs, this is the place to do it. Excellent location, near Santisouk Restaurant and Nam Phou Fountain. Singles with A/C and bathroom with hot water $15, with TV $20. Doubles $25. Laundry service. Planning to build a back room for backpackers. Ask about student discounts. Helpful maps of the city.

Lani Guest House #1, 281 Thanon Setthathirat (tel. 214 919 or 216 103; fax 215 639). From the airport, it's on the left past the Chao Anou intersection, opposite Wat Ong Teu; set back from the road, so look for the sign. Used to be a house—a mansion, in fact. Quiet patio surrounded by bamboo and palm trees. Uniquely decorated rooms with hardwood floors have A/C, hot water, and telephones. Singles 19,500kip, for more floor space and a fridge 23,400kip. Doubles 23,400kip and 27,300kip. Popular with aid workers and diplomats; make reservations 2-3weeks in advance by phone, letter, or fax. Laundry service. AmEx, Visa, MC.

FOOD

Vientiane's decidedly cross-cultural flavor is reflected in its tantalizing culinary options, which permit you to indulge in flights of gastronomic ecstasy. Where else can you start your day with a traditional breakfast of *Khao jii pâté* and finish with a hearty repast of venison steak with all the trimmings? For cheap eats head for **Thanon Heng Boun** and **Chao Anou** where noodle shops and street vendors peddling savory yummies from grilled chicken to "Vietnamese sandwiches" abound. Vendors also set up shop along **Quay Fa Ngum** overlooking the river, north of the Mixai Restaurant. Stalls are heavy on desserts—fruitshakes and juices—and you can sample *lao khao* (rice whiskey), a national obsession, for about 500kip per shot.

LAOS

Restaurant Ha-Wai, 74-76 Thanon Chao Anou (tel. 214 664). Just east of Heng Boun intersection on the right. A culinary microcosm of Vientiane. For Francophiles there's *filet mignon* (2800kip); for Vietnam aficionados, a wide assortment of *pho* soups (1500kip); and from China, grilled Cantonese duck (4000kip). Open daily 11am-2pm and 6-10pm.

Santisouk Restaurant, 77/79 Thanon Nokeo Koummane (tel. 215 303), opposite the Lao Revolutionary Museum. Sometimes referred to by its pre-revolution name "Cafe La Pagode," this place is praised far and wide for its cheap, tasty steaks—some of the most savory meat you'll find in these parts. Decor isn't fancy, but icy A/C and quiet atmosphere are wonderfully relaxing. Sizzling T-bones (6000kip). Miserly carnivores can sink their mandibles into a juicy venison steak with green beans and fries (3800kip). "Wild pig steak" (3500kip); oink, oink. Assorted western and Chinese/Thai/Lao dishes (700-5000kip). Open daily 7am-11pm.

Just for Fun, 51/2 Thanon Pang Kham (tel. 213 642). Near the fountain, opposite the Lao Aviation office. This quirky eatery lives up to its name with a jovial white and lime-green color scheme, Richard Marx on the stereo, and Lao handicrafts for sale. Specializes in vegetarian food and herbal tea. Most dishes 1000-1400kip. Try sweet peanut curry with bean curd, or morning glory vines with rice (1400kip). Two-page list of teas 500kip. Lao coffee 400kip. Open Mon.-Sat. 9am-10pm.

Sweet Home Bakery, 109 Thanon Chao Anou (tel. 214 742). Heading west toward the river, it's on the right just beyond the Heng Boun intersection. Popular with locals and expats for its inexpensive and delicious pastries. Enjoy a breakfast of Lao coffee and pastry for 500kip. Sit at one of the sidewalk tables and watch young women and men take offerings to the area's many wats. Iced coffee (300kip). Ice cream (300-350kip). Open daily 7am-10:30pm.

The Taj, 75/4 Thanon Pang Kham (tel. 212 890), opposite Nakhorn Luang Bank, just before the fountain. Groove to the kickin' sitar music as you devour mouthwatering north Indian cuisine. Specialties include *tandoor* chicken (300-5500kip), *malai kofta* (3500kip), and *roti* (500kip). All-you-can-eat lunch buffet 2800kip. Open daily 11am-2:30pm and 6-10:30pm. All major credit cards.

Vanh Mixay, 004 Thanon Nokeo Koummane (tel. 214 160). From Nam Phou head north on Setthathirat, and take a left at the corner of Wat Mixay, with the Banque Setthathirat on the other corner. It's on the right before Tai Pan Hotel. The miser's choice for Thai food. No-frills decor, but there are tables outside. Most dishes 1000-1500kip. Chicken and cashew nuts (1000kip). Thai omelette (500kip). Open daily 10am-10pm.

La Souriya, 31/2 Thanon Pang Kham (tel. 215 887 or 212 660). This intimate little French restaurant opposite Lao Aviation near the fountain was started by a Hmong princess; the cuisine is certainly fit for one. An interesting blend of architectural media—brick, bamboo, and plaster—all represented in one room. Most dishes are 2200-4500kip. Chicken curry (4500kip). Divine French onion soup (2200kip). Specialties include veal tongue in mustard sauce. Open daily 6:30-11:30pm.

Namphu Garden Restaurant (tel. 216 775). This pleasant beer garden has a monopoly on Nam Phou Fountain. Thankfully food and drink are cheap. A variety of Indian, Chinese, and Lao food; most patrons just come for a beer by the fountain and head elsewhere for serious vittles. Beer Lao 1800kip. Mug of draft beer 500kip. Open daily 11am-11pm.

SIGHTS

Vientiane's featured attractions are all located within 1km or less of the **Nam Phou Fountain** and can easily be visited in a single day, especially with the aid of a bicycle. A number of temples and some of the best-preserved colonial architecture can be found along tree-lined Thanon Setthathirat and Quay Fa Ngum near the Mekong River. The quiet residential district south of the city is ripe with excellent bike rides.

Vientiane's pre-eminent wat, like Bangkok and Phnom Penh, is **Wat Pha Kaew,** or Temple of the Emerald Buddha (tel. 212 621), on Thanon Setthathirat. The original temple was built in the mid-16th century by King Setthathirat to house the Emerald Buddha he brought from Lannathai in Chiang Mai, Thailand. (See "History" on page 125.) Two hundred years later, in 1778, the game of musical Buddha continued when the Thais stole it back again. Sacked by the Thais in 1827, the wat was restored to its original grandeur (minus its namesake) in the 1940s. The two ornately carved wooden doors at the temple's north and south entrances are all that remain of the original structure. Inside, the temple houses a fine collection of statuary from all over Southeast Asia including Lao, Khmer, Thai, and Burmese styles. Bronze Buddhas in the "calling for rain" stance—standing erect, hands at their sides—guard the entrance. Highlights of the collection include a replica of the Pha Bang, the most sacred Buddha image in Laos (the small gold figure in the middle of the room), a Burmese-style wooden meditating Buddha, and a wooden door adorned with a ceramic tile entitled "The Atom Struck Tile," which comes from a temple destroyed at Hiroshima. A jar from the Plain of Jars sits in the garden surrounding the wat. Open Tues.-Sun. 8-11:30am and 2-4:30pm. Admission 200kip. Photography prohibited inside the temple. Just north of Wat Pha Kaew is the **Presidential Palace,** now closed to the public but visible from the temple grounds.

Across the street from Wat Pha Kaew, on the corner of Thanon Setthathirat and Lane Xang is Vientiane's other major wat, **Wat Sisaket,** built by King Anou in 1818. The temple was completed just ten years before the Thais plundered the capital. In a display of sensibility not often seen in pillagers, the army spared Sisaket; today however, nature and lack of funds are accomplishing what the Thais failed to do, and the wat is in desperate need of repair. A small collection of Lao and Khmer statuary is inside the cloister which surrounds the temple. Within the central sanctuary some 2052 Buddha images stand in small niches chiseled into the walls. A series of faded murals decorates the lower sections. Outside the temple to the right of the entrance is a small library with a large wooden chest that may have been used to house the wat's collection of scriptures. Open Tues.-Sun. 8-11:30am and 2-4:30pm (tel. 212 622). Admission 200kip. Photography prohibited inside the temple.

About 1km east of Wat Sisaket on the opposite end of Thanon Lane Xang is one of Vientiane's most distinctive landmarks, the **Anousavari Monument,** also called the Pratuxai, or Victory Gate, today a popular hangout for Vientiane's teens. To take in the view from the top is to fully appreciate just how small Vientiane is: rice fields begin less than 2km from Thanon Lane Xang, and many of the residential districts to the south and east disappear beneath a canopy of trees. To the east, the golden spire of That Luang and the triangular roof of the National Assembly can be seen. To the north is the gold dome of the National Opera House. Open daily 8am-5pm. Admission 200kip; 100kip more to park a bike.

Beyond the Anousavari Monument on Thanon That Luang is **That Luang,** the towering golden stupa that is one of the most important religious symbols in Laos. The statue in front of That Luang is of King Setthathirat, who built the temple in 1566. Twice raided during the 18th century (by the Thais and the Chinese), the shrine was refurbished by King Anou, who added the walls which currently encircle the stupa. The 30m-high stupa consists of two levels, with an entrance on each side. Originally four wats surrounded the stupa, one on each side, but today only the north and south wats remain. Open Tues.-Sun. 8-11:30am and 2-4:30pm (tel. 412 516). Admission 200kip. Just to the north of That Luang is the **National Assembly** with a distinctive triangular-shaped roof. At the far end of the parade ground opposite the stupa is the **Revolutionary Monument,** dedicated to the Pathet Lao guerillas who died during the war.

Another of Vientiane's important wats is **Wat Ong Teu,** a large religious complex at the north end of Thanon Setthathirat, at the corner of the Chao Anou intersection. The largest temple in the capital, it is home to one of the country's most prestigious Buddhist schools. A massive statue of the Buddha, weighing several tons, meditates in celestial harmony within the main sanctuary. If the *sim* is locked, one of the young student-monks in residence may be able to open it for you in exchange for a few minutes of English practice.

Wat Sokpaluang, a large forest temple south of the city center, is worth a visit for its traditional **Lao herbal sauna.** The saunas are built in elevated bamboo huts and steamed from beneath by a boiling water/herb mixture whose vapors rise up into the hut. The saunas are touted for their reputed medicinal value. Do not bathe for 3-6 hours after your sauna, to allow the fragrant herbs to enter your skin, enhancing the health benefits. Open daily; a 1500kip donation expected; saunas last two hours. To get to Wat Sokpaluang head south on Thanon Tha Dua, pass the concrete water tower (ouch!), and take a left onto Thanon Khou Vieng, opposite a Lao State Fuel Co. gas station. Follow Khou Vieng for about 700m and take a right onto Thanon Sokpaluang, the first major road. The wat is on your left.

Wat-weary sightseers who feel ready to throw themselves off the Friendship Bridge if they have to tour another temple should check out the amusingly propagandistic **Lao Revolutionary Museum** (tel. 212 460/1) on Thanon Samsenthai, northeast of Nam Phou. Two huge flags, one the hammer and sickle on red of the now-defunct Soviet Union, the other the Lao PDR flag, greet you at the entrance. The first floor chronicles the country's natural wonders through photography: waterfalls, mountains, the Plain of Jars, etc. The second floor documents the "victorious struggle" of the Lao people against first the French colonialists and then the American imperialists. Each room is liberally sprinkled with photos and busts of great communist leaders like former Premier Kaysone Phomvihane, Ho Chi Minh, and Lenin. Exhibits range from the macabre—torture devices used by the French—to the downright bizarre—Kaysone Phomvihane's exercise spring. Open Tues.-Sun. 8-11:30am and 2-4:30pm. Admission 200kip. No photography.

L'Arc de Triomphe Oriental?

Inspired by Paris's famous monument, the former royal government erected Anousavari in memory of those who died during Laos's war for independence. When builders ran out of concrete, they used cement donated by the American military for the construction of Wattay International Airport to complete the memorial in 1969, thereafter known as the "vertical runway."

ENTERTAINMENT

In keeping with its mellow, laid-back character, Vientiane boasts a number of excellent bars and beer gardens where Laotians and expats alike gather for cold beer and stunning sunsets along the Mekong River. There is little raucous nightlife here (bars and clubs must shut down at midnight) and die-hard disco-junkies might be disappointed. In a move no doubt intended to maintain the strength and purity of the Lao proletariat, the Lao People's Revolutionary Party, in its infinite wisdom, has **banned karaoke** from most public venues in the capital.

Sala Khounta, on Quay Fa Ngum about 2km north of the center of town. The beer garden is 100m beyond the hot-pink striped Riverview Hotel. This little watering hole, built of bamboo, has some of the finest sunset vistas anywhere. Tables hewn from single logs, chairs made of driftwood, and fishing nets hanging from the ceiling complete the tropical-paradise atmosphere. Beer Lao 1200kip. Lao snacks like *khao niaw,* spring rolls, and fried pigeon. Open daily noon-10pm.

Samlo Pub, 101 Thanon Setthathirat (tel. 222 308), near Wat Mixay. A newcomer to the Vientiane nightscene and wildly popular; trendy decor with abstract paintings by local artists on the ground floor. Hang out at the bar or shoot pool on the 2nd floor; a 3rd floor loft is stocked with Lao pillows for people who have had too much fun. Great western music. Bar is stocked with Kahlua, tequila, and other liquors you won't find anywhere else in Laos. Open Mon.-Sat. 5:30pm-midnight.

Mixai Restaurant, 31 Quay Fa Ngum. A large wooden open-air restaurant on the river. Popular with locals and expats. Stereo blasts remakes of 1960s rock. Most people just come to drink and watch the sunset but the inexpensive Lao food is highly recommended: *tom yam* (2000-4000kip), *laap* (2000kip). Beer Lao 1200kip. Open daily 8am-10pm.

Salongsay Restaurant (tel. 214 114), a part of Lane Xang Hotel, opposite the hotel on Quay Fa Ngum. Traditional Lao music and dance are performed nightly. Menu is pricey, but soda (300kip) and beer (600kip) are not. Performances 7-9:45pm.

SHOPPING

As a rule, most former Soviet-bloc countries are not known for their shopping—unless you are in the market for busts of communist leaders or 15kg calculators. Vientiane, on the other hand, if not quite a shopper's wonderland, isn't a shopper's gulag either. No city block seems complete without at least one store peddling "Lao Handicrafts," a vague term encompassing everything from carved teak elephants and hand-hammered silver jewelry to yes, busts of communist "head" honchos. Vientiane is an excellent place to purchase traditional *ikat* silk and cotton fabric, named for the painstaking process by which cloth is bound and dyed a number of times to achieve vivid patterns.

Talat Sao, the morning market, is the only one of Vientiane's many markets with a large handicrafts section. If you picture the market as shaped like an "E" lying on its side, the leg farthest from the river holds most of the silk and cotton stalls. A dress-sized piece of cotton fabric similar to that worn by virtually every adult woman in the city starts at about 4500kip and increases with the quality and complexity of the pattern. Other non-specialized handicraft shops to try include:

Kanchana Lao Handicrafts, 102 Thanon Samsenthai (tel. 213 467). Large selection of mostly women's clothes and *mut-mee* silk from Pakxe, starting at 6000kip per meter. Also rents bikes 1500kip per day. Open daily 9am-7pm.

Lao Textiles by Carol Cassidy, 84 Thanon Nokeo Koummane (tel. 212 123; fax 216 215). Begun by an American fashion designer, combining modern patterns with *ikat* techniques. The result is some of the finest silk in Southeast Asia. Ms. Cassidy has shown garments and wall hangings in galleries all over the world as well as in the *New York Times* and *Vanity Fair.* The showroom occupies an entire colonial mansion. Prices begin around $100 for a handkerchief-sized piece of *ikat.* No set hours; call for appointments, or just go and hope they're open. All major credit cards.

Lao Cotton Company (tel. 215 840) on a dirt side street off Thanon Luang Prabang, about 800m past the statue of the three elephants on the right—look for signs. Started with the help of the Lao Women's Union and the UN Development Program, Lao Cotton employs some 200 women weavers in villages around Vientiane, while allowing them to remain at home with their families. Observe the weaving process from beginning to end. The showroom sells men's, women's, and children's silk and cotton clothing. Cotton fabric can be purchased for 4250kip per meter. Open Mon.-Sat. 8am-5pm. All major credit cards.

■ NEAR VIENTIANE

THA DUA

Travelers who were entranced by the fantastical Wat Khaek in Nong Khai should pay a visit to **Xieng Khonane,** Wat Khaek's pre-1975 counterpart. The sculpture park was built by the same Lao monk/mystic who designed the Sala Kaew Ku, before he fled Laos following the communist victory 20 years ago. Visitors to both parks will recognize the same unique combination of Hindu and Buddhist themes, although most agree that Xieng Khonane is not nearly as grandiose. Tha Dua is easily reached by bus from the central bus station (5 daily, 50min., 200kip).

NAM NGUM LAKE

Ninety km northeast of Vientiane, nestled in a valley surrounded by serpentine ridges and lush hardwood forests, lies **Ang Nam Ngum,** a vast man-made reservoir formed following the damming of the Nam Ngum River in the late 1970s. Today the dam's hydroelectric powerplant supplies electricity to much of Laos, and every year large amounts are exported to energy-starved Thailand.

The natural setting is nothing short of spectacular. Jagged ridges slope steeply down to the crystal clear lake. During the wet season, their peaks are often obscured by clouds, creating vistas reminiscent of a high alpine lake, when in fact the reservoir is only a few hundred meters above sea level. Nam Ngum is dotted with hundreds of emerald islets, some of which were used as prisons and political "re-education" camps during the early 1980s. Stories of attempted escapes from these Laotian Alcatrazes abound. One famous case involved a convict who escaped from his work camp yet was sucked under the dam by the current., only to turn up, in one piece, on the other side! Stupefied guards, convinced they had witnessed a miracle, let the charmed prisoner go.

Travelers seeking some voluntary solitary confinement of their own can find it on idyllic **Santipap Island,** site of a dilapidated, but endearing government-owned **guest house.** Don't expect creature comforts like electricity and running water here; food is prepared over charcoal stoves and bathing water comes straight from the lake. Nonetheless, the scenery is breathtaking, and the clear, warm lake provides unparalleled swimming opportunities. Government-owned but you'd never know it; friendly, easy-going management. *Lao khao* and "Lao cigarettes" are on the house. Doubles 2500kip. Dorm beds 2000kip.

To get to Nam Ngum Lake take a bus from the central bus station to **Ban Thalat** (7:10, 9, 11am, 3, and 3:30pm, 1-½hr., 500kip), a logging town. From Ban Thalat songthaews run to the lake for 400kip. On the way you will pass the **dam complex** itself. While rather unimpressive, the government considers it to be one of the Lao people's greatest technical triumphs and photography is strictly prohibited.

Floating Logs

At the tiny port on Nam Ngum you will notice the piles of massive logs and perhaps wonder where they came from. The answer is, from the bottom of the lake. Nam Ngum Reservoir is the site of what may be the world's most unusual logging operation. Hurrying to complete the dam, no one thought to harvest the vast tracts of forest that were soon covered in 20m of water. Lao loggers, with the help of Thais, developed special underwater chainsaws and lumberjacks and quickly traded in their boots for flippers to get at the lucrative hardwoods.

At the port, **Nam Ngum Restaurant** is worth a stop for lunch. It's to the left of the elevated pier, surrounded by ferns and potted plants. Fresh lake fish 2500-3000kip. Longtail boats make the 30-min. trip to Santipap Island for around 3000kip. A convenient way to see the lake and spend a night on the island is to include it on a trip to **Vang Vieng.** Make arrangements for a longtail to meet you the next morning to continue on to **Tha Heua** on the northern shore of the lake (3hr., 15,000kip) from which regular buses run to Vang Vieng (2hr., 500kip).

LAO PAKO

South of Nam Ngum Lake and about 50km north of Vientiane, hidden away on the bank of the Nam Ngum River is the small resort of **Lao Pako.** Billing itself as an "eco-tourism" lodge, Lao Pako consists of a central longhouse and several individual bungalows all constructed with local materials in that endearing *faux Île de Gilligan* style. Nestled in the jungle on an isolated stretch of river accessible only by boat, Lao Pako caters to adventure-seekers. The Austrian owner, Mr. Pfabigan, organizes pfabulous treks, river-rapfting expeditions, horse-back riding, and pfisists to nearby pfillages pfor the guests. Hammock potatoes can enjoy less active pursuits, such as chess, checkers, and reading (Lao Pako has a small library) from the comfort of the main lodge's thatched-roof veranda, which affords spectacular front-row views of the setting sun and the Nam Ngum River. The **Lao Pako Bar and Restaurant** is a popular watering hole for expats living in the capital who want to get away from the hustle and bustle of that hectic, fast-paced Vientiane life—at least that's what they say. Rooms start at 5000kip for a bed in the dorm. Doubles with private bathroom 15,000kip. Bungalows 20,000kip. If you wish to "Enjoy your life at Lao Pako" as the fliers in Vientiane proclaim, stop by the **Burapaha** office, 14 Quay Fa Ngum (tel. 216 600), to reserve a room; there is no telephone service at the resort.

To reach Lao Pako, hop on a Pakxap bound bus at the central bus terminal (daily 6:30, 11am, and 3pm, 1hr.) and ask to get off at the village of Som Sa Mai. From the village take a longtail to the resort (25min.).

■■■ VANG VIENG

As the bus leaves the flat plains of the Mekong River valley behind and begins wheezing up steep mountain grades, and swooshing down winding switchbacks, the scenery grows more beautiful with each passing km. Rolling foothills give way to jagged peaks inlaid with terraced rice fields; by the time it reaches the tiny district seat of Vang Vieng it is awe-inspiring. Sheer limestone cliffs, or karsts, tower above the sleepy village on the west bank of the Song Nam River, like spikes on the back of some massive slumbering dragon. Locals call them Phou Daeng, or Red Cliffs, in reference to the distinct pinkish tinge of the limestone. They are honeycombed with caves, some of which spread for km through twisting subterranean corridors; a spelunker's dream, a mother's nightmare. During the Vietnam War this area was a stronghold of General Vang Pao's Hmong guerillas, recruited by the CIA to fight a costly war against the Laotian communists (Pathet Lao). Today there are many easily accessible Hmong and Yao villages near Vang Vieng.

The town itself consists of a single main road. During the evening, when the cows come down from pasture, the gentle bovines rule the streets and motorbikes pass at their own risk. Light is provided by generators and candles; as yet there is no regular supply of electricity, though a new power station should come on line next year.

ORIENTATION AND PRACTICAL INFORMATION

From the **market,** where the bus from Vientiane leaves you, the **Song Nam River** is to the west, and beyond it the sheer face of Phou Daeng. To the east is **Thanon Luang Prabang (Rte. 13),** Vang Vieng's main drag. Several guest houses and a dilapidated wat are located north of the market along this road. A few hundred meters later the town ends and the road winds through the mountains past Lao and hill-tribe villages, reaching the town of **Kasi,** 70 bone-jarring km later. South on Thanon

Luang Prabang, about 50m from the market, is the **post office** (tel. 213 398; fax 213 488), which provides **overseas phone** service (about 12,500kip per min.), open Mon.-Sat. 8-11am and noon-4pm. Opposite the post office is the rarely used **airstrip**. About 800m beyond the post office is the turnoff to the Vang Vieng Resort and **Tham Chang** cave. Heading south from the market along the river you will pass the Phou Ban Guest House on the left and, 30m later, the turnoff to ford the river en route to **Tham Pourke** cave. The **district hospital** is also on this road.

Five to six **buses to Vientiane** leave daily from the market (5:50, 6:10, 6:30, 7, 7:30am, and 1pm; 4-½hr., 1300kip). Buses to **Kasi** also leave from here (11am-noon, 2hr., 800kip). **Bicycles** can be rented from a shop three doors up (toward Thanon Luang Prabang) from the Siripangna Guest House near the market.

From **Kasi** it is possible to continue by road to **Luang Prabang.** Be aware that, under the best of circumstances, the road conditions are abysmal. During the rainy season the narrow road becomes a sheet of mud and accidents—often resulting in 300-m plunges down steep mountain gorges—are frequent. The trip, which normally takes 12 hours, can take anywhere from 20 to 48 hours during the wet season. There are no regularly scheduled public buses, but trucks leave daily from Kasi, and travelers can pile in, for an average fee of 5000 kip. One final caution: the region between Vang Vieng and Luang Prabang is occasionally raided by Hmong rebels who continue to wage a guerilla war against the government. Still, the locals consider the roads themselves far more dangerous than insurgents.

ACCOMMODATIONS AND FOOD

There are several adequate, inexpensive guest houses to choose from, the best of which is the **Phou Ban Guest House** on the river road just south of the market. A large wooden house with a pleasant garden and plenty of seating on the covered patio, it's an ideal place to recuperate after a hard day's cave exploration. Rooms (all with two beds) are spacious with mosquito netting and fans (3000kip). Electricity is available between 6:30 and 10:30pm. Peruse the guest book on the second-floor coffee table; it's chock full of helpful tips on exploring the caves and ethnic villages in the area. Asian-style bathrooms behind the main house. Laundry service and bicycle rentals available. A small restaurant serves basic Lao dishes.

On the opposite end of the market from Phou Ban Guest House, near Thanon Luang Prabang is **Siripangna Guest House,** the other popular backpacker hangout (for the handful that are here, that is). Cramped but spotless rooms (all doubles) with concrete floors, private toilet, and shower 3000kip. The friendly proprietress speaks decent English and is a good source of information on the area.

South of the market just off Thanon Luang Prabang behind the post office is **Vieng Samanh Guest House,** in an elevated Lao house. Comfortable rooms with mosquito netting and fans, 3000kip (singles and doubles). Bathrooms are outside the rooms. Request a room on the second floor for the wooden floors. Check-out 10am.

Vang Vieng boasts a number of small street-side noodle shops and a few small restaurants. **Nang Bot Restaurant** (tel. 213 514) is opposite the market on Thanon Luang Prabang. The limited French and English menu lists the usual dishes (noodle soups, fried noodles, omelettes, and fried rice) all between 800-1000kip. They do serve more Lao food, though it is not listed. Yummy *laap kai* 1000kip. This is also the place to meet Mr. Keo, a local guide who takes travelers to the caves and hilltribe villages. Open daily 6am-9pm.

SIGHTS

Vang Vieng is a caveman's arcadia. The chief attractions are the limestone caves that riddle the cliffs outside town. With the exception of the touristy Tham Chang, the caves are largely unspoiled, which means that not only are they beautiful but also difficult to find and quite easy to get lost in. If you get lost, simply ask for directions:

"Tham yuu sai?" For inexperienced adventurers who feel uncomfortable exploring caves alone, search out Mr. Keo at Nang Bat Restaurant, a veritable Indiana Jones who will take small groups through the caves and to hill-tribe villages for about 4000kip per person for a five-hour expedition. Flashlights are a must for serious caving and can be purchased at the market for 800kip.

Closest to town is **Tham Chang,** an overpriced tourist trap on the grounds of the Vang Vieng Resort. Expect to pay 200kip to enter the compound and 2000kip more to see the cave lit up with cheesy colored lights. The view of the village and surrounding rice fields from the mouth of the cave is almost worth the price. Almost.

Also west of the Song Nam River are Tham Pourke and Tham Phou Kham. **Tham Pourke** is closer to town. Head north from the market along the river and cross about 30m upstream. The cave is about 1km west of the river across several rice fields. To get to **Tham Phou Kham** (Cave of the Golden Crabs) head south from the market; the turn-off to ford the river is 50m down on the right. During the rainy season you may have to hire a fisherman to take you across (200kip). The cave is approximately 4km west (head for the small hill in front of the larger cliffs); the entrance faces town. If you are lucky you may catch a glimpse of the "golden crabs" which inhabit the subterranean pools. A **Hmong village** lies 3km west of the cave.

Twelve km north of town are the **Elephant Caves (Tham Xang)** off Rte. 13, near the village of Ban Tham Xang. To get there hop on a jumbo tuk-tuk heading north from the market (2000kip per person). The driver will drop you off at the dirt access road (on the left); walk down it. A few rice paddies later, villagers run an informal ferry service (200kip) across the Song Nam River. The first elephant cave rises dramatically out of the rice fields in the center of the village like the dorsal fin of a huge shark. Inside the cave, actually more of a grotto, are numerous Buddha images, one of the Big Guy's footprints, and a stalactite bearing an uncanny resemblance to an elephant's head. Two larger caves lie at the foot of the cliffs, west of the village. The larger of the two is known as the "Snail Cave" because of the odd swirling rock formations on the floor which, to some imaginative chap, looked like snail slime.

Vang Vieng's largest cave, **Tham Nang Phomhorm** (Cave of the Fragrant-haired Woman) is about 4km past Ban Tham Xang. Take the turn-off on the right at the village of **Ban Patthana.** The cave, with two levels, is another 15km down this road. On the way you will pass **Ban Nam Yen,** a Yao hill-tribe village 3km before the cave entrance. Another Yao village, **Ban Samsavath,** is 6km north of Ban Tham Xang.

South of Ban Tham Xang about 2km west of the bridge is a sprawling **Hmong village** of some 300 households, comprised of repatriated refugees from Thailand. The United Nations High Command for Refugees (UNHCR) oversees their reassimilation into Laos, providing them with housing and training them to farm without resorting to swidden techniques. In contrast to Lao dwellings, which are often built on stilts, Hmong houses are built on the ground, resembling traditional Hmong homes in the highlands where there is no threat of flooding. Keep in mind that the inhabitants may not take kindly to photo-happy *farang.* Indeed, there are reports of villages requesting the police to confiscate the film of particularly obnoxious shutterbugs.

■■■ LUANG PRABANG

Luang Prabang is virtually synonymous with Lane Xang, the magnificent "Kingdom of a Million elephants" that once stretched across most of northern Indochina. Stand atop Mount Phousi at sunset, and for a few fleeting moments you almost believe you are back in the golden age of Laos. Substitute palanquins and pachyderms for bicycles and tuk-tuks and the city, physically, hasn't changed that much. The graceful gold-leaf encrusted peaks of Luang Prabang's many wats glint through the canopy of palm trees that shelter the old quarter of the city. Monks, their saffron robes glowing like embers, add pinpricks of color to the streets below.

Luang Prabang was built by King Fa Ngum, the unifier and first king of Lane Xang, on a rocky spit of land at the confluence of the Mekong and Nam Khan Rivers. The tiny city (present pop. 20,000) was lavished with gorgeous wats by the royal family, who maintained a palace there after King Setthathirat moved the capital to Vientiane in 1556. This shift proved to be a blessing for Luang Prabang, which remained largely isolated from the country and the world until well into the 20th century. As a result the city is widely regarded as the best-preserved in Southeast Asia.

For travelers, Luang Prabang can be a springboard for explorations of the remote northern provinces. The city itself retains a strong ethnic flavor—Hmong women in brightly colored traditional garb frequently visit the Dara Market. With unspoiled natural and architectural splendor and unparalleled possibilities for adventures even farther afield, Luang Prabang will surely be the highlight of any visit to the land of a million elephants.

ORIENTATION

Luang Prabang is a small city in terms of population and area, and finding one's way around is not difficult. Don't bother trying to decipher the city's incomprehensible system of street names; it stumps the locals too and besides, there are no street signs, Lao or otherwise.

The main road, running roughly southwest-northeast from the soccer stadium to the **Nam Khan River,** is **Thanon Sisavangvong,** which becomes **Thanon Phalongxay** at the southwest end and **Thanon Sakkarine** at the northeast end. The **post office, tourist office,** and a number of important sights, including the national museum and Wat Xieng Thong are along this road. Just southwest of the statue of **Ma Torani,** on the left, is **Thanon Souvanaphouma.** West of Thanon Sisavangvong is **Thanon Manthathourath,** which runs along the **Mekong River.** Boats headed north and south leave from quays along the south end of this road.

The other main street, **Thanon Kitsalat Setthathirat,** intersects Sisavangvong at the tourist office just south of **Mount Phousi.** The **Dara Market** is on this road, and one intersection south of the market is **Thanon Wisunalat;** the Rama Hotel and several good restaurants line the eastern leg of this road.

PRACTICAL INFORMATION

Tourist Office: Luang Prabang Tourism, 72 Thanon Sisavangvong (tel. 212 198 or 212 379). Friendly staff, but not fountains of knowledge. Good for practical questions; the only place with city maps 1500kip. Will arrange pricey (of course) tours to outlying sights ($35 average). Open Mon.-Sat. 7:20-11:30am, 1-5pm.

Tours/Travel Agency: Most run non-budget trips to the caves and waterfalls. $70 and up for one person to Pak Ou; prices drop a little for groups. **Inter-Lao Tourism** (tel. 212 034), on Thanon Kitsalat Setthathirat opposite Dara Market. The friendly folks will extend visas for $1 per day, plus a small processing fee, a helpful service as the immigration authorities do not speak much English. Open Mon.-Sat. 8am-noon, 2-5pm. **Diethelm Travel,** (tel. 212 277), on That Xieng Thong, opposite Wat Sop. Open daily 8am-noon and 2-5pm.

Immigration Office: (tel. 212 453), on Thanon Wisunalat. From the Kitsalat Setthathirat intersection, take a left onto Wisunalat; the office is on the right, opposite Rama Hotel. Will extend visas 700kip per day (up to 15 days). Allow 1-2 days for processing, but it usually takes 20min. Open Mon.-Sat. 8-11am and 2-4pm. A **2nd office** (tel. 212 334) on Thanon Mahin Quakham behind the post office directly to the left of the wide concrete steps leading to the river. Open daily 8-11:30am and 2-4:30pm. **Before leaving Luang Prabang you must "check-out" with the immigration authorities at either office 300kip tax.**

Currency Exchange: Lane Xang Bank, 90/8 Thanon Sisavangvong (tel. 212 185/6; fax 212 411). A few stores down from the tourist office on the left. Cashes traveler's checks. No credit cards. Open Mon.-Sat. 8:30am-3:30pm. **Exchange booth** (tel. 212 105) in the Dara Market; same rates and hours as the main office.

Post/Telephone Office: (tel. 212 288; fax 212 024), on Thanon Sisavangvong, just north of Nam Phu on the left, in a large yellow building. Overseas telephone and fax service. Cash only, no collect. Open Mon.-Sat. 7:30-11:20am and 2-5pm. **Postal code:** 0600. **Telephone code:** 71.

Airport: Luang Prabang Airport (tel. 212 173), on Thanon Phetsarath. A new terminal is slated to be finished in late 1996, at which time Lao Aviation hopes to begin direct service to and from Chiang Mai, Thailand. Upon arrival register at the immigration desk and have the internal travel paper you received at the airport in Vientiane stamped. Daily flights to: **Vientiane** (1-5 flights per day, 40min., 35,730kip); **Houixay** (55min., 32,800kip); and **Oudomaxi (Muang Sy)** (40min., 19,700kip). Wed. and Fri. to **Phonsavan** (35min., 24,600kip). The official schedule bears little resemblance to reality. If not enough tickets are sold, flights may be cancelled. **Lao Aviation** (tel. 212 172; fax 212 406), on Thanon Wisunalat. Head south on Thanon Kitsalat Setthathirat and take a right on Wisunalat; the office is on the left about 500m down. Purchase tickets (cash only) at least 1 day in advance. Re-confirm 1 day before. Open daily 7:30-11:30am and 2-4pm.

Buses/Trucks: At present there is no bus service to Vientiane, but this should change with the renovation of Rte. 13. Travelers can catch trucks to **Kasi,** halfway to Vientiane (12-48hr., 5000kip). Trucks leave downhill from the Naviengkham Market (but not every day). Visit the truck stop, on the left with the massive mud-caked Russian trucks, several days before you plan to leave.

Local Transportation: Songthaews and **tuk-tuks** can be hired from the Naviengkham Market to: **Khouang Si Waterfalls** (2hr., 8000kip); **Ban Phanom Pottery Village** (15min., 1000kip); **Ban Hat Hien** (10min., 500kip); and the **airport** (10min., 1000kip). **Bicycles** remain your best bet.

Boats: Boats leave from the quay behind the post office on Thanon Mahin Quakham to **Vientiane** (rainy season 3 days, dry season 5 days, 10,000kip, bring provisions). Check the quay early and often for vessels beginning several days before you wish to depart. Be ready to leave on short notice; riverboats run on a schedule mere backpackers cannot understand. Boats north up the Nam Ou River to **Nambak** leave from the concrete steps to the river behind the post office (daily, 8am, 5hr., 5300kip). Speedboats (2hr., 20,000kip) can be hired at the quay behind the Royal Palace. From Nambak, pick-up trucks run to **Muang Sy.** Always check river conditions. To **Pakbeng** on the Mekong (8am, 9hr., 6000kip), continuing to **Houixay.** Tickets are sold at the bottom of the staircase to the left of the immigration office from 7:30am and sell out fast. To **Pak Ou caves** (speedboat 1hr., slow boat 2hr.; 15,000kip). Fishing boats run a continuous shuttle service to and from **Ban Chiang Man** across the river, gateway to Wat Long Khoune and Wat Tham (5min., 100kip). To **Ban Chan Pottery Village** (20min., round-trip 2000kip).

Car Rental: Luang Prabang Tourism, 72 Thanon Sisavangvong (tel. 212 198 or 212 379). With driver $30 per day.

Bicycle/Motorbike Rental: Vannida and **Boun Gning Guest House** 2000kip per day. **Phou Vao Hotel** (tel./fax 212 194), on Thanon Phou Vao, on the outskirts of the city. Bikes (3900kip per day) and ancient Chinese-made motorbikes (11,700kip per day). Inquire at your guest house.

Markets: Dara Market, at the corner of Thanon Kitsalat Setthathirat and Wisunalat. Everything from live armadillos to *lao khao*. Minders will watch your bike for 50kip, though its hardly necessary. Open daily 6am-5pm. **Naviengkham Market,** on Thanon Phothisane, south of Kitsalat Setthathirat on the eastern outskirts of town is also worth a visit. Open daily 6am-5pm. **Tha Heua Market,** also known as **Talat Noi** (small market) is along the river behind the post office. As close to a food market as Luang Prabang gets.

Pharmacies: Stock-up on important drugs in Vientiane.

Hospital: (tel. 212 123), on Thanon Kitsalat Setthathirat. A few doctors speak French. Does not meet modern standards of hygiene. In the event of a serious health emergency, return to Vientiane A.S.A.P.

Police: Provincial Headquarters (tel. 212 151), on Thanon Wisunalat on the right before the Lao Aviation office. Some French spoken.

ACCOMMODATIONS

Luang Prabang only recently became accessible to independent (read budget) travelers, and 25,000kip ($25)-a-night hotels still outnumber more inexpensive lodgings by a hefty margin. This is changing rapidly, however; at the time of this year's research, two guest houses had opened in a span of three months. More budget digs are no doubt on the way.

Boun Gning Guest House, 109/4 Thanon Souvanaphouma (tel. 212 274). Across a small sides street from the Vannida Guest House. Recently built, and everything has that freshly scrubbed, brand-new look. Take your breakfast (400kip) on the lovely 2nd floor veranda. Shared bathrooms with hot water. Singles 5460kip. Doubles 6240kip. Discounts to guests who stay 3 days or longer. Laundry service. Doors locked at 11:30pm.

Rama Hotel (tel. 212 247), on Thanon Wisunalat. Heading south on Kitsalat Setthathirat, take a left onto Wisunalat; the hotel is on the left. An excellent no-nonsense budget hotel that is popular with backpackers. Basic rooms with hot water and western toilet. Singles $8. Doubles $10. Laundry service. Owner speaks decent English. Check-out flexible. Disco next door open 9-11:30pm.

Vannida Guest House, 87/4 Thanon Souvanaphouma (tel. 212 374). Heading west (away from Mount Phousi) from the Nam Phou sculpture, Souvanaphouma is the next left. It's about 100m on the right. Once the home of a Lao prince; envision his Lord and Lady munching bon-bons in the high-ceilinged be-columned dining room where hungry backpackers now wolf down breakfast. Energetic staff maintains a clean, fresh establishment. Singles 5000kip. Doubles 7800kip, with A/C 11,700kip. Laundry service. Talk to ambitious owner about trekking and excursions to Pak Ou Caves and Khouang Sy waterfalls. Check-out noon.

Vieng Kao Guest House (tel. 212 271), on Thanon Kitsalat Setthathirat south of Wisunalat, on the right. A slightly rundown, colonial-style building. The best part is the 2nd-floor balcony with ferns and comfy chairs. Check-out noon. Unbeatable rates: singles 3500kip, doubles 5000-6000kip. Shared bathrooms are a bit grungy. Popular spot, so singles fill up quickly. Small restaurant next door serves Lao food (1500-3500kip).

FOOD

Fans of authentic Lao food will find Luang Prabang a garden of succulent (and spicy) culinary delights and may have difficulty tearing themselves away from the city's excellent and inexpensive restaurants. Signature Luang Prabang dishes include watercress salad, *laap kai* (spicy chicken salad), and mountain-grown brown sticky rice. The budget-conscious should head for **Talat Tha Heua.** Vendors selling *kai ping* (grilled chicken-on-a-stick), sweet sausage, fried fish, and *khao jii pâté* sandwiches abound. The market is bustling before noon, tapers off in the afternoon, and then picks up somewhat in the evening, closing at about 8pm. A few noodle vendors and *khao jii pâté* sellers hang out at **Dara Market** as well. Vegetarians in search of fresh fruits and vegetables should look no further than **Naviengkham Market** on Thanon Phothisane.

Restaurant Luang Prabang (tel. 212 387), on Thanon Wisunalat, on the right past Rama Hotel and opposite Wat Wisum. Sit on the sidewalk amidst lush hanging plants or inside surrounded by Lao handicrafts and pictures of recent Miss Luang Prabangs. Extensive menu with Lao, Chinese, Vietnamese, and French food; small vegetarian selection as well. Large portions at moderate prices. Open daily 7:30am-10pm. Live, traditional Lao music nightly 7-8pm.

Yong Khoune Restaurant, 145/1 Thanon Wisunalat. Heading south on Kitsalat Setthathirat, take a left on to Wisunalat, right across from Rama Hotel. This simple street-side eatery dishes up large helpings of savory Lao and Thai food at agreeable prices. Vegetarians will salivate over the "Luang Prabang salad," a green salad topped with sliced eggs and crushed peanuts (700kip). Fried chicken in chili and basil leaves (1500kip). Most dishes 500-1500 kip. Open daily 6am-11pm.

Maylee Lao Food Restaurant, 5/6 Thanon Phou Vao. From Naviengkham Market head south and take a right at the bottom of the hill. The restaurant is beyond Muang Sua Hotel on the left. Connoisseurs of Lao food should make tracks for the pleasant Maylee on the quiet southern outskirts of town. Signature dishes include *laap* (2000kip) and fried bamboo shoots stuffed with minced pork (1500kip). The gutsy can try cow viscera soup (1500kip). Open daily 6-10pm.

Sala Khem Khane Restaurant, 14/2 Thanon Khem Khane. Head east on Thanon Rathsavong from Dara Market. The restaurant is on the left, opposite the back entrance to Mount Phousi. The 1st-class setting and unparalleled view make this place worth a visit. Sit beneath thatched pavilions on stilts over the river and watch fishermen tend their nets, with the golden spire of Wat Tao Hai and the mountains in the background. Stereo blasts an eclectic mix of music from Bill Haley to the Doors. Smorgasbord of Lao, Vietnamese, and French dishes 1000-2000kip. Fine chicken curry (2000kip). Open daily 7am-10pm.

View Khem Khong (tel. 212 471), on Thanon Manthatourath. From the river bank behind the National Museum the restaurant is about 50m up-stream on the left. Look for the satellite dish. Another restaurant boasting thatched pavilion built on stilts over the river; gorgeous vistas at sunset. Popular with the city's fledgling yuppies. Menu is too hip to list prices, but most dishes a low 1000-2500kip; *tom yam paa* (3000kip). Open daily 7am-11pm.

SIGHTS

The glory years of Lane Xang may have faded into the distant past, but Luang Prabang retains the trappings of a great capital, most notably in the vast number of wats (some 33 of the original 66 remain). These superb temples remain the city's chief attractions. Many of the most important wats line Thanon Sisavangvong, the road that runs down the center of the peninsula. If you can only handle a few sights, be sure to visit Wat Xieng Thong, Wat Wisunalat, Wat Mai, Wat That Luang, Mount Phousi, Wat Prabouthabat, and of course, the Royal Palace. Often wats are locked to prevent theft of valuable statues, but a polite request will usually open them.

Opposite the Provincial Hall on Thanon Phalangxay is the statue of **Ma Torani,** depicted as a young maiden washing her hair. According to Buddhist legend Ma Torani (Mother of the Earth) protected the Buddha from the demon Devarade by washing her hair, the water from which swept the demon away. Her image can be seen stenciled on wats all over town.

Stroll down Thanon Sisavangvong to **Mount Phousi** (Marvelous Mountain), the craggy hill which dominates the city. At the top stands **Wat Chom Phousi,** whose glittering gold stupa is visible for miles in every direction. In the evening there is no better spot from which to take in Luang Prabang's spectacular sunsets, a natural light show unmatched by the most sophisticated Hollywood special effects. A booth on the Thanon Sisavangvong side of the hill charges a scandalous 500kip admission fee to climb to the top; duck the charge by entering from the Thanon Khem Khane side along the Nam Khane River bank, via Wat Tham Phousi.

North of the tiny chapel, in a bizarre contrast to the peaceful wat, is the skeleton of an old anti-aircraft gun which no one seems eager to lug down. A narrow, partially overgrown path leads from the right of the A-A gun down the eastern slope to **Wat Tham Phousi,** the entrance to which is framed by 2 US-made bomb casings that have found a peacetime job as flowerpots. A jolly, rotund Buddha sits in a grotto next to the cave entrance inside of which is a large collection of Buddha images in varying stages of decay. Beyond the pavilion is a deep footprint of the Buddha.

Directly opposite Mount Phousi on the left side of Thanon Sisavangvong is one of Luang Prabang's most beautiful wats, **Wat Mai.** Seventy years in the making (finally completed in 1788) the temple was home to the sacred Pha Bang Buddha between 1894 and 1947. The entire northside of the wat is adorned with a gorgeous bas-relief covered entirely with gold leaf, depicting the story of Phravet, an incarnation of Gautama Buddha; included in the masterpiece are several highly detailed processions and scenes of village life. Inside is one of the largest Buddha images in the city.

Next door to Wat Mai is the **Royal Palace,** home to the **National Museum,** one of the most well-presented, eclectic, and engrossing collections in Southeast Asia. The palace was built by King Sisavangvong in 1904 (his statue stands on the front lawn). It remained the home of the royal family until the monarchy was abolished in 1975, and several former princesses of the *ancien regime* still live in Luang Prabang, minus their birthrights of course. One highlight of the collection is a copy of the **Pha Bang,** the golden Buddha that is Laotian Buddhism's most revered image. A gift to Lane Xang's first king from the Angkor court in the 1300s, the original is made of 50kg of pure gold and now resides in a Vientiane bank vault. Currently displayed in the royal family's private chapel, the replica will soon be moved to **Wat Ho Pha Bang,** the temple to the right of the entrance gates, when it is completed in 1996. Directly beyond the entrance hall is the grand throne room, marked by the distinctive seal of a three-headed elephant on the back of the throne. The elephant symbolizes the three kingdoms that were unified under Lane Xang: Luang Prabang, Champassak, and Vientiane. The encased crystal and gold Buddhas to the right and left of the throne were originally stored in That Mak Mo stupa at Wat Wisunalat, but were moved to the palace for safekeeping. Behind the throne room are the royal family's private quarters which have been left largely untouched since the monarchy was abolished.

The National Museum (tel. 212 122 or 212 470), is currently open for very limited hours, Mon.-Sat. 8-10am. Tourists are required to procure a 100kip permit to visit the museum at the Information and Culture Service Office (tel. 212 044), on Thanon Sisavangvong, diagonally opposite Lane Xang Bank. Open Mon.-Sat. 8-11am and 2-5pm. Admission tickets purchased at the palace cost 100kip and include an English- or French-speaking guide. With luck, this maddening, inefficient, and quintessentially communist system will have passed on by 1996, at which time the museum plans to adopt regular hours (Mon.-Sat. 8-11 and 2-5pm) and permits will no longer be necessary. Photography is strictly prohibited.

Head north on Thanon Sisavangvong, which becomes Thanon Sakavongsa, to get to the *grande dame* of Luang Prabang's many temples, **Wat Xieng Thong,** or Copper Tree Temple. Widely regarded as the crowning achievement of Lao religious architecture, it is set back from the road amidst a well-manicured tropical garden. A flight of broad marble steps lead from the western edge of the compound down to the Mekong River. Built in 1559 by King Setthathirat, the graceful temple was lavished with money from the royal coffers until 1975, explaining its excellent condition. The base of the wat glitters with thousands of emerald-green mosaic tiles; gold leaf stencils adorn the outside walls. On the back wall of the temple is a mosaic depicting Wat Xieng Thong's namesake. Inside, the jet black walls and columns contrast magnificently with the overlaying, vivid gold stenciling. Swirling *dharma* wheels adorn the ceiling, while a massive Buddha takes in the scene with a sleepy, eternal gaze. Behind the temple is a small side chapel housing a bronze reclining Buddha (an attitude rare in Lao Buddhist art). Just to the right of the gate as you enter is a large pagoda housing **King Sisavangvong's funeral chariot.** A 12-m high float surrounded by writhing golden *nagas,* it brought the king's funerary urn to the cremation site following his death in 1959. Open daily 8am-5pm. Admission 250kip.

Luang Prabang's other "most important wat," **Wat Wisunalat,** is on Thanon Wisunalat past the Rama Hotel on the left. Built in 1523, it was razed by Chinese mercenaries and then rebuilt at the turn of the 19th century. The towering *sim* houses a treasure-trove of Buddhist art, watched over by the largest Buddha in the city. Stacked haphazardly along the walls are hundreds of Buddha images of various sizes and styles, some over 400 years old. To the right of the altar are several Sanskrit stelae. Wat Wisunalat, like many large temples, houses a number of novice monks who will be glad to tell you "Wat's up" in exchange for some English conversation.

Across Thanon Wisunalat from the temple is the Luang Prabang branch of the Lao Red Cross, which operates a **traditional Lao herbal sauna** similar to those at Wat Sokpaluang in Vientiane. Open Wed.-Fri. 5-7pm, Sat.-Sun. 9-11am and 5-7pm. Soak yourself for 1500kip. Bring your own towel. Also opposite the temple is the bulbous **That Mak Mo stupa,** sometimes referred to as the "Melon Stupa" because of its rounded top. Constructed in 1504, it once held many priceless Buddha statuettes now on display at the National Museum. Open daily 8am-6pm. Admission 250kip.

A few meters farther down on the left is the turn-off to Ban Phanom (if you pass the Mitthaphap Restaurant you've gone too far). Down the dirt road is the **Santichedi,** part of **Wat Phnom Phao,** whose golden spire is visible from Mount Phousi. The temple was modeled on a large wat in Rangoon, Burma, but the result is a mix of wannabe-Buddhist-monumentalism and Victorian kitsch.

Heading south from the statue of Ma Torani on Thanon Phalongxay, behind the soccer field is **Wat That Luang,** another of Luang Prabang's don't-miss wats. It's the final resting place of many royals, including King Sisavangvong, whose ashes are entombed in the golden stupa across from the entrance. The temple itself lacks the richness of other wats, but is beautiful in its austerity. A large gray stupa whose corners are adorned with kneeling ascetics and lotus flowers contains "relics" from the Buddha.For sunset watchers, That Luang is surpassed only by Mount Phousi.

Farther down Thanon Phalongxay, on the right opposite a Shell station is **Wat Prabouthabat,** the crazy Aunt Matilda of Luang Prabang's temple family. Built in the 1950s with money supplied by the local Chinese and Vietnamese communities, the impression is of a temple designed by Walt Disney and colorized by Ted Turner. The bright pastel reds and blues that predominate always seem a tad off. Concrete pavilions hold several rotund Buddhas. Open daily 8am-6pm. Admission 250kip.

SHOPPING

The region around Luang Prabang enjoys a long tradition of weaving excellence, dating back to the days of the monarchy, when the royal family was a great patron and Luang Prabang's weaving villages flourished. Today many of the woven goods sold in Vientiane are produced in Luang Prabang Province, and bargain hunters will delight in the vast array of colorful, high-quality cloth and finished garments for sale. Some textiles can be found at the **Dara Market,** but a number of handicraft shops in town, such as **Lao Handicrafts and Antiques Shop,** 49/6 Thanon Sisavangvong and **The Antique Shop,** 2/22 Thanon Sisavangvong (tel. 212 500), carry much larger, eclectic selections. Prices start around 5000kip for a 1m-long piece of fabric. Finished, off-the-rack garments including Hmong vests (distinguished by the colorful embroidery) 2000kip. All prices are negotiable.

■ NEAR LUANG PRABANG

ACROSS THE RIVER

For those hearty wat-goers who crave additional temples, the other side of the Mekong River boasts some impressive wattage. In terms of setting, few can match **Wat Long Khone's** location within a tranquil tropical garden on a high bank above the river. The delicate temple dates from the 1700s and is in excellent condition thanks to recent renovation efforts. Restorers have left the frescoes that decorate the interior and exterior walls of the chapel in their original, if faded, grandeur. Behind the wat are several traditional wooden monks' quarters.

Just 20m up the path from Wat Long Khone is **Wat Tham** (temple cave). This subterranean chapel is filled with Buddha images, many of them human-size, in varying stages of decay. Beware, it can be quite a shock when the termite-ridden face of a golden statue suddenly appears in your flashlight beam! A labyrinthine passageway twists and turns some 50m underground, ending at a glittering quartz stalactite as thick as a tree trunk. A flashlight is a must for exploring the cave; wizened, old monks will gladly lead you through it, pointing out Buddha statues and rock formations along the way.

To get to the opposite bank, take one of the fishing boats (100kip) that shuttle back and forth across the river when the small canoes are full. Boats leave from the second set of concrete stairs upstream from the Lao State Fuel Co. gas station.

CRAFT VILLAGES

Each of the three craft villages near Luang Prabang specialize in the production of a specific item: weaving, knives, and pottery. All make interesting excursions, as visitors view the village's industry from raw materials to finished products.

By far the most interesting is **Ban Phanom,** a weaving village roughly 4km east of the city. Located on the banks of the Nam Khan River, the 300 year-old village is inhabited by members of the Lu tribe, originally from southern China. Historically Ban Phanom enjoyed considerable royal patronage, and many villagers served as the royal family's personal weavers and tailors. Partially as a result, Ban Phanom's weavings are of high quality and are sold in handicraft shops in Vientiane as well as Luang Prabang. Goods are sold in the market on the banks of the Nam Khan. Open daily 8am-5pm. It's best to come early, before the package tour groups arrive.

To get to Ban Phanom by bicycle head east on Thanon Vatniuenna, passing the bridge over the Nam Khan; the dirt turnoff to the village is about 10m past the entrance to Wat Pha Na Theup on the left. If you reach Mitthaphap Restaurant you've gone too far. Ban Phanom is about 1km farther down. By tuk-tuk 1000kip.

Well-beyond Ban Phanom on the same dirt road near the Nam Khan River is the **grave of Henri Mouhot,** the French adventurer who "rediscovered" Angkor Wat in 1860, only to die of malaria a year later in Luang Prabang. The grave is difficult to find (in fact, the grave itself wasn't "rediscovered" until 1990); ask a local to point you to it or risk a long, frustrating search.

As you enter **Ban Hat Hien,** about 5km northeast of town near the airport, the clanging of hammers against anvils announces that this is Luang Prabang's knife-making village. Craftsmen begin with pieces of scrap, cut them into knife-sized pieces and pound them flat. Next the metal is heated in coal fires and pounded repeatedly to create an edge. Some craftsman use old propellant canisters from American-made artillery pieces to make human-powered bellows that fan the coal fire. Other villages crack open old car batteries and melt the lead down to make a shot. During January and February when the water in the Nam Khan is low, the village harvests aquatic weeds and dries them to make *khai pen,* a popular snack food.

By bicycle, cross the bridge off Thanon Vatniuenna as if heading to the airport. The turn-off to Ban Hat Hien is on the right just before the old terminal. By tuk-tuk 500kip. Both Ban Phanom and Ban Hat Hien can be visited in a single morning.

South of Luang Prabang about 4km, on the opposite side of the Mekong, is **Ban Chan,** a pottery-making village. The entire village participates in the production of large *thongs* or water jugs, and clay roofing tiles. While the jugs may be a bit heavy for the average backpacker, visitors can observe the entire process from the grinding of clumps of clay into fine sand to throwing the pots on hand-turned pottery wheels, and finally baking the pots and tiles in large, underground kilns. A visit to Ban Chan can easily be combined with an excursion to the temples across the river from Luang Prabang. Hire a boat from Luang Prabang or Ban Chiang Man 2000kip.

PAK OU CAVES

At the confluence of the Mekong and the Nam Ou Rivers, 25km upriver from Luang Prabang, are the Pak Ou Caves, an important religious site for 500 years. For those travelers not intending any extensive river expeditions while in Laos, the two-hour boat trip (one hour return trip) is an excellent way to get a taste of a mode of transport as old as Lane Xang itself. The scenery is splendid as the chocolaty Mekong snakes its way between rolling hills and craggy, serrated peaks soaring 60m above the water. The caves are buried on the left bank of the river, opposite the village of Ban Pak Ou; there are two caves, Tham Ting (the lower one) and Tham Phum (the upper one). Every April, during Phimai, the Lao New Year, thousands of devotees flock to the caves to pray, a practice once followed by the kings of Lane Xang, allegedly dating back to the caves' discovery in the 1500s by King Setthathirat.

Tham Ting, featured prominently on many postcards and travel brochures is packed with hundreds of Buddha images. Clamber up to the ledge on the right for a great profile of the entire collection. The second cave, **Tham Phum,** is reached by a steep brick staircase leading from the river bank (someone has thoughtfully erected two small rest houses at the top and bottom of the path, no doubt for winded *farang*). A flashlight, or at least a candle, is necessary to fully appreciate the vast collection of Buddha images in various postures and conditions, some of which date back to the 16th century. Taller Buddhas cast eerily beautiful shadows on the roof of the cavern. Several of the large wooden statues are inlaid with colored glass mosaic tiles. Admission 700kip for both caves.

Ask your skipper to take the boat up the mouth of the Nam Ou River a ways for a close-up of the magnificent **limestone cliffs** before heading south again. There are several worthwhile sidetrips along the way. About 3km south of Pak Ou at a bend in the river is **Wat Don Khoun.** Scarcely visible from the water, the small temple has been abandoned to the jungle, though several crumbling Buddha images remain.

No river excursion is complete without a visit to **Xang Hai village,** famed for its *lao khao* (rice whiskey) distillation industry. Locals brew the potent firewater from sticky rice in large oil drums along the river bank. Four hundred kip should purchase half a bottle-full of still-warm moonshine, more than enough to put a little hair on anyone's chest. Village children delight in watching camera-clicking *farang* hop nimbly off the boat on arrival, and teeter back 10 minutes later. Tip the captain an extra 200kip if he is considerate enough to install a bamboo handrail for re-boarding or at least manage not to hoot with laughter if you fall in.

Boats can be hired from the landing behind the Royal Palace for about 13-15,000kip for a large boat with a roof (desirable, as the sun is brutal). Be sure to decide upon any additional stops beforehand. Longtailed speed boats (1500kip), which roar up and back in well under an hour each way, gather at the narrow concrete stairs just upriver of the Lao State Fuel Co. gas station.

KHOUANG SY WATERFALL

Located 30km south of the city; in this case getting there is at least half the fun: the rugged dirt road winds through rolling hills, their slopes notched with terraced rice fields, and increasingly rare teak groves, identifiable by their distinctive broad leaves and ram-rod straight trunks. As your tuk-tuk chugs through tiny villages, it exerts a magnetic attraction on local children who will drop their games to smile and wave.

In terms of sheer grandeur, the falls (admission 700kip) are hardly Niagara-like, but swimming in the series of sapphire-blue pools below them is not to be missed. A popular tourist destination for Lao and *farang,* Khouang Sy crawls with vendors who congregate near several cabanas. Bring a picnic and sit at tables near the cascades. Steps cut into the clay slope run up the right side of the falls beneath lush jungle, to the first tier; here it is possible to cross the river and continue up a series of natural steps eroded by the water, to the top. Not for the equilibrium challenged.

■■■ PHONSAVAN

Geographically, Xieng Khouang Province, northeast of Vientiane along the Vietnamese border, is something of an anomaly. The terrain is a mix of rugged mountains and beautiful rolling hills, more reminiscent of County Cork, Ireland than Indochina. Its high elevation (average over 1000m) ensures cool, at times down-right chilly, temperatures all year long, and produces what many westerners would consider paradoxes, such as terraced rice fields rising out of pine forests. During November and December the mountainsides near the border are ablaze with poppy blossoms; opium, grown by the hill tribes, is the province's chief cash crop.

Historically, the province has been under Vietnamese hegemony, and the Vietnamese influence remains strong, though the population is equal parts Hmong, Kamu, and lowland Lao. To travelers, Xieng Khouang is best known for Thong Hay Hin, the Plain of Jars, the mysterious collection of massive 3000-year-old stone vessels scattered across the region. More recently Xieng Khouang was one of two Lao provinces most heavily bombed during the Vietnam War. Scarcely a town survived unscathed, and a number simply vanished all together. The former provincial capital, Xieng Khouang City, was so hard hit that after the war the provincial seat was moved to Phonsavan, 36km to the north. The landscape is pockmarked with craters and thousands of cluster bombs still litter the countryside, exacting a gruesome toll in lost lives and limbs from the local population. The skies over Phonsavan are still not silent; Soviet-made Mig-21 fighter planes from the airbase outside the city scream overhead while on training flights. Every morning the all-women Lao army parachute stunt team can be seen practicing their daredevil aerial acrobatics.

ORIENTATION

Finding your way around Phonsavan is easy; the town consists of two main streets. Running south from the Phudoi Hotel to the market is **Thanon Phonsavan** with a small spit of grass and a large gold urn in the middle. Rte. 7 runs east-west and crosses the north end of Thanon Phonsavan, like a "T" at the market. The budget hotels and guest houses line the east leg of Rte. 7. South of **Phudoi Hotel** Thanon Phonsavan turns west, passing the hospital on its way to the airport. Upon arrival at bustling **Phonsavan Airport,** take a tuk-tuk to your guest house (1000kip).

PRACTICAL INFORMATION

Tour/Travel Agency: Sodetour Travel (tel. 130), at the corner of Thanon Phonsavan and Rte. 7, organizes day-long trips with car, driver, and guide, about

30,000kip. English spoken. Hmong-run with highly praised tours of the Hmong villages. Open daily 8-11:30am and 1-5pm. **Inter-Lao Tourism** (tel. 156), on Thanon Phonsavan, on the left around the bend from the Phudoi. Rents unstoppable Russian jeeps with driver 30,000kip, with guide 50,000kip. Arranges day-long itineraries including Plain of Jars, Hmong villages, and Tham Phyu cave. Only the director speaks English. Open daily 8am-noon and 2-5pm. **Lane Xang Travel and Tour** (tel. 144). Off-road vehicles for about 30,000kip per day, depending on the distance. English spoken.

Currency Exchange: Aroun May Bank (tel. 187). South end of Thanon Phonsavan, opposite Phudoi Hotel. Dollars or baht to kip. No traveler's checks or credit cards accepted. No English. Open Mon.-Sat. 8am-4:30pm.

Post Office: Post and Telegram Office (tel. 166), at the corner of Rte. 7 and Thanon Phonsavan across from the market. Open daily 8-11am and 1:30-5:30pm. No overseas phone calls.

Airport: Phonsavan Airport, 5km west of town off Thanon Phonsavan. "Terminal" consists of a single woven bamboo shed with immigration checkpoint. To **Vientiane** (daily, 40min., 35,100kip) and **Luang Prabang** (Wed. and Fri., 35min. 23,400kip). Arrive at least two hours before your flight to avoid being dumped from the flight list. **Lao Aviation** (tel. 284), on a dirt side street off Rte. 7. From the market head east on Rte. 7, turn left at the Hay Hin Hotel, the office is on the left. Tickets must be confirmed one day before departure. Cash only. Open daily 7am-noon and 2-5pm.

Buses: Ramshackle buses and trucks to the rest of the province leave from the empty lot on Rte. 7, adjacent to the market. Buses to: **Ban Thatcho** (24km, noon and 3pm, 1hr., 400kip); **Muang Kham** (22km, noon and 4pm, 500kip); **Xieng Khouang** (36km); and **Nong Het** (120km).

Local Transportation: Tuk-tuks are almost as plentiful as bomb canisters; they will take you anywhere in town for 3-600kip, as well as **Hay Hin I,** the first Plain of Jars site 10km west of town (5000kip) and **Ban Thatcho,** 24km east of town.

Taxis: For hire at the bus stop next to the market on Rte. 7. During the dry season they can reach all three **Plain of Jars** sites (20,000kip), although during the rainy season you have to walk several km. To: **Tham Phyu Cave** (56km, 22,000kip); **Ban Nam Horn** (76km, 25,00kip); and **Ban Thatcho** (17,000kip).

Car Rental: Cars, 4-wheel drives, or sedans from the tour companies. Average price 30,000kip with driver. No self-drive. Or check at your hotel/guest house.

Markets: Phonsavan's **central market** at the north terminus of Thanon Phonsavan, opposite the post office. Open daily 5am-6pm. A small **Talat Vietnam** (Vietnamese market) is on Rte. 7 north of town past the Vinh Thong Guest House. Imported Saigon beer, plastic pith helmets, and shrimp chips.

Hospital: Xieng Khouang Provincial Hospital (tel. 240), on Thanon Phonsavan, southwest of town past the provincial hall on the right. Doctors speak some French and a little English and Russian.

Police: Xieng Khouang Provincial Police (tel. 141), on Thanon Phonsavan, a 2-story concrete building in a field opposite the hospital. No English.

ACCOMMODATIONS

A number of guest houses and hotels have opened in Phonsavan in recent years, hoping to cash in on the hoards of tourists that were expected following the easing of internal travel restrictions. The *farang* masses have yet to materialize, and until they do, rooms remain as cheap as any in Laos. Perhaps the only drawback is that Phonsavan only has electricity from 7-10pm, so your late-night letter writing will have to be by candle-light.

Dok Khoune Guest House (tel. 162), on Rte. 7. Head east from the market, the guest house is in a 2-story stucco building on the right, about halfway down the street. A real house, with hospitable owners. The interior decorating is *très-Xieng Khouang,* with an assortment of defused bombs in the corner of the lobby and expended cartridges posing as key chains. The rooms are all freshly painted and well-kept. Upstairs rooms 3000kip. Downstairs (all have two beds) with bathroom and western toilet 5000kip. All rooms have netting. Laundry service.

Vinh Thong Guest House (tel. 181), on Rte. 7. Just past the Dok Khoune on the right, next to the Muang Phuon. Not much from the outside, but the rooms are cheap and clean, with netting. Cluster bomb ashtrays in the lobby. Doubles 3000kip, with private bath 4000kip. Popular with backpackers. Convivial Vietnamese owner and his Lao wife have a go-anywhere Land Rover and will **organize trips** to the Plain of Jars, Tham Phyu, and opium fields (in season), a steal at 10,000kip per day. Laundry service.

Phudoi Hotel (tel. 238), at the south end of Thanon Phonsavan, opposite Aroun May Bank. The jaundiced yellow Soviet-style building is an abomination; rooms are only slightly more attractive, but clean and bright just the same. Basic double with bathroom and western toilet 7000kip. Triples 7000kip, 6000kip for one person. Breakfast included. Friendly, English-speaking owner can **arrange excursions** to outlying areas. Laundry service.

FOOD

Don't expect much in the way of fine, or even just O.K. dining in a city with three hours of electricity per day. The **food market** (open 6am-7pm) behind the post office sells fruit, vegetables, and French bread, and some prepared snack foods, particularly Vietnamese pastries and noodle soups. There are a few **noodle stands** as well and a few more across the street in the **main market.**

Sanga Restaurant, on Rte. 7 east of the market on the left before the Hay Hin Hotel. Serves cheap, basic Lao food, conveniently displayed on an English menu. Most dishes 1000kip: chicken curry, beef *laap*, and cucumber salad. Fried rice (700kip). Open daily 6am-10pm.

Inter-Lao Restaurant (tel. 156), on Thanon Phonsavan. Past Phudoi Hotel and around the bend about 20m past the provincial hall on the left. Run by the manager of Inter-Lao Tourism, this joint is as chic as Phonsavan gets, with cloth napkins, clean glasses, and Lao music at only moderately irritating decibel levels. "French" and Lao food, but only the French section is in English. Decent Lao food 800-1500kip. Chicken, pork, or beef *laap* (1000kip). Open daily 10am-8pm

■ NEAR PHONSAVAN

THE PLAIN OF JARS (THONG HAY HIN)

The principle sight around Phonsavan is, of course, the **Plain of Jars.** The romantic name conjures up visions of a vast rolling field littered with thousands of massive stone urns, an image the National Tourism Authority and tour companies encourage through clever photography. Alas, reality, as is usually the case, is far less dramatic. The Plain of Jars actually consists of about 300 jars scattered across the countryside around Phonsavan in clusters ranging from 50 jars down to one measly urn.

The origin and function of the jars has baffled archaeologists for decades. They are believed to be between 2500 to 3000 years old, although even this is debatable. According to one theory the jars are primitive kegs left over from a rollicking rice-wine bacchanal thrown by a now extinct race of giants. A more widely accepted theory holds that the jars are funerary urns used to inter bodies of the deceased. This hypothesis was strengthened by the discovery of human remains in one of the jars in 1963. Some archeologists believe the jars, which were hewn from solid stone, may have been made by ancestors of the Kamu people who, well into this century, continued to place the remains of their dead in jars.

Three groups of jars are readily accessible from Phonsavan. The first, **Hay Hin I,** is 12km west of town near the airbase and reachable by tuk-tuk (5000kip). It consists of about 50 jars on two levels. Next to the first group is a large bomb crater. Down the hill on the left is a cave used by Pathet Lao as shelter from those very same bombs during the war. The site is a bit touristy; pavilions hawking much smaller aluminum jars of soda and beer are considerably less than 3000 years old. Open daily. Admission 1000kip.

The other two sights, **Hay Hin 2** (24km) and **Hay Hin 3** (32km) are accessible only by a thrill-a-minute car ride, and at times during the rainy season only by Russian jeeps. Although not as large a collection as #1, both 2 and 3 remain untouched by the hand of tourism and afford a sweeping view of the Lao highland landscape. The remote sites are certainly worth it if you can find enough people to make it economical. By taxi from the market 17,000kip; during the rainy season it may be necessary to cover the final few km on foot. Off-road vehicles with driver can be rented from Sodetour or Inter-Lao Tourism for about 25,000kip.

While the areas immediately surrounding the jars have been cleared of landmines, the rest of the countryside cannot be considered safe. Exercise caution and stick to well-trodden paths.

There are several rarely visited **Hmong villages** in the region, including one at **Ban Dong Dan** near Hay Hin 2. The only signs of the area's tragic recent history are cluster bomb canisters which serve as pig troughs. Twenty-four km east of Phonsavan is the large Hmong village of **Ban Thatcho,** a frequent stop for package tour groups. It is easily reachable by tuk-tuk (8000kip), taxi (15,000kip), or bus (noon and 3pm, 400kip).

MUANG KHAM DISTRICT

Of course no Lao tourist area would be complete without at least two caves. Fulfilling the quota, **Tham Phyu** lies 56km from Phonsavan in Muang Kham district. During the war the cave was used as a bomb shelter for civilians until one day in 1968 an unidentified aircraft fired a rocket into the cave, killing several hundred people. Most historians point to the Royal Lao Airforce, but the Lao government insists it was an American plane. Bone fragments are still scattered around the cave, a gruesome testament to the tragedy of war. Muang Kham district has achieved some degree of notoriety for the local population's ingenious use of the flotsam of war—bomb casings, artillery shells, and scrap metal from downed aircraft—in their building projects. There are also several **Hmong villages** near Tham Phyu. For travelers who do not speak Lao but who want to get a good look at Hmong village life, it is best to go with a guide who can translate for you, as the villagers tend to be quite shy and suspicious of foreigners. The Phonsavan branch of **Sodetour Travel** is entirely Hmong-run. Their tours are highly recommended by travelers for the high degree of interaction between themselves and the villagers. A one-day trip to Tham Phyu and several Hmong villages costs around 27,000kip ($30) for car, driver, and guide. Sodetour also organizes 3-day treks into **the mountains near the Lao-Vietnamese border,** where trekkers sleep in remote Hmong villages

■■■ SAVANNAKHET

Savannakhet or "Savan," as it is sometimes called locally, perches on the west bank of the Mekong River nearly 500 buttock-bruising km south of Vientiane. The commercial hub of the central Laotian panhandle, Savannakhet is a town on the make. As the high-rise hotels across the river in Mukdahan, Thailand testify to, the region is gearing up for an economic boom now that Laos and Vietnam are both opening capitalism's Pandora's box. Savan, only a day's bus ride from Hue and Da Nang on the central Vietnamese coast, looks to take advantage of the expected boom. If Thai business interests have their way and a second "Friendship Bridge" is built here, Savan's stock will rise even higher.

For travelers en route to Vietnam or the splendors of the "Emerald Triangle" to the south, a night in Savan is considered to be something akin to a night in purgatory, and the city suffers from a not-entirely-fair reputation as an uninspiring pitstop. To many who don't give it a chance, Savannakhet's wonders are limited to "I wonder when the bus leaves." While the sights may not rival those in the enchanting deep south, there is a certain charm to the city's unabashed blue-collar atmosphere and narrow, cluttered streets. The population is far less reserved than those in northern cities, and visitors can expect plenty of cheerful "*Sabai-dee*"s and giggling children eager to clown around with the goofy *farang.* So rest your road-weary bones, spend an afternoon exploring Savannakhet's plebeian attractions, and then forge ahead, where greater wonders beckon.

ORIENTATION

Savannakhet runs north-south along the **Mekong River** (which is always to the west) and is laid out in an uneven grid. Three main roads run parallel to the river: **Thanon Tha Heua,** along the bank, **Thanon Khanthabouli,** and **Ratsavongseuk.** They're linked by a number of streets running east-west, the largest of which, **Thanon Oudomsin,** passes the **market** in the north section of town; **Thanon Makhavena,** in the south section, leads to the **airport** on the southwest outskirts of town. The **immigration pier,** a number of cheap restaurants, and the Hotel Santyphab are clustered near the **St. Teresia Catholic Church,** five long blocks south of the market off Thanon Khanthabouli. The **bus station** is on the extreme northern end of town. Take a tuk-tuk to your hotel (1000kip). Lao National Tourism Authority maps can be purchased at the Savanbanhao Hotel (1500kip).

LAOS

PRACTICAL INFORMATION

Tours/Travel Agency: Not particularly helpful; their job is not to set up tours, but to handle package tours from Vientiane. **Savan Travel and Tour,** in the Savanbanhao Hotel, 644 Thanon Senna (tel. 212 202; fax 212 733). Will rent car and driver for city tours and environs $38 per day. Open Mon.-Sat. 8-11:30am and 2-4pm. **Lane Xang Travel and Tours,** 385 Thanon Ratsavongseuk (tel. 212 804; fax 212 266), opposite the market. Mostly package tours bound for Vietnam. Open Mon.-Fri 7am-noon and 2-5pm, Sat. 7am-noon. **Sodetour** (tel. 212 445), on Thanon Kanvoravong. Organizes excursions to the dinosaur remains at Ban Namo, Phalan District. Open Mon.-Sat. 8-11:30am and 2-4pm.

Consulate: Vietnam (tel. 212 418; fax 212 182). From the north end of the market head west on Thanon Oudomsin, take the first right, onto Thanon Sisavangvong. The embassy is 1-½ blocks on the right. Visas issued for crossing at Lao Bao US$70; allow 3-5 days for processing. Open Mon.-Sat. 8-11:30am and 2-4:30pm.

Immigration: The office is at the pier, but unlike in the northern provinces, where travelers must register with the police in each province, these rules are not strictly enforced in the south. Try to get it stamped anyway. Immigration will stamp travel sheets for those entering by bus.

Currency Exchange: Banque Pour le Commerce Exterieur Lao, (tel. 212 722 or 212 261; fax 212 723), opposite the market. Visa, MC, AmEx traveler's checks and cash advances available. Open Mon.-Sat. 8am-3:30pm. **Lao May Bank,** 23 Thanon Khanthabouli (tel. 212 508; fax 212 836). Traveler's checks, credit card cash advances. Open Mon.-Sat. 8am-noon and 1-3:30pm. **Exchange booths** near the market exchange cash for cash.

Post/Telephone Office: (tel. 212 296), on Thanon Khanthabouli. From the intersection with Thanon Simuang, head south. The post office is 1 block down on the right. Look for the massive radio tower. Exchange booth (cash only) open during business hours. Cash only overseas telephone and fax service; open daily 7:30am-10pm. Post office open Mon.-Sat. 7:30-11:30am, 2-5pm. **Postal code:** 1300. **Provincial telephone code:** 041.

Airport: One airstrip and a rickety wooden "terminal," at the southwest end of town at the intersection of Makhavena and Sisavangvong. To: **Vientiane** (daily, 1hr., 47,000kip) and **Pakxe** (Mon. and Fri., 30min., 31,600kip). Purchase tickets up to 1 day before and confirm. Cash only. **Lao Aviation Office** (tel. 212 140), in the terminal. Open daily 7-11:30am and 2-5pm.

Buses: Bus station (tel. 212 140), at the intersection of Thanon Sisavangvong and Visouthat, in the north end of town. Daily buses to: **Vientiane** (5 and 11am, 12hr., 7000kip; via **Thakhek** 2500kip, **Song Hong** 3500kip, **Num Thone** 4000kip, and **Nam Ngum** 6500kip); **Pakxe** (5 and 6am, 6hr., 3200kip); **Thakhek** (5am, 6hr., 1700kip); and **Lao Bao** (5am, 7hr., 2800kip). To **Vietnam: Da**

Nang (Mon., Tues., Thurs., and Sat., 2am, 16hr., 5300kip); **Hue** (Wed. and Fri., 2am, 12hr., 4000kip); and **Hanoi** (4th day of the month, 2am, 72hr., 10,700kip). Buses to the border and Vietnam fill up fast; arrive a few hours early.

Ferries: Leave from the pier next to the customs office, at the west end of Thanon Simuang at the intersection with Thanon Tha Heua. Those arriving in Laos must have a visa from the Lao embassy in Bangkok and must register at the customs office (1500kip). To: **Mukdahan,** Thailand (Mon.-Sat. 9, 10, 11am, 1:30, and 2:30pm, Sun. 10:30am, 20min., 850kip).

Local transportation: Tuk-tuks roam the streets in large numbers; from the bus station to the center of town (1000kip). To **That Inheng** (40min. each way, 4000kip round-trip) and **That Phon** (2hr., 15,000kip).

Car Rental: Savan Travel and Tour, rents sedans with driver 30,000kip per day.

Bike Rental: French Food Restaurant, 31 Thanon Chaleunmuang (tel. 212 792), next to the pier. 1000kip per day with passport deposit. **Phonepaseud Hotel** (tel. 212 258), on Thanon Santisouk. Heading north on Sisavangvong from the intersection with Thanon Oudomsin, take your first right; hotel is on the right. 1700kip per day. Inquire at your guest house for this service.

Markets: The **central market** occupies a large city block at the intersection of Thanon Oudomsin and Ratsavongseuk. Well worth a wander. Little of interest to shoppers, save a few textile stalls and jewelry shops. Large central food area, produce stalls outside carry a cornucopia of fruits and veggies, as well as fresh-baked French bread in the morning. Open daily 6am-6pm.

Swimming Pool: Across the street from Phonepaseud Hotel. A large, clean pool with slide and diving board. Open daily 6am-8pm. Admission 850kip.

Pharmacy: Pharmesco, 236/1 Thanon Ratsavongseuk (tel. 212 313). Near the market. Carries French-made anti-malarial pills. Open daily 8am-6pm.

Hospital: Savannakhet Provincial Hospital (tel. 212 131), on Thanon Khanthabouli 3 blocks south of the post office on the right. Some English spoken. In case of emergencies get to Thailand as soon as possible.

Police: (tel. 212 212), on Thanon Khanthabouli, 1 block south of the intersection with Thanon Simuang, opposite the post office. Little English spoken.

ACCOMMODATIONS

Sayamungkun Hotel, 186 Thanon Ratsavongseuk (tel. 212 426). From St. Teresia Church head east away from the river, and turn right on Ratsavongseuk. The hotel is on the right, 1 block down; an unassuming 2-story, yellow, colonial-style house with "Welcome" in vertical letters on the front gate. A rarity in Savan, this hotel combines value and character. Towering ceilings and hardwood floors; lovely 2nd-floor screened patio. Clean doubles with fan and western bathroom 4000kip, with A/C 8000kip. Owner speaks French and some English. Laundry service.

Hotel Santyphab (tel. 212 177), on Thanon Chaleunmuang. From the pier, head east, passing the French Food Restaurant; the Santyphab is on the right about 20m farther. Savan's premier backpacker lodge. Dirt cheap (or cheap dirt) room wouldn't pass Mama's white glove test, but at least the rooms are poorly lit. Great view of the river and Mukdahan, especially at sunset. With shower and western "toilet" doubles 3000kip, triples 3500kip. With A/C doubles 5000kip.

Savanbanhao Hotel, 644 Thanon Senna (tel. 212 202). Senna runs along the west side of the market. From the market head south; the hotel is two blocks on the right. Locals sometimes call it the "Silan Hotel." Popular with package tour groups; ideal place for a quick fix—doubles with A/C 5000kip, and bathroom 7000kip, plus TV and Free Willy's bathtub 8700kip. Laundry service.

FOOD

Food is certainly one of Savan's bright spots; the city is practically afloat in *pho*, or noodle soup, due to the strong Vietnamese influence. One of the most popular shops is adjacent to the Hotel Santyphab. It's usually packed from 6-9am. Large bowl 500kip; add tea 800kip. The market also boasts a large food section where vendors hawk *pho* (500kip), spring rolls (200kip each), *pho, kai ping, pho, khao jii pâté,* and other Lao and Vietnamese snacks.

Savanhlaty Food Garden, at the intersection of Thanon Simuang and Khanthabouli, just east of Hotel Santyphab. Not exactly a night market, and not exactly a restaurant either, but it has the best meal deal in town. Sit at tables surrounded by a peaceful garden, while hawkers serve you basic Thai and Lao food standbys such as fried rice (800kip), *pad thai (*800kip), and a kaleidoscopic array of savory noodle soups (600kip). Top it off with a fruit shake (300kip). Open daily 4-10pm.

French Food Restaurant, 31 Thanon Chaleunmuang (tel. 212 792). At the corner with Tha Heua close to the immigration office. Owner and chef serves up excellent Euro and Asian dishes. Popular with travelers and locals, who thump the tables and sing along drunkenly to old French ballads as the night goes on. Monstrous portions. Steak and fries 2500kip. *Sukiyaki* and Korean-style grilled beef also popular. Specialties include other-worldly *Nem Nuong* (grilled pork balls with starfruit, plantains, and veggies, wrapped in rice paper, 15-3500kip). Cannabis soup should be ordered in advance. Open daily 11am-10:30pm.

Mekong Riverside Restaurant (tel. 212 522), on Thanon Tha Heua, north of Wat Sayaphum, about 50m past the ramp going down to the river on the left. Look for the Christmas lights. Built directly out over the river bank with excellent views of Thailand and the lights of Mukdahan; this is the place to be in the evening when the sun bids a fiery farewell to the day. Sit inside or on a deck surrounded by brightly flowering tropical plants—kitschy but pleasant. Fresh river fish (2000-2500kip). Mixed seafood salad (2000kip). Open daily 10am-10pm.

SIGHTS

The city's most interesting sight is the **Savannakhet Provincial Museum** on Thanon Khanthabouli, one block south of the hospital. The front lawn of the 1920s colonial-style mansion is littered with rusting artillery pieces and the carcass of a downed warplane. The first floor of the endearingly eclectic and jumbled museum features the pride and joy of the province: the discovery of dinosaur fossils near Ban Namo east of the city. The bones were first found by a French paleontologist in the 1930s. A large room on the second floor documents the province's military history during the Vietnam War, including a large diorama of the route of Lam Son 719, a disastrous American-backed invasion of southern Laos by the South Vietnamese army in 1971. The rest of the collection documents the successes of the province (and the Party) since 1975. Savannakhet has close ties to the revolution; it was the home of Kaysone Phomvihane, first premier of the Lao PDR. The museum is usually empty and helpful curators will guide you, explaining the exhibits, most of which lack English titles. Open Mon.-Sat. 7:30am-12:30pm and 2-4pm. Admission 500kip.

The only wat of historical significance, **Wat Sayaphum,** turns 100 years old this year. On Thanon Tha Heua, north of the pier, the complex contains two main *sims,* the largest of which is a gymnasium and is decorated on the inside with murals depicting scenes from the Buddhist epic *Ramakien.* The smaller, older temple just to the right is the older of the two and is an interesting blend of Lao and Thai styles. Both buildings are encrusted with bas-reliefs..

About 15km north of the city is **That Inheng,** the city's most revered religious shrine. The gray 25m-high stupa, adorned with ascetics and fanciful creatures, is all that remains of the ancient city of Sikhottabong. Women are not permitted to enter

That Phon

About 60km south of Savan on Rte. 13 is a tall, blocky white stupa that, while not overly awe-inspiring, is sacred to the Lao. Dating from the Angkor period, the story behind its construction is perhaps one of the most unusual Buddhist anecdotes. According to legend, the Buddha was in the middle of a particularly "moving" sermon when nature's call came on strong. Not content to use the local facilities and exercising the prerogative of a major deity, he had a *naga* build a toilet for him on the spot (anyone spending some time in rural Laos can certainly sympathize). That Phon's white spire now commemorates the site, proving that perhaps someone really can "shit bricks."

That Inheng's tiny chamber, which allegedly contains the Buddha's spinal chord (alas, his backbone is nowhere in sight). An empty, crumbling cloister surrounds the stupa on three sides, surrounded by a large religious community. The road is in deplorable condition and biking is not advised

■■■ PAKXE AND THE SOUTH

After traveling literally hundreds of km against a virtually seamless backdrop of rice paddies, palm groves, and very little else, the terrain begins to change as the bus bumps and bangs its way along the final km to Pakxe. High mesa-like hills, their slopes cloaked in verdant jungle, rise in the distance, marking the foothills of the Bolovens Plateau, to the north and east of the city.

Here, in the region known as the "Emerald Triangle" (where the borders of Laos, Cambodia, and Thailand meet), the rugged natural beauty of Laos reaches a magnificent crescendo of remote mountain idylls, deep narrow gorges, and countless tiny islands populated by a rich, colorful mix of ethnic groups. The gateway to these wonders is Pakxe, a quiet port city some 680km south of Vientiane in Champassak Province. Historically, Vietnam and Cambodia have exercised an inordinate influence on the region, far more than northern Laos. In the 11th century, the Khmers built a grand temple city at Wat Phu, 40km south of Pakxe. From 1948 until 1975, Pakxe, which stands at the confluence of the Mekong and Xedone Rivers, was the capitol of the quasi-independent Kingdom of Champassak.

As the commercial and transportation hub of southern Laos, Pakxe makes an ideal base for forays into isolated Saravane and Attapu provinces to the north and east, and the "land of 4000 islands" to the south. The city itself is pleasant, but unremarkable. Enjoy its peaceful, largely car-less streets and roam the fascinating market, but don't dawdle long—the many jewels of the Emerald Triangle await.

ORIENTATION

Pakxe, the capital of Champassak Province, is 685km south of Vientiane along **Route 13,** at the confluence of the Xedone and Mekong Rivers. Most budget hotels, restaurants, and shops are clustered along several narrow streets near the central market and waterfront. The main thoroughfare does not run through the center of town but passes north of it. From the airport west of town, Rte. 13 crosses the one-way **Xedone River Bridge,** passes the Champassak Palace Hotel (formerly the palace of Prince Boun Oum), and continues east, past the stadium and the bus station about 2km east of the hotel. All of the streets have numbers as well as names; most addresses use the numbers. The NTA (National Tourism Authority) publishes a helpful map of the city, available in Vientiane or at the Champassak Palace Hotel gift shop (2000kip).

PRACTICAL INFORMATION

Tourist Office: National Tourism Authority, Champassak Province Branch, 461 Thanon 12 (tel. 212 021). Just off Rte.13 near the Xedone River, opposite the Phonsavanh Hotel. Seems to have a policy of denying information to anyone who might be a tourist. Decent English spoken by a few staff members but tour companies will probably be more helpful. Open Mon.-Sat. 8-11:30am and 2-4pm.

Immigration Office: (tel. 212 000), at the police station. Open daily 8-11am and 2-4pm. English and French spoken.

Post Office: Office of Post and Telecommunications (tel. 212 056 or 212 612; fax 212 650), on Thanon 8. From the pier and ferry, Thanon 8 begins at the Lao State Fuel Co. gas station. The post office is 50m down on the right at the intersection with Thanon 1. Open daily 8am-5pm. **Overseas telephone** and **fax** service (cash only). Open 8am-10pm. **Postal code:** 1600. **Telephone code:** 031.

Tour Companies: Inter-Lao Tourism (tel. 212 226), on Rte.13 next to the Phonsavanh Hotel. Pick-ups that seat 4 people can be rented for 38,500kip per day with driver. Open Mon.-Sat. 8am-noon and 2-5pm. **Dafi Travel and Tour,** 146/

148 Rte.13 (tel. 212 239), across from Phonsavanh Hotel. Has pick-ups and mini-buses, but rates are exorbitant. Open Mon.-Sat. 7:30am-noon and 1:30-4:30pm. **Sodetour** (tel. 212 122; fax 212 765), on Thanon 8. Past the gas station on the right. Conducts 2-day package tours of southern Laos, $500 and up for 2 people. Open Mon.-Sat. 8-11:30am and 2-4:30pm.

Embassies and Consulate: Vietnam (tel. 212 658), on Thanon 24. Heading west (toward the Xedone River) from Champassak Palace Hotel, Thanon 24 is just past Ketmany Restaurant on the right. Visas to Vietnam issued $70. Takes at least 5 days. Open Mon.-Fri. 7:30-11am and 2-4:30pm, Sat. 7:30-11am.

Currency/Exchange: Banque Pour Le Commerce Exterieur Lao (tel. 212 770; fax 212 771), at the corner of Thanon 10 and 5, opposite the market and near Pakxe Hotel. AmEx traveler's checks. Visa, MC, and AmEx cash advances. Open Mon.-Fri. 8:30am-3:30pm, Sat. 8:30-10am. For higher exchange rates (cash only), a number of **jewelry shops** near the market will exchange dollars for baht or kip.

Airport: Pakxe Airport, on Rte.13, about 1km west of the Xedone River Bridge. To: **Vientiane** (daily 10am, 1-¼hr., 74,000kip); **Savannakhet** (Mon. and Fri., 45min., 31,600kip); and **Dong Khone Island** (Thurs. and Sun., 20,450kip). **Lao Aviation office** (tel. 212 252; fax 212 751) is just before the airfield on the left. Purchase tickets up to 1 day in advance, cash only, confirm 1 day before. Open Mon.-Sat. 7-11:30am and 2-4:30pm, Sun. 7-11:30am. Take a tuk-tuk.

Buses: Pakxe Bus Station (tel. 212 428), on Rte. 13 about 2km east of Champassak Palace Hotel, past the stadium on the left. To: **Vientiane** (daily 6, 7, and 8am, dry season 13hr., rainy season 18hr., 11,000kip); **Savannakhet** (daily 5 and 6am, 6hr., 3,200kip); **Champassak** (daily 9 and 10am, 1hr., 700kip); **Saravane** (daily 7, 9, and 11am, 2hr., 1500kip); **Attapu** (daily 8am, dry season 5hr., rainy season 12hr., 3000kip, includes ferry across the river); and **Khong Island** (daily 6 and 7am, 5hr., 1500kip, includes ferry). **Songthaews** leave frequently for **Pakxong** (1hr., 1000kip). Catch the ferry and cross the river, where **songthaews** make the 45min. trip to the **Vang Tao/Chong Mek** border crossing (660kip). **Share taxis** (1000kip per person) also make the trip. Songthaews and taxis leave about 400m up the road from the pier.

Ferries: Car and truck ferries run between Pakxe and the opposite bank (approximately every 15min., first boat 7am, 1000kip). To **Champassak,** taxi boats leave from the waterfront area near the ferry to the other side of the river (1hr., 500kip). No set schedule, the first boat usually leaves at 8am. Get there early since the seats fill up fast.

Market: The **central market** sprawls over a large block in the middle of town. Open daily 6am-6pm. A second, smaller market sells mostly food and produce next to the bus station on Rte. 13. Open 6am-7pm.

Pharmacy: Phone Souk Pharmacie, 33 Thanon 5 (tel. 212 440). Carries anti-malarial drugs. Open daily 7:30am-8pm.

Hospital: (tel. 212 042; 212 041 **emergency**), opposite the market across from Pakxe Hotel. A small **pharmacy** to the right of the entrance. Open 7am-10pm.

Police: (tel. 212 145), on Thanon 10 directly across the street from the northeast end of the market.

ACCOMMODATIONS

As the gateway to gorgeous southern Laos, Pakxe supports a number of hotels, most of which are empty nearly all of the time. The budget digs are all within a five-minute walking radius of the center of town.

Pakse Hotel, 112/113 Thanon 5 (tel. 212 131). It's the hulking yellow monstrosity in the center of town opposite the market. Rooms are bright and clean with towering ceilings. Singles with fan 4400kip, with A/C 6400kip and up. Doubles with fan and private bath (western toilet) begin at 6400kip, with A/C 8800kip; price goes up with size and other perks in the room. Laundry service.

Phonsavanh Hotel, 294 Rte. 13 (tel. 212 842). At the western end of Rte. 13, on the right just before the Xedone River Bridge; near Wat Luang. A basic budget motel. Rooms are a bit shabby but the congenial manager keeps them clean.

Cramped, spartan singles with fan 4000kip. Doubles with more elbow room 5000kip. Triples with sink 6000kip. All have shared bathrooms. Laundry service.

Saksumran Hotel, Thanon 10 (tel. 212 002), on the corner, across a small park from Wat Luang. Almost 3 years old, Saksumran still retains that "new" look. Rooms are neat and clean, but scrunched and bare for the price—you pay for the A/C and hot water that graces every room. Singles 10,000kip, doubles 12,000kip. Laundry service. Upscale restaurant (by Pakxe standards) next door.

FOOD

Despite southern Laos' growing popularity with tourists, Pakxe has yet to develop a decent restaurant scene. Bring your appetite for *pho* soup. Pakxe has the largest Vietnamese population in Laos and *pho* shops are everywhere. There may not be much variety but at least you can eat cheaply. The **central market** features a cavernous food vending pavilion selling *kai ping, khao niaw,* fried fish, spring rolls, and enough noodle soup to refill the Grand Canyon.

Sedone Restaurant, 110 Thanon 5 (tel. 212 155). Two shops down from Pakse Hotel opposite the market. A pleasant cafe-style restaurant; the lengthy page-and-a-half menu is about a page and a half longer than most in town. Tasty Lao, Thai, and Vietnamese dishes 500-1000kip for regular size portions, 1000-1500kip for bigger portions. Fried rice with veggies 700kip, with meat 800kip. *Tom yam plaa* (1000kip). Fried or fresh spring rolls (1000kip). Open daily 6am-10pm.

Ketmany Restaurant, 227 Rte. 13 (tel. 212 615), at the end of the long block west of Champassak Palace Hotel, equidistant between the palace and Xedone River. As trendy as Pakxe gets—Ace of Base throbs on the stereo while teens eat ice cream and watch Thai-dubbed American movies. Check out the psychedelic Buddhist shrine above the door. Does brisk business in *pho* (500kip). Iced Ovaltine (300kip). Small baked goods selection. Ice cream 500kip. Open daily 8am-5pm.

Dornsokdee Restaurant, 94/95 Thanon 6 (tel. 212 332). From Pakse Hotel follow the sidewalk around the block; the restaurant is on the opposite side, near the Thanon 10 intersection. Sit at tables set out on the sidewalk and chat with the owner's myna birds who boast an impressive vocabulary—after all, if they don't learn quick they might become grilled partridge (1000kip). Specializes in *sukiyaki* (5000kip, feeds 3-4), "instant *sukiyaki*" is really just *pho* in disguise (1000kip, feeds 1). Most dishes 1000-2000kip. Open daily 11am-11pm.

SIGHTS

Pakxe itself offers little in the way of attractions save the stunning natural scenery. The city's principal wat, **Wat Luang,** erected on the east bank of the Xedone River in 1830, is worth a visit, if only as an example of renovation gone awry. The temple, which stands at the west end of Rte. 13 just before the bridge, was refurbished in 1991, and the lovely carved original wooden doors and shutters are almost lost in a swarm of brightly painted, cartoonish reliefs and gaudy *nagas.* A large golden Buddha dominates the interior, an island of serenity in a writhing mess of plaster kitsch.

At the top of a small hill on Rte. 13 in the middle of town is one of the most bizarre landmarks in Laos, the **Palace of Boun Oum,** former residence of the prince of Champassak. Construction of the massive six-story palace began in 1969, and was not yet completed when the communists deposed the prince in 1975. Until recently the structure stood in its unfinished state; it now houses the Champassak Palace Hotel (basic singles start at $40 per night). Visitors can take the elevator to the top floor to take in the **truly awesome view** of the Bolovens Plateau, whose table-top flat hills rise to the north and east, while the city spreads out like a diorama below.

During the colonial years, Pakxe was a French outpost and a number of fine **colonial buildings** remain, in varying stages of decay. The best examples are near the river along Thanon 8, 1, and 10. In the evening, the point just beyond the post office along the river bank is a superb spot to watch the **sunset.**

Whether or not you intend to buy anything, Pakxe's **gargantuan covered market** is well worth a browse—it may well be the best "sight" in town. The first floor overflows with everything the well-equipped backpacker needs: antler horn extract for the libido, imitation Soviet watches, and puffed shrimp chips of an unnatural pastel hue. Upstairs is solely fabric and clothing, with cotton prints but no silk. Produce, electronic, and toy stalls crowd the lot outside. There's so much "local color" here that even the baby chickens come in different colors (green, pink, or yellow, 100kip each). Buy a string of live toads (300kip) to plop a few in your traveling companion's *pho* when he or she isn't not looking.

Lying 13km west of town off Rte. 13 is the weaving village of **Ban Saphay,** renowned for its *ikat* silk and *mat-mi* cotton cloth. The patterns tend to be more complex, with brighter colors than northern weavings. You won't find the cloth in the local market—most of it is sold wholesale, but two shops along the main road carry a large assortment of fabrics, sold by the meter, with a few ready-made garments. One is operated by the **Lao Women's Union,** but the privately owned **Lao Home-made Silk Skirt Shop** (nary a skirt in sight) carries a better selection. *Mat-mi* cotton begins at about 7000kip per meter, *ikat* silk at 3000kip per meter. To get to Ban Saphay, take a tuk-tuk from the central market (30min., 4000kip).

■ NEAR PAKXE

WAT PHU

The small town of **Champassak** lies 38km down river from Pakxe, sandwiched between the Mekong and a string of steep, craggy limestone hills. The town itself would hardly be worth a visit were it not for the ruins of an ancient Khmer temple 7km to the south. Known as **Wat Phu** (Hill Temple), or simply Muang Kao (Old City), many structures are still in good condition, and it is considered one of the finest examples of Khmer art outside Cambodia.

Archaeologists believe that the site might date back to the 6th century, during the Chenla period. Wat Phu itself was built at the end of the 11th century by King Suryavarman II, when the power of the Angkor court was at its zenith. The temple bears many stylistic similarities to Angkor Wat, King Suryavarman's *magnum opus,* and may actually have served as a model or trial run for Angkor Wat.

Following the sacking of Angkor Thom in the 13th century Wat Phu was abandoned to the jungle until a French expedition "rediscovered" the complex in 1866. Today the temple is in desperate need of renovation; to this end UNESCO is planning a major project. Be aware that some of the walls are not entirely stable, and exercise caution when poking around the ruins; a three-ton laterite block landing on your head might obligate you to unbutton your fly to wipe your nose.

The temple access road skirts a large man-made lake or *baray,* which symbolized the waters of the earth and also helped irrigate the surrounding rice fields. Originally visitors would enter the complex by crossing a long causeway lined with *naga* balustrades, as at Angkor Wat. Today the causeway is fenced off. Two large rectangular galleries—the one on the right made of laterite, the one on the left of sandstone—stand on either side of the entrance. Lintels above the entrances depict Kala, the Hindu god of time, a sea monster with writhing serpents streaming from his mouth.

At the top of a series of moss-covered laterite tiers is the small, almost delicate central sanctuary, an example of Khmer art and architecture at its best. Lithe *apsarases,* the celestial nymphs synonymous with Khmer sculpture, grace both sides of the entrance. Above it, a perfectly preserved lintel depicts Vishnu the Destroyer astride his trademark three-headed elephant. The temple has been reconsecrated to Buddhism and now a large, rather incongruous Buddha sits where the *lingga* once did.

Take a few minutes before descending to admire the tremendous view of the perfectly symmetrical temple complex, and, beyond it, acres of emerald rice fields and the silvery band of the Mekong River. The Bolovens Plateau, which from a distance looks like a massive purple wall, looms on the horizon. The temple complex is open daily 8am-4:30pm. Admission 300kip, with camera an additional 700kip, though the ruins are a good 500m from the pavilion and nobody checks. (For more on Khmer art, see Cambodia "Architecture" on page 71 and Angkor "History" on page 96.)

Wat Phu is easily visited as a daytrip from Pakxe. Champassak is accessible by bus and boat from Pakxe. The latter is by far the more relaxing and scenic of the two options as the Mekong passes picturesque hills and limestone cliffs. Boats bound for Champassak leave when they are full from the area just upriver from the ferry landing. The trip takes about an hour and a half; standard fare 500kip. Buses leave from the station on Rte. 13 (9 and 10am, 1hr., 700kip). The boats and buses should drop you off outside **Hotel Sala Wat Phou,** Champassak's one and only hotel. Singles with fan 12,000kip, with A/C 18,000kip. Doubles with fan 18,000kip, with A/C 21,000 kip. Insist on big discounts (7000kip for a single with fan) during the low season. Motorized cyclos can be hired to go the rest of the way to Wat Phu for 4000kip round-trip. The hotel rents bicycles for 3000kip, but plan on spending the night if you wish to ride to the temple. To get to Wat Phu, head south (downriver) along the main dirt road through Champassak and past several rice fields. The large reservoir and the gates of a more recent temple will be visible to the right after about 7km. Ask a local for directions: *"Muang Kao yoo-sai?"*

As of this writing, there were no buses to Pakxe after noon; however, boats heading upriver are frequent. There is no main landing; boats normally stop at the landing near Hotel Sala Wat Phou and about 1km farther upstream. The trip back upriver takes about 45 minutes longer and costs 500kip.

THAD LO

Set amidst the stunning backdrop of the Bolovens Plateau, 90km northeast of Pakxe, is idyllic Thad Lo. Built on a bend in the Xedone River, downstream from a series of tumbling waterfalls, the area is downright utopian, where travelers can soak road-weary bodies in fantastic natural swimming pools/jacuzzis, explore ethnic villages, or just kick back in gorgeous, though pricey, riverside bungalows, lulled to sleep by crashing waterfalls.

The handful of collapsing bamboo huts clustered along the main road to Saravane where the bus will drop you off is unimpressive. Patience. About 1km down a dirt road (follow the signs), is charming Thad Lo village, where the decidedly un-shy inhabitants will greet arriving *farang* with broad smiles and cheerful *"sabai-dees!"* Continuing through the village and bearing right takes you to a small bridge just below Thad Heng falls. A path to the left of the bridge leads to **Thad Lo Resort,** a collection of bungalows grouped around a large main lodge. The six-year-old government-run resort is in excellent condition and the location is enchanting. Unfortunately, a night in this little corner of paradise, as elsewhere in the Bolovens region, isn't cheap. Two-bed bungalows (with electricity and western bathroom) start at 12,000kip. More lavishly furnished bungalows across the river, literally within spitting distance of the falls, cost 24,000kip. The open-sided lodge with high ceilings, wicker furniture, and bamboo bar is a classic tropical hangout. Slightly cheaper rooms can be had at the **Saise Guest House** across the bridge. Clean simple rooms with fan (bathroom outside) 10,000kip for one person, a ridiculous 20,000kip for two. Demand discounts or head for the resort and pay 2000kip more for nicer digs.

The Thad Lo Resort has a Land Rover for exploring the surrounding countryside. A more exotic, if slightly hokey, option is to get around by elephant (3000kip per person per hr.). An hour trek on one of the slightly cantankerous pachyderms will take you past Thad Lo, the upper falls, and across the river to an Alak animist village.

Thad Lo can be visited in a daytrip from Pakxe if you leave early (first bus departs Pakxe 7am, 2hr., 1200kip). Arriving at 9am, there is plenty of time for an elephant foray, an exploration of the falls, a swim, and lunch at a noodle shop in the village or at the Resort's pricey restaurant (1200-3000kip). Truck-buses pass through Thad Lo on their way to Saravane. The last official bus to Pakxe reaches Thad Lo at 2pm. It is possible to obtain transport from Pakxe-bound trucks, but there are no guarantees.

THE BOLOVENS PLATEAU

The ruggedly beautiful, isolated, and somewhat mysterious **Bolovens Plateau,** which rises dramatically to the north and east of Pakxe, is certainly one of Southeast

Asia's last frontiers, still largely untainted by environmental desecration or tourist proliferation. Physically, its natural splendors are unsurpassed; the region is laced with white-water rivers, steep, narrow gorges, and remote valleys. The plateau is home to a plethora of ethnic minorities, many of whom were forced to flee their ancestral homelands in the Annamite Cordillera near the Lao-Vietnamese border during relentless American bombing campaigns in the 60s and early 70s. Among the larger groups are Ngai, Suk, Katou, and Alak. Most are animists and still practice shamanism in villages largely untouched by the long arm of modernity. Finally, the Bolovens Plateau possesses some of the world's most fertile soil, and is one of Laos' agricultural centers. Tea, coffee, fruit, and cardamom are grown in abundance on plantations founded by French *colons* at the turn of the century.

This vast plateau stretches across the provinces of Champassak, Saravane, and Attapu; its primary towns are **Saravane** and **Tataeng,** about 100km northeast of Pakxe, and **Pakxong** just 50km to the east of Pakxe. Both Saravane and Pakxong are readily accessible by bus and songthaew from Pakxe. Along the "Coffee Road" to Pakxong is **Tad Phi,** a 120-m-long cascade (one of the biggest in Southeast Asia). Several Katou and Alak villages dot the landscape in this vicinity.

From Tataeng, in Saravane Province, just south of the capital city of the same name, it is possible to take boats down the Khong River to **Attapu,** passing through mountain gorges as spectacular and inviolable as any in the world. As of this writing, there were no regularly scheduled buses to Tataeng from Pakxe. Travel conditions in Laos are changing at warp speed, however, so check at the bus station. If not, you will need to take a bus to Saravane city and then transfer to Tataeng. Until recently, independent travel in south Laos was banned completely and no one ever accused the Bolovens Plateau of being an easy place for *farangs* to explore. Travel here requires time, patience, flexibility, and cash, as many towns with accommodations are used to only package tour group customers and charge high rates for simple, at times rudimentary, rooms. Nevertheless, the rewards for those who come are more than worth the price. As Laos' draconian tourism regulations and transportation infrastructure improve, the Bolovens Plateau will become a hot tourist attraction and a prime locale for industries eager to take advantage of its myriad natural resources. But for now, the plateau remains a bastion of unsullied natural splendor ripe for exploration and adventure.

THE 4000 ISLANDS REGION

As the Mekong winds its way south from Pakxe it undergoes a Jekyll to Hyde transformation from lethargic, mild-mannered river to raging, white-water torrent. Here, in the extreme southern tip of Laos over 140km south of Pakxe, the river widens to as much as 10km from bank to bank, while at other times surges through a series of dramatic cataracts on its way to the Cambodian border. Thousands of small islets, many of which are only above water during the winter, dot the complex web of branches and tributaries the Mekong becomes, earning the region its nickname: **Sii Phan Don,** meaning 4000 islands.

The largest island, and the most logical starting point for explorations of the region, is **Don Khong.** There are several hotels in Muang Khoune, the island's main village, accessible by ferry from the town of **Ban Hat Xay Khoune** on Rte. 13. From Don Khong, boats brave the south to **Don Khone** at the southwest tip of which is **Li Phi Falls,** one of the area's two major waterfalls. Don Khone is notable as there is a small, 5-km railroad line (now inoperable) built by the French to bypass the un-navigable stretch of rapids. South of Don Khone, off Rte. 13, is **Khong Pha Phing,** the "Voice of the Mekong," a spectacular cascade that is the **largest in Southeast Asia.**

The 4000 island region is targeted for tourist development, and the accommodation scene is changing rapidly; check with tour companies in Vientiane or in Muang Khoune for the latest information. **Buses** run daily between Pakxe and Muang Khoune (daily 6 and 7am, 5hr., 1500kip, ferry included). **Lao Aviation** also flies to Don Khong airfield (Thurs. and Sun., 24,500kip).

PENINSULAR MALAYSIA

The beguiling scent of modernization fills the air and dusts the streets of Malaysian cities as the country flexes its economic muscles to leap frog over its Southeast Asian counterparts into the 21st century. For first-time visitors a preponderance of English-speaking Malays is a welcome result of this development. Even in rural areas, lost travelers sporting their most endearing helpless look may find English-speaking aid on its way. However, economic success also makes for high designer-label costs and conspires with basic Islamic notions about propriety to make neat dress mandatory for tourists within Malay borders. Islam is a powerful force in Malaysian life, especially on the more conservative east coast, where hotel rooms often come complete with signs pointing toward Mecca. Travelers should be particularly sensitive in regard to local, religious, and cultural taboos.

Despite its booming economy, Malaysia is still predominantly well-suited to budget travel. Although Pulau Langkawi and Taman Negara National Park cater to a higher-class Malaysian and Singaporean clientele, the average cost of living for budget travelers in Malaysia is probably just a little higher than in Thailand.

How does the traveler to Peninsular Malaysia plan an itinerary? Going from north to south or vice versa is the obvious solution, but you may be constrained to choose either the east- or west-coast route. The inland rainforest mountain ranges allow few crossing points in between. Concentrating on one coast and taking in the best sights can realistically be accomplished in two weeks or less. This makes for a truly difficult decision—the west coast has historic Melaka and Penang, the capital city Kuala Lumpur, and the beautiful island of Langkawi. The east coast is more sedate and representative of traditional Malay culture, particularly Kota Bharu; peaceful fishing villages dot the hundreds of kilometers of clean beaches along the South China Sea, and the gorgeous Perhentian and Tioman Islands provide an idyllic escape. Another important stop is Taman Negara, the largest national park in the country, renowned for its appeal to experienced jungle trekkers and trekking novices alike.

ESSENTIALS

GEOGRAPHY

Malaysia's 13 states cover 329,750sq. km of land stretching from the isthmus of southern Thailand to the island of Singapore, just across the narrow straits of Melaka from the Indonesian island of Sumatra. The country then hops over and picks up the states of Sabah and Sarawak which share the island of Borneo with Brunei and the Indonesian state of Kalimantan. To get a picture of Malaysia's size, imagine taking New Mexico from opposite corners and stretching it until it was shaped like a giant smile, with a few missing teeth in the middle (to represent the ocean).

WHEN TO GO

Rain is one of the biggest factors for traveling in Malaysia. If you dig wearing a poncho and think that rain is, in fact, a romantic, life-giving force, then you may want to plan accordingly. The rainy season in Malaysia differs from coast to coast. On the east, rain storms hit most frequently between November and February, and on the west coast the rains are less frequent and less intense but generally last from May to September. Schools go on vacation from late February to early March, mid-May to early June, early August to mid-August, and late October to early December; popular tourist destinations tend to fill up faster during these times.

■■■ GETTING AROUND

BY PLANE

Airport tax is RM5 on domestic, RM20 on international flights. From the **Subang Kuala Lumpur International Airport,** Malaysia Airlines (the national carrier) flies to 95 locations in Malaysia and worldwide. For flight info, call 746 1014.

BY BUS OR TRAIN

Both A/C and non-A/C **buses** run between major towns at reasonable prices. Fares are higher for express buses and vary with distance. **Malayan Railways,** or Keretapi Tanah Melayu Berhad (KTM), runs throughout Peninsular Malaysia, but service is much more developed for west coast travel. KTM railpasses allow unlimited travel on passenger trains in Malaysia and Singapore for 10 days (US$55, children 4-12 US$28) or 30 days (US$120, children 4-12 US$60). For those under 30 with an ISIC, YIEE Card, or Youth Hostel Card, a 7-day KTM pass is US$32. The **jungle train** from Jeantut to Wakaf Baru, near Kota Bharu, is a slow, but scenic touristic option.

BY CAR

Inter-city **taxis** connect all major towns and cities; they are shared-fare, taking 4 passengers (fares are fixed, and a private cab costs more). Local taxis are sometimes unmetered, in which case you should agree on a price beforehand—the driver will often quote you a figure before you get in, giving you a chance to decline politely. Metered cabs are RM1.50 for the first 2km and increase by RM0.10 per 200m. Additional surcharges apply for taxis booked by phone (RM10), trips between midnight and 7am (50%), and trips carrying 3 (RM0.20) or 4 (RM0.40) passengers.

To **rent a car,** you must have an international driver's permit or a license issued by your government to drive in Malaysia. In addition to rental companies, some hotels rent cars. Expect to pay RM70-RM200. Remember that vehicles drive on the left side of the road, and that, by law, the driver and all front-seat passengers must wear seatbelts. Rains in the monsoon season may make east coast travel difficult.

■■■ MONEY

US$1=RM2.50 (ringgit)	**RM1=US$0.401**
CDN$1=RM1.835	**RM1=CDN$0.545**
UK£1=RM3.877	**RM1=UK£0.258**
IR£1=RM3.952	**RM1=IR£0.253**
AUS$1=RM1.839	**RM1=AUS$0.544**
NZ$1=RM1.636	**RM1=NZ$0.611**
SARand1=RM0.682	**RM1=SARand1.465**

The legal tender for Malaysia is the **ringgit,** and comes in denominations of RM1, 5, 10, 20, 50, 100, 500, and 1000. Each ringgit is divided into 100 **sen,** which are issued in coins of 1, 5, 10, 20, and 50 sen. There are also bulky RM1 coins. A 10% service charge is automatically added to most restaurant and hotel bills, so **tipping** is not considered necessary. On the other hand, it's not considered rude either, so feel free to do so if service is exceptional.

■■■ KEEPING IN TOUCH

The Malaysian **postal system** does quality work. Airmail across the globe should take under one week, but larger parcels may take up to two weeks. The important

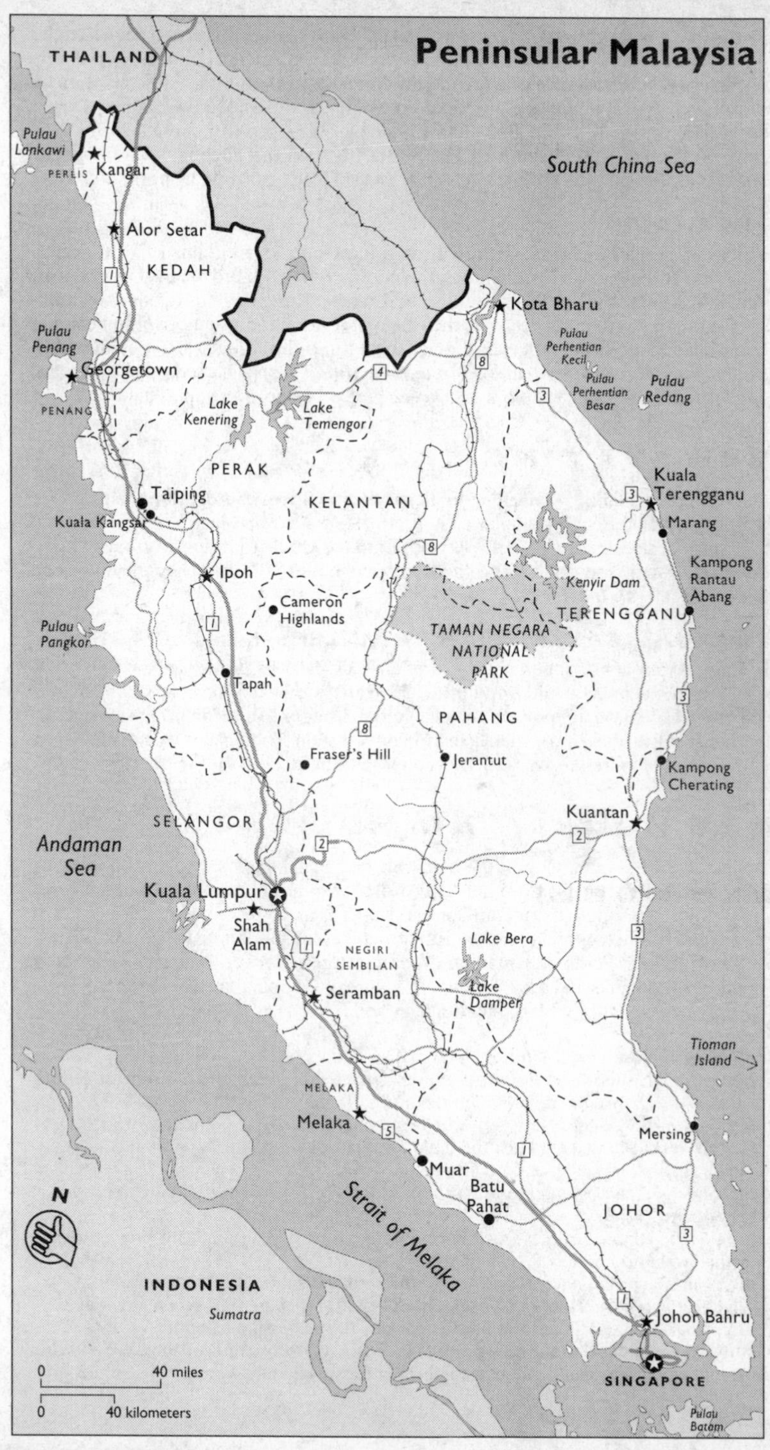
Peninsular Malaysia
THAILAND
South China Sea
Pulau Lankawi
PERLIS
Kangar
Alor Setar
KEDAH
Kota Bharu
Pulau Penang
Georgetown
PENANG
Lake Kenering
Lake Temengor
Pulau Perhentian Kecil
Pulau Perhentian Besar
Pulau Redang
PERAK
Taiping
Kuala Kangsar
KELANTAN
Kuala Terengganu
Marang
Ipoh
Kenyir Dam
Kampong Rantau Abang
Cameron Highlands
TERENGGANU
Pulau Pangkor
TAMAN NEGARA NATIONAL PARK
Tapah
PAHANG
Fraser's Hill
Jerantut
Kampong Cherating
SELANGOR
Kuantan
Andaman Sea
Kuala Lumpur
Shah Alam
NEGIRI SEMBILAN
Lake Bera
Lake Damper
Seramban
Tioman Island
MELAKA
Melaka
Mersing
Muar
Batu Pahat
JOHOR
Strait of Melaka
N
INDONESIA
Sumatra
Johor Bahru
SINGAPORE
0 40 miles
0 40 kilometers
Pulau Batam

part is that it will almost definitely reach its final destination. Malaysia's **country telephone code is 66.** *Let's Go* lists telephone codes in the Practical Information section of each city. Long-distance calls are usually easiest at card-phones; cards can often be purchased at local telephone offices or convenience stores. **Home Country Direct Numbers:** British Telecom, 800-0044. Canada Direct, 800-0017. New Zealand Telecom, 60 700 6401. Telecom Australia, 800-0061. Telecom Eireann, 800-0053. Telekom South Africa, 800-0027. US: AT&T, 800-0011; MCI, 800-0012; Sprint, 800-0016.

THE MEDIA

Across Malaysia English-language DJ's crank out music programs of all varieties. Only one of the 3 major TV channels, the commercial TV3, broadcasts in more than occasional English, with British series and Chinese Kung-Fu films (frequently interspersed with ads to compete with the other government-run stations.) You can get English-language newspapers and magazines throughout Malaysia, including *The New Straits Times, The Business Times, The Malay Mail,* an afternoon paper, and *The Star,* a weekly news tabloid. *Asiaweek* is also available most places.

■■■ STAYING SAFE

One thing is certain: **"Trafficking in illegal drugs carries the death penalty."** This warning, and others very similar to it, are plastered across Malaysian tourist literature, and for good reason—Malaysia does not take kindly to drugs. Don't use them, don't buy them, and don't bring them into the country. **The emergency number for all of Malaysia is tel. 999.**

BISEXUAL, GAY, LESBIAN TRAVELERS

Homosexuality is no longer a criminal offense in Malaysia; however, just two years ago homosexual acts could bring up to 20 years in prison and/or whipping. Open displays of affection are not a good idea, and neither is discussing homosexuality; it is a taboo topic both in the media and in conversation. For Malays, legally subject to Islamic law, open homosexuality is even more difficult than for the traveler.

■■■ HOURS AND HOLIDAYS

Businesses are generally open 9:30am-7pm, but banks only stay open until about 3pm, and supermarkets and other large stores may not close until 10pm. Government offices are open about 8am-1pm and 2-4:15pm. In most parts of the country offices and businesses are closed on Sunday, and close at noon or 1pm on Saturdays. In Johor, Kedah, Perlis, Kelantan, and Terengganu, however, buildings are closed on Friday, and banks and government offices are often open half-days on Thursdays.

Approximate dates of Malaysian holidays and festivals in 1996 include:

January 1: New Year's Day.
January: Thaipusam, in honor of Hindu deity Lord Subramanian. A day of repentance and thanksgiving, in which devotees pierce various body parts.
February 19: Chinese New Year, a 15-day lunar festival.
March 1: Hari Raya Aidil Fitri, the end of Ramadan.
May 1: Labor Day.
May: Wesak Day, commemorating the Buddha's birth, death, and enlightenment.
May-June: Hari Raya Aidil Adha, a Muslim day of sacrifice.
June 5: the King's birthday; mostly celebrated in Kuala Lumpur with processions.
June: Awal Muharam.
July: Hari Raya Haji. Pilgrims celebrate the return from the Hajj to Mecca.
July: Festival of the Hungry Ghosts. Candles with faces are burned on street altars.
July: Maal Hiraj, commemorating the first day of the Muslim calender.
August: Mooncake/Lantern Festival. Marks the overthrow of the Mongols with the exchange of mooncakes and the lighting of festive lanterns.

August 22: Maulid Nabi Muhammad (birthday of Muhammad).
August 31: Hari Kebangsaan, or National Day.
October: Kiew Ong Yeah, involves mediums supposedly possessed by spirits of the 9 emperor gods, and culminates with a fire-walking ritual
November: Deepavali, a Hindu festival of lights.
December 25: Christmas Day.

■■■ POTPOURRI FOR $100, ALEX!

Malaysia is **8 hrs. ahead of GMT.** This puts Malaysia one hour ahead of Thailand to the north and Sumatra to the south, which can be confusing for border crossings.

A few common geographical terms can come in handy, especially since *Let's Go* uses them. **Pulau** is an island; and on that pulau, each beach is a **pantai,** each bay is a **teluk,** and each hill is a **bukit.** Large cities often have **kota** (or city) preceding their name, such as Kota Bharu, small villages are **kampung,** like Kampung Juara. **Kuala,** as in Kuala Lumpur, means river estuary, and **kra** is, of course, both a crab-eating Macaque and the peninsula that includes Southern Thailand, Malaysia, and Singapore. Most streets in Malaysia are labeled **jalan** (abbreviated Jl.), as in Jalan Laksamana or Jl. Merdeka, and many (such as Jalan Hospital) are named after an important location on the road. Many smaller side-streets, often called **lorongs,** share the name of the larger road they stem from. Both small and large streets are also sometimes called **lebuh,** like Lebuh Chulia. Most important of all, however, is **cinta,** or love.

LIFE AND TIMES

■■■ HISTORY

For thousands of years the Malaysian peninsula, or **Malaya,** has been crisscrossed by traders and navigators who left behind a unique conglomerate of cultures and a multi-layered ethnic diversity. As with much of the region, writing a complete history of modern Malaysia would mean incorporating the histories of countless empires which seem to have had no respect for modern colonialist borders. Tragically, this makes it unreasonably difficult for editors of Southeast Asian guidebooks to write concise histories of contemporary boundary-defined nations.

The peninsula's first inhabitants, the aboriginal Malays, or **Orang Asli,** (Authentic People), probably arrived more than 10,000 years ago. The ancestors of the **Ethnic Malays,** the proto-Malays, probably arrived around 6000 years later, perhaps from southern China. Most of Malaysia's pre-history, however, is simply conjecture.

EARLY KINGDOMS

From at least the first centuries AD, the **Straits of Melaka** have linked China and India through trade. Control of these ports was a boon for local rulers on the west peninsular coast and Northern Sumatra, while the Orang Asli of the interior remained relatively isolated. Throughout the 4th, 5th, and 6th centuries Malaysia's resources, gold and tin, were highly sought after, and its ease of access by water provided safety while nomadic hordes in Central Asia ravaged overland trade routes. Through these early years of trade, the northern states of the peninsula, extending south about as far as Kedah, were loosely known as the **Langkasuka** kingdom. Subsequent contact with Indian traders brought strong cultural and religious traditions to the peninsula including Hinduism, Buddhism, Brahman priests, and a hereditary dynasty of divine kings. The Sumatran state of **Srivijaya,** which encompassed Malaya from the 7th century until the rise of **Melaka** almost 800 years later, spread this Indic influence throughout Southeast Asia; the empire was ruled by Indian style Maharajas and was a revered center of Buddhist thought (See Indonesia: History).

After buttressing attacks from both India and Siam around the end of the first millennium the Srivijayan empire weakened, leaving Malaya as fragmented states under the nominal rule of the Javanese **Majapahit** empire. This regional subservience ended with the establishment of Melaka in early 15th century, and the factors of its founding reveal the complex stew of interaction within Southeast Asia. According to 15th century writings a Malay prince, **Sri Paremesvara,** was fleeing the wrath of local Majapahit rulers in Java as well as his own Javanese father-in-law. Upon reaching modern day Singapore, Paremesvara made alliances with the small kingdoms in the archipelago and killed the governing Thai vassal, but was soon driven to the north by reinforcements from Siam. Founding Melaka in legendary style (see Melaka), Paremesvara was supported by both the **Orang Laut** (literally, sea people, also known as sea gypsies) who controlled the straights, and the Ming Dynasty in China, who saw Melaka's position on the straights as an excellent opportunity to monitor sea traffic. Protected by its large neighbors to the northeast, Melaka quickly grew as a naval port and trading center; as it grew, the powers of the Majapahit empire continued to wane.

THE RISE OF ISLAM

As with any good story the happy ending was just a beginning. Paremesvara converted to **Islam,** and was renamed **Iskandar Shah** to accompany a marriage alliance with the Muslim ruler of the Sumatran state of Pasai. The incredible spread of Islam among the Malay thus began with his reign. Conflicts after his death regarding whether Islam or the Indic influences would prevail in Melaka eventually led to the ascension of **Muzaffar Shah,** a devout Muslim. Melaka was declared a Muslim state, and Muzaffar refused to pay the traditional tribute to the Buddhist Thai kingdom. Under the leadership of his Prime Minister, **Tun Perak,** Melaka pushed the Thai vassals off of the peninsula. By the reign of Melaka's last shah, **Mahmud Shah,** at the end of the 15th century, Melaka's domain included all of Peninsular Malaysia, Singapore, and parts of Thailand and Northern Sumatra

The western "age of exploration" brought the ever-diplomatic Europeans to the region, but the **Portuguese** invasion in 1511, along with their occupation of Melaka did little to keep the Orang Laut or the rest of the peninsula from being faithful to the Shah dynasty, who fled south and established the state of **Johor.** The Muslim Indonesian state of **Aceh** began vying for trade ports as well, creating a three-way foundation of war and intrigue. The two outside forces and the state of Johor twisted and turned for over a century. In 1699, however, the last true heir of the Melakan ruling family, a cruel Marquis De Sade type, was killed by his own well-meaning court. Although perhaps understandable, the assassination of a member of the dynasty, still believed to be divine, was considered a terrible act against God. The Malay world did in fact fall into greater and greater disarray through the 18th century. Chaos and piracy in the straight marked the next hundred years, and the lack of order brought the kingdoms of the Buginese and Minangkabu north from Sulawesi and Sumatra. These new forces set up powerful states on the peninsula and competed with both the Sultan of Johor and the **Dutch**, who had replaced Portugal in Melaka during the late 1600's. In the north, the Thai kingdom continued its pressure for tribute and territory as well.

COLONIAL RULE

The Dutch ceded the island of **Penang** to the **British** at the end of the 18th century as independent traders formed ties with local rulers. So began the stabilizing, but oppressive, colonial presence in Malaya. The primary city of Penang, **Georgetown,** imported the teachings of Adam Smith, and absorbed regional trade quickly, upsetting both the Thai and the Dutch. Through political alliances and entrepreneurial maneuvering the British eventually moved into Melaka, Indonesia, and Singapore. It was only with this intervention that modern Indonesia and Malaysia became formally differentiated, through the famous **Anglo-Dutch Treaty of 1874.** The kingdom states of Malaysia fell under British eye, and Sumatra under Dutch. With the

Treaty of Pangkor British power was strengthened, as the southern states acquired British "counselors" who dealt out indirect rule. By World War I, Malaysia had been divided into five federated and four non-federated states. More independent, but less developed, than the five federated states, the four states to the north politely declined counselors, after being nominally transferred to Britain by Thailand. However, in 1919, the last of these states, Terengganu, was compelled to accept a powerless, but symbolic, British General Adviser. Colonial occupation of Malaysia continued until World War II and was marked by economic advances as well as uprisings and subsequent suppressions. More subtle anti-colonialist feeling was growing, and throughout the 20s and 30s the Malay press and intelligentsia began to increase political consciousness, creating small political organizations which educated individuals to anti-colonialist possibilities, especially as they related to current Islamic thought from the Middle East and Turkey.

FORGING A NATION

During WWII the **Japanese** moved swiftly into Malaysia, returning the northern states to Thailand and exploiting Malaya's resources and strategic location. With the end of the war, a few years later, the British, who had turned tail and left the country defenseless, came back but were unable to return the country to its former docility. Protests began from politically active movements in reaction to decades of direct outside interference as well as the Japanese's inspiring, if hollow, anti-colonialist rhetoric. In the late 1940s, **UMNO, the United Malay National Organization,** formed to combat the unacceptable British plan for refederation and forced a continuing dialogue. This led to an increasing frequency of local elections in the 1950's. The military arm of the **Malay Communist Party** added guerilla tactics and other violent forms of pressure which, although not politically popular, kept Malaya in a state of emergency throughout the decade and created incredible difficulties for the British. The steady movement toward independence culminated on **August 31, 1957,** with the establishment of the independent **Federated States of Malaya.**

The 1960s provided a rollercoaster of excitement for the newly independent country. Joining with Singapore and the states of Sabah and Sarawak on Borneo, Malaya put together a complicated package of immigration rights and ethnic balance, as well as an "si", to become Malaysia on September 16, 1963. This infuriated Malaysia's new international neighbors as the Philippines were holding onto an ancient claim to Sabah, and Indonesia believed Malaya's action to be covert neocolonialism under the auspices of the British. Indonesia's president, **Soekarno,** declared a **Confrontation,** supporting protests and revolts in Malaysia's eastern states. This led to extreme tensions, bordering on war, between the two until 1966, when Suharto and his New Order came to power in Indonesia.

Within Malaysia as well, ethnic tensions continued to grow. The diverse nation was home to a proud Malayan majority who dominated politically, but remained behind economically. The administrative attitude toward Singapore's predominantly Chinese population as ethnically and politically "balanced" by the Malay majority states on Borneo, only created more policy problems for the Malay-oriented government, which had established Islam as the official religion and Bahasa Malaysia as its language. As Singapore attempted to gain federal political footholds in the new nation, the peninsular government grew increasingly apprehensive, and by 1969 a teary-eyed **Lee Kuan Yew** withdrew Singapore from Malaysia, while Britain finally severed its deep ties, leaving Malaysia in the hands of the peninsula. In May of that year, ethnic riots erupted in the capital city, **Kuala Lumpur.** The riots occurred after the Malay majority party, the **Alliance** (the joining of the UMNO with the conservative Malayan Chinese Association) lost a significant number of seats to non-Malay supported parties for the first time since its founding in 1952. "Victory" parades among non-Malay groups led to racial epithets on both sides. Many Malay interpreted this as a movement by "infidels" to question their political superiority. Malay political leaders called mass meetings, and quickly lost control of the riled mobs, many of whom came armed. The ensuing riots left many dead and over 5,000

Chinese homeless. **Prime Minister Tunku Abdul Rahman** was blamed for the riots by more militant Malay politicians and elites, such as **Dr. Mahathir bin Mohammed,** who demanded a firm "Malay sovereignty," but was quickly thrown out of the UMNO for questioning Tunku Abdul's leadership. Malay response, in general, however, blamed the riots on concessions to non-Malay groups, rather than Malay racial attitudes, and the Prime Minister was supplanted by **Deputy Prime Minister Tun Abdul Razak** along with a temporary ruling council which ruled by decree. The council prohibited public discussion of issues such as Malay special status and the status of Bahasa Malaysia as the only official language. These issues were deemed too "sensitive" for public discussion and continue to be censored.

Tunku Abdul retired in 1970, leaving Tun Abdul Razak to become Prime Minister with the dissolution of the ruling council. Under his rule, UMNO gained increasing power, and the country continued to pander to Malay interests. Further political alliances increased the status and political clout of Malay citizens relative to their non-Malay counterparts, and economic policies were implemented to support Malay business ownership under the assertion that democracy can only work under relative economic equality. The old Alliance gained support from other parties and reformed as the *Barisan Nasional*, or **National Front.** Malaysia continued to expand its international relations, especially to communist nations which were much closer in proximity than the US or Europe. In 1971 the status of Malay citizens was given a further boost, through the creation of the **National Culture Policy** which defined National Culture as indigenous tradition, informed heavily by Islam. Ironically, indigenous tradition referred only to that of the Malay people. It disregarded not only the Chinese and Indian traditions, which influenced Malaya before Islam, but also ignored the Orang Asli who had populated the region thousands of years before the proto-Malay. Policy makers insisted on education in Bahasa Malaysia alone and provided federal support for a "National Culture," which only included ethnic Malay art and literature. With Tun Razak's unexpected death in 1976, his deputy and brother-in-law, **Hussein Onn,** came to power with a small political base and poor health. Though the country's confidence wavered, he steered the nation toward greater development until 1981, when his heart forced him to retire. Into Hussein's shoes stepped his unlikely deputy, Dr. Mahathir, who had slowly risen in the ranks since his original expulsion. Mahathir's administration began an increasing movement to Islamicize Malaysia. Islam became a part of Malaysian education, and Bahasa Malaysia words found in Islam, including those for God or religion, fell under a religious copyright and were only allowed to be used by Islam. Throughout the 1980s Mahathir pushed religious fervor along with rapid growth and industrialization. In 1987 Mahathir's re-election was surrounded by controversy which included the court's declaration that the UMNO was unconstitutional. Mahathir prevailed, however, organizing the **UMNO Baru** (or New UMNO), and in April of 1995 was elected to his fourth term. His National Front coalition currently holds a constitutional majority, as well as political majorities in 10 of the 11 states. As long as Mahathir pushes for Malay political and economic advantage, support for him will likely remain strong.

■■■ MALAYSIA TODAY

Historically, each ethnic group has been separated by trade and often by geography. Malays have lived in the countryside, subsisting on agriculture. Chinese-Malaysians were the merchant class, and Indian-Malaysians were the laborers, particularly on rubber plantations. Today, with majority rule (and thus a Malay-dominated government), the authorities are eager to see Malays take on an equitable share of the nation's wealth, formerly concentrated in the hands of the Chinese. Government propaganda assures the people that happy Malaysians are working together harmoniously in pursuit of mutual prosperity and development, while the grumblings about discriminatory policies and the old cultural-stereotyping continue.

The modern government is a constitutional monarchy similar to Britain's, with executive power resting with the Prime Minister and a parliament composed of an upper and lower house. More distinctive to the Malaysian Government is the **Conference of Rulers** and the **Yang di-Pertuan Agong,** or **Supreme Ruler.** The Conference of Rulers is comprised of the nine hereditary sultans of the region who determine 27 of the 63 senators and select the country's titular monarch from among the senior sultans. The current Agong, **Ja'afar ibni Abdul Rahman,** was selected in April of 1994. Each Supreme Ruler is elected for five years, appoints Supreme Court Justices, and performs other governor-like duties, such as signing pardons and constitutional amendments. The Agong is also able to declare a national state of emergency, so that all legislative powers are given to the executive branch, as occurred during the 1964 Confrontation, after the 1969 riots, and in Kelantan during riots in 1977.

Malaysia is a rapidly developing nation, and although not as advanced as Singapore, it provides more modern facilities for tourists than either Indonesia or Thailand. Under Mahathir's administration, the country has moved away from dependency on tin and rubber, and toward industrialization, and there is less poverty and unemployment here than in most developing nations. Development fever has embraced the entire nation, and the people are mobilized to achieve "developed nation status" by the year 2020. The downside of this is severe **environmental degradation.** Much of the land that is not protected or valued as a tourist attraction has been damaged. Bus rides are rarely scenic because of hills scarred by mining, huge monocrop plantations of rubber or palm, and wastelands of factories and construction sites. Environmental awareness has only recently gained popularity, but much of it is little more than rhetoric.

With rapid industrialization, it seems logical that Malaysia might become more westernized, like so many other developing nations. This is only partially true; Dr. Mahathir has espoused a **"Look East" policy** when seeking foreign investment and trade partners, some of which is due to the anti-western attitude that has accompanied the rise of Islamic fundamentalism. Other aspects of Mahathir's policies are based on ethnic stereotyping which leads him to believe that training by Korean and Japanese firms will aid the "Malay work ethic." However, even as Malaysia continues forward with AFTA, the new Asian Free Trade Agreement, which includes Indonesia, Singapore, Thailand, Brunei, the Philippines and Vietnam, the United States continues to be second only to Japan as a foreign investor. Predominantly Muslim states in Malaysia discuss implementing Islamic *hudud* laws to replace the secular courts; newspapers question the moral integrity of western TV programs imported and aired on Malaysian television. These are reactions to the perceived cultural imperialism that the west wages on the Third World. Even the English street names have been Malaysianized, but old street names die hard, resulting in oodles of confusion for the tourist. As often as not what all of this means is that western-style ads with rock stars and fast cars still appear and work their mind-numbing magic, but are quickly removed or "edited" by the government's Censorship Board. For a small country with a high economic growth rate and an increasing international market, "Look East" often gives way to "Growth at any Cost." Ah, the best of both worlds.

■■■ THE PEOPLE OF MALAYSIA

Malaysia has a population of 19,283,157, of which about 15 million live on the peninsula, the rest inhabiting Sabah and Sarawak to the east. The distinctions between Malaysian, Malayan, and Malay are very important. Malaysian is a political term, referring to anyone who is a citizen of the country. Malayan refers geographically to anyone from the peninsula. Malay is an ethnic term referring to the Malay people. Moreover, most Malays are Muslim. Non-Malays? Mostly not, although there are Malaysian-Indian-Muslims. The similarity between these terms should give even the most unfamiliar an idea about the cultural biases inherent in the nation's structure.

MALAY

Ethnic Malays constitute 50% of the nation's population. Although many argue that their migration thousands of years ago puts their ancestry in China, the favored status granted to the Malay, *bumiputra* (Sons of the Earth), qualifies them as indigenous Malaysians. Barely comprising a majority, the birthrate of the Malay people has been an important consideration in government planning. Attempts to create favorable conditions for large Malay families (including the "Go for five!" campaign) are working, at least indirectly, as the gap between Malay and other ethnic groups is widening.

CHINESE

Chinese-Malaysians make up about one-third of the population, and began arriving in the 1400s; the influx stepped up during the 1800s, as immigrants came to work for the colonial tin-mining industry. This direct connection to British industry gave the Chinese an advantage in industrial dealings, and over the years, the Chinese have come to dominate Malaysian commerce while making political concessions to the Malay majority. Many early Chinese immigrants married Malay women giving birth to the **Baba-Nyonya** culture, perhaps most easily recognized in Nyonya food, a mix between Chinese and Malay styles. Today, the large Chinese population is among the most vocal for increasing the definition of National Culture to include other religious and ethnic traditions, such as the Chinese Lion Dance. A pocket created by British influences on migration, the city of Georgetown still has an authentic yet prosperous Chinatown with some of the country's best food.

INDIAN

The next largest percentage of Malaysians (9%) are **Indian-Malaysians,** many of whom are descendants of the Hindu Tamil laborers brought over by British rubber plantation owners earlier this century. The influence of Indian trade over the centuries, however, means that some Indian ancestry, however distant, is probable among many inhabitants of the peninsula. The status of the Indian culture and population as non-indigenous and non-national is perhaps more ironic than that of the more populous Chinese, due to the Indic influence found in Southeast Asia long before Islam and other cultural traditions left their marks. Indian-Malaysian communities are found in almost every decent-size city, particularly on the more cosmopolitan west coast, where almost every city has its own "Little India."

ORANG ASLI

The singular term **Orang Asli,** to refer to the aboriginal Malaysis, in fact, misleading, as Orang Asli refers to a diverse set of predominantly animist tribes who inhabit the peninsula. The two major groups are the Semang (or Negritos) in the north, and the Senoi in the south, but many other small tribes exist within the interior. They are rarely seen outside of their remote rainforest and highland settlements, and comprise only a minute fraction of modern Malaysia's population.

■■■ CUSTOMS AND CULTURE

GETTING ALONG IN MALAYSIA

Westerners traveling to Malaysia automatically suffer strikes against them because of the perceptions of immorality that are attached to western culture. Travelers would do well to be sensitive to these issues, and do everything they can to respect local customs and etiquette. Remember that you are a guest in Malaysia and act appropriately. Losing your temper or arguing is considered poor breeding and will only make you the loser in any dispute. Take a deep breath and remain calm. Misunderstandings are the source of most disputes. Unless you speak fluent Malay, realize you may be misreading a situation that is perfectly clear to everyone else. When you become irate, you will look like a self-centered fool. Learn to say thank you—it lubricates bureaucratic wheels and makes people smile.

Non-Muslim women are not expected to keep their heads and legs covered the way most Malay women do, but wearing pants or a long skirt and a t-shirt that covers the shoulders (and a bra) is presentable enough. Shorts, even baggy ones, are not acceptable. Men should dress equally neatly and modestly. Shorts are only acceptable at the beach. Shave daily and keep long hair tied neatly. Dressing presentably can make a surprising difference in the way Malays treat you; you will be treated with as much respect as it appears you give to yourself. This not only displays respect for local sensibilities, but it avoids potential hassles and harassment and smooths the way to more congenial encounters with the local population.

Women traveling alone should be especially careful, since local perceptions assume that women alone are definitely up to no good. Some other points to look out for: don't give or receive anything with the left hand; don't point with your feet; don't point with your index finger, especially at people—make a fist, push your thumb against it and gesture; and avoid touching people on the head. Ask permission to enter mosques. For **mosque visits,** take off your shoes, stay off prayer rugs, dress appropriately, and avoid going on Fridays.

RELIGION

Malaysia's cultural hodge-podge pervades all aspects of life on Peninsular Malaysia, not least of which is religion. Muslims predominate as most Malays are Muslim and Islam is the official religion. During its arrival to the peninsula, **Islam** was molded by earlier Hindu-Buddhist influences, as can be seen in the dynastic Sultanates and contemporary Malay presentations of the Ramayana. The Modern Malaysian Agong is not simply a monarch figure; he is also the final authority on all religious issues, just as the Sultans who comprise the Conference of Rulers are in charge of religious affairs for their own states. This mix of church and state creates special liabilities and advantages for Muslims, including penalties for disregarding prayers or drinking liquor, and even the appearance of a man and women alone together. On the other hand, all religious festivals *are* national holidays. The 1970s saw a revival of fundamentalism among some Malaysian youth with the *dakwah* movement. Such fundamentalism is viewed questionably by Malaysian Muslims and non-Muslims alike. There is a strong sense of freedom of religion in Malaysia, but there is an uncomfortable tension between this freedom and the granting of superior status to Islam, especially considering how closely religious lines parallel ethnic ones. Nonetheless, Islam continues side-by-side with temples and churches, in a peaceful understanding, and religious extremes are often viewed as threats to this fragile stability.

Chinese-Malaysians practice an incredible mix of **Mahayana Buddhism, Taoism,** and **Confucianism** built on a strong tradition of ancestor worship; temples rear their elaborate heads in just about every city, often incorporating more than one tradition. It is a religion of the community and family; the Goddess of Mercy and local deities are important, and family rituals are usually given priority. Tamil-speaking Indian-Malaysians predominantly practice **Hinduism;** most are followers of God and Protector, Vishnu (Vaishnavaites) or the great ascetic, Siva (Shaivites). Indian-Malaysians from northern India are likely to practice Islam, however. A small percentage, about 3%, of Malaysians are **Christian,** although the majority of these are on the island of Borneo, not on the peninsula.

WOMEN IN MALAYSIAN SOCIETY

Women in Malaysia have a relatively high autonomy, both socially and economically. Women hold land, own businesses, are occasionally heads of households, and make up the majority of the large semi-skilled working class. However, this autonomy is due in part to a Malaysian man's ability, according to Malay Islamic law, to divorce freely or practice polygamy at will. Women, therefore, often find themselves with an economic autonomy they were not planning on.

Men are certainly viewed as superior to women in Malaysia, at least in theory. Whereas hierarchies of age and wealth often take precedence over those of gender, according to Malay Islam, men simply have a greater capacity for reason. Women, on the other hand, are deemed emotional and susceptible to spirits. In rural areas, women are brought up to be shy and reserved, but once they are married, women have more freedom, as their sexuality is not in danger of being "stolen." Those women who have moved into the factory life in urban areas are often stereotyped, unfairly, as fast, "loose," and influenced by western ideas.

Governmental Islamic organizations monitor many of these urban Muslim women, often threatening them with arrest for appearing with men in "suggestive" ways or for walking alone at night on the street. Revivals of fundamentalism are also encouraging greater modesty among women, including veiling, a practice that is much less prominent in Malaysia than in Middle Eastern Islamic countries. Many men and women support the idea of increased modesty as much to create a sense of Malay pride as for religious virtue. Women, in general, do dress modestly, covering most of their bodies, and are encouraged to abstain from western styles.

■■■ THE ARTS

LITERATURE

Traditionally, the *Sejarah Melayu* is given credit for being the first significant piece of Malay literature. This work, written in the 15th century, chronicles the Melakan Sultanate, and includes the legends of its founding. Like the court chronicles which followed it, the *Sejarah* also describes court traditions, and weaves them together with anecdotes that put legend before history, making it an excellent cultural resource, similar to the Hindu *Mahabarata.* Much of Malay literature is influenced by a fairy tale/folk tale style that exemplifies the central role of magic and the supernatural in Malaysian culture. Malay stories, called *hikayat,* come in a wide range of styles, and the term itself is less a genre than an overarching principle of "Storytelling." Many *hikayats* are highly influenced by styles and stories from other regions, such as the *Hikayat Seri Rama,* which retells the *Ramayana* in Malay without a great deal of Malay influence. A more definite genre of Malay folk tales is the *penglipur lara* story, or "soother away of cares." These stories are usually hero stories, taking into account ancestries and lineages. There is a clear distinction here between Malay literature and literature written in Malay by writers from other ethnic groups. There are strong movements of Arabic Islamic and Chinese Indonesian writings in the Malay language as well.

Modern Malay literature began in the 1920s with Syed Sheikh Al-Hadi's 1925 novel *Faridah Hanum.* The founder of popular Malay newspapers, Al-Hadi was an important distributor of contemporary Islamic thought from the Middle East and Turkey. His and his colleagues' writings in the 20s and 30s contributed to increasing pre-war activism, and helped re-ignite the pride and achievements of Malay writers.

DRAMA AND DANCE

Malaysian dance and drama are very closely related. This is exemplified with the **Ma'Yong,** a uniquely Malay dance-drama art form. Over 400 years old, it gained prominence as a court tradition. At the same time that Shakespeare was filling all his roles with men, the presenters of Ma'Yong were reserving all the roles for young women, except for the role of the buffoon, which only a man can play. In the courts, the play might continue for days, only taking breaks at the Raja's convenience. Without scenery or other conventions attention is placed directly on the movements of the actresses. The stories themselves are romantic dramas, involving seemingly universal conventions: boy (who is played by a girl) meets princess; boy loses princess; boy meets ogre; boy miraculously kills ogre; boy saves princess, becomes hero, and amasses a great fortune. The most famous, **Dewa Muda,** involves magic kites, cloud princesses, fatal arrows, and rejuvenation; in the end Dewa Muda and the princess live happily ever after. Unlike other forms of drama, the classic canon is all originally Malay. Slow dances and intensive solos by the actresses are broken up by long comedic interludes by the actors, all of which is accompanied by musicians playing curious polyphonic tunes, elaborate costumes, improvisation, and formality.

The **Malay Shadow Play** is a form of the ancient mix of puppetry and theater which is found across Southeast Asia. Although the shadow play almost certainly has its roots in Java, many of the Malay conventions are more easily traced to the Khmer style, which in turn may have been brought from Java by **Jayavarman II** (see Cambodia: History). The central story of the shadow play is the **Ramayana,** the great Hindu Epic relating the journeys of Vishnu's incarnation Rama, and his travails against the demon-king Ravana in order to rescue the lovely Sita. The continuing popularity of this Hindu story reflects the lasting, if underappreciated, Indic influence in the now Muslim nation. In the Malay shadow play, a *dalang,* or puppeteer sits behind a long cotton screen with two-foot tall figures. He gracefully moves these behind the screen, usually two at a time, in order to tell the story through the gray shadows cast on to the screen by a small lamp. Although the colors are not seen by the audience, the puppets are brightly and ornately decorated. To provide comic relief, most localities also provide a character or two from outside the traditional story. For more serious scenes, characters are often stood upright by being stuck into the trunk of a banana tree. Accompanying the production is a small orchestra led by the melancholy oboe, which provides the sound of battle, the songs of love, and the emotional background to a lonely king's soliloquy.

Malay dance comes in many popular forms—court dances, seasonal dances, the Melakan *Ronggeng,* the Arabic *Zapin*—most important for the Malay in almost all dance, however, is the graceful movement of the arms and hands, exemplified by the word **Tari**. Most famous of the court dances is perhaps the **Ashek,** a three-part dance with 11 young women, where the lead dancer weaves her way among the other stationary women. The **Ronggeng** involves two lines of dancers who may approach each other, but not touch. They dance to the tune of a fiddle or rebab, while a gong keeps time. Unlike other dances, the complicated and precise steps are most important. The **Zapin** is a much faster dance which is very difficult to execute well; it also involves pairs of line dancers. As the accordion music increases in tempo the dancers are encouraged to improvise. **Malay folk dances** revolve around crop production or the harvesting of fish and are open air dances used to appease spirits and bring in good crops. Most involve a female lead dancer and a chorus line of other young males and females.

MUSIC

Malay music takes some of its influence from Cambodia, India, and the Middle East, but the sounds of Malaya are unique. Those instruments which are given greatest recognition are considered to have some connection to magic. Among the most widely recognized is the **spike fiddle,** or *rebab,* an adaptation of a similar Middle Eastern instrument. The neck of the instrument resembles the spike of a Malay top, and the three silver strings stretch down to a body which is shaped like half an apple. Its produces a very nasal sound, and leads the orchestra for the Ma'Yong. Its mystical abilities are ambiguous, but powerful. Don't mess with one of these babies unless you're trained. The Arabic **gendang,** large drums that usually come in pairs, provide tempo for most Malay drama and dance events, as well as for *silat* demonstrations. The *gendang* lays on its side across the percussionist's lap when played. The larger "mother" drum and the smaller "child" are tuned to provide a quick punch, and are usually tapped by hand. Although most Malay music highlights percussion, the Malay oboe, **serunai,** has achieved more popularity than other wind instruments and leads the orchestra for shadow plays. At other times Chinese **tawak** gongs will lead a group of drums and a *serunai* to accompany dances or *silat.* Other important instruments in Malay music include the violin played like a rebab (by way of Portugal), and a wide range of smaller upright drums.

Popular singing styles include **pantum,** an evolution of Islamic devotionals which consist of improvisational duets; **ghazals,** a mournful style, reminiscent of Islamic love songs; and the classical singing which accompanies the powerful, percussion-heavy **dondang.** The Europeanization of Malay music took place with **P. Ramlee,** the famous crooner of Malaysia, whose shorter romantic ballads and western instruments transformed the *dondang* style.

ARCHITECTURE

Few things can really be described as distinctive to Malay architecture. Many buildings, past and present, are marked with wood-carvings of Islamic calligraphic designs. Other conventions, such as buildings raised on piers and high-tiered roofs, are no longer as evident. The great popularity in early Malay history of impermanent wooden structures, even for palaces and mosques, makes a tour of "ancient" Malaysian architecture much less impressive than in Cambodia or Thailand. In many cities the surviving "historic" architecture retains a strong Dutch and Portuguese influence; however, the domed mosques represent the retention of many Islamic conventions among the region's building styles.

BATIKS

Batik is a process of covering cloth with wax or resin-like pastes so that it becomes resistent to dye which is then used to decorate it. As some dye soaks and the rest is repelled, the process creates vibrant colors and brilliant patterns. Within Malaysia the definition of *batik* applies more to the design than the process of its creation. Although the Malay people have been wearing *batik* sarongs for centuries, Malaysian *batik* differs from other parts of the region in that it is really a modern activity. *Batik palangi* (rainbow) uses the Indonesian formal process of *batik*, and was probably first used in Malaysia in the late 18th century. The other forms of *batik (cap* which involves block printing, and *tulis,* which uses hand-drawn designs) came about even later. The "traditional" Malay pattern involves an abundance of tropical leaves and vines abstracted into curves and lines across the material, and is similar to those used on the ornamented Malay kites. *Batik* is considered an ethnic Malay art-form, and is therefore given government support. As with many forms of traditional art, much of its production is centered in Kelantan and Terengganu.

■■■ RECREATION

Many sports are popular in Malaysia, from the traditional *sepak takraw* to soccer, hockey, and cricket. **Sepak takraw** is very similar to the Thai *takraw* (see Thailand: Recreation), and basically means *takraw* ball. With the burgeoning tourist industry in Malaysia, all the classic tourist sports are rampant as well: scuba, snorkeling, golf, tennis, windsurfing; you name it. **Outdoor treks** are also possible throughout much of the country, although they are not as easily accessible as in Northern Thailand. The **Betel Nut,** Malaysia's own mild stimulant, could perhaps be considered recreation as well. *(The Betel nut is not considered an illegal drug by the Malaysian government. Let's Go does not condone the use of illegal substances. The use or possession of illegal drugs in Malaysia is punishable by the death penalty.)*

KITE-FLYING

Let's Go: Fly a Kite / up to the highest height. This great little ditty is nowhere more appropriate than in Malaysia, where kite flyers and decorators are well-regarded for their abilities, and kites fill local legend, saving princes and performing miraculous feats. Although the tradition no longer maintains the popularity it once did, it still flourishes in the eastern states of Kelantan and Terengganu. Most kites are about seven feet tall and six feet wide, and the most common, the **Moon Kite,** *wau balau,* somewhat resembles an eye with a north-facing crescent below it; others include the Bird, Fish, Cat, Peacock, and the simple Thai-influenced "Kite from the West."

Large kites may take two weeks to make and are usually finished in conjunction with the rice-harvest. Flying these large ornaments takes two people; landing them takes both skill and luck.

The four most popular kite-flying contests are highest-flying, skill in handling, most ornamental, and humming. The majority of kite styles are weighted to accommodate a bow across the top which makes a light humming sound when it flies. The quality of sound is judged over a fifteen minute period for the humming contest, and the effect is electrifying. In the past, kite fighting was a contest as well, but the tensions between contestants became greater than that of a kite line and contestants kept flying off the handle. The government now frowns upon such face-offs.

TOP SPINNING

To compare western tops with Malay **gasing** is to compare Free Willy with Moby Dick. They may be the same animal, but the similarities end there. As the esteemed "top" expert Jesse Grayman says, "Top-spinning in Malaysia ain't no kid stuff!" In fact, even teenagers are discouraged from participating because their muscles are not developed enough. Adult men spend weeks fashioning perfectly balanced and proportioned tops from the trunks of specific trees which provide good wood for tops. The center of the top is a short steel spike with a rim of lead; finished products usually have the circumference of an Olympian's discus and weigh a bit less than a shotput. Tops are spun by coiling one end of a thick rope around and around the top's head and the other end around the spinners wrists. The top spinner throws it as if cracking a whip. The top then whirls onto a raised and hardened dirt surface. Men compete with each other by throwing their tops at rival tops to knock opponents off the dirt mound, or play for time with slightly lighter tops – setting them to spin for hours on a holder. Contests continue all day, and even magic is called upon, in the form of "top doctors," to gain important victories.

In the fighting contests two teams face off, attackers and defenders. Each attacker must hit only one of the other team's tops. Those tops that are still spinning from both sides are then placed on holders. Like volleyball, if the attackers have the last top spinning they gain a point; if the defenders have the last spinner they do not get a point, but get to "serve." Although less exciting, the "spinning" contest is also very complex. The top, once thrown, has to be immediately but incredibly smoothly scooped off the ground with a long flat piece of wood and placed into the holder. The better the top-spinner-scooper team, the longer the top will spin.

SILAT

The Malaysian form of Martial arts, *silat* supposedly originated in Sumatra, but has been changed and perfected on the Peninsula for hundreds of years. Its creation occurred, as with all great Malaysian events, according to legend. As the story goes, three Malay brothers travelled to Sumatra in the 13th century to study Islam. One of them, **Aminuddin,** was getting water from a pool at the base of a waterfall. As he watched the water he noticed a small flower riding the waters ripples. As the water approached it would retreat, and as the water retreated it would approach, remaining buoyant all the while. Encouraged by a mysterious voice, Aminuddin decided to form a style of self-defense from the flower's movements.

Silat is a graceful art using crouches, rolls, hand blows, and kicks. It is often demonstrated in public, especially at wedding ceremonies, when young men may take classes to learn just enough for their weddings. Many of the secrets of *silat,* however, are not allowed to be demonstrated, and its history is filled with stories of magic powers passed down from masters to promising students. Until the latter half of this century *silat* existed in many different styles under many local teachers. Since WWII there has been an increasing movement toward uniformity. Although this has brought a greater professional recognition to *silat,* along the lines of Tae Kwon Do and Karate, it has perhaps removed some of the local charm which its individualized graceful movements provided.

■■■ FOOD AND DRINK

No one eats or drinks in Malaysia. It is a special quality of the Malay people. Unfortunately this makes dining very difficult for the budget traveler. Okay, this is not true, but if it were, it would explain why so much of Malaysian cuisine has been imported or influenced by other countries. The Chinese and Indian population both contribute to the national dinner plate, and each group's cooking style feeds off the other's. Ethnic Malay dishes are not exactly pristine either, dishes such as *mee jawa* (Javanese Noodles) have obvious roots in Indonesia, and most of its specialties are regional specialties such as *sate,* the well-known grilled meat dish served with a spicy peanut sauce.

Coconut milk, fish pastes, peanut sauces, boiled eggs, and rice dishes, or *nasi,* are very popular in Malaysia. *Nasi lemak* is rice cooked in coconut milk with cucumbers, peanuts, and boiled egg, with an anchovy condiment *Nasi kerabu* brings out a wide variety of colors you never thought possible in rice, topped with fish condiments, along with spices and coconuts; *nasi padang* has even more coconut, tuna, and its own unique sauce. For the West Sumatran *nasi padang*, servers bring you a big bowl of rice and then display a wide variety of dishes for you to choose from and mix with your *nasi.* The dishes can include everything from the spicy meat *rendang,* to cow brains. The choice is yours. *Nasi briyani* is an extremely tasty Indian addition with meat, cooked in ghee and spices; *nasi kandar* is a hot and spicy rice and chicken dish with the more enigmatic *kandar* sauce. Both are happily eaten across the land. There are many Chinese rice dishes as well, but they aren't called *nasi.* Claypot Chicken, or *ngah poh fan,* is one example; chicken and rice are cooked in a clay pot with vegetables and sausage.

Malaysia is also known for a style of Chinese cooking known as **Nyonya,** which borrows heavily from Southeast Asian cuisine, especially the use of coconut milk, found most predominantly in Penang and Melaka. *Kwae teow,* Chinese flat noodles, are also popular, especially in Ipoh.

Indian cuisine in Malaysia includes dishes that are also popular throughout Indonesia. *Rojok* is an excellent salad, with shredded cucumbers, fruit, and often seafood. Although equally spicy, its peanut sauce is much sweeter than that of *satay* or other spicy dishes. *Roti canai* can be found everywhere for an excellent breakfast of pancakes with curry or lentils. For noodles, *mee goreng,* with chili, tomato, egg and shrimp, is popular.

Perhaps the greatest addition to Malaysian cuisine, however, is the Chinese **bubur cha-cha.** The coconut, shaved ice, yams, and rice "gummies" leave the tasty *cendol* in the dust and are almost worshipped by past researchers to the region. If you pass up *bubur cha-cha,* you may find yourself singing gastronomic versions of Paul Simon tunes twenty years down the line. To wash it all down try the *teh tarik,* the Indian vanilla tea that is poured from cup to cup to cool it, quite a sight to see. Remember that Malaysia is a Muslim country, so alcohol is less likely to be served in restaurants that are not used to a large tourist industry.

The best Chinese food is found in Penang and Ipoh, and premier Malay food is in the northeast, particularly at the night market in Kota Bharu. Just about every town has at least one excellent Indian restaurant. Try it all, and remember the golden rule of dining...if you don't know what to get, see what everyone else is eating and point at whatever looks good.

WEST COAST

■■■ KUALA LUMPUR

Somewhere between its self-proclaimed splendor as the "Garden City of Lights" and its literal English translation, "Muddy River Mouth" lies the true capital of Malaysia,

Kuala Lumpur. Visitors and residents tell tales of both extremes, and the city often seems to fit both descriptions. Despite its heavy traffic, teeming streets, and intense humidity, KL (as it's almost exclusively called) has somehow retained the appeal of a tropical metropolis. Its daunting monoliths of finance and exhaust-laden air are offset by the beauty of its lush vegetation and the green, as well as by the stunning mix of colonial and Islamic revivalist architecture.

As a hub of international commerce and the capital of a country hell-bent on developed status by the year 2020, KL seems to be constantly expanding, implementing, and metamorphosing. It's a city of movement; express buses from Johor Bahru, Melaka, and Ipoh race around wide highways and take the winding streets of Chinatown at the same velocity. Relentless pink minibuses mow down anything in their path, and fearless pedestrians dart in and out of streams of traffic, happily ignoring "no crossing" signs. So devoted is this town to progress and action that in mid-1994 the government declared war on *lepakking,* or loafing (defined, apparently, as hanging out with friends at a place other than home or the library). Parents were urged to rethink their life-styles, and to retool schools to provide intellectual and athletic activities that would keep kids away from malls and snooker joints.

While the government continues to wrestle with image problems, over a million Malay, Chinese, and Indians keep the city running and the tourists coming. What their remarkable efforts have produced is the fascinating confluence of three rich heritages—making Kuala Lumpur the consummate Malaysian experience.

GETTING THERE AND AWAY

By Air

For flight information and general inquiries, call 746 1014. **To get to and from the airport,** take blue bus #47 from Klang Station on the edge of Chinatown; the same bus also travels from the airport into the city (RM2). Taxis take about 45min. to go from the city center to the airport and cost about RM25.

By Train

The railway station (tel. 274 74 42) is on Jl. Sultan Hishmuddin across from the National Art Gallery and the Kuala Lumpur Visitor's Center. Trains leave for: **Butterworth** (7:30am and 2:15, and 10pm, 1st-class RM67, 2nd-class RM30); **Bangkok** (1:40pm, RM77.50); **Johor Bahru** (7:45am and 2:25pm, 1st-class RM64, 2nd-class RM33; 10:35pm, 1st-class RM86, 2nd-class RM39); and **Singapore** (7:25am, 2:35pm, 1st-class RM68, 2nd-class RM34; 10:25pm, 1st-class RM87, 2nd-class RM40).

By Bus

The long-distance bus station is the **Pudu Raya Station** on Jl. Pudu. Dozens of express bus companies sell tickets for destinations all over Malaysia; their offices are either within the station itself or across the street near the 7-Eleven store and the Kuala Lumpur City Lodge. As always, beware of touts and scam artists, many of whom hang around the station and literally drag travelers off to their particular company's booth. **Ekspres Nasional** (tel. 238 81 85) is a reputable company whose office is located just inside the station, immediately in front of you as you debark from the pedestrian overpass. Open 6am-11pm. To: **Butterworth** (10am, noon, 10, 10:30pm, and midnight; RM17.20 adults, RM8.60 children); **Johor Bahru** (9:30, 11am, 1, 2, 4:30, 10:30, 11pm, and midnight; RM16.60 adults, RM8.30 children); **Singapore** (9am and 10pm; RM17.80 adults, RM8.90 children); and **Kuantan** (9, 10:30, 11:30am, 12:30, 2:30, 4:30, 5:30pm and midnight; RM12.10 adults, RM6.10 children). The **KL-Melaka Ekspress** runs at 8, 9, 10, 11:30am, 1, 1:45, 3, 4:30, 6, and 6:30pm (RM6.75 adults, RM3.40 children).

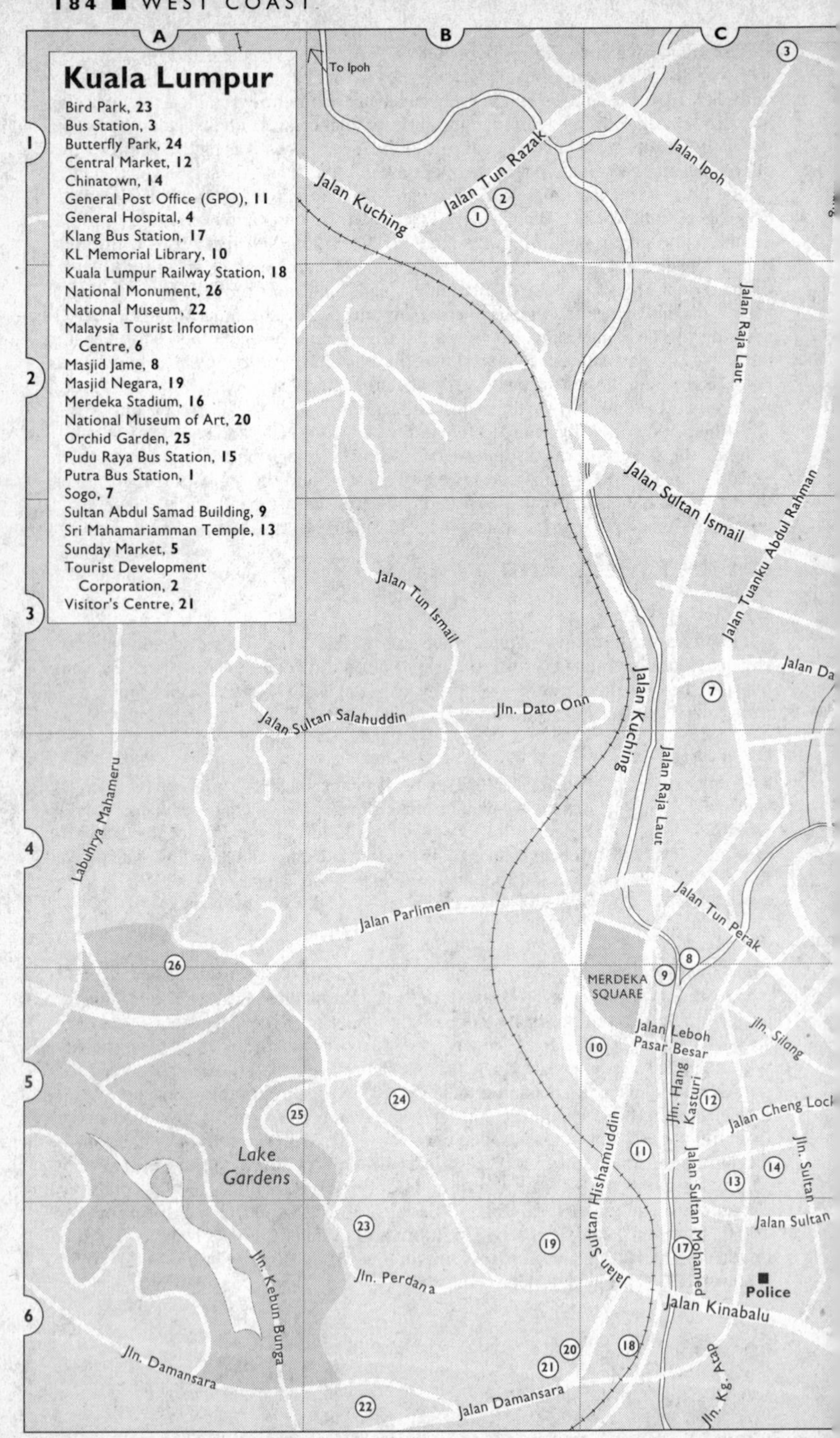
Kuala Lumpur
Bird Park, 23
Bus Station, 3
Butterfly Park, 24
Central Market, 12
Chinatown, 14
General Post Office (GPO), 11
General Hospital, 4
Klang Bus Station, 17
KL Memorial Library, 10
Kuala Lumpur Railway Station, 18
National Monument, 26
National Museum, 22
Malaysia Tourist Information Centre, 6
Masjid Jame, 8
Masjid Negara, 19
Merdeka Stadium, 16
National Museum of Art, 20
Orchid Garden, 25
Pudu Raya Bus Station, 15
Putra Bus Station, 1
Sogo, 7
Sultan Abdul Samad Building, 9
Sri Mahamariamman Temple, 13
Sunday Market, 5
Tourist Development Corporation, 2
Visitor's Centre, 21
To Ipoh
Jalan Tun Razak
Jalan Kuching
Jalan Ipoh
Jalan Raja Laut
Jalan Sultan Ismail
Jalan Tuanku Abdul Rahman
Jalan Tun Ismail
Jalan Da
Jalan Sultan Salahuddin
Jln. Dato Onn
Labuhrya Mahameru
Jalan Parlimen
Jalan Tun Perak
MERDEKA SQUARE
Jalan Leboh Pasar Besar
Jln. Silang
Jln. Hang Kasturi
Jalan Cheng Lock
Jalan Sultan Hishamuddin
Jalan Sultan Mohamed
Jln. Sultan
Jalan Sultan
Lake Gardens
Jln. Kebun Bunga
Jln. Perdana
Jalan Kinabalu
Police
Jln. Damansara
Jalan Damansara
Jln. Kg. Atap

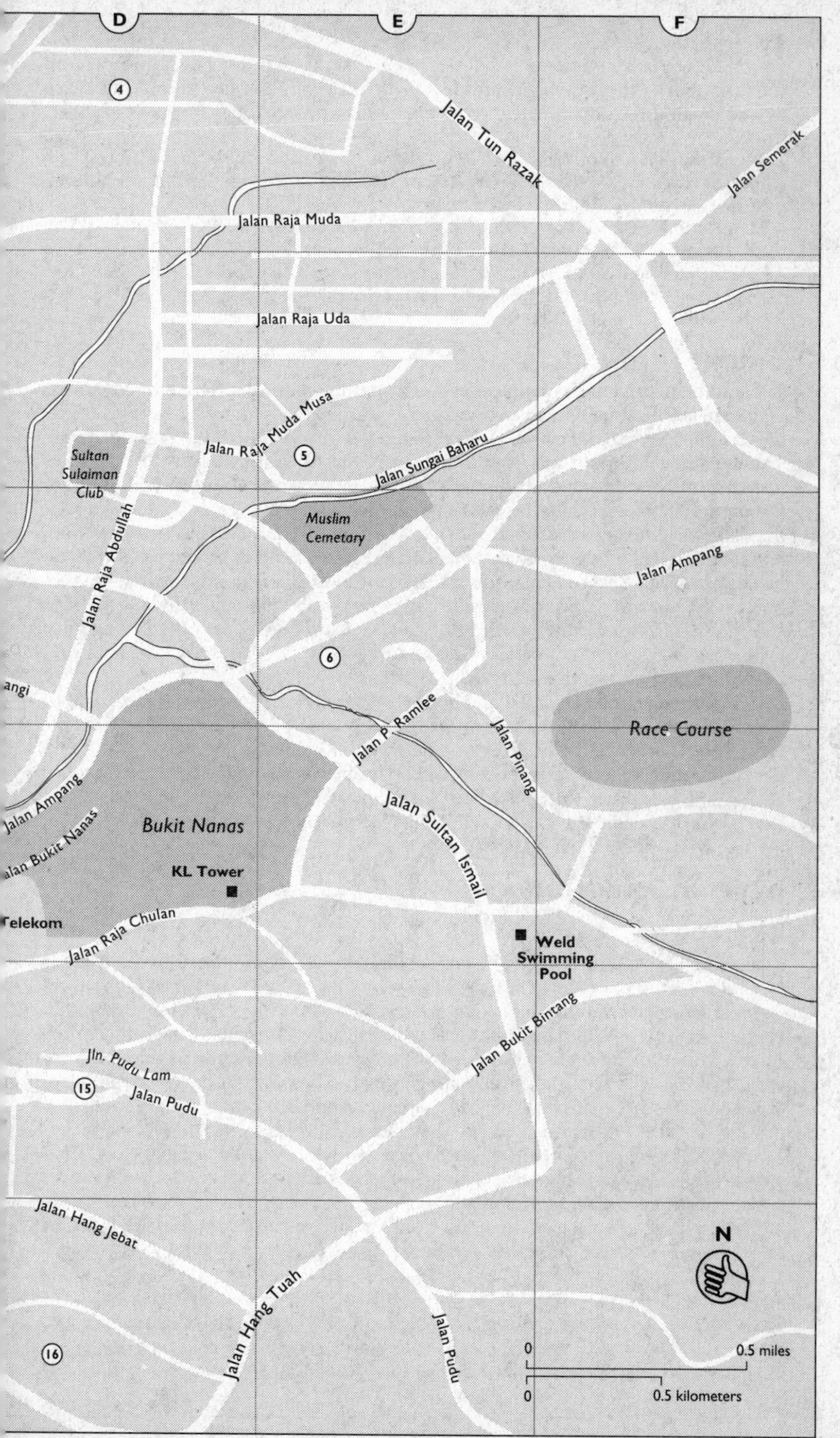
D
E
F
4
Jalan Tun Razak
Jalan Semerak
Jalan Raja Muda
Jalan Raja Uda
Jalan Raja Muda Musa
Jalan Sungai Baharu
5
Sultan Sulaiman Club
Jalan Raja Abdullah
Muslim Cemetary
Jalan Ampang
6
Jalan P. Ramlee
Jalan Pinang
Race Course
Jalan Ampang
Bukit Nanas
Jalan Bukit Nanas
Jalan Sultan Ismail
KL Tower
Telekom
Jalan Raja Chulan
Weld Swimming Pool
Jalan Bukit Bintang
Jln. Pudu Lam
15
Jalan Pudu
Jalan Hang Jebat
N
Jalan Hang Tuah
Jalan Pudu
16
0
0.5 miles
0
0.5 kilometers

By Taxi

Four different taxi companies handle service to various regions of the country from the floor above the buses. If you are alone, you will most likely be sharing your inter-city taxi with three others. The price is higher for a private cab.

Persutuan Kebajikan (tel. 232 65 04). Travels to west and south Malaysia. To: **Johor Bahru** (RM36, with A/C RM38); **Melaka** (with A/C RM17); and **Muar** (RM17, with A/C RM21).

Persutuan Pemandu (tel. 232 50 82). Travels to the eastern parts of Malaysia. To: **Kuantan** (RM25), **Kuala Terangganu** (RM25), and **Kuala Bharu** (RM35).

Persutuan Teksi (tel. 238 02 13). Runs to the North. To: **Ipoh** (RM20, RM80 for the whole car, plus RM2 toll) and **Butterworth** (RM36 per person, RM144 for the whole car, plus RM6 toll).

ORIENTATION

There is no method to the madness of Kuala Lumpur's streets. It's best to remember certain major thoroughfares and to peruse a city map before arriving with your first destination in mind. The railroad runs through the west part of the city proper. **Jalan Tuanku Abdul Rahman** and **Jalan Raja Laut** run north-south parallel to each other just east of the railroad, then merge at their southern ends to form **Jalan Sultan Hishamuddin,** along which lie the General Post Office, the National Mosque, and the National Art Gallery. **Chinatown** sits just east of **Jalan Sultan Hishamuddin,** bounded roughly on the north by **Jalan Cheng Lock** and on the south by **Jalan Kinabalu. Jalan Raja Chulan** begins just north of the **Metrojaya** shopping center on the border of Chinatown and runs east through glitzy malls and office towers. A short street called Jl. Gereja runs north off Jl. Raja Chulan, then veers east turning into **Jalan Ampang,** sometimes called "Ambassador's Row" for the many colonial mansions-turned-embassies along this road.

Jalan Sultan Ismail makes a grand northwest to southeast sweep, connecting the **Gobak River** in the west with Jl. Ampang and Jl. Raja Chulan on the east. Finally, **Jalan Tun Razak** carves a wide semi-circle around KL's eastern perimeter and hosts as many embassies as Jl. Ampang, while **Jalan Ipoh** serves as the main route for tourist-filled buses heading to sights north of the city. Most sights are in the west half of Kuala Lumpur, while the east contains many luxury hotels, shopping malls, office towers, embassies, and nightclubs.

GETTING AROUND

Buses

Kuala Lumpur's bus system can be fairly difficult to decipher. Bus stops are usually labeled with the numbers of the buses that stop there, and sometimes with more detailed information about individual routes. Fares are RM0.20-2. **Pink minibuses** charge a flat rate of RM0.60 regardless of the distance traveled; they run shorter routes within the city. They also display their routes prominently inside the front windshield, so you can see it well enough in advance to flag it down (always flag buses—drivers will often cruise by a designated stop if they think no one wants to get on). Be on the lookout as well for silver **"Interkota"** buses, which will soon take over as minibuses are phased out. Larger red and white buses (often labeled **"Cityliner"**) travel longer distances extending to KL's satellite towns. If you aren't sure which bus to take, go to a station and ask. The **Klang Bus Station** is conveniently located in Chinatown across the street from the Starlight Hotel on Jl. Hang Kasturi. Most minibuses stop at Central Market, and bus stops are everywhere.

Taxis

Taxis may or may not be metered. If unmetered, agree on a price beforehand; the driver will often quote you a figure before you even get in the car, giving you a chance to decline politely. Metered cabs start at RM1.50 and increase by RM0.10

per 200m. Additional surcharges apply for taxis booked by phone (RM10), trips between midnight and 7am (50%), and trips carrying 3 (RM0.20) or 4 (RM0.40) passengers. To book a cab by phone, call **Telecab** (tel. 211 10 11), **Kuala Lumpur Taxi Driver's Association** (tel. 221 52 52), or **Federal Territory and Selangor Radio Taxi Association** (tel. 293 62 13). All are open 24 hrs. Taxi hotline: tel. 255 33 99.

PRACTICAL INFORMATION

Tourist Information: Malaysian Tourist Information Complex (MATIC), 109 Jl. Ampang (tel. 242 39 29). From the Pudu Raya express bus terminal, cross the pedestrian overpass, turn left, and walk past the Metrojaya shopping center on the left. Turn right onto Lorang Raja Chulan, then turn left onto Jl. Gereja in front of the Telekom office. Jl. Gereja turns into Jl. Ampang. MATIC is on your right just past the intersection with Jl. Sultan Ismail. A tin magnate's mansion, this is the most elaborate tourist information center in town. The office is as much a **museum** (9am-5pm) of Malay culture as it is a **Malaysian Air** office, an **Ekspres Nasional bus** counter, and a **Telekom** branch (Mon.-Thurs. 9am-1pm and 2-5pm, Fri. 9am-12:30pm and 2:45-5pm, Sat. 9am-1pm). Information desk open 9am-9pm. **Kuala Lumpur Tourist Association and Kuala Lumpur Visitor's Center,** 3 Jl. Hishamuddin (tel. 238 18 32), next door to the National Art Gallery, across the street from the railway station. Friendly and helpful staff. Open Mon.-Fri. 8am-5pm, and Sat. 8am-12:45pm. **Kuala Lumpur Railway Station Branch** (tel. 274 60 63), on Jl. Sultan Hishamuddin. On the same side of the station as platforms 1, 2, and 3, near the A&W Restaurant. Open 9am-9pm. **Subang Airport Branch,** Terminal 1 (tel. 746 57 07). Open 9am-10pm. **Jl. Parlimen Branch** (tel. 293 66 61/4), right behind Merdeka Square. Open 9am-9pm.

Tourist Police: 12th floor, Police Tourist Unit, Jl. Hang Tuah (tel. 249 69 53).

Budget Travel: MSL Travel, 66 Jl. Putra (tel. 442 47 22; fax 443 37 07), just off Jl. Chow Kit, next to the Grand Central Hotel. A veritable gold mine of budget travel goodies, including the Eurotrain Explorer Pass for unlimited travel on KTM-Malayan Railway (from RM88) or SRT-State Railway of Thailand (from US$32). Discount travel passes, and ISIC cards. Open Mon.-Fri. 9am-5pm, Sat. 9am-1pm.

Embassies and Consulates: Australia, 6 Jl. Yap Kwan Seng, 50450 (tel. 242 31 22, after hours 242 39 42; fax 241 44 95). Open Mon.-Fri. 8am-12:30pm and 1:30-4:30pm. **Canada,** 7th floor, Plaza MBF, 172 Jl. Ampang, 50450 (tel. 261 20 00, after hours 261 20 31). Open Mon.-Fri. 8am-4pm. **Indonesia,** 233 Jl. Tun Razak, 50400 (tel. 984 20 11; fax 984 79 08). Open Mon.-Thurs. 8:30am-1pm and 2-4:30pm, Fri. 8:30am-1:30pm and 2:30-4:30pm. **Laos,** 108 Jl. Damai (tel. 248 38 95). **New Zealand,** 193 Jl. Tun Razak, 50400 (tel. 248 64 22 or 248 65 60; fax 241 30 94). Open Mon.-Fri. 8am-12:30pm and 1:30-4:30pm. **Singapore,** 209 Jl. Tun Razak (tel. 261 62 77). **Thailand,** 206 Jl. Ampang, 50450 (tel. 248 83 33 or 248 83 50; fax 248 65 27). Open Mon.-Fri. 9am-1pm and 2-5pm; consular section open Mon.-Fri. 9am-1pm. **UK,** 185 Jl. Ampang, 50450 (tel. 248 21 22 or 248 08 00; fax 244 77 66 or 248 08 80). Open Mon.-Fri. 8:15am-1:15pm and 2-4pm. **US,** 376 Jl. Tun Razak, 50400 (tel. 248 90 11, fax 242 22 07). Open Mon.-Fri. 7:45am-12:30pm and 1:15-4:30pm. **Vietnam,** 4 Persiaran Stonor (tel. 248 40 36).

Immigration Office: Pusat Bandar Daman Sara, Jl. Semantan (tel. 255 50 77), near the Road Transport Dept. Block I. Open Mon.-Thurs. 8am-12:45pm and 2-4:15pm, Fri. 8am-12:15pm and 2:45-4:15pm, Sat. 8am-12:45pm.

Currency Exchange: MayBank (Malayan Banking Berhad), Menara MayBank, Bukit Mahkaman, 100 Jl. Tun Perak, 50936 (tel. 230 88 33), a short walk from the Pudu Raya Express bus terminal, across from Metrojaya. RM5 per transaction for cashing traveler's checks, plus RM0.20 charge per check. Open Mon.-Fri. 9:30am-4pm, Sat. 9:30-11:30am. **Hong Leong Bank,** 57 Jl. Hang Lekiu (tel. 232 32 11), opposite the Telekom office. 1% commission (minimum RM2) plus RM0.15 per traveler's check. Open Mon.-Fri. 10am-3pm, Sat. 9:30-11:30am. **Bank Simpanan Nasional** (tel. 238 83 77) at Pudu Raya Bus Station. A hefty price for the convenience. The rate is about RM0.10 less for traveler's checks than for cash, plus RM5 commission and RM0.15 charge per check. Open Mon.-Sat. 9am-4pm and Sun. 9:30am-12:30pm.

Credit Card Companies: American Express, 2nd floor, MAS Bldg., Jl. Sultan Ismail, P.O. Box 12269, 50772 (tel. 261 00 00; fax 262 10 50). Mail should be marked "client mail" and addressed to this office; it will be held free for card-holder for three months. Open Mon.-Fri. 8:30am-5:30pm, Sat. 8:30am-noon. **Diner's Club** customer service (tel. 261 10 55); emergency card replacement (tel. 261 13 22 or 261 12 66).

General Post Office: Jl. Sultan Hishamuddin 9 (tel. 274 11 22). **Poste Restante** is at the information counter. Open Mon.-Sat. 8am-6pm.

Telephones: Pusat Telekom, Jl. Raja Chulan (fax 230 25 69). From the Pudu Raya express bus terminal, cross the pedestrian overpass, walk left to the MayBank tower. Turn right after the tower onto Lorong Raja Chulan. The Telekom Office is on the left just after the Hong Leong Bank. Open 24 hrs. Soundproof phone booths and Home Country Direct phones. Pricey **fax** and **telegram** services. **Telephone code:** 03. **Directory Assistance:** 103. **Assisted International Calls:** 108. **General inquiries:** 102.

Car Rentals: Avis, 40 Jl. Sultan Ismail (tel. 242 35 00). Daily rates from RM165; weekly from RM990. Insurance RM15 per day. Open 7:30am-7pm. **National,** Ground floor, President House, Jl. Sultan Ismail (tel. 248 05 22). From RM138 per day, RM828 per week. Insurance RM15 per day. Open Mon.-Sat. 8am-6pm.

Luggage Storage: At the Pudu Raya Express Bus Terminal, **Akijaya Enterprise** (tel. 230 53 34), near the Ekspres Nasional counter. RM1 per bag per day. Open daily 8am-10pm. At the railway station on platform 4, **Matang Luggage Service** (tel. 274 55 61), RM1.50 per bag per day. Open 7am-10pm.

English Bookstore: MPH Bookstore, Metrojaya Sinar Kota, Level 3, Jl. Tun Perak (tel. 232 83 03), inside the Metrojaya shopping center. Fiction, self-help books, and glossy entertainment mags. Open 10am-10pm. **Popular Book Company,** 34-6 Jl. Jang Lekir (tel. 230 06 87/9). In the heart of Chinatown. English, Chinese, and children's books, and an extensive selection of travel guides. Open 9am-9pm.

Libraries: Pustaka Peringatan Kuala Lumpur (Kuala Lumpur Memorial Library), 92 Jl. Raja (tel. 293 29 08). See map. Tourists may browse but may not check out books. A formal affair—note-taking is not tolerated. No sleeveless shirts, shorts, or slippers allowed. Open Mon. 1-5pm, Tues.-Fri. 10am-5pm, Sat. 1am-4:30pm, Sun. 10am-1pm. Closed public holidays. **Australian Information Library** (tel. 242 31 22), on Jl. Yap Kwan Seng.

Cultural Organizations: Alliance Française, 15 Lorong Gurney (tel. 292 59 29). Open Mon.-Fri. 9am-6pm. **British Council,** Jl. Bukit Aman (tel. 298 75 55). Open Mon.-Fri. 8:30am-12:30pm and 1:30-5:30pm. **Goethe Institute,** 1 Langgak Golf (tel. 242 20 11). Open Mon.-Fri. 8am-1pm and 4-6pm. **Japan Cultural Center,** Wisma Nusantara, Jl. Punchak, off Jl. P. Ramlee (tel. 230 663). Open Mon.-Fri. 8:30am-12:30pm and 2-4:30pm.

Supermarkets: UDA Ocean, Lot PT1, Section 24, Jl. Sultan (tel. 202 12 01). Open 10am-9:30pm. **Sogo Supermarket** (tel. 298 21 11), on Jl. Tuanku Abdul Rahman in the basement of the Sogo Department Store. Imported Japanese foodstuffs like *donburi*. Open Mon.-Thurs. 11am-8pm, Fri.-Sun. 11am-9pm. **Yaohan** has three locations: the mall on Jl. Putra (tel. 293 72 55), Jl. Awan Mendung (tel. 783 05 88), and Plaza OUG, Taman OUG (tel. 782 24 88).

Laundry: While there are over 20 laundromats in KL, your best bet is to use the services offered by most guest houses (RM5-10 per load; same day service). To save RM1-2 try: **Wah Li Drycleaners,** 72-1 Jl. Putra (tel. 443 93 28), across the street from the Grand Central Hotel. From Sogo, walk up Jl. Tuanku Abdul Rahman, turn left onto Jl. Chow Kit, and the shop is on the left. Clothes brought in before noon are returned the same day. Charges by the piece. Open Mon.-Sat. 8:30am-8pm, public holidays 10am-3pm. **YMCA Laundromat,** 95 Jl. Padang Belia. Located in the YMCA complex; take bus #33 or #46, or minibus #12. Wash and dry RM4 per 5kg. All proceeds go to benefit the deaf. Open Mon.-Sat. 8:30am-1pm and 1:45-7pm, Sun. 9am-1pm and 1:45-3pm.

Public Toilets, Showers, and Swimming Pools: The Pudu Raya Express bus terminal and the railway station have **public toilets** (RM.10) and **showers** (RM1). There is a **swimming pool** in the Chinwoo Athletic Association compound (tel. 232 46 02) on Jl. Hang Jebat. From the Rex Cinema on Jl. Sultan, turn left, walk

PENINSULAR MALAYSIA

past the Furama Hotel, and take a left onto Jl. Hang Jebat. Take a right onto the small road running uphill on your right, near Gereja Gospel Hall. Open Mon.-Fri. 10am-12:30pm and 3-8pm, Sat.-Sun. and public holidays 9:30am-8pm. Adults RM2, under 18 RM1.

Pharmacies: The area around Jl. Sultan-Jl. Cheng Lock is crammed with pharmacies. **Apex Pharmacy,** Ground floor, Metrojaya Sihar Kotak, Jl. Tun Perak (tel. 232 77 35). Also at Kompleks Kota Raya, Jl. Cheng Lock (tel. 232 25 80). Open 10am-10pm.

Hospital: Kuala Lumpur General Hospital, Jl. Pahang (tel. 292 10 44). **City Medical Center,** 413-425 Jl. Pudu (tel. 221 12 55; fax 221 43 72).

Emergency: tel. 999.

Early Closing Days: Many offices close for lunch from 1-2pm. On Fridays, some offices—especially government bureaus—close for prayers, generally from 12:15-2:45pm. Banks and large shopping centers typically stay open.

ACCOMMODATIONS

Kuala Lumpur's Chinatown is a prime hunting ground for cheap accommodations. A number of inexpensive Chinese hotels and a few dorm-style hostels lurk in the area's winding streets. The stretch of Jalan Tuanku Abdul Rahman, northeast of Chinatown, between the intersection with Jalan Tun Perak and the Sogo Department Store, contains several cheap Chinese hotels.

Backpackers Travelers Inn, 60 Jl. Sultan (tel. 238 24 73). Turning onto Jl. Sultan from Jl. Cheng Lok, the conveniently located Backpackers Travelers Inn is on your right; look for the red sign. "Stevie (the) Wonder Host," his wife, and the highly professional staff have turned this hostel into *the* place to stay in Kuala Lumpur. Budget travelers convene from all corners of the globe and immediately sense the tightly knit family atmosphere. Extremely clean. The A/C lounge has nightly movies at 9pm. Laundry refreshments, lockers, and tour reservations. Dorms RM8, with A/C RM10. Singles and doubles RM22-30, with A/C RM40-50. Check-out noon, but RM2 buys luggage storage and a shower later in the day.

Ben Soo Homestay, 61B, 2nd floor, Jl. Tiong Nam (tel. 291 80 96 or 010 332 70 13). Easy access to the major bus route on Jl. Raja Laut. Call Ben Soo for a free pick-up upon arrival in KL, and he'll take you to his accommodations on the north side of the city, behind Jl. Raja Laut and close to the main sights. Budget travelers will enjoy being part of a family, rather than a customer of another KL business. Avoid the mayhem in Chinatown and snuggle in an dorm (RM10). Or get your own digs: Single RM25. Double RM30. Separate showers and baths. All with fans. Sight-seeing, car rental, bus, and plane ticketing arranged with a smile.

Kuala Lumpur International Youth Hostel, 21 Jl. Kampung Attap (tel. 273 68 70), on your right at the very end of the street. Dorms actually have spring mattresses, and the pink tile bathrooms are absolutely spotless. Laundry facilities, kitchen, TV rooms, and a prayer room for Muslims. Linen provided; lockers free. The staff is wonderfully friendly. With an approved (6 stamp) IYH card, dorms are RM15 for the first night and RM12 for subsequent evenings. They sell cards for RM15 to Malaysians, RM30 to others. Alcohol not permitted. Doors locked at midnight. Make reservations 1 month in advance. Check-out noon. MC.

Riverside Lodge, 80 Jl. Rotan (tel. 201 12 10). One of the newest and best additions to the "Travelers" family. Riverside boasts a quiet, secluded location off Jl. Kampung Attap, a 5-min. walk from Chinatown across Jl. Kinabalu. Detailed city and travel information, laundry service, and neat rooms which are emptied and scrubbed on each weekly cleaning day. Dorms RM8. Single bed RM20. Double bed RM23. Double bed with balcony RM25. RM5 per additional person.

Twin Happiness Hotel, 44 Jl. Silang (tel. 238 76 67 or 238 95 28), just past the Travelers Home. Newly renovated rooms with rumpled flooring, but furniture and guaranteed clean sheets. Free filtered cold water and hot water on request. Central location and friendly, helpful proprietors. Dorm RM8. Doubles RM30. Doubles with bath RM38. Doubles with A/C RM38. Triples with A/C and bath RM48. Quads with A/C and bath RM58. Check-out noon.

YMCA Hostel, 95 Jl. Radang Belia (tel. 274 14 39; fax 274 05 59). Inconveniently located far south of the city center; take bus #33 or #46 or minibus #12. Fantastic facilities and comfortable rooms. Your chance to play "traveling in style" in the hotel-quality AC rooms with TV. The non-A/C rooms are less impressive—no carpet and old brown budget motel blankets. The bathrooms are old but spotless. Singles RM30, with A/C and bath RM60. Doubles RM43 with A/C and bath RM73. Triples RM50. Quads RM69. Non-YMCA members pay a surcharge of RM3 per person per week. Prices include breakfast. Restaurant open 7:30am-9pm. Gym open 7am-9pm. Laundromat. Transport to airport RM17. Unmarried couples may not share a room. Check-out noon. MC, Visa.

Travelers Home, 42A Jl. Silang (tel. 201 35 46). A few paces closer to the bus station than Travelers Moon Lodge, Travelers Home is owned by the same family. Larger, cleaner, and perhaps even a bit friendlier. Singles RM20. Doubles RM23-25. Laundry service and bus ticket booking.

Travelers Moon Lodge, 36C Jl. Silang (tel. 230 66 01). Crossing Jl. Cheng Lok from the bus station and continuing past McD's and Metrojaya, the lodge is on your right, past Travelers Home and Twin Happiness. Typical inexpensive hostel, with dorm beds and bathrooms that have seen better days. Dorms RM8.50. Doubles RM25. Includes free breakfast of toast, coffee, and tea. Kitchen facilities. Laundry RM6. Reception 24 hrs. Check-out noon.

YWCA Transient Hostel, 12 Jl. Hang Jebat (tel. 230 16 23 or 238 32 25). Take Jl. Sultan from Jl. Cheng Lok and the bus station/Metrojaya area. Turn left onto Jl. Jang Jebat, and the YMCA is on your left, past Jl. Wesley. Comfortable hardwood-floored rooms are Puritan-plain; the airy lounges are a comfortable hangout, and there's an eclectic library on the first floor. *Women and married couples only.* Rooms have fans and separate baths. Singles RM30. Doubles RM50. Triples RM70. Quads RM80. Check-in 24 hrs. Check-out 10am. Make reservations during the summer and December.

Starlight Hotel, 90/92 Jl. Hang Kasturi (tel. 238 98 11). From Jl. Cheng Lock after crossing Jl. Petaling and Jl. Tun H.S. Lee, turn left onto Jl. Hang Kasturi. The Shell station will be on your right; the hotel is on your left just past the Konica shop. A jazzed-up Chinese hotel with plain but well-scrubbed rooms. A touch pricey for its age. Doubles RM60-68. Quads (2 double beds) with bath and A/C RM80. Laundry service. Coffee shop next door. Call for reservations, with your arrival time.

Tivoli Hotel, 136-138 Jl. Tuanku Abdul Rahman (tel. 292 41 08). From the Sogo, exit onto Jl. Tuanku Abdul Rahman and turn right; you'll pass Kowloon Hotel on your right and the giant Glove Silk Store on your left; the hotel is across from Disney Babyland. The slightly musty, cement-floored rooms have something of a warehouse feel, but are spacious and the prices are hard to beat. Singles RM24. Triples RM30, with bath and A/C RM45. Check-out 1pm.

FOOD

There's no shortage of good food in Kuala Lumpur; the mixing of cultures over the years has produced a brilliant medley of cuisines. In the evenings, **Jl. Sultan** and **Jl. Hang Lekir** host an open-air carnival of steamboat restaurants, *sate* sellers, and exotic-fruit juice vendors, while the **Chinatown night market** rages along Jl. Petaling. Jl. Sultan restaurants take on a much more festive atmosphere after dusk when the tables move onto the street. Restauranteurs assemble their stalls just as the sun slips past the horizon, generally closing around midnight.

The Kampung Bahru Sunday Market, located near the Muslim cemetery on Jl. Sungai Baharu in the northern part of the city, is another trusty place to search. The muddy Kelang River slaps up against several tourist restaurant-pubs behind and outside the **Central Market,** which offers romantic dining under the stars. The third floor boasts a small hawker's center that is largely ignored and a few mid-range restaurants serving Malay, Indian, and Thai food.

The Kapitan's Club, 35 Jl. Ampang (tel. 201 02 42 or 201 06 37). From the 24-hr. Telekom office, turn right and follow Jl. Gereja as it turns into Jl. Ampang. Nyonya and Malay food served in an airy, colonial-style building, complete with decorated tile floors. An almost Casablanca-esque ambiance of somnolent ceiling fans and artistically unfinished walls is dimmed a whit by the Top 40 blaring from the speakers. Kapitan chicken RM7.50. Beef *rendang* RM7.50. Portuguese baked fish RM15.50. Try the *bubur cha-cha* for RM3.50 or the *ice kacang,* a dessert made of sweet red beans, corn, *cendol,* and peanuts on a base of shaved ice and ice cream, all topped with rose syrup—it will change your ideas about permissible taste combinations (RM3.50). Open 11am-11pm. Happy hour(s) 4-8pm. AmEx, DC.

Restoran Insaf, at 2 locations: 116 Jl. Tuanku Abdul Rahman (tel. 293 97 37), from Merdeka Square, at the south end of the street on your left; and 158 Jl. Tuanku Abdul Rahman (tel. 291 28 06), a bit farther down the same street opposite the Globe Silk Store. The classy blue and white china distinguishes these cafés from the other Malay-Indian eateries along Jl. Tuanku Abdul Rahman. Excellent *nasi lemak* and *murtabak* for breakfast; old favorites like *briyani* and *mee goreng* for lunch and dinner. Open Mon.-Sat. 8am-9pm, Sun. noon-4:30pm.

Coliseum Café, 98-100 Jl. Tuanku Abdul Rahman (tel. 292 62 70), at the south end of the street, on the left as you approach from Jl. Melayu or the railway station. The grand old dame of Kuala Lumpur restaurants, this legendary restaurant-bar has been serving sizzling steaks and hearty western food since British colonials first chowed with fancy cravats and lace parasols. During the Japanese occupation, it was the hang-out of high-ranking officers of the Emperor's army. The continental decor has remained intact for the past seven decades. Sizzling steak with potatoes, tomatoes, sprouts, and salad RM23.90. Grilled fish RM6.30. Roast chicken, veggies, and chips RM7. Look for William, the genial waiter who's been around almost as long as the restaurant. Open 10am-10pm.

Restoran Ramzan, 11-13 Lebuh Pudu (tel. 201 39 70). Tucked away in front of the Central Market, Ramzan has spacious seating and a central location which keeps this joint constantly full. Ramzan offers a wide range of subcontinent dishes and staples ranging from *thosai* and *roti* to North Indian *naan* and *capati*. Save room for the Tandoori chicken (RM4) and the quickly devoured *Nasi briyani* (RM2.50). Open 6:30am-10:30pm.

Bangles, 60A Jl. Tuanku Abdul Rahman (tel. 293 01 00), at the extreme southern end of the street, near Merdeka Square. On your left, up a flight of stairs. Over 25 years old, this quiet, North Indian restaurant has a penchant not only for glass bracelets and anklets (hanging from the ceiling), but also menu poetry—"what a pity if in this city, you do not have our *naan (*RM1.90) and *roti*." Vegetarian dishes RM6-10. Try the fish *tikka masala* sizzler (RM14.90) and the double-braised orange-prawn (RM9.90). Open noon-11pm.

Restoran Rasa Utara (tel. 274 59 08 or 274 12 79), in Central Market. It would be like dining in a chalet on Tioman Island if it weren't for the Central Market surroundings. The Sunday buffet (11am-2:30pm) gives a sampling of the delicious Malay repertoire (RM14.90 adults, RM7.90 children), but the tea special (Mon.-Fri. 3-6pm) is cheaper, featuring hawker specialities like *nasi lemak* (RM2.50) and *mee goreng* (RM2.20). Open daily 8:30am-10pm. AmEx, DC, MC, Visa.

Hard Rock Café, 2 Jl. Sultan Ismail (tel. 244 41 52; fax 244 11 09). In the basement and ground floor of the Wisma Concorde. The 27th incarnation of the international burger-and-rock paraphernalia chain attracts more westerners than you've seen since that last Monster Trucks race in Boise. Fajitas RM26.50, Cajun blackened fish RM17, nachos RM12.50, all in portions big enough to feed a busload. Open Sun.-Thurs. 11:30am-2pm, Fri.-Sat. 11:30am-3am. All major credit cards.

SIGHTS

Most of the big tourist attractions lie west of the railroad. The **Kuala Lumpur Railway Station** on Jl. Sultan Hishamuddin, built in 1900, is a magnificent jumble of domes, minarets, and archways that looks more like a sultan's palace than the hub of modern Malaysia's public transportation system. **The Malayan Railway Headquarters Bldg. (KTM),** across the street, is in much the same style; a plaque outside proudly proclaims that it has 97 gothic arches on the first floor alone. Next door to the railway headquarters is the **Balai Seni Lukis Negara** (National Art Gallery; tel. 230 01 57/8), an eclectic collection of impressive artwork by Malaysian artists. The first floor features standard Chinese watercolors and scrolls of brush-stroked Chinese characters, while the second and third floors house a fantastic collection of mostly modern, multi-media works. Open 10am-6pm; Fri. 10-noon and 3-6pm. From the National Art Gallery, turn left and walk down Jl. Damansara past the Kuala Lumpur Visitor's Center and the Duty-Free Emporium to get to the **Muzium Negara** (National Museum; tel. 282 62 55), which houses exhibits of Malay weapons, musical instruments, and household utensils, a whole room of stuffed indigenous animals, and that staple of every Malaysian museum: dioramas of traditional Malay, Indian, and Peranakan wedding ceremonies. The most interesting attraction is hidden in the weapons room behind all the *keris* and spears—an "amok catcher," a two-pronged pitchfork used by British colonials to catch Malays who had "run amok." Open daily 9am-6pm. Admission RM1, under 12 free.

The **National Mosque** is on Jl. Sultan Hishamuddin; from the National Art Gallery, turn left and the mosque will be on your left past the intersection with Jl. Perdana. This modern, metallic center of the Islamic faith in Kuala Lumpur is a stark contrast to the Masjid Jame across the river. Built on two levels, the upper deck houses the main prayer hall and a reflecting pool. Visitors must dress properly: no shorts or short sleeves. If you borrow a robe (and a scarf for women) in either mosque, you can explore them entirely, sliding around in your socks. Open Sat.-Thurs. 9am-noon, 3-4pm, and 5:30-6pm, Fri. 3-4pm and 5:30-6pm.

On the western edge of the city is the 91.6 hectare **Lake Gardens,** an oasis of green just beyond Kuala Lumpur's congested freeways. From the National Art Gallery, turn left and walk up Jl. Sultan Hishamuddin, then turn left onto Jl. Perdana and follow it until you reach the gardens. The biggest draw here is the **Taman Burung** (Bird Park), an outdoor aviary housing over 100 species of tropical birds, including the strange looking Malaysian hornbills, who spend most of their time gnawing on each other's necks, feet, and the banana-shaped horns protruding from their beaks. Open 9am-6pm. Admission RM3 adults, RM1 children. Other attractions in the garden include the **Taman Orkid dan Bunga Raya,** or Orchid and Hibiscus Garden (open 9am-6pm; free); the **Deer Park,** where hordes of screaming mothers and children yell "Bambi! Bambi!" at perplexed and timid mouse-deer (open Mon.-Thurs. 10am-noon and 2-6pm, Fri. 10am-noon and 3-6pm, Sat.-Sun. and public holidays 10am-6pm; free); and the **Butterfly Park** (open Mon.-Fri. 9am-5pm, Sat.-Sun. and public holidays 9am-6pm; admission RM5 adults, RM2 children). **Boats** can be rented on the lake in the gardens (tel. 298 32 53) at RM3 per hour.

Off Jl. Parlimen in the northern section of the garden is the **National Monument,** dedicated to Malaysians who died in the two world wars and the Emergency of 1948-1960. The main sculpture was inspired by Felix de Weldon, the sculptor of the Iwo Jima Memorial.

East of the railroad tracks are some of the city's more colorful sights. **Central Market** (tel. 274 65 42, after 10am) lies on Jl. Hang Kasturi across the river from the GPO; there is a footbridge connecting the post office complex with the market. Formerly Kuala Lumpur's produce market, this Victorian building was refurbished and stuffed with three floors of souvenir shops and restaurants. Mobbed daily by locals and tourists, the market has become a symbol of Kuala Lumpur's tourist industry and a magnet for backpackers taking a break from pounding the city's very hot pavement. Open 7:30am-10pm.

The **Masjid Jame,** as curvaceous as the National Mosque is angular, stands on a lush island of palm trees at the confluence of the Kelang and Gombak Rivers behind Central Market. Built in 1907 on the site where the first settlers landed in Kuala Lumpur, the mosque is one of the most stunning sights in the city, with its multitude of grand domes, dainty minarets, and meticulous greenery.

The nearby **Sri Mahamarlamman Temple,** one of the rare Hindu temples, often overlooked for its magnificent Islamic neighbors, symbolizes religious harmony in Kuala Lumpur. From Central Market, walk down the part of Jl. Hang Kasturi that is open to traffic, turn left onto Jl. Sultan after the Starlight Hotel, and take another left onto Jl. Tun H.S. Lee across the street from the UDA Ocean shopping center. The temple is on your left. The focus of this 121-year-old temple is a silver chariot that occupies a prominent position in the procession to the Batu Caves during the Thaipusam festival. Open 6am-9pm.

The area immediately south of the Masjid Jame and east of Central Market is the most exciting and lively place in Kuala Lumpur: **Chinatown.** At dusk, the central part of Jl. Petaling becomes a night market crammed wall-to-wall with cheap clothing, inexpensive videotapes of the most recent box office smashes, top pop albums, and tourists. Food stalls and open-air restaurants roll their tables into the street on Jl. Hang Lekir and Jl. Sultan.

ENTERTAINMENT

The Jump, Wisma Inai, 241 Jl. Tun Razak (tel. 245 00 46). This brand-new pub/restaurant is the hottest sensation on the KL scene. Decorated with an interesting mix of Tiffany lamps, carousel horses, and a lone dentist's chair that doubles as drink-mixing equipment. "Performance bartending" is the attraction here, as the bar staff juggles and tosses bottles and glasses a la *Cocktail.* Copious serving of barbecue and Tex-Mex at dinner. Chicken fajitas RM23.90. Sunday champagne brunch (11am-4pm) RM125 for all-you-can-eat and drink, or RM65 for 1 glass of champagne and all-you-can-eat. Food served until midnight; dancing after 11pm. Open Sun.-Thurs. 11:30am-2am, Fri. and Sat. 11:30am-3am. Happy hour Mon.-Sat. 11:30am-7:30pm, Sun. 5pm-2am. All major credit cards.

Boom Boom Room, 11 Lorong Ampang (tel. 232 69 06/7). From the 24-hr. Telekom office, turn right; it's the blindingly blue building set away from the street on your right. A massive, hopping disco with some odd decor; check out the oriental carpets on the pillars. The front door proclaims "Dress code: GQ/Vogue." R&B downstairs; bands perform upstairs at 10:45 and 12:15pm. The staff is proud of the Monday night Miss Malaysia beauty pageant, and tourists flock to see the popular transvestite shows. Cover RM15 weekdays, RM20 weekends; includes one drink. Open Sun.-Thurs. 8pm-3am, Fri.-Sat. 8pm-4am. All major credit cards.

Barn Thai Jazzaurant, 370B Jl. Tun Razak (tel. 244 66 99), across from the Micasa Hotel apartments on the east side of the city; in a traditional Thai-style house. An eclectic collection of knickknacks—old typewriters and sewing machines, Thai wooden horses, posters of American jazz greats, teakwood bird cages—adorns the interior. Live bands every night. Good Thai cuisine on which to sober up. Beer RM8.50-14, cocktails RM12-29. Open Mon.-Thurs. noon-1am, Fri. and Sat. noon-3am, dinner only Sun. Happy hour 5-9pm. All major credit cards.

■ NEAR KUALA LUMPUR

The most famous attractions outside the city center are the **Batu Caves** (tel. 689 62 84). Hindu devotees descend on the caves in the hundreds for the annual Thaipusam Festival, armed with *kavadis,* hooks and needles used to pierce the skin. For the rest of the year, the caves lie open to the public and provide a home for the burgeoning community of docile, but extremely hungry, wild monkeys. Climb the 272 steps to the main cave for free or pay RM0.50 to view the Gallery Cave's paintings of Hindu mythology. Take the #11 minibus from Central Market, Sri Jay Bus #349 from Lebu Ampang Bus Stand, or Len Omnibuses #69 or 70 from Pudu Raya Terminal. open 7:30am-6:30pm.

The **Royal Selangor Pewter Factory,** 4 Jl. Usahawan Enam, Setapak Jaya (tel. 422 100), makers of the world's most famous pewter goods, has the world's largest pewter tankard. Amiable guides take you through the whole pewter production process, serve you cold drinks from the finished product, and hover attentively—suggesting expensive goblet sets and tea services from their well-stocked souvenir showrooms. Open Mon.-Sat. and public holidays 8:30am-4:45pm, Sun. 9am-4pm. Take buses W12 or W10 from the Lebuh Ampang bus stand (RM0.70). The fascinating **Orang Asli Museum** (tel. 689 21 22) houses exhibits relating to Malaysia's indigenous people. Take bus 174 from the Lebuh Ampang bus stand (RM1). Open Sun.-Thurs. and Sat. 9am-5:30pm; free. See what 500 species of animal and fish call home at the **National Zoo and Aquarium** (tel. 408 34 22); the exhibits of feathered and hairy creatures are the most worthwhile. Take Bus #170 (RM0.80). Open daily 9am-

5pm. Admission RM5 adults, RM2 children. The new **Mines Wonderland** amusement park (tel. 948 74 02 or 942 50 10) in Sri Kembangan, 20min. away from Kuala Lumpur, proudly advertises itself as one of the very few (maybe the only) places in Malaysia where Malays can experience the severe chills of less fortunate climes for a few brief moments, and thank their lucky stars afterwards. The Wonderland's Snow House features artificial snow and ice, while the Spring Garden tries to recreate the feeling of that unheard of season in Malaysia with fake waterfalls, wall murals and a fog machine. Take a cab. Open daily 11am-11pm. Admission Mon.-Fri. RM6 adults, RM3 children; Sat.-Sun. and public holidays RM10 adults, RM5 children.

■■■ MELAKA

Sometime in 1440, a mouse-deer trapped by hunting dogs decided not to accept its fate gracefully and instead turned and kicked one of the hounds into the river. An exiled Sumatran prince—the dog's owner—witnessed the event and, taking the deer's unusual bravery as an auspicious omen, promptly founded the city of Melaka on the site. Over the next 500 years, Melaka grew into a major port; its rulers had close dealings with China's Ming emperors and were visited by merchants and emissaries from India and the Middle East. The Portuguese arrived not long after in 1509 and conquered the city two years later; 130 years of Portuguese rule (and energetic Christian conversion efforts of the Muslim locals by St. Francis Xavier and others) followed. The Dutch attacked Melaka and defeated the Portuguese defenders in 1641, but after Holland's defeat at the hands of Napoleon in 1795, Dutch leaders turned Melaka over to their British allies to prevent it from falling into French hands. Briefly returned to Holland in 1818, the city was permanently signed over to the British and remained a British colony until its independence in 1957.

Reminders of European rule, in the form of churches, government buildings, and graveyards, exist all over Melaka, but the legends and heroes of the pre-Portuguese days live on in the popular imagination. Streets bearing the names of indigenous heroes, alongside their European names, are one testament to this period. Lorong Hang Jebat in old Melaka and Jl. Hang Tuah in the main business district, for example, are named for two early heroes whose story has become a symbol of the greatest period in Melaka's history. Two blood brothers, Hang Jebat and Hang Tuah, saved a prime minister from assassination and, after being rewarded with positions in the royal household, were quickly caught up in palace intrigues designed to discredit him. Spirited away by the prime minister, Hang Tuah narrowly escaped execution, but his brother Hang Jebat rebelled in his anger, causing the sultan to flee. The ever faithful courtier Hang Tuah promptly challenged his brother to a duel and killed him after three days of fighting. To Melakans, Hang Tuah represents loyalty and Hang Jebat justice, and their duel the clash between these two virtues.

Despite its burden of history and its eclipse by Singapore and Kuala Lumpur, Melaka remains a lively town with plenty of hotels, cafés, and night markets. History buffs will find what they're looking for, but Melaka is no ghost town. It may, in fact, offer Malaysia's happiest medium between urban activity and small-town charm.

ORIENTATION

The city sprawls across both sides of the **Melaka River,** which winds its way southwest as it empties into the **Straits of Melaka.** While several of the main thoroughfares have different names in different parts of the city, the visitor still should have little trouble with navigation. The bulk of Melaka's historic attractions, for example, are grouped along the water, at the mouth of the river. On the **northwest side** of the river's mouth are the Buddhist temples, antique shops, and Baba-Nyonya homes of **"Old Melaka,"** running along **Jalan Tun Tun Cheng Lok** and **Jalan Hang Jebat,** both parallel to the coastline. At their far end, **Jalan Kubu** runs perpendicular and connects these two roads to **Jalan Hang Tuah-Jalan Munshi Abdullah,** which also runs parallel to the coastline farther inland and around which Melaka's business district thrives.

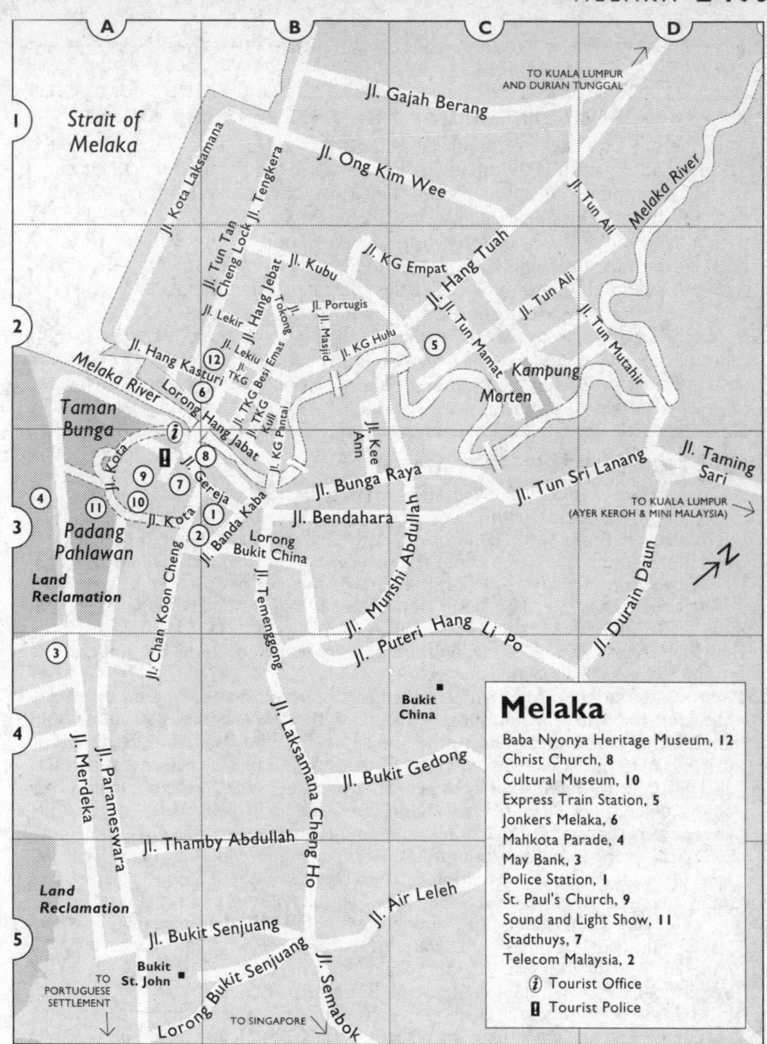

Jalan Bendahara-Jalan Laksmana intersects this street and runs along the river to the coast on the south side of the river. The **southeast** side of the river mouth is prime shopping grounds for the sightseer and is easily recognized by the bright red **Christ Church** and the **Stadthuys.** The traffic circle next to the river also boasts a tourist office, and the gateway to backpacker heaven—**Jalan Merdeka.** Take this street in front of the offensively large and pink Mahkota Parade mall to **Taman Melaka Raya,** a series of side-streets off Jl. Merdeka which offer some of the best values for budget accommodations in all of Malaysia.

The town is almost unbearably hot between noon and 4pm. The best time to see the outdoor attractions is before 11am, saving the museums for the hotter part of the day. The town is easy to traverse on foot, and trishaws stand ready near the tourist office should your feet fail you.

The Life of Sir Stamford Raffles: Part the Third

With the fundamentals of Colonialist philosophy under his belt, Stamford Raffles, the young stud of the civil service, moved from Penang on to Malacca where he promptly became Agent to the Governor-General of Malaya. During this time, through his unparalleled foresight and powers of persuasion, he single-handedly saved Malacca from complete destruction by the British. He was quickly, but not surprisingly, promoted to Secretary to the Governor-General. Never above mixing with natives, Raffles quickly learned the Malay language, which afforded him greater interaction with the local people. He even had friends among the Malay, one of whom, the Sultan of Sambar in Borneo, gave him a pet orangutan which Raffles dressed in trousers, a coat, and hat. Yes, good Sir Raffles was always trying to improve the lot of poor, unfortunate souls. (To hear what Sir Stamford did next, see page 665.)

PRACTICAL INFORMATION

Tourist Office: Melaka Tourist Information Center (tel. 283 65 38; fax 249 686), on Jl. Kota near the bridge connecting Jl. Laksamana and Lorong Hang Jebat, across the street from the Stadthuys and the clock tower. Limited selection of pamphlets, but be sure to pick up the silver *American Express-Melaka Heritage Trail* brochure, which maps out a guide to a number of monuments (it's especially good for Old Melaka). Open Mon.-Thurs. 8:45am-5pm, Fri. 8:45am-12:15pm and 2:45-5pm, Sat. 8:45am-5pm, Sun. 9am-5pm.

Tourist Police: (tel. 270 32 38), on the "pedestrian mall" section of Jl. Kota, across from the tourist information center.

Tours: The tourist information center runs 45-min. boat tours up and down the Melaka River. The schedule varies; check with the tourist office. RM6 adult, RM3 children. If you don't have any specific sights in mind, you can hire a trishaw driver (RM15 per hour) who will take you to some of the major tourist attractions and probably throw in some commentary as well. A normal trishaw can seat two adults; bigger parties can hire several trishaws and go in a cavalcade.

Currency Exchange: OCBC Bank, 6 Lorong Hang Jebat (tel. 282 48 12; fax 247 525), just over the bridge from the tourist office. Open Mon.-Fri. 10am-3pm, Sat. 9:30-11:30am. **Malaysian Banking Berhad (MayBank),** 6 Jl. Hang Tuah (tel. 282 24 77), is close to the bus and taxi stations. Turn left as you emerge from the small street leading to the station; the bank is on your left. **ATM services.** Open Mon.-Fri. 9:30am-4pm, Sat. 9:30-11am. **Bank of Commerce,** on Jl. Melaka Raya. Open Mon.-Fri. 9:30am-3pm, Sat. 9:30-11:30am.

Post Office: GPO (tel. 283 38 60) on Jl. Bukit Baru. Take bus #19 from the local bus station. Open Mon.-Sat. 8am-6pm, Sun. 10am-1pm. Use the mini-post for buying stamps and mailing letters or packages: **Pos 2020** (tel. 284 84 40) on Jl. Laksamana. Located behind and to the left of Christ Church. **Poste Restante** must explicitly say this office or it will go to the GPO. Open Mon.-Sat. 8am-5pm. **Postal code:** Jl. Merdeka and the hostel 75000; Old Melaka 75200; business district 75100.

Telephones: Telekom, Jl. Banda Kaba (tel. 284 91 91). Up the alley between Christ Church and Stadthuys, turn right, walk past the Dutch graveyard, and hang a left at the sign for Jl. Banda Kaba just past the cemetery. Not a full-service Kedai Telekom office, but a booth on your left sells phonecards; nearby are cardphones. Open 24 hrs. **Telephone code:** 06.

Train Station: The nearest train station is at Tampin, 38km north of Melaka; Melaka office (tel. 282 30 91).

Bus Station: The express bus station is on Jl. Tun Ali; long-distance buses are run by private companies, whose tiny offices circle the station. The **Kuala Lumpur-Melaka Express,** 324 Jl. Kilang (tel. 282 25 04), has buses to **Kuala Lumpur** (every hour., 8am-6pm, RM6.75). The **Johora Express** (tel. 282 52 01) runs to

Singapore (8, 9, 11am, 1, 3, 5, 7 and 8pm, RM11). **Express Mutiara** runs to **Butterworth** (9:30pm, RM23).

Taxi Station: On Jl. Tun Ali, at the opposite end of the road from the express bus station. A cab to **Kuala Lumpur** costs RM17, to **Muar** RM5, and to **Batu Pahat** RM10. A trip to **Port Dickson** costs RM45 for the whole car, but the fare can be split with other passengers.

Local Transportation: The town is compact enough to cover on foot. **Trishaw** drivers congregate around the tourist office and the Stadthuys; it should cost about RM5 per one way trip or RM15 per hour.

Bike Rental: Muhibbah Enterprise (tel. 283 06 31), on Jl. Munshi Abdullah, in the Intan Plaza Shopping Arcade in the Plaza Inn. RM5 per day. Open 10am-6:30pm.

Supermarket: Parkson Supermarket, (tel. 283 95 23) in the basement of Mahkota Parade. It's the huge pink complex on Jl. Merdeka. Open daily 10am-6pm.

Pharmacies: Guardian Pharmacy, (tel. 282 94 99) on the ground floor of Mahkota Parade. Everything you could possibly need, from condoms to contact lens solution. Open daily 10am-10pm. **Apex Pharmacy,** 83A Jl. Munshi Abdullah (tel. 282 52 96), on your left as you approach from the bus station. Open 9am-7pm.

Laundry: Pusat Dobi Ace, 122 Jl. Munshi Abdullah (tel. 238 155), across from the Melaka Renaissance Hotel. RM5.60 per kilo, ready same day if you come in the morning. Open 9am-7pm. Most guest houses have laundry for RM4-6 per load.

English Bookstore: Sykt Buku Thai Kuang, (tel. 282 05 11) on the 2nd floor, Mahkota Parade. Best-selling novels and glossy fashion mags. Open 10am-10pm.

Hospital: (tel. 282 23 44). Take bus #19 from the local bus station.

Emergency: tel. 999. **Fire:** tel. 994.

ACCOMMODATIONS

An amazing number of clean and comfortable rooms are available. Most of the least expensive options are off Jl. Merdeka, just beyond the Mahkota Parade Mall. There is another set of budget hotels on the small streets off Jl. Munshi Abdullah on the other side of town. Don't worry about the hoard of guest house owners and "runners" who will greet you at the bus terminal. Most are not there to cheat you, but to tell you about their place, hand you a flyer, show you pictures, and subsidize your taxi or trishaw ride if you choose their establishment.

Malacca Town Holiday Lodge, 148/149B Taman Melaka Raya (tel. 284 88 30). Well, penny pinchers, it doesn't get much better than this. MTHL stands alone when it comes to cleanliness, comfort, and a conscientious attention to detail. The matriarch, Mrs. Lee, her charismatic husband, and the personable, professional staff offer the maximum value for your ringgit. The cool and airy building is in the heart of the city's sights, and the entire building seems to be religiously scrubbed every day, until it's dirt and pest free. Singles RM12 and RM15. Doubles RM15 and RM18. Doubles with a combination of attached bathroom and A/C RM25-RM40. Restaurant with tasty breakfast, under RM3. Kitchen, laundry service, bicycles for rent. Common room with TV. Travel tips, city info, and guided tours of the city.

Malacca Town Holiday Lodge #2, 52 A,B,C Kampong Empat (tel. 284 69 05). Located in the Wine and Spirits Association building off Jl. Kubu, MTHL2 is the larger and newer sibling of the original. Farther from the historical sights, it is still within walking distance and is close to the bus terminal. Three breezy floors of spacious rooms. Same rates and amenities as MTHL1. Look for the helpful Mr. Paul Lim or Mrs. Lee herself at the bus terminal.

Eastern Heritage, 8 Jl. Bukit China (tel. 283 30 26). One of Melaka's best, but dorm lovers could do better elsewhere, as the attic dorm is hot and a bit cramped (RM6). Singles (RM12-18) and doubles (RM15-20) are clean and the dark-wood interior is exquisite. In the heart of Chinatown and close to the historic district. Impressive array of extras: laundry service, indoor "dipping" pool, city tours, and evening excursions for groups.

Robin's Nest Guest House, 205B Taman Melaka Raya (tel. 282 91 42). Pass Mahkota Parade on Jl. Merdeka, turn right at the first intersection and look for the newly renovated and relocated Robin's Nest on the right. Convenient location for sights, banks, and food stalls. Has lockers, laundry service, and kitchen facilities. The Nest fills up quickly as a hang-out for guests of all nations, so call before arriving. Dorms RM7, singles RM12-15, doubles RM18. All with fans and common bath. Rooms with A/C cost RM30-35.

Traveller's Lodge, 214/215B, Taman Melaka Raya (tel. 010 666 80 62). The atmosphere is a bit more subdued a few doors down from the bustling Nest. While quiet and laid-back (listen for the Jim Croce), the Traveller's Lodge has quality accommodations. The owners will remind you that this is "simply our home" as you retreat to a small, clean, inexpensive room. Terrific if you're arriving from the chaos of a KL or Singapore hostel. Dorms RM6, singles RM12, doubles RM15, triples RM21. Baths for 3 rooms, and no squat toilets. Laundry RM4 per load.

Sunny's Inn Guest House, 270A/B Taman Melaka Raya (tel. 283 79 90). Sunny is more than energetic, he is an astute businessman and an excellent host, having established one of the friendliest atmospheres around. In addition to his prime location, Sunny provides hot and cold showers, international telephone and fax services, bicycle, motorbike, car and van rentals, laundry and kitchen facilities, and updated travel info. His pride and joy are the two movies shown nightly in the living room. With fan: dorms RM6-7, singles RM12-18, doubles RM15-20, triples RM21-28. With A/C RM9-10, RM20-22, RM25-35, and RM 32-37, respectively.

Melaka Youth Hostel, 341 Taman Melaka Raya (tel. 282 79 15). If you really like the dorm-scene, this is the place. Eighty beds! With fan RM10, with A/C RM12, for the first night. RM7 and RM9 for each additional night. Also has common room with TV, dining room, laundry service, and the always useful—bathrooms. Separate accommodations for men and women; only open for YHA or HI members.

FOOD

Melaka's multi-cultural community and long history of interaction with other countries means that quality Malay, Chinese, Indian, Portuguese, and Nyonya cuisine all dwell happily side by side. There are **hawkers' stands** in the streets between the Plaza Hotel and Jl. Bunga Raya (open 5pm-10pm). There are also **food stands** on Jl. Bunga Raya itself, near the intersection with Jl. Munshi Abdullah, and on Jl. Merdeka near the river, at the opposite end of the road from the hostel area. Many travelers opt for a light, western guest house breakfast, grab lunch at a superb Indian restaurant, and save the Chinese feasts for the evening.

Rasturan San Pedro, 4D Aranjo Rd. Ujong Pasir, Portuguese Settlement (tel. 284 57 34 or 284 21 70). Take bus #17 from the local bus station to Medan Portuguese, walk down the main road and turn right when you see the sign. A rustic wooden cabin, San Pedro's is famous throughout Melaka for its excellent seafood and unbeatable atmosphere—a statue of the Virgin Mary and a garrulous English-speaking bird greet visitors in the foyer. The romantic might want to try the intimate "Cabana de Amor" section. Portuguese fried *sotong,* or honey-fried *sotong* RM8-10; prices for fish and crab vary with season and availability. Open daily noon-2pm and 5:30-10:30pm.

Restoran Veni, 34 Jl. Temenggong (tel. 284 95 70). From the tourist info center walk down Jl. Laksamana, heading away from the historic part of town. Turn right onto Jl. Temenggong just after the Public Bank; Restoran Veni is about ½-block on your right. A spotless and very friendly place whose walls are smothered in plaques proclaiming it one of the best restaurants in the area. Plain *dosai* RM.40. *Masala thosai* RM1.20. *Biryani* RM3.50 Open daily 7am-9:30pm.

Lucky Famous Restaurant, 578 Taman Melaka Raya (tel. 284 00 31). The first choice of guest house proprietors and local Chinese in-the-know, Lucky Famous offers Chinese dishes of unparalleled variety and quality. Don't be fooled by the Americanized name. Gather a group from your guest house, or tag along with its owners; Lucky Famous caters to large groups eating several courses. Dishes, RM10 on average, feed several people. Open 10am-2:30pm, 6-11pm.

Restoran Vazhai Elai (Banana Leaf Restaurant), 42 Jl. Munshi Abdullah (tel. 283 16 07). If you're looking to explore Melaka and to delve your hands into a heap of white rice and *dall,* head to one of the best Indian joints in town, a short walk on Jl. Munshi Abdullah, heading toward the river from Jl. Bunga Raya. Enjoy yourself amidst the catchy Tamil music and the curious stares from children who wonder why you're using a fork and spoon. As authentic and delicious as it gets. More than you can eat will cost you less than RM5.

Jonkers Melaka, 17 Jl. Hang Jebat (tel. 283 55 78). From the tourist information center, cross the bridge and go down the road; the restaurant is on your left about 10 doors down. Nyonya and western cuisine served in a genuine *peranakan* house; small tables and a quiet setting make for an intimate atmosphere. Set of four Nyonya dishes RM16. Also serve a weekend special, usually delicacies such as Portuguese baked fish. Open daily 10am-5pm.

Madras Café, 50 Jl. Temenggong (tel. 283 07 40), a few doors down from Restoran Veni, on the corner of Jl. Temenggong and Lorong Bukit China. An extremely popular Indian café mobbed at every hour of the day and night. Those in the know claim it dishes up the best *murtabak* (RM2.50) in town. Open daily 7am-10:30pm.

Restoran Kerala, 197 Taman Melaka Raya (tel. 284 52 64). This South Indian restaurant across from Malacca Town Holiday Lodge serves up scrumptious *briyani* and fish-head curry as its specialties, always according to Indian custom, on banana leaves. *Roti*, *capati*, and *tandoor* also available. Friendly service, tasty cuisine, and a street-side location make this ideal for watching the tourists go by. Dishes RM1-4. Open 8:30am-9:30pm.

SIGHTS

Melaka has no shortage of sights. Across from the tourist information center, the bright pink Stadthuys, built by the Dutch in the mid-1600s as the official residence of the Governor of Melaka, now contain the **Melaka Ethnographical and Historical Museums** (tel. 284 19 34). The **Ethnographic Museum** houses exhibits of porcelain, weaponry, stamps, medals, and coins used in Melaka over the centuries, as well as dioramas of scenes from a traditional Malay wedding and a costume gallery depicting the garb of the various groups in Melaka. One glass case holds the boxing gloves of Mohammed Ali. The **Historical Museum** traces Melaka's development from the fateful mouse-deer kick to the present day. Interesting for those who relish Melakan history, but the Ethnographic Museum is quite a bit livelier. One ticket buys admission to both museums (RM2 adults, RM1 children). Open Sat.-Thurs. 9am-6pm, Fri. 9am-12:15pm and 2:45-6pm.

Christ Church, next door to the Stadthuys, was built by the Dutch in 1753 to commemorate the occupation of Melaka. Though reconsecrated as an Anglican church by the British (from the original Dutch reform), services have never stopped being held since 1753—not even (the fathers proudly note) during the Japanese occupation. Some of the tombstones in the floor are even older than the church itself and nobody knows exactly where they came from, though it is assumed they were moved from St. Paul's. The large, well-preserved stone in the center aisle attracts the most attention. It belonged to an Armenian merchant and bears a rather sentimental inscription in Armenian and a no-nonsense, just-the-facts-ma'am one in Dutch. Open Thurs.-Tues. 9am-1pm and 3-5pm, Wed. 9am-1pm.

Around the bend from the Stadthuys, in the heart of the historic district, is a steep flight of stairs leading up to a well-known graveyard within the ruins of **St. Paul's Church.** Built in 1521 by the Portuguese as a Catholic chapel, the church was appropriated and reconsecrated as Protestant by the Dutch when they acquired Melaka in 1641. Dozens of tombstones, once laid in the floor, are now lined up against the crumbling walls. In the back, where the altar normally would be, is an open (and empty) tomb covered with a wire cage. It was here that St. Francis Xavier's supposedly "incorrupt" body was buried for nine months before being sent on to its permanent resting place in Goa, India. People have taken to tossing small change into the tomb for luck. There is a beautiful view of the Straits of Melaka from the hilltop.

Another flight of steps leads down the hill to the **Porta de Santiago,** part of the fortress **A Famosa,** built by the Portuguese when they took over Melaka in 1511. When the Dutch came into power, they stamped the coat of arms of the Dutch East India Company on the entrance and archway, the Porta de Santiago, where it remains today. Some 150 years later, the British demolished most of A Famosa while Melaka was in their hands to ensure that Dutch military strength in Melaka would not be able to challenge British power in Southeast Asia. The Porta de Santiago was saved by Sir Stamford Raffles, who (as if founding modern Singapore weren't enough) intervened to stop the destruction which, unfortunately, was already in its last stages. The inside of the archway is now covered with graffiti and is occupied by the odd hawker or two selling cold drinks.

Around the bend from this is the **Cultural Museum** (tel. 282 07 69), housed in a luxurious wooden replica of the old Sultan's Palace. Dioramas depict the Sultan's audience chamber, with everyone from the Prime Minister (the Bendahara) to a condemned criminal in his proper place, and the Sultan's bedchamber, from which even the queen was excluded without permission. There is also a diorama showing the epic duel between Hang Tuah and Hang Jebat. Open Sun.-Thurs. and Sat. 9am-6pm, Fri. 9am-12:15pm and 2:45-6pm; admission RM2 adults, RM1 children. The meticulously manicured garden in front of the palace is the site of the **nightly sound and light show,** a multi-media extravaganza depicting Melakan history. Daily hour-long shows take place at 8pm in Bahasa Malaysia and 9:30pm in English. During the month of Ramadan, there is one show daily, in English, at 8:30pm. Admission RM5 for adults and RM3 for children under 15. Tickets are sold at the Cultural Museum's ticket booth at the entrance to the complex.

Across the river from the historic European buildings is what is commonly known as **"Old Melaka,"** a district of narrow winding streets and old Chinese shopfronts. The fascinating **Baba Nyonya Heritage Museum** is at 48-50 Jl. Tan Cheng Lock (tel. 283 12 73); from the tourist information center cross the bridge and turn left when you see the OCBC Bank. Take a right at the next intersection and the museum is on your right, about 1-½ blocks down the street. The building was constructed in the 1890s as a private residence of a prominent Baba Nyonya (Chinese-Malay) family and was converted into a museum in 1985 when the fourth generation decided to build a house of their own. The ancestral shrine on the ground floor contains photographs of the founder of the family, a Chinese trader, and the Malay lady he married. Their son (a Baba, or male of Chinese-Malay descent) and his wife (a Nyonya, or woman of Chinese-Malay descent) are pictured in the entrance hall. The rest of the building contains the original furnishings—canopied beds, carved wooden chairs made by Chinese artisans, and an overwhelmingly large collection of knickknacks from all over the world, placed more or less as they were when the building was a private home. There are few explanatory plaques, so it would be wise to take the free guided tour and then go back to see items of particular interest. Open 10am-12:30pm and 2-4:30pm; admission RM7 adults, RM4 children.

Farther away from the historic part of town is **Bukit China,** a hill that was originally designated the residence of the hundreds of attendants that accompanied Princess Hang Li Poh to Melaka when she came from China to marry the sultan. The hill is now a Chinese Graveyard. Locals use the hill as a jogging trail, ignoring the elaborate 10,000 and more graves lying about. At the foot of the hill is Hang Li Poh's well, built for her after she became Queen of Melaka. Legend has long held that anyone who drinks from the well is guaranteed to return to Melaka; the Dutch and the forces of the Johor Sultanate proved this wrong by poisoning the well during the wars of the 1500s-1600s to kill their enemies. Nowadays, people toss coins in through the grate covering the well to ensure a return trip to Melaka.

The descendants of marriages between Portuguese colonists and local Malays live in a settlement south of the historic area. The **Portuguese Settlement** is hot and somnolent during the day; the main attractions are the seafood restaurants around the Medan Portugis (Portuguese Square). On Saturdays at 8:30pm, Portuguese dance troupes perform in front of the Restoran de Lisbon (tel. 284 80 67). Check with the tourist office for details about the **Festa San Pedro.**

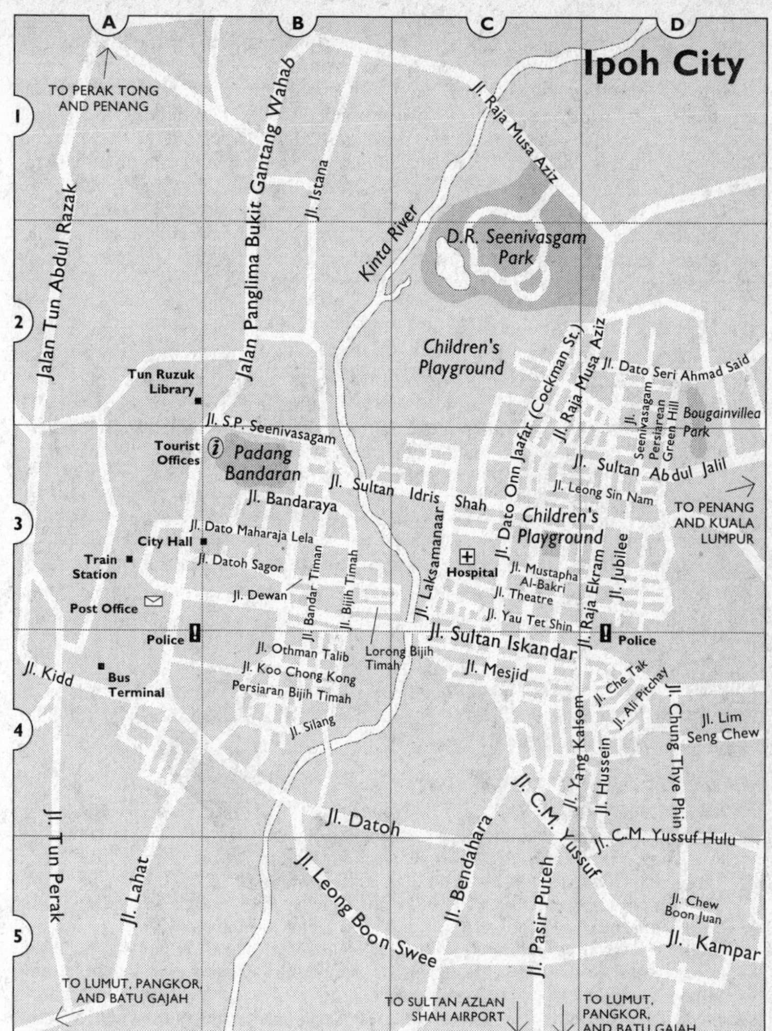

■■■ IPOH

Names such as "The Tin City" or "The Bougainvillea City" hardly do justice to the capital of this bit of Perak. While this large and still growing city along the Kinta river has maintained and cultivated its flora and it doubtless owes it historical boom to the first mining of tin in 1890, Ipoh's origins extend much farther back, and its appeal is more than just pretty flowers. Ipoh began as a small village harbor administered by a Sultan-appointed territorial chief, through which junks from the Straits of Melaka would pass en route to the Perak River. The name comes from the Ipoh tree, indigenous to the Kinta Valley, which produced a poisonous latex used by native hunters for their blow-pipe darts.

The English, French, Chinese, and Indians began a mass migration to Ipoh in 1890, and in 1905 the city spilled across to the east side of the Kinta River. In a few years, the village grew into a town, the town into a city, and today Ipoh covers 171 sq.km with over half a million people within its borders.

Now that the tin mines have all been shut down, very little colonial influence remains, except for some architecture, exemplified by the train station and city hall and a few die-hard institutions, such as the Majestic Ipoh Hotel and the FMS Bar and Restaurant. Ipoh is a modern Malaysian capital and a major transportation hub, spanning both sides of the Kinta River and exhibiting the usual *melange* of Chinese, Indian, and Malay cultures. While its newer east side has cornered the market on dining, shopping, and urban practicality, its historic west boasts grand architecture and stately gardens. Just beyond Ipoh's border, fascinating sights, including Buddhist cave temples, hot springs, and ghostly castles and towns, are all within reach.

ORIENTATION

Ipoh is 205km north of Kuala Lumpur along the main highway, Highway #1, halfway between KL and Penang. The **Kinta River,** running north-south, splits Ipoh roughly in half. The **bus** and **train stations** are on the far west side of town, and the Town Hall is across the street from the train station on **Jalan Panglima Bukit Gantang Wahab.** The tourist information office is behind it and to the left, on **Jalan Bandar.** Exiting the bus terminal, the Southeastern Hotel is to the right, on the corner and across **Jalan Lahat.** Following Jl. Lahat into town, you'll pass through Ipoh's "Little India" and then Chinatown.

Much of Ipoh's commercial activity takes place on the east side of town. The **Central Market** takes up a whole city block bounded on the west by **Jalan Laxamana,** and on the east by **Jalan Dato Onn Jaafar.** The city's main thoroughfares form a grid, and for an easy understanding of its layout, consider six streets running north to south. From the bus station going east you hit Jl. Panglima Bukit Gantang Wahab, **Jalan Sultan Yussuf,** the Kinta River, the short Jl. Laxamana, Jl. Dato Onn Jaafar, **Jalan Raja Musa Aziz,** and **Jalan Raja Ekram.** Its northernmost cross street is **Jalan Sultan Idris Shah,** and parallel to it is **Jalan Sultan Iskandar Shah.** A taxi will take you across the city for about RM4.

PRACTICAL INFORMATION

Tourist Office: There are two tourist offices: **DBI Tourist Information Center** (tel. 532 800), on Jl. Bandar near the Town Hall and Padang Ipoh should be able to answer your questions and provide you with maps *ad nauseam*. Open Mon.-Thurs. 8am-12:45pm and 2-4:15pm, Fri. 8am-12:15pm and 2:45-4:15pm, Sat. 8am-12:45pm. For regional information, **Perak Tourist Center** (tel. 532 800) is on Jl. Dato Sagor, near the State Mosque and Birch Memorial Tower.

Currency Exchange: Assar Trading, 15 Jl. Lahat (tel. 538 389), located in "Little India." Open Mon.-Sat. 9am-4:30pm. There are banks all over town where money can be changed for a RM5-6 surcharge.

Post Office: Pejabat Pos Besar (tel. 548 555), next door to the train station. Open Mon.-Sat. 8am-8pm. **Postal code:** 30670.

Telephones: There are 2 **Telekom Malaysias** with Home Country Direct. **Kedai Telekom,** Jl. Dato Onn Jaafar (tel. 549 292, ext. 164), south from the central market. Open Mon.-Sat. 7am-10pm, Sun. 7am-1pm. Also on Jl. Sultan Idris Shah, near the Kinta River (tel. 253 77 88). Open Sat.-Thurs. 8:30am-4:15pm, Fri. 8:30am-12:30pm. **Telephone code:** 03.

Airport: Sultan Azlan Shah Airport, Jl. Lapangan Terbang (tel. 312 47 70; 24-hr. reservation hotline 746 30 00). 7km outside town. Flights carry an airport tax of RM5. MAS flights to: **Kuala Lumpur** (30min., RM66 one-way) and **Singapore** (90min., RM244). **MAS Office,** Lot 108, Bangunan Seri Kinta, Jl. Sultan Idris Shah (tel. 241 41 55, at airport 312 24 59). Open Mon.-Fri. 8:30am-5pm, Sat. 8:30am-3pm. Taxis to the airport cost RM10.

Trains: KTMB Ipoh (tel. 254 79 87 or 254 04 81), on Jl. Panglima Bukit Gantang Wahab. Trains to: **Kuala Lumpur** (express, 10:30am and 5:30pm, 3-½hr, RM22; mail trains, 12:30pm, 4-½hr, RM7.80) and **Butterworth** (express, 10:40am, 2:20, and 5:40pm, 3-½hr., RM21; mail trains 1:30am, 5hr., RM6.90).

Buses: Medan Kidd Bus Terminal, on Jl. Kidd, in the southwest corner of town. Buses going nearly everywhere. **Kuala Lumpur** (every hour, RM8-8.50). Buses to **Lumut,** the launching town for Pulau Pangkor, (every hour, RM3.80) leave from across the street from the main terminal.

Taxis: A ride from one side of town to the other usually costs RM4. The **taxi stand** is at the Medan Kidd Terminal, but these are mainly for long distance travel. They can be hired for local sight-seeing at RM15 per hour. Expensive, but convenient.

Car Rental: Avis Rent-A-Car (tel. 313 65 86), at the Ipoh Airport. Open Mon.-Sat. 7:30am-7pm, Sun. 7:30am-5pm. **Hertz** (tel. 313 71 09 or 313 38 22).

Library: Perpustakaan Tun Razak, Jl. Panglima Bukit Gantang Wahab. Follow the road north from the train station; it's a new building on the left before a church. Air-conditioned. Open to browsing, but not borrowing, by foreigners. English books on the 3rd-floor Open Tues.-Sat. 10am-8pm, Mon. 9:30am-8pm.

Markets: The big **central day market** is on the east side of town bounded by Jl. Laxamana and Jl. Dato Onn Jaafar.

Pharmacy: Apex Pharmacy, Lots 11-12, Yik Foong Complex (ground floor), Jl. Laxamana (tel. 253 86 55). Open 10am-9pm.

Hospital: (tel. 533 289 or 533 612) on Jl. Hospital, on the northeastern outskirts.

Emergency: tel. 999.

Police: (tel. 501 736 or 535 522), on Jl. Sultan Iskandar.

ACCOMMODATIONS

Out of a whole range of accommodations in Ipoh, few guest houses are geared toward backpacking travelers. Hotels can be found all over town, however, and many offer prices reasonable to even the most frugal journeyman.

YMCA of Ipoh, 211 Jl. Raja Musa Aziz (tel. 254 08 09 or 253 94 64). Nestled in the green countryside extending from D.R. Seenivasagam Park—just a little farther than you'll want to walk—this establishment offers everything from tennis to Tae-Kwon-Do, from Japanese to Jazzercize, from...well you get the picture. Cheap, clean rooms to boot. Single with A/C and attached bath RM43. Doubles RM51 and up according to size and TV. A temporary membership of RM1 per week is required for non-members.

Tokyo Hotel, 159-161 Jl. Raja Musa Aziz (tel. 254 20 05/6 or 254 00 84). A short walk into town from the YMCA. Convenient location. The Tokyo rents impressive, clean and large "singles" with 2 beds and full baths RM25, with A/C RM40. TVs for RM5. Their card proclaims: "The Warmth Welcomes you a Tokyo Hotel."

Cathay Hotel, 88-94 Jl. C.M. Yussuf (tel.241 33 22 or 241 36 28). The endearing Chinese owner gives good advice on what to do in Ipoh. Unfortunately, the Cathay is not in a good location at the southeast corner of town—a good 10-min. walk from the center. Single/double with fan and shared bathroom RM18.90, with private bath RM21.90. Double with bath RM26.40, and A/C RM31.90.

The Majestic Ipoh, (tel. 255 56 05 or 255 33 93) on Jl. Panglima Bukit Gantang Wahab. The expensive alternative, but worth every ringgit. This hotel has the unique feature of being above the train station in a restored colonial structure. Take the old-style elevator up to the 3rd floor, where the reception desk presides over an immense balcony with a view of City Hall, Ipoh, and the mountains beyond. All rooms have A/C. Standard doubles are RM80.50, triples RM100, 4-person room RM120. International phone service. Locomotive Coffeehouse on the ground floor. All major credit cards. Prices fluctuate, but rugged backpackers may be able to bargain for lower rates with sad tales about living on a tight budget.

FOOD

Ipoh is reputed to have some of the best Chinese food in Malaysia. Of particular renown is *kway teow,* a dish of flat rice-noodles, chicken, vegetables, and seafood that can be fried or served in soup. Ask for it in any of the Chinese coffee shops (*kedai kopi*) in town, many of which are concentrated in Chinatown around **Jalan Leech** (now called Jl. Bandar Timah, but most Chinese seem reluctant to use the new name). For Malay food, the **Pusat Penjaja Padang Kanak** on Jl. Raja Musa Aziz is a food center with at least 40 different stalls serving up inexpensive and delicious meals and desserts.

Kedai Kopi Kong Heng, 75 Jl. Leech. Join the hordes lunching at this popular Chinese restaurant. Try the *kway teow,* or whatever the person next to you is having (everything looks great). Join in the din by yelling out your order. Open 8am-4pm.

Restoran Kader, 71 Jl. Sultan Yussuf (tel. 253 44 41), located in "Little India," the south end of Jl. Sultan Yussuf. The specialty is *nasi kandar,* a spicy concoction of curry, chicken, fish, and vegetables served over rice. At lunchtime, see the suits come in and dig right into their lunch with their hands. It tastes better that way. *Roti canai* is served for breakfast and throughout the day. Open 7am-9pm.

The F.M.S. Bar and Restaurant, 2 Jl. Sultan Idris Shah (tel. 254 05 91 or 254 08 63), on the corner of Jl. Sultan Idris Shah and Jl. Sultan Yussuf, near the large "Padang Bandaran" common. The F.M.S. stands for "Federated Malay States," and the restaurant is a remnant of the colonial era when it served as a watering hole for resident British officials. Today, it's where Chinese businessmen come to get hammered with their buddies. Most dishes cost RM5-10, though steaks can cost as much as RM17. Open Thurs.-Tues. 10am-10pm.

SIGHTS

Ipoh's most significant sights are on the west side of the river, and they're mainly architectural. On Jl. Panglima Bukit Gantang Wahab you'll find colonial buildings like the train station and the Town Hall, surrounded by well manicured gardens. On the veranda above the train station, you can catch a brilliant view of the city. Next to the Town Hall is the unexciting **State Mosque.**

Approximately 100m from the Town Hall, on the right side of Jl. Panglima Bukit Gantang Wahab, heading north, the **Muzium Darul Ridzun** houses a collection of artifacts tracing both the natural and industrial histories of Ipoh. Flashy charts and graphs illuminate tin mining and forestry statistics, while stuffed animals, models, and photographs of jungles and waterfalls reside upstairs. Open 9:30am-5pm, Fri. 9:30am-noon and 2:30-5pm. Free.

For the museum-weary, try a stroll with that significant fellow budget traveler in **D.R. Seenivasagam Park.** Covering the broad expanse between the YMCA and the traffic circle on Jl. Raja Musa Aziz, it offers soccer fields, shady gazebos, shady trees, and fish-filled ponds. The newly designed Japanese Garden adds a certain flair to this somewhat characterless facility.

The shops of **Chinatown** and **Little India** are easily identifiable by the covered sidewalks (formed by the overhanging second floors supported by archways every 15 ft.). Ipoh is good for a daytime stroll, when the town goes about its urban activities with much vigor. In Little India, the incense burns, the Indian music blares, and colorful clothing and Hindu religious icons adorn the sale displays. At night, most of the city shuts down, except the occasional karaoke bar and eatery.

The limestone hills surrounding Ipoh temporarily inhabited by the tin-mining industry earlier this century are now home to an extensive network of natural **caves.** With the immigration of the Chinese into the region, the caves were used as Buddhist temples. There are three cave temples within the area worth noting: north of Ipoh on the road of Kuala Kangsar is **Perak Tong,** a temple best known for its paintings and the seemingly endless stairwell that leads to the top of the caves. Open daily 8am-5pm; steps open 9am-5pm; it can be reached on the Kuala Kangsar bus. Another cave temple of interest is **Sam Poh Tong Temple** south of Ipoh on the main road 6km out of town, which can be reached on the Kampar bus. It is the oldest in the region, built 128 years ago, and shelters ponds brimming with hundreds of fish and turtles. Some are active, some have lost their zest for life in captivity and sit motionless, while others are optimistic about their children's futures and are actively copulating. Open 9am-5pm. Its direct neighbor, **Kek Lok Tong,** is just before Gunung Rapat and is also accessible on the Kampar bus. Built over a century later, it offers much of the same, including more turtles. Open 9am-5pm.

A bit out of the way but accessible either by taxi or a short bus ride from Butu Gajah on the Gopeng bus (Butu Gajah is accessible by bus from Ipoh's main terminal) is **Kellie's Castle,** the rapidly decaying remnant of William Kellie Smith, a wealthy Scottish planter who died during the building's construction in 1926. If you can scrounge RM0.50 and stomach the tacky restaurant and Pepsi billboards, take a quick peak at the castle's empty rooms, rubble walls, and narrow arches.

A final sight in the vicinity of Ipoh is the tiny town of **Papan,** a fascinating piece of living history. Built as a mining town in the 1890s, Papan has one road which leads to the now closed tin mine. Since the fall of tin (yes, it made a clunking sound), Papan has remained virtually untouched and rather ghost-towny. The inhabitants of Papan are Chinese and the only activity that goes on here is limited to the few coffee shops along the road. Any uninhabited building is left to fall to pieces, reclaimed by the vegetation. Even the buildings that are still inhabited are barely maintained. A relic of Malaysian history, Papan should be seen before it decays entirely.

Getting to these regional sights may be difficult unless you hire a taxi at RM15 per hour from the taxi stand at the Medan-Kidd Bus Terminal. Try to get a taxi driver who is knowledgeable about the sights that you want to see. If you have a bit more time to spare and are looking to hold onto your ringgits, buses from the Medan-Kidd terminal *do* reach all of the sights. Seeing the sights by public bus will take a full day, but will only run you about RM5.

■■■ KUALA KANGSAR

Dwarfed by both its northwestern neighbor, Taiping, and the state capital of Ipoh to the southeast, Kuala Kangsar has remained a smaller and quieter town with majestic grace and royal dignity worthy of the Sultan of Perak himself. Indeed, since 1931, Muslim heads of state have inhabited the palace of Istana Iskandariah overlooking the Perak River on the outskirts of town, lending Kuala Kangsar its reserved and peaceful aura and perhaps preventing its capitulation to the forces of physical expansion and modernization. The city's few main streets capture Malaysia's distinct ethnic mix by providing homes for Chinese, Muslim, and Indian entrepreneurs, while its more distant gardens and sidewalks afford lofty river views and shady retreats. The sights in Kuala Kangsar can be seen within a few hours. Their digestion, however, and the soothing effects of a quiet night's stay off the main drag, beg infinitely more time from the weary traveler.

ORIENTATION

The several short streets that make up Kuala Kangsar's commercial center revolve around the **clock tower** at the intersection of **Jalan Taiping** and **Jalan Kangsar**. The train station is on the northwest outskirts of town, approximately 2km from the center clocktower or a 15-minute walk down either **Jalan Tun Razak** or Jl. Taiping. The bus station is toward the end of **Jalan Raja Bendahara,** between its intersection with Jl. Taiping and the traffic circle where it meets Jl. Kangsar. Curving left as it comes downhill from the traffic circle, Jl. Kangsar meets the clock tower, and becomes **Jl. Daeng Selili.** It serves as Kuala Kangsar's central thoroughfare, with shops and restaurants located on it or along the short side streets it meets. The town's major tourist sights—the Ubudiah Mosque, Istana Iskandariah Palace, and the Royal Museum—are all found over the bridge and under the gate visible just behind the clock tower.

PRACTICAL INFORMATION

Tourist Information: The police, train station, and post office can be helpful sources of information, but one must often look to friendly English-speaking residents for assistance.

Post Office: (tel. 776 45 55), on Jl. Daeng Selili, at the clock tower. Open Mon.-Sat. 8am-5pm. **Postal code:** 33000.

Telephone Office: Telekom Malaysia (tel. 776 92 92), on Jl. Raja Chulan. Phone cards can be purchased here; the only cardphones are right outside the door. **Telephone code:** 05.

Currency Exchange: UMBC, 6-7 Jl. Daeng Selili (tel. 776 17 62). Open Mon.-Fri. 9:30am-3:30pm, Sat. 9:30-11:30am. **Bank Bumiputra,** 39 Jl. Kangsar (tel. 776 52 20/1). Open Mon.-Fri 9:30am-5pm. Sat. 9:30am-1pm.

Trains: (tel. 776 10 94), on Jl. Stesyen about 2km northwest of town (down Jl. Taiping or Jl. Tun Razak). To: **Kuala Lumpur** (2nd class: 9:30am, RM26; 4:30pm, RM22; and 1am, RM10) and **Butterworth** (11:30am, RM13 and 6:30pm, RM17—tickets are RM9 if purchased the same day).

Buses: The **bus station** is on Jl. Raja Bendahara, between the intersection with Jl. Taiping and the traffic circle with Jl. Kangsar. To: **Taiping** (every 30min., RM2.05) and **Ipoh** (every 10min., 7am-6pm; every 20min., 6-9:30pm; RM 3.05).

Taxis: The taxi stand (largely for inner-city transport) is at the bus terminal.

Laundry: Kedai Dobi V. Singaram-The Indian Pinmen Laundry, 45 Jl. Kangsar. Language barrier a problem here, but these kind men are eager for business. Dry cleaning is the specialty. Shirt RM2. Pants RM2.50. Open Mon.-Sat. 7am-6pm.

Pharmacy: Farmasi Kangsar, 29 Jl. Kangsar (tel. 776 41 57). Open Mon.-Sat. 9am-5pm.

Hospital: (tel. 776 33 33), on Jl. Sultan Idris Shah, from the clocktower, a right off Jl. Taiping.

Emergency: tel. 999

Police: (tel. 776 22 22), on Jl. Raja Chulan.

ACCOMMODATIONS

Rumah Rehat Kerajaan-Government Rest House (tel. 776 38 72), on Jl. Istana. While not quite the Sultan's palace nearby, the Rest House provides choice accommodations in town. Perched on the hillside overlooking the Perak River. Cozy double rooms, all with A/C RM50; with water heaters RM60.

Double Lion Inn, 74 Jl. Kangsar. The restaurant is defunct, but the Inn stands proud as a clean, convenient, and cheap alternative to the more elegant Rest House. Roomy single with fan and bath RM20.

Hai Thean Hotel, 25 A Jl. Daeng Selili. The truly determined bargain hunter will pass the Double Lion, continue down Jl. Kangsar past the clock tower, and try his luck at this street-corner establishment. Food is served on the street level, while upstairs their RM15 buys a single bedroom with separate bath. Doubles RM25.

FOOD

Despite its diminutive size, Kuala Kangsar is brimming with gastronomic temptations in typical Malaysian style. Chinese and Indian/Muslim restaurants abound along Jalan Kangsar and in the market area between Jl. Kangsar and the bus station.

New Kassim Restaurant, 25 Jl. Daeng Selili (tel. 776 73 09). A lively and affectionate Muslim couple welcomes you. Let Maimun fuss over you like a mother, bringing forth plates of *mee goreng* or *roti*, while her husband, Ramli, keeps the books. Traditional Muslim fare, reliably delicious for RM1-3. Open 7am-9pm.

Meng Kee Restaurant, 11 Bandar Baru Fasa III (tel. 776 49 07). Located in the row of shops behind the bus station and above Jl. Kangsar. Serves up a small menu's worth of exceptional Chinese food. Rice dishes for RM1.50-2 are served with chicken, pork, vegetables, or curry. Open Sat.-Thurs. 11am-3pm and 5-8:30pm.

SIGHTS

Thrusting its gold onion domes to the sky along Jl. Istana, **Masjid Ubudiah** was commissioned in 1917 by Sultan Idris Murshidul'adzam Shah I, the 28th Sultan of Perak, as thanksgiving for his recovery from a chronic illness. Its construction was plagued by difficulties; once, the Sultan's two elephants allegedly ran over and ruined the mosque's imported Italian marble tiles. It remains an impressive landmark, though it's constantly being renovated.

Continuing along the same road for about 10 minutes brings you to **Istana Iskandariah,** the Sultan's Palace, a grand and monolithic tribute to Muslim royalty. Barricaded by a wrought-iron fence, it's closed to the public, but easily admired from the road which encircles it. It began serving as the royal home in 1933, and was given an added annex in 1984 to contain a banquet and ceremonial hall. Make sure to follow the road around to the front of the palace for a better photo of the building and a good view down the Perak River.

Passing the palace and heading to Jl. Istana, you'll see the **Royal Museum** on the left, an apparent architectural *non sequitur* built without a single nail and in the shape of a sword. Inside you can trace the history of Perak's royal families, admire the royal regalia (medals, gowns, jewelry, and instruments), and learn about the heyday of the Perak state. Once known as Istana Kenangan, the memory palace, the structure actually served as the home of the 39th Sultan, Iskandar Shah, as he awaited the construction of the present Istana Iskandariah. Remember to take off your shoes. Open Sat.-Wed. 9:30am-5pm, Thurs. 9:30am-12:45pm. Free.

A short and scenic walk from the clock tower to Jl. Istana takes you over the Perak River and back to an era when Kuala Kangsar served not only as a royal home, but as an administrative center on the forefront of colonial Malaya's most important industry—rubber. Strolling back into town and up Jl. Tun Razak toward the train station, the stately **Malay College** sits on your right, set back from the road by its sprawling green playing fields. Opened in 1905 as the Malay Residential School for the children of the Royal Family and Malay dignitaries, it changed its name to Malay College in 1909, but has retained the feel of an English manor house. During the Japanese occupation of World War II, the college served as a Japanese administrative office, where those thought to be against the army were interrogated and often beheaded.

■■■ TAIPING

Translated, the Chinese word "Taiping" means "town of everlasting peace"; and so it was after the British intervened to put an end to the Larut Wars (skirmishes among Chinese gangs over the tin and opium trade) and made the city one of their administrative hubs in the mid-1800s. From that time onward, Taiping has had a string of firsts to claim for itself: the first central market, rest house, airstrip, swimming pool, court house, Malay school, hospital, prison, telegraph office, railway station, museum, and more. Today Taiping is known for its lovely lake garden at the east end of town and the nearby hill retreat of Bukit Larut.

ORIENTATION

"Downtown" Taiping, the central part of the city, is set up in a grid pattern. The main drags go east-west and lead "uptown" to the east where the government offices, lake gardens, zoo, museum, and library are located. These east-west roads, from south to north, are **Jalan Panggong Wayang, Jalan Kota, Jalan Pasar, Jalan Taming Sari, Jalan Barrack,** and **Jalan Stesyen.** It takes less than 10 minutes to walk from Panggong Wayang to Stesyen. The **express bus terminal** and taxi stand are on **Jalan Iskandar** between Jl. Kota and Jl. Panggong Wayang.

PRACTICAL INFORMATION

Tourist Police: 293 Jl. Iskandar. Next to the Express Bus/Taxi stand, this office will enthusiastically provide you with a sketch map of the city, directions, phone numbers, and advice.

Currency Exchange: Bank Bumiputra Malaysia Berhad, Jl. Kota (tel. 807 245), next to the pink clock tower. Open Mon.-Fri. 9:30am-4pm, Sat. 9:30am-noon. **Money Changer** at **Fulahm Touring Agency,** 25-E Jl. Kelab Cina (tel. 804 30 69), off Jl. Panggong Wayang. Open Mon.-Fri. 9am-6pm, Sat. 9am-1pm.

Post Office: Jl. Barrack (tel. 807 75 55), located uptown past the last major intersection, Jl. Istana. Open Mon.-Sat. 8am-5pm. **Postal code:** 34000.

Telephone Office: Kedai Telekom (tel. 808 92 92), on Jl. Barrack, next to the post office. You can buy a Telekom card for RM3, 5, 10, 50 but Telekom "Kardfons" are hard to find. The orange Uniphones have International Direct Dialing. Yellow booths are domestic. **Telephone code:** 05.

Trains: Stesyen Keretapi Taiping (Taiping Train Station tel. 807 25 91), on Jl. Stesyen, located about 500m west from the downtown area. 3rd- and 2nd-class fares to: **Kuala Lumpur** (4:15 and 11:10pm, 7hr., RM16 and RM28) and **Butterworth** (12:20 and 7:40pm, about 2hr., RM3.60 and RM7).

Buses: The **Stesyen Bus** (Bus Station) is at the west end of Jl. Panggong Wayang. To: **Kuala Kangsar** (every hour, 7am-6pm, RM1.65). The **express bus terminal** on Jl. Iskandar between Jl. Panggong Wayang and Jl. Kota has buses to **Butterworth** (roughly every 30min., 7am-8:30pm, RM4) and **Kuala Lumpur** (roughly every hour, RM13-14).

Taxi: To the right of the express bus terminal. Share-taxis to other parts of Malaysia cost more than the buses. Rides around town are a rip-off; they'll demand RM3 just to drive the 10-min. walk across town.

Library: Perpustakaan Awan Taiping (Taiping Public Library), on Jl. Kota (tel. 808 80 14), uptown past Jl. Istana and the other government buildings. English news magazines available. Open Tues.-Sat. 10am-5pm, Sun. 9am-1pm.

Public Market: The **day market** stretches across the center of town, going from Jl. Taming Sari all the way past Jl. Panggong Wayang. Stalls with fresh, delicious food, and bargain-clothing you probably wouldn't wear at home.

Public Bathrooms: At the market on Jl. Panggong Wayang (RM0.20).

Pharmacy: Farmasi Kota, 125 Jl. Taming Sari (tel. 806 32 66). Open 9am-9:30pm.

Hospital: on Jl. Taming Sari (tel. 808 33 33).

Emergency: tel. 999.

Police: (tel. 808 22 22), on Jl. Taming Sari, uptown, past Jl. Istana.

ACCOMMODATIONS

No guest houses exist here, just a bunch of Chinese hotels of varying quality in town and a "new" rest house uptown.

Peace Hotel, 30 & 32 Jl. Iskandar, on the corner with Jl. Panggong Wayang. The cheapest place in town, fraught with oodles of character. Stained-glass windows and decorated porcelain tiles on the outside of the building adorn this clean-kept hotel. Large rooms have fans but no private bathrooms. Rooms for 1 or 2 RM12. Rooms for 2 or 3 RM15-16.

Rumah Rehat Baru (New Rest House), #1 Jl. Sultan Mansur Shah (tel. 807 20 44), uptown, just north of the lake gardens, but hard to find, even with a map. Idyllic setting away from the city. Very popular with locals and foreigners alike; book in advance. Enjoy drinks on the veranda, then sleep well in your comfortable A/C room with private bath. Singles/doubles with fan RM31.50; with A/C RM36.75. Triples with fan RM44.10; with A/C RM49.35.

Swiss Hotel, on Jl. Panggong Wayang, across from the express bus terminal and next to the public bathrooms. The convenience attracts quite a few tourists. Singles with fans RM18. Doubles RM25, with A/C RM34.

Hotel Malaysia, 52 Market Square (tel. 807 37 33 or 807 37 55). In the heart of Taiping, next to the day market and express bus terminal. Clean singles with attached bath RM20, with A/C RM28. Doubles with A/C RM32.

FOOD

Everywhere you look, there are **hawker stalls** set up in clumps, or big markets full of 'em. The **Pusat Penjaja food center** is on Jl. Tupai (going uptown on Jl. Panggong Wayang, turn right); keep adequate room in your stomach for the clay-pot *nasi ayam* (chicken rice) stall at the end of the row. Another food center is near the express bus terminal and taxi stand, beneath Fajar Supermarket on Jl. Panggong Wayang. Other hawker stalls are set up at either end of the day market (open at night, too).

Bismillah Restaurant, 138 Jl. Taming Sari, on the corner of the intersection with Jl. China. Built and opened in 1932, this Indian-Muslim restaurant is a Taiping institution. Marble-topped tables, framed Arabic calligraphy, and a colorful clientele give the place a character that the recently constructed cement monstrosities can't match. Enjoy *roti canai* for breakfast or *nasi briyani* on Mondays, before it runs out. It will cost you RM3; other dishes are RM2 or less. Open 6am-9pm.

Restoran Tom Yam Taiping/T. Brek Caterer, 120 Jl. Taming Sari (tel. 806 82 26). Muslim women glide among the tables at this recently opened Taiping favorite. Let them serve you one of the 10 dishes of *nasi* (RM2.50-4.50), *mee* (RM1.50-2.50), or *ayam* (RM2.50). If you hanker for something familiar, try a western dish such as steak, fish and chips, or lamb chops. Clean, air-conditioned, and loaded with choices.

SIGHTS

Taiping has Malaysia's first museum, the **Musium Perak**, built in 1883. Far uptown on Jl. Taming Sari, it's on the left side of the road across the street from the prison, easily spotted with its massive walls topped with barbed wire. This museum has historical and cultural exhibits, as well as displays of wild animal and plant life. Free. Open Saturday through Thursday 9am-5pm, Friday 9am-12:15pm and 2:45-5pm.

At 62 hectares, the **Taiping Lake Gardens and Zoo** is one of the biggest and most beautiful parks in Malaysia. Located at the east end of the city and accessible via Jl. Kota or Jl. Panggong Wayang, it offers lush gardens and a winding lake with freshwater fish. Visiting hours for the zoo are 10am-6pm. Admission RM2.

Malaysia's oldest hill station, **Bukit Larut,** formerly known as Maxwell's Hill, lies 1250m above sea level in the mountains that form Taiping's scenic background. It is popular for its cool temperatures and mountain greenery similar to the Cameron Highlands, but has the added attraction of seclusion and peace. The only way to get to Bukit Larut is by taking the government-operated Land Rovers which leave every hour, on the hour, 8am-6pm from the base in Taiping on Jl. Air Terjun, just past the northeast end of the lake gardens (RM3). Up in Bukit Larut there are several accommodations available at rest houses and bungalows ranging in price from RM80-200. Some have cooking facilities, and most have simple western and Malaysian meals available. The tourist police recommend calling ahead to verify that the Land Rovers are making the ascent, as recent landslides have interrupted their schedules. For more information and to make reservations (best done in advance) call the Officer in Charge at the Bukit Larut Hill Resort, 34020 Taiping (tel. 807 72 43).

■■■ PULAU PANGKOR

The small and neglected stepchild of Penang and Langkawi, Pangkor has lived through historic bullying at the hands of the Dutch and English and now rests safely in the hands of some 23,000 Malaysians, mostly Chinese fisherman. Covering only about eight sq.mi. and hugging the Perak coastline about seven km from the port of Lumut, Pangkor provides a convenient getaway for local daytrippers and weekend holiday-makers but is often overlooked by western visitors. What Pangkor lacks in dazzling tourist sights it makes up for with cheap beach accommodations, tasty Chinese food, and roads for scenic motor bike cruising. There's not a whole lot to do here except laze away on the warm beaches and eat fresh seafood, but who's complaining, other than the fish?

GETTING THERE AND AWAY

Pangkor Island is just off the coast of Perak State, southwest of Ipoh. The launching town on the coast is Lumut, which can be reached by **bus** from Tapah, Taiping, Butterworth, Ipoh (about every 45min., RM3.80), and Kuala Lumpur (about every 30min., until 6pm, RM13). There's a **tourist information center** in Lumut at Bangunan PPP Lumut (tel. 934 057), in the same area as the bus station and the ferry to Pangkor. Open 9am-5pm. From the bus terminal, the ferry jetty is a 5-minute walk toward the water. The **Lumut-Pangkor ferry** is operated by **Pan Silver Ferry Sdn. Bhd.,** 1A Main Road 23200 (Pangkor tel. 685 10 46 or 685 10 82; Lumut tel. 683 55 41; fax 685 17 82). From **Lumut** to Pangkor (every 20min., 6:45am-8pm, and 9pm). The ferry stops at **Sungai Pinang Kecil** and **Pangkor Town,** but the sights are more accessible from Pangkor Town. Save your ticket stubs for the return trip from Pangkor Town (every 20min., 6:30am-7:10pm and 8pm) or Sungai Pinang Kecil (every 20min., 6:45am-7:20pm and 8:15pm).

ORIENTATION

The whole island is small; riding around the circular road route takes less than an hour. On the east side of the island is a string of Chinese fishing villages and towns. The main town is **Pangkor,** where ferry passengers disembark and find a few dingy hotels. The island's main attractions—its lovely beaches—are on the west coast. A **bus** at the jetty takes passengers to the other side of the island for RM0.50. Whether you take the bus, a taxi (RM2), or a motorbike, you'll traverse the island at its south end, along **Jalan Pasir Bogak,** reaching the approximately 200-m strip of road and beach known as **Pasir Bogak** after about 2km. Continuing on will lead to mountainous terrain and quieter beaches such as **Teluk Nipah** and **Coral Beach.** Beyond Coral Beach, at the north end of the island the road passes the **airport** and the Pan Pacific Resort, which lies on the Golden Sands beach of **Teluk Belanga.** Passing **Teluk Daram,** another beautiful and secluded inlet, the road makes a steep and winding descent from the mountain back into **Sungai Pinang Kecil** and then Pangkor Town, where the road finally rejoins Jl. Pasir Bogak.

PRACTICAL INFORMATION

All vital services are on Jl. Pasir Bogak. The **post office** (tel. 685 12 81; open Mon.-Sat. 8am-5pm; **postal code:** 32300; **telephone code:** 05) and the **Hospital** (tel. 685 12 84) are on the right side of Jl. Pasir Bogak. The **currency exchange** is located on the left side in the **Wonderful Jewelry and Souvenirs Shop,** 146-A Jl. Pasir Bogak (tel. 685 14 99). Open Mon.-Sat. 9am-9:30pm, Sun. 9am-2pm. **Police:** tel. 685 12 22.

Shops abound in Pangkor Town and along Pasir Bogak for **motorbike and bicycle rentals** (RM25 and RM10); try **Khoo Holiday Resort** for starters. A motorbike is preferable if you're planning to climb the steep northern road.

ACCOMMODATIONS

Pangkor Anchorage, Lot 7, Jl. Pasir Bogak (tel. 685 13 63), across the street from the beach. Run by a savvy Chinese woman (who is contemplating selling it), Anchorage is by far the cheapest and most popular deal around. Rooms can be cramped, but the 30 A-frame huts, bathrooms, garden, and reception area are all kept meticulously clean. Huts for one person RM11.50; for two RM18.40. A few 6-person huts for RM62. Travel information. Lights on at 6:30pm, off at midnight.

Joe's Fisherman Village, 4452 Teluk Nipah (tel. 685 23 89), at Teluk Nipah (Nipah Bay) a beach about 6km up from Pasir Bogak. The huts are off the main road (turn right at the Bayview Café). A-frame huts for RM20 per day; discounts can be arranged for longer stays. Nipah Bay is quieter and more peaceful than Pasir Bogak. A small snack menu and nightly dinners for around RM6.50. Traveling information dispensed by the helpful and friendly management.

Standard Pangkor Camp, Lot 53 Jl. Pasir Bogak (tel. 685 18 78), south of Anchorage, past the seafood center. More costly A-frame huts: RM31.50 for 1 or 2 people. A group of 10 can stay in a cabin with 10 bunk beds for RM8.40 per person.

FOOD

The intersection of laid-back resorts and Chinese fishing villages influences Pangkor's culinary offerings distinctly. Food is either Chinese seafood in Pangkor Town or light, hawker-style Malay fare along Pasir Bogak or Teluk Nipah. Don't expect to titillate your taste buds, but the **Pusat Penjaja** (food center) on Pasir Bogak beach, across from the Standard Pangkor Camp and Pangkor Anchorage, serves up reliable Malay (and a bit of Indian food). Several other stalls offer similar food at the far end of Pasir Bogak, heading west toward Teluk Nipah. Nipah Bay itself offers hawker-stall food from **vendors** clustered around Joe's Fisherman's Village. **Restoran Pangkor,** Lot 12 Jl. Pasir Bogak (tel. 685 21 62), on the small road just off Jl. Pasir Bogak near the Standard Pangkor Camp, has ample seafood dishes ranging from RM3-6, but mostly RM6. Open 2-11pm.

SIGHTS

The Pan Pacific Resort has a virtual monopoly over **Golden Sands Beach** at Belanga Bay, considered to be the most beautiful beach at the northwest corner of the island. The place is off-limits to non-guests, and would-be sun-bathers must choose from the three other beaches further south along the west coast; in order from the south they are Pasir Bogak, Nipah Bay, and Coral Bay. **Coral Bay** is probably the best beach for snorkeling, but the water isn't perfectly clear. The beaches get increasingly less crowded as you move north from Pasir Bogak. The small, 2-person kayaks for rent at the end of Pasir Bogak for RM6 per hour are perfect for a little off-shore exploration. Circling the island is best on a motorbike, and carefully, since the less developed and mountainous roads at the north end of the island are tough to maneuver. Moving up the west coast along the main road (mainly along the beach-strips, especially up by Coral Bay) there are little dirt paths which go off-road to the beaches. Stopping at one of these may lead to that uncharted and secluded beach you've been looking for.

If the beach scene is too tame for you, the trail network that goes into the mountainous jungle interior of Pangkor Island can add a little thrill. Stop at the **Jungle Information Center** past Pasir Bogak on the right side of the road before coming to Nipah Bay; one of the trails starts right there. Another starts just south of Standard Pangkor Camp on Jl. Pasir Bogak. Stay away from these trails if it has rained recently—read: mud and leeches.

To get to the old Dutch fort of **Kota Belanda,** make tracks down the road that branches off the main road to Pasir Bogak from the post office in Pangkor Town. You will pass the two villages of **Kampung Teluk Kecil** and **Kampung Teluk Gedung** on the way. The fort dates back to 1670 when it was used to store tin supplies and guard against piracy in the Straits. Across the street from the fort, slightly farther down the road, is **Batu Bersurat** (Sacred Rock), an 11m long, 5m wide, and 4.5m tall boulder carved with the faint inscription "1743 IFCRALO," memorializing the disappearance of a Dutch officer's daughter. According to Dutch legend, the rock was used by the child for a last desperate plea for help while being eaten by a tiger. More likely, rebellious Malays kidnapped the child, in an act of defiance to the despised Dutch presence.

Before Sungai Pinang Kecil jetty on the way from Pangkor Town, an easily missed left hand turn after the Petrol Station takes you to **Taman Foo Lin Kong.** Don't expect too much, as no statues of the Buddha yet reside in this temple-under-construction. While the temple itself may still be shrouded in scaffolding, however, the fish and turtle ponds, monkeys and birds, and the miniature Great Wall of China salvage the heavily advertised tourist sight. Worth a quick look, especially as the temple nears completion. Free, but a contribution to the temple fund is appreciated.

PULAU PENANG

Off the northwest coast of Peninsular Malaysia gleams Penang Island, a favorite of tourists, epicures, and sun worshippers alike. Interesting sights in the city of Georgetown and relatively nice beaches make for a mob magnet; Penang's immense popularity is both a boon and a bust. On the one hand, streetside commotion preserves the exciting atmosphere that was once the norm in Chinese trading cities but that Singapore, for one, has lost since modernization. On the other hand, the traffic and noise can get tiresome, fast.

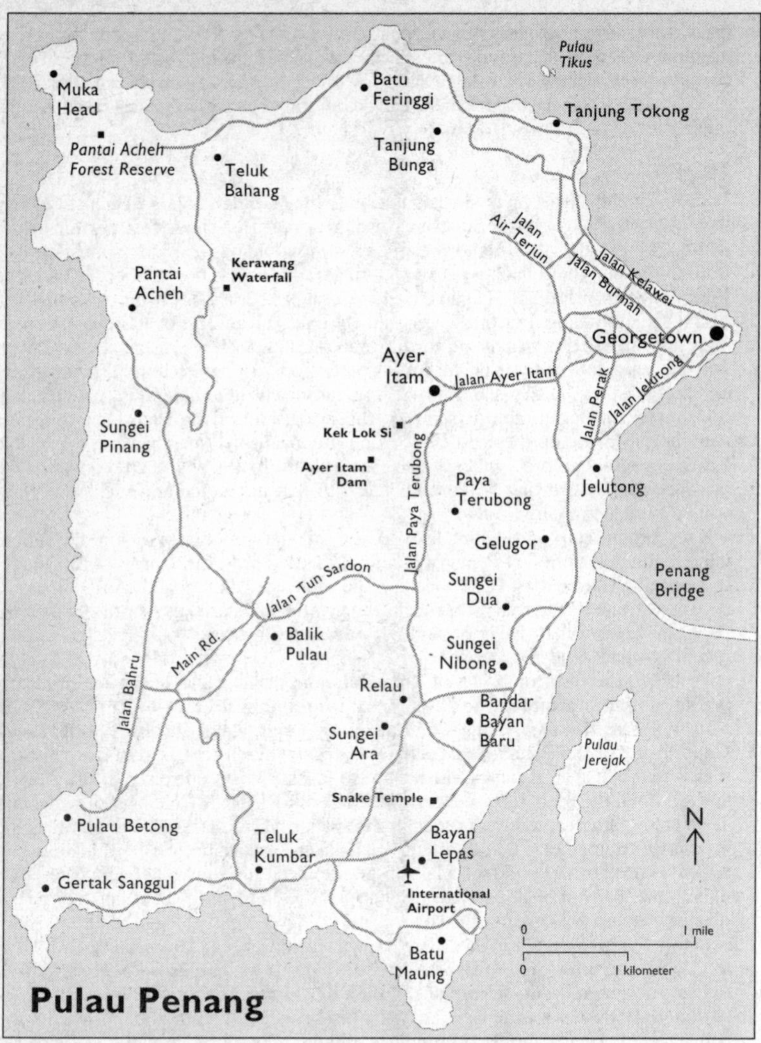

Linked to the mainland by the Penang Bridge and a 24-hr. ferry service, the island is home to Malays, Chinese, and Indians. Its history of successive colonial influences dates back to Francis Light's 1786 establishment of a British East India Co. trading post on what was then known as Prince of Wales Island. The British named the island's capital Georgetown, after King George III, and remained in control until its incorporation into the Independent Federation of Malaya in 1957.

Nature-lovers will be impressed with the Pantai Acheh Forest Reserve in the northwest corner of the island, where trails, silent beaches, campsites, and unusual plants and wildlife tempt the adventurous. Regardless of the superficial mediocrity of Penang's other attractions, the swarms of travelers that flock here testify to the enduring allure beneath the island's surface. Besides, the food is just scrumptious.

The Life of Sir Stamford Raffles: Part the Second

Recognized as a shining star in his first years with the East India Company, Sir Stamford Raffles, the veritable savior of Southeast Asia, was appointed to his first overseas position as Assistant to the Chief Secretary in Penang. He arrived there in 1805 with reckless enthusiasm and his wife Olivia. A true renaissance man, Raffles once again astounded and outdid his peers by not only thriving in commerce and politics (his primary duties as a servant to the EIC), but by pursuing his passion for exotic Eastern philosophy, history, religion, art, linguistics, botany, and zoology. He also immediately developed a powerful paternal instinct to protect the natives under his empire's dominion; this would serve him well throughout his illustrious career. (To continue on the path of this consummate Orientalist, see page 196.)

GETTING THERE AND AWAY

Penang is easily reached from Butterworth, the launching point from the mainland, which in turn is accessible by bus and train from all over Peninsular Malaysia.

Airport: Bayan Lepas International Airport (tel. 834 411), 20km south of Georgetown. Take yellow bus #83 (every hr. on the hr., 6am-10pm). **Malaysian Airline System (MAS)** (tel. in town 620 011, at airport 830 811) runs 24 daily flights to Singapore, Bangkok, Hat Yai, Phuket, Medan, Xiamen (China), and Madras (India). Call MAS for schedule information.

Trains: At the ferry landing in Butterworth. To: Kuala Lumpur (7:30, 8:45am, 2:50, 8:30, and 10:30pm). Trains from Butterworth also head north to Alor Setar, Padang Besar, and across the Thai border to Hat Yai and Bangkok.

Buses: At the ferry landing in Butterworth. Almost every location on the western seaboard of Malaysia has frequent buses to Butterworth.

Ferries: Between Butterworth and Georgetown (every 15min., 24 hrs. per day, 40¢ to Penang, free to the mainland).

ISLAND ORIENTATION

Getting around Penang Island on your own is easy—there are only a few main roads and they are well-marked. You will arrive in Georgetown, which takes up the northeast corner of the island. Heading west from there along the north coast, there's **Gurney Drive,** a popular eating and relaxation spot off the main road. Several km farther loom the countless luxury beach resorts of **Batu Ferringgi,** an over-developed strip of coastline. Penniless pilgrims continue in pursuit of **Teluk Bahang's** budget accommodations and more laid-back atmosphere.

Blue bus #93 takes you along the north coast from Georgetown to Batu Ferringgi and Teluk Bahang. Yellow buses #76 and #66 travel the west and south coasts of the island, while #1 and #8 patrol the interior. While the farms and small villages of the west offer little to the traveler, the central-northern city of **Ayer Itam** (via the #1 and #8 buses) is a popular launching point for sight-seeing.

■■■ GEORGETOWN

Mosques; the British garrison at Fort Cornwallis; and streets filled with Indian hawkers, Chinese merchants, and crowds waiting to see the latest Hollywood film combine to make Georgetown a city which wears its cultural influences like a tattoo on its forehead. Named after Britain's King George III and once a bastion of western influence, Georgetown today serves as Penang's seat of administration and as the commercial hub of the state. While its debris and screeching street noise seem to mar Penang's tropical resort feel, Georgetown not only offers a fascinating cultural dynamic but also affords the budget traveler the services—mail, laundry, shopping, and money changing—that only a major city can. To reach Georgetown, take the

15-min. ferry ride from Butterworth or the 30-min. trip from Bayan Lepas Airport on yellow bus #83.

ORIENTATION

The layout of Georgetown is not easy to follow and definitely requires a map, available at the tourist office, at local hotels, or in Butterworth.

The **ferry terminal** is on Pengkalan Weld Rd., which runs the short length of the perimeter of Georgetown on the coast. Turning right onto Pengkalan Weld and walking about 1km will lead to the **post office** on the left. The **tourist office** is a few blocks past, on a traffic circle with a clock tower in the center.

The main drag for cheap accommodations, money changers, and funky tourist-oriented restaurants is **Lebuh Chulia,** which meets Pengkalan just to the left of the terminal. Lebuh Chulia cuts through Georgetown for nearly 2km and ends at **Jalan Penang** (not to be confused with Lebuh Penang, another major thoroughfare). In the north, Jl. Penang meets **Lebuh Farquhar** at the E&O Hotel, right next door to the Asrama Belia Youth Hostel. In the south, Jl. Penang meets the ever-visible KOMTAR Plaza, the very tall shopping and office complex which, when you get your bearings in Georgetown, will always be a good way to orient yourself in town.

PRACTICAL INFORMATION

Tourist Offices: Malaysian Tourism Promotion Board, 10 Jl. Tun Syed Barakbah (tel. 619 067 or 620 066). This office gives info on Malaysia in general. (Open Mon.-Fri. 8am-4:15pm, Sat. 8am-12:45pm.) For maps and specific information regarding Penang go to the **Penang Tourist Association,** just 5 offices down around the circular Penang Port Commission Bldg., ground floor, Pesara King Edward (tel. 616 663; open 8am-5pm). English spoken in both offices. *Shopper Magazine* lists good restaurants and useful info on Penang (free).

Tourist Police: (tel. 615 522).

Budget Travel Office: MSL Travel Sd. Bhd., Ming Court Lobby, Jl. Macalister (tel. 372 655). Offers the Malay and Thai equivalents of the Eurailpass, available to students with an ISIC. Other packages also available.

Foreign Consulates: France, Wisma Rajab, 85 Lebuh Bishop (tel. 629 707). **Indonesia,** 467 Jl. Burma (tel. 374 686). **Japan,** 2 Jl. Biggs (tel. 368 222). **Thailand,** 1 Jl. Ayer Rajah (tel. 379 484). **UK,** c/o Price Waterhouse, UMBC Building, Lebuh Pantai (tel. 625 333).

Currency Exchange: At any of the many money-changers on Jl. Chulia or the major banks along Lebuh Pantai. Banks may take a small service charge, but their rates are slightly better. A fair money changer works out of the coffee shop on the ground floor of the Tye Ann Hotel, 282 Jl. Chulia (tel. 614 875). He also rents out motorcycles and jeeps for a good price.

Post Office: GPO Penang, Lebuh Downing (tel. 619 222), on corner of Lebuh Downing and Pengkalan Weld. Open Mon.-Sat. 8am-6pm. Poste Restante open Mon.-Sat. 8am-5pm. **Postal code** (for the post office only): **10670.**

Telephones: Central Telegraph Office, Syarikat Telekom Malaysia, Jl. Burma (tel. 373 273). Jl. Burma starts at KOMTAR and goes west. The **Telekom office** is on the left a few blocks down the road (open 24 hrs.). Home Country Direct service available here and at Bangunan Tuanku Syed Putra, Lebuh Downing, ground fl. (tel. 610 791; open 24 hrs.)**Telephone code** for Penang: 04.

Local transportation: All **buses** pass through KOMTAR. Coastal buses leave just north of the ferry terminal on Pengkalan Weld. MPPP city buses leave from Gat Lebuh Pasar, the street leading away from the water at the ferry terminal. **MPPP city buses:** #2 to **Wat Chayamang Kalaram,** #1 to **Kek Lok Si** temple; from there, #8 to the trolley car which goes up Penang Hill, #7 to the **Botanical Garden.** Fares vary according to distance (RM0.20-0.70). **Coastal buses** are either blue or yellow. Blue bus #93 runs the north road through **Batu Ferringgi** to **Teluk Bahang,** but you might have to switch to another blue bus #93 to make the whole trip. Yellow buses loop around the rest of the island. Yellow bus #83 to the **airport** every hr. on the hr. Yellow bus #66 to **Balik Pulau** every 30min.,

PENINSULAR MALAYSIA

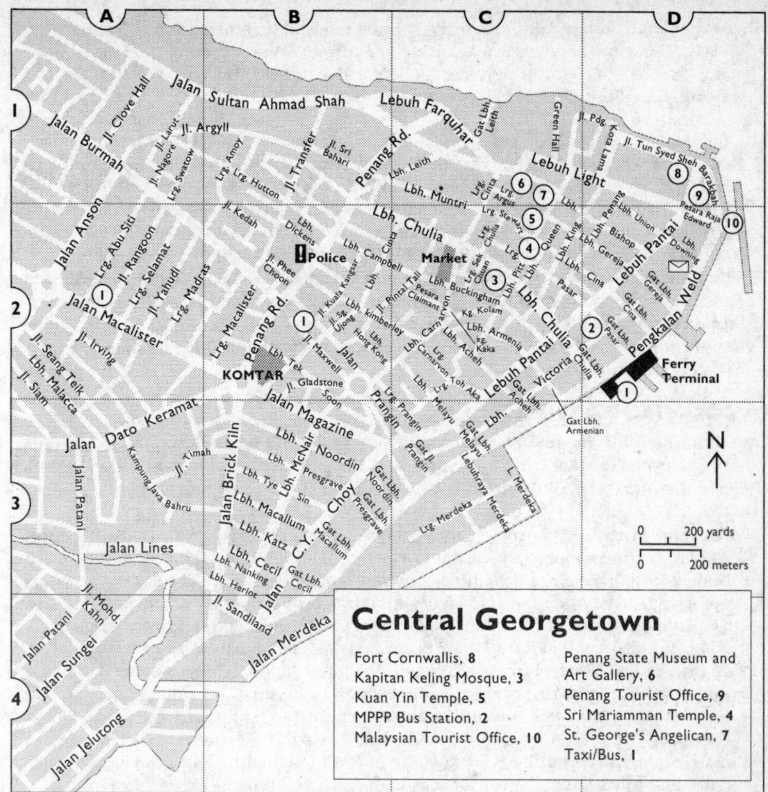

6am-midnight. Use either #83 or #66 to the **Snake Temple.** Yellow bus #76 takes the long ride to Teluk Bahang by looping round the island every 2-¼hr., 7am-4pm.

Ferries: To **Butterworth** (every 15min., 24 hrs, RM0.40, cars RM5). Two express services operate out of the same building as the tourist offices. **KPLFS Company** (tel. 625 630/1; fax 625 508) goes to **Medan** (Tues., Thurs., and Sat., 9am, RM90 one-way, RM160 round-trip) and **Langkawi** (9am and 6pm, RM35 one way, RM60 round-trip). **Ekspres Bahagia** (tel. 631 943 or 635 255; fax 631 944) goes to **Medan** (Mon. at noon and Wed. and Fri. at 10am; same rates as KPLFS).

Taxis: Charge grossly immodest fees—RM6 for a cross-town trip. The cheaper, slower, and more scenic way to get around is by **trishaw,** or by pedaled vehicles called **becak** (pronounced "bay-cha"). Haggle aggressively over prices; initial demands for RM30 for an hr.-long tour quickly become pleas for RM10.

Car Rental: International Driver's License required for all car rentals. **Avis Rent-A-Car** has 3 outlets: E & O Hotel, Lebuh Farquhar (tel. 631 685), Rasa Sayang Hotel Lobby (tel. 811 522), and Bayan Lepas International Airport (tel. 839 633). **Kasina Rent-A-Car** (tel. 641 18 42; fax 852 500) has vans and 4WD vehicles (from RM109 per day, from RM654 per week). **Ruhanmas Rent-a-Car,** 76-C-1 and 157-B, Batu Ferringgi (tel. 881 17 60 or 881 1023) offers the same cars at about half the price (RM69 for a Nissan "Sunny").

Bike/Motorbike Rental: Along Lebuh Chulia or from the money-changer at the Tye Ann Hotel, 282 Lebuh Chulia (tel. 614 87; motorbikes RM15 per day). Rates at Batu Ferringgi and Teluk Bahang aren't as good as those on Lebuh Chulia.

English bookstores: Along Chulia there are several used bookstores; many have travel guides. The **N.J. Books Centre,** 425 Lebuh Chulia, next to the Swiss hotel, (tel. 261 61 13) is large and well organized. They sell an array of literature, and also change money, rent motorbikes, book bus and boat tickets, and arrange Thai visas. The same services are available at **Parvez Book Store,** 419 Lebuh Chulia (tel. 262 23 14). Both open 9am-8:30pm. For new books try **Syarikat United Book,** Sdn. Berhad at 213 Jl. Penang (tel. 626 890/1; fax 626 892), near the intersection with Lebuh Chulia. Open Tues.-Sun. 9:30am-9:30pm. Most stores have English magazines like *Time, Newsweek International,* and *Asia Week.*

Public Market: The bustling, hectic, and colorful **morning market** on Lebuh Carnavon between Lebuh Chulia and Lebuh Campbell persists until around 11am. The location of the night market changes every few weeks; check *Shopper Magazine* or call the Penang Tourist Association for current locations.

Laundry: Kwong Sun Loong, 80 Lebuh China (tel. 631 920). Open 9am-6pm.

Pharmacy: Guardian Pharmacy, Ground Floor, KOMTAR, Lebuh Tek Soon (tel. 631 119). Open 10am-10pm.

Hospital: General Hospital, Jl. Hospital (tel 373 333).

Emergency: 999. **Fire:** 994. **24-hr. Information Hotline:** (tel. 373 737).

Police: Jl. Panang (tel. 999).

ACCOMMODATIONS

Accommodations are many and inexpensive in Georgetown. Most budget rooms are on or around Lebuh Chulia, though the cheapest accommodation is the Asrama Belia at the north end of town on Lebuh Farquhar (for HI members only).

Wan Hai Hotel, 35 Lorong Cinta ("Love Lane"; tel. 616 853). Just off Lebuh Chulia, Lorong Cinta is a pleasant street of old shophouses. This straightforward budget hotel has a friendly Chinese owner who speaks enough English to get his guests what they need. A message/notice board in the lobby details bookings to Thailand and points of interest in Malaysia. Cold drinks and light breakfasts available. Laundry service. RM2.50 for dorm beds, RM16 for singles/doubles.

Asrama Belia (Youth Hostel), 8 Lebuh Farquhar (tel. 630 558), where Jl. Penang meets Lebuh Farquhar. Stand facing the E&O; the hostel is immediately to the right on the 2nd fl. of a white building. The office is toward the back. Dorm rooms are ventilated by fans and sea breezes and bathrooms are clean. Open noon-midnight. Dorm beds or nothing at RM5 per night. Cold drinks, mosquito coils, and toilet paper for sale at reasonable prices. HI members only.

Broadway Hostel, No. 35F, Jl. Masjid Kapitan Keling, a.k.a. Lebuh Pitt, (tel. 628 550/60; fax 619 525). Just north of the mosque, on the corner with Lebuh Pasar. New, with clean rooms, all with shared bathroom and fan. Within walking distance of ferry terminal buses. Dorm beds $7. Singles $15. Doubles $25.

Swiss Hotel, 431-F, Lebuh Chulia (tel. 620 133 or 620 306). Coming from the ferry terminal, the Swiss Hotel is down Lebuh Chulia past Jl. Masjid Kapitan Keling (Lebuh Pitt) on the left, set back from the road. Popular with travelers and often full because of its swell location. Singles RM16.50. Doubles RM19.80.

Y.M.C.A. International Hostel, 211 Jl. Macalister (tel. 362 211; fax 365 869), in the suburbs far from the parts of town where you want to be. From there, city buses go into town (50¢). Big and clean and, despite its inconvenient location and size, often full; make reservations in advance. Doubles with fan RM35; with fan and TV RM40; with A/C RM45; with A/C, TV, and hot water RM60. Triples RM70. RM2 off for single occupancy. Non-YMCA members RM2 extra. Café on the ground floor open Sun.-Tues. 7:30am-10:30pm.

Tye Ann Hotel & Coffee Shop, 282 Lebuh Chulia (tel. 614 875). A favorite hangout in backpacking circles. A coffee shop on the ground floor offers breakfast and light meals (RM1-3.80), while Mr. Ah-Chew (*Gesundheit!*) and proprietor Mr. Tan rent motorbikes (RM15), change money, and arrange Thai visas. Treacherously steep stairs lead to clean rooms with fan and window (RM16). Dorm beds RM6.

Hotel Hong Ping, 273-B Lebuh Chulia (tel. 262 52 43/4). Opposite Tye Ann, hidden behind and above Coco Island Pub and Café. More upscale digs at reasonable rates. Rooms have A/C and private bath. (Single RM46, double with TV RM55.)

FOOD

The food in Penang... ah, the food in Penang. The island, especially Georgetown, is a mecca for gourmets and gourmands. Some great **food centers** are found at the west end of Gurney Drive (on the outskirts of town on the way to Batu Ferringgi) and at the west end of Jl. Tun Syed Sheh Barakbah; both in pleasant north coast locations. The listing below is just a sampling of what's available.

The regional dishes most often associated with Penang are *nasi kander,* a spicy curry dish with chicken or mutton, served at most Indian Muslim coffee shops, and *laksa*, fish soup with rice noodles, most often found at hawker stalls. One of the most unique and scrumptious desserts found around Penang is *bubur cha-cha,* a sweet coconut-milk concoction with chunks of fruit and yams mixed in with colorful rice-flour "gummy things" and ice. *Bubur cha-cha* is an ecstasy rivalling sex—try to have several per day.

The Tandoori House, 34-36 Lorong Hutton (tel. 619 105). Lorong Hutton (no relation to the proud-to-be-middle-aged, gap-toothed model) is off Jl. Penang about 2 blocks from where it meets Lebuh Chulia. Prices are steep by Malaysian standards, but how much wouldn't you pay for gourmet North Indian food? Check out the varieties of *naan* (plain or with garlic, cheese, meat, or vegetables) and rice, then move on to the fruit *lassis.* An average meal (including 5% service charge) costs around RM20. Open daily 11:30am-3pm and 6:30-10:30pm. Major credit cards accepted.

Nyonya Corner, 15 Jl. Pahang (tel. 228 14 12; fax 228 14 13) outside the center of town. Follow Jl. Penang past the KOMTAR complex; it will change to Jl. Dato Keramat. About 7 blocks later, turn right onto Jl. Pahang; Nyonya Corner is about 200m down. "Nyonya," a hybrid of the Chinese and Malay cuisines, is popular in Penang. As one customer put it, "It tastes like Chinese food with coconuts." Everyone likes creamy coconut "curry kapitan" chicken, while the "wood fungus salad" satisfies the discriminating palate. Go for the *Bubur cha-cha* or ice cream for dessert. Beware: the nuts, tea, and wash towel are not complimentary. An average meal including the 5% service charge and dessert costs about RM17. Open Tues.-Sat. 11:30am-3pm and 6:30-10pm. Major credit cards accepted.

Restoran Kassim Mustafa, 12 Lebuh Chulia (tel. 620 629). From the ferry, Kassim Mustafa is on a corner on the right side of the road before Jl. Masjid Kapitan Keling. One of the better Indian Muslim coffee shop-style restaurants in Georgetown. Come in the morning for *nasi kandor* or *roti canai*; later fresh curries are ladled from huge saucepans onto your plate of rice. No alcohol allowed. Most meals RM4-5. Open daily 5:30am-11:30pm.

Green Planet, 63 Lebuh Cintra (tel./fax 616 192). Lebuh Cintra, not to be confused with Lorong Cintra, runs parallel to Jl. Penang, 2 blocks east of it. Look for the big green sign. A friendly Christian Chinese family serves freshly prepared western dishes to the Occidental crowd that gathers nightly. Notebooks filled with honest travel advice from the hundreds who have passed through are available for perusal on the tables. Neither dirt cheap nor expensive. Open 9am-2:30pm and 7pm-midnight. Closed Sun. mornings.

Tzechu-Lin Vegetarian Food Centre, 229-C Jl. Burma (tel. 373 357), on the left side about 0.5km past the telephone office. Way beyond the center of town, but worth it. Caters mainly to the Chinese Buddhist crowd, negotiating the rigors of religious faith with bean curd products. Extensive menu of fake meat and some real vegetables, too. A bit pricey; meals average RM9. Open daily 10am-9:30pm.

Coco Island Pub & Cafe, 273 Lebuh Chulia, across from the Tye Ann Hotel. This backpacker's hot spot offers both western food (chicken, pork chops, bacon and egg sandwiches RM3-9) and simple Chinese meals (RM3 and up). Tiger, Guinness, and Anchor beers and ice cream all pushed heavily. Coco Island also runs buses to Ipoh (RM10), Singapore (RM35), and Bangkok (RM70). Buses run frequently each day; times are clearly posted. Open daily 2pm-midnight.

SIGHTS

For a bit of colonial history and some insight into the international politics of the past few centuries, visit Britain's original headquarters on Penang, **Fort Cornwallis,** at the northeast corner of the city a few meters from the tourist offices. A museum recounts Briton Captain Francis Light's acquisition of Penang from the Sultan of Kedah in 1786. Old cannons are still in position, the largest one having been transformed (destruction leading to procreation) into a fertility shrine. The extensive souvenir shop is worth a browse, if only for the A/C. (Admission to Fort Cornwallis RM1; open daily 8:30am-7pm.)

Georgetown shelters a diverse representation of world religions. An hour-long walk in the old quarter of Central Georgetown affords a sampling of the various houses of worship. **St. George's Anglican church,** the oldest Anglican church in the Far East, has occupied the corner of Lebuh Light and Jl. Masjid Kapitan Keling since 1817. Next door, the **Penang State Museum and Art Gallery** reputedly has historic memorabilia and paintings; both were closed for renovation at the time of writing. Just around the corner down Jl. Masjid Kapitan Keling, Georgetown's Chinese Buddhists pay their respects to the Goddess of Mercy at the **Kuan Yin temple.** Clouds of incense in the pigeon-filled front clearing blanket the city's other pungent odors, and magnificently detailed porcelain figures decorate the tiled roof.

Continue down Jl. Masjid Kapitan Keling to the back of the Hindu **Sri Mariamman Temple,** on the left just before the intersection with Lebuh Chulia. See the front of the temple one block over on Lebuh Queen. Mornings here are busy with Hindus worshipping at the shrines of the major deities. Crossing Lebuh Chulia and walking one more block down Jl. Masjid Kapitan Keling will bring you to **Kapitan Keling Mosque,** an Indian mosque graced with ochre-yellow domes and minarets. Before waltzing in, obtain permission from the mosque official and make sure you are modestly dressed. A covered lane near the mosque has food stalls reputed to have the best *nasi kandar* in town.

West on the main road to Batu Ferringgi is a peaceful, low-walled cemetery on Jl. Sultan Ahmad Shah, not more than a km past the intersection with Jl. Penang. Georgetown's founder, Francis Light, is buried here along with countless other colonial officials. Out of walking distance but accessible by MPPP city bus #2 is **Wat Chayamang Kalaram,** a Thai Buddhist temple just off the main road to Batu Ferringgi on Lorong Burma (not to be confused with Jl. Burma). The reclining Buddha is the largest in Malaysia and reputedly the third largest in the world. Come to this temple to get an architectural preview of what awaits in Thailand. If you've just come from Thailand, you can probably skip this one and not lose any sleep, though the wheel of fortune inside gives amazingly accurate predictions for just 20¢.

■■■ TELUK BAHANG

Past Batu Ferringgi is **Teluk Bahang,** a peaceful fishing town that doesn't see much action aside from some homegrown attractions. From here, the Pantai Acheh Forest Reserve, the Butterfly Farm, the Forest Park, and a batik factory are all within walking distance. Besides, local docks make excellent vantage points and the coastline is dotted with fishing boats. Privacy, inexpensive services, and quietude make Teluk Bahang well worth the trip. Take blue bus #93 from Georgetown (45 min.).

ACCOMMODATIONS

Rama's Guest House, 365 Mk. 2, Teluk Bahang (tel. 885 11 79). Coming from Batu Ferringgi, turn right at the traffic circle in Teluk Bahang. Rama's is on the right about 100m down the road leading to the beach. Rama and his happy family fuss over guests and make them feel at home. Every now and then, Rama's wife will cook up a fantastic dinner. Close quarters in their home, which could serve as a Hindu shrine to the elephant-headed deity, Ganesh. Guests stay upstairs, the family lives downstairs, and everyone, including the neighbors, hangs out in the living room and front porch. Dorm beds RM6, singles RM12.

Miss Loh's Guest House, turn left at the Teluk Bahang traffic circle, take your first right, and continue over the bridge. Miss Loh can be reached at her bus-stop store, 159 Jl. Teluk Bahang (tel. 885 12 27). Enjoy the lively company of an international cast of characters that return to Miss Loh's every year. Family atmosphere, well-kept accommodations, and unparalleled peace and privacy make Miss Loh's a reliable favorite among backpackers. Singles RM12, doubles RM20.

FOOD

You really can't go wrong in this village—food stalls and restaurants abound, even around the small traffic circle. Hours are generally the same from place to place, and full meals can easily be had for under RM5.

Sun Stall, (tel. 885 14 69), on the right side of the main road just before the traffic circle. A Malay and Indian Muslim Restaurant whose *nasi briyani* is guaranteed to send you to heaven. There are also plenty of curries to choose from; just point to what you need. (Open daily 7am-10pm, except Fri. 7am-1:30pm.)

Hassim Brothers, next door to Sun Stall. This family establishment offers similarly delicious Malay fare at great prices. Beef and chicken *murkabans* make for a hearty meal, while the traditional *nasi goreng* and *bihun goreng* are tremendous. In addition, the Hassims pour an especially tasty "Milo Ice."

Restoran Ibrahim, a Muslim restaurant across the street, provides steady competition with its consistently tasty *roti* bread and Malay dishes.

Jawi Corner, take a left at the end of Miss Loh's street or walk straight through the traffic circle for approx. 1km; Jawi is on your left. Some of the best *Chaw Koay Teow* on the island for only RM1.50. No dish costs more than RM2, and all are scrumptious. Don't miss this gastronomic delight.

End of the World Restaurant. It is unclear whether good food and a beautiful ocean view justify the long walk, inflated prices, and less-than-charming service. A favorite of many tourists, this seafood joint requires at least RM8 for a full meal.

■■■ ISLAND SIGHTS

Heading west from Georgetown along the north coast, signs direct visitors to the **Botanical Garden,** a pleasant forested park hugely popular with the locals for picnics and exercise. Trees from all around the world grow here, and there are special pavilions devoted to specific greenery. Monkeys roam free and visitors have recently been forbidden from feeding them, though many local tourists flagrantly toss food to them anyway. The park is generally crowded all the time but most people don't stray far from the entrance and the main paths; you should. Go in the early morning or late afternoon when it isn't too hot. Take MPPP city bus #7; or signs along the main road will lead you there easily if you're going solo.

Near Teluk Bahang are the Penang Butterfly Farm and the Pantai Acheh Forest Reserve. The **Penang Butterfly Farm** is at 830, Mk. 2, Jl. Teluk Bahang (tel. 811 253 or 812 053; fax 812 011; telex MA 40380). Coming from Batu Ferringgi, turn left at the traffic circle; it will be on your left. The farm is a lovely freak show of amazing tropical butterflies and creeping insects that think they're branches, twigs, and leaves. All the exhibits are contained in a well-landscaped atmosphere resplendent with flowing streams. (Admission RM4; open Mon.-Fri. 9am-5pm, weekends and holidays 9am-6pm.) Several km past the Butterfly Farm is the **Air Terjung Kerawang** (Kerawang Waterfall), a cool freshwater respite from the warm salty seas.

Hard-core nature enthusiasts satisfy their sylvan urges at the **Pantai Acheh Forest Reserve**. The trail begins at the End of the World Restaurant; to get there, follow the road along the north coast in Teluk Bahang. From the trailhead, walk for about 30 minutes to a campsite with a wooden shelter near a swaying footbridge. At this campsite, the trail forks. To the right, it leads to a **lighthouse** at the northwest tip of the island; the left trail goes to **Keracut Beach,** where there are more camping facilities. Bring your own food if you plan to camp at any of the sites.

The hike to the lighthouse is rewarding, but often downright treacherous. The four-part walk should take no more than two hours. Beginning at the campsite, the trail is pretty good until you reach the first beach, where there are a biological field station and a dock. Pass along the shore to the next patch of forest, where the path turns dangerous: broken walkways traverse huge boulders and I-can-see-hell-at-the-bottom crevices; twisting roots and hanging vines assist you in bridging these crumbling chasms. The most dangerous part of the trail, a la Hansel and Gretel, has been marked with white squares of paper pointing out the best way to climb onward.

When the white squares end, the roughest part is over. The trail then spills out over more boulders onto an empty, undeveloped beach approached only by day-trippers on boats. The path resumes just beyond the abandoned bungalow at the end of the beach. A rusty, out-of-date "Do Not Enter" sign depicts a cop shooting a trespasser, but hikers now go up, up, and up the crumbling asphalt trail to the lighthouse without crossing the law. The lighthouse operator lives alone at the top; he'll let travelers in, give them water, and maybe even take them to the top for a view of the island. Those who take the hike should bring plenty of drinking water.

From Ayer Itam, one can walk to **Kek Lok Si Temple,** the largest Buddhist temple in Malaysia and an impressive work of Chinese Buddhist architecture. The steps leading up to it are surreal or annoying depending on your mood and energy level; an endless row of souvenir hawkers and their canopies turn the stairwell into a tunnel. At the entrance is a turtle pond and past it, an expensive vegetarian restaurant. The peaceful sanctuaries here are Nirvana compared to the mayhem passed en route. Take your shoes off at the central sanctuary and do not take pictures of the monks, although other photography is permitted. In the stunning main sanctuary, thousands of Buddhas on individual platforms line the walls, and deities fly about the ceiling in colorful relief.

A funicular (RM4) goes to the top of **Penang Hill,** the island's highest peak and an incredible vantage point with views of Georgetown and the entire island. To get to the hill, take red bus #8 from Ayer Itam or a RM5 taxi ride. All around, t-shirt vendors and food hawkers attempt to trap tourists.

Close to the airport and accessible by yellow bus #66, Penang's **Snake Temple** allows visitors to watch and play with harmless, incense-entranced snakes. These poisonous pit vipers are said to be servants of the deity Chor Soo Kong, whose temple is also known as the Temple of the Azure Cloud. Free.

PULAU LANGKAWI

The gorgeous island of Langkawi, just off the northwest coast of Peninsular Malaysia, is the most recent target of the Malaysian Tourism Promotion Board. Heavily marketed as the "Isle of Legends," Langkawi has recently seen some of the most rapid development in all of Malaysia, including the construction of an airport runway to accommodate 747s by the year 2000. Fortunately, the ceaseless construction of resort getaways and other tourist facilities has not yet detracted from the island's beauty: superb beaches, green rice fields, forested mountains, and amazing waterfalls. Development has left the whole island a bit more expensive than the rest of Malaysia, and the fact that Langkawi is duty-free (largely to attract wealthy local visitors) means little to the budget crowd.

The hype surrounding the "Isle of Legends" is based principally on a local story about the lovely Mahsuri Binti Pandak Mayah, daughter-in-law of the island's chieftain and representative to the Sultan of Kedah. Wrongly accused of adultery by her jealous mother-in-law and sentenced to death, she was tied to a tamarind tree and stabbed with her own spear. To the amazement of the spectators, white blood gushed forth from her body, symbolizing her innocence. In her dying breaths, she uttered a curse banning prosperity from the entire island for seven generations. Indeed, over the next 200 years the island was subject to Thai and Acehnese

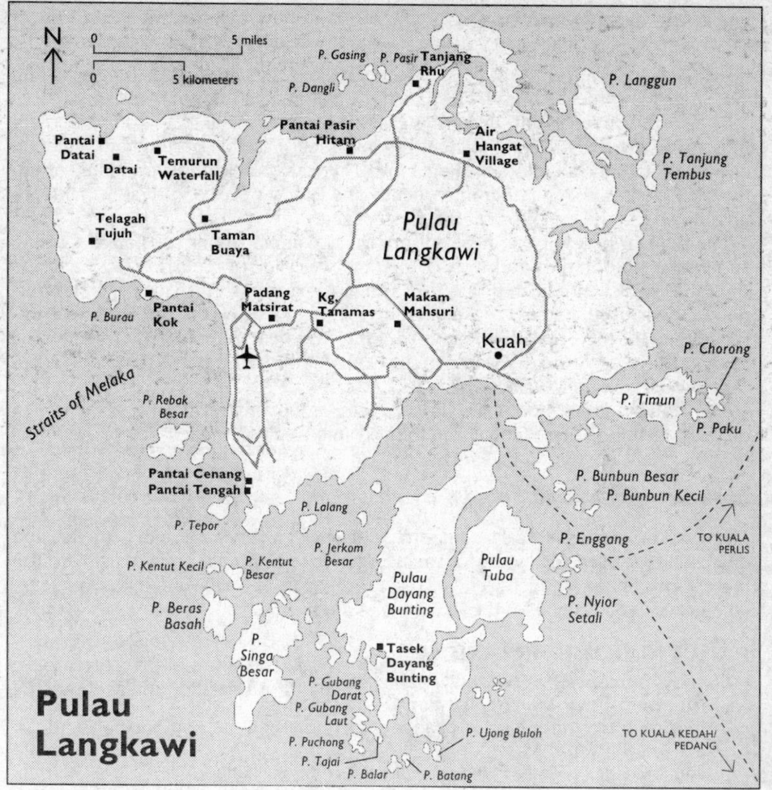

marauders, crop failure, and little economic activity…until now. With the seven generations now passed, Langkawi is undergoing a spectacular transformation from haunted fisherman's outpost to breathtaking island treasure.

GETTING THERE

Kuah, Langkawi's main town, is accessible by boat from Kuala Perlis and Kuala Kedah on the mainland, and from Pulau Penang to the south. Boats also arrive at Kuah from Satun, the southernmost town on the west coast of Thailand. Kuala Perlis is reachable by **bus** from **Kangar,** on the mainland, (every 30min., 80¢) and **Butterworth** (11am, 2, 4, and 6pm, RM6.20).

Ferries run to Langkawi from: **Kuala Kedah** (8, 10, 11am, 1:30, 3, 4:30, and 6:30pm, RM13); **Kuala Perlis** (9, 9:15, 10, 11:15am, 1, 2, 3:30, 4:20, and 6:20pm, RM11); **Penang** (8am and 6pm, RM35); **Satun** (8:30, 10am, 2, and 5pm, RM16). Other islands off Langkawi are accessible only from the main island and for a handsome price. If you get stuck in Kuala Perlis because you missed the last ferry over, the only place to stay is **Pens Hotel** on Jalan Kuala Perlis, the main road in town (tel. (04) 985 41 22; fax 985 41 31). Singles go for RM63-81; doubles RM75-93.

Malaysian Airlines (tel. (03) 746 30 00, (04) 966 86 21/3, or (04) 966 66 22) offers flights from **Kuala Lumpur,** direct and via Penang. Langkawi airport is at Padang Mat Sirat, about 20km from Kuah and 14km from Pantai Cenang.

PENINSULAR MALAYSIA

ISLAND ORIENTATION

The Langkawi island group consists of 104 islands off the northwest corner of Peninsular Malaysia, only three of which are inhabited. The main island is Langkawi, and visitors arrive at the port town of **Kuah** in the southeast corner of the island.

The roads are excellent, making it easy to get around Langkawi on your own; motorbikes are an efficient choice. Every intersection is well posted with direction boards, so it's almost impossible to get lost. There are public buses trundling 'round the island, but they run rather infrequently and almost never on schedule; taxis are ubiquitous and their high prices are mostly fixed.

The popular beaches that host most of the accommodations are **Pantai Cenang** and **Pantai Kok** on the southwest corner and west side of the island, respectively. **Pantai Tengah,** immediately south of Pantai Cenang, also provides accommodations. On the north end of Langkawi, sights include **Teluk Datai, Air Terjun Temurun** waterfall, the **crocodile farm, Tanjung Rhu** beach, and the fabricated **Air Hangat Village. Mahsuri's tomb** is in the center of the island near Kuah, and **Telaga Tujuh** waterfall is near Pantai Kok.

The Tourism Promotion Board has a counter at the ferry terminal, and their main office is one of the first buildings on the way into Kuah on the left side of the road.

■■■ KUAH

The town of Kuah is basically a one-street affair, but a very long one. Crowded and dirty, it's best used for money-changing, laundry, shopping, and day trips to the more scenic and peaceful beaches. To get to any part of Kuah from the arrival jetty, you'll have to take a taxi for the fixed rate of RM4.

PRACTICAL INFORMATION

Tourist Office: (tel. 966 77 89), on Persiaran Putra, coming from the jetty into Kuah. On the left side. Helpful staff. Open 9am-6pm.

Currency Exchange: Money changers can be found all over Kuah. There are banks on Jl. Pandak Mayah; turn right off Jl. Persiaran Putra, across from the taxi stand. Outside of Kuah, Padang Matsirat has money changers.

Post office: (tel. 966 27 21), 500m before the tourist office on the right side of Persiaran Putra. The only one on the island. Open 8am-5pm, Fri. 8am-noon. **Postal code:** 07000.

Telephone Office: Kedai Telekom, Jl. Pandak Mayah 6 (tel. 966 61 91), off the main road a few blocks. Open Sat.-Wed. 8:30am-4:30pm, Thurs. 8:30am-1:15pm. International service available. Telekom Malaysia phone cards are available for RM5, 10, 20, and 50. They are necessary for international calls from the island and only work at Telekom Malaysia Cardphones. **Telephone code:** 04.

Buses: Buses going around **Langkwai** are irregular and very infrequent. The Kuah station, a big dirt lot, is across from the hospital on Jl. Kisap, the main road going to the north. To: **Pantai Cenang** (9:10, 10:40, 11:25am, 1:10, 2:40, and 4:40pm, RM0.70) and **Pantai Kok** (8:10, 10:40am, 2:10, and 4:40pm, RM1.70).

Ferries: To: **Kuala Perlis** (8, 8:30, 10, 11:30am, 12:30, 2, 3, 5, and 6pm, RM10); **Kuala Kedah** (8:10, 9:20, 11:30am, 1:30, 3, 5, 6:30pm, RM13); **Penang** (6:15pm, RM35); and **Satun,** Thailand (8:45am, noon, 3:30, and 5pm, RM15).

Taxis: All fares are fixed. From the jetty to Kuah town (RM4). From Kuah to **Pantai Cenang** (RM12.50) and **Pantai Kok** (RM15).

Car Rentals: At most major resort hotels for about RM70-80 per day.

Markets: Night Markets weekly in Kuah (Wed.) and Padang Lalang (Fri.). Cheap dinners and fruits to be found aplenty.

Laundry: Island Laundry Service and Dry Cleaning, 56 Pusat Dagangan Dan Pelancongan Kelana Mas (tel. 966 00 07), on the right side of the detour that runs in between and parallel to the shore and the main road. One load RM7.50, ready in a few hours. Open 9:30am-9pm

Pharmacy: MNY Multi-Pharmacy, 102 Persiaran Mutiara, Pusat Dagangan Kelana Mas (tel./fax 966 00 66). From the jetty, on the left side as you enter the detour to the left off the main road. Open 9am-11pm.

Hospital: (tel. 966 63 33), on Jl. Leboh Kisap on the corner of the main road and Jl. Langgar Kisap.

Emergency: tel. 999

Police: (tel. 966 62 22), on Jl. Leboh Kisap across from the hospital.

ACCOMMODATIONS

Budget travelers staying in Kuah must search long and hard for mediocre rooms at about RM20. Kuah is not aesthetically pleasing—if you can, stay elsewhere on the island.

Hotel Langkawi, 6-8 Persiaran Putra (tel. 966 62 48). Clean, friendly, and near the tourist office, it's a convenient place to shack up for the night. Singles RM15, doubles RM28, triples RM35, all with fan and separate bath. Rooms with attached bath, A/C, and TV are RM40 for 2 single beds, RM50 for 1 double and 1 single bed, RM75 for the deluxe suite.

Hotel Malaysia and Restaurant, 66 Jl. Mahsuri (tel. 966 62 98), on the main road out of Kuah; and 39 Pusat Masmeyer (tel. 966 80 87 or 966 62 98), in Chinatown, a left hand turn off Jl. Mahsuri. Both branches, located about 100m from each other on opposite sides of Jl. Mahsuri, offer excellent bargains for the budget traveler. The main location: singles RM25, with A/C RM30; triples RM35; quads RM50. Chinatown location: dorms RM20 and up, singles RM65, doubles RM75, all with A/C.

FOOD

Kuah has restaurants and coffee shops everywhere, but they're not very good, and all charge inflated prices. The 7-Eleven-style mini-markets are fine for snacks, bottled water, and other necessities.

Sari Seafood (tel. 966 61 92), on Jl. Putra. Attracting Langkawi islanders as well as droves of German and Japanese tourists, this seaside restaurant serves up an amazing number of dishes from a reasonably priced Malay and Thai menu. Under the airy, beamed ceilings of the porch overlooking beautiful Kuah Bay, choose from 10 delicious dishes of crabs, prawns, fish, and chicken. Extensive drink and dessert menus. Basic Malay noodle and rice dishes RM3-5; seafood RM7-15.

Ghoz's Café (tel. 966 29 92), on Jl. Putra, across from the fire station and beside the taxi stand. Ghoz's offers casual dining and snacking at reasonable prices, with a beautiful view of the harbor. Many varieties of *roti canai* (RM0.50-2), freshly squeezed watermelon or tamarind juice, and a familiar western breakfast. Waffles, pancakes, eggs, or ice cream all RM0.80-2.

Restoran Alam Ria, Lot 85, Pusat Dagangan Kelana Mas (tel. 966 83 52), on the detour between the beach and main road. Decent Indian and Malay food at reasonable prices, mostly for RM2 and up. Specialties include *nasi briyani* on banana leaves and, if you're lucky, the special *nasi tomato*. Open 7am-9pm.

■■■ PANTAI CENANG

Pantai Cenang is nestled in the southwest corner of Langkawi Island and is a welcome alternative to the din and flying dirt of Kuah. It is easily reached via Jl. Mahsuri/Matsirat, the one main road leaving Kuah. Accommodations, restaurants, and motorbike rentals abound here, along with a few water sports and camping outlets. The beach itself is pleasant, and the water is warm and green but not clear. Explore the mud flats and sandbars that appear when the tide recedes during the late afternoon and at sunset; they're best over at the Pelangi Beach Resort. Thousands of harmless fiddler crabs trundle about among the shells. The flats stretch out over 100m from the beach; standing on a distant sandbar during a late afternoon shower is magical—all is temporarily covered by a thin sheet of water created by the rain, and it looks as if you're walking on water.

ACCOMMODATIONS

AB Motel (tel. 955 13 00; fax 955 14 66). Has well-kept wooden huts on the beach, about midway down the main Pantai Cenang road. Motorbikes for rent (RM25 per day), and a cheap "island-hopping" tour is available (RM30). Fan huts with bath RM30 and RM35; extra beds RM6. A/C huts RM50 and RM60; extra beds RM7.

Delta Motel (tel. 955 22 53; fax 955 13 07), the last place on the beach before the rocky headland dividing Pantai Cenang from Pantai Tengah, has roomy A-frame huts at reasonable prices. The restaurant has some of the most budget-friendly fare at Pantai Cenang. No alcohol allowed on the premises. Singles and doubles with fan RM35, quad RM50; with A/C, up to 3 people RM65.

Twenty Twenty Chalet and Restaurant, Lot No. 2014, Jl. Leboh Pantai Cenang (tel. 955 28 06; fax 955 28 10), toward the end of the Pantai Cenang strip. The huts are cleaner, brighter, and more furnished than elsewhere. Dorm beds in the long house RM25 for 1 or 2 people, RM35 for 3. RM40 for 4. Huts with fan and bath RM35; with A/C RM70. Deluxe hut with TV, A/C, and hot water RM90.

Sandy Beach Motel (tel. 955 13 08 or 955 16 62), on Jl. Pantai Cenang. Overlooking the waters of Cenang Beach, a short walk from its neighbors, the Delta and AB motels. The Sandy Beach offers clean and affordable chalets and bungalows. Standard A-frame hut with fan RM35, with A/C RM80. Other huts as high as RM100.

FOOD

Delta Restaurant, in the motel of the same name, boasts the cheapest food you'll find in town. Mostly Malay-style food with plenty of chicken, fish, and veggies. Good coconut curries with chili peppers. They charge by weight—specify how much food you want. No alcohol. Most Malay dishes under RM3.

Hot Wok Restaurant, Lot 1584 Jl. Pantai Cenang (tel. 955 29 26), across from the beach, next to the Backofen German restaurant. Specializes in putting local seafood on your plate. Fair prices (RM10-15) for the freshest, most delicious seafood around. Amiable Indonesian waitstaff. Open 3:30pm-midnight.

Bon Jon at the Beach (tel. 955 36 43), on Jl. Pantai Cenang, past the Pelangi Beach Resort on the way to Pantai Kok, this "restaurant gallery" offers an amazing feast for the senses. Treat yourself to its "East/West Island food with local Malay specialties" as you sit under a stately tiled roof and watch the waves roll in. Lunch runs from noon to 3pm for RM8-14 and features a superb toasted jaffle and tomato, avocado, basil, and mozzarella salad. Dinner from 7-10:30pm creeps into the RM10-20 range, but is even more scrumptious. Tea from 3-7pm. Rich desserts all day. Call for transportation and reservations. Open 11am-11pm.

Backofen, 1584 Jl. Pantai Cenang (tel. 955 16 67). Next door to the Hot Wok, this Austrian restaurant serves not only Euro dishes, but also local fare. Most entrees are pricey (RM9-20), but try the specialties for something tasty and reasonable. Cheeseboard (RM15) and cold cuts with sausage, bacon, cheese, and bread (RM16.50) Free transportation to and from your hotel.

ENTERTAINMENT

A few beach bars spring up nightly behind the hotels along Pantai Cenang, but that's about it for nightlife in this area.

Oasis Bar and Restaurant (tel. 955 31 90), on Jl. Pantai Tengah. Turn right at the end of Jl. Pantai Cenang at its border with Pantai Tengah. Chairs and tables spill out onto the beach from under an open, high-ceilinged hut with hanging Chinese lamps and fans. The kitchen opens at 6pm, but the drinking begins with happy hour, 5-7pm. Fruity mixed drinks around RM7.50

Safari Bar And Restaurant (tel. 553 57 11). At Pantai Tengah, with signs on the road pointing the way. If you're staying anywhere at Pantai Cenang or Pantai Tengah, they'll pick you up in the "Free Shuttle Safari," the only tiger-striped van this side of the island. Offers a western menu (fish 'n' chips, black pepper steak, and spaghetti) supplemented by local standbys (fried rice, fried noodles). Live music by the two British managers. Imported beers from RM4.50, cocktails from RM6. Open 6pm-2am; happy hour 6-7pm. Local beer RM2.50. Kitchen closes 1am.

■■■ PANTAI KOK

On a 30-minute, RM15 taxi ride from Kuah and a short but circuitous motorbike ride from Cenang, the clear ocean water and white sand of secluded Pantai Kok at once remind you why you came to Langkawi. Easily reached by following signs for Burau Bay and Teluga Tujuh from Pantai Cenang, Pantai Kok lies at the bottom of a windy descent through Langkawi's dense jungle, along a road visited by frolicking monkeys. The beach itself is a fairly short and curved strip, an inlet sheltered by palm trees with the forested mountains looming behind.

Accommodations and Food While more than eight establishments offer beachside huts and longhouse rooms on Pantai Kok, only a few stand out. Food is standard, and generally limited to the restaurants at each hostel.

Wholly honest nomenclature is employed at the **Last Resort** (tel. 955 10 46), on Jl. Teluk Burau. One of the last places on the beachside of the road going toward Telaga Tujuh. But this place is more than just a hotel with clever name. Its tasteful wooden huts on a quiet beach provide a rather idyllic setting, and there's a relaxing restaurant with comfortable atmosphere and decor. Private rooms in the longhouse with fan cost RM30, huts with fan on the beach cost RM35-40, with A/C RM50, and a hut for two to four people with A/C goes for RM70.

Country Beach Motel and Restaurant (tel. 955 12 12), on Jl. Teluk Burau, has a prime piece of real estate on the middle of Pantai Kok. Offers clean rooms, a conscientious staff, and a reliable restaurant. Single chalets with fan RM30, with A/C RM65, with A/C for 4 RM85. A bonus for backpackers is the single with fan and separate bath RM18. Restaurant open 8am-midnight.

Currently on the beach behind the Mila Beach Resort, **The Original Jungle Bar at the Beach,** has been known to relocate as it rents new property. Bamboo and plastic furniture clusters around a small makeshift bar and spills out onto the sand in typical beach-bar fashion. Most beers cost RM2. The extensive menu ranges from peanuts to fried squid (RM1-6), light meals such as fried eggs and chips (RM3), seafood *tom yam* with rice (RM7), and a broad selection or seafood and curry dishes (RM6-18), with the special, 100g of daily fresh lobster for RM8. Hang around late enough and watch the waiters pull out guitars for an impromptu show.

■■■ ISLAND SIGHTS

There's little to see in Kuah, but the rest of the island is full of lovely beaches and waterfalls. Traveling around the island is simple, thanks to the excellent roads, directional signs, and minimal traffic outside of Kuah.

Heading west from Kuah, one of the first sights of any interest is **Mahsuri's Grave** (*Makam Mahsuri*) a clearly marked right hand turn-off (Rte. 118) off the main road from Kuah (Rte. 112), opposite the Langkawi Island Golf Club. After the turn-off, keep an eye out for the patch of road whose original marble pavement is intact. The grave of Mahsuri is a tourist event: the complex includes not only her grave (with her curse inscribed on the marble), but also a traditional Malay house and a well where she supposedly drew water. Remove shoes before entering the mausoleum or house. Open 8am-6:30pm; admission RM1.

Heading northeast from Pantai Kok, there's a turn-off to the northwest corner of the island which passes the **Crocodile Adventureland** (Taman Buaya), home to 15 ponds of sleeping crocs. If you're into watching prehistoric reptiles do fancy tricks, the much-hyped shows are at 11:15am and 2:45pm every day; feeding sessions occur every 30 to 45min. The highlight of the show's stunts is when the trainer puts his fist into the largest crocodile's open mouth. The show is full of dramatic effect, replete with music lifted from *Star Wars* and *Hawaii 5-0*. Open 9am-6pm; admission RM5 adults, RM3 children under 12.

A better value exists farther down the road past Pantai Kok. Rather than following signs for the first right, Rte. 113 and the Crocodile Farm, take the second right to **Telaga Tujuh,** the Seven Wells Waterfall. While the hike is steep and dangerously dehydrating during the dry season, a splendid view of the waterfall can be found at its bottom, less than 300m from your starting point. For the more adventurous, the full hike affords spectacular views of Langkawi, refreshing swims in the fall's seven wells, and close contact with the monkeys. Beware the effects of Malaysia's dry summer months: the waterfall dries up and becomes a hang-out for local ne'er-do-wells. Donkey rides also available (RM10). Parking charge RM1 per car, RM0.50 per motorbike.

Head farther to **Teluk Datai** and the road meanders dreadfully, yet remains marvelously paved. This majestic and serene inlet arrests the attention of any passer-by. Continuing on the road, steep paved side-roads lead to secluded beaches of unsurpassed beauty. The home of only two resorts, this gorgeous locale will doubtless become the next target of Malaysian tourist development. The trip to Datai from Pantai Kok is not without its own attractions either; **Pantai Pasir Tengkorak** and **Air Terjun Temurun** (Temurun Waterfall) both offer magnificent vistas and nature at its most impressive.

For those who want to see some of the **islands around Langkawi,** it's possible, but at great cost. Many hotels along Pantai Cenang ally with boat owners of small companies along the beach to offer island-hopping day tours for around RM30. Four-hour trips, leaving at 9:30am and 2:30pm, feature snorkeling around Pulau Beras Basah, the wildlife park on Pulau Singa Besar, and the Lake of the Pregnant Maiden on Pulau Dayang Bunting. Many of the hotels also offer **watersports** such as water-skiing and jet skiing, but prices can be unreasonably high.

CAMERON HIGHLANDS

The Cameron Highlands offer travelers a cool, refreshing, and relaxing respite from the hot and dusty life at sea level. The comfortable day climate, cool nights, and beautiful mountain scenery will rejuvenate any traveler moving through equatorial Southeast Asia. Named after William Cameron, a government surveyor who charted the region in 1885, the Cameron Highlands are known for its rolling tea plantations, fruit and vegetable farms, flower gardens, and an intricate network of jungle trails. Varying in difficulty and doubtless the most popular recreational site for visitors to the Highlands, these jungle walks gained notoriety in 1967 with the disappearance of American Thai-silk tycoon Jim Thompson, a mystery that was never solved.

While tourists and locals alike continue to flock to the highlands, the government seeks to monitor its rapid course of development, both to preserve the area's serenity and to offset the threat of landslides, such as that which rocked the Genting Highlands in June of 1995. Not to fear, Cameron Highlands have remained a safe and relaxing paradise for the traveler, both tastefully and only moderately developed.

There are three towns in the Cameron Highlands; in increasing distance from Tapah they are Ringlet, Tanah Rata, and Brinchang. Brinchang is the biggest of the three, but Tanah Rata is the main town with most of the facilities. Ringlet is the lowest and least convenient of the towns.

■■■ TANAH RATA

Nestled in the clouds 14km farther than Ringlet and about 8km before Brinchang, Tanah Rata is reached only by way of an infamously hair-raising ride along a steep and winding road. This same road becomes Tanah Rata's main drag, with a monopoly on the main facilities of the Cameron Highlands—many of which offer bargains to the budget traveler. The street can be busy and noisy, but things quiet down just outside the developed area in the environs of Tanah Rata's cozy guest houses.

ORIENTATION

On the right side of the road the **bus station** and numerous **Malay food stalls** stand, while the left side of the road fronts restaurants, hotels, and shops. Everything in town lies within a stone's throw of everything else. Past the main part of town the road continues up to Bala's Holiday Chalets 2km away and then onto Brinchang.

PRACTICAL INFORMATION

Tourist Information: Tanah Rata Tourist Bureau, on the main road coming from Tapah, next to the large, often empty Tandoori Restaurant at the beginning of town. The small, white building has no identifying sign, but offers plenty of information. Open 8am-5pm, but known to open and close arbitrarily.

Currency Exchange: Hong Kong Bank, 31-32 main road (tel. 491 12 17). Open Mon.-Fri. 10am-3pm, Sat. 9:30-11:30am. **Maybank,** 20-21 Main Road (tel. 491 16 16 or 491 15 42). Open Mon.-Fri. 9:30am-4pm, Sat. 9:30-11:30am.

Post office: (tel. 491 10 51), on the shop side of main road near the Oriental Hotel. Open Mon.-Sat. 8am-4:30pm. **Postal code:** 39000.

Telephone: There is no Telekom Malaysia office, but International Telekom cardphones are on the bus station side of the main road across from the second block of shops as well as across from the Hospital. **Telephone code:** 05.

Buses: From the station halfway down the main road, the **Regal Transport Co.** (tel. 901 485) operates local routes. To: **Tapah** (every 30min., 8am-6pm, RM3.50, A/C RM3.70); **Brinchang** (every hour, 6:40am-6:45pm, RM0.50); and **Boh Tea Estate** (10:45am, 3:15, and 5:15pm). **Kurnia Bistari Express** (tel. 491 29 78) runs buses to: **Kuala Lumpur** (8:30, 10:30am, and 1:30pm, RM10.10) and **Penang** via **Ipoh** and **Butterworth** (9:30am and 2:30pm, RM14.10).

Taxis: Next to the bus station. RM15 per hour (max. 2hr.). A quick ride to **Brinchang** will cost RM2.

Markets: Both the **day market** and the **Saturday night market** are rather uninteresting. Coming from the bus station, go left on the main road and turn right at the Federal hotel. The market is on the left.

Laundry: Highland's Laundry & Dry Cleaning (tel. 491 18 02). Across from the taxi stand. Open 9am-6pm. Will charge RM5 per load, wash and dry. Many guest houses also provide washers and clotheslines.

Public Bathrooms: Next to the taxi stand. A big, white sign leads the way. Toilets RM0.20. Bath RM1.

Hospital: (tel. 491 19 66), past the row of shops on the left side of the main road. During office hours (8am-4:15pm), patients should check in at the registration room. **24-hr. emergency room.**

Emergency: tel. 999

Police: (tel. 491 12 22), just past the hospital as you leave the main part of town.

ACCOMMODATIONS

Your best bet in Tanah Rata is to choose among one of the many family-run, reasonably priced guest houses. Nearly all provide attractive services, including bus reservations to major destinations in Malaysia, international phone service, hot water (you'll need it up here), kitchen facilities, and tourist information.

Father's Guest House, P.O. Box 15, Tanah Rata (tel. 491 24 84), an oldie but goodie. Turn-off just before the bridge which is just before the tourist office coming from Tapah. Follow the signs up the many stairs to the house, named for the French priest who once inhabited the premises. Some rooms are in the old monastery; most are in enormous, corrugated iron tubes converted into dorm space and private rooms. Kitchen menu, garden area, and fantastic library. Dorm beds RM6. Singles and doubles RM16, with shower RM25. Weekly rates available.

Cameronian Holiday Inn, 16 Jl. Mentigi (tel. 491 13 27). A rising star in the competitive world of Highland guest houses, it seems destined for success. Friendly, family-run, and priced well, the Cameronian has already gained a faithful following via word-of-mouth. Telephone service, laundry, tours, travel arrangements, and TV. Dorms RM6. Clean and quiet singles and doubles RM16, with attached bath RM25. Probably the most private guest house still convenient to town, it also boasts a restaurant with an extensive menu. Call for free pick-up.

Bala's Holiday Chalets, Lot 55, Tanah Rata (tel. 491 16 60), 2km up the road from town (a sign indicates the turn-off). The distance from town is an inconvenience, but they shuttle guests to and from their lovely colonial-style house with fine Highland vistas. Give a call upon arrival in Tanah Rata for pick-up. Quiet and peaceful. Fresh roses on the tables, tea and scones in the afternoon, and a super dinner menu. International phone service, laundry and mail service, maps, travel info, hot water, bus reservations, and a small library available. Wide range of rooms: dorm beds RM6-7, singles from RM14, with bath RM25; doubles RM14-20, with bath RM30-60. Family rooms RM80-120.

Twin Pines Chalet, 2 Jl. Mentigi (tel. 491 21 69). Set back to the left off the main road, just after Father's. The serenity here may soon be threatened by the monstrosities being erected at its doorstep. An international consortium of backpackers convenes here, and Twin Pines offers an amazing array of services: bus/taxi arrangements, laundry, tours, international calls, books, TV, and a restaurant. RM16 for a bunk. Interior doubles RM18. Sun-lit side doubles RM22. Rooms with a single bed and a double RM27. Two double beds RM32. All have separate baths.

Rumah Rehat (Rest House) (tel. 491 12 54). A short walk off the main road, across from the hospital, this accommodation is well worth the ringgits. Old English fireplaces, sitting rooms, and gardens are present but not overly pretentious. The dining area has photographs documenting bygone eras in Tanah Rata. All rooms have attached bathrooms. Doubles RM60. Triples RM80. Quads RM100. Make reservations in advance since rooms are often booked.

FOOD

Good food at inexpensive prices can be found almost anywhere in Tanah Rata. Entering town, there are cheap food stalls on the right side of the road before the bus station serving standard Malay and Chinese fare. Several good Indian and Chinese restaurants are on the left side of the road. Guest houses have menus as well.

Excellent Food Centre/Fresh Milk Corner, G. 19 Main Rd., are the first stalls on the right if you're coming from the Tapah end of town. True to their names. Dish of fried noodles RM2.20. Open 7am-5pm. For dessert, order some fresh dairy beverages from the adjacent Fresh Milk Corner. The Cameron Highlands is Malaysia's only producer of dairy products, so get it fresh while you're here. Strawberry milkshake RM2. Open 8am-5pm.

Restoran Thanam, 25 Main Rd. (tel. 491 16 45). This excellent Indian-run restaurant on the left side of the road is open for breakfast, serving *roti* with fruit and fresh juices (orange, carrot, lemon, watermelon). Most of the rice dishes on the English menu cost under RM3. For dessert, slurp on a shake or ice cream. Beers are RM4 and RM8. Open 6:30am-10:30pm.

■■■ BRINCHANG

Only eight km closer to heaven than its less-elevated neighbor, Brinchang is easily reached from Tanah Rata via bus (RM0.50) or taxi (RM1-2). Larger, pricier, and a bit more industrial, Brinchang lacks Tanah Rata's charms, but the Highland's sights are accessible from the town, which is also host to one of the best Indian restaurants in all of Malaysia.

ORIENTATION

There is no bus station in Brinchang—just a bus stop along the main road at the central square. In the square there's a playground, the **Pasar Seni** (art market), and **Malay food stalls.** West of the square, behind the Hong Kong Hotel about 20m is **"Bandar Baru,"** with the laundry, bank, and drugstore.

PRACTICAL INFORMATION

The **Public Bank Berhad,** MDCH 41-43 Bandar Baru (tel. 491 15 90 or 491 26 82), exchanges currency. Open Mon.-Fri. 9:30am-3:30pm, Sat. 9:30am-noon. The **GPO** is on Main Rd. (tel. 491 10 16) past the central square on the left. Open Mon.-Sat. 8:30am-12:30pm and 2pm-4:30pm. **Postal code:** 39100.

The bus stop is on Main Road next to the Hong Kong Hotel and restaurant. Catch a **public bus** (50¢) or a **share taxi** (RM1-2) from there down to Tanah Rata where all other important connections can be arranged at the bus station.

The **day market** is held in Bandar Baru. The **night market** capitalizes there as well on Saturday nights and public holidays, and is larger and more interesting than the one in Tanah Rata. The arts/souvenir market stalls in the central square all sell the same tacky plastic flowers. **Sakuni Laundry,** a.k.a. Shan Laundry, No.3A, Bandar Baru, washes 5kg for RM8. Open 8am-8pm. **Highland Health Shop,** 12 Bandar Baru (tel. 491 28 48) is the closest thing in town to a pharmacy. Open Mon.-Fri. 9:30am-9:30pm, Sat. 9:30am-1:30pm.

ACCOMMODATIONS

Hotel prices in Brinchang run the gamut from dungeon-cheap to indulgent.

Hong Kong Hotel, No. 5 Main Rd. (tel 491 17 22), right across from the bus stop on the corner. Clean rooms have two double beds with an attached bathroom. At RM25 a night, it's a real bargain if you are traveling in a group of 2 to 4 people.

Highlands Hotel, 29-32 Jl. Besar (tel. 491 15 88), Close to Shal's Curry House. Carpeted rooms with attached baths. Singles and doubles RM37. Quads RM42.

Chua Gin Hotel, 11 Main Rd. (tel. 491 18 01 or 491 27 82), is on the left if coming from Tanah Rata. Clean rooms with separate baths. One double bed RM35, two double beds RM45, "deluxe" sleeps 5 at RM55.

FOOD

There could very well be over 100 restaurants in Brinchang; just walk around for a few minutes until you happen upon something that looks good. The **Malay food stalls** are in the central square.

Shal's Curry House, 25 Main Rd. (tel. 491 24 08), is definitely worth a try even if you're staying in Tanah Rata. On the opposite side of the square from the main road, it has a green sign with the logo of a fish head in a clay pot on a banana leaf. Shal's serves South Indian cuisine on banana leaves. Locals come here to sup on breakfast of *roti* and tea for only RM1.20. The more worldly clientele can sample flavored Cameron Highland teas and the unique versions of *roti* or *thosai* with peanuts and honey or butter and coconut. Apprehensive visitors can savor the fish head claypot meal with slices of fish meat instead of an actual head. Vegetarian dishes aplenty. A full meal costs RM7-10. Open 7:30am-10pm.

Restaurant Hong Kong, No.5 main Road (tel. 491 17 22), below the Hong Kong Hotel and facing the bus stop. Fits the bill for those craving Chinese. Serves a few simple western items such as sandwiches and breakfast foods. Plate of fried noodles RM2.50. Open 7am-1pm and 4pm-8:30pm.

■ CAMERON HIGHLAND SIGHTS

The sights in Cameron Highlands are accessible from Tanah Rata and Brinchang, though cheap transport may be hard to come by if not on a tour. Visits to tea plantations, vegetable farms, flower nurseries, jungle walks, butterfly- and bird-watching, and Buddhist temples are all popular with tourists.

Bala's, Twin Pines, and the Cameronian arrange tours which generally stop at Boh Tea Estate, Rose Valley, Butterfly Garden, the strawberry farm, the bee farm, the vegetable farm, the market, and Sam Poh Buddhist Temple. Usually a group of 2-10 from the guest house, and led by knowledgeable guides, these excursions cost

RM15 (plus RM3 for the Butterfly Garden, and extra for any tea purchases) and take about 4-½hrs.

Hiking is doubtless the traveler's favorite pastime while in the Highlands. Trail maps are available at most guest houses. Some trails are more difficult than others, but the maps have descriptions of each one, so you can choose accordingly. Don't overestimate your energy or endurance, however. Count on each hike being more difficult than its description. Equip yourself with water and comfortable hiking boots, and don't make the same mistake Jim Thompson made: bring companions.

INTERIOR PENINSULAR MALAYSIA

■■■ JERANTUT

Jerantut is relevant to your itinerary only if you plan to go to Taman Negara, as it's the official gateway to the national park. The town is small, harmless, and a little disheveled. Poor city planning has left Jerantut with no clear city center, and facilities are set up in random locations. It does have a bundle of beauty parlors, however, perhaps a strange yet noble instinctive response to the environment—"Though we are disheveled, we try to better ourselves." One night in Jerantut is plenty; get a good night's rest, pick up some supplies, and rise early the next morning to begin your exploration of Taman Negara National Park.

Orientation and Practical Information Jerantut is in the middle of both Pahang State and Peninsular Malaysia. There are only two roads of significance: **Jalan Besar** and **Bandar Baru.** The **bus station** is on Bandar Baru, and Hotel Chet Fatt is across the street. Turn left from the bus station, and the **post office** (tel. 266 62 01; open Mon.-Sat. 8am-5pm) is at the end of the street. **Postal code:** 27000. Head right, past Hotel Chet Fatt, and turn left, make the next right and you're on Jl. Besar, facing the **police station** (tel. 266 22 22). The Emporium is on the right. Green Park Guest House is farther down.

While many people rely on **taxis** to get to the Kuala Tembeling pier (easily arranged by many guest houses), **buses** in Jerantut also go there to catch the 9am and 2pm boats for Taman Negara. Local buses run to: **Kuala Tembeling** (8:15, 11am, 1:30, and 5:15pm, 30min., RM1.20) as well as **Kuantan** (7, 9, 11am, 1:15, 3, and 4:30pm). **Tanjung Keramat** has express buses to **Kuantan** (8:30, 10:20am, 2, and 3pm, 3-½hr., RM8.50). Express buses to **Kuala Lumpur** are run by **Perwira** (8:30, 10:30am, 2:30, 4, and 5pm, RM9) and **Orient** (9:30am, 1:30, 3:15, and 5:30pm, RM9). If the Jerantut station doesn't have your destination, try the station in Temerloh, a bigger town about an hour south. Buses to **Temerloh** depart every hr., 6am-6pm, RM2.40. The **train station** (tel. 226 22 19) is on Jl. Station. Trains run daily to **Wakaf Bharu** (near Kota Bharu; 5:30am, 6-½hr., RM12.60) and **Singapore** (9:15pm, 9hr., RM14.80). Express trains also run to **Singapore** (Sun., Tues., and Thurs., 1am, 7-½hr., 2nd-class RM28, sleeper: top RM35.50, bottom RM38). **Taxis** zoom to **Kuala Lumpur** (RM17 per person) and **Kuantan** (RM15 per person).

Upon arrival at the train station, turn right on the barren road and walk the 100m to the intersection with Jl. Besar. To get to **Bandar Besar,** turn left. To get to the **hospital** (tel. 266 33 33) follow Jalan Besar out of town and turn at the last left. Keep to the right and follow the signs for about 0.5km.

Accommodations and Food A large overhead sign marks **Hotel Chet Fatt,** 2nd floor, Lot 2755 Jl. Diwangsa, Bandar Baru (tel. 266 58 05), across the street and to the right of the bus station. The friendly Chinese owner manages immaculate rooms with flip-flops for the shower, towels, soap, and soft pillows and blankets. Second-floor rooms are designated by movable floor dividers. Clean bathrooms are numerous. Hot and noisy front rooms mean your laundry will dry more quickly! They also mean you will have to stroll through the TV room on the way to the shower. Double with fan RM15, A/C rooms range RM20-28.

Guest house fever is finally starting to hit Jerantut. The **Green Park Guest House,** Lot. 34 Jl. Besar (tel./fax 09 266 38 84), is on the last left as you head out of town on Jl. Besar. If you reach the mosque, go back about 30m. The owners grew up in one of the villages on Taman Negara's boundary and are a wealth of info. Spartan rooms have plenty of windows and clean shared bath. Can arrange transportation (boat, bus, and train) and accommodations in Taman Negara. Dorms (4 beds per room) RM8 per person. Singles RM12. Doubles RM20. Triples RM27.

Stock up on supplies for Taman Negara at either the **day market** next to the bus station or at the **Emporium** on Jl. Besar. The **night market** on Saturday nights behind the day market (just before sundown-10:30pm), doesn't sell great food—unusual for a Malaysian night market. In other parts of town, *roti canai* stands are set up for late night snacks.

■■■ TAMAN NEGARA

A glance through the comment book in the small library of Taman Negara, Malaysia's first and largest national park, gives two distinct impressions: that Taman Negara is one of the world's best kept tropical rainforests and that it is on the brink of ecological disaster owing to the recent privatization of park facilities. The truth is hard to figure, but this shouldn't keep you from the ultimate jungle experience, though it may require extra effort to separate yourself from the crowds of people that mill about Kuala Tahan, Taman Negara's resort town, and its environs.

Taman Negara was under government administration from 1937 until a few years ago when the park was allowed to join the development frenzy gripping the rest of Malaysia. Investors created the Taman Negara Resort in Kuala Tahan and the Nusa Camp. A combination of increased river traffic, land development, and noise pollution ensure that wildlife stay far away from the resort areas. Visitors who come to Taman Negara regularly testify that the rivers are not as clean as they used to be and that the wildlife is more elusive. Fortunately, escape is only a half-hour walk in any direction away from the park facilities. Just before dawn is the best time to hike out and see the natural beauty of the place; the air is cool and the wildlife, especially the magnificent birds, are more likely to venture out. "Hides" around the park's salt licks allow guests to quietly observe larger animals. Diehard adventurers can make the leisurely nine-day trek to and from Tahan Mountain and the nearby four-tiered waterfall (where "day two" consists of climbing about 23 hills and crossing the river seven times), but planning the trek and the expense of the mandatory guide can prove even more daunting than the summit. Still, there's no better way to appreciate Taman Negara in all its splendor.

For now, the pollution, crowds, and noise are concentrated in one part of the park. Talk of new routes and gateways to the park, even an airstrip, are causes for concern, however, and criticism aimed at developers in Taman Negara is justified.

GETTING THERE AND AWAY

Taman Negara can be reached only by boat on the Tembeling River. To get to the boats, you must first get to Jerantut and then catch a bus (RM1.20) or share-taxi (RM4 per person) to the village of Kuala Tembeling, where boats leave every day at 9am and 2pm (RM18, one-way; boats return to Kuala Tembeling from Taman Negara at the same times). If you want to make the 9am boat, renting a taxi is the surest way to make the 40min. trip since the 8:15am bus from Jerantut often runs late. The boat ride lasts 3-4 hours depending on the depth of the river. Keep your eyes peeled for monkeys, lizards, and colorful birds on the shores.

Visitors to Taman Negara should make reservations in advance for their boat ride (either with the resort or Nusa Camp) and accommodations, especially during Malaysian/Singaporean holiday seasons. The forestry department requires all visitors to buy an entry permit (RM1), and photography (RM5) or fishing (RM10) permits if you plan to partake. Put these in a safe place—you'll be asked to produce them when you leave. Now that the park is private, it stays open all year; visitors, however, have a miserable time of it from November to January, because the rains prevent outdoor activities. Bring lots of water, fruit, and snacks to Taman Negara. Snacks at the mini-market are more than three times as expensive as in the rest of Malaysia, and only slightly less so in the village across the river. The Emporium, in Jerantut, is a good place to stock up on goods before heading to the park.

ORIENTATION

Taman Negara, literally "national park," is roughly in the center of Peninsular Malaysia, taking in remote corners of Pahang, Terengganu, and Kelantan States with a total area of 4343 sq.km. **Taman Negara Resort** is in **Kuala Tahan** on the left of the river; on the right is a village of cheap hostels and restaurants. Boats shuttle back and forth across the river for free. Upriver a few km is **Nusa Camp,** a cheaper alternative to the resort that's popular with foreigners. Good **maps** with trails and points of interest are available at most tourist offices in Malaysia. Clearly **marked trails** and **directional arrows** make it difficult to get lost. Most local accommodations sell a more detailed book about the park and its paths for RM4. If you are undertaking a lengthy hike or are not particularly experienced in jungle trekking, you may consider hiring one of the many expensive, but congenial and knowledgeable, guides.

PRACTICAL INFORMATION

Currency Exchange: Change all the money you need before going to Taman Negara. The reception desk at the resort will exchange money, but they'll rip you off like you've never been before.

Post Office: The reception at the resort sells stamps. **Postal code** for Taman Negara environs (Kuala Tahan, Kuala Tembeling, Jerantut, etc.): 27000.

Telephones: Again, at the resort's reception desk, they'll rip you off some more.

Trains: See Jerantut (Practical Information).

Buses: If you take the 9am boat from Taman Negara to Kuala Tembeling, you'll be able to catch a bus back to Jerantut; if you take the 2pm boat you won't make the connection and will have to take a taxi to Jerantut (RM4).

Boats: Nusa Camp runs **riverbus** routes within the park that are much cheaper than chartering your own, when rates can range RM30-290 per day. Nusa Riverbus routes go from Nusa Camp to Kuala Tahan (RM5), and Kuala Trenggan (RM5), and from Kuala Tahan to Kuala Trenggan (RM10), and Kuala Tahan to Blau Yong Cave (RM3) several times a day. Guests at Nusa Camp ride the riverbus from Nusa Camp to Kuala Tahan for RM3.

Taxis: When you return to Kuala Tembeling from Taman Negara, share-taxis will take you to the following destinations at fixed prices (split the total fare by the number of people in the taxi; max. 4 passengers): **Jerantut** RM16; **Kuala Lumpur** RM100; and **Kuantan** RM100.

Library: There's a small A/C library at the resort with a small but informative selection of books about Malaysian ecology, flora and fauna, and natural history. Friendly staff keeps an amusing comment-book. Open daily 9am-5pm, 6-10:30pm. A video room next door shows nature films daily at 10am, 3:30, and 9pm.

Rental Equipment: At the resort office next to reception you can rent hiking and camping gear at daily rates: binoculars RM10, fishing rod RM7, sleeping-bag RM3, boots RM2.5 (up to size 9), flashlight RM2 (no batteries), small backpack RM3, large backpack RM6, canoes RM25, 2-person tent RM8, 4-person tent RM14.

ACCOMMODATIONS

Kuala Tahan's cheap accommodations are across the river from the resort. Ferries will take you there for free from the resort's dock. The two cheap places facing the river are the yellow Liana Hostel and the brown Teresek View Village. Aside from these, there's just the Taman Negara Resort and Nusa Camp.

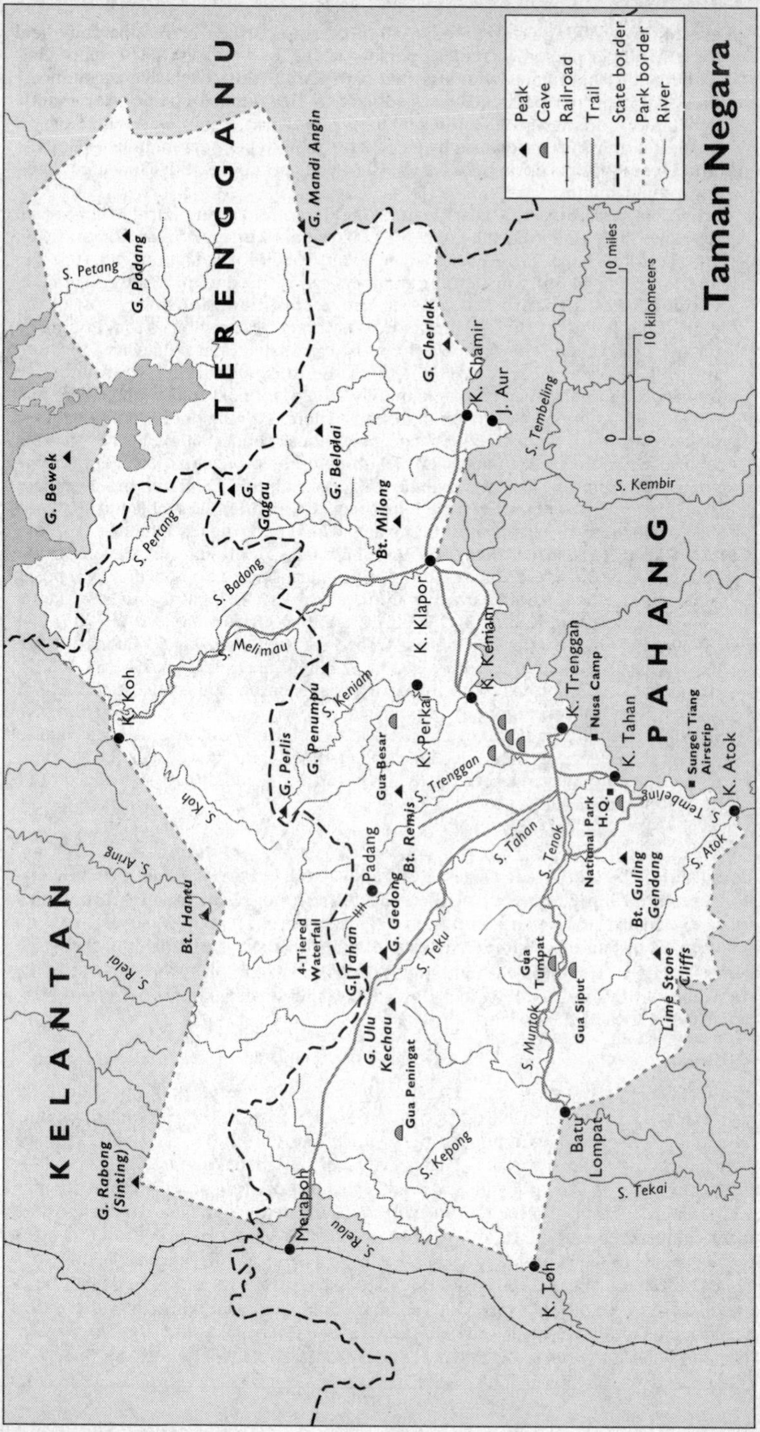

Taman Negara

Peak
Cave
Railroad
Trail
State border
Park border
River

0 10 miles
0 10 kilometers

TERENGGANU
KELANTAN
PAHANG
G. Bewek
S. Petang
G. Padang
G. Mandi Angin
S. Pertang
G. Gagau
G. Belolai
G. Cherlak
K. Chamir
J. Aur
S. Tembeling
S. Kembir
S. Badong
Bt. Milong
K. Klapor
S. Melimau
K. Koh
G. Perlis
G. Penumpu
S. Keniam
K. Perkai
Gua Besar
K. Keniam
K. Trenggan
Nusa Camp
K. Tahan
Sungei Tiang Airstrip
K. Atok
S. Koh
S. Aring
Bt. Hantu
S. Relai
G. Rabong (Sinting)
4-Tiered Waterfall
G. Tahan
Padang
G. Gedong
Bt. Remis
S. Trenggan
S. Tahan
S. Tenok
National Park H.Q.
S. Tembeling
Bt. Guling Gendang
S. Atok
S. Teku
G. Ulu Kechau
Gua Peningat
Gua Tumpat
Gua Siput
S. Muntok
Lime Stone Cliffs
Batu Lompat
S. Kepong
S. Tekai
Merapoh
S. Relau
K. Toh

Teresek View Village (tel. (09) 266 30 65). Camp on their barren, parched field for RM2.50 per person, or rent a 2-person (RM12) or 4-person (RM14) tents. Hostel beds RM10. A-frames with attached bath RM30. More exclusive accommodations RM50-60 per night. All rates subject to 10% service charge. Not exactly idyllic forest quarters, but features include a mini-mart, equipment rental, prayer mats, and transport to Jerantut by jeep (2 hrs., RM20 per person, min. 4 people).

Liana Hostel. Offers dorm beds for RM10 (4 beds per room), but there are limited bathroom facilities.

Taman Negara Resort, Kuala Tahan, 27000 Jerantut, Pahang Darul Makmur (tel. (09) 266 35 00 or 266 22 00; fax 266 15 00). **Kuala Lumpur Sales Office:** Lot 6, 2nd fl., Hotel Istana, No. 73 Jalan Raja Chulan, 50200 Kuala Lumpur (tel. (03) 245 55 85; fax 245 54 30). Any of these numbers can be used to make advance **reservations for the boat** to Kuala Tahan and **accommodations.** For most of the year, call a few days ahead. During local holidays, reservations should be made further in advance. The resort is the most expensive (and expansive) place to stay, but also the most convenient, with the most facilities. The grounds are immaculately landscaped and look awfully discordant next to the jungle, like putting a push-up bra on the Statue of Liberty. There is a range of accommodations: hostel with dorm beds RM20.70. A/C guest house rooms, single RM120, double RM150. Standard chalet, single RM170, double RM200. Deluxe chalet (with balcony, river, minibar, and A/C), single RM260, double RM290. The big bungalow suite for 4 with a kitchen, RM520. Extra beds RM25. All prices subject to 10% service charge and 5% tax, except the hostels which have the tax included.

Nusa Camp, Jerantut Office, 16 LKNP Building, 27000 Jerantut, Pahang Darul Makmur (tel. (09) 266 23 69; fax 266 43 69). At the Jerantut bus station, and poses as a tourist office. **Kuala Lumpur Office:** Express National Counter, Malaysia Tourist Information Center, 109 Jl. Ampang, 50450 Kuala Lumpur (tel. (03) 264 39 29, ext. 112). **Kuala Tembeling Office** (at the jetty): No. 5, Taman Negara Jetty, Kuala Tembeling, Jerantut, 27000, Kuala Tembeling (tel. (09) 266 304 3). **Reservations for boats** and **accommodations** can be made at the above addresses and phone numbers. Down river from the Resort, Nusa Camp also provides a complete package of facilities and activities, but at more reasonable prices. Malay cottage RM60; A-frame chalets RM40; and dorm beds RM9 (4 to a room). Restaurant serves set meals: breakfast RM5, lunch RM7.50, and dinner RM8.50. All rates subject to 5% tax.

FOOD

Both Nusa Camp and Taman Negara Resort have their own restaurants, but the ridiculous prices will frighten your pockets. Even the "budget cafeteria" is three times more expensive than what you would pay elsewhere. Thankfully, several reasonably priced restaurants line the river. One floats on the resort side, and three are across the river. The middle restaurant on the other side is said to be the best. With the constant turnover of guests they don't aim to please; they know you're just there because the food is cheaper.

SIGHTS

Mother Nature's majesty is the park's *raison d'être*. The network of trails is clearly marked so it's easy and safe to slip away from the resort in the early morning and surround yourself in virgin jungle. Spend a night at one of the many hides (*"bumbun"* in Malay) to spot wildlife. The large, nocturnal mammals such as elephants, tigers, rhinos, leopards and wild cattle rarely visit human-frequented areas of the jungle. Though only appropriate for those fit for the challenge, the **nine-day trek** to and from Gunung Tahan (at 2187m, Peninsular Malaysia's highest peak) and a nearby four-tiered waterfall is probably the best way to take in the diversity and ecological riches of Taman Negara. The trip requires massive planning. All food and camping materials must be brought to Kuala Tahan. You must consult with park authorities beforehand, and hire a guide (RM500 per week, RM50 per day after the first week). The info desk at the resort often has postings from people willing to share the costs of a trek to the peak. Though not a problem on most paths, leeches can be a concern; locals recommend spraying BAYGON (in the green can) on shoes and pants.

For a fresh perspective, take a stroll on the recently built **"canopy walk"** about 2km away from park headquarters (9am-noon, RM2). Suspended by a web of woven ropes, wires, cables and wooden planks along the tree-tops, the canopy walk is safer than it looks and provides a tremendous Tarzan's- eye view of the jungle, although the thrill of being so high above the ground would be enough in itself. Bring a camera! Authorities test the safety of the walkway daily (hence the short hours), checking stress points and the integrity of the whole delicate structure.

PERHENTIAN ISLANDS

Pulau Perhentian Besar (Big Island) and Pulau Perhentian Kecil (Small Island) are a pair of oceanic twins bathing in the warm tropical waters of the South China Sea. About 20km off the mainland coast, the 1½-3hr., boat ride to their shores provides plenty of eye candy for expectant travelers as the islands' smooth green contours and sparkling beaches come into view with agonizing slowness. Upon arrival, your first steps through soft water and onto beaches whose sand does delightfully intimate things to bare feet will prove that these islands are no mirage. However, word of the Perhentian's exquisite charms is spreading like wildfire through travelers' circles. Don't be surprised if during your trip the view is ominously eclipsed by mattresses, plastic chairs, and building supplies. Things are getting more crowded, but for many, these two nautical oases still embody the tropical ideal.

The islands are one of Malaysia's newest marine parks. Fishing is prohibited within two nautical miles, as are spear-fishing, souvenir collecting of any sort, and littering (take your garbage bag back to the mainland). Do not touch or accidently step on any coral. The exquisite but extremely fragile reefs have already begun to show signs of damage; one touch can destroy an entire branch. Items to bring for an extended stay include mosquito repellant, a flashlight, batteries, toiletries, toilet paper, and condoms (the isles are ruthlessly romantic). Accommodations are closed Nov.-Feb., except Petani Beach House, due to monsoons.

GETTING THERE AND AWAY

The islands are reached by boat from **Kuala Besut.** From Kota Bharu, catch a southbound bus to Pasir Putih, and from there catch another bus to Kuala Besut. From Kuala Terengganu, catch a northbound bus to Jertih, and from Jertih catch another bus to Kuala Besut. The largest of the various boat services, **5P** (Persatuan Pengusaha Pelancongan Pulau Perhentian) (tel. (09) 691 91 89), next to the jetty, beneath a large "Information Center" sign, has 16 boats that leave when they have 12 booked passengers (daily, 8am-5pm, round-trip RM30). The tourist office in Kota Bharu sells tickets for **Tanjung Enterprise** (tel. (09) 691 01 89 or 010 983 72 89), to the left of the jetty for the same price. Boats leave the island at 8:30am and 2pm; let your guest house owner know the day before you leave. Travel time 1½-3hr.

■■■ PULAU PERHENTIAN KECIL

Currently the favored twin, with Long Beach as the island's most popular stretch of sand to snuggle into for UV caresses. Its sandy bottoms are perfect for swimming, while rocky edges blaze with coral. There is not much to see at the village; smiling children on bikes dodge bedraggled goats and oil drums on the beach.

ISLAND ORIENTATION

Long Beach is on the east coast, and moving counter-clockwise from south to north are Rock Garden, Cempaka, Long Beach Chalets, Mata Hari, and Moonlight. Isolated D'Lagoon is on the next beach to the north, it boasts some of the island's best coral accessible only by boat. On the west coast, almost opposite Long Beach and accessible by a 15-minute jungle walk, is **Coral Bay.** A quiet beach with memorable sunsets, its waters are spiked with dying coral. Raja Wali, Au Beach Chalets, and Coral Bay Chalets shack up along these shores. Continuing farther south, in a **small cove** with a private beach, is Mira. A 30-minute walk on south is larger **Petani beach,** with Petani Beach house. **Perhentian village** is at the southeast tip of the island.

PRACTICAL INFORMATION

Currency Exchange: D'Lagoon. Poor rates. RM5 service charge.

Post Office: Most guest houses will deliver mail to the post office in the village. **Mata Hari** sells stamps. For important missives, it's best to wait to return to the mainland. **Postal code:** 22200.

Telephones: D' Lagoon. International, RM10 per min. Local, RM2 per minute.

Local Transport: Fiendish **motorboats** shriek through the waters hitting turtles. Long Beach Chalets to: Besar RM10, D'Lagoon RM10, Mira RM15, Petani RM15.

Clinic: (tel. 011 971 14 23), behind the police station, across a small bridge to the right. Nurse cleans up coral cuts and routine infections. More serious problems are sent to the mainland. Open Sat.-Wed. 8am-4pm, Thurs. 8am-12:45pm.

Police: Blue building, along the beach behind a rusting 10-ft. fence. Mainly for filing insurance claims. Open Sat.-Thurs. 8am-4pm.

ACCOMMODATIONS AND FOOD

Most travelers set their sights on the powdery charms of Long Beach, with a five o' clock shadow of palm trees stubbling its broad curves. The limited accommodations fill up quickly. By noon most have hoisted their red no-vacancy flag on the beach. If you are dumped on Long Beach and everything is full, hike to Coral Bay or hire a small motorboat to bring you to one of the smaller beaches or the big island. Many accommodations face water shortages during peak season (June-August).

Long Beach

Mata Hari, the most coveted digs on the beach. Solid, spacious, well-crafted bungalows (RM18) set back from the dunes within a cool green enclave, and garnished with sailfish arching from roof eaves and dragons scrambling up handrails. Hammocks sway from shady front porches. Each bungalow has a different wood-carved railing and a view of the ocean. Shared bath with real showerheads. Recycles cans and bottles. Restaurant open 7am-midnight serves 3 specials and the regulars, such as ginger beef (RM6) and chocolate shakes (RM3). No alcohol allowed. Snorkel trips. Snorkel, mask, and fins RM12 per day, less than 3hr. RM7.

Rock Garden. The cheapest on Long Beach. Active, cheap-fun attitude, with a penchant for recycling. Dorm RM5. Older A-frame huts RM10. Newer huts with bathrooms nearer the beach RM12. Spontaneous volleyball tournaments and frisbee matches are common outside their beatniky, funky beachside restaurant. Super-friendly wait staff operates on a first name basis, hollering at people on the beach. Breakfast 8-11am, lunch 1-4pm, and a luscious buffet dinner at 7:30pm RM6-8. Boats to Perhentian Besar (RM5) and other destinations.

Moonlight (tel. 010 984 20 65), isolated at the north end of Long Beach. Thatched A-frames (RM15) peer at azure waters from beneath the canopy while larger bungalows (large bed RM22, family-size RM40) perch precariously on verdant hillsides. The restaurant (open 7am-very late) and surf-side deck are favorites among cocobutter-clad sun bunnies in search of a fruit shake (RM3) or banana pancakes with chocolate syrup (RM3). Group meals (RM7) served by lamp light at 7pm. No alcohol allowed. Taxi to big island (round-trip RM12) and the village (RM10).

D'Lagoon (tel. 011 970 631). In a placid cove on the isolated northeast tip of the island, D'Lagoon is accessible only by boat. Travelers willing to forgo Long Beach's social frolicking will be rewarded with a private beach facing one of the best snorkeling sites on the island. In the evenings try the 10-min. hike through winding jungle paths to the isolated west coast beaches for idyllic sunsets. Dorms RM6, A-frames RM15, room with bath RM40. The popular tree-house is a small hut 15ft. up in the arms of a giant tree. Camping RM5. Clean shared baths, with showers. Snorkeling equipment RM12 per day. *Batik* lessons RM25. Restaurant open 7:15am-3:30pm and 7-10pm. Razak, the fisherman-manager, offers 7 set breakfasts. Group dinner (usually fish) for RM6.

Coral Bay

Rajawali Island Resort (tel. 010 980 52 44). Claiming a rocky hilltop, Rajawali sports intoxicating views on 3 sides. A brief walk behind the huts and down the slope leads to a string of secluded beaches and excellent snorkeling. A-frame huts (RM15) among trees, with two floor mattresses and mosquito nets. Electric lighting in every hut and shared showers. Veranda restaurant's (8:30am-midnight) incandescent sunsets add spice to rice and noodles. Snorkel gear RM10 per day, RM3 per hr. Trips to Rawa island (RM20 per person, 3hr.) or locally (RM15, 3hr.), not including equipment. Boats to the village (RM10) and the big island (RM15).

Coral Bay Chalets is a relaxed, family-run establishment. A-frame huts (RM15) with mosquito nets and well-water baths. Young naked children frolic with pet crabs on a string, until they wake up grandpa under the mango tree. Uninspired restaurant is offset by the kind waitstaff who offer guests free fried bananas and fresh jackfruit, or a cup of tea and toast the morning they depart.

Mira is reachable only by boat or by hiking for about 2hr., from Coral Bay Beach. A bohemian feel, where the navel rings outnumber the navels. Hillside rooms surround a small stretch of sandy-bottomed beach and coral farther out. Robinson Crusoe aesthetic, reflected in twisted driftwood cots set amongst wild ginger and banana trees. Elegant Malay long-house with broad balconies. All RM15. Camping space RM5. Restaurant open 7:30am-11pm. Steaming banana pancakes RM2.50. Ginger tea RM1. Set dinners RM6. Snorkel equip. RM12 per day, RM4 per hour.

Petani Beach House (tel. 010 881 24 44; in KL (03) 757 09 12), is sandwiched between Mira and the village. Petani is a meticulously landscaped affair, with pyrotechnic flowers and a sizable stretch of beach. Five bungalows with bath (RM 45, RM30 low season) and 2 "semi-detached" rooms with shared bath (RM30, RM20 low season) available year-round. Upscale rooms have lighting and fans. Restaurant specialty is fish (RM10 and up). The village is a 15-min. walk away. Snorkeling equip. RM12 per day. Reservations recommended.

ENTERTAINMENT

"Old man, old boat, no teeth" is how locals describe **Hamzah,** a village fisherman. Amiable Hamzah will take you on his boat to the island's best snorkeling sites; he'll even let you spend as much time as you like exploring. At RM15 per head (not including gear) it's a great deal compared to tours that race around the island at a break-neck pace. Ask at Mata Hari for tours.

If floating above extraordinary coral gardens is not enough, consider a **SCUBA course.** The friendly and knowledgeable staff of **Coral Sky** (tel. 011 977 963), next to Mata Hari on Long Beach, offers PADI courses, including open water certification. The 4-day course (RM650) includes SCUBA theory, confined water training, and 4 dives and results in international certification. Other PADI courses offered are advanced certification, rescue, and dive master training. Qualified divers can explore local dive sites for RM120 for 2 dives or RM95 with your own equipment. Staff can relate the wonders of the Perhentian's waters. Visa, MC (3% service charge), and traveler's checks. The staff at **Turtle Bay Divers** (tel. (60) 11 337 514; fax 603 40 51) is also on Long Beach, next to Moonlight Chalets. Offers similar services and prices, and will pick up interested travelers on the big island. Visa, MC.

Hikers yearning to scuff their boots might consider the **2-hr. trek to the village.** The trail begins at the south end of Coral Bay just behind the half-finished frame of a wooden house on the hillside. The path disappears periodically; when in doubt, follow the coastline. Stop for a milkshake at Mira Beach. From here the path to Petani often wanders in what seems the wrong direction for a lovely view of the sea. From

Petani Beach House, the village is only 15-minutes away; you can take a boat back in clear weather. Bring some water; morning is the best time to make the trip. For those too sunburned to contemplate any more UV, the **turtle hatchery** in front of Mata Hari allows travelers to admire newly hatched turtles as they make their moonlit trek to the waves. Beginning in June, drop by at 11pm to see if they are being released (no noise, flashlights, or flash photography).

■■■ PULAU PERHENTIAN BESAR

Balinese Batik and Indian weaves wave cheerfully in the seabreeze like international backpacker's banners along the big island's shores. The larger island is a brief, but butt-bruising speed boat ride across the waves of the narrow channel separating the two islands. Most accommodations here lounge along the talcum lengths of the west coast. Below the upscale resorts to the north and isolated from other budget lodgings farther south by a tumble of large wave-swept rocks is Mama's Place. Proceeding south, beyond the rocks are Coco Hut, Ibi's, and Abdul's. Rounding the forested tip of the island, via a 30-min. walk, brings you to the southside fringe of beaches, inhabited by a few large establishments and the intimate Seashell's Chalet.

PRACTICAL INFORMATION

There is no official tourist office. Most places can answer basic questions and provide **postal service,** but Mama's Place is a good source of info; also **sells stamps** and offers **currency exchange** for a RM5 service charge. **Check point,** just past Coco Hut and before Ibi's, changes currency for similar rates and is the closest thing on the islands to a **store,** with a pricey selection of sunscreens, toiletries, and souvenirs. Also offers 2 for 1 **book exchange, haircuts** (RM5), and **boat trips (**round-trip rates: Mama's Place RM4, Resort RM8, Blue Lagoon RM16, Pelangi RM12, Village RM4, Petani RM8, Mira RM14, Coral Bay RM14, and D'Lagoon RM16). Open 9am-6pm, when they go for beers at Seahorse.

ACCOMMODATIONS

Pulau Besar boasts refined accommodations with plenty of bath water, amenities, and a budding night life. Stunned by the fickleness of tourist migrations, establishments have redoubled advertising efforts and managers are often willing to dicker discreetly over upscale rates. Sand and surf aplenty. Jump right in!

Mama's Place (tel. 010 984 02 32 or 010 981 33 59). A perennial favorite; finding a room can be difficult. Candy-coated pastel beachside bungalows with shared bath RM15. Prance through Mama's papaya patch to upscale digs with fan and attached bath RM25-35. Patrons congregate in the tiny restaurant. Before 5pm ask Mama to include you in the 7:30pm dinner, or order from the menu. No alcohol in the restaurant. Small book exchange and some beach needs. Sea canoe rental and trips to Sasudara island.

Abdul's (tel. 010 983 73 03). The southernmost digs, Abdul's has intimacy and a more coral-free beach. Shack up in a ferocious, acid green bungalow (RM12, RM15 for beachside) or a wooden chalet with fan and bath (RM40). Electricity 7pm-8am. Restaurant has engaging view of the village. Seaside fireball (deep-fried ice cream with strawberry sauce) RM5. Open 7am-11pm. Snorkel gear RM10 per day. Overseas calls RM10 per min.

South Shore

Isolated from the west coast's social scene, the south shore picks up the trash from offshore-fishing. Most hotel staff keep their areas clean, however, and the relatively undeveloped length is perfect for evening strolls. Locals say the rocks to the far right of the beach are a great place to snorkel; you're guaranteed to see a shark or two. In the next cove is **the famous spring** that gave the Perhentian's islands their name, "stopping place" for boats to fill up on fresh water.

Seashells stands all by itself. The very basic palm thatch A-frames with mosquito nets (RM10) share a common shower and bath, but most of the guests spend their days in the beach-side hammocks, stirring only to walk 10m for a burger (RM2.50) and beer (RM6) in a nook made from an old ship's prow. Camping space RM5. Multi-lingual manager. Snorkel gear RM10. Inquire about trips to other islands or about renting the 2 larger motor-boats. Plenty of water.

ENTERTAINMENT

For a touch of romance, pack your snorkeling gear and lunch for two and head to Blue Lagoon, a deserted beach on the north shore. Check Point will arrange round-trip transport for RM16. In the evening mosey over to the **Sea Horse Cafe** (tel. 010 984 181), just behind Check Point. Cowboy-esque decor and country music, with a few fishnets to remind you you're at the beach. Grilled mackerel and chips (RM7) over tequila toasts (RM4). Unpack that guitar for beach-side bonfires. Open 7:30am-2:30pm and 7:30pm-1am. There are several dive centers around the island as well.

Check Point, Rents sea canoes (singles RM25, doubles RM35), fishing rods (RM15), and snorkel sets (RM15). Also arranges group fishing tours for RM25 per person with one day notice. Overnight stays on **Rawa Island.**

A.N.D. Dive (tel. 011 971 762), on the south beach at Pelangi Chalets. Two dives for RM120 or RM80 with your own gear. PADI open water certification (RM650) and other courses offered as well. Open daily 8:30am-6pm. No credit cards.

Perhentian Island Resort (tel. 60 11 345 562) has similar aquatic adventure but more stylish wetsuits. 2 dives RM195; PADI certification RM700. Windsurfers (RM15 per hr., RM20 with instructor). Sailboats (RM30 per hr., RM40 with instructor). Sea canoes (singles RM7 per hr., RM30 per day; doubles RM12 per hr., RM45 per day). Open daily 9am-6:30pm. Major credit cards accepted.

EAST COAST

■■■ KOTA BHARU

Dubbed by many as the heart of traditional Malay culture, Kota Bharu is one of the most attractive urban centers in Malaysia. The capital of the Kelantan State, it is the largest city within a few hours of the Thai border, and thus a sensible stopover if you're coming from or going to Sungai Kolok or Ban Taba in Thailand.

Perhaps the local cultural pastimes have been slightly over-hyped and glossed up for tourists (top-spinning, kite-flying, *silat*—Malay martial art, drum-beating, dancing, and the puppet theatre), but the various daily performances are certainly worth a visit. Just as memorable are the colorful and busy day and night markets held in the center of town. Padang Merdeka ("Independence Square") is surrounded by historic architecture and museums. With these assets, the city itself provides a good place for a few days of touristic distraction, not to mention the sights outside town. The fantastic selection of budget accommodations and restaurants are sure to make a stay here even more pleasant.

ORIENTATION

Kota Bharu is built on the east side of the Kelantan River, and the streets follow an imperfect and confusing grid of one-ways. Buses from the border arrive at the local bus terminal in the center of the city. The K.B. Inn Guest House is across the street on **Jalan Padang Garong,** and the **New Central Market** and **night market** are nearby. Maps of the city are at the tourist info center on **Jalan Sultan Ibrahim,** near the traffic circle with the **clock tower.** Many of the guest houses are likely to have maps, or can offer you good directions to where you want to go. The long-distance **express bus terminal** is in the southern outskirts of town on **Jalan Pasir Putih.** Some long-distance buses stop at the local terminal anyway. If you arrive at the express terminal, consider taking a taxi or trishaw into town.

PRACTICAL INFORMATION

Tourist Office: Tourist Information Center, Jl. Sultan Ibrahim (tel. 748 55 34 or 748 35 43; fax 748 66 52), in a bubble-gum pink building near the traffic circle with the clock tower. Very helpful staff; excellent English spoken. Brochures, maps, and souvenirs are available. Open daily 8:30am-12:45pm and 2-4:30pm. From Jan. until the end of Ramadan, open regular hrs. Sat.-Wed., Thurs. 8-11am.

Currency Exchange: Hong Kong Bank (tel. 748 14 51), on Jl. Padang Garong, cashes traveler's checks. Accepts Visa and MC. Open Sat.-Wed. 10am-3pm, Thurs. 9:30am-11:30pm. **Azam Restoran/Money Changer/Guest House,** 1872-D, Jl. Padang Garong (tel. 744 17 86). Good rates. Open Sat.-Thurs. 7am-8pm. **Bank Simpanan National,** 61 Jl. Pintu Pong (tel. 748 44 66) is the only bank open on Fri.—come if you desperately need some ringgit, but rates can be poor. Accepts AmEx traveler's checks and Visa card, not Visa checks. Open daily 9am-4pm.

Royal Thai Consulate: (tel. 782 545 or 745 266), on the right side of Jl. Pengkalan Chepa on the way out of town toward the airport. Open Sun.-Thurs. 9am-12:30pm and 2-4pm. Closed on Malaysian and Thai holidays. Will grant one tourist Visa extension, but requires 24 hrs. to process; bring 2 photos.

Post Office: GPO, (tel. 748 40 23), on the left side of Jl. Sultan Ibrahim, farther away from the clock tower traffic circle heading out of town past the tourist office and the police station. Open Sat.-Thurs. 8am-5pm. **Postal code:** 15670 (for post office only).

Telephones: Kedai Telekom (tel. 744 66 09), on Jl. Doktor in the center of town, not far from the local bus terminal. Home Country Direct. Accepts MCI, Sprint, AT&T, but no credit cards. Open Sat.-Wed. 8:30am-5pm, Thurs. 8:30am-noon. **Telephone code:** 09.

Trains: The nearest train station is at **Wakaf Baru** (tel. 719 69 86), where the jungle trains depart for Malaysia's interior. It's a hassle to use this to get to Kuala Lumpur, but might be a good option for **Jerantut,** the launching point for Taman Negara National Park (daily 6:30am, 8-½hr; 3:12pm, 6-¼hr.). To continue on to **Kuala Lumpur** or **Singapore,** you must change at **Gemas station.** The **Timuran Express** departs on Wed., Fri., and Sun., at 7:10pm direct to Singapore, arriving at 8:05am the next day.

Buses: From the local bus terminal to: **Kuala Terengganu** (8:30, 10am, 12:45, 1:45, 4, and 5:30pm, RM7.40). From the Express Bus Terminal (also known as Langgar Station) outside town on Jl. Pasir Putih to: **Kuantan** (8, 10am, noon, 3, and 11pm, RM15.80); **Kuala Lumpur** (9am and 9pm, RM20, 8pm, RM25); **Singapore** (8pm, RM30); and **Penang** (9am and 10pm, RM19.40). It is recommended that you make a reservation at least one day before you plan to leave, especially for long-distance journeys. Reservations can usually be made at either bus station, regardless of departure location. There is also a network of regional buses that leave from the main bus station or within its vicinity. Heading for the **Thai-Malaysian border,** bus #29 leaves every hour from the central bus terminal and goes to the border town of Rantau Panjang.

Local Transportation: Trishaws ply the street of Kota Bharu. The average ride within town costs RM2-3.

Taxis: The long-distance taxi stand is right next to the main bus station in the center of town. Taxis depart as soon as they've found 4 passengers, who split the fare to: **Kuala Terengganu** (RM12 per person); **Kuantan** (RM25 per person); **Kuala Lumpur** (RM35 per person); **Butterworth** (RM30 per person); **Wakaf Bharu** (RM2.50 per person); and **Kuala Besut** (RM5 per person).

Car Rental: Avis Rent-A-Car (tel. 748 44 57). Operates out of the Perdana Hotel on Jl. Mahmud. Rates run RM125 and up per day. Weekly packages also available. Passport deposit and International Driver's Permit required.

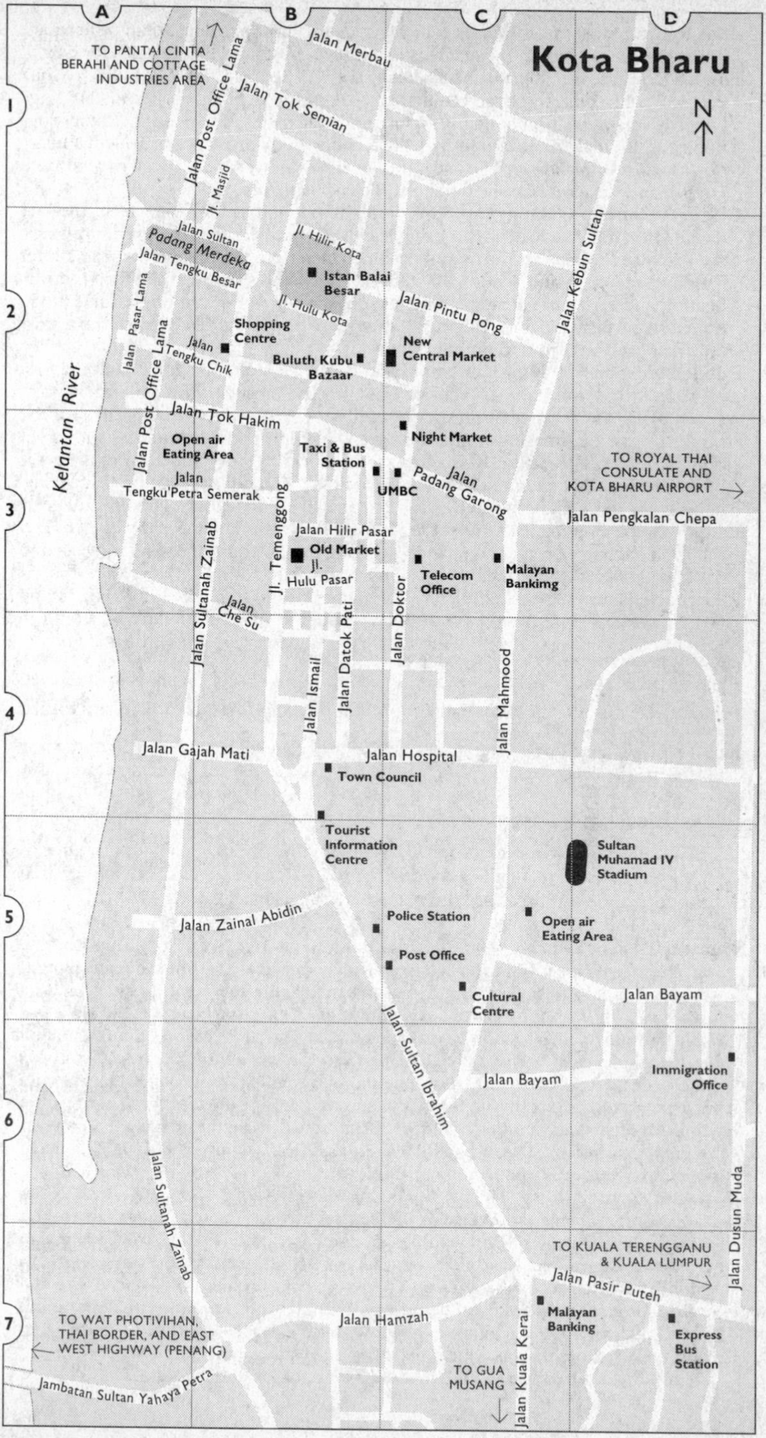

Kota Bharu
N
A
B
C
D
1
2
3
4
5
6
7
TO PANTAI CINTA BERAHI AND COTTAGE INDUSTRIES AREA
Jalan Merbau
Jalan Tok Semian
Jalan Post Office Lama
Jl. Masjid
Jalan Sultan
Padang Merdeka
Jalan Tengku Besar
Jl. Hilir Kota
Istan Balai Besar
Jl. Hulu Kota
Jalan Pintu Pong
Jalan Kebun Sultan
Jalan Pasar Lama
Jalan Post Office Lama
Shopping Centre
Jalan Tengku Chik
Buluth Kubu Bazaar
New Central Market
Kelantan River
Jalan Tok Hakim
Night Market
Open air Eating Area
Taxi & Bus Station
UMBC
Jalan Padang Garong
TO ROYAL THAI CONSULATE AND KOTA BHARU AIRPORT
Jalan Tengku'Petra Semerak
Jalan Pengkalan Chepa
Jl. Temenggong
Jalan Hilir Pasar
Old Market
Jl. Hulu Pasar
Telecom Office
Malayan Bankimg
Jalan Sultanah Zainab
Jalan Che Su
Jalan Doktor
Jalan Datok Pati
Jalan Ismail
Jalan Mahmood
Jalan Gajah Mati
Jalan Hospital
Town Council
Tourist Information Centre
Sultan Muhamad IV Stadium
Jalan Zainal Abidin
Police Station
Open air Eating Area
Post Office
Cultural Centre
Jalan Bayam
Jalan Sultan Ibrahim
Jalan Bayam
Immigration Office
Jalan Sultanah Zainab
Jalan Dusun Muda
TO KUALA TERENGGANU & KUALA LUMPUR
Jalan Pasir Puteh
Malayan Banking
Express Bus Station
Jalan Hamzah
TO WAT PHOTIVIHAN, THAI BORDER, AND EAST WEST HIGHWAY (PENANG)
Jambatan Sultan Yahaya Petra
TO GUA MUSANG
Jalan Kuala Kerai

PENINSULAR MALAYSIA

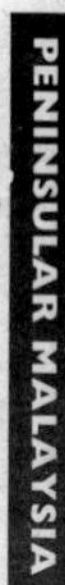

Bike Rental: Most guest houses rent bicycles for RM5 per day. Some other guest houses, such as Mummy's Hitec Hostel, will let guests use the bicycles for free.

English Bookstore: Toko Buku Rakesh, Lot 731 Section 9, Jl. Cik Kadir (tel./fax 748 35 75), behind the large Hankyu Jaya Department Store on Jalan Post Office Cama. A small selection of English books and magazines. Check out the humorous books in the magazine section by LAT, a comic-book artist popular for his hilarious "Scenes of Malaysian Life" strip in Malaysian newspapers. He writes in both English and Bahasa Malaysia. Open Sat.-Thurs. 9am-9pm.

Cultural Center: Gelanggang Seni, Jl. Mahmud, across the street from the Perdana Hotel. Join the locals who bring their kids here for the free evening shows; see traditional Malay art forms and pastimes in action. During the day, the center is open Sat., Mon. and Wed. 3:30-5:30pm. when top-spinning, kite-flying, drum-beating and *silat* martial arts can be seen. From 9 to 11:45pm on Sat. and Wed., there are performances of dancing and *wayang* puppetry. Check with the tourist information center to find out what's on.

Public Markets: The **New Central Market** is in a 3-story octagonal building, just off Jl. Doktor, Pintu Pong, or Tengku Chik. It's the most colorful and orderly market in Malaysia. Foodstuffs on the ground floor; arts, crafts, and clothes on the upper levels. An amazing **night market** is in the parking lot across the street 6pm-midnight. The **Buluh Kubu Bazaar** is another 3-story arts and crafts center off Jl. Tengku Chik and next to Istana Balai Besar. The **old market** on Jl. Temenggong Putra Semerak between Jl. Dato Pati and Jl. Temenggong is less exciting.

Laundromat: Pertama Laundrette, 4261-D Jl. Kebun Sultan, mid-way between the Jalan Padang Garong and Jalan Pintu Pong intersections. RM4.50 to wash and dry a load of clothing (roughly 5kg). Open daily 9am-10pm.

Pharmacy: Kian Farmasi, 2981 B-C Jl. Padang Garong (tel. 748 39 06; fax 748 64 50), in the center of town next to A&W Family Restaurant and across from the K.B. Inn Guest House. Drop by for snow cones. Open 9am-10pm. Closed Fri.

Hospital: (tel. 748 55 33) at the end of Jl. Hospital.

Emergency: tel. 999. **Fire:** tel. 994.

Police: (tel. 748 55 22), on Jl. Sultan Ibrahim between the post office and tourist information center. Some officers speak English.

Early Closing Day: Kelantan State is Islamic. Most establishments are closed Fri. instead of Sun., and some places close early on Thurs. afternoon.

ACCOMMODATIONS

Kota Bharu is a haven for budget travelers looking for cheap, clean, and fun places to stay. Guest houses are a dime a dozen. The following places each have their own special perks, and you can afford the place that appeals most.

Mummy's Hitec Hostel, 439-B Jl. Pengkalan Chepa (tel. 744 47 60), opposite the Thai Consulate. It's a 10-min. walk from the center of town, but the management will pick you up for free if you call; or you can take bus #4 or 9 opposite the Hong Kong bank on Jl. Padang Garong. Get off at the Thai Consulate; on the right is a small "Mummy's" sign. Mummy was a legendary party lover who opened the first guest house in K.B. in the early 70s. She passed away about 3 years ago and has since been succeeded by Boy the Dog and Asean, an old friend of Mummy's who keeps everything exactly the same as Mummy had it, only cleaner. There isn't a whole lot of structure to this enterprise. The house is pretty laid back. Free breakfast, tea, and coffee. Dorm beds RM5. Singles RM8. Doubles RM10. Beds have mosquito nets. Guests have free use of bicycles.

K. B. Inn Guest House, 1872-D Jl. Padang Garong (tel. 744 17 86), next to the Azam Money Changer and close to the central bus station and night market. The location—in the center of everything—is a selling point, but the street traffic can be noisy. The owner, Nasron, is famous for his hospitality and the lengths to which he will go to for his guests. The latest creature comfort is access to the rooftop for great views of the city, especially at night. Hot rooms with fans are not very bright, but there's a common room with a TV, books, and lots of travel information. Shared bathrooms. Dorm beds RM4, private rooms RM10-12. Free breakfast, coffee, tea, cold water, and do-it-yourself cooking and laundry facilities.

Ideal Traveler's House, 3954 F-G Jl. Kebun Sultan (tel. 744 22 46). From the bus station follow Jl. Doktor past the New Central Market and turn right onto Jl. Pintu Pong. Pass the Pantai Timor Shopping Center and go 1 block. On the left, before the major intersection with Jl. Kebun Sultan, is a sign down a small, paved road to the House at the end of the street on the right. In a peaceful neighborhood, Ideal Traveler's House is popular with backpackers and families. Airy, clean, and comfortable rooms with wooden floors. Shaded tables in the back in a green, garden-like space. Breakfast available for a price, but you can bring food back and use the dishware. Lots of travel info, and they book tickets to the Perhentian Islands. 2 single beds RM10; 1 double bed RM12; 1 double and 1 single RM18; double bed with balcony and private bath RM25. All have fan. Bicycle for rent RM4 per day.

Town Guest House, 4959-B Jl. Pengkalan Chepa (tel. 748 51 92; fax 744 94 03), located out of town one block past the Caltex gas station on the left side of the road, just past the bus stop but not beyond the Royal Thai Consulate. Facilities galore: motorbike and car rental; ticketing by bus, train, air, or boat; laundry service, book exchange, safety deposit locker, and more. Roof-top restaurant. Rooms have carpeting and fan. Dorms RM4, rooms without bath RM8-12. Rooms with bathroom RM12-15, and A/C RM20-25. MC.

FOOD

Without question, the place to eat in Kota Bharu is the **night market** held across the street from the main bus terminal in the parking lot of the New Central Market (daily, 6pm-midnight). Walk around and take stock of your options before committing to a meal. The inspired can choose from a basic array of Malay dishes and visit the fruit vendors, who sell piles of whatever's in season for dessert. Adventurous stomachs should sample the local specialties, including *ayam percik*—chicken grilled on sticks similar to the delicious *gai yang* popular in northeast Thailand, *nasi dagang*—coconut-based rice topped with tunafish cooked in a special sauce, and *nasi kerabu*—rice topped with an unusual combination of salted fish, coconut shaving, and an array of pungent spices. *Nasi kerabu* can be had with different colored rice and it's a mystery how vendors get it to turn pastel shades of blue, pink, and violet. Most dishes run for less than RM2, usually RM1-1.50. The banana-leaf-wrapped desserts are none too shabby either (RM0.25 or RM0.50).

Hawker stalls inhabit the river end of the **Padang Merdeka,** the ground floor of the **Old Market,** and a few sat the upper levels of the New **Central Market.** For Chinese, seek out **Jl. Kebun Sultan,** near Ideal Traveler's House. **Jl. Gadjah Mati,** the road heading west (toward the Kelantan river) from the clock tower traffic circle, is known for its tasty Indian eateries.

Qing Liang Vegetarian Restaurant, 3400-H Jl. Zainal Abidin (tel. 748 27 66), located on a small side street that connects the main thoroughfares of Jl. Sultan Ibrahim and Jl. Sultanah Zainab. Not so fancy, this vegetarian restaurant offers a good value for great food. All the food is on display in the back; the manager will give you a bowl of broth and a plate of rice topped with what you point to. 3 toppings plus a beverage RM4. No English. A/C splendor. Open daily 11:30am-9pm.

Restoran Nasi Kandar, 2952-J Jl. Post Office Lama. The road runs parallel to the river starting from Padang Merdeka; Nasi Kandar is 8 stores down from Lido Cinema, on the left. Their specialty, surprise surprise, is *nasi kandar.* They ladle the spicy *kandar* sauce from a huge cauldron at the front of the shop near the shelves. Clean, and friendly too. *Nasi kandar* and beverage around RM3.20. Open Sat.-Thurs. 11am-5pm.

Family Cake House and Restaurant, 1964-A Jl. Dato Pati (tel. 748 38 08). Close to the Jl. Hospital intersection, with an impressive English sign. Immaculate facilities and A/C breezes are popular with locals at lunch. The delectable house specialty is platefuls of *nasi dagang* with plenty of cakes. Wash it down with a tall glass of iced star fruit juice (RM1.50). Open Sat.-Thurs. 11am-9pm, Fri. 11am-6pm.

Meena Curry House, 3377-G Jl. Gajah Mati (tel. 747 09 59). As you walk toward the river, it's on the left just before the intersection with Jl. Sultanah Zainab. Fistfuls of gastronomic fun abound at Meena, one of the "banana leaf" restaurants that dot Malaysia's landscape. Customers hunker down before a clean banana leaf and a bedrock of solid rice, which is then drenched with ladles of chicken and fish curry. Chicken RM3.50, fish RM2.80, or vegetarian RM2.50. Silverware is considered poor form; use your right hand. Open daily 11am-3pm and 6-9:30pm.

SIGHTS

A trip to Kota Bharu would be incomplete without inspecting some of the markets, visiting the Gelanggang Seni Arts Center, and taking a stroll about the city's cultural and historical center, the Padang Merdeka. Kota Bharu's **New Central Market,** bounded by Jl. Pintu Pong, Doktor, and Tengku Chick, pulses with energy during the day. The octagonal, three-story building has a semi-translucent dome that lets in plenty of light while keeping out the leaf-wilting heat. The ground floor is the "wet market" where fresh produce, meat, and last night's catch are neatly organized. Veggies and fruits are the centerpiece of the market—bright yellow bananas, burning red peppers, and greens of all shades are arranged in neat patterns. Fabrics, handicrafts, and stacks of spices are sold around the perimeter of the building.

If you're into fabrics and handicrafts, the **Buluh Kubu Bazaar,** next door to the Istana Balai Besar at the east end of the Padang Merdeka, is an excellent outlet for bargain hunting. You might also try the top floor of the **Old Market** bounded by Jl. Dato Pati and Temenggong Putra Semerak. For more specific Malay handicrafts such as *batik,* kites, and wood-carvings from the Kelantan region, there are handicraft shops strung out along the road to Pantai Cinta Berahi (10km north of the city).

The **Gelanggang Seni** (Cultural Center) on Jl. Mahmud across from the Perdana Hotel is a great place to witness local art forms and pastimes. The set-up is a bit contrived, but foreigners are usually outnumbered by locals. From 3:30 to 5:30pm on Saturdays, Mondays and Wednesdays, visitors are likely to see top-spinning, kite-flying, drum-beating, and *silat* demonstrations. On Saturday and Wednesday nights (9-11:30pm), there are traditional performances of *wayang kulit* (shadow-puppet shows), dancing, and traditional drama. Check with the tourist office to see what's on the schedule. All exhibitions and performances are free—there's no excuse to miss this exciting bundle of fun. (See Malaysia: "Recreation" on page 180).

Padang Merdeka means "Independence Square," a reminder of the Malay struggle against British rule. Tok Janggut, who organized rebellions against the colonial tax system in the early 1900s, was killed by the British and displayed here as a warning to other malcontents. The square is surrounded by monuments to the Malay heritage in Kota Bharu. At the east end of the rectangle, away from the river, is the Istana Balai Besar, a large wooden hall built in 1844. No entrance or photography is allowed, as the building is used strictly for ceremonies. Nearer the river on the right side of the square are the royal museum, an art and handicraft museum, and a war museum. The surplus of museums has somewhat diluted the quality of the individual collections. If you're in the mood, the **State Museum** next to the tourist information on J. Sultan Ibrahim is worth a gawk for its beautiful cultural exhibits. Most museums charge RM2 and are open Sat.-Thurs. 10:30am-5:45pm.

Outside Kota Bharu there are several places to visit. **Moonlight Beach** is a pleasant beach with plenty of cheap accommodations and small restaurants (look for homes with signs that say "*tempat penginapan,*" "*asrama,*" or "budget accommodations"). The beach used to be named **Pantai Cinta Berahi,** the Beach of Passionate Love, but the conservative Kelantan state decided that was just too suggestive. Most people still refer to it by the old name, however; to get to "PCB" take bus #10 (RM0.70), which departs every 30min. from in front of the royal museum.

River cruises through the jungles and isolated villages surrounding Kota Bharu are an option to be explored. A recommended tour is done by Roselan "Fabulous" Hanafiah, an award-winning and cheerfully chatty guide who works at the tourist information center. His half-day river cruise (10am-1pm, min. 3 people, max. 10) through the canals and rivers in Kelantan makes a stop for tea; RM65. Check the tourist center for the specifics of the tour, and meet Roselan for yourself. Travelers on a smaller budget can take their own cruise on a public transportation river boat and then return to Kota Bharu by bus. Most boats depart from Kuala Krai, which can be reached by bus from the central terminal.

You can make reservations through Mr. Roselan to stay with a local family in their village through a program called **The Kampung Experience.** Visitors are allowed to choose the families they stay with (kite and *batik* makers, fishermen, potters, etc.) and are able to learn about their profession as well as daily life in a Kelantan village. For three days and two nights RM160 per person (children under 12 stay free). Reports have been glowing and it's the only program of its kind in Malaysia.

■■■ KUALA TERENGGANU

Capital of a decidedly conservative Islamic state, Kuala Terengganu unfurls between the restless pounding of the South China Sea to the east and the brackish eddies of the Terengganu River to the west. Little more than a fishing village in the past, the city is once again turning to the sea with the discovery of off-shore petroleum deposits. Fed by oil, concrete, air-conditioned high-rises loom over more picturesque, weathered structures from yesterday's economy. It's not a four-star destination, but burrowing for bargains in the Central Market, puttering about the boat yards of Duyong Island, and strolling in the expansive Istana Tengku Long Museum might be enough to distract beach-bound travelers for at least a little while.

ORIENTATION

Kuala Terengganu follows a basic scheme that's somewhat crumpled by sea and river at the edges. **Jalan Sultan Zainal Abidin** runs east-west along the seaward tip of the city. Its center is marked by the **express bus terminal,** across from which is the Seri Pantai Hostel. Located on the street's west half is the tourist information center next door to the post office, and at the far east end is the **Tourism Malaysia** office. **Jalan Sultan Ismail** is the city's commercial spine and runs parallel to Jl. Sultan Zainal Abidin. Its west edge begins with the **Hotel Terengganu,** while its center is dominated by **Maybank,** and to the east lie the police station and immigration office. **Jalan Dato Isaac** is sandwiched between these two streets. **Jalan Tok Lam** stretches from the city's center north to its shores and connects all three boulevards. Parallel to the west is **Jalan Massid Abidin;** travelers walking from Jl. Sultan Ismail successively encounter the taxi station and the local bus station. **Duyong Island,** bobbing placidly in the waters of the west coast, is accessible by ferry from the west shores.

PRACTICAL INFORMATION

Tourist Office: Tourist Information Center (tel. 09 622 15 53), on Jl. Sultan Zainal Abidin. Maps of Kuala Terengganu. Open Sat.-Wed. 9am-5pm, Thurs. 9am-12:45pm. **Tourism Malaysia,** 2243 Ground Floor Wisma MCIS Building (tel. 09 622 14 33), also on the east half of Jl. Sultan Zainal Abidin. Maps of the city. Open Sat.-Wed. 8am-4pm, Thurs. 8am-12:45pm.

Immigration Office: (tel. 622 14 24), on the 2nd floor of the 13-floor Wisma Persekutuan building, at the intersection of Jl. Pejabat and Jl. Sultan Ismail. Same-day visa extensions. Open Sat.-Wed. 8am-4pm, Thurs. 8am-12:45pm.

Currency Exchange: Bank Bumiputra (tel. 09 622 26 11), on the corner of Jl. Masjid Abidin and Jl. KG Dalam accepts Visa, MC, AmEx, and traveler's checks. Foreign currency exchange upstairs, next to the **ATM.** Open Sat.-Wed. 9:30am-5pm, Thurs. 9:30am-1pm.

Post Office: (tel. 09 622 85 55), on Jl. Sultan Zainal Abidin. Facing the river, it's about 100m left of Jl. Masjid Abidin. Poste Restante. Open Sat.-Thurs. 8am-5pm.

Telephone: Telekom office (tel. 09 623 15 84), on the corner of Jl. Sultan Ismail and Jl. Banggol. Overseas calls. No credit cards or calling cards. Open Sat.-Wed. 8am-5pm, Fri. and holidays 8:30am-noon. **Tourist Information Center** has an international service booth.

Airport: (tel. 666 42 04), 13km out of town. **Malaysian Airlines,** 13 Jl. Sultan Omar (tel. 09 622 76 54). To **Kuala Lumpur** (3 daily, 4 on Sun., RM109). Visa, MC, AmEx. Open Sat.-Wed. 8:30am-4:30pm, Thurs. 8:30am-2:30pm.

Buses: Local **buses** and **minibuses** leave from the large terminal at the intersection of Jl. Masjid Abidin and Jl. Syed Hussain. To: **Marang** (every 30min. 7:30am-6pm, RM1.20); **Rantau Abang** (every 30min.; RM3.30); **Duyong** (every hr., RM.50); and **Dungun** (every 30min., RM4.20). **A/C buses** leave from the **Express Bus Station** near the Jl. Sultan Zainal Abidin and Jl. Tok Lam intersection to: **Kota Bharu** (8:30, 10am, noon, 1:30, and 5pm, 3hr., RM7.50); **Kuala Lumpur** (9:30, 10am, and 9:30pm, 8hr., RM21.70); **Mersing** (8:30am, 8:30, and 9:30pm, RM16.10); and **Kuantan** (8, 9, 11am, 12:30, 1:30, 2:30, and 4:30pm, 3-½hr., RM9.20). Warisan Express to: **Kuala Lumpur** (9am, 8hr., RM20) and **Kuantan** (9pm, 3-½hr., RM8). Bumi Express to: **Melaka** (10pm, 8-½hr., RM20.10). Santanara Express to: **Singapore** (8:30am and 9:30pm, 11hr., RM23).

Local Transport: Trishaws ply the streets for RM2-3 per trip.

Taxis: On Jl. Masjid Abidin, north of the Jl. Sultan Ismail intersection. Max. 4 people to: **Mersing** (RM120, A/C RM160); **Marang** (RM10, A/C RM15); **Kuantan** (RM60, A/C RM80); and **Kota Bharu** (RM48, A/C RM70).

Laundry: Pusat Dobi Seri Pantai, 1-A Jl. Tok Lam (tel. 624 15 92). Toward the water, on the left side of the last block. Wash and dry: shirts RM.50, pants RM.60, jeans RM1.20. Open daily 9am-9pm.

Pharmacy: Dew Ma, 10-D Jl. Tok Lam (tel. 622 02 00), near the north tip, with a large English sign. Open Sat.-Wed. 9am-10pm, Thurs. 9am-6pm.

Hospital: Big and pink, it looms south of the Turtle rotary on Jl. Sultan Mahmud.

Police: (tel. 622 22 22), on the corner of Jl. Sultan Omar and Jl. Sultan Ismail.

ACCOMMODATIONS

Awi's Yellow House, along the shores of Duyong Island. Accessible by boat from the jetty across from the Tourist Info Center or behind the Seri Malaysia Hotel on Jl. Bandar. Upon reaching Duyong, walk upriver until the sea wall stops. Cross the small bridge and continue along the shore until you reach a large boat yard. Awi's is four houses farther, past the *batik* shop on the left side. It's not yellow, but it does face a yellow house. The "house" is a tiny suburb of huts with woven walls, roosting above the Terengganu River. The charming complex is interconnected by boardwalks strewn with fishing nets and trailing plants. Dorms RM5. Singles RM8. Doubles RM14. Family room for 6-7 RM25. Cooking facilities. Boats to the city stop around 6pm, but city buses stop at the bridge every hour until 11pm.

Ping Anchorage Traveler's Homestay, 77A Jl. Dato Isaac (tel. 622 08 51; fax 622 80 93). Just off the Jl. Tok Lam intersection; from the mosque it's on the right with a small English sign. Despite aloof staff, rooms are bright and airy. Roof-top café open 8am-10pm. Shared bath with sinks that leap off the wall, and travel service. Dorms RM5. Singles with fan RM15. Doubles with fan RM20. Rooms with bath RM30. Reception open 8am-10pm; gate locked at 10pm.

FOOD

For a quick lunch try the cluster of cheap **food stalls** on the first floor of the local bus station on Jl. Syed Hussain. For late night excursions, the **night market** stacks up just around the corner at Jl. Tok Lam. Head to the shores of **Pantai Batu Buruk** on the east coast for similar fare in saltier, seaside settings.

Restoran Cheng Cheng, 224 Jl. Bandar (tel. 09 623 22 24). About 100ft. south of the Dragon Gate, next to a parking lot. Step up to an extensive buffet of Chinese dishes, including vegetarian selections. To calculate your bill, colored clothes pins are affixed to the edge of your plate, one for each entree, but managers often forgo this embarrassing, yet colorful ritual. Open daily noon-3pm and 5-8:30pm.

Restoran Zainuudin, 79C Jl. Tok Lam (tel. 09 623 37 79). From the local bus terminal, walk to the Jl. Tok Lam intersection and turn left. The restoran is on the left. Plush, fuzzy blue menus in this occasionally A/C establishment. Managers say dishes are "Thai-inspired," but Thais would refer to them as "Malay-inspired." Denied by both parents, the unclaimed culinary orphan of Jl. Tok Lam packs in the locals. Ginger chicken RM3. *Tom yam campur* RM4. Open daily 7am-11pm.

SIGHTS

West of the city at the intersection of Jl. Kota and Jl. Bandar, the **central market** entices visitors with hours of intrepid bargain-hunting pleasure.

Gelanggang Seni, the cultural center, is on the east shore of Terengganu, off Pantai Batu Buruk. Locals stroll the beach in the evenings before wandering over to watch amateur troupes perform *silat* and traditional dances. Showtimes are Fri., 5pm and Sat., 8:30pm, but schedules are erratic; contact info centers for details.

Boats to restful **Duyong Island** depart from behind the pink and grey Seri Malaysia Hotel at the south tip of Jl. Bandar, as well as from the jetty across from the tourist info center on Jl. Sultan Zainal Abidin (about RM0.50, 15min., last boat 6pm). Along these quiet shores locals still slowly **construct boats** of all sizes without plans or diagrams. The wood is aged for ½ yr. before the planks are fitted together using wooden pegs and sealed with a resin derived form local swamp trees. If you have some time and a spare RM500,000, cruise home in your own custom-built yacht.

■■■ MARANG

The photogenic visage of Marang, one of a dwindling number of coastal fishing villages that still makes its living off fishing, can be found on postcards throughout the peninsula. The picturesque, palm-fringed coastline with Kapas Island and the harbor nearby make this conservative community a relaxing getaway.

ORIENTATION AND PRACTICAL INFORMATION

In Terengganu State, Marang (not to be confused with Merang) is immediately south of Kuala Terengganu, the state capital. Marang can only be reached by the Marang or Dugan bus or share-taxi by the Terengganu-Kuantan Highway. The **bus stop** is the highway, and if you cross the bridge you've missed Marang. Most people get dropped off at the new 4-way intersection next to the giant statue of the lobster and cuttlefish in day-glo colors struggling to emerge from a frothy cube of blueberry jello. When you leave town, find a place to sit with some locals and they'll help you flag down your bus. Also on the highway, on the side away from the shore, is the **post office** (tel. 618 22 15), which is open Sat.-Thurs. 8am-5pm. **Postal code:** 21600. The Marang **clinic** (tel. 618 22 16) is located between the two. Open Sat.-Wed. 8am-4pm, Thurs. 12:45pm-2pm. The main part of town pulses on **Jalan Lama,** the street parallel to the highway, running close to the river and beaches. It turns toward the highway at the southern end of town where the river starts to meet the sea. Jl. Lama ends at a small set of steps leading to the highway. The **police station** is at the very end of Jl. Lama on the highway side (tel. 618 22 22). Heading in the opposite direction on Jl. Lama will take you past the town's shophouses, two footbridges, and bring you to the better budget accommodations.

Offshore is Kapas Island, a popular resort spot. There are fine beaches here, but overdevelopment has destroyed most of the coral. Boats cost RM15 round-trip, last boat 1pm. Last boat from Kapas is at 3-4pm. Guest houses and several agents in Marang can arrange your crossing, or you can just swim there; every year in July there is a 7km swim race to the island. First one on the beach lands RM2000.

ACCOMMODATIONS AND FOOD

There are plenty of places to stay in Marang, and most have their own eateries. Although the food situation here is not as attractive as the accommodations, there's an exciting Sunday and Wednesday **night market** which occupies most of Jl. Lama in the main part of town. For such a small town, Marang's market is big on activity and epicurean amazement.

Island View Resort and **Island View Inn,** Lot 1507 and 1506, Kg. Paya (tel. (09) 618 20 06). North on Jl. Lama between the 2 footbridges, and across the street. Recently expanded, with a wider range of accommodations and a shiny veneer. The prices, however, have stayed the same. Open-air common space with TV near the reception area is a comfort. Home Country Direct phone next to reception is super-convenient. The restaurant has only a breakfast menu, but the Seafarer Restoran is nearby. Dorm beds RM5, comfortable rooms with bath and fan RM12, 15, and 18. Rooms with A/C and bath RM40, with TV and hot water RM50.

Kamal's Guest House, on Jl. Lama, just past Island View Resort toward the second footbridge. An older establishment that creaks around the joints, but friendlier and more lived-in than its neighbors. Wonderful, quiet courts and shady trees. Beds are outfitted with gloriously delirious *batik* sheets. Dorms RM5. Singles with fan (no bath) RM10. Private chalet RM13.

Sri Marang Guest House and Restaurant, No. 35A, Jl. Lama, Bandar Marang. In the center of town on the side of the road away from the water, in one of the old shophouses. Ranks as one of the best deals in town. Up a steep wooden stairway (watch your head!), rooms with two beds costs RM5 for one person, RM10 for two. Makeshift, corrugated tin-walled bathrooms are downstairs in the kitchen behind the restaurant. "Chinese style" menu has dubious western selections.

Seafarer Restoran, Lot 1507, Kg. Paya, Marang (tel. 618 28 54). Expensive, tourist-oriented, with great tropical fisherman decor. Limited selection of western and Malay dishes. Black pepper steak (RM20), *spaghetti bolognese* (RM8.50). Fish comes straight from the docks. It's not on the menu 'cause they never know what's going to be available. Four species of beer. Open daily 9am-1am.

■■■ RANTAU ABANG

Even smaller than Marang, Rantau Abang, another popular sun-and-surf destination on the east coast, hardly qualifies as a village. The east coast's shoreline stretches for hundreds of kilometers from Kuantan to Kota Bharu, and Rantau Abang would be only a blip on this lengthy stretch if it weren't for the giant leatherback turtles, which draw hundreds of tourists annually. As the currents, tides, and turtle instincts would have it, the roughly 5km stretch of beach at and around Rantau Abang is the favorite site of female leatherbacks, who come to lay their eggs between May and September, with the peak months being July and August.

ORIENTATION AND PRACTICAL INFORMATION

Rantau Abang's most visible landmark is the **Turtle Information Center** (tel. (09) 844 169) to the left (beach side) of the highway if you are coming from points north. The highway is the only road in town. The Center has decent exhibits documenting the decline in turtle landings of recent decades, the cruelties (accidental and otherwise) that have affected the population of these Chelonian reptiles, and general explanations of turtle wildlife in Malaysia, particularly the sea-faring variety. There is a free video presentation daily at 9:30, 10:30, 11:30am, 2:30, 3:30, 5, 5:30, 8:30, 9:30, and 10:30pm. From May through August, the center is open Sat.-Thurs. 9am-1pm, 2-6pm, and 8-11pm, Fri. 9am-noon and 3-11pm. From September through April, the center is open Sat.-Wed. 8am-12:45pm and 2-4pm., Thurs. 8am-12:45pm. To leave Rantau Abang for the south, catch a bus to **Dungun** (RM1, last bus 5:30pm). For long-distance travel catch a bus to **Kuantan** and transfer there. Practically any bus heading north will stop in **Terengganu,** where you can change buses.

ACCOMMODATIONS AND FOOD

Along the highway, there are **food stalls** next to the Turtle Information Center; here, the tortoise-loving backpacker will find the town's two guest houses right on the beach. Cross a boardwalk over a swampy area to access them. With your back to the highway Ismail is just right of the Turtle Information Center, and Awang's is a few hundred feet farther to the right. The Thursday **night market scene** in nearby Dungun is reputed to be one of the best in Malaysia.

Ismail Beach Resort (tel. (09) 843 293), has dim rooms without fans and somewhat damp bathrooms for RM10. A double bed and electric fan costs RM12. A slightly larger, cleaner version with ceiling fan runs RM15. Separate "chalet-style" structures, one single bed and one double bed, cost RM30, and two double beds cost RM50. Kindergarten nostalgics can swoosh through the air on the funky wooden swing. The restaurant, **Siri Rantau,** grooves to Malay love songs and has a decent breakfast and lunch/dinner menu with more variety, but slightly higher prices than the food stalls on the highway. Restaurant is closed 3-6pm.

Awang's Beach Bungalows (tel. 843 500). Rooms are a bit more spacious, but more austere-looking. With bath, but no fan, RM6 for single bed, RM20 for a double. Rescue your sanity in a room with fan: singles RM15, doubles RM20. Room with A/C RM60. Serve and dive at the beach volleyball net or putter at *batik* making (RM15-20). Restaurant serves Malaysian, Chinese, and western dishes.

SIGHTS

Weighing up to 500kg and having a length of nearly 1.5m, the leatherback females lumber onto the beach past the high tide using their immense flippers to move about. On land, they dig a hole 60-80cm deep, lay 60-120 tennis ball-sized eggs in the nest, and bury them before returning to the sea to swim gracefully away. One female may do this 4-5 times in one season. The eggs hatch after about 55 days, with a success rate varying from 40 to 80%. A baby turtle's chance for survival to adulthood is about the same. In the 1950s, records show, leatherback landings at Rantau Abang in one season numbered in the high hundreds, but the count in recent years has dwindled to fewer than one-hundred. It seems clear that this drop in landings is a direct consequence of human disturbance of the leatherback's reproductive strategies. Crowds of up to 100 people gather around, shining lights and taking flash pictures, as the turtle makes her way up the beach to do her job. Some spectators have been known to sit on the turtle's back. In the past, the eggs were eaten as a delicacy.

Today the situation has improved significantly, though the numbers haven't been restored to their former level. The government has taken an active interest in the survival of the species and the preservation of Rantau Abang as a site for the turtles' egg laying. The wildlife department has set up different zones of limited or no access to visitors and eggs are collected from the sand and nurtured in hatcheries where their survival chances are much better. Upon hatching, the babies are set free into the wild seas, hopefully to return in the future to lay more eggs. What remains disappointing is that tourists flagrantly ignore new regulations prohibiting visitors from coming within 5m of a pregnant turtle, using flashlights, or flash photography. If violators are caught there is a fine of up to RM1000 or 6 months in prison. Let's Go recommends following these simple rules at the beach in Rantau Abang: Keep at least a 5m distance from the turtles; no lights; no flash photography; no campfires; no noise; and no litter.

Turtle-watching is a mini-industry in town. "Agents" patrol the beaches at night and when a turtle lands, word spreads like wildfire, and the agents bang on everyone's door to wake up all interested tourists. If the turtle is more than a kilometer away from where you are, rides will be offered and a total of RM5 will be charged to you for the ride and wake up call. You get trucked out to the living attraction and the exploitation begins.

On the whole, it is probably both easier and cheaper to check with the turtle hatchery next to Awang's Beach Bungalows at night to see if they have any newly hatched baby turtles to release into the sea. The same strict rules apply, but the impact of the tourist is lower and the sight is inspiring.

■■■ CHERATING

Another tiny beach resort town on the east coast, Cherating seems to consist solely of guest houses, restaurants, and souvenir shops. The good news: the town is relatively inexpensive, and gift shops promote local arts and handicrafts (many offer do-it-yourself *batik* lessons). The bad news: the endless strip of tourist-oriented facilities coupled with the overwhelming population of foreigners makes the community rather tiresome. Cherating is less than perfect if you're looking for real peace and quiet. It's a party town with plenty of spirit and spirits to last the night.

Orientation and Practical Information Cherating is less than 50km north of Kuantan, the capital of Pahang State. By bus, it costs RM2.50 to or from Kuantan. From Rantau Abang and other northern towns public buses stop at Dungun and connections must be made to Kemaman (RM4.30). A bus from Kemaman going to Kuantan will make the Cherating stop (RM0.90), right on the highway.

The town itself has two main roads: the **Kuantan-Terengganu Highway,** and the road parallel to it which runs along the beach. These main thoroughfares are connected by two perpendicular roads (each only 300m long). Cherating is contained within the borders of this rectangle. Mak Long Teh's Guest House is on the highway right behind the bus stop. At the corner of the northern cross street and the beach road is the Cherating Beach Mini Motel. All along the beach road are guest houses and restaurants suited to varying budgets, as well as **Travel Post** (tel. 09 581 91 34), a de-facto **tourist information office** offering tours, travel tips and packages, international phone service and money exchange. This is not a government tourist office, and thus may charge for its services. Open daily 9am-10pm.

Accommodations and Food Guest houses and restaurants are packed like sardines along the beach road. They're all the same, offering either A-frame style or small chalet-style huts (RM10-60). The restaurants service western patrons, with plenty of movie videos while you eat, but prices are higher than the average Malaysian restaurant. When you tire of the beach scene, try one of these alternatives.

Mak Long Teh Guest House (tel. (09) 581 92 90), on the highway behind the bus stop, is the best deal in town. Traditional wooden rooms are raised on piles; fans and mosquito nets keep your tender body cool and protected; and shower and toilets in the backyard have excellent water pressure. While the chickens and goats on the grounds compete for scraps, guests are stuffed with amazing all-you-can-eat home-cooked breakfasts and dinners, included in the bare-bones price of RM12. From 8-10am and at 6:30pm sharp, guests savor *roti canai,* fried dough, toast with butter and jam for breakfast; chicken curry, fried fish, mixed vegetables, prawn crackers, and bananas at dinner. There's also tea, coffee, and cool water on tap. For those not interested in eating, the room costs RM5. If Mak Long Teh's is full, try **Mak De's** next door for similar pampering at comparable prices.

The Moon (tel. (09) 581 91 86), on the northern cross street and on the left, is at once the most bizarre and beautiful spot in Cherating. The sign on the road boasts "we are different...even a bit peculiar." Perched up on a hillside, hidden among trees, the location is lit with pale lights at night. Beer is served at "The Deadly Nightshade...the Restaurant at the End of the Universe." The lounge area belies a chic New York aesthetic mixed with pervasive witchcraft themes, and the wooden construction of the main area and the other huts blends well with the forest surroundings. Theatrics aside, the basic principle is that less concrete and more nature makes for a better guest house. Chalets cost RM30-35 depending on the season; rooms in the longhouse are RM10. Prices are negotiable and weekly, even monthly rates can be arranged, especially for people who are handy with tools and willing to help out.

Entertainment Located surfside, **Cherating Sports Center**—a strange combination of bar and watersports rental—offers a variety of equipment for rent: wind surfer RM15 per hr., RM20 with instructor, canoes RM10 per hr., and a jetski RM40 per 15min. of fun. Beers are RM4.50 and the salt water is free. Daily volleyball matches at 5pm and nightly bonfire at 9:30pm. Bring your guitar.

■■■ KUANTAN

If you've been sticking to the east coast, Kuantan, the capital of Pahang, will seem refreshingly modern and cosmopolitan. On the surface at least, the city appears to have more in common with the west coast. Malaysia's three predominant ethnic groups (Malay, Chinese, and Indian) are well represented in this urban community where religious conservatism predominates. Kuantan's new State Mosque is one of Malaysia's most beautiful, combining the architectural styles of Moghul North India and Disney's Magic Kingdom. Just outside Kuantan is Teluk Chempedak, a pleasant beach resort worthy of a daytrip or even a few nights' stay.

ORIENTATION

The heart of Kuantan is the **State Mosque.** Nearby, the two main roads, **Jalan Mahkota** and **Jalan Besar,** run parallel to the **Kuantan River. Jalan Bukit Ubi** crosses both and passes the city's **padang,** a recreational field in front of the mosque. Farther past the *padang*, Jl. Mahkota becomes **Jalan Abdul Aziz.**

PRACTICAL INFORMATION

Tourist Information Office: (tel. 513 30 26), on Jl. Mahkota across the street from the Kompleks Terantun and the police station, next to the pedestrian overpass that crosses Jl. Mahkota. Very helpful and informative staff. Come here for info on Taman Negara National Park and a map of Kuantan. Open Mon.-Fri. 9am-12:15pm and 2:45pm-5pm, Sat. 9am-1pm.

Immigration Office: (tel. 521 373), on Wisma Persekutuan. Same-day visa extensions. Open Mon.-Fri. 8am-4:15pm.

Currency Exchange: Hong Kong Bank, 1 Jl. Mahkota (tel. (09) 524 66 66) is about one block behind the mosque on the left. Accepts Visa, MC, and traveler's checks. ATM machine in front accepts Visa. Open Mon.-Fri. 10am-3pm, Sat. 9:30-11:30am. If banks are closed try **Hamid Bros.,** 23 Jl. Mahkota (tel. 521 119), across from the mosque. Open 9am-9pm, Sun. 10am-2pm; don't confuse with the Hamid Bros. Store down the road and closer to the tourist office.

Post Office: Pejabat Pos Besar, (tel. (03) 521 032), on Jl. Abdul Aziz past the mosque and close to the intersection with Jl. Merdeka. Open Mon.-Sat. 8am-5pm, but they "actually work" 8:30am-4:30pm.

Telephones: Kedai Telekom, (tel. (09) 513 92 92), next door to the post office. Home Country Direct. Open Mon.-Sat. 8:30am-5:45pm, Sun. 8:30am-1pm.

Airport: (tel. 538 12 91), west of town. Take the bus (every hr., 7am-5pm) from the local terminal or rent a taxi (RM15-20). **Malaysian Airlines** (tel. 555 05 55; fax 552 870) on the ground floor of the Wisma Bolasepak Building on Jl. Gambut, has flights to Kuala Lumpur (daily, RM79 one way) and Singapore (weekly, Wed., Fri., Sat., and Sun., RM166 one way). Open Mon.-Fri. 8:30am-5:30pm, Sat. 8:30am-12:30pm. On Sun. and holidays call 03 746 3000. Visa, MC, AmEx, DC.

Buses: Local bus terminal, on Jl. Haji Abdul Rahman, about1 block in from Jl. Mahkota, and services **Cherating** (every hr., RM2.50); and **Kemaman** (every hr.). The new **express bus terminal** looms off the Jalan Tun Ismail and Jl. Bukit Sekitau intersection. It's in a vacant lot in front of the stadium. Most buses are run by private companies. Buses to: **Kuala Lumpur** (every hr. until midnight, RM12) and **Kuala Terengganu** (every hr. until 7pm, 3-½hr., RM9). **Mara Holding** (tel. 515 67 40) runs buses to: **Singapore** (9am and 11pm, 7hr., RM16); **Kuala Besut** (2am and 2pm, RM17); and **Jerantut** (9, 10am, 1, and 2pm, RM8.40). **Utama Ekpress** (tel. 515 60 02) runs to: **Ipoh** (9:30am and 9pm, RM21.10) and **Butterworth** (5:30 and 8pm, 12-½hr., RM26.75). **CEPAT Express** (tel. 515 66 78) runs to **Melaka** (8am and 2:30pm, 5hr., RM14.50). **SKMK** runs to **Kota Bharu** (8, 10am, noon, 2:30, 3:30, 10, and 11pm, RM16).

Taxis: From the **city taxi stand,** on Jl. Besar close to the pedestrian overpass, taxis whizz through the streets and go anywhere in town for RM4. **Share-taxis** also leave from the stand and travel the peninsula (min. 4 passengers). Sample fares are per person, to: **Kuala Lumpur** (RM25); **Jerantut** (RM15); **Cherating** (RM5); **Rantau Abang** (RM15); and **Kota Bharu** (RM25.

Car Rental: Hertz Rent-A-Car (tel. (09) 528 041) at Samudra Riverview Hotel on Jl. Besar. Rates average RM150 and up; weekly packages also available. Open Mon.-Fri. 8am-6pm, Sat. 8am-3pm. Accepts all major credit cards.

English Bookstore: Hamid Bros., 23 Jl. Mahkota (tel. 521 119). A gold mine of romance novels, including one by Margaret Thatcher.

Hospital: Hospital Besar Kuantan (tel. 513 33 33), on Jl. Tanah Putih. Head out of town on Jl. Besar (going southwest, away from Teluk Chempedak) and the road changes name to Jl. Tanah Putih. It is on the right.

Emergency: tel. 999.

Police: (tel. 513 22 22), on Jl. Mahkota.

ACCOMMODATIONS

New Capitol Hotel, 57-59 Jl. Bukit Ubi (tel. 505 222 or 507 276). Turn onto Jl. Bukit Ubi from Jl. Mahkota and it's a few blocks past the *padang,* on the left next to the cinema, above a Chinese coffee shop. Clean, quiet, and relatively private rooms have sinks. The common baths are reasonably clean and have squat toilets (with a view!) separate from the showers. Rooms start at RM18, with private baths RM25-30. Kung Fu movies and Chinese films of dubious merit shown.

Kuantan Planet Hotel, No. 77, 1st and 2nd floor, Jl. Bukit Ubi (tel. 513 98 52). On the last side street on the left before the Jl. Tun Ismail intersection. Not even the congenial manager seems to know where the name came from, but most of the basic rooms here do offer a window facing west so you can peer at the sunset and the rising stars. Convenient 24-hr. check-in, and some of the best rates in town. Singles RM11. Doubles RM15. Triples RM17, with A/C RM28.

Min Heng Hotel, 22-24 Jl. Mahkota (tel. 504 885), located above a steak restaurant opposite the tourist information center. The elderly structure (circa 1926) has a balcony overlooking the other shopfronts of Jl. Mahkota. Like most cheap Chinese hotels, there is little privacy and no perks; the rooms are little more than a bed and sink. Singles RM13. Doubles RM14, with A/C RM28. Triples RM17.

FOOD

The **food stalls** are to be found on Jl. Mahkota near the State Mosque and by the river behind the express bus terminal. They specialize in *nasi ayam* (chicken rice, RM2.50) and *sate*. Kuantan has a disproportionate number of bakeries; look for one on any street and enjoy pastries at a fraction of the cost you'd pay at home.

Restoran Chan Poh, 52 Jl. Bukit Ubi (tel. 527 678), across from the cinema and a few stores down. The evening roar of their steamers (almost) drowns out the noise on the busy street and makes you fear a Death Star-style explosion is about to occur. Very popular with locals for late night *dim sum.* No English, but if you are patient they will bring you a selection of the evening dishes. Point with your thumb, not your disgusting forefinger. Open daily 8am-1:30pm, and 6-11:30pm.

Lotus Vegetarian Hotel, 1394-8 Jl. Dato Lim Hoe Lek (tel. 514 48 72), away from the city center past the stadium on the ground floor of the L.A. Exclusive Hotel. Tuck into succulent Chinese vegetarian food in a spotlessly clean, spacious setting, cast in shades of green and white with pleasant arboreal scenes adorning the walls. The waitstaff recommends the mock fish-head curry (RM7) or try the fried "goose" with mixed fruit salad. Don't accept the "refreshing towel" if you don't want the extra RM0.30 tacked on to your bill. Open daily 7am-10pm.

Parvathy Restoran, 75 Jl. Bukit Ubi (tel. 514 31 40). In a neighborhood of Indian restaurant/coffee shops, heading away from Jl. Mahkota it's seven stores past the cinema on the left. Prepares a daily selection of vegetarian dishes or try the old standbys: *thosai, roti, chapati,* and *nasi briyani,* plus a host of curry selections. Owners are much friendlier than their jaded waitstaff. Open daily 7am-11pm.

SIGHTS

The creamy white walls of **Masjid Negeri** climb breathlessly into the air of central Kuantan city, providing a foundation for the graceful curves of the eggshell blue and green central dome. Not a subtle setting, as the white of purity, the green of Islam, and the blue of peace are surrounded by screaming-pink bougainvilleas. The fragile four corner minarets soar elegantly, challenged only by the lewd red and white communications tower next door. Tilted to face Mecca, the substantial complex is riveting from the outside; inside, the lace-like curtains of concrete block that clothe the arches create a mosaic of light and shadow throughout the courtyards, halls, and prayer spaces. Too bad inferior construction only 5 years ago has taken its toll—the walls are stained with water, and tiles have faded and popped out.

Visitors are allowed in the mosque if they are quiet and respectful, dressed appropriately (no shorts or bare shoulders), and do not walk on the carpeted areas or into the offices. No pictures allowed. Early morning is the best time to visit, but at night the exterior provides a beautiful backdrop, except for the smoldering red warning lights on top of the minarets to ward off planes coming in for a better view.

The nearest and most popular attraction around Kuantan is **Teluk Chempedak,** just 4km out of town on the east coast shore. Teluk Chempedak's sandy 1-½ mile beach is bounded by rocky headlands. The developed part is at the north end of the shore where a promenade passes by restaurants, souvenir shops, and a cheap food stall center. Walk over the bridge at the north end of the beach and explore the trails through the forests. Past the rocks is another, much smaller beach, which offers a secluded respite from the madding crowd. Budget **accommodations** can be found at **Sri Pantai Resorts,** 2 Jl. Sim Lim (tel. 525 250; fax 527 268), where rooms with fan but without bath cost RM25. Rooms with bathroom and A/C start at RM60. Visa, MC, and AmEx. Get to Teluk Chempedak by taking **bus #39** from the bus stop by the State Mosque on Jl. Mahkota (7am-9pm). One way fare is RM0.60.

■■■ MERSING

Beyond the travel agencies, budget hotels, and beach-gear shops, Mersing is a tiny fishing village trying to cope with its dubious status as *the* gateway to Malaysia's islands in the South China Sea. Busloads of tourists pass through, but few stay more than a few hours; they're all headed for Tioman Island or one of the other white-sand, tropical resort isles to the east. Residents have grown a little callous toward these flocks of passers-through, and they just keep harvesting ringgit, just as they've fished the sea for years. Locals gather in the few open-air restaurants to chat and watch their favorite television dramas, but by 8pm the streets are virtually deserted. Warnings about the conservative east coast are, for the most part, true. Avoid wearing shorts to help ward off the "hello my darling" legions. Solo women travelers should expect a constant onslaught of stares, come-ons, blown kisses—the works.

ORIENTATION

The two main thoroughfares, **Jalan Abu Bakar** and **Jalan Ismail,** meet the road from Johor Bahru at a roundabout with a huge sculpture of two crossed swords. The tourist office and the **wharf** both lie along Jl. Abu Bakar. Next to the wharf is the blue-and-white tile **Plaza R&R,** a tourist center containing an **express bus terminal,** travel agencies, restaurants, and an information booth. Taxis and the **local bus station** are on **Jalan Selenium,** a short street one block north of Jl. Abu Bakar.

PRACTICAL INFORMATION

Tourist Office: Mersing Tourist Information Center (METIC) (tel. 799 52 12), on Jl. Abu Bakar; on the left from the roundabout, about 100m before Plaza R&R. Friendly staff has all the answers. Open Mon.-Fri. 8am-4:45pm, Sat. 8am-2:15pm.

Currency Exchange: Bank Bumiputra Malaysia Berhad, 4-5 Jl. Ismail (tel. 799 16 00). Changes traveler's checks; RM2 charge. Visa, MC accepted (RM4 service charge). Open Mon.-Fri. 9:30am-4pm, Sat. 9:30am-noon.

Post office: (tel. 799 10 31), on Jl. Abu Bakar. Open Mon.-Sat. 8am-5pm.

Telephone office: On Jl. Dato Timor has 6 cardphones and sells phonecards. Open Mon.-Fri. 8:45am-4:15pm, Sat. 8:45am-12:15pm. **Telephone code:** 07.

Taxis: (tel. 799 13 93), on Jl. Suleiman. From the roundabout, walk down Jl. Abu Bakar. Left at the 1st intersection, then right at the end of the road. Cabs depart regularly for points on the peninsula.

Buses: Private express **long-distance buses** depart and arrive either at the Restoran Malaysia or the Plaza R&R, up Jl. Abu Bakar. Purchase tickets at either venue for daily buses to: **Kuala Lumpur** (noon and 10pm, RM16.50); **Singapore** (12:30pm, RM15); **Melaka** (9:30am and 1pm, RM11.20); **Kuantan** (1 and 11pm, RM9.10); and **Penang** (5pm, RM35).

Market: Parkson Ria Supermarket, on Jl. Ismail next to the Mersing Inn. Open daily 10am-10pm.

Public toilets/showers: in Plaza R&R.

Pharmacy/Hospital: Kelinik Mersing, 16 Dato Muhammad Ali (tel. 799 12 70), fills prescriptions and performs medical exams. Open daily 8am-6pm; doctors in 10am-6pm. **Hospital Daerah** (tel. 799 33 33) is at the far end of Jl. Ismail, a 15-min. walk out of town; handles more serious ailments.

Emergency: tel. 999.

Police: tel. 799 22 22.

ACCOMMODATIONS

Omar's Backpacker's Hostel, on Jl. Abu Bakar, just beyond the post office as you walk toward the pier. Refreshingly intimate with only 10 beds. Spartan rooms. Shared bath, just beyond a community kitchen. Small balcony. Dorms RM6. Doubles RM14. Congenial Omar also offers a tour of 3-4 islands on his boat for a bargain RM50 (including lunch and snorkeling gear; 4 person min., 12 max). Also offers accommodations on nearby Sibu Island for RM10 and up.

Hotel Embassy, 2 Jl. Ismail (tel. 799 35 45; fax 799 52 79), near the roundabout, two doors down from Bank Bumiputra. Unlike many Chinese hotels, this hotel has walls that go all the way up to the ceiling. Best value in town. Double with common bath RM16, with private bath RM25, with A/C RM35.

FOOD

Small **open-air restaurants,** many specializing in seafood, abound along Jl. Abu Bakar. Try the **market** across the street from the taxi and local bus station on Jl. Suleiman for overflowing baskets of durian, bananas, mangos and pineapples. **Plaza R&R** has stands selling traditional Muslim and Chinese dishes. Sign says the plaza is open 24-hours, but most restaurants close before 7pm. **Loke Tien Yuen Restaurant,** 55-56 Jl. Abu Bakar (tel. 799 16 39), at the intersection with Jl. Dato Timor, has a fiercely loyal following among locals; many have been coming for generations. English menu. *Charsiu* rice RM2.50. The specialty is steamed fish; price varies. Open daily noon-9pm; sometimes closed in the afternoon to prepare for banquets.

TIOMAN ISLAND

The tourist board touts Tioman as "the last paradise on earth," and—rarely as it happens—they're not too far off. 50km from Mersing, it's the largest and best-known of a dozen little islands scattered off the east coast of Malaysia. The sandy beaches are superb, and the water is almost perfectly clear to a depth of over 30ft. A few yards beyond the beach, rampant jungle takes over, not quite obliterating the trails that wind through the mountainous center of the island. The beaches vary widely with the season. During Malaysian and Singaporean public and school holidays, they get mobbed by city folk; high season comes in August. During the annual monsoon season (Nov.-Jan.), the island is nearly deserted and prices become negotiable. June and July are probably ideal: the seas are calm, the crowds haven't arrived, but there's still enough company around to stave off boredom.

GETTING THERE

By far the most popular way of getting to Tioman Island is by **boat** from Mersing. In the past, boats were labeled "fast," "medium," and "slow," and were priced accordingly; today, all boats are called fast, but vary widely in speed and air-conditioning.

The fare is RM25 for adults and RM15 for children. Ask what time you will arrive at your chosen beach and what kind of climate-control the boat has when you buy your ticket in **Plaza R&R** in Mersing. The best boats arrive at the first stop on Tioman 1-½hr. after departure. **Do not buy a return ticket beforehand,** as it may not be honored by the ferry company that takes you back. **Do not buy tickets from touts. Do wear long pants,** because the 1-2hr. trip can get mighty cold.

Tioman Island's **airport** is located near Kampung Tekek, and Pelangi Air has daily flights from Singapore.

ISLAND ORIENTATION

Most of the popular beaches lie on the west coast. The ritzy **Berjaya Tioman Beach Resort** reigns over this side of the isle and is about midway between the north and south extremes. **Kampung Tekek** (Tekek Village), the largest village on the island, is about a 20-minute walk north of the resort. **Kampung Air Batang,** popularly known as ABC—or "Air Batang Chalets," is a hotel at the far north end of the beach. A smaller and more isolated beach is at **Kampung Salang,** a 45-minute sea-bus ride from Air Batang. For some real solitude, seek out **Kampung Juara,** on the east coast of the island, where a half-dozen smallish hotels dot the largely deserted beach and fierce waves beat the shoreline. Juara is a 2-hr. sea-bus ride from Tekek (or a 2-hr. walk along a jungle trail). South of the resort, **Paya, Genting,** and **Nipah Villages** also boast fine beaches but tend to be neglected by westerners, and more often cater to tour groups. The south end of the island boasts two impressive natural formations: the **Asah waterfall** and **twin mountains** that have earned themselves the epithet "Mukut" or "grandmother" for their resemblance to an old woman's face.

■■■ KAMPUNG TEKEK

Tekek is the largest village on Tioman Island and has the most amenities, including a money changer, post office, and police station. Once an extremely popular destination, Tekek is now avoided by tourists who spurn its commercialized image. The beach stretches on and on, but litter is more of a problem here than elsewhere, and a new concrete embankment near the jetty has done little to improve the appearance. The nearby airport also adds an insidious dose of noise pollution. Still, the long expanse of white sand farther south is fine for swimming and sunbathing, and the rocky regions north of the jetty are good snorkeling spots.

Orientation and Practical Information Tekek is one of the first ferry stops on Tioman. A bridge connects the jetty with the **airport-hotel road** that ends just before Nazri's Place in Air Batang to the north and at the resort to the south. It's about a 20-min. walk either way. On the left, just past the bridge, is a small plaza, **Komplek Terminal Kampung Tekek.** The airport is to the left (north) of the plaza.

There is no official tourist office. The Komplek Terminal Kampung Tekek has a **money changer.** Open Mon.-Sat. 9am-4:30pm; checks only, and no service charge. On Sundays and after hours, catch the free resort bus from the airport and head to the cashier's counter in the Tioman Resort lobby. (RM5 surcharge for non-guests.) **Post office** and **telephones** are located 10 min. south of the jetty (turn right as you get off), just past the Sri Tioman signs along the road. Look for the blue cardphones along the left side of the road; there is no sign. Open Mon.-Fri. 8:30am-12:30pm and 2:30-4:15pm, Sat. 8:30am-12:45pm. **Telephone code:** 011. Just to the right of the jetty is the **clinic.** Open Mon.-Thurs. 8am-12:45pm and 2-4:15pm, Fri. 8am-12:15pm and 2:45-4:15pm, Sat. 8am-12:45pm.

Turn left as you get off the ferry for the **airport** (tel. 344 038). Flights go to: **Singapore** (9:20, 11:20, 11:45am, and 3:55pm, RM132); **Kuala Lumpur** (1:20, 3:50, 3:55, and 4:10pm, RM146); and **Kuantan** (9:45am, RM77). **Pelangi Air Office,** at the resort, is open daily 9:30am-12:30pm and 2:30-5pm. **Berjaya Air Office** is there too, with flights for **Kuala Lumpur** (10:20am and 2:30pm, RM125). These flights are full weeks in advance. **Ferries** daily to Mersing (7:30, 8:30am, RM25, children RM15.)

Contact your accommodation for tickets. Schedules vary with the season, weather conditions, and tides. **Sea buses** sail to: **ABC** and **Salang** (9:45, 11:15am, 2:15, and 5:45pm, RM3 and RM8); **Juara** (9:15am, RM15); and the **Resort** (9:15, 10:45am, 1:45, 3:45, and 4:15pm, RM3). Buy tickets at the jetty or from the hotels.

There are **bicycles for hire** at the Komplek Terminal Kampung Tekek, 2nd fl., for a hefty RM5 per hour. The **RND Mini Mart,** a 10-min. walk to your right as you get off the jetty, across the road from Liza Restaurant, stocks an impressive inventory of all you'll need on Tioman Island, including the all-important flashlight for those pitch-black nights. Open daily 7:30am-11pm.

Accommodations and Food **Mango Grove** (tel. 952 032) is the last establishment at the north tip of Kampung Tekek. To save yourself a 20-minute walk, ask the boat captain to drop you off at the Fisheries Department's pier next door. The grove has little chalets with bare wooden floors and mosquito nets. A *batik* shop lets guests design their own t-shirts (RM25) and the mango, papaya, and guava trees can be harvested free of charge in August. Snorkeling equipment (RM10 per day) and boat tickets. The beach in front is too rocky for swimming or sunbathing, but there's fine snorkeling off the coast. Restaurant open daily 8-11am and noon-10pm. Double chalet RM10-12, with bath RM20-40. Trips to Coral Island. Laundry service.

Wake up to superb breakfasts (including banana porridge) at the **Sri Tioman Chalets & Café** (tel. 414 518 9). Turn right from the jetty and walk until you pass Liza Restaurant on your left. Look for a faded blue sign on the right pointing the way down the road to the hotel. The pleasant chalets are on your right, with mosquito netting and clean bathrooms. Doubles in the back of the compound with bath RM25, in the middle RM30, with sea view RM35. Restaurant open 7:30am-10pm.

PENINSULAR MALAYSIA

Sights and Entertainment The best option here is an excursion to nearby **Coral Island,** where reefs and abundant marine life invite you to get your snorkeling gear on. The friendly folks at the **Mango Grove** arrange **guided tours** to the island. The **Babura Dive Shop,** located within the Babura Chalet complex just beyond Coral Reef Holidays, charges RM140 for two dives complete with equipment. Open daily 9am-6pm. The **round-island sea bus** is a good way to combine swimming and snorkeling with sight-seeing. The boat leaves from the Tekek jetty at 9:15am and goes around the southern coast, passing the twin mountains known as "Mukut" ("grandmother") and stopping at **Asah Waterfall.** The sea bus makes a lunch-stop at Juara and then continues on to Teluk Dalam, in the north of the island, for **snorkeling.** The trip takes an entire day and costs RM35 without equipment.

Jungle trekkers might consider making the two-hour walk to **Juara.** The trail is clearly marked (beginning north of the Tekek jetty, just past Riley Bungalows) and cement steps have been built over much of it to facilitate progress over the thickly forested hillsides. Monitor lizards are everywhere but most are bashful and scamper away at the sound of approaching footsteps, unless you look like Bon Jovi.

A walk along the beach to Air Batang takes about one hour; from the jetty, walk north along the beach and as you approach the forested headland, follow the very short trail which emerges at Nazri's Place.

■■■ KAMPUNG AIR BATANG

New accommodations are springing up all over Kampung Air Batang. Many of the new chalets have A/C, which jacks the price up threefold. Many hotels have their own restaurants, although those in the know journey to ABC for meals and to Nazri's Place, at the south end of the beach, for nightlife.

Accommodations and Food **ABC (Air Batang Chalets)** (tel. 349 868), at the very end of the road to your left as you get off the jetty, is so famous that Air Batang itself is now usually known as ABC. The hotel is a lively place frequented by backpackers of all nationalities; their basketball court and restaurant, widely regarded as the best in all of Air Batang, are both constantly hopping. Doubles (2 mattresses on the floor) RM10, with baths RM15, and with fan RM20, and with sea view RM45. Nap in the giant tree with hammocks. Restaurant open 7:30am-10pm, last order 9pm. Snorkel gear RM10 per day.

To reach **Nazri's Beach Cabanas** (tel. 011 349 534), turn left off the jetty and walk 12 min. to the end of the road. The new branch of Nazri's Place is the most romantic on Air Batang. Spacious, widely spaced chalets for two nestle in the hillside and feature hardwood floors, mirrored dressers and sparkling bathrooms. Hill-view doubles RM25. "Twin peaks" doubles with mountain views RM55. Sea-view double RM65. The excellent restaurant offers set dinner specials, such as prawns in soy sauce with fried vegetables and fruit platter (RM15). Laundry service. **Nazri's Place** (tel. 349 534) is at the far south end of the beach; turn right as you get off the jetty and walk to the end of the path, passing TC Beach Chalets and Mokhtar Place. Nazri's has rooms arranged in blocks, making for close-knit neighbors and a friendly atmosphere. Tile bathrooms shine and let you escape the usual chalet mildew. Rooms in the Rosita Villa contain one double bed and one bunk, plus private bath, fan, and a large veranda (RM55). The Anita Villa has smaller verandas and an inferior view (RM30). Doubles with attached bath in the sea-view wing RM95. Double huts without electricity (RM10). The **restaurant** turns into a hopping night hangout. Open 7:30-11am and noon-3pm; drinks only 3-7pm and 7-11pm. Snorkeling equipment (RM12), boat tickets, and laundry service. Reception closes 11pm.

■■■ KAMPUNG SALANG

Salang, at the north tip of Tioman Island, is the last stop on the ferry from Mersing. The extra 20-minutes on the boat necessary to reach this dreamy beach, with its stretch of white sand blending into palm trees and jungle, is well-spent. Salang is popular with dive-shop owners (and divers), but you have to take a boat to any dive site. Most of the hotels rent snorkeling equipment.

Orientation and Practical Information The beach and budget accommodations stretch out on both sides of the pier, although the right of the jetty, as you arrive, is more popular with swimmers and sunbathers and has most of the restaurants and cafés. Most budget hotels serve as **currency exchanges.** The rates, however, tend to be mediocre. Try **Salang Sayang** (Zaid's Place) (tel. 719 820), halfway between the pier and the rocks on the right-hand side of the beach. International (RM13 per min.) and long-distance **telephone** calls can be made for a price from the reception desk. **Telephone code:** 011. **Sea buses** set out daily at 8:30, 10am, 1, 3, 3:30 (except Fri.), and 5pm to: **ABC** RM6, **Tekek** RM8; **round-island** 8:30am, RM30; and **Juara** 8:30am, RM15. **Ben's Diving Center** (tel. 717 014) offers snorkeling trips for RM30, diving courses in English and German, daily diving excursions, and rental equipment. One dive RM90, including all equipment, and two, RM110. MC, Visa, travelers checks. **Dive Asia,** across from the Mini Mart, does shore dives (tank, weight, and guide RM40; full scuba set and guide RM60) and night dives (full scuba set and guide RM80; tank, weights, torch, and guide RM50). Day-trips (with 2 dives) RM90-110; snorkeling RM30. Rental equipment and diving courses are available. Open 8:30am-6:30pm; AmEx, MC, Travelers checks, Visa.

Accommodations and Food There are around half a dozen inexpensive hotels in Salang, all lined up along the beach. Most have restaurants, which serve Malay, Chinese, and western seafood fare. **Salang Pusaka (Khalid's Place)** (tel. 953 421), on your right as you get off the jetty and follow the signs, is set back from the beach across a wooden bridge. Aristocratic monitor lizards strut majestically through the laundry lines in the small green courts. Ultra-clean rooms without A/C have fake-stone floor. A/C rooms are classier, with tile bathrooms. Dorms RM10. Doubles with bath RM25. Quads with bath RM70, and A/C RM90. Quints with bath RM60, and A/C RM120. Laundry service. Pleasant restaurant open 7:30am-10pm.

Ferry tickets and trips to Coral Island RM25. **Salang Sayang (Zaid's Place)** (tel. 719 820), is to the right as you get off the jetty (follow the signs). This hotel has it all, even a tiny library (RM3 per book for 3 days; RM20 deposit). Rooms are compact with pink mosquito netting. Towels and soap. Dorms RM7. Singles RM20. Doubles RM40-60 depending on size and view. Family room (quad) RM80. All with attached bath. Traveler's checks cashed. Safety deposit box. Restaurant open daily 8am-5pm and 7-10pm. Reservations recommended for August. Check-out 10:30am.

■■■ KAMPUNG JUARA

Juara, on the east coast of Tioman Island, is quiet and isolated. Long, undeveloped parcels of palm-lined real estate still stretch along the beaches, and locals hope to keep it that way. The sea thrashes the white sand with an intensity unknown on the west coast; during the monsoon season it's positively ferocious.

Orientation and Practical Information Chalets spread out on both sides of the rickety jetty. The road is set back from the beach; the jungle trail to Tekek meets it south of the jetty. **Happy Café,** next to the jetty, will **exchange** traveler's checks and major currencies, but rates are unpredictable. Happy Café also sells ferry and sea bus tickets. The **ferry** departs for Mersing daily (8:30am, RM25) while the **sea bus** heads off to Tekek, Air Batang, Salang and Berjaya Resort (3pm, RM15, to the resort RM20). The **Mini Mart** at Atan's Place is open 7:30am-11:30pm.

Accommodations and Food **Atan's Place and Turtle Café** (tel. (07) 799 23 09), to the left as you get off the jetty, is an attractive dark wood chalet with blue and white tile baths (RM15). The restaurant is one of the best in Juara. No alcohol is allowed; open daily 7:30am-11:30pm. Try one of their snorkeling or trekking trips. **Juara Mutiara Chalets** (tel. 799 48 33) is a few minutes walk past Atan's Place, and has pretty chalets with green tile bathrooms. Ask for a fan. The restaurant is absolutely swarming with cats. Doubles with bath RM20; for four RM25; for six RM30. Laundry service. Restaurant open daily 7am-10pm.

SINGAPORE

One of the four mighty industrial and financial "dragons" of Asia (in addition to Hong Kong, Taiwan, and Korea), Singapore is often accused of filing down its ethnic talons in order to present a well-groomed, western-style appearance. Indeed, nostalgics seeking to recover the historic charm of the old Orient will be disappointed in the Occidentalized urban barnyard of this modern-day Animal Farm. Even though some of the city's neighborhoods have retained the quaintness of the pre-economic-boom era, cynics point out that this self-conscious preservation has been carried out for the benefit of tourists and sentimental locals. Sci-fi author William Gibson, writing for *Wired* magazine, describes the brave new world of Singapore as "a relentlessly G-rated experience, micro-managed by a state that has the look and feel of a very large corporation." And indeed, there is a slightly fascist cloud looming over the Lion City, a state which bans gum-selling and constantly bombards its workers with well-funded pleas to be cheerful and courteous.

ESSENTIALS

■■■ GETTING THERE

BY AIR

Changi Airport (arrival and flight info tel. 542 1234) is about 10km east of the city center. Two terminals are connected by the zippy **Skytrain.** Hawkers sell pan-Asian specialties in air-conditioned luxury (S$1.50-4). To get to a food center in Terminal 2, go to Parking Garage C, 6th floor. Airport tax is S$15. Bus #16 shuttles to and fro (45min.; S$1.30, exact change or fare-card). Bus 16E runs to the airport in the morning and back in the evenings. The closest stop to the **Bencoolen St.** area is in front of the National Museum on Stamford Rd. To the airport, board anywhere on **Bras Basah Rd.** To the **Geylang Rd. area,** take #16 to the first stop on Panang Rd., 1-½ blocks after the National Museum. Next, go to the Dhoby Ghaut MRT station between Panang Rd. and Orchard Rd., and take the MRT to Kallang or Aljunied stops. To **Chinatown,** take #16 to the intersection of Stamford and North Bridge Rd.; from there, catch #174, 179, or 182 to the blue China Point building. **Taxis** are perhaps the most efficient means of transport (Bencoolen St. S$15, Chinatown S$20, less to the Geylang Rd. area; S$3 airport charge).

BY TRAIN

The **railway station,** Keppel Rd. (tel. 222 5165), is on the south tip of the main island across from Brani Island, 20 minutes from downtown by bus. **Buses** run every 5-15 minutes to and from the Raffles Hotel (buses #84, 97, 100, 131); Selegie Rd. (buses #97, 131); Chinatown (buses #84 and 145); and Little India (buses #97 and 131). The train station has fetid bathrooms (20¢), showers (S$1), luggage storage (S$1 per bag per day, open daily 7am-11:30pm), phones, a newsstand that sells phone cards, and food stands (S$1-3). Open daily 6am-11pm. **Trains** for **Kuala Lumpur,** Malaysia (7:30am, 3pm, and 10:30pm, 1st-class S$68; 2nd-class S$34). No visa or tax necessary. Check with **STA Travel** for great deals (see Budget Travel).

BY BUS

Luxurious but jarring buses leave from the Golden Mile Complex, Beach Road. From the bus stop at the intersection of Seah St. and Beach Rd. behind the Raffles Hotel, take buses #82, 100 or 181. **To: Bangkok,** Thailand (daily, early afternoon,

S$68); **Hat Yai,** Thailand (S$32); **Butterworth,** Malaysia (every night, S$30); **Kuala Lumpur,** Malaysia (3 daily, S$22). Most agents are open daily 8am-9pm and accept cash only. Other buses leave from the Lavender St. bus station in Little India.

BY FERRY

Most ferries dock at the **World Trade Centre,** Keppel Rd., across from Sentosa Island, and cruise to Singapore's islands, Indonesia, and Malaysia. Ferry companies moor inside the Centre on the second floor. The World Trade Centre is served by buses from Bencoolen St. (#97 and 131), from Bras Basah Rd. (#97 and 131), from North Bridge Rd. (#61, 84, and 145), and from Orchard Rd. (#143). **Ferrylink** (tel. 733 4866) makes regular trips to **Tanjong Belungkor,** Malaysia (9am, noon, 4:15pm; one-way S$15, round-trip S$24). Make reservations and arrive one hour before sailing. Trips to **Indonesian** beaches, greenery, and generally less cement and steel are: **Batam Island** (every hr., about 8am-6pm, 30min., round-trip S$26) and **Tanjung Pinang,** Bintan Island (1 daily, 2-½hr., S$51, round-trip S$73).

■■■ ORIENTATION

Linked by bridge to the southern tip of the Malaysian peninsula, Singapore's skyscrapers rear their bristly heads from a collar of rain forest. The island is oblong, longer from east to west than from north to south. The **airport** roars in the far east corner and three **MRT** (underground subway) tentacles run north, east, and west from the city center. The Kallang and Aljunied stops (three and four stops away on the east-west line from City Hall) are gateways to neighborhoods brimming with inexpensive guest houses.

The city can be divided haphazardly into six areas. The budget-friendly **Bencoolen St.** area is enclosed by Bencoolen St. on the west, Rochor Rd. on the north, Beach Rd. on the east, and Bras Basah Rd. on the south. The neighboring **Raffles Hotel area** showcases colonial architecture and imposing high-rises and extends from the Bras Basah Rd. side of the Raffles Hotel south to the Singapore River, bordered to the southeast by the Nicoll Highway and to the northwest by the Dhoby Ghaut MRT station. **Orchard Rd.** runs from the Dhoby Ghaut MRT station in the east to Scotts Rd. in the west. Floundering **Chinatown** clamors south of the Raffles Hotel area and is bordered by Pearl's Hill City Park, Boat Quay near the river, Cecil St., and the loop comprising Keong Salk Rd., Craig Rd., and Wallich St. It's served by the Outram Park and Tanjong Pagar MRT stations on its southern edge. **Little India** lies north of the Bencoolen St. area. Outside the city center is the **Geylang Rd. area** (northeast of Arab St. and across the Kallang River), and the East Coast Parkway (due east of the city between the Geylang River and the Singapore Straits).

Sir Stamford Raffles himself would get lost in modern Singapore without a **map.** The tourist office hands out two free varieties: *The Singapore Visitor* and the more detailed *Map of Singapore.* Map fiends can wrestle with the larger *Map of Singapore* (available in bookstores and newsstands, S$12.65).

■■■ GETTING AROUND

BUS

Local buses miss scarcely an inch of Singapore and run 6am-midnight. Snazzy yellow- and orange-roofed stops brandish info boards listing buses by street, price, and destination. Downtown, fares are about 50-70¢ (regular) and 60-80¢ (A/C). State your destination when boarding and pick up your receipt from the machine.

While buses are cheaper than the MRT in the long run, their routes and numbering system require too much brainpower. Locals hoard the limited-edition annual *Bus Guide,* without which, the system is almost indecipherable. You may be able to buy one (S$1) at bookstores, MRT stations, or the Singapore Bus Service's head office, 205 Braddle Rd. Otherwise, ask the tourist office, locals, or bus drivers for

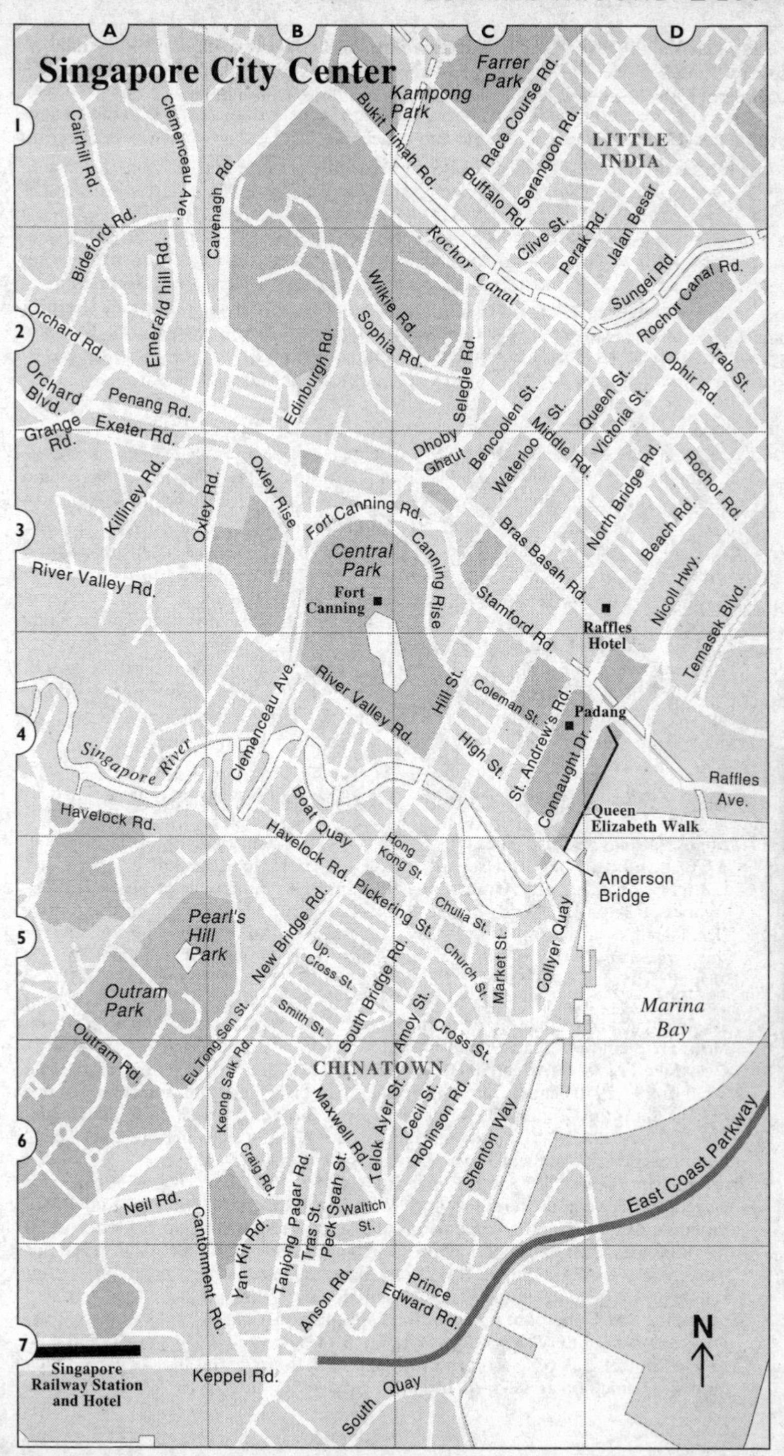

Singapore City Center
A
B
C
D
1
2
3
4
5
6
7
Cairhill Rd.
Clemenceau Ave.
Cavenagh Rd.
Kampong Park
Bukit Timah Rd.
Farrer Park
Race Course Rd.
Serangoon Rd.
LITTLE INDIA
Buffalo Rd.
Bideford Rd.
Emerald hill Rd.
Rochor Canal
Clive St.
Perak Rd.
Jalan Besar
Wilkie Rd.
Sungei Rd.
Rochor Canal Rd.
Orchard Rd.
Sophia Rd.
Edinburgh Rd.
Selegie Rd.
Arab St.
Ophir Rd.
Orchard Blvd.
Penang Rd.
Queen St.
Grange Rd.
Exeter Rd.
Dhoby Ghaut
Bencoolen St.
Middle Rd.
Victoria St.
Waterloo St.
Killiney Rd.
Oxley Rd.
Oxley Rise
North Bridge Rd.
Rochor Rd.
Fort Canning Rd.
Bras Basah Rd.
Beach Rd.
Central Park
Canning Rise
River Valley Rd.
Fort Canning
Stamford Rd.
Nicoll Hwy.
Raffles Hotel
Temasek Blvd.
Clemenceau Ave.
River Valley Rd.
Hill St.
Coleman St.
St. Andrew's Rd.
Padang
Singapore River
Clemenceau Ave.
High St.
Connaught Dr.
Raffles Ave.
Havelock Rd.
Boat Quay
Queen Elizabeth Walk
Havelock Rd.
Hong Kong St.
Anderson Bridge
Pickering St.
Chulia St.
New Bridge Rd.
Pearl's Hill Park
Up. Cross St.
South Bridge Rd.
Church St.
Market St.
Collyer Quay
Outram Park
Smith St.
Eu Tong Sen St.
Amoy St.
Cross St.
Marina Bay
Outram Rd.
Keong Saik Rd.
CHINATOWN
Maxwell Rd.
Telok Ayer St.
Cecil St.
Robinson Rd.
Shenton Way
Craig Rd.
East Coast Parkway
Neil Rd.
Tanjong Pagar Rd.
Tras St.
Peck Seah St.
Waltich St.
Cantonment Rd.
Yan Kit Rd.
Anson Rd.
Prince Edward Rd.
N
Singapore Railway Station and Hotel
Keppel Rd.
South Quay

SINGAPORE

directions. Buses have the same number for both directions on their route. On one-way streets, buses return on the next parallel street. Bypass exact change hell with a **Farecard** (S$12, including S$2 for the card; you can add credit up to S$50) at any MRT stop. Insert the Farecard into the machine on your right as you face the back of the bus, punch in the correct fare, and collect the card and receipt from the bottom of the machine on the right. **Bus hotline** (tel. 1 (800) 287 2727).

MASS RAPID TRANSIT (MRT)

Singapore's Mass Rapid Transit System (MRT) is the ultimate panacea for your transportation blues. Two main lines lead you by the hand to virtually any destination (6am-midnight). The north-south route overlaps the middle of the east-west line at the **City Hall** and **Raffles Place** stops, and extends only one stop farther south of Raffles Place. The system resembles an upside-down three-pronged fork. 60¢ fare for the three stops closest to where you board; 70¢-S$1.20 for more. Skip the hassle with a Farecard from any MRT stop's ticket office. Same as for buses. Nice.

TAXIS AND TRISHAWS

Taxis are to Singapore what the J. Crew catalog is to style-deprived college students: safe, convenient, and overpriced. Flag one down or head for the nearest taxi stand (in front of office buildings and malls). The meter starts at S$2.40; most city fares will be S$3-7. Beware the late-night 50% surcharge (midnight-6am). Other charges are S$2.20 for phone-booked taxis, S$1 charge for trips originating in the Central Business District (CBD) Mon.-Fri. 4-7pm and Sat. noon-3pm, S$3 from Changi Airport, and S$2-4 for going through the Central Business District. To order a taxi, call 474 7707, 452 5555, or 481 1211. Yellow cabs accept Visa. Airport to Raffles Hotel S$15. **Taxi Lost and Found:** tel. 450 5349.

Trishaw drivers, surgically attached to their vehicles, are parked on the edges of Bras Basah Park across from the YMCA on Orchard Rd. They wear bright-green or orange jerseys, and give tours of the Orchard Rd.-Little India region (S$20). Call Trishaw Tours (tel. 545 6311 or 828 3133) for an official tour package.

■■■ PRACTICAL INFORMATION

Tourist Offices: Scotts Branch, 02-02 Scotts Shopping Centre (tel. 1 (800) 738 3778/9). Take the MRT to Orchard; cross Orchard Rd. to Scotts Rd.; it's in the 2nd complex on the right. Open daily 9:30am-9:30pm. Fluent English. **Raffles Branch,** #2-34, 328 North Bridge Rd. (tel. 1 (800) 334 1335/6), in the Raffles Hotel Arcade, at the top of the staircase. Free *Singapore Official Guide.* Ask for the *Singapore Budget Hotels.* Staff gives directions. Open daily 8:30am-8pm.

Budget Travel: STA Travel, 1 Tanglin Rd., 02-17 Orchard Parade Hotel (tel. (65) 734 5681; fax 737 2591; telex RS 555 74). Student/youth-rate plane tickets, youth ID, ISIC cards, and excellent train packages for Thailand and Malaysia. Open Mon.-Fri. 9am-5pm, Sat. 9am-noon. MC, Visa, 3% service charge. **Singapore Comfort Travel Service,** 5001 Beach Rd., 01-11 Golden Mile Complex (tel. 294 9450 or 297 2910), faces onto Beach Rd. Open daily 8am-8pm. International bus tickets. Shop the Golden Mile of ticket dealers. **Sin Seng Guan,** 28 Weld Rd. (tel. 293 237; fax 292 2874), amid auto parts in the Weld Rd. flea market area. Travel equipment can be bargained way down. Open Mon.-Sat. 9am-5pm.

Immigration Office, 95 South Bridge Rd. (tel. 532 2877 or 1 (800) 538 5400 for visa info). Between Pickering St. and North Canal Rd. on the 7th and 8th floors of Pidemco Centre. Handles extensions. To avoid the hassle, pop back across to Johor Bahru, Malaysia, get a new passport stamp, and galumph back in. Take bus #170 (every 15min., 35min., 80¢) from the stop near Rochor Centre on Rochor Rd., near the head of Bencoolen St. Open Mon.-Fri. 8am-5pm, Sat. 8am-1pm.

Embassies and Consulates: Australia, 25 Napier Rd. (tel. 737 9311). Open Mon.-Fri. 8:30am-4:30pm. Visa services Mon.-Fri. 9-11:30am and 2-3:30pm. **Canada,** 80 Anson Rd. (tel. 225 6363), on the 14th and 15th floors of the IBM Towers. Open Mon.-Fri. 8am-noon and 2-4pm. **India,** 31 Grange Rd., (tel. 737 6777). Open Mon.-

Fri. 9am-5:30pm. **Indonesia,** 7 Chatsworth Rd. (tel. 737 7422). Open Mon.-Fri. 9am-4pm. **Malaysia,** 301 Jervois Rd. (tel. 235 0111). Open Mon.-Fri. 8:45am-3:30pm. **New Zealand,** 319A Orchard Rd. #15-06 Ngee Ann Tower A (tel. 235 9966). Open Mon.-Fri. 8:30am-4:30pm. **Thailand,** 370 Orchard Rd. (tel. 737 2644). MRT to Orchard, 1-½ bl. down Orchard Rd. away from downtown on the right. A tourist visa to Thailand costs S$28 for 2 months (re-entries are extra) and will usually be stamped in your passport by 2pm the next business day after your application. Expect a 30min. wait. Open Mon.-Fri. 9:15am-4:45pm; for visas 9:15am-12:15pm. **UK,** 325 Tanglin Rd. (tel. 473 9333). Open Mon.-Fri. 8:30am-4:30pm. **US,** 30 Hill St. (tel. 338 0251). Open Mon.-Fri. 8:30am-noon and 2-3:30pm. Visa service Mon.-Fri. 8:30am-noon. **Vietnam,** 10 Leedon Park (tel. 452 5938). Open Mon.-Sat. 9am-noon.

Currency Exchange: Money changers offer marginally better rates than banks and hotels. Open daily 9am-9pm and often on public holidays. **Banks** are open Mon.-Fri. 9:30am or 10am-3pm, Sat. 9:30-11:30am. **American Express Bank,** 16 Collyer Quay (tel. 439 1085), near Anderson Bridge. $US for $US traveler checks, 2% commission. No cardmember services. Open Mon.-Fri. 10am-3pm. **Saj Drug Store Money Change,** 01-09 Raffles City Shopping Centre (tel. 339 1723), at City Hall MRT stop. Open daily 8:30am-9pm. **United Overseas Bank,** 11 Empress Pl. (tel. 338 9393), in Victoria Concert Hall on the Raffles Hotel side of the Anderson Bridge. Open Mon.-Fri. 9:30am-3pm, Sat. 9:30-11:30am.

American Express Office: 3 Killiney Rd. (tel. 235 8133, after hrs. 235 8133; fax 235 2736), on the 1st fl. of the giant, rose-pink Winsland House building on the corner of Somerset Rd. 1 block toward the city centre from the Somerset MRT stop. Mail held 1 month for AmEx card or traveler's check holders. Replaces cards and cashes cardmember's personal checks. Open Mon.-Fri. 9am-5pm and Sat. 9am-1pm for cardmember services; financial services Mon.-Fri. 9am-4:30pm.

Post Offices: Telecom post offices have extensive phone (card, coin, and credit card), fax, telex, and telegram services. The GPO is not a Telecom office, but is the only one with **Poste Restante. Postal codes:** Bencoolen St. 0718; Little India 0820; Chinatown 0106. **Postal Helpline:** tel. 165. **GPO** (tel. 165 or 169), in the Fullerton Building on the corner of Fullerton Rd. and Collyer Quay. Leave the Raffles Place MRT station, Battery Rd. exit. Turn right onto Battery Rd. It's near the end of the road across from the Hong Kong Bank skyscraper. Open Mon.-Fri. 8:30am-6pm and Sat. 8:30am-2pm. **Raffles City Branch,** in the Raffles City Shopping Center, at the corner of North Bridge and Bras Basah Rd. MRT: City Hall. Telecom office as well. 5 soundproof phone booths.Open Mon.-Fri. 9am-6:30pm and Sat. 9am-2:30pm.

Telephones: Card phones and coin phones decorate hostels, hotels, malls, MRT stations, and Telecom post offices. Buy cards at newsstands, post offices, and anywhere with a "phone cards sold here" sign. Use the "follow" button on cardphones to milk those extra minute scraps. Coin phones beep when it's time to insert another 10¢. Local calls are free in the transit lounge of Changi Airport with a new arrival ticket. **Directory assistance:** tel. 161. **International access code:** 005. **Home Country Direct** phones at Telecom. **ComCentre,** Exeter Rd. (tel. 169), across from the MRT stop, Open 24 hrs. **Country code:** 65. **Telecom Helpline:** tel. 169. **Home Country Direct numbers:** British Telecom, 8000-440-400. Canada Direct, 80000-100-100. New Zealand Telecom, 65 1308 64 0000. Telecom Australia, 800-6100. Telecom Eireann, 800-353-353. Telekom South Africa, 8000-27-0270. US: AT&T: 800-0111-111; MCI, 8000-112-112

Luggage Storage: Train Station, S$1 per day per piece. Open 7am-11:30pm. **Changi Airport,** S$3-4 per day. Follow the "left luggage" signs. Open 24 hrs.

English Bookstores: Evernew Bookstore, 231 Bain St. #1-07 Bras Basah Complex (tel. 338 1753; fax 334 4898), on the corner near the Raffles Hotel. Steamy romance and paperback sci-fi. Rental S$3, deposit S$7. Open Mon.-Sat. 11am-8pm, Sun. 11am-6pm. **MPH,** 71-77 Stamford Rd. (tel. 336 3633), at Armenian St.; 2-½ blocks from City Hall MRT. Marble-trimmed, wood floors of classics, Singapore literature, and children's books. Fit for browsing. Open daily 10am-9:30pm.

Libraries: The National Library, Stamford Rd. (tel. 332 2645), at the beginning of Waterloo St. next to the National Museum. Check your own books at the door; even notebooks are prohibited on upper floors. Tourists can browse, but not check out items. Open Mon. 11am-8pm, Tues.-Fri. 9am-8pm, Sun. 1-5pm. Reference section open Mon.-Sat. 9am-8pm.

Newspapers and Magazines: *International Herald Tribune, Straits Times, Business Times,* and *The International Express* available at newsstands. Other periodicals can be found in **Times** bookstores. Censorship has taken its toll; don't expect to get much news, and don't expect it to be entirely accurate.

Laundromats: Laundry Land, International Plaza #01-78, 10 Anson Rd. (tel. 225 7161). Open daily 8:45am-5:30pm. T-shirt S$1.50, pants S$4, jacket S$8. **Express Laundry Service,** 18 Liang Siah Rd. (tel. 339 7390). Free pick-up and delivery in most downtown areas. Costly S$3.50 per kg. Open Mon.-Sat. 9am-7pm.

Public Toilets and Showers: Mall toilets are generally the cleanest and most likely to have toilet paper (20¢). Shower at public pools (S$1-2). Passengers can bathe at the airport transit lounge (S$5), or at the train station's foul bathrooms (S$1).

Swimming Pools: The River Valley Swimming Complex, River Valley Rd. (tel. 337 6275), across from the red-brick New Otani Hotel. Open daily 8am-9:30pm. S$1 for 2hrs. Call the Singapore Sports Council (tel. 345 7111) for other locations.

Pharmacy: Guardian Raffles City Pharmacy, Raffles City Shopping Centre #03-09), 252 North Bridge Rd. (tel. 339 2137). MRT: City Hall. Open Mon.-Thurs. 10am-9:30pm, Fri. and Sat. 10am-10pm, Sun. 10:30am-6pm for prescriptions. Over-the-counter services open daily 10am-10pm.

Hospitals: Government clinics and hospitals have 24-hr. emergency rooms. **Raffles Medical Group Clinic,** Changi Airport Terminal 2 (tel. 543 1118), in the basement. Open 24 hrs. for consultations (S$30) and stocks its own (legal) drugs.

Helplines: Samaritans of Singapore: tel. 221 4444. **Women for Action and Research:** tel. 293 1011. **Alcoholics Anonymous:** tel. 338 2791. **Counseling and Care Centre:** tel. 337 7748. **Teensline:** tel. 221 4949.

Emergency: Police: tel. 999. **Ambulance:** tel. 995. **Fire:** tel. 995.

■■■ HEALTH AND SAFETY

The **water,** as if you had any doubt, is safe. Hearty backpackers yearn for cold showers in the steamy **climate** (average 80°F, 26.6°C with at least 80% humidity). Invest in one of the millions of cheap umbrellas in Chinatown for the cursory daily downpours. Bug spray and loose, light clothing also go far toward maintaining morale.

Crime is scarce in Singapore and for good reason. Big Brother doles out high fines, serious jail sentences, "strokes of the *rotan,*" vapulation, and the death penalty. Michael Fay, the American juvenile delinquent/graffiti artist, learned his lesson the hard way in 1994—from the business end of a swiftly descending cane. Still, wear a money belt. **Women traveling alone** find Singapore relatively safe , but for *joss* (luck), go out in groups after dark. Sexual harassment does occur, but is mostly restricted to stares and less-than-subtle comments. If ignoring them doesn't work, mentioning a boyfriend or husband usually bursts their boorish bubble.

Singaporean law has absolutely no sense of humor; do not jaywalk within 50m of a crossing ($50 fine), import or sell **chewing gum,** litter, smoke in enclosed public areas (mass transit, malls, air-conditioned restaurants, etc.), or eat or drink on the MRT. Most offenses carry hefty fines of S$500-1000. The rewards of importing **illegal drugs** involves some combination of rotting in jail, multiple caning lacerations, and death. Foreign embassies cannot intervene. For more information, contact any of Singapore's embassies, refer to the *Singapore Official Guide,* or read *1984.* Though not illegal, heterosexual public displays of affection will really irritate locals.

Disabled travelers can maneuver around malls and office buildings, but will find Chinatown, Little India, and many hostels and little shops difficult to navigate. Write The Singapore Council of Social Services (at 11 Penang Lane; tel. 336 1544 or 331 5417) for a guide to accessible attractions.

BISEXUAL, GAY, AND LESBIAN TRAVELERS

Like most everything else, homosexuality is illegal in Singapore. Not surprisingly, homosexual acts face strict punishment—10 years to life in prison. There are few to no specifically gay nightspots. Even in mixed clubs, always keep in mind that Big Brother is watching you, and police are rumored to discriminate.

■■■ MONEY

US$1=S$1.422	**S$1=US$0.703**
CDN$1=S$1.046	**S$1=CDN$0.956**
UK£1=S$2.210	**S$1=UK£0.453**
IR£1=S$2.253	**S$1=IR£0.444**
AUS$1=S$1.048	**S$1=AUS$0.954**
NZ$1=S$0.933	**S$1=NZ$1.072**
SARand1=S$0.389	**S$1=SARand2.571**

The unit of currency used in Singapore is the Singaporean dollar (S$) which is divided into 100 cents.

Tipping is "officially discouraged." Taxi drivers, hawkers, and waiters don't expect it. Clubs, bars, and classier restaurants and hotels label themselves either "plus" which means that you pay a 10% service charge, or "plus plus" where you will pay 10% plus a 4% tax. Check the menu or ask. **Bargaining** in outdoor markets and many shops in Chinatown and Little India as well as for trishaw rides is okay, but don't go hog wild. Don't haggle in nice clothing stores or other upscale shops.

■■■ LANGUAGE

Singapore has a progressive *four* official languages: Mandarin, Bahasa Malaysia, Tamil, and English, although *Bahasa Malaysia* is the national language. (The distinction is symbolic at best.) To navigate this sea of linguistics, most people speak both the language of their family and English, the unofficial language of business.

■■■ HOURS AND HOLIDAYS

Banks are open 8am-4pm. Shopping centers and large stores will stay open from 9am-9pm or 10am-10pm. Smaller stores and businesses pull the ol' 9am-5pm shift.

Holidays for 1996 are:

January 1: New Year's Day
January 14: Ponggal, The Harvest Festival
February 4: Thaipusam
February 19&20: Chinese New Year
Februray 20: Hari Raya Puasa
April 4: Qing Ming
April 28: Hari Raya Haji
May 31: Vesak Day
June 22 &23: Dragon Boat Race (celebrating the Dragon Boat Festival)
August 9: National Day
August 14-September 12: Festival of Hungry Ghosts
September 27: Mooncake Festival
September 28: Brithday of Monkey God
October 12-20: Festival of Nine Emperor Gods
October: Navarathiri
October: Thimithi (Fire Walking Festival)
October 12- November 10: Pilgrimage to Kusa Island
November 10: Deepavali
December 25: Christmas.

LIFE AND TIMES

■■■ HISTORY

ISLAND COLONY

Although the modern history of Singapore begins with Sir Stamford Raffles, its existence far predates European incursion. The first known account of the island comes from the Chinese in the 3rd century, who, with incredible originality, called it **Puluochung,** "island at the end of the peninsula." By the 13th and 14th centuries the island state of **Tumasik,** or "sea town," was established and already trading and warring with Siam to the north. Some legends say Tumasik was founded by a Srivijayan prince who claimed descent from Alexander the Great. According to another 15th century legend, the island was named by the son of the union between an Indian Rajah and the daughter of the sea god. Believing he saw a lion on the horizon, the divine prince called it **Singhapura,** or "lion town." Raids by the Majaphit, Siamese, and Portugese quickly took their toll, however, and in the early 15th century the once-thriving port city reverted back to jungle, inhabited only by the Orang Laut.

Although the Dutch and British struggled to control Singapore for its position along important trade routes, the island remained little more than a pirate's pit-stop, free of European intervention, until the 19th century. The first drastic changes came when that Brit errant, **Sir Stamford Raffles,** took an interest in Singapore and convinced the British government to support him. Raffles worked with the two local powers of the time, **Sultan Hussein** and **Temenggong,** a Malay chief, and transformed Singapore into a thriving port city, and eventually, a British colony.

Waves of immigration followed, and the island developed the curious mix of Chinese, Indians, Javanese, Bugis, Arabs, Malays, and Europeans that characterizes it today. Piracy, intrigue, trade, exploitation, and prosperity waltzed through the area during the 19th century. As British expats strolled the *padang,* lacy parasols in hand, Chinese traders grew rich off Malayan exports, and indentured Indian convicts built St. Andrew's cathedral and other local edifices. By the time Ngiam Tong Boon invented the **Singapore Sling** for the Euro-chic clientele of the Raffles hotel in 1915, opium addiction had become a serious problem. The government, already intent on cleaning up Singapore by funding public works and improving social services, took on the drug problem by controlling the opium market and cracking down on the subversive mafia-style activities of the Chinese Triad secret societies.

Sir Stamford Raffles has been lauded by guidebooks and historians more than perhaps any other figure in the history of island Southeast Asia. His influence is undeniably extensive, but to overhype Raffles just a bit more (as if that were possible), the following short mocking history travels across Southeast Asia with the Quintessential Colonialist himself.

The Life of Sir Stamford Raffles: Part the First

No mere mortal has contributed more to the history, politics, and knowledge of island Southeast Asia than the dashing Sir Stamford Raffles. The son of a slave trader, Raffles was born July 5, 1781 on a boat off Jamaica. Lay Raffles-enthusiasts are amused by the irony that the man who shaped the East Indies was actually born in the West Indies. Astute Raffles-historians point out, however, that Raffles' glory was destined all along, as his ancestry has been traced back to Sangiran, Central Java, where fossilized DNA residue of Java Man show unmistakable similarities to the Raffles' lineage. At the young age of 15, Raffles, the Mozart of Orientalism, received an incredibly important entry-level position with the East India Company (EIC) as an office clerk, but this was only the beginning...(Wait, I want to know more! Then see page 213.)

The Japanese turned the little colony into a living hell on **February 15, 1941** when an inept British garrison was caught off guard by the invasion and quickly surrendered the colony. Europeans (including author James Clavell, whose novel *King Rat* described his internment experience) were carted off *en masse* to Changi Prison; and the Japanese army raped, pillaged, and slaughtered the local Chinese population. Singaporeans today happily pluck the yen from the pockets of Japanese tourists, but haven't forgotten the bloodbath, commemorated in the National Museum.

SINCE INDEPENDENCE

After the war, a battered Singapore fell into political disarray, and it was not until the electoral victory of the left-leaning **People's Action Party** and the subsequent rise of **Lee Kuan Yew** to Prime Minister in 1959 that Singapore embarked on its path to stabilization and modernization. The PAP sought to dissolve its ties to Britain and pursued an alliance with the strongly nationalist **Federation of Malaya.** This uneasy partnership, however, culminated in a bitter divorce, and Singapore assumed its present form in 1965, fully independent from its much larger neighbor to the north.

The Cambridge-educated lawyer Lee became a *de facto* and then a *de jure* benevolent dictator, masterminding Singapore's miraculous transformation into a full-fledged, modern city-state and an economic powerhouse with all the social service trimmings. The price of this progress has been paid in the freedoms of speech and press. In order to transform the swampy fishing villages of the island into an icon of modernity, Lee maintained that although democracy and free speech are important, they mean little to the individual with nothing to eat and nowhere to live. The government regularly files (and wins) libel suits against its critics. In 1987 nearly 100 political activists were tossed into the slammer without a trial (100% legal under Internal Security Act). Though not technically censored, only a few copies of newspapers critical of the government have been allowed into the country. The older generation explains these restrictions as the penalty for extremely rapid modernization. The younger generation has never experienced the hardship and deprivation of the pre-Lee Kuan Yew years and has grown up in a clock-work organization of hyper-efficiency, state-subsidized housing, and bargain health care.

The government's steely fist may be slowly unclenching: Lee stepped down in 1990, succeeded by **Goh Chok Tong,** whose administration re-admitted political exiles. Lee Kuan Yew remains active in the cabinet, however, and his popularity has waned little since his resignation. Although opposition parties continue to grow, many people eye Lee's son as a dynasty waiting to be. .

SINGAPORE TODAY

Singapore, as many modern cities, places education, cultural pursuits, and economic growth as high priorities for the next millennia. Unlike many cities, however, Singapore's overarching government has the power to establish and fund National Arts Councils, "Sports For All" programs, universal health care, and a variety of other positive programs. The flip side of this government activity is Singapore's Big Brother persona; the city runs like a machine, with its citizens as well-oiled cogs, just as Lee Kuan Yew believed it should be.

The thousands of expatriates living in Singapore love the city's western convenience. Everyone under 50, as well as many over, speak excellent English. Most signs use English and dandy little icons. Public phones, air-conditioning, and toilets abound in malls. For sight-seeing, cuisine, and survival tips, pick up the free **Official Guide** of the Singapore Tourist Promotion Board (STPB) at the Tourist Office.

■■■ THE PEOPLE OF SINGAPORE

Singapore is over 75% **Chinese.** It's a population that has been migrating to the island since the 1300s, but most Singaporeans are descendents of migrants from the British occupation in the 19th and 20th century. Only recently have the majority of Singapore's inhabitants been native-born. The **Malay** population hovers around 14%

and has been living on the island the longest, due to its proximity to the peninsula. The official language is *Bahasa Malaysia,* in part as a gesture of respect to their seniority. **Indians,** who stopped off at the island on their way to Malaysia as laborers for the British, make up 7%. As on the peninsula, the majority are Tamil. European ethnic minorities abound as well, leftovers from Singapore's colonial past.

After its population explosion in the 1960s, primarily caused by high immigration, the government worked toward getting all families, especially immigrant ones, to "Stop at Two." Now, however, similar to Malaysia's campaigns, Singapore has implemented "Go for Three" policies to maintain a high percentage of the Chinese population, and reach a healthy population of 4 million by 2020.

■■■ CUSTOMS AND CULTURE

Singapore attempts to maintain two faces: one face being truly cosmopolitan, the other attempting to stay rooted in the traditions of its citizens. As a British port which has only flourished in the 19th and 20th century, however, its attempts to "go back to its roots" often become Disneyesque in presentation.

The government continues to instill values of family over self, society over family, and nation above all, into the character of its young population. Understandably, many, especially non-Chinese, remain apprehensive of this steady movement away from individuality. The government's incredible emphasis on education, technology, employment, and community, works alongside its silent control over the city-state; there is a frightening irony to Singapore's attainment of multiple "Best Workers" awards from international business organizations. One could almost say it's part of Singaporean culture not to disobey authority; one could also say that a quick S$500 fine for small infractions simply teaches you to know better.

RELIGION

Singapore's status as a cultural crossroads has brought followers of many religions and the ensurance of religious freedom. The large Chinese population makes **Buddhist** temples perhaps the most noticeable, but **Islam** is also widely practiced as well. The non-sectarian government, with its wise and effective yet bureaucratic and paternalistic qualities is most highly influenced by **Confuscianist** philosophy.

■■■ THE ARTS

Specific cultural art forms aren't Singapore's strong point. The art is predominantly modern art, although certain genres are influenced by older Chinese styles, such as the traditional pen and ink. Some other traditional forms from across the region can be found in local cultural presentations, including the Malay shadow plays and kite flying or the Chinese lion dance.

Western and Chinese drama are both popular, but **films** take center stage. Western and Chinese action blockbusters can be found along with popular Malay and Indian films. For a more "cultural" evening the Chinese opera, or **Wayang,** is one of your best bets, combining high (melo-) drama with elaborate costumes.

Architecturally, Singapore captures both the old and new. While many of its older regions, fishing villages, and bungalow-style *kampongs* have undergone urban renewal, conservation has maintained some classic structures and neighborhoods, which often combine western, Indian, Arabic, Chinese styles into unique and eclectic forms. Others buildings stick to one style, such as the Raffles Hotel, but are nonetheless extraordinary buildings. The skyscrapers of Singapore are more difficult to miss. **I.M. Pei's** architectural wizardry dots the landscape. Clean and gleeming against the few remnants of a diverse past, these engineering and technological feats are perhaps the most apt metaphor for the city-state itself.

■■■ RECREATION

To hear the government tell it, Singapore is *the* city for sports and recreation. Of course, to hear the government tell it, Singapore is *the* city, period. Nonetheless, Singapore provides all the modern forms of recreation including golf, tennis, squash, sailing, water skiing, and of course, snooker. The recreational *tour de force* for locals and tourists alike, however, is **shopping.** Another inescapable Singaporean pastime is **karaoke;** its popularity seems to rise exponentially each year. So fill those bags, grab a mike, and go craaazy!

■■■ FOOD AND DRINK

Food enthralls the Singaporeans—it's one of the only topics they can discuss freely. It is occasionally considered a recreation in itself, and many proclaim the city-state to be the food capital of Asia. Sampling the Chinese, Indian, Malay, Indonesian, and even Japanese and western foods from the **hawkers centers/wet markets** is nothing less than a national hobby. Everyone has an opinion on where to get the best *mee* (noodles), *congee,* or chicken rice (both about S$2), and will offer it with the utmost conviction. The government regularly inspects the stands, keeping them safe for even the soft-bellied tourist. That killer smell snarling in these markets is **durian,** the green spiky fruit with a sweat-like stench so potent that MRT stations and many hotels post "No Durians" signs. **Open-air Chinese** and **Indian vegetarian restaurants** are similarly priced sources of palate-pleasing proteins and carbohydrates (about S$2 per dish, including rice). Manipulating the **drink** situation is tougher than extracting the truth from Newt Gingrich. Alcohol sells for S$6-9 in clubs and only slightly less in bars. Singaporeans favor Tiger Beer and booze-less beverages like chrysanthemum tea and Indian milk tea (both S70¢).

Like most of Singapore, the more heavily trod restaurants and hawker centers have adapted all too well. "Local food centers" marked on the tourist map are gussied up for visitors—**Lau Pa Sat's,** south of Raffles Place in the financial district, proudly vaunts an info booth stocking *This Week Singapore,* maps, and brochures detailing the history of the market site. For a more genuine grazing experience, tenderfeet can trot over to an **HDB (Housing Development Board)** high-rise off any suburban MRT stop. Generally off-white and architecturally mind-numbing, these stables are actually an ingenious response to formerly atrocious living conditions. Look for zillions of stacked cubbyhole apartments spiky with laundry-draped bamboo poles. Residents chow down at economical chuckwagons for breakfast, dinner, and often lunch. Their discriminating stomachs keep the vittles worthy. Stalls open as early as 6am. Some hit the hay at 3pm, but most keep cooking past 10pm. Some of the new apartment buildings in Little India also corral hawkers' stands or open-air restaurants on the first floor. *The Guide to Singapore Hawkers* by James Hoi (available in bookstores) can help round up and lasso these mavericks.

SLINGIN' AROUND SINGAPORE

■■■ BENCOOLEN STREET

Wander the wasteland that is Bencoolen St. for uninspiring alternatives to Singapore's pricey pads and fancy eats. Stretching from the National Museum of Brah Basah Rd., past the gigancitc Aiwa sign to the Rochor canal, this is the cheapest and most convenient place to stay, within walking distance of Little India, the Raffles Hotel, and Orchard Rd.'s credit card chaos. Bargain-basement prices, unfortunately, do not make up for its aesthetic blandness. Look elsewhere for tourist attractions and the "real Singapore." On the other hand, you're much more likely to meet other backpackers around Bencoolen St.—milk them for all the travel tips they can spare, and then treat them to a Hello Kitty pen-and-pencil set.

ACCOMMODATIONS

Goh's Homestay, 169-D Bencoolen St. (tel. 339 6561; fax 339 8606). Across from the outdoor market under the red- and white-striped tent. Immaculate dorms (A/C at night) and private rooms with garish murals of street scenes. Rooms are named; the luxury-minded can stay in "Raffles" while the curious might try the ominous-sounding "Bird Cage." All feature glossy sinks and tile floors. Dorms S$12. Singles S$28. Doubles S$40-42, with A/C S$44-46. Triples S$52. Lockers. Laundry facilities. Reservations recommended. Travel info and 2 cardphones.

Lee Traveler's Club, 75 Beach Rd. #6-02 Fu Yuen Bldg. (tel. 339 5490), 2-½ blocks past Raffles Hotel. Look on the left for the polished brown elevator (6th floor reception). Jolly manager and fellow backpackers make for one big slumber party every night. Pick from airy dorms S$6, with A/C S$8. Doubles S$25, with fan S$30, with A/C S$35. Coffee, tea, and toast included.

San Wah Hotel, 36 Bencoolen St. (tel. 336 2428), 4 buildings from Bras Basah Rd., and across from the Asia Radio Building in an old-style colonial house crowned by fuchsia flowers. Extremely conscientious staff is steaming mad at dirt, wielding Lysol daily. Don't expect any English, although the hospitality and warmth of the Chinese owners shines through their Cantonese. Showers in outdoor stalls. Doubles S$45, with A/C S$45. Discounts for over 5 days. Laundry service.

Peony Mansion Traveler's Lodge (Green Curtains), 46-52 Bencoolen St. (tel. 338 5638), next to Bay View Hotel. On the 4th floor of Peony Mansion. Circle around back to the elevator. Pleasant, airy lobby masks a maze of mediocre dorms and private cells that are more or less hygienic, but short on bathrooms. TV, in-house movies, and tea, coffee, and toast (8am-10am) included. Dorms S$7. Singles S$18-22, with sink S$25. Doubles S$25-35, with A/C S$49, with private bath S$50. Additional person S$7. Luggage storage. Visa, MC for S$20 and up.

Why Not Homestay, 127 Bencoolen St. (tel. 338 8838). From the National Museum, it's past Middle Rd. on the left. Reception in the corner of Kevin's Restaurant. Hodge-podge of dorm beds make for close-knit roommates. Pooped pilgrims plop down in the open-air 1st-floor restaurant for Hindu Indian food. Dorms with A/C S$30. Doubles S$35. Coffee, tea, and toast. Key deposit for dorms S$5.

FOOD

At night, many hawker courts transmogrify into open-air restaurants. The bigger your crowd, the cheaper the meals—large portions cost little more than small ones. One set of these courts is in the alley next to **North Bridge Rd.** (across from the Lido Hotel and a few meters toward Beach Rd. on Middle Rd.). Tables stay out from around 6 to 10pm. **Bencoolen St. Market** unfurls from the red- and white-striped tents on Bencoolen St. all the way to Victoria St. with few gaps. The area around Bugis St. holds court at night, and all four blocks overflow with locals on Sunday afternoons. Sweets are the area's specialty. Treat yourself with the peanut paste ball (S$0.50) and various Peranakan (Chinese-Malay) treats. Open daily 8am to 10pm.

■■■ RAFFLES HOTEL

The Raffles Hotel stands majestically in the southeast corner on Beach Rd. and marks the beginning of a herd of government buildings extending to the south, including the National Archives and Parliament House. City Hall MRT station, and St. Andrew's Cathedral lie in wait farther south along Stamford Rd., as do the National Museum and Art Gallery and the National Library.

FOOD

Satay Club, on the corner of Connaught Dr. and Raffles Ave., is within easy striding distance of Raffles Hotel. Those in the know congregate here to feast among cute blue-domed booths and lush park environs, sucking up the sweet air of peanut *sate* (about S$0.30 per stick). Open daily 2pm-1am.

Yet Con, 25 Purvis St. (tel. 337 6819), 2 blocks north of the Raffles Hotel. Still going strong after 50 years, this crowded Hainanese restaurant continues to dish up the same chicken and *charsiu* roast pork (S$2) that earned it a fanatical following. Specialty is the steamboat, where patrons cook their own food in a boiling pot and dip it into sauces. Vegetarian dishes available. Open daily 11am-9:30pm.

SIGHTS

First plan of attack: the **Raffles Hotel,** a huge white tank occupying the entire block between North Bridge Rd. and Beach Rd. along Raffles Blvd. Blast through the third-floor **Raffles Hotel Museum,** which traces the history of the hotel from its founding in 1887 all the way through New Year's Eve 1993, dwelling on the golden years of the 1920s and 30s. Open daily 10am-9pm. **The National Museum and Art Gallery** (tel. 330 0971) on Stamford Rd. at the origin of Bencoolen St., swaggers with more history than art. Open Tues.-Sun. 9am-5:30pm; admission S$3, children S$1. The lovely 128-year-old **Empress Palace Museum,** 1 Empress Place (tel. 336 7633), near the southern mouth of the Singapore River, tries to compensate for Singapore's pitiful art scene with visiting collections from artsier China. Open daily 9am-7pm. The art gallery, antique gallery, and Queen's Room on the first floor are free; the rest are S$6, children S$3.

The Life of Sir Stamford Raffles: Part the Sixth

In 1819, Sir Stamford Raffles was between positions and had a little spare time on his generous hands, so he declared his intention to do something truly eternal. Thus was born the city of Singapore, which amassed a population of 5000 in just 3 months. Lacking the time to wait for approval from Europe, he returned to Bencoolen and made further foundational contributions in the fields of zoology, archaeology, and geology, among others. A witness to Raffles' brilliant forethought, in three years Singapore grew to over 10,000 people, with a booming economy exceeding Penang and Malacca combined! Pleased with his most recent *magnum opus,* Raffles founded the Singapore Institution, where Malays were allowed to receive an Enlightened Western Education. A series of masterfully executed treaties with the Dutch ensured the survival of Singapore, the founding of the lordly Raffles Hotel, and a path through which the exotic riches of the Far East could be tapped. Hard times hit Raffles soon after, but amidst health problems, legal controversies, and the death of 4 of his 5 children, Raffles still found the time to open the London Zoo and re-establish himself at the forefront of high society before he died on July 4, 1826, a day before his 45th birthday. An essential link in the transformation of the Far East, Raffles reputation stands not just as the founder of one of Southeast Asia's largest cities, but also as the world's greatest humanitarian and natural scientist and as The Consummate Orientalist and Colonialist. Who can imagine what Southeast Asia would be like today without his efforts on the part of the West? (To return to the beginning of Sir Stamford's life, and follow his illustrious journeys, see page 266).

ENTERTAINMENT

Sail away from nightlife on a **Chinese junk ride,** operated by Watertours, 3-A Clifford Pier (tel. 533 9811 or 535 7743). It docks at Kusa Island in the straits, so passengers can walk up to a "holy" hilltop with a view (pier departures 10:30am and 3pm; fare S$20, children S$10; dinner cruise leaves at 6pm, 2-½hr., S$34, children S$17).

The Long Bar, on the 2nd floor of the Raffles Hotel. Birthplace of the famed Singapore Sling (S$12), a fruity "lady's drink." The "tangy, bittersweet" Million Dollar Cocktail appeared in Somerset Maugham's bar-side tale, "The Letter," making it (temporarily) hot stuff on the Singapore scene. Now it trails a distant 2nd to the more palatable Sling, a must for every Singapore first-timer. Open Sun.-Thurs. 11am-1am, Fri.-Sat. and eves of public holidays 11am-2am.

■■■ GEYLANG ROAD AREA

The city's northeast district is like a Malay noodle floating in Singapore's simmering broth of Chinese and Muslim-Indian ethnicities. Many Malay hold down the area around Geylang Road and authenticity struggles on its last legs at the market. From the Paya Lebar MRT, continue along Sims Ave. to the bazaar. Tracking down East Coast Road will lead architecture hounds to lovely Peranakan-style structures.

ACCOMMODATIONS

Wads of guest houses (most around S$50) are stuffed between Geylang Rd. and Sims Ave. Tiny streets *(lorong)* cut across the two main roads and form the rungs of this ladder-shaped district. Watch your step around the idiosyncratic numbering system: odd numbers through 31 between Geylang Rd. and Sims Ave., even numbers on the other side of Geylang Rd. The MRT stops at Lorong 1 (MRT: Kallang) and Lorong 25 (MRT: Aljunied).

Lai Ming, 432 Geylang Rd. (tel. 744 2038 or 744 6707), near Lorong 24. This beautiful, tan stucco home rests behind a hedge-shaded circular drive on the main drag. Spacious A/C rooms with sink and shower in the corner and beds the size of plane runways. "Singles" could easily house two, the doubles three or four or more. Go wild. Cheerful English-speaking managers will help you with just about anything. Dank hall bathrooms. Singles with shower and A/C, S$50. Doubles with shower and A/C S$60. Laundry service. 24-hr. reception.

Yen Hua Boarding House, 44 Lorong 25A (tel. 748 6466 or 748 8562). Exit the Aljunied MRT station, take a left, then take another left onto Lorong 25A; on the left. Ultra-clean cubicles with shower tucked in a corner, but share hall bathrooms. "Doubles" come with 2 beds and A/C. A beautiful Buddhist shrine near the back. Doubles with shower S$35, extra person S$5. Reception closes midnight.

Yew Lian Hotel, 549 Lorong 29 (tel. 748 7689). A blue-and-white sign advertises the entrance, on the right as you approach from the MRT. 3rd-floor reception. Bantam-sized Buddhist shrine at every landing to help you up the stairs. Plaid sheets, A/C, and a view jazz up your tidy quarters. Doubles Mon.-Fri. S$45, Sat.-Sun. S$50. 3 guests S$55; S$5 for each additional guest. Free washer and kitchen. 24-hr. reception.

SINGAPORE

FOOD

Many a poor fish eventually flops its way to the seafood-rich beach area off **East Coast Parkway,** halfway between downtown and the airport. Take bus #14 from Bras Basah Rd. (60¢) to Mountbatten Rd. The **UDMC Seafood Centre** to the right and **East Coast Lagoon Food Centre** to the left, are known for the ocean views, squirming seafood, and pre-industrial Singaporean atmosphere. Geylang locals toss down *dim sum,* seafood, chicken rice, and just about any other indigenous treats at non-tourist prices in the smattering of sit-down, **open-air eateries.**

Kiat Seng Hainanese Chicken Rice, on the corner of Geyland Rd. and Lorong 23. Ultra-clean, ultra-efficient chicken-rice joint leaves customers satisfied, if not deafened by blaring TV. Chicken rice (S$2-4). *Dim sum* (S$1.20-1.80). Open 24 hrs.

Chang Ghiang Eating House, on the corner of Geyland Rd. and Lorong 16. Follow your nose along the trail of exotic whiffs from this hectic open-air restaurant. Spiced pig's trotter (S$3). Black mushroom and chicken feet (S$3). Culinary cowards can munch on *mee* and chicken rice. Open daily 7am-6:30pm.

■■■ ORCHARD ROAD

Mobbed with shoppers, anathema to backpackers, the sidewalks of Orchard Rd. lead to pricey boutiques, five-star hotels, and mall, after mall, after huge A/C mall. Orchard Rd. caters to the caviar tastes of jet-setters who never leave its safe shores. Cultural attractions read like Ivana Trump's Rolodex: Burberry's, Cartier, Chanel, Christian Dior, Ferragamo, Rolex, Tiffany. Not for the uninitiated; proceed with extreme caution. At the junction of Orchard Rd. and Fort Canning Rd., you'll see Le Meridien Hotel on the right and the Phoenix Hotel on the left. About 2-½ blocks west of the Phoenix is the giant Ngee Ann City/Takashimaya Shopping Center. Just beyond Scotts Rd. is a cluster of foreign embassies and still more luxury hotels.

ACCOMMODATIONS

YMCA, 1 Orchard Rd. (tel. 336 6000 or 337 3444; telex RS 55325, YMCA; fax 337 3140), in the Bencoolen St. area., across the road and visible from the National Museum. MRT: Dhoby Ghaut is hidden across from the church next door. Pricey but posh dorms have 4 bunk beds each, a call-in only phone, A/C, TV, private bath, and key lockers. Carpeted private rooms equipped with the amenities of a major hotel. Pool and weight room. 24-hr. reception. Dorms S$20. Doubles S$90. Family rooms S$105. Reserve 6 wks. ahead or hope for (rare) cancellations. Major credit cards. S$5 YMCA membership required of non-members.

Madam Lim's Place, Cavenagh Rd., Cavenagh Garden Block 73, 3rd fl. (tel. 737 4600). From the Phoenix Hotel, cross Orchard Rd. and head through the block of open-air restaurants and past the Holiday Inn. Cross the highway on the pedestrian overpass, turn left, and head up the hill. Look for the clearly labeled Cavenagh Garden complex on the left. Block 73 is on the far side. Possibly the cleanest guest house in Singapore, Madam Lim's is a 3-room, 2-dorm-bed affair. Dorm beds are on the screened and fanned balcony. Toast, coffee, and tea included. Dorms S$10. Triples with bath S$70. Reservations highly recommended.

FOOD

Most malls have basement-level A/C "food courts," a little like eating in a K-Mart. **Emerald Food Court,** in the basement of the Orchard Emerald Shopping center, has Indonesian and Chinese stands vending everything from congee to *mee* (S$3.60). **Cuppage Road Wet Market** is just across Orchard Rd. from MRT: Somerset, and down Cuppage Rd., past the classy open-air restaurants. The market sloshes on the 3rd floor in a pseudo-parking garage building. The usual Chinese, Hokkien, and Muslim fare, plus a number of excellent fruit and dessert stands aching with lychee juice and shaved ice treats. Open daily 7am-8pm.

Orchard Peach Garden Noodle House, 22-24 Orchard Rd. (tel. 339 9755 or 338 6115), at the beginning of Orchard Rd., next to the Singapore Manufacturers Association House and across the street from MRT: Dhoby Ghaut. A glorified hawker's stand and the cheapest of the Orchard Rd. restaurants. Noodle dishes (S$4.50-5). Congee (S$4.80). Coast on a glucose high after ingesting sea coconut lemon and honey or the water chestnut cream (S$2.20). All-you-can-eat lunch deal (S$9.80) daily 11:30am-2:30pm. Open daily 11am-11pm.

Maharani North Indian Cuisine, 5th fl., Far East Plaza, Scotts Rd. (tel. 235 8840). The Plaza is the 4th building to the right as you turn from Orchard Rd. The Maharani ("queen") is consistently voted one of Singapore's best restaurants and for good reason. Delicious curries, *vindaloos,* and breads in a hushed setting. Set dinner (S$29.50). Set lunch (S$13.50). Fish head curry (S$19.90). Chicken *vindaloo* (S$12.90). Open daily noon-10pm.

ENTERTAINMENT

Young Singaporeans have a zest for gyrating into the wee hours that the "filial piety" generation cannot fathom. Witness the spectacle of any pricey (cover S$15 and up, usually including a couple of drinks) disco. Check *This Week Singapore* (free at tourist offices) for a frank analysis of what's hot and what's not. Clubs, bars, and pubs such as **Fire, Brannigan's,** and **Tornado** lambada shamelessly near the intersection of Scotts Rd. and Orchard Rd.

■■■ CHINATOWN

Chinatown seems to have had its character scrubbed away by the tidy government. Newly "restored" with garish paint, Chinatown is about as authentic as Cher's nose. Don't expect the bustle, flavor, and excitement of Chinatowns all over the world; though over 70% Chinese, Singapore has not preserved its heritage in this neighborhood. Instead, Chinatown brings you close to spending sprees, yet affords some peace and quiet on sidestreets of pastel-trimmed rowhouses. Landmarks include the Pearl's Centre Mall along Eu Tong Sen St. and the Maxwell Market Food Center, which is smack in the middle at the intersection of South Bridge and Maxwell Rd. The financial district ferments to the northeast of Chinatown, starting at Collyer Quay, across the Singapore River from the Raffles Hotel area, and extending down Shenton Quay to Cross St.

ACCOMMODATIONS

Metropolitan YMCA Singapore, 70 Palmer Rd. (tel. 222 4666; fax 222 6467). Take the MRT to Tanjong Pagar, exit on Cecil St. and turn right. Palmer Rd., off Anson Rd., is the 3rd street after the intersection with Choon Guan St. Turn left and walk past the 2 temples. You should see "YMCA" painted in large letters. Less-than-new private rooms with attached toilet-shower-sink. Dorm and common baths are for men only. A/C for those Village People sing-alongs. Expect a 10% service charge and 3% goods and service tax. Dorms S$18. Singles S$30. Doubles with bath S$50. Triples with bath S$65. Extra bed S$10. Non-refundable deposit of 1 night's room rate. Check-in after 1pm.

Airview Hotel, 10 Peck Seah St. (tel. 225 7788 or 225 6688). From MRT Janjong Pagar, it's across Wallich St. and up Peck Seah St. on the left. Well-ventilated with A/C, TV, baths, and phone in each room. Amusement park-style elevator—you can see the whole shaft as you whoosh to your room. Doubles S$60. Triples S$75.

Chinatown Guest House, 325D New Bridge Rd., 5th fl. (tel. & fax 220 0671), opposite Pearl's Centre Mall on the southwest edge of Chinatown. From MRT: Outram Park, exit right. Turn left and follow the signs to Eu Tong Sen St. Cross the median strip to New Bridge Rd. and turn left. In a small block of shops. Slightly bedraggled, but balconies open out over a park. Communal kitchen. Eggs, toast, coffee and tea for breakfast; amiable proprietor, Johnny, claims guests eat more than they pay in rent. Open 24 hrs. Laundry service. Free luggage storage. Free lockers. Dorms S$8. Singles S$25. Doubles S$35, with A/C S$40.

FOOD

Chinatown usually means an express lane to exceptional edibles. Not so in Singapore. Chinatown's best bargain banquets come from the hawkers' centers, notably the **Outram Park** apartment complex behind the Pearl's Centre on Eu Tong Sen St. Singaporean upper-crust jet to nearby **Murray Terrace Food Alley** to partake of the famous Asian food joints such as **New Indian Restaurant** (12 Murray St.), **Moti Mahal** (18 Murray St.), and **Moi Kong** (22 Murray St.). Swanky establishments swathed in linen and charm-oozing waiters terrorize the street, but more down-to-earth eateries continue to hold their ground. Take the MRT to Tanjong Pagar, follow Peck Seah St., heading away from the distant IBM skyscraper, until the end of the street. Turn left, then left again after the Bank of China. A plethora of culinary delights also reside in the **Maxwell Market Food Center** at the intersection of Maxwell Rd. and South Bridge Rd. The immense hawker center boasts traditional Chinese fare and a startling supply of fish heads, duck, and durian. Open 8am-10pm.
People's Park Centre, on Eu Tong Sen St. in Chinatown. Take buses #81, 83, or 103 from Bencoolen St. or the Raffles Hotel, or take the MRT to Outram Park, exit on the right, turn left and follow green signs to Eu Tong Sen St. The People's Park Centre is beyond the Pearl's Centre Mall. A huge venue with special emphasis on duck, Chi-

nese bacon 'n' sausages, and fruit. Open daily 10am-10pm. **Amoy St. Food Center** is near MRT: Tanjong Pagar, at Telok Ayer and Amoy St. Cross Maxwell Rd. and veer leftish down Telok Ayer. Fruit and vegetarian, Indian, Hokkien, and Cantonese. Open Mon.-Sat. 9am-7:30pm, Sun. 10:30am-7:30pm.

SIGHTS

Only a few years ago, Chinatown was a sea of idol carvers, fortune tellers, calligraphers, and herbalists. Today, there's not much activity other than a trickle of tourists and devotees through the scattered temples and the souvenir shops peddling bamboo back-scratchers and "I Love Singapore" T-shirts.

The **Chinatown Historic District** is designated as Telok Ayer St., a quiet avenue running parallel to Amoy St. and coming dangerously close to financial behemoths at its east edge. Home to Chinese and Malay immigrants in the 19th century, it became the Chinese commercial district from 1850-70, and served as a hub of the slave trade due to its location on the original shoreline. Urban renewal efforts to resuscitate the gasping area include the application of gaudy pastel makeup to the traditional shopfronts and temples built by immigrants in thanksgiving for safe journeys—a renovation tactic as successful as dropping a saltwater creature into a freshwater aquarium.

Three temples along Telok Ayer St. between Boon Tat St. and McCallum St. can be zapped in a jiffy, but only the Escher-ian **Thian Hock Keng Temple,** or **Tian Fu Gong Temple** ("Temple of Heavenly Happiness") merits a more than a cursory pause. The statue of Ma Cho Po, goddess of the sea, was installed in 1840. Sailors donated tile and ironwork, plus a spate of stone dragons who slink on the roof, the pillars, and the walls, much to the delight of M.C. himself. Open daily 6am-5:30pm.

At the southeast end of Temple St., the **Sri Mariamman Temple,** 244 South Bridge Rd., an old Hindu temple, stokes up a 4m pit for **Thimithi,** the **Firewalking Festival.** Hindu stalwarts wrap their toes with faith alone for the yearly October stroll. The frescoed, columned temple escaped much of the brash decor of temples built in wealthier eras. From MRT: Outram Park, follow Eu Tong Sen St. past Pearl's Centre, the Central Police Station People's Park complex, then turn right onto Temple St. and walk to the end of the road. Open daily 6am-12:30pm and 4-9:30pm.

■■■ LITTLE INDIA

Scrubbed and purified in Singaporean manner, this neighborhood's restaurants, shops, and overall panache have somehow maintained their vitality to a far greater degree than those of Chinatown. Still, don't look for Calcutta here. The district's two broad thoroughfares, Serangoon Rd. and Jalan Besar Rd., run north-south, parallel to each other near the Raffles Hotel and the Orchard Rd. area. Zhujiao Centre, with its annexed food center and market, nibbles at the southern end of Serangoon Rd. Three blocks north waxes the crayon box of Kali Amman temple, its high dome graced with tiny sculptures of humans, deities, and animals.

ACCOMMODATIONS

Ali's Nest, 23 Robert's Lane (tel. 291 2938), off Serangoon Rd., across from Serangoon Plaza. Accessible by bus #16 or 16E from the airport and #97 or 103 from the library, Ali's is near the Broadway Hotel. "A New Place for Backpackers" and "A Family Guesthouse," its flyers proudly proclaim; budgeteers have certainly responded. Clean and quiet rooms with sundeck for a sweaty sunbath. Free breakfast. Rooms from S$6-S$25. Call for a free ride if you're lost.

Little India Guest House, 3 Veerasamy Rd. (tel. 294 2866; fax 298 4866). Head down Serangoon Rd. with Zhujiao Centre on the left. Veerasamy Rd. is the 6th street on the right; the guest house is blazing orange as you round the corner. Wake with the dawn, courtesy of an over-enthusiastic rooster who crows from 5-9am. Clean and comfortable, with plenty of hall showers. Rooms have fans, TV, and baths. Lockers, iron, medicine, and umbrellas available. Singles S$38. Doubles S$50. Triples S$62. Call ahead (or break out that fax machine).

FOOD

Serangoon Rd. buzzes with mouth-watering Indian vegetarian food. A string of restaurants, specializing in fish-head curry, *tandoor,* and other Indian recipes compete for the prize along Race Course Rd. **Zhujiao Centre** (Kangdang Kerbau Wet Market), on the corner of Serangoon Rd. and Buffalo Rd., wobbles on the edge of Little India. Breakfast at one of the Indian Muslim hawker stalls is always a thrill. Festive, early-morning crowds froth for their daily fix of *paratha* with curry (S$1), milk tea (S$0.50¢), and fruit (S$0.30-0.50). Open daily 7am-9pm.

Komala Vilas, 76-78 Serangoon Rd. (tel. 293 6980), around the corner from Upper Dickson Rd. A cornucopia of south and north Indian vegetarian food. Use your right hand when eating. Try the *masala dosai,* a sassy mix of sauces (from coconut to chick-pea) and spices, scooped up with a huge pancake rolled around a potato base (S$1.20). Except for the relatively tame burnt-milk candy (S$0.50), sweets require taste-testing bravado. Open daily 7am-10pm.

Madras New Woodlands Restaurant, 12-14 Upper Dickson Rd. (tel. 297 1594). Approaching from the Zhujiao Centre at the south end of Serangoon Rd., turn onto the 4th street on the right. Combustible vegetarian food at mind-blowingly low prices. On Sunday evenings, the little café gets hectic, and lumping small parties at one big table makes for a sociable evening. Open daily 7:30am-11:30pm.

Bobby-O Claypot Curry, 35 Jalan Besar (tel. 298 3876; fax 299 6991), at the south end of the street across from Sim Lim Tower. Yo, daddy-o! Cool cats sip sweet glasses o' *lassi* in the open air while penning beatnik lyric poetry. Claypot curry (S$3-3.50). *Naan* (S$.80-2). *Tandoor* (S$2-5.80). Open daily 7:30am-9:30pm.

SIGHTS

As the spirited cheerleader of the city, **Little India** makes the rest of Singapore look plastic and comatose. Roughly bounded by a road-box made up of Bukit Timah Rd., Race Course Rd., Lavender St., and Jalan Besar Rd., the area's main events square off the six blocks northeast of the Rochor Canal between Clive St. and Race Course Rd.

The Chinese moniker of the **Zhujiao Centre** distinguishes this Sino-bazaar from its surroundings. The market is swamped by local crowds on Sunday afternoons; come nightfall, neighbors and friends network near the ground-floor hawker center. Clothes and knick-knacks are on the second floor. Shops near **Serangoon Rd.** launch skyrocketing clouds of fragrant incense and freshly ground spices. Proprietors fuss with displays of jewelry, gold, *saris* (from S$8 up to S$3000 for those woven with gold thread), and Hindu gods resting on velvet. August gentlemen ask parrots to draw fortunes from a stack of invariably pleasant forecasts for S$1. Around Upper Weld Rd. mayhem reigns as men haggle with a vengeance over second-hand treasures ranging from walkmans and foreign coins to jade figurines and bamboo bongs. In the afternoon, a quiet glass of Indian milk tea smooths the psyche as streams of traders drift home.

Sri Veerama Kali Amman Temple, 141 Serangoon Rd. (tel. 293 46 34 or 295 4538), at the corner of Belilios Rd., draws power- and luck-seeking sadists to its statues of Kali, the multi-limbed goddess of destruction. The most extreme representation of her shows two hands ripping open a man's belly, one lifting his entrails to her lips for a little snack, one squeezing the life out of a baby, and one foot trampling a woman. For jewelry, she wears a garland of skulls. Considerate of her tastes, devotees sacrifice chickens to the revered deity. (Perhaps a happy pill would be more appropriate.) Open daily 7am-12:30pm and 4-9pm.

At 397 Serangoon Rd., just after Perumal Rd., the **Sri Srinivasa Temple** (tel. 298 5771) is a blue complex guarded by a thicket of barbed wire. The broken coconuts in the inner courtyard are for the elephant-headed Vinayagar, who is revered for his filial piety and worshipped first upon entering the temple. The temple is the launching pad for the **Thaipusam Festival** pilgrimage. At the beginning of the year, devotees honor Lord Subramaniam by carrying a huge metal cage, called a *kavadi,* from this temple to the Chettiar Hindu Temple. Not only is the *kavadi* decorated with offerings, but it also bristles with hooks and spikes which masochistic worshippers use to pierce their skin so the *kavadi* can hang freely from their flesh. But that's not all—they also stick tiny lances through their cheeks and tongues, and walk on nails. During the procession of self-mutilation, the zealots never bleed, a phenomenon thought to be due to their trance-like state. Check the newspaper a day ahead for the pilgrimage route, (so you can pick another one). Only worshippers are allowed to approach the main altar; anyone can stick nails in his or her cheeks, however. Open daily 6:30am-noon and 5-9pm; Fri. and Sat. open until 9:30pm.

The flashy **Sakaya Muni Buddha Gaya Temple** (Temple of 1000 Lights), north of Perumal Rd. at 366 Race Course Rd. and just behind the line of tour buses, is webbed with yards of little lights and features a sleepy-eyed Buddha, so enormous that it nearly outsizes the tiny temple. Open daily 7:30am-4:45pm.

Labeled with Malaysian street names, the Muslim neighborhood around **Arab St.** unwinds east of Little India and north of the Bencoolen St. area. Plan ahead and pick up stocking-stuffers here, including *batik,* printed sarongs, baskets of all dimensions, jewelry boxes, and other crafts.

AROUND SINGAPORE

Red-line your thrill-o-meter and send your blood pressure through the roof as you gun up the engine and vamoose out of the city center to catch Singapore's most exciting sights. The **Singapore Zoological Gardens,** 80 Mandai Lake Rd. (tel. 269 3411), are a perennial favorite; traditional zoo cages have been replaced by moats and cleverly concealed wire barriers, giving the illusion of freely roaming peacocks and monkeys like you would find in the rest of Southeast Asia. Pour out a tall glass of orange juice for a hungry **orangutan** at **breakfast** or scarf down a scone with the big apes at **high tea** (breakfast daily 9am, S$15, children S$8; reserve in advance). The zoo also has a rare collection of four **Komodo dragons,** which are publicly fed at 2pm, two Sundays per month to the great delight of the audience and the carnivores themselves. Elephant rides are offered Mon.-Fri. from 1-4pm, Sat.-Sun. 1-2:30pm and 4-5pm. Travel there in luxury on the Zoo Express from Orchard Rd. hotels (tel. 292 2388). Or, jump on the MRT to Ang Mo Kio station and then transfer to bus #138. Open daily 8:30am-6pm; admission S$9, ages 3-16 S$4. Creatures of the night can visit the **night safari exhibit** and tour a patch of rainforest after dark, prying into the nocturnal affairs of their favorite beasts. Take the tram (covering about 75% of the exhibit) or, for the truly tireless, walk. True to Singaporean form, there's a restaurant in the middle of the forest where you can dine while watching a herd of giraffes doing the same. Open daily 7:30pm-midnight; admission S$15, children S$10. Zoo and night safari **package admission** S$20, children S$12.

Also popular is **Jurong Bird Park,** Jalan Ahmad Ibrahim (tel. 265 0022; fax 261 1869), containing over 450 species of birds, including the cassowary from Papua New Guinea, which is known for its startling ability to charge humans and rip their hearts out with its bare claws. For a more cheerful way to start your day, have **breakfast with the birds** (daily 9-11am, S$12, children S$10), and no, you don't have to eat what they eat (and hopefully they'll not eat yours or your heart). Take the MRT to Boon Lay Station and transfer to bus #251, 253, or 255 at the bus interchange. Open daily 9am-6pm; admission S$9, children S$3.

Crocodiles are to Singapore what the Victoria's Secret catalog is to American males aged 12-59. "Crocodiles are fun to look at! Come especially at feeding time to see them devouring pig's lungs and fish. Even the little ones show no mercy to prawns, cockles and mussels" declares one brochure. Browse through the biggest, laciest collection at **Jurong Crocodile Paradise** (tel. 261 8866), next to Jurong Bird Park, featuring crocodile wrestling at 11:45am, 2, and 4pm. Open daily 9am-6pm;

admission S$4.50, children S$2.50. Perhaps the quirkiest (and certainly the only free) crocodile attraction is the **Singapore Crocodile Farm,** 790 Upper Serangoon Rd. (tel. 288 8910 or 288 9385), where 300 crocodiles are raised and then turned into handbags, shoes, and belts right in the middle of a Singaporean residential area. The place is littered with "Enter at your own risk" signs (now you know why it's free), and the crocs lie in shallow pools just a little more than an arm's length away. Don't make any sudden moves unless you want your fingers on a pair of boots. Feeding time is Tues.-Sun. at 11am. Take buses to Upper Serangoon Rd. which stop opposite the farm. Open daily 8:30am-5:30pm.

The less lethal Chinese and Japanese Gardens, Jurong Park, Yuan Ching Rd. (tel. 264 3455; fax 265 8133), are built on a pair of islands in Jurong Lake connected by an elegant, carved white stone footbridge. The **Chinese garden** features pagodas, gazebos, and structures with romantic names like "Moon Inviting Boat" and "Moon Receiving Tower," and other bits of Bernardo Bertolucci-esque sets that eclipse the ascetic **Japanese garden.** Take the MRT to the Chinese Garden station and follow the signs. Open Mon.-Sat. 9am-6:30pm, Sun. and public holidays 8:30am-6:30pm. Last admission 6pm. Admission S$4.50, children S$2.

■■■ SENTOSA ISLAND

Dubbed "Singapore's Discovery Island" by the tourist bureau, this small isle just south of the peninsula is the number-one attraction recommended by eight out of 10 locals. Meddling kids may want to snoop around the **Asian Village,** the **Pioneers of Singapore and Surrender Chambers Museum,** and the **Butterfly Park.** There are nature trails through a "jungle area," a tree-lined promenade, big beaches, and **Underwater World,** where you can walk through an 100m underwater acrylic tunnel and get all misty-eyed as over 2000 species of fish swim around over your head. Thrillseekers can beat the heat at **Fantasy Island,** a giant water park offering wading pools for children, white water rapids, tube slides, a heart-stopping underground plunge, and almost every conceivable maritime activity in between. The island is run like a giant amusement park, with a basic admission charge of S$5 and S$3 for children, plus separate fees for all the attractions. To get there, take the bus to the World Trade Center and transfer to Sentosa Bus Service A, Sentosa Ferry (one way S$0.80, round-trip S$1.20), or cable car (S$5, children S$3). Or, take the MRT to Tiong Bahru and get on Sentosa Bus Service B or C. Call 743 8668, 270 7888, or 270 7889 for information. For **camping** on the island make reservations (472 5130 or 270 7889) three days in advance. Four-person tents S$14; 8-person tents S$19.

THAILAND

Thailand attracts a variety of tourists, drawn by the country's savory cuisine, brilliant temples, ample jungles, beaches, or natural preserves. As the only Southeast Asian people never ruled by a western power, Thais possess a unique and independent cultural heritage. Thailand's rapid industrialization and growing presence on the international economic scene makes it a challenge for the nation to maintain a specifically Thai identity as it seeks a more assertive role in the world community.

The country consists of six distinct regions: Bangkok, Central, East, North, Northeast, and South. Urbanites seek shelter in the capital's maelstrom of towering high-rises and mammoth shopping complexes. Meanwhile, tourists devote days in the South and the East to soaking up tropical sun and frolicking on the famous sandy white beaches. The rugged head to the North on mountain treks to meet hill tribes who have inhabited the region for centuries. Archaeology buffs and fans of tranquility tour the Northeast and Central regions, picking through crumbling ruins and exploring the cradles of Thai civilization, which now repose in silent majesty.

ESSENTIALS

■■■ GEOGRAPHY

Sweltering in Southeast Asia, Thailand (pop. 58.6 million) claims an area of 514,000 sq.km, about the size of Texas. The central region (known as the "rice bowl") is extremely fertile, thanks to the large Chao Phraya River, but the southern part of the region bursts at the seams with Bangkok, the capital and hub of Thailand (pop. 6-8 million). The east is graced with miles of sand, surf, and sky, before reaching the Cambodian border. Mountains and river valleys that spread across Burma and Laos festoon the north, the largest region. Also known as Khorat Plateau or Isaan, the northeast is underdeveloped, sparsely populated, and little-explored, with only the Mekong River seperating it from Laos. The tropical south is sprinkled with beaches and slowly melts away into the Malaysian peninsula.

■■■ WHEN TO GO

Thailand is generally hot, sticky, and humid, with an average annual temperature of 28°C (83°F). The air is cooler in the mountainous north than in the tropical south. Thailand has three seasons. The cool season, October-February, brings high prices and high tourist density, but lower temperatures—especially in the north, where nighttime temperatures can dip to 11°C (52°F). The hot season, March-May, means summer highs near 38°C (100°F) throughout the country; traveling costs often plummet as tourism winds down. The rainy season, June-September, hits its peak in August when the rains just keep on coming. In May and October, heavy monsoons pummel the southern isthmus, making flodding an annual experience. Travelers come in greater numbers during this season, hoping to avoid the cool season's crowds and the hot season's unbearable heat. Except for in the south, the rainy season can be ideal for traveling; prices will still be much better than in the cool season.

■■■ GETTING AROUND

BY PLANE

THAI Airways International holds a near-monopoly on commercial flights within Thailand and offers 22 flights from Bangkok to various destinations in the north, northeast, and south, plus flights within and across regions outside Bangkok. More popular routes are serviced by Airbus jets; other routes are serviced by smaller propeller planes. The only alternative to THAI is **Bangkok Airways,** a small start-up whose major route is between Bangkok and Ko Samui. Thailand has a 200฿ **airport tax** (per person) on international flights.

BY TRAIN

The Thai government, through the **State Railway of Thailand,** operates an efficient and inexpensive rail system that reaches many locales throughout the country. The four main train routes in Thailand start in Bangkok and run north to Chiang Mai, south to Malaysia, northeast to Nong Khai, and east to Ubon Ratchathani. The minor routes connect Bangkok to Kanchanaburi and cities north of the eastern seaboard. Thailand has three different types of trains: **ordinary, rapid,** and **express.** Ordinary trains offer the cheapest fares and basic services, and they stop at every station. Rapid trains offer slightly better cabins and speedier service, but rarely roar past more than a stop or two. For quickest service, hop on board an express or even a **special express** train.

Most trains have a **third class,** offering the hard bench, and a **second class** with individualized cushioned chairs. Only express trains really have **first class,** offering comfortable, air-conditioned private cabins. Some ordinary trains offer only third class. Sleeper accommodations, separated from the passageway by curtains, are usually available on rapid and express trains. Train **tickets** for departures from Bangkok or for transportation between two other cities can be purchased up to 90 days in advance from the Hualamphong Railway Station in Bangkok. Though this does not always guarantee you a seat; it save you the hassle of buying a ticket on board.

■■■ MONEY

US$1=25.11฿ (baht)	**1฿=US$0.040**
CDN1$=18.47฿	**1฿=CDN$0.054**
UK£1=39.03฿	**1฿=UK£0.026**
IR£1=39.78฿	**1฿=IR£0.025**
AUS$1=18.51฿	**1฿=AUS$0.054**
NZ$1=16.47฿	**1฿=NZ$0.061**
SARand=6.87฿	**1฿=SARand0.146**

The Thai monetary system is based on the **baht** (฿). The *baht* is divided into 100 *satangs,* although the *satang* is rarely used in transactions. All Thai currency has a picture of the King on it—do not deface any money or you'll quickly find your booty, and your booty, in jail. Thailand has a 7% VAT (value-added **tax**) on most items, including hotel rooms and food; it is usually tacked onto stated prices. Rarely is the VAT added onto a final bill; the menu, tariff sheet, etc. should specify if this is the case. **Tipping** is not customary. With cab drivers the fare can be rounded off to an even number. Upscale restaurants often have a 10-15% service charge, but in nice restaurants without a service charge, it is appropriate to leave something (3-5%). Do not tip maids or service staff, especially in your guest house. Valets and luggage carriers should receive a small tip (5-20฿).

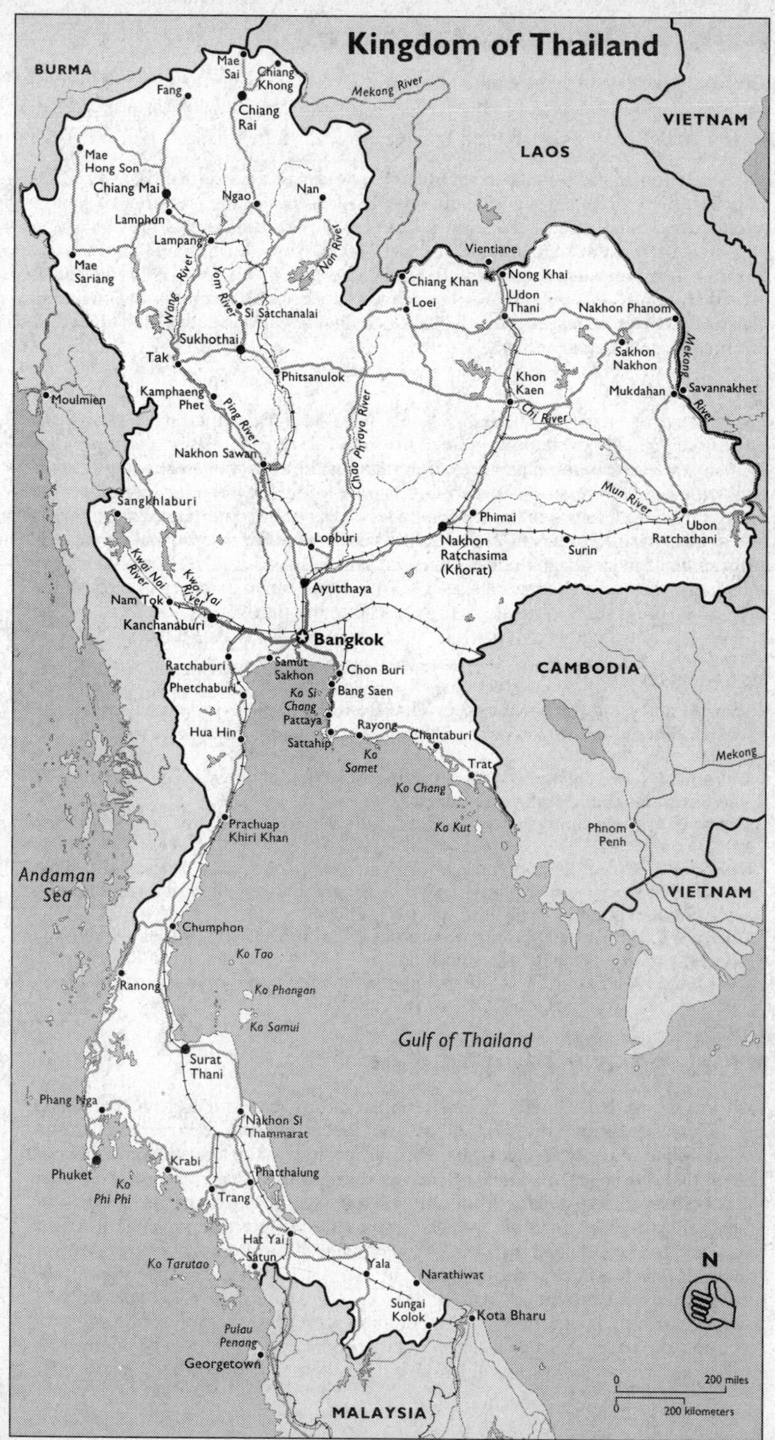
Kingdom of Thailand
BURMA
LAOS
VIETNAM
CAMBODIA
MALAYSIA
Andaman Sea
Gulf of Thailand
Mekong River
Mae Sai
Chiang Khong
Fang
Chiang Rai
Mae Hong Son
Chiang Mai
Ngao
Nan
Lamphun
Lampang
Nan River
Mae Sariang
Wang River
Yom River
Si Satchanalai
Sukhothai
Tak
Phitsanulok
Moulmien
Kamphaeng Phet
Ping River
Nakhon Sawan
Chao Phraya River
Vientiane
Nong Khai
Chiang Khan
Udon Thani
Loei
Nakhon Phanom
Sakhon Nakhon
Khon Kaen
Mukdahan
Savannakhet
Mekong River
Chi River
Mun River
Phimai
Ubon Ratchathani
Surin
Nakhon Ratchasima (Khorat)
Sangkhlaburi
Lopburi
Kwai Noi River
Kwai Yai River
Nam Tok
Kanchanaburi
Ayutthaya
Bangkok
Ratchaburi
Samut Sakhon
Chon Buri
Phetchaburi
Bang Saen
Ko Si Chang
Pattaya
Hua Hin
Rayong
Chantaburi
Sattahip
Ko Samet
Trat
Mekong
Ko Chang
Ko Kut
Prachuap Khiri Khan
Phnom Penh
Chumphon
Ko Tao
Ranong
Ko Phangan
Ko Samui
Surat Thani
Phang Nga
Nakhon Si Thammarat
Krabi
Phuket
Ko Phi Phi
Phatthalung
Trang
Hat Yai
Satun
Ko Tarutao
Yala
Narathiwat
Sungai Kolok
Kota Bharu
Pulau Penang
Georgetown
N
0
200 miles
0
200 kilometers

THAILAND

■■■ KEEPING IN TOUCH

The Thai **postal system** is extremely efficient for a country on the verge of becoming a Newly Industrialized Country (NIC). Airmail across the globe from Bangkok generally takes between seven and 10 days. Overseas mail from rural areas may take up to two weeks to arrive, but almost always makes it to its destination. For three-day overseas mail the postal service offers **Express Mail Service (EMS),** available at all post offices in Bangkok and many other post offices in the country. Thailand's **telephone country code** is **66. Home Country Direct numbers:** British Telecom, 001-99-944-1066. Canada Direct, 001-999-15-1000. New Zealand Telecom, 66 120 64 0000. Telecom Australia, 001-999-611-000. US: AT&T, 0019-991-1111; MCI, 001-999-2001; Sprint, 001-999-13-877. For domestic telephone information (including Malaysia and Vientiene, Laos) dial 101. *Let's Go* lists telephone codes in the Practical Information section of each city.

PRINT MEDIA

Thailand has two major English-language dailies: **The Nation** and the **Bangkok Post.** They hold virtually even shares of the market. The *Bangkok Post,* established in 1946, is the leader in the reporting of international news stories and its quirky style. *The Nation,* once the struggling upstart, is now said to have better local coverage than its rival. Both newspapers have good local events and entertainment sections.

The **International Herald Tribune,** the **Asian Wall Street Journal** are readily available English language bookstores (such as Asia Books and DK Books) and first-class hotels at tourist destinations. as is **USA Today,** which manages to publish the latest U.S. sports scores and stock prices despite the time difference. Most papers publish U.S. news with a two-day time delay, but USA Today cuts it to one.

TELEVISION

The non-cable stations broadcast in Thai from Bangkok. For listings, check the Focus section of *The Nation* or the Outlook section of the *Bangkok Post.*

Channel 3, privately owned, offers a varied selection of movies, Thai soap operas, and cartoons. Daily 4pm-past midnight.

Channel 5, the military network, mainly airs variety shows and documentaries. Daily 4pm-1am.

Channel 7, also military-owned, but private companies lease time on the air. A favorite of stock market players; daytime programming is often interrupted with current market news. Daily 4pm-around midnight.

Channel 9, the national public television station, broadcasting variety shows and documentaries. Daily 6am-around 1am.

Channel 11, the Ministry of Education channel, with an emphasis (surprise!) on educational programs. Daily 5:30am-midnight.

■■■ STAYING SAFE

Travelers report that crime in Thailand is often more clever and creative than direct and violent. Scams abound. Taxi and tuk-tuk drivers, guest house operators, fellow travelers on trains or buses, and those friendly students at the museum have all been known to attempt various kinds of cons or outright thefts. We have heard stories about people who feign illness and lure a hapless good samaritan into a car to be robbed; a nice young man who claimed he wanted to practice his English over a meal, only to leave before the check arrived; English-speakers who start conversations with travelers in airports, waiting to be asked to watch their bags for a minute. Keep these warnings in mind, but don't just take *Let's Go's* word for it; talk to fellow travelers about their experiences. Use common sense, and keep on your toes.

Many of the larger Thai cities have separate **tourist police** forces in addition to the local police. They should speak English, and are there to help you, so don't hesitate to contact them. They roam busy neighborhoods at night in vans, waiting for tourists to come to them with problems. With crimes such as pickpocketing, there is often little they can do, but report the crime anyway. **Drugs** in Thailand are always illegal, regardless of what that guest house owner may say, and penalties can be very stiff—up to life in prison.

The emergency tourist police number for all of Thailand is 1699.

One of the most common cons is the selling of gems. Touts will accompany you to temples, invite you to dinner, and make it seem like you were the one who brought up the subject of gem trade. Before you realize it, you have "ended up" at a gem shop, and your new friend has gone home with a tidy commission. The most common line is that there is a one-week government special on gems, and you will not be charged tax if you buy today. There is no such special and there are no "government export agencies". If you buy expensive items, especially gems, you are taking a great risk with your money.

BISEXUAL, GAY, AND LESBIAN TRAVELERS

Thai people, at least in Bangkok, seem to offer a benign but guarded tolerance of gay men and lesbians. There is no legally mandated discrimination against homosexuals, and Thailand seldom witnesses the grotesque hate crimes against gays and lesbians that plagues much of the west. People seem to feel that homosexuality is an individual practice that need not concern others, much less the state or society at large.

Still, sexual orientation is a taboo topic; most gays and lesbians remain more or less closeted. Public discussion and displays of affection or attraction are avoided by homosexuals and heterosexuals alike. In the home of the world's largest sex industry, Thais keep their sexuality buttoned up. What goes on behind closed doors is nobody else's business, and the doors must be fully and firmly closed.

Although gay and lesbian nightlife does exist, much of it is closed to *farang,* who the Thais feel misrepresent their lifestyle by participating in the sex trade. Apart from *de facto* brothels it is hard for *farang* to find a gay or lesbian bar or club scene.

While Thai customs permit female friends to hold hands or put their arms around each other's shoulders, and male friends often have one hand on the other's shoulder, Thais do not believe that westerners, especially men, share these customs. You may not be openly harassed for holding hands, but you may receive plenty of stares. More explicit displays of affection will be frowned upon. However, you can generally feel safe walking together. Unpleasant incidents can still occur, even in *laissez-faire* Thailand, and gay or lesbian travelers together in public should be aware of what is going on around them.

■■■ PROSTITUTION AND AIDS

Women and children make up the majority of Thai prostitutes. Many are poor, lured into the industry with false promises of money, gifts, and respectable jobs in the city; others are kidnapped and forced to work for nothing. Countless more are sold into prostitution by their families to cover debts and escape abject poverty. In rural areas, where yearly incomes are about one-eigth those in Bangkok, community members may sell their daughters at 11 or 12 years old. Some women are brought from Burma, worked as prostitutes, then sent back to the border where they may be turned away or arrested for their "crimes." Most prostitutes die young from disease or other causes related to their occupation.

Estimates on the number of women employed in prostitution range from 200,000 to 2,000,000 (in a country of 58 million people). Understandably, prostitution has been illegal in Thailand since 1960 and carries stiff penalties (up to and including death). Nonetheless, tourism and the industry are mutually reinforcing. Two-thirds of all foreign visitors in Thailand are male. The U.S., Japan, Europe, Australia, South Korea, and Taiwan, all have organizations that send sex tours to Thailand, but laws in many of these same countries now allow them to arrest their own citizens for sex crimes abroad. You will have to decide whether your money will join other foreign cash supporting this exploitative, dangerous, and illegal industry. **Sexual offenders face 1-7 years of prison in Thailand and fines of up to 140,000฿. Forced prostitution can bring a life sentence. Any involvement with the trade in women or children can bring sentences of 1-10 years and fines of 200,000฿.**

AIDS is decimating workers in the sex industry and the population at large; estimates of HIV-positive prostitutes range from 15% to more than 50%. Every day 1000 Thais are infected, and the World Health Organization calculates that by the year 2000, 2-4 million Thais will have HIV. The Thai government's campaign against AIDS—now said to be the best and most progressive in Asia—had less than auspicious beginnings. Initially ignoring the problem, then blaming it solely on foreigners, the state hatched a scheme to inspect and officially certify uninfected prostitutes. When this proved ineffective, the Thai government in 1990 took land set aside for a leper colony to build a detention center for HIV-positive people who ignored government restrictions on their activity and movement.

The man most responsible for changing the direction of the government's AIDS policy is **Meechai Viravaidya,** widely known as "Mr. Condom." Until the fall of 1992, Meechai led the national anti-AIDS program until the fall of 1992, spearheading innovative PR techniques including mandatory radio and TV AIDS commercials and ATM machines that flash AIDS warnings. The Thai government budgeted nearly US$45 million for AIDS education in 1993, and AIDS education has been placed on the public school curriculum. Thais now use condoms—known as Meechais—in record numbers (as many as 80% of all brothel customers now use them, up from 20% in the mid-80s). On the legal front, there have been proposals to attack the sex industry and question the traditional immunity of the customer. Skeptics claim that even if these measures pass the male-dominated, foot-dragging legislature, they will not be enforced in any meaningful way; optimists, however, see them as a first step. As a result of other initiatives, including rural education and increasing publicity of the conditions of prostiution, fewer Thai women are entering prostitution, while

Population and Community Development Association

Founded in 1974 by Meechai Viravaidya to pursue community development projects, mainly with refugees in the wake of the Vietnam War, the Population and Community Development Association (PDA) has become the largest—and possibly most successful—non-governmental organization in Thailand's history. Their unique and aggressive social action campaigns are refreshingly frank, using phrases such as "Make Love, not Babies" in radio, TV, and print ads. It has taken more than catchy slogans, however, to achieve the triumphant decrease in the average number of children per family: from seven to two in twelve years. By working to increase individual standards of living, PDA's comprehensive programs promote behavior beneficial to society as a whole. They have garnered several awards for their efforts, including a UN prize for being one of the most successful family planning programs in the world.

In the 1980s, PDA began to use its high-profile techniques in the fight against AIDS. In this vein, they opened the Cabbages and Condoms restaurant, with the goal of making condoms as easy to obtain as cabbages. Many of these programs are based in Northern Thailand, where a combination of less education and more prostitution (15 customers per night vs. 2 per night in Bangkok) has made AIDS a severe problem. Recently, PDA has further expanded their work to include environmental sanitation and occupational programs in rural villages and hill-tribe communities. Thai businesses have become involved through the Thai Business Initiative for Rural Development (TBIRD) program. These projects are tailored to village needs and vary from school lunch prgrams to promoting sustainable hill-tribe tourism.

more and more Burmese women are being brought across the border to meet the demand of Asian and western males.

The AIDS crisis has put a damper on Thailand's sex trade; however, it has also pushed the business farther into the countryside, where it is believd the women are less likely to be infected and do not press for condom use. Hustlers for brothels in town now recruit from the hill-tribes and the borderlands. Furthermore, AIDS awareness has increased the demand for child prostitutes, who are supposedly too young to have contracted the disease, a trend that has led to increased punishment for those involved in child prostitution.

Critics of the government's AIDS program argue that money and manpower would be better spent elsewhere. Others feel that bad publicity on Thailand's AIDS situation will jeopardize the nation's US$5 billion per year tourist industry. Meechai, however, argues that the only way to save the industry is to tackle the disease; his fight is with AIDS, and not with the plague of prostitution, which he sees as too mixed up with politics, law enforcement, and big business to ever be shut down.

■■■ HOURS AND HOLIDAYS

Many public holidays commemorate a royal event or recognize a Buddhist holy day. Banks, government offices, and firms close on these dates. Many holidays coincide with festivals, and all of them involve some sort of revelry. See regional listings for details on festivals. In 1996, the official holidays are:

January 1: New Year's Day.
March 3: Makha Bucha, commemorating Buddha's address to 1250 monks.
April 6: Chakri Day, marking the 1782 founding of the current Thai dynasty.
April 12-14: Songkran, the water festival, celebrating the Thai New Year.
May 1: Labor Day.
May 5: Coronation Day, honoring the 1946 coronation of the King and Queen.
May 10: Royal Ploughing Ceremony, kicking off the rice-planting season.
May 31: Visakha Bucha, celebrating the birth, enlightenment, and death of Buddha.
July 12: Asanha Bucha, commemorating Buddha's first sermon and the beginning of Khao Phansa (the Buddhist Lent).
August 12: Queen's Birthday.
October 23: Chulalongkorn Day, marking the death of Thailand's revered leader.
November: Loi Krathong, cleansing of mind and spirit beneath the full moon.
December 5: King's Birthday.
December 10: Constitution Day.
December 31: New Year's Eve.

Many Chinese businesses close for the Chinese New Year (Feb. 19, 1996), and some international firms close for Christmas. In general, government offices and banks are open Mon.-Fri. 8:30am-noon and 1:30-4:30pm. Regular shops usually stay open until 5, 7, or 9pm, depending on the size of the shop and the city.

■■■ POTPOURRI FOR $100, ALEX!

DATE AND TIME

Military time is widely used in addition to the standard western scheme. The cycle begins at 0001 hrs. (12:01am) and goes to 2400 hrs. (midnight).

In the oral system, there are four base hours: 1 at night (*dee neung*) which corresponds to 1am in western time, 1 in the morning (*neung moang chao*) which corresponds to 7am, 1 in the afternoon (*bai moang*) which corresponds to 1pm, and 1 in the evening (*thoom neung*) which corresponds to 7pm. Thus, a meeting at "three in the morning" in the spoken language, will occur at 9am in western time.

Finally, calendars in Thailand use the Buddhist Era to determine the year. To convert the year from the Christian Era to the Buddhist Era, add 543 years to the current year. Thus, 1996 is the year 2539 in the Buddhist Era.

A STREET BY ANY OTHER NAME

In Thai towns and cities, areas are divided according to the following system: **nakhon** or **muang** is the overall city, **amphoe** is a city district, **tambon** is a precinct within a district, and **mu** is a small neighborhood within an amphoe. A street, road, or boulevard is usually known as a **thanon.** Side streets are called **soi** and are often accompanied by a number (i.e., Soi 12 off Sukhumvit Rd.). Sometimes they are named, as in Soi Asoke. A soi will almost always be followed by the name of the street from which it branches.

LIFE AND TIMES

■■■ HISTORY

PRE-HISTORY

Some argue that the ancestors of the Thai people migrated from Mongolia or north China. Driven by the Chinese, these peoples moved south to Yunnan, where the various tribes coalesced and established the kingdom of **Nanchao** in 651 AD. Counter-theorists, however, argue that the Thai people originated in what is now northeast Thailand. Recently discovered human remains in **Ban Chiang** (see Around Udon Thani) on the Khorat Plateau suggest that early farmers settled in the area around 4000 BC and lived there until the beginning of the Christian era. These tribes left for southern China in 651 AD, setting up Nanchao.

During the four centuries that followed the establishment of Nanchao, various tribes of the Tai-Kadai linguistic group moved farther south into the hilly, northern areas of Burma, Thailand, and Laos in search of greater independence from their powerful neighbor. These people became known as the Shan, Thai, and Lao and founded minor kingdoms and city-states. By 1000 AD, the Chinese had subjugated the original Thai group in Yunnan, and in 1253 AD, Kublai Khan conquered the remnants of the Nanchao lands and incorporated them into the Mongol Empire. Fifteen years earlier, two chiefs from the southern Thai tribes had moved into the central plains of what is now Northern Thailand. They quickly founded the new Sukhothai kingdom under the tutelage of neighboring **Angkor.**

SUKHOTHAI AND AYUTTHAYA

In 1275 **King Ramkhamhaeng the Great** ascended the throne. Under his active rule, **Sukhothai** reached its zenith in power and size, incorporating present-day Laos, Thailand, Singapore, and Malaysia. In 1283, King Ramkhamhaeng contributed to the cultural consolidation of the Thai people by introducing the **Thai alphabet** to his subjects. It remains, with relatively few changes, the alphabet used by Thais today. Other major accomplishments of Ramkhamhaeng's reign include the abolition of slavery (the first of a series of attempts), the codification of laws, and the introduction of **Theravada Buddhism.** The strength and compassion of this John F. Kennedy of Sukhothai held the kingdom together, and made him a much sought-after lover; but his shoes proved too large to fill, and his Camelot crumbled within two generations of his death.

The son of a Sukhothai princess, **King U Thong**—later dubbed **King Ramathibodi I**—inaugurated the **Ayutthaya** period by founding the island city of the same name that served as the nation's capital for the next 417 years. Under **King Ramathibodi II,** two generations later, diplomatic relations with the Portuguese over the disputed territory of Melaka brought the first Europeans to what was then known as Siam; the Spaniards, Dutch, English, and French soon followed.

In 1584, after a 15-year period of Burmese occupation, **King Naresuan,** the son of a vassal-king, rose to become the greatest warrior-monarch in Thai history. Appointed by King Burengnong of Burma, Naresuan was given military training in Burma to prepare him to be a Burmese puppet ruler. Instead, Naresuan organized an army, ignited a revolution, and reclaimed the city of Ayutthaya. Legend has it that as the Burmese were soundly defeating the Thais, King Naresuan engaged the prince in an epic duel on elephants. After much fighting, Naresuan beheaded the crown prince. Demoralized, the Burmese retreated, and their empire fell soon after.

Ayutthaya became an important trading crossroad between Europe and East Asia until a series of misunderstandings and intrigues led to the brutal massacre of Japanese palace guards in 1632, ending relations with the Japanese for 200 years. Trade between Ayutthaya and Europe, however, continued to boom. Under **King Narai,** Ayutthaya reached its pinnacle with a population greater than London's. But in 1688, while the king was seriously ill, **Constantine Phaulkon,** your average Greek-adventurer-turned-Thai-Prime-Minister, was accused of conspiring to replace King Narai with a puppet-king loyal to France. The Thai nobility arrested Phaulkon and executed him. Relations with the French were cut off, and virtually all foreigners were expelled from the kingdom.

The trumpets of Jericho sounded for Ayutthaya in 1767. After laying siege for over nine years, the Burmese finally broke through and stormed the once-great capital. Everything was put to the torch, the king was killed, and mass slaughter ensued. Of a community of more than one million, only 10,000 people survived. **General Phraya Taksin** and a few hundred followers managed to escape the carnage. Regrouping on the east coast of Thailand, Taksin led an army of several thousand men to reclaim the nation and expel the Burmese. Within 15 years, he had achieved this goal and also captured Chiang Mai, Cambodia, and parts of Laos. It seems, however, his superhuman exertions drove him over the edge. Insanity struck the new King Taksin, who declared himself the reincarnation of Buddha.

Commander-in-Chief **Chao Phraya Chakri** found himself named king by the country's nobles and generals. He made his first two decrees in strict accordance with Siamese law. King Taksin was executed in royal fashion: he was placed in a sack and beaten to death so as not to spill royal blood. The general who had handed Chakri the helm was killed for committing treason against the former king. Not being of royal blood, he was swiftly beheaded. Chakri was given the title Rama I.

THE DYNASTY OF RAMA

Feeling that Thon Buri was too vulnerable, **King Rama I** moved the capital across the Chao Phraya River to the village of Bangkok. There he built the **Grand Palace** and the **Royal Chapel** (Temple of the Emerald Buddha) and consolidated the kingdom's various fiefdoms into a unified nation. He overhauled the Buddhist priesthood and created the "Law of the Three Seals," which set rules on economic, political, and military affairs.

The reign of King Mongkut, or **King Rama IV,** is probably one of the most significant transition periods in contemporary Thailand. Unfairly portrayed as a flippant and licentious monarch in Margaret Landon's novel, *Anna and the King of Siam,* Mongkut was actually a progressive and serious man. His 27-year stint as a monk vested him with a thorough knowledge of Buddhism, its principal languages, Pali and Sanskrit, as well as extended exposure to the commoners' livelihood. Mongkut actively sought out western missionaries and from them learned English, western history, mathematics, and astronomy.

Mongkut anticipated the danger of western imperialism and met the challenge squarely with deft diplomacy and an active program of domestic modernization. In 1855, to strengthen the nation and to silence western critics, Siam negotiated a foreign trade treaty with the British—reversing 150 years of virtual isolation—and quickly imported western technologies. Mongkut's rule was cut short when, in

1868, he contracted malaria while leading dignitaries into marshy countryside to view a solar eclipse he had predicted. The reins of government fell into the able hands of his son, **Prince Chulalongkorn,** who was crowned **King Rama V.** His 42 years of rule were characterized by numerous reforms in Thai government and society, and a courageous foreign policy in an era of aggressive European colonialism.

The latter half of the 19th century witnessed Britain's seizure of Burma and the French colonization of Indochina to the east. A showdown between the two powers over the fate of Siam was imminent. In 1893, after prolonged tensions between France and Siam in the northeast, two French gunboats shelled Siamese defenses at the mouth of the Chao Phraya River and sailed into Bangkok. Thanks to the swift diplomatic action of **Prince Devawongse,** the Siamese foreign minister who greeted the arriving ships and congratulated the captains on their prowess and skill, war between the two countries was narrowly averted. Siam was established as a buffer state, guaranteeing its independence. By the time of his death in 1910, King Rama V had become the most revered Thai monarch in modern history.

THE RISE OF THE MILITARY

During the Great Depression, the Thai treasury nearly went bankrupt from public works projects. Prominent academics and intellectuals were demanding a **civil constitution.** On June 24, 1932, government workers and the military launched a bloodless coup. Proclaiming themselves the People's Party, the revolutionaries, led by **Major Luang Pibulsongkhram** and **Dr. Pridi Banomyong,** moved quickly to occupy high government posts. **Phraya Manopakorn Nitthada,** a former Supreme Court justice, became Thailand's first Prime Minister, and for the next three decades, Pibul and Pridi were the dominant forces in Thai politics. A 1933 attempt at counter-revolution was quickly suppressed.

Thailand did not enter World War II until December 1941, when Japan demanded that its forces enter the country. Pibulsongkhram, then Prime Minister, gave in against strong opposition. When things went badly for the Japanese, Gen. Pibul resigned as Prime Minister and **Khuang Aphaiwongse** secretly allowed Allied forces into the country to help repel the Japanese. Thus, when the war ended in 1945, the United States resumed normal relations with Thailand, declaring as void the country's earlier declaration of war.

The year 1946 was marked by gruesome royal intrigue. On June 9, King Rama VIII, **Ananda Mahidol,** who had returned from school in Switzerland just the year before, was found shot to death in his bed. Conspiracy buffs maintain that the king was a victim of a political design. Others remember the king as an avid gun collector and believe that he died when his favorite revolver accidentally discharged. Currently popular is the theory that he committed suicide. With the death of the young king, his younger brother, **Bhumibol Adulyadej,** ascended the throne, and Pibul returned to power. Thailand developed economically through the late 40s and early 50s and moved toward more democratic practices. Despite this progress, however, the government was riddled with corruption.

In 1957, the military seized an opportunity to stage a *coup d'état* during the rigged general elections. **Field Marshall Sarit Thanirat** took over. The crooked police force was purged, drug dealers were imprisoned and executed, and communist propaganda was suppressed. By the time Sarit died in 1963, Thailand had become a staunch U.S. ally in Southeast Asia; under his successor, U.S. forces were permitted to build air bases in Thailand to support the American war in Vietnam. In 1967, Thailand helped create the Association of Southeast Asian Nations (ASEAN), and in the next two years a new constitution was drafted, and the much-awaited elections were held.

Unfortunately, the elections proved to be generally meaningless. In June 1973, university students fed up with fifteen years of political repression led thousands of demonstrators into the streets, calling for a constitution to guarantee a truly democratic government. The more radical individuals left the cities to join the communist guerrilla forces. In October, the government responded, sending troops into Thammasat University to quell demonstrations, and more than 100 people were killed in what was called the **October Massacre.**

TOWARD DEMOCRACY

Before the October Massacre erupted into a full scale conflagration, **King Rama IX** intervened. Although he had no legal authority, he commanded great respect and loyalty among the people. Swayed by the king's reproach, **Prime Minister Thanom Kittikachorn** and other high-ranking officials went into exile. An interim government was established and soon drafted a new, democratic constitution. The tenth Thai constitution provided for national suffrage for men and women over the age of 20 and a certain amount of freedom of speech and religion.

Thailand's first general election in six years was held on January 26, 1975. After a year of political instability, however, the military and influential elites had come to see democracy as a dangerous experiment, and were determined to end it.

In a series of Reichstag fire-type maneuvers, the military and its conservative supporters reclaimed the government. Military leaders cited staged demonstrations as evidence of resurgent socialist and communist tendencies nurtured by democratic lassitude. A stand-off between students and police at Thammasat University, Thailand's favorite hot-bed of political activism, exploded on October 6, into another bloody assault on the campus. In the ensuing violence, scores of people were killed, and the military once again took control of the government.

After 16 *coups d'état* since World War II and long years of economic hardship, public dissatisfaction and shrinking military support led to the end of military rule and general elections in 1988. Peace and freedom from overt military domination, however, proved short-lived. The army launched a successful bloodless coup under the leadership of **General Suchinda Kraprayoon** in February of 1991. Citing general corruption in the government; he abolished the 1978 constitution, dissolved the legislature, and curtailed various freedoms, including the freedom of assembly.

While preparations were made for elections and constitutional revision, a military government of sorts was created under the title of the National Peace-Keeping Council (NPKC), and a civilian, **Anand Panyarachun,** was selected as the interim Prime Minister. Critics accused the army of influencing the framing of the constitution in order to institutionalize its rule. After a series of protests over this new constitution and the possibility of General Suchinda's leadership, thousands—including many members of the new middle class—took to the streets one more time on May 17, 1992. Suchinda ordered the military to clear them out, and between 100 and 1000 people died, many of them before Bangkok's Democracy Monument and western television cameras. King Bhumibol pushed Suchinda out of office and brought back Panyarachun to serve as a transitional Prime Minister.

■■■ THAILAND TODAY

On August 1, 1992, Anand fired the top four military officers in a bold move that signaled a new era in Thai politics. Their replacements promised to distance the military from politics. With the next Prime Minister, **Chuan Leekpai,** the leader of the Democratic party, the military still had substantial control over television, radio, and some state-owned industries. In July of 1995, Leekpai was defeated by **Banharn Silparcha,** head of the Thai Nation Party, a party long tied to corruption and vote-buying. Although the new party is pushing for powerful six-party alliance, it is likely nothing will change, as there is little to no difference between the political stances of Silparcha and Leekpai, and although Leekpai may be more honest, Silparcha is believed to be more competent. Most important, perhaps, is that the military finally kept its promise to stay out of the elections entirely.

Approximately two-thirds of Thais still work in agriculture, but the current shift is toward low-wage industrial work with vile factory conditions and few safety measures. Many feel that the western and Japanese producers who sub-contract Thai work should be responsible for safety measures and regulations. But with the tourist industry reigning as the largest source of foreign money, the government is working to maintain its reputation in the international community. The Thai tourist industry has had negative effects. Child prostitution and environmental degradation have been nationally and internationally decried. Western countries have begun working with the government to crack down; as with the recent arrest of a Swedish tourist by his own government for sex crimes in Thailand. (see Prostitution and AIDS, page 283). In order to curtail environmental damage, the government has declared areas where beautiful countryside has been replaced by concrete resorts and other projects, to be damaged zones, and has restricted their use accordingly.

■■■ THE PEOPLE OF THAILAND

TAI

The word "Thai" is a political/geographical designation that refers to the citizens of Thailand, as the country has been known since 1939. Tai, however, refers to the ethnic Tai-Kadai people who speak Tai-based languages, many of whom live outside the borders of Thailand, in China, Laos, and Burma (where they were known as the Shan). Ethnically, Thailand is 75% Tai, and the word Thai is often used in its stead when referring to the people of Thailand. These people are divided into numerous sub-groups with somewhat different dialects and cultures. Previous to 1939 the country was known as Siam, from the Khmer name for the Tai people, Syam.

CHINESE

Ethnic Chinese make up only 10-15% of Thailand's population, yet their presence extends back for centuries. In fact, many scholars believe that the Tai people came from China. Assimilating more easily than some other ethnic groups, the Chinese have a strong influence in Thailand. As in Malaysia, their leadership in commerce is much greater than their small population would suggest.

OTHER ETHNIC MINORITIES

Malays constitute about 4% of the population; the rest is composed largely of Vietnamese, Mon, and Khmer. Thailand has traditionally been home to refugees—Burmese, Vietnamese, Laotians, and Khmer fleeing political violence. Religious freedom, a relatively stable domestic situation, a growing economy, and a laissez-faire culture attract minorities to Thailand.

HILL-TRIBES

Over 550,000 hill-tribe people, or *Chao Khao,* live in north Thailand. The six major groups are the Karen (*Kariang* or *Yang*), the Hmong (*Meo*), the Yao (*Mien*), the Lahu (*Mussur*), the Akha (*Kaw*), and the Lisu (*Lisaw*). The Akha, Lisu, Lahu, and the Southern Chinese Mien all migrated from Yunnan province in this century. Other small tribes include the Lawa, Kha-mu, H'Tin, and Yumbri (*Mlabri*). There are believed to be only 140 *Mlabri,* all living in Nan Province. The Lawa, perhaps Thailand's oldest remaining inhabitants, are remnants of an ancient Mon-Khmer kingdom in Northern Thailand. Though the Shan people, or *Thai Yai,* have their own distinct language, they are not included among the hill-tribes since they have never really been a nomadic people. Like the Karen, they have been struggling for autonomy from the Burmese government for years. The largest hill-tribe populations are in the Chiang Mai, Chiang Rai, Mae Hong Son, and Tak provinces.

■■■ CUSTOMS AND CULTURE

GETTING ALONG IN THAILAND

The ideal of Thai behavior can be summarized in a two-word phrase: *jai yen.* Literally, it translates as "keep a cool heart," but in a more important sense, it encompasses calmness, patience, kindness, compassion, generosity, and grace. *Jai yen* is the Thai key to a peaceful life, free from the struggles that harm both the body and the soul. The companion to *jai yen* is *mai pen rai,* or "it doesn't matter," "it's all right," "no harm done." This all-purpose phrase is used generously by Thais to lubricate the friction points of social interaction. If someone has committed a social *faux pas,* and immediately recognizes the mistake, you might prevent that person's obvious embarrassment by saying "*mai pen rai.*"

Another gesture that serves to achieve and perpetuate *jai yen* is the Thai smile. This ubiquitous, yet enigmatic, grin, which earned the country its reputation as the laid-back, friendly land of smiles, is not merely a sign of pleasure. The smile sidesteps conflict and shows sympathy or embarrassment. However, the arrival of millions of tourists has sparked the development of an economy that both serves and preys on foreign visitors. Those sweet, beamy songthaew drivers, waiters, hotel staff members, and even officials in private tour agencies may be ripping you off. Be observant, persistent, and stubborn whenever money is involved.

Casual physical contact is distasteful to Thais. Tapping a waitress on the shoulder may draw horrified stares from other patrons. The head is considered the most sacred part of the body, and it is considered rude to pat or touch anyone, even children, on the head. Exemptions are granted to husbands and wives or to a mother and her child. Feet are the most impure part. Never point the sole of your foot at anyone or at a religious symbol. Foreign visitors often do this accidentally when they cross their legs. Do not step over people, food, or books. Displaying significant amounts of skin is also frowned upon. Travelers should avoid unnecessary exposure. Nude sunbathing is illegal and is considered disrespectful and perverted.

The proper method of greeting is to *wai.* To perform a *wai,* puts your hands together as if praying. Bring your thumbs to your lips and bows your head. When greeting a person superior in age or status, bow deeper than normal, and bring the hand higher. Do not *wai* anyone of "lower" social standing. For example, it is not considered proper to return a *wai* to a beggar to whom you have just given some change. A slight nod or smile suffices.

Most Thais realize that foreign visitors cannot know and understand all local customs. Nevertheless, travelers should be acquainted with the core customs and practices given here in order to avoid inadvertently offending the local population or accidentally landing in jail.

For more information consult *Culture Shock! Thailand,* by Robert and Nanthapa Cooper (Portland: Graphic Arts Center Publishing Company, 1990).

BARGAINING

Thailand is a wonderful place to practice your bargaining skills. Taxi fares (nonmetered) and items in outdoor markets are fair game for haggling. Don't bargain on prepared foods (on the street or in restaurants) or on items marked with a price tag. Although, in smaller, family-run stores it might not hurt to try. Be prepared to pay what you offer; it is considered outrageous to refuse to purchase something after coming to a compromise with a merchant. Start by offering half the stated price and let your charismatic powers do the rest.

THE MONARCHY

King Bhumibol Adulyadej is not merely the longest-reigning living monarch in the world, the longest-reigning Thai King, and the composer of the royal anthem (*Falling Rain*). He is not revered in the Thai people's hearts simply for his dedication to the underprivileged, his role in resolving government conflicts, and his selfless commitment to the peace and unity of his country. He is considered nearly if not fully divine. **Travelers to Thailand must take special care never to insult the monarch in any way.** Stand when the Royal Anthem is played (usually before movies and other events); do not speak disparagingly of Royal Family members; and avoid defacing currency and licking stamps (both carry the King's portrait); in short, don't mess with the man, whose name means "Strength of the Land, Incomparable Power."

RELIGION

Thailand enforces some of the strictest laws regarding religious respect. The majority of the nation (around 95%) is deeply devoted to Theravada Buddhism and the religion plays a vital role in the Thai community. Understandably, defacing or harming religious objects and buildings is a definite no-no and punishable by jail terms. Take special care to avoid insulting the religion in any way and try to learn the customs and beliefs of the Thai people.

Visit temples in appropriate attire. Men should wear slacks and a dress shirt; women should wear either a long skirt or pants, with a blouse. Shorts, miniskirts, and tank tops are inappropriate. Shoes may be worn on monastery grounds, but not inside the *bot,* where the principal Buddha image is kept.

Buddha images and amulets are sacred objects and should be treated carefully. Their exportation is prohibited. As fun as it may look, it is unconscionable to climb on a giant Buddha. This will quickly send the offending traveler (and the friend taking a picture from the ground) to jail. It's happened before, so don't be a beanhead.

Buddhist monks are forbidden to come into physical contact with women. Women travelers should always avoid sitting next to Buddhist priests. Women should not hand anything directly to a monk either. She should first hand the object to a man, who will then give it to the priest. If no intermediary is available, the priest may produce a saffron robe on which the woman may place the item.

Muslims, Christians, Jews, Hindus, Sikhs, and Mahayana Buddhists (the other major sect of Buddhism) comprise the remaining five percent of Thailand's population. The religious rights of these groups are, and have always been, despite social upheaval and martial law, guaranteed by the Thai government.

Although not registered as official religions, ancestor worship, Confucianism, (especially among ethnic Chinese) and animism (among the hill-tribes) are also pervasive in Thai society, and complement other beliefs.

WOMEN IN THAILAND

In Thailand, as in most societies, women are not fully equal to their male counterparts and are hemmed in by a variety of legal, religious, and cultural restrictions. Women travelers in the country will find themselves beset by prejudices and double standards. Traditionally, women are expected to remain chaste until marriage, although men can be promiscuous before and after wedlock. Abortion is only available in cases of rape, or in the case of a serious health risk to the mother. "Respectable" women do not go out on the town alone, and unaccompanied women are assumed to be prostitutes. Robert and Nanthapa Cooper observe, in their book *Thailand! Culture Shock,* that women are still referred to as "'the hind legs of the elephant'—which implies that they are just as important as men in terms of economic contribution but that their proper role is at the back, behind their men and supporting them." Restrictions on female advancement in the public sector have driven women into business, where some have been quite successful. The developing economy will probably continue to provide more and more women with opportunities to increase their social standing. Such economic empowerment could well be followed by cultural changes, but until then, the society remains one in which women are subordinate to men.

■■■ THE ARTS

LITERATURE

A recognizably Thai literature emerged at around 1345 AD with the writing of *Traiphum* (or *Traiphumikhatha, Three Worlds*), a Buddhist text based on apocrypha. The foremost work in Thai literature, however, is the *Ramakien,* the Thai interpretation of the Indian epic *Ramayana* which recounts the kidnapping of the consort Nang Sida from her king Phra Ram by a 10-headed, 20-armed demon King Thotsakan. Assisted by the monkey-warrior Hanuman and other allies, the king and his brother Phra Lak travel to Longka (Sri Lanka) to reclaim Nang Sida. **King Rama I** himself authored the longest of three present versions of the Ramakien, incorporating elements of court and contemporary life in Ayutthaya into the story. The other two versions of the Ramakien were composed by King Rama II for the theater.

In contrast to the *Ramakien,* the work *Khun Chang, Khun Phaen* has uniquely Thai origins. This epic love triangle was set in the Ayutthaya period, and its detailed information on Thai customs of that period established it as an important cultural document for scholars. Other classics include *Phra Aphai Mani* and the *Nirats* by the literary giant **Sunthon Phu.** Renowned for his stories written in the vernacular, Sunthon Phu was known throughout the country during his lifetime, an uncommon feat for a man whose profession was normally limited to pleasing the upper echelon of Thai society.

The *nirat* (Travels, or Poem of Farewell) is the most popular genre in classical Thai literature. Early predecessors to the *Let's Go* series, these poems chronicle the journeys of laymen and left a prominent mark on Thailand's literary landscape.

The 20th century has seen a number of important Thai writers. **Dokmai Sot** (b. 1906) was one of two great woman writers who emerged early in this century. Her novels, including *The Good Citizen,* were harsh indictments of modernity, criticizing its impact on traditional Thai life. **K. Surangkhanang** (b. 1911) was also a social critic, but her work focuses on specific problems presented by modernization. *Ying Khon Chua* (*The Prostitute*, 1937) is probably her most important piece. The subtle and elegant novels of **Malai Chuphinit** (b. 1906) discuss humanity's experience with nature. His *Rising Flood* is available in *Thai Short Stories* (Bangkok, 1964). **Srirat Sathapanawat** (b. 1918), journalist, essayist, and fiction writer, has written many works of social criticism focusing on the plight of women and the poor.

A number of new translations and critical studies of Thai literature have appeared in the last few years. Readers may wish to consult *Modern Thai Literature,* by Herbert Phillips (Honolulu: U. of Hawaii Press, 1987) or *Modern Thai Literature: The Process of Modernization and the Transformation of Values,* by Mattani Mojdara Rutnin (Bangkok: Thammasat University Press, 1988). Those interested in writings on Thailand might enjoy Steven Runciman's *A Traveller's Alphabet,* Anne Harriette Leonowens's *The Romance of the Harem,* or George Brewer's *The Siamese Tales.*

DRAMA AND DANCE

Thai classical drama and dance are complementary. The three main types of dramatic media in Thai culture are the *khon,* the *lakhon,* and the *likay.* The first two forms are usually attended by the Thai upper classes, while the *likay* is a phenomenon among poorer Thais, making it the most popular form of the three.

The **khon,** or masked dance drama, is based on Indian dancing and ritual; its various stories come exclusively from the *Ramakien.* During the Ayutthaya period, it was performed only by men; women could not appear on stage until the middle of the 19th century. With the exception of the leading male and female characters, all actors wear elaborate masks. Similar to Greek drama, their verses are recited by a chorus that sits next to a small band. The *khon* is performed with a great deal of stylized action; the movements are suggested by motifs in the music. The original *khon* productions lasted over twenty hours; sleepy audiences and overworked actors prompted later playwrights to shorten their works to a mere three hours.

The **lakhon** is a less structured form of drama but shares some characteristics with the *khon.* Human characters in a *lakhon* do not wear masks; the masks are reserved for monkeys, demons, and other non-human, non-celestial creatures. Like the *khon,* the *lakhon* is derived from the *Ramakien,* but it also adds stories from Thai folk tales and Buddhist *Jakatas.* Dance movements in the three styles of the *lakhon* are far more relaxed than those of *khon. Lakhon chatri* is a simple play usually performed at shrines for the benefit of gods. *Lakhon nai,* traditionally given by women, dramatizes romantic stories and focuses on gentle and graceful movements. The word *nai* means "inside" in Thai, and refers to the fact that performances occurred inside the palace. *Lakhon nok* (*nok* meaning "outside") were once performed by men only and took place beyond the palace walls. It is characterized by quick movements, fast-paced music, and humor. Today, men and women perform in both *lakhon nai* and *lakhon nok*.

In contrast to the *khon* and *lakhon* which are formal and highly stylized, the **likay** is bawdy and humorous. There are no masks, no exquisite costumes, and no tear-jerking scenes—just loud, sharp music, lyrics strewn with lewd innuendos, and on-the-spot improvisation by the performers. *Likay* is often performed at festivals, combining local and court stories to create a workable plot.

MUSIC

The Thais created unique musical instruments and gave them onomatopoeic names such as *krong, chap, ching, krap,* and *pia.* Simpler instruments were combined to create more complex ones. When Thai music assimilated elements of Indian, Mon, and Khmer styles, still more instruments were developed.

The oldest surviving Thai songs were composed during the Sukhothai period. One noteworthy tune, still well-known today, is *Phleng Thep Thong.* In the Ayutthaya period, music was decreed an official part of court life. Imperial expansion brought instruments and musical styles from neighboring regions such as Burma, Malaya, and Java into the court. During this period, the rules defining musical form were introduced. Songs were composed in a form called **Phleng Ruang,** literally a music story, but actually a suite of melodies.

After the fall of Ayutthaya, the growth of Thai music was halted, but the Bangkok period initiated a musical revival: Thai literary masterpieces were translated into musicals, and poets added lyrics to music composed in the Ayutthaya period. The latter half of the 19th century saw the introduction of western instruments, including the violin and cello. Contemporary Thai music has taken all sorts of forms. Local and regional folk music, less studied than Thai classical music, is exceedingly common. One of the most popular styles is **luk thung,** Thai country music, which has developed into fast-paced electronic versions. The northeastern **mo lam** is a well-known folk style; it's fast-paced and features a male and a female vocalist who sing as if courting one another, accompanied by a *khaen.* Younger Thais groove to Thai-style rock 'n' roll and trendy western music.

ARCHITECTURE

During the early part of the Sukhothai period, Thai architecture was greatly influenced by the Khmer in the central and eastern parts of Thailand. Sandstone was the primary building material until brick and later stucco took over. Structures were covered with carved stone and held together with vegetable glue. Ornate thin gold sheets, mother-of-pearl inlay, and porcelain also covered the buildings. In the north, teak and other forms of lumber were the predominant construction materials.

The best examples of Thai architecture are found in Buddhist monasteries. Each age has contributed important structures to the monastery grounds. The *bot* (*ubosoth*), or main chapel, is a tall, oblong building with three highly sloped, superimposed roofs whose highest corners end in sharp points called *chofas.* These *chofas* represent swans, the carriers of Brahma. The *bot,* the most magnificant structure, houses the principal Buddha image and serves as the site of most ceremonies. The *wiharn* is similar in style to the *bot* but holds lesser Buddha images and is primarily used for meetings, meditation, and sermons. The *sala* is an open, gazebo-like structure used for meditaton and preaching.

Some monastic compounds contain a tower called the *phra chedi.* Derived from the Indian *stupa,* the *chedi* is a tapering, spire-like structure with a round or rectangular base that houses the possessions and cremated remains of important people: high priests, members of royalty, and Buddha. *Phra Pathom Chedi* rises 127m above the ground in Nakhon Pathom and is the largest *chedi* in the world.

PAINTING

Thai painting was once limited to murals inside the temples and palaces of Ayutthaya. Little of this work remains, however, as the city was torched by the Burmese in 1767. Thus, the vast majority of extant murals comes from the present Bangkok period. Thai murals are unsigned, and the artists remain unknown.

The scenes in murals are taken either from the *Jatakas* or significant events from contemporary Thai life. Figures are drawn in two dimensions without shadows, and the size of the character determines its relative importance in the story being told. Certain stylistic conventions designate social rank. Members of royalty and celestial beings are given peaceful, majestic forms and stately countenances, while the depiction of commoners is less flattering and more realistic. The emotional gestures employed by muralists resemble those found in *lakhon* and *khon* drama forms.

By the middle of the 19th century, Thai artists imported pigments, greatly enhancing the color and detail of their paintings. In 1933, King Rama VI brought Corrado Feroci to Thailand to establish the country's first art institute. Today, beautiful mural works adorn larger temples, including Wat Phra Kaew and Wat Arun.

■■■ RECREATION

Along with more traditional forms of recreation, Thailand has excellent facilities for all your warm-weather vacation needs. The east coast and the south are especially blessed with water for **sailing, windsurfing, snorkeling, boating,** and **scuba diving.**

MUAY THAI (THAI BOXING)

Muay Thai was developed to keep Thai soldiers battle-ready in the 15th and 16th centuries. The first boxer to win historic recognition was **Nai Khanom Tom.** Captured by the Burmese, he won his freedom after dispatching a dozen Burmese soldiers in a boxing challenge. When word of his amazing feat reached Thailand, King Naresuan and his generals made *Muay Thai* a mandatory part of military training.

Fights are full of ritual, music, blood, sweat, and violence. Every blow imaginable is legal with the exception of head-butting. Fighters go at it for five three-minute rounds, with the winner either knocking his victim into a dizzying malaise or taking the bout by points. Surprisingly, most bouts are decided in the latter manner.

There are 12 weight divisions, and according to aficionados the best action is in the welterweight division. Fights are packed with screaming fans, many of whom have a financial stake in the match. While some provinces have venues, most of the best fighting occurs in Bangkok's Ratchadamnoen Stadium and Lumpini Stadium.

TRADITIONAL PASTIMES

Every year during the hot season, a strong southerly wind allows people to fly their handmade kites high over Bangkok. Kites are often shaped to represent animals such as serpents, fishes, and owls, and are sometimes flown against one another in games of aerial tag. **Kite fighting** is even patronized by the King.

Another popular sport is **takraw,** the only traditional team sport and the only Thai sport that uses a ball. It's somewhat similar to volleyball; players try to hit the ball over a high net and land it on an opponent's side of the court. The difference is that players must use only their feet, knees, elbows, and heads to hit the ball.

In certain regions of the country, crowds watch and bet on **Siamese fighting fish.** The fish are extremely ill-tempered and, when let loose in a tank with another, will battle to the death in a flurry of fins and scales. The fish are so aggressive that they will often kill themselves trying to attack other fish in neighboring jars or tanks. Similar events are staged with cocks.

HILL-TRIBES AND TREKKING

Northern Thailand is home to a diverse group of hill-tribe peoples. Only recently has organized "trekking" become big business, with trips arranged by tour agencies and guest houses in the region. A "trek" is usually a several-day trip into the jungle, combining trucking, hiking, elephant-riding, rafting, and stops at hill-tribe villages.

The flood of camera-toting tourists has spoiled many hill tribe villages, turning them into bastions of ugly commercialism. Be wary of tour guides advertising "newly discovered" or "non-touristy" villages. Ask around when picking a company and talk to fellow travelers; any decent operation will make reports from former customers available. Treks affiliated with guest houses are generally safer bets than the packages arranged by independent organizations. The best expeditions are led by guides who have established a relationship with the residents of a particular village.

In an effort to regulate this industry, the TAT publishes a list of trekking agencies, indicating those that use licensed guides (guides who have studied at the Tribal Research Institute in Chiang Mai). New TAT regulations also require that trekking companies, guides, and customers be registered with the tourist police. They will file a copy of your passport photo page before you set out. Reputable companies are also members of the Jungle Tour Club of Northern Thailand. Make sure your guides speak English and the languages of the villages on your itinerary.

Trek costs vary, depending on duration, destination, starting point, and the number in the group traveling. In Chiang Mai, a three-day, two-night trek including elephant-riding and rafting will cost around 1800฿. From Pai, the same trek could cost 900฿. As insurance becomes mandatory, prices may rise. Begin treks as close as possible to where you want to go. Pure hiking treks are the cheapest.

Most companies provide insurance, food, sleeping arrangements, transportation, and extra supplies like small backpacks, but **check beforehand.** Buy water along the way. Go in a group of eight or fewer; smaller groups are less disruptive to the isolated social systems you will be visiting. If you can afford it, the best way to learn about hill-tribe culture is by hiring a personal guide (about 500฿ per day).

A visit to the Chiang Mai University Tribal Research Institute's museum and library should help acclimate you to the trekking situation, and local bookstores may have good information as well. A particularly good title is John Davies' *A Trekker's Guide to the Hill Tribes of Northern Thailand.* You will benefit more from your experiences if you inform yourself before leaving.

Health and Security

Try to gauge how rigorous the different treks are and check about first aid. Bring a personal kit (even if the company claims they provide it), sunscreen, a hat, mosquito repellent, and long clothing. Some regions contain malarial mosquitoes.

Bandits have been known to raid trekking groups. Before taking a trek, try to find a safe place to leave your valuables while you are gone. The TAT recommends that trekkers leave their valuables in a bank safety deposit box; there have been numerous reports of credit cards being lifted from guest house "security" boxes. Give bandits your belongings if they ask. They've been known to use force when rebuffed.

Opium is a controversial feature of many treks. The fact that it is illegal seems irrelevant in the middle of the jungle, and it may seem cool to try it. Always consider the legal consequences of illegal drug use, however. Remember too that your one-time adventure is an addictive routine for the young men who offer to share with you.

TAT discourages independent trekking. Unfriendly bandits and hill-tribes, KMT, and Shan United Army poppy cultivators get very angry when people wander into their fields. Periodic battles in the border areas are unpleasant places to pick up a little extra shrapnel. Some people have accidently wandered into Burma, and have had great trouble getting back out.

Trekking Etiquette

Don't expect to be welcomed into a village like a long-lost friend. Most villages have seen their fair share of foreigners, and many guides make no attempt to establish any sort of bond with the villagers. Hill-tribes have no control over the organization and staging of treks, though they are the main attraction. **Always ask before taking photographs.** Some people or even whole villages may object. Even if your guide says it's OK, ask permission of the specific people you want to photograph or record on video. Respect people, space and things—particularly hill-tribe beliefs, and be careful about what you touch. For example, the gate at the entrance to Akha villages marks the point past which spirits may not enter; don't touch this. Also, don't wander into people's homes just because there is no door. Ask your guide about particular taboos before entering a village. Be careful about offering gifts; don't give them your Mighty Morphin' Power Rangers t-shirt unless you want them to start looking like you do. Learn how to say "hello," "good-bye," and "thank you," and say these phrases often; consider what it would be like if tourists began to trek through your living room every three days. *The Hill-Tribes of Northern Thailand,* which has a phrasebook section, is available at the Tribal Research Institute, and Lonely Planet puts out the useful *Hill-Tribe Phrasebook.*

The hill-tribe societies are rapidly being integrated into Thai society. Their unique, centuries-old cultures are changing, and there is no question that tourism speeds the process. Many trails are littered with plastic water bottles and trash. Bring bags to pick up after yourself and others.

When to Go

Of Northern Thailand's three distinct seasons, the cool season (Nov.-Feb.) is the best time to go trekking. The vegetation is at its lushest, and temperatures are usually in the mid-20s by day, falling to near freezing at night. In the rainy season (July-Oct.) the paths are muddy, and the raging rivers make rafting fun, but more dangerous. In the hot season (March-June) the land is parched and the air is dry.

■■■ FOOD AND DRINK

In food as in geopolitics, Thailand has always been an independent power. Thai cooking is a tasty blend of Chinese and Indian styles. You can see the Chinese influence in the enthusiasm for stir-frying and in the penchant for bringing together contrasting flavors: sweet, sour, bitter, hot, and salty. Countless curries and stewed dishes provide ample evidence of the cuisine's Indian legacy.

As in most Asian countries, steamed rice is the basis of the traditional Thai meal and is usually accompanied by five to six courses. Any given setting will usually include a clear soup, a curry, a stir-fried dish, and a hot salad, all of which are shared. After dinner, a sweet dessert (perhaps glazed bananas or coconut ice cream) and fresh fruits cap off the meal. The selection of Thai **fruits** is prodigious. Some of the local favorites are jackfruit, lychee, longan, and the pungent durian.

Chilies form the backbone of flavor. They come in all sizes and colors, and vary greatly in their degrees of spiciness. The yellow-orange *phrik luang,* found on plates of the more intrepid Thai epicures, ranks as one of the hottest chilies in the world. *Phrik khi nu,* ("mouse-shit pepper") is also commonly used. Affectionately named for its small size, this slender green chili is slightly less hot than *phrik luang,* and is often a garnish in popular dishes such as *gai phut bai grapao* (chicken with basil leaves), wreaking havoc on the taste buds of the uninitiated. Milder chilies include *phrik yuak* and *phrik chi fa. Phrik thai,* known throughout the world as ground white pepper, rounds out the torrid arsenal and is the most commonly used.

Along with the chilies, the most important spice is coriander. Ginger and garlic often appear in meats or soup bases. Other spices include basil, lemon grass, cloves, cardamom, pandamus, and, in the southern regions, tumeric. For sauces, peanut sauce, stinky fish sauce, shrimp paste, and tangy tamarind sauce are favorites.

Throughout Thailand, food vendors clog sidewalks and alleys, hawking sweets like *kluay buat chii* (banana in coconut milk) and meats like *moo satay* (skewered, barbequed pork). Dirt-cheap restaurants often serve single-entrees like *pad Thai* (fried noodles with egg, meat, peanuts, and vegetables in a light sweet and sour sauce) and *guay tiaw rad naa* (noodle dishes).

Different regions of Thailand boast their own local specialties. The north lays claim to *naem,* a chili-filled sausage of raw pork, and also specializes in dishes like frog curries and roasted beetles. The northeast is known for hearty feasts of *som tam* (papaya salad seasoned with lime, shrimp, chilis, and garlic), *gai yang* (grilled chicken), and *khao niaw* (sticky rice). The south cooks up coastal creations and savory seafood specialties like jellyfish salads and oyster omelettes. The Muslim presence there also brings to the southern table the irrefusable *roti* and various kebabs.

Gaengs, are one of the best known groups of Thai dishes. They vary in spiciness, the meat involved, and curry color, and include coconut milk. *Gaeng* nomenclature is based upon these differences and the intended flavor. Thus, *gaeng kiaw wan gai,* means "green, sweet chicken curry."

Soups and broths represent another large group of dishes. *Gaeng jeut,* literally "bland curry," and *tom yam,* a hot, spicy Thai soup, are the most common. *Gaeng jeut* consists primarily of a chicken soup base with pork, chicken, or vegetables, and is virtually devoid of spices and chilies. On the other hand, *tom yam,* a favorite among Thais, does not shy away from the hotter flavors and is known for piping spiciness tinged with a sour splash of vinegar; *tom yam gung,* with shrimp, lemon grass, and mushrooms, is by far the most prevalent variety.

Noodle dishes, the Asian version of a Big Mac, come in two categories. *Guay tiaw* is a flat, white rice noodle, while *ba mii* is the yellow, chow mein-style noodles with which westerners are more accustomed. Dishes usually come drenched in broiled meats, roasted meats, barbequed meats, or a thick gravy of fried meats.

As for meal-time etiquette, Thais use spoons and forks: it is rare to find a knife on the table. The spoon is considered the main utensil, with the fork pushing food onto the spoon and, occasionally, spearing hard-to-get morsels. Eating with a fork alone would be viewed as uncouth. When eating a shared meal with Thai friends, avoid dropping rice from your plate into the communal entree.

Restaurants sometimes display a *shell chuan chim,* "Shell invites you to eat," sign. A few years ago, the Shell Oil Company combed the nation looking for exceptional, inexpensive restaurants and awarded signs to establishments that impressed. These round signs are written in Thai, but you can spot them by their pointy "S" logo.

DRINK

Officially prohibited from drinking by Buddhism, Thais still indulge in their fair share of liquor, although not at meal time. Despite the protests of local fans, it's safe to say that the nation has not developed any exceptional proficiency in brewing, distilling, or fermenting. The two main beers in Thailand are Singha Beer and Kloster Beer. Singha is the cheaper of the two, the leader in sales and that great formaldehyde taste. Iced coffee with cream is a soothing dessert drink, as are shakes and *lassis* (a sweet fragrant refresher derived from the Indian drink of the same name). Energy drinks like Lipovitan are popular among bus drivers and Bangkok taxi jockeys. The liquid comes in a small bottle packed with enough vitamins, sugar, and caffeine to fight off the drowsiness that comes with carbon monoxide poisoning.

Central Thailand

The fertile central region of Thailand, also known as the Chao Phraya River Basin, stretches from Hua Hin in the south all the way up to Nakhon Sawan in the north. The people of the region speak the central Thai dialect, which is considered normal conversational Thai. As a region, its people are the wealthiest, in large part because Bangkok is its major metropolis.

Historically, the area has supported great cultures and civilizations with its fields of rice, but has also strained under the devastation of numerous wars. World War II and numerous conflicts with the Burmese have redefined borders several times and left ruins, both ancient and modern, strewn about the countryside. The area now

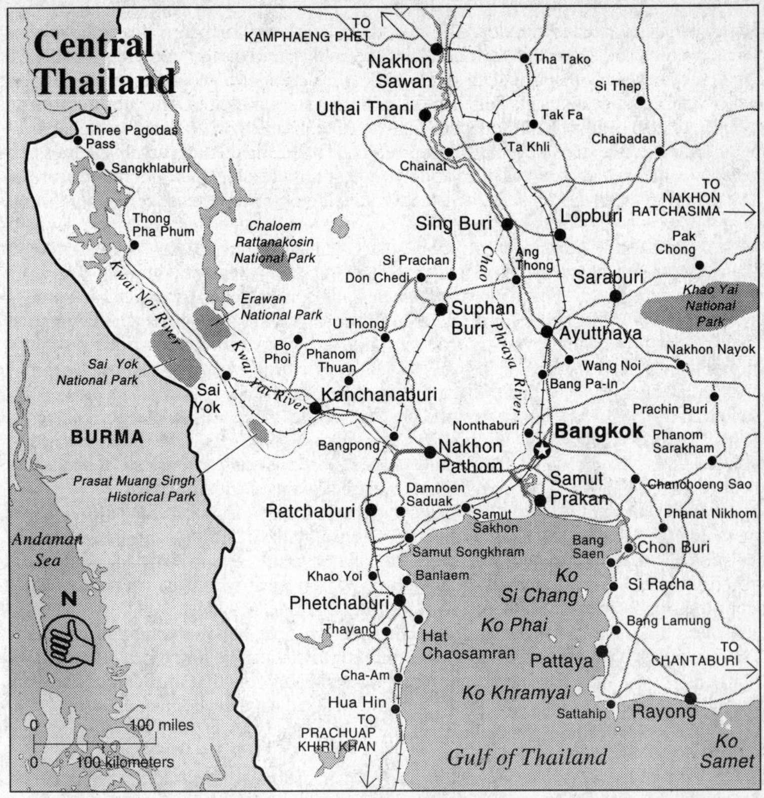

seems to have entered a period of relative calm and prosperity. There is talk of opening the border between Burma and Thailand—an amazing leap of progress, considering the long tensions between the two. But in the shadow of high diplomacy, the Mon and Karen people wage an unacknowledged struggle for survival as their culture and existence continue to be eroded by political oppression, economic modernization, and, in the past decade, touristic invasion.

Ayutthaya constantly inspires awe with the magnitude of its temple ruins and monuments. Lush green landscapes fanning west of Bangkok are the background for Kanchanaburi, which attracts travelers to the banks of the River Kwai and the province's many national parks. Southbound buses and trains wind their way through the beginnings of peninsular Thailand, a teaser for the snady playgrounds of the south. Due to the proximity to Bangkok, the beaches here attract local travelers and are not overrun with *farang*. In the middle of it all, Bangkok serves as the region's, and the country's, hub—the massive brain, for the body that is Thailand.

■■■ BANGKOK

Bangkok's Thai name, Krung Thep, means "City of Angels." Like its American equivalent, however, it often seems a few cherubs short of the celestial city. Whole showrooms of BMWs and Mercedes meet at each intersection, spewing carbon monoxide. Seething legions fight for territory on the sidewalks and protrude from the orifices of every bus. The unsleeping, predatory heat and humidity reduce crisp clothing to saline sludge in seconds, coating exposed skin with a sweat-soot gel.

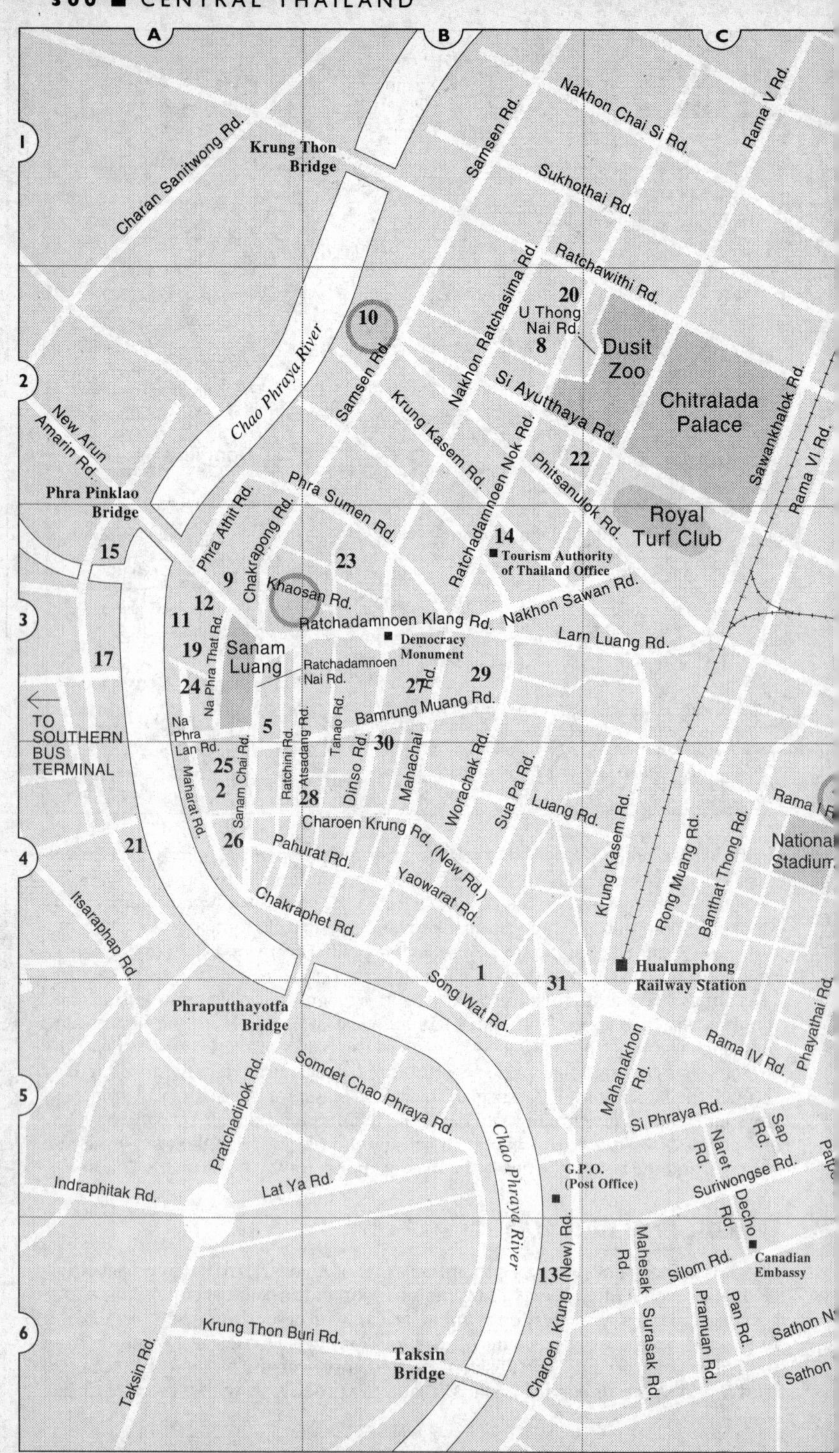

A
B
C
1
2
3
4
5
6
Krung Thon Bridge
Charan Sanitwong Rd.
Samsen Rd.
Nakhon Chai Si Rd.
Rama V Rd.
Sukhothai Rd.
Ratchawithi Rd.
Nakhon Ratchasima Rd.
20
U Thong Nai Rd.
8
Dusit Zoo
10
Chao Phraya River
Samsen Rd.
Krung Kasem Rd.
Si Ayutthaya Rd.
Chitralada Palace
Sawankhalok Rd.
Rama VI Rd.
New Arun Amarin Rd.
Ratchadamnoen Nok Rd.
22
Phitsanulok Rd.
Phra Pinklao Bridge
Phra Athit Rd.
Chakrapong Rd.
Phra Sumen Rd.
Royal Turf Club
14
Tourism Authority of Thailand Office
15
23
9
Khaosan Rd.
Ratchadamnoen Klang Rd.
Nakhon Sawan Rd.
12
11
Larn Luang Rd.
Democracy Monument
19
Na Phra That Rd.
Sanam Luang
17
Ratchadamnoen Nai Rd.
29
24
27
Rd.
TO SOUTHERN BUS TERMINAL
Na Phra Lan Rd.
5
Bamrung Muang Rd.
Ratchini Rd.
Atsadang Rd.
Tanao Rd.
Dinso Rd.
30
Mahachai
Worachak Rd.
Sua Pa Rd.
25
Sanam Chai Rd.
2
28
Maharat Rd.
Luang Rd.
Krung Kasem Rd.
Rong Muang Rd.
Banthat Thong Rd.
Rama I Rd.
National Stadium
21
26
Charoen Krung Rd. (New Rd.)
Pahurat Rd.
Yaowarat Rd.
Itsaraphap Rd.
Chakraphet Rd.
1
31
Hualumphong Railway Station
Song Wat Rd.
Phraputthayotfa Bridge
Mahanakhon Rd.
Rama IV Rd.
Phayathai Rd.
Pratchadipok Rd.
Somdet Chao Phraya Rd.
Si Phraya Rd.
Sap Rd.
Naret Rd.
Suriwongse Rd.
G.P.O. (Post Office)
Indraphitak Rd.
Lat Ya Rd.
Decho Rd.
Chao Phraya River
Canadian Embassy
Charoen Krung (New) Rd.
Mahesak Rd.
Silom Rd.
13
Surasak Rd.
Pramuan Rd.
Pan Rd.
Krung Thon Buri Rd.
Taksin Rd.
Taksin Bridge
Sathon

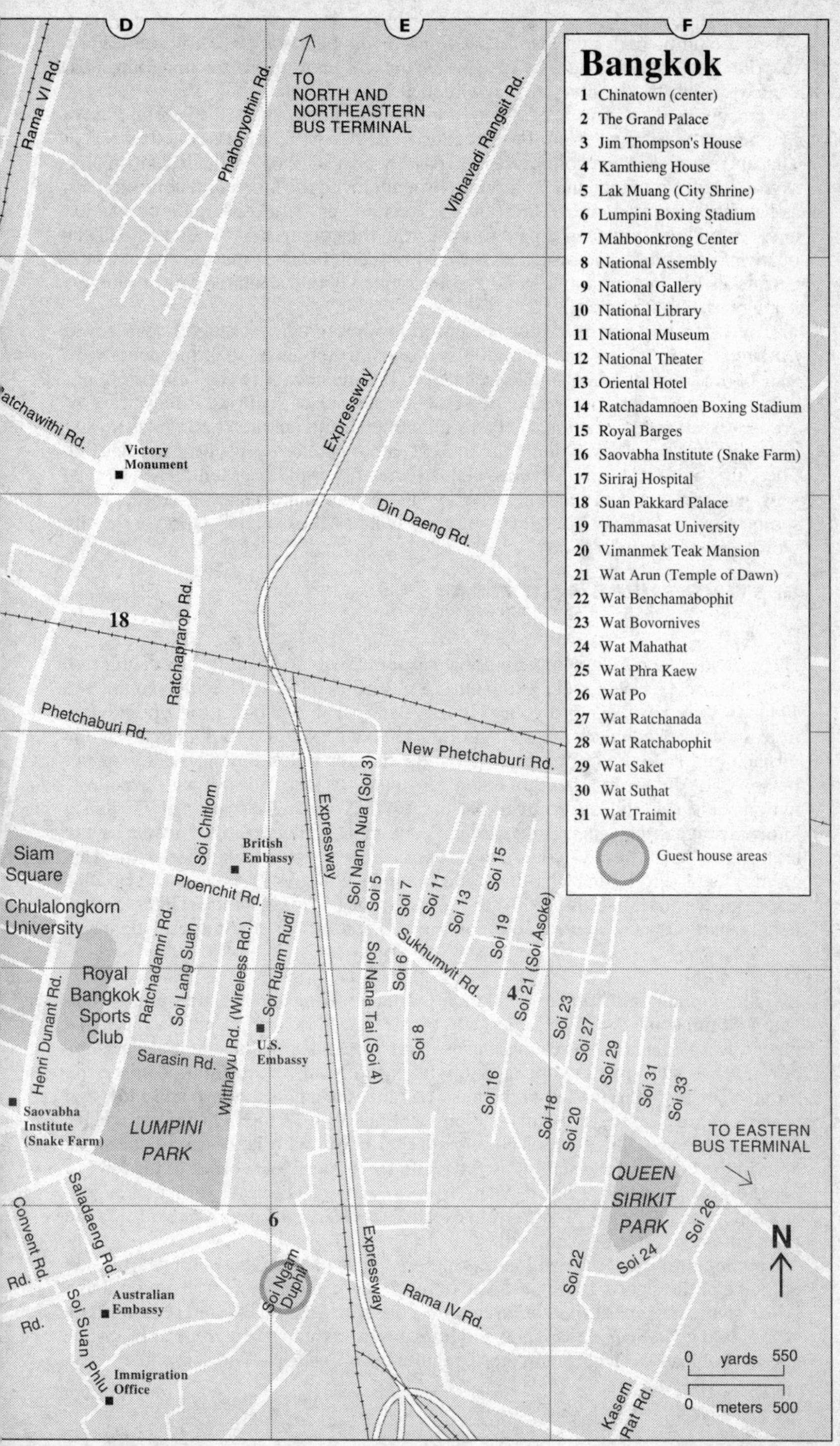

D
E
F
Bangkok
1 Chinatown (center)
2 The Grand Palace
3 Jim Thompson's House
4 Kamthieng House
5 Lak Muang (City Shrine)
6 Lumpini Boxing Stadium
7 Mahboonkrong Center
8 National Assembly
9 National Gallery
10 National Library
11 National Museum
12 National Theater
13 Oriental Hotel
14 Ratchadamnoen Boxing Stadium
15 Royal Barges
16 Saovabha Institute (Snake Farm)
17 Siriraj Hospital
18 Suan Pakkard Palace
19 Thammasat University
20 Vimanmek Teak Mansion
21 Wat Arun (Temple of Dawn)
22 Wat Benchamabophit
23 Wat Bovornives
24 Wat Mahathat
25 Wat Phra Kaew
26 Wat Po
27 Wat Ratchanada
28 Wat Ratchabophit
29 Wat Saket
30 Wat Suthat
31 Wat Traimit
Guest house areas
Rama VI Rd.
Phahonyothin Rd.
TO NORTH AND NORTHEASTERN BUS TERMINAL
Vibhavadi Rangsit Rd.
Ratchawithi Rd.
Victory Monument
Expressway
Din Daeng Rd.
18
Ratchaprarop Rd.
Phetchaburi Rd.
New Phetchaburi Rd.
Soi Chitlom
British Embassy
Soi Nana Nua (Soi 3)
Soi 5
Soi 7
Soi 11
Soi 13
Soi 15
Soi 19
Soi 21 (Soi Asoke)
Siam Square
Chulalongkorn University
Ploenchit Rd.
Sukhumvit Rd.
Royal Bangkok Sports Club
Henri Dunant Rd.
Ratchadamri Rd.
Soi Lang Suan
Witthayu Rd. (Wireless Rd.)
Soi Ruam Rudi
U.S. Embassy
Soi Nana Tai (Soi 4)
Soi 6
Soi 8
4
Soi 16
Soi 18
Soi 20
Soi 22
Soi 23
Soi 27
Soi 29
Soi 31
Soi 33
Sarasin Rd.
Saovabha Institute (Snake Farm)
LUMPINI PARK
TO EASTERN BUS TERMINAL
QUEEN SIRIKIT PARK
Soi 24
Soi 26
6
Convent Rd.
Saladaeng Rd.
Soi Ngam Duphli
Rama IV Rd.
N
Rd.
Rd.
Australian Embassy
Soi Suan Phlu
Immigration Office
Kasem Rat Rd.
0 yards 550
0 meters 500

When the umpteenth tout insists that your life will be incomplete without his tuk-tuk ride, his Thai massage, or his sister, you will be forgiven for imagining that Bangkok is just modernity gone haywire in a muggier climate.

Certainly Bangkok was not fashioned in a design studio under the careful gaze of planners; it was hewn from unsuspecting paddies by the double-edged sword of Thailand's burgeoning economy. In the past two decades, the standard of living has skyrocketed: Nintendo, and Lexus have brought joy to the lives of millions of Thais, as have modern medicine, education, and technology. An ever-surging population of seven million, however, saps resources from the countryside, swamps the inadequate infrastructure, and brutalizes the environment. Bangkok may be one of Southeast Asia's leading economic centers, but the newly built high-rises must pierce a smoggy haze to find the sky.

The city's idiosyncratic modernization is something of a marvel. Wide-eyed *farang* witness trigger-happy Buddhist monks preserving Kodak moments with state-of-the-art camcorders, while well-heeled businessmen set aside cellular phones to pray at wayside shrines. As the permanent residence of the Royal Family, the government seat, and the nation's center of commerce and culture, it comes as no surprise that this tinsel town offers the most creature comforts anywhere in Thailand. The city's sights are impressive as well: an array of magnificent temples, historical sites, parks, monuments, and museums will stall your camera shutter. And in more serene moments, the open-minded observer will find the everyday fabric of the city worthy of thoughtful scrutiny.

GETTING THERE AND AWAY

By Air

Flights land at **Don Muang International Airport**, 25km north of the city center (tel. 535 1254 or 535 1386 for departure info.; 535 1301 or 535 1310 for arrival info.; 535 1111 for directory). To find your way into Bangkok, buy a ticket for a public taxi from an authorized vendor to the left of the left-hand exit (200-300฿ per car). A limousine counter to the right of the left-hand exit offers rides to any hotel (500฿ per person). For the thrifty, the right exit leads to the bus stop. A list of bus fares, destinations, and schedules is available at the **TAT (Tourist Authority of Thailand) information center** (open 8am-midnight), the middle counter in the row near the exit. Across from the TAT counter are several currency **exchange booths**; the Thai Military Bank and Krung Thai Bank are open 24 hours. A **24-hour tourist police booth** near the right-hand exit offers English-speaking assistance. Flights out of Bangkok are subject to **taxes**: 200฿ for international and 30฿ for domestic flights.

By Train

All trains coming into Bangkok end their journies at Bangkok's **Hualamphong Railway Station,** Rama IV Rd. (tel. 223 7010 or 223 7020). Hualamphong is a perpetual madhouse. The dearth of seating means that travelers sprawl on the floor; remember never to step over anyone as that will expose your feet to the person on the ground. Inside and to the left of the main entrance are a **police booth** and a **luggage storage center** (open daily 4am-10:30pm; 20฿ per day). To the right are newspaper stands and food stalls. There is an **information booth** with English schedules and fares in the center of the station by the platforms. Around the corner to the left is a Bangkok Bank **exchange booth** (8am-6:30pm) with a 24-hour ATM that takes Visa and American Express for cash advances. There is also a small **post office** outside the main entrance (open 8:30am-5pm).

Hopping into one of the numerous metered taxis or tuk-tuks waiting at the side entrance of the station is the best way to reach town. Otherwise, walk down Rama IV Rd. (which begins at the station) to find a bus stop. A/C bus #1 and regular buses #25 and 40 go to Siam Square and continue down Sukhumvit Rd.; regular bus #109 goes to Robinson's Department Store; regular bus #53 goes to Banglamphu.

Ignore touts offering free advice outside the station; there are rip-off artists everywhere looking for plump foreign wallets.

By Bus

The national bus transportation system is cheap and extensive. For virtually every destination, there is the choice of either an A/C (blue) or a non-A/C (orange) bus. Doing without A/C will typically halve the cost of traveling, but you will pay with your health. Hours of sucking up car exhaust fumes and being bombarded by raucous sounds can be excruciating. Fares listed are for A/C buses; non-A/C is approximately half. Outbound buses leave from four different terminals in Bangkok depending upon the destination. Beware of touts and other artful dodgers at bus stations, and safeguard your valuables.

Eastern Bus Terminal, Sukhumvit Rd., before Soi 42 (for A/C tel. 392 9227 or 391 9829; for non-A/C tel. 391 2504 or 392 2521). Take local A/C bus #1, 8, 11, or 13, or regular bus #2, 25, 38, 40, 48, or 98. Open 24 hrs. To: **Trat** (14 daily, 6-7hr., 140฿); **Si Racha** (every 40 min., 5:40am-8pm, 2hr., 52฿).

Northeastern Bus Terminal, Phahonyothin Rd. near Chatuchak Park (for A/C tel. 279 4484, through -87; for non-A/C tel. 271 0101, through -05). To get to the terminal take local A/C bus #2, 3, 9, 10, 12, or 13, or regular bus #26, 34, 39, 63, 104, or 112. To: **Nakhon Ratchasima (Khorat)** (every 15min., 7:15am-10:30pm, 5-6hr., 115฿); **Khon Kaen** (18 daily, 8-9hr., 193฿); and **Ubon Ratchathani** on the new route (7 daily, including 1 VIP bus at 8pm; 9-11hr.; 287฿, VIP 400฿).

Northern Bus Terminal, same location and phone number as Northeastern Bus Terminal. To: **Chiang Mai** (15 daily, 10-11hr., 352฿); Sukhothai (3 daily, 7hr., 218฿); and **Ayutthaya** (every 30min., 6am-6:30pm, 1-½-2hr., 40฿).

Southern Regular Bus Terminal, Boromat Chonnani (Pinklao-Nakhonchaisi) Rd. (tel. 434 5557-58). To get to the terminal take regular bus #124 or 127. To: **Phuket** (daily, 6 and 8pm (1 VIP); 14hr.; 380฿; VIP 570฿) and **Kanchanaburi** (every 15min., 5:30am-8pm, 2hr., 62฿).

In Bangkok, **beware of people selling gems.** This is one of the most common cons, especially in heavily touristed areas, such as Khaosan Rd. and the Grand Palace Compound. Touts may befriend you and present themselves as sincere, trustworthy folks who just happen to know about a great one-week no-tax deal on gems. There are no such government specials, and government export agencies do not exist. Your new friend may accompany you to temples and restaurants, until you "end up" at the gem store, and they receive their commission. If you buy expensive items in Bangkok, especially gems, you are taking a big risk.

ORIENTATION

Bangkok's raw urban sprawl lacks any formal districting, making navigation a daunting challenge for the uninitiated. Tourists can make sense of the most important areas of the city by thinking of it as roughly L-shaped. The northernmost district of interest is **Dusit.**. Lying farther south along the **Chao Phraya River** is the **Banglamphu/Ko Rattanakosin area,** the original part of the capital built by King Rama I in 1782. Ko Rattanakosin normally refers to the southern half of the district, thick with palaces and temples, while Banglamphu describes the enclave of cheap lodgings around Khaosan Rd.. Farther south along the river lurks the **Yaowarat/Pahurat area,** otherwise known as Chinatown and Indiatown. Gold shops and Chinese-owned guest houses adorn the area on and around Yaowarat Rd., while a sizeable Indian community has settled in the area around Chakraphet Rd. The southernmost district along the Chao Phraya is **Silom,** or the **Financial District,** centering on Silom Rd., which runs east-west, home to raunchy Patpong Rd. Turning the corner of the L and moving north and east of Silom, you will encounter the **Siam Square/Pratunam area,** Bangkok's prime shopping district, straddling Rama I Rd. Farther east, the last main area of Bangkok is the **Sukhumvit Road area,** named for the road that is the extension of Rama I Rd. Many wealthy Thais have built homes on side streets off this main thoroughfare. Eventually, Sukhumvit turns into Sukhumvit Highway and travels toward Samut Prakan.

GETTING AROUND

Maneuvering in the city is a nightmare on wheels. Transit authorities are feverishly brainstorming on plans to relieve the horrendous traffic congestion. In the works are more expressways, more highways, and a light rail system. For now, every hour is rush hour, and you can expect to be bogged down in a vehicular morass even at 3am. Avoid the gaping jaws of the traffic monster by traveling between 10am and 4pm during the day, and after 7pm for your evening jaunts. Tangled tie-ups occur between 4pm and 7pm, when traffic moves an average of 4km per hour and the fumes are so thick you can (and will) eat them.

By Bus

The shiny, happy bus system, run by the Bangkok Metropolitan Transit Authority (BMTA), supplies the most inexpensive and efficient means of transportation. Routes are extensive and usually serviced by a large number of buses, meaning minimal waiting time for the next bus. There are three types of buses: blue-and-white regular buses (no fan or A/C), red-and-cream regular buses (fan-cooled), and dark blue-and-white A/C buses. The fare on the blue-and-white bus, which is slowly being phased out, is 2.5฿, while the more common red-and-cream bus charges 3.5฿. The fare on an A/C bus depends on the distance traveled (6-16฿). Pay all fares to the uniformed officer who walks through the bus.

The fiery orange-red and the pea-green buses (3.5฿ and 2.5฿ respectively), also run by the BMTA, are smaller, pernicious contraptions with no published routes. Since route numbers are often duplicated, make sure you get on the right type of bus, not just the right route number. Grrr.

Airport buses run 6am-8pm; most other buses run 5am-midnight or a bit later. Night services charge more, but they are few and far between.

When boarding a bus, only the quick and surefooted survive: bus drivers sometimes pull off as soon as the last passengers are through the door, which is often left open. Sit (or, more likely, stand) near the front of the bus; it will be easier to get off and to avoid pickpockets. Since traffic travels on the left side of the road, sitting on the left (curb) side of non-A/C buses lessens the risk of asphyxiation. If you need help identifying your destination, ask the fare collector (not the driver). The following is a list of the major bus routes:

Regular Buses (Light Blue-and-White)

#1: Wat Po—Yaowarat Rd. (Chinatown)—General Post Office—Oriental Hotel.

#15: Banglamphu (Phra Athit Rd., Phra Sumen Rd.)—Sanam Luang—Democracy Monument—Wat Saket—Siam Sq.—Ratchadamri Rd.—Lumpini Park—along Silom Rd.

#18 and 28: Vimarnmek Teak Museum—Dusit Zoo—Chitlada Palace—Victory Monument.

#25: Wat Phra Kaew—Wat Po-Charoen Krung Rd.—Rama IV Rd. (near Hualamphong Railway Station)—Phayathai Rd.—Mahboonkrong Center—Siam Sq.—World Trade Center—Ploenchit Rd.—Sukhumvit Rd. to outer Bangkok.

#48: Sanam Chai Rd. (just east of Wat Po)—Bamrung Muang Rd.—Siam Sq.—all along Sukhumvit Rd.

#53: Samsen Rd. (National Library)—Phra Athit Rd.—Sanam Luangt—Wat Po—near Pahurat and Yaowarat.

#59: Airport—Victory Monument—Pahonyothin Rd. (American Express office)—Phetburi Rd.—Lanluang—Democracy Monument—Sanam Luang.

#74: Rama IV Rd. (outside Soi Ngam Duphli)—Lumpini Park—Ratchadamri Rd.—World Trade Center—Pratunam-Ratchaprarop Rd.—Victory Monument.

#115: Silom—Rama IV Rd. (near Soi Ngam Duphli)—all along Rama IV Rd. until it meets Sukhumvit Rd.

#116: Sathon Nua Rd.—all along Rama IV Rd. (passes near Soi Ngam Duphli)—Sathon Tai Rd.

#204: Victory Monument—Ratchaprarop Rd.—World Trade Center—Siam Sq.—Bamrung Muang Rd.

Air-Conditioned Buses (Dark Blue-and-White)

#1: Wat Po—Charoen Krung Rd.—Rama IV Rd. (near Hualamphong Railway Station)—Phayathai (Mahboonkrong Center)—Siam Sq.—along Sukhumvit Rd.

#8: Sanam Luang—Bamrung Muang—Rama I—Ploenchit—Sukhumvit to outer Bangkok.

#10: National Assembly (Ratchawithi Rd.)—Dusit Zoo—Chitlada Palace—Victory Monument—Phahonyothin Rd. (American Express office)—Don Muang International Airport.

#11: Banglamphu Guest House Area (around Chakrapong Rd.)—Phra Sumen Rd.—Democracy Monument (Ratchadamnoen Klang Rd.)—Phetchaburi Rd.—World Trade Center—Sukhumvit.

#15: Silom Rd. (corner of Silom and Charoen Krung)—Patpong and Bangkok Christian Hospital—Lumpini Park and Chulalongkorn Hospital—Ratchaprarop Rd. (near Victory Monument)—Din Daeng Rd.

By Taxi

Formerly, all fares were negotiable, but a 1992 law banned most bargaining and introduced metered cabs (35฿ for 1km and 2฿ for each additional km or each minute spent stuck in traffic). Non-metered taxis are still around; but they are rapidly disappearing as more passengers. Unless you insist otherwise, taxi drivers may shut off the meter and attempt to bargain for a set fare; this can be particularly problematic for farang.

By Tuk-Tuk

Like taxis, tuk-tuks (motor-tricycles) abound, and usually idle at the same locations as their four-wheeled brethren. Nimble tuk-tuks can slither through dense traffic that brings taxis to a halt. Skillful negotiators can find fares that are at least 30% cheaper than taxi fares, but risk contracting an acute case of "black lung" from exposure to Bangkok pollution.

By Motorcycle Taxi

Motorcycle taxis in Bangkok are usually identifiable by their drivers, who wear brightly colored vests. Located where taxis and tuk-tuks congregate, motorcycle taxis can zip through stand-still traffic and cost 10-25% less than tuk-tuks. Riding on a motorcycle taxi can be a risky affair, though. A helmet is provided for passengers, for what it's worth.

By Car

Renting a car in Bangkok is not a bright idea, considering the ghoulish traffic and the perils of metro-motoring. A small sedan typically 1000-1500฿ per day. Weekly rates run around 6000-8000฿. Insurance is extra (around 250฿). An international driver's permit and major credit cards are required. **Avis,** 2/12 Witthayu Rd. (tel. 255 5300, through -04). **Hertz,** 420 Sukhumvit Rd. 71 (tel. 391 0461). **National,** Maniya Building, 518/2 Ploenchit Rd. (tel. 255 6837).

By Boat

The most convenient, expedient, and peaceful way to travel along the Chao Phraya River is by river-taxi—wooden boats along the back canals of the city. Boats run on a set route (every 10 min.) from early morning until 7pm. Fares are 4-6฿ in most of downtown areas. The main stops, from north to south, are: **Thewet** (for the National Library and Dusit guest houses), **Phra Athit** (for Khaosan Rd.-Banglamphu), **Rot Fai** (for Thonburi Railway Station and Royal Barges), **Chang** (for Wat Phra Kaew and Royal Palace), **Tiei** (for Wat Pho), **Ratchawong** (for Chinatown and Hualamphong), **Si Phraya** (for GPO) and **Oriental** (for the Oriental Hotel and Silom). Don't confuse river taxis with smaller ferries which shuttle across the river from each landing for 1฿. A small sign identifies each pier (*tha*). State your destination to a ferry-worker or local—they will tell you where to disembark. Other services run as far upstream as Nonthaburi and Ayutthaya. Ask at any pier for details.

PRACTICAL INFORMATION

The Latest Edition Tour 'n Guide Map to Bangkok, Thailand, available at DK Book House (see English Bookstores) and at many tourist shops and guest houses, is a don't-leave-home-without-it map of Bangkok (35฿). It includes all city bus and boat routes as well as important sights and landmarks. See Media below or Essentials for more information.

Tourist Information: TAT, 372 Bamrung Muang Rd. (tel. 226 0060, 226 0072, 226 0085, or 226 0098; fax 224 6221). Take regular bus #15 or A/C bus #8; get off as soon as it turns onto Bamrung Muang heading away from Banglamphu. The office is at the intersection, inside the main courtyard underneath the water tower. A staff blessed with more enthusiasm than knowledge or resources dispenses glossy leaflets with gay abandon. Open daily 8:30am-4:30pm.

Tourist Police: Division I, Unico House, 4th fl., 29/1 Soi Lang Suan, Ploenchit Rd. (tel. 652 1720). Take regular buses #25, 40, 48, which stop near the corner of Ploenchit and Soi Lang Suan. English-speaking staff totals 500 and is vested with the same powers as the regular police. Also handles lost and found Open daily 8am-4pm. **24-hr. booth,** opposite Dusit Thani Hotel in Lumpini Park (tel. 253 9560/1). Regular bus #141, A/C bus #4, 5. **24-hr. booth,** Don Muang International Airport (tel. 535 1641), 1st-floor lobby. Vans roam popular areas 24 hrs. **Emergency:** tel. 1699. **Tourist Assistance Center:** tel. 282 8129 or 281 5051; daily 8am-midnight.

Budget Travel: Many areas of Bangkok, especially tourist centers such as Khaosan Rd. and Soi Ngam Duphli, are replete with budget travel offices, which are often a part of or affiliated to a guest house. In Thailand, a truly legitimate "budget" travel agency, however, is as hard to come by as cheap Barbra Streisand concert seats. "VIP" tickets, often costing hundreds of extra baht, may actually only mean a spot at the front of the bus. **STA Travel,** Wall St. Tower, 14th fl., 33 Suriwongse Rd. (tel. 233 2582 or 233 2626). Take regular bus #15 or A/C bus #5 to Silom Rd.; cut through Patpong Rd. to Suriwongse. Open Mon.-Fri. 8:30am-5pm, Sat. 8:30am-noon. **Branch office** at the Thai Hotel on 78 Prachathipathai Rd. (tel. 281 5314/5). **ETC Travel,** Royal Hotel, Rm. 318, 2 Ratchadamnoen Klang Ave. (tel. 224 4800-02 or 224 0043; fax 287 1478), near Atsadang Rd. Take regular bus #15. Member FIYTO. Open Mon.-Sat. 8:30am-5pm. **Branch offices** also at 180 Khaosan Rd., next to BKK Photo Lab and at 5/3 Soi Ngam Duphli, near the Quality Hotel.

Embassies and Consulates: Australia, 37 Sathon Tai Rd. (tel. 287 2680; fax 287 2029). Regular bus #17, 22, 62, 67, 106, 116, 149. New passport 1880฿ for adults, 950฿ for children. 3-day processing. Open Mon.-Fri. 8:15am-12:15pm. **Cambodia,** 185 Ratchadamri Rd. (tel. 254 6630). Consular services around the corner off Sarasin Rd. on the 1st soi on the left. Open Mon.-Fri. 8-11am. **Canada,** 11/F Boonmitr Bldg., 138 Silom Rd. (tel. 237 4126; fax 236 6463). Regular bus #115; A/C bus #2, 4, 5. Consular services Mon.-Fri. 8-11am. New passport 640฿; 1 week for processing. **Indonesia,** 600 New Phetchburi Rd. (tel. 252 3135-40). Open Mon.-Fri. 8:30am-noon and 1:30-3:30pm. **Ireland,** 205 United Flour Mill Bldg., 11th fl., Ratchawong Rd. (tel. 223 0876). Take a cab. New passport 1900฿, extension 600฿; 2 week processing. Open Mon.-Fri. 9am-noon and 1:30-4pm. **Laos,** Soi Rankapeng 39 Open Mon.-Fri. 9am-noon.Visa 300฿. 2-day processing. **Malaysia,** 35 S. Sathorn Rd. (tel. 286 1390-02). Open Mon.-Fri. 8:30-11:30am. **New Zealand,** 93 Witthayu (Wireless) Rd. (tel. 251 8165; fax 235 9045). Regular bus #13, 17, 62, 106. New passport 1800฿ for adults, 900฿ under 16; 1-week processing. Open Mon.-Fri. 8:30-11:30am. **Singapore,** 129 S. Sathorn Rd., (tel. 286 2111; fax 286 1434). Open Mon.-Fri. 8:30am-noon. **South Africa,** 6/F Park Palace, 231 Soi Sarasin, Ratdamri Rd., (tel. 253 8473-5; fax 243 8477). **UK,** 1031 Witthayu

(Wireless) Rd. (tel. 253 0191). Regular bus #13, 17, 62, 76. Consulate on the 2nd floor. New passport 720฿, subject to change. 1-week processing. Open Mon.-Thurs. 8-11am, Fri. 8am-noon. **US,** 95 Witthayu (Wireless) Rd. (tel. 252 5040-09; fax 254 2990). Regular bus #13, 17, 62, 106. Consular services Mon.-Fri. 7:30-10am. New passport 1375฿; 3-day processing. **Vietnam,** 83/1 Wireless Rd., (tel. 251 7202; fax 254 2990). Open Mon.-Fri. 8:30-11:30am and 1:30-4pm. Visas 1200฿ 3-4 day processing.

Currency Exchange: At least one exchange booth on every block in tourist areas; stiff competition keeps their rates almost equal. **Union Bank of Bangkok (Banglamphu),** in the middle of Khaosan Rd. next to Grand Guest House; also under the Vista Travel sign near Chakrapong Rd. Open daily 7:30am-9pm. **Bangkok Metropolitan Bank Money Exchange (Silom/Financial),** corner of Suriwongse Rd. and Patpong 2 Rd. Open daily 1-11pm (for night owls). **Bangkok Bank (Sukhumvit Rd.),** Soi 4 (Nana Tai) Sukhumvit Rd., at the mouth of Nana Plaza. Open daily 7am-10pm.

American Express Office: Head office in IBM Building, 388 Pahonyothin Rd. (open Mon.-Fri. 8:30am-5pm, tel. 273 0044 or 273 0033); **branch office** and all **mail holding** at **Sea Tours Co. Ltd,** Siam Center, Suite 413-414, 965 Rama I Rd. 10330 (tel. 251 4862 or 255 2080). Mail held for 60 days; no packages accepted. Open Mon.-Fri. 8:30am-noon and 1-4:30pm, Sat. 8:30-11:30am. Credit card authorization: call 273 0022 (24 hrs.). Lost traveler's checks: call 273 5296.

General Post Office (GPO): on Charoen Krung Rd. (tel. 234 9530 or 233 1050). Regular bus #1, 16, 35, 75, 93. To pick up **poste restante** mail (held for 2 months), bring picture ID, passport number, and 1฿ per letter. Poste restante open Mon.-Fri. 8am-8pm, Sat. 8am-1pm. Have friends address letters: John SCHOELLERMAN, beach king (or name of addressee), c/o Poste Restante, General Post Office, Bangkok, Thailand 10500. **Packaging booth.** Boxes of varying sizes 5-35฿. open Mon.-Fri. 8:30am-4:30pm, Sat. 9am-noon. **Express Mail Service (EMS),** to Europe in 1-3 days, North America in 2-3 days. **EMS** and **normal mailing hours** are Mon.-Fri. 8am-8pm, Sat.-Sun. 8am-1pm. Next to the packaging booth is the **telegram office,** an A/C oasis in the midst of a busy, hot post office.

Branch post offices: Banglamphu, on the soi behind Sweety Guest House, parallel to Ratchadamnoen Klang Rd. near Khaosan Rd. Open Mon.-Fri. 8am-5pm, Sat. 8am-noon. Overseas telephone office on 2nd floor; go up the stairs outside the back of the building. Open daily 7am-11pm. **Silom/Financial,** 113/6-7 Suriwongse Center Rd., near Soi Than Tawan. Overseas phone. Open Mon.-Fri. 8:30am-4:30pm, Sat. 9am-noon. **Sukhumvit Rd.,** 118-122 Sukhumvit Rd. (tel. 251 7972), between Soi 4 (Nana Tai) and the Landmark Plaza. Small and always crowded. EMS and overseas calls. Open Mon.-Fri. 8:30am-5:30pm, Sat. 9am-noon. Another is at Soi 23, Sukhumvit Rd. (tel. 258 4197), on the right. EMS and overseas calls. Open Mon.-Fri. 8:30am-5:30pm, Sat. 9am-noon.

Telephones: To make **domestic calls,** look for "Fonepoint" (coin) or "Cardphone" (card) booths, usually clustered in business and tourist centers. Make **international telephone calls** at hotels, businesses, and some post offices (see above) or at the **Communications Authority of Thailand (CAT) Telecom Center,** Charoen Krung Rd., next to the GPO. Open 24 hrs. The CAT Telecom Center has fax and telex services. **Telephone code** (including Nonthaburi, Samut Prakan, and Pathum Thani): 02.

Luggage Storage: Hualamphong Railway Station, Rama IV Rd. (tel. 223 7010-20). Regular bus #25, 29, 34, 40, 53, 109. 20฿ per day. Open daily 4am-10:30pm. Also at most guest houses (for guests only) for 5฿ per day; security may be iffy.

English Language Visual Media: The Nation and the **Bangkok Post** are the two national dailies (12฿). Decent foreign news, good local events listings and entertainment coverage. Available at most newsstands in the city. Also available are the Singapore edition of the **International Herald Tribune,** the **Asian Wall Street Journal,** and **USA Today.** Sold primarily in major English-language bookstores (Asia Books and DK Books) and first-class hotels (35฿). **Time** (80฿) and **Newsweek** (90฿) can be found too. Bop to the latest music videos on **Star TV** and see the world through Rupert Murdoch's eyes.

English Language Aural Media: Bangkok has over 40 FM radio stations and just about as many AM stations. A few offer English programming; consult the **Bangkok Post** *Outlook* section or **The Nation** *Focus* section. **Smile Radio 4 (107 FM)** cranks out imported Top 40 (daily 5am-2am). The DJs speak a combination of English and Thai. **Smooth 105 (105 FM)** operates daily 5am-2am. Older listeners prefer the lilting, heavily English-accented DJs. **Lite 97 (97 FM)** competes with Smooth 105 (daily 6am-2am). **Gold 95 (95.5 FM)** targets jazz and oldies lovers with hits from the '60s and '70s (daily 5am-2am). **Chulalongkorn University's 101.5 FM** plays classical music (daily 9:30pm-midnight).

English Book Stores: Many department stores, such as Central Department Store, sell English books. **Elite Used Book Store,** 593/5 Sukhumvit Rd., between Soi 33 and 35 (tel. 258 0221). From Siam Sq., take A/C bus #8 or regular bus #48. Wide selection of used books, magazines, and newspapers from all over the world; emphasis on English-language titles. Open daily 10am-8pm. **Asia Books,** Peninsula Plaza, 2nd fl., Ratchadamri Rd. (tel. 253 9786-88). Find the *Let's Go* guide of your choice, along with recent best-sellers, maps, picture books, and some used books. Open daily 10am-8pm. Also at Thaniya Plaza, 3F, Silom Rd. (tel 231 2106). Open daily 10am-8pm. **DK Book House,** 244-246 Siam Sq., in passage between Sois 2 and 3. (tel. 251 6335). Regular bus #15, 25, 40, 48, 54, 73, 204; A/C bus #8 and 1. Similar to Asia Books. Open daily 9:30am-8pm.

Libraries: Neilson Hays Library, the best English-language library in Bangkok. **Chulalongkorn University Library,** comfortable, with A/C and some English magazines. Open Mon.-Fri. 9am-4:30pm. See Sights: Siam Square. **National Library,** chockfull o' books on Samsen Rd. near Si Ayutthaya Rd. Coming up Samsen Rd., take bus #16, 30, 32, 49, or 64 or A/C bus #5; all stop frequently in front of the library (open daily 9:30am-7:30pm except on national holidays; free). Hang out in the A/C periodicals room.

Cultural Centers: Alliance Française, 29 Sathon Tai Rd. (tel. 213 2122/3). French language courses, French movies and French and Thai food. Library open Mon.-Fri. 8:30am-6pm, Sat. 8:30am-12:30pm and 1:30-4:30pm. **AUA (American University Alumni),** 179 Ratchadamri Rd. (tel. 252 8170-73). Offers 5-week courses in Thai. Cultural programs with an emphasis on things American. Videos and CD-ROM for members (200฿). Library open Tue.-Fri. 8:30am-5pm, Sat. 9:30am-4:30pm. **British Council,** 428 Soi 2, Siam Sq., Rama I Rd. (tel. 252 6136-38). Will move soon, but will remain in Siam Square. Cultural events, and bully kidney pie. Library open Tues.-Fri. 10am-7:30pm, Sat. 10am-5pm.

Convenience Stores: For the bare necessities. In Banglamphu, **New World Dept. Store,** corner of Chakrapong and Phra Sumen Rd., 5th fl. Open daily 8am-8pm. In Silom/Financial, a plethora of options. **Mini-Market,** Khaosan Rd. near Bowonniwet Rd.; open 24 hrs. **7-Eleven,** corner of Suriwongse and Patpong I Rd.; open 24hrs. **Robinson Dept. Store,** Silom Rd., next to Rama IV Rd., basement level. Food court. Open daily 10am-midnight. Along Sukhumvit Rd.

Swimming Pools: Budget travelers are welcome at many fitness clubs with swimming pools. Admission is usually 50฿. **Soi Klang Racquet Club,** 8 Soi 49 Sukhumvit Rd. (tel. 391 0963). From Siam Sq., regular bus #25 or 48 or A/C bus #8. Members-only tennis courts; all who wear swim caps may paddle in the pool (40฿, under 12 30฿; open daily 8am-9pm).

Pharmacies: A dime a dozen in Bangkok, but most are only open daily from 9am to 8pm. Plan ahead and stock up for medicinal or contraceptive needs. **New World Dept. Store (Banglamphu),** Krai Si Rd. entrance, 1st fl. Open daily 8am-8pm. **Robinson Dept. Store (Silom/Financial),** Silom Rd., ground fl. Open daily 10am-midnight. **Drug Store (Sukhumvit Rd.),** corner of Soi 21 (Asoke) Sukhumvit Rd. Open daily 8:30am-9pm.

Hospitals: The following have English-speaking doctors: **Bangkok Christian Hospital (Silom/Financial),** 124 Silom Rd. (tel. 233 6981-89). Regular bus #115, A/C bus #2, 4, and 5. A 600-bed hospital with 24-hr. ambulance service. **Bamrungrad Hospital (Sukhumvit Rd.),** 33 Sukhumvit Rd. Soi 3 (Nana Nua) (tel. 253 0250 or 253 0269; fax 255 6622). One of the best private hospitals in Thailand. Open 24 hrs. **Chulalongkorn Hospital (Sukhumvit Rd.),** Rama IV Rd. (tel. 252 8131 or252 8139), on the corner of Ratchadamri Rd. Come here if bitten by a poisonous snake. Ambulance service. **Siriraj Hospital (Thonburi),** 2 Pran Nok Rd. (tel. 419 7000). Take regular bus #19 from Sanam Luang. Thailand's best public hospital and largest, it is the site of daily total chaos. **24-hr. ambulance service.** Cheapest vaccinations at **Red Cross Society's Queen Saovabha Institute** on Rama IV Rd.

Emergency: Tourist Police: tel. 1699, for a guaranteed English speaker. **Police:** tel. 191 or 123. **Fire:** tel. 199. **Ambulance:** tel. 252 2171-75.

ACCOMMODATIONS

The distinction between a classy guest house and a run-down hotel is a fine one. Whatever your quarters, confirm the price what it includes, and check the room carefully. In the summer, a fan is essential. Most decent, economical lodgings fill up quickly and often don't take reservations, especially during the high season.

Banglamphu/Ko Rattanakosin

Every year thousands of travelers make a pilgrimage to the mecca of guest houses in Banglamphu, **Khaosan Rd.** Generally, the farther you move from Khaosan Rd., the more peaceful the area and the more regulations against alcohol, smoking, and prostitution (which is illegal anyway). In terms of choice, accessibility, economy, and safety-in-numbers, Khaosan Rd. is where it's at. To get to the Khaosan Rd. area from the airport, take regular bus #59, which stops near the Democracy Monument. From Siam Square and Silom, regular bus #15 stops at Ratchadamnoen Klang Rd. near the Democracy Monument, Phra Athit Rd., and Phra Sumen Rd. (All within walking distance of guest houses.)

Budget Accommodations:

Peachy Guest House, 10 Phra Athit Rd. (tel. 281 6471). Regular bus #15 stops right across the street. Surrounding a pleasant courtyard, it offers the best value for A/C rooms with trimmings. Large, fastidious rooms and spotless baths. Towels, toilet paper, and cable TV also available, plus a writing table, chair, and dresser. Singles 85฿. Doubles 130฿, with A/C and shower 230฿, with A/C and private bath 300-500฿. 50฿ deposit for key. Restaurant dishes 30-60฿. Reserve during high season.

J & Joe Guest House, 1 Trok Mayom, Chakrapong Rd. (tel. 281 2949). Turn left from Khaosan Rd. onto Chakrapong Rd. and take the 1st alley left. Ideal, inexpensive digs for those seeking tranquility and cleaner air. Beautiful old teakwood house, tastefully decorated in pink and mauve, with frilly gingerbread trim. Your elderly aunts would drool. Singles 90฿. Doubles 150฿. Breakfast 25-35฿. Laundry service. No reservations.

Sweety Guest House, 49 Ratchadamnoen Klang Rd. (tel. 280 2191; fax 280 2192), near the Democracy Monument. Walk through the traditional Thai massage shop. The Volkswagen Beetle of guest houses: compact, cheap, reliable, and charming. "Compact and cheap" refers to the boudoirs, while the beflowered rooftop terrace is downright "charming," and, er, "reliable." Quiet and exceptionally well-maintained. Closes at midnight; ring bell to get in. Singles 60฿. Doubles 80฿, more expensive with window or bath. Laundry service. Barber shop.

Apple 2 Guest House, Trok Kai Chae, 11 Phra Sumen Rd. (tel. 281 1219). Turn left from Phra Sumen Rd. into a narrow alley, walk 200m to the end. Lobby is the downstairs of a quiet, old, teakwood home. "Mama," though a friendly manager, is definitely in charge here, treating all her guests like family (yells at you to turn off a light). Smallish but sanitary salons; common bathrooms are also well-scrubbed. Dorms 50฿. Singles 80฿. Doubles 100฿. Restaurant. Laundry service. Reservations recommended during high season.

Chada Guest House, 216/6 Khaosan Rd. (tel. 280 1318), near Tanao Rd. Walk through Friendly Restaurant, turn right. A mainstay in Khaosan area yet small enough to escape the "institutional" feel of other guest houses in the area, Chada Guest House is like a traveler's old friend. Some rooms have natty floral sheets and vanity tables. Shared bathrooms are scoured 4 times a day. Closes 2am, ring to get in. Singles 75฿. Doubles 150฿, with A/C 250฿. Triples with A/C 300฿. Laundry service.

Hello Guest House, 63-65 Khaosan Rd. (tel. 281 8579). One of the original guest houses along Khaosan Rd. and one of the most popular. Strict management runs a tight ship despite throngs of backpackers and busy location. Sanitary common bathrooms include shower and flush toilet. Singles 90฿. Doubles 140฿, more with window or A/C. Bustling restaurant downstairs is perhaps the best place to meet fellow travelers in Bangkok (dishes 25-60฿). No alcohol or smoking in room. Cops will be called if drugs are suspected or found. No reservations.

More Expensive Accommodations:

Marco Polo Hostel, 108/7-10 Khaosan Rd. (tel. 281 1715), down alley to the left of Bank of Asia exchange booth. Spacious 2-tier foyer houses a restaurant made popular by daily movie marathons (dishes 25-60฿). A/C and bath in all rooms; rates depend on size. Singles 250-300฿. Doubles 250-300฿. Reservations during high season.

Orchid House, 323/2-3 Rambuttri Rd. (tel. 280 2691). Take a right from Khaosan Rd. onto Chakrapong Rd. and then go right on quieter Rambuttri Rd. Spotless lobby with nifty wicker chairs compensates for the smallness of the squeaky-clean quarters with private bathrooms. Closes 10pm. Singles 300฿, with A/C 350-400฿. Doubles 300 ฿, with A/C 450-500฿. Small restaurant (dishes 35-85฿). Reservations during high season.

Khaosan Palace Hotel, 139 Khaosan Rd. (tel. 282 0578). Take the alley to the right of Nita's Boutique. May be the best digs on Khaosan Rd. Certainly the most expensive. Large private bath in each well-outfitted chamber. Singles 250฿, with A/C 400฿. Doubles 350฿, with A/C 450฿. Triple with A/C 600฿.

Dusit/Government Center

Home to various government ministries and agencies, as well as the Royal Family, the area has only limited accommodations for the proletariat. A cluster of friendly, offbeat, and clean guest houses offering much-needed quiet has popped up behind the National Library on **Si Ayutthaya Rd.** Since most are relatively new, they are generally in good condition. Management in is more laid-back, blending well with the Dusit atmosphere.

Bangkok Youth Hostel (HI), 25/2 Phitsanulok Rd. (tel. 281 0361; fax 281 6834). About 300m from the intersection with Samsen Rd. The only hostel in Bangkok, the fan-cooled building has acceptably sanitary dorm-style bunk beds (70฿) and spacious, pristine singles/doubles (200฿). The newer A/C building has awesome dorm-style, sex-segregated rooms (90฿), as well as narrow singles (250฿) and twin doubles (300฿). Private rooms have small, clean, personal baths, but only A/C rooms have hot showers. Go to the old building for singles/doubles, and the new one for dorms. Overseas calls. No smoking or alcohol. HI members only (non-members can buy a year-long membership, 300฿). No reservations.

Shanti Lodge, 37 Si Ayutthaya Rd. Soi 16 (tel. 281 2497). Thrives on the 'make salad, not war' philosophy. Restaurant serves only veggie food, and all the staff are vegetarians. Aquarians will delight in the fish pond with turtles. Don't trample the shower foliage. Popular and often full. Closes 9pm. Dorm 60฿. Singles and doubles 150-170฿. No smoking or alcohol. Laundry service. No reservations.

Paradise Guest House, 57 Si Ayutthaya Rd. (tel. 282 8673 or 282 4094). At the end of Soi 16. Short on character, but long on congeniality, cool, and calm, with a cushioned teakwood sitting area in the lobby/restaurant. Fastidiously kept rooms and common Thai-style baths. Useful info. board. Curfew 11pm; ring to get in. Dorms 60฿. Singles 80-100฿. Doubles 120฿. Laundry service. No reservations.

Sawatdee Guest House, 71 Si Ayutthaya Rd. Soi 16 (tel. 281 0757). Where Marx would stay in Dusit. Slightly worn walls are made attractive by low rates and free fruit and drinks given to departing guests. Towels at front desk. Closes 10pm. Dorms (A/C when full) 40฿. Singles 80฿. Doubles 120฿. Restaurant. Overseas calling in lobby. Laundry service. No smoking or alcohol in rooms. Call ahead for vacancy info. in the winter, but no reservations.

Chinatown/Pahurat/Hualamphong

Little has changed around here in the last few decades—still the same frenzied commerce, busy sidewalks, and ungodly population density. Traffic policemen sport face masks to protect their respiratory systems, and travelers and locals alike keep one hand on their money belts. Stroll along Yaowarat Rd. if you're looking for gold jewelry and watches, along Pahurat Rd. and Chakraphet Rd. for cheap clothing and fabrics. Take bus #1 from Suriwongse Rd. (Silom area), #40 (Siam Sq. and Sukhumvit), #73 (Siam Sq.), or #9 or 10 from Dusit and Banglamphu.

Walk down **Yaowarat, Pahurat, Chakraphet,** or **Rong Muang Rd.** to scope out the guest house and hotel options. Some are rip-offs; in some Asians are more welcome than westerners; and many, especially those near the Hualamphong Railway Station, are what the Thais call "lizard hotels" (short-term, no-tell motels). This is not the safest area of town, but there are some acceptable places to stay.

TT2 Guest House, 516-518 Soi Sawang, Si Phraya Rd. (tel. 236 2946; fax 236 3054). From Rama IV Rd. by Hualamphong, turn right on Mahanakhon Rd., then take the 1st left, and walk 10min. to the end of the soi. Set deep within a quiet residential neighborhood. This place has achieved cult status among tourists, in part due to the signs plastered on each lamp post within a 1-mile radius, but also for its spotless facilities and friendly management. Lobby doubles as a restaurant, complete with fish tank and classical music. Open 5:30am-midnight. Small singles with mattresses on the floor 120฿, larger ones with bed 140฿. Doubles (2 twin-sized beds) 180฿. Dorm 90฿. Overseas calling and fax from the lobby. Pulp fiction books lent for 2฿ per day. Restaurant serves home-made yogurt. Reserve 2-3 wks. ahead in high season.

New Empire Hotel, 572 Yaowarat Rd. (tel. 234 6990), near Ratchawong Rd. Convenient location, full amenities, and **wheelchair access.** Both staff and clientele speak more Cantonese than Thai. Pleasant lodgings offer telephones, A/C, and passable bathrooms with bathtubs. Singles and doubles 440-495฿, with TV 550฿. Triples 600-660฿. Laundry and fax services. Reserve 1 day ahead in high season.

Krung Kasem Srikrung Hotel, 1860 Krung Kasem Rd. (tel. 225 0132; fax 225 4705). Less than 5min. from Hualamphong by foot. Well-liked by *farang* for its cavernous triples and 6pm check-out. Every room has a balcony, TV, phone, fan, A/C, and a tidy bathroom with hot water. Doubles with twin beds 550฿. Competitively priced triples 750฿, jam-packed with fridge, mini-bar, and huge bathroom. Restaurant open daily 6:30am-11pm. Room service. Laundry, fax, and copy services. Reserve a couple days in advance, at least a week for a triple.

Silom/Financial District

A couple of decades ago, Silom Rd. still charted its course through rice paddies. But economic boom days in the '80s made it the financial center of Thailand, with a pack of glitzy hotels in tow. Even the bottom-tier lodgings here entice travelers with air-conditioning and other amenities. Be warned: luxury has its price. The wallet-friendly guest house is still alive and well, but many are quickie crash pads renting rooms by the hour. Keep your eyes open and you'll be able to separate the good from the bad and the ugly. Most budget establishments are located 2km from Silom Rd. along **Soi Ngam Duphli** and **Soi Si Bamphen,** which are off Rama IV Rd. near the Lumpini Tower. Take regular bus #115 from Silom Rd. (to get to Silom, take regular bus #15 from Banglamphu or Siam Sq.).

Sala Thai Daily Mansion, 15 Soi Si Bamphen (tel. 287 1436). Across the street from Quality Boutique, enter through the alley next to Lee 3 Guest House. Sunny home run by a patient bibliophile. Rooms are smaller than the name implies, but have a desk, bookshelf, and wall-mounted fan. Sitting area with cable TV on each floor. Breezy rooftop terrace with plants, flowers, and garden tables. Many guests stay for months. Closes at 9pm. Singles and doubles 150฿, larger rooms 200฿. Restaurant (dishes 25-40฿). Laundry service. No reservations.

Lee Guest House #2, 21/38-39 Soi Ngam Duphli (tel. 286 2069). Walk down the soi for about 50m and turn left down an alley just after Anna G.H. Immaculate rooms have double beds and the common baths, shared by 3 rooms, are outfitted with flush toilets. Legions of Thai tots at the nearby school learn epics by repeating them aloud from 8am-4pm. Plug your ears or chant along. Doubles 140฿. Suites with dresser, sturdy queen-sized bed, and balcony 200฿. Laundry service. Locked baggage area. Reserve suites at least 1 week ahead. Also Lee #1, 3, and 4 around the Soi Ngam Duphli area.

Anna Guest House, 21/30 Soi Ngam Duphli (tel. 286 8830). Left-hand side coming from Rama IV Rd. Rooms are tidy, fairly large, and some have precipitous balconies, but nothing out of the ordinary. Colorful Anna, however, brightens up the place. Prices negotiable. Singles 80฿, for larger room 100฿. Doubles 120฿, with balcony 150฿, with bath 180฿. Laundry service.

YMCA Collins International House, 27 South Sathon Rd. (tel. 287 1900; fax 287 1996). Next to Thai Wah Bldg. From Silom Rd. go down Convent Rd. to Sathon Nua Rd., then cross over the overpass and turn left on Sathon Tai. The YMCA aspires to join the ranks of other first class hotels, but it's still the best value in Bangkok for its price range. Soft pastels, wood grains, hot water, plenty of gadgets, and swimming pool. Singles 1170฿, deluxe 1450฿. Doubles (twin beds) 1290฿, deluxe 1650฿. Extra bed 250฿. **Wheelchair accessible.** Non-smoking floors available. Laundry service. Restaurant. All major credit cards.

Siam Sq./Pratunam

Basking in the glow of Bangkok's biggest shopping malls, you'd expect the accommodations around the Siam Sq. area to deliver some luxuries. And they do: private baths , towels, toilet paper, soap, blankets, telephones (for overseas and local calls), dressers, writing tables, hot water, and at some places, satellite TV and refrigerators with mini-bars. Most of the better lodgings are on **Soi Kasem San I** off Rama I Rd., across from the National Stadium Complex and less than 100m from Mahboonkrong Center. Much quieter than Khaosan Rd. and practically tout-free, the soi claims a loyal following of travelers who swear they'd never stay anywhere else.

Pranee Building, 931/12 Soi Kasem San 1 (tel. 216 3181). Another entrance is through the Wat Watana Yonta Co. on Rama I Rd., at the bus stop near Soi Kasem San 1. The lobby is located in a car-park, but we mean that in the best possible sense. Frolic amongst the floral bedspreads and flower pictures on the walls in good-sized, pristine rooms. Rooms with A/C are a much better value, since they have a balcony and western-style flush toilets. Security guard at night. Singles and doubles 300฿, with A/C 350฿, with hot water and A/C 400฿. Doubles with twin beds, A/C, and hot water 500฿. Triples with 1 large and 1 small bed 600฿. Laundry service. No alcohol in rooms. Reserve 1 week in advance Nov.-Feb.

The Bed and Breakfast, 36/42-43 Soi Kasem San 1 (tel. 215 3004). A family-run establishment—the kind of place that will lend you an umbrella when it rains. Swell ambience and a hushed location. All rooms have A/C, contain homey fixings, and are very clean, but many are a bit small. Bathrooms have hot water and overhead fans. Savor satellite TV and complimentary continental breakfast in the bright dining room. Fax service. Lock up at 11pm; after that, rely on the night guard. Singles 380฿. Doubles (with 1 larger bed) 480฿. Triples 600฿. Laundry service. No alcohol. Call 3 days ahead for reservations Nov.-Feb.

Sukhumvit Rd. Area

The side-sois off Sukhumvit Rd. bear many of Bangkok's trendiest nightspots. But like Siam Sq., the Sukhumvit area has few guest houses and high prices, but in Sukhumvit the payoff is slimmer. Everything is accessible from Siam Sq. or Banglamphu by A/C buses #8 and 11, and regular buses #25 and 48. Consider staying in the area if you plan to take a bus down the east coast, since the Eastern Bus Terminal is at the Ekamai intersection, a few km down Sukhumvit Rd. and easily accessible by A/C bus #8 or regular bus #48.

S.V. Guest House, 19/35-36 Soi 19, Sukhumvit Rd. (tel. 253 0606). 100m down on the left. One of the better deals in Bangkok. Pleasant but subdued atmosphere.

Each of the large, neat rooms sports a dresser, parlor area with mirror, flip-flops, firm springy bed, and a phone for local and overseas calls. Hygienic tiled common bathrooms. Singles 250฿. Doubles all with A/C 300฿. Three rooms with bath for an extra 50฿ are always full. Some French and German spoken. Breakfast 60฿. Laundry service. Call for reservations during high season (Nov.-Feb.).

Uncle Rey's Guest House, 7/10 Soi 4 (Nana Tai), Sukhumvit Rd. (tel. 252 5565). On the left across from Nana Hotel. Follow the signs through the alley with the food vendors, then walk to the back left corner of the parking lot. Genial front-desk personnel and great location. Roomy chambers labeled with hippie flower names include dresser, small wicker sitting area, well-kept bath with hot-water shower, and spine-tingling A/C. Phone for local and overseas calls and bathtubs in most rooms. Singles and doubles 3rd and 4th floors 350฿; 1st and 2nd floors 400฿, with twin beds 400฿. Laundry and fax service. Reserve 2 days ahead.

FOOD

Everywhere in Bangkok, delicious victuals can be had at rock-bottom prices from street vendors and tiny, no-name restaurants. Learn the appellation of a few simple dishes, or point, and let your palate run wild. You can get streetwise experience in the low-pressure, A/C surroundings of supermarket food courts. The places we list aren't necessarily any better in terms of culinary quality, but provide variety, calm, comfort, atmosphere, English-language menus, and (sorry) higher prices.

Banglamphu/Ko Rattanakosin

This area is bursting with cheap eats, served up by both sidewalk vendors and restaurants. For good food stalls, stroll down **Soi Rambuttri, Krai Si Rd.** (in the evening), or **Phra Chan Rd.** across from Thammasat University (during the day). On weekends, the area around **Sanam Luang** is also a popular hang-out for street-side peddlers of edibles. Nearly every guest house has its own restaurant, with varying degrees of menu selection. Khaosan Rd. has over 20 such restaurants with dishes running 25-60฿, or head to the **New World Department Store Food Center,** for Thai and Chinese dishes at prices so low you'll almost feel guilty (corner of Chakrapong Rd. and Phra Sumen Rd., 8F, open daily 8am-8pm).

Wang Nar Restaurant, 17/1 Phra Athit Rd. (tel. 224 8552), under the Phra Pinklao Bridge. Thai-Chinese seafood restaurant snuggled on the riverside. Dine in the A/C upstairs or the open-air downstairs, overlooking the river. Staffed by a fleet of yellow-polyester-clad waitresses and packed with Thai and Chinese patrons. Extremely spicy curries served in decent portions. Most dishes run 60-80฿; more exotic seafood dishes up to 600฿. Menu in English, Thai, and Chinese. Dinner reservations recommended. Open daily 10:30am-11pm.

Royal India Restaurant, 57 Khaosan Rd. (tel. 281 5116). In the alley to the left of Hello G.H. Small, spartan curry joint packs in the Indian tailors and *farang.* Tasty vegetable curry (35฿) and other **vegetarian** dishes (30฿) provide some of the only fleshless fare in Banglamphu. Meat dishes 30-90฿. Stuffed to the gills during high season. English menu. **Wheelchair accessible.** Open daily 11am-11pm.

Yod Kum, 365/1 Phra Sumen Rd. (tel. 281 7186), across from Wat Bovornives. Strictly middle-class clientele in a shoebox-sized restaurant decorated with western memorabilia from the 20s and 30s. Ooh and ahh at the glass cabinet with crystal and old toys. Hot-as-hell Thai curries, soups, and chili-paste dishes as well as some Chinese fare. Rice dishes 35-50฿. Curries 80-140฿. Beer and whiskey. English menu. Open daily 11:30am-11pm.

Tang Teh, 269-271 Samsen Rd. (tel 281 9426), on the left at the 1st major intersection coming from Banglamphu. Airy, modern-artsy dining room, and dishes that will make your taste buds sing. Try *yam pla dook foo* (fried catfish with cashews and chili sauce, 65฿). Rice with olives and pork is...unique (50฿) as is the stellar homemade ice cream (rum raisin, green tea, and cherry Bordeaux, 20฿ per scoop). English menu. Open daily 11am-2pm and 4:30-11pm.

Vijit Restaurant, 77/2 Ratchadamnoen Klang Rd. (tel. 282 0958), at the Democracy Monument. No English sign, look for cafe-style tables lining the sidewalk.

Live music at lunch and dinner packs in locals who slurp on beer and whisky while talking loudly over the synthesizer beat. Chinese and Thai food knock the socks off Japansese and Vietnamese offerings. Most dishes 40-80฿. Soured crab with coconut mil is popular (48฿). How about frog curry (60฿)? 10% service charge after 6pm. Open daily 11am-11pm.

Dusit/Government Center

There are very few restaurants, and they are generally sub-par. Start your search for cheap eats at the market packed with noodle stands on Si Ayutthaya Rd. across from the guest houses.

Thai Youth Hostel Association Cafeteria, 25/2 Phitsanulok Rd. (tel. 282 5559). Sign on the door simply says "Thailand." A full-fledged restaurant, it may be the only hostel cafeteria in the world that attracts more cellular telephones than backpacks. Decor consists of carved-wood mirrors and national flags. Amuse waitresses by seizing your home emblem and planting it squarely on your table. Extensive menu loaded with various Thai dishes and a few western favorites of the soup/salad/sandwich variety such as "horse derves" and "chili fried hog." Dishes 25-60฿. English menu. Open daily 7am-11pm (kitchen closes at 10pm).

Baan Khun Luang, 131/4 Khao Rd. (tel. 241 0521; fax 243 5375). Take bus #3, 30, 32, 33, or 64, or A/C bus #5 or 6 to the Samsen Rd. stop nearest Sukhothai Rd. Walk along Sukhothai Rd. toward the river; turn left on Khao Rd. Tour groups overrun this mammoth restaurant overlooking the river to take advantage of the impressive 100฿ buffet in the cafeteria-style dining hall. The spread includes a multitude of Thai and Chinese dishes, seafood, and some "American" specimens like salad, bread, and deli meats. English menu with tons of entrees in the 40-95฿ range. Last page of Chinese section has vegetable dishes. Open daily 9:30am-11:30pm (buffet daily 11am-2pm). All major credit cards.

Chinatown/Pahurat/Hualamphong

Richard Simmons and Jenny Craig would go nuts in this gastronomically fixated part of town. For Chinese food, duck into one of the tiny, bustling restaurants that crowd **Yaowarat Rd.** For Indian curries head to the **Prahurat** area. To stock up on Thai noodles or sweets take your pick from the hundreds of food stalls in **Hualamphong.** Not many places have English menus, so use your instincts.

White Orchid Coffee Shop, 409-421 Yaowarat Rd. (tel. 226 0026; fax 225 6403). On the second floor of the White Orchid Hotel. Smoky don't-ask-what's-going-on-in-the-back room atmosphere made even more sinister by Chinese '80s music. The restaurant's claim to fame is its 120฿ lunch buffet (tax and service included) of mostly Chinese food. Thai and European offerings include curries, green salads, buttered fish with tartar, and deli meats. Beer, whiskey, and various cocktails. Open daily 11am-2pm for brunch. All major credit cards.

Royal India Restaurant, 392/1 Chakraphet Rd. (tel. 221 6565), through the small alley off Chakraphet Rd., between Saphan Han (the bridge) and Yaowarat Rd. The progenitor of the Royal India on Khaosan Rd., this is one of the best Indian restaurants in Pahurat. Extensive bread selection. Vegetarians will like the 14 meatless items (20-45฿). *Tandoori* chicken is popular, and the most expensive (110฿). Try the *pakoras*—potatoes, peas, and mild spices in pastry. Open daily 9am-10pm.

Silom/Financial District

During the day the neighborhood caters to the appetites of the business elite. Local noodle vendors, the original fast food dispensers, compete for lunch-time baht with their western counterparts. Look for local fare along **Convent Rd.,** and deep inside **Soi Ngam Duphli**. By night, **Silom Rd.** is flooded with street-side stalls, especially near the two Patpong Roads and Thaniya Rd. A steady stream of hungry souls flows through this district until the early hours (around 3am). A stroll down these roads yields everything from Vietnamese to Mexican, but prices are generally higher.

Cheaper to Moderate Places:

Silom Restaurant, end of Silom Soi 15 (tel. 236 4268). Huge, inexpensive Chinese and Thai dishes make this place a favorite with workers and families in the Silom area. Gorge on a large selection of fish and prawn dishes. Service reflects the prices (they schlep the food; don't ask for more). Regular-sized (huge) dishes 60-90฿. The chicken curry (65฿) contains the most tender chicken imaginable. English menu. Open daily 11am-10pm. No reservations, but it fills up at lunch.

Charuvan Duck Shop, corner of Silom Rd. and Soi Silom 4 (tel. 234 2206). Noodles, rice, vegetables, and, as the sign says, "a lot of fat duck to eat." Spartan eating conditions keep overhead and food prices low: nearly everything goes for 25-35฿ a plate. English menu. Open daily 9am-9pm.

Sukol Thros Bakery, 14 Silom Rd. (tel. 233 2680), near Robinson Dept. Store. No English sign—look for pointy 'S' logo. A 30-year Thai institution with *shell chuan chim* recognition. Popular with workers in the Silom area by day and couples by night. Decent selection of Thai hot and sour salads *(yam)* and delicious *pad Thai.;* some western fare. Dishes 25-90฿ (most are 30-40฿). In-house bakery makes a wide variety of cakes, meat pies, and Thai/Chinese goodies. No reservations, but good luck trying to find a seat at lunch. Open daily 7am-9pm.

Mid-range Places:

Thai Room, Plaza Bldg., Patpong II Rd. (tel. 233 7920). Go to the entrance of the Pavilion Place Hotel and take a right down the narrow corridor. Serving westerners coming out of Patpong bars for 28 years, the Thai Room is an institution among tourists, many of whom come back to see if it is still in business (it is, and bustling, too). The A/C interior is clean, with a slight lounge-lizard, 1970s feel. Scope out the funky blue, green, and red wall lights, man. Wear anything, especially Hawaiian floral shirts. The English menu lists over 400 selections, including Mexican, Italian, Chinese, Thai, and American food. Stick to the Thai and American selections. Most dishes 35-80฿. Open daily 10am-2am. All major credit cards.

Somboon Seafood, 169/7-11 Suriwongse Rd. (tel. 233 3104). Open 4pm-midnight—the day is devoted to unloading fresh seafood shipments from the Gulf of Thailand. The evening is for feasting on an extensive yet inexpensive array of seafood. Glossy atmosphere plays host to the occasional Thai or Hong Kong movie star, complete with entourage. The most famous dish is the fried crab with curry powder (120฿), although there is a wide selection of crab, shrimp, shellfish, abalone, etc., to point to on the menu, as well as meat and 9 vegetarian dishes. Non-seafood and cheaper seafood dishes 30-120฿. More exotic seafood 100-800฿ (per kg for lobster). Ample servings. English menu. Service charge 5฿ per person.

Fifth Floor Lunch Buffet at Silom Plaza Hotel, 320 Silom Rd. (tel. 236 0333; fax 236 7566), near Mahesak Rd. Remarkable deal for the ravenous at an all-inclusive 120฿. Choose from Korean, Thai, and Japanese food, noodle dishes, shish kebab, cold cuts, and salads. Tea and coffee included. 5th floor view enhances the pleasant hotel restaurant surroundings. Open daily 11am-2pm. AmEx, Visa.

Siam Sq./Pratunam

Finding food in this area is as easy as walking down the street. In the afternoon and early evening, food vendors hawk their goodies in front of the **National Stadium** on Rama I Rd., at the mouth of **Soi Kasem 1,** and along the network of sois weaving through **Siam Sq.** In Pratunam, vendors and sidewalk restaurants dot **Ratchaprarop Rd.** and **Soi Wattanasin** across from the Indra Regent Hotel.

Western fast food places skirmish with regular restaurants for territory. **Mahboonkrong Center** harbors a giant Food Center, with a variety of Thai meals on the 6th floor (most dishes around 35฿, open daily 10am-9:30pm). Many restaurants, though, have been pleasing Bangkokites for decades. Without gouging the wallet (Silom) or jumping to adopt the latest culinary trend (Sukhumvit), these places offer consistently good food at manageable prices.

UFM Noodle House, 230/17-18 Siam Sq. Soi 2 (tel. 252 7187), on the same soi as the Kirin Restaurant. Other locations at 182-184 Siam Sq. Soi 1, in front of the

Scala Movie Theater, and at Amarin Plaza, 4th floor. Sign says "Noodle Shop" with a pair of chopsticks. Youngish crowd flocks to this shiny, colorful place for Thai, Chinese, Japanese, and Italian noodle dishes made fresh daily (30-50฿). No alcohol. 5% service charge. Open daily 11am-9pm.

Tota Restaurant, 63/12 Soi Lang Suan off Ploenchit Rd. (tel. 252 2455). Regular bus #48 and A/C bus #8 pass by the soi on Ploenchit Rd. Pleasant, A/C restaurant with pink walls, blue-tinted window panes, plants, and framed bird pictures. Serves spicy Thai cuisine that is as authentic as it gets. Most dishes 30-50฿. *Som tam* (25฿) and *yen tao fo* (30฿) are spicy specialties. Ice cream and fruit for dessert cool off tingling tongues. English menu. Open daily 10am-11pm. MC, Visa.

Oldies Goldies, 4th fl., Siam Center, Rama I Rd. (tel. 252 2717). Recreate the 50s in this cute take on the American diner. Bobby-soxers hang out in the pink and cream booths listening to hits and looking at memorabilia from the era. Obligatory picture of Elvis in his prime. Juke boxes and so-so American food (45-90฿). Better Thai food (30-55฿) and even better beverage list, with its unbeatable selection of tea drinks, coffee drinks, and fruit juices, including brandy iced coffee and cantaloupe juice. 10% discount for *Let's Go* users on food only. Service 5%. Tax 7%. English menu. Open daily 10am-11pm.

Seefah Restaurant, Siam Sq., behind the little fire station, near the Novotel (tel. 251 5517). The success of this legend (opened in 1936) comes from delicious, skillfully prepared food at reasonable prices. Large windows between the 1st-floor dining room and the preparation area allow diners to see how the food is concocted. Fried fish cakes *(tod mun plaa)* are popular starters (50฿), while the sweet and sour shrimp on a sizzling platter (100฿) looks, smells, and tastes amazing. Dishes 35-80฿ for most non-seafood dishes, more for seafood. Open daily 9am-11pm.

New Light Coffee House, 426/1-4 Siam Sq. (tel. 251 9591), next to the Hard Rock Café. With bizarre green mood lighting and a vinylized A/C ambience testifying to its 60s vintage, New Light lives on today with good international offerings. The menu covers lots of ground: Thai (cheapest, at 40-80฿), Chinese (60-350฿), and European/American (40-135฿). Spring for fried pigeon with vegetables. Cheap and extensive sandwich selection. Open daily 8am-12:30am. AmEx, MC, Visa.

Coca Restaurant, 416/3-8 Siam Square (tel. 251 6337), facing Henri Dunant Rd. Bangkok's most popular *sukiyaki* joint. You choose the meats and vegetables, and they are promptly dunked in a steaming cauldron before your eyes. Meats 20-40฿; vegetables 9฿ for each variety. Or, choose from a variety of cheap but good noodle and rice dishes (most around 30฿). English menu. Open daily 11am-11pm.

Sukhumvit Rd. Area

Along with Siam Sq. and Silom, Sukhumvit forms part of Bangkok's triumvirate of culinary powerhouses. Some of the best restaurants were set up by expatriate chefs trying to cook up a name for themselves on the Bangkok scene. Travelers with a hankering for Euro, Indian, Chinese, Californian, or simply good Thai cuisine will be satiated—but the price of satisfaction is usually steep. For those with less demanding palates, the **Ambassador Food Center** serves up a variety of Asian dishes (20-70฿) with some vegetarian options (right side of the Ambassador Hotel parking lot near Soi 13 off Sukhumvit Rd., open daily 10:30am-11pm).

Cabbages and Condoms, 10 Soi 12 Sukhumvit Rd. (tel. 229 4610), behind the Population Development Building. Between the non-scalpel vasectomy center and the sterilization clinic—hint, hint. The brainchild of Dr. Vichit, a leading family planning advocate, the restaurant was established in 1986. All proceeds go to charitable organizations. Decorated with Thai wicker-work and framed newspaper articles on the AIDS crisis. Decent Thai food; *gaeng nua* (beef curry) is a specialty. Pick up condoms in lieu of post-prandial mints. Most dishes 50-90฿, with seafood dishes costing 100฿ or more. Open daily 11am-10pm. Reservations recommended on weekend evenings. All major credit cards.

Maharajah's Restaurant, 19/1 Soi 8 Sukhumvit Rd. (tel. 254 8876). Elegant Indian restaurant furnished with A/C, curvy-backed chairs, and a grandiose red-purple-green color scheme; and livened up with Indian classical hits on the sound sys-

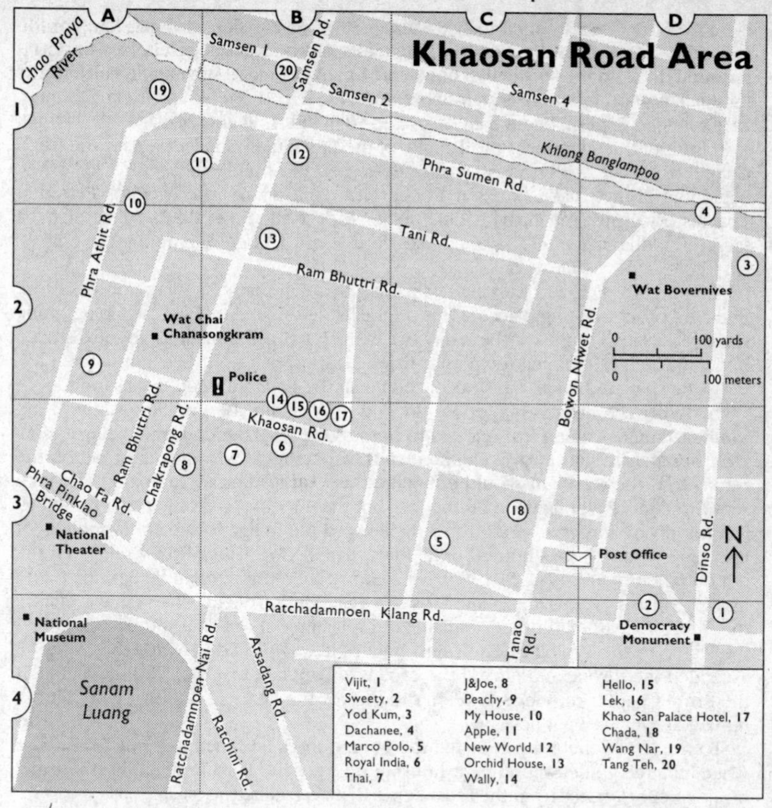

tem. *Tandoori* and kebabs; large selection of vegetarian dishes (50-70฿). Enormous servings, especially the *biryani* dishes and breads (20-50฿). Most dishes 60-120฿. *Lassi,* champagne, wine, cocktails. 10% service charge. Open daily 11am-11pm. English menu. All major credit cards.

Bei Otto Bakery, Butchery, and Restaurant, 1 Soi 20 Sukhumvit Rd. (tel. 258 1495). Bangkok's premier German restaurant and priced that way; those on a tight budget should head straight past the restaurant to the bakery and deli. Good deals on cold cuts and home-made pastries, breads, and pickles. Load up on chicken or sausage pies (15฿ each) or sandwich fixin's. Cold cuts include knockwurst and veal sausages (20-55฿). Sweets (5-45฿) and breads are baked daily. Bakery open daily 8am-midnight, restaurant open daily 11am-3pm and 6-11pm. English menu. All major credit cards.

Suda Restaurant, 6/1 Sukhumvit Soi 14 (tel. 252 2597). No frills, open-to-the-winds office worker lunch joint. Fried tuna with cashews and chili paste like your mother could never make (60฿). Rice and noodle dishes aplenty (30฿). Open daily 11am-midnight.

SIGHTS

Banglamphu/Ko Rattanakosin

Wat Phra Kaew (the Temple of the Emerald Buddha) and the **Grand Palace** (tel. 222 0094, ext. 40) are the preeminent sights in all of Bangkok. Many buses find their way here, including regular bus #3, 6, 9, 15, 19, 30, 31, 32, 33, 39, 44, 47, 59, 64, 70, 80, 90, 91, 201, and 203. A/C bus #6, 8, and 12 also make the pilgrimage. Buses stop around the compound and across the street at Sanam Luang, but the entrance gate is on Na Phra Lan Rd. (open daily 8:30am-3:30pm; admission for Thais free, for foreigners 125฿). Proper dress (shirts, long pants, skirts, blouses, semiformal shoes) is required. Pick up the small guidebook and a map (included with admission). Inside the main compound there is an info booth on the left, 100m past the ticket counter. Free tours, in English, begin daily at 10 and 10:30am, 1:30 and 2pm.

In front of the entrance is the Temple of the Emerald Buddha, originally the Royal Chapel of the Chakri Dynasty. It took three years to build, starting in 1782 at the beginning of the Chakri Dynasty (the current dynasty) and the Bangkok Period in Thai history. Inside the main chapel building (bot) is the **Emerald Buddha,** the most sacred Buddha image in Thailand. Take your shoes off before entering the chapel. No photography is allowed.

The itinerant Emerald Buddha has passed through many halfway houses before finding a proper resting place. It was originally discovered in 1434, when lightning shattered a chedi in the northern city of Chiang Rai. Inside, an abbot found a stucco Buddha. Later, he noticed the plaster flaking off, revealing a green substance. Curiously, he sloughed off all the stucco, and voilà! the Emerald Buddha was found.

Following the discovery, people flocked to worship the priceless statue. King Samfangkang of Chiang Mai yearned to possess the little Buddha, and, being a monarch, summarily sent a royal elephant to transport it. At a fork in the road on the return trip, the elephant would only take the road leading to Lampang. The king sent three more elephants to do the job, but they, too, would only go to Lampang. Sensing divine forces at work, the king allowed the image to remain in the city of Lampang, where it was housed until 1468, when King Tiloka finally relocated the hot commodity to Chiang Mai. Nearly a century later, the peripatetic figurine found its way to Laos, where it remained for 214 years until General Chao Phraya Chakri, the future Rama I, captured Vientiane and reclaimed it for Thailand. He carted off the statue to the capital of Thon Buri, where it was placed in Wat Arun. After he ascended the throne and moved the capital to Bangkok in 1782, King Rama I built the Royal Chapel, known as Wat Phra Kaew, for the Emerald Buddha, where it has remained ever since. Whew.

To the left of the temple, inside the compound's entrance, is **Phra Sri Ratana Chedi,** a large golden monument housing relics of the Lord Buddha. **Mural drawings** depicting scenes from the Indian epic Ramayana line the walls.

Next door to the temple is the **Grand Palace,** accessible through a gate connecting the two compounds. After turning right inside the gate, a stroll down the path leads past many important buildings on the left. The first, **Amarinda Vinichai Hall,** was the location of important court ceremonies (open Mon.-Fri.). Next, **Chakri Mahaprasad Hall,** the residence of King Chulalongkorn, is a hybrid of European and Thai architectural design. Today, the reception areas and central throne hall are still used for certain royal ceremonies, although it's off-limits to ordinary folks. Farther on, **Dusit Hall** is a symmetrical building of Thai design whose audience hall houses a mother-of-pearl throne (open Mon.-Fri.). Admission to Wat Phra Kaew and the Grand Palace entitles the visitor to free admission to Vimarnmek Palace in Dusit with your admission slip.

After leaving the Grand Palace compound, a right turn past the gift shop leads to the **Wat Phra Kaew Museum.** The first floor contains relics and parts from buildings that originally stood in the compounds which have been replaced, as well as the bones from a white elephant, which are considered good luck. The second floor is air-conditioned and contains hundreds of Buddha images along with enamel and crystal wares (open daily 9am-3:30pm; free).

From Wat Phra Kaew, a walk around the block (three left turns from the entrance) brings you to **Wat Po,** known to westerners as the **Temple of the Reclining Buddha** and officially called Wat Phra Chetupon in Thailand. Wat Po is the oldest and largest temple in Bangkok. Its grounds are split in two by Soi Chetupon: one side is home to the monastery, while the other contains temple buildings. Wat Po was built in the 16th century during the Ayutthaya Period when the area around present-day Bangkok was little more than a fishing village. King Rama I enlarged the temple's grounds and made improvements on its structures; his grandson, King Rama III, built the wiharn that houses the Reclining Buddha. The statue measures 46m in length and 15m in height; the feet alone are 3m long. Don't give in to the temptation to clamber onto this laid-back giant (open daily 8:30am-5pm; admission 20฿). Wat Po is currently undergoing major renovations, which may account for the recent increase in the admission fee.

Wat Po is famous not only for the variety and abundance of its Buddhas, but also as the home of what can be considered Thailand's first university. While it has never officially been called a "university," about a century before the founding of Bangkok, a monastery was founded at Wat Po to teach Thai medicine. In the past three centuries, it has developed into a world-famous school of traditional Thai massage. Today, this technique is still taught and administered on the temple grounds.

After visiting the Reclining Buddha, a short walk to the eastern part of Wat Po leads to the **Medical Hall.** Peek inside and you will probably find over a dozen masseurs kneading their customers. If you knead some revitalization after a hard day of sight-seeing, you can get a massage for about 180฿ per hour, 280฿ with herbs. On the other hand, if you want to learn how to give this therapeutic massage to someone you love, or want to love, sign up for the 15-day course (3000฿). For further therapy, fortune tellers and palm readers abound.

To get to **Wat Arun** (the Temple of Dawn) from Wat Po, take a right from Chetupon Rd. onto Maharat Rd., and a left at Tani Wang Rd. This takes you to Tha Tien, a pier on the Chao Phraya River. From an adjacent pier, ferries make frequent crossings to the wat (1฿). The name of Thailand's second-most-famous wat is derived from Aruna, the Indian god of dawn. Wat Arun was founded in the Ayutthaya period, which explains its Khmer architecture. During King Taksin's short reign in Thon Buri, Wat Arun served as the Royal Chapel. Today, as a royal temple, Wat Arun is visited once a year by the King, who conducts a merit-making ceremony.

While Wat Arun is famous for its size and majesty, it was not until the reign of King Rama II that the idea of building a great prang, the steeple-like structure atop the bot, came into being. However, King Rama II did not live to see his dream realized, since the wet Thon Buri soil delayed completion of the construction until the reign of King Rama III. Finished, the prang towered 81m over the temple grounds. Built in the Khmer style, it is inlaid with millions of ceramic tiles and porcelain, much of which was donated by villagers. It is an awesome sight to behold at sunrise, when solar beams make the temple glitter brilliantly and project its reflection onto the Chao Phraya River. The best view of the wat is from the Bangkok side of the river early in the morning, and the top of the prang affords a beautiful view of the water (open daily 8:30am-5:30pm; admission 10฿ to enter the prang area and climb the prang's steep, narrow stairs).

To go to **Siriraj Hospital** from Wat Arun, head down Arun Amarin, walk to the nearest bus stop, and take regular bus #19, 57, or 83. The largest public hospital in Thailand, it is also noteworthy for its **forensics museum,** where the public may view the embalmed body of **Si Oui,** Thailand's notorious child serial killer, as well as other pathologies, skeletons, and gunshot wounds. Morbid kiddies come to see gruesome examples of human death and disease. The museum is at the back of the hospital complex (open daily 8:30am-3pm; free).

The **Royal Barge Museum** (tel. 424 0004), is a short bus or taxi ride away. Located on Arun Amarin Rd. under the bridge over Khlong Bangkok Noi, it is accessible by regular bus #19. From the inconspicuous entrance, walk 300m along a winding path, following the arrows and signs through a riverside residential neighborhood, to get to the museum. If you're coming from Banglamphu, take the ferry from Tha Phra Arthit to Tha Phra Pinklao on the opposite bank (1฿). Take the first left on Phra Pinklao Rd., after the big school underneath the green arch. Follow the signs about 500m through the neighborhood to the museum. The most impressive barge in the museum is undoubtedly the **Suphannahongsa,** a 46m-long stiletto of a vessel reserved exclusively for the Royal Family. Its bow is carved into the shape of a mythical bird called the *hongsa.* Getting the Suphannahongsa moving in the water requires 50 oarsmen and an accompanying crew of 13 to transport the King and Queen in a royal procession (open daily 8:30am-4:30pm; admission 10฿).

Starting again from the entrance to Wat Phra Kaew, a walk across Na Phra Lan Rd., a left turn, and a stroll past the souvenir sellers along the street leads to the front entrance of **Silpakorn University** (tel. 221 3841), Thailand's foremost university specializing in the fine arts. The school was founded in 1933 by expatriate Italian sculptor Corrado Feroci, who had been personally invited to join the Royal Fine Arts Department by King Rama VI. The university gallery is just inside the main entrance. Gallery open Mon.-Fri. 9am-7pm, Sat.-Sun. 9am-4:30pm; free.

Walking through the small campus past the statue of Silpa Bhirasri leads to the university's side entrance. A left turn, followed by a right just down the road at Phra Chan Rd. brings you to Na Phra That Rd., with **Thammasat University** (tel. 225 7517) on the left and **Wat Mahathat** (tel. 222 2835) on the right. Thailand's second university, Thammasat is the country's premier institution of higher learning in political science and law, and the traditional hotbed of student activism. In the past two decades, the campus has been the sight of two of the bloodiest student demonstrations in Thai history. In October 1973, demonstrations against the Thanom regime provoked a violent military reaction in which scores of students were killed. In October 1976, the scene repeated itself when police and the army stormed the campus to break up demonstrations protesting the return of Thanom to Thailand as a monk. More students were killed; many of the survivors had to swim across the river to escape death. Today, campus activism has cooled down, but Thammasat maintains its reputation as one of the top universities in the nation.

An extremely old monastery, built before Bangkok became the nation's capital, **Wat Mahathat** is also known as the Temple of the Great Relic. Not surprisingly, the main chapel houses a large sitting Buddha (open daily 9am-5pm). The wat was the home of King Rama I, who was a monastery abbot before he did an about-face and took up military campaigns as a way of life. These days, the temple is known as a center of Buddhist teaching and the home of Wat Maha Chulalongkorn University, one of Thailand's two Buddhist colleges .

Back at Na Phra That Rd., look across the street and see **Sanam Luang,** the "national common" of Thailand. In the old days, criminals convicted of particularly heinous crimes were lined up here and shot. Although public executions have been discontinued, summer kite fighting contests are going strong, as competitors from all over descend upon the grass. The large kites are "males" called chula, while the smaller kites are "females" known as the pukpao. The goal of the chula is to catch the pukpao, and the goal of the pukpao is to avoid capture. For a few baht, sate your testosterone-driven, kite-fighting urges and compete.

Walking on Na Phra That Rd. farther away from Wat Phra Kaew, you will pass Thammasat University campus to the left. Immediately after Thammasat, the **National Museum** (tel. 224 1396) is in the compound to the left of the sidewalk with a guard booth at its entryway. This Bangkok branch is the crown jewel of Thailand's national museum system, and the largest museum in Southeast Asia. In 1874, King Chulalongkorn started the museum when he opened a public showroom inside the Grand Palace to exhibit royal collections from the reign of his father King Rama IV. However, Smithsonian or British Museum devotees will sneer at the dusty, cluttered displays and hokey waxworks. Time-conscious travelers should take the free 90-min. museum tour given by English-speaking guides on Wed. and Thurs. at 9:30am (other tours are offered in French, German, and Japanese). Each guide is a specialist in a field of Thai art (museum open Wed.-Sun. 9am-4pm, tickets sold until 3:30pm; admission 20฿).

At the end of Na Phra That Rd., you will arrive at Ratchini Rd. Take a left, walk under the Phra Pinklao Bridge, and turn onto Chao Fa Rd. The **National Theater** (tel. 221 0171 or 221 9838) is through the first gate on the left of Ratchini Rd. Dedicated in 1965, the National Theater has regularly scheduled drama and dance shows (See drama and dance page 293). On the second weekend of each month (Sat. and Sun.), lakhon is performed (10am and 2pm). Khon is performed on the third weekend of each month (10am and 2pm). The last Friday of each month is reserved for a special cultural show at 5:30pm. The theater is also home to the **Thai National Orchestra,** which plays for the public the first Fri. of each month at 5:30pm. When there are no state-sponsored shows, other performance companies may use the National Theater. Ticket prices run 40-80฿ for the regularly scheduled government-sponsored shows. The box office (tel. 224 1342) opens Mon.-Fri. 8:30am-4:30pm and one hour prior to performances.

On Chao Fa Rd., straddling eight lanes of traffic, is the **National Gallery** (tel. 281 2224) which contains classical and contemporary works by prominent Thai artists as well as the **National Film Archives**. The two air-conditioned rooms display paintings of scenes from epic stories (such as the Ramayana) and classical plays. One of the rooms shows four rare watercolors done by King Rama VI (gallery open Wed.-Sun. 9am-4pm; admission 10฿).

A good 10-minute walk along the continuation of Chao Fa Rd., Ratchadamnoen Klang Rd. will bring you to the **Democracy Monument.** Commemorating Thailand's transition from an absolute monarchy to a constitutional monarchy with the Revolution of 1932, it was the site of bloody demonstrations during May 1992, when many students and middle-class citizens took to the streets to protest the dictatorial rule of General Suchinda Kraprayoon. When the protesters refused to back down in a stand-off with police, Gen. Suchinda ordered the army to attack. Dozens were mowed down by machine-gun fire. The general's move backfired, however, as the King and the public were outraged. Suchinda eventually resigned in disgrace and disappeared into exile before he could be arrested and put on trial.

On Worachak Rd. is **Wat Saket,** noteworthy for its **Golden Mount** soaring 80m into the sky (accessible by reg. bus #15). The mount was formerly the highest point in the city, and today its breezy, high location and 360° panoramic view make it a very popular place for the energetic. The nimble-limbed are rewarded with a tall golden chedi at the final destination (admission to the top 5฿; open daily 7:30am-5:30pm). The main chapel stands within an enclosed set of corridors; the perfectly symmetrical design is stunning. The temple grounds provide a restful spot for contemplating the other 42 sights on your whirlwind itinerary.

Going down Worachak Rd. to Bamrung Muang Rd., **Wat Suthat** and its famous **Sao Ching Cha (Giant Swing)** lie to the right (accessible by A/C bus #8). In the past, Sao Ching Cha was the scene of Brahmin rituals, when a priest would swing high to try to catch money suspended 25m in the air in his *teeth!* Many priests lost their lives attempting this feat, and a law passed during the reign of King Rama VII prohibited this exciting but dangerous ritual. King Rama I began construction on the temple, but it was not finished until King Rama III's reign. One of the largest wats in Bangkok, it is the only one without chedi or stupa (open daily 9am-5pm; free).

A 10-minute walk to the left along Bamrung Muang Rd. will lead back to Wat Phra Kaew and Sanam Luang, right at **Lak Muang** (the City Pillar). Walk to Na Hap Phoei Rd.; the gate is on the right. Lak Muang was built by King Rama I at the founding of Bangkok to house the spirit of the city. Worshippers still come daily to pay their respects, bringing offerings of food and drink (open daily 5:30am-7:30pm; free).

Wat Bovornives, on the corner of Phra Sawn Rd. and Bowon Nivet Rd. in North Banglamphu, is only a short walk from the Khaosan Rd. area; it is also accessible by A/C bus #11. King Rama IV spent 27 years here as a monk and an abbot before ascending to the throne. Wat Bovornives is also the home of the second Buddhist college in Thailand, **Mahamakut University.** If you want to flee the hordes of tourists, drop by and admire the main chapel's magnificent ornamental borders and Chinese-style stone guardian statues (open daily 9am-5pm; free).

Dusit/Government Center

The two most important numbers for a traveler in this area to remember are 70 and 72. Bus #70 runs along the entire lengths of Ratchadamnoen Nok Rd. and U Thong Nai Rd. and beyond, while bus #72 traverses the entire length of Si Ayutthaya Rd. Between the two, you can reach all the sights in this part of town.

Traveling north, away from the center of town from the point where Ratchadamnoen Klang Rd. and Ratchadamnoen Nok Rd. meet, the roads widen and traffic subsides. Trees spring up more frequently, and buildings fronted by security guards and the occasional armed trooper begin to appear. This is the Dusit area, the governmental center of the city and country.

Past the Si Ayutthaya Rd. light, Ratchadamnoen Nok Rd. opens into **Suan Amphon,** site of the revered **statue of King Chulalongkorn on horseback.** The beloved King Rama V ruled from 1868 to 1910 and is remembered for abolishing slavery, modernizing Thai society, and fending off mad British and French colonialists.

Behind the statue, guarded by an iron fence and a well-kept garden, stands the former **National Assembly,** or **Parliament Building.** The gigantic and venerable domed building was commissioned by King Chulalongkorn in 1908 to replace his old residence. This new Royal Palace, called Anandasamakhom, was patterned after St. Peter's Basilica in Rome, which explains its white marble and Italian Renaissance construction. In 1932, revolutionaries ended the absolute monarchy in a bloodless coup and seized the palace from King Rama VII, designating it as the new National Assembly building. Today it is referred to as the "old Parliament building," since the Assembly has been moved to another location in Dusit.

Ratchadamnoen Nok Rd. bends around the Assembly building to the right and becomes U Thong Nai Rd. On the right side of the road is the **Dusit Zoo,** the largest zoo in Thailand. Regular bus #70 conveniently stops right across the street from the U Thong Nai Gate. There are also gates on Rama V Rd. (accessible by bus #5) and Ratchawithi Rd. (bus #18, 28, and 108 or A/C #10). Visitors to the Dusit Zoo are soothed by the lush greenery and tall trees, amused by the playfulness of the Malaysian sun bears, and relaxed by steering a paddleboat on an artificial lake. Follow the zoomorphic signs to see the animals of your choice; you can grunt at the American bison donated by the city of Seattle (open daily 8am-6pm; admission 20฿, seniors over 60 10฿, and children under 10 5฿).

Farther up U Thong Nai Rd. past Dusit Zoo is an entrance to **Vimarnmek Palace,** on the left. When a constitutional crisis is brewing (which is most of the time in Thailand), this gate is locked to keep out the protestors who threaten to bring the country to its knees by playing bad folk music and pounding the ground with empty mineral water bottles. Take bus #70. Vimarnmek was built during the reign of King Chulalongkorn, and its L-shaped structure is made of golden teakwood; curators claim that it is the largest teakwood mansion in the world. It has 81 rooms on four floors—impressive enough, but the most remarkable feature of the building is that it was constructed without nails.

Vimarnmek Palace contains numerous pieces of ancient art from various countries. Tours of the palace are given in English every half-hour. The one-hour tour is very detailed, and goes through the most important rooms of the palace, including the throne room and the King's personal quarters. Check out the **King's bathroom,** considered technologically advanced for its day (open daily 9:30am-4pm, last admission 3pm; admission 50฿, for children 5-15 20฿, under 5 free). Admission to Wat Phra Kaew (Temple of the Emerald Buddha) and the Grand Palace entitles the visitor to free admission to Vimarnmek Palace if the admission slip is kept. Free display of Thai dancing daily at 10:30am and 2pm. No shorts or sleeveless shirts.

Following the route of bus #72 down Si Ayutthaya Rd., shortly after it passes the Ratchadamnoen Nok Rd. intersection, the grounds of **Wat Benchamabophit,** or Bangkok's famous **Marble Temple,** will appear on the right. Its perfectly symmetrical architecture and pure white Carrara marble walls were built in 1899 by (who else?) King Chulalongkorn. Every morning, monks chant inside the main chapel. The cloisters of the courtyard are splendidly lined with 52 bronze Buddhas, representing the styles of Buddha images from different periods. After visiting the main chapel, take a stroll around the garden and see the sacred turtles, which are given to the temple by its faithful worshippers (open daily 8am-5:30pm; admission 10฿).

Past Wat Benchamabophit and Rama V Rd. on the left is a walled compound protected by a moat and specially trained soldiers. The compound is **Chitlada Palace,** official home of the Royal Family, and the assault-rifle-toting blue-uniformed troops are the King's Royal Guard. The palace is not open to the public. Do not attempt to enter. You will be shot. May our fearlessly thorough researcher rest in peace.

Chinatown/Pahurat/Hualamphong

When Bangkok was founded in 1782 by King Rama I, Chinese immigrants came to settle in this area to the southeast of the royal center along the Chao Phraya River, which has remained home to the ethnic Chinese community for over two centuries. Today, this area is called **Yaowarat** (after the road which runs through Chinatown), or **Sampeng.** In Chinatown there are no sights in the traditional sense, but what the area does offer is a slice of life, seen through a lens unchanged for decades. Although modern conveniences have intruded, the lifestyle of the inhabitants has remained rather constant—witness the number of shops peddling dried frogs.

Near Yaowarat, in an area marked by Pahurat Rd., Chakraphet Rd., and countless alleys around and in between, is the **Pahurat** district of Bangkok, the traditional home of the ethnic Indian population. While it is a bit smaller than Yaowarat, Pahurat's streets are no less chaotic, filled with lively sidewalk and street markets. Inexpensive clothing sold by both Sikhs and Hindus is the big draw here .

The only major temple in the Chinatown/Pahurat/Hualamphong area is the famed **Wat Traimit,** home of the **Giant Golden Buddha,** a three-meter, five-ton, 100% gold Sukhothai-style statue. Really. When the Burmese sacked Ayutthaya, the people of the ancient capital saved the statue by covering it with stucco, a cheap but successful trick. Its true identity remained a secret until 1955, when the statue slipped from a moving crane as it was being transported to Wat Traimit and cracks developed in the plaster, revealing traces of glittering gold. The stucco was removed, and —eureka!—the Golden Buddha, over 700 years old, was rediscovered. Today it is housed in a small room above a currency exchange booth and gift shops. A small sitting area next to the ticket office has a tape recording of the history of the temple and of the Golden Buddha played in three languages: English, Chinese, and Japanese (open daily 8:30am-5pm; admission for Golden Buddha 10฿). The main entrance is on Yaowarat Rd. near where it meets Charoen Krung Rd., but there is also a smaller entrance on the short Traimit Rd., which is accessible by bus #73.

Silom/Financial District

Believe it or not, the area around Silom Rd. offers more than just the moth-eaten-ragtag-down-at-heel-sleazy-whore-houses-cum-go-go-bars which line Patpong Rd. **Lumpini Park,** the largest park in Bangkok, is an oasis of lush greenery amid the gas fumes and dusty roads which coat the greater portion of the capital. Bordered by Ratchadamri, Rama IV, Sarasin, and Witthayu Rd., the park has man-made lakes, wide roads, and paths overrun by joggers, as well as some of the largest trees in Bangkok. In the mornings, elderly Chinese go through the slow motions of tai chi, the ancient exercise designed to promote health and prolong life. For a little pseudo-exercise, rent a paddleboat and cruise along the lakes (20฿ per 30min.; boat rentals daily 7am-7pm). The park is accessible from Silom by regular bus #15, 77, and 115; from Siam Sq. or Banglamphu by regular bus #15; from Sukhumvit take regular bus #25, 40, or 48 to Siam Sq. and make the connection to #15.

From Lumpini Park, a five- to ten-minute taxi ride brings you to the Red Cross Society's **Queen Saovabha Institute,** on the corner of Rama IV and Henri Dunant Rd., home of the famous **snake farm** (tel. 252 0161-64). The farm was established in 1923 as a center for the milking of poisonous snakes for the production of local antivenin. Today, the farm displays a variety of non-poisonous and poisonous serpents, including the king cobra and various vipers (open Mon.-Fri. 8:30am-3:30pm, Sat.-Sun. and holidays 8:30-11am; admission 70฿, free for children under 10). Admission is good for the whole day; the snake farm closes for lunch hour at noon. Various lectures and snake-handling demonstrations take place on weekdays (10:30am-2pm); weekends and holidays (10:30am). The snake farm also has a small museum.

One of the world's most famous hotels, **The Oriental Hotel** (tel. 236 0400 or 236 0420), is located five minutes from the library, at 48 Oriental Ave. along the Chao Phraya River. Walk down Charoen Krung Soi 40 toward the river; it will be on the right. Founded in 1876 by two Danish sea captains, Evie Jarck and Buck Salje, The Oriental was a classy hotel from the start. H. N. Andersen built the original, grand Italianate building in 1887, and it still stands as the **Authors' Residence** wing of the hotel, which shelters some of the finest and most expensive rooms. The famous guest list of The Oriental includes: Joseph Conrad (1888), King Chulalongkorn (1890), Carl Fabergé (1912), W. Somerset Maugham (1922), Prince Charles and Princess Diana (as their marriage was headed down the slippery slope in 1988), Prince Philip (1989), and Emperor Akihito (1991). Contemporary authors John Le Carré, Gore Vidal, Peter Ustinov, and Henry Nguyen have also been pampered at The Oriental.

Siam Sq./Pratunam

This area is famed for its munificent temples of conspicuous consumption, where faithful worshippers bearing credit cards pay homage (or cold hard cash) to the gods of Gucci. Some sights are worth checking out, but it will take time and patience to traverse this area, home to the city's most gargantuan traffic delays.

The most noticeable landmark on Rama I Rd., aside from the Mahboonkrong Shopping Complex and the Siam Sq. Shopping Center, is the **National Stadium** complex. Anyone may freely enter the grounds and run about like a fiend or join a pick-up game of soccer or takraw.

Across from the National Stadium complex, at the end of Soi Kasem San 2 and to the left, is **Jim Thompson's House,** 6 Soi Kasem San 2 (tel. 215 0122), which which houses one of Thailand's best collections of Ayutthaya and Rattanakosin period art. The one-hour English language tour (included in admission) is interesting. The guide discusses various ingenious architectural oddities found in Thai houses and shows visitors a shallow cup designed to prevent people from getting drunk too quickly (open Mon.-Sat. 9am-4:30pm; admission 100฿, for those under 26 40฿). Proceeds from ticket sales go to various Thai charities.

Farther along Rama I Rd. around where the street name changes to Ploenchit Rd. are **Amarin Plaza** and the famous **Erawan Shrine,** built after several workers lost their lives in mysterious accidents during the construction of the Erawan Hotel on Ratchadamri Rd. Devotees flock to give offerings to the Brahma figure housed within the small, glittering display. This shrine is believed to house especially influential and powerful spirits. Thai dancers hired by grateful worshippers whose prayers were answered by the deity often perform around the shrine.

Less than 2km away on Si Ayutthaya Rd. is **Wang Suan Pakkard** (tel. 245 4934), otherwise known as Lettuce Farm Palace. No lettuce can be found here now, but five traditional Thai wooden houses set on teakwood stilt-like columns struggle to take the place of the impressive Lactuca sativa. An immaculately kept garden with plants from all over the world surrounds the buildings. In the back of the garden is the Lacquer Pavilion, which is filled with porcelain, statues of Buddha, and painted pottery from Ban Chiang. Perhaps the biggest attraction at Wang Suan Pakkard, however, is the relative calm it offers those weary of the Bangkok heat and congestion (open Mon.-Sat. 9am-4pm; admission 80฿, for students 20฿). To get there, take regular bus #54, 73, or 204 from Siam Sq. past the Indra Regent on Ratchaprarop Rd. Get off near the corner of Ratchaprarop and Si Ayutthaya Roads, and turn down Si Ayutthaya. The palace will be on the left, behind a wooden fence.

One of the more **arousing** sights in Bangkok is the **Goddess Tuptim Shrine,** or the **Phallic Shrine,** near the Hilton International Hotel on Wireless Rd. The shrine is known for the large numbers of **priapic** objects around its spirit house, brought there by couples seeking help for infertility. These offerings vary in **size** and **composition;** some are marble, but most are **woody.** According to history, when the hotel was founded, a spirit house was **erected** for the Goddess Tuptim, whose spirit was said to live in a nearby tree. Slews of people had **come** to the shrine bringing gifts and eventually someone hit on the idea of a **phallic gift.** Soon, worshippers with fertility problems began making the trip to the shrine with their own **tubular** offerings. To see this **unusual** shrine, take a tuk-tuk or taxi to the Hilton, or get on bus #76 from Silom to its farthest point on Witthayu (Wireless) Rd., and walk the rest of the way (5min.). Once at the Hilton, take a right turn before the entrance, walk down the path, go downstairs and through the parking lot, pass the staff entrance, and go out into the clearing.

Missing: One Silk Magnate. Answers to Jim.

It can be argued that the mystique surrounding James H. W. Thompson, O.S.S. (the pre-C.I.A. American intelligence organization) officer, and the father of the modern Thai silk industry, draws more visitors than the house itself. Jim Thompson was born in Greenville, Delaware, U.S.A. in 1906 and was an architect before enlisting in the U.S. Army during World War II. He was stationed in Thailand at the end of the war, and loved the country so much that he left his wife in America for an extended stay. Intrigued by the hand weaving of silk cloth, he spent his time and money creating the modern Thai silk industry and making Thai silk famous around the world. Thompson's mansion, a testament to his financial success and great love for things Thai, was built in authentic Thai style and decorated with antique Thai art, including some of the oldest known Thai paintings. On March 27, 1967, Thompson disappeared while tiger hunting in Malaysia. Numerous theories, enough to keep Oliver Stone happy, have been advanced about his fate. The unimaginative believe he was eaten by a tiger, but others think that he was exposed as a C.I.A. operative and deep-sixed, or that he was involved in a shady business deal that got out of hand. In any event, Thompson left the legacy of the Thai silk industry, as well as a beautiful house.

Sukhumvit Rd. Area

Sukhumvit Rd., with its overwhelming number of sois, restaurants, and tailoring shops, may not enthrall the tourist . One of the few real sights is **Kamthieng House,** at 131 Soi 21-Asoke (tel. 258 3491), an ethnological museum and the home of the **Siam Society,** a Thai cultural society supported by the royals. Built in the mid-19th century, the Kamthieng House was originally on the east bank of the Ping River in Chiang Mai, where it was owned by an ancestor of the wealthy and well-known Nimmanahaeminda family. The museum attempts to reconstruct the daily life of 19th-century Thais, with exhibits on tools, utensils, and other objects. (open Tues.-Sat. 9am-5pm; admission 20฿, students 10฿).

Those seeking a respite from the confusion of town without actually leaving Bangkok can go to the **King Rama IX Royal Park** on Soi 103 Sukhumvit Rd. Grab A/C bus #8 from Siam Center to Soi 103 and take a taxi to the park. Here, the magnificently sculpted 200-plus acres dwarf the more natural Lumpini Park. The land was donated to the King by a wealthy lady during the mid-1980s; the king then donated it to the public, hence the name. Exhibits detailing the life of King Rama IX in his various roles – philanthropist, sportsman, family man, model/actor, etc. line the perimeter of the octagonal building in the park center. Each weekend, families and couples converge to picnic and frolic among the smooth grassy hills, neatly arranged flower beds, and manicured foliage. Paddleboats on the man-made lake rent for 20฿ per 30min. A 20-min. trolley ride around the park is 10฿ (open daily 6am-6pm; admission 10฿; use of bathroom in the main building 2฿). The best time of the year to come to the park is during the first 10 days of December, when flowers and decorations commemorate the King's birthday (Dec. 5).

ENTERTAINMENT

As the song from the musical Chess says: "One night in Bangkok makes the hard man humble. Not much between despair and ecstasy." Bangkok may be full of appalling and prurient opportunities, but pubs, discos, markets, and cultural shows are an active, if under-publicized, surrogate nightlife. Bangkok has impressive cabarets in the **Calypso Cabaret,** Ambassador Hotel, entrance on Soi 11 Sukhumvit Rd. (tel. 261 6355, -56 from 9am-6pm or 254 0444 from 6-10pm), featuring well-costumed transvestite performers whose gender is betrayed only by their singing voices. Acts range from wistful torch singing to parodies of famous artists. Calypso is performed in a 200-seat theater and is Bangkok's longest running and most popular show of its kind. Reservations must be made the day of the show. Two 80-minute shows daily at 8:30pm and 10pm. Admission (390฿; all major credit cards) includes one free drink. Additional drinks cost 80-180฿.

Bars and Pubs

"Bars" in Bangkok are rarely aimed hanging out, nor do they cater to a singles scene. In Thai culture, it is acceptable for men to head around the block for a bottle of Singha, but not for women. Traditional, "respectable" Thai women rarely frequent bars informally; it would cast doubt on their characters.

Bars come in three types. First and most atrocious are the infamous go-go bars, which are a mainstay of the international Thai prostitution industry. Women and children (of both genders) from all over Thailand are sold into slavery by their impoverished rural families and sent to work in Bangkok go-go bars, which are fueled by the bucks funneled in by overseas visitors. These are not listed.

The second type is the "hostess bar," where attractive women are hired by the management to serve your drinks and sit with you. Some of these bars are fronts for prostitution, some aren't. These too are not listed.

Finally, there are the few pubs where people can get together and drink without participating in the skin trade in any way. Despite the romping nightlife in Bangkok, this last type of bar is amazingly difficult to encounter.

In Thailand, "bar" generally designates an establishment connected to the sex industry. "Pub" refers to a standard reputable drinking hole. The bars listed below are "pubs." Some reputable establishments are located in not-so-reputable entertainment areas. Use common sense when choosing where to go: the nature of a particular bar may change overnight, for better or for worse.

Bobby's Arms, inside the parking garage, Patpong II Rd. (tel. 233 6828). Established in 1975, this is Thailand's oldest British pub. It has a wide following of English-speaking expatriate workers, especially those from Britain. Get a dose of cribbage, backgammon, darts, and other staple British pub games amid the warm wood tones and overwhelming British paraphernalia. Flight crews of many airlines (particularly from Britain and the US) come here and get bombed out of their minds. Laugh, and feel secure knowing that you won't be on their 6am flight the next morning. Beers and ales (including Foster's, Guinness Stout) 40-85฿. Spirits 55-75฿. Cocktails 65-95฿. Numerous liquored coffees. Happy hour daily 5-7pm (15% off all drinks). Open daily 11am-1am. Live music Fri.-Sat. 8:30-11:30pm. Dixieland jazz Sun. 8-11pm.

Jool's, 21/3 Soi 4 (Nana Tai) Sukhumvit Rd. (tel. 252 6413), 175m down the soi on the left. This joint with a lively atmosphere and the choicest pub food competes fiercely with its cross-town rival, Bobby's Arms. The smaller Jool's is usually packed with Brits of both genders who find it easy to get to know each other in the scrunched surroundings. Getting a stool can take hours. Those not into conversation can leaf through a stack of magazines and photo albums just inside the entrance or peruse the walls crammed with pictures of customers. Stucco walls and a ceiling made of wooden planks give the bar an underground feel. Beer (Carlsberg, among others) 50฿ and cocktails.

Woodstock, 210-213 Nana Plaza, 3rd fl., Soi 4 Sukhumvit Rd. (tel. 258 2565). Yes, the owner was at Woodstock. Pleasantly seedy, this place packs graying ZZ-Top fans around pool tables in a haze of passive smoke. It was established in 1984 as a go-go bar, but the owner changed his mind and made it into a rock 'n' roll bar paying homage to the '60s and '70s. Fans of Hendrix, Dylan, the Allman Brothers, CCR, and the Eagles should be forever grateful. Beers 60฿. Cocktails slightly higher. Happy hour (11:30am-8pm) offers beers at 45฿ (all other drinks 20% off). Open daily 11:30am-2am. Free popcorn. Real food (60-110฿) includes burgers.

The Bar at Bei Ottos, 1 Soi 20 Sukhumvit Rd. (tel. 258 1495, -96). The cozy bar, pictures of Germany, beer mugs, and other *München* motifs can cure some expatriates' homesickness and create it for others. The sturdy black wooden slab bar has cushy vinyl to protect the predominantly German customers' midsections as they imbibe. See the Thai waitresses look uncomfortable in their St. Pauli girl outfits. Oktoberfest celebrations here raise chugging to a new level. Beers and ales include local brands, as well as Foster's, Guinness Stout, Carlsberg, and the German D.A.B. Beers start at 60฿ and go all the way to 220฿ for a 1.25 liter boot! Cocktails 85-110฿. Open daily 10:30am-2am.

Cheap Charlie's, Sukhumvit Soi 11, inside the first little soi on the left on Soi 11. Basically a street kiosk with a few chairs. The mixed clientele is almost as eccentric as the western death motif in the decor; admire the skulls, antlers, and live bats. Open daily 3pm-2am.

Discos

The disco in Bangkok is what you would expect anywhere: a cavernous building for frenetic dancing, decked in gaudy decorations, a booming sound system and flashing video screens. Throughout the night, music shifts between live bands and a DJ spinning Euro and American fad-ish music. Discos stay hot for about six months to a year before the crowds find a newer, cooler place. The hordes of disco-seekers can make it nearly impossible to get into popular spots on weekends. Discos in Bangkok are not always the safest night-spots—some of the seedier ones can get scrappy.

Cola Concert Hall, 906 Soi 40 Sukhumvit Rd. (tel. 391 1105). Michael Wong, the handsome and popular Hong Kong-born singer who appeared in a series of Thai Chivas Regal ads, sang a few songs here, and the rest was history. Mike may no longer hang here, but Cola's popularity is holding strong among well-dressed teens and yuppies thanks to its large dance space, laser lights, and mix of pop and techno. Cover charge 400฿ (includes 2 drinks), 500฿ when a hot artist comes to perform. Open daily 8pm-2am. Look 18.

Rhino Music House, 215/2 Soi Thong-Lo 1, Soi 55, Sukhumvit Rd. (tel. 392 3291). A popular cross between disco and live music bar—but no dance floor. The more sedentary professional crowd gazes at video screens or live bands. Cover Sun.-Thurs. 100฿ (1 drink), Fri.-Sat. 250฿ (2 drinks). Open daily 7pm-2:30am. Look 18.

NASA Spacedrome, 999 Ramkhamhaeng Rd. (tel. 314 4024). It keeps going, and going, and going...the undisputed winner of the disco longevity award. It has been pumping out hits since Culture Club. An enormous dance floor allows all ages and backgrounds to work out life's frustrations under a cloud of billowing fog and flashing lights. Open daily 9pm-2:30am. Cover Sun.-Thurs. 200฿ (2 drinks), Fri.-Sat. 250฿ (2 drinks); 300฿ (2 drinks) when a hot band comes to play.

Live Music

First popping up in the mid-80s, live music bars have held Bangkok's attention by providing good bands in a low-pressure, festive atmosphere. Especially on Friday and Saturday nights, they've become the entertainment of choice for many office workers, businesspeople, middle-class students, and high society party-goers. There are as many musical options as there are live music bars: ranging from Thai music, jazz, or country to heavy metal. Bands generally start around 8pm, but things get cooking around 11pm or midnight.

Brown Sugar, 231/19 Sarasin Rd. (tel. 250 0103 or 250 1826), opposite Lumpini Park. A Bangkok favorite, it plays the sweetest jazz and pulls in its well-dressed clientele even on weeknights. Pubby feel created by the heavy emphasis on brick and pictures of past performers. Famous past guests include Willem Dafoe, Gregory Hines, and Spyro Gyra. Some food (60-360฿, most under 100฿). Beer 120-150฿. Cocktails 140฿. Happy hour 11am-6pm, all drinks 15% off. Cover 150฿ Sun.-Thurs; 180฿ Fri.-Sat. after 8pm (1 drink included). Open Sun.-Thurs. 11am-

1am, Fri.-Sat. 11am-2am. Music every night from 9:30pm until closing time. All major credit cards.

Old West, 231/17 Sarasin Rd. (tel. 252 9510), near Brown Sugar. The premier spot to take in live folk and country music. Head into the saloon through the swinging doors and sip Jack Daniels or Jim Beam amidst Wild West kitsch such as saddles, cattle skulls, and pictures of cowboys and Native Americans. Beer 60-70฿. Cocktails 80฿. Small food menu (40-80฿). No cover. Open daily 5pm-1am. Two bands per night play from 8:30pm until closing time. MC, Visa.

Thai Classical Dance Dinners

The highlight of some people's visits to Bangkok is a night at a Thai restaurant with a classical dance show. Because the National Theater schedules infrequent performances of Thai classical dance, some restaurants have tried to fill the gap. Most Thai classical dance dinners put on half a dozen traditional dances in an hour-long show (the dinner lasts another hour). Shows usually include khon dances from the Ramakien. No shorts, sandals, or tank-tops allowed. Reserve at least a day in advance.

Ruen Thep, Silom Village, Silom Rd. (tel. 234 4581). Better-than-average ambience for a Thai classical dance dinner. Doors open daily at 7pm. Thai dinner served at 7:30pm amid pools of carp and turtles. Performance 8:30-9:30pm. Includes 7 dance styles (changed monthly). 350฿ per person. All major credit cards.

Sala Rim Nam, Charoen Nakhon Rd. (tel. 437 3080), across the Chao Phraya River from the Oriental Hotel. When money is no object. This show has no equal (in elegance, quality of performance, or steepness of price). Restaurant opens at 7pm. Show with 6 dances performed 8:30-9:30pm. 820฿ per person, includes ferry from the Oriental Hotel across the river to restaurant. All major credit cards.

Maneeya's Lotus Room, 518/5 Ploenchit Rd. (tel. 252 6312). The most inexpensive classical dance dinner around—performances are still decent. Dinner begins at 7pm, and the 45min., 6-dance show (350฿) starts at 8:15pm. MC, Visa.

Cinema

Thais have a remarkable penchant for mainstream American films. Recent hits include Pulp Fiction and Die Hard With A Vengeance. One notable drawback about movies is that the censor board can shred the film, blurring some love scenes and cutting others altogether. Check the newspaper for comments on the nature and extent of the censorship in a particular movie. Before every movie, the royal anthem is played, and it is required of moviegoers to stand at attention during the song. All English films are subtitled in Thai. For more info and movie times for all major theaters in Bangkok, refer to the Focus section in The Nation.

Scala Theater, Siam Sq. Soi 1 (tel. 251 2861). One of Bangkok's older and larger English-language theaters From hits to artier, less commercial features.

MacKenna, 117/2 Phayathai Rd. (tel. 252 6215). Medium-sized theater usually shows the most popular film of the moment.

Ground Floor, Mahboonkrong Center, ground fl., Rama I Rd. (tel. 217 9436). One of the new mall theaters invading Bangkok, it shows popular US movies.

Washington Theaters, opposite Soi 33 Sukhumvit Rd. on Sukhumvit Rd. (tel. 258 2045). Popular English-language films.

American University Alumni (AUA), 179 Ratchadamri Rd. (tel. 252 7067, -68, or -69). Infrequent showings of older American films.

Muay Thai (Thai Boxing)

Muay Thai goes on every single day of the week in Bangkok at one of two venues. On Sun., Mon., Wed., and Thurs., the action gets hot and heavy at the **Ratchadamnoen Boxing Stadium,** Ratchadamnoen Nok Rd. (tel. 281 4205). To get there, take regular bus #70 from Sanam Luang. Bouts start at 6pm on Mon. and Wed., 5pm on Thurs., and 4pm on Sun. On Tues., Fri., and Sat. at 6pm, fighters bomb away at each other at the **Lumpini Boxing Stadium,** Rama IV Rd. near Lumpini Park (tel. 251 4303). To get there, take regular bus #115 from Silom Rd. Bouts here start at

6:20pm. Tickets at both stadiums are sold at the gate. Prices currently run from 150฿ to 500฿ depending on which of three classes of seats you get. First-class seats are those at or near ringside, usually purchased by government officials and wealthy fans, while the muggy third-class seats are favored by gamblers and other regulars. See Life and Times for more information.

SHOPPING

The frenzy that is Bangkok shopping occurs both in department stores and malls, where prices are fixed, and in street markets, where bargaining rules the day. While most department store wares (especially clothing and handicrafts) are also sold on the street, the quality can be much lower. The street markets are the places for knock-off designer watches and clothing (from Polo to Levis) and pirated cassette tapes and videos. Since street markets are the domain of the haggler, weak bargainers will be chewed up and spit out.

The **weekend market** at Chatuchak Park is a bargain-hunter's dream. Hundreds of covered stalls form a labyrinth of shopping delight, selling everything from regular street market clothes to military surplus equipment. The weekend market is notorious for its adept pickpockets; guard your wallets and purses carefully.

The market is actually open every day of the week from dawn to dusk, but the excitement and the vendors do not come out in full force until the weekend. The weekend market was formerly located at Sanam Luang near Wat Phra Kaew, but restrictions on space for the ever-growing market eventually forced it to move to its present site at Chatuchak Park on Phahonyothin Rd., which is near the Northern Bus Terminal. Take regular bus #3 from Sanam Luang or A/C bus #2 from Silom. The bus ride could take up to three hours if traffic is grisly.

Every region of Bangkok has its own **street markets,** and individual street vendors are ubiquitous. Some markets are open only in the morning; but typically, most vendors emerge during the late afternoon and early evening. The markets with relatively few tourists have the best deals (Yaowarat, Pahurat, and Banglamphu), but it really depends on what you are looking for (food is always cheap at street markets).

The **Banglamphu Market** branches out onto Chakrapong, Krai Si, and Tani Roads, while a more tourist-oriented street market pops up along Khaosan Rd. A mostly late-afternoon and early-evening market, the frenzied Banglamphu Market's best deals include food, leather products, and no-name clothing, in addition to Levis, Ralph Lauren, and Benetton spin-offs. It is one of the most convenient markets, with the widest range of products and the lowest prices. **Thewet Market** is on Krung Kasem Rd. near the pier; it's in the area north of Banglamphu next to **Dusit** and along the Chao Phraya River. Vendors hawk most of the usual street market items, although it is best known for its flowers and plants.

The **Yaowarat** area contains the **Sampeng Market,** while Pahurat, naturally enough, is home to the **Pahurat Market.** Both of these markets are well-known for their inexpensive cotton and silk fabrics, no-name clothes, shoes, housewares, fake watches, and other fake (and sometimes real) jewelry items. In the Pratunam area, a lively street market (the **Pratunam Market**) operates during the day along Ratchaprarop Rd., around and across the street from the Indra Hotel. Once again, clothes are big here, although there is also a wide selection of knick-knacks, including toenail clippers, sunglasses, and fake braids.

In the **Silom** area, the street market scene is pretty sedate during the day. After nightfall, however, vendors set up stalls along **Patpong Rd.,** giving travelers a legitimate reason to go to Patpong. They sell fake designer clothing, lighters, pewter, wood carvings, counterfeit cassette tapes, and souvenirs, among many other things. Prices are generally hard to bargain down because of the market's touristy nature.

The Siam Sq. and Silom areas are packed with most of Bangkok's major **department stores and shopping centers.** Most are open daily between 10am and 9pm and remain open even on most national holidays.

The undisputed heavyweight of all of Bangkok's shopping centers is **Mahboonkrong Center,** on the corner of Rama I and Phayathai Roads in the Siam Sq.

area. A six-tiered shopping Goliath, Mahboonkrong houses the Tokyu (not Tokyo) Department Store as well as hundreds of other shops and restaurants.

Across Phayathai Rd., **Siam Square** is connected to Mahboonkrong Center by a footbridge over the street. Siam Sq., Thailand's first shopping center, spreads over a network of sois. Today, it contains two movie theaters and a hotel. Across Rama I Rd. from Siam Sq. is the **Siam Center,** a self-appointed "House of Boutiques." These "shoppes" cater mainly to young, chic Thais.

Amarin Plaza is farther up Rama I Rd. at the intersection of Rama I with Ratchadamri Roads. About 200m down Ratchadamri Rd. is the relatively small **Peninsula Plaza,** the site of Northwest Airlines' ticket office and a branch of Asia Books. Up Ratchadamri Rd. toward Phetchaburi Rd. is the **Zen World Trade Center,** vying for Mahboonkrong Center's spot as the mama of all shopping centers, but offering more open space than anything else.

In the Silom area, on the corner of Silom and Rama IV Roads, the **Silom Center** prominently displays a large "R" (for Robinson Department Store). The **Silom Complex** is farther down on the left, sheltering the popular **Central Department Store**.

In Banglamphu, convenient to Khaosan Rd., the **New World Department Store,** the poor man's Mahboonkrong, has the best deals on manufactured goods.

For quality **handicrafts** and the satisfaction of helping a cause, head directly to **Narayana-Phand** at 127 Ratchadamri Rd. (tel. 252 4670, through -72). Take A/C bus #15 from Dusit, reg. bus #2 from Sanam Luang, or reg. bus #204 from Siam Sq. Narayana-Phand was established by the Thai government and the private sector around 50 years ago to support traditional handicrafts. The two-story shop sells an extensive array of artifacts and handles all necessary paperwork with the Fine Arts Department for goods which need approval for export (open daily 10am-8pm; all major credit cards). There are also branches at Sogo Department Store in Amarin Plaza and Isetan Department Store in the Zen World Trade Center. **Central Department Store,** on the corner of Soi Chitlom and Ploenchit Rd., also carries an impressive selection of handicrafts (open daily 10am-9pm; all major credit cards).

From the end of March through the first part of April, the annual **Arts and Crafts Fair** exhibits Thai handicrafts for sale. It is held at the Exhibition Hall on Ratchadaphisek Rd. and sponsored by the Department of Export and Promotion.

To purchase **leather goods** such as belts, wallets, purses, and briefcases, go to **Medlep Leather Products,** 178 Silom Rd. (tel. 234 0146), near the Narai Hotel. Their prices tend to be lower than those in the western world. On sale, leather briefcases come to around 1200฿ and a full-length leather overcoat may not be a total pipe-dream (open Mon.-Sat. 10am-7:30pm).

■ NEAR BANGKOK

SAMUT PRAKAN

The center of Thailand's leather industry, Samut Prakan is about 30km south of Bangkok next to the Gulf of Thailand. Besides its numerous unentertaining factories, the town holds two popular attractions, the **Samut Prakan Crocodile Farm** and **Muang Boran,** the Ancient City. To get to both, take regular bus #25 from Bangkok to Pak Nam, the boisterous and crowded shopping area of Samut Prakan. Get off at the first stop after **Wat Phichai Songkhram,** a major temple in the heart of Pak Nam. To get to the Crocodile Farm, walk forward from the bus stop, along with the one-way traffic, toward the next street-corner, where a line of light blue songthaews marked with a capital "S" waits to go to the Crocodile Farm (3฿). To go to Muang Boran after getting off the bus, walk back approximately 100 ft. against the flow of traffic from the bus stop to the street corner at the Bank of Ayudhya. Along the side street, a row of songthaews lines up to go to Muang Boran (3฿).

The **Crocodile Farm,** (tel. 703 4891) is a small zoo with an emphasis on crocodiles. Witness two young trainers taunting and teasing the reptiles. Much to the delight of the bloodthirsty crowd, one of the trainers even places his head into a crocodile's mouth. This "wrestling" extravaganza takes place on the hour 9-11am and 1-4pm daily. On Saturdays, Sundays, and holidays, shows are added at noon and 5pm. Included in the admission is an elephant show in which audience members are invited to lie down on the stage while an elephant or two steps daintily over their bodies. Other exciting attractions include an aviary full of exotic, mysterious birds, snake pits, tigers, go-carts, and, if that's not enough, a train will take you on a joyride around the compound for a mere 20฿ per adult and 10฿ per child.Open daily 8am-6:45pm; admission: 200฿, children 120฿, Thai citizens 30฿.

Muang Boran (tel. 323 9253), Km33 on the Sukhumvit Highway, is proudly described by its owners as the largest open-air museum in the world. Not counting ancient ruins, they are probably right, as Muang Boran covers hundreds of acres of land. The museum contains replicas of famous Thai historical monuments and some authentic structures laid out in the geographical shape of Thailand. The most striking sights at Muang Boran are the **Sanphet Prasat Palace**, the **Dusit Maha Prasat Palace**, and the **Khao Phra Wihaan**, the top of which has a spectacular view of the surrounding countryside and the Gulf of Thailand. For a complete description of all the monuments and other sights within Muang Boran, buy the Muang Boran book in English or Thai for 50฿. Bring all your desert gear because Muang Boran is scorching-hot. Open daily 8am-5pm; admission 50฿, children 25฿.

NONTHABURI

One of the nation's oldest provinces, Nonthaburi is about 20km north of Bangkok, on both banks of the Chao Phraya River. The town of Nonthanaburi, on the east bank, is believed to have been part of the great Ayutthaya Empire; now it's known for its fruit and earthenware. On the west bank of the Chao Phraya, in Amphoe Bangkluai, stands a magnificent, newly renovated temple called **Wat Chalerm Phra Kliad Wora Wihaan,** known to locals simply as Wat Chalerm. The temple had been neglected for years and was deteriorating markedly when King Bhumibol donated 20 million baht of his personal cache to renovate it. When renovations were completed, the king and queen attended a rededication fête on Jan. 12, 1993.

Chinese styles strongly influence the statues around the grounds, as well as the ceramics and flowering decorations adorning the temple. Inside the cool main chapel sits a large golden-colored Buddha in a sash given by His Royal Majesty. Pictures of the King's 1993 visit line the walls. Chinese artists patiently handpainted the excruciatingly intricate designs on the walls. Open daily 9am-5pm; free. The rabbit on the doors outside the chapel is a sign that the temple was built by King Rama II for his queen, whose birth year was the year of the rabbit. (Other famous rabbits include King Bhumibol.) The small artificial cave on the temple grounds has a path set atop the waterway and a naga head sticking through the hill above the cave.

The best way to travel to Wat Chalerm is by the **Chao Phraya River Express ferry,** which terminates at the Nonthaburi Pier. From here, take a small ferry to the west bank of the river (1฿), then hire a motorcycle to Wat Chalerm (5฿). Convenient places to board the ferry (5-15฿) are Tha Chang near the Temple of the Emerald Buddha, Tha Phra Arthit near Banglamphu, and Tha Thewet by the National Library.

RATCHABURI

Damnoen Saduak Floating Market is one hour out of town, on the road to Ratchaburi. Catch bus #78 (15฿) at the bus stop in front of the Chinese headstone store 200m down on your left when you turn right out of the chedi's south exit. From Damnoen Saduak town, grab a yellow songthaew (3฿) on the main road across from the post office to take you the 2km to the floating market. Upon arrival, people will quickly approach you about water-taxi tours that will fleece you out of 200฿. If you want to do the tourist thing, get a boat for 50฿. But you'll get equally good pictures by walking along the canals. Either way, you'll be confronted by souvenir peddlers, but at least they're not as pervasive as in Bangkok. The market is only on one stretch of water, with unimpressive houses and boat-rocking speedboats along the other side. Peak activity in the markets is between 9am and 10pm, with its centers at the

Hia Kui and Thom Khan markets. Head out early if you want to see all the loot-laden boats; they return home at noon after all the tourists have disappeared.

■■■ AYUTTHAYA

Ayutthaya's lengthy history and integral role in the development of the country distinguished the town in the hearts of most Thais. The Ayutthayan empire was founded in 1350 by Prince U Thong and lasted more than four centuries. In that time, the capital city raised 33 kings to the throne, withstood 23 invasions by Burmese troops, and extended its rule as far west as Pego in Burma and as far east as Angkor in Cambodia. The empire was a dominant power in Southeast Asia with all the trappings of its position: arts, trade, technology, literature, and commerce.

In 1767, on their 24th time around, Burmese troops succeeded in breaching Ayutthaya's defenses and, when they found that they could not hold the city, burned it to the ground. They took scores of prisoners and destroyed the wats, palaces, libraries, and *chedis*. They melted Buddha images for gold and slaughtered the king along with many Thais. Forced to abandon the location, the remainder of the Thai military moved the capital to Bangkok, where it has been located ever since. For more information, see History and Politics, page 287.

Today, Ayutthaya is a mainstay on the Thailand tourist circuit. As you clamor over crumbling ruins you'll witness the city's latest invasions: Asian "holiday-makers," European air-conditioned adventurers, and, of course, busloads of Thai school children perhaps more interested in *farang* visitors than ancient temples. Amidst all this, it's easy to forget that Ayutthaya is a bustling provincial capital in its own right, a face of the city perhaps best seen in the lively Chao Phrom market where the agricultural abundance of the fertile central river valleys appears for sale everyday.

Many Thais still view the sacking of Ayutthaya as the greatest tragedy in the country's history. A re-enactment of the battle preceding the fall of Ayutthaya, complete with elephants, swords, kings, foot soldiers, and explosions, is staged annually to commemorate the event. After a day at the monuments, take a look at life behind-the-scenes of Ayutthaya's well-orchestrated tourist industry. Spinning ghost stories is a favorite pastime in this dry-as-a-bone town. When tour buses have headed back to Bangkok and tuk-tuk drivers have given up their zealous search for foreign fares, locals claim to hear the cries of fallen soldiers and their massacred families among the charred ruins.

ORIENTATION

Ayutthaya proper is located on a roughly oval-shaped island, about 3km across at its widest point, that sits in the intersection of three major rivers, the **Chao Phraya, Pa Sak,** and **Lopburi. U Thong Road** travels the island's circumference, intersecting at some point all the island's major roads which run north-south and east-west. **Buses** pull in from Bangkok and elsewhere next to the **Chao Phrom market** at the corner of **Naresuan** (also known as Chao Phrom Rd.) and U Thong Rd. in the northeast corner of the island. Most budget accommodations can be found off Naresuan Rd. in this area. The train station is located east of the island near the **Pridi Damrong Bridge.** While Ayutthaya's array of sights is spread across the island several of the major ones are centrally located near the **TAT office** on **Si Sanphet Road.**

Between 11am and 3pm, Ayutthaya gets very hot, arid, and dusty—not the best time for sight-seeing. Visit the temples (and capture them best on film) in the early morning and the early evening. Most major temples can be seen in one day if you've snagged motorized transportation. For a more leisurely tour, rent a bike (guest houses will usually rent a beat-up, antique model for about 50฿ per day) and examine the sights over the course of a couple of days.

PRACTICAL INFORMATION

Tourist Office: Tourism Authority of Thailand (TAT) (tel. 246 076/7; fax 246 078), on Si Sanphet Rd. beside the Chao Sam Phraya Museum. Now in a traditional

THAILAND

Ayutthaya

1 Chan Kasem Palace
2 Chao Sam Phraya National Museum
3 Elephant Kraal
4 Mosque
5 Phet Fortress
6 Phu Khao Thong Temple (Golden Mount Chedi)
7 Queen Suriyothai Memorial Pagoda Stirlings Library
8 St. Joseph's Cathedral
9 Wang Luang (Royal Palace)
10 Wat Chai Wattanaram
11 Wat Hasadawat
12 Wat Kasatthirat
13 Wat Khudi Dao
14 Wat Khudi Thong
15 Wat Kok Phaya
16 Wat Lokaya Sutha
17 Wat Mae Nang Pleum
18 Wat Mongkhon Bophit
19 Wat Na Phra Meru
20 Wat Phanan Choeng
21 Wat Phra Mahathat
22 Wat Phra Ram
23 Wat Phra Si Sanphet (Old Palace)
24 Wat Phrom Niwet
25 Wat Phutthaisawan
26 Wat Pradu Sogtham
27 Wat Ratburana
28 Wat Rong Khong
29 Wat Sala Pun
30 Wat Somana Kotharam
31 Wat Suwan Dararam
32 Wat Suwannarat
33 Wat Thammikarat
34 Wat Thin Tha
35 Wat Yai Chai Mongkhon

wooden Thai house on stilts, but scheduled to move to more modern digs across Si Sanphet Rd. from its current spot. English spoken. Open daily 8:30am-4:30pm.

Tourist Police: (tel. 1699 or 242 352). Currently across from TAT on Si Sanphet Rd., but will share the new buildling next door with the TAT in 1996.

Tours: You can arrange professional tours with **A/C bus** and English-speaking guides through Bangkok travel agencies. **Long-tailed boats** and **cruisers** can be hired at the Chantharkasem Palace pier, north of the post office on U Thong Rd. for a 1-hr. trip around the island. A long-tail boat holds up to 8 people (300-400฿).

Currency Exchange: Bangkok Bank (Hua Raw), 20 U Thong Rd. (tel. 252 652), across from the school near the Ayutthaya Post Office. **Krung Thai Bank,** 8-10-12 U Thong Rd. (tel. 245 364). **Thai Farmers Bank,** 6/24 Mu 4 Naresuan Rd. (tel. 423 791). All three banks open Mon.-Fri. 8:30am-3:30pm with 24-hr. ATM.

Post Office/Telephones: 123/11 U Thong Rd. (tel. 251 233). Handles regular mail, EMS express mail, telegraph service, and overseas calls. Open Mon.-Fri. 8:30am-noon and 1-4:30pm, Sat. 9am-noon. **Postal code:** 13000. Overseas telephone office on the 2nd floor of the GPO. 30฿ service charge for collect calls or dial "Home Direct" for free. Open daily 7am-10pm. **Telephone code:** 035.

Train station: (tel. 251 521), east of the island. Tuk-tuks go into town (30฿). Trains to: **Bangkok** (every 30min., 1:20am-5:30pm); **Chiang Mai** (8am, 4:15, 7:20, and 11:20pm); **Lopburi** (5:45, 6:05am, 5:50, 6:14, and 7pm); and **Saraburi** or **Pak Chong** (8:14, 9am, 5, and 8pm). Baggage storage (pick-up 5am-10pm).

Bus station: (tel. 241 025). From Chao Phrom market, buses go to **Bangkok** (regular every 15min., 4:30am-7:15pm, 20฿; with A/C every 30min., 6am-7pm, 30฿) and **Saraburi** (regular every 30min., 6am-5:30pm, 2-½hr., 18฿) for points in the northeast. To **Kanchanaburi,** take a non-A/C bus to **Suphanburi** (every 30min., 4:50am-6:15pm, 18฿), and transfer at the station to bus #411.

Boats: Chao Phraya Express Boat (tel. 222 5330; fax 433 9425) offers the most affordable cruise option. Boats leave from Maharat Pier at 8am and return at 5:30pm every Sunday and include the Royal Folk Arts and Crafts Center at Bang Sai (lower deck 190฿, upper deck 250฿). **Horizon Cruise,** River City Pier (tel. 538 3491; fax 538 2465). Daily tours start at 8:45am and return by 5pm, going by cruiser and returning by A/C bus (900฿, includes lunch).

Local Transportation: Mini **songthaews,** or glorified 8-person tuk-tuks, serve as buses on the island, traveling all the main roads. They do not have set routes; flag one down going in your general direction and pay 3฿ when you get out. If you are alone or in a group traveling to a specific sight, expect to pay 30-40฿ for the trip. Hire a **tuk-tuk** by the hour for 150฿. The cheapest way to the train station is the **ferry** (1฿) from the intersection of U Thong and Horattanachai Rd., near the Chao Phrom market. A final option is to rent a **bicycle,** throw some suntan lotion and a bottle of water in your pack, and hit the road in pollution-free style.

Hospital (U Thong): (tel. 241 027), at the intersection of Si Sanphet and U Thong Rd. at the south end of the island.

Emergency: tel. 199.

Police: tel. 241 001, 241 663, or 241 608.

ACCOMMODATIONS

Boost your self-empowerment skills. The key thing to remember when heading to a guest house in Ayutthaya is that you decide where you stay—not your mother, your therapist, or the in-your-face tuk-tuk driver at the train station or bus terminal. One thing you can't decide for yourself is the room rate, which will skyrocket during festival season (around December)—that is, if you can find a room.

Ayutthaya Youth Hostel (Ruenderm YH), 48/2 U Thong Rd. (tel. 241 978), north of the Pridi Damrong Bridge, at the intersection of U Thong and Pathon Rd. Look for the funky wooden house with the lit sign in English. The best-looking place in town, although U Thong Rd. traffic and long-tail boats on the river make late-morning sleep impossible. Gorgeous traditional Thai-style teak house with 1st-floor restaurant and lovely views. With only 5 rooms, the place fills up fast; all have double beds draped with lace canopies and mosquito screens, a fan, wood floors, and high ceilings. Large, Downy-soft towels. Rooms 200฿, for IYH member

150฿. Office open 10am-11pm. Restaurant and main door close at 11pm; another entrance remains open 24 hrs. Check-out noon. Call for reservations. Visa.

Ayutthaya Guest House, 16/2 Naresuan Rd. (tel. 251 468), next door to the Old BJ. Large, comfortable, and festively decorated eating area. Friendly manager moonlights as the guitarist for a local 70s rock band and loves to party and socialize with guests. Stellar central location, and the noise level is tolerable. Rooms have clean, well-lit shared baths. Singles 80฿. Doubles 100฿. Bike rental 50฿ per day. Office open 7am-10pm. Check-out noon.

Old BJ Guest House, 16/7 Naresuan Rd. (tel. 251 526), near the end of the soi, across from the bus terminal off Naresuan Rd. Coming from U Thong Rd., take a right when you see Siam Commercial Bank on your left. Follow the signs 100m. Snug rooms with wood floors and common bath. Singles 80฿. Doubles 100฿. *Farang* menu downstairs is more expensive than market fare (3-min. walk away). Bike rental 50฿. Little English spoken. Office open 6am-10pm. Check-out noon.

New BJ Guest House, 19/29 Naresuan Rd. (tel. 251 512), on the same road as Chao Phrom market, to the right before ancient Wat Phra Mahathat and Wat Ratburana. Much like the Old BJ, except floors here are concrete. Ring the bell if you come in late. Dorms 60฿. Rooms (1 large bed) 100฿. The restaurant area is a great place to meet fellow travelers and pick up tips. About 40฿ for a full meal. Laundry service. Get a shampoo, cut, and dry for 50฿ at the beauty room downstairs. Basic English spoken. Check-out before noon (don't worry about oversleeping—a noisy rooster, sans snooze button, has taken over the 1st-floor restaurant area).

U Thong Hotel, 86 U Thong (tel. 251 136). Enter on the right side of U Thong Rd., across the street from the post office. A 20-minute walk from Chao Phrom market. U Thong Rd. ruckus will probably keep you up late and wake you up early. Impersonal hotel aura. Room with double bed, private bath, and river view 180฿, with TV 220฿, with A/C 300฿. 2 double beds with bath and view 250฿.

FOOD

Looking for a place to consume some carbos before your marathon sight-seeing session? A good place to start is the row of **food stalls** inside the **Chao Phrom market.** To get there from the guest houses on Naresuan Rd., walk toward U Thong Rd. and enter the market building to the right, just after the small Buddhist shrine on the sidewalk. Open 7am-7pm. Just across is the Amiporn Department Store, home to the 3rd floor **Amiporn Food Center.** Expect to pay just a bit more than market prices for a wide variety of dishes (20฿ for basic rice and chicken, 30฿ for more exciting concoctions). Open 9am-9pm.

Ruanderm, 48/2 U Thong Rd. (tel. 241 978), north of the Pridi Damrong Bridge, where U Thong meets Pathon Rd. If the hostel's room prices are too much to swallow, at least treat yourself to a meal here. This floating restaurant on the banks of the Pa Sak River is a favorite among locals for its open-air atmosphere. Wagon wheels, lanterns, and private eating alcoves are assembled among antique furniture and tons of plants. The food is downright delectable even though it's a bit pricey (60-80฿ per entree). Bilingual menu. Open 10am-11pm. MC, Visa.

Riverside Seafood Grill (tel. 944 9239), on U Thong Rd., 100m before the post office across the street from the Rodeo Saloon. Chanup, the owner of this riverside restaurant, is armed with a devastating culinary weapon: special sauce. Pick a fish (priced by the gram) and they will grill it up with the killer flavoring that makes you froth with pleasure. Open 4-11pm.

Thai House Restaurant (Ruenthai Maisuay Restaurant), 8/2 Mu 3 Klongsuanplu District (tel. 245 977; fax 245 979), farther down the road from Wat Yai Chai Mongkhon, around the bend and on the right. Set atop stilts in an old-style, wooden Thai house. The restaurant serves up moderately priced traditional Thai food, including an assortment of *yams* (a salad with meat or seafood and a lot of spices) and curried soups (50-60฿). Stop here for lunch between seeing Wat Yai Chai Mongkhhon and Wat Phanam Choeng. Open daily 11am-10pm.

SIGHTS

Ayutthaya's claim to fame is its rich history, and there is plenty of evidence lying around to back it up. Before you run off to see the ruins, take an educational trip to the **Ayutthaya Historical Study Centre,** the modern Thai building on Rotchana Rd. near the Chao Sam Phraya National Museum. This US$8 million research institute, funded by the Japanese government, has an excellent high-tech exhibit on the ancient city's domestic political developments, trade relations with foreign countries, and the traditional life-style of its inhabitants. The explanations are written both in Thai and English. If none of that sounds interesting, it's still worthwhile to see for the detailed miniature reconstructions of Ayutthaya at the height of its power, and for the Thai chants that greet you as you trip off hidden light sensors. Open Wed.-Sun. 9am-4:30pm; admission 100฿, 50฿ with student ID. The **Chao Sam Phraya National Museum** is across the street and to the left about 100m. The two galleries here illustrate all you just learned at the Historical Study Centre. On the first floor of the main building is a collection of old wooden door panelings and pediments with high relief images of demons, deities, and religious events. Farther back you'll find delicate ceramic work and examples of ancient Thai lacquerware. The second floor is where the shiny and glittery stuff is kept. A vault-like room on the east side displays gold treasures found in an excavation of Wat Ratburana. This collection of valuables includes swords, scabbards, and delicately worked headgear worn by queens and other noble ladies. Relics from Wat Mahatat are in the western side of the second floor. In the second exhibition hall, you'll see maps of the trade routes from India to Southeast Asia and a funky fake wood stove ablaze. Open Wed.-Sun. 9am-4pm; second exhibition hall open Wed.-Fri. 9am-4pm; admission 10฿. On the eastern side of the island next to the post office is **Chan Kasem Palace National Museum** (open Wed.-Sun. 9am-noon and 1-4pm; admission 10฿). The artifacts here don't size up to the Indiana Jones-type findings at Chao Phraya, but if you're at the post office, you might as well inspect the offerings.

If you've only got an afternoon to blast through the ruins of Ayutthaya, there are three main locations to target. **Wat Phra Si Sanphet,** on the west side of the island, was the largest temple in Ayutthaya's heyday, as well as the king's palace (admission 20฿, also includes the Ancient Palace just north). The line of three large fire-charred *chedis* is the trademark image of this site. Now empty, they once held the bones of the successive Ayutthayan kings: Rama I, II, and III. Next to this site is **Wihan Phra Mongkhon Bophit,** which shelters one of Thailand's largest Buddha images. Look for sarong-wrapped *Bodhi* trees. Locals place broken images of Buddha under these trees; it is unholy to keep damaged Buddhas at home. Halfway between Wat Phra Si Sanphet and Chao Phrom Market are **Wat Phra Mahatat** and **Wat Ratburana.** King Borom Rachathirat II (Chao Sam Phraya) had these two pagodas built after his two brothers (Chao Ai and Chao Yi) killed each other in a brawl atop elephants.

The second important site to visit is **Wat Yai Chai Mongkhon,** which is located southeast of the island. The temple is known for the big (*yai*) *chedi* visible from miles away. Built in 1357 by King Naresuan when he won a duel atop an elephant, *yai chedi* shows its age with an impressive tilt. If you climb up into the *chedi,* you'll enter upon an eerie scene of eight golden Buddhas serenely meditating in a circle around you. On the grounds of this temple there is a meditation garden where each tree is adorned with politically incorrect bits of food for thought like " to have a wife is the ultimate suffering; to have independence is bliss." Admission 20฿.

Just down the road and across the train tracks to the left of Wat Yai Chai Mongkhon is **Wat Phanan Choeng.** Built in 1325 before the establishment of Ayutthaya as the capital of Siam, the wat is believed to have been the work of the Khmers. The 19-m Buddha sits in the main *wiharn.* You can get here by catching a ferry at the Phet Fortress or walking from Wat Yai Chai Mongkhon.

Ayutthaya is the site of one of the country's largest **Loi Krathong festivals** which usually take place in November or December on the full moon. Thais gather around **Beung Phra Ram,** the large lake in the center of the island, to see fireworks, watch *li-kay,* Thai folk dance-drama, and groove to Thai pop stars on stage. The traditional ceremony of the holiday, the floating *(loi)* of small, lotus-shaped paper boats with candles and incense on top *(krathong),* takes place at the **Chan Kasem Pier** across from the Chan Kasem Palace Museum and post office. Legend says that couples who launch their *loi* together are destined to become lovers. Get moving.

ENTERTAINMENT

Late-night options in this town are fairly limited. Sneaking into the ruins after dark to drink and listen for ghosts from the past is highly recommended by locals; however, lone women may not be comfortable among the men there. In a distant second are:

Knock on Wood, 51/213 Rojana Rd. (tel. 336 104), across the street from the Ayutthaya Grand east of the railway station. Nightly live bands play reggae, folk, blues, 70s rock, as well as country. Get here after 10pm to catch the action. The proprietor of Ayutthaya Guest House also owns this place. Check with him about organizing a tuk-tuk load of *farang* who want to hit the party area around Ayutthaya Grand. One tuk-tuk load 40฿. Beers start at 60฿. Open daily 6pm-2am.

Rodeo Saloon and Restaurant, 79-81 U Thong Rd. (tel. 251 616), across from the Riverside Seafood Grilled Restaurant before you get to the post office. Look for the Jack Daniels sign, all lit up and ready to take you on. The *other* western bar in town, it boasts *Bonanza* decor, posters of Elvis, live music, and karaoke. Drink prices comparable to Knock on Wood, but a more extensive and expensive menu. Pepper steak 70฿. Open daily 5pm-midnight, but the band normally doesn't get jumping until 9 or 10pm.

Thai Massage (tel. 244 582), at the Chao Phrom market bus station. Sample the "good taste" massage (2 hrs. of traditional Thai bodywork, 200฿). The masseuse will first wash your feet and give you a pair of satin slippers. Then you'll change into snazzy polka-dot pajamas and take your place in an A/C cubicle. Be prepared to be stretched out and have every muscle in your body firing by the end. Pamper yourself—this travel stuff is hard work. Open 10am-midnight.

■■■ KANCHANABURI

Kanchanaburi, Thailand's fourth largest province, spreads over nearly 20,000 rather mountainous sq. km and borders Burma to the west of Bangkok. The provincial capital of the same name, 129km to the northeast of Bangkok with a population of approximately 33,000, was originally founded by King Rama I to serve as a first line of defense against Burmese attacks through the vulnerable Three Pagodas Pass area. Situated in a luxuriant valley at the confluence of the Kwai Yai and Kwai Noi Rivers, Kanchanaburi is also one of the most fertile areas in Thailand; sugar cane, maize, tobacco, wheat, and cotton are grown in abundance here.

Kanchanaburi is also home to the bridge over the River Kwai, immortalized by World War II, the author Pierre Boulle, and the American movie (actually filmed in Sri Lanka). Over 100,000 people died building a railway supply line over this bridge for the Japanese, who wanted clear passage between Burma and Thailand through Three Pagodas Pass. The bridge still stands today, thanks to post-war reconstruction, and is certainly disappointingly tiny for a bridge shored up by so much lore.

Kanchanaburi's low-key attitude and natural beauty—plus its proximity to Bangkok—make it a popular destination for both Thais and foreigners. Many services here are geared toward tourists and the TAT is a good place to start. Travel agencies hawk one-to-three day tours of the outlying sights, which are spread over the province, but guest houses are good sources of information for those who want to go it on their own. Many travelers come to Kanchanaburi while they wait for Vietnam or Laos visas to go through in Bangkok. Indeed, several have just decided to stay in Kanchanaburi and forget the rest of Thailand.

ORIENTATION

Two daily trains follow the **southern rail line** from Bangkok to Kanchanaburi, but a faster and more frequent jaunt is by bus (from Bangkok's Southern Bus Terminal).

Kanchanaburi's main drag is **Saeng Chuto Road,** connecting the train terminal at the north end of the city to the **Ban Noue Village** 2km away in the southeast—an area home to the bus terminal, market, and TAT. The **Kwai River** also meanders toward the southeast, paralleling Saeng Chuto Rd. Most of the guest houses are situated along the river (actually, many float in the river) close to the train station at the north end. The **bridge** (yeah, the famous one) is 2km north of the train station, an easy walk or bicycle ride from most accommodations.

PRACTICAL INFORMATION

Tourist Office: Tourism Authority of Thailand (TAT) (tel. 511 200), on Saeng Chuto Rd., a 5-min. walk from the bus station: exiting the front of the station turn left 2 short blocks onto Saeng Chuto Rd.; the TAT is 100m to your left. From the train station: take a left onto Saeng Chuto Rd. and walk 20min. or catch a songthaew. Friendly advice, English maps and brochures. Open daily 8:30am-4:30pm.

Tourist Police: (tel. 512 795). Next to TAT office. Speedy 24-hr. assistance in case of emergency. You can also get some cool water, use the toilets, or leave your heavy backpack with them. English spoken. A tourist police mini-station is near the stadium and conference hall on Song Kwai Rd. Open 8am-5pm.

Tours: Border Tour Travel, Rong Heeb Oil Rd. 2. (tel. (01) 922 8589 or (034) 624 203). Gives very competitive prices for package trips (e.g. to Sangkhlaburi). **KTT Tours,** in front of Jolly Frog Backpacker, also offers package tours.

Immigration Office: (tel. 513 325) on Mae Nam Mae Rd. From TAT, follow Saeng Chuto Rd. away from the Ban Noue Village area and turn right at City Hall. Watch for the English signs on the 4-km trek. If you can't bear to leave Kanchanaburi, this is the place to get a visa extension. Open Mon.-Fri. 8:30am-4:30pm.

Currency/Exchange: The TAT recommends 3 banks for foreign exchange services. The others also have exchanges and ATMs, which generally operate 7am-10pm. **Thai Military Bank,** 160/35 Saeng Chuto Rd., Ban Noue Village (tel. 511 677). **Bangkok Bank,** 2 U Thong Rd., Ban Noue Village (tel. 511 111, 511 212, or 512 710). **Thai Farmers Bank,** 160/80-2 Saeng Chuto Rd., Ban Noue Village (tel. 511 203 or 511 774). Banks open Mon.-Fri. 8:30am-3:30pm.

Post Office: GPO (tel. 511 131), on Saeng Chuto Rd. From Ban Noue Village, 1km beyond TAT on the left. Poste Restante. Open Mon.-Fri. 8:30am-4:30pm, Sat.-Sun. 9am-noon. **Local branch** on Lak Muang Rd. at the corner of Phraek Rd. by town gate. From TAT office head right, take your 1st left and walk about 500m. Open Mon.-Fri. 8:30am-4:30pm, Sat. 9am-noon. **Postal code:** 71000.

Telephones: Long-distance and overseas calls on 2nd floor of GPO (tel. 511 131). Open daily 7am-10pm. **Telephone code:** 034.

Trains: Kanchanaburi Railway Station (tel. 511 285), on Saeng Chuto Rd. To: **Bangkok** (#171 at 7:31am and #197 at 3:21pm, 3hr., 25฿) and **Nam Tok via the River Kwai Bridge** (#353 at 6:10am, #171 at 10:55am, and #197 at 4:25pm, 2hr., 17฿). Additional trains may make the Bangkok-Kanchanaburi-NamTok trip on weekends and holidays when tourist demand is high; check with the TAT. For the best view of the "Death Railway" section on the way to Nam Tok, sit on the left.

Buses: The **bus station** (tel. 511 182) is in the heart of Ban Noue Village. Proceed quickly from the station area—peddlers and samlor drivers are good at spotting *farang* (it's not that hard, really). Locals say that to go see the waterfalls, it is more *saduak* (convenient) to go by bus (or even songthaew) than by train. To: **Bangkok** (#81, every 10min., 3:30am-6:30pm, 3hr., 35฿; with A/C, #81, every 20min., 4am-7pm, 2hr., 62฿); **Ratchaburi** connecting to destinations in the **south** (#461, every 15min., 5:10am-6:15pm, 2-½hr., 26฿); **Suphanburi** connecting to **Ayutthaya** (#411, every 20min., 5:25am-5pm, 2-½hr., 25฿); **Sai Yok Noi, Sai Yok Yai,** and **Thong Pha Phum,** (#8203, every 30min., 1-3hr., 18-39฿); **Erawan National Park,** (#8170, every 50min., 8am-4pm, 2hr., 19฿); and **Sangkhlaburi** (#8203, 6:45, 9, 10:45am, and 1:15pm, 4-6hr. depending on road conditions, 60฿). **A/C minibus service** departs from behind the bus terminal (every hour, 7:30am-4:30pm, 3 harrowing hr., 100฿ and a numb backside).

Local Transportation: Songthaews run up and down Saeng Chuto Rd. frequently (10฿ or less). **Motorbike taxis** or **samlors** will be 10-20฿ (from railway to TAT). Many places (including bungalows) rent **bikes** for 20฿ per day. A scenic

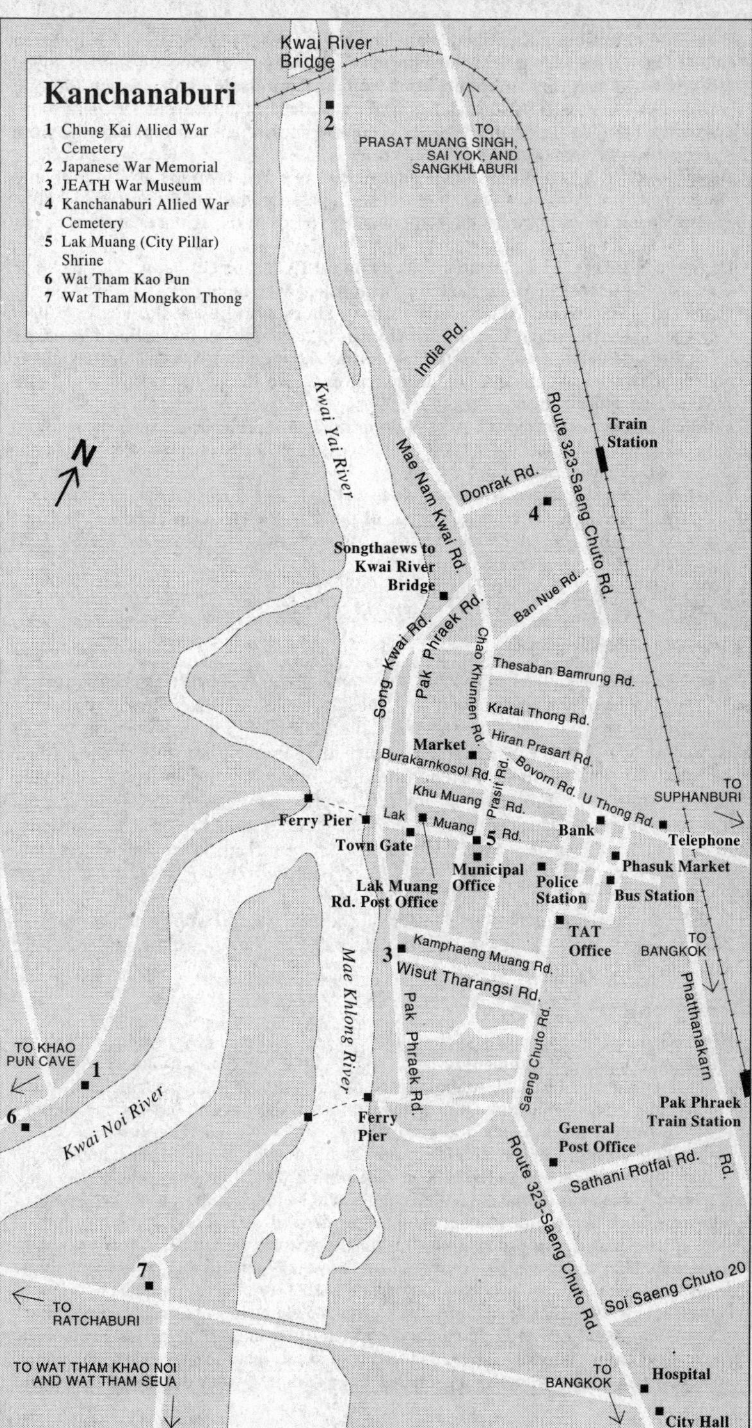
Kanchanaburi
1 Chung Kai Allied War Cemetery
2 Japanese War Memorial
3 JEATH War Museum
4 Kanchanaburi Allied War Cemetery
5 Lak Muang (City Pillar) Shrine
6 Wat Tham Kao Pun
7 Wat Tham Mongkon Thong
Kwai River Bridge
TO PRASAT MUANG SINGH, SAI YOK, AND SANGKHLABURI
N
India Rd.
Kwai Yai River
Mae Nam Kwai Rd.
Route 323-Saeng Chuto Rd.
Train Station
Donrak Rd.
Songthaews to Kwai River Bridge
Ban Nue Rd.
Song Kwai Rd.
Pak Phraek Rd.
Chao Khunnen Rd.
Thesaban Bamrung Rd.
Kratai Thong Rd.
Hiran Prasart Rd.
Market
Burakarnkosol Rd.
Prasit Rd.
Bovorn Rd.
U Thong Rd.
TO SUPHANBURI
Khu Muang Rd.
Ferry Pier
Lak Muang Rd.
Bank
Telephone
Town Gate
Phasuk Market
Municipal Office
Police Station
Bus Station
Lak Muang Rd. Post Office
TAT Office
TO BANGKOK
Kamphaeng Muang Rd.
Wisut Tharangsi Rd.
Mae Khlong River
Phatthanakarn Rd.
TO KHAO PUN CAVE
Saeng Chuto Rd.
Kwai Noi River
Ferry Pier
Pak Phraek Train Station
General Post Office
Sathani Rotfai Rd.
Route 323-Saeng Chuto Rd.
Soi Saeng Chuto 20
TO RATCHABURI
TO WAT THAM KHAO NOI AND WAT THAM SEUA
TO BANGKOK
Hospital
City Hall

THAILAND

way to get to Chung Kai Allied War Cemetery or Wat Tham Khao Pun is by **ferry** (2฿), leaving the pier at the intersection of Lak Muang and Song Kwai Rd. If speed is what you need, hire a **speed boat** from any waterside establishment (around 100฿ per hour with driver). For a more lackadaisical jaunt, rent a **raft** (2500฿) which will hold 20 or more. Smaller groups or individuals can rent a **canoe** from some guest houses (around 50฿ per hour).

Bike/Moped Rental: Bikes are a standard 20฿ per day. **Mopeds** go for 200฿ and less for 24 hrs.; you may have to put down a passport and 500฿ deposit. Motorcyclists should be *very* careful on Kanchanaburi roads. Inexperienced motorcyclists should stick with bicycles.

Luggage Storage: At the Tourist Police behind TAT. It's free!

Catholic Church: On Phrak Paek Rd., near Allied War Cemetery.

Market: In Ban Noue Village. Labyrinth of shelves and glass showcases full of clothes, toiletries, toys, bags of *phrik kii nuu*, and slabs o' meat. **Food vendors** line the side facing away from the bus terminal. Open 7am-6pm. After they close, a **night market** keeps cookin' along Saeng Chuto Rd. at the north end of Ban Noue village until about 11pm.

Public Toilets and Showers: Across from the floating restaurants near the stadium on Song Kwai Rd. (tel. 013 120 667). Toilets (2฿) and showers (5฿); bring your own towel. Open 6am-10pm.

Hospitals: Paholpolpayuhasena Hospital (tel. 511 507), on Saeng Chuto Rd. 1km past the GPO when heading out of the city. **24-Hr. Clinic:** From the guest houses on Song Kwai Rd., head south. At the tourist police box, take a left and go 3 blocks. The clinic will be on your left.

Emergency: tel. 191 or 1699 for tourist police.

Provincial Police Headquarters: (tel. 511 540) across from TAT.

ACCOMMODATIONS

When you arrive at either the bus or train station, you will be accosted by many a samlor driver hoping to escort you to a guest house on the river. If you're too hot and bothered to walk, pay them no more than 20฿ (10฿ for a motorcycle taxi). If you do choose to hoof it, head left from the front entrance to the bus station, after 2 short blocks cross straight over Saeng Chuto Rd., and follow Lak Muang Rd. past the town gate until you hit the river. From here, Nita's is to your left and all the rest are a five- to 15-minute walk to your right. From the train station, cross Saeng Chuto Rd. and head down the small street labeled by a P.S. Guest House sign. Follow this until you hit the waterworks. Jolly Frog's will be to your right, while the rest are to your left along the river.

Although the river guest houses offer the best views and opportunities to meet fellow travelers, they are also the most vulnerable to the intense booming beat of the floating discos on weekends.

Along the River Kwai

River Guest House, 42 Rong Heeb Oil Rd. (tel. 512 491). A 10-min. walk from train station or 15฿ samlor ride from TAT. Simple wood-box rooms are afloat on the river, a hazard for late night trips to raid the honor-system refrigerator, but a convenience for spur-of-the-moment River Kwai dips. A laid-back scene. Singles 40฿. Doubles with fan, net, and bath 100฿. Check-out noon. Laundry service.

Jolly Frog Backpacker's, 28 Mae Nam Kwai Rd. (tel. 514 579). Call and they'll pick you up for free from the bus or train station. This 45-room guest house, built around a large garden next to the river, caters to independent travelers and tour groups. Both the friendly owners and fellow *farang* are full of helpful information about the area. A big production, but on the whole, well done. A few good bargains in Thai and western food (big breakfast 25฿). Concrete n' drywall single 50฿. Double 90฿. 2 twin beds with private bath 130฿. Bicycle rentals.

Nita Raft House, 27/1 Phra Phrak Rd. (tel. 514 521). A 10-min. walk to bus station. Sit on comfy pillows and open a good book in the restaurant if you get tired of the river-and-mountain view. An occasional boat wake will lull you to sleep until the floating disco barges begin their nightly river circuit. Owner dispenses videos and sight-seeing info. Tasty victuals (rice with fried veggies 25฿). Shoe box single with mattress on floor 40฿. Double 60฿. Add 10฿ for fan. Bed frame 100฿. Two single beds with fan and private bath, a steal at 150฿. Laundry service at 3฿ per article!

P.S. Guest House, 48/4 Rong Heeb Oil Rd. (tel. 513 039). Floating bungalows in a meditation-ready setting among reeds and water lillies. Single with private porch on the river 50฿. Double 80฿, with fan and private bath on the hillside 120฿.

Rick's Lodge, 48/5 Rong Heeb Oil Rd. (tel. 514 831). Between P.S. and River G.H., bi-level bungalows cling to the hillside and include full western bath and a ladder up to the loft bedroom. River tourboat parked out front doubles as dock for sun-seekers. Restaurant boasts great river sunset views, a 5pm happy hour, and satellite TV for sports and news. Bungalows away from the river 250฿, riverside 280฿.

Sam's Place (tel. 513 971), on Song Kwai Rd. 15-20฿ motorbike ride from stations on the south side of the wat. Pristine, well-decorated floating rooms with plants everywhere. Trade-off for aesthetics is nightly disco action passing by. Bungalows for two 100฿, with bath 150฿. Large, A/C room 250฿, even larger 300฿.

Away from the River Kwai

V.L. Guest House, 18/11 Saeng Chuto Rd. (tel. 513 546), across from River Kwai Hotel, 1km to the right of TAT on Saeng Chuto Rd. Spacious rooms all have desk and private bath with squat n' flush toilets like no other. Staff may serenade you with Thai pop tunes, if you're a good guest. Very clean, but it's on the riotous main drag. Doubles 150฿, with A/C 300฿. Check-out 2pm. Laundry service.

FOOD AND ENTERTAINMENT

Finding a place to calm your stomach growlies is as easy as finding a samlor driver (or having one find you) in Kanchanaburi. Near the bus terminal in Ban Noue Village, food stalls and simple open-air eateries are unavoidable. Similar oases abound along Saeng Chuto Rd., but the highest concentration of restaurants is along Song Kwai Rd., many with karaoke, live bands, and wide selections of seafood (*aahaan talay*). If you just want to dine and sleep on a full stomach, most accommodations serve good meals for about 25฿.

Near the bus station, three places offer an A/C haven. Going counterclockwise around the terminal from the theater, there is the **Freeway Restaurant** (tel. 513 063) on the corner next to the theater. The specialty is *gai neung manao* (85฿), which is a small whole chicken marinated in hot lime sauce. Dishes go as low as 20-25฿. It's a popular hangout at night where Chivas Regal reigns and Thai-style karaoke fills the air. Open 9am-1am. **Chut Ice Cream** (tel. 512 672) offers regular fare as well as relief for the sweet tooth—dig into corn cream (14฿) and jelly (20฿) flavors. Open 10am-10pm. For the pastry-lover, **Si Fa Bakery** (tel. 512 317), next to the large watch store, serves up cakes, snacks, and even pizza. Open daily 7:30am-8:30pm. Along the river, between Nita's and Sam's Place, many restaurants cater to townspeople with various combinations of food and entertainment.

Mem (tel. 513 851), on the corner of Song Kwai and Burakarnkosol Rd. No English sign, but it's the first of a series of restaurants north of the tourist police booth and white convention center. Isaan specialties. Fried fish cakes go for 30฿, most salads 40฿. Open until midnight.

Jukkru, 3 restaurants up the street from Mem. Again no English sign, but fab, spicy food makes it worth the extra effort to find. Individual rice and meat dishes 20฿. Super-spicy (read: typical Thai) seafood plates 40-60฿. Open 4-11pm.

Mae Nam (tel. 512 811). The floating restaurant closest to the ferry on Song Kwai Rd. Squid's the draw here (40-60฿), served up by sailor-garbed waitstaff. English menu. Afternoon and evening music. Open until midnight.

Aree Bakery, toward Saeng Chuto Rd. on Burakarnkosol Rd. (between the conference center and the stadium). Take the 1st right on Pakpreak Rd.; it's 100m down on the left. Friendly couple used to work in the Thai embassy and speak great English. Apple pie *à la mode* 23฿. Coconut cakes 10฿. Open 7am-9pm.

SIGHTS

Renting a bike is the easiest and most wallet-friendly way to take in all the sights. The **bridge over the River Kwai** about 3km north of the train station, is Kanchanaburi's most well-known memorial to those who lost their lives here during World War II. The current tourist attraction is actually a reconstruction of the original "Death Railway Bridge," which was bombed by the Allies. During the war, engineers predicted that it would take five years to construct the bridge, but the Japanese army, in its eagerness to dominate Asia, forced POWs and local laborers to complete the railway in 16 months. In the process, tens of thousands died from disease, starvation, punishment, and exhaustion. Laborers were buried where they fell. The first (wooden) bridge was finished in February 1943. Two months later, a bridge of steel was completed, but construction on the railroad continued from both ends until they met just short of the Three Pagodas Pass by Sangkhlaburi. For 20 months, the Japanese moved supplies in and out of Burma and Thailand until the Allies destroyed the bridge in December 1945.

On the bridge's eastern approach is a small **Railway Museum** (open 8:30am-5pm, 25฿) where train aficionados can examine vintage steam locomotives and a peculiar hybrid road/railcar. During the first week of December, a spectacular nightly light and sound show commemorates the Allied destruction of the hated Japanese bridge. Legions of tourists throng to the event; plan ahead to witness it firsthand.

Also near the bridge are the **Japanese War Memorial,** riverside restaurants, and handicraft and jewelry shops. The new **Art Gallery and War Museum** (tel. 513 478 or 511 523; admission 30฿), 500m toward town from the bridge, is an outstanding museum that illustrates the major leaders of World War II and unflinchingly examines wartime atrocities. Along the wall of the smaller building are hand-carved replicas of Hitler, FDR, and Churchill, among others. Inside the marble-floored building are well-preserved weapons, uniforms, photographs, and displays on archaeology, war, and stamps. Artistically impressive are the glass-encased **Tomb of the Unknown Soldier** who lost his life working on the Death Railway and the five-story building documenting the history of Thai warfare. On the lower level, visitors can see the original lookout tower and a section of the bridge over the Kwai River.

On the way back into town is the **Kanchanaburi War Cemetery,** across from the train station. Here 6,982 Allied prisoners-of-war lie buried beneath the well-kept grounds. Burial plaques carry remembrances of the fallen, with their names, military ranks, and short epitaphs. A memorial service is held for them every year on April 25. The graveyard is open daily 8am-5pm.

On the other end of town along Lak Muang Rd. lie the **town gate** and **city pillar shrine** of this youthful provincial capital (founded in 1831). Less than 1km away down Pak Phraek Rd. is the **JEATH War Museum,** established in 1977 by the chief abbot of **Wat Chaichumphon (Wat Dai** to locals) to honor victims of the Death Railway Bridge, or as the entrance announces, "To Forgive But Not Forget." JEATH stands for Japan, England, America/Australia, Thailand, and Holland, the nations that met in battle at Kanchanaburi. The thatched detention hut with cramped bunks contains photographic, pictorial, and physical memorabilia, including items donated by several POW survivors. Most notable is a disturbing series of paintings that vividly underscores the inhumanity of war. Information sheets are available. Open 8:30am-4:30pm; admission 20฿.

Across the river, 2km south of town, the **Chung Kai Allied War Cemetery** is a smaller version of the Kanchanaburi War Cemetery on the former site of the Chung Kai POW Camp. Take a ferry across the river from the pier by Lak Muang Rd.

For wat-lovers, there are three major sites in the area besides Wat Chaichumphon. **Wat Thavasatkhalam** on Jiao Naen Rd., in the middle of town, is an active temple that is the most frequented by townspeople. **Wat Tham Khao Pun,** 1km beyond the Chung-Kai War Cemetery, boasts a cave and beautiful Buddha images. Finally, 4km across the river, **Wat Tham Mongkon Thong** (The Cave Temple of the Golden Dragon) is famous for its magnificent cave site and its renowned **"floating nun,"** a venerable old lady who can meditate while supine on water without sinking. People come here from all over Thailand in order to receive her blessings; early weekend mornings are usually the best time to catch her in action, coinciding with the arrival of the tour buses. Otherwise, make a 200฿ donation to the wat and she'll give you a private demonstration.

Behind the *bot,* steep steps lead up the mountain side and into the limestone cave, affording spectacular views of the surrounding mountains and valleys. A white-bearded, camera-shy Chinese hermit sells old remedies in front of the cave.

■ AROUND KANCHANABURI

The best thing about Kanchanaburi Province is not the capital town (Muang Kan, as it is known)—gorgeous national parks, historical sites, and the area around Sangkhlaburi are what really make the trip west worthwhile. The parks contain waterfalls of all sizes from the five-minute photo-opportunity **Sai Yok Noi Waterfalls** to the most popular, multi-tiered **Erawan Waterfalls** and **Huay Khamin Waterfalls.** Cave cravers delight in the grottoes scattered throughout the province, especially **Phra That Cave.** For animal lovers, the green valleys created by the Kwai Noi-Kwai Yai River system shelter diverse forms of wildlife. **Muang Singh City** and the **Ban Kao Museum** open a window to an ancient time, with some Neolithic artifacts. But the hidden gem is serene **Sangkhlaburi,** hours away from the floating discos of Kanchanaburi and the bedlam of Bangkok.

Routes 3199 and 323 split the province and are good jumping-off points. Buses leave regularly from Kanchanaburi town along these two arteries (see Kanchanaburi: Practical Information: Buses). Trains go nearer than the buses to Prasat Muang Singh and Ban Kao historical area, but they usually run behind schedule.

R. 3199 is a well-paved passage to Erawan, easily traversed by motorbike as well as by bus. Those who wish to go beyond Erawan to Huay Khamin or Phra That Cave should plan to use their own transportation (durable motorcycle or pick-up truck); otherwise, find a group to split the cost of hiring a boat or minibus. Before exploring the region, make bank and phone stops in Kanchanaburi town. Currency exchangers are rare, and long-distance calls may be prohibitively costly on the road.

As R. 323 heads west to Sangkhlaburi and the border, lonely stretches and sharp curves wind ahead. The bus or minivan is the best option for insecure motorists. If you do take your own wheels, drive during the day and keep a careful eye on the fuel gauge. Thong Pha Phum is the most commonly used pit stop before running to the border. Bring extra money—many visitors stay longer than expected once they discover the pleasant weather and beauty of Sangkhlaburi. Also, it is home to some of the country's best deals on jewelry, cloth, and hand-crafted wooden furniture.

ALONG ROUTE 3199

Bo Phloi

Blue sapphires and semi-precious stones such as onyx are extracted from the open cast mines here. Not many tourists make the trip, but the TAT says they're hoping to develop the area to allow visitors to see the process from mining to polished gem. Rather than risk your wad buying gems in a random market, invest in a gem from Bo Phloi Ltd., which comes with a certificate of authenticity so you won't get ripped off as so many travelers are. Open Mon.-Sat. Bus #325 from Kanchanaburi will bring you straight there (every 30min., 6:30am-5pm, 1-½hr., 50km, 14฿) or you can follow the blue and white gem signs. Bo Phloi is actually on Rte. 3086, branching north from Rte. 3199, and is along the way to Chaloem Rattanakosin National Park.

Erawan National Park

If you can only see one place around Kanchanaburi, this should be it. The seven levels of waterfalls seem landscaped by some master architect, but the cascading water, natural pools, and bamboo groves were there long before humans ever discovered this paradise (open daily 6am-6pm; the first check-point doesn't allow people in after 4:30pm and you can't climb beyond Level 2 after 4pm; admission for *farang* 25฿, for motorcycles 5฿, for cars 30฿). The money goes to the upkeep of the very well-managed and beautifully maintained Eden.

Before setting off, check the **visitor center** for their English maps (and a slide presentation in Thai if you happen to be there with a group of 10 or more). Lovely slides are set to a musical soundtrack and accompanied by a talk on the Kanchanaburi national parks and the increasingly influential environmental movement.

The first three levels of the waterfalls are an easy 5-10-minute walk from the trail head. Bring swim gear for a refreshing dip. If you feel a nipping at your legs, don't worry; it's just the fish *(plaa wien)*. The name in Thai indicates the fish are naturally protected—you'll get a headache if you dare eat one. Fishing is illegal as well.

The higher up the falls you go, the more challenging the trail. The payoff in climbing the steep concrete stairs and crossing the bridges is the clearer water and the 0.5m-long fish. Then there's the legendary eighth level. Only those that know the way can make it from level 7 (one of the park rangers has only been there himself 3 times in 4 years). Tigers and monkeys cohabit in the untouched jungle around this crystal-clear pool. Talk to the headquarters people if you're interested; maybe you'll be one of the handful of people who have experienced level 8. Be prepared to swim if you are so fortunate—it's part of the membership. Don't try to get there alone; there are stories of wanna-be Rambos trying to scale the falls but falling instead. Most likely you'll turn around at the 2.2km point and head back downhill. The other seven levels can be seen easily in a 2-hour round trip, but do add on another two hours for frolicking in Erawan's waters.

In the park, re-energize at the **food** stalls, a short walk from the visitor center. A simple rice dish and drink will cost about 20฿. Bathrooms are here as well as along the trail. **Accommodations** range from camping (bring your own tent; 5฿) to dorms (no beds, common bathroom; 10฿) to bungalows (with 4 beds and bath; 250฿).

The park makes a perfect daytrip from Kanchanaburi; use **public bus** #8170 (every 50min., 8am-4pm, 2hr., 65km, 19฿). The last bus returns to Kanchanaburi at 4pm. **Songthaews** that also make the trip pass by the river houses at 9am and return from Erawan at roughly 4pm (round-trip 60฿).

In emergencies, make a bee-line for the **National Park Headquarters.** It's the building straight through the check-point where the bus drops people off. They have no telephone here, but they can reach police and medical services in the park by walkie-talkie. There is a phone at the station near the market 1km back down the mountain. The park has an excellent safety record, considering it is the most popular park in Thailand. During the rainy season, the paths can be slippery but manageable. Peak season is November to January, when the visitors fill the pools. New Year's Day and major holidays will also see hordes of (occasionally drunk) people.

To continue on to Huay Ma Khamin Falls in Sri Nakharin National Park or Phra That Cave in Erawan, get information on road and travel conditions from the headquarters or visitor center. You must have a private vehicle (and good directions from Erawan Headquarters) to reach these sights.

Phra That Cave, well-known for its monumental stalagmites, is the largest and most popular spelunking sight in Kanchanaburi. Lanterns are provided at the cave entrance; 5-10฿ is a reasonable donation. There is no regular transportation over the 10km to the cave. Groups can hire songthaews (around 300฿), or you can jam up there on the motorbike you rented in Kanchanaburi.

Tha Thung Na Dam is along the road before reaching Erawan. Eager beavers can also head upstream to **Sri Nakharin,** 2km above Erawan.

Sri Nakharin National Park

This park is rather inaccessible, especially compared to Erawan, but those who brave the challenge emerge with tall tales. The park headquarters is 105km from Kanchanaburi, but it is best to visit the park and **Huay Ma Khamin Waterfalls** on a daytrip from a base at Erawan National Park or the Sri Nakharin Dam area. The seven-level falls are the centerpiece of the 1532 sq. km area. A Disney menagerie of deer, elephants, and tigers are hidden in more remote areas. The park also contains **Phra and Niramit Caves** and a reservoir where fishing is allowed in some sections.

Bring your own food, but three bungalows are available in the park at 100฿ per person. To get to the park headquarters, take a 40-km dry-weather road parallel to the reservoir; it is passable only by motorcycles, pickups, and 4-wheel-drive vehicles. Or take a 45- to 70-minute boat ride from the **Tha Kradan** pier, 24km northeast of the Sri Nakharin Dam, 5km past Mongatet Village. The trip to Huay Ma Khamin Falls allows glimpses of deciduous forest and bamboo groves full of bee-eaters, hornbills, babblers and other winged critters. Split boat costs 1000฿ among a group.

Si Sawat

If you're looking to get away from it all and willing to sleep on the floor to do so, head for Si Sawat on the banks of the Sri Nakharin Reservoir, five-to-six hours from Kanchanaburi on R. 3199. In this sleepy fishing village you can probably crash at the temple; ask the English-speaking school teacher for assistance. Fish on the lake—you're sure to catch a whopper. To get there, take #8170 from Kanchanaburi (10:30, 11:45am, 1, or 2:30pm, 40฿). Or pick up the bus in the afternoon after an early morning trip to Erawan.

ALONG ROUTE 323

Prasat Muang Singh Historical Park

For the average backpacker, Prasat Muang Singh may not be worth the inconvenience of getting there, but archaeologists will be in seventh heaven. The walled "City of Lions" is situated along the Kwai Noi River and contains skeletal remains and artifacts dating back 2000 years. Dominating the four groups of ruins, Prasat Muang Singh (Tower of the City of Lions) is believed to have been the westernmost outpost of the Angkor-centered Khmer empire. Art from Cambodia, as well as the Thai Dvaravati period, decorates the tower. Laterite bricks give way to the inner shrine where the four-armed Bodhisattva images were housed 800 years ago.

For more information, go to the **visitor center** (tel. 572 573) to the right of the main ruins upon entering. The chief English-speaking administrator has articles about Muang Singh's history. Open daily 8am-5pm; admission 20฿.

Most visitors arrive by motorbike or car (admission 10฿ extra for cars), and the park can be seen by following the road winding through it.

Trains come closer to the park than the bus. The train goes twice daily from Kanchanaburi to Thakilen (the stop for Prasat Muang Singh). Theoretically, it's supposed to depart at 6:10 and 10:55am, but in the real world, trains run 15 to 30 minutes behind schedule (1hr., 10฿). From the train station, walk 1km to the main road and then walk another km to the right. Trains head back to Kanchanaburi at 6:25am, 2:14, and 4:31pm.

Bus #8203 stops 7km from the park, and transportation for the extra leg may be hard to find. When it's time to head back to Kanchanaburi, buses on R. 323 are best caught before 5pm.

Sai Yok Noi Waterfall

This waterfall, as its name suggests, is small *(noi),* and it will be a drip in the bucket compared to Erawan. It's right off R. 323, across the road from the market area where the bus stops. The cascades are best experienced during the tail end of rainy season. They lie 60km away from Kanchanaburi and 30 minutes before the **Sai Yok Yai National Park** entrance. If you want to stop here *en route* to Thong Pha Phum or Sangkhlaburi, the **Sai Yok Noi Bungalow** (tel. 512 279) is a bit off the highway, 500m south of the falls. Fan rooms for one or two are 120฿, three to four people 200฿, with A/C 250฿ and 350฿. There are good deals for groups of 10 or larger. Check-out is at noon, and they have laundry service.

Trains leave from Kanchanaburi at 6:10 and 10:55am (expect it to run late; 17฿). Get off at the end of the line (Nam Tok) and walk or hop on a songthaew or motorcycle to the falls 2km northwest of the station. The #8203 bus will cost about the same for a faster trip, but the train ride is more relaxing and rather scenic. Trains back to Kanchanaburi leave Nam Tok Station at 5:25am, 1:15, and 3:10pm.

Wang Badang Cave

For intrepid tunnelers yearning for serious adventure, head to this cave, a 3km walk from the station, or just 2km off R. 323. Turn right 100m south of Sai Yok Noi. Bring a flashlight and good shoes; your rubber thongs won't hold up here.

The Lawa Cave

This, the largest cave in the Sai Yok Yai National Park area, is most accessible to larger groups. A 10- to 12-person boat can be hired (1000-1200฿) at **Pak Saeng Pier** in Tambon Tha Sao southwest of the Sai Yok Noi Waterfall. Boats will also go by the Sai Yok Yai Waterfalls and the **Dao Wadung Caves** (4hr. round-trip).

Sai Yok Yai Waterfall and National Park

"Sai Yok" (literally "quaking fig tree") refers to a giant fig tree that fell in the Kwai Noi River over 100 years ago. The park stands at the forefront of a campaign to reverse the ecological havoc wreaked by the logging and stripping of Thailand's forests. The government has initiated replanting projects, but its valiant push for public awareness may be an uphill battle.

Celebrated in Thai poetry and song, the Sai Yok Yai Waterfall dribbles unimpressively except between July and September, when the 500 sq. km park has more to offer. Barking deer, blue-winged pittas, gibbons, limestone wren babblers, wild pigs, and wreathed hornbills inhabit the deciduous forests. Holy rodents, Batman! Some of the world's smallest mammals, the Kitti hog-nosed bats, live here in the **Bat Cave,** accessible by trails. Rumor has it that Jim Carrey dynamited the area, forcing Val Kilmer and Chris O'Donnell elsewhere...Oh wait, wrong cave. The park is open daily 6am-7:30pm; admission 25฿.

Pick up English maps and leave your hefty gear at the **tourist center** desk. **Accommodations** are limited to camping (5฿) and rooms for one or two over the river (200฿); a better option may be the Sai Yok Noi-area hotels. Swing by the park on a daytrip that can include the **Hellfire Pass** and **Burma-Thailand Death Railway Memorial** along the connecting section of R. 323. Hike along a trail to the original tracks constructed by the Allied POWs under the Japanese.

The actual National Park entrance is 30 minutes from the Sai Yok Noi Falls. Scramble onto any bus or songthaew heading north (about 15฿) and tell them where you are going. It will then be a 3-km walk or 10฿ motorcycle lift to the visitor center. Bus #8203 goes from Kanchanaburi (30฿); you'll still have to get a motorcycle taxi to the information center.

Hin Dat Hot Springs

These two sights don't garner an English road sign, but their turnoff is about 127km from Kanchanaburi and before Thong Pha Phum. Most tourists come on 2- or 3-day tours organized in Kanchanaburi. The natural springs bubble away in a hollow 3km northeast of Route 323. One pool stays a constant 40°C, while the other fluctuates from 35 to 38°C—hot, any way you cut it. If you can haul yourself out of these pools of bliss, the waterfall (your basic tri-level cascade) is 10km ahead.

Thong Pha Phum

This town really doesn't have much to offer but fuel to those *en route* to and from Sangkhlaburi. Road signs along Route 323 clearly lead to Thong Pha Phum. About 153km out of Kanchanaburi, it lies 6km from the **Khao Laem Dam,** a scenic reservoir for fishing and boating. This 1019m-long dam offers superb views of Khao Laem Lake.

The **Sri Thong Bungalow** (tel. 599 058) is a 10฿ motorcycle jaunt or a short walk (left down the main road with the bus stop behind you). Turn left at the red arrow with their phone number on it across from the Polaroid store. Their driveway is the first on your right. Rooms for one or two people are 130฿, with A/C 240฿. No English is spoken. Park your motorbike beneath the carport of your room. Laundry service. Check-out 10am.

Sunyataram Forest Monastery

Folks come from far and wide to hear the teachings of Phra Ajaan Yantra Amaro, one of the most revered monks in Thailand, whose picture adorns most of the buses in the province. He leads one of the 15 major meditation centers in Thailand; if you're interested in learning the Buddhist way, three-day stays are allowed (donations would be a good show of reciprocity). Visitors are invited to join in strict, ritualized days of meditation and learning while observing the precepts of a clean and devout life. For more information and booklets, write: P.O. Box 20, Thong Pha Phum, Kanchanaburi Province 71150, Thailand. Or, simply hop off the bus on your way to Sangkhlaburi when you see the monastery's ornate gardens on your right.

Thung Yai Sanctuary Park

This national park, a UNESCO World Heritage sight, is living proof of the environmental groups' continued role in Thailand's future. The large area of forested mountains and high plains lying west of Sangkhlaburi is a safe harbor for protected wildlife species including tigers, elephants, bears, otters, tapirs, gibbons, and peacocks. Only four-wheel-drive vehicles can traverse the terrain, even during the dry season; special permission is required for entry. Contact the Kanchanaburi TAT Office (tel. 511 200) for road conditions, accessibility and entrance requirements; or talk to Armin at the Burmese Inn in Sangkhlaburi for details and possible jeep-with-driver rental.

■■■ SANGKHLABURI

An escape for the tourist who yearns to escape from tourists, Sangkhlaburi is situated about 225km northwest of Kanchanaburi, on the northern edge of the reservoir created by the Khao Laem Dam. The 70km route from the dam to town runs parallel to the reservoir, passing raw limestone mountainsides, verdant valleys, and several raft complexes harbored among partially submerged trees. Visitors come mainly for Three Pagodas Pass, Chedi Phuthakaya of Wat Wang Wiwekaram (say that five times fast), and the markets and villages along the border. Even now, the Mon village is a source of conflict between Burmese "displaced persons" and the Thai government. During the dry season (Nov.-April), Sangkhlaburi offers opportunities for swimming in waterfalls, adventuring along the border, or simply relaxing and enjoying the fresh air and countryside.

Orientation To get there, **bus** #8203 from the Kanchanaburi bus station takes four to six hours depending on road conditions (6:45, 9, 10:15am, and 1:15pm, 60฿). A speedier A/C minivan service leaves every hour 7:30am-4:30pm (3½hr., 100฿) and stops in Tong Pha Phum (70฿ to get off here). Ask for the *rot tuu* at the Asia Sai Yok Company in Kanchanaburi (tel. 513 151), to the right of the theater behind the bus station. The van drops you at Sree Dang Hotel in Sangkhlaburi.

The regular bus arrives one block away from the market area with its many food stalls. The Sree Dang Hotel is nearby while the Burmese Inn and P Guest House are about a kilometer down the road to your right from the bus stop. If you're not in the walking mood, ask a motorcycle driver to take you (10฿).

When it's time to head back, the regular bus #8203 leaves at 6:45, 8:15, 10am, and 1pm. To take the *rot tuu* to Kanchanaburi, buy your ticket at the desk in Sree Dang Hotel (every hour, 6:30-11:30am and at 1, 2:30, and 3:30pm; check for additional trips in the dry season, 100฿).

Practical Information Your **currency exchange** needs can be handled at **Siam Commercial Bank** (tel. 595 076). From the bus stop, walk 2 blocks to your right, then take a left. Open Mon.-Fri. 8:30am-3:30pm. To get to the **post office** from the bus stop, head 3 blocks to your right. At the photo lab, take a left and walk 2 blocks. Turn left and the post office will be on your left. Open Mon.-Fri. 8:30am-4pm, Sat. 9am-noon. **Postal code:** 71240. **Overseas telephone calls** can be made at the post office. P Guest House will also place your call for a 50฿ charge. **Telephone code:** 034. In case of medical emergencies, contact the local **hospital,** across from the post office (currently under construction, but should be open soon), or the **Missionary Hospital,** 18km from Sangkhlaburi in Huay Malai, which has a western doctor. The **police** can be reached at tel. 595 031. **Motorbike** rides to the guest houses cost 10฿; from the market to the Mon temple 15฿.

Accommodations and Food Follow the signs to the two rival guest houses, 15 minutes apart on the same road. The **Burmese Inn** (tel. 595 146) is 1km to your right from the bus station. Armin (Austrian), Meo (Thai), and their lovely baby Alissa have created a clean, comfortable, bungalow-style guest house nestled amid wild orchids. Meo prepares Thai, European and Burmese food at reasonable prices. Armin offers helpful and interesting information and maps about the border area. Alissa spits up on the floor. Motorbike rental 150฿ per day. Singles with net 45฿. Doubles 60฿. Add 10฿ for a fan. Room with private bath, fan, and desk 100฿; doubles 130฿. Laundry service. Check-out noon. The **P Guest House,** 81/1 Tambon Nong Loo (tel. 595 061), 1km beyond the Burmese Inn, is run by Duranee Yen Jai and her husband, who maintain a beautiful restaurant and garden overlooking the lake. The view of the Mon village, wats, and wooden bridge is unbeatable, although the single rooms are small and the thin mattresses even smaller. Honor system lets you raid the 'fridge at leisure. Multilingual Duranee organizes daytime boat, elephant, and raft tours for 700฿ per person, including a room for the night. Motorbike 150฿ per day. Overseas calls for a 50฿ charge. Single cot 30฿, double mattress 50฿. Room with private bath 120฿. Laundry service. Check-out noon. The third option in town is the **Sree Daeng Hotel,** (tel. 595 039), near the central market, where the A/C minivan drops you 2 blocks straight from the bus station. Look down the street to your right for the English sign. Well-scrubbed rooms and hardwood floors compensate for the dearth of river views. Two single beds, fan, and private bath 180฿, with A/C 350฿. Deluxe room with fridge, TV, carpet, and A/C 700฿. Restaurant proudly displays a "clean Bill of Health" certificate. Laundry service. Check-out noon.

Sights One of Sangkhlaburi's two basic tour packages whisks you off to the cave, Three Pagodas Pass, the bridge, the temple, and the Mon market and village. The jaunt is occasionally guided in English and costs about the same as a do-it-yourself expedition (two days 750฿, three days 950฿), but eliminates the hassle of hailing songthaews and motorcycles. "Jungle trekking" tours inflict considerable wallet wounds, due to their inclusion of long-tail boat, elephant-back, and bamboo raft experiences. After two hours, expect the "seats" on the elephants to be uncomfortable and the romance of the jungle to become routine. Going with a group keeps things lively; you'll be astounded at how the elephants negotiate steep slippery slopes (they sort of kneel-and-slide). Wear long clothing or slather on sunblock. Tours organized in Kanchanaburi include transportation to and from Sangkhlaburi, visits to the sights, accommodations, and some meals.

THE MON VILLAGE

Across the **Khao Laem Lake** created by the dam near Thong Pha Phum is the **longest wooden bridge in Thailand.** The Mon constructed this 400m trestle bridge to connect their camp with the main part of the city, and it has a spectacular panoramic view of Sangkhlaburi. Walk from your guest house across the bridge to the Mon village or take a motorbike taxi for 15฿ to the Mon Temple across the bridge.

The Mon people are not quite refugees—they do not have Thai citizenship, but some have obtained work permits from immigration. Most of them have fled the shackles of slave labor in Burma. For years, the Mon have fought the Burmese for the right of self-determination, claiming land that now comprises the eastern states of Burma. Some Mon have joined the Karen army to further their aims. It has long been feared that the people here would be sent back to Burma if it weren't for the protection of the elderly Luang Phaw Utama, who watches over the temples in the area. Rumor has it, however, that the Thai government has negotiated with the aged village abbot, so that the Mon people will not be deported once he dies.

Luang Phaw Utama, the abbot of Wat Wiwekaram and Chedi Phuthakaya in the village, is active in the protection of the Mon people. When Old Sangkhlaburi was flooded and destroyed in 1981, the Thai government gave Luang Phaw Utama land to rebuild the temple and 500 Mon households. Now about 1000 households sit beneath the gaze of the two new temples. When you cross the bridge into the Mon Village, head straight back to the paved road; follow this road left until you reach the wat's gate. From here the *chedi* and handicraft market are to the left, opposite the game-show-glittery Wat Wang Wiwekaram. The wat is the center for Mon worship, whereas **Wat Somdet** (before entering Sangkhlaburi) and **Wat Si Sewan** (between Burmese Inn and P Guest House) are respectively the Thai and Karen temples.

The highly revered Mon temple is architecturally derived from Indian, Burmese, and Thai styles. Constructed in 1985, the red-tiled *chedi* was modeled on the Mahabodha stupa in Bodhgaya, India. The top of the pagoda is caked with 6kg of dazzling gold, and a thousand Buddhas adorn the sides. One of the monks is said to have healed many chronic pain sufferers by walking across their backs.

At the base of the *chedi*, the **Mon market** deals in sapphires and other gems, jewelry, fabric, and wood carvings. You'll think you are getting a good deal for that egg-sized, pigeon-blood ruby—think again. If you really want to buy gems of dubious quality, stay home and order from the QVC home shopping network. If you want the real thing, go to Bo Phloi.

■■■ BORDER CROSSING: THREE PAGODAS PASS

One-day tours from local inns leading up to this sight often make the Three Pagodas Pass and the border area an emotional letdown. The diminutive **Three Pagodas** at the border sit benignly on a patch of grass around which vehicles turn around to head back. The location was in one of the rowdiest regions during the Thai-Burmese War. One story says that the pagodas got there when, as the wars were winding to a close near the end of the Ayutthaya period (1350-1767), the King laid down three stones to mark the border between the two countries (since that time, the border has shifted). The flanking stones represented Thailand and Burma, while the middle one signified unity and peace. Villagers later constructed the three pagodas (*Chedi Sam Ong*) over the original legendary stones, and the middle shrine has been used by monks to pray for peace.

Between 6am and 6pm, Burmese border control allows *farang* to enter the country for two hours (130฿). However, the money goes to support the Burmese regime and certainly does not help the Mon or Karen people. Moreover, the black market on the other side isn't all that special; the market developing on the Thai side will soon have similar goods, and almost everything here is sold in the Mon market for comparable prices. On your way to the border, you can visit the **Wang Badon Cave.** What the plain façade doesn't reveal are the **limestone caves** that have been carved by thousands of years of trickling water etching out caverns, tunnels, and spectacular rock formations. Acrophobics won't make it too far, since getting up the mountain and around the caves means scampering up bamboo ladders and edging along narrow ledges. Monks come to meditate in the niches of the caves, so don't whoop too loudly. To get to the caves, catch a green songthaew from

Sangkhlaburi market heading to Three Pagodas (hourly, 7am-6:30pm, 30฿). Get out 1.5km before the border at the bus stop on your right. Walk 1km down the dirt road and turn right before the timber mill; the cave entrance is 500m down on your right. When you've finished scaling, catch the next songthaew to the border at the bus stop or walk the 1.5km. Local guest houses can take you to the caves, the Mon Village, and the border for 100฿, five person minimum. During the dry season, hire a jeep with driver (500฿ for up to six people) from the Burmese Inn to chauffeur you for the day. This trip includes **Takien Thong Waterfall** in the Thung Yai Park area. Alternatively, you can rent a motorbike to hit the road solo.

■■■ PHETCHABURI

Although the TAT tags Phetchaburi as the "little-known province on the way to Hua Hin," romantics might prefer its usual label, "City of Diamonds," bestowed when gems were found nearby in the Chao Phraya River. You won't trip over any Liz Taylor-sized rocks in the brown muck of the river, but you may find hidden golden Buddhas in the mazes of Khao Ban Da It and Khao Luang Caves. Most *farang* don't bother stopping here on their way to the southern beaches—don't be surprised if people whisper to each other as you stroll along Phetchaburi's busy streets. The town (pop. 35,000) chugs along regardless of outsiders—people rush to work in the morning, school children in uniforms flood the streets at 5pm, and by 9pm, everyone is at home, hanging with the family unit.

ORIENTATION

Nobody actually calls the city of Phetchaburi by its full name. "Phetburi," "Muang Phet" or simply "Phet" are common monikers. Located 135km south of Bangkok, Phetburi can be reached on buses and trains to the south in 2 to 2-½ hours.

The center of town and a good reference point is the **Chomrut Bridge** (Saphan Chomrut) over the Phetchaburi River, which runs north to south. **Pongsuriya Road** crosses the river at Chomrut Bridge and runs west to east. The large roads intersecting Pongsuriya and running parallel to the river on the west bank are **Rachadamnern Road** and **Damnernkasem Road.** On the east bank, **Punich Jaren Road, Suranluchai Road,** and **Matayawong Road** each intersect Pongsuriya Rd. from east to west respectively. **Ratwithi Road** in the north end of town intersects Damnernkasem Rd. at the General Post Office and its red and white communication tower. The west side of Ratwithi Rd. ends at **Khao Wang mountain.** Phetkasem Highway is on the west side of the mountain and **Khao Luang Caves** are 4km outside of town to the north.

PRACTICAL INFORMATION

Tourist Office: Phetburi is served by the **TAT office** in Cha-Am. If you're coming to Phetburi from the south, you may want to stop there, although the information on Phetburi is pretty sparse.

Currency Exchange: On the west bank, **Siam Commercial Bank** (tel. 425 303), on Damnernkasem Rd. south of the GPO. On the east bank, **Thai Farmers Bank,** 1 block beyond Chomrut bridge on the corner of Pongsuriya Rd. and Suranluchai Rd. Both banks open Mon.-Fri. 8:30am-3:30pm.

Post Office: GPO, at the intersection of Ratwithi and Damnernkasem Rd. Head toward the red and white communications tower. Open Mon.-Fri. 8:30am-4:30pm, Sat.-Sun. 9am-noon. **Postal code:** 76000.

Telephone/Telegraph: 2nd floor of the GPO for long-distance calls and other services. Open daily 7am-10pm. **Telephone code:** 032.

Trains: To **Bangkok** (7 trains daily, 2:21am-3:28pm). The bus is quicker and more convenient.

Buses: The **regular bus station** on Phetkasem Hwy. is on the opposite side of Khao Wang mountain from downtown. Buses to **Bangkok** roll out every 15min. (3-½hr., 30฿). From the station, motorcycle taxis ride into town (20฿). If walking, continue down the road and turn left at the first major cross street, Noke Rd. With the mountain to your left head straight into downtown about 1km. Cross the Phetchaburi River and go left on Punich Jaren Rd., walking until you reach Pongsuriya Rd. just east of Chamrut Bridge. **A/C buses** use a terminal just east of the GPO on Ratwithi Rd. Two companies offer service to **Bangkok** (every 30min., 5am-8pm, 2-½hr., 50฿). To intercept A/C buses headed **farther south,** and try your luck on Phetkasem Hwy.; ask for help at either bus station first.

Local Transportation: Your feet should take you anywhere in the downtown area or take **samlors** (10฿) or **motorcycles**. The **tram** on the far side of Khao Wang saves you the hike up to the 2 peaks (20฿ adults, 10฿ children). To get to **Khao Luang Caves,** go to Ratwithi Rd. at the mountain base and hire a *rot lenk* (a small pick-up) or tuk-tuk (10฿).

Hospital: Phetchaburi Hospital (tel. 428 082) on Rot Fai Rd. North of town.

Emergency: tel. 191.

Police: Phetchaburi Police Station (tel. 425 500) on Ratwithi Rd. Near the GPO. 24-hr. mini station at the base of Khao Wang mountain.

ACCOMMODATIONS

The lack of *farang* tourists to Phetburi makes finding guest houses a little tricky—most signs are in Thai. Room rates are higher than in Thailand's backpacker meccas, but the cheap, generous servings of market food and genuine smiles should make up the difference. Fret not, the places listed below are happy to have a foreigner sign in their guest book.

Rabieng Rinnum Guest House, (tel. 425 707). A dark teakwood house, just on the west side of the Chomrut Bridge. White sign says "Guest House." Popular restaurant with a young, hip Thai crowd, has added 4 fan-cooled doubles (200฿), two common baths, and some sunny patio acreage overlooking the Phetchaburi River. Friendly staff speaks good English and plays western music, even though the clientele is mostly Thai. Central location. Prawns in spicy coconut milk (50฿) and other bona fide Thai dishes served until midnight. Laundry service.

Ratanaphakdi Hotel (tel. 425 041), two blocks west of Chomrut Bridge on Pongsuriya Rd. Look for the golden letters in Thai above the door and a 12-person table in the entrance area. Lovingly preserved wooden stairs lead to an upstairs hideaway. Blue tile bathroom with western toilet down the hall. Singles 100฿. Doubles 200฿. Laundry service.

Day King Long Hotel (tel. 425 023). From Chomrut Bridge, go east on Pongsuriya Rd. At Thai Farmers Bank, turn right onto Suran Luchai Rd. and take your first left. Day King Long is the 2nd to last entrance on the left, past the shoe store. No-frills lobby (an empty 3-car garage with TV) belies chambers with marble-patterned floors, phone, and desk area catering to Thai business people (140฿). Laundry.

Khao Wang Hotel, 147/1-3 Ratwithi Rd. (tel. 425 167), at the base of Khao Wang. the hotel is down the driveway in front of the green-topped phone booth on your left. The less you pay, the higher you'll have to climb, but it's quieter at the top of this five-story complex. Much like Day King Long Hotel, but here TVs substitute for desks. Singles 180฿, with A/C 280฿. Laundry service.

Chom Kow Hotel (tel. 425 398), at the east side of Chomrut Bridge, with the red-lettered Thai sign. The cheapest place in town, and it shows (hard beds). Double bed and fan 120฿, hall bathroom 80฿. Large German Shepherd in lobby does not like late arrivals. Laundry service.

FOOD

There's no such thing as low blood sugar in Phetchaburi. The usual Thai spread is complemented by delectable desserts created by local bakeries. Palm sugar abounds in Thailand's crown jewel of sweet-making. A cluster of stores sells pre-packaged sweets along Phetkasem Rd. at the base of Khao Wang, but you'll have no problem finding vendors walking the streets around the temples. Downtown near the clock tower and Wat Ko Kaew are a **market area** and bakeries such as **Lamiet** and **Khodi.** They also have *salapao* (meat-filled steamed dough) and kebobs to warm you up.

Once you recover from the sugar rush, you might be ready for an after-dessert meal. Try the food courts tucked on the side streets of Pongsuriya Rd., or Suran Luchai Rd. **Rabiang Restaurant** just west of Chomrut Bridge has a long menu of classic Thai plates and soups (40-80฿), and the chef will tone down typically psycho-spicy Thai meals for sensitve *farang* taste buds. Their English menu makes your immediate existence less stressful. The owner puts Santana, B.B. King or Dire Straits on the stereo as you sip your banana/papaya shake (15฿). Open daily 10am-midnight. If the heat has taken over your head, ease on down to the A/C **mall.** This stark-white, triple-decker acropolis is hidden away on your first left east of the stoplight at Pongsuriya Rd. and Matayawong Rd. A plate of nourishment runs about 20฿ and a Thai-style ice cream sundae is only 5฿ at the second-floor food gallery (buy with tickets). Open 9:30am-9pm.

SIGHTS

Phetchaburi's chief tourist lures, **Khao Wang Historical Park** and **Phra Nakhon Khiri Palace,** lie west of the river (open daily 8am-5pm). To get to the palace, walk up the hill where it meets Ratwithi Rd. Although the path is steep, it is paved and the view from the top is a definite reward for your sweat and aching hamstrings. If you really don't want to walk, take the **tram** from the west side of the mountain (20฿ round trip, 10฿ for kids). The tram runs 8am-5pm.

Built in 1858 during the reign of King Rama IV (King Mongkut), this was the first hilltop palace in Thailand. Furnishings and architecture are a blend of Chinese, Thai, and European styles. Phra Thinang Phetphum Phairon Hall of the royal palace is now a **museum,** displaying art and antiques including the royal throne and materials used at the royal household (open daily 9am-4pm; admission 20฿). The observation tower gives a stunning wide-angle view of the province; don't hit your head on the low beam as you ascend the platform. Owww.

The walk to the other peak takes you past a towering *chedi* between the temple and the palace. The temple is supposedly modeled after the Royal Chapel in Bangkok, and even shares the name **Wat Phra Kaew.** Climbing to the base of the smaller gray *chedi* affords spectacular views of Phetburi, which include the large *chedi* and palace in one direction and a glimpse of the Gulf of Thailand in the other.

More than 30 wats lie within a 10km radius of Chomrut Bridge. Many of these Buddhist temples date back to the Ayutthaya period, when Phetburi was an artistic mecca. Some of the most visited wats are listed below, although just walking down Damnernkasem Rd. south of the bridge will treat you to many shrines.

Wat Yai Sawannaram, on the right-hand side of Pongsuriya Rd., is a 10-minute walk east of Chomrut Bridge. Enter at the vanilla-colored arches. The large compound features some amazing examples of Ayutthaya art and architecture, dating back 500 to 600 years. Two wooden buildings demand special attention here; find someone in the dormitory area in the back of the temple grounds who has the keys.

The wooden red **Teaching Hall** was actually built in Ayutthaya and transported here by boat 300 years ago. Door panels feature elaborately carved interweaving floral designs; the great slash in them is believed to have been left during a Burmese attack. If you duck under the hall and go roadside, you will notice that two central window carvings are different from the others, representing the King and Queen.

As you follow the monk who has the keys (proper etiquette demands that you stay behind him), you will come to the main *bot.* Passing through the first locked door of the new white outer wall, you enter a courtyard rimmed with golden Buddha images. The unusual windowless *bot* then has a locked door of its own. Entering through this wooden portal brings you back half a millennium. Wooden rafters reveal the underside of the tiled roof, and the murals depict humans and mythical creatures paying their respects to the large Buddha under the white *chat.* The inside panels of the doors show *farang* in awe of the power of Buddha. The *bot's* columns and the objects within it revolve around the number six. Look in the back for the Buddha with six toes on one foot.

Continue down Pongsuriya Rd. and turn right before the train tracks; walk 500m, past the Esso station, to reach the 12th century **Wat Kamphaeng Laeng.** If the front gate is locked, turn right on the road just after the wat and enter at the gate on your right. The five laterite block structures which house Buddha images are suggestive of the Angkor-style *bot*. If it's closed, ask for the key to peek inside. **Phra Khruu Yanwitmon,** who is *Luang Phaw Phet* (the venerable monk of Phetchaburi), resides here and is much revered in the province. The belief that he possesses healing powers draws many to pay respects and seek his blessing.

Wat Mahathat is a five-peaked Khmer-influenced temple built around eight centuries ago. To go to Wat Mahathat, head south on Damnernkasem Rd. until you spot the huge white *prang.* Within the biggest *prang* lie relics of Buddha which were presented by the king in 1954. This active wat is the temple used by the Thais of Phetburi for worship and religious ceremonies.

The **Khao Ban Da It Caves** are hidden beneath the three communications towers on top of the hill, about 4km west of town on the other side of Phetkasem Hwy. The entrance to the compound is on the right side of the road past the series of three ornate shelters which are maintained by the monks of Khao Ban Da It. Skip up the steps between the two gray elephant statues to get to the caves. Bring a flashlight so you can really explore this underground labyrinth and find the 'thousand buddhas' tucked away into crevices. A *rot lenk* or tuk-tuk from town should run about 20฿. Donations are welcome. Open 8am-6pm.

Promoted by the TAT everywhere and over-run by tourists are the **Khao Luang Caves,** 4km to the north of town. They are best seen between 11am and 2pm, when sunlight filters through two openings at the top of the cave, sparkling off the collection of golden Buddha images and a red-tiled floor. Bring bananas to feed the caves' ravenous monkeys. Take a 10฿ tuk-tuk or *rot lenk* ride from Ratwithi's intersection at Khao Wang mountain and then follow the 500m path uphill. Donations are accepted to preserve the site.

■ NEAR PHETCHABURI

Thailand's largest national park, **Kaeng Krachan National Park,** stretches out on the western half of Phetchaburi province. It envelops a whopping 3000 sq. km of land between Burma and the Gulf of Thailand, most of which is "steep and deep" tropical rainforest. Plant and animal life are especially diverse because species from both continental Asia and the Malaysian peninsula mix here. Since the park's opening in 1981, four white elephants, for centuries considered divine symbols of royal prestige and fortune, have been captured here and given to the current king. If you like shooting rapids, the Phetchaburi and Phanburi Rivers are good for **rafting.** Sometimes park rangers lead **3-day hikes** in the high season for a 200฿ per day fee (with food added in, 352฿) for four people. If you are car-less and want to visit the park, things could get pretty pricey unless you're content hanging out at the headquarters on the 45-sq. km **Kaeng Krachan Lake.** Four-person bungalows are 300฿, or you can pitch a tent for 50฿. The restaurant also overlooking the lake not only has a bird that chirps *"Sawadee,"* but also features fried rice and chicken (15฿) or sweet and sour pork (40฿). To get to the park, follow signs 25km west from Tha Yang, south of Phetchaburi. Beyond the main gate, take your first left and then cross the bridge. The road hairpins to climb the dike face; at the top, turn left and drive about 2km to the park headquarters. If you shun the driver's seat, take a minibus from Phetkasem Hwy. at Tha Yang to the park headquarters. The trip should cost no more than 20฿.

Chao Samran Beach is a 10฿ songthaew ride. Minibuses leave from the station along Mattawayong Rd. (parallel to the Phetchaburi River, and two blocks east). It's quieter than the bigger beaches to the south, but people pack the place when the weekend rolls around. Songthaews usually stop running around 6pm.

■■■ CHA-AM

Picture a small road that runs straight for several kilometers. On one side, place a long beach overlooking wide-open water, dotted with an occasional boat or jet ski. Sprinkle some beach chairs, umbrellas, casuarina and pine trees, and mini police stations beside the road. On the other side, spread hotels, guest houses, bungalows, seafood restaurants, snooker joints, and gaudy beach-wear shops. That's Cha-Am.

Thais flock to Cha-Am to hide-out from the stress goblins of the city, work, and school. Most make the 173km trip from Bangkok for a weekend of *hat* (beach), the *phra athit* (sun), and the *sanuk* (fun). Bikini-clad *farang* who let it all hang out will feel a bit out of place on the beach. But all in all, Thai vacationers are happy to share their slice of the good life.

ORIENTATION

About 3-½ hours from Bangkok, Cha-Am is easily reached by southern bus and train lines. It's only a half-hour more to Hua Hin. The **TAT** is right along **Phetkasem Road** (Route 4), the main highway. A few streets run to the beach, but the main intersection is with **Narathip Road** which meets the beach at one end and the train station at the other. Between the train station and Phetkasem Highway are the post office and police station. Narathip Rd. runs to a T-intersection with **Ruamjit Road,** the beachside street. Turning left will point you due north, and going right (south) brings you to many places to eat and stay without as many shops along the way. The street parallel to Ruamjit Rd. away from the beach is **Chaolai Road,** which also has some guest houses. Motorcycles will save you a blistering walk to the beach (10฿).

PRACTICAL INFORMATION

Tourist Office: Tourism Authority of Thailand (TAT), 500/51 Phetkasem Rd. (Route 4) (tel. 471 502 or 471 005-06). Ask the bus to drop you off there or walk 20min. from the train station (out to the highway and turn right). The inviting, bright white building has plenty of useful brochures and maps for the local area as well as for Hua Hin, Ranong, Prachuap Khiri Khan, and Phetchaburi. Open daily 8:30am-4:30pm.

Tourist Police: 24-hr. TAT (tel. 471 502 or 471 005-06).

Currency Exchange: Banks line Phetkasem Hwy. and are open Mon.-Fri. 8:30am-3:30pm. **Exchange booths** are at the intersection with Narathip Rd. and Ruamjit Rd., generally open 9am-8pm.

Post/Telephone Office: GPO (tel. 471 252), on Narathip Rd. midway between the train station and the main intersection. Open Mon.-Fri. 8:30am-4:30pm, Sat.-Sun. 8:30-noon. **Postal code:** 76120. **Telephone code:** 032.

Trains: The station (tel. 471 159) sits at the end of Narathip Rd., away from the beach. To **Bangkok** (7 daily, but 4 pass by before 5am, others at 6:30, 6:50am, and 2:50pm, 4hr., 40฿). Cha-am is a minor stop, so confirm times with station officials and be ready to jump on when the train zooms past. Motorbikes go from the station to the beach (10฿).

Buses: The A/C terminal (tel. 471 654) is the small blue building past Aruntip Bungalows on Ruamjit Rd. South. Open 7:30am-5pm. To and from **Bangkok** (every 2hr., 8am-5:30pm, 82฿). On weekdays you can generally just buy a ticket and board, but on weekends and holidays buy at least 1 day in advance. **Regular** buses also run to **Bangkok** (every 30min., 45฿) and to **Hua Hin** (every 30min., 10฿). Flag these down on Phetkasem Hwy.

Local Transportation: You can walk from Phetkasem Rd. (Route 4) to Ruamjit Rd., but it's about 1.5km. Generally, motorcycles (10฿) will take you along this stretch as well as along the beach.

Bike/Moped Rental: Along Ruamjit Rd. Make sure the bike fits before renting it; many places have kiddie-sized Day-Glow pink or green BMX bikes. Rentals 20฿ per day. Mopeds should run about 100-150฿ per day.

Public Bathrooms/Showers: Several along Ruamjit Rd. Quality varies, but prices are standard (showers 5฿, for kids 3฿; toilets 2฿).

Weather and Peak Season: In the dry season (Nov.-May), crowds are sparse. In April and May hot weather and no school mean big crowds. In the off-season the town relaxes and awaits the rains. Prices drop in June, an ideal time to visit before the monsoons hit.

Hospital: (tel. 471 007), on Klongtien Rd. Go north 200m on Phetkasem Hwy. from the intersection with Naratip Rd. Klongtien Rd. will be on the right where the highway bears left, and the hospital is about 1km down the street on the right.

Emergency: tel. 191. **24-hr. TAT/Tourist Police:** tel. 471 502 or 471 005-06.

Police: (tel. 471 321) on Narathip Rd. next to the post office.

ACCOMMODATIONS

The Count on *Sesame Street* would work himself into a numeral frenzy trying to total up all the places to stay in Cha-Am. During the off-season and on weekdays (except in April and May), you'll have many options, but no real bargains. Cha-Am is a Thai family getaway—not a *farang* resort. Many of the crash pads in town are meant to be rented as two- or three-room bungalows (600฿ and up). Expect some of the prices listed below to as much as double during popular months and holidays, but if they're empty when you arrive, you may be able to get a discount. "Ruamjit Rd. North/South" corresponds to a left/right turn off Narathip Rd. All places generally allow check-in at any time and have noon check-out and laundry service.

Pratarnchok House, 240/3 Ruamjit Rd. North (tel. 471 215 or (01) 918 2946). The 4th guest house from the intersection (look for the English sign). No doubt inspired by Banana Republic: subtle tan color scheme pervades the place, and the management is friendly. Room with shower and Thai-style toilet 200฿, 150฿ for stays of 4 nights or longer most of the year. Rooms with A/C 300฿.

Cha-Am Villa Hotel, 241/1 Ruamjit Rd. North (tel. 471 086). You can't miss the bold English sign about 5 guest houses north of Pratarnchok House. Each spacious room has a large and comfy bed with firm pillows to give your back a break. western toilet and Thai shower combination guarantees a wet seat. Rooms 200฿, with A/C 300-400฿, with refrigerator and hot water 500฿.

Nalumon Bungalows, Ruamjit Rd. South (tel. 471 440). Look for the English sign. Smooth wooden balconies shade each upstairs bungalow from the unrelenting sun. Rooms with king-size bed and western bath 250฿.

J. J. Guest House, 277/1-2 Ruamjit Rd. South (tel. 471 231). The 1st guest house when you turn right off Narathip Rd. Spacious rooms with sparkling white sheets 300฿, with A/C and alpine mountain paintings 500฿.

FOOD

Not only is Ruamjit Rd. lined with places to stay; it is also a haven for inexhaustible eaters. At most of the food carts or **street vendors,** you can get snacks for 15-20฿. The restaurants will cost you a bit more, but may be worth it for their wide selections of seafood. As you approach the five-star Methavalai Hotel on the north end of the **beach,** there are several restaurants with seaside patios and mm-mm tasties for your tummy at about 50฿. The **mini-mart** just north of Prathanchok House is open daily 8am-11pm. If you're making a post office run or heading for the train, stop 100m beyond the highway at the intersection of Narathip Rd. with the small Soi Sa-Ad Eiam ("sparkling clean alley"). Here you'll enter **Ice Cream Land,** where a double chocolate sundae runs 17฿, and a satellite dish of rainbow-hued ice cream blasts you into gastronomic orbit for only 35฿. Open daily 10am-10pm.

SIGHTS AND ENTERTAINMENT

If you've come to Cha-Am expecting to do anything more than kick back on the beach, you have made a serious mistake. Thai college students make MTV's Beach Party look like a Tupperware gathering, with their non-stop action on Cha-Am's beaches between April and May.

The **Fisher Pub** on the north end has purple and white-garbed Thai hostesses to help you with your **snooker** game. To show your stuff at one of their six tables in the large A/C hall you'll have to shell out 80฿ (open 6pm-midnight). It might be more pleasant just to sit back on the beach in one of the chairs across from a well-lit restaurant and watch the world go by.

At sunrise or sunset, take the kilometer stroll up the north end of the beach to **Wat Neranchara.** Here you'll see the Buddha as you have never seen him before: he has six arms covering his face, ears and his lap. The Gulf of Thailand crashes before him and the cool breezes caress him, but he is blithely oblivious to it all; nothing interrupts his meditations.

■■■ HUA HIN

Long, Long Ago, before Phuket and Pattaya launched into the international jet-set travel scene, Hua Hin was catering to the upper crust from Thailand and abroad. In the 1920s King Rama VII deemed the spot worhty of royal relaxation and ordered up a summer palace, Klai Kangwon (Far From Worries), still in use today. Soon after, the State Railway Co. laid tracks to Hua Hin for an opulent train service from Bangkok. The Thai nobility has since exchanged fan-toting servants for air-conditioning and afternoon tea for karaoke, but many Bangkok families with a few baht to burn still own estates along the coast to the south of Hua Hin.

The town itself, with its upscale guest houses and pier-side seafood restaurants, caters to sun-seeking Thais and foreigners with slightly more proletarian incomes. Compared to over-developed, X-rated Pattaya, Hua Hin is a laid-back PG, gracefully welcoming both the worn-out backpacker and the expat golfer. With a long stretch of *clean*, white sand (increasingly rare in Thailand) reasonably priced accommodations, and some of the best seafood in the country, it's no surprise that a great variety of Bangkok-embattled beach-goers head to Hua Hin.

ORIENTATION

Hua Hin (head rock) is 232km from Bangkok and is a popular stop on the route of buses and trains heading south. Both the Phetkasem Hwy. and train line parallel the beach; three major streets cross the highway and head to the sand. From north to south: **Chomsin Road, Dechanuchit Road,** and **Damnoenkasem Road.** The roads that parallel the shore are (from the beach) **Naresdamri Road, Poonsuk Road, Phetkusern Hwy.,** and **Srasong Road.**

Foot force is the easiest way to explore the tadpole-size town. From the bus or train stations, head for the guest house, bar, and restaurant-lined sois connecting Poonsuk Rd. and Naresdamri Rd. The sand is a five-minute walk away, with thatched umbrellas and beach chairs awaiting your presence. For good swimming, walk about a km or so from the fishing pier to where the pebbles are less profuse.

PRACTICAL INFORMATION

Tourist Office: Tourist Information Service Center, 114 Phetkasem Rd. (tel. 511 047), on the 1st floor of the municipal building at the intersection with Damnoenkasem Rd. Open daily 8:30am-noon and 1-4:30pm.

Tourist Police: In the little white building on the left side of Damnoenkasem Rd., just before the beach. Open 24 hrs.

Tours: Travel agents line Phetkasem Rd. and are in the Damnoenkasem Rd. area. They arrange trips to sights around Cha-Am as far as Phetchaburi and the Damnoen Saduak Floating Market.

Currency Exchange: Banks and associated exchange booths stay open until around 9pm. They are along Phetkasem Hwy. as well as at the intersection of Damnoenkasem and Naresdamri Rd.

Post Office: GPO (tel. 511 063), on Damnoenkasem Rd. as soon as you turn off Phetkasem Rd., across from the police station. Open Mon.-Fri. 8:30am-4:30pm, Sat.-Sun. and holidays 9am-noon. **Postal code:** 77110.

Telephone: (tel. 511 350). Office next to GPO handles international calls, fax, telex, and even sells stamps. Open daily 8am-midnight. **Directory Service:** 13. **Telephone code:** 032.

Airport: Hua Hin Airport is about 5km north of the city. To **Bangkok** (daily, 8am and 5:30pm). All flights through **Bangkok Airways,** which has an office in Hua Hin (tel. 512 083 for reservations; open daily 9am-5pm). AmEx, MC, Visa. Bangkok office: tel. (02) 253 8942.

Trains: (tel. 511 073) at the end of Damnoenkasem Rd. away from the beach. Tickets sold 30min. before departure, but reservations should be arranged in advance. Open for reservations Mon.-Fri. 8:30am-12:30pm and 1:30-4pm, Sat.-Sun. and holidays 8:30am-noon. Fares are listed for 3rd-class. To: **Bangkok** (8 daily, 5hr., 44฿); **Chumphon** (10 daily, 4hr., 49฿); **Phetchaburi** (9 daily, 1hr., 13฿); **Prachuap Khiri Khan** (9 daily, 1-¼hr., 19฿); and **Surat Thani** (10 daily, 7hr., 74฿).

Buses: Regular bus station, on the corner of Dechanuchit Rd. and Srasong Rd. (tel. 511 230). Open 24 hrs. Regular bus tickets to Bangkok's Southern Terminal (every 15min., 4hr., 51฿) can be pre-purchased or bought on the bus. During the day, regular buses stop at the station, but at night the orange buses will look for flag-stops by the bus station or clock tower on Phetkasem Rd. Check beforehand at the bus station. To **Cha-Am** (every 30min., 10฿). Regular buses to the **south: Chumphon** (every 40min., 8am-midnight, 5hr., 66฿), **Prachuap Khiri Khan** (every 20min., 7am-2:20am, 2-½hr., 25฿), **Surat Thani** (16 daily, 12:35am-11:55pm, 8hr., 112฿). **A/C Bus Station** (tel. 511 654 or 512 543), 1st floor of Siriphetchkasem Hotel Building on Srasong Rd. near Dechanuchit Rd. Open daily 4am-8pm. To: **Bangkok** seats should be reserved in advance (every 30min., 3am-9pm, 3-½hr., 92฿) and **Cha-Am** (every 15min., 30฿). To the **south:** All north-south buses to and from Bangkok go through Hua Hin, but A/C buses going far south are normally non-stop from Bangkok; flagging them down on Phetkasem Hwy. is iffy at best. If you want A/C, book with a tour office.

Local Transportation: Samlors and **motorcycle taxis** serve the main part of Hua Hin (10-20฿). Hire only drivers wearing vests with identification numbers. Local green **buses** run from the regular bus station to **Krilas** and **Takiab Hills** (every 20min., 6am-5:50pm, 5฿).

Taxis: From Phetkasem Rd., in front of Chatchai Market (round-trip) to: **Khao Sam Roi Yod National Park** (600฿), **Krilas,** or **La-U Waterfall** (600฿).

Bike/Moped Rental: Damnoenkasem Rd., opposite Hua Hin Bazaar. Bikes are 50฿ per day. Motorbikes or mopeds 150-290฿ per day plus deposit.

Public Toilets and Showers: Right as you come off the beach onto Damnoenkasem Rd. Shower 3฿.

Hospital: Red Cross Institute (tel. 511 024), on Damnoenkasem Rd. between the train station and highway. Next to the tourist information office. Open Mon.-Fri. 8am-4pm, Sat.-Sun. and holidays 8am-noon. For major medical problems, the **Thonburi Hua Hin Hospital** (tel. 520 841), 4km north of town on Phetkasem Hwy. Open 24 hrs.

Emergency: tel.191.

Police: (tel. 511 027) on Damnoenkasem Rd. toward the beach off the highway. At this number, the police can radio the tourist police.

ACCOMMODATIONS

The guest houses that flourish in the area between Poonsuk Rd. and Naresdamri Rd. are cheap, clean, and within spitting distance of sizzling seafood. During high season, the places fill up quickly and prices may shoot up. Be careful in choosing a guest house if you're serious about catching some deep zzzs—many are adjacent to rambunctious bars.

All Nations Guest House, 10-10/1 Dechanuchit Rd. (tel. 512 727). Look for the sign as you head toward the beach. It's a shiny, white-tile world at this easily accessible guest house, popular with the international set. Each floor has 2 rooms which share a mammoth bathroom. Ground-floor restaurant and bar beckon you to hang out, 24 hrs. a day. Singles 130-150฿, with king-size bed 250฿.

M.P. Guest House, 6 A/2 Soi Kaanjanomai (tel. 511 344). Take a left turn off Damnoenkasem Rd. onto Poonsuk Rd. and then take your 1st right onto a quiet alley, Kaanjanomai Rd. Hostess Poo keeps the place clean and pest-free. The 4 upstairs rooms lead to a peaceful and secluded balcony which begs you to sit under its fan and read a book. Spacious rooms have queen-size beds, although you'll have to be democratic and share the potty. Rooms 100-150฿.

Pattana Guest House, 52 Naresdamri Rd. (tel./fax 513 393). Take a left off Dechanuchit Rd.; look for the elephant backpacker logo on your left near the fishing pier. Beautiful Thai-style architecture with Dutch doors and open patio areas. Rooms 170฿, with bath 250฿.

Moti Mahal Guest House, 152 10/1 Naresdamri Rd. (tel. 513 769). At the intersection of Soi Bintabart and Naresdamri Rd., this white 5-story building looks like a Lego brick stood on end. Downstairs restaurant serves Indian food 9am-10pm. Bombay native Mahadeb speaks flawless English. Doubles with bath 150฿, with view and massive sofa 200฿. Big discounts in low season.

Joy Guest House, 6/5 Soi Bintabart (tel. 512 967), three blocks from Dechanuchit Rd., off Poonsuk Rd. Boost your spirits at this Dutch-run establishment that features a first-class pool table, imported beer and liquor, and a front-row view of Hua Hin's night life. Singles and doubles 150฿, with breakfast 175฿. Large rooms 200฿. All have shared bath.

FOOD

Seafood reigns supreme here. The **night market**, at the intersection of Dechanuchit Rd. and Phetkasem Hwy., is a prime place to net a plate of fried clams *(hoi tawd)* for 10฿. It's quite lively, inexpensive, and not very touristed during the off-season. Almost all the guest houses serve dinners for around 40฿; **Moti Mahal** on Naresdamri Rd. (see Accommodations) tends to the *tandoori* and *masala* crowds until 10pm. **Headrock Pub and Restaurant** at 1541 Naresdamri Rd. (tel. 514 002) provides MTV, A/C, and Aussie steaks. Try your hand at snooker. Look for the pot of gold at the end of their visually and physically stunning "Rainbow" cocktail.

When the sun goes down, the doors open at several excellent family-run seafood shops next to All Nations, with 10฿ bowls of *khao tom* (rice soup) plus whatever seafood you desire (add 5-15฿ more). Across the way, a restaurant makes incredible *plaa biew-waan* (sweet-and-sour fish) as well as *plaa raad phrik* (fish cooked in semi-sweet chili sauce).

To ease your early morning hungries, slurp a bowl of rice soup in the **Chatchai market area** (off Dechanuchit Rd. near the bus station), open 5am-6pm.

SIGHTS AND ENTERTAINMENT

Hua Hin Beach rolls along for kilometers in either direction from town. The daily catch arrives at the **fishing pier** (at the base of Chomsin Rd.) when most people are still asleep. The best **swimming** requires a 1km walk south of the pier where it's less rocky and smelly. Folks wander the sand offering massages, food, and pony rides.

If you stroll north along the beach (past Melia Hotel and the pier), the **Klai Kang Won Palace** comes into view. The palace became a royal summer residence in the 1920s, and it was even designed by one of the King's grandsons. Naturally, this residence is closed to the public, but the mere presence of royalty ensures that the area surrounding it remains respectable and clean.

At the southern end of the beach, you can stroll through the scenic grounds of the **Sofitel Central Hotel,** whose entrance is at the bottom of Damnoenkasem Rd. Originally the Railway Hotel, it was built in 1922 by Prince Purachatra (then Director General of State Railways). This place earned its 15 minutes of fame in the film *The Killing Fields,* playing Phnom Penh's leading hotel. Rooms here run 19,000฿. Barge in for high tea and meander through the gardens where foliage has been dutifully trimmed to resemble elephants and peacocks. A frightening piece of the past, its servers kneel to the ground when they give you tea. Outside the hotel on Damnoenkasem Rd. is the **Hua Hin Bazaar** where vendors sell handicrafts of wood, shells, and straw. Nearby tailors sell fabric and will custom-make suits at off-the-rack prices.

South beyond **Wat Amphala** on Phetkasem Rd. are the twin hills of **Khao Takiab** and **Khao Krilas.** If you don't go by motorbike (the most convenient way), snag a local bus from the Dechanuchit Rd. station (2฿ to Khao Takiab Village, 5฿ to the hill; last returning bus at 5pm). **Khao Takiab** (Chopsticks Hill) features a wat overlooking the sea, with a view of pine tree-lined **Suan Son Beach.** Farther south is **Khao Tao** (Turtle Hill), while inland is **Khao Krilas,** each with spectacular views.

Live rock 'n' roll is featured occasionally at the **Rock Walk Pub;** off Dechanuchit Rd. Along Poonsuk Rd., the **Muay Thai Garden** serves up Isaan dishes and holds **Thai boxing** matches several times a month (200฿ cover charge).

■ AROUND HUA HIN

The area between Hua Hin and the Thai-Burmese border boasts spectacular natural sights for the rambler. **Maps** are in the guide at the TAT in Hua Hin and Cha-Am.

The **Tanao Sri range** forms the border and backdrop for **Pa-La-u,** an untamed jungle in the **Kaeng Krachan National Park** (see also Near Phetchaburi). Within the jungle are the twin waterfalls *(nam tok),* **La-u Yai** and **La-u Noi,** that merge as **Pa-La-u Waterfall.** Nam Tok Pa-La-u consists of over nine levels of cascades; it takes three days to reach the source. A one-day trip brings you to the first few levels. Longer stays require a guide (100฿ per day) and camping equipment (camping is 10฿ per night per person). The park rents out tents or bungalows are available, but will start at 300฿ for the simpler accommodations. Visit November to April.

Overnight trekkers should contact the **Sub-Forestry Office** 7-10 days in advance by writing to: Kaeng Krachan National Park, Pa-La-u Hua Hin, Prachuap Khiri Khan 77110. A songthaew from Chomsin Rd. in Hua Hin takes you to Fa Prathan Village (53km) on local highway 3219 (20฿), departing at 11:30am, 1, and 3pm, return at 6:30, 8, and 9am. From the village to the Sub-Forestry Office you can take the 4km hike or hire a songthaew. From the office to the first cascade, there is official transport for 10-20฿ round trip. Hiring a *rot lenk* from Hua Hin to the waterfall (700฿ per day) or renting a motorcycle are the best options if you want to make a one-day trip.

On the way to Pa-La-u on Rte. 3219, three caves lie 27km from Hua Hin near Nongphlab Village. The **Dao, Lablae, and Kailon Caves** offer exciting spelunking possibilities. The caves are 500m, 2.5km, and 3.5km from the main road, respectively; ask the local police for more directions. The Pa-La-u mini-bus goes there for about 10฿. About 15km from Fa Prathan Village, taking the opposite fork from the one to Pa-La-u will bring you to the Karen Village, where Burmese refugees have settled.

Khao Sam Roi Yot National Park lies 63km southwest of Hua Hin off Highway No. 4 to Prachuap Khiri Khan. Stunning limestone hills rise from the sea and marsh. Evergreens clump densely in the forest and surrounding coastal waters where porcupines, leopards, barking deer, dolphins, crab-eating macaques, dusky langurs, serow (a rare goat-antelope beast), and 300 species of birds make their home. Park bungalows sleep 2-20 people and cost 300-1000฿.

The East Coast

Thailand has focused almost all its new industrial development in the "eastern seaboard" region within 150km of Bangkok. Shiny new oil refineries, power stations, and petrochemical plants line up along the coastline, and pipelines criss-cross the inland rice paddies. Along the highways, the air is thick with diesel grit from the streams of freight trucks shuffling goods between Bangkok and the deep sea ports at Si Racha and Rayong. Two hours south of Bangkok in the middle of all the hubbub, Pattaya sits on an astonishingly dirty beach rolling in bundles of sex-industry cash. Nowhere is the harried pace of Thailand's economic development more evident.

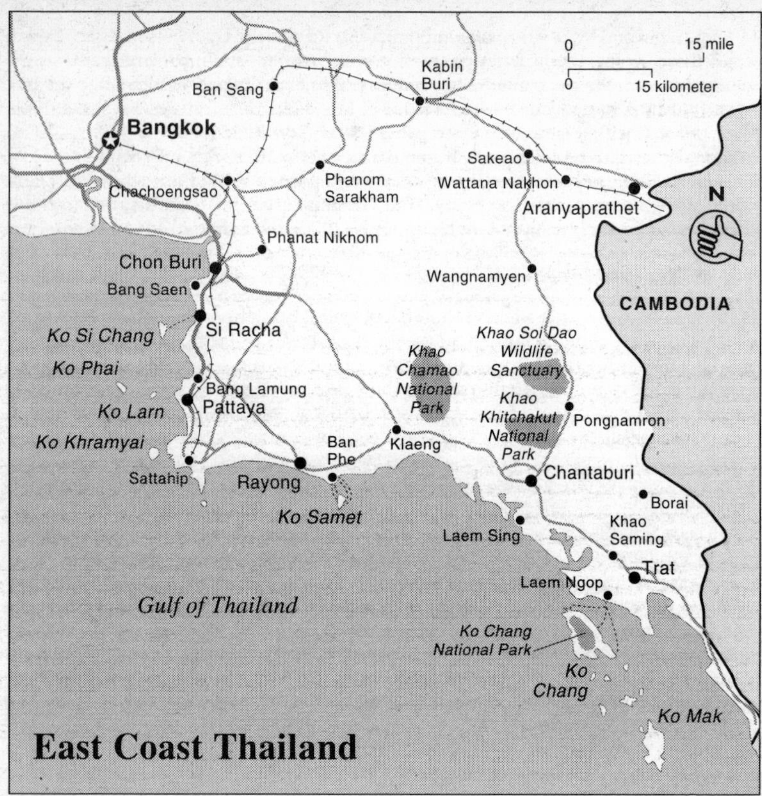

East of Rayong to the Cambodian border, the face of Thailand's coastline undergoes a striking shift back a decade or two in time. As the burger joint-and-smoke stack strips disappear and the main highway sheds several lanes, tradition becomes the rule and western holiday-makers the exception. To the north, jungled limestone hills rise suddenly out of the coastal plains. Groves of mangosteen, rambutan, and durian encroach on a few remaining patches of rain forest. Elusive gem-traders smuggle Cambodian stones through small border towns.

Off the coast of the far eastern province of Trat, the largely undeveloped island of Ko Chang lifts thick rain forest high above the calm cobalt waters. Closer to Bangkok but just out of reach of the sweeping industrialization, Ko Samet hosts a steady flow of sun-seekers. And in the middle of a fleet of freight ships and oil tankers off the coast at Si Racha, the tiny Ko Si Chang seems immune to changing times.

■■■ SI RACHA

With its characteristic aesthetic insensitivity, the Thai tourist industry has hit beautiful Si Racha. But the resilient little fishing village has retained its charm despite a tenfold population growth. Just a block toward the sea from commercialized Sukhumvit Rd., weathered wooden warehouses and colorful fruit peddlers are not selling out. Even the freighters off the coast blend comfortably with decades-old fishing boats. Presiding over this hamlet is Ko Loi Temple on Ko Loi (a pile of rocks poking out of the sea and connected to the land by a causeway), a decidedly gaudy structure, with shining turquoise mirror tiles. The unabashedly eccentric motorcycle-powered "taxis" and hotels mounted on stilts prove that industry can come and go, but Si Racha will do its own thing.

ORIENTATION

Buses from Bangkok or from points to the east pull up next to the Raemton Department Store on **Sukhumvit Road,** the principal north/south highway of the area. To get to the heart of the village and the ferries to Ko Si Chang, cross Sukhumvit Rd., and follow **Surasak Road** for 10min. until it runs into **Jermjompol Road,** Si Racha's main street. The whole of the Jermjompol Rd. downtown, bounded in the south by a market and a clock tower and in the north by a park and the causeway to Ko Loi, is less than ¾-km long. The hotels are over the water, down the tiny sois off Jermjompol Rd.

PRACTICAL INFORMATION

Currency Exchange: Bangkok Bank, at Jermjompol Rd. and Tesaban 1 Rd. (tel. 311 916, 311 223, or 311 599) changes traveler's checks at a pleasing rate. It's just across the main drag from the Siwichai and Siri Watana hotels. Open Mon.-Fri. 8:30am-3:30pm.

Post Office: (tel. 311 202 or 312 611), near the road out to Ko Loi at the north end of Jermjompol Rd., a 10-min. walk from the hotels. A riotous bunch of fellows handle telegrams, mail, and parcels, and manage the **international telephone** network (collect 30฿; cash, MC, and Visa calls) while birds nest in the ceiling. Open Mon.-Fri. 8:30am-3:30pm. **Postal code:** 20110. **Telephone code:** 038.

Buses: To **Bangkok,** frequent departures from a stand at 81/4 Jermjompol Rd., just north of Tesaban 1 Rd. (face the water and it's to the right of all listed hotels).

Tuk-tuk: Jaunts around town cost 10-20฿.

Markets: Outdoor markets are on Surasak Rd., near the clock tower at the south end of Jermjompol Rd. Open daily 5am-6pm. **Raemton Department Store,** 135/99 Sukhumvit Rd. (tel. 322 870 or 352 390), has a bona fide **modern supermarket** on the first floor, with western goods. From the Soi 10-14 waterfront, head straight toward Sukhumvit Rd. and look for the Dunkin' Donuts sign. The market is at the back. Open daily 10am-9pm.

Laundry service: 1/17 Surasak 1 Rd. (tel. 323 749), about 100m from Jermjompol Rd. on the left. Items washed 10฿ per piece. Open Mon.-Sat. 8am-6pm.

Pharmacy: Pramuan Bhesat Pharmacy, 147 Jermjompol Rd. (tel. 311 962; after hours 260 018), on the south side of town, is across from Soi 18 and two stores toward the clock tower (uphill). Look for green lettering over the door. They have antibiotics and excellent English-speakers. Open daily 9am-10pm.

Clinic: Polyclinic, 135/10-12 Sukhumvit Rd. (tel. 312 288 or 323 405; fax 312 287), on the other side of the Dunkin' Donuts in the Raemton Department Store. MC, Visa. Open 24 hrs.

Emergency: tel. 191.

24-hr. police box: (tel. 311 111 or 191), at corner of Jermjompol Rd. and Soi 10.

ACCOMMODATIONS

When the waters are less than ship-shape, staying in an ancient wooden hotel on stilts is hardly an experience to savor. All are about a 15-20 min. walk from Sukhumvit Rd. bus stop and 5 min. to the left of the Jermjompol Rd. stop.

Siri Watana, 35 Soi Siriwatana (tel. 311 037), 1 block north of Soi 10. A maze of cheery sky-blue houses extends way out to sea. Catch spectacular sunsets from picnic areas dense with potted plants. Surprisingly good food 20-30฿. The Thai guests and the hordes of little dogs are sociable and the Ratanaliem family speaks English, creating a wonderfully chatty atmosphere. Rooms with 1 double bed near the sea 120฿, closer to land 100฿. Rooms with 2 double beds are 200/250฿.

Samchai Hotel, Soi 10 Phulphiphat (tel. 311 800 or 321 130), is at the end of the soi (across Jermjompol Rd. from Surasak Rd.) A festive spot, complete with swings and bunting, it has more modern bathrooms. Very clean and comfy. Singles 140฿. Doubles 180฿.

FOOD

Si Racha is famous for its seafood and spicy (some say tangy, but it's hot) sauce.

Sri Racha Seafood Restaurant, (tel. 311 563), Jermjompol Rd., on town-side of the park with a gravel parking lot. Complements an ocean view with red tablecloths and flowering vines. The menu lists prices, which run from 45฿ for crispy catfish to 180฿ for steamed white snapper in lime juice (open daily 8am-9pm).

Hua Huat Restaurant, (tel. 311 047), on Jermjompol Rd., is across from the Bangkok Bank ATM machine, a few doors south of Soi 10. Hovering, venerable old ladies proudly display lettuce, loofah, and bags of dried fish. Over 20 shrimp dishes, plus stir-fry crab and vegetables for 50฿.

Seaside Restaurant, Soi 18 (tel. 312 537), all the way at the end of the pier. All three of Si Racha's Mercedes huddle in the well-groomed parking lot. Delicious spicy shrimp and cashews (95฿) is a memorable experience. Open daily for coffee and tea 8-10am and for the whole mouth-watering shebang 10am-10pm.

■■■ KO SI CHANG

The islanders here fight tooth and nail to ward off an international port which would engulf the southern end of their tiny paradise. The east side's horizon has already been marred by dozens of freighters carrying Vietnamese metal to the unsightly mint just south of Si Racha. The west coast retains its natural landscape; its craggy, dramatic coastline covered with wind-stunted shrubs is interrupted only by the sandy crescent of Tampong Beach. Eclectically painted fishing boats part the sea from the sky. King Rama V and countless monks discovered the island's charm and left a fascinating handful of sights, but winds, tides, and varying levels of effluence turn the beaches to occasional wastelands of litter and livid green water. Ko Si Chang is more of a spot for local-color lovers than for beach bums.

GETTING THERE

Ferries for Ko Si Chang depart Si Racha's main pier, at the end of Jermjompol Rd., Soi 14, (tel. 321 680), daily at 7, 9, and 11am, and 1, 3, 5, and 7pm. When the tide is low, the ferry departs from Ko Loi Island. Returning boats leave Ko Si Chang's Ta Bon Pier (at the north end of town) daily at 6:30 and 9am, noon, 3 and 5pm. The trip takes 30min., unless the driver feels like picking up passengers from the freighters parked off-shore (20฿ one way).

PRACTICAL INFORMATION

Currency Exchange: Thai Farmers Bank, 9-9/1-2 Atsadang Rd. (tel. 216 132), on the main road near the center of town. Open Mon.-Fri. 8:30am-3:30pm.

Post Office: (tel. 216 227) A brand-spankin' new white building at the north end of Atsadang Rd. (the main drag) near the Chinese temple. Open Mon.-Fri. 8:30am-4:30pm, Sat. 9am-noon. **Postal code:** 20120.

Telephones: At the post office. Pull up a stool and call collect for 100฿; to the US 184฿ for 3min. **Tiew Pai Guest House** at the other end of town on Atsadang Rd. has **24-hr. telephone service** and offers operator rates for 70฿ collect. **Telephone code:** 038.

Motorcycle Rental: Motorcycles (and a little red motor scooter) can be rented for 150฿ per day at Tiew Pai Guest House. Helmets available for the conscientious.

Laundry: Tiew Pai Guest House, Atsadang Rd. (tel. 216 084, -85), at the south end of town. Next-day service; 5฿ per piece.

Pharmacy: 8 Mu 3 (tel. 216 122), between the Talang (southern) pier and Tiew Pai. Stocks most of the basic items. Try local remedies like pomegranate leaf tea for an upset stomach. Open 6am-11pm.

Hospital: (tel. 216 100), on the northern continuation of Atsadang Rd. next to the giant gray hotel with cupids over the entrance. Open 24 hrs.

Emergencies: Police (tel. 216 192), about ½-km south (uphill) on Atsadang Rd. from Tiew Pai Guest House, labeled Marine Police. They have a super speedboat to get to the mainland hospital in 15min.

ACCOMMODATIONS

Tiew Pai Guest House, (tel. 216 084, -85), on Atsadang Rd. at the south end of town. The sailor-tongued manager separates karaoke-singing Thai guests from low-key *farang,* who shack up around a sunny courtyard to listen to the wind in the bamboo. Freshly tiled and painted rooms range from fan-cooled (single or double, 100฿) to A/C bungalows with bathroom and sitting area (500฿).

Benz Bungalows (tel. 216 091), on the road to Tha Wong Beach, 1km south of the pier, past Tiew Pai. Each bright, green bungalow enjoys its own view of the off-shore freighter fleet. Single or double with private shower 200฿, with A/C 600฿.

Sripitsanu (tel. 216 034), 1km up an alley to the right, just past Tiew Pai. Continue straight when the path forks at the Development Spiritual Center. Cluster of bungalows high above a secluded cove with unusually clean water. Facilities and accommodations are sparse; you're paying for stunning sunset views. Bare room with double bed and Thai-style toilet 400฿. Better equipped ones, up to 800฿.

FOOD

Ko Si Chang's food won't earn a Michelin Guide star anytime soon, but you'll survive. A few food vendors of the folding-table-beside-the-road variety congregate around the piers and along Atsadang Rd. south of the town. **Tiew Pai Guest House** cooks up a tasty western breakfast (40฿) and the staple rice dishes (30-40฿). The closest thing to a real restaurant may be **Thong Chai,** the seafood joint opposite the Marine Police Station south of Tiew Pai on Atsadang Rd. Christmas lights and ornaments delight the eye, while talented cooks appease your stomach with shrimp and cashews for 50฿. Huge crab and shrimp dinners are 100฿ tops.

SIGHTS

Motorcycle tuk-tuk drivers will buzz you through the maze of roads and paths for a tour (set prices are 150฿ for a glimpse at the main sights, 250฿ with a few hours of swimming at Hat Tampang beach). To go it on your own, study the wall map in the Tiew Pai restaurant.

The east side's two beaches are the easiest to reach. From town, go straight south down the main road. Head through the gates to the Aquatic Resources Research Institute and down to the water. The beach to the right is the narrow and rocky **Hat Tha Wong,** ideally situated to capture a variety of refuse from passing ships and barges. Nearby is the hillside site of **King Rama V's summer palace,** marked by cracked balustrades and wall foundations. Best-preserved is the elegant little swimming pool now filled with green ectoplasm slime. One of the few English public signs warns tourists not to take a dip.

The other side of the hill looks down on **Hat Sai Kaew,** a pleasant beach that attracts the picnicking and camping crowd. Farther south along the coast, the limestone **caves** should be explored with a flashlight and a stick to beat back snakes.

The beautiful **Hat Tampang** is the west side's only sandy beach. It is accessible by a red dirt road that forks off Atsadang Rd. near Benz Bungalows. The beach has relatively clear turquoise water and only a modest audience of fishermen on fine days, but occasionally the tide washes in whole landfills of non-biodegradable junk, which it deposits beyond the reach of petroleum-laced waves.

The south end of the island has a confusing network of 10-ft. wide reddish dirt paths which end in spectacular panoramas, if nothing else. Anyone who endures the ferry ride and pesky taxi drivers deserves to wander around the blissfully isolated southern tip of the island. Keep an eye out for the **"white squirrel,"** a little yellow beast that lives only on Ko Si Chang.

The even more spectacular west and northwest coasts alternate between lush greenery and dramatic gray stone. Not accessible by motorcycle and most bicycles, it's one of the few areas to explore where you won't run into anyone.

The town itself is surrounded by several hillside sights you can't miss. The 10m **Yellow Buddha** on the hill to the west is perched on top of a maze of tunnels and caves inhabited by a group of monks. Ask politely and they may let you explore their limestone abode that inspired John Schoellerman to proclaim, "Asceticism kicks ass!" The **Chinese Temple** overlooking the north end of the town receives throngs of pilgrims each New Year. Farther on is yet another **Genuine Buddha Footprint** (the holy one puts even the best-traveled backpackers to shame).

■■■ KO SAMET

Ko Samet is a 6km-long, key-shaped splash of emerald jungle in the (usually) clear waters of the Gulf of Thailand. When kicked, the fringe of powdered sugar sand squeaks like the wet rim of a crystal glass, giving the spot its original name: Ko Kaew Phitsadan, "island of amazing crystal". Less romantic types renamed it after the indigenous Samet tree used for firewood and fishing boats.

Weary urbanites stumble onto Samet every Friday evening, quickly easing into a weekend vacation of boombox pop, spicy seafood, and low-key boozing. During the week, the island is left to scantily clad *farang* backpackers who sunbathe, windsurf, snorkel, and swim, happily oblivious to the ebb and flow of the weekenders. Despite complaints that it's neither as clean nor as friendly as Ko Samui, people return to the island for its (relative) proximity to Bangkok and its uncanny ability to stay bone-dry when torrential monsoons strike the mainland.

As you set foot onto Samet the local park rangers will extract the 50฿ entrance fee. It's an oft-debated question what the park service actually does with this money, but someone has thus far managed to fend off the Pattaya plague of monolithic hotels and seedy bars. Even at the busy north end of the island, bungalows and restaurants linger behind the tree line and visitors can frolic on wide-open, largely litter-free white sand. Meanwhile, the southeast has achieved a balance of marginally modern comforts (running water for at least a few hours a day) and virtual desertion, especially during the low season (April.-Oct.). Seclusion-seekers can rest assured that the wind-chime hawkers and noodle-vendors don't stray far from the northern crowds.

GETTING THERE

Ferries to Ko Samet depart from **Ban Phe** and arrive at **Na Dan Pier** (9 daily, 7am-5pm, 30฿), at **Ao Wong Duan** (8 daily, 9am-5pm, 30฿), and at **Ao Wai** (8 daily, 30฿). Though fares are constant throughout the year, the schedules are prone to change, with far fewer boats making the trip in the off-season (May-Oct.).

To reach the northern beaches (**Hat Sai Kaew, Ao Hin Khok,** and **Ao Phai**) take a ferry to Na Dan Pier, and then head south on foot. To get to the beaches in the middle of the island (**Ao Tup Tim, Ao Nuan, Ao Cho,** and **Candlelight Beach**), catch a ferry to Ao Wong Duan. For southern destinations (**Ao Wai** and **Ao Kiu**) look for the **Samet Ville Ferry** to Ao Wai.

Several tour companies (try **Rimtalay Express** and **Sea Horse Tour**) transport revelers from Bangkok's Khaosan Rd. to Ko Samet by A/C minibus and connecting ferry for reasonable prices. Otherwise, take a bus to **Rayong,** where you can find a songthaew to drop you in Ban Phe (10-20฿ if full).

ISLAND ORIENTATION

From Na Dan, at the northeast corner, a dirt road leads south, slightly inland, along the east coast, where all but one of the island's beaches border the surf. They are, in order, the heavily developed Hat Sai Kaew, the quieter and cheaper Ao Hin Khok and Ao Phai, the slightly wan Ao Tup Tim (Ao Pudsa), the charming and secluded Ao Nuan, the squalid Ao Cho (Ao Tawan), the unspeakable Ao Wong Duan, the decent Candlelight and Lung Dum beaches, the upmarket Ao Wai, and the deserted and pristine Ao Kiu. One beach graces the west coast for sunset-grubbers: the mildly run-down Ao Phrao, which can be reached by a spur which parts company with the main road just behind Ao Phai. Beaches are listed below starting from Na Dan and going clockwise around the island.

PRACTICAL INFORMATION

Tourist Office: The **ranger station** on the road between Hat Sai Kaew and Na Dan Pier has park information and free maps. Open daily 8am-4:30pm. There is also a small station on Ao Wong Dong. You'll meet the park rangers upon arrival, since they greet each boat to collect 50฿ from all foreign vacationers.

Travel Agencies: Rimtalay Express, the travel agency at the beginning of the road to Na Dan Pier (and another stand at Ao Tup Tim at the Pudsa Bungalows Restaurant—open during high season), deals in domestic and international airplane tickets, minibuses to the airport, Ko Chang, and Bangkok, and snorkeling trips to Ko Kuti and Ko Thalu (250฿). They also have currency exchange, stamps, aerogrammes, telegrams, and international phone service (collect 70฿). Open daily high season 8:30am-6pm; low season 10am-5pm. MC, Visa. **Sea Horse Tour,** Ao Wong Duan (tel. (02) 353 3072) or, in Bangkok, 23/12 Si Ayutthaya Rd. (tel. (02) 282 1574 or 281 3412; fax 281 3412), offers the same services as Rimtalay Express, plus mini-bus rides to Chiang Mai, Phuket, Hat Yai, Surat Thani, Samui, Penang, and Singapore. Snorkeling trips are 250฿. Open daily 7:30am-8pm. MC, Visa, and traveler's checks.

Currency Exchange: For decent exchange rates, use the bank in **Ban Phe** (open Mon.-Fri. 8:30am-3:30pm). See travel agencies above for Ko Samet exchanges, or look for the clumps of them on Hat Sai Kaew and the road to Na Dan Pier.

Post Office: GPO (tel. 321 0732) in Naga Bungalows, Ao Hin Khok, has Poste Restante. Open Mon.-Sat. 8:30am-3:30pm. **Postal code:** 21160-101.

Telephones: Most bungalow operations have **international phones** for cash or collect calls (50-100฿ service charge). Ao Phai Hut (tel. 353 2644), between Ao Phai and Ao Hin Khok, has an international phone at the reception (collect 80฿; open 7am-10pm). **Telephone code:** 01.

Buses: Buses from Ban Phe's coast road (5min. east of the pier) to Bangkok (every 2hr., 5am-6pm, 90฿, 120฿ round-trip). Regular buses connect Ban Phe to **Chantaburi** (every 15min., 7am-6pm, 30฿). In Ban Phe, flag down the bus on Sukhumvit Rd. at the intersection with Salasan Khasi Rd. Songthaew or motorcycle to the intersection is 10฿. To or from **Ko Chang,** the **Sea Horse Tour** (see above) has A/C minibuses and will ease you onto a connecting ferry. It's cheaper (but more of a pain) to catch a regular bus to Chantaburi, connect with a bus to Trat, and then ferry to Ko Chang. Songthaews also leave from the pier in Ban Phe for **Rayong** (30min., 10฿).

Local Public Transportation: Songthaews from Na Dan Pier go to: **Hat Sai Kaew** (10฿); **Ao Phai** (20฿); **Ao Tup Tim** (20฿); **Paradise Beach (Ao Phrao)** on the west side of the island (30฿); and **Ao Wong Duan** (30฿). If there are fewer than 10 people, a songthaew can be hired for 150-200฿. It's only a ½-km stroll on a nice dirt road from Na Dan to Hat Sai Kaew. From Ao Wong Duan, walking to Ao Phai takes 30min. with a steep rocky part just before Ao Tup Tim.

Motorcycle Rental: Room 63 Aladin, on the little road from the dock and on the right just before the gate. Motorcycles can go as far south as Ao Kiu, but the walk along the coast is stunning. Rental is 100฿ per hr., 600฿ per day; passport deposit required. Open daily from first to last ferry arrival.

English Bookstore: Most bungalow restaurants have a collection of English and German books for rent (10-30฿) with a deposit (150฿).

Markets and Supermarkets: A little restaurant next to Na Dan Pier has an abbreviated **convenience store** that sells toothpaste, toilet paper, instant noodles, bread, rice, whiskey, batteries, and more. Open daily from first to last ferry arrival. Ban Phe's **market** has usurped the whole pier area. Open daily from 5am until the last boat's arrival. Rayong's market, adjacent to the bus station, caters to all your epicurean fantasies.

Laundry Service: Every major beach has a few entrepreneurial launderers. Hat Sai Kaew is awash with them near the road to Na Dan Pier.

Public toilets and showers: On the road to Na Dan Pier, there is one near Hat Sai Kaew and one ¼-km farther toward the pier. Not quite Budapest-quality baths, but you'll live (10฿).

Hospital: The island's only **clinic,** midway along the road between Sai Kaew and Na Dan Pier, opens daily 8:30am-4pm. People with a fever should get checked for malaria, although it's now extremely rare on the island. The doctor leaves the island at night and emergency transport to Ban Phe is more dangerous than most emergencies. If you need emergency help on Ko Samet, go to the nearest bungalow reception (Hat Sai Kaew, Ao Hin Khok, and Ao Phai have the best English-speakers).

Police: On the road between Na Dan Pier and Hat Sai Kaew.

Emergency: tel. 191.

ACCOMMODATIONS

When you reach the pier in Ban Phe, a welcoming committee of touts awaits you. Ignore them—you're bound to be taken to some sordid little hovel while charming bungalows sit empty. Even in high season, when rooms are scarce and steep, you're better off relying on your own resources. Accommodations are generally bungalows on thick cement bases or stilts with a front porch, complete with a broom to combat the sand. Private bathrooms, screens, fans, and beds (versus mattresses on the floor) elevate prices. Several shoddy operations make a killing off their proximity to the ferry; the island isn't long enough to make the extra baht worthwhile. Check the bathrooms before paying—keep walking if anything bubbles or squirms on the shower floor. Bungalows with functional shared bathrooms, floor mattresses, and mosquito netting (no screens) should run 60-80฿, with attached shower 100-120฿; proper beds, screens, fan (electricity only at night), and private shower will be 150-200฿. Prices fluctuate depending on the season. Reservations during public holidays could save you a sandy night on the beach. See Beaches below for specific accommodations listings.

FOOD

Every bungalow operation has a restaurant with the standard inflated Ko Samet prices (open 7am-10pm—11pm if you're lucky). Imported food costs about twice the mainland prices (water 10฿, meat dishes 30-60฿, Muesli with milk 30฿); bring food from Ban Phe or Rayong to skip the island rates. Samet's seafood merits serious if not nightly appreciation, since villagers drag in boatloads of shrimp, squid, and fish each morning. Lemon and mint seafood fondue (60-100฿) is a feast fit for the gods. Restaurants never advertise the catch of the day; consult the waitstaff. There is a grocery store near Na Dan, and a fruit stand near the pier sells premium-priced pineapples, bananas, and seasonal treats. Finally, the women who trudge along the beach with pots of noodles will happily fix you a meal for a few baht. Skip the grilled chicken and eggs on the beach if you're averse to salmonella poisoning. See Beaches below for specific food listings.

ISLAND SIGHTS AND ENTERTAINMENT

Snorkeling trips to the "coral islands," Ko Kuti and Ko Thalu, run daily from most major beaches. Ao Phai Hut, Rimtalay Tours, and Sea Horse Tour Express do full-day tours for 250฿, which includes snorkeling equipment, lunch, drinks, and boat. Talk to them a day in advance; most trips leave at 9 or 11am. **Game fishing** swamps the budget at 2500฿ per day for a boat at Vong Duern Villa on Ao Wong Duan (tel. (038) 651 741 or 652 063). Avoid jet skiing; it destroys the fragile coral and the skulls of swimmers who might get in the way.

Motorboats hang out off Hat Sai Kaew and Ao Wong Duan (200฿ per hr., 250฿ around Ko Samet, 350฿ to Ko Kuti and Ko Thalu). In Ban Phe, Ban Phe Travel, Sunkankhamai Rd. (tel. (038) 651 159), just 10m from the pier, rents speedboats with a driver for 200฿ per hr. and a 15-person boat for 1500฿ per day.

On the northeast corner of the island (just north of Diamond Beach Island Resort), an over-14m concrete **sitting Buddha** dwarfs the more delicate black Buddha by his right knee. Neither are in danger of landing in the Louvre. To get there (to the enlightened ones, not the Louvre), go along the Na Dan Pier-Hat Sai Kaew road and take the dirt road that leads from the east side of the primary school, around the Pineapple Beach Bungalows, to the Buddhas.

You'll have to make your own **nightlife** on Ko Samet after the restaurants close at 10pm. Whiskey and Cokes on the beach are as wild as it gets among this incorrigible early-bird crowd. On weekends, the **Silver Sands Resort** on Ao Phai pulls out all the stops with a beachside disco showcasing forty-something slaves-to-the-rhythm; on weekdays it reverts to bar status. Other bars on Hat Sai Kaew, Ao Wong Duan, and the road to Na Dan pull in a few devotees. Sip Singhas to the sound of the surf, or, for slightly better prices, try **U Konička,** just before the ranger station on the way to Hat Sai Kaew from Na Dan. Probably the only Czech-run establishment on Ko Samet, it offers beers (sadly not Czech) for 40-50฿, as well as food, rooms, the *Bangkok Post,* and Connect Four. Open daily 9am-late.

BEACHES

Hat Sai Kaew

A 10-min. walk from Na Dan Pier, Hat Sai Kaew—the widest band of sand between tree-line and sea—was Ko Samet's first bungalow, bar, and restaurant magnet. Though the famous sand stays litter-free, plastic bags and straws ride the slightly milky waves at respectable intervals. Travel agents and vendors of beach paraphernalia cluster along the road running from mid-beach to Na Dan Pier. During low season, the 1km of beach has no more bodies per square foot than the smaller beaches as far south as Wong Duan, but its size gives it a less secluded feel. Wave riders (who destroy the coral), motor boats, and inner tubes ruin the view.

Diamond Beach Island Resort (tel. 321 0814) takes up serious acreage with well-spaced huts and very thirsty plantation-style gardens. The once-primitive bungalows facing the rocky banana beach are receiving facelifts, but will still total up to less than the 300฿ modern-convenience bungalows facing Hat Sai Kaew.

White Sand (tel. 353 2566), at the south end of the beach, has wood huts with peeling white paint; shrouds budget travelers in king-size mosquito nets. Huts with showers are 100฿, cement version with screens 350฿. A huge, fully furnished beach-front bungalow with barred glass windows is 400฿.

The **White Sands Restaurant,** on the south end of the beach, barbecues scrumptious fresh seafood nightly (40-50฿). Open daily 8am-10pm. The **Saikaew Villas Restaurant,** a blue and white plastic-chaired restaurant south of the road from Na Dan Pier, coats even the biggest stomachs with slightly greasy vegetable fried rice (25฿), meat curries (40฿), and seafood (60-100฿). Open daily 7am-10pm.

Ao Hin Khok and Ao Phai

A half-eroded relic of a cement mermaid graces the rocky point between Hat Sai Kaew and the smaller but just as stunning **Ao Hin Khok.** According to Sunthon Phu's epic, the irresistible prince Phra Aphaimani was forced to consort with a repulsive giantess until a lovely Ariel arrived and dragged him from his underwater prison up to Ko Samet's shores, where they lived happily ever after. Today, topless European sunbathers on Ao Hin Khok's beach keep the aquatic lady from feeling out of place. **Ao Phai,** just to the south, shares its neighbor's mellow, secluded tone, Eurovisitors, and beauty. Seasoned backpackers' bargain radars will pick up some of the island's best value accommodations here. For bars, Hat Sai Kaew is a short walk away on the beach-side dirt road.

Naga (tel. 353 2575) has achieved an admirable repose beneath rustling trees; home-made cakes and breads (10-20฿) silence the jaws of restless guests. Furthermore, the establishment has spurned the cheap satisfaction of showing violent, beefy, mealtime videos—Arnold's grunts and Jean-Claude's squawks won't perturb the casual diner. Pizza (small 75฿, large 150฿) is a Naga specialty. Veteran British proprietor Sue will do anything for her guests, short of performing minor surgical procedures. Thatched bamboo huts march up the hillside on stilts. Mattresses sit unceremoniously on the floors, but intact mosquito nets and well-scrubbed showers with 24-hr. water lure an international Anglophone clientele. Huts are 50-150฿.

Little Hut, immediately south of Naga on Ao Hin Khok, shows a decent-by-Samet-standards movie every night at 6pm. Luxurious thatched wood huts with shelves and a sprawling raised bed keep the sand where it belongs. Separate showers and toilets, with 24-hr. water (except for a few minutes when fresh water is being pumped in), and the restaurant's the cheapest around. Bungalows are 60-80฿.

Ao Phai Hut (tel. 353 2644) is behind the narrow rocky jetty separating Ao Hin Khok from southern Ao Phai. Little Buddhas sit complacently over the doors to the solid, bamboo-covered wooden huts. They have shelf space, dark wood interior with raised beds, private showers (24-hr. water), and fans (electricity 5:30am-6:30pm). Porch-sitting enthusiasts rhapsodize about the bamboo chairs. The excellent restaurant suffers from the video plague: morning BBC, afternoon MTV, a violent movie or two at night, and on special occasions, a Madonna extravaganza. Small bungalows cost 100฿, larger 150฿. International phone service (collect 80฿, AT&T card and cash accepted), snorkeling trips (250฿, minimum 10 people), and books (10฿ for 3 days) including Toni Morrison's *Song of Solomon* (100฿ deposit).

Sea Breeze, at the south end of Ao Phai, has fairly spacious thatched wood huts well-removed from the sea but not from each other. They have separate showers and toilets. Huts with a mattress on the floor are 70฿. Sturdy, screened huts with private showers and knee-level bed are 150฿, with two double beds 300฿. Home to **Rimtalay Express 2,** where you can **fax,** rent from the extensive **book collection** (20฿ per week, 150฿ deposit), and arrange future wanderings and squanderings.

Ao Tup Tim (Ao Pudsa)

The formerly lush hillside has become a barren testimonial to the power of trampling feet. Sand and sea sparkle on, as yet undaunted by the Ao Cho and Ao Wong Duan ferry scum. Definitely a better place to picnic than to live.

Tup Tim, the nicer of the two places to stay, has a collection of woven reed-walled bungalows with well-worn floor mattresses and mosquito nets for 70฿, with tacked-on shower room 150฿. Water flows round-the-clock; electricity 5pm-3am. White frame bungalows complete with shower, platform bed, and screens are an overpriced 300฿.

Ao Nuan

A slip of powdery sand emerges from the headland between Ao Tup Tim and Ao Cho before the cove swings back into stone. Nuan is the only truly secluded beach left on the north half of the island. The rock path from Ao Tup Tim to Ao Cho has a seaward branch leading down to this charming spot's sole sleeping quarters.

Nuan Bungalows is a landscaper's masterpiece, complete with floating lily pads, a collection of folk masks hanging on the open-topped, rock-walled shower, and ferns aplenty. Rugged, picturesque wood huts with floor mattresses cost 100-200฿. Guests can sink into cushions in the *tatami*-matted restaurant (open 8am-9pm). Perfect for moon-gazing and meditating. Nothing but sea, sun, sand, stars, and the 10฿-per-week library to keep you company.

Ao Wong Duan

Recent commercialization has made the once-stunning piece of sand attractive only to the rich and lazy. Water supply hoses criss-cross the bay between ferry boats. Incredibly pricey "resorts" line the beach with bland little bungalows, some of which are air-conditioned. Only one row of decrepit wood shacks falls below 300฿.

Ao Thian and Hat Lung Dum

A sparse crop of *farang* squash into 40m of white sand. Check under trees and behind books for more. They occasionally refocus their eyes on the gulls hypnotically circling the rock island just off shore. Get here on the wide smooth path in back of the miniature golf course at the south end of Ao Wong Duan (south, 5min.).

Candlelight Beach Bungalows (tel. 321 1934) fills each bamboo hut with a king-size mattress. Thatched roofs accommodate the very tall or claustrophobic; practice for a Twister tournament by tackling the obstacle course of flimsy bamboo slats on the front porch. Relatively sweet-smelling toilets and showers on the hill behind the huts enjoy a sea view. Water flows 24 hrs.; electricity 6pm-midnight. Huts 80฿, high season 100฿; with bath 300฿, high season 500฿.

The eccentric **Lung Dum Hut** (tel. 038 651 810) is located on **Hat Lung Dum** (the south part of Ao Thian). Even more remote and mellow than its northerly neighbor, it is still on the well-beaten (and fairly well-lit) path to the bars of Ao Wong Duan. Choose either the "love shack" (the tree house on the beach) or one of the rainbow of cinder-block bungalows. There's 24-hr. running water in the separate, rustic showers. Electricity zaps from 6pm-4am. Ask for a fan. Hovel for one 100฿, for two 120฿. Tents available.

The **Candlelight Beach Restaurant** (tel. 651 223) has fallen prey to the culinary shortage on Ko Samet. It shares a menu with the **Candlelight Kitchen** at the north end of the beach, but occupies a much less frenzied position between the two sets of bungalows. Sink your teeth into sumptuous sandwiches and chicken fried rice (each 30฿). The bamboo-tabled patio catches the breeze and is close enough to the sea for proper wave contemplation. Seafood costs 60-80฿. Open daily 8am-11pm. Closed during the off season.

Ao Wai

Get some Robinson Crusoe action here. Translucent water and coral-strewn sand are worth every second of the 20-min. walk from Ao Wong Duan. Take the path marked "To sunset" to the main road from the Candlelight Beach (or the main road from Ao Wong Duan). At low tide, scramble over the coastal boulders scarred by crystalline salt pockets, but it's nearly impossible to tiptoe around the razor-sharp shells cemented to the rocks at water level. The **Samet Ville Ferry** makes the trip to Ban Phe and back at least once a day in low season (50min., 40฿), and more often in high season. Ferret out the times at the Ban Phe Pier or in Bungalow Koa Kaew about 400m east of the Ban Phe Pier on the coastal road. Otherwise, call the Bangkok information office (tel. (02) 246 3196, 247 1090, or 321 1284). The **Samet Ville Resort** (tel. 321 1284) monopolizes the silvery beach and does not advertise on Khaosan Rd. Small, multi-roomed bungalow-houses come in 2-, 4-, 5-, and 13-person dimensions for a whopping 700฿ per person including meals, dipping slightly to 600฿ during low season.

Ao Kiu

The ultimate Ko Samet beach makes even Ao Wai (just a 15min. rock scramble away) look muddy. If you open your eyes under water, every grain of sand appears in relief. Shells and chunks of coral (including the brain variety) join the palms in decorating the otherwise naked beach with perhaps the snowiest sand around. Ao Kiu is situated on the skinny end of the island, so the west coast is across the lawn—just wade through the dogs and roosters. Farther along, **Ao Pakarang** (about 15min. over the rocks) has gone to the dogs, literally. A few weathered men "tend" a couple of old wooden bungalows hidden amidst piles of discarded water bottles.

The friendly women at **Ao Kiu Bungalows/Restaurant** (tel. 321 1231) flash more smiles than you can keep up with, but don't speak a word of English. There are no worries for anyone except the finicky of palate who will need to learn how to say "ease off the black pepper." Seafood is 80฿, pineapple 30฿, shrimp and rice soup 35฿. They are not likely to have many guests during much of the year; bring a book or a friend. The stilted, thatched huts are barely distinguishable from haystacks and have meter upon meter of elbow room (100฿, with shower 150฿). Water runs 8-9am and 6-7pm.

Ao Phrao

Although some ferries lie hither in the *haute saison,* for most of the year, the view across the waves to the sunset and the mold-and-pour development at Khao Laem Ya stands uninterrupted. Best for dinner against an orange and amber backdrop, the beach greets you with several bungalow outfits at the end of the 30฿ songthaew ride from Na Dan. The **Ao Phrao Resort** (tel. (01) 941 8652) has clean, well-appointed beach-front bungalows with private bath, all decked out in wood and wicker for 250฿. The next-door **Dome** (tel. (01) 321 0768) and **Ratana** bungalows have some basic rooms with primitive shared bathrooms for 150฿. All three have attached restaurants with standard Sametian fare.

■■■ TRAT

At 400 bumpy kilometers from Bangkok, Trat is a frontier town. It is the last outpost before the misty rain forests along the southern Thai-Cambodian border. Patchwork groves of durian, rambutan, and papaya fan out through the gentle valleys to the north, and coastal marshlands meet the Gulf of Thailand to the south. Trat's municipal market overflows with the region's rich produce and seafood harvests, making it one of Thailand's best. Across the ill-defined border, the Khmer Rouge wages sporadic war against the Cambodian government, and traveling conditions are uncertain at best. Peasant miners from both countries are rumored to traipse through the mine fields blanketing the Cambodian mountains to smuggle sapphires into Thailand. Trat's transportation connections, great market, and friendly backpacker-oriented guest houses make it an ideal base from which to explore the region or rest up before catching a boat to Ko Chang, just off the coast.

ORIENTATION

A 400-km (on the coast road) or 315-km (by the new interior highway) bus ride from Bangkok, Trat is just a few km from the Cambodian border. **A/C buses** from anywhere north or west of town shudder to a halt on the east side of **Sukhumvit Road,** the main drag. (Some regular buses stop on a quiet little street parallel to Sukhumvit Rd.) From north to south, **Trat Hospital,** the **A/C bus stop,** the **night market,** the **Municipal Market** (across from the Trat Department Store), and the south end's traffic light squeeze into six blocks along Sukhumvit Rd.

PRACTICAL INFORMATION

Currency Exchange: Thai Farmers Bank, 3 Sukhumvit Rd. (tel. 511 569, -71), across from the A/C bus stop, offers decent rates. Open Mon.-Fri. 8:30am-5:30pm.

Post Office: On Tha Reva Jong Rd., 10min. from the Municipal Market. Turn left (north) onto the road in back of the market. Turn right where it ends in front of the gas station; walk 2 blocks to the 4-way intersection with traffic lights; turn left and the post office is 100m ahead on the right. Telegraphs, parcels, and Poste Restante. Open Mon.-Fri. 8:30am-4:30pm, Sat.-Sun. 9am-noon. **Postal code:** 23000.

Telecommunications Office: Located above the post office. Positively wired with telex, international calls (cash; collect costs 30฿), and a fancy selection of radio communications. Open daily 7am-10pm. **Telephone code:** 039.

Buses: To **Bangkok** (9 daily, 7am-4:45pm and 2 at night, 6hr., 140฿) stop in Chantaburi (1-½hr., 50฿).

Songthaews: To **Laem Ngop** leave from Sukhumvit Rd. just south of the Municipal Market (10฿). To **Bo Rai,** they wait up to an hour for 10 people, and are nestled against the market's front (north) corner in the little driveway between the building and Sukhumvit Rd. (35฿). To **Khlong Yai,** they leave from the back of the market (25฿); last songthaew back to Trat leaves Khlong Yai at 5pm.

Taxis: 10-15฿, although almost everything's within walking distance.

Supermarket: Inside **Trat Department Store** opposite the municipal market. Open daily 9am-9pm.

Pharmacy: Osoph-Charoen Pharmacy, (tel. 511 085), across from municipal market on Soi Sukhumvit (off the main Sukhumvit Rd.) is a dandy place to pick up malaria pills before a jaunt to Ko Chang. Passable English spoken. Open 7am-9pm.

Hospital: Trat Hospital, Sukhumvit Rd., sits beyond the traffic light at the north end of town. Open 24 hrs. but expect to wait at least 2-3hr. A **clinic** (across the street and a few doors toward Sukhumvit Rd. from the Foremost Guest House) employs an English-speaking doctor who pops in and out all day until 7pm.

Emergencies: tel. 191.

24-hr. Police: Santhisuk Rd. (tel. 511 239), corner of Wiwathana Rd. about a block past the turn-off for the post office on the right (across from the soccer field).

ACCOMMODATIONS

Foremost Guest House, 49 Thon Charoen Rd. (tel. 511 923), has a house, complete with windows, inside another larger house. This mellow place works on the honor system. Walls are papered with info about Trat province, Isaan, Cambodia, and Vietnam. Plentiful showers, including a hot one, are separate. Along with Lars, the congenial and well-informed Swedish owner, A/C lobby, stereo, Poste Restante service, and self-serve tea/coffee/toast (7฿) contribute to an authentic home feel. Laundry service. Free luggage storage for guests. Safe-deposit box. Dorms 30฿. Singles 50฿. Doubles 70฿. Triples 90฿.

Windy Guest House, 63 Thon Charoen Rd., is just before Foremost as you're walking from Sukhumvit. You'll feel like you've moved in with the family, since the house has only three guest rooms, and they'll insist that you use the TV, the stereo, and the single bathroom. Built on stilts over a small river. Single or double with fan, 80฿.

FOOD

There's no excuse for not eating in the **market.** Stands compete mightily for customers, so a hearty vegetable noodle soup costs just 5฿. Elaborate versions with meat or fish set you back 10-15฿; for fresh mussels, shell out 15฿; various rice dishes can be had for 10-25฿. Pastry, fruit, and dessert stands sweeten the meal deal. The whole operation moves to the open square two blocks north of the municipal market building for the **night market,** lasting 7pm-midnight. Otherwise, there is **Khokasuki Sukiyaki Restaurant,** 43 Sukhumvit Rd. (tel. 511 051 or 511 618). On the 2nd floor of the Trat Department Store. Dunk raw meats and veggies into a steaming pot o' stew on your table. Windows overlooking the road distract you from the sterile surroundings and raucous Thai pop music. Ideal for those ready to sell their first-born for a gasp of air-conditioning. Fresh crab 60฿, chicken 21฿, veggies 5฿ each, noodles 20-30฿.

Sights and Entertainment There is little to do in Trat aside from strolling off to the market or catching a flick at the Sukhumvit Rd. cinema. Groups solvent enough to shell out 1000฿ for a day's rental of a ten-person fishing boat can go to sea from the Municipality Pier *(tha reva)* 2km outside town on Tha Reva Jang Rd. For those of modest means, the Foremost and Windy Guest Houses run frequent **sightseeing trips** in the high season involving a tour of the border market at Ban Hat Lek, a stop at a local beach, and a visit to a former Cambodian refugee camp, all for a reasonable 100฿.

■ NEAR TRAT

This is the place to witness nature at her jungled best and spy on the gem and hardwood smuggling subculture prowling around the Thai-Cambodian border. The **Seaview Resort** (tel. (01) 521 0055 or (039) 597 143) on Ko Chang's Kai Bai beach plans day trips to Cambodia during high season (8am-5pm, 2hr. each way, 500฿ round-trip). Of course, this depends on the current situation in Cambodia.

LAEM NGOP

A sleepy seaside village with an increasingly chaotic pier, **Laem Ngop** is a fine place to spend the night or stock up on essentials before boarding the ferry to Ko Chang. Trat, however, is much hipper, and just a quick songthaew ride away (20min., 10฿). Laem Ngop is now home to the Immigration Office, where you can get visa extensions and listen to the "official" line on **visiting Cambodia.** The office is on the ground floor of a white building about a 15-min. stroll up the main road from Ban Phe to Trat. **Thai Farmers Bank** (tel. 597 0456), 300m from the pier on the Trat-Laem Ngop Rd., is open Mon.-Fri. 8:30am-3:30pm. **Chut Kaew Guest House** (tel. 597 088), near the bank, offers a row of cement-floored rooms (1 shower serves 3 rooms). Singles cost 60฿, doubles 100฿. Their patio **restaurant** doles out Euro and Thai food (open daily 7am-10pm). On the pier, **Rimsapan Restaurant** provides a pleasant (though somewhat overpriced) dining diversion for prospective ferry-goers. A wee plate of fried rice costs 25฿. Open daily. **Boat trips** to the islands off southern Ko Chang cost 1700฿, including food and a night's lodging.

■■■ KO CHANG

Stalwart nature lovers may find a new (if not improved) Eden in Ko Chang. The fabled garden had one serpent; Ko Chang is blessed with seven poisonous varieties—the golden tree snake, the copperhead racer, caboia, blue krait, Malaysian moccasin, the run-of-the-mill cobra, and the dramatically hooded king cobra, reported to reach a thickness of two hand spans at maturity. But neither the risky approach (on an overloaded ferry or in a jeep or motorcycle traversing a precipitous road) nor the immediate threat of malaria (natives get tested every two weeks) seems to be saving the park from destructive tourism. In 1997, electric wires will ring the island and oust the kerosene lamps. The environmental consequences of burning plastics and draining sewage into the ground will inevitably wilt the flowers of this paradise.

A hike in the jungle will increase your chances of crossing paths with dozens of endangered species such as barking deer, stumped-tailed macaque, silver langur, small Indian civet, Javan mongoose, and flying fox. The less adventuresome can take the horseshoe-shaped main road through spectacular strips of jungle and rubber, coconut, banana, durian, rambutan, and mangosteen plantations. Strap on an armory of mosquito repellents—this island is part of a malarial region.

Much of the 39-island archipelago off the south shore remains isolated. If you manage to find your way here by boat, the villagers are said to be very helpful to *friendly* visitors as far as bed (or floor space) and food are concerned; the deserted beaches of glittering sand and crystal waters are rumored to be exquisite.

GETTING THERE AND AWAY

To reach **Ko Chang,** take a bus to Trat, then a songthaew from the front of the Municipal Market on Sukhumvit Rd. to **Laem Ngop Pier** (25min., 10฿), and a ferry to the island. Ask carefully about the ferry's destination; they'll say anything to get you on the boat.

Getting to your destination on Ko Chang from Laem Ngop Pier will cost 70฿. In the rainy season (May-Oct) the trip consists of a ferry to Al Saparot Pier (40฿) followed by a jeep ride down the island (30฿) to the west coast beaches. In the high season, the west coast's waves peter out, allowing ferries from Laem Ngop to drop off travelers right on the beaches. Daily ferries depart year-round from Laem Ngop at 9am, noon, 1 2, 3, and 4pm. In high season the noon and 3pm ferries go directly to west coast beaches, and the 2pm goes directly to Hat Sai Kaow; the others go by way of Al Saparot Pier, as in the low season. There is also a daily ferry to **Ko Chang's east coast,** stopping at **Dan Mai, Than Mayon,** and **Salapet** (1pm, 70฿). Return ferries depart A Saparot Pier daily at 7:30, 9am, noon, and 4pm; expect a jeep taxi to pass by each of the west coast beaches within an hour of the ferry's departure (30฿). Additional ferries may pick up passengers directly from west coast beaches in the high season; ask any bungalow crew for details. Remember, traveling to Ko Chang is still an inexact science; if you're the only one on the boat, don't expect it to budge.

ISLAND ORIENTATION

Bearded with tropical rainforest, the oblong island of Ko Chang runs lengthwise from the southeast to the northwest tip. Its east side slopes parallel to the mainland of Trat Province, but most beaches line the west coast and are inaccessible to ferries during the stormy season (May-Oct.). During this time, ferries dump you at **Ao Saparot pier** on the northeast corner of the isle, from which a jeep will fray your nerves for the 15-min. ride to **Hat Sai Kaow (White Sand Beach)** as it plows through stunningly beautiful but treacherous terrain along the northern cliffs. In the rainy season, tourists would be well-advised to stand at the back of the pick-up so they can bail if it loses control in the mud. Ring Rd. is scheduled to encircle the island in 1997; for now it remains Horseshoe Rd. (which has a large gap at the south end of the island and an impassable bridge along the southern half of the east coast). As a result, **Bang Bao** on the southwest coast (a 3-hr. walk from the road) and **Hat Sai Yao (Long Beach)** are accessible only by boat. Several bungalow companies have mainland offices on and around the Laem Ngop Pier that may provide island information and maps, but beware of committing yourself to anything you have not seen first-hand.

PRACTICAL INFORMATION

Tourist Information: Ko Chang National Park Headquarters (tel. (039) 521 122) in Than Mayom, a town at the midpoint of the east coast, 20km from Hat Sai Kaew on Horseshoe Rd. These two wooden cottages stay open 24 hrs., displaying wildlife and coral and dispensing info.

Currency Exchange: Get your legal tender in Laem Ngop or Trat before leaving the mainland. A few resorts change money, but at hefty commissions. **Sun Sai Resort** at the south end of Hat Sai Kaow charges only 3%.

Post Office: On the road running through the village to the pier. Telegrams and post are open Mon.-Sat. 8:30am-4:30pm. Usually. **Postal code:** 23120

Telephones: International phones are encroaching on Ko Chang's Hat Sai Kaow in the **White Sand Resort,** and on Hat Khlong Phrao in **Magic Bungalows** (tel. 329 0408). **Telephone code:** 01 (for cellular phones *on* Ko Chang); 039 (for phones in Laem Ngop).

Local Transportation: Taxis, the misnomer for jeeps and motorcycles, drain your wallet and endurance (from Ao Saparot to Hat Sai Kaow 30฿, to Hat Kai Bai 50฿).

Motorcycle Rentals: Those with off-road experience and some extra baht can rent motorbikes at some resorts (about 500฿ per day, 700฿ with driver). Contact Graham or Sunan in the small house opposite Phlamoa Cliff Resort, south of Hat Sai Kaow, to rent a motorbike (400-600฿ per day) and get info on island conditions.

Ferries: If you *really* need to leave the island outside of scheduled departures, fishermen will charter their boats (1000-1500฿). **Emergency trips to the mainland** cost 3000฿ in a speedboat from Sea View Resort on Hat Kai Bai (tel. 521 0055).

Markets: Buy food in Trat's bitchin' **municipal market** before departing the mainland to pare down the restaurant bills on the island. Ko Chang has no markets.

Hospitals: The government-run hospital in Trat handles Ko Chang's serious medical problems (See Trat: Practical Information). The island's four **clinics** do provide an important service: **malaria testing.** They are located at Khlong Phrao on the west coast, Khlongson in the north, Dan Mai on the east coast, and the southern village of Salapet. All open Mon.-Fri. 8:30am-4:30pm.

THE WEST COAST

The north end of the west coast is spiked with soaring cliffs rising vertically from the water. The west's gorgeous beaches are the most heavily trafficked part of the island. The ultimate stretch of silica is a 15-min. walk through the jungle from the cove at the south tip of Hat Kai Bai. It has no facilities (yet).

Hat Sai Kaow

Misnamed "White Sand Beach," the grey grit scatters along choppy surf on the northwest coast. Deserted at dawn, the beach gets congested in the afternoons during high season. Backpackers congregate on the porches of bungalows to watch the sunset and bemoan the big, bad encroachment of guest house VCRs.

The White Sand Beach Resort and its neighbor, a cement bungalow operation, swallow up lots of space, but are not the only accommodations. **Ban Rung Rang** (tel. (01) 329 0464) at the north end has typical Ko Chang budget digs of thatched bamboo bungalows with common baths (singles 50฿, doubles 80฿; in high season 80฿ and 150฿ respectively). Ditto **Cookie Bungalow,** just to the south. Farther south **Sunsai** (tel. (039) 597 078) is a bit more removed from the socializing. Canadian owner Dave can happily answer *any* question about Ko Chang. Simple bungalow 80฿, with bath 150-200฿; discounts in low season. At the southernmost point, the **Phlamoa Cliff Resort** (tel. (01) 323 0164 or tel./fax (039) 597 060) has two rows of thatched bamboo huts perched over the rocky point just south of Hat Sai Kaow (250฿ high season, discount in low season) in addition to more pricey concrete rooms with electricity in the evening and private bath (400฿+ in high season).

Hat Khlong Phrao

More peaceful than its northern neighbor Hat Sai Kaow, Hat Khlong Phrao practically hibernates during the rainy season. Bungalows here are spaced farther apart, so the population density of beach-goers seems lower even when the island is crankin' (though the density of angry dogs seems high year-round). Inland from Hat Khlong Phrao, a one-hour walk from **Horseshoe Road** brings you to a waterfall. Under the cascade, a pool too deep to fathom refreshes salt-water-logged beach bums.

Coconut Beach Bungalows, (tel. (01) 329 0432), about 4km south of Hat Sai Kaow, at the north end of Hat Khlong Phrao, plants its huts on a spread of grassy lawn behind a rocky portion of the beach. Singles or doubles 120฿, with bath 300฿; discounts in low-season. **K.P. Bungalows** (tel. (01) 327 0225) located in the middle of the beach, is a 10-minute walk south of the river mouth that splits Hat Khlong Phrao—expect to ford some knee-deep water if you choose to walk down the beach instead of following Horseshoe Rd. K.P. offers standard grass-roof bungalows with mosquito nets and views of the beach through the palms (100฿, low season 50฿) as well as one of Khlong Phrao's only operational **restaurants** in the low season (fried rice or spicy soups 25-35฿). **Magic Bungalows** (tel. (039) 597 231 or (01) 329 0408) at the southern end of the beach has a bevy of well-maintained huts for 100฿, with attached shower 150-300฿ (closed June-Oct.). If you have brought your **camping** equipment, the management at most resorts will let you set up your tent nearby and use toilet/shower facilities for a small daily fee (10-20฿).

Hat Kai Bai

Some visitors to Hat Kai Bai bemoan its small rocky patches of swimming beach. Others call it Ko Chang's most beautiful length of coast, making it their island home for weeks or months on end. Like Hat Khlong Phrao, Hat Kai Bai virtually shuts down in the rainy season. Most bungalow owners are still happy to rent you a room, but don't look for much in the way of food or social life.

Nangnual Resort, near the north end of the beach, peers out from its fringe of vine-choked trees and hanging plants. Myna birds and Thai TV provide the soundtrack. The bamboo huts are just a five- to 10-minute walk from the swimming beach (100฿, June-Oct. 30฿). Snorkel and mask rental costs 40฿ per day. The popular **Kai Bai Beach Bungalows** have recently joined the video brigade. Bamboo huts run 100฿, with shower 200฿; June-Oct. 50฿, with shower 100฿. **Siam Bay Resort** (tel. 213 6923), at the south end of Kai Bai just before the sandy cove, has electrified stucco bungalows for 400฿, June-Oct. 200฿. Open 6pm-midnight. As on Hat Khlong Phrao, most bungalow owners accommodate campers for a daily fee (10-20฿).

Hat Kai Bai also houses the **Wind Eagle School of Taiji.** *Farang* Jessy Boxer has studied and taught taiji (tai chi) as a form of meditation for 30 years, and offers both 2-½hr. (200฿) and one-month courses (3000฿) in a gorgeous wooden dance room.

A man named **Alpha** rents out a couple of **bamboo huts** (with showers 100฿, June-Oct. 50฿), **books,** and **hammocks** at the north end of the beach. He'll give you the low-down on the park's environmental disintegration in a **bar** straight out of a Dr. Seuss book—the chairs are tilted to best observe the colorful ceiling. A sedated version of Hat Sai Kaow's social scene lurches along at the few restaurants and at this outlandish bar (open 10am-2am).

THE EAST COAST

Gently picturesque, but short on beaches, the east coast has yet to be stormed by backpackers. In the north end, staid colonnades of rubber trees with collection bowls strapped to their trunks alternate with fruit orchards. Bayous riddle the swampy southerly coast, necessitating stilt houses. The east coast is accessible by motorcycle taxi as far as Than Mayom, where a lone plank bridges a ravine, and the road continues as far south as Salapet (but cuts inland away from Long Beach).

Ao Saparot

At the northernmost point of the east coast, Ao Saparot's crescent of gold is usually just an *hors d'oeuvre* for the west coast beaches. In monsoon season (June-Oct.), the ferry terminates in this tiny village, but most people pray for the good luck to survive the "taxi" ride (30฿) and head for even fairer shores.

The Central Area

Sai Thong won't slow you down much, but **Dan Mai** hides a path to **Tok Khonansi** (a waterfall), a 30-minute walk inland. **Than Mayom,** 4km to the south, has plenty of roosters but no beach, and is home to **Than Mayom Resort** and its corrugated plastic-roofed five-person bungalows (1600฿). The **National Park Headquarters** (tel. (039) 521 122) keeps a line of typical thatched-bamboo **huts** (100฿, June-Oct. 70฿), free **public toilets** (bring your own tissue), and Thai-style **showers.** Nearby **Tok Mayom,** a favorite of that waterfall buff King Rama V, still bears his initials. Freezing clear mountain water gushes over a 7m vertical coppery rock into a jungle pool.

Hat Sai Yao (Long Beach)

On the west side of the peninsula jutting from the southeast corner of the island, Hat Sai Yao is remote and remarkable. Check with the Information Office on Laem Ngop Pier for the current scoop on accommodations, and ask the captain of the ferry to Salapet to make a special trip, since there are no direct ferries.

Salapet

On the bay at the southeast tip of the island, Salapet is Ko Chang's most energized fishing village. Accessible by ferry (to Laem Ngop 6am, return 1pm, 70฿), it is also the place to charter boats to the southern archipelago (at least 1000฿).

■ NEAR KO CHANG

THE SOUTHERN ARCHIPELAGO

The isolated group of islands off Ko Chang's south coast is famous for fishing, coral, rock formations, bird nests, and bat guano. Scuba dive at **Ko Rang.** The deep, flickering water is home to coral, tons of fish, and toothy sharks. To get there, charter a boat in Salapet or check at Ko Chang bungalows for scuba or snorkeling tours.

Ko Wai, a less-remote version of Ko Rang, is surrounded by a necklace of coral, and the fishing is legendary. **Ko Bhrao** has an archetypal palm tree-studded beach with only group lodgings. **Ko Lao Ya,** now accessible during the low season, is known for its coral and clear water (sound like a trend?) and has some bungalows. Budget travelers can head to an Israeli guest house on **Ko Maak,** but new accommodations appearing on **Ko Kut** may be prohibitively expensive. Ask at Foremost Guest House in Trat for details.

Northern Thailand

Confident and poised, Northern Thailand receives visitors with easy graciousness, inviting them to uncover what lies behind the commercialized caricature the country presents elsewhere. Once the home of the prosperous and independent Kingdom of Lanna, the land runs over heavily forested hills, which are interspersed with farms, rice paddies, and poppy fields. Many people share this space: hill-tribes predominate in certain regions, Chinese immigrants proudly display pictures of the Thai Royal Family in shop windows, and refugee camps swell with Burmese, escaping the repression of a military government back home. The unique dialect, cuisine, dance, and wat architecture of Northern Thailand owes much to the fusion of these ethnicities, which continue to enrich and expand the meaning of "Thailand."

Potential visitors are simultaneously drawn to serene border towns and repelled by the presence of rebel camps, involved in sporadic, often violent disputes just across the border. However, even travelers oblivious to the culture surrounding them cannot ignore the ineffable natural scenery and fresh, cool air. Despite its relative remoteness, the region is incredibly easy to navigate and explore. The mountains of the north are the lowest extremities of the Himalayan foothills, and the Mekong River forms the border with Laos, while the Salawin River flirts with Burma before eventually draining into the Bay of Bengal. The Ping River cuts through Chiang Mai and in earlier times connected the North with central Thailand.

Chiang Mai stands at the door to the north provinces, which fan out on all the major compass points from the city's central location. To the south is antique-laden Lamphun. The west province of Mae Hong Son borders Burma and is thick with forest and hill tribes. North of Chiang Mai is Chiang Rai, the traditional gateway to the opium-laced Golden Triangle. Finally, to the east, snuggling up next to Laos, is Nan, often-ignored, yet perhaps the loveliest province in the North, if not all of Thailand.

One way to see the north is to go overland on Hwy. 107 from Chiang Mai, north to Fang and Tha Thon. From Tha Thon, an excellent new road leads up to Mae Salong, a village whose inhabitants are a mixture of Yunnanese, hill-tribe, and Thai. Many people prefer to take a long-tailed boat trip on the Kok River from Tha Thon to Chiang Rai and then use Chiang Rai as a base for venturing into the Golden Triangle to see Mae Salong, Mae Sai, Chiang Saen, and Sop Ruak.

Another approach is to detour from Hwy. 107, taking Route 1095 to Pai and into Mae Hong Son, then back-track to Hwy. 107 and head up to Tha Thon. Some people loop south from Mae Hong Son to Mae Sariang, then go past Doi Inthanon National Park and back to Chiang Mai. Or head southwest from Chiang Mai along Hwy. 108 to Mae Sariang first, then on up to Mae Hong Son and around. These routes offer choice mountain scenery and assured contact with hill tribes.

Growing regional integration is continually increasing possible crossing points into Burma and Laos. Check with any immigration office for the latest details. A land route to China is in the works, and weekly flights connect Chiang Mai and Kunming.

See "Hill-Tribes and Trekking" on page 295 for more information.

■■■ CHIANG MAI

Who would have thought that mice scurrying down a hole beneath a *bodhi* tree would lead to all this? But that was the omen that convinced King Mengrai in 1296 to build Nopburi Si Nakhon Ping Chiang Mai on a virgin stretch of land 696km northwest of present-day Bangkok. Mengrai's kingdom of Lanna ("million rice

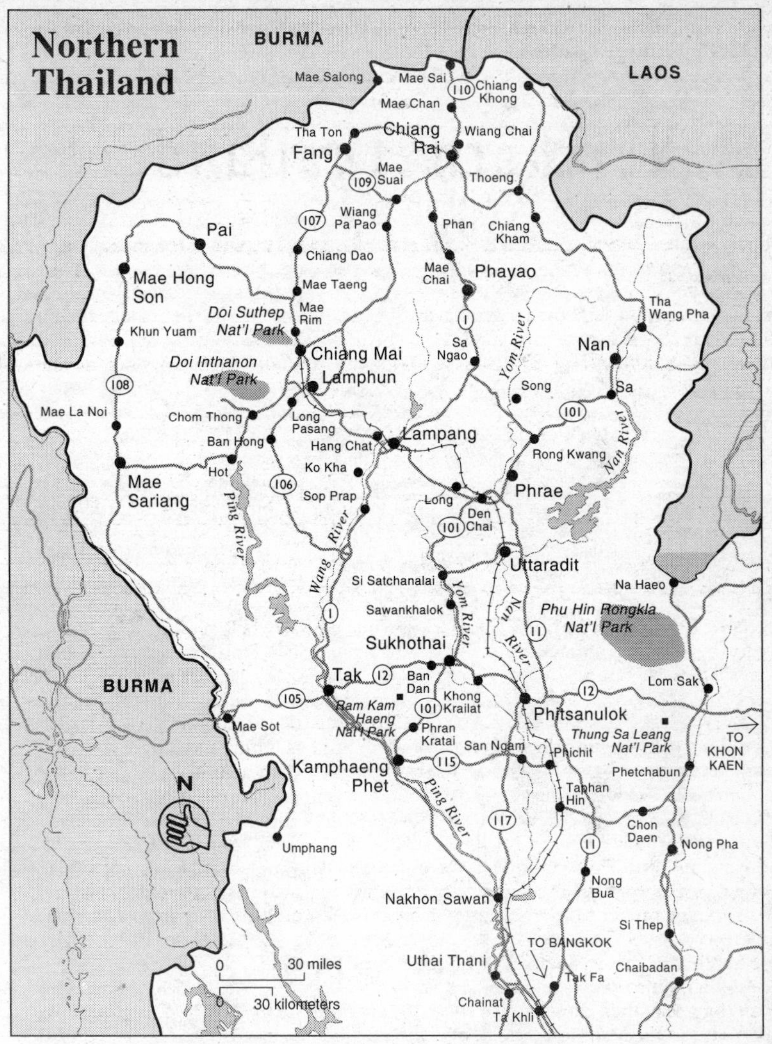

fields") was contemporaneous with the dominions of Sukhothai and Ayutthaya, and clashed with them through the 14th and 15th centuries. During this period, Ayutthaya expanded, taking over Sukhothai and pressing against Lanna's southern border. But in 1556, the kingdom's northern neighbors, the Burmese, took the initiative and captured Chiang Mai, occupying the city for over 200 years while dismantling the Ayutthayan Empire. King Taksin re-claimed the city in 1775 with a Thai army.

Despite formal incorporation into Thailand, Chiang Mai retained a large measure of independence—commanding its own army, and great latitude in the governance of its people. Separated from Bangkok by mountainous terrain, dense jungle, and many kilometers, the city could be reached only by an arduous river trip or a several-week-long elephant journey. Even with the introduction of the railway, the journey still took two or three days—the trains, like the elephants, needed to rest at night. The region was only truly integrated in the 1930s, when improved transport and communication systems brought all of Thailand firmly within the capital's reach.

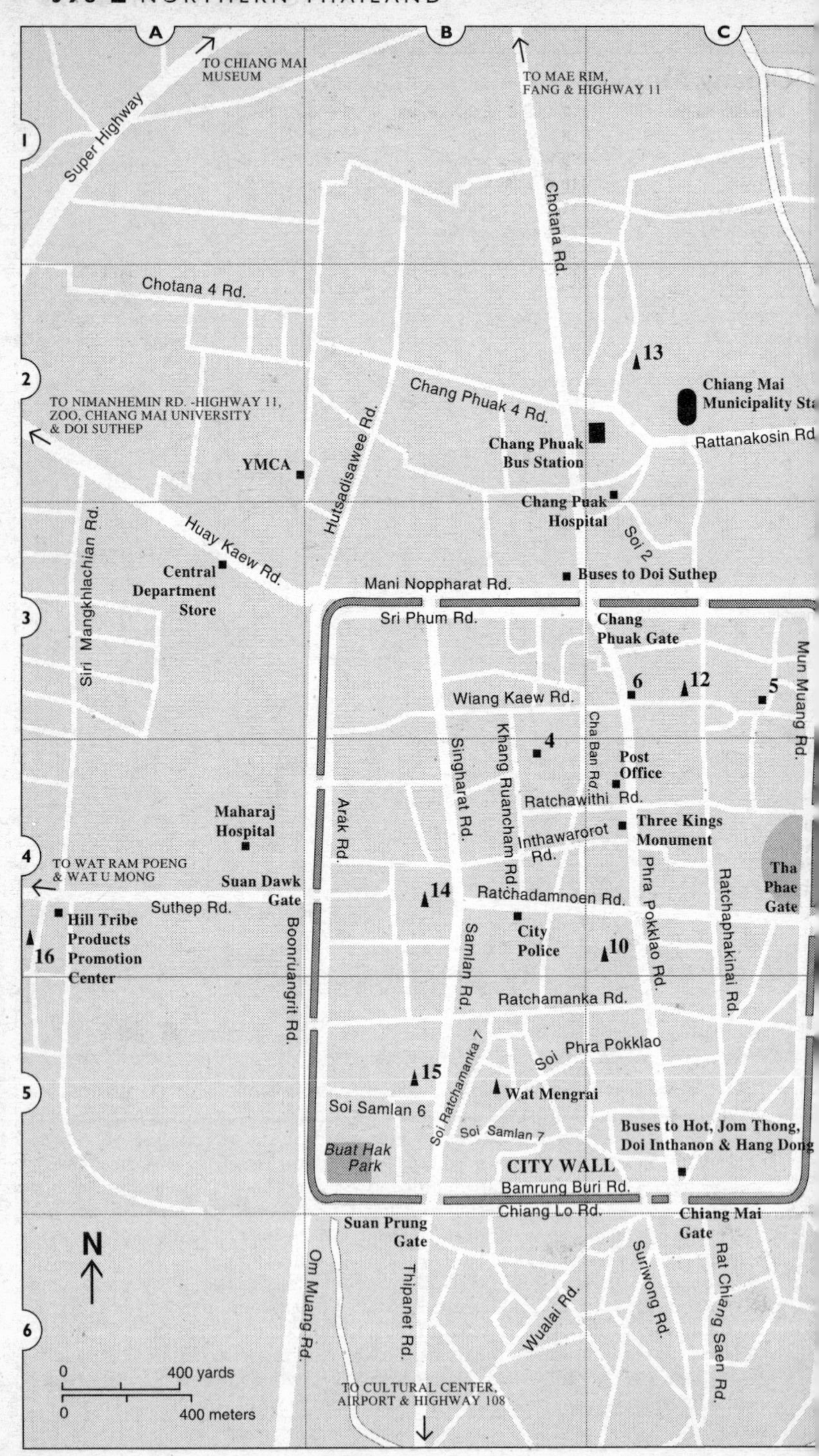

A
B
C
1
2
3
4
5
6
TO CHIANG MAI MUSEUM
TO MAE RIM, FANG & HIGHWAY 11
Super Highway
Chotana Rd.
Chotana 4 Rd.
13
Chiang Mai Municipality Sta
Chang Phuak 4 Rd.
TO NIMANHEMIN RD. -HIGHWAY 11, ZOO, CHIANG MAI UNIVERSITY & DOI SUTHEP
Hutsadisawee Rd.
Chang Phuak Bus Station
Rattanakosin Rd
YMCA
Chang Puak Hospital
Soi 2
Huay Kaew Rd.
Central Department Store
Buses to Doi Suthep
Mani Noppharat Rd.
Sri Phum Rd.
Chang Phuak Gate
Siri Mangkhlachian Rd.
6
12
5
Wiang Kaew Rd.
Mun Muang Rd.
4
Cha Ban Rd.
Singharat Rd.
Khang Ruancham Rd.
Post Office
Ratchawithi Rd.
Maharaj Hospital
Arak Rd.
Three Kings Monument
Inthawarorot Rd.
TO WAT RAM POENG & WAT U MONG
Suan Dawk Gate
14
Ratchadamnoen Rd.
Tha Phae Gate
Ratchaphakinai Rd.
Phra Pokklao Rd.
Suthep Rd.
Hill Tribe Products Promotion Center
16
Boonruangrit Rd.
Samlan Rd.
City Police
10
Ratchamanka Rd.
Soi Ratchamanka 7
Soi Phra Pokklao
15
Wat Mengrai
Soi Samlan 6
Soi Samlan 7
Buses to Hot, Jom Thong, Doi Inthanon & Hang Dong
Buat Hak Park
CITY WALL
Bamrung Buri Rd.
Chiang Lo Rd.
Suan Prung Gate
Chiang Mai Gate
N
Om Muang Rd.
Thipanet Rd.
Wualai Rd.
Suriwong Rd.
Rat Chiang Saen Rd.
0
400 yards
0
400 meters
TO CULTURAL CENTER, AIRPORT & HIGHWAY 108

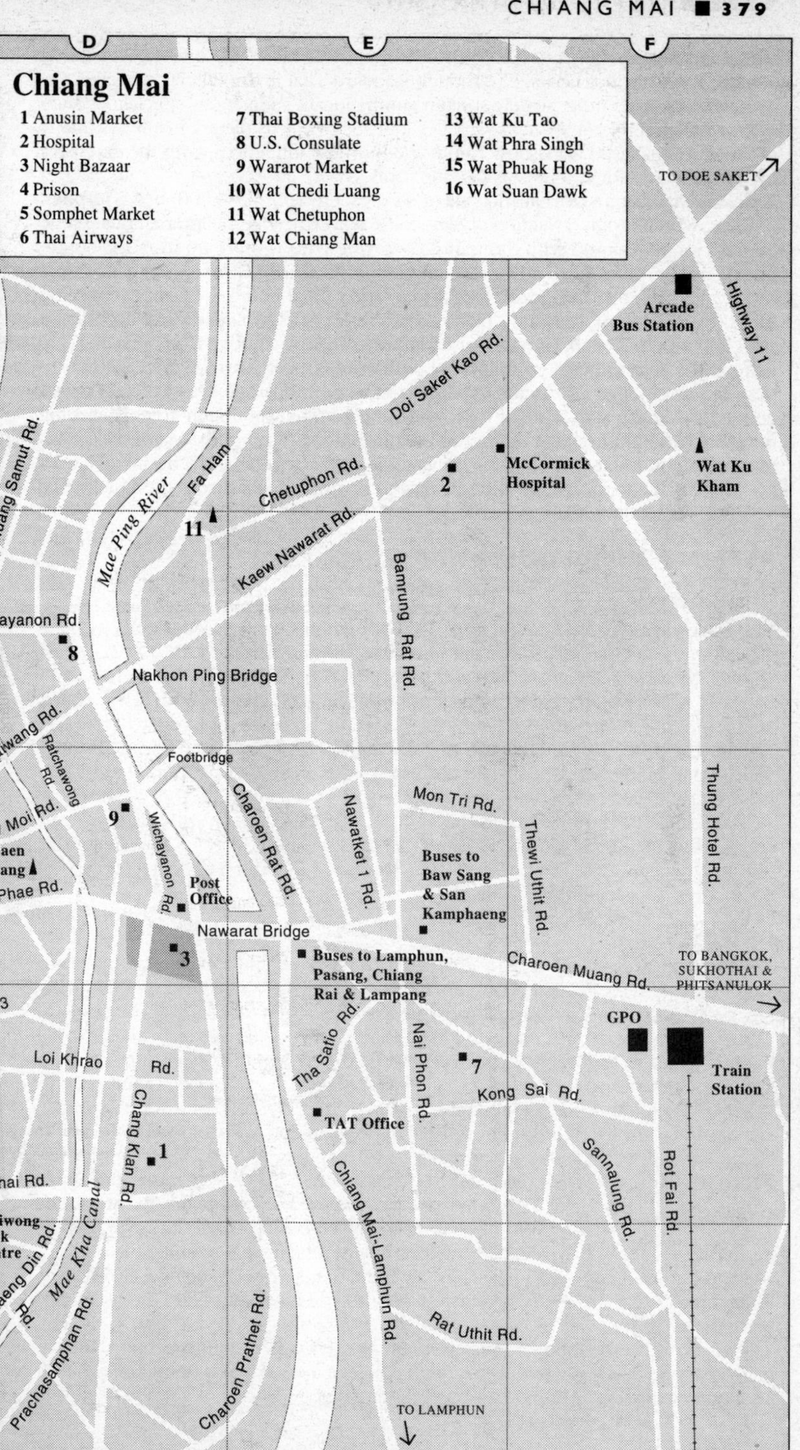

D
E
F
Chiang Mai
1 Anusin Market
2 Hospital
3 Night Bazaar
4 Prison
5 Somphet Market
6 Thai Airways
7 Thai Boxing Stadium
8 U.S. Consulate
9 Wararot Market
10 Wat Chedi Luang
11 Wat Chetuphon
12 Wat Chiang Man
13 Wat Ku Tao
14 Wat Phra Singh
15 Wat Phuak Hong
16 Wat Suan Dawk
TO DOE SAKET
Arcade Bus Station
Highway 11
Doi Saket Kao Rd.
McCormick Hospital
Wat Ku Kham
Muang Samut Rd.
Fa Ham
Chetuphon Rd.
Mae Ping River
Kaew Nawarat Rd.
Bamrung Rat Rd.
Nakhon Ping Bridge
Footbridge
Ratchawong Rd.
Mon Tri Rd.
Thewi Uthit Rd.
Thung Hotel Rd.
Charoen Rat Rd.
Nawatket 1 Rd.
Buses to Baw Sang & San Kamphaeng
Wichayanon Rd.
Saen Fang
Post Office
Nawarat Bridge
Buses to Lamphun, Pasang, Chiang Rai & Lampang
Charoen Muang Rd.
TO BANGKOK, SUKHOTHAI & PHITSANULOK
GPO
Train Station
Tha Satio Rd.
Nai Phon Rd.
Loi Khrao
Rd.
Kong Sai Rd.
TAT Office
Chang Klan Rd.
Sannalung Rd.
Rot Fai Rd.
Chiang Mai-Lamphun Rd.
Mae Kha Canal
Prachasamphan Rd.
Charoen Prathet Rd.
Rat Uthit Rd.
TO LAMPHUN

Though north and south have become one, denizens of Chiang Mai steadfastly cling to their distinct heritage. Although standard Thai is the official language, the northern dialect is more widely spoken among locals. Indigenous specialities such as *khao soi* noodles and *naem* sausages join sticky rice as dietary mainstays. Many of the more than 300 wats show Lannu and Burmese influences, with the extensive use of teakwood for columns, walls, and roofs.

Chiang Mai's status as Thailand's second-largest city (pop. 250,000) belies its physical size, which is only a fraction of Bangkok's. Nevertheless, the international scene here is vibrant, infused with thousands of *farang* who venture up from the South, drawn by the promise of adventure and a cooler climate. Far too many of them, however, come to Chiang Mai, take a trek, and return home, without ever seeing the rest of Northern Thailand's beauty. Chiang Mai speaks English, but even those who know only French, German, or Japanese have little trouble. Hundreds of establishments cater to every tourist need, and competition knocks prices down to obscene levels. The enormous expansion in these industries, however, increases concerns that the stampede of tourists through certain mountain areas is eroding both hill-tribe culture and the natural environment. Trump-like visionaries with mountain condo fantasies and trekking entrepreneurs now clash frequently with growing local environmental and social action groups, but for now the Chiang Mai valley is still accommodating everyone.

GETTING THERE AND AWAY

By Plane

THAI Airways, 240 Pokklao Rd. (tel. 210 042) with branches around the city, handles all domestic flights into **Chiang Mai International Airport** (tel. 270 222), just 3km southwest of the city on Sanambin (Airport) Rd. Nine flights arrive daily from Bangkok's Don Muang and often sell out in advance (7:10am-10pm, 1hr., coach 1650฿ plus a 20฿ airport tax). From Chiang Mai flights leave to: **Bangkok** (13 daily, 7:15am-10:45pm, 1hr., coach 1650฿); **Chiang Rai** (6:30am and 6:45pm, 40min., 420฿); **Mae Hong Son** (5 daily, 40min., 345฿); **Phitsanulok** (1:15pm, 1hr., 650฿); **Phuket** (11:50am, 2hr., 3455฿); and **Kunming,** China (2:30pm, 2-½hr., 3450฿).

To get into town, you have several options. The THAI Airways shuttle service to your Chiang Mai destination is 40฿; a tuk-tuk ride will cost 30-40฿. Cheaper still are the songthaews (15฿). Dirt-cheap rides are provided by bus #6 (5฿), which departs 200m away, on Sanambin (Airport) Rd.

By Train

The most popular means of shuttling between Bangkok and Chiang Mai, trains are safe, quick, and clean. Trains pull up at **Chiang Mai Railway Station,** 27 Charoen Muang Rd. (tel. 245 363/4; open 6am-9pm), on the eastern outskirts of the city.

Sprinter trains are the fastest (11hr.), followed by **express trains** (12-13hr.). **Rapid trains** are, ironically, the slowest (13-14hr.). Only second and third-class are available. Reserve one to two days in advance; many guest houses can also book tickets. Bangkok to **Chiang Mai** (rapid 6:40am, 3, and 10pm; express 6pm; sprinter 8:10am; and the posh Nakornping Special Express 7:40pm); Chiang Mai to **Bangkok** (rapid 6:35am, 3:30, and 8:40pm; express 4:40pm; sprinter 7:50pm; and Special Express 9:05pm). In each direction: third-class 121-171฿; second-class 255-305฿, with A/C 305฿; sleepers 355฿ and up. Expect a 30-80฿ surcharge on all tickets.

All trains leaving after 3pm have sleepers; reserve these far in advance. Lower berths are pricier but are ideal for the morning mountain view coming into Chiang Mai and for late-night toilet forays. Most of these trains from Chiang Mai also stop in **Phitsanulok** (7hr., 3rd-class 35฿, 2nd-class 136฿) and **Lampang** (2hr., 3rd-class 23฿, second-class 48฿).

Upon arrival at the train station, ignore the booth marked "information," which is really manned by a tout. To get into town, you can take a samlor or tuk-tuk for 20฿, a songthaew for 5฿, or hop on a #1 west-bound bus.

By Bus

To Chiang Mai from **Bangkok's Northern Bus Terminal,** the cheapest deal and the roughest ride are the four non-A/C buses (6, 6:30, 7am, and 5:30pm, 190฿). A/C buses (5 daily, 9:10am-9:30pm, 10hr., 242฿).

Buses serving outside of Chiang Mai province go to and from **Arcade Bus Station** (tel. 242 664), on the northeastern outskirts of town on Kaew Nawarat Rd. near the superhighway; a tuk-tuk, songthaew, or west-bound buses #1 or 3 take you to the old city. To get to the station, catch an east-bound yellow #3 bus on Chiang Moi Rd. To: **Bangkok** (#18-orange, 12:30pm, 11hr., 190฿; A/C #18-blue, 5 daily, 237฿); **Chiang Rai** old route: (#148-green, every 30min., 6am-4:30pm, 6hr., 83฿), new route: (#166-green, 13 daily, 4hr., 57฿; A/C 3 daily, 79฿); **Mae Hong Son** via **Mae Sariang** (#170-orange, 8 daily, 6:30am-9pm, 115฿/59฿), via **Pai** (#612-orange, 6 daily, 7am-4pm, 115฿, 45฿); **Nan** (#169-green, 4 daily, 6hr., 83฿; A/C 3 daily, 115฿); **Phitsanulok** (#155 or #623-orange, 5 daily, 6hr., 104฿; A/C 5 daily, 6hr., 146฿); **Mae Sai** (#619-green, 5 daily, 5hr., 71฿; A/C 6 daily, 5hr., 127฿); **Lampang** (#152-green, every 30min., 6am-10pm, 2hr., 29฿).

Buses within Chiang Mai province are served by **Chang Phuak Bus Station** (tel. 211 586), north of the old city beyond Chang Phuak Gate on Chang Phuak Rd.; catch south-bound bus #2 to get within the moats. To get to the station, take bus #2 from Tha Phae Rd. To: **Bo Sang** and **Sankampang** (#225-red and white, every 30min., 5:30am-5pm, 20min., 5฿); **Tha Thon** (#1231-orange, 5 daily, 4hr., 50฿).

Many private services offer discounted bus tickets between cities. You will usually get exactly what you pay for, and you may be expected to stay at an affiliated guest house upon arrival. **Keep all valuables, especially credit cards, securely on your person during any bus trip.**

ORIENTATION

Chiang Mai is actually very easy to navigate. There are just two landmarks to know: the Ping River and the old city, enclosed by a moat. The heart of Chiang Mai is the **old city,** and within its square moats are its winding streets and alleys. **Bamrung Buri Ave.** runs just inside the southern moat and has two gates, **Suan Prung Gate** to the west, and **Chiang Mai Gate** to the east. **Arak Road** runs along the western moat and has **Suan Dawk Gate. Sri Phum Road** follows the northern moat and has **Chang Phuak Gate. Moon Muang Road** follows along the eastern moat and has **Tha Phae Gate.** The gates, remnants of the walls once surrounding the city, are now undistinguished brick ruins. Lining the length of Moon Muang Rd. and parallel streets are the highest concentration of accommodations, restaurants, and bars. **Ratchadamnoen Road** bisects the old city east to west. Within the old city, the east-west soi numbers increase as you go north (with traffic on Moon Muang Rd.).

At Tha Phae Gate, Ratchadamnoen Rd. changes names to **Tha Phae Road** and courses 1.5km east to the **Ping River.** Tha Phae Rd. is rich with banks and currency exchange counters, as well as travel ticket agencies and film developing shops. After crossing the Ping over Nawarat Bridge, Tha Phae Rd. plays the name game again, becoming **Charoen Muang Road** This road then runs straight for 1km, to the **train station,** on the right, with the General Post Office next door. Tha Phae Rd. is intersected on the west bank of the Ping by **Charoen Prathet Road** which runs north to south and is lined with a few restaurants and guest houses. Also intersecting Tha Phae Rd., and running parallel to Charoen Prathet Rd. on the old city side, **Chang Klan Road** is home to the Night Bazaar, some banks, and more places to eat.

The road running along the Ping on the river's east bank is **Charoen Rat Road** when it is north of Nawarat Bridge, and **Chiang Mai-Lamphun Road** when it is south of the bridge. On Charoen Rat Rd., there is a smattering of guest houses and on Chiang Mai-Lamphun Rd., 0.5km south of the Nawarat Bridge, is the TAT.

Chang Phuak Road extends north from Chang Phuak Gate; the **Chang Phuak Bus Station** lies 1km from town along it (buses arriving from points in Chiang Mai province). A **superhighway** rings the entire city. The **airport** is located on the superhighway in the city's southwestern corner, about 3km from the old city.

GETTING AROUND

Although not the sticky car jams of Bangkok, diesel fumes overpower the local oxygen. Your feet, the most ancient means of transport around, are the best option if you want to explore the Tha Phae Gate area and the 2km-square old city at a leisurely pace. Use caution when strolling at night. For long-range missions, rent a motorcycle or a car. If all else fails, there are always the hungry packs of songthaews, tuk-tuks, and samlors eager to lighten your load.

By Bicycle

Chiang Mai is a compact city and most sights are easily reached by bicycle. Random places in the Tha Phae Gate area have a few cycles—look for the row of bikes parked outside. An average bike rental shouldn't cost more than 30฿ per day. You'll need to leave your passport or a 500฿ deposit (far more valuable than the aged two-wheelers). **Jaguar,** 131 Moon Muang Rd. (tel. 419 161) has mountain bikes for the same price as the Jessica Fletcher versions available elsewhere.

By Motorcycle and Moped

If you're going anywhere east of the river or a few km from the old city area a moped might be the best rental option—especially in the hot season (March-June) when pedaling a bike can be torturous. Moped rentals will be around 150฿ per day, and a motorcycle about 200฿. Insurance should be included in the price; a helmet will cost an extra 10฿ and is well worth it. A passport or hefty deposit is required. Make absolutely sure who is responsible in cases of theft or accident. Without insurance, you'll have to fork over thousands of baht, if the bike is stolen or damaged. Rental shops abound in the Moon Muang and Tha Phae Gate areas.

By Car

Traveling in a group or farther outside Chiang Mai with a lot of gear may require a car rental (1200฿). Many rental shops on the streets are of questionable legitimacy, but there are two American car offices in Chiang Mai: **Avis,** Orchid Hotel, 14/14 Huay Kaew Rd. (tel. 221 316); and **Hertz,** 90 Sri Donchai Rd. (tel. 279 474).

By Songthaew, Tuk-tuk, and Samlor

A songthaew safari beats any roller-coaster ride in terms of price (5฿) and hair-raising lurches. Tell the driver where you're going. If he shakes his head and speeds away, this means that your destination was not on his route. Don't fret, another one will come by soon enough. Tuk-tuks and samlors are omnipresent (20฿ or more, depending on your bargaining skills).

By Bus

Local buses service most places. Bus #1 runs east and west along Suthep Rd. and from Tha Phae Gate to the train station. Bus #2 runs north and south to/from Chang Phuak Gate. Bus #6 circles the city and goes by the airport. Bus routes appear in the **Tourist Map of Chiang Mai** (30-60฿ at many stores). Buses run 6am-6pm, and pass a stop every 15 minutes. Flag one down, and cheer for the rock-bottom fare (3-5฿).

PRACTICAL INFORMATION

Get a copy of *Trip Info,* a comprehensive listing of virtually all traveler-oriented establishments in Chiang Mai (available at the TAT, restaurants, and guest houses).

Tourist Office: TAT, 105/1 Chiang Mai-Lamphun Rd. (tel. 248 604 or 248 607; fax 248 605), 0.5km south of the Nawarat bridge, on the left. A resource for maps and brochures. Gather all you can about the rest of northern Thailand; the only other TAT office in the north is in Chiang Rai. Open daily 8am-5pm. TAT booths like the one at the airport are scattered around town.

Tourist Police: Next to TAT (tel. 248 974, 24-hr. line). International direct-dial phone, no surcharge for overseas collect calls. Open daily 6am-midnight.

Immigration Office: 97 Sanambin (Airport) Rd. (tel. 272 510). To extend your visa, bring 500฿, 3 passport photos, and 2 copies of your passport photo page, visa page, and arrival/departure card. Open Mon.-Fri. 8:30am-noon and 1-4pm.

Consulates: China: 111 Chang Lo Rd. (tel. 276 125). Open Mon.-Fri. 9-11:30am and 2:30-5pm. Visas in mornings only. **UK:** 54 Village 2, Tambon Suthep (tel. 211 474). **US:** 387 Vitchayanon Rd. (tel. 252 629 or 252 665). Open Mon.-Fri. 8-11:30am.

Currency Exchange: Plenty of places scattered around town. **Siam Commercial Bank** (tel. 273 171) on Chang Klan Rd., near the intersection with Tha Phae Rd. **24-hr ATM** accepts all major cards. Open daily 8:30am-4:30pm.

American Express: Sea Tours Company, 2/3 Prachasamphan Rd. (tel. 271 441). Only AmEx connection in northern Thailand. Mail held for 3 months, free for check or card-holders. Open Mon.-Fri. 8:30am-4:30pm, Sat. 8:30-11:30am.

Post Office: (tel. 245 376) on Charoen Muang Rd., next to the Railway Station. Anywhere along Chiang Moi Rd., hop on bus #1 going east. Open Mon.-Fri. 8:30am-4:30pm, Sat.-Sun. 9am-noon. Telex and fax services. **Branch Office:** On Phra Pokklao Rd. just north of the intersection with Ratwithi Rd. in the old city. Open Mon.-Fri. 8:30am-4:30pm. Other branches at Chiang Mai University, the airport, and the basement of the night bazaar. **Postal code:** 50000.

Telephones: Red phones for local calls (1฿). Blue phones for calls within Thailand. For overseas calling card or collect calls, use home country direct phones (IODC) located at the TAT, the airport, the post office, Tha Phae Gate, or the THAI Airways office. These phones connect you to operators in your home country. Accommodations will place international calls for a hefty surcharge. Overseas calls 24 hrs. in telecommunications office around the side and upstairs from the GPO. **Telephone code:** 053.

Directory Assistance: In Chiang Mai: tel. 13, outside Chiang Mai: tel. 183.

Luggage Storage: The train station has a cloak room with luggage storage (5฿ per day per piece for the first 5 days, 10฿ per day after that—check for time limit). Open daily 6am-6pm. Most guest houses will store luggage for free.

English Bookstores: Suriwong Book Center, 54/1-5 Sri Donchai Rd. (tel. 281 052). Good selection of maps as well as numerous English magazines. Open Mon.-Fri. 8am-7:30pm, Sun. 8am-12:30pm. **Book Exchange,** 21/1 Ratchamanka Soi 2 (tel. 278 518). Maps, guides, and fiction. Open Mon.-Sat. 9am-6pm. **D.K. Bookstore,** 234 Tha Phae Rd. (tel. 251 556). English books. Open daily 9am-8:30pm.

English Libraries: USIS/AUA Library, 24 Ratchadamnoen Rd. (tel. 278 407). Lots of English newspapers and magazines. Open 7:30am-noon, 1pm-4:30am.

Local Publications: Besides *Trip Info,* pick up free copies of *The Chiang Mai Newsletter, What's On..., Where to Go Chiang Mai, Welcome to Chiang Mai and Chiang Rai,* and *Chiang Mai and Beyond,* available at TAT and around town.

Radio: FM 93.25 Radio Thailand (tel. 275 293). English show 6-8:30am 'n' pm.

Swimming Pools: The closest place to plunge is the **Top North Guest House,** 15 Moon Muang Rd. Soi 2 (tel. 227 890). Open daily 8am-8pm; admission 50฿. **Sara Health Club,** 109 Bunruangrit Rd. (tel. 244 371), east of the old city. Open daily 8am-noon, 1pm-7pm; admission 50฿. **Suan Dawk Hospital** pool at CMU Faculty of Medicine (tel. 221 122), on Suthep Rd., is the cheapest at 8฿; open Mon.-Wed. and Fri.-Sun. 9am-8pm.

24-hr. Pharmacy: Both hospitals listed below have pharmacies that will fill your prescriptions in the middle of the night in case of emergency.

Hospitals: McCormick Hospital, Kaew Nawarat Rd. (tel. 241 107), **ambulance.** Some English spoken. **Chiang Mai University, Maharaj Hospital,** Suthep Rd. (tel. 221 122), **ambulance.** Both have **24-hr. emergency pharmacies. Malaria Center,** 18 Bunruangrit Rd. (tel. 221 529), near Maharaj Hospital just north of Suan Dawk Gate on the west side of the old city. Open Mon.-Fri. 8:30am-4:30pm.

Emergency: tel. 191.

ACCOMMODATIONS

Moon Muang Rd., the area across the moat (the southeast corner of the old city), and the Ping's east bank, teems with guest houses. Basic rooms start around 60฿ and go up depending on the amenities. Spend 20-50฿ more if you're in town during the cool season (Nov.-Feb.) or at festival times.

Transportation and accommodation deals made in Bangkok often stipulate that you trek with an affiliated guest house. Many smaller inns support themselves with tour funds—refusal to comply with trekking arrangements often means denied lodgings. While trekking, leave your baubles in a bank safety deposit box (see Practical Information) rather than in safekeeping at your guest house. There have been reports of missing belongings and maxed-out credit cards. The TAT office hands out a list of Chiang Mai Guest House Association lodgings, all of which pay government taxes. These places may be slightly more secure for storing your prize troll.

Tha Phae Gate Area—Within Moat

Libra Guest House, 28 Moon Muang Rd. Soi 9 (tel. 210 687), near the northeast corner of the old city. This family-run guest house puts others in its price range to shame. Freshly renovated, spacious, and spotless rooms, all with fan and private bath, tip the scales in Libra's favor. Energetic owners serve up delicious food, and their good cheer has won the place a far-reaching reputation. So popular that trekking is almost a requirement. No loss, reports on their treks are excellent. Singles 80฿. Doubles 100฿. Check-out 10am.

Julie Guest House, 7/1 Phra Pokklao Rd. Soi 5 (tel. 274 355). Look for the sign on Ratchaphakinai Rd. Beneath the spectacular Julie's Roof Garden Restaurant (see Food section). Classy, clean place. Bright lights, colorful bedding. Singles and doubles 50฿, with cold shower 120฿, with hot shower 200฿.

Rose Guest House, 87 Ratchamanka Rd. (tel. 276 574), on the corner with Ratchaphakinai Rd. The bamboo restaurant below promises more than the spartan rooms with shared bath actually deliver, but console yourself with the few baht saved by staying here. Singles 60฿. Doubles 80฿. Check-out 9am.

Moon Muang Golden Court, 95 Moon Muang Rd. (tel. 212 779). Above and beyond the standard guest house, but still a decent deal for those weary of their usual dank quarters. Rooms range from 130฿ (1 big bed, cold water, fan) to 280฿ (2 big beds, hot water, A/C) with a variety of permutations in between.

Top North Hotel, 41 Moon Muang Rd. (tel. 278 531). If all the cheap places are full and you must stay within the city moats, dig deep into your pockets for this top-notch hotel. Right in the thick of things, this ritzy joint lets folks flit from bar to restaurant to TV lounge to ping-pong table to small pond without ever leaving the building. Every trimming from A/C to stocked refrigerators. Higher floors have full views of Doi Suthep and Chedi Luang. Singles 500฿. Doubles 650฿.

Tha Phae Gate Area—Outside Moat

Lek House, 22 Chaiyaphum Rd. (tel. 252 686). A backpacker favorite, Lek is cloistered off a soi with a garden and tree canopy. A hut to the left of the entrance is the most interesting place to stay. All rooms have private baths (common hot shower 10฿); the ones upstairs are decadently larger. Singles 80฿, upstairs 100฿. Doubles 100฿, upstairs 120฿. Popular steak house has banana flambée (25฿).

Daret's House and Restaurant, 415 Chaiyaphum Rd. (tel. 235 440), at Tha Phae Gate. Enjoy fans and private baths in this condominium look-alike. Balconies on each floor. Weight machines and a ping-pong table to pass the time. Singles 80฿. Doubles 100฿. Check-out 10am.

Ping River—East Bank

Lanna River Hut, 75 Chiang Mai-Lamphun Rd. (tel. 241 016), near the TAT. Bamboo huts with mosquito nets and private baths set in a flowery garden lend flavor to this guest house. Spacious common area and hardwood floors distinguish the regular building. Immense teak rooms with common bath. Singles 40฿. Dorms 50฿. Doubles 60฿.

Sriprakard Hotel, 35 Chiang Mai-Lamphun Rd. (tel. 241 272). Reportedly the oldest lodge in Chiang Mai (at least by the looks of it). The center of this complex is a big sixtysomething teak house that the owner built for his family; later they decided to take in lodgers. During World War II, it was used as a hospital. Time has taken its toll on this historic structure, but it's close to the train station. Singles 150฿. Doubles 180฿.

Pun Pun Guest House, 321 Charoen Rat Rd. (tel. 243 362). Pardon the location (1km north of the Nawarat Bridge). A peaceful respite for those with a motorbike. Quiet bungalows are raised on stilts over the river. Gaily decorated rooms have hot water. Singles with common bath 60฿, with private bath 120฿. Doubles with bath 120฿.

FOOD

Chiang Mai has a tremendous number of restaurants, offering a colorful range of culinary styles spanning the spectrum of American, European, Chinese, Middle Eastern, and Thai gastronomy. Only in Bangkok could you do better. Strong Chinese and Burmese influences imbue the hearty cuisine of north Thailand with a unique flavor. Sticky rice is preferred over regular steamed rice, and noodle dishes are fortified with vitamins, minerals, and coconut cream. One don't-miss dish is *khao soi,* a noodle dish in a potent mixture of coconut cream, curry sauce, red onions, and lemon.

The **Sompet Market** between sois 6 and 7 on Moon Muang Rd., and the **Wahorat Market** near the Ping River at the end of Chiang Moi Rd. offer the standard set of grilled *saba*, fresh *rambutan*, sticky-sweet *roti*, and fried noodles. At night, head to the nocturnal **Anusarn Market,** between Chang Klan and Charoen Prathet Rd. just north of Sri Donchai Rd., an excellent snack zone. Those heading into rural territory may want to make a "last chance" stop at the **Hard Rock Café,** 6 Kohtchasarn Rd. or a fast food joint in **Chiang Mai Pavilion** or **Chiang Mai Plaza,** on Chang Klan Rd.

For a serious culinary experience, try out a traditional *khantoke* dinner. In this formal northern meal, diners sit on the floor and use their hands to eat from bowls placed on a low lacquer table. The dinner typically consists of glutinous rice, two meat dishes, and two vegetable dishes. The well-frequented **Old Chiang Mai Cultural Center,** 185/3 Wualai Rd. (tel. 275 097), about 1.5km south of the old city from the Chiang Mai Gate area on Chiang Mai-Hang Dong Rd. offers dinner accompanied by traditional northern dancing from 7pm to 10pm nightly. Call ahead for reservations.

If you get hooked on Chiang Mai-style food, the **Chiang Mai Thai Cookery School,** 1-3 Moon Muang Rd. (tel. 206 388), opposite the Tha Phae Gate feeds your addiction with one- to three-day classes (600-1500฿). Course also supplies English recipe book with substitutions, since durian isn't sold in most western supermarkets—darn.

Listings here are skewed toward the *farang* hangouts because the whole area is skewed toward *farang*. To join the locals, head for the stands at the Sompet Market off Moon Muang Rd.

Tha Phae Gate Area—Within Moat

Vegetarian Food Restaurant, 65 Moon Muang Rd. (tel. 278 315), at Tha Phae Gate. Inconspicuous location, predictable name, but delicious food. Sai Baba and his incredible hair preside over the operation. Dig into the chunky vegetables in northern curry (25฿), or the acrobatic Healthy Vegetable Soup (20฿) with mushrooms, ginger, pumpkin, squash, and spinach. Open daily 8:30am-2pm and 5-9pm.

J.J.'s Bakery (tel. 211 069), under the Montri Hotel at Tha Phae Gate. A western transplant into the heart of the city. Start your day off right with ice cream, baked goods, and western breakfasts. A full meal will run you 60-150฿. Refreshingly air-conditioned. Open daily 6:30am-10:30pm.

Julie's Roof Garden Restaurant, 7/1 Phra Pokklao Rd., Soi 5 (tel. 274 355). Perched atop the guest house of the same name, this eatery joins Parisian flair with back-woods foliage, producing an aura of distinct *je ne sais quoi.* Waterfall and flora distract you from sweaty t-shirt woes. *Poulet sauce forestière* 85฿. Delectable *ananas* juice. Open daily 9am-11pm.

Tha Phae Gate Area—Outside Moat

Aroon Rai, 43-45 Kotchasarn Rd. (tel. 276 947). This open-air restaurant has been a local favorite for over 33 years. Wondrous array of Thai, Chinese, and Chiang Mai-style dishes. Schmooze with Thais and *farang* alike under the multitudinous portraits of His Ubiquitous Majesty. Scrumptious chicken with coconut milk (30฿). Open 10am-8pm.

Croissant, 318 Tha Phae Rd. (tel. 252 418). Western food, coffee, and TV—a purist's nightmare, a homesick backpacker's dream. Espresso (30฿) with a buttery croissant (chocolate filled, 30฿) will prepare you for your next excursion. Cable movies several times a day. Open 7am-10pm.

Kuey Tio Pikgalian, Tha Phai Rd. (tel. 276 638) at the intersection with Soi 6 near Tha Phae Gate. Nothing fancy, just fast, delicious noodles at dirt cheap prices (15-20฿). Even the ice is a bargain (1฿). Open 10am-10pm.

Near the Ping River

Antique House, 71 Charoen Prathet Rd. (tel. 276 810). Teakwood house? Retail store? Eatery? Answer: all of the above. Entrees run 40-120฿; everything in the place, including your table and placemat, is for sale. Candlelight dinners accompanied by classical Thai music with a river view. Open daily 11am-midnight.

The Whole Earth, 88 Sri Donchai Rd. (tel. 282 463), east of Chang Klan Rd. Hungry heathens can find "Heaven on Earth...at the Whole Earth." Offering health education classes and serving divine food, the Whole Earth's chief aim is to transform the world by means of the "same intelligence that creates a lotus from the mud." Thai and Indian dishes for veggies and carnivores alike. Special Flavor Bean Curd (70฿). Open daily 11am-2pm and 5-10pm.

Shere Shiraz, 23-25 Charoen Prathet Rd. Soi 6 (tel. 276 132), off of Chang Klan Rd., down the alley near Porn Ping Tower. Pakistani, Indian, Arabic, and Thai food. Everything is made from scratch, and they cater to individual tastes, adding a pinch here and there, as you wish. This policy translates into extended preparation times, but the place is right in the middle of the Night Bazaar so you can kill time amid the stalls. Feast on a set meal of *tikki*, curries, *tandoor* chicken, breads, dessert, and tea (150-250฿). Open 9:30am-11:30pm.

SIGHTS

As in any other heavily touristed area, travelers in Chiang Mai must filter the genuine sights from the wretched yet prolific tourist traps. No spot has escaped the commercializing touch, but Chiang Mai will still reward you with the precious gems of its long history. Chiang Mai has over 300 wats, similar to the number found in Bangkok, but more densely packed. Even the sparkling, exhaustively researched prose of *Let's Go* cannot hope to capture the allure of local shrines. As it is, they tend to blend into each other. To maintain sanity, you could break with tight-wad tradition and hire a guide or take an organized tour (arranged by your guest house).

Wat Chiang Man, the oldest wat in Chiang Mai, is in the northeastern part of the old city off Ratchaphakinai Rd., near Chang Phuak Gate. King Mengrai built this wat in 1296 when he founded Chiang Mai and made it his humble abode. With its extensive use of teakwood and its architectural harmony with the surrounding forest, the temple is a classic example of northern Thai design.

Inside the grounds, you will first be drawn to the *bot,* with its huge teak columns and neighboring *wiharns.* The one on the right is home to two very ancient and sacred Buddhist images. **Phra Sae Tang Kamani** ("Crystal Buddha") is thought to have come from Lopburi about 1800 years ago. The second important Buddha image is **Phra Sila,** or the Stone Buddha, imported from India or Sri Lanka some 2500 years ago. Visitors can enter daily 9am to 5pm. Rows of sturdy elephant buttresses support a *chedi* outside the *wiharn,* representing the mythical era of unity between man and animals.

Wat Phra Singh lies on the western side of the old city, near Suan Dawk Gate, at the end of Phra Singh Rd. Construction on this wat began in 1345 under the supervision of King Pha Vu, seventh ruler of Chiang Mai. Its chief attraction is the bronze

Phra Singh Buddha in the finely decorated **Phra Wiharn Lai Kam.** Although locals will assure you otherwise, experts are not sure as to whether this is the true Phra Singh Buddha—there are identical statues in Bangkok and Nakhon Si Thammarat. The image is the focal point of Songkran festivities each April 13-15, when it gets a bath from adoring monks.

Occupying the old city's southwest corner, **Buak Hat Public Park's** fountains, palm trees, and grassy stretches make a relaxing rest stop. To get there, walk down Moon Muang Rd. to the southern moat, take a right on Bamrung Buri Rd., and go 2km to the western moat. Rent a mat, if you don't want those pesky little grass stains (10฿). Open 5am-10pm.

Down Phra Singh Rd. from Wat Phra Singh and Buak Hat Park, at the Phra Pokklao Rd. intersection lies **Wat Chedi Luang,** built by King Saen Suang Ma in 1401. The temple walls hold the remains of Chiang Mai's largest *chedi,* which once rose 86m above the ground. It was destroyed by either an earthquake in 1545 or by cannon fire in 1775 during King Taksin's battle with the Burmese.

But the fun isn't over yet. A *naga* staircase adorns the front porch of the *bot;* nestled within are the **standing gold Buddha** and 32 *Jataka* story panels depicting scenes from Buddha's life. Popular lore claims that Wat Chedi Luang was home to the Emerald Buddha during its short stay in Chiang Mai. A nearby **sacred gum tree** supports the legend that as long as it stands, so will Chiang Mai.

Considering its proximity to noisy Tha Phae Rd., **Wat Saen Fang** is amazingly intimate and secluded. The entrance path is lined with two extremely long and wavy snake *nagas.* Inside, you can see an elegant multi-colored spire and eight dogs protecting the four corners of the *chedi*.

Beyond the Old City

To venture into new territory, start at Chang Phuak Gate ("White Elephant Gate") on the north side of the moat. From here, grab a west-bound songthaew or #3 bus.

In the west part of town, **Chiang Mai University** sprawls over 600 acres just north of Suthep Rd. Serving the school's 10,000 students, the **university library** includes many English sources on all subjects. Upstairs, the staff will copy them for you for 0.5฿ per page. The **Chiang Mai Arboretum** is located 4km from the main entrance of the university, along Huay Kaew Rd. Studded with rare trees, this is a relaxing place to take a break from a hectic schedule. There's also an exercise park here; your lungs will certainly get a workout pumping in enough clean air to counteract gasoline fumes from the road. Next door, the **Chiang Mai Zoo** (tel. 221 179) houses thousands of animals in their natural habitat surrounded by hilly, forested terrain with lakes, waterfalls, and well-groomed gardens. Open 8am-6pm. Admission 20฿.

On the southwest corner of the campus is the **Tribal Research Institute,** which has a small museum with excellent exhibits on the various minorities inhabiting the mountainous area of northern Thailand (open Mon.-Fri. 8:30am-4:30pm). Wander to the southwest corner of campus or, alternatively, head west on Suthep Rd. from Suan Dawk Gate. Turn right into the Chiang Mai Universtiy gates. At the clock tower go left, right, left (all on paved roads) and the institute is on your left. Those interested in learning more about the hill tribes can go next door to the **library,** which sells books and cassettes of hill-tribe music and maintains a sizeable collection devoted to hill-tribe studies. Open Mon.-Fri. 8:30am-noon and 1-4:30pm.

Also off Suthep Rd., **Wat Suan Dawk** ("Temple of Flower Gardens," also known as Wat Buppharam) is just west of the gate. King Ku Na constructed the shrine in 1383; the enormous Chiang Saen-style bronze building inside the *bot* dates from 1504. Originally, the grounds served as a pleasure garden for the first kings of Chiang Mai, but later became a cemetery for their graves.

Wat U Mong lies farther along Suthep Rd., off to the south. Located on the outskirts of town, this peaceful forest temple is another remnant of King Mengrai's building spree. The grounds contain serene footpaths through the trees (which bear pithy phrases of wisdom) and two surprising sculptures of a nose and ear.

A gallery by the entrance displays modern religious art created by resident monks. The wat also has its own little library (open 8:30am-4pm). Tunnels leading into the hill are lined with niches housing Buddha figures. Farther along, **Wat Ram Poeng** is the location of the **Northern Insight Meditation Center** (tel. 278 620), where you can practice *vipassana* meditation. Saffron-robed monks, white-clad nuns, and lay practitioners quietly inhabit the grounds. Both wats are a bit off the beaten track, but can be reached by heading west from the city along Suthep Rd. Once you cross the canal, take the third left, then follow the signs to Wat U Mong. Wat Ram Poeng is about 2km ahead.

The **Chiang Mai National Museum,** located in the northeast sector of town, is due to re-open in October, 1996. Follow Chang Phuak Rd. to the superhighway intersection, take a left, and continue about 1km. The northern Thai-style museum is on the right, with showcases devoted to (who else?) Buddha. Upstairs are exhibits on northern Thai life, complete with tribal tools and household effects.

Wat Chet Yot is 500m farther west on the superhighway. Inspired by the design of the Mahabodhi temple in Bodhgaya, India, King Tilokaraja built this shrine in 1455. Each of the *chedi's* spires represents one of the seven weeks that the Buddha spent in Bodhgaya, India after attaining enlightenment there. Wat Chet Yot also has important historical significance: in 1477, the Eighth World Buddhist Council met here to revise the *Tripitaka* scriptures of Theravada Buddhism. The two **Bo trees** are said to be descendants of the one the big guy himself sat under during his epiphany. The smaller *chedi* nearby reputedly holds the ashes of King Tilokaraja.

SHOPPING

As Thailand's main center for handicrafts, Chiang Mai is a hard-core shopper's paradise. Just strolling past stores on the street or shuffling through night markets, you'll see a great variety of antiques, silver jewelry, hill-tribe embroidery, Thai silks and cottons, parasols, lacquerware, pottery, basketry, furniture, and wood carvings for sale. The main hunting grounds are Tha Phae Rd. and Chang Klan Rd.

The **night bazaar** occupies practically the entire length of Chang Klan Rd. from Sri Donchai Rd. to Tha Phae Rd. Merchants set up their wares and throw their advertising pitch out to the crowd of shoppers, browsers, and hangers-on. Moving from stall to stall, disregard any price tags—bargaining is the norm, but never back out of a price you have offered. Thai silk shirts priced at 150฿ can easily be had for 100฿ if you haggle. Leave the dubious silver and jewelry booths to discerning experts.

In Chiang Mai there are a couple of places that will satisfy your itch to buy hill-tribe wares. The **Hill Tribe Handicraft Project,** 1 Moon Muang Rd. (tel. 274 877) on the southeastern corner of the old city, sells audiotapes of Karen, Lisu, Akha, Lahu, Yao, and Hmong music, as well as quilts, bags, pouches, pullovers, shoes, and more. The administration hopes to shift tribal economies from opium cultivation by providing another means of income. Open Mon.-Sat. 8:30am-4:30pm. The more well-known **Hill Tribe Promotion Center,** 21/17 Suthep Rd. (tel. 277 743) is located next to Wat Suan Dawk. Also government-run, this is a bigger place with a greater selection of traditional and innovative crafts. Open 9am-5pm.

ENTERTAINMENT

The **British Council,** 198 Bamrung Rat Rd. (tel. 242 103), shows free British movies on Thursday evenings at 7pm. **Alliance Française,** 1238 Charoen Prathet Rd. (tel. 275 277) shows French films subtitled in English on Tuesdays at 4:30pm and Fridays at 8pm (free to members, 10฿ for students, 20฿ for others). The **USIA/AUA,** 24 Ratchadamnoen Rd. (tel. 211 973), has free American movies on Saturdays at 7pm.

If you're sore from all the temple jaunts, luxuriate in a traditional Thai massage. Two centrally located options are **Suan Samoonprai,** 1/11 Chaiyaphum Rd. Soi 1 (tel. 252 706; open 9am-9pm), and **Garden of Many Herbs,** 2/2 Chang Moi Rd. Soi 3 (tel. 232 089; open 9am-9pm). Both offer seven-day courses (2000฿). The **Old Medicine Hospital,** south of the old city at 78/1 Soi Moh Shivaya Komarapaj (tel. 275 085), also garners praise for its deep-tissue massage. Some guest houses can arrange for a practitioner to pay a room call (no funny business here—just a massage). A session usually runs 100฿ per hour.

Nightlife

Chiang Mai corners the market on bars and live music. Perhaps the most popular amongst *farang* and Thais alike is the **Riverside,** on the Ping's east bank at 9-11 Charoen Rat Rd. (tel. 243 239). Every night they serve up live western music, usually folksy, and good food (open daily 10am-1am).

Bars, bars, and more bars line Moon Muang Rd. and the Tha Phae Gate area. You'll easily get a feel for where you want to go. A popular place for Thai music is the **Ruan Come Garden,** on the eastern moat at 59 Kotchasarn Rd. (tel. 276 095; open daily 9am-1am). On some nights, the crowd energetically joins in with the singing. Duck into **Linda's Bar and Snooker,** at 3 Loi Kroa Rd., off Kotchasarn, to play a few games. Open noon until "really late, sometimes all night." Another good place off Kotchasarn Rd. and down Soi 2 is **The Moon Garden,** with pool and darts in a bungalow atmosphere. They also serve delicious food at decent prices. Open 9am-2am.

German Hofbrauhaus House (tel. 821 273) is a beer and food joint near the night bazaar on the corner of Chang Klan Rd. and Loi Kroa Rd. Also serves liquid blankets like Jägermeister and Schnapps. They have an extensive, good menu in six languages. Open daily 11am-11pm. **German Beer Garden** is near the river on 48 Charoen Prathet Rd. (tel. 276 179). This *biergarten* is the place for open-air drinking (open noon-2am), but if the mosquitoes are bugging you, retreat to the bar inside (open until 3am).

TREKKING IN CHIANG MAI

Trekking is to Chiang Mai what gambling is to Atlantic City: it's what people are here to do. Although Mae Hong Son and Chiang Rai are closer to the action, the concentration of trekking companies in Chiang Mai has driven prices down. Most organized treks last from two to seven days, and provide transportation, food and equipment. Karen, Hmong, Akha, Yao, Lisu, and Lahu villages are all accessible from Chiang Mai. Most treks aim for the area northwest of Chiang Dao. In general, the farther out one drives to begin a trek, the more isolated and less touristed the area will be. Be skeptical of treks which drive only two hours or less out of the city, and favor the ones which skirt the Burmese border. Treks to the Mae Tang River region and Mae Hong Son area are preferable to those to Chiang Rai. Don't expect to break new ground or discover a lost village; all trails are well-trodden.

New TAT regulations require that trekking companies, guides, and customers register with the tourist police. They need to file a copy of your passport photo page before you set out. Companies should also be members of the Jungle Tour Club of Northern Thailand; look for guides who belong to the Chiang Mai Guide Association, and who can speak both English and the relevant tribal languages.

Some independent spirits choose to set out on their own in rented jeeps or motorbikes. This could lead to disaster or, conversely, the best experience of your life. In any case, check with the tourist police for the latest regulations. Potential trekkies should visit Chiang Mai University's Tribal Research Institute (see "Sights").

Not to be overlooked in the swarm is **The Trekking Collective,** 22 Ratchadamnoen Rd (tel. 419 080; mail to P.O. Box 142 Mae Ping Rd.), near Tha Phae Gate, which offers a variety of treks, from the standard to the not-so-standard, up to 10 days. Especially good for the experienced trekker, they're willing to break the "hike-bamboo raft-elephant ride" mold if you assemble your own group (5-6 people). Animal watching (deer, gibbons, wild elephants, boars, and birds) and bike tours as well as "survival" treks for the more adventurous. If you want to "give a little back," **Chiang Mai Green Tour and Trekking,** 29/31 Chiang Mai-Lampun Rd. (tel. 274 374) donates a portion of its proceeds to a conservation program, and the **Chiang Mai Youth Hostel,** 63 Bamrung Buri Rd. (tel. 276 737) gives medical supplies, educational materials, and haircuts (for children) to the hill tribe people.

Diary of a Researcher-Writer's Trek with Mr. T: Day 1

Rafting through proper jungles. Saw monkeys, but no major rapids; passed several small waterfalls, some with streams, others just looked like the rocks were weeping. Some fine meals but vegetarians and others with special diets should make sure it is understood before they depart. Camping under a rock, pitching tents, fire, etc. Eight guides, leader speaks English fairly well. Others are passable but couldn't go it alone. Traveling with two Americans and five Danish. Lots of vines. Feels like Tarzan may come along at any moment. The mosquitoes are unrelenting. Not too hot, but rains lightly a lot. Guides are a crazy, but fun bunch. The guys (the Americans—the Danish don't speak English so we're not bonding) love them. (To see what happens on Day 2, turn to page 397)

■ NEAR CHIANG MAI

DOI SUTHEP AND DOI PUI

Wat Phra That Doi Suthep, seated majestically on Suthep Mountain, is unparalleled among the many possible excursions from Chiang Mai and remains one of the most sacred pilgrimage sites in the country. The centerpiece of the wat is a brilliant gold *chedi* visible from the city below. The word "*doi*" is a northern Thai word meaning "mountain," and *"suthep"* derives from the Pali word "*Sudevoy*," the name of the hermit who inhabited the area before the shrine was built. *"Phra That"* refers to the Buddha's relics.

Buddha's anvil (or *incus*, a teeny anvil-shaped bone in the middle ear) was discovered by a Sri Lankan monk in Thailand who was guided to it by a dream. A few years later, in 1383, while in the safe-keeping of King Ku Na the relic (so the story goes) spontaneously self-replicated. One anvil was enshrined in Wat Suan Dawk, while the other left on a special journey: it was placed on the back of a white elephant that promptly made three trumpet-like noises and walked out of the city via the soon-to-be-named White Elephant Gate (Chang Phuak Gate). The beast climbed 100m to the wat's present location, trumpeted three more times, made three counter-clockwise circles, and knelt down. This omen convinced the king to dig a pit and place the stone-enclosed relic in the ground, along with other sacred objects.

Dress appropriately to enter this sanctified spot; de rigueur *couture* means long pants or a long skirt, and no tank tops or ragged shirts. Complimentary loaner pants and skirts are available if you're guilty of a fashion *faux pas*. To participate more fully, purchase a flower with attached incense sticks and gold leaf paper (5฿); watch others to see what to do with it. If you can't handle the hike up the hill, take the trolley adjacent to the stairs (5฿). Conventional wisdom states: those who go to Chiang Mai without visiting Doi Suthep are no better than those who have never been to Chiang Mai at all.

Five km up the mountain past the wat is **Phu Phing Palace,** the winter residence of the royal family (hence off-limits to you). Lavishly landscaped gardens and ancient trees offer peaceful strolling on weekends. Appropriate attire is mandatory; the sartorially challenged can rent pants for 10฿. Picnic on the palace grounds.

Moving 3km around and down the mountain to the valley tucked below, you will come to the **Doi Pui Meo Village,** inhabited by the Hmong ("Meo" is a derogatory term for this hill-tribe). Somewhat of a tourist trap, there are shops selling hill-tribe jewelry and handicrafts everywhere, though traditional dress and housing still pervade the place.

The places around Doi Suthep are easily accessible. Winding mountain roads are fun to navigate by scooter or motorcycle and the terrain and vistas are beautiful, but keep your eyes on the road. **Songthaews,** leaving from Chang Phuak Gate and Chiang Mai Zoo, also ascend the mountain. They charge 30฿ for the 30minute ride up to the wat, and 20฿ back down. Hand over an additional 20฿ each way to reach the palace, and 20฿ more to the village and back (130฿ total). You can rent a motorbike and buy your freedom (possibly your death) for 150฿. If you want everything done for you, take one of the sight-seeing tours offered by guest houses. Huay Kaew Rd. (Hwy. 1004) follows the mountain to the three main sights and is lined with turn-off viewpoints and waterfall routes. Just before the road rises up the mountain, the monument on the left is the revered **Kruba Srivichai shrine.** Kruba Srivichai was the monk who inspired thousands of volunteers to build the road to Wat Phra That in 1934. Pause to pay respects to ensure your safety up and down the mountain.

A few km up the road, a sign marks the turn-off for the **Huay Kaew Falls.** It's a very romantic spot, but even solitary sojourners can appreciate the shady and relaxing area at the base of the falls, 3km from the main road.

Doi Suthep-Pui National Park encompasses the entire area: a wide variety of plants, animals, and birds, plus waterfalls and the aforementioned sites. A project begun in 1987 by a professor from Chiang Mai University has so far collected 2062 species of vascular plants in the park, more than can be found in all of verdant Britain. Unfortunately, the park's flora and fauna are being edged up the mountain as Chiang Mai expands; teak trees, various legumes, and other commercially valuable trees have almost completely disappeared from the lowlands of Doi Suthep.

Spare some time for the drive to **Doi Pui's summit,** which rises 1685m and is only a few km past the Doi Pui village turn-off. Head right at the turn-off, follow the road on up, and bear left at the next branch-off for the short ride to the summit. The road will end and you'll have to hoof it the rest of the way to the peak. The top, surrounded by pine trees, is a good place to hike. Stop at the **park headquarters** (tel. 248 405) between the wat and the palace to get some information before you set out on any long walks. Camping costs 5฿ per night, and tents are available for 40฿ per night. If you're with a group, you can rent a guest house at the park headquarters compound, complete with a grocery store and eating facilities. The Suan Son guest house, for example, can sleep 12 people for 1000฿ per night, and the Mon Tha accommodates 45 for 2500฿ per night.

MAE SA VALLEY

Another possible day trip is an excursion to the **Mae Sa Valley.** The area's rural beauty barely compensates for the heavily tourist-oriented attractions here. Head north out of the city along Chang Phuak Rd. (Hwy. 107) and pass through the tiny town of Mae Rim. Right after the town (17km from Chiang Mai), take the turn-off to the left, Mae Rim-Somoeng Rd./Hwy. 1096. Numerous signs guide you to the abundance of sight-seeing opportunities. At the **Mae Sa Elephant Training Center** (tel. 236 069), the elephants and their riders put on a show every day from 9:30 to 11:30am. The anything-but-Dumbos demonstrate their strength and dexterity by handling teak logs, and reveal their grace and balance by maneuvering their huge bodies into surprising contortions (admission with show 40฿, without 10฿). Buy some bananas (10฿) and feed them to the elephants, but they may snatch the fruit before you get a chance to dole them out yourself. Post-show, there's an **elephant-back jungle tour** (40฿ for a short ride, 1000฿ for an hour). Similar fun can be had at the **Mae Rim Elephant Farm,** 3km down the road, or at the **Pong Yaeng Elephant Training Center** 9km farther.

Much of the Mae Sa Valley is also part of Doi Suthep National Park; in this end of the park there is another tribal village as well as some waterfalls. The best cascades tumble at the 10-tiered **Mae Sa Falls.** Only a few kilometers from the Mae Sa Elephant Center, the falls has a visitor center right before it, with a map of the area for further explorations. Entrance fee 5฿; 30฿ per vehicle. Touristy snake shows display the local deadly species. Slightly more genuine are the orchid and butterfly farms (10฿), which feature "exotic hybrids."

Bus #2 (3฿) can take you from Chang Phuak Rd. north of Chang Phuak Gate to Mae Rim district and from there grab the rare songthaew or motorbike taxi (30฿). Many backpackers end up hitching to the sights. Songthaews (6฿) to Mae Rim leave from the Chang Phuak Gate. Guest house tours to the valley are easy to arrange and often include stops at an elephant center, an orchid farm, and the falls (300฿).

DOI INTHANON NATIONAL PARK

The 188km route from Chiang Mai to Mae Sariang along Hwy. 108 is ruggedly scenic. The drama picks up speed as the mountains huddle near **Chom Thong,** 58km away, which is a good place to stop because **Doi Inthanon National Park,** home to **Thailand's highest peak,** is accessible from here. Blue buses from Chiang Mai leave the Chang Phuak Station (every 30min., 6am-6pm); they also stop for about 15 minutes in the Chiang Mai Gate southern moat area. The fare to Chom Thong is 11฿.

Built in 1451 and expanded in 1516, **Wat Phra That Si Chom Thong** is neatly contained on Chom Thong's main road. The intricate, Burmese-style teak *bot* that is the temple's centerpiece is regarded as one of the most beautiful in the north. The altar holds the right side of Buddha's skull.

From Chom Thong, songthaews can be harnessed for transport to the national park and Mae Klang Waterfall, an 8-km ride up to the Hwy. 1009 turn-off (10฿). A trip to the **summit of Doi Inthanon** is 50฿; band together and divy up the 500฿ private rate. A summit-bound songthaew leaves the Mae Klang Waterfall area every two hours. But a motorbike—like an associate editor—makes life infinitely easier. Strike your best Brando pose and pick up some wheels for 120฿ per day in Chom Thong at N.P. Travel and Service (tel. 341 220). AEs, needless to say, are priceless.

The 1km path above the falls to the visitor center can also be reached by driving through the park's vehicle entrance, a few hundred meters past the Mae Klang turnoff (admission for motorcycles 10฿, for cars 30฿). **Mae Klang Waterfall,** with places to eat, swim, and picnic, is the Andy Williams of this park's cascades—the only one of three worth seeing. Its big brother, Mae Ya waterfall, is not; it's a 28km side trip. Admission to walk around and see Mae Klang costs 25฿, children 15฿.

A little-known place of intense beauty lies near Mae Klang Waterfall. Just above the eating spots, cross the bridge and take a left. After 1km, there's a driveway entrance into stunning gardens. The grounds are home to a branch of the Wittayalai Sung Kamphaeng San, the **Monk's College of Kamphaeng San,** based near Bangkok. It's up on a hill that commands a panoramic view of the surrounding mountains amidst meticulously maintained green grass, lovely flowers and trees, walkways, a fish pond, a temple, and lodgings for the seven monks who live there.

Just before the visitor center, a 1km path directs you to **Borichinda Cave,** which has a skylight to the surface in its sizeable entrance chamber. Guided tours can be arranged at the visitor center, which also has information and exhibits on local animal life, including the **nocturnal pangolin,** whose Gene Simmons-like tongue is 50% longer than its head and body, enabling it to consume 73 million ants per year.

Wachiratan Waterfall, the most powerful fall, is the next stop, at the 20.8km mark. Set up your picnic too close to the falls and enjoy the uniquely refreshing sensation of eating your *pad thai* under a lawn sprinkler.

At the 31km mark, the elegant cascades of **Siriphum Waterfall** appear to be sliding down glass. The lane leading to it winds through the park's Royal Project, which encourages local hill-tribes to replace opium production with strawberry and flower cultivation (which, unfortunately, is not as lucrative). The program also seeks to halt slash-and-burn agricultural methods, which have depleted the park's vegetation.

The road bids farewell at **Doi Inthanon's summit,** 48km from Chom Thong, which is usually shrouded under a misty blanket due to the monsoon climate. Nevertheless, the best time for viewing (and bird-watching) is the cool season. The average park temperature is 12°C—bring a warm jacket and rain protection, especially if you intend to climb. Even without hiking, the drive up with its lush terraced valleys and distant vistas is definitely worthwhile. The park has **guest houses** available from 300-2,000฿, and a **restaurant** at park headquarters just past Siriphum Falls.

■■■ MAE SARIANG

Mae Sariang (pop. 7400), on the Yuam River near the Burmese border, promises a quiet retreat from the blaring percussion of more popular cities, and a proximate base for fearless adventurers. Surrounded by hill-tribe villages, this nondescript town is modernizing with its profits from border trade (both illicit and legitimate) through the southern part of Mae Hong Son Province.

ORIENTATION

Mae Sariang is bordered by the **Yuam River** to the west and **Hwy. 108** to the east. **Wiang Mai Road** lies between these two landmarks. **Laeng Phanit Road** runs parallel and closest to the river; one block to the east and parallel to it is **Mae Sariang Road** The highway is 1.5km from the river, and everything in town is situated between, with activity concentrated around the river. From Chiang Mai, buses bound for Mae Sariang depart eight times per day (4hr., 70฿); from Mae Hong Son, seven buses leave daily (4hr., 61฿).

PRACTICAL INFORMATION

Immigration office: (tel. 681 339), on Mae Sariang Rd. next to the police station. Open 8:30am-4:30pm.

Currency Exchange: Thai Farmers Bank, 150/1 Wiang Mai Rd. (tel. 681 339), between Laeng Phanit Rd. and Mae Sariang Rd. Open Mon.-Fri. 8:30am-3:30pm.

Post/Telephone Office: 31 Wiang Mai Rd. (tel. 681 356), 1km from the river. Open Mon.-Fri. 8:30am-noon and 1-4:30pm., Sat.-Sun. 9am-noon. **Postal code:** 58110. **Telephone code:** 053.

Buses: (tel. 681 347), the terminal is 100m north of Wiang Mai Rd., across from gas station. To: **Chiang Mai** (7, 9, 10:30am, 12:30 and 1:30pm; A/C 3pm, midnight, and 1am, 4hr.); **Mae Hong Son** (7 and 10:30am; A/C 1:30, 3:30, and 5:30pm, midnight, and 1am, 4hr.). Buses to **Bangkok** depart from across the street at the gas station. Yan Yong Tours (tel. 681 532) offers **shuttles** (6pm, 15hr.; A/C, 4 and 7pm, 13-14hr.).

Songthaews: To **Mae Sot** (every hour, 6:30am-12:30pm, 5hr., 150฿).

Pharmacy: 172/1 Wiang Mai Rd. (tel. 681 606), next to Renn Restaurant. Open 6am-10pm.

Hospital: (tel. 681 027). On Wiang Mai Rd. 200m off Hwy. 108.

Emergency: tel. 191.

Police: (tel. 681 038), 200m south of Wiang Mai Rd. on Mae Sariang Rd.

ACCOMMODATIONS

See View Guest House, (tel. 681 556), off Wai Seuksa Rd. Follow the signs from the bus station or walk to the south end of Laeng Phanit Rd., turn right, cross the bridge, and turn left. The concrete bomb shelter has large if dreary chambers with hot water. Great view of the giant Buddha across the valley. Organizes treks. Singles in old teak house 80฿, in new building with private shower 120฿.

Riverside Guest House, 85/1 Laeng Phanit Rd. (tel. 681 188), 300m north of Wiang Mai Rd. Watch the river flow and the sun set over the mountains in simple rooms with common bath. Singles 80฿. Doubles 100฿.

FOOD

Nong Bou Farm, (tel. 681 237) on Mae Sariang-Mae Sam Laep Rd. Head toward See View Guest House. When you cross the bridge, go straight for 1km until you see the blue sign. It should be a shame to come to Mae Sariang and miss this gem. Personal-size straw gazebo dining areas surround a peaceful pond. Thai menu and indigenous food is their specialty. *Yum sumoon prae* (fried pigskin in lemon juice and herbs) is good (it is!), as is the fried chicken with ginger and cashews. Dishes 40-50฿. Open daily 11am-10pm.

Renu Restaurant, 174/2 Wiang Mai Rd. (tel. 681 171), is in the center of town, clearly marked with an English sign. A long-running favorite with long-running hours. Nut hatch curry 30฿ is not the vegetarian dish you may imagine. Open daily 6am-midnight. MC, Visa.

■ AROUND MAE SARIANG

Because Mae Hong Son province edges Burma, there are sometimes border skirmishes between Karen independence fighters and the Burmese army. December and January mark peak battle season, so make sure an area is safe before hitting the road. If you plan to venture out of town, check with the police for the latest safety update and border status. Transportation here is unreliable and sporadic; short trips can stretch unavoidably into days.

There aren't many ways to fritter away your time in Mae Sariang proper. In fact, Mae Sariang is a great town to leave; use it as a base for semi-risky adventures in the country side. The lazy drudgery disappears in the surrounding border wilds. See View arranges excursions during the high season, but the area around Mae Sariang calls for an independent and intrepid spirit.

Cut-rate teak furniture crosses the Salanin River from Burma into Thailand at **Mae Sam Laep,** but the machine-gun-toting policemen and army commandoes aren't there to turn back the piles of wooden chairs. About 46km west of Mae Sariang, Mae Sam Laep allows *farang* an insider's glimpse of the jungle-obscured action. Take a songthaew to Mae Sam Laep (50฿). Most Mae Sariang guest houses can arrange for one to pick you up at a pre-arranged time on their daily route. You can also snag one in the morning on Laeng Phanit Rd. They leave approximately hourly. When one approaches, gesticulate like crazy. The first leaves Mae Sariang at 6am, and the last returns in the mid-afternoon. Motorboats carry the multi-ethnic locals and transnational trading goods up and down the river. **Sop Moei** lies 50km (2hr.) down the river. Boats cost 500฿ per day; stingier and braver souls risk the impossibly confusing and infrequent 30฿ passenger boats. The village headman operates a big guest house 100m from the river (rooms 100-150฿).

As always, beware of those offering to take a group over the border on a hush-hush spree. It may seem like the adventure of a lifetime, but once there, you're at their mercy, and the return fare is often substantially higher. **Pha Ma Lo,** 3km east of Mae Sariang toward Chiang Mai, is a large White Karen village known for its reasonably priced hand-woven **fabrics.** Songthaew it both ways (50฿).

North of Mae Sariang, rural villages abound which can be visited on daytrips, or in transit from Mae Hong Son, 160km away. Past the halfway point is **Khun Yuam,** about the same size as Mae Sariang (pop. 6500), where the bus stops for a welcome break. Every November they host the **Bua Tong Blossom Festival** here in celebration of the beautiful, wild sunflower blossoms that pop up everywhere. Just before the bus stop, signs indicate the direction of **Ban Farang Guest House.** There are other guest houses in this potential jumping-off point. South of Khun Yuam are the **Mae Ha Cave** and **Mae Na Hot Springs,** both worth a look if time permits. **Nam Tok Mae Surin National Park,** 30km from Mae Hong Son, contains the **Mae Surin Waterfall,** the highest waterfall in Thailand.

■■■ MAE HONG SON

A popular subject of postcard portraitists, Mae Hong Son's setting, on the grassy banks of a quiet lake stocked with an overabundance of small fish, is ideal for practitioners of pastoral escapism. Nearby, unassuming wats combine Burmese and Thai architecture in a peaceful and fetching aesthetic, offering spiritual uplift to weary pilgrims of a certain fat, yellow budget guide.

Following the formula of any good Hollywood thriller, the idyllic scenery gives way to a more sinister side. Opium deals, smuggling, and other illegal border action, like the Bates's motel murders, are never viewed directly, but lurk within the shadows, often alluded to and mentioned in hushed tones.

According to local lore, Mae Hong Son was born out of an elephant *kraal.* King Puthawongse had sent out a party to capture wild elephants, and the hunters traveled all the way to this area before they managed to seize an adequate number. Not wanting to herd them back, the party built a *kraal* and a city eventually flourished.

In the early part of this century, Mae Hong Son was converted into a city of exile, a *kraal* for criminals, recalcitrant officials, obstreperous editors, and other troublemakers. Although modern-day residence is now voluntary, the town's past doesn't seem too far-removed. Thrice-daily flights to Chiang Mai cost only US$15, a figure which apparently contradicts all laws of supply and demand, until the non-governmental subsidy in the cargo hold is factored in. Efforts to promote tourism here have yielded excellent services and a beautiful town. It doesn't get much better than this.

ORIENTATION

Mae Hong Son is 348km from Chiang Mai via the southern route through Mae Sariang (on Hwy. 108) and 247km from Chiang Mai via the northern route through Pai (on Hwy. 107 and 1095).

Mae Hong Son is easily navigable. Buses stop on **Khunlum Praphat Road,** which runs north and south through the center of town. Turning left out of the bus station and heading south, the second street is **Singhanat Bamrung Road** (oriented east-west). One block south **Udom Chao Nithet Road** is dotted with guest houses and borders the lake (which is east of Khunlum Praphat Rd.) **Chamnansathet Road** runs along the south side of the lake.

PRACTICAL INFORMATION

Tourist Police/Information: 1 Ratchadamaphitak Rd. (tel. 611 821), on the corner of Singhanat Bamrung Rd. Stop by and grab a map. Little English spoken.

Immigration Office: (tel. 612 106), on Khunlum Praphat Rd. 1km north of the bus station. Visa renewals with 2 photos, copies of photo and visa page from passport, and 500฿.

Currency Exchange: Bangkok Bank, 68 Khunlum Praphat Rd. (tel. 611 275). Open Mon.-Fri. 8:30am-5pm. **24-hr. ATM** accepts AmEx, Visa, and PLUS.

Post Office/Telephones: Mae Hong Son Post Office, 79 Khunlum Praphat Rd. (tel. 611 888). Open Mon.-Fri. 8:30am-4:30pm, Sat.-Sun. 9am-noon. **Postal code:** 58000. **Overseas phone** (cash, collect, or home-direct for calling card calls; tel. 611 711), telex, telegram, and fax. Open daily 7am-11pm. **Telephone code:** 053.

Buses: 33/1 Khunlum Praphat Rd. (tel. 611 318). To **Chiang Mai,** via **Mae Sariang** (fan: 8, 10:30am, 8, and 9pm; A/C: 6, 9am, and 9pm; 4hr. to Mae Sariang, 50฿; 8-½hr. to Chiang Mai, 115฿); via **Pai** (fan: 7, 8:30, 10:30am, and 12:30pm; A/C: 7 and 8am; 3hr. to Pai, 42฿; 8hr. to Chiang Mai).

Airport: Mae Hong Son Airport, (tel. 612 057), on Nivit Pisan Rd. Go to the end of Singhanat Bamrung Rd. and turn left at the hospital. Transforms into an exercise park in the evening. To **Chiang Mai** (10:30am, 12:50, 3:10, and 5:30pm, 345฿). **THAI Airways** 71 Singhanat Bamrung Rd. (tel. 611 297), near Tourist Police. Open 8am-noon, 1-5:30pm.

Motorbike Rental: P.J. Motorbike, 28 Singhanat Rd. (tel. 611 291). 120-200฿ per day. Open daily 8am-6pm.

Car Rental: In addition to **Mae Hong Son Travel, Rose Garden Tour,** 7/1 Singhanat Bamrung Rd. (tel. 611 681), rents Suzuki 4-wheel drives.

Hospital: Sri Sangwarn Hospital (tel. 611 378), at the very end of Singhanat Bamrung Rd. near the airport.

Clinic: Dr. Sunit Boonyasong operates a **small clinic,** 32 Khunlum Praphat Rd. (tel. 611 622), near the bus station. Open Mon.-Fri. 5-9pm, Sat.-Sun. 9am-9pm.

Ambulance: tel. 611 378.

Emergency: tel. 1699 (tourist police emergency number).

Police: Mae Hong Son Provincial Police, south of the post office on the road to Mae Sariang (tel. 611 239).

ACCOMMODATIONS

Take time to smell the roses in Mae Hong Son. Gardens burst into bloom at most guest houses. In addition to flora, accommodations here also offer hot shower facilities and trekking arrangements. The nearby lake teems with aquatic scenery.

Bus Station Area

Mae Hong Son Guest House, 295 Makasantee Rd. (tel. 612 510). Turn right out of the bus station, then left 1km down the 1st street. Follow the signs. For those weary of the main town's frantic Bangkokian pace, this friendly, family-run establishment features bungalows in a large garden setting. Owner speaks English, and is very helpful. Excellent reports on their treks. Singles 50฿. Doubles 80฿, with private bath 200฿.

Sawasdee Guest House, 18 Khunlum Praphat Rd., 150m north of the bus station; turn right and go 200m at the road with a Sawasdee sign. Perhaps the most authentic northern home-style accommodations in town. Every night, resident Shan couple cooks or fetches tasty dishes from the market. Guests can pitch in and help. Eating until satisfied sometimes means trying as many as 10 different selections (20฿). Singles 40฿. Doubles 60฿.

Jong Kham Lake Area

Rim Nong Guest House, 4/1 Chamnansathit Rd., (tel. 611 052). A friendly mini-complex with various rooms tucked into every cranny, all at affordable prices. Supan throws parties for Christmas and Thai New Year. Lake-front side decorated with an odd, yet appropriate homage to Singha beer. Dorms 40฿. Singles 50฿. Doubles 70-100฿ depending on size.

Prince Guest House, 37 Udom Chaonithet Rd., northside (tel. 612 256). Formerly the Cheer Pub. Retains the expansive deck with nice view over the lake and Wat Jong Klang, but there's nothing palatial about these proletarian digs. Singles 40฿. Doubles 60฿, with cold shower 80฿.

Johnnie House, 5 Udom Chaonithet Rd., northside. A few rooms, all rather blah. Hip young staff chill on the porch waiting for backpackers to wander by. Offers a "jungle craft" trek where you learn to live in the jungle. Singles 50฿. Doubles 70฿.

Jong Kham Guest House, 7 Udom Chaonithet Rd., northside. Not where we'd want to stay or take a tour.

FOOD

Aladdin Home, on Khunlum Praphat Rd., across the street and just south of the bus station. Arguably the best restaurant in town. Special *khao soy*, a northern Thai coconut curry (20฿) is spectacular. Open 6am-10pm.

Kai Muk Restaurant, 23 Udom Chaonithet Rd. (tel. 612 092). Excellent open-air place for Thai or Chinese food, served up by eager, uniformed youngsters. Tongue-scorching fried duck in crispy basil leaves is popular among locals (small 60฿, large 90฿), as is the late-night drinking. Open daily 10am-3am. AmEx, Visa.

Restaurant Holland, Khunlum Praphat Rd., at Singhanat Bamrung Rd. Expat Dutchman brews the best coffee for miles. Western standards for the curry-jaded. Burgers 30฿. Open 7am-11pm. May be closed during the low season.

Fern Restaurant, 87 Khunlum Praphat Rd. (tel. 611 374). Runs the gamut from Thai to Chinese and European. Hanging plants, rattan chairs, and no-meat selections include pumpkin patties (40฿). Pai river fish (120฿). Sublime chrysanthemum drink. Open daily 7am-2pm, 4:30-10pm.

Ban Buatong Café, 34 Khunlum Praphat Rd. (tel. 612 187), near the bus station. Melting pot of Mexican, Italian, Greek, Middle Eastern, and Indian food as well as Thai. American breakfasts and good vegetarian menu. Shepherd's Pie with kidney beans, potatoes, etc. 45฿. Open 6:30am-9pm.

SIGHTS

Asserting itself 474m above the town on a mountain peak is **Wat Doi Kong Mu,** the best place for snatching a panoramic view of the city. Built in 1874, this Shan-influenced temple is Mae Hong Son's most important wat. Two *stupas* contain remains of monks, and the place is lit up like a Christmas tree in the evening. According to a government report on Mae Hong Son province, "tourists enjoy walking up the hill as a source of exercise," so strap on those boots. Move west on Udom Chaonithet Rd. Turn left at the end until you see the wat road on your right. It's 1.5km up.

Another nearby shrine is **Wat Phra Non,** just slightly north of the Doi Kong Mu turn-off road. The wat houses a 12m reclining Burmese-style Buddha and the ashes of Mae Hong Son's kings guarded by two massive stone lions.

Fitness buffs might enjoy the exercise track lining **Jong Kham Lake.** Not for the inflexible or self-conscious. The small stand on the southwest shore sells bags of fish food for 2-10฿, great for stirring up a feeding frenzy among the athletic fish that somersault out of the simmering water.

On the lake's south side, two wats draw scores of visitors. **Wat Jong Klang** is the one on the right, with glass paintings and wooden puppets brought from Burma about 100 years ago. Formerly it was a rest stop for journeying monks; today, most pilgrims are tourists. Open 8am-6pm. Next door is **Wat Jong Kham,** built in 1827, so named because its pillars decorated with gold leaf, were originally silver plated. All the wats request appropriate attire. No one will drag you out if you don shorts and a tank top, but be respectful.

TREKKING IN MAE HONG SON

Some of the best hiking in Thailand awaits you in Mae Hong Son. Many Chiang Mai-based treks come here. Surrounding hills support village after village of Lisu, Lahu and Karen tribes, in addition to Shan and Kuomintang (KMT) zones. The KMT are members and descendants of the nationalist party which once ruled China. Other party hotshots went to Formosa and formed the Taiwanese government—these guys took a wrong turn and wound up in Thailand.

Most of the treks are hiking only and can take you as far as Chiang Mai, although the standard version including rafting and elephant riding is also available. The treks offered by **Mae Hong Son Guest House** have received favorable reports. Drop by their office in town at 20 Singhanat Bamrung Rd. (tel. 620 105).

In the low, rainy season, Mae Hong Son hosts fewer travelers than Chiang Mai. This drop in regular business drives prices up and availability down. To get around this predicament, put your own group together and/or shop around.

Numerous villages lie along roads accessible by car or motorbike. Pick up a map from the tourist police and roam if you want to.

Diary of a Researcher-Writer's Trek with Mr. T: Day 2

3 hours trekking. First hour uphill then down for a bit. So muddy, I don't know which was more difficult. Poorly made path will ruin your sneakers. Wear sturdy boots or footwear you're willing to lose. Hopefully better trekking tomorrow. Tee Lor Su falls are about 25 minutes away from our camp. Breathtaking—possibly the most fantastic sight I've seen in Thailand. Three main falls and a massive area covered by smaller ones; some are quite deep, good for diving. Very secluded. How do I know this? Because I got lost. Seriously lost. I was with Mike, one of the two Americans; we had separated from the group on our way up. Then we saw them at the top. When we returned an hour later they had left. Instead of back-tracking we decided to follow their path but we never found it. Instead, we took a rather precarious route down steep (90°) falls working our way down on the roots, and swam through 8-ft. deep pools, trying to find a path. At some point we apparently overran the path and ended up at a pool below the camp level. After attempting to cut through the jungle at a couple of places (our only other choice was to swim), Mike found a path through some miracle of God. We had no idea where it went, but we hoped. About 20min. along, we ran into an American from North Carolina, towel around his neck with a flashlight. He asked us which way to the falls. We asked where the hell we were. Two hours after we left the falls, we made it back. (See day 3, page 419)

THAILAND

Warning: Remember that quick trips across the border are illegal, dangerous, and a good way to pay big bahts to get back into Thailand.

■ AROUND MAE HONG SON

Mae Hong Son is a Thai enclave, surrounded by clusters of hill tribes, Shan, KMT, and Burmese refugees. Directly across the nearby border is the Karenni (Red Karen) state in Burma; just north of that lies Khun Sa's headquarters and Shan state. Border politics dominate outlying areas of Mae Hong Son province. Uniformed policemen regularly stop and search buses for refugees fleeing Burma, where the situation is so dismal that fugitives now cross over the western border into Bangladesh.

No tourist should have any problem on the rural routes here, unless they're stashing drugs or carrying a Burmese refugee as passenger. In fact, almost no other city in Thailand makes it so easy to experience such array of ethnic cultures and political backgrounds. 150฿ for a motorbike provides access to Karen, Lisu, Hmong, and Lahu hill-tribe villages, Shan towns, and KMT camps. The population of Mae Hong Son province is 51% highlanders of various tribal cultures and languages. Most guest houses and all trekking companies offer guided daytrips. Be prepared for embarrassment, however, when you realize that you are just one of the hordes of tourists who gawk at the villagers as if they were zoo animals.

Most trekking companies also offer **rafting and boating trips.** From Mae Hong Son, most paddle (or motor) down the Pai River to the Burmese border (3-4hr.) where the Pai merges with the Salawin. Some head up to Pai, but it's more common for Pai folks to come the other way.

There is no way a traveler in Thailand can make it as far as Mae Hong Son province without hearing of the **Long-Necked Karens.** In addition to Hollywood-esque tour company billing, the faces of the long-necked women are often featured on tourist maps and guide books. Entering the touristy village costs 250฿, and the necks are not even stretched; the effect is achieved by squashing the rib cage and collar bone. Remember, however, these people are Burmese refugees who are not allowed to own land and farm. Besides trinket sales and day labor, this is their only means of support. So if you have an inkling to see them, think of your baht as going toward a good cause.

Before leaving Mae Hong Son behind, you might want to visit the **Nam Hu Hai Chai Hot Springs,** 12km south of the city, which are very inviting in the winter.

HIGHWAY 1095 TO PAI

Some of Thailand's most stunning scenery adorns Hwy. 1095 between Mae Hong Son and Pai (111km). The road follows mountain peaks that crest above the sky and dive below the cloudy waves. Twisting and turning the whole way, the views change, but the two constants are *buena vista* and nausea. About 35km from Mae Hong Son and 20km before the turn-off to Mae La Na, two great round-topped summits appear, shorn away from their brethren. Nearby reposes the **Sunnyata Forest Monastery.** A spectacular row of jagged tree-topped pinnacles comes up 15km later, and at their base lies a village.

Heading out from Mae Hong Son on the left, a couple of km before the Fish Cave, is a road marked with numerous Thai signs. This lane leads through Shan and Hmong villages, a waterfall, and mountain panoramas, terminating at the KMT village of **Mae Aw,** 1-½ hours from the Hwy. 1095 turn-off. Mae Aw is situated along a mountain top right on the Burmese border, sheltering remnants of Chiang Kai-shek's Kuomintang army, which retreated to northern Thailand over four decades ago after defeat at the hands of Chinese Communists led by Mao Zedong. Occasional skirmishes break out between the KMT in Thailand and the Shan United Army in Burma. These are probably drug-related battles; the SUA is headed by Khun Sa, an elusive drug lord/Shan rebel leader who has evaded security forces from around the world for decades. He's a controversial figure; no one can pin down his motives. During the 1970s, while still rising to power, he offered to stop producing opium if the U.S. government would compensate him. The offer was ultimately rejected, although Khun Su has yet to retract it, supporting the opinion that his primary interest is in freedom for his people from the Burmese dictatorship. Ask about the situation at trekking companies or tourist police offices before going.

Including Mae Aw in a journey to the Fish Cave (see below) requires motorbike or car rental. A songthaew leaves Mae Hong Son from Singhanat Bamrung Rd. near the telephone office daily at 8am (100฿ one way). A regular motorbike will suffice for most of the year, but in the muddy rainy season, a 4-wheel-drive or motorcross bike (and driving skills) are necessities.

Tham Plaa (Fish Cave), 20km north of Mae Hong Son, makes a scenic daytrip that you can handle solo. Fish food sellers will badger you at the entrance—since the guppies here are sacred, you might as well capitulate and treat them to a snack of dried bugs, or save the bugs and fry them for your friends back home. The Shan villagers who look after the fish never catch them, believing that the spirit of the mountain protects them from harm, and will hex violators. Among knotty and twisted *taawon* trees stands a statue of the long-haired hermit who meditated here long ago. Recently, a scuba-outfitted Australian camera crew penetrated the depths of the pool discovering a waterfall and open air for several km. Enhancing the *Journey to the Center of the Earth* mystique, it is said that Japanese soldiers retreating from Burma buried treasure in caverns throughout the mountain.

The fish cave is about a 30min. drive and only takes a short while to enjoy, barring a nap on the grass at the lazy stream or a descent into the depths. To get there, hop on a Pai-bound bus and signal the driver to stop at the cave. Don't pay the full Pai fare; the jaunt costs no more than 10฿.

SOPPONG

Midway between Mae Hong Son and Pai, the miniscule metropolis of **Soppong** provides a scaled-down version of both. While it has fewer services and scintillating sights, less might be more in this case. **Tham Lod Cave** is the main event here, but relaxation and excellent hiking are the real reasons to come.

New Soppong skirts the highway, where the buses stop. Most guest houses are here, on or off the highway. Turning right from the bus station, old Soppong dozes along the road which branches off to the left.

The best accommodations and a beautiful restaurant both fall under the **Kemarin Garden.** Turn right out of the bus station and then take another right. Bungalows with private bath and balconies with town views run 80฿ for a single, 100฿ for a double. *Sans* private bath, singles fetch 50฿, doubles 60฿. Owner, Udom, doubles as a fantastic chef and triples as the best source of information on Soppong. He'll even provide you with a map, flashlight, and letter of introduction to the hill-tribes if you want to head out on your own. You pay the hill-tribe headman directly for your accommodations and food. Udom doesn't get a cut. If you want to check other options, there are a handful of guest houses near the bus station with bungalows running from 50-100฿.

Buses to: **Mae Hong Son** (8:30, 10am, 2, 4, and 5pm, 2hr.) and **Pai** (9, 10:30am, noon, 2:30, 4 and 5:30pm, 1-½hr.). All run on "Thai Time" (give or take 10min), and all but the last two, which may not run during low season, continue to Chiang Mai (6hr.).

As an alternate hiking base, Soppong is in the immediate vicinity (10km radius) of several Lisu villages, the concentration increases as you move east from Soppong toward Pai; there are also Karen and Lahu villages nearby. Just as you were thinking that all of those opium stories were a thing of the past, you run into Sunny's treks out of **Jungle House** (turn left out of the bus station; it's about 200m on your left). *Let's Go* does not recommend experimentation. Read the letters and live vicariously. North of town, a laterite road leads to **Tham Lod** 8km away, and beyond it to a Karen village. A river runs through Tham Lod; though getting wet is unavoidable, the cave is interesting to explore. Prehistoric remains have been found among its colorful stalagmites and stalactites. Avoid renting the kerosene lamps which are not only expensive (100฿), but harsh on the cave environment. Instead, bring your own flashlight or try to get a loaner from your guest house. To get to the cave, hunt up a rare songthaew from the bus station (20฿), or catch a motorbike taxi (30฿). Alternately, make use of your bi-pedal power and walk. It's 1-½hr. straight down the road from old Soppong.

■■■ PAI

Pai has somehow managed to weather the blows of an immense annual load of tourists and a megalomaniac associate editor exceptionally well. Its charm derives from its combination of high-country quiet and a booming tourist industry that has so far managed not to be too intrusive. The surrounding nature gushes with hot springs, waterfalls, and the Pai River which courses from the northern mountains. *Farang*, ethnic Thais, and a strong Muslim community contribute to Pai's cultural diversity and editing expertise. Regional day tours pass through KMT, Lisu, Shan, and Lahu villages.

ORIENTATION

Pai is 136km northwest of Chiang Mai and 111km from Mae Hong Son. Hwy. 1095 cuts through town, but Pai is shifted in such a way that much of the traffic is channeled away from the center of town and only skirts the western border formed by **Ketkerang Road.** At Pai's south end, the highway turns east and forms the southern border. The eastern border of Pai is naturally set by the **Pai River,** while the northern border is **Chaisongkhram Road,** more practically known as the road where the bus station is located. To the west, this road leads to the hospital, waterfall and local hill-tribe villages. Within these borders, everything is easily accessible by foot, which is fortunate because there is a noticeable lack of public transportation. **Rungsiyanon Road** leads south from the bus station and crosses the east-west **Ratchadamrong Road** 200m down.

PRACTICAL INFORMATION

Currency Exchange: Krung Thai, on Rungsiyanon Rd. Open Mon.-Fri. 8:30am-3:30pm.

Post Office/Telephones: (tel. 699 208), on Ketkerang Rd. on the southwestern edge of town. International telephone, fax, and telegrams. Open Mon.-Fri. 8:30am-4:30pm, Sat. 8:30-11:30am. **Postal code:** 58130. **Telephone code:** 053.

Buses: Pai Bus Terminal, on Chaisongkhram Rd., just east of the intersection with Rungsiyanon Rd. Because Pai is the center of the universe in this part of the world, buses to **Mae Hong Son, Chiang Mai,** and **Soppong** all leave at the same times: 7, 8:30, 11, and 11:30am; A/C 12:30, 2:30, and 4:30pm. To: **Chiang Mai** (3-½hr., 45฿, A/C 90฿); **Mae Hong Son** (3hr., 42฿, A/C 84฿).

Motorbike Rental: Northern Green, 87 Chaisongkhram Rd. (tel. 699 099). Honda Dreams for 100฿ per day.

Bicycle Rental: Duang Guest House, 5 Rungsiyanon Rd. (tel. 699 101), across from the bus station. Mountain bikes 30฿ per day. For the same price, the gears on the bikes at **Own Home** (see "Food" below) are supposedly better.

Pharmacy: Rungsiyanon Rd., near Ketkerang Rd. Open daily 8:30am-10pm.

Hospital: (tel. 699 031), on Chaisongkhram Rd., about 0.5km west of the bus station.

Ambulance: tel. 699 031.

Police: 72 Rungsiyanon Rd. (tel, 699 217) 0.5km south from the bus station.

Emergency: tel. 191.

ACCOMMODATIONS

Accommodations in Pai, like evidence from celebrity court cases, surface all over town, clustering near the bus station, by the river, and outside the city.

Mountain Blues Huts, 174 Chaisongkhram Rd., an 8-min. walk after turning right from the bus station. Though the lake seems to exist for no other reason than to necessitate bungalows built on stilts, it nonetheless creates a relaxing aesthetic lost on most guest house architects. With a stellar restaurant, pool table, and live acoustic music from 8-10pm every night, you'll never have to leave the property. Mosquito nets and hot water to boot. Bungalows 40฿ for one person, 70฿ for two.

Charlie's House, 9 Rungsiyanon Rd. (tel. 699 039), about 100m from bus station. Pleasant courtyard area. Hot-water showers outside, spartan rooms inside. Sink into your super-soft mattress and let your cares drift out into space. Dorms 40฿. 2-bed singles 50฿. Doubles 80฿. Special lodgings: Romantic House, Sweet House I, and Sweet House II, add private shower, fridge, and bigger bed, respectively.

Pai River Lodge, off Ratchadamrong Rd., near the Pai River. Follow the signs. Set scenically by the river with 2nd-floor sitting area. A microcosm of Pai itself; relax in a shady hut and let the soothing rhythm of the river carry your spirit to meditative nirvana. Mosquito nets and hot water in the cold season. They'll return half your money if you see other groups on their treks. Singles 60฿. Doubles 90฿.

Duang Guest House, 5 Rungsiyanon Rd. (tel. 699 101), across from the bus station. Convenient, clean, friendly, and cheap. Displays a superb wall map showing greater Pai. Mrs. Duang can arrange visits to her kindergarten class—bone up on Barney trivia. Money exchange, laundry facilities, free tea; they even throw a party on Christmas. Dorms 40฿ and 50฿. Singles downstairs 50฿, upstairs 60฿. Doubles 70-100฿. Rooms with private shower 150฿.

FOOD

Although Pai's restaurants dish up perfectly good fare, locals tend to ignore professional efforts in favor of the **night market** munchies along Rungsiyanon Rd.

Own Home Restaurant, (tel. 699 125), on the corner of Rungsiyanon and Ratchadamrong Rd. The most popular with the *farang,* but in this case, with good reason. Outstanding vegetarian menu, both Thai and western. Lasagna 40฿. Homemade brown bread with cheese 20฿. Also hosts a book exchange, predictably pulp-fictionish. Open daily 7:30am-11pm.

Homestyle Restaurant, on Ketkerang Rd., near Chaisongkhram Rd. intersection. Burmese, Thai, and local food. *Tom yam gai* (spicy chicken soup) is tasty at 20฿. Occasional Thai cooking lessons. Open daily for breakfast, lunch, and dinner. May close in the low season.

Thai Yai Restaurant, 12 Rungsiyanon Rd. (tel. 699 093). Thai name for the Shan people. Bread made from whole wheat flour from nearby Shan village. Real coffee and butter. Brown bread with butter and honey 15฿. Peanut butter and banana sandwich 20฿. Carrot and ginger cake 15฿.

La Pet (tel. 699 162), in front of Happy Rabbit. Delicious Isaan dishes. Do you have the, uh, *guts* to try the oxen penis salad (20฿)? Roasted pig chin 20฿. Minced bitter uncooked cow liver 20฿. Better than you might think. Really. May close in the low season.

Chez Swan, 13 Rungsiyanon Rd. (tel. 699 111). Who would have suspected to find such an authentic French transplant right in the middle of Pai. *Quiche Lorraine* 50฿. *Camembert avec du pain* 45฿.

■ AROUND PAI

Wat Phra That Mae Yen takes up residence on a hill complete with a penthouse view of the city. Rent a vehicle or take a very long stroll. Head east on Ratchadamrong Rd. and cross the Pai River. It's visible from the bridge. Cross the Mae Yen River (a veritable stream, actually); soon you'll come to the stairs to the top. It's just 1km to the wat, but negotiating the 360-stair climb may prove more difficult than gazing upon a *lederhosen*-clad David Hasselhoff without incurring severe gastrointestinal disturbance.

Rafting along the Pai River is a staple ingredient of Pai treks. This waterway, the longest (180km) in Mae Hong Son, starts north of town, then turns west below Pai, and back-tracks north through Mae Hong Son, eventually emptying into the Salawin

River on the Burmese border. River trips starting north of Pai usually take only a few hours, but there are multiple-day rafting treks from Pai to Mae Hong Son. The area between the Pai River and Hwy. 1095 is seldom charted on maps, but there is a network of interconnected Karen, Lahu, and especially Lisu villages.

North of Pai, there are also several Lisu, Karen, and Lahu villages; Pai expeditions frequently meander up here for hiking and rafting. Some excursions are done in the Soppong-Mae La Na area, and Pai serves as an alternative stop to Mae Hong Son. The country northeast of Pai is rarely touristed, but it's possible to travel as far as **Ban Pang Luang** near the border, and south from there to **Wiang Haeng,** both sizeable by village standards. Alternatively, this area can be accessed via the more well-trodden roads from **Chiang Dao.** East of Chiang Dao, the area is heavily trekked from Chiang Mai. Whatever the plan, it's easy to pick up multiple maps of the Pai area from guest houses and some restaurants. The information these places offer usually conflicts; the truth lies somewhere in between.

Despite its proximity to trekking areas, Pai doesn't entertain many visitors. Form a group to cut costs in the low season. Most guest houses can arrange daytrips and longer treks. **No Mercy Trekking,** 9/1 Rungsiyanon Rd. (tel. 699 024) goes to the Soppong area on hiking trips, but also has raft and elephant options.

■■■ THA TON

Situated 220km north of Chiang Mai, Tha Ton is a departure point for boat trips down the Kok river to Chiang Rai. The sleepy town still seems a bit surprised by its popularity, but local capitalists provide services to accommodate the influx of tourism. The town, however, remains very hushed, interrupted only by boat traffic. Trekking opportunities and the Lisu, Karen, Lahu, Akha, and Yao villages nearby are missed by most *farang* who rush off to Chiang Rai.

Orientation and Practical Information Buses leave for Chiang Mai from the lot on the northern side of the bridge (6:25, 8, 9:25, 11:30am, 1, 2:25, and 3pm). The main road in Tha Ton is **Route 1089,** which continues across the river to Mae Chan, 62km away. Tha Ton is 43km from Mae Salong, 92km from Chiang Rai, and 175km from Chiang Mai. Along the river by the pier, shops sell souvenirs and clothes. A Buddha surveys his domain from a hill-top lookout point.

Long-tailed boats with huge propeller shafts depart for Chiang Rai daily at 12:30pm (3-5hr., 160฿). Along the way, the vessels stop at the villages of Phra That, Ban Mai, Mae Salak, Phatai, Jakue, Kok Noi, Pha Khang, Pha Keau, Hadwauodem, and Ruammit. Chartering a private craft (seats 8) costs 1600฿; the last boat leaves before 3pm (the ride becomes dangerous after dark).

There are no banks or currency exchange booths, but **Tha Ton Tour** near the pier may exchange a small sum. The **post office** is on the main road near Thip's Traveler's House but it deals only in very basic postcard and letter service. Open Mon.-Fri. 8am-4:30pm, Sat. 8am-noon. There is no overseas telephone. **Postal code**: 50280. **Telephone code**: 053.

Tha Ton Tour rents **motorbikes** for 200฿ per day, and a car with driver for 1000฿ per day. The closest **hospital** is in Mae Ai, 9km south of Tha Ton (tel. 459 036). In case of emergency, call your guest house or the tourist police (tel. 1699) for transportation to the hospital—they're faster than the ambulances. A **tourist police box** is just before the pier. Sign in before leaving Tha Ton so they can keep precise tourist statistics. No phone, but a 24-hr. officer is stationed there.

Accommodations and Food Guest houses and resorts scatter along both sides of the river, but higher-priced quarters reside on the north bank. The few places to eat in town are usually affiliated with the lodgings. **Thip's Traveller's House,** (tel. 459 312) right by the bridge, organizes treks and is the closest to songthaew and bus drop-off points. Private showers are cold and common ones are hot; elevated "King's throne" squatters suit you up royally (singles 80฿, doubles

100฿). The adjoining restaurant is a small-time hangout on weekends. Open daily 7am-9pm. **Chankasem Guest House,** by the river past the pier, answers plenty of questions and arranges rafting trips. Glow-in-the-dark switches in downstairs rooms compensate for lack of natural lighting (with cold showers singles 80฿, doubles 100฿; common hot shower costs 10฿). Upstairs, some 200฿ rooms come with hot showers, bookshelves, sinks, and big bathrooms (and even have a **map** of the Golden Triangle for 20฿). The restaurant serves basic sustenance and is right on the water. Open daily 7am-9pm. **Apple Guest House** (tel. 459 315), has new bamboo rooms with hot common showers (singles 150฿, doubles with private bath 250-300฿), and serves fair fare. It's right by the river and just a step from departing boats.

Across the river, **Mae Kok River Lodge** (on a mini-lychee and coconut plantation) provides an idyllic setting for a relaxing pre-trip lunch. Study the information about Thai cuisine and meal manners. Isaan dishes 50-75฿. Along the north shore of the river, the restaurant-*cum*-fancy hotel doubles as a reserve where jungle animals are re-acclimated for the wild.

Sights **Wat Tha Ton** showcases a highly visible Buddha—it's that 12m-tall white colossus sticking out of the hill. **Boat rides** to Chiang Mai are the main town industry. The Mae Kok River originates in the high mountains of the Shan states in Burma, enters Thailand above Tha Ton, and flows 200km to meet the Mekong River in Chiang Saen. In the past, bandits posed a considerable security risk, holding up boats in broad daylight. Armed guards began accompanying the tourist freighters and such Jesse James bravado decreased, but at least one tourist was killed by a sniper, supposedly aiming for the guard. No such incidents, however, have transpired since 1988. See "Orientation" for boat info.

Rafting up and down the length of the Kok gives you a moving base for exploring riverside hill-tribe villages. Trips usually last two to three days (400฿ per person, including meals and sleeping arrangements). In Tha Ton, contact Chankasem Guest House, Tha Ton Tour, or Thip's Traveller's House. Mae Salak, Phatai, and Ruammit are popular stops that can also be easily reached via the public boat. **Mae Salak,** with a large Lahu population, is the biggest village along the way and is the starting point for journeys south into the Wawi area, with its numerous Lahu, Lisu, Hmong, Akha, Karen, and Yao hill-tribe villages, waterfalls, and hot springs. **Phatai** is a Black Lahu village on the north bank and **Ruammit,** near Chiang Rai, is heavily touristed. Rafters at the end of their trips and tour groups at the beginning of shopping sprees gather here to enjoy the guest houses, elephant riding, and the nearby Temple Cave.

Some travelers favor road trips to **Mae Salong** from Tha Ton, lured by the well-conditioned pavement and exceptional scenery. Songthaews depart regularly (7am-3pm, 1hr., 50฿) from near the police box. Make sure the songthaew doesn't head south, since the ones to Fang look the same (yellow). Go in the morning—in the afternoon, songthaews only go about two-thirds of the way to the junction of the road leading to Mae Salong and the road to Mae Chan (35฿). If you get stranded here, there are two options: some spend 100฿ to enlist another songthaew's services, while others hop into the back of a passing (and consenting) pick-up truck. If you want to go to **Mae Chan** from Tha Ton, stop at this junction and change songthaews—this is where Chiang Mai and Chiang Rai songthaews meet, and they seldom penetrate each other's provinces. The fare is around 60฿, and there are more rides in the morning. It is also possible to rent motorbikes in Tha Ton, or in Chiang Rai via Mae Chan.

Along the route to Mae Salong, overnight stays are possible at **Lota's Guest House** in a **Lisu village.** Just mention "Lisu," to the songthaew driver and you'll be dropped off about 1km away from the inn. Mention "Karen," and you'll be delivered near the Karen village where beds can be found at **Fanya's Guest House** (a 1-km walk, and very close to the Lisu village).

■■■ CHIANG RAI

Poor Chiang Rai. The provincial capital (pop. 70,000) has always played second fiddle to its southern neighbor of similar appellation. King Mengrai built the city in 1262, using it as command central for three decades before he founded Chiang Mai and left his old pals face-down in the dust.

The city basks in the poppy glow of the Golden Triangle, the 60sq.km convergence of Thailand, Laos, and Burma famous for its opium-producing activities, and serves as a springboard for visiting the area. The guest house-trekking and budget tour scenes here are healthy, but alas, Chiang Mai remains *el número uno* in these (and most other) departments.

ORIENTATION

The **Kok River** flows west to east, forming the town's north border. Accommodations can be found on the two big islands in the river. **Singhaklai Road,** site of the TAT office and guest houses, skirts the river. In the east, this street passes the **King Mengrai Monument** which hails visitors arriving from the airport. The active north sector of town lies between Singhaklai Rd. and **Banphraprakan Road,** 500m south and parallel to it. The town's most helpful landmark, the puny **clock tower** (*haw nariga*), occupies the middle of Banphraprakan Rd. **Jet Yod Road** (with lots of good food) leads south from the clock tower. **Phahonyothin Road** runs parallel, one block to the east (it has the **bus station** and the **night market**).

PRACTICAL INFORMATION

Tourist Office: TAT Office, 448/16 Singhaklai Rd. (tel. 717 433; fax 717 434), just west of Ratanaket Rd. Important border crossing and trekking information. English spoken. Open 8:30am-4:30pm.

Tourist Police: (tel. 717 779), at the TAT. English spoken. Open 24 hrs.

Budget Travel/Trek: Chat House, 3/2 Soi Sangkaew Trirat Rd. (tel. 711 481). Day tours to **Doi Tung, Mae Sai,** and the **Golden Triangle** (600-1200฿ depending on group size). River boats, elephant rides, and longer overnights.

Currency Exchange: Thai Military Bank, 870/12 Phahonyothin Rd. (tel. 715 657), next to the bus station and THAI Airways. Open daily 8:30am-9pm. **Siam Commercial Bank,** 573 Ratanaket Rd., just south of Thanalai Rd. Open 8:30am-3:30pm. **ATM** accepts MC, Visa, Cirrus, and Plus. Open 6am-11pm.

Post Office: 486/1 Mu 15 Uttarakit Rd. (tel. 713 685), 150m straight south of the TAT; 250m north of the clock tower. Open Mon.-Sat. 8:30am-4:30pm, Sun. and public holidays 9am-noon. **Postal code:** 57000.

Telephone: Telecommunications Office (tel. 715 711), Ngam Muang Rd., at the west end of town. Telex, fax, and overseas calls. Open daily 7am-10pm. Several small offices are scattered around town. **Telephone code:** 053.

Airport: Chiang Rai International Airport (tel. 793 048). 9km out of town on Hwy. 110 to Mae Sai. To: **Bangkok** (6 daily) and **Chiang Mai** (2 daily). **THAI Air Office,** 870 Phahonyothin Rd. (tel. 711 179). Open Mon.-Fri. 8am-5pm, Sat. 8am-noon.

Buses: Chiang Rai Bus Station, Phahonyothin Rd., across from the night market. Regular and A/C buses (tel. 711 224). VIP buses (tel. 711 369). To: **Bangkok** (new route, 21 daily, 7am-7:30pm, 11hr., 189-525฿; old route, 8 daily, 7:30am-8pm, 199฿); **Chiang Mai** (new route, 24 daily, 6am-5:30pm, 3-4hr., 57฿; A/C 102฿; old route via **Lampang,** every 20min., 5:20am-4:30pm, 6hr., 83฿, for Lampang, 5hr., 50฿); **Mae Sai** (every 15min., 6am-6pm, 1-½hr., 17฿); **Chiang Saen** (every 15min., 6am-5pm, 1-½hr., 17฿); **Chiang Khong** (every 45min., 4:45am-5:45pm, 3hr., 31฿); **Nan** (9:30am, 6hr., 104฿); and **Phitsanulok** via **Sukhothai** (5 daily, 6hr., 104฿).

Boats: Longtail boats to Tha Ton leave once a day at 10:30am (170฿) from the pier near Dusit Island.

Local Transportation: Songthaew stand is 50m west of the post office. Within the city, fares should be 2-5฿. 10-30฿ should get you anywhere within a 10-15km radius. Across from the post office is a **samlor/tuk-tuk** stand. From the bus sta-

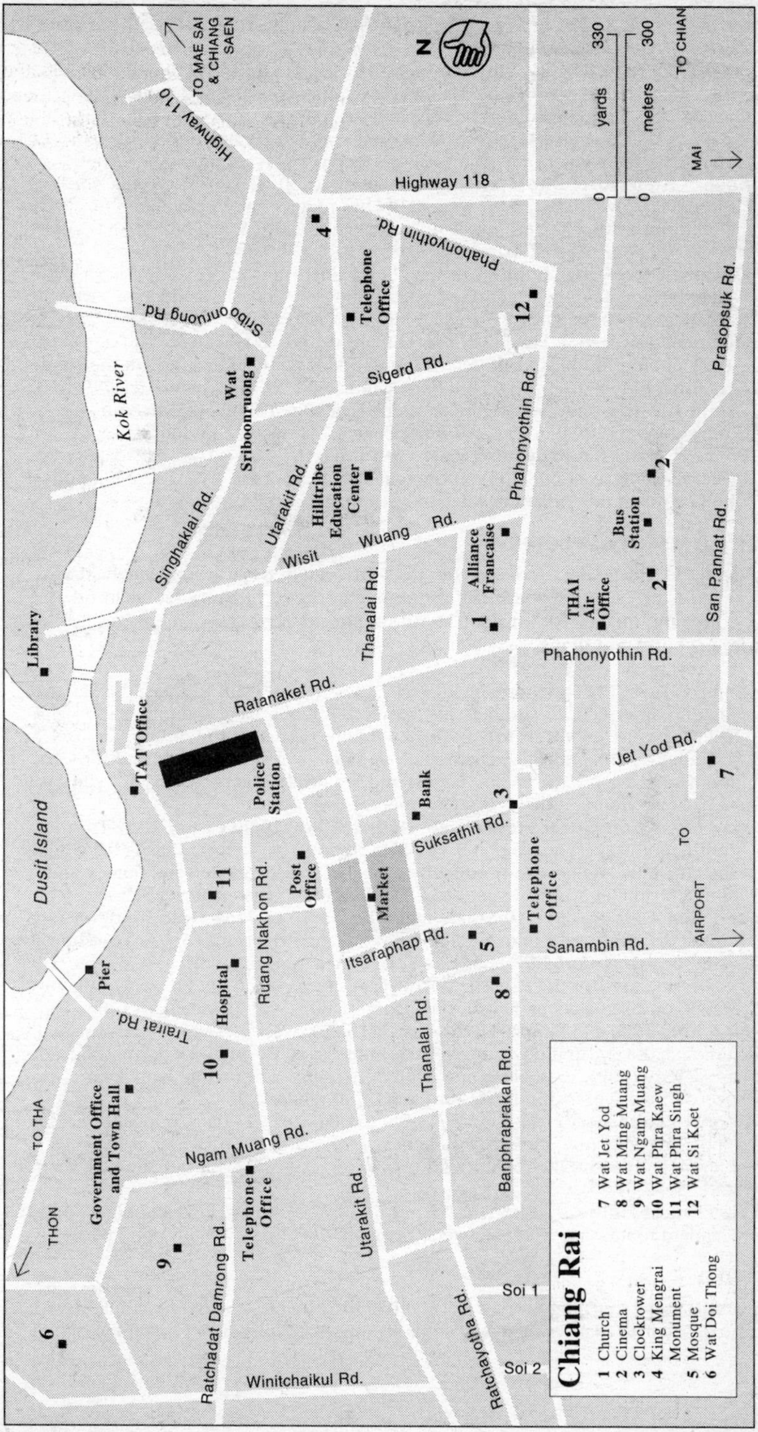
Chiang Rai
1 Church
2 Cinema
3 Clocktower
4 King Mengrai Monument
5 Mosque
6 Wat Doi Thong
7 Wat Jet Yod
8 Wat Ming Muang
9 Wat Ngam Muang
10 Wat Phra Kaew
11 Wat Phra Singh
12 Wat Si Koet
TO MAE SAI & CHIANG SAEN
Highway 110
Highway 118
N
0 yards 330
0 meters 300
TO CHIANG MAI
Phahonyothin Rd.
Sriboonruong Rd.
Telephone Office
Sigerd Rd.
Kok River
Wat Sriboonruong
Singhaklai Rd.
Utarakit Rd.
Hilltribe Education Center
Wisit Wuang Rd.
Alliance Francaise
Bus Station
San Pannat Rd.
Prasopsuk Rd.
Library
Thanalai Rd.
THAI Air Office
Ratanaket Rd.
TAT Office
Police Station
Dusit Island
Bank
Jet Yod Rd.
Suksathit Rd.
Post Office
Market
TO AIRPORT
Ruang Nakhon Rd.
Sanambin Rd.
Itsaraphap Rd.
Pier
Hospital
Trairat Rd.
Banphraprakan Rd.
TO THA THON
Government Office and Town Hall
Ngam Muang Rd.
Ratchadat Damrong Rd.
Soi 1
Soi 2
Ratchayotha Rd.
Winitchaikul Rd.

THAILAND

tion near the center of town, fares anywhere will be 10-20฿. From the airport, expect to pay at least 50฿.

Motorbike Rental: Practically every guest house rents the same bikes for the same prices (150฿ and up). Also try Teepee Hippie Happy (see Entertainment).

Car Rental: Chiang Rai Agency Center, 428/10 Banphraprakan Rd. (tel. 717 274). **P.D. Tour and Car Rental Services,** 834/6 Phahonyothin Rd. (tel. 711 164), near the Wang Come Hotel. A day's jeep rental is around 800฿.

English Bookstore: Pho Thong, 202 Thanalai Rd. (tel. 711 239), 100m north of the clock tower, and 200m west. Also has maps. Open daily 6am-9pm. **D.K Bookhouse** (tel. 752 288), on Banphraprakan Rd. near Sanambin Rd., has guidebooks, dictionaries, and maps. Open daily 10am-9:30pm.

Library: Chiang Rai Public Library, Singhaklai Rd. (tel. 711 673), across the bridge from TAT. Small section of English newspapers and a random assortment of books. Open Mon.-Fri. 8:30am-4:30pm.

Hospital: Overbrook Hospital, 444/3 Singhaklai Rd. (tel. 711 366), 150m west of TAT. **Chiang Rai Hospital,** (tel. 711 300) on Sathan Phayaban Rd., in the southern area of town near Jet Yod Rd. **PDA Clinic,** 620/25 Thanalai Rd. (tel. 719 167), at the Hill-tribe Museum. English-speaking staff. Open Mon.-Fri. 9am-8pm.

Emergency: tel. 1699 or 191. **Ambulance:** tel. 711 366 or 711 300.

Police: Chiang Rai Provincial Police Station (tel. 711 444), on Rattanakhet Rd. Near the Singhaklai Rd. intersection, one block east of the TAT. There is a **police box** on the corner of Rattanakhet and Banphraprakan Rd.

ACCOMMODATIONS

Lodgings in Chiang Rai dwell either in the north end of town around Singhaklai Rd. near the river, or in the south half of town, comprised of Banphraprakan Rd., Jet Yod Rd., and Phahonyothin Rd. The north is residential and quieter, but farther from the buses and shops.

Chian House, 172 Sriboonruang Rd. (tel. 713 388), east from TAT past the Rattanakhet Rd. intersection. Turn left, just past Wat Sriboonruang and follow the signs. 1km from the center of town. The pool here makes all the difference. Yes, a swimming pool and cheap rooms side by side—lion and lamb. Private showers, too, and self-serve ice cream, yogurt and icy drinks. "Is this heaven?" you ask. "No, Chian House." Singles 60-80฿. Doubles 100-150฿.

Mae Hong Son Guest House, 126 Singhaklai Rd., 100m east of TAT. Turn left (north) at the guest house sign. Like Chian House, a haven from Chiang Rai within the city limits. Achieves the effect by means of a shady garden and homey atmosphere. Bathe in private. Singles 60฿. Doubles 80฿. Very small menu.

Ben Guest House, 351/10 Sankhongnoi Rd. (tel. 716 775). Head south on Sanambin Rd., turn right onto Sankhongnoi Rd. then right onto Soi 4. Teak house with clean, comfortable rooms, and hot water. Amazingly friendly owner will constantly toss out the English colloquialisms he's picked up. Free lift to the bus station on your way out. Singles 60฿. Doubles 80฿. With private bath 120฿.

Mae Kok Villa, 445 Singhaklai Rd. (tel. 711 786), west of TAT. Not HI-affiliated, although the registration form gives this impression. Hospital-like dorms, only not as sanitary (40฿). Passable rooms with double bed and private bath 150฿. Gorgeous rooms with bathtub, western toilet, and vanity 190฿.

Boonbundan Guest House, 1005/13 Jet Yod Rd. (tel. 717 040), opposite Wat Jet Yod. Row after row of clean, if impersonal, rooms. Eager-to-please management. Bicycle and motorbike rental. With cold showers 120฿, with hot showers 250฿ and 350฿.

Tip's Guest House, 100 Jet Yod Rd. (tel. 716 672). Close to food and night spots. Standard rooms, hot water showers, and a pot o' coffee 150฿ for 1 or 2 people.

FOOD

Breakfast at the **morning market** just south of the post office and the tuk-tuk/samlor stand or the **fruit market** next to the bus station. Practically all of Chiang Rai's good eating spots are on or south of Banphraprakan Rd. along Jet Yod Rd. and Phahonyothin Rd.

Cabbages and Condoms, 620/25 Thanalai Rd. (tel. 719 167), downstairs from the Hill-Tribe Museum. Raising money and awareness for Meechai Viravaidya's anti-AIDS campaign. C&C also cooks up a mean chicken curry (50฿). Condoms (both "Thai" and *"farang"* styles) for after-dinner entertainment. Open Mon.-Sat. 8am-midnight.

Golden Triangle Restaurant, 590 Phahonyothin Rd. (tel. 711 339), on the section running east to west. Scan the clearly organized Thai food eating guide, and learn about *yams* (salads) and *tom yams* (soups) before you dig in. Tasty *gaeng kiaw wan* (green sweet curry) is 50฿. Open 7am-midnight.

Hawnariga Restaurant, 402/1-2 Banphraprakan Rd. (tel. 711 062). The popular "clock tower" restaurant has moved 200m west. Garden with fish-laden moats. Vegetarian menu on request. Spicy, sour Vietnamese sausage salad 50฿. Open 8am-8pm.

La Cantina, 528/20-21 Banphraprakan Rd. (tel. 716 808). Down the "L"-shaped soi on the corner of Jet Yod Rd. and Banphraprakan Rd. *Primo* Italian food. Get your money's worth out of the **"Giant American Breakfast":** fresh juice, unlimited coffee and tea; unlimited toast or hot rolls with butter and jam; 4 eggs any style; 4 slices of bacon, sausage, or ham; and home-fried potatoes 110฿. Plenty of meaty or veggie pastas. *Spumone di Torrone* for dessert. Open 10am-11pm.

Bierstube, 897/1 Phahonyothin Rd. (tel. 714 195), 200-300m south of Banphraprakan Rd. This beer joint delivers on its German promise. Hearty meat dishes. Not for the vegetarian or the kosher. Pork cutlet 75฿. Sausage 85฿. Knuckles 105฿. Open 9am-midnight.

SIGHTS

Wat Phra Kaew, originally known as Wat Pa Yier, is on the west end of town across the street from Overbrook Hospital. When the *stupa* was struck by lightning in 1434, an **Emerald Buddha** inside was revealed. To commemorate the discovery, the *wat* was renamed Wat Phra Kaew ("Wat of the Crystal Buddha"). Today, the precious figurine sits in Bangkok's Wat Phra Kaew. Farther west is **Wat Ngam Muang,** on top of a hill with the same name. Its *stupa* contains King Mengrai's ashes and relics. Close by these two, 50m west of TAT, **Wat Phra Singh,** dating from the 1400s, is representative of classic Lanna architecture. **Wat Jet Yod,** named for the seven (*jet*) pointed chedi, is down toward the end of Jet Yod Rd., south of all the eateries. Use the side entrance. The area alongside the Wang Come Hotel between Jet Yod and Phahonyothin Rd. is where the rather sparse **night market** murmurs with activity between 6 and 11pm.

Though many trekking companies in Chiang Rai focus on daytrips to the Golden Triangle, the northern forests and many hill-tribe villages await in the vicinity. The TAT office distributes a useful guide to possible trekking itineraries and registered companies as well as the appropriate prices. Many tours follow the river and visit the villages along its banks. The area is dominated by the Lahu, Karen, Yao and Akha tribes. Some companies offer trips into Laos and Burma, even China. Before making that great leap forward, check the company with the TAT and/or Tourist Police. Prices are approximately the same as in Chiang Mai.

The Population & Community Development Association (PDA), 620/25 Thanalai Rd., 150m east of Phahonyothin Rd., offers treks and tours similar to other groups, but you have the advantages of an exceptionally knowledgeable guide who has a relationship with the hill-tribes other than traipsing through with gazing *farang*. Your money goes to the funding of rural development and AIDS education/treatment/prevention programs to boot. They charge standard TAT prices (1600฿ for three days with a group) and show all trekkers a 25-min. slide show about hill tribes prior to departure. If for you choose to trek with someone else, stop by the **Hill-tribe Museum and Handicraft Exhibit** at PDA before striking out. The museum should sensitize visitors to the culture of the hill-tribes and the role that tourists can play in preserving or destroying it. The slide show is well-worth the 50฿ (for those not trekking with them).

ENTERTAINMENT

Most of Chiang Rai's bars at least hint at sleaze. Take shelter from rented love at **Tee pee Hippie Happy Bar,** 542/4 Phahonyothin Rd., south of Banphaprakan Rd. It doubles as an American West decor shop, and hosts an occasional acoustic blues band made up of self-termed "long-haired Thais." Shake some booty at **Where Else** in the Saen Phu Hotel, a crowded dark bar with a sound system entirely too large for its size, on Banphaprakan Rd. and Sanambin Rd. (tel. 717 300). When Thais want to break loose, they head to the upscale **Par Club** at the Inn Come Hotel (172/6 Rajbamrung Rd., tel 717 850, southeast of the city center).

The Golden Triangle

For Thais and foreigners alike, the Golden Triangle connotes one thing: opium. Geographically designated as the area where Laos, Burma, and Thailand meet the region's reputation is well-grounded in historical fact. While Thailand has been largely successful in controlling opium production within its borders, politics in the Golden Triangle continue to be dictated by the poppy. Drug money supplies the livelihoods of hundreds of impoverished hill-tribes and is the lifeblood of nearby paramilitary organizations.

Increasingly, a new financial force has entered the *realpolitik* equation—tourism. The poppy fields are all well-hidden, but tour companies still manage to entice bus-loads of tourists here with the mere hint of the Hollywood-esque drug legends. Trekkers are led to villages and convinced that opium smoking is an integral part of tribal culture when it is actually considered as shameful among the young and healthy as it is in the west. The scenic river and majestic views of Burma make the area enticing nevertheless.

■■■ MAE SALONG

There is a lot of talk in the Golden Triangle these days about a land route opening up between Thailand and China. In a sense, though, one has already been pioneered. The village of Mae Salong sits on the western leg of the Golden Triangle, atop a mountain of the same name. Members of the Nationalist Chinese Army (Kuomintang), 93rd Division, who fled China after the 1949 revolution, settled here with their families after being driven by the Burmese military from that country's mountains, where they had initially sought refuge. The few former KMT soldiers still alive in Mae Salong today are *very* old. Regardless, the Chinese identity of the village refuses to dissipate; Thai is taught in schools, but Chinese is the predominant language. Homemade herbal liqueurs made from tree bark and flowers are popular (half a shot a day is standard, taken at night before sleeping) and Chinese medicines and balms, legal and illegal, find their way here.

Orientation and Practical Information Mae Salong can be reached from Tha Ton and Chiang Rai (via Mae Chan and Ban Pasang). In Chiang Rai, take a bus heading east on Singhaklai Rd. (east of Ratanaket Rd.) or at the bus station to Mae Sai (every 15min., 6am-6pm, 1hr., 17฿) and get off 2km past the center of Mae Chan at Ban Pasang and the junction with Route 1130. From there, catch a blue songthaew (1hr., 50฿) to Mae Salong. From Tha Ton, catch a yellow songthaew heading north from the police box (7am-3pm, 1hr., 50฿). Songthaews return to both destinations until 3 or 4pm.

The **main road** through Mae Salong is a continuation of the roads from Tha Ton and Mae Chan. The town is roughly 3km long; the Tha Ton end is marked by the Khumnaiphol ("protect the General") Resort, while the Mae Salong Villa signals the Ban Pasang end. The center of town, **songthaew** central, has some daytime **food**

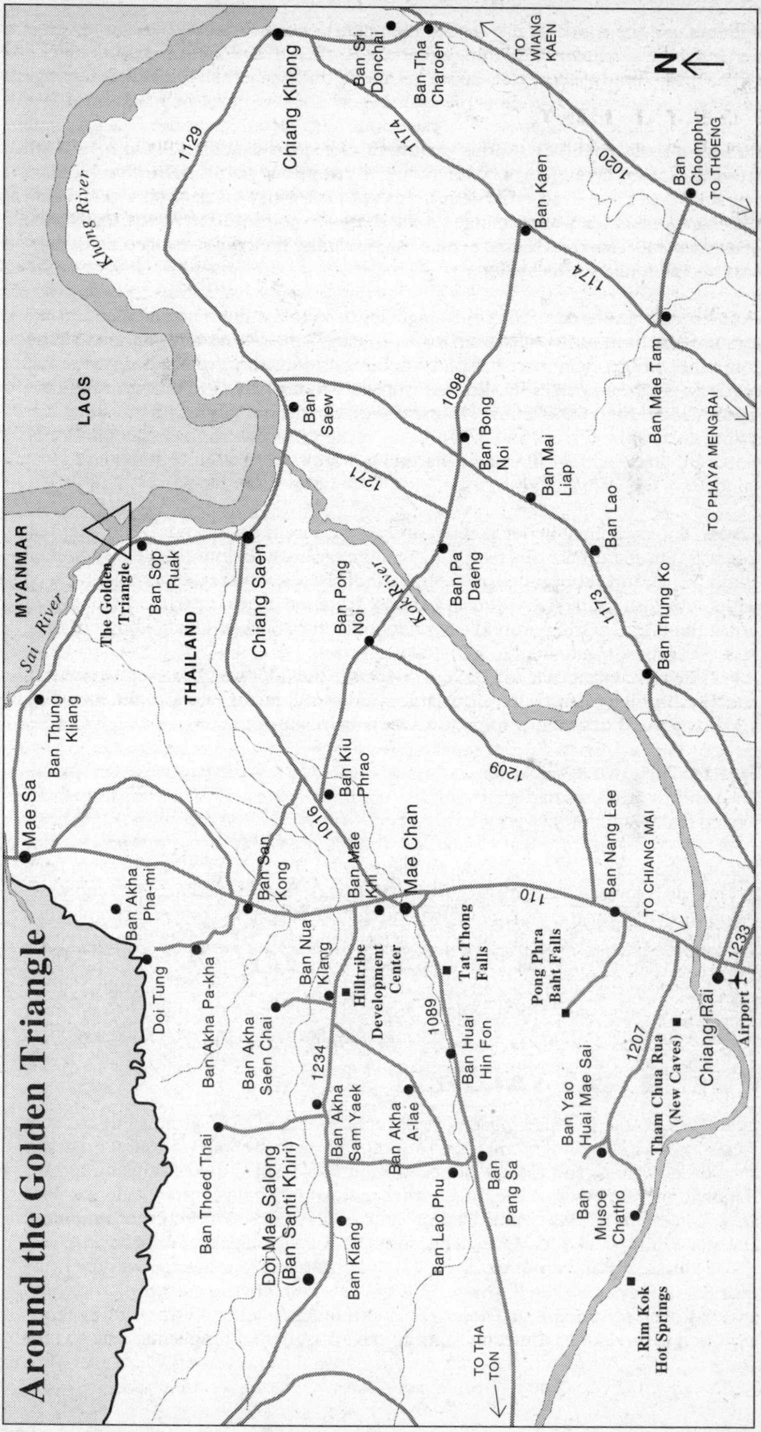
Around the Golden Triangle
N
MYANMAR
LAOS
THAILAND
Sai River
Khong River
Kok River
The Golden Triangle
Ban Sop Ruak
Chiang Saen
Ban Saew
Chiang Khong
Ban Sri Donchai
Ban Tha Charoen
TO WIANG KAEN
Ban Kaen
Ban Chomphu
TO THOENG
Ban Mae Tam
TO PHAYA MENGRAI
Ban Bong Noi
Ban Mai Liap
Ban Lao
Ban Pa Daeng
Ban Pong Noi
Ban Thung Ko
Ban Thung Kliang
Mae Sa
Ban Kiu Phrao
Mae Chan
Ban Mae Khi
Ban San Kong
Ban Akha Pha-mi
Doi Tung
Ban Akha Pa-kha
Ban Nua Klang
Hilltribe Development Center
Tat Thong Falls
Ban Nang Lae
TO CHIANG MAI
Pong Phra Baht Falls
Chiang Rai
Airport
Ban Akha Saen Chai
Ban Thoed Thai
Ban Akha Sam Yaek
Ban Akha A-lae
Ban Huai Hin Fon
Ban Yao Huai Mae Sai
Tham Chua Rua (New Caves)
Doi Mae Salong (Ban Santi Khiri)
Ban Klang
Ban Lao Phu
Ban Pang Sa
Ban Musoe Chatho
Rim Kok Hot Springs
TO THA TON
1129
1174
1020
1098
1271
1173
1209
1016
110
1233
1089
1234
1207

vendors and the **mosque,** not far from the guest houses. The Mae Salong Resort is above these, and above everything is the *chedi.*

The Mae Salong Resort (tel. 765 014) above the village may be able to **change money.** The **telephone code** is 053, but overseas calls cannot be made from Mae Salong. The **clinic,** 200m above the Mae Salong Guest House near the Thai flag, handles minor ailments. For serious treatment, the nearest hospital is in Mae Chan (transportation arranged on your own). A couple of part-time **police** have an unmarked spot, but in an **emergency,** try your luck with a local, or go to a resort so they can contact the police in Mae Chan. There are police boxes on the roads from Mae Chan and Tha Ton. Nights in Mae Salong during the cool (Nov.-Feb.) and rainy seasons call for added insulation.

Accommodations From the songthaews, scale the hill. The guest houses are arranged harmoniously, all within 100m of each other. **Gold Dragon,** before the Shin Sane, off the main road, has pleasant bungalows with private hot showers and porches, 200฿. Fireplaces, in the larger upstairs rooms, are comforting in the cold season, 250฿. **Shin Sane Guest House,** just off the main road near the mosque, has sitting areas among trees and a pond—an escape from worn, bare sleeping cells. Concrete chambers with grungy shared bath 50฿ per person. Significantly nicer bungalows with private western facilities, 100฿ per person.

Food Put away the Perrier and sip on *tsa,* the locally produced Yunnanese tea, instead. Ginseng drinks *(ginseng juo)* will energize you before the next mountain climb or daunting shopping foray. Street shops stock whiskey and vodka brewed with herbs (ask for *woh yao juo* and choose from red, black, or white varieties). As usual, the prime grazing ground can be found at the **market.** Quaff a bowl of *meeghun,* a Chinese white noodle soup (6฿).

F-1 Minirestaurant (tel. 765 035), is on the second floor near the songthaew stop. A bit of a hospital cafeteria look, but large windows allow for a view of the surrounding mountains. Fried yellow tofu, 30฿. Open daily 8am-10pm.

Sights The town is a sight for wat-weary eyes—witness the tea and coffee plantations and the fruit orchards cresting the mountain. (Imagine what this must have looked like when poppies grew everywhere—or see *The Wizard of Oz.*)

As you come up from Ban Pasang, the three most visible structures on Doi Mae Salong are a radio tower, a pagoda, and a mosque. The dozen Chinese Muslim families in Mae Salong built their place of worship with Iranian funding. Each morning, the *mullah* mounts the minaret to give the call for a pre-dawn prayer, accompanied by a chorus of roosters and howling dogs. Hill-tribes in the area include the Akha, Lahu, and Lisu, and in smaller numbers, the Hmong and Yao.

From before dawn until about 7am, all ethnicities mingle at the morning market near Mae Salong Guest House. Camera buffs should remember that Akha women, while beautifully outfitted in native regalia, are quite averse to being photographed.

■ NEAR MAE SALONG

In addition to the hill-tribe villages, pockets of Shan and KMT groups line the Burmese border and are interconnected by footpaths. Don't set out on your own in this area; drug dealings and clashes between Khun Sa's Shan United Army and the Wa National Army (as well as the Thai border patrols) make this a potentially perilous area. As recently as 1989, Khun Sa sent some of his troops to the northern slopes of Doi Mae Salong to abduct villagers because of opium smuggling conflicts.

The village of **Ban Hin Taek,** about 15km northeast of Mae Salong, was the headquarters of the Shan United Army and Khun Sa's home in the early 80s. Today the area has been renamed **Ban Thoed Thai** (Thai Independence Village) and is generally open for trekking; Khun Sa claims to have abandoned drug smuggling to concentrate on his political struggle. Check out the situation in advance and go with a knowledgeable guide—the area is not entirely safe.

Opium and Independence

The most notorious insurgent group in Burma is the Shan State, led by Khun Sa, in northeast Burma across from Mae Salong. Khun Sa allegedly funds his people's struggles by trading in opium and other illegal goods. He was captured 1966, only to be released seven years later in a hostage trade. During the 1970s, while still rising to power, he offered to stop producing opium if the US government would compensate him, asserting that it was independence, not drug smuggling that interested him. The offer was ultimately rejected, although Khun Sa has yet to retract it. Since then he has incurred the wrath of the US through drug smuggling. After he escaped from 800 Border Patrol troops in 1981 with a 200-mule caravan loaded with opium, the Thai government slapped a 500,000฿ price tag on his head. Khun Sa responded by offering money for the death of US Drug Enforcement Agency agents. Over a four-month period, eight DEA officials were killed, and Khun Sa was untouched. He may lose out in the end, however. In late 1995, it was rumored that he may be forced to step down as the Shan State's political chief and head of the tens of thousands of Mong Tai Army soldiers. Those plotting the bloodless coup claim that Khun Sa's reputation is obstructing the state's program toward independence.

■■■ MAE SAI

Although a sign still proclaims Mae Sai to be the northernmost point in Thailand, in fact, the Sai River, marking the Burmese border, curves farther upwards as it heads east. The erroneous sign symbolizes the town's efforts to sell itself. While Mae Sai remains one of but two land links with Burma, the area often open to tourists is many figurative miles removed from the true Burma; it is rather a Thai-ilyzed zone neutered by government propaganda operations. Still, beneath all that is false on both sides of the border lies a pair of truly genuine and enjoyable towns.

The border, open to Thais and Burmese for years, was opened to *farang* in October 1992 then closed in March 1995. Border opening and closing is generally determined on the Burmese side. When it is open, tourists can cross into Burma and stay in Thachilek, or travel 167km north to Keng Tung with a tour group. Coming attractions include a land bridge between Keng Tung and the Yunnan province in China, but whether the border will reopen next week or next year is anyone's guess.

ORIENTATION

Mae Sai is 61km from Chiang Rai, 68km from Mae Salong, and 35km from the Golden Triangle. Its centrality makes it a solid alternative to Chiang Rai for exploring the far north. Buses leave from Chiang Rai (every 15min. 6am-6pm, 1-½hr., 18฿) and Chiang Mai (5 daily, 5hr., 71฿; 5 A/C, 4hr., 127฿). From Mae Salong, take a blue songthaew to Ban Pasang, and change there to a green one heading north (10฿), or flag a bus for the same price. Songthaews also run to and from Mae Chan.

The **bus park area** is farther south than you'll want to be. The **border crossing** is 1km ahead, where Hwy. 110 terminates. In town, the highway is called **Phahonyothin Road** and basks in a carnival climate as *farang,* Thais, and Burmese browse, bargain, buy, and beg. **Silamjoi Road** jogs along the river; heading west from the bridge brings you to the vicinity of many guest houses.

PRACTICAL INFORMATION

Budget Travel: K.K. Guest House, 135/3 Silamjoi Rd. (tel. 733 055). Trips to Burma, regional treks, excursions to Doi Tung Sop Ruak. **Anada Travel,** 22 Mu 7 Phahonyothin Rd. (tel. 731 038), 500m from the bridge. Tours to Keng Tung.

Currency Exchange: Several banks on Phahonyothin Rd. **Krung Thai Bank,** 23 Phahonyothin Rd. (tel. 731 624), about 300m from the border, accepts MC and Visa. Open 8:30am-5pm. (Remember to get the US$5 needed to cross the border.)

Immigration Office: Phahonyothin Rd. (tel. 731 288), near the hospital. Open Mon-Fri. 8am-noon and 1-4:30pm. See Near Mae Sai for border regulations.

Post/Telephone Office: Mae Sai Post and Telegraph Office, 68 Phahonyothin Rd. (tel. 731 402), 2km south of the bridge. A long, long walk past the hospital and virtually everything else. Open Mon.-Fri. 8:30am-4:30pm, Sat.-Sun. 9am-noon. **Postal code:** 57130. Fax, telex, calling card, collect, and cash calls through the side door (tel. 731 727). Open 7am-10pm. More convenient are guest house phones and the small **telephone office** beneath the bridge on Silamjoi Rd. Open 8am-10pm. Both charge 50฿ service fee for collect or credit card calls.

Buses: Mae Sai Bus Park, 1km south of the bridge along Phahonyothin Rd. To: **Chiang Rai** (33฿) and **Chiang Mai** (71-127฿) 14 daily, 6am-3:30pm. Several private companies around the bus park offer direct buses to **Bangkok** ranging from 200฿ to 500฿. Most depart early morning or late afternoon.

Songthaews: Leave for **Chiang Saen** via **Sop Ruak** from Thai Farmers Bank (30฿).

Local Transportation: Motorcycle taxis smother Mae Sai, and wear official numbered orange jerseys. Tuk-tuks and samlors too. 10-20฿ for anywhere in the city.

Motorbike Rental: Thong, on Silamjoi Rd., 150m from the bridge. Honda Dreams 150฿ per day. Open 7am-6pm.

Hospital: Mae Sai Hospital (tel. 732 276), off Phahonyothin Rd. at 101 Mu 1 Pomathalat Rd. Turn-off near the Immigration Office, 2km from the bridge, before the post office. Some English spoken. **Ambulance:** tel. 731 300.

Emergency: tel. 731 444 or 733 616.

Police: Mae Sai Police Station, on Phahonyothin Rd. 200m south of the bridge.

ACCOMMODATIONS

Big spenders surrender their gold cards at the Phahonyothin Rd. hotels, located close to the main action. Scenic inns flank Silamjoi Rd. west of the river; the best places are clustered at the end of the road, where the river becomes narrow enough to throw a rock into Burma. Just past these guest houses, the border crosses the river, a fact that is indicated only by the frantic gestures of nearby residents as you approach that invisible line.

Mae Sai Guest House, 688 Wiengpangkam Rd. (tel. 732 021), at the end of Silamjoi Rd. about 1km. On the river and removed from urban jungle, spacious bungalows with back-friendly beds and hot water, in a manicured oasis of lawn and butterfly-attracting flower beds. Staff is a bit militaristic, but at least they take the same attitude toward cleaning. Spend evenings watching bats swoop over the river. Singles 60-70฿. Doubles 100฿, with shower 150-300฿.

Mae Sai Riverside Guest House, 690 Phahonyothin Rd., at the end of Si Lanjoi Rd., just before Mae Sai Guest House. Beautiful, well-appointed rooms with cold shower and a porch overhanging the river. Friendly service and fab fare at the restaurant on premises. Rooms with double bed, 100฿.

Mae Sai Plaza Guest House, 386/3 Silamjoi Rd. (tel. 732 230), about 350m down the river west of the bridge. How this multi-level complex of colorful cottages remains affixed to the steep hillside remains a mystery to even the most astute *Let's Go* researcher. Rooms are a bit rough around the edges; opt for the private bath. All rooms are doubles 80฿, with cold shower 120฿, with hot shower 150฿.

THAILAND

FOOD

Get your vital nutrients at the **night market,** 200m south of the Thai Farmers Bank on the opposite side of Phahonyothin Rd.; it serves traditional Thai food 7pm-10pm. Peek down the sois to catch market activity, then use your nose. Restaurant options are fairly bleak. Try your guest house or head to Mae Sai Riverside.

Jo Jo's, Phahonyothin Rd. (tel. 731 662), just north of the bus stop; big English sign. American breakfasts, Thai curries, and veggie selections. Extraordinary ice cream includes "Jelly Boys" (ice cream heads with jello hats, 25฿). Fried chicken on yellow rice 25฿. Rainbow Parfait 38฿. Open 6am-6pm.

The Border Pub, at the end of Silamjoi Rd. A sedate place to spend an evening hunched over mealtime Mekong. Attentive service. Proximity to guest houses means you won't have to stagger too far to get home. Open noon-1am.

■ NEAR MAE SAI

The best sights are away from the border to the south, easily accessible from the highway. Rented motorbikes are the optimal exploring companions, and allow for unobstructed eyeballing of the mountains as they rear up from the flat valley.

About 5km south of Mae Sai off Hwy. 110 lurks **Tham Luang,** or Great Cave, 2.5km off the highway down a paved road. A well-run park, Tham Luang encompasses the Buddha Cave (a small formation predictably housing a Buddha) and the larger Royal Luang Cave (which is 7km deep). Bring a flashlight or rent a lantern from the park office. Open 6am-6pm.

Three km farther south (8km from Mae Sai), a road unfurls 2km farther west to **Khun Nam Nang Non** (Sleeping Lady Lagoon). The undulating rock formations resemble a reclining female figure. The only sign on the highway faces northbound traffic, so check over your shoulder for the brown English sign. Open 6am-6pm.

The exit to **Tham Plaa** (Fish Cave) lies 1km south (13km from Mae Sai). Fresh water surges through the cave, also called "monkey cave" due to the proliferation of gamboling primates; hold onto your belongings. Bribe them with bananas (5฿).

The first road off their respective access roads connects the cave and **Sao Hin Lake.** A few hundred meters south of the cave, it is an awesome green reservoir surrounded by steep verdant cliffs. Pedal boats are rented here (10฿) and small restaurants broadcast merciless Thai pop. Across the lake and accessible only by boat, the Sao Hin Cave is known for its multi-colored limestone formations.

When the border is open, you can cross from Mae Sai to Thachilek, Burma. The border has been closed since March 1995 with no plans to reopen it.

■■■ CHIANG SAEN

Only the dysfunctional histories of talk-show guests eclipse Chiang Saen's tumultuous past. This small town on the Mekong was founded in 1328 by the grandson of King Mengrai, King Saen Phu, who made it the capital of the Chiang Saen Kingdom; however, scattered ruins provide stone-faced testimony to the existence of pre-11th-century civilization. The city was destroyed again in 1803 by Rama I to save it from Burmese subjugation and the district in distress did not begin to recover until the beginning of this century, when people started to resettle.

More visitors are scheduled for imminent arrival. Plans for regular passenger service along the Mekong between Thailand and China will bring *farang* and Chinese. As the Golden Triangle is being forced to sever its drug connections, the TAT steps up its aggressive efforts to push the region on tourists. During the day, Chiang Saen is extremely sedate, but at night the whole river boardwalk rages deliriously with food vendors, whiskey pit stops, guitar strummers, singers, and occasional dancers.

Orientation From Chiang Mai buses stop in Chiang Saen (6:30am and 2:30pm, 5hr., 73฿; A/C, 8am and 3pm, 130฿) on the way to Sop Ruak. From Chiang Rai, buses go through Mae Chan and Mae Sai (every 15min., 6am-5pm, 1-½hr., 17฿). Songthaews also run to and from Mae Sai until 3pm (30฿). By car or motorbike it's more scenic to head east directly out of Mae Sai. Follow the sign 2km south of the Sai River that indicates Sop Ruak is 35km away. Another, unmarked road has better views. To find it, move south from the bridge/border area; take the first road east after the Thai Farmer's Bank. The road more or less follows the Sai River, through small villages, rice paddies, and around the hills, meeting the marked road for the last 3km. It passes through Sop Ruak first, then it's 11km to Chiang Saen.

The center of town is in the shape of a "T". The top is formed by **Rimkhong Road,** north to south along the **Mekong River.** Across the river to the east is **Laos.** The tail of the "T" is **Phahonyothin Road** which terminates at the river. Most sights and businesses are on Phahonyothin Rd. including the **bus park area** 200m from the river.

Practical Information 300m from the river, **Siam Commercial Bank,** 116 Phahonyothin Rd. (tel. 777 041-3) exchanges currency and has a **24-hr. ATM** that accepts AmEx, Plus, and Cirrus. Open Mon.-Fri. 8:30am-3:30pm. The **Chiang Saen Post and Telegraph Office** (tel. 777 116) is 600m from the river. Open Mon.-Fri. 8:30am-4:30pm, Sat. 9am-noon. **Postal code:** 57150. There are no overseas telephone facilities. **Telephone code:** 053. J.S. Guest House has **bike rentals** 30฿. A nameless shop on the same road (36/1 Soi 1) south of Phahonythin Rd., rents **motorbikes** (108฿ per day). Open 7am-7pm. The **Chiang Saen Hospital** (tel. 777 017) stands 1km from the river. The **police** (tel. 777 111) on the corner of Rimkhong and Phahonyothin Rd., face the market.

Accommodations and Food From the river, turn right before the post office; the **J.S. Guest House** (tel. 777 060) is a few hundred meters away, run by Suree and her Swiss husband. Both speak English. More like crashing in your friend's spare bedroom than a guest house. Rooms 50-100฿.

The **Siam Guest House,** 295 Rimkhong Rd. sits on the river, 300m north from Phahonyothin Rd. Plush garden. Great mosquito netting in otherwise anemic rooms. Free map of the area north of Mae Chan. Fan-less singles 60฿. Equally warm doubles 70฿. Rooms with cold shower 120฿.

On the river, **Chiang Saen Guest House,** at 45 Rimkhong Rd., 22m north of Phahonyothin Rd., has an admirable concern for the environment, wallpapering with "green" editorials. Plain rooms with double bed 50฿, a slightly classier single 70฿, double 90฿. Bungalows with cold shower singles 100฿, doubles 120฿.

Decent Thai dishes and the best atmosphere can be found at riverside restaurants. Try **Sak Thai** south of Phahonyothin (open 8am-11pm) or the **Mekong Riverside** just north (open 8am-10pm).

Sights At the entrance to the city from the Chiang Rai side is the **Chiang Saen National Museum,** a warehouse of artifacts from the Chiang Saen and Lannathai periods, in addition to hill-tribe clothes and tools. Some objects displayed date from the Neolithic period. Ancient ruins on the museum grounds are a taste of sites found in the province. Open Wed.-Sun. 9am-4pm. Admission 10฿.

Next to the museum, a massive 13th-century brick *chedi* dwarfs **Wat Chedi Luang.** Back then it was the tallest Lannathai monument (58m). Today it's so overgrown with shrubbery that it looks like a hill. Off Rimkhong Rd., 3km north of the town entrance, the remains of Chiang Saen gate, is the uninspiring **Wat Chom Kitti.** The hilltop here offers a compelling view of the Mekong River and Laos.

■ NEAR CHIANG SAEN

SOP RUAK

Sop Ruak may be the official name of the village, but this place is better known by its 24-carat pseudonym, the **Golden Triangle (Sam Liam Tongkham).** Here, the narrow Sai River, separating Thailand from Burma, joins the Mekong. The wider Mekong sequesters Burma, Laos, and Thailand from each other; the triangle where the three countries come together is invisible, in the middle of the tributary.

This infamous town ranks with Woodstock '94 and Michael Jackson's *HIStory* as contenders for the Top Ten list of over-hyped, over-priced attractions. Busloads of corpulent, sunburned westerners might be entertaining in their own right, but many prefer to stop only long enough to snap a photo of the rivers. The river is spectacular, but capitalist inclinations have transformed the town into one immense souvenir shop. Relax on a Golden Triangle Boat Ride (300฿) after a night of tossing and turning at Golden Triangle Resort, where rooms fetch 2,000-12,000฿ (uneasy lies the head who must foot the bill). Budgeteers can make a beeline for **PK House** (tel. 784 061) across from the "Golden Triangle" sign. Singles with cold showers are a bargain at 150฿. Doubles with hot showers start at 250฿. The few guest houses by the river have been bulldozed in anticipation of the economic boom expected to hit the region, now named the **Golden Quadrangle** (China has been added). Soon it may be possible to go to China via Thailand by boat; a land route through Mae Sai is being developed as well.

The **House of Opium** (don't get your hopes up) is a poppy museum with exhibits about various stages of production, as well as pipes, scales, and books. No samples are given out, but pipes are sold. (Penalties for using them are stiff—see "Staying safe" on page 282). Open daily 8am-8pm; admission 10฿. If you need moolah to pay for a hookah, the **Thai Farmers Bank** just outside changes money 9am-5pm daily. To reach Sop Ruak from Chiang Saen, go north 11km along the river, easily accomplished on a Mae Sai-bound songthaew from a stand across from the bus stop.

■■■ CHIANG KHONG

The tiny district of Chiang Khong, located on Thailand's northern boundary, has formerly garnered fame only for the *plaa beuk*, giant catfish snared from the depths of the Mekong River. However, the recent opening of the border, allowing non-Thai foreigners to cross the Mekong into Laos and the trading port of Ban Houie Sai, threatens to overshadow the aquatic felines as the main tourist attraction. There are also a number of Hmong and Yao villages nearby, but trek operators have yet to tap into this potential source of income.

Orientation and Practical Information Chiang Khong can be reached by car or motorbike from Chiang Saen—just follow the river. There will be a fork at Ban Saew. Route 1129, on the right, is shorter, but going left is the scenic route along the river, around 15-20km longer. The trip can also be made by boat (1200฿!, 1-½hr.) or by grabbing one of the green songthaews off of Rimkhong Rd., just south of Phahonyothin Rd. They leave whenever it suits the driver's fancy from about 8am to 2pm (40฿, 2-½hr.). From Chiang Rai buses leave every 45min. (4:45am-5:45pm, 3 hr., 31฿). From Chiang Saen, Rte. 1129 terminates at the town's main drag, **Saiklang Road** which runs along the river. Turn right (southeast) to get to everything. Heading southeast, past the town center, Saiklang Rd. turns into Rte. 1020 where the bus stops. Out of the bus station, turn left to get to town. Once you're there, everything is in walking distance.

From the bus stop, heading northwest on Saiklang Rd., the **immigration office** (tel. 791 322) is first up on your right. You'll need to stop here to get a re-entry visa if you intend to go to Laos and return to Thailand for longer than the allotted transit visa. Bring 500฿, two photos, and photocopies of your passport. Next door is the **police station** (tel. 791 437). A few hundred meters farther is **Thai Farmers Bank,** 416 moo 2 Saiklang Rd. (tel. 791 111-3) where you can exchange money or get a cash advance off your MasterCard or Visa. Farther north, past the wat, is the **post office** (tel. 791 325) which also has an **overseas telephone office.** Open Mon.-Fri. 8:30am-4:30pm and Sat. 9am-noon. **Postal code:** 57140. **Telephone code:** 053. At the northwest end of town is **Soi 1** which has the town's two guest houses. **Yooparach Hospital** (tel. 791 206-7) is 2km out of town on Rte. 1020.

Accommodations and Food **Ban Tammila** (tel. 791 350) off Soi 1 which has simple bungalows with mosquito nets and outside, hot showers for 100฿. Nicer bungalows with private showers go for 150-400฿. The friendly owner speaks English and can arrange visas to Laos. Next door is the expensive **Ruan Thai Sopaphan** (tel. 791 023) which has austere rooms with private hot showers and fans for 200-300฿. Bungalows on the river are 500฿. Near the intersection with Rte. 1129, the **Chiang Khong Hotel,** 68 Sai Klang Rd. (tel./fax 791 242) is near the pier and has basic, impersonal rooms with hot showers and fans for 120฿. There are several indistinguishable **noodle and rice shops** along Saiklang Rd. For a better view, dine at one of the guest houses or at one of the riverside restaurants, **Rinan** (open 8am-11pm) and **Rimkhong** (tel. 791 105; open 9am-midnight) between Sois 7 and 9. Nibble fishcakes (70฿) and fried rice (15฿) while gazing at the buildings in Laos.

Sights Relax by the majestic **Mekong River** or head 1km south to Ban Had Klai to catch a glimpse of the *plaa beuk*, the immense freshwater catfish that can weigh up to 300kg (if you're in town during the angling season, late April to early June).

Ban Houie Sai across the river is now an official point of entry to Laos. A visa is simple to obtain. **Ann Tour,** 6/1 moo 8 Saiklang Rd. (tel./fax 791 218) near Soi 1 can arrange a 15-day visa in half a day (2000฿) with just your passport. They also offer car and boat tours. You can take a ferry on your own from the pier north of the intersection with Rte. 1129 for 20฿. From here you can travel across Laos to Vietnam. Inquire at Tammila Guest House for details.

■■■ NAN

Less than 80km from the Laotian border the hills tuck away the charming town of Nan. Formerly called Woranakorn ("excellent city"), the town was founded in the mid-13th century, contemporary with the establishment of Sukhothai. By the next century, Nan was one of the nine provinces of the early Lanna kingdom, and the architectural style of that era is evident in the town's wats and monuments.

During the 1960s and 70s, the region's isolation made it a safe haven for smugglers and the People's Liberation Army of Thailand (PLAT), communist rebels who periodically destroyed roads to keep the government at bay. While the PLAT's struggle failed dismally, their ghosts have nonetheless managed to fend off tourism, the capitalist vanguard, for more than a decade. The surrounding province conceals a myriad of unmarred and spectacular sights. Even the bus trip into Nan is delightful, taking you on a magic carpet ride past small farming communities, lush green forests, and fog-covered mountains.

ORIENTATION

Nan, like its name, is short and sweet. Buses (arriving from the north) arrive at the station on **Ananthaworarittidet Road,** which runs roughly east-west through the center of town. A block to the south is **Mahawong Road,** which leads over the town's bridge and harbors the post office. Two blocks farther south is **Suriyaphong Road.** The **police station,** the **city hall,** and many sights flank this road. Four blocks east of the northern bus station is the **Nan River,** which forms the town's eastern border. One block in, **Sumonthewarat Road** is the town's main street and runs parallel to the river. Parallel and two blocks farther in is **Pha Kong Road. Nora Department store,** a useful point of reference, is on the corner of Ananthaworarittidet Rd. and Sumonthewarat Rd.

PRACTICAL INFORMATION

Travel Agency: Fhu Travel Service, 453/4 Sumonthewarat Rd. (tel. 710 636), 1 block south and across the street from the Dhevaraj Hotel. English-speaking manager leads treks and day tours starting at 1500฿ per person. Open 8am-8pm.

Currency Exchange: Thai Farmers Bank, 434 Sumonthewarat Rd. (tel. 710 248), just north of Mahawong Rd. Open Mon.-Fri. 8:30am-3:30pm.

Post Office/Telephones: GPO, 70 Mahawong Rd. (tel. 710 176). Open Mon.-Fri. 8:30am-4:30pm, Sat.-Sun. and holidays 9am-noon. Overseas telephone and fax on 2nd floor. Open daily 7am-10pm. **Postal code:** 55000. **Telephone code:** 054.

Buses: The bus station (tel. 710 027) is on Ananthaworarittidet Rd. To: **Chiang Mai** via **Lampang** (green bus opposite the station, 7hr.: regular, 8:30, 9, 11am, and

2pm, 83฿; 2nd-class A/C, 10am and 3pm, 115฿; 1st-class A/C, 8am, noon, and 10:30pm, 148฿); **Chiang Rai** (blue bus, 6-7hr.: ordinary, 9am, 97฿; A/C, 9am, 136฿). Government buses to and from **Bangkok, Phitsanulok,** and **Sukhothai** arrive and depart from the station on Kha Luang near the river, 1 block north of Ananthaworarittiket Rd. The old route to Bangkok passes through **Sukhothai;** the new route, through **Phitsanulok.** To **Bangkok:** by new route (VIP, 7 and 8pm, 445฿; 1st-class A/C, 8am, 6:30, 6:45, and 7pm, 289฿; 2nd-class A/C, 7 and 10:15pm, 225฿; regular, 9am, 7:30, 8, and 8:30pm, 180฿); by old route (1st-class A/C, 8:30am and 6pm, 319฿; regular, 8:30am, 5:30, and 6:30pm, 177฿).

Flights: THAI Airways, 34 Mahaphrom Rd. (tel. 710 077). English spoken.

Bicycle/Motorbike Rentals: Overseas, 488 Sumonthewarat Rd. (tel. 710 258). Mountain bikes 50฿ per day, motorbikes 150-200฿ per day. Open 8am-5:30pm.

Swimming: The **Nan Stadium** has a running track, tennis courts (you did bring your racket, didn't you?), an exercise course, and a swimming pool. The pool is open daily 7am-7pm (admission 50฿). Unlike some of Thailand's fetid city rivers, the **Nan River** is also safe for swimming. The park just south of the bridge and the army camp in the north part of town are ideal spots for a dip.

Pharmacy: 345/5 Sumonthewarat Rd. Open 8am-10pm.

Hospital: Nan Provincial Hospital (tel. 710 138), on Sumonthewarat Rd., near the bend 1.5km north of downtown.

Emergency: tel. 191. **Fire:** tel. 199.

Police: (tel. 710 033) on Suriyaphong Rd., opposite City Hall.

ACCOMMODATIONS

Doi Phuka Guest House, 94/5 Sumonthewarat Rd. (tel. 771 442), outside town. Take a samlor from the bus terminal (20฿). Or walk north toward the night market (the 1st left after turning left from the northern bus station), then left at the intersection. A sign directs you up a soi, past the wat on the left. A splendid teak house with authentic decor. Singles 70฿. Doubles 90฿. Free use of bicycles.

Nan Guest House, 57/16 Mahaphrom Rd. (tel. 771 849), a 10-min. walk from the bus station. Turn left onto Ananthaworarittidet Rd. and walk past the municipal market to the 1st major intersection with Pha Kong Rd. Turn right and walk 2 blocks. When you pass Wat Hua Khuang on your right, turn right and follow that road to the THAI Air Office. Go to the end of the soi opposite the office. Trying to find it is half the fun. The other half is reveling in your peaceful, cozy room. Trek and local attractions info on the walls. Singles 60฿. Doubles 80฿. Laundry service.

Wiangtai House, 21/1 Sumonthewarat Rd. (tel. 710 247), off a soi north of the intersection with Ananthaworarittidet Rd. Basic, impersonal rooms with a huge four-post bed and hot water. With shared bath 120฿. With private bath 150฿. Not for those who like to sleep in; check-out 10am.

FOOD

During the day, **produce markets** set up near the bus terminal and in the soi opposite the Dhevaraj Hotel on Sumonthewarat Rd. A passable **night market** convenes at the corner of Ananthaworarittidet Rd. and Pha Kang Rd. **Food vendors** gather along Sumonthewarat Rd. and the sois that branch off it. The stand to the south on Sumonthewarat Rd., where it meets the river, serves stupendous curries over rice and noodles in the afternoon and evening. Nan retires around 10pm but burners of the midnight oil can enjoy company and treats with the Indian man who sells *roti* with jams and sauces (4฿) on Sumonthewarat Rd. near Wat Hua Wiangtai. Riverside restaurants are 1.5km north of town, reachable by songthaews scrambling up and down Sumonthewarat Rd.

Suan Isaan, 2/1 Anantaworarittidet Rd. (tel. 710 761). From the Dhevaraj Hotel, turn left and take the left after Bangkok Bank. It's 100m down the soi. Recommended by locals for its spicy Isaan food. Even waif Kate Moss would *lahp* up the wide range of *yam, yang,* and more (dishes 25฿). English menu. Open 9am-9pm.

Pin Pub Restaurant, 438-440 Sumonthewarat Rd. (tel. 772 640), in the Nan Fah Hotel. One of the town's few nightspots. Live Thai folk music and admirable array of Thai and western dishes 45฿ and up. The specialty is *ho mok ma plaw oun talang* (seafood curry inside a young coconut 55฿). Open 6am-midnight.

Ruen Kaew Restaurant, 1/1 Sumonthewarat Rd. (tel. 710 631), at the north end of town, on the river. Go by songthaew. Caters to tour groups (read: expensive), but exceptional *gai op grawp* (crispy baked chicken) and fish specialty (*plaa shon ruen kaew*). Open 10:30am-10pm. MC, Visa.

Suriya Garden Restaurant, 9 Sumonthewarat Rd. (tel. 710 687), near Ruen Kaew. Overlooks the river. Live music after 7pm. If you haven't been reading enough lately, cuddle up with their nearly 300-item menu. Tongue-peeling curries are not toned down for *farang.* Staff derives gentle amusement from your discomfort. Entrees 40-60฿. Open 11:30am-midnight. MC, Visa.

SIGHTS

Wat Phumin, on Pha Kong Rd., 200m southwest of the police station and city hall, is the 400-year-old jewel of Nan town. The cruciform *wiharn* with heavy teak doors surrounded by flame carvings is the undisputed star of the show. The famous murals depicting the culture of the Lanna people are slightly water-damaged, and preservation efforts ban photography. Down the street from Wat Phumin and across from Wat Phra That Chaeng Kham, is the **Nan National Museum** (open Wed.-Sun. 9am-noon and 1-4pm; admission 10฿). Exhibits on the ethnic groups that inhabit the province feature jewelry, royal regalia, weaponry, and large wax figures in traditional clothing. A second-floor vault encloses a prized black-ivory tusk held up by a wooden goblin. This tusk and the murals at the wat now symbolize the area in the popular imagination. Sneak by the six elephant statues guarding the *chedi* at **Wat Phra That Chang Kham,** across the street from the museum.

Wat Phra That Chae Haeng, the oldest temple in the region, sprawls 2km beyond the Nan River bridge. Nearly 700 years old, the highly revered wat has a bronze-tipped *chedi,* Buddha image, moat, and wall. Water from this canal was used in King Rama IX's (the current king's) wedding ceremony. Equally captivating is the statue of Say Jao Wang Tao Kha Khaong, the first king of old Nan. There's a wooded area perfect for picnics, and a small zoo. Among the animals held captive in pathetically small cages are, inexplicably, chickens.

Southeast of the town, **Wat Pra That Khao Noi** offers sweeping views of the entire valley cradling the town. Head out onto Hwy. 101 to Phrae. Just after the bridge as you leave town, turn right (marked by a green English sign). The wat is 3km further down the road, past Wat Phayawat on the left. To the left, just before the bridge on the way to the shrine, villagers shape bricks by hand—the blocks are scattered everywhere as they bake in the sun.

The **Thai Payap Project** sells Hmong, Yao (Mien), H'tin, and Khmer **handicrafts** from its showrooms on Sumonthewarat Rd. north of the Dhevaraj Hotel. All proceeds help fund community development projects in the surrounding rural areas (open 8:30am-5pm).

THAILAND

■ NEAR NAN

Even accounting for the history of guerilla insurgency, it is astounding that relatively few travelers have glimpsed the mountainous back country of Nan province. Incredibly wealthy in hill-tribe culture and natural scenery, Nan is waiting in the wings for its moment in the package-tour spotlight. Virtually all of Nan is now safe, but a few mines remain buried in the most remote areas. This should not deter anyone; the risks are negligible, but stick to roads or trails when way off the beaten path. There is a greater danger of getting lost in these parts due to the lack of English signs—it may help to have the Thai names of your destination in writing before departing.

Fhu Travel Service, 453/4 Sumonthewarat Rd. (tel. 710 636), one block south and across the street from the Dhevaraj Hotel, leads excellent expeditions around the province. The Fhus speak English and personally guide customers. Day trips and treks start at 1500฿ per person, depending on the number of people in the group. A trek with Mr. Fhu is now the only way to visit the **Mrabi people** (also known as Phi Toong Mang, or Spirit of the Yellow Leaves), a small nomadic tribe.

Doi Phukha National Park monopolizes a huge expanse of Nan province, and is home to the Hmong and Mien who are permitted to live within the park. Dozens of waterfalls and caves remain hidden, waiting to be claimed as a personal haven for those apocalyptic fruitopian moments.

Hop on your Harley (or Suzuki, rather) and take Hwy. 1080 from the northeast corner of the city of Nan (pass an Esso station on the left as you leave town) for 60 beautiful countryside kilometers to **Pua.** In Pua (gas, food), turn left just before the police box, then left again 100m up the road at the English sign for the park. From here, follow the main road and the Thai signs of the same yellow/brown color scheme. The road stretches 47km over a mountain peak through the park to **Ban Bor Kleua.** The drive along this road thrusts you into the chilly mountain air and past some of Thailand's highest and most magnificent mountains. Twenty-five km up the road is the park office which has huts (100฿). Camping in the park is free, but be prepared for freezing temperatures (below 0°C) in the cool season, and penetrating wetness in the rainy season. Songthaews also speed to **Pua** from the local bus station in Nan (20฿); one leaves from the market in Pua in the morning for Ban Bor Kleua and can drop you off at the park office (30฿).

A few km past the park office is the prized **Chomphu Phukha tree** *(Bretschneidera sinensis).* Though it is not the only specimen in the world as locals claim, it is extremely rare. A symbol of the province, the tree blossoms once a year in February, when hordes of Thais come to see it. A few hundred meters past the tree stands a grove of "ancient" palm trees. These distinctive trees, which look more like giant ferns, are relics of Jurassic National Park. From here it is only a few km to the road's highest point and the long, winding descent into Ban Bor Kleua, which features much-lionized salt wells. Turn left off the highway and north from Ban Bor Kleua, however, and a road leads to **Ban Supan,** 6km away. After crossing the bridge just before the village, turn right onto a dirt road to reach the **Supan Waterfall,** off the road to the right and marked by a red Thai sign and a small English one. The gazebo marks the spot where a trail leads to all three levels of the falls. While the few hundred meter journey requires bushwhacking and numerous river crossings, the secluded upper falls are worth the adventurer's efforts.

You can loop back from Ban Bor Kleua. Head south to Ban Phak Heuak, then west on Hwy. 1081. Swerve south after Ban Huai Lek Lai (the hilly route) or just before Ban Nam Yao (the flat route). Turn right onto road 1225 from either, then left onto 1169, which heads south to Nan.

Diary of a Researcher-Writer's Trek with Mr. T: Day 3

Eggs for breakfast every morning. I'll die of a cholesterol heart attack by the end of this trip. The trek was much better today. Proper path through proper jungle. Crossed a crystal clear river to get to the village. We seemed to have little impact on the villagers. They went on with everyday life while we sat at the head person's home and had dinner. Cute children taught us string tricks around citronella candles. Slept in a teak/bamboo hut on stilts. Didn't sleep for shit. Roosters at 5:30am again. Mountains engulfed in mist surround us. Quite a beautiful town. (For the exciting conclusion to this journey, please turn to page 435)

THAILAND

■■■ LAMPANG

Lampang (pop. 50,000) is one of the North's oldest settlements, inhabited as far back as the 7th century, during the Dvaravati period. The horse-drawn carriage is the symbol of this community; colorful, flower-bedecked carriages still clip-clop through the town's streets, bearing starry-eyed local couples and Thai tourists. Only 100km from Chiang Mai, Lampang has always played underdog to its larger, better-known neighbor. Every dog has its day, though, and Lampang is getting the last laugh as its slowly developing tourist facilities have begun to lure overflow and through-traffic from *farang*-saturated Chiang Mai. Though it lacks an abundance of sights and a raging nightlife, Lampang's active market and friendliness are sure to please all but the most cynical.

ORIENTATION

Most major roads radiate from the **clock tower rotary** near the town center. **Boonyawat Road,** which points directly east, will take you past many of the town's hotels, shops, and banks to city hall. In the opposite direction, **Thakhraonoi Road** runs past the Aswin Market. **Suren Road** goes directly to the train station. **Chatchai Road** and **Ban Chiangrai Road** branch out from the station, heading toward the **Wang River** and intersecting **Thipchang Road,** a commercial avenue running parallel to Boonyawat. Across the river, the town turns residential. The bus station, right off **Asia I Highway,** is on **Jantsurin Road** about 2km from the traffic circle. Start at Kim Hotel, about 1km down Boonyawat, to get to less expensive accommodations.

PRACTICAL INFORMATION

Tourist Information: (tel. 218 823) Past all the hotels and banks, behind the main city hall building on Boonyawat Rd. They have the maps necessary to find the sights. Open Mon.-Fri. 8:30am-4:30pm.

Currency Exchange: Banks line Boonyawat Rd. Most open Mon.-Fri. 8:30am-3:30pm; **Bangkok Bank,** 36-44 Thipchang Rd. (tel. 228 135) has an **ATM** that accepts AmEx, Visa, and Plus.

Post Office/Telephones: GPO (tel. 224 069) is on Thipchang Rd. Follow Boonyawat past all the hotels to the city hall; turn left on Praisanee. Open Mon.-Fri. 8:30am-4:30pm, Sat.-Sun. and holidays 9am-noon. **Overseas calling and fax.** Open daily 8am-8pm. **Postal code:** 52000. **Telephone code:** 054.

Airport: (tel. 226 258), on Sanambin Rd. **THAI Airways,** 314 Sanambin Rd. (tel. 217 078). Open daily 8am-5pm. Daily flights to and from **Bangkok** via **Phitsanulok,** 1395฿.

Trains: Lampang Railroad Station (tel. 211 024), on Prasanmaitri Rd., 2km out of town. Songthaews run there frequently. A regular stop on the Bangkok-Chiang Mai line; 6 trains to **Bangkok** (8-12hr. depending on service, 3rd-class 106฿) and **Chiang Mai.**

Buses: (tel. 227 410). Station is off Asia 1 Highway, several km out of town. Go by songthaew (10฿). Avoid samlors, who will charge up to 50฿. Buses running the Nan-Phrae-Denchai-Lampang-Lamphun-Chiang Mai route come through town 9 times daily in both directions. Goes to **Nakhon Ratchasima** (7 daily) and **Bangkok** (10 daily). Private lines and through-buses for Bangkok and points along the way are also available.

Local Transportation: Blue songthaews go to the "Rop Wiang" line (around the circle), will take you anywhere in town for 10฿. **Horse-drawn carts** gather near the entrance to city hall, and offer tours (short trip 50฿, circuit of town 80฿).

Car Rental: 359/21-22 Chatchai Rd. (tel. 217 682), about 1-½km from the clock tower rotary. Covered jeeps 1000฿ per day, driver 200฿ extra. Arrange through No. 4 Guest House, and you may be able to arrange a discount. Open 8am-10pm.

Hospital: Lampang Provincial Hospital (tel 217 045), on Phahonyothin Rd.

Police: (tel 217 108), on Boonyawat Rd.

ACCOMMODATIONS

No. 4 Guest House, 54 Thanon Phamai Rd. (tel. 321 070 or (01) 472 4690), northeast of the town center, across the river. Take a songthaew, or follow Boonyawat almost to its end. Turn left on Thama-O Rd. Cross the bridge and turn left on the next block. It's on your left about halfway down the street. The well-kept teak rooms will appeal to the ascetic. **Sudarut Tour and Travel** on the premises provides tour and information service. The tour to Wat Phra Kaew Don Tao and the Elephant Conservation Center costs only a tad more than if you ventured out on your own (250฿ each, for 5 or more includes transport, admission, and lunch). Near the lively No. 4 Restaurant. Singles 80฿, doubles 120฿.

Riverside Lampang Guest House, 286 Talat Kao Rd. (tel. 227 005). From the Kim Hotel with Wat Suan Dok on your right, walk past the Pin Hotel and the 1st intersection. At the T-intersection, turn left. On the right side, look for the wooden gate just before the street ends. Pure class. Many of the large, gorgeous rooms have balconies and bathtubs; all have hot showers and western toilets 300฿. Breakfast with the Wang River on the veranda. Laundry service.

9-Mituna Hotel, 285 Boonyawat Rd. (tel. 222 261), 100m from the clock tower. Small, well-furnished rooms. Bathrooms have squatters and hot showers. Singles 160฿, with tub and A/C 330฿. Doubles 220฿, with tub and A/C 380฿. Hotel café open 9am-midnight. Check-out noon.

FOOD

Two fantastic markets gather up near the center of town around 6am and dissolve around 7pm. **Tesaban Market I** sets up across the street from city hall along Praisanee Rd. **Aswin Market** (Tesaban Market 2) is on Thakrownoi Rd. off the town's traffic circle. Follow Boonyawat Rd. to the traffic circle and take the street straight ahead. After you pass the luxury Thip Chang Hotel, walk a little farther and enter through any of the side streets on the left. After 7pm, the **night food stalls** move in and stay until midnight, serving dirt-cheap fried oysters, *roti, sukiyaki,* and everything in between. Look for **Star Heaven,** which sells 19 flavors of *roti.* The blueberry is spectacular.

Ban Chom Wang, 276 Talat Kao Rd. (tel. 222 845), behind a house, on the river. From the Kim Hotel, take Suan Dok Rd. toward the river, past the 1st intersection. Turn left and walk 100m. Look for the Thai sign with the Pepsi logo. Staff dons traditional Thai outfits to serve Isaan dishes. Behold stunning sunsets from the multi-tiered deck overlooking the river. Fried shrimp with garlic and pepper eases crustacean cravings. No English menu. Open 4pm-midnight.

Riverside Restaurant (Ban Rim Nam), 328 Thip Chang Rd. (tel. 221 861). From the Kim Hotel, walk along Suan Dok Rd. in the direction of the Pin Hotel, toward the Wang River. Take the 1st left, and walk about 300m. Alternatively, look for the sign on Boonyawat Rd., which points down an alley, and hang a left. The restaurant is on your right. Wide range of Thai and Euro classics. Speedy service with a loving smile. Pizza (60฿) and *tiramisù* (45฿). Open daily 10am-midnight.

No. 4 Restaurant, 54 Thanon Phamai. Look for the guest house of the same name. Overshadows the accompanying guest house. Indoor and garden dining. Live music after 7pm. Up-and-coming local hangout. Open 5pm-midnight.

Jeu Jao Kao, 1256-1257 Praisanee Rd., across from the post office. Family-run noodle shop is known for its excellent pork noodles. Fastest bowl of soup this side of the Mekong. Open daily 6am-2pm.

SIGHTS

Wat Phra Kaew Don Tao, in the northeast corner of town, in a residential area by the river, housed the Emerald Buddha during the reign of King Anantayot (1436-68). A typical horse-cart tour stop, the wat has a Burmese-style pagoda in front of its *chedi.* The *wiharn* is open to visitors on certain holidays only. Wat open daily 6am-6pm. Admission 10฿. **Wat Si Chum,** on Si Chum Rd. past Phahonyothin Rd., south of town, was the victim of a fire due to an electrical mishap a few years ago. During the early evening, tots frolic in the charred remains next to the *chedi.*

Analyze the **market** conditions. The open-air produce shops, where the atmosphere is galvanized and exciting, are wise investments of your time. Gasping fish and freshly butchered meat may send your sight-seeing appetite plummeting.

■ NEAR LAMPANG

West of Lampang (38km), the **Thai Elephant Conservation Center,** also known as the Young Elephant Training Center, mounts the highway between Chiang Mai and Lampang, a few km outside Thung Kwian Forest. Elephants begin their training here when they are five years old, and continue with one master until they are 67, when they can legally retire, and are returned to the wild. Exhibitions show them walking in procession, carrying teak logs, and *sawasdee*-ing the crowd (daily at 9:30, 11am, and 2:30pm). Admission is 50฿; a bundle of sugar cane to feed the elephants costs 10฿ more. For an extra 100฿, you can take a 30-minute elephant-back trip into the surrounding forest; 200฿ for an hour. During peak season, the shows are held 0.5km from the highway. At all other times, the show moves to the school's main grounds. To reach the elephants, take a Chiang Mai bus and ask to be let off at the center. Catch a bus back along the highway.

The **Thung Kwian Forest Market** (open 5am-4pm), a few km down the road from the elephant training ground, sells a wide range of forest products. Arrive early for the choicest selection of fried crickets, disemboweled lizards, and cow placenta.

The **Kew Lom Dam** is a popular relaxation spot among Lampang youth. The island with bungalows and a beach in the middle of the reservoir can be reached by boat (50฿). North of the dam, another oft-visited spot, the **Jae Sorn Waterfalls** crash in **Jae Sorn National Park.** The six-tiered cascades are cloaked in lush tropical forest. Camping is permitted (8am-5pm, admission to the falls 20฿); food stalls and hot springs make a steamy combination.

A web of **songthaews** and **mini-buses** to these sights queue up in several spots in Lampang. To get to Jae Sorn Falls or any stop along the way, look for the dirt parking lot in the soi off Thip Chang Rd., one block from Bangkok Bank. To Khoka and passing Wat Phra That Lampang Luang (4 daily, 30฿), go to the line next to Oomsin Bank, one block from city hall, and across Boonyawat Rd. from a local clinic. For Kew Lom Dam (15฿), find a songthaew on Phahonyothin Rd. near Krung Thai Bank, across from the vocational school. From city hall head toward the Kodak photo shop and turn left on Phahonyothin Rd.

WAT PHRA THAT LAMPANG LUANG

About 18km southwest of Lampang, in the small town of **Khoka,** is **Wat Phra That Lampang Luang,** one of the North's finest displays of religious architecture. The main compound, surrounded by thick plaster walls, dominates a hill and must be entered through one of the four gates. To the left of the front entrance, stalls sell drinks and trinkets, and a small model of the wat bears English labels.

Through the main gate, the central *wiharn* is a large, open-air, Lanna-style structure, supported by 46 laterite columns. Constructed in 1486 by Muen Kum Reg, a vassal of Chiang Mai and ruler of Lampang, the chapel houses two important Buddha images: Phra Jao Lan Tang, cast in 1563, is enclosed in a golden *mondop* near the rear of the temple; and Phra Jao Tan Jai, who sits behind the *mondop.* The 19th-century wall panels give behind-the-scenes glimpses of court life.

To the right of the main temple, **Wiharn Ton Kaew** was built in 1476 (its excellent condition can be attributed to 1967 renovations), and its neighbor **Wiharn Naamtaem,** dating from 1501, displays murals.

Directly behind the main *wiharn,* the main **chedi** was built in 1449 by Chao Haan Sri Tue Thong, but was reconfigured into its present form in 1496 by Chao Haan Sri. Buddha's hair and ashes from the right side of his forehead and his neck are stashed here. The structure is 24m wide and 45m high, and is made from brass-coated bricks and copper plates. The base is scarred by a bullet hole left by a Burmese soldier in 1739, during the occupation of the Lanna region.

The 700-year-old Buddha image inside **Phra Phuttha Wiharn** looks mighty spry for his age. Behind that structure, in the small white building named **Haw Phra Phutthabat** (1149), is a replica of Buddha's footprint. The **sacred tree** growing near the bells is believed to have sprouted from a pole a local used to carry offerings to Lord Buddha. Beyond the back wall of the compound, a lackluster shrine actually showcases the temple's most valuable Buddha image, a jade (erroneously called emerald) Buddha from the Chiang Saen period (1057-1757 AD). Legend relates that the jade was found in a melon by a local woman named Suchada. She consulted an abbot who decided that it should be sculpted into a Buddha image. Less pious members of the community spread rumors that the abbot was carrying on un-monklike relations with Suchada. For this, she was beheaded. In her death she was vindicated, because her blood spurted upwards and vanished into the sky. The abbot fled to this *wat* with the image. To the left of the main temple compound, the *wat's* "museum" contains Buddha images, photos of monks, and paintings from years past. Open daily 9am-noon and 1-5pm. Admission 10฿.

■■■ PHITSANULOK

Phitsanulok was once an important satellite of Sukhothai (as Sawng Kaew). Ayutthaya kings trained here to become military leaders and coached their armies to fight the Burmese. King Naresuan the Great and his brother Prince Ekathotsarot were both Philok natives. Since then the city has maintained a military tradition, but has submerged its history in a morass of modernity. From the late 1960s through the early 1980s, the Third Army of Thailand was stationed in Philok to combat the communist rebels in the hills of Nan. The recent Cobra Gold exercises between Thai and American forces took place here, perpetuating the town's military tradition. Friendly and conveniently located, Phitsanulok is a popular stopping point on the way north. Home to one of the world's most fabulous Buddha images and birthplace of the famed "flying vegetable" dish, Phitsanulok merits a day on the itinerary.

ORIENTATION

Roughly shaped like a ladder, the center of Phitsanulok (usually referred to by locals as "Phitlok" or "Philok") is west of the Nan River and is densely clustered between the two legs: **Ekathotsarot Road,** running north-south in front of the train station, and **Phutta Bucha Road,** which streams along the east river bank and contains the night bazaar. A number of important streets, namely **Naresuan Road** (straight out of the station), **Sairuthai Road** (south of the station), and **Phra Ong Dam Road** (north of the station), run perpendicular, forming the rungs. South of the train station (at the TAT office), **Borom Trailokanat Road** runs between the two main ladder legs before veering off into Phutta Bucha Rd. Behind the train station, two major roads run parallel (north-south) to the train tracks: **Wisut Kasat Road** and **Sanambin Road.** Both roads can be reached by crossing the tracks south of the station on Ramesuan Rd. Walking around here can sap vital forces. The youth hostel and folk museum are on this side of the tracks. A postman's nightmare, the building numbers have little order. Use for identification but don't depend on them for direction.

PRACTICAL INFORMATION

Tourist Office: TAT, 209/7-8 Surasi Trade Center, Borom Trailokanat Rd. (tel. 252 742/3; fax 252 742). Turn left out of the train station and follow Ekathotsarot Rd. for 3 blocks. After you pass the S-curve, take the 1st right at Borom Trailokanat Rd. The office is in the middle of the block on the right. Good and necessary maps. Open daily 8:30am-4:30pm.

Tours: Phitsanulok Tour Center, 55/45 Srithammatraipidok (tel. 242 206), near TAT office. Arranges English-language tours. **Car rentals.** Open daily 9am-5pm.

Tourist Police: (tel. 251 179) on Borom Trailokanat Rd., near the TAT.

Currency Exchange: Thai Farmers Bank, 144/1 Borom Trailokanat Rd. (tel. 258 599). Open Mon.-Fri. 8:30am-3:30pm. Many more banks on Naresuan Rd.

Post/Telephone Office: Phutta Bucha Rd., 0.5km north of Naresuan Bridge. Open Mon.-Fri. 8:30am-4:30pm, Sat.-Sun. and holidays 9am-noon. **Overseas calling and fax** next door, open daily 7am-11pm. **Telephone code:** 055.

Buses: Phitsanulok Bus Station, (tel. 242 430) on Phitsanulok-Lomsak Rd. The city is a popular transfer point for those entering and departing the north, northeast, west, and Bangkok. City bus #1 goes between the train and bus stations. To: **Bangkok** (27 daily, 7am-11pm, 5hr., 72฿; A/C 171฿); **Chiang Mai** (every hour, 6:25am-2am, 5-½hr., 67฿; A/C 117฿); **Chiang Rai** (3 daily, 11:10am, 1, and 3:50pm, 6-½hr., 81฿; A/C, 8:30am, 110฿); **Khon Kaen** (every hour, 10am-2pm, 5hr., 76฿; A/C 106฿); **Nakhon Ratchasima** (8 daily, 9:30am-1am, 6hr., 81฿; A/C 146฿); **Loei-Udon Thani** (4 daily, 9am-1:30am, 4-7hr., 104฿; A/C 91฿/164฿);

Sukhothai (every 30 min., 5am-6pm, 1hr., 16฿); **Tak** (every hour, 6:20am-5pm, 3hr., 36฿); and **Mae Sot** (12:30pm, 5hr., 83฿).

Trains: Phitsanulok Train Station, (tel. 258 005) on Ekathotsarot Rd. Most trains on the Bangkok-Chiang Mai route will stop in Philok. To: **Bangkok** (13 daily, 6hr., 3rd-class 69฿) and **Chiang Mai** (6 daily, 7hr., 3rd-class 65฿).

Airport: Phitsanulok Domestic Airport, Sanambin Airport Rd. (tel. 258 029). Flights to Bangkok (920฿) and Chiang Mai (650฿) run at least once per day. **THAI Airways,** 209/26-28 Borom Trailokanat Rd. (tel. 258 020). Near the TAT office. Open daily 8am-5pm.

Local Transportation: A well-marked bus system makes getting around town pretty easy. Bus #1: city bus center on Naresuan Rd. Take a left out of the train station to reach the Philok Bus Station (5฿). Bus #4: city bus center to airport (3฿). Buses stop around 6pm.

Motorbike Rental: Lady Motorcycle Rental, 168/10 Ekathotsarot Rd. Scooters 150฿ per day.

Luggage Storage: at the train station. 24 hrs., 5 ฿ per day up to 5 days.

Hospital: Provincial Hospital, (tel. 258 812) Srithammatraipidok Rd.

ACCOMMODATIONS

Low-priced hotels are scattered around the town center (80-100฿). Those who can't stand such shabby quarters should head farther out to the hostel or fork out the extra dough for a mid-priced hotel.

Phitsanulok Youth Hostel (HI), 38 Sanambin Rd. (tel. 242 060). Take bus #4, which goes to the airport. After the bus crosses the train tracks and turns right onto Sanambin Rd., look for the hostel on the left. Extraordinarily beautiful teak-furnished common area set in an equally exquisite garden. Well-kept rooms are simply furnished. Romantic private rooms have a teak four-post bed and mosquito net. Friendly owner speaks fluent English. HI membership is mandatory, but a one-night stamp can be purchased for 50฿. Six stamps and you're a member. All ages. Dorm 40฿. Singles 90฿. Doubles 120฿. Check-out 11am.

Asia Hotel, 176/1 Ekathotsarot Rd. (tel. 258 378). Take a left from the train station and walk 500m. The hotel is on the left. Innocuous rooms, but all the usual social disadvantages of an impersonal hotel. Clean bathrooms with western toilets. Singles 150฿. Doubles 220฿. A/C rooms 350฿-450฿. Check-out noon.

FOOD

Decent Thai cuisine can be had almost anywhere in town. However, three areas of town claim a particularly high food-joint-to-person ratio. The neighborhood around the mosque on **Phra Ong Dam Rd.** is full of Muslim cafés where you can enjoy thick, hot *roti* (5฿). In the evening, the southern section of **Phutta Bucha Rd.** along the river is ablaze with the **night bazaar.** It features the mega-publicized *phak bung loi faa* (floating-in-the-sky morning-glory vine), where your meal is launched into the air and caught on a plate by your waiter. Flanking **the northern half of the river** is a touristy collection of floating restaurants, where for a few extra baht you can dine while cruising up the muddy Nan River.

Sawng Ahung, 26/25 Sanambin Rd. (tel. 251 935), south and across the street from Naresuan University. Look for the pavilion, partially obscured by the bushes. A local favorite for breakfast and lunch. Rice-topped curry soups are popular, as are the excellent desserts. Open 6am-2pm.

Beef Ball Noodle, Sairuthai Rd., near the Chaloen Phon movie theater. Look for the cow. Best and cheapest *guay tiaw luk chin* (noodles with meatballs, 12฿). Open 5pm-midnight.

Fakara, 52/1 Pra Ong Dam Rd., near the mosque. Muslim café run by an English-speaking Pakistani-Thai woman who is related to 300 of the town's 400 Muslims. Beat the heat with arctic A/C and a long, tall *lassi* (10฿). Open 6am-8:30pm.

Pak Boong Hern Fah and **Pak Boong Loi Fah,** Nan Riverside, Phutta Bucha Rd. Look for the flying vegetable trucks. Both branches are owned by the same family and sit together in front of the night bazaar. Another place where they throw the food around before serving it; consider the costumed participants live entertainment and enjoy the land-bound version for 30฿ less. Open daily 7pm-midnight.

SIGHTS

A gorgeous Buddha image preens in **Wat Phra Si Ratana Mahathat** (Wat Yai). The spectacular Phra Buddha Chinnarat (Victorious King) was cast in 1557 during the reign of Sukhothai's King Mahatammaracha. Encircled by a golden flame-dragon halo, it is one of the most duplicated of all Buddha images, and can be seen glimmering far outside the mother of pearl trimmed doors of the *wiharn*. Open 7am-5pm. Appropriate dress required. Part of the temple has been turned into a small museum. Open Wed.-Sun. 9am-4pm; admission 10฿. The red #5 city bus which leaves every 10 minutes from the city bus terminal halts at Wat Yai (3฿).

Near the base of the river are **Wat Ratburana** and **Wat Nang Phraya,** two other temples from the same period, which are pretty, but not nearly as striking as Wat Yai. **Wat Chulamani** is 7km outside of town and can be reached by the green #5 city bus. Built in 1464 by King Borommatrailokanat, who quit his throne to become a monk here, the temple is the oldest in the area.

The **Buranathai Buddha Image Factory,** 20/8 Wisut Kasat Rd. (tel. 259 228), handcrafts bronze Buddhas ranging from small figurines to huge wat-sized behemoths. The factory (open daily 8:30am-5pm; free) is in the backyard of Dr. Thawee's house. He has opened a fabulous **folk museum** across the street; if you only go to two museums, make this one of them. Dr. Thawee's dedication to the preservation of traditional artifacts has yielded one of the most comprehensive records of daily village life. Museum open daily 8:30am-4:30pm; donations accepted.

ENTERTAINMENT

Nightlife in Philok is better than in most small tourist towns. Plenty of pubs and cafés have live music; the requisite karaoke bars and some discotheques are great places to audition your newest pick-up line. Pubs are clustered on the far north end of Borom Trailokanat, near the Pailyn Hotel. If you want an alcohol-free muscle relaxant, go to **Bualang Thai Traditional Massage,** 57/59-60 Phra Ong Dam Rd. (tel. 259 235). The Wat Poh method (perfectly legit) is practiced here for 100฿ per hour. Make funny faces at the shark in the lobby tank. Open daily 11am-1am.

Folkway Pub, 20/2 Sanambin Rd. (tel. 21 120), across from Naresuan University, near the youth hostel. Students pack into this tiny restaurant/pub to listen to live performers croon western pop in incomprehensible English. Play "name that tune" all night. Open 7pm-1am.

Chopin City Steak House and Pub, 33 Borom Trailokanat Rd. (tel. 244 086), north from the city center, past Pailyn Hotel. Mellow atmosphere to relax with a Singha and a 180฿ peppered steak at the keyboard/bar. Open 7:30pm-1:30am.

DJ Complex, 214/21 Borom Trailokanat Rd. (tel. 243 546). Head south, on the other end of town from other clubs. A favorite among local teens—there's often a line out front. Black-clad kids dance and flirt under the watchful gaze of video screens. Karaoke bar upstairs. Open daily 8pm-3am.

Studio 54, 38 Borom Trailokanat Rd. (tel. 252 411), in the Pailyn Hotel basement. Classy disco with dark corners and private tables. Cover 80฿, includes 1 drink. Open daily 9pm-2am. Come after 11pm.

■ NEAR PHITSANULOK: PHU HIN RONG KHLA

The area surrounding Phitsanulok was once the sight of frequent clashes between the Thai army and the military branch of the Communist Party of Thailand, the **People's Liberation Army of Thailand (PLAT).** From 1967 to 1982, PLAT was able to survive in the hills, thick forests, and strange rock formations of the countryside.

Phu Hin Rong Khla, 123km from town and 30km from the Laotian border, was the Communists' headquarters and training ground, and the town filled with recruits after the bloody crackdown on student demonstrators in Bangkok in 1976. Unable to dislodge the Communists with the combined strength of the army, air force, navy, and national guard, the government finally struck a decisive blow by offering amnesty to all students who joined the movement after 1976. The government over-ran the area in 1982 and turned it into a national park. A war monument was erected on **Khao Kur,** a hill 100km from town and the site of the army artillery base. The road to Khao Kur is a knock-out; Hwy. 12 whisks you past rice paddies, teak forests, and gently rolling hills. Drop by TAT to pick up a map. From Phitsanulok, buses (to Kakhon Thai) leave every hour 6am-4pm. From there catch a songthaew to the park or rent a scooter for the day to see it all. You can also book **bungalows** rented out by the Forestry Department for a night in Phu Hin Rong Khla. For more information contact the Forestry Department in Bangkok (tel. (02) 579 0529) or Golden House Tour Co. in Phitsanulok (tel. 259 973).

■■■ SUKHOTHAI

In 1238, having just sealed an alliance with the Mon people to form the Lanna Thai ("million Thai rice fields") kingdom, the Thais established a new capital city on fertile land near the Yom River, driving the area's former residents, the Khmers, to the east. Named Sukhothai ("Dawn of Happiness"), this city marked the birth of what is now considered the first Thai nation. Although the era of Sukhothai rule was brief, its former glory is reflected in its art and architecture (now the "classic" Thai style), preserved in spectacular ruins. The famous historical park in the old city is especially breathtaking when the ruins bask in the light of hundreds of floating candles launched during the Loi Krathong Festival in mid-November.

Sukhothai's phenomenal guest houses will make nights pleasurable and days relaxing, while the ruins will fill your imagination with images of life 700 years ago.

ORIENTATION

New Sukhothai city is 12km to the east of the old city (*muang gao*) historical park. The new city is located in an L-shaped elbow of the Yom River. **Charot Withi Thong Road** runs along the Yom River and then makes a sharp turn to cross it at **Praruang Bridge,** in the corner of the "L," before heading out to the old city. **Nikhon Kasem Road** runs along the other leg of the Yom River "L." **Singhawat Road** runs parallel to Nikhon Kasem Rd., one block away from the river, and intersects Charot Withi Thong Rd. at the city's largest intersection, at the corner of the "L," near the Praruang Bridge. **Pravet Nakhon Road** runs parallel to Nikhon Kasem Rd. on the opposite bank of the river. All the guest houses in town provide maps, or stop by Chinawat Hotel and purchase a comprehensive map of the new city, historical park, and Si Satchanalai for 10฿.

PRACTICAL INFORMATION

Currency Exchange: Most banks handle foreign currency and traveler's checks. Open Mon.-Fri. 8:30am-3pm. **Thai Farmers Bank,** BA Charot Withi Thong Rd. (tel. 611 932), at the base of Praruang Bridge. Others are on Singhawat Rd. Look to the rooftops for all the bank logos.

Post/Telephone Office: GPO, 241 Nikhon Kasem Rd. (tel. 611 752), 1km from the bridge. Open Mon.-Fri. 8:30am-noon, 1-4:30pm, Sat.-Sun. 9am-noon. **Postal code:** 64000. **Overseas calls** can be made 7am-10pm. **Telephone code:** 055.

Buses: Government buses along with several private companies cluster in town near the cinema on Prasertpong Rd. Government buses to: **Bangkok** (106฿), and **Chiang Mai** (91฿). Win Tour Agency Ramkhamphaeng Rd. (tel. 611 039) has A/C buses to: **Bangkok** (A/C 10 daily, 5hr., 190฿; VIP 4 daily, 210฿); **Chiang Mai** (4 daily, 6hr., 91฿); and **Phitsanulok** (every 30min., 6am-6pm, 1hr., 14฿). Guest houses have printed schedules. Otherwise, investigate deals in town.

Local Transportation: The new town can be traversed easily by foot. Samlor rides cost 10฿ if you need them. To get to the old city, catch a songthaew (last one at

6pm, 5฿) at the terminal across the bridge, about 100m on your right toward the old city. Win Tours has buses to **Si Satchanalai Historical Park** (20฿).

Bike and Moped Rental: Bikes at the Historical Park go for 20-25฿ per day. Motorbikes are available at Sky Tours, Prasertpong Rd. (tel. 611 175), near the cinema (130฿ per day).

Market: If you cut through the wat at the base of the bridge, Sukhothai's day market greets you with durian, funky fish, and big smiles.

Hospital: (tel. 611 782 or 622 701) is on the road to the old city.

Police: (tel. 611 010), on Nikhon Kasem Rd. Police boxes are at the old Sukhothai bus stop across the bridge and at the 2nd traffic light to the east of the bridge.

ACCOMMODATIONS

New Sukhothai is blessed with an abundance of hotels and excellent guest houses, and the competition keeps prices low. With a little wheeling and dealing, it is even possible to stay cheaply in a luxury hotel, but the guest houses are so good that it almost seems like a waste of time. All listings are within walking distance of the bus station—don't fall prey to the rickshaw drivers. Reasonably priced meals are available at all guest houses.

Ban Thai Guest House, 38 Pravet Nakhon Rd. (tel. 610 163), across the Yom River from the main bus stop. Take a left after the bridge at Thai Farmers Bank and walk about 300m. In between Somprasang and Yupa Guest Houses, Ban Thai is the best of the three by a thin margin. Patio in the well-kept garden overlooks the river. Bungalows with private bath 150, with A/C 300฿. Singles in the refurbished antique house 60฿. Doubles 80฿. Check-out noon. Laundry service.

No. 4 Guest House (B), (tel. 610 165) on Rajithanee Rd. From the bus station head to the wat at the base of the bridge. Exit the wat's compound and out the back gate. Walk through the market stalls along the river and then see a sign for the guest house about 100m on the right. Magnificent teak guest house on the river has large, pillow-strewn common rooms adorned with baskets and straw hats, clean shared bathrooms, and mosquito-netted bedrooms. Your hosts, Sun and Lin, will bend over backwards to make your stay enjoyable. Thai cooking lessons available. Loads of information in the encyclopedic guest book. Scrumptious meals. Singles 60฿. Doubles 80฿. Triples 120฿. Family cabin 350฿. Check-out noon. Laundry service. If it's full, make sure Sun or Lin point you to No. 4 (A).

Somprasong Guest House, 32 Pravet Nakhon Rd. (tel. 611 709), near Ban Thai. Immaculate rooms, quiet atmosphere, and a porch with a view of town. Tidy Thai- and western-style facilities have hot water. Singles 50฿. Doubles with bath 80฿. Triples 120฿. Check-out noon. Fab kitchen fare 20-30฿.

Chinawat Hotel, 1-3 Nikhon Kasem Rd. (tel. 611 385), across the river from Somprasong. From the bus station, take a right and walk along the river, following the signs. Like a tourist center: maps (10฿), luggage storage, money exchange, motorcycle rental (120฿ per day), tickets for tour buses, videos at 7pm nightly, and German and English books for sale or swap. Fan rooms in back are the quietest. All rooms have private baths. Singles 80฿, with A/C 180฿. Doubles 140฿, with A/C and carpet 250฿. Check-out noon. MC, Visa. Some English spoken.

FOOD

The best meals you'll find in town are in your guest house—the public eating scene is rather bleak. The sluggish **night market** (about 5pm-3am) occupies only a thin sliver of street near the local government bus terminal. Furthermore, nearly all the sit-down restaurants (most of which are in the big hotels) are over-priced and serve Thai dishes flavored for wimpy tourists. Outside of the **day market,** along the wall of Wat Ratchanee, a handful of food stalls hawk decent noodles or fried rice (20฿).

Dream Café, 86/1 Singhawat Rd. (tel. 612 081), is past all the banks and across from Bangkok Bank, 2 blocks from the traffic light. Relax in this terribly hip spot amidst antique knick-knacks. The guiding maxim here is "the best coffee is as black as the devil, as hot as hell, pure as a fairy, and fragrant as love." Amen. Cappuccino 45฿. Ten secret formula drinks available as well, guaranteed to cure anything from aches and pains to feeble libido (15฿). Open daily 10am-10pm. A smaller version of Dream Café is on Ramkhamhaeng Rd. next to Win Tours. Open daily 7am-10pm.

SIGHTS

Old Sukhothai Historical Park

The **historical park** lies within the triple-layered walls of the old city, and outside of it, fragments of wats and *chedis* intermingle with current homes, and can be explored along any of the paths branching out from the park's four main gates.

To the left of the park's main entrance, at **Kamphaeng Hak (Broken Wall) Gate,** a **museum** contains, among other things, a knock-off of the stone inscribed by King Ramkhamhaeng in Thai script, his own invention, describing the town of Sukhothai. Also worth checking out are a large white elephant taken from the walls of Wat Chang Rop in Kamphaeng Phet, and a model of a 13-14th century Thai kiln. Museum open 9am-4pm; admission 10฿.

But of course, the museum is just a warm-up bout for the heavyweights inside the old city (open 6am-9pm; admission 20฿, good for the whole day). The grand centerpiece of the town is **Wat Mahathat,** one of the first ruins you'll run into coming from the museum. The main *chedi* here is known for its lotus-bud shape—you'll see it in the background of many TV commercials advertising Thailand.

Nearby **Wat Si Sawai** is an ancient Hindu shrine that was later converted into a Buddhist temple. The three *prangs* are not as large as those at Wat Phra Phai Luang, but they are in better condition. Poke around in the holes at the base of the *stupas* left by archaeological digs.

Just north of Wat Mahathat on an island named **Traphang Traguan,** surrounded by a reflecting pool, is **Wat Sa Si.** The *chedi* is in the Lanka style, and the Buddha in front sits in the Maru Vichai posture. A lovely spot for an early evening picture.

The **bronze statue of King Ramkhamhaeng** sits on a throne called *Phra Thaen Manangkhasila Asana.* His right hand holds a sacred text, while his left is up in a teaching gesture, not subtly flipping the bird. The statue is meant to symbolize the king's love of benevolence, justice, and decisiveness. Citizens would ring the massive bell outside the gate when they wanted the king to settle a dispute.

Farther north, 500m outside of **Sara Luang Gate,** is **Wat Phra Phai Luang,** the second most important wat in the region. Lying on an island encircled by a moat, the ruins have not been renovated to the extent that others in the area have. The magnificent Lopburi-style stupas are the most prominent feature of the site, while the crumbling plaster reliefs of Buddha are just hanging on for dear life. To the west of Wat Phra Phai Luang, you'll come to **Wat Sri Chum,** a square *mondop.* Inside you'll glimpse the massive Buddha sitting serenely as his face seems to drip with mascara streaks. Head 2km back toward New Sukhothai and hang a left at the small green sign leading to **Wat Chang Lom.** The wat has a large Lanka-style *chedi* buttressed by a force of 36 large white elephants. For those who can't navigate the sandy road to Wat Chang Lom, **Wat Sorasek** is within walking distance of the northern gate, and though smaller, is structurally similar.

To get to the historical park, catch a songthaew on the west side of the river (5฿). Once you've traveled the 12km to the park, you can rent a bike for 20-25฿ and tool around. If you want to walk, heck, you can do that too. Bring sunscreen and water.

■ NEAR SUKHOTHAI: SI SATCHANALAI

During the 13th century, along with Phitsanulok and Kamphaeng Phet, **Si Satchanalai** completed the triangle of power and influence surrounding the capital. The city's fortunes waxed during this period, bringing a wealth and sophistication comparable to that of Sukhothai. As the capital waned in the following century, political power went south to Ayutthaya, and the thriving metropolis of Si Satchanalai sunk into anonymity (literally, losing its name).

With the recent and marvelous success of Sukhothai as a tourist attraction, history is repeating itself for the city. The old city continues to rival its former capital in aesthetic appeal. The outlying ruins are diamonds in the rough, yet to be liberated from the jungle soil.

Start at the **Visitors Information Center,** clearly marked by signs from the roads entering the park. The headquarters contains a scale model of the entire area and a comprehensive museum, detailing the history and architectural significance of the important ruins. They have an English brochure with excellent pictures and an incomprehensible map here as well (5฿).

Backtrack to the main road running along the river and turn left. The old city ruins edge the southwest bank of a turn in the Yom River. The entrance is past Don Laew Gate. Go left at the entrance. Just ahead on the right is **Wat Chang Lom,** the city's central wat. According to the ancient inscriptions, King Ramkhamhaeng ordered the temple's construction in 1287 AD; the style was imported from Sri Lanka concurrent with the introduction of the island's brand of Buddhism.

Opposite Wat Chang Lom is **Wat Chedi Chet Thaew,** which features a lotus-shaped *chedi* similar to those found in Sukhothai and a meditating Buddha beneath a flared serpent. The 33 surrounding *chedi* of various styles are said to contain the relics of various Si Satchanalai rulers.

Khao Phanom Phloeng and **Khao Suwan Khiri,** the two hills within the city walls, offer slightly occluded but splendid views of their surroundings. Atop the former is a monastery built on a site originally designated for fire worship. The latter features a Lanka-style *chedi* and better views. A brick path extends from the entrance road at the foot of Khao Phanom Phloeng (the shorter hill closer to the river), spiraling up and over both hills.

Lying 2km east of the park entrance is the town of Chaliang, which was settled in the 10th century. In the center is **Wat Phra Si Ratana Mahathat,** with a Sinhalese-style *chedi* stared down by two sitting Buddha images. A miniature market gathers near the thrilling **suspension footbridge.** Unfortunately, electrical wire surrounds the ruin, frustrating those seeking good camera angles.

Five km in the opposite direction, ruins of ancient kilns are found at **Ban Ko Noi.** The unearthing of 200 kilns here destroyed archaeological misconceptions of ancient Thai economic isolation and technological simplicity. The city's kilns produced advanced celadons for export to countries as far away as what is now the Philippines. Kiln #61 has an adjacent museum, displaying ceramics dating back hundreds of years. Open daily 8am-4:30pm; admission 20฿.

Si Satchanalai is best visited from Sukhothai. **Win Tours** has buses at 6:40, 9, 10, and 11:30am (last bus around 5pm, 1hr., 20฿); a **government bus** leaves at 4:30pm.

Buses deposit you at the highway exit across the river from the park. Bicycles can (and should) be rented here, for 20฿. Luckily for those born to be wild, a **motorbike** is the best transport for seeing Si Satchanalai. From new Sukhothai, take Hwy. 1195 (across the river and preferable to Hwy. 101 on the Sukhothai-side of the river), in the direction of Old Sukhothai. Follow this road 31km to its end, turn left and continue for 1km, then right at the sign. Go 15km up to a sign which directs you left to the park. Follow signs to Si Satchanalai Historical Park (not the Si Satchanalai National Park or Si Satchanalai city which is 11km to the north of the ruins). For an interesting detour, stop and check out the wacky **Wat Tawet** 6km out of new Sukhothai on Hwy. 1195. There's a light-green water tower on the left around the 6km mark; go about 200m more and take a right onto the small paved road.

If you cannot return to Sukhothai, shell out big-city bucks to stay at resort-level "bungalows" just outside the park, or take a songthaew from the bus stop 12km south to Sawankhalok. **Muang Inn Hotel** is at the intersection of Hwy. 101 and Kasemat Rd. near the Win Tours Agency in town (tel. 642 622). All rooms have fan and private bath. Singles 100฿. Doubles 140฿. **Food** is available from stands at Wat Phra Si Ratana Mahathat or restaurants between there and the park entrance.

■■■ KAMPHAENG PHET

In the Sukhothai period, Kamphaeng Phet (a member of the Sukhothai Triad along with Phitsanulok and Si Satchanalai) played an important role in the defense of the Thai empire against the Burmese to the west. Standing high on the banks of the Ping River at an elevation of 976m, the fortified city was supposedly impenetrable—hence its name, Diamond Wall. The town has shrunk considerably since its heyday, and now occupies a strip of riverside property just south of the old city. If ruins are your groove thang, Kamphaeng Phet's award-winning historical park is sure to put a serene-Buddha smile on your face. You might even have all the old temples to yourself because not many *farang* make the bus journey out here. Instead, they zip up to Chiang Mai on the train and miss out entirely.

ORIENTATION

The **bus station** is on the southern side of the Ping River. Once you cross the river, the old town and all the ruins are to the left; the new town is to the right. In the new part of town, the three main roads, **Thesa, Ratchadamnoen,** and **Wichit,** run parallel to the river and are connected by smaller sois. These sois are clearly labeled with numbers which escalate as you head east, away from the traffic circle. You'll find most of the banks and shops on Wichit Rd., farthest away from the river, and the hotels and restaurants on the other two. Ratchadamnoen, the middle road, will take you straight into the old city to the main historical attractions. The **market** is on Thesa between Soi 11 and 13.

PRACTICAL INFORMATION

Tourist office: Tourist Information Center (tel. 713 050), in the folk crafts store on Thesa Rd. across from the market. Not terribly useful, but near the hotels, so pick up a glossy, color brochure. No English spoken. Open daily 8am-8pm.

Currency Exchange: Bangkok Bank, 6 Charoen Suk Rd. (tel. 711 014), on the corner of Ratchadamnoen between Thesa Soi 11 and 12. Open Mon.-Fri. 8:30am-3:30pm. 24-hr. **ATM** accepts VISA.

Post/Telephone Office: GPO, 23 Thesa Rd. (tel. 711 729), 100m from the traffic circle toward the new city. Open Mon.-Fri. 8:30am-4:30pm, Sat.-Sun. and holidays 9am-noon. **Postal code:** 62000. **Overseas phone** and fax are on the second floor. Open daily 7am-10pm. **Telephone code:** 055.

Buses: To: **Tak** (songthaews, 6am-5pm, 1-½hr., 33฿); **Sukhothai** (every hour, 8am-7pm, 1hr., 23฿); **Chiang Mai** (every hour, 6am-3pm, 6hr., 122฿; A/C 280฿); and **Bangkok** (regular 8am-11pm, 87฿; A/C 9am, 3:20, 10, and 11:20pm, 157฿).

Local Transport: Songthaews shuttle regularly from stops along Thesa Rd. in the new city to the bus station, stopping at the traffic circle. Samlors can be hired at the corner there to take you around the monuments for 100฿.

Hospital: 47/1-2 Thesa Rd. (tel. 711 865).

Police: (tel. 711 199) on Thesa Rd.

ACCOMMODATIONS

Cheap, decent places to stay are hard to come by in this town. All of the hotels are in the new section of town, a good place to be in the evening for food and entertainment. Don't come to Kamphaeng Phet expecting to really dig your temporary digs.

Gor Choke Chai Hotel, 7-31 Ratchadamnoen Rd. (tel. 711 247 or 711 531). Actually on Ratchadamnoen Soi 6. From Thesa Rd., take Thesa Soi 12 to the left of the market. Walk through the intersection; look for the red and white sign and the coffee shop on the 1st floor. Excellent location. Clean, freshly painted rooms; majestic western-style potties repose in massive private bathrooms. Check-out noon. One double bed 170฿. Two beds 190฿, with A/C 230฿. Laundry service.

Ratchadamnoen Hotel, 114 Ratchadamnoen Rd. (tel. 711 029 or 711 766), right before the newly constructed Wat Bang. Look for the yellow English sign on your right. The hardwood floors are cared for but that doesn't mean the same attention is paid to the cleanliness of your room. Ask for a towel at the desk. Rooms 100฿, with showers and Thai-style squatter 170฿, with A/C 220฿. Two twin beds 190฿, with A/C 250฿. Check-out noon. Café on the 1st floor stays open until 3am.

FOOD

Every evening, street-side **vendors** set up shop along the low numbered sois off of Wichit Rd. and on Ratchadamneon near the traffic circle. *Khao tom,* fried rice, and various Thai desserts can all be had for under 20฿. Avoid the over-priced, air-conditioned cafés on Thesa Rd. that serve expensive food in meager portions. Sample the fruit, especially the small *kluay khai* (egg banana), a sweet, delicious treat. A festival each year in late September or early October celebrates these tasty finger foods.

Gundad, 84/1 Thesa Rd. (tel. 713 873) between Soi 7 and 9. Look for the black and white sign with a coffee pot and mug, about 200m toward the traffic circle from the Nissan sign. Great A/C place with amusing decorations and English-speaking owner. Antique bottles and dusty books abound. Most dishes 20-60฿, beer 30฿. Menu with pictures. No smoking. Open daily 10am-10pm.

Malai Restaurant, 77/1 Thesa Rd. (tel. 711 630), within walking distance of the Chakungrao Hotel. Head for the old city along Thesa Rd. Look for the shop with the red sign next to the Nissan building. Delicious Isaan dishes (20-30฿). No English. Open daily 7am-9pm.

SIGHTS

Registered since 1991 in UNESCO's World Heritage List for its outstanding historical value, Kamphaeng Phet's **historical park** offers about 40 magnificent, well-preserved wats and *chedis* from the Sukhothai and Ayutthaya periods. These sights rival and perhaps surpass those in Ayutthaya. The park is divided into two sections: the city area inside the walls and within walking distance of the town traffic circle, and the Aranyek area to the northwest of the city's fortifications. One fee of 20฿ permits entrance to both areas.

If you head straight from the traffic circle and then left on Ratchadamnoen Rd., you'll get to the **Historical Park Information Center.** Although no English is spoken here, the wall-size map gives you an idea of the park's enormity. From the information center you can walk to **Wat Phra Kaew.** Centuries of rain and wind have smoothed the features of these brick Buddhas. Conscientious worshippers have piled stones on several headless Buddhas. The hole in the back of one of the larger images was made by treasure hunters looking for riches rumored to have been buried near the heart. The famous Emerald Buddha was kept at this wat from 1375 to 1389. About 100m away is **Wat Phra That,** with a well-preserved *chedi.*

Farther down Ratchadamnoen Rd. is the entrance to the Aranyek area. Ignore the huge green Kamphaeng Phet Historical Park sign, and look for the B&W sign on your left. Less manicured than its neighbor, this section of the park retains more of the original look and feel of the site before the Fine Arts Department got hold of it. The two notable sights here are **Wat Chang Rop,** a monastery surrounded by a herd of trunk-less elephants, (climb to the highest point for a majestic view of the surrounding hills), and **Wat Phra Nan,** near the exit, within whose *wiharn* stand huge pillars made of the largest pieces of laterite stone in the world. The park opens around 6am and closes at dusk (around 6pm). The ideal way to see the Aranyek section is to hire a motorized samlor (100฿ or less depending on your bargaining skills). If you decide to walk, take plenty of water.

The **Kamphaeng Phet National Museum,** behind the historical park information center, houses a tedious display of Buddha images and ceramic pottery collected from the sites. Open Wed.-Sun. 9am-4pm; admission 10฿.

■■■ MAE SOT

People come to Mae Sot expecting border action, mystery, and intrigue. To their surprise, they stumble onto fabulous foliage, friendly folk, and phenomenal bargains instead. Lying 7km from the Burmese border, Mae Sot is one of three trading zones between Thailand and Burma. South of Mae Sot, Um Phang sits barely touched by tourism, offering opportunities for wilderness adventure. The drive from Tak to Mae Sot takes you through splendid mountain scenery and lands you in the middle of *marveloso.*

ORIENTATION

Parallel to **Asia Road** run Mae Sot's two major roads. **Intirakiri Road** has one-way traffic heading east and **Prasatwithi Road** has one-way traffic heading west toward **Moei Market** and the **Burmese border** 7km away. The large **city market** is off Prasatwithi Rd. around Siam Hotel. Mae Sot is small enough to explore by foot.

PRACTICAL INFORMATION

Tourist Information: Stop by **Myawaddy Café** or **West Frontier Restaurant** to pick up guides and rap with owners.

Tourist Police: 738/1 Intirakiri Rd. (tel. 532 960), next to Guest House No.4.

Currency Exchange: Bangkok Bank, 124/8 Prasatwithi Rd. (tel. 531 639) **24-hr. ATM** takes AmEx, PLUS, and Visa. **Thai Farmers Bank,** 94/9 Prasatwithi Rd. (tel. 531 020). Open Mon.-Fri. 8:30am-3:30pm.

Post/Telephone Office: (tel. 531 227), on Intirakiri Rd. Facing the police station, head right. Open Mon.-Fri. 8:30am-4:30pm, Sat.-Sun. 9am-noon. **Postal code:** 63110. **Overseas calls** can be made 8:30am-4:30pm. **Telephone code:** 055.

Airport: 3km to the west of town. **THAI Air** office, 110 Prasatwithi Rd. (tel. 531 730). Open daily 9am-5pm. Shuttle is 20฿. Flights leave Tues., Thurs., Sat., and Sun. to: **Chiang Mai** (5:15pm, 590฿) and **Bangkok** (2:40pm, 1405฿).

Buses: There are 4 bus stations in town. The bus station to and from **Bangkok** (10 buses daily, 6-10hr. depending on class, ordinary 125฿, A/C 224฿, VIP 345฿) is on Asia Rd. next to the Michelin Man sign. To get to town, head right with your back to the station and walk through the white concrete apartment complex and market. Go over the wooden footbridge in the right-hand corner of the market and then follow the road until you reach the police station on your left and Intirakiri Rd., which runs one way to the left. Buses to **Mae Sariang** are actually songthaews which leave from the market area behind the police station (5hr., 150฿). Songthaews to **Um Phang** leave from the southern side of town (4hr., 80฿). To find the bus to Um Phang, walk away from Myawaddy on Prasatwithi Rd. Turn right at the Fiji film store. Just past Haji Yusoof & Sons, you'll see a blue sign with an arrow to your left. Follow it. Orange and white mini-vans to **Tak** leave from the station across from Mae Sod Plaza just off Intirakiri Rd. 1 block west (against traffic) of the police station (1-½hr., 28฿).

Local Transportation: You can walk anywhere in town. To get to **Moei River Market** and the **border,** catch a navy-blue **songthaew** across from Myawaddy Café on Prasatwithi Rd. (last one back at 6pm, 7฿).

Bike Rental: Myawaddy Café rents bikes for 30฿ per day. Guest House No. 4 rents bikes for 25฿ per day.

Trekking Companies: Rather than have a company take you down to Um Phang, consider going down yourself and booking a tour in Um Phang with Mr. T at Trekker Hill. If you want to book in Mae Sot, Mr. Wiboon at B&B House runs **Mae Sot Conservation Tours.** His wife, Boong, is a reporter and is well informed about border events. In 1996, they expect to take trekkers across to Burma. A TAT-approved outfit, Mr. Wiboon is friendly and recognizes Um Phang's need to protect its environment. **Mae Sot Travel Center,** at S&P Guest House (tel. 531 409, in Bangkok 573 7942) has TAT-approved treks to the north or south.

Pharmacy: Mae Sod Siam Pharmacy, 137/1-2 Prasatwithi Rd. at the intersection of Tang Kim Chiang Rd. Open daily 8:30am-8:30pm.

Hospital: 1km south of town (tel. 531 224).

Police: (tel. 191) at the intersection of Tang Kim Chiang and Intirakiri Rd.

ACCOMMODATIONS

Neighborhoods on Intirakiri and Prasatwithi Rd. play host to the majority of Mae Sot's crash pads. Guest houses are relatively inexpensive since proprietors organize treks for their main income, but you'll be "teaked out" by the time you leave.

B&B House, 415/17 Tang Kim Chiang Rd. (tel. 532 818; fax 544 726). At the police station on Intirakiri Rd., head toward the Pim Hut sign. B&B is a few doors beyond. Orderly and hygienic chambers. Hot water flows lavishly in the exceptionally clean, common bathrooms. Dorm 50฿. Private room with 2 single beds 100฿. Mr. and Mrs. Wiboon speak perfect English and are ready to help travelers.

S&P Guest House, 14/21 Asia Rd. (tel. 531 409, in Bangkok 573 7942). From the Bangkok bus terminal, walk west on Asia Rd. for about 10min. You'll see wagon wheels proclaiming the guest house just beyond the radio telecommunications tower on your left. Because this place is a bit out of the way, the owners will come pick you up, and bikes are loaned *gratis.* Meditate in the splendid garden; don't let Asia Rd. traffic intrude on your mantras. Common bathrooms have hot water. Rooms 30฿ per person.

Guest House No. 4, 736 Intirakiri Rd. Facing the police station, head left about 600km. Unwind in the common room with cable TV. Futons in the all-teak dorm room 30฿. Private singles 60฿. Doubles 80฿. Common bathrooms with hot water.

FOOD

Mae Sot's ethnic melting pot ladles out a multicultural stew of culinary delights. Family-run restaurants along Prasatwithi and Intirakiri Rd. serve up Muslim, Thai, and Chinese food, but the **night market** makes for mighty slim pickin's.

West Frontier, 350 Intirakiri Rd. (tel. 533 820). Facing the police station, proceed to your right. Fresh flowers and teak decor hand-carved by the owner adorn the restaurant. Feast on delectable spicy Thai dishes (can be modified upon request). Half-priced coffee happy hour (5฿) until 9am. Open daily 7am-midnight.

Myawaddy Café, 100/22 Prasatwithi Rd. (tel./fax 532 549). Head west (with traffic). On your right, past all the banks. Doi and Roger sell Burmese lacquerware in one half of the shop, and western food in the other. Tastefully decorated place with equally scrumptious food. Nightly western meal—salad, garlic bread, the works (100-180฿). Mornings feature all-you-can-drink coffee 15฿. Open Thurs.-Tues. 7am-9pm. They also have maps of the area and like to give out information. Roger has an extensive library and is happy to exchange or sell his books.

SIGHTS

In Mae Sot town, **people-watching** qualifies as a "sight." You'll spot Chinese, Burmese, Indian, Mon, and *shazam!* even Thai people doing business and simply going about everyday life. This cross-cultural scene extends to the **Moei River market** at the Burmese-Thai border 7km west of town, where you'll find cheap products imported from Burma. Hoist yourself onto a blue songthaew on Prasatwithi Rd. across from the Myawaddy Café (7฿). Open daily from around 8am-6pm. Riding a bike to the market takes you by rice paddies and makes for a pleasant half-day trip.

Between Mae Sot and the town of Tak, is **Lan Sang National Park,** where clear water cascades down gneiss rock steps. From the visitors' center, the first fall may have up to 10,000 visitors a day (in April), but few walk on to the third and most serene fall, Pha Te. The path snakes 8km through dense forests, terminating in Mon, Karen, and Lisu villages. To be an educated observer ask to see the 20-minute slide show before beginning your trip. Bungalows available 150฿; restaurant is open daily from 8:30am-5pm. Take the Tak minibus (28฿) to the entrance. From the Tak-Mae Sot highway, try waiting for a songthaew (30฿) or walk the 3km to the visitors' center, though some visitors have found it easier to just hitch this short stretch. You'll pass the Park Headquarters and camping area (5฿ per night) on your way up. The park is open for day visitors from 8am-4:30pm; admission 5฿, with a vehicle 20฿.

■■■ UM PHANG

Um Phang is a cultural delight waiting to be discovered. The pint-size polis hosted only 500 trekkers last year, compared with the 6000 visitors stomping around Chiang Mai. Statistically speaking, Um Phang gives off good vibrations: the 3000 Mon and Thai people are welcoming and the nature around them is awe-inspiring. A four-hour songthaew ride snakes through rice paddies, corn fields, chili plantations, banana groves, and over 1500m-high peaks, finally landing you 164km south of Mae Sot, only 30km from Burma. Change money before you head here—there are no banks. Mosquitoes and the night chills can be unrelenting; bring insect repellent and some warm clothes. Otherwise, Um Phang does nothing but allow you to do whatever you darn well please.

Orientation and Practical Information Um Phang is small—very small. Two parallel roads make up the main arteries of this mini-metropolis. **Pravesphywan Road** leads you into town, and there is another street to the west of it. Songthaews leave Mae Sot between about 7:30am-4pm to make the four-hour journey (80฿). Most of the songthaews back to Mae Sot leave between 6am-9am (so people can do business in Mae Sot and then return home that night) but a bus will leave at around noon. As you enter town, you'll pass the **post office** on your left (open Mon.-Fri. 8:30am-4:30pm, Sat. 9am-noon; **postal code:** 63170), and then the electrical power center. This generator produces all the electricity for little Um Phang. Taking your first left onto the paved road heading uphill, you'll come to the **morning market** on your left and the **hospital** on your right in about 200m. Back on the main road, the **pharmacy** is open daily 7am-9pm. The **police station** (tel. 561 112) is on the road parallel to Pravesphywan Rd. Turn right down the dirt road past Trekker Hill, then left. There are **no banks** and **no overseas telephone** operators in Um Phang (**telephone code:** 055). Change that *dinero* in Mae Sot!

Accommodations and Food Guest houses in Um Phang are rapidly popping up as locals realize that *farang* are in need of lodging, and that lodgings translate into baht. There isn't much city planning involved in this development, and problems arise for tourists when they try to book a trek with their guest house: either the tour guide speaks no English or the tour company isn't registered with the TAT. The **Trekker Hill** (tel./fax 561 090) company, however, has both bases covered. Mr. Jantawong (Mr. T) has built a wonderful Thai-style teak shelter decked out with futons, mosquito nets, and toilet paper. The dorm goes for 50฿ per person, or you and your mate can shack up in a private mini-bungalow for 100฿. Mr. T's motley troupe of fun-loving guides will escort you through dense jungles, placid hill-tribe villages, and the breathtaking **Tee Lor Su** waterfalls by raft, elephant-back, and on foot. Food and service so fabulous you'll almost feel guilty. (Those with special diets should let it be known in advance.) Bring sturdy footwear (the trek will ruin your sneakers) and an adventurous attitude. If you telephone ahead and join a group you'll save some baht. Mr. T's is open to organizing whatever you need. Look for the Trekker Hill sign as you enter town on the left, just past the power center.

To explore Um Phang's other options, go past Mr. T's on the main street, and take a right at the wat. **Um Phang Guest House** (tel. 561 021) will be first up on your left, with basic rooms and a woefully common wash area for 50฿. Next up is **Um Phang House** (tel. 561 073). Bungalows range from grimy to grand. Ask to see your potential pad first. All go for 100฿ per person with a 300฿ minimum. Farther down the road are more expensive locales for the more fastidious traveler.

Most guest houses will rustle up chow for 25฿, or you can head to an open-air restaurant on the main street. Get there early—proprietors shut down at 10pm.

Sights The buzz of crickets, the hum of the river, the green hills, and the smiles of the townfolk will soothe your soul. If the hills, jungle, and river aren't enough to send your mind a-wandering, then book a trek and take that body on an adventure.

The TAT has made an effort to have trekking companies register with the government. This way, Thailand can keep tabs on trekking companies, ensuring that they adhere to safety and environmental rules, as well as to national hiring practices—Burmese Karens are not allowed to work as guides. As a tourist, support the TAT, even if it means paying a few more baht. Guides are probably too polite to admonish you for littering, but treat Um Phang (and the rest of Thailand) as if it were your own living room—watch where you prop your feet and discard candy wrappers.

Diary of a Researcher-Writer's Trek with Mr. T: Day 4

Elephant ride from hell. Six hours. Cold. Raining. I'm going to get sick. Luckily the Thais think Halls throat drops are candy so they sell them everywhere. Great food continues. Got stuck in Mae Sot with Jason and Mike (the two Americans from Yale) because we ran late. Apparently this happens a lot. Danish people stayed another night at Mr. T's and enjoyed Mrs. T's great cooking, I'm sure.

Oh, and did I mention the parting gifts the guides gave us? These brilliant guides can make *anything* out of bamboo—guns, toilet paper holder, utensils, cups, soups—you name it. They gave us bamboo cups which we excitedly carved with our pocket knives. Mine has the Let's Go logo and says *Let's Go: Southeast Asia 1996* below it, of course!

Northeast Thailand

Thais call it "Isaan," denoting prosperity and vastness. This expansive plateau encompasses about one-third of Thailand's total land mass, supporting an equal proportion of the nation's population. Among Thais, Isaan has a reputation as an economic and cultural backwater. They have it half right.

Isaan *is* one of the country's poorest regions, and the lifestyle remains largely agrarian. The people of this arid country earn their livlihood the old fashioned way, "face to the earth, back to the sky." They dry season is always excruciatingly hot and dusty, with many water shortages, and the rainy season does not always deliver relief. Many towns and villages appear to be devoid of young adults: males leave home to earn more money as tuk-tuk jockeys or construction workers in urban areas, while numerous women are forced into prostitution.

In all other respects, however, this negative attitude is simply a misperception, stemming from differences in history, geography, and culture. In the past, the giant plateau has been isolated geographically from the rest of the Kingdom, and the people have a greater cultural and genealogical kinship with the Laotians and Khmers across the Mekong River. Life in Isaan is further enhanced by the crossroads of dialect and culture (Thai, Lao, Khmer, Viet, and Suay, an indiginous people famed as elephant hunters and trainers), particularly in Surin.

Isaan's four largest cities (Nakhon Ratchasima, Ubon Ratchatani, Udon Thani, and Khon Kaen) were used as U.S. Air Force bases during the Vietnam War. The U.S. military presence helped trigger a period of rapid economic growth in these areas, which remain centers of transportation, commerce, and education. Perhaps nowhere else is there more of a disparity between the modern and the traditional: saffron-robed monks share 7-11 slurpees and occasionally even the frenetic pace of Khon Kaen's rush hour traffic grinds to a halt to allow an elephant to cross a busy intersection.

Unlike other parts of the country, Isaan has yet to trade in its homespun essence for a more commercially appealing countenance; its appeal cannot be captured in some glossy travel brochure. Perhaps as a result few tourists are willing to brave the region's rudimentary infrastructure and vastness, but those who come are rewarded with a human beauty that is fast disappearing in more developed regions. Here it's not what you have, its what you can give away.

Avid hikers and gourmands will find the region a treasure trove of delights. Pristine national parks and wildlife preserves possess no shortage of trails, scenic mountain tops, cliffs, and waterfalls. The Mekong affords infinite possibilities for river adventures along the Laotian border and magnificent relaxation. Signature Isaan cuisine includes *som tam* (salad of sliced unripe papaya, lime, shrimp, chilis, and garlic), *gai yang* (grilled chicken), *laap* (a spicy salad made from various meats), and *khao niaw* (sticky rice), which is eaten with the hands. The divine *plaa beuk* or "giant golden catfish," a true leviathan of the Mekong River frequently weighing 300kg or more, is the answer to a ravenous back packer's prayer.

■■■ KHAO YAI NATIONAL PARK

If you've got a few days left in Thailand and want to rescue your lungs from the clutches of Bangkok fumes, Khao Yai National Park and its gateway city, Pak Chong, are your salvation. Consecrated as Thailand's first national park in 1961, Khao Yai remains the forerunner of Thailand's extensive and impressive national park network. *Let's Go* was not able to visit Pak Chong and Khao Yai National Park in summer 1995; some information may be out-dated by one year.

PAK CHONG

Stocked with good food and shopping, Pak Chong is the jumping-off point for trips to Khao Yai National Park. The town extends on either side of **Mittaphap (Friendship) Highway.** Streets branching off the highway have blue signs in Thai and English and are named **Tesaban Road** followed by a number. That applies on both sides of the main road. The entire town is only about 1km long. The **day market,** starting from Tesaban 21, extends one block from the main road from dawn until about 4:30pm, and is stocked with flashlights, dead fish, some camping gear, and more. A **supermarket,** on Tesaban 17 sells similar wares daily 9am-10pm. After 4:30 the **night market** (Tesaban 17-19) is the place to be for dinner and people-watching. **Thai Farmers Bank** (tel. 311 501 or 311 481) with its large green English sign, is next to the day market near Tesaban 18. **24-hr. ATM** takes Visa, MC. Traveler's checks and western currency exchange Mon.-Fri. 8:30am-3:30pm. **Post office,** on the corner of with Tesaban 25, handles telegrams, money and postal orders, faxes, **international phone calls** (collect for 30฿ and cash), and parcels Mon.-Fri. 8:30am-4:30pm. **Postal code:** 30130. Privately run **phone center,** beside the post office. Can place Home Direct calls; 30฿ service charge. Open daily 6am-10pm (if later, ring the bell). **Telephone code:** 044.

The **train station** (tel. 223 3762 or 223 0341) sits at the end of Tesaban 15. Trains to **Bangkok** via **Ayutthaya** (7 daily, 7:30am-1:49am, 4-½hr., 40฿). At the **regular bus station** near Tesaban 18 catch buses beneath the pedestrian overpass to: **Chiang Mai** (daily, 3, 5am, and 3pm); **Nakhon Sawan** via **Lopburi** (#121 6:30, 8:20, 11:20am, and 1:20pm); and **Sukhothai** (#572, 7:10, 9:20, 10:20, and 12:20pm). **A/C bus terminal** is beyond the post office next to the Shell station. You can catch A/C buses, however, at Tesaban 19, catty-corner to 7-Eleven. To **Bangkok** (6am-2am, 80฿); and **Chiang Mai** via **Phitsanulok** and **Lampang** (8, 9am, 6, 8, and 8:30pm).

Light-blue **songthaews** leave for **Khao Yai National Park** (40km, 20฿) from the highway when they have collected a sizable group of passengers.

Your best bet is Tom and Maew's **Jungle Guest House,** 63 Tesaban 16, Kongvaksin Rd., Soi 3 (tel. 313 836). From the bus terminal, head right to the stoplight at Tesaban 17. Take a left and, when the road forks, veer left. A huge sign announces the guest house about 50m on your right. From the train walk down Tesaban 15 until you hit the highway. Hang a left, then a right at the stoplight. 70฿ gets you a

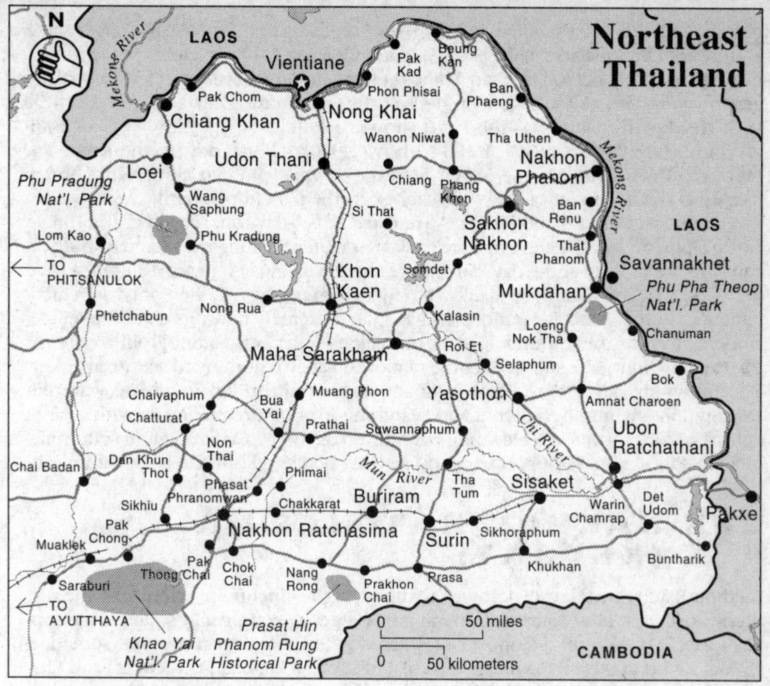

firm mattress, sheet, fan, western toilet, separate showers, small breakfast, and coffee. Extra tea, coffee or water any time (5฿). Toilet paper (10฿). Run the 1-½ day Jungle Adventure tours in Khao Yai National Park.

THE PARK

Khao Yai National Park, home to one of the last wild elephant herds, has over 40km of gorgeous hiking trails, mostly through rainforest and grasslands. Outlandish reptiles, insects, and vines crawl through it all, with hornbills, gibbons, and rhesus monkeys screeching several meters up in the canopy. The waterfalls alone are worth the trek. Don't mind the leeches—just stay clear of the brownish water.

Tigers, though rarely spotted, still reign in Khao Yai. Wild boar, deer, Asiatic black bears, Malayan sun bears, leopards (always spotted), Siamese hare, Asian wild dogs, and dozens of other species share the spectacular terrain arrayed over parts of four provinces. Night driving with a giant spotlight turns up quite a few deer, and the occasional elephant, but they're groggy and not much more than ghostly outlines. The civets, cat-like mammals, are in top form, though.

Better luck spotting Elvis here than catching sight of a pachyderm. Determined naturalists spend a night or two in the park, hiking during the wee hours (around 4am). If you do see elephants, keep a safe distance; they may charge. Recently, a monk got in so good with a herd that he could actually pat their trunks. And that was exactly what the last picture showed in the camera found next to his mangled body. If an elephant does charge, be warned; they can beat the fastest mountain bike. Local wisdom is to stand your ground, stiffly and silently. If the big one is bluffing, it will turn away just before goring you. Otherwise, it would have caught you anyway. Ha ha.

There are two strategies for exploring the park. The bold should stay in the park and explore with a pal. Otherwise, take a day tour. The park is open daily 6am-midnight (admission 10฿). Hitchhiking is common in the park (but *Let's Go* does not recommend this nefarious activity). Pick up a road and trail map (5฿) or hire a guide at the Park Headquarters and Visitors' Center (at least 200฿ per group per trip).

Nasty relations between Khao Yai and encroaching resorts have left two rustic **accommodations.** A long wooden house (10฿) where the floor awaits you is near Park Headquarters and has food and shower facilities (10฿). 3km east, a campground has tents (upwards of 100฿, showers 10฿). For **food,** try the **Khao Yai National Park Club House** (open Mon.-Fri. 6am-11pm, Sat.-Sun. 8am-10pm), located at the mid-point of the road that bisects the park north-south.

A simpler method is the **Jungle Adventure,** a 1-½-day tour, based at the Jungle Guest House in Pak Chong. Trips are daily at 3pm, terminating the next day, but you can split the full day and ½day. Adventures usually begin at a nearby Buddhist cave network. While you explore the down under, Tom teaches a lesson or two on meditation and other tools for tranquility. Next, an extremely rigorous climb up a limestone cliff yields the astounding sight of millions of bats streaming from a cave for the evening hunt. The sunset over the rainforest valley is nothing to sneeze at either. The following day (9am-11pm) is an action-packed thriller, involving waterfall exploration, swimming, hiking, and searching for nocturnal animals with a large light. The tour moves at a blistering pace and costs 650฿. Only fruit and soft drinks included; food runs 40-60฿. Bring good walking boots, a flashlight, and swim wear.

■■■ NAKHON RATCHASIMA (KHORAT)

Nakhon Ratchasima, locally known as Khorat, is the chief point of entry to the rest of the northeast. Most tourists drop in on this large, geographically strategic metropolis (pop. 205,000) for a stopover on their way to other attractions, but some use Khorat as a home base for daytrips to places such as Phimai, Dan Kwian, and Phanom Rung. Nakhon Ratchasima is also famed for its silk; bargain-hunters scavenge here for textile deals.

The regal Thao Suranari Memorial, honoring Khorat's hometown heroine who saved the city from encroaching Lao armies in the 19th century, presides over the central square. A series of moats in the eastern section mark Khorat's original boundaries. Today this area is home to gargantuan air-conditioned shopping malls and numerous hotels and restaurants. Unfortunately, many travelers view Khorat as they might a trip to the dentist's office—a necessary evil. This reputation is unfair, for *sabaii,* the unique blend of warmth and generosity for which Thailand is justly famous, remains alive in Khorat to a degree not seen often in cities of its size. Consider Khorat a gentle introduction to Isaan before pushing on to the heart of this enchanting region.

ORIENTATION

Located 256km northeast of Bangkok, Khorat is on the main corridor to all other destinations in northeastern Thailand. Herds of buses and trains stampede back and forth from Bangkok to Khorat every day.

Khorat is laid out on an east-west grid, divided by **Ratchadamnoen Road;** a rectangular moat surrounds the east side of town. **Chumphon Road** runs parallel to Ratchadamnoen Rd., not to be confused with **Chomphon Road** directly behind the **Thao Suranari Memorial.** The Memorial is an excellent landmark and is located smack in the middle of these roads; locals consider it the center of town.

The **train station** is on the west side of town on **Mukkhamontri Road,** and the **Fah Saeng Hotel** is a short walk to the right on the other side of the road. The **TAT office** is on the highway-sized **Mittraphap Road,** which runs along the northern edge of the moat and finally curves south along the western edge of town. The office is across the road from the intersection with Mukkhamontri Rd., and a little to the left. Bus #1, 2, or 3 (3฿, A/C 5฿) go the distance to Mittraphap Rd. This is also the way to the **Khorat Doctor's House,** the only guest house in town. Get off the

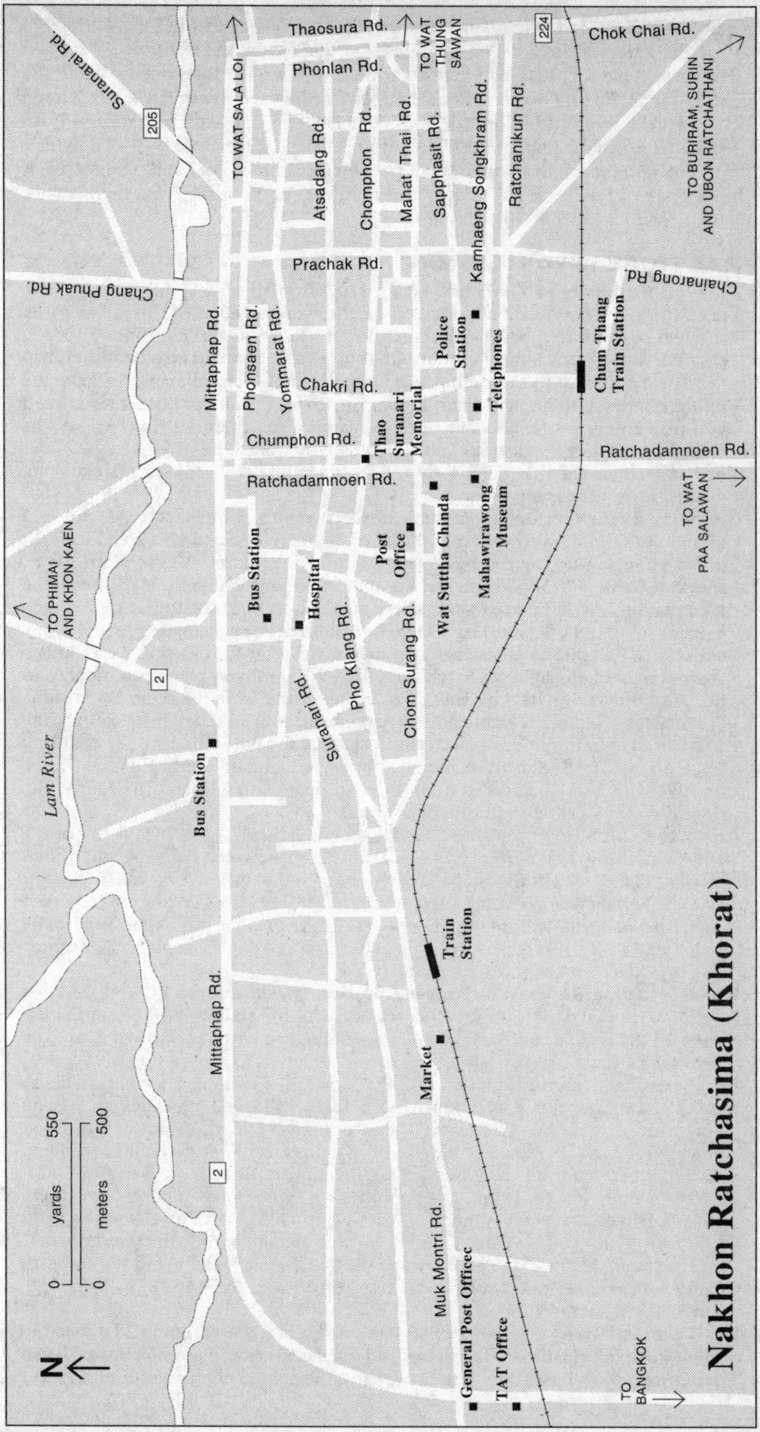

Nakhon Ratchasima (Khorat)

N

0 yards 550
0 meters 500

Thaosura Rd.
Phonlan Rd.
Suranarai Rd.
205
TO WAT SALA LOI
TO WAT THUNG SAWAN
224
Chok Chai Rd.
Atsadang Rd.
Chomphon Rd.
Mahat Thai Rd.
Sapphasit Rd.
Kamhaeng Songkhram Rd.
Ratchanikun Rd.
TO BURIRAM, SURIN AND UBON RATCHATHANI
Prachak Rd.
Chang Phuak Rd.
Chainarong Rd.
Mittaphap Rd.
Phonsaen Rd.
Yommarat Rd.
Police Station
Chum Thang Train Station
Chakri Rd.
Thao Suranari Memorial
Telephones
Chumphon Rd.
Ratchadamnoen Rd.
Ratchadamnoen Rd.
TO WAT PAA SALAWAN
TO PHIMAI AND KHON KAEN
Bus Station
Hospital
Post Office
Wat Suttha Chinda
Mahawirawong Museum
Pho Klang Rd.
Chom Surang Rd.
2
Suranari Rd.
Lam River
Bus Station
Train Station
Mittaphap Rd.
Market
2
Muk Montri Rd.
General Post Officec
TAT Office
TO BANGKOK

bus at **Sueb Siri Road** (the wanna-be highway that comes just before Mittraphap Rd., on the left), walk to Soi 4 on the right side, and follow the signs.

The eastern part of Mukkhamontri Rd. forks into three roads before it reaches the moat: **Suranari Road, Phoklang Road,** and **Jomsurangyard Road.** These roads intersect Ratchadamnoen Rd. close to the Memorial. The **Bangkok bus station** is on **Burin Lane,** north of Suranari Rd. Tokyo Hotels #1 and 2 are close by to the right.

The **bus station for the upper Isaan provinces,** such as Loei and Nong Khai, is Khorat's newer Bus Terminal #2, just north of town on Route 2. From there, take a tuk-tuk or samlor (30-50฿) into town.

PRACTICAL INFORMATION

Tourism Authority of Thailand (TAT): 2102-2104 Mittraphap Rd. (tel. 213 666; fax 213 667). Inconveniently located on the western edge of town, but easily reached by bus #1, 2, or 3 from Mukkhamontri Rd., Suranari Rd. (bus #2), Phoklang Rd. (bus #1), or Jomsurangyard Rd. (bus #3). Get off and cross at Mittraphap Rd. The TAT is just to the right of Sima Thani Hotel. Helpful map of Khorat and info on Buriram, Surin, and Chaiyaphum province. Check the border situation if you plan to enter Cambodia at Chong Kham village in Surin; the TAT says its closed indefinitely. English spoken. Open daily 8:30am-4:30pm.

Tourist Police: Directly behind the TAT office (tel. 213 333). English spoken. Open 24 hrs. **Emergency number:** 1699.

Currency Exchange: Bangkok Bank of Commerce, 30 Phoklang Rd. (tel. 244 288), in the center of town. From the Thao Suranari Memorial, it's about ½ block down Phoklang Rd. on the right. Open Mon.-Fri. 8:30am-3:30pm. **Siam Commercial Bank,** 306 Mukkhamontri Rd. (tel. 251 356 or 245 536). As you exit the train station, it will be across the street and a short distance to the right. Open 8:30am-3:30pm. Both banks have large blue 'currency exchange' signs.

Post Office/Telephone: 48 Jomsurangyard Rd. (tel. 259 483). Facing the Thao Suranari Memorial, go right on Ratchadamnoen Rd. until you reach Jomsurangyard Rd. Turn right and pass the Klang Plaza center; office is on the right. Open Mon.-Fri. 8:30am-4:30pm, Sat. 9am-noon. **Overseas phone,** Mon.-Fri. 8:30am-3pm (tel. 242 046). For better hours, place calls upstairs at the post office on 371 Assadang Rd. From the Thao Suranari Memorial, follow Assadang Rd. for 2½ blocks. On the left side with a red mailbox in front. International phones open daily 7am-11pm. **Postal code:** 30000.**Telephone code:** 044.

Airport: South of town on Dejudom Rd. (tel. 255 425). A 50-70฿ tuk-tuk or 80-100฿ songthaew ride. 20฿ airport tax. Daily flights between Bangkok and Khorat (40min., 540฿). Flight times change frequently; contact THAI Air in Bangkok or Khorat. **THAI Airways** is at 14 Manaf Rd. (tel. 257 211-13; fax 244 214) between Mahatthai and San-Pasit Rd. Open Mon.-Fri. 8am-5pm, Sat. 8am-4pm, Sun. noon-4pm. AmEx, MC, Visa (cash sales only at the airport). English spoken. Transportation provided from airport to their office.

Trains: Nakhon Ratchasima Railway Station, Mukkhamontri Rd. (tel. 242 044 or 245 037, ext. 515). From the center of town, the station is 500m on the left once on the road. 2 trains daily for Ubon Ratchathani. 10 trains daily to Bangkok (8:07am-12:10am, sleeper 40฿).

Bus Terminal 1: Burin Lane (tel. 242 899, for A/C 245 443). Serves travelers to Bangkok and nearby towns and provinces. Take city bus #2 onto Suranari Rd. and get off near the Tokyo Hotels. Walk east toward the town center and turn left onto Burin Lane. Station is a block up. Ask drivers and street vendors milling around where your bus is. Buses are number-coded. Regular to: **Bangkok** (#21, every 20min., 4:50am-10pm, 64฿); **Phimai** (#1305, every 30min., 5am-10pm, 16฿); **Surin** (#274, every 30min., 2:30am-11pm, 50฿); and **Pak Chong** (#1310, every hr., 6am-6pm, 24฿). A/C buses located behind terminal: **Bangkok-A/C** (every 20min., 24 hrs., 115฿); **Buriram** (80฿); **Chiang Mai/Chiang Rai** (3 buses daily, 3, 6am, and 3pm, 180฿); A/C buses: (#635, 6 daily, 4:15, 8, 9:45am, 6, 8, and 8:30pm, 325฿-400฿).

Bus Terminal 2: (tel. 256 007 or 256 009), north of town on Route 2 beyond the Takhong River. Handles A/C coaches and regular buses going to the **upper Isaan provinces.** Most buses are on their way from Bangkok; no guarantee of a vacant seat. **Nong Khai** (on the hour, 3am-10pm, 157฿); **Ubon** (2 daily, noon and 2pm, 150฿); **Udon** (every 30min., 8:30am-3am, 135฿); **Mukdahan** (2 daily, 11:30am and noon, 180฿); **Khon Kaen** (every 30min., 8:30am-3am, 86฿); and **Loei** (2 daily, 1 and 3am, 174฿)

Local Transportation: Samlors and tuk-tuks are omnipresent; bargain hard. From the TAT to the Thao Suranari Memorial should not cost more than 40฿. Take the city buses around town (3฿, A/C 5฿)—they're just as convenient (5am-10pm). Buses #1, 2, and 3 start on Mukkhamontri Rd. near the TAT office; they all go into the center of town. They split when Mukkhamontri forks into Suranari Rd. (#2), Phoklang Rd. (#1), and Jomsurangyard Rd. (#3). Exact change for regular bus #2. TAT city map has bus routes. Songthaews run these routes (3฿) with greater frequency. Bus stops are clearly indicated. Traffic is too heavy for safe bicycling.

Tour company: Khorat Business Corporation, Ltd., 37-39 Buarong Rd. (tel. 258 631 or 258 632). Offers 2 full-day tours 6am-6pm, covering Phimai, Phanom Rung, and Muang Tham. Car and driver 1500฿, English speaking guide 500฿. Also complete travel agency; tickets to Bangkok. Excellent English spoken.

Markets: Day market, in the center of town on Suranari Rd., across the street from Wat Sakae and extends to the other side of the block on Phoklang Rd. A wide array of Isaan food including *gai yang* and enough sticky rice to fill Klang Plaza. Open daily at 7am and shuts down around 9pm. The **night bazaar** on Manat Rd. between Chompon and Mahatthai Rd., developed by the TAT, is small and organized. Food stalls are skewed toward yummy desserts, but there's plenty of Isaan food as well. *The* place for Marky Mark bootlegs. Open daily 6-10pm.

Laundry: Mr. Clean Laundry and Dry Clean Service, 107 Mahatthai Rd. (tel. 242 277), on the corner of Washara Sit Rd. Slacks 10฿, jeans 15฿, shirts 10฿, suits 60-90฿. Open daily 7am-7pm.

Swimming Pool: Janya Pool (tel. 252 305, 244 425, or 356 358), Sueb Siri Rd. Soi 3. Past the Doctor's Guest House, cross the train tracks and take first left onto Soi 3. Follow this soi to the end and take another left and go past a heavily forested wat on the right. Pool is about 100m past the bus stop on the right. Very clean and largely deserted during the week; half the 10-year-olds in Khorat frolic here on the weekends. Open daily 6am-8pm. Admission 30฿.

Pharmacy: Amarin, 122 Chumphon Rd. (tel. 242 741), right in the center of town behind the shrine and a short walk to the left. The owners speak enough English. "Rx" on the glass doors. Open 7am-9pm. For contact lenses, **Jok Su Eye Clinic,** 742-744 Ratchadamnoen Rd. (tel. 242 250). Facing the shrine, turn right onto Ratchadamnoen Rd. and walk 1 block until it meets Jomsurangyard Rd. Cross the street, and the shop is on the corner. 350ml disinfectant solution 160฿, enzymatic cleaner (24 tablets) 241฿. Open 8:30am-8:30pm.

Hospitals: St. Mary's Hospital, 307 Mittraphap Rd./Route 2 (tel. 242 385, 243 642, or 244 211). 50m south of Bus Terminal #2. Private hospital with excellent English-speaking staff. **Khorat Memorial Hospital,** 348 Suranari Rd. (tel. 230 215), past the Sri Pattana Hotel on the right as you walk from the Thao Suranari Memorial. Sign is a green cross on the roof. English spoken. Visa. Open 24 hrs.

Emergency: tel. 191. Contact tourist police first (tel. 1699).

Police: Nakhon Ratchasima Police Station, on Sapphasit Rd. between Washara Sit and Chainarong Rd. (tel. 242 010 or 242 045). Try the tourist police's emergency number first (tel. 1699); they speak English.

ACCOMMODATIONS

Hotels in Khorat are blighted by the cookie-cutter syndrome. Symptoms include a functional toilet, token furniture, A/C options, and a creaky bed all against a backdrop of vintage two-tone pastel paint. Hotels of this model are all over town, so at least you can choose by location.

Khorat Doctor's Guest House, 78 Sueb Siri Rd. Soi 4 (tel. 255 846). From the train station, go left on Mukkhamontri Rd. When you reach Wat Amphawan, turn left onto Sueb Siri Rd. Soi 4 is a short way down the road on the right. If you cross the railroad tracks, you've gone too far. A sign on the corner directs you to the Doctor's. The proprietress, Rachel Sue, a nurse in Illinois for 20 years, speaks excellent English and is a sage on the area, though the daughter Penny now oversees much of the day-to-day running of the place. Maps, pamphlets, and a log book with travel advice. 2 shared bathrooms with hot water. Recently renovated. Near a swimming pool, C&C Restaurant, and TAT office. Lock-out at 10:30pm; make advance arrangements for late arrival. Singles around 100฿. Doubles around 130฿. Triples 180฿. Bed in 3-person dorm room 60฿. Breakfast (2 eggs and toast) 30฿. Laundry service. 6 rooms fill up during the high season. No reservations.

Siri Hotel, 688-690 Phoklang Rd. (tel. 242 831), about 350m down Phoklang Rd. after Mukkhamontri Rd. forks into the 3 roads leading to the center of town. On the left side of the street, next door to the VFW cafeteria and opposite a basketball court. Hike and thou shall be rewarded—rooms on the fourth floor are cheapest. Little English spoken, but a sign explains the dizzying array of accommodation permutations. Heed the signs in every room which say "Sorry no lepers allowed." Singles with fan 120-140฿, with A/C 280฿. Sumptuous "special room" with TV, A/C, and fridge, a cool 500฿. Laundry service. Check-out noon.

Sri Chompol Hotel, 133 Chompol Rd. (tel. 252 829, 242 460). A short walk down Chompol Rd. from the statue. The hotel is on the left, opposite a Buddhist paraphernalia shop. If you reach the Thai Farmers Bank, you've gone too far. A relative rarity in Khorat: cheap hotel *and* rooms that don't make you feel as if the last occupant was a wanted felon. Freshly painted walls will brighten your day; bathrooms with flushing Thai-style toilet are so fine. Single with fan 130฿, with A/C 200฿; double with fan 200฿, with A/C 300฿. Check-out 11am.

Sirivijaya Hotel, 9-11 Buarong Rd. (tel. 242 194), down Suranari Rd. from Ratchadamnoen. Just past the day market on the left, turn onto Buarong Rd.; hotel on the left. Definitely a step up (though you won't have to—there's an elevator). Relax in a comfy *faux*-leather armchair in front of the TV or on the western toilet in every room. Order in from the Lai Thai restaurant next door. Singles with fan 200฿, with A/C 350฿; double with fan 200฿, with A/C 400฿. More decadence? Try the VIP suite, 500฿. Laundry service 10฿ per piece. Check-out noon.

FOOD

Mouth-watering cuisine is as plentiful as broad smiles and Thao Suranari statuettes in Khorat. There are about 15 restaurants on every street and the markets proffer a kaleidoscopic array of fresh, exotic fruits and scrumptious local delicacies. Good restaurants for all budgets congregate in the center of town near the shrine and along Ratchadamnoen and Chumphon Rd. For the really lame (or homesick), the fast food joints are at the Klang Plaza II shopping center on the northwest corner of Jomsurangyard and Ratchadamnoen Rd.

The markets are fine places to sample regional specialties. It might be a good idea to try Isaan food in Khorat (where antacids are close at hand) before moving on to more remote territory. **Warning: eat *som tam Thai* made without crab.** The crabs may contain parasites, which make unfriendly internal pets. When in doubt, don't eat. See Practical Information for day and night markets. Vegetarians can enjoy **Ran Ahaan Jay Con Im,** 191/2 Suranari Rd. (tel. 252 726). Open 7am-6pm.

Dok Som, 130 Chumphon Rd. (tel. 252 020), behind the Monument and on the left, with a Thai sign. Walk past Amarin Pharmacy. Wood-paneled, the ceiling is strung with white Christmas lights. A more-than-satisfying dining experience if you can stomach Lionel Richie and Richard Marx. The menu is bilingual, but the staff isn't. Thai and Chinese dishes with European items, and for the adventuresome, a page of Isaan cuisine. The spicy label is no joke. Cool your smoldering mouth with a dish of coconut milk ice cream (10฿). Sit in the covered central courtyard below a leafy bamboo canopy where the din of Chumphon Rd. seems a million miles away...that's because Lionel is an inch from your ear. Entrees 20-80฿. Open 10am-midnight. MC, Visa.

Cabbages and Condoms (C&C Restaurant), 8611 Sueb Siri Rd. (tel. 258 100), just a few steps past Soi 4 and the Doctor's Guest House; look for the tiny bridge on the right. Brainchild of PDA, a non-government group that funds social welfare projects, including AIDS awareness/education programs. Hence the name and framed Thai condoms. Look for the prancing prophylactics! A clean joint with an impeccable English menu. Sit on the spacious 2nd floor balcony to avoid the "skeeters" and bask in a cool Isaan breeze. Try the "chicken in herb leaf bikinis" (60฿) or steamed rice cooked in a pineapple (55฿). Profits fund PDA projects. Open daily 10am-10pm. AmEx, Visa/MC.

Suan Pak, 540 Chumphon Rd. (tel. 255 877), behind the shrine and to the left, past Dok Som. Heavily tinted glass windows give the impression of dimly lit interiors with relaxing atmosphere. Wrong! Bright whiteness and waves of Thai pop music, punctuated by the tap-tap-tap of the waiter's platform shoes, bombard the senses. Join the teeny-bopping in the A/C front, or loll on the back patio. A peeing boy fountain strategically placed in front of the *hawng nam* adds a touch of class. It's mainly a local hang-out, but there's a separate English menu, and some of the gregarious waiters, clad in spiffy electric blue vests and bowties, speak English very well. Thai and Chinese entrees 20-100฿. Open 10am-midnight. MC, Visa.

The VFW Cafeteria (tel. 256 522), immediately to the right of the Siri Hotel on Phoklang Rd. A slice of displaced Americana straight from the silver screen, exemplifying the cinematic "bar-and-grill"/GI hangout in every Vietnam War flick, down to the lazy ceiling fans and Miss February pinups. The bar girls are now long gone, but regulars nurse pot bellies with their Singha and complain about the government full-time. Foul American food, but worth a gawk—a chunk of living history, covered with a thick patina of hamburger grease. Dartboard. Tossed salad 10฿, cheeseburger 28฿, and fries 10฿. Open 8am-9:30pm. MC, Visa.

Super Seafood Restaurant, 915/2 Jomsurangyard Rd. (tel. 246 706 or 246 946). Located just beyond the large fork, heading into town, it's on the right past West Cheng Nai. A large tree grows through the awning. Look for a yellow oval sign in Thai. The warehouse-like setting belies what may well be the best seafood joint in Isaan. Locals throng here to slurp up shellfish and wolf down heaping platters of prawns (the specialty) and lobster. By the end of a meal, tables tend to look like the crustacean equivalent of the St. Valentine's Day massacre. English menu boasts pages of prawn dishes: sauteed mixed veggies with prawns 60฿, baked prawns with red wine 80฿. Most dishes 30-150฿. Open daily 5pm-midnight.

SIGHTS

While the province's main attractions lie beyond the city limits, Khorat proper is home to several intriguing sights that can be visited in a single, unhurried afternoon.

The **Thao Suranari Memorial,** in the center of town, is the symbol that captures the spirit of Khorat best. Built in 1934, over the city moat between Ratchadamnoen and Chumphon Rd., the bronze statue depicts the heroic Khun Ying Mo, wife of Khorat's deputy governor, who in 1826 rallied the citizens (including 300 women volunteers) in the city's defense against Laotian invaders. Locals reverently refer to her as 'Yah Mo' (Grandmother Mo), wrap the shrine in ribbons, and burn copious amounts of incense. When prayers are answered, they sing their thanks in the local Khorat dialect or hire young women to dance in her honor. An annual **Thao Suranari Fair** (March 23-April 3) draws thousands of admirers.

Directly behind the shrine is **Chumpol Gate.** In the wooden rooms above the gate, monks used to chant for the safe homecoming of soldiers who passed underneath. Walking through the gate ensures your return to Khorat one day.

If you're weary of seeing the same old wats all over Thailand, **Wat Sala Loi** offers a chance to set sail for new spiritual horizons. Located on the Takhong River a few hundred meters down a small road off Mittraphap Rd. at the northeast corner of the city moat, the wat has a bot shaped like a Chinese junk, symbolizing the passage of the devoted to Nirvana.

Every city in Thailand has its sacred city pillar, from which all distances are measured. Khorat's is enshrined at **Wat Phra Narai Maharat** on Prachak Rd. (between Assadang and Chomphon Rd.) inside the city moat. This wat contains one of Khorat's most sacred objects, a sandstone image of the Hindu god Narayana. Marvel at the five-story mural depicting Khorat's history, made from Dan Kwian clay tiles.

The **Mahawirawong Museum,** (tel. 242 458) Khorat's branch of the National Museum, is on Ratchadamnoen Rd., two blocks south of the shrine on the right. Its small collection contains artifacts from the Angkor and Ayutthaya periods. Highlights include a beautifully ornate wooden gable from the Ayutthaya period and wooden sitting Buddha covered with gold leaf and inlaid with sparkling stones. Open Wed.-Sun. 9am-noon and 1-4pm. Admission 10฿.

ENTERTAINMENT

Rumors that Elle, Claudia, and Naomi might open a branch of their "Glamour Café" here aside, there is little unique entertainment open to foreigners, save the **Khorat Night Bazaar,** where you can join flocks of painfully hip Thai youths for a stroll down Manat Rd. (open 6-10pm). The karaoke plague has reached epidemic proportions in Khorat, with little sign of a cure. For temporary relief, the **Simi Thani Sheraton Hotel,** (tel. 213 100) directly to the left of TAT, holds performances of Isaan music and dance. Tues.-Sun. 7-9pm. Admission about 200฿. Shows are outdoors, so rain means you're out of luck. (Don't worry, there's a k'oke bar around the corner, any corner). For those with a taste for more gladiatorial entertainment, **Thai Boxing** kicks off at Khorat's stadium on weekends. Inquire at the TAT office.

Khorat also has the standard array of movie theaters, nightclubs, and discotheques. **Klang Plaza II,** on the corner of Ratchadamnoen and Jomsurangyard Rd., offers Thai Top 40 and consumptive diversions.

Music Bank, on Mahatthai Rd. at the corner with Washire Rd. Coming from the center of town, on the right, look for the wooden façade and flashing Christmas lights of the restaurant next door. Dodge City meets Gilligan's Island in this marvelous C&W bar. Choice of decor is intriguing: lush tropical plants outside with fountains on the windows, and bamboo walls inside for the log cabin feel, complete with plastic horse heads and antelope horns. Country music starts at about 9:30pm; before that it's Thai ballads. Singha 85฿, enough whiskey to wet any outlaw's whistle. Munchies also available (40฿), though it's hard to imagine ole Tex bellying up to the bar and ordering a plate o' chicken feet along with his firewater. Open daily 6pm-midnight.

Elite 2002, (tel. 260 154), on Jomsurangyard Rd. next to Scanners and across from Klang Plaza. *Psst!* Menudo has resurfaced and they're now playing at the Elite! Live Thai music is worth a trip, though the place is a forest of bar stools and difficult for dancing; save your Saturday Night Fever routine for Scanners, the disco next door. Open daily 9:30pm-4am. 1 drink minimum (80฿).

Cocoon Beer House, on Jomsurangyard Rd. Opposite Klang Plaza, just to the left of the Elite 2002. Water buffalo skulls and old rifles adorn the walls of this small, open-air pub made entirely of packing crates. Rather enigmatic accordion completes the decor. Remarkably peaceful, considering it faces the dynamic duo of Elite 2002 and Scanners. An excellent spot for people-watching on a Saturday night. Single beer 35฿, 150฿ for a pitcher of Carlsberg. Small snack menu; still can't escape the chicken feet though. Open daily 7pm- 6am.

■ NEAR KHORAT

DAN KWIAN VILLAGE

Tiny **Dan Kwian village** has long been famous for its distinctive rust-colored pottery, incised with detailed geometric patterns. The crafts are quite beautiful—but also heavy and breakable. Still, vendors sell plenty of beads, necklaces, and belts, which fit nicely into luggage pockets. Take a half-day trip there, and visit Mr. Pomsinsab, who produces pottery behind his shop and allows discreet visitors to wander.

Follow Chomphon Rd. behind the Thao Suranari Memorial and turn left on Chainarong Rd. At Khorat's south gate, do not exit. Turn left onto Kamhaeng Songkhram Rd. and walk past the herds of vendors. Just beyond, on the right you should see a small blue-striped bus (#1307, 30min., 5฿). Indicate to the driver the destination. Disembark when the small road forks into three lanes lined with little shops. To return, wait on the left side of the road back to Khorat. When the bus comes, gesticulate wildly and make kooky gorilla noises. They will stop for you. Or not.

PHANOM RUNG AND MUANG THAM

The ancient Khmer temples of **Phanom Rung** and **Muang Tham** are the tourist magnets of lower Isaan. Phanom Rung is larger, completely restored, and more impressive than Muang Tham. Transportation is not overly difficult, but start early in the morning. From **Khorat** or **Surin,** catch bus #274 and get off at **Ban Ta-Ko** (about 20฿), which is clearly marked as the turn-off for Phanom Rung and Muang Tham. Here you will be accosted by the 'motorcycle mafia,' but if you are just going to Phanom Rung, you can catch a **songthaew** here (around 15฿, double-check the destination before getting in). If you would like to see both Phanom Rung and Muang Tham, **motorcycle drivers** will take you to the temples and wait while you tour the grounds. A round trip to both temples should cost 150-200฿. Do not pay all at once! This arrangement is especially recommended during the off-season or weekdays, when transport back can be unpredictable. Heading back to Surin or Khorat, try to be back at Ban Ta-Ko before 5pm, as the buses plying the highway here run less frequently after that.

Prasat Hin Khao Phanom Rung Historical Park

Phanom Rung lies 383m above sea-level atop an extinct volcano. This superb temple, the closest thing in Isaan to Angkor Wat, was built between the 10th and 13th centuries AD and is among the largest of Khmer monuments, with some of the most detailed architecture and sculpture of its kind in Thailand.

Once inside the complex, climb the three terraced earthen platforms up to the "white elephant hall," a partially reconstructed stone structure on the right directly ahead. In front is the 160-m promenade leading to the main complex and its stairway. This avenue is lined with lotus bud-shaped pillars. You'll encounter the first of three *naga* bridges (a platform flanked by many-headed mythical serpents). The stairs to the main complex are not too much of a chore; at the top is the eastern side of the main gallery. Once through the hallway of the gallery, you'll be standing on the third bridge and facing the east portico of the chamber leading to the main sanctuary. The lintel above this entrance is perhaps the most famous door fixture in all of Thailand. It was stolen, then resurfaced in the Art Institute of Chicago, and was eventually returned in 1988. The **Phra Narai Lintel** shows the reclining Lord Narayana in the Hindu creation myth. A lotus flower, upon which rests the god Brahma, is growing out of his navel. Open daily 7:30am-6pm; admission 20฿.

Muang Tham

Muang Tham does not match the splendor of Phanom Rung, but some aspects of it provide an eerie glimpse of what the temple must have looked like before its restoration. For the best effect, see this and then go on to Phanom Rung. The Fine Arts Department has begun renovation of Muang Tham, but it will be a few years before the project is complete. Open daily 7:30am-6pm; admission 20฿.

■■■ PHIMAI

The lethargic little town of Phimai, northwest of Khorat, boasts only two main streets, but has the good fortune (or the savvy town planning) of having grown up around an impressive Angkor-period Khmer temple. The ruins, now largely restored, constitute the **Prasat Hin Phimai Historical Park.** The recently opened **Phimai National Museum,** in addition to being an architectural triumph, provides an engaging compliment to the temple. A few kilometers east of the town center is Phimai's third don't-miss attraction: Sai Ngam, or "beautiful banyan," a leafy behemoth that dwarfs its arboreal brethren. Two first-rate guest houses and an excellent restaurant make a night in this narcoleptic village worth your while. If not, all three sights can be covered with the aid of a bicycle in about five hours.

ORIENTATION AND PRACTICAL INFORMATION

Buses leave from Khorat's Bus Terminal 1, platform 17 (#1305, every 30min., 5am-10pm, 1-½hr., 16฿). The bus will deposit you next to the police pavilion with the clock tower on top. (Those in town for only a few hours can leave bulky packs with the friendly officers there). Facing west, **Juenkao Road** runs right past the front gate of the park. Phimai's main drag **Chomsudasapet Road** intersects Juenkao here, forming a T shape. From the middle of Chomsudasapet you will see the towering *prang* of the temple complex to the north, and the town's old south gate. At the other end, heading south on Chomsudasapet, the **Old Phimai Guesthouse** and the **S & P New Phimai Guest House** are on a side-street, **Mu 1,** to the right. If you pass the **Thai Farmer's Bank** (open Mon.-Fri. 8:30am-3:30pm; tel. 471 352), you've gone too far. A little farther is the laterite-block **Baiteiy Restaurant,** an informal **tourist information center.** The Khorat **bus station** is farther down Chomsudasapet on the right, opposite a wat. The **post and telegraph office** (123 Wonprang Rd., tel. 471 342), on the left side of Wonprang, also places **international phone calls** and telegrams (open Mon.-Fri. 8am-4:30pm, closes Sat. and Sun. at noon. **Postal code:** 30110). To get there, heading west on Juenkao, **Wonprang Road** is the first right past the historical park and runs the length of the western edge of the park. **Bike rental** available at The Old Phimai Guest House or the S & P New Phimai Guest House (8฿ per hour, 25฿ per day). Bikes allow easy access to Sai Ngam, about 2 kilometers east of town.

ACCOMMODATIONS AND FOOD

Phimai's modest tourist traffic supports two fine guest houses, located about 2m from one another on either side of a narrow dirt alley off Chomsudasapet Rd., just close enough to pass the Grey Poupon. A **night market** springs up every evening on Juenkao Rd. east of the police clock tower on the way to Sai Ngam.

Old Phimai Guest House, 214 Mu 1 Chomsudasapet Rd. (tel. 471 918). Heading south on Chomsudasapet Rd., the alley is on the right just before an Agfa film shop. A wonderfully airy, bright wooden house overseen by a cheerful English-speaking family. Rooms are palatial. Take your breakfast (omelette 5฿) on the rooftop terrace. Singles 90฿, with A/C 250฿. Doubles 120฿, with A/C 300฿. Triple 170฿. Rooms in the 6-bed dormitory 70฿. Discounts for HI members: (dorm 60฿, single 80฿, double 100฿). Overseas phone service: 75฿ per minute, 30฿ fee for collect calls. Helpful information board with directions to major cities in the northeast and guest house cards. Tours of Phnom Rung and Muang Tham available: 400฿ per person, 4 person minimum. Laundry service.

S & P New Phimai Guest House, 213 Mu 1 Chomsudasapet Rd. (tel. 471 797). Across from the Old Phimai Guest House. In a wooden Thai-style house, only not nearly as bright as the Old Phimai G.H. The most interesting thing here is the large plaster wall decorated by the guests, who sign their names, draw the flag of their home country, and leave a pithy quote. Rooms are so big the owner could double his occupancy by dividing them in half. Small balcony so you can swap jokes with the guest across the street. Singles 80฿. Doubles 100฿. Triples 150฿. Cramped dorm rooms 60฿. Helpful traveler info on the walls downstairs. Laundry 10฿. Breakfast 25฿.

Baiteiy Restaurant, 246/1 Chomsudasapet Rd. On the right past the turnoff to Old Phimai and S&P Guest Houses, before the Thai Farmer's Bank. Unique laterite construction, a restaurant as the ancient Khmers might have built (minus the A/C and durian ice cream). This place bills itself as an **"information center"** though the English language section is skimpy and not very informative. Your best resource is the staff, some of whom speak English. No trip to Phimai is complete without a plate of Phimai style fried noodles (25฿). Extensive English menu boasts a variety of Thai foods (20-100฿). Fried mixed veggies 30฿, Singha 30฿, Coke 10฿. Open daily 7am-midnight.

SIGHTS

Phimai's *raison d'être* are the stately Khmer ruins smack in the middle of town, now the **Prasat Hin Phimai Historical Park.** At its zenith, the Angkor empire (802-1431) spread from Malaysia and Burma in the west to the Vietnamese coast in the east. Testimonies of its power and wealth can be seen in the hundreds of temples that still dot the region. The site situated at Phimai was an important post, from which the Khmer god-kings established suzerainty over northeast Thailand. At one time, a laterite highway linked the city with the empire's magnificent capital, Angkor Thom, 225km to the south. The temple was built in a style similar to that of Angkor Wat in the late 11th century, probably during the reign of Jayavarman VII, the most prolific builder of the god-kings. The park's immaculately manicured lawn gives the impression that the Khmers chose to erect their temple in the middle of a golf course. Unfortunately the archeologists from the Fine Arts Department went a bit overboard with their "Restoration," hence the abundance of cement and the incongruous plaster ceiling in the central sanctuary. On the right as you cross the stone causeway with *naga* balustrades is a collection of faded sandstone lintels. While initially dedicated to Hinduism the temple was later re-consecrated to Buddhism, and many of the lintels still depict mythical Hindu creatures or scenes from the epic poem the *Ramayana*. Marvel at the Khmer's strategic placement of ashtrays and floodlights. The best preserved carvings can be found on the central tower or *prang,* which rises 28 meters above the ground. Surrounding structures, such as libraries (another feature of Khmer temples) have not been restored. Most of the buildings are built of soft red sandstone. Open daily 6am-6pm, admission 20฿. North of the park about 0.5km along the road that runs past the east perimeter of the temple complex is the **Phimai National Museum,** on the right in a large white building with a red tiled roof. The museum is well worth a visit; not only does it include an extensive collection of Khmer and Dvaravati art, but it also houses interesting anthropological exhibits documenting the social, political, and economic history of the Isaan region. The downstairs collection focuses on Phimai itself, explaining the restoration process. The most impressive piece by far is a magnificent statue of Jayavarman VII found at the Phimai Prasat. The upstairs houses the social exhibits. Tour guides available. Open Wed.-Sun. 9am-4pm (tel. 471 167). Admission 10฿.

For a less cerebral diversion, **Sai Ngam,** the largest banyan tree in Thailand, stands on the bales of the Moon River about 2 km east of town. A 10-min. bike ride tops; head east on Juenkao Rd. past the clock tower and follow the signs, sticking to the main rust-tinged dirt road. Descending under Sai Ngam's thick green canopy is like entering some J.R.R. Tolkien-inspired netherworld. Vines brush against your face, and even at high noon much of the brutal tropical sun is filtered out by the leaves. Wizened old men sit at card tables and will read your palm for a few baht. At the center stands a small pagoda, which houses the spirit of this 360-year-old miracle. A long pavilion at the entrance to Sai Ngum houses a number of noodle stalls and souvenir stands. Other attractions in this pleasant pavilion include a traditional Isaan house built on stilts, a flower garden, and a statue of **Sock Prasat Hin,** a famous Thai boxer from Phimai. A relief behind the bronze figure depicts the champ pummeling his hapless opponents.

■■■ SURIN

Fifty-one weeks out of the year, Surin remains a rare stop on most traveler's itineraries, since many prefer to press on to the Mekong River. Their loss is your gain, for those who do venture to this delightful provincial capitol (pop. 40,000) find themselves witnesses to a slice of Isaan life the omnipresent Thai tourist industry has yet to devour (the absence of a TAT office is proof of this). The many tongues you are bound to hear spoken at the market are a testament to the cultural crossroads Surin has become; Thai, Lao, Khmer, and Suay (an indigenous people famed for their prowess as elephant hunters and trainers) mix and mingle, their rich individual cultures combining to form a social fabric as colorful and varied as a bolt of Surin's renowned silk. Surin is also known for its rice production, specifically jasmine rice. One week a year, at the end of November, Surin has her 15 minutes of fame, when hordes of tourists, Thai and *farang,* flood the town for the annual **Surin Elephant Roundup.** Fantastic markets (home to some of the finest Isaan cuisine in the land), restaurants, pubs, and a great guest house only sweeten the payoff for those lucky few who visit. The many small Khmer ruins that dot the province make fine day-trips. Most have been looked over by the Fine Arts Department in all their enchanting, if crumbling, grandeur.

ORIENTATION

The provincial capital of Surin is 452km from Bangkok and easily reached by bus or train from Bangkok, Nakhon Ratchasima, and Ubon Ratchathani. The **bus** and **train stations** are relatively close to each other at the north end of town. From there it's a short samlor ride (about 20฿) to **Pirom's Guest House** at the end of **Krung Sri Nai Road. Thornsarn Road** is the main thoroughfare, running north-south and ending at the elephant statues in front of the train station. A traffic circle and many hotels and banks line this street. To the east of Thornsarn Rd., the next major north-south street is **Chit Bam Rung Road,** which runs behind the bus station. Two blocks west of Thornsarn is **Tessabarl 3 Road,** which passes the **market** (at the corner with Krung Sri Nai Rd.) and the turnoff to Pirom's Guest House. **Tessabarl I Road,** running east-west, crosses Thornsarn Rd. at the traffic circle about 4 blocks south. **Lakmuang Road,** the other major east-west thoroughfare, also intersects Thornsarn. Needless to say, a map will be indispensable during your stay in Surin; pick one up at the TAT in Khorat, at Pirom's Guest House, or at the Tarin Hotel.

PRACTICAL INFORMATION

Currency Exchange: Bangkok Bank, 252 Thonsarn Rd. (tel. 511 443). Walking down Thonsarn Rd. from the train station, the Bangkok Bank is just past the traffic circle on the right. Near the bus station is the **Siam Commercial Bank,** 415 Chit Bam Rung Rd. (tel. 512 061). Turn left onto Chit Bam Rung Rd. The bank will be a brief walk down this street, on the left. Both are open Mon.-Fri. 8:30am-3:30pm.

Post Office/Telephone and Telegram: Surin Post Office (tel. 511 009), on the corner of Thornsan and Tessabarl 1 Rd. at the traffic circle. Open Mon.-Fri. 8:30am-4:30pm, Sat.-Sun. 9am-noon. Phone (7am-10pm) and telegram services (8am-6pm) open daily. **Postal code:** 32000. **Telephone code:** 044.

Trains: Surin Railway Station (tel. 511 295), on Nongdoom Rd. To **Ubon,** (10 daily, 3 hr).

Buses: Surin Bus Terminal (tel. 511 756), Chit Bam Rung Rd. on a side street which opens into the bus station. #274 runs to and from **Khorat** (approx. every 30 min., 4 hr., 50฿). To **Ubon** (10 daily, 3hr., A/C 85฿).

Local Transportation: Tuk-tuks and samlors. Samlor from the bus station to Pirom's Guest House is about 25฿. Pay a little bit more for tuk-tuk rides.

Bicycle Rental: Pirom's Guest House rents for 7฿ per hour or 30฿ per day.

Market: Surin's **day** and **night markets** are in the same location along Krung Sri Nai Rd., between Tessabarl 3 and Thonsarn Rd. During the day, you can buy anything from clothes to durian, but at night, most of the non-food vendors pack up, leaving some of the best Isaan (and Thai) food around until 3am.

Swimming Pool: The Tarin Hotel, 60 Sirirath Rd. (tel. 514 281-88; fax 511 580). 60฿ per day. Open 3pm-midnight.

Pharmacy: Virat Pharmacy, 6 Chit Bam Rung Rd. Heading north on Thonsarn, take a right at the elephant statues and follow Mitari Rd. until it intersects Chit Bam Rung. The Pharmacy is on the left at the corner. Open daily 6am-9pm.

Hospital: Surin Hospital, Lukmuang Rd. (tel. 511 006 or 511 757); the government hospital. **Ruam Paet,** Tessabarl Rd. (tel. 513 192). Private, and more expensive. English-speaking doctors. Thai sign with a red arrow directs you left.

Emergency: tel. 191.

Police: Surin Police Station, (tel. 511 007), Lukmuang Rd. The police station is next to the Red Cross Health Station (it has a pink neon "red cross" symbol high up in the air), on the corner of Lukmuang and Chit Bam Rung Rd.

ACCOMMODATIONS

Surin's hotels are mostly empty year-round except during the elephant round-up festival in November, when rates can go up as much as 50% and finding a room can be nearly impossible. During the off-season, when rooms are more plentiful than silicon at a Bel Air cocktail party, try wrangling a discount at the hotels.

Pirom's Guest House, 242 Krung Sri Nai Rd. (tel. 515 140), at the far west end of the road before it begins to curve south, 2 blocks past the market. An art history major in school and a government social worker for 25 years, Mr. Pirom is a historical and cultural resource like none other. When not working, he gives **tours** (much cheaper than travel agents') that are famed for their spontaneity and the interaction between guests, Mr. Pirom, and the villagers. Trips to silk-weaving villages, Khmer ruins, and Suay elephant-training villages around October and November. Their comfortable, Thai-style home has a beautiful pond, which is actually part of the old city moat and the source of all the mosquitoes you'll find here—fear not, the chambers have fly nets and repellent incense coils. Spotless rooms with fan. Shared bathroom. Dorm beds 50฿. Singles 70฿. Doubles 120฿. Laundry 5฿ per piece. Restaurant service. Gate is locked at 10:30pm.

New Hotel, 6-8 Thonsarn Rd. (tel. 511 322; fax 511 971), immediately outside the train station on the right side of the road. The staff is helpful and hospitable, with limited English. Basic and conveniently located. Singles 150฿, with A/C 360฿. Doubles 230฿, with A/C 430฿. Triples 300฿, with A/C 750฿. A/C rooms have warm water. Laundry 10฿ per pants/shirt combo. Check-out noon.

Santhong Hotel, 279-281 Thornsarn Rd. (tel.512 009; fax 514 329). Heading north, it's on the right, just before the traffic circle, opposite the Bangkok Bank. Clean and well maintained, if rather institutional rooms. Bedsheets so crisp any drill instructor would be proud. Singles 180฿, with A/C 320฿. Doubles 280฿, with A/C 400฿. An extra 100฿ gets you TV so you can catch up on any Thai soaps you missed while touring more remote areas of the province. Laundry: pants 10฿, shirts 8฿. Small kiosk and breakfast nook. Check-out noon.

FOOD

Surin has some of the best Isaan food around, especially at the **market** (at the intersection of Tessabarl 3 and Krung Sri Nai Rd.) which is open almost 24 hours. If Isaan food ain't up your soi, pardner, then rustle up the best hamburgers in all of Thailand, cooked just the way you like 'em by a Texas cowpoke.

Pai Ngen (tel. 512 151) on Soi Poi Tanko, off Krungsrinai Rd. As you leave Pirom's Guest House, head east toward the market and make the first right. 100m down to the left. Look for the newly painted green fence, and an illuminated Pepsi sign. Popular with the locals, and it's no wonder—their Thai and Isaan food is delicious. *Laap* 25-30฿, *nua nam doag* 25-30฿. Thai menu. Mr. and Mrs. Pirom can recommend dishes to those who can't read Thai, or simply close your eyes and point—it's a gastronomic gamble you can't lose! Prices are moderate, but worth it. Open 9pm-midnight. MC, Visa.

Country Roads Café and Samlor Bar, 165/1 Sirirat Rd. (tel. 515 721), on the dusty outskirts of town. From the bus station, instead of walking onto Chit Bam Rung Rd., go in the opposite direction. At the end of the road (about 150m, with a gate), turn left. Passing the Tarin Hotel, it is at the end of the road on the left corner. Owned and run by a native Texan and his Thai wife, this restaurant/bar sports an English menu with authentic hamburgers, pizza, and fries for the homesick. Country and '50s music, if not movies on the VCR, provide the ambience. The bar includes liquors rare in Thailand (Kahlúa, Malibu, etc.). Heart-shaped pizzas available for those Hallmark moments (up to 250฿). Open 10am-3am.

Wai Wan Restaurant, 44-46 Sanitnikhomrat Rd. (tel. 511 614). From the train station, take the second left onto Sanitnikhomrat Rd. Wai Wan will be halfway down the block. Look for the wood paneling. Inside, the waitstaff scurry among framed French Impressionist prints and bunches of dried flowers. Triple your pleasure with three-colored rice (sausage, olive, and crab) or three-colored cake (vanilla, strawberry and *bai duey*). Steaks (90-250฿) or more traditional Thai rice dishes (30-40฿) available. Impressive dessert menu includes coffee rum raisin cake (28฿) and durian sundaes (Yum). English menu and A/C. Open 9am-10pm.

SIGHTS

Surin is a pleasant place to relax and enjoy Isaan life, but there's not much in the way of "official" sights, unless you're there for the annual **Elephant Round-Up** at the end of November (check with TAT for exact dates). The stars of this two-day festival are the 200 pachyderms who perform spectacular feats of strength and skill, reaffirming their slot as the national animal. Highlights include a battle re-enactment, fought in the ancient style, and a staged "elephant hunt" exhibiting traditional Suay techniques. The finale features a soccer match played by the surprisingly agile beasts, who would give Pelé a run for his money (or crush him to a bloody pulp anyway). Touristy, but not something to be passed up.

ENTERTAINMENT

Turruars Maintain, 618 Thonsarn Rd. At the extreme south end of Thonsarn Rd. From the intersection with Lakmuang Rd. walk past the massive Isuzu dealership. The bar is about 150m farther, on the right just before the large water tower. The exterior is nearly obscured by a swirling tangle of roots, ropes, and a large parasol. An eclectic assemblage of bull skulls and pop-culture icons including Marilyn Monroe and Ozzy Osbourne. Attracts a young, hip, and very friendly crowd. Bone up your Eagles and CCR trivia, since they will pump you for info not even Kurt Loder knows. Beer 60฿, Coke 15฿. Open 6pm-2am. Music starts at 9pm.

■ NEAR SURIN

Anyone can go to one of the local silk-weaving villages, but don't expect to be taken around by the hand to see the entire silk-making process, especially given the communication barrier (if you don't speak Thai) and the fact that Thai villagers are wary of strangers, especially *farang*. This is where Mr. Pirom's tours (see above, Pirom's Guest House) come in handy. Pirom knows the people well, and as a go-between for travelers and locals, he makes learning about rural Thailand easier. Take his tours to places like **Ban Ta Klang,** a Suay village where elephants are trained and kept as pets, **Ban Khaosinarin,** traditional silk-weaving villages, and numerous Khmer ruins and temples such as **Prasat Srikhoraphum.**

If you are going solo to the villages, walk toward the train station on Thonsarn Rd. After the traffic circle, enter the second alley on the left. Trucks here ferry people the 20-odd km. Get here early to avoid a wait or an overnight in the village.

In the past, travelers have used Surin as a staging ground for trips **across the border into Cambodia at Chong Chom.** Presently, however, the territory on the Cambodian side has fallen into the hands of the **Khmer Rouge** and the border remains sealed with no immediate plans to re-open it. Don't expect any change until Cambodia's tragic situation works itself out. Inquire at the TAT for the latest details.

■■■ UBON RATCHATHANI

Ubon Ratchathani (pop. 100,000), the 'Lotus City,' is known simply as "Ubon" to Thais. One of the larger metropolitan centers in the country, Ubon is the commercial magnet for this corner of Thailand. Despite a small collection of temples, a noteworthy museum, and its renowned silk and cotton cloth, this city does not attract many travelers, except during the **Candle Festival,** celebrating the start of Buddhist Lent in August. The holiday is a time of great pageantry and rejoicing, and is well

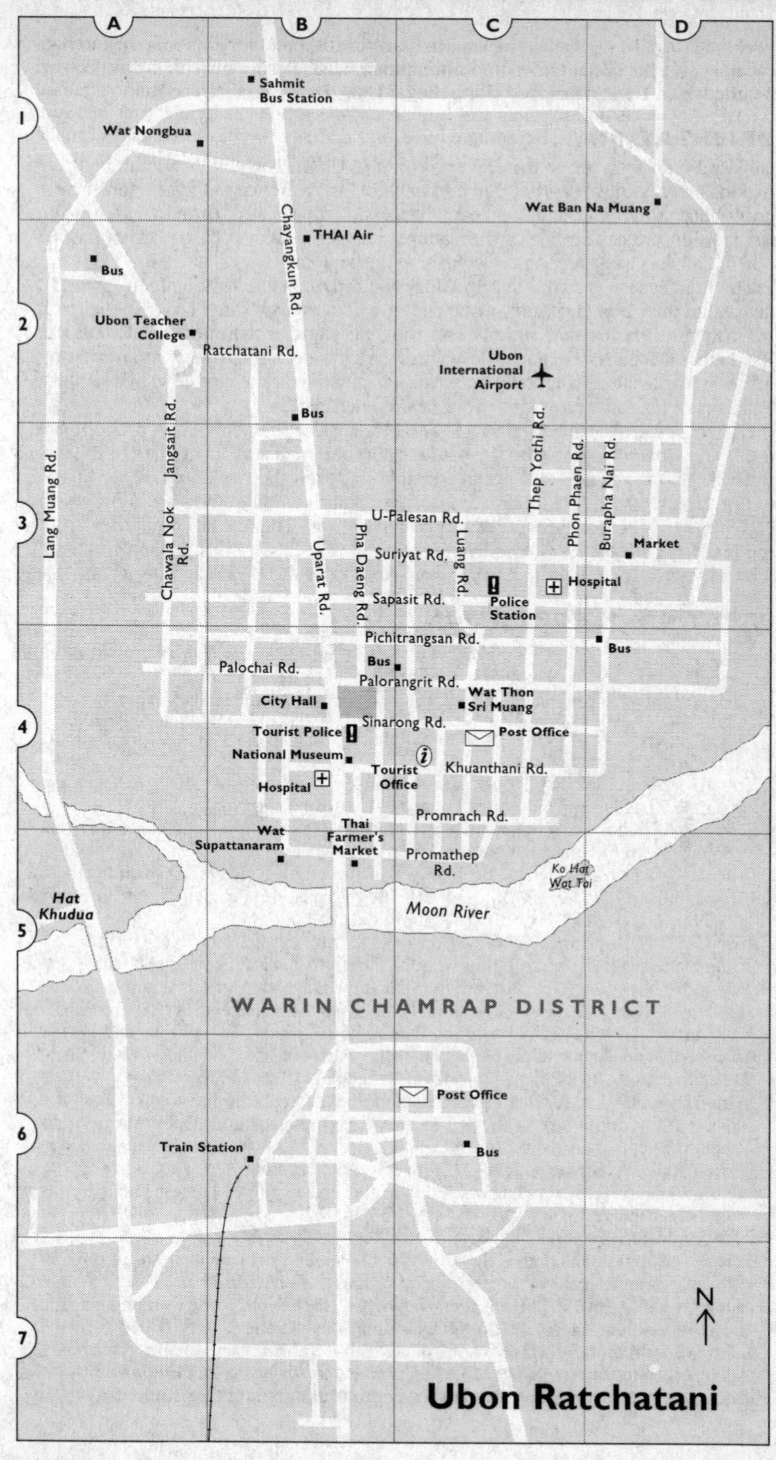
A
B
C
D
1
2
3
4
5
6
7
Sahmit
Bus Station
Wat Nongbua
Wat Ban Na Muang
THAI Air
Bus
Chayangkun Rd.
Ubon Teacher
College
Ratchatani Rd.
Ubon
International
Airport
Bus
Jangsait Rd.
Lang Muang Rd.
Thep Yothi Rd.
Phon Phaen Rd.
Burapha Nai Rd.
U-Palesan Rd.
Chawala Nok Rd.
Uparat Rd.
Pha Daeng Rd.
Luang Rd.
Suriyat Rd.
Market
Hospital
Sapasit Rd.
Police
Station
Pichitrangsan Rd.
Bus
Palochai Rd.
Bus
Palorangrit Rd.
Wat Thon
Sri Muang
City Hall
Sinarong Rd.
Tourist Police
Post Office
National Museum
Tourist
Office
Khuanthani Rd.
Hospital
Promrach Rd.
Wat
Supattanaram
Thai
Farmer's
Market
Promathep
Rd.
Ko Hat
Wat Tai
Hat
Khudua
Moon River
WARIN CHAMRAP DISTRICT
Post Office
Train Station
Bus
N
Ubon Ratchatani

worth the trip. Ubon makes an excellent jumping-off point for exploring the archaeological sites, national parks, and charming villages (many of which can only be reached from Ubon) sprinkled along the Mekong River region to the East.

ORIENTATION

Laos and Cambodia are to the east and south of Ubon. The corner where the three nations meet is known as the "emerald triangle," in reference to the lush forests that grow here. Although the city is readily accessible by air, bus, or train, Ubon is the last stop on the eastern leg of the national railway network. To go farther east or north, travelers must rely on the confusing bus system.

The train station is in the **Warin Chamrap district** south of the Moon River. To get within the Ubon city limits, catch city bus #2 or #6 (3฿). After crossing the river, stay on the bus for two blocks and then go right on **Khuanthani Road;** the Ratchathani Hotel is two blocks down on the right side of the road. If you're arriving in Ubon by bus, then you could be arriving in any one of the city's five bus stations. Take a taxi, tuk-tuk, or samlor to your desired destination.

City maps are available at the TAT. The **Moon River** separates Ubon proper from the Warin Chamrap district to the south, site of the train station and one of the bus stations. Ubon proper is laid out in a simple grid, and the city buses weave in and out of the streets, making their ways north or south. Luxury hotels are at the north end of town; other lodgings are scattered throughout. The main thoroughfare, from the bridge north to the previously mentioned first-class hotels, is **Uparat Road,** which eventually changes to **Chayangkun Road** after the U-Palesan intersection.

PRACTICAL INFORMATION

Tourist Office: Tourism Authority of Thailand (TAT), 264/1 Khuanthani Rd. (tel. 243 770; fax 243 771). From the train station, bus #2 crosses the river, goes up Uparat Rd. for 2 blocks, and then turns right. It's at the end of the 2nd block on the left. Carries city map with bus routes and brochures on neighboring provinces. Friendly staff, some of whom speak decent English. Open daily 8:30am-4:30pm except major holidays.

Tourist Police: (tel. 245 505, emergency 1699), on the corner of Uparat and Sinarong Rd. English spoken, so call here before dialing the police.

Currency Exchange: Thai Farmers Bank, 211 Promathep Rd. (tel. 243 47; fax 255 675). After crossing the Moon River from Warin Chamrap, Promathep Rd. is the 1st road on the right. The bank is on the right. **Krung Thai Bank,** 40-46 Uparat Rd. (tel. 242 280), on the right side just past the Promathep Rd. intersection. Both open Mon.-Fri. 8:30am-3:30pm except holidays.

Post Office/Telephone: GPO (tel. 254 000), Sinarong Rd. Exit left from the TAT office, and walk to the 2nd intersection. Turn left. Walk north 1 block to the Sinarong intersection. The post office is on the right hand corner. Open Mon.-Fri. 8:30am-4:30pm, Sat.-Sun. 9am-noon. Telephone and telegram service open daily 7am-11pm. Accepts AmEx, Visa/MC. **Postal code:** 34000. **Telephone code:** 045.

Airport: Ubon Ratchathani International Airport (tel. 243 037), Thep Yothi Rd. Two flights every day to and from Bangkok on THAI Airways (1hr., 1345฿). The **THAI Airways** office, 364 Chayangkun Rd. (tel. 313 340-43) is across the street, a few min. walk to the left from the Pathumrat Hotel. Open Mon. 10am-4pm, Tues.-Sun. 8am-4pm. Visa/MC.

Trains: Railway Station (tel. 321 878; advance ticketing 321 004), Sathani Rd., Warin Chamrap district. The station is at the end of the Northeast line. 6 trains run daily from Bangkok (6:55, 7:10am, 1:55, 4:50, 5:55, and 7pm, 13hr., 3rd-class: 95฿, rapid 115฿, express 175฿).

Buses: The nightmare that is the Ubon Bus terminal system will soon be only an unpleasant memory; a new, centralized terminal is being built and is set to open sometime in early 1997. Until then, however, there seem to be as many bus stations in Ubon as there are possible destinations. At the far north end of town along Chayangkun Rd. (take bus #2 or #3) is the **Sahmit bus station.** Four buses leave every morning (5:45, 6:15, 7:45, and 8:15), stopping at **Mukdahan** (43฿) and ending at **Udon Thani** (106฿). Direct to **Mukdahan** (11am, noon, and 1pm,

43฿) and **Nakhon Phanom** (6, 7, 8, and 10am, 67฿). This station is particularly confusing—always double-check with other passengers before getting on a bus. At the northwest end of town along Jangsanit Rd., 2km beyond the traffic circle, is the **Sayan Tour bus station.** Daily buses to **Udon Thani** (97฿) stop in **Khon Kaen** (70฿), leaving at 5:30, 6, 6:30, 7, 7:30, 8, 9, 10am, 5:50, 10:30, 11:14pm, 12:30, and 2:30am. Next to Pathumrat Hotel, buses leave for **Bangkok** (tel. 241 831; 10 daily, 5am-7pm, 159฿; A/C: 8am, 5:40, 6, and 7pm, 223฿, 400฿). Two blocks east of the Uparit intersection on the northeast corner are mostly A/C buses to: **Bangkok** (8 daily, 8:15am-9:30pm, 278฿, VIP 325฿); and **Chiang Mai** (6 daily, 12:15-6:30pm, 445฿, VIP 500฿). Buses to **Mukdahan** (53฿), **Phibun** (32฿), and other points in the province leave along Buraphani Rd., one block east of Sapasit Hospital. Buses leave from **Warin Champrap bus station** south of the Moon River (take bus #1, 3, 6, or 7, 3฿) to **Phibun** (every 15min., 6:20am-5:30pm, 12฿).

Local Transportation: City buses cover Ubon and Warin Chamrap. TAT map has bus routes. Buses are 3฿ (4฿ for long-distance trips) and run 6am-6pm. Tuk-tuks and samlors also, but they can be expensive. Samlor trips shouldn't go beyond the river. With non-metered taxis, bargain hard or get seriously ripped off.

Car/Moped Rental: Cho Watana, 39/8 Suriyat Rd. (tel. 242 202 or 241 906), one block west of the Uparat/Suriyat intersection in the north of town. Motorbikes cost 250฿ per day, cars 1200฿ and up. A 500฿ deposit for bikes; 5000฿ for cars. Any accidents and it's bye bye baht. International drivers permit required.

Markets: Several markets in Ubon; the largest is near the bridge on the north side of the river, behind Promathep Rd. It only takes 1 hr. off each day; the day market becomes the night market at 5pm, with a break from 4am-5am.

Laundry: If your hotel doesn't have the service, try **Gow Chang** (tel. 242 029), Khuanthani Rd. Located a few stores to the left of the Chiokee Restaurant. Pants and jeans 10฿, shirts 7฿.

Swimming Pool: Provincial Sports Complex (tel. 313 480), several hundred meters past the Ratchathani Rd./Chayangkun Rd. intersection heading north. On the left side of the road, opposite the Shell station. The pool is in back. Open Mon. 3:30-7:30pm, Tues.-Fri. 5:30-9am and 3:30-7:30pm, Sat.-Sun. 5:30-10am and 3-7:30pm; adults 20฿, children 10฿.

Pharmacy: Chaiwit Pharmacy, 87 Promathep Rd. (tel. 254 077). Turn right onto Promathep Rd. after crossing the bridge. It is 4 blocks down the road on the right side on a corner. Open Mon.-Sat. 7am-7:30pm, Sun. 7am-noon. **Contact Lens Supplies:** 222-224 Promrach Rd. (tel. 244 676; fax 244 871). At the Chaiwit Pharmacy intersection, turn left instead and walk 1 block north to Promrach Rd. Look for the giant eyeglasses above the sign. Open Mon.-Sat. 8am-8pm, Sun. 8am-5pm.

Hospitals: Sapasit Hospital (tel. 244 660 or 255 970), about 100m east of the intersection of Thebyotee and Sapasit Rd. Public hospital. **Rom Klao,** 123 Uparat Rd. (tel. 244 658, -60). 2 blocks down Uparat Rd. from the bridge, on the left, just before Khuanthani Rd. Private service, English-speaking doctors. Cash only.

Emergency: tel. 191.

Police: (tel. 254 216 or 255 117), on Sapasit Rd. at the Thebyotee Rd. intersection. Contact the tourist police first (tel. 1699).

ACCOMMODATIONS

There are two decent guest houses in **Khong Chiam,** a small town 60km due east of Ubon near the Laotian border, and one in **Warin Chamrap,** only a few kilometers south. The hotel scene in the city is pretty gloomy.

Ratchathani Hotel, 297 Khuanthani Rd. (tel. 244 388; fax 243 561). A small step above the rest. If you can only afford a fan room, at least you can relax in the A/C lobby with Peace Corps volunteers who flock here on their off-days. Color TV, cold drinking water, and western bath with hot water. Lame, high-priced restaurant in the back. Conveniently located near the TAT and relatively close to the National Museum, the post office, good restaurants, the day/night market, and a few bars. Singles 280฿, with A/C 450฿. Doubles 400฿, with A/C 600฿. VIP rooms 800฿. Laundry 15฿ for shirt/pants combo. Visa.

River Moon House, 43-45 Sisaket 2 Rd., Warin Chamrap (tel. 322 592). Exit left on the main road in front of the train station, walk 1-½ blocks until the road merges with Sisaket Rd. With your back to the train station, it's across the street and left of the fire station. If you reach the highway you've gone too far. Built over a century ago, River Moon is held together by wood dowels. Republicans will feel right at home: the emphasis is on family and tradition. Local hand-woven baskets are used as lampshades, while conical, straw farmer hats and Ubon's woven fish traps adorn the walls. An abundance of musical instruments provides the tools for an Isaan jam session. Attractive, freshly painted rooms with monster double beds and traditional Isaan furniture (100฿). Free breakfast eaten family-style downstairs. Laundry 5฿ per item. Ideal for those in Ubon for just a day or so.

Tokyo Hotel, 320 Uparat Rd. (tel. 241 739; fax same), on the right side of the road on the block past Pichitrangsan Rd. Look for the small red 'hotel' sign next to Siam Commercial Bank. Conveniently located near a market. Cheaper than most, but bathrooms are small, Thai style, and while clean, have seen better days. Ceiling fans will keep you cool, but hang a little low. Anyone over 6 ft. risks an impromptu lobotomy. Singles 150฿, with A/C 230฿. Doubles 200฿, with A/C 280฿. Laundry service 8-10฿ per piece. Check-out noon.

FOOD

As is the case with most towns in Thailand, you can't throw a book out of a tuk-tuk without hitting an eatery. For cheap dining use the **market,** off Promathep Rd. east of Leparit Rd. Open virtually 24 hrs. to serve your stomach. At night, **vendors** also gather off Khuanthani Rd. on Rachabut Rd. near the Ratchathani Hotel. Several Chinese restaurants nearby on Khuanthani Rd., are open well past midnight.

Bua Boo Cha Mangsawirat, 11 Sri Saket Rd., Warin Chamrap (tel. 323 360). From the Warin Chamrap train station, walk straight ahead and turn right onto Uparat Rd. at the 4th large intersection. Walk 1 block to the next intersection past the Bangkok Bank of Commerce. Turn left and it's on your immediate right. Look for an abundance of potted plants and a small sign with 'vegetarian' written in English. A large round clay well, framed with gnarled roots, dominates the room. Herbs and flowers dangling from the walls make a pleasing potpourri. Popular with devout Buddhists (hence the religious literature), as the Thai and Lao veggie cuisine is first-rate. Each topping is 6฿ and served over special *koklan* rice (whole-grain mixed with wheat grain). Salads 10฿. Open Mon.-Sat. 6:30am-8pm.

The Fern Hut Bakery and Restaurant, 17 Ratchathani Rd. (tel. 244 305), in the north of town, just off Ratchathani Rd. With your back to the traffic circle, it is on the first small soi on the right next to a gas station. You can see the English sign from Ratchathani Rd. Truly an enigma: nary a fern in sight and the feel of a Vermont ski lodge—right down to the varnished wood ceiling and stone fireplace. No hot cocoa, but extensive (and expensive) menu boasts delicious Thai cuisine. Fried rice is possibly the best in Thailand (35฿). *Laap* (60฿). Roast duck with baby broccoli (house special, 100฿). Deadly bakery: Black Forest cake (25฿) and pastry almost too pretty to eat. Almost. Open daily 8am-10pm. Visa/MC.

Chiokee Restaurant, 307-317 Khuanthani Rd. (tel. 254 017 or 291-244). With your back to the Ratchathani Hotel, turn left and cross the small intersection. The restaurant will be a few stores down on the left, across the street from the National Museum. Really popular, especially in the mornings. Breakfasts 20-50฿ (fresh OJ, 15฿). Voluminous menu has large Thai and western selections. A bit pricey, but worth it. Noodle and rice dishes 25-40฿. Meat dishes (pork, cricket) 40-100฿. western standards (25-40฿), but the burgers are rumored to suffer from "Where's the Beef" syndrome. Open daily 6am-9pm.

Villa Food, 115 Polpan Rd. (tel. 243 680). Exit Sapasit Hospital and turn left. Walk to the first intersection and turn right onto Polpan Rd. Continue walking south for 1 block until you reach the Pichitrangsan intersection. Villa Food is on the right corner. No spooky Thai interpretations of Italian cuisine here. This is the real thing made by a bona fide Italian from Milan. Seven styles of pasta, eight types of pizza (80-250฿, depending on size), and 6 types of spaghetti (50-70฿), plus other western and Thai favorites. *Tutto è 'squisito!* Round off the evening with a glass of wine or a cappuccino (40฿). A/C. Open Tues.-Sun. 11:30am-10pm.

SIGHTS

The **Ubon Ratchathani National Museum,** considered one of the best in the country, documents the geology, paleontology, archaeology, history, and culture of the region. Most of the exhibits have excellent English translations, and there is even a small replica of the prehistoric paintings at Pha Taem if you can't make it all the way out to see the real thing. The museum is on the left side of Khuanthani Rd. immediately after turning right off Uparat Rd. The one-story building, built in 1873, was formerly the Governor's office (tel. 255 071; open Wed.-Sun. 9am-4pm).

Ubon is famous for its silk and its cotton cloth. Two stores that sell clothing made from the area's unique handwoven cotton are the **Maybe Cotton Hut,** 142 Sinarong Rd. (tel. 254 932), and **Peaceland,** 189 Thepyotee Rd. (tel. 241 821). Maybe is a block east of the post office, open daily 7:30am-9pm. To get to Peaceland, exit right from Sapasit Hospital and walk to the first intersection. Turn left and walk south on Thepyotee Rd. It's on the corner of the first alley on the right, underneath the huge pink flowering bougainvillea vine. Watch your wallet, as Peaceland's large selection of beautiful shirts, pants, hats, and dresses, all made of hand-spun cotton cloth, are a sure way to get rid of all those little red-100 baht notes in your money pouch. Cloth is also sold, and the owner may let you peruse the hundreds of bolts stacked in the back (which are shipped all over the world, even to your house). Take the cloth and a pattern idea to any tailor for a one-of-a-kind wardrobe. Open daily 8am-8pm.

For a more general selection of local handicrafts, try **Ban Phan Chat,** 158 Ratchabut Rd. (tel. 243 433). Exit right from the TAT office and turn right again at the first intersection. The store will be to your immediate right. Open every day except Wednesday 9am-8pm. Ban Phan Chat also carries a greater selection of cotton outfits for children.

Wat Thon Sri Muang is on Luang Rd. opposite the provincial kindergarten school. Built during the Chakri Dynasty, this wat is over 200 years old, and the interior walls have paintings (some erotic) depicting life in ancient Ubon. The topaz Buddha image attracts tourists to **Wat Sri Ubon Ratanaram (Wat Sri Thong)** on Uparat Rd. **Wat Nong Bua** on Chayangkun Rd. is modeled after Bhodgaya Chedi in India, where Lord Buddha attained his Enlightenment; the architecture is thus quite different from the traditional Thai-style wat.

Two relaxing spots on the Moon River are popular with locals. **Ko Hat Wat Tai** is an island surrounded by a village of *Gilligan's Island* huts perched on stilts above the water. During the dry season (Dec.-April), the island can be reached by a bamboo footbridge. When the bridge is closed, the island is inaccessible and closed to the public. Locals order food from the restaurants on the island and picnic in the small thatched huts. Come and watch the sunset over the Moon River, but don't forget the mosquito repellent. If you walk east to the end of Promrach Rd. and then turn right and walk down to the river bank, you'll see the island and the bridge. Similar to Ko Hat Wat Tai in terms of what it has to offer, **Hat Khudua** is on the north bank of the river 12km west of town. Food and drinks are available on bamboo rafts.

ENTERTAINMENT

Green Peace, 185-187 Jangsanit Rd. (tel. 311 299), in the northwest corner of the city, past the traffic circle on the road to Yasothon, opposite the Esso gas station. The self-styled music studio and art gallery is a favorite among Ubon's expat community and roving environmental crusaders. A good rendition of a SoHo loft, complete with abstract, activist paintings and tinfoil on the ceiling, but the leather hides on the wall seem oddly inappropriate. Excellent live music. Open 8:30pm-1am; music starts at 9:30pm. Singha 50฿, Coke 25฿.

Country Saloon (tel. 243 389). Located off Chayangkun Rd., one block past the Tokyo hotel. In a narrow alley on the right, just before a FIAT dealership. Clearly visible from the sidewalk—look for the white Christmas lights. A classic Thai-style C&W bar. 10-gallon hats adorn the walls, and countless framed Marlboro Man pix add a western flavor. Large and very popular on weekends. Menu lists pricey Thai food (40-200฿). Come for the music—CCR anyone? Drink your Singha from a boot-shaped mug. YEE-HAA! Open daily 8pm-2am; music starts at 11pm. Visa.

The Cave, #377 Chayangkun Rd. (tel. 247-501, ext. 118). Directly north of the Pathumurat Hotel, before the Siryat intersection. The place to see and be seen in Ubon; no sleazy dive, this disco/nightclub may be the best in the region. Walls are decorated with "cave paintings" that look more like amoebas than antelopes. Live music on weekends; band plays unusually good Thai pop and a smattering of English tunes. Whopping 140฿ cover gets you two drinks. Open 9pm-5am.

■ NEAR UBON RATCHATHANI

For those with a hunger for genuine world-famous Isaan silk, try the **Women's Weaving Cooperative** in the village of **Ban Pa-Ao,** 17km north of Ubon. Begun by CARE international with a staff of three, the cooperative has blossomed into an award-winning operation, with 10 full-time weavers, and six part-time. Their traditional mutmee silk in a kaleidoscopic array of colors and patterns is breathtaking, and as is often the case, money-taking as well. Prices begin at 650฿ per meter, and run well into the thousands. All the looms are hand-operated, and the process of creating the final product, thread by thread, is painstaking. Weavers will be happy to perform demonstrations upon request. The showroom also sells clothes, mostly women's blouses and skirts, starting at around 450฿. Special tailoring available. Open daily 8am-5pm. Any bus heading north from the Sayan Tour bus station passes Ban Pa Ao. Just tell the ticket collector to drop you off there (10฿). From the main road, the cooperative is about 3km east; motorcycle taxis can take you the rest of the way for 10฿. To return to Ubon, simply flag down any bus heading south to the city or catch a songthaew directly from the village (6฿).

Not far outside Ubon city (about 12km on the way to Si Saket) is **Wat Paa Nanachat Beung Wai,** a forest monastery with predominantly western monks. English is spoken here, so any foreigner studying meditation and the Buddhist religion should visit this wat. Visitors can stay as long as they like, provided they participate in the daily activities of the wat community (waking up at 3am, chanting, meditating, keeping up with group maintenance chores, and having one meal a day). Men who stay longer than three days will be asked to shave their heads and wear the clothes of a novice. Strict rules regulate separation of the sexes. The monastery is behind a peaceful rice field off the highway to Si Saket, near Beung Wai village. Catch a Si Saket-bound bus or songthaew from the Warin Chamrap bus terminal and ask to get off at Wat Nanachat (4฿). The best time to visit is before 11am.

Along the southern border of the province with Cambodia is the large, ancient Khmer temple complex of **Khao Phra Wiharn.** It is far away and difficult to access, but can be reached from either Ubon, Si Saket, or Surin. Before making the trip, check at the TAT office to see if it is currently open, since periodic fighting makes things dangerous. To date it has been closed since June 1994, when Khmer Rouge forces won control of it, and the situation still looks grim. However, if it is open and the site is deemed safe, you will still have to pass through Thai and Cambodian military checkpoints before entering and pay about 100฿ at each one. Visitors must not stray from the designated paths, since these are the only areas which are sure to be cleared of land mines. The temple, dating from Angkorian times, has been semi-restored. It is built on a 500m-high escarpment overlooking the Cambodian jungle, which explains its strategic military value. To get there, catch a bus to Kantharalak from the Warin Chamrap bus terminal, and from there ride a songthaew to the temple. It's at least a three-hour trip one way.

KHONG CHIAM

Sixty kilometers east of the city, at the confluence of the Moon and Mekong Rivers, lies the tranquil hamlet of Khong Chiam. To local young people it's "Sticksville," but to the traveler, weary of the heat and dust of larger metropoli, it's paradise lost (*or regained?*). Only the two main streets are paved, and children squeal and hide when a sweaty *farang* toting a heavy backpack trudges up the road. The simplest way to get here is to take a bus from the Warin Chamrap bus station to Phibun Mangshan. From the Phibun market, take a samlor to the songthaew station near the Moon River (10฿). Songthaews leave approximately every 30 min. (12฿). Check with the driver to make sure he's headed to Khong Chiam. The Apple Guest House has a list of departure times and destinations of songthaews leaving from the market.

The town is shaped like a parrot's beak, jutting out into the two rivers. **Klaewpradit Road** runs from the market and bus stop straight through the center of town, ending at a wat. Walking across the temple grounds will take you to a small pavilion that affords an excellent view of the spot where the two rivers meet (called the Two-Color river in reference to the different levels of silt dispension in the water, a phenomena clearly visible from shore). The **post office** and a small branch of **Krung Thai Bank** are located along Klaewpradit Rd. near the Apple Guest House. **Rimkheng Road** runs along the Mekong River just north of Klaewpradit Rd. Here a stone tablet opposite the police station identifies Khong Chiam as the **easternmost point in Thailand.** Several good restaurants line Rimkheng Rd. farther down, all affording excellent views of the river, with Laos on the other side.

Khong Chiam supports several fine guest houses of which the **Apple Guest House,** 267 Klaewpradit Rd. (tel. 351 160), is tops. From the market head right on Klaewpradit Rd. It's about 300m down the road, past the bank and opposite the post office on the right. Signs are sprinkled along the road. Large, clean rooms (singles and doubles) are 80฿ and 250฿ with A/C. Communal Thai-style bathrooms; A/C rooms have private bath. The small restaurant in front contains a helpful information board with bus schedules to Phibun and Ubon, directions to the parks, and a map of the village. Laundry service. Motorcycles rented for 150฿ per day.

The **Khong Chiam Guest House,** 355 Pakumchai Rd. (tel. 351 079) is located off Klaewpradit Rd. From the market take a right onto Klaewpradit, then another right, just before the VIP restaurant. Fairly new, spotless rooms with bath 100฿, with A/C 250฿. Laundry service. Motorcycles rented for 150฿, bicycles 50฿. Light sleepers beware: with little traffic to drown them out, Khong Chiam's roosters can be deafening at 6am.

To the north of Khong Chiam is the recently designated **Pha Taem National Park,** where a 200m stretch of prehistoric rock paintings, dating back over 3000 years, has been found. There is no public transport to this park, but you can get there easily with a map and rented wheels from either guest house in Khong Chiam. Road signs direct you as well. Once you are at Pha Taem, it's a 500-m walk to the paintings, which were drawn on a cliff face with a magnificent view of the Mekong River and Laos on the other side. Trails along the top of the cliff offer gorgeous views of the river and Laos. **Tana Rapids National Park** is about 3km south of Khong Chiam on the Moon River.

BORDER CROSSING: CHONG MEK / VANG TAO

Before the opening of the Friendship Bridge linking Nong Khai with Vientiane, the tiny, remote village of **Chong Mek** was the only location from which travelers could enter Laos on foot. From the even more minuscule village of **Vang Tao** on the Lao side, it is a short ride to **Pakxe,** an excellent springboard for exploring southern Laos. Other than the border crossing itself, there is little of interest to travelers here, unless you come on Saturday or Sunday, during which a lively market springs up on both sides of the border. Located in the boonies, 44km southwest of Phibun, Chong Mek can only be reached form Phibun. From Ubon, take a bus from the Warin Chamrap station to Phibun. At the Phibun market, locals can direct you to songthaews heading to Chong Mek (80 min., 13฿). Get to Phibun early; songthaews are more frequent on the weekends when the market is open.

The Thai market is much larger, though it consists largely of commercial goods, with little in the way of souvenirs or handicrafts (baby ducklings 10฿!). Only on these two days are foreigners allowed to cross the border freely, but they can proceed no more than 250m onto Lao soil. The smaller market on the Lao side consists of a few stalls proffering an array of wicker baskets, lacquer boxes, and rotgut Vietnamese whisky. Several small open-air restaurants sell traditional Lao food, but little English is spoken. **Warning:** the people apparently use meat to flavor their chilis.

Travelers intending to officially enter Laos here must first obtain a visa, stamped with the appropriate entry point (i.e. Vang Tao), from the Lao PDR Embassy in Bangkok. **Visas obtained in Nong Khai are not valid here.** Before crossing the border you must officially register your departure from Thailand at the Thai immigration office on the right, about 30m before the fence. Once in Laos, present your visa to the Lao immigration office, also on the right just beyond the border (entry tax 10฿). From Vang Tao, a songthaew can take you to Pakxe for 10฿.

■■■ MUKDAHAN

Mukdahan was carved out of Ubon Ratchathani and Nakhon Phanom provinces in 1982. It lies midway along the eastern border of Isaan with the Mekong River to the east, directly opposite the Lao city of Savannakhet. There is a strong Lao flavor to this small, dusty provincial capital, whose population speaks a fifty-fifty mix of Thai and Lao. While admittedly not Ansel Adams territory (good luck finding a postcard in Mukdahan), some beautiful vistas can be had along the river at twilight. Beyond that the appeal here is a human one—few *farang* make it out this way, and those who do can expect a few stares and chuckles, as well as many genuine attempts at conversation. Students on motorbikes cajole you into practicing English with them,; older street workers will remind you not to get ripped off by tuk-tuk jockeys.

ORIENTATION

The town of Mukdahan is right on the river, and with the Mekong always to the east, you would think that orienting yourself would be easy—it's not. When you arrive in town, grab a tuk-tuk ride to your hotel (5฿). The town is laid out on a grid, with streets running roughly parallel to (north-south) and perpendicular to (east-west) the river. Get to know the river's location well; it is your friend, and with the limited number of English speakers in Mukdahan, the most valuable guide. At the center of the town is a **traffic circle.** The road running east-west (toward the river) is **Chaiyankan Road; Phitak Phanomket Road** runs parallel to it. Standing at the traffic circle facing the river, the hospital stands behind you on Chaiyankan. The police station will be to your left on Phitak Phanomket. **Samran Chaikhong Road** runs down the length of the river and has several decent restaurants. The **Indochina Market** is there during the day. **Samut Sakdarak Road** is the next road over. **Song Nang Sathit Road** intersects these roads, running east-west straight to the Immigration and Customs buildings at the pier. The expensive Mukdahan Hotel is on the outskirts of the town going south on **Mukdahan-Dontan Road,** from which songthaews leave for Phu Pha Theop National Park, 16km south of town. Pick up a map of town at the **Pith Bakery** on Phitak Phanomket Road near the police station.

PRACTICAL INFORMATION

Currency Exchange: Bangkok Bank of Commerce, 141 Samut Sakdarak Rd. (tel. 611 098), across from Hua Nam Hotel. **Thai Farmers Bank,** 222 Song Nang Sathit Rd. (tel. 611 056), 2 blocks up the road from the pier that is across the street from the **Bangkok Bank**. Open 8:30am-3:30pm, except holidays.

Post Office: Mukdahan Post and Telegram Office, Chaiyankan Rd. (tel 611 065). From the traffic circle, walk west *(away* from the river) 500m, passing the hospital to your right. At the motorcycle dealerships and the sign for the Ploy Palace Hotel, take a right. The post office faces the market. Open Mon.-Fri. 8:30am-4:30pm, Sat.-Sun. 9am-noon. **Postal code:** 49000

Telephones: 191/1 Song Nang Sathit Rd. (tel. 611 697), on the outskirts of town. From the pier, walk through town, pass the banks on the left, pass the field in front of city hall on the right; it's on a small dirt soi on the left. Small office with a very tall antenna. Open daily 7am-10pm. **Telephone code:** 042.

Buses: Mukdahan has no central bus station; locations of the stops vary according to the destination and the bus company. There are 2 major companies that operate in Mukdahan. One is **999VIP** (tel. 611 478), whose main stop is located a few stores to the right of the intersection before the night market, opposite the police box. To: **Bangkok** (ordinary bus 4:30 and 7:30pm, 164฿; VIP bus 5:30pm, 445฿); **Nakhon Phanom/That Phanom (**every hour 6am-5pm, Nakhon Phanom 29฿; That Phanom15฿); and **Ubon** (every 30min., 6am-2pm). The other company is **927 Tour Co.** (tel. 611 813), across from the City Pillar Shrine on Song Nang Sathit Rd. To **Bangkok** (3 VIP buses per day 8am-5:30pm, 287฿).

Local Public Transportation: Tuk-tuks around here look more like a cross between a mini-songthaew and a regular tuk-tuk. Standard fare 5฿. (If someone charges you more, write his license down and give it to the police.)

Laundromat: If your lodgings don't have laundry service, try **Sa-Art Laundry,** 77-77/1 Samut Sakdarak Rd. (tel. 611 188), 1 block past Foremost Restaurant and on the left heading south out of town. Pants 7฿, shirts 5฿. Open daily 7am-9pm.

Swimming Pool: Tempting as the chocolate-brown Mekong may look, swimming is not advised. Try the **Ploy Palace Hotel**, 40 Chaiyankan Rd. (tel. 611 329 or 612 150). Near the day market and the post office. Maybe the tallest building in the city. Tough to miss. Pool open daily 9am-5pm; 30฿.

Markets: Day market, off Chaiyankan Rd. about 0.5km west of the traffic circle on the right. In the middle of a small square bordered by the post office and the Ploy Palace Hotel. Mostly clothes, with a few excellent Vietnamese soup stalls. **Night market:** Mukdahan's fabulous night market alone is reason enough to spend the night. Beginning at about 6pm, 75m of Song Nang Sathit Rd. in front of the City Hall is cordoned off. Locals congregate to chat and feast on Isaan delectables. A highlight in this blue-collar riverine town. Shuts down by 11pm.

Pharmacy: Huan Hong Osoth Pharmacy, 38 Samut Sakdarak Rd. (tel. 612 002), on the corner opposite Hua Nam Hotel. Open daily 6am-8pm.

Hospital: Mukdahan Hospital, Chaiyankan Rd. (tel. 611 285), on the road west of the traffic circle, away from the river. As you walk away from the circle, the hospital is 2 blocks down on the right. No English spoken.

Emergency: tel. 191.

Police: Mukdahan Police Station, Phitak Phanomket Rd. (tel. 611 333), near the post office. No English spoken.

ACCOMMODATIONS

The only downside to Mukdahan's lack of *farang* visitors is a paucity of decent guest houses of the type that typically grace this region of Isaan. For 120฿ you can get a simple, clean room with a ceiling fan and a communal Thai-style bathroom (character and originality not included).

Hua Nam Hotel, 36 Samut Sakdarak Rd. (tel. 611 197 or 611 137), on the corner of Samut Sakdarak and Song Nang Sathit Rd., one block from the pier/immigration area. Couch turnips can bask in the glow of the boob tube in the downstairs restaurant. Owners take care of the necessities; rooms are clean and comfortable. Centrally located. Singles with shared bath 120฿, with private bath 220฿, with A/C 300฿. Doubles with shared bath 200฿, with private bath 220฿, with A/C 400฿. All A/C rooms have hot water and telly. Laundry 14฿ per shirt/pants combo.

Mukdahan Hotel, 8/8 Mukdahan-Dontan Rd. (tel. 611 619 or 611 629), on the outskirts of town, on the road to Phu Pha Theop National Park (Route 2034 or Samut Sakdarak Rd.). Either a doghouse or a palace. Rover's singles or doubles with shared, unisex bathroom 150฿. Request a room upstairs for the best view in town. Regular A/C 300฿, tack on 50฿ for a TV. Rama IV's singles or doubles with A/C, TV, fridge, and spacious private bath 500-600฿.

Ban Phun Muang Guest house, 128 Phitak Santikrat Rd. (tel 632 478), located south of the traffic circle on the right, in a large white building with dark blue balustrades on the balconies. Small street-level sign reads "Guest house." Recently opened and currently the only guest house in town, although the rooms are rather motel-ish. 6 freshly painted, fastidiously neat rooms. Small rooms 120฿, large corner rooms with 2 windows 180฿. Rooms open onto the narrow balcony with a decent view of the burg. Some English spoken. 2 Thai-style bathrooms.

FOOD

The riverside restaurants are all quite similar. When the sun goes down, tables are set up outside so that diners can enjoy the cool breeze off the Mekong while the lights of Savannakhet begin to wink in the twilight. The Suwa Blend Restaurant and Pub stays open much later than the night market.

Foremost Restaurant, 74-74/1 Samut Sakdarak Rd. (tel. 612 251). Exit Hua Nam Hotel and walk past Huan Hong Osoth Pharmacy on the right for 1 block. It will be across the next intersection on the right corner. Elevator music seeps through the A/C air while trendy Thais tap their feet approvingly. New and pretty, with a glass wall facing the street for 360° rubber-necking at the *farang*. The pseudo-translated menu has Thai food and even some western selections. The Thai language section of the menu is 3 times as long as the English section. If there's something you want that is unlisted, inquire; chances are they have it. Cashew chicken 50฿, Singha 65฿, Coke 10฿. Open daily 7am-11pm. MC, Visa.

Pith Bakery, 102 Phitak Phanomket Rd. (tel. 611 990). From the pier walk to the Bangkok and Thai Farmers Bank intersection. Turn left. It will be a short distance down Phitak Phanomket Rd. on the right with an English sign, before the police station. Pick up their map of Mukdahan and gulp down a chocolate brownie. Besides baked goods and ice cream, breakfast is also available with freshly ground coffee (30฿ for eggs, bacon, and coffee). A wide selection of blends ranging from 'Blue Mountain' to 'Dunkin Donut' (10฿). Open 7am-8:30pm.

SIGHTS

Don't count on a whirlwind tour of excitement in Mukdahan, but you might as well check out **Wat Si Mongkan Tai** on Samran Chaikhong Rd and the daily **Indochina market** (*talaat Indochina* in Thai) by the pier, so named because of the many Lao and Vietnamese vendors who peddle their wares here. Many people come over from Savannakhet, Laos to sell their goods, bringing bounties of...stuff. Mostly gaudy, petroleum-based products too functional to be first-class kitsch. Hum along with clocks tinkling the *Young and Restless* theme. If you're in the market for a dining room set, you'll hit the jackpot here. Monumental, intricately carved tables and chairs with mother-of-pearl inlays are sold at criminal prices. Weekend markets feature an even larger selection of...stuff.

■ NEAR MUKDAHAN

Known for its interesting rock formations and caves, **Phu Pha Theop National Park** also has lots of barely visible prehistoric rock art, varied landscape (unusual rocks, bare plateaus, cliffs, valleys, waterfalls, forests, and streams), protected nature (barking deer, birds, monkeys, wild boar, civets, and late-blooming flowers), and trails throughout. The rangers here know the area quite well, and one speaks English. Trail maps in English are available upon request from the park office at the entrance.

The collection of huge, oddly shaped rocks at the main entrance to the park are the chief crowd-pleasers. The undersides of many overhanging rocks are decorated with prehistoric paintings resembling those at Pha Taem. They are 3000 years old and are mostly handprints, enigmatic geometric patterns, shapes of animals, and some indications of calligraphic characters. They're all very faint, so ask one of the park rangers to point some out.

The main 2km hike to the **Buddha Cave Waterfall** goes straight past the rocks. Most of the other trails are short side hikes offering mountain and cliff scenery as well as more weird rocky areas. The trails aren't always easy to follow; explore carefully. Signs in Thai direct you right, left, and ahead; the arrows pointing straight ahead lead to the waterfall, past a slightly inclined rock plateau. The arrows then pass through to the forested area, down a mountain and up the next one, with beautiful scenery and foliage all along the way. If you come during the rainy or cold season, you will hear the cascades of the waterfall as you approach. During the dry season, the waterfall is likely to have dried up to a pathetic trickle. Take the rickety wooden stairs leading to the **Buddha Cave,** which is to the left at the top. The large Buddha image here is surrounded by a coterie of thousands of smaller crumbling Buddhas carefully placed on the rock ledges by devout followers. If you return to the stairs you will find more steps leading to the rocky summit. Even during the peak of hot season, there are refreshing pools of water here where you can rinse off (don't drink it). Buy water for the hike.

Phu Pha Theop National Park can only be reached from Mukdahan by blue trucks and songthaews leaving town on the Mukdahan-Dontan Rd. (Route 2034) past Mukdahan Hotel on the right (2 trucks depart per hour; last bus to Mukdahan 6pm; 5฿). Tell the driver to let you off at Phu Pha Theop (poo-PAH-tayp). You'll be dropped off on the main road next to a large 'Mukdahan National Park' sign on the left. The entrance is a 15-min. walk down a small paved road on the right. Go as early as possible because it gets mighty hot while hiking in these parts. On the weekends the park is crowded with Thai tourists who clamor to have their pictures taken with gorgeous you. Open 8am-6pm daily.

■■■ THAT PHANOM

That Phanom is a tiny town in the southern part of Nakhon Phanom province. Like the provincial capital, it lies on the Mekong River, but the similarities end there. That Phanom is famous throughout Thailand and Laos for its historic **Wat That Phanom.** The temple's stunning gold leaf-covered *chedi*, rising nearly 60m above the ground, glints like a 24-carat needle in the noon-day sun, and at night, illuminated by flood lights, it appears like some divine rocket ship bound for *nirvana*. The Laotian and Vietnamese presence in town is apparent in the town's architecture, temples, and markets for which merchants cross the river to sell their goods. Expect small-town Mekong living here; many travelers end up staying much longer than they had planned. Accommodations fill up during the February Festival, when room prices inflate faster than a baboon's ass in heat—plan accordingly.

ORIENTATION

That Phanom is roughly equidistant (53km) from Nakhon Phanom to the north and Mukdahan to the south, and is easily reached from either town by bus or songthaew (about 15฿). The main drag where buses and songthaews pick up passengers is **Chayangkun Road.** Wat That Phanom is on this road and is visible from almost anywhere in town because of its soaring *chedi*. The road leading directly away from the wat to the river is **Kuson Ratchadamnoen Road,** passing under a Laotian arch of victory. After the arch there is **Phanom Phanarak Road.** The Chaiuon Hotel is to the left, and most of the town's budget spots are located off or further down this road. Everything is about a 15-min. walk from wherever you get dropped off on Chayangkun Rd., but tuk-tuk drivers will take you anywhere for 5฿.

PRACTICAL INFORMATION

Currency Exchange: Thai Military Bank, 99/13 Chayangkun Rd. (tel. 541 008). Facing Wat That Phanom on Chayangkun Rd., it's to the right, on the right side of the road, about 1-½ blocks away. Open Mon.-Fri. 8:30am-3:30pm.

Post Office: GPO (tel. 541 159), sits way outside of town on Chayangkun Rd. After a long walk from Wat That Phanom, past the bank, past the songthaews, it's on the left side of the road. Open Mon.-Fri. 8:30am-4:30pm, Sat.-Sun. 9am-noon. **Postal code:** 48110. **International phone service** available during business hours. **Telephone code:** 042.

Buses: Leave and arrive from Chayangkun Rd., mostly at its north end. To: **Mukdahan** or **Nakhon Phanom** (1-½hr., 15฿); **Bangkok** (regular: 8am and 5pm, 167฿; A/C 7:30am, 5:30, 5:45, and 6pm, 301฿); **Udon Thani** (6 daily, 10am-2:40pm, regular 62฿, A/C 105฿); **Mukdahan** (5 daily, 7am-12:10pm, 1-½hr., 15฿). **Songthaews** run to **Nakhon Phanom** (every 10min., 15฿). Both guest houses have detailed listings of bus schedules and destinations.

Bicycle Rental: Niyana's Guest House or **E-SAN Guest House** (25฿ per day).

English Books: Niyana's Guest House has a small but interesting lending library. Many of her guests just sit around for days reading her books.

Markets: The **day** and **night markets** are on Chayangkun Rd. Facing Wat That Phanom, they are a brief walk to the left and on the left side of the road. Delicious Isaan classics here. The **Laotian market** takes place on the banks of the river just north of town. Open Mon. and Thurs. mornings. Vendors cross the river to sell anything from herbal medicine to livestock to electronics and even clothing. Police and customs officials wander about to make sure that peddlers aren't selling *ganja* to *farang*.

Hospital: (tel. 541 255, -56). Two kilometers west of town on the highway.

Emergency: tel. 191.

Police Station: (tel. 541 266). Far north of town, on the right side of Phanom Phanarak Rd.

ACCOMMODATIONS

Niyana's Guest House, 65 Soi Wee Tee Saw Ra Chon, Rimkhong Rd. From the victory arch, facing the river, turn left onto Phanom Phanarak Rd.; about 1-½ blocks down the road, there are signs pointing down a small soi on the right to the guest house. Niyana is the free-spirited proprietress who manages the place by herself, and still finds time to bake an occasional pie, or just chat with her guests. Books, a copious selection of audiotapes, and an English menu with a full page of **vegetarian** selections. On the weekends she teaches local school children English; guests are welcome to help (1hr. of your time gets you a free curry dinner—a more than fair deal). Thai cooking lessons available. Common bathrooms upstairs and downstairs. Dorms 40฿. Singles 60฿. Doubles 90฿. Laundry service.

E-SAN Guest House, Soi Wee Tee Saw Ra Chon, Rimkhong Rd., opposite Niyana's Guest House. Recently purchased by Ms. Niyana, which is great news for travelers since there are now 6 more rooms under her divine care. Singles 60฿, doubles 90฿.

Chaiuon Hotel, 38 Phanoum Phanarak Rd. (tel 541 391). Standing at the arch facing the river, it's on the left about 20m down, just before the turnoff to Niyana's Guest house. An excellent alternative if That Phnom's two guest houses are full (a frequent occurrence during the high season). Really a guest house in hotel clothing, Chaiuon has clean rooms in a large wooden house with an airy upstairs sitting area. Singles with shared bath 80฿, with private bath 100฿. Double with communal bath 120฿, with private bath 150฿. The manager went to high school in Milwaukee, Wisconsin and speaks excellent English. Food available. Laundry service.

FOOD

Besides Niyana's kitchen, some of the best food is right at the markets on Chayangkun Rd (20฿ will get you a savory stick of *gai yang*, a heaping mound of sticky rice, and a bowl of Vietnamese *pho* soup). Several good restaurants lie on Phanom Phanarak Rd. and serve standard Thai and Chinese fare. If you don't feel like walking, head to **Somkhane** (tel. 541 028). Walking east from the temple toward the river, it's on the right immediately before the arch. English menu and photos of monstrous *plaa beuk* (giant golden catfish) on the wall; yes, they really are that big. (And yes, they really are that expensive: 250฿). Dishes 15-80฿. Open 6am-9pm.

SIGHTS

The town's main attraction is **Wat That Phanom,** a symbol of Northeast Thailand and one of the region's most revered temples. This Laotian-style shrine has been restored a total of seven times since its initial construction 1500 years ago, most recently in 1978, after heavy rains in 1975 caused the 57m-high *chedi* to collapse. Every year at the beginning of February is the seven-day **Phra That Phanom Homage Fair,** when thousands of devotees come to pay their respects, accompanied by vendors and entertainers. If you make the journey to Wat That Phanom seven times and "sleep near the Buddha," you are guaranteed passage to heaven. Behind the shrine and to the left is a small two-story museum where you can peruse the gifts brought to the temple over the centuries, including several large meteorites. A series of painted murals with Thai and English captions offer fascinating commentaries on Buddhism and Isaan custom and tradition. Open daily 8:30am-4pm.

About 15km northwest of That Phanom is the tiny silk-weaving village of **Renu Nakhon**. Travelers desperate for a culture fix can observe **traditional Isaan music and dance** (a rare opportunity outside of the major cities) at the **Renu Nakhon** wat every Saturday afternoon during the high season. (Niyana's Guesthouse has helpful information on performance times; check with her before making the trek as the schedule is by no means set in stone.) To get there, take any Nakhon Phanom-bound songthaew and ask to be left off at the Renu Nakhon junction 8km north of That Phanom; from there hire a tuk-tuk.

Supernatural Stupa?

That Phanom is a holy town, a *Sathanii Saksit,* blessed with a temple which radiates tremendous power. Many townspeople claim that just as the temple can grant everlasting happiness to those who worship there, so too can it bring tragedy to those who defile it. Residents here often point to 1975 as a remarkable year of misfortune for many of their neighbors. That year, the magnificent *chedi* collapsed following torrential rains. Some locals rushed to remove chunks of the fallen stupa as tokens of luck and benediction. Not long afterwards, unsolved accidents and inexplicable illnesses befall the culprits and their families. To this day there remain many abandoned houses whose owners have died or ran away.

One late June night last year, the townspeople again witnessed another show of divine power. A young songthaew driver, unable to pay his rent, clambered up the scaffolding around Wat That Phanom, intending to swipe the three large diamonds embedded in the *chedi.* Unable to get back down, he was spotted in the glare of floodlight that illuminates the temple. Word spread like wildfire through the sleeping town and a crowd soon gathered on the street below, including the police.

One officer, convinced that the thief was an illegal Lao immigrant, drew his pistol, and pulled the trigger. *Click!* The exploding sound never came. Again he pulled the trigger, but nothing happened. Exasperated, he grabbed another gun, but had the same result. Perhaps the divine one had taken pity on the would-be burglar and protected him. The hapless bandit was finally dragged down and officers had to forcefully restrain irate townspeople intent on lynching him. Keep in mind that nothing, not even the most innocuous looking pebble, can be taken beyond its gates. If you inadvertently do so, return it immediately. If not, sleep lightly, and don't say we didn't warn you.

■ NEAR THAT PHANOM: NAKHON PHANOM

The capital of Nakhon Phanom province is a sleepy town, whose magnificent view of Laos along the Mekong River even rivals the view from Pha Taem National Park. The range of jagged emerald peaks across the river are often shrouded in mist during the rainy season, as if lifted straight from a Chinese landscape painting. In the not-too-distant future it may be possible to enjoy breakfast along the Mekong in Nakhon Phanom and dinner on the South China Sea in Vietnam. A second bridge (similar to Nong Khai's "Friendship Bridge") is being planned, as is a highway linking the Thai border with the Vietnamese port of Vinh, a scant 300km to the east. If you are traveling through the province, spend a few relaxing nights in That Phanom to the south, and make a day trip to Nakhon Phanom for the scenery.

Most buses and songthaews arrive in the west end of town along **Apibanbuncha Road,** home to the **banks,** and the **provincial hospital** (tel. 511 422; at the Tespradit Rd. intersection. English-speaking doctor.) Others stop along Fuang Nakhon Rd., and Bam Rung Muang Rd. Ask the TAT office or a tuk-tuk driver to find the one you want. To: **Mukdahan** (3 daily, 29฿); **Khon Kaen** (6 daily, 72฿, with A/C 128฿); **Nong Khai;** and **Khorat.** Buses to and from **Udon Thani** may go out of the way to pass through **Nong Khai,** an interesting 9-hr. bus ride. **Songthaews** leave south of Thai Farmer's Bank on Apibanbuncha Rd. to **That Phanom** (every 15min., 1hr., 15฿).

The street adjacent to the river is **Sunthon Wichit Road.** The **TAT office** (tel. 513 490; fax 513 492); **post office** (tel. 512 945; **Postal code:** 48000); and **police station** (tel. 511 266) are clustered here, at the north end of town. Continuing south along the Mekong River will bring you to the **clock tower,** where Sunthon Wichit Rd. continues along the river and **Si Thep Road** branches diagonally to the right. The **Grand Hotel** is at 2210 Si Thep Rd., a couple of blocks after the fork on the right side. A strange menagerie of wood-plaster-*papier maché* critters congregates in the lobby. Singles 160฿, with A/C 350฿. Doubles 230฿, with A/C 490฿. Continuing further down Si Thep Rd. on the right side is **Wat Si Thep,** which is worth a quick visit if you're here for the day. **Tuk-tuks** will take you just about anywhere for 5฿.

Nakhon Phanom's restaurants specialize in **"giant golden catfish"** straight from the Mekong River. This denizen of the deep (often weighing 350kg or more) is growing quite rare in the Mekong and no more than 35 are caught each year along the entire stretch of the river. The fishing season is during the winter; as a result, restaurants are known to pass off other less valuable fish as *plaa beuk* during the rainy season. **New Suan Mai** (open 10am-10pm) and **Golden Giant Catfish Restaurant** (open 7am-10pm) are next to each other just south of the clock tower on Sunthon Wichit Rd, serve scrumptious food, and do not engage in catfish fraud. At Suan Mai, if *plaa beuk* isn't on the menu, just ask, but at both places it should cost 160-250฿. Other less baht-busting yet equally delicious local fish are *plaa juke* and *penang*.

■■■ NONG KHAI

For a heavy dose of Isaan relaxation and good cheer, ease up to Nong Khai province, where weary travelers lose themselves in any one of the towns along the Mekong River. Indeed, many *farang* have decided to put down stakes and work in some of the guest houses, restaurants, and bookstores around here. Despite the foreign presence and the border-crossing traffic heading toward Laos, the city and the rest of the province refuse to cede any of their original character. Nong Khai province claims several interesting, sometimes bizarre wats (particularly Phu Thawk and Sala Kaew Ku). With 300km of the provincial border along the Mekong (and hence the Laotian border), a significant Lao-French influence pervades the area, and an abundance of trade (under and above the law) goes back and forth across the river.

ORIENTATION

In the long and narrow town of Nong Khai, all the main roads run parallel to the river (which runs west-to-east), and are interconnected by a web of sois. Because street numbers were assigned haphazardly according to when the buildings were built—not by location—addresses can be confusing. A better way to orient yourself is using the 19 wats in Nong Khai as landmarks; rest assured there is a temple within 5 minutes of your destination. Good maps are available at all of the guest houses. The **train station** is in the far west end of town on **Kaeworawut Road,** the road closest to the river at that point. As Kaeworawut Rd. runs toward the center of town from the west, it becomes a dirt road which intersects **Haisok Road** (heading to the river). In the east end of town, **Rimkhong Road** is the closest parallel to the river and is where the Mekhong Guest House, the handicrafts market, the immigration pier, and several restaurants are located. **Meechai Road, Prachak Road,** and **Highway 212** run parallel to Kaeworawut and Rimkhong Rd. Highway 212 forms the southern border of the town. The **bus terminal** is on the eastern end of Prachak Rd.

PRACTICAL INFORMATION

Currency Exchange: Thai Military Bank, 580 Prachak Rd. (tel. 420 562 or 420 564; fax 420 562), across from the bus terminal. **Thai Farmers Bank,** 929 Meechai Rd. (tel. 411 058 or 411 669), in the town center. Open Mon.-Fri. 8:30am-3:30pm.

Post Office: GPO, Meechai Rd. (tel. 411 521). Open Mon.-Fri. 8:30am-4:30pm, Sat.-Sun. 9am-noon. **Telephone** service open daily 7am-10pm; telegram office open daily 8am-6pm. **Postal code:** 43000. **Telephone code:** 042. Visa, MC.

Trains: Nong Khai Railway Station, Kaeworawut Rd. (tel. 411 592), on the far west end of town. Trains pass through **Khorat, Khon Kaen,** and **Udon Thani** on their way to **Bangkok** (7:40am rapid train: 3rd class 133฿, 2nd class 245฿; 5:40pm, rapid train: 3rd class 133฿, 2nd class 245฿; and 7pm express train: 3rd class 153฿, 2nd class 265฿.). Always book in advance.

Buses: Nong Khai Bus Terminal on Prachak Rd., at the east end of town. Green buses to **Pak Chom** and **Loei** (#507 roughly every hr., 6am-4pm, 7hr., 61฿) pass through **Si Chiang Mai** (2hr., 15฿) and **Sangkhom** (3hr., 25฿). To get to **Chiang Khan,** switch buses at **Pak Chom**. Buses to **Bangkok** (every hr., 5:30am-7pm,146฿) pass through **Udon Thani, Khon Kaen,** and **Khorat.** To **Udon Thani** (every 30min., 45min., 15฿); **Nakhon Phanom** (4 daily, 7hr.). A/C buses to Bangkok leave from the back of the bus terminal (4 daily, 7:30am, 7:30, 8, and 8:30pm, 263฿).

Local Transportation: Tuk-tuks, or "skylabs" as they're called in this part of the country, are everywhere and shouldn't cost more than 5฿. Since the town is a tourist enclave, drivers will often demand as much as 50฿. Bargain like a banshee, but be ready to settle for 10-15฿.

Bike/Motorcycle Rental: Mut-mee Guest House rents bicycles (40฿ per day) as does the **Mekhong Guest House** (30฿ per day). For motorcycles, try **Nana Motor,** 1160 Meechai Rd. (tel. 411 998) opposite Chayaporn Market. Motorbikes start at 200฿ per day. Helmets included. Open daily 6:30am-6pm.

English Bookstore: The Wasambe Book Shop, 1121 Kaeworawut Rd. (tel. 460 717), on the same soi as Mut-mee Guest House, just off Kaeworawut Rd. The Swahili name means "timeless." Besides international crafts and incense, a huge selection of quality, multi-lingual books to buy, trade (for a discount on purchases), or borrow (20฿ per day). Go from Richard Wright to the Bröntes to Eastern religions. New books average 200฿-300฿. You won't find newly printed English books for less anywhere else in Thailand, and this is the only heavy-duty reading outlet in Isaan. Open daily 9:30am-8pm. *Carpe librum!*

Market: Chayaporn Market, in the west and bordered by Kaeworawut, Meechai, and Talat Chayaporn Rd. **Pochai Market** is by the bus terminal. No night scene.

Laundromat: Siamsaghaeng, 209 Prachak Rd. (tel. 411 830). Exit left from Banterngjit Rd. onto Prachak Rd. A few stores down, look for the "209" on the store wall. Across from a motorcycle shop and next door to a photo lab (don't confuse it with 205 Prajak Rd., twice as expensive). 6-10฿ per piece. Open 7am-7pm.

Pharmacy: Tong Tong Pharmacy, 382/2 Meechai Rd. (tel. 411 690). Exit left from the post office; it's on the corner, a short walk away. Open 7am-9pm.

Hospital: Nong Khai Hospital (tel. 411 504), on Meechai Rd., close to Mut-mee Guest House and across the street from the police station.

Emergency: tel. 191.

Police: Nong Khai Police Station (tel 411 020, -01), on Meechai Rd.

Visas to Laos: With the opening of the "Friendship Bridge" a few years back and a growing business and tourist interest in Laos, companies offering visas to Laos have multiplied faster than lemmings in Nong Khai. Be wary when choosing an outfit, since a number of them (particularly those along Rikhong near the immigration pier) are rather shady, fly-by-night affairs *and are best avoided.* Your best, and most legitimate, option is to acquire a visa through the Lao Embassy in Bangkok (which will save you piles of baht too). In Nong Khai, count on spending between 2700-3000฿ for a 15-day tourist visa. Many travelers and the folks at Mut-mee Guest house recommend the **International Meeting Place** (tel. 421 223) on 1117 Soi Chuen Jitt off Meechai Rd. (heading east, the soi is on the right just before Wat Srichomchuan). It is a guest house run by an expat Australian and his Thai wife, who can arrange same-day visas for 2700฿ (a 200฿ surcharge is added for travelers from the US, Australia, France, and Japan, for reasons only a bureaucrat in the Lao Foreign Ministry knows). The staff are helpful and the office is chock-full o' maps, accommodation suggestions, and travel advice. The International Meeting Place is affiliated with an accredited travel agency in Vientiane. For those who feel more comfortable dealing with a genuine travel agency, try **Song Fung Khong Tour,** 613 Rimkhong Rd. (tel. 412 294; fax 411 158). 20m east of the immigration pier, look for the large plastic THAI Airways sign. Visas 3000฿, allow 2 days processing. Note that visas purchased in Nong Khai are only valid for crossings from Nong Khai; to enter Laos from anywhere else (i.e. Nakhon Phanom, Mukdahan, or Chiang Khong) you must purchase a visa in Bangkok.

ACCOMMODATIONS

Several excellent guest houses (and some inexpensive hotels) make it hard to choose where to hang your knapsack. These spots (particularly the riverside lodgings) are so enticing that a modern-day Odysseus could easily fall under their siren spells, staying in all day and never venturing out to the real Nong Khai.

Mut-mee Guest House, 1111/4 Kaeworawut Rd. On the river, 100m off Kaeworawut Rd., at the end of a soi. Arguably the most popular guest house in Northeast Thailand, it's not just a place to relax—for some it's a religious experience, for others it's a big clique. Cheerful, professional staff has guest house management down to an exact science; service is always quick and attentive despite Mutmee's size (25 rooms for up to 50 guests). Delicious variety of food; portions are generous. Beautiful riverside sitting and eating areas in the lush garden. Dorms 60฿. Singles 70-100฿ depending on location. Doubles 100-160฿. Laundry service and bicycles for rent. During the high season teachers-in-residence hold drawing, *tai chi*, and yoga classes. Inquire for details.

Sawasdee Guest House, 402 Meechai Rd. (tel. 412 502; fax 420 259), about 5 blocks past the post office heading east. Across from the white gate to Wat Si Khun Muang. Courtyard garden and remarkable rooms (some have A/C) compensate for lack of river proximity. New and clean, and kept that way. Actually the home of a Thai family, so it comes closest to the true meaning of the words "guest house;" the front room is jammed with traditional art. Ideal for travelers who shun the sort of self-imposed withdrawal from Thai life that occurs at larger, more social guest houses. Singles 80฿. Doubles 120฿, with A/C and hot water 280฿. Twin room 120฿, with A/C and hot water 320฿. English spoken. Self-service snack bar and laundry service. Bicycles for rent. Especially safety-conscious; guests are given a key to the back gate since the main entrance is locked at 8pm.

Mekhong Guest House, 519 Rimkhong Rd. (tel. 412 119; fax 411 073 or 411 546), a few stores west of the immigration pier. Where Bacchus would stay if he were a backpacker; the central location pumps up the street-traffic volume. A popular late-night hangout, as is the restaurant next door. Neat, well-kept rooms on two floors with porches that sport expansive views of the river, Laos and the Friendship Bridge. You don't have to pay through the nose to get a glimpse either: Singles start at 50฿, doubles 70฿. First floor view rooms are a bit more. Bike rental.

FOOD

Profit from Nong Khai's epicurean overkill and feast at a riverside eatery. Most have English menus, decent food, and beautiful scenery, but they're none too gentle on the expense account. Prices drop significantly as you move away from the river.

Udom Rod, 423 Rimkhong Rd. (tel. 421 014), next to the immigration pier. Standard restaurant with deluxe view. Bony, budget-decimating, but bursting-with-flavor Mekong River fish dishes (the house specialty). Also renowned for its Vietnamese cuisine; try the fried spring rolls. Most dishes 25-50฿; for fresh fish expect to pay 70-140฿. Open 2pm-8pm.

Reuan Pae Haisok, (tel. 412 211). Floating restaurant behind the dilapidated Wat Haisok, near Mut-mee Guest House. Not only is this place genuinely *on* the river, it takes diners on an hour-long spin every evening (5:30pm, 20฿ extra). On a clear day, you'll savor a succulent sunset in addition to a close-up view of the new Friendship Bridge. The food does not meet the exacting standards of penny-pinching gourmets (fried rice and veggies 40฿). Open daily 10am-10pm.

Mekhong Restaurant, 519 Rimkhong Rd. (tel. 412 119). Part of the Mekhong Guest House. A marginal place with a sitting area right over the river. Tasteful interior decorating features lovely climbing vines and unobtrusive ceilings. Usual Thai menu, though the pig knuckles with sauerkraut and broccoli (80฿) manages to raise a few eyebrows. Prepare to pay 45-60฿ per dish. Open 7am-10pm.

Thai Thai Restaurant, 257/1 Banterngjit Rd. (tel 420 373). View-deprived, but friendly family ownership dishes up delicious Thai and Chinese fare at more than agreeable prices (*pad thai* 15฿, chicken and cashews 30฿). For those who get lonely without a view of the river, bring a postcard and prop it up against your Singha (55฿). Popular with locals. Open daily 2:30pm-3:30am.

SIGHTS

A **market** on Rimkhong Rd., east of the immigration pier, hawks everything from chicken statuettes with genuine feathers and beaks (15฿) to fuzzy striped steering-wheel covers (80฿), with an occasional Communist Bloc goodie to be discovered. Ginseng extract is available in just about every imaginable form, from candy to tea to whiskey. Flagging libido? Ground deer-antler tea may be just what the doctor ordered. Coffee addicts can also root out all the necessary supplies to brew a real cup o' java: ground Laotian coffee beans (80฿ per kilo), coffee strainers, and electric heating coils. Seekers of hand-woven *mut-mee* fabrics can visit **Village Weaver Handicrafts**, 786/1 Prachak Rd. (tel. 411 236; fax 420 333). The goal of this 13-year-old project is to "promote the professional and social welfare of disadvantaged artisans and families." More specifically, the aim is to promote local industry and prevent young Isaan women from seeking their fortunes in the brothels of Patpong or Pattaya. Traditional cloth is woven on looms in the back of the shop and sold off the bolt or as off-the-rack clothing, hand bags, and other practical items. Bring a pattern or just a picture and the seamstress can make-up tailor-made outfits in just a few days, a sure-fire way to satisfy all those greedy relatives for whom ya foolishly promised to "buy something." Don't worry about trying to fit your lovely purchases into your rucksack—the Village Weaver will ship anywhere in the world at reasonable prices. Open Mon.-Sat. 8am-5pm, Sun. 9am-3pm. MC, Visa.

A few km east of Nong Khai on Hwy. 212, **Sala Kaew Ku,** also known as Wat Khaek, is one of the most bizarre temples in all of Thailand. The grounds are populated with towering, concrete statues of Hindu and Buddhist figures narrating scenes from the cycles of life: the good and the evil, the mundane and the fantastic, the innocent and the downright freaky—all the brainchild of an octogenarian Lao mystic. Of these massive images looming high overhead, the newest and most magnificent is a seven-headed, tongue-lashing serpent rearing over a Buddha as he meditates on its coiled lengths. The most bizarre scenario depicts an elephant strolling through a pack of whiskey-drinking, poker-playing, car-driving dogs who snap jealously at its enlightened heels. To get there, bike along Rte. 212, pass "St. Paul Nong Khai School" on the right. Wat Khaek is just two turnoffs later. The turnoff (to the right) has a small English sign that says *"Salakeokoo."* You can also catch any of the buses going east and ask to be let off at the turnoff, or hire a tuk-tuk for about 100฿ (or less) round trip. Open daily 8am-5pm; admission 10฿.

■ NEAR NONG KHAI

SANGKHOM

Ninety-five km upriver from Nong Khai, nestled in a range of rolling, jungle-shrouded hills, sits the drowsy hamlet of Sangkhom. The area's mountainous setting not only creates some stunning vistas, but jealously hordes many natural wonders—multi-tiered waterfalls and breathtaking cliffs plummeting straight down to the river below—from the rest of the province and all but the most intrepid *farang*. Rest assured as you gaze across the mighty Mekong toward the rugged, untamed forests of Laos on the opposite bank, that you are about as far from 7-Elevens, karaoke bars, and other signs of industrialization as is possible in Thailand.

Despite its isolation, Sangkhom is home to several fine guest houses, first and foremost the **Bouy Guest House,** 60 M.4 Sangkhom (tel. 441 065). Romantic bamboo bungalows (singles 60฿, doubles 80฿), all in tip-top shape, perch on stilts along the banks of a small stream. A wooden footbridge leads to additional huts set amongst a grove of papaya trees. The remarkable Mrs. Toy, owner and chef, prepares gargantuan portions scrumptious Thai and Lao specialties. Don't miss the "jungle curry." Laundry service, a wealth of tourist info, and motorcycles for rent (180฿ per day). Just west of the Bouy Guest House is the brand-new **TXK Guest House,** forced to relocate due to devastating erosion. "Mama," the eccentric and warm-hearted proprietress, is famous for her Thai and Lao feasts on which guests can gorge themselves for 45฿ per mouth. Single bungalows 80฿. Doubles 100฿. The **post and telegraph office** is 100m north of the Bouy Guest house on the left (open Mon.-Fri. 8:30am-4:30pm, Sat.-Sun. 9am-noon, tel. 441 069). Also has **overseas telephone** service. **Postal code:** 43160. **Telephone code:** 042.

Sangkhom is an ideal spot to kick off the Tevas and rest your road-weary feet (a bottle of *lao khao,* the local firewater, never hurts either). The surrounding wilderness is dotted with caves and waterfalls, all of which are marked on a helpful map provided by Bouy Guest House. Particularly impressive are the **Than Thip falls,** about a 30-minute motorbike ride west of town. Signs on the highway will direct you to the dirt turnoff. The cascades' second level contains a swimming hole. East of Sangkhom are the **Than Thong Falls** which, while larger than the Than Thip Falls, are a Thai tourist trap. The designated "scenic area" just before the falls is a beautiful spot to watch a sleepy sun retire for the evening. **Wat Hin Maak Peng,** a monastery set among large boulders and bamboo graves, is well worth a visit for the spectacular river views. Remember to dress respectfully.

To get to Sangkhom, take the small, green #557 bus which wheezes and chugs its way from Nong Khai to Loei, stopping in Sangkhom (every hr., 25฿).

BAN AHONG

About 185km east of Nong Khai lies the small town of Beung Kan. The town itself offers nothing commendable (picture a scaled-down, Thai-style Newark, NJ), but the tiny village of Ban Ahong in the Beung Kan district is worth a visit. Don't expect any frills like banks, post offices, police stations, tuk-tuks, or *samlors;* this lonely bus stop on Hwy. 212 consists of a single dirt road and traditional houses on stilts. A sign even reads "Welcome to the middle of nowhere." All told the population consists of "84 roofs" (the traditional Thai manner of census taking), or about 800 souls.

The Mekong River narrows here, and often mist-shrouded mountains on the Lao side fall away dramatically to the shore. In the evenings Lao fisherman sing folk songs as they pull in their nets, providing an authentic soundtrack to this spectacular Shangri-La on the Mekong. For travelers with an insatiable urge to take the path less traveled, Ban Ahong is home to the **Hideaway Guest House.** The English- and German-speaking proprietor, Mr. Saksil, opened this romantic bamboo retreat two years ago with the hopes of attracting travelers who want the real scoop on rural village life. (Singles 70฿, doubles 100฿.) Mr. Saksil's venture has been a resounding success, most notably because the sudden influx of *farang* has done little to change the pace of life here, which crawls along slowly, even by Isaan's lethargic standards. The village is quite friendly; the chief's house, just upriver from Hideaway, is the center of social activity, where men go to drink home-brewed moonshine and smoke "Lao cigarettes." The women and children chat nearby, in their own circles.

Just downriver from Hideaway across a small brook is **Wat Ba Ahong** ("Forest Temple of Ahong"), an enchanting place dotted with massive boulders worn smooth by the river in eons past, and shielded by massive leafy trees. Stop in for a mug of traditional Lao medicinal tea brewed from sundry twigs, herbs, and roots and keep hot all day. Check out the temple's furniture, made from gnarled bamboo roots. Other than just kicking back and watching the river flow, the list of activities in Ahong is pretty slim: Mr. Saksil will arrange boat trips downriver to visit several islets (50฿ per hr.), and during the dry season you can join village children cavorting in a fine swimming hole amongst boulders on the bank. Ban Ahong is definitely a worthwhile stop on the long trek between Nakhon Phanom and Nong Khai and is reasonably close to the breathtaking Phu Thawk monastery. To escape the clutches of civilization from Nong Khai take a bus bound for Beung Kan (2hr., 35฿)—make sure the driver knows you're going east to Ban Ahong. From Nakhon Phanom first catch a bus to Beung Kan (57฿). Some will continue on past Ban Ahong (ask the ticket seller) and if not, switch at Beung Kan to a bus going to Nong Khai (7฿); ask to be let off at Ban Ahong.

WAT PHU THAWK

Although it is one of the northeast's most awe-inspiring sights, Wat Phu Thawk is so far removed from any regular tourist destination that is virtually ignored by all foreign pilgrims. In the Isaan dialect, *"Phu Thawk"* means "single mountain." A mountain range runs behind it, but the shrine stands alone on a massive red sandstone outcropping riddled with caves and ledges.

A wooden staircase twists its way to the top of the rocky shelf, with seven levels representing the stages of enlightenment. Level five contains a sanctuary built into the cliff face and adorned with a regal Buddha image that glows softly at dusk. On the opposite side of the mountain is a unique hermitage built on a rock pinnacle, nestled underneath a huge boulder that threatens to topple any second and smash the entire affair. This island of stone can only be reached by a narrow ridge, with spectacular views falling away to either side. To reach the top, forge through the cool green quiet along the expansive paths on the back of the mountain. Or tiptoe across the hot, gritty, sandstone cliffs of the mountain front on boardwalks clinging improbably to the rock face, with all of Nong Khai's splendor before you. Along the walkways you will find small, wooden platforms and huts for meditation. The top level, mostly forested, is a maze of trails. Fortunately for the faint of heart, the summit is only accessible via the innocuous lanes on the back side of the mountain. The monastery's founer, Ajaan Juan, died in a plane crash a few years ago, and a newly built pagoda at the foot of Phu Thawk houses his relics.

Visit Phu Thawk as early in the morning as possible, preferably with your own transportation, a good set of directions, and a healthy tolerance for potholes. By public transportation, go first to Beung Kan; from there you can sometimes catch a songthaew to Ban Siwilai (about 10฿)—sit on the left side of the bus and look for the "Ban Siwilai" sign in English. From there, catch another songthaew to Phu Thawk (another 10฿). Monday to Friday, morning, noon, and evening, you may be able to share a ride with the local students on their way to and from school. Otherwise, you may have to hire a tuk-tuk for about 100฿ to take you the 20km to the mountain and back. Pay a little more if you make him wait while you explore; settle on a round-trip price before you get in the tuk-tuk. Remember: this is not Disney World, and gravity always wins. Use caution when exploring. Closed April 12-16.

■■■ CHIANG KHAN

Of all the riverside towns on the Isaan-Laos border, Chiang Khan comes closest to embodying the term "border town." It's not just the river and surrounding mountains that contribute to the atmosphere of this one-horse village; the town itself is composed of just two parallel roads, lined from end to end with old wooden structures evoking the spirit of American pioneer days. Unfortunately, it's likely that many of these buildings will slowly be replaced. Chiang Khan's halcyon has attracted the attention of investors; land values have increased tenfold in the past few years, with parcels near Kaeng Khut Khu rapids fetching as much as 2 million baht per acre. In the meantime, however, life is still slow and relatively isolated from the clutches of the world.

ORIENTATION

Chiang Khan is on the northern border of Loei province, 50km from the provincial capital and just across the Mekong River from Laos. Heading east along the river, there is the small town of Pak Chom (with Sangkhom and Nong Khai province just beyond it); to the west is Tha Li district with several small villages (Ban Nong Phu, Ban Pak Huay, Ban Ahii) on the Heuang River. Chiang Khan can be reached by songthaew from either Loei (every 30min., 6am-6:30pm, 1hr., 14฿) or Pak Chom. Those headed to Chiang Khan from Nong Khai province must take the Nong Khai-Loei bus to Pak Chom and switch there for a songthaew to Chiang Khan.

The town of Chiang Khan has two significant parallel roads, **Chiang Khan Road** (the highway passing through town) and **Chai Khong Road,** which runs along the river. These two roads are connected by sois 1-21, from west to east. Buses from Pak Chom drop passengers off around **soi 18.** From Loei, passengers disembark at the **songthaew station,** just outside the west end of town.

PRACTICAL INFORMATION

Currency Exchange: Thai Farmers Bank, 444 Chiang Khan Rd. (tel. 821 381-4). Open Mon.-Fri. 8:30am-3:30pm.

Post/Telephone Office: Chiang Khan Post and Telegraph Office, (tel. 821 011) Chai Khong Rd., at the far east end of town. Open Mon.-Fri. 8:30am-4:30pm, Sat.-Sun. 9am-noon. **Postal code:** 42110. **Telephone code:** 042.

Buses: To **Loei,** buses leave from the west end of town. Walk west out of town with the Thai Farmers Bank on your left; turn left onto the highway at the next 3-way intersection. Buses leave across from the gas station a few hundred feet farther down. Last bus 5pm. Buses to **Pak Chom** leave (every 30min., 6am-5pm, 1hr., 15฿) from the east end of Chiang Khan Rd., near soi 20.

Local Public Transportation: Tuk-tuks putt around town (5฿).

Bike/Moped Rental: Nong Sam Guest House rents mountain bikes (30฿ ½-day, 50฿ full-day). Zen, Nong Ball, and Chiang Khan Guest Houses rent regular bicycles (30฿ per day) and motorbikes (200฿ per day).

Markets: The **morning/day market** is 1 block south of Chiang Khan Rd. near soi 9 and 10. The very small **night market** is on Chiang Khan Rd., between soi 17 and 18. It gets going at sundown and lasts until around 9pm.

Laundry: Nong Ball Guest House, 15฿ per kg. Nong Sam Guest House and Suksombun Hotel, 5฿ per item.

Hospital: Chiang Khan Hospital (tel. 821 101), on Chiang Khan Rd., past soi 21, on the eastern outskirts of town.

Emergency: tel. 191.

Police: (tel. 821 181), on a soi off Chiang Khan Rd. on the outskirts of town, past the hospital on the right, a few hundred feet farther on the left side of the road.

ACCOMMODATIONS

Suksombun Hotel, 243/3 Chai Khong Rd. (tel. 821 064), near soi 8 and 9. A weathered wooden building right on the river. The preferred choice of many a weary traveler. Some rooms have swell sunset views. Friendly owners arrange a variety of **boat trips** on the river (including a visit to Kaeng Khut Khu); prices vary according to the number of people and destination. Double bed with shared bath 100฿. Rooms with a view (and private bath) 150฿.

Nong Ball Guest House, 204 Chai Khong Rd. (tel. 821 056), on the river side, near soi 16. The 2nd-floor rooms have a view and a small balcony. Vintage establishment sports a peaceful kitchen veranda and common hot shower. Grab one of the ubiquitous cats in one hand and a cup of coffee in the other as you sit down to watch the colorful Laotian boats float by. Singles 70฿. Doubles 120฿.

Nong Sam Guest House, 407 Nam Pon Najan Rd. (tel. 821 457). Follow Chiang Khan Rd. straight out of town past soi 1 (on the road to Ban Nong Phu) for about 1km until the wooden sign in English appears on the right. Remote location facilitates tranquil riverside contemplation. Singles 120฿. Doubles 150฿. Bike rental and boat trips. Only breakfast during the rainy season; day-long food service resumes during the busy tourist season.

Zen Guest House, 126/1 Soi 12 (tel. 821 119). Owners take Buddhist minimalism and the art of low-pressure maintenance to new levels, spending precious little time on the property. Signs posted throughout this do-it-yourself guest house tell guests what to do in the hosts' absence. Religious (mostly Zen) imagery and maxims on the walls. A few shelves of books (for lending only) in English. Singles 50-60฿. Doubles 100฿. Self-serve coffee and snacks.

FOOD

Ask any Chiang Khanian where to eat, and they'll tell you to go to soi 9. Ask them what is good to eat, and they'll tell you to get the unique local twist on *pad thai*.

Prachamit Restaurant, 263/2 Chiang Khan Rd, in the southwest corner of Chiang Khan Rd. and soi 9. One of several restaurants on soi 9 serving good *pad Thai.* Owner recommends *kow mun gai,* a chicken 'n' rice dish with special sauce (12฿). Cheap and friendly too. Open 8am-7pm.

Mekhong Riverside Restaurant, 328/10 Chai Khong Rd. (tel. 821 351), on the river; spot the English sign. Nice porch with tables in back. A bit posh for Chiang Khan; the elegant English menu is more expensive than the restaurants on soi 9 (dishes 30-50฿). Impressive selection isn't always available. Isaan handicrafts for sale in front. Open 9am-midnight.

SIGHTS

About 3km east of town, a turn-off leads left to the **Kaeng Khut Khu rapids.** Follow the sign to Wat Thakhaek and continue another kilometer. A long row of covered picnic areas make for good rapids-watching. The cascades are best in the dry season, but the mountain scenery is always stupendous. Vendors sell Isaan standards, *som tam, gai yang,* and sticky rice. They've also got two local specialties: *gung thawt* (batter-fried prawns stuck together like a big ole shrimp cookie) and *gung ten* ("dancing shrimp"), consisting of live wigglies bathed in a spicy sauce. Chug-a-lug! Some guest houses and hotels in town provide transportation by boat to the rapids (see Accommodations). Otherwise, you can take a songthaew from Chiang Khan Rd. (5฿) or a tuk-tuk for about 40฿ round-trip.

■■■ LOEI

As you enter the provincial capital of Loei, the big billboard on Highway 201 near the hospital greets you with, "Welcome to Loei, Land of the Sea of Mountains and Coldest in All Siam." Grammar aside, the billboard has neatly captured the essence of this seldom-visited but pulchritudinous province. Indeed, wherever you go in Loei, you'll be surrounded by verdant mountain ranges, and some parts of the region (like Phu Reva) have regularly recorded night-time temperatures below freezing in December and January. Little else is known about this relatively isolated part of Thailand, and life in Loei carries on without much outside intervention—often a shady existence, especially along the northern border with Laos in towns such as Tha Li and Chiang Khan, where smuggled goods sneak into Thailand.

At the end of June, you can be tricked or treated into attending the **Phi Ta Khon Festival,** the region's own version of Halloween. This annual three-day festival takes place in **Dan Sai,** in the west end of the province. The festival originated when Prince Vessandorn, the Buddha's penultimate incarnation, returned to the city and was greeted by a procession so jubilant and festive that spirits got in on the action. During the festivals, young men don giant colorful masks with long pointy noses and parade around town.

The town of Loei itself has little to offer tourists, but it's the perfect base from which to explore the rest of the province. In the evenings, Loei's surprisingly numerous late-night restaurants and pubs are relaxing stops after a rough day of gallivanting about the mountainous countryside.

ORIENTATION

Loei town is at the center of Loei province, bordered by Laos to the north and, clockwise from northeast to west, Nong Khai, Udon Thani, Khon Kaen, Phetchabun, and Phitsanulok provinces.

The petite provincial capital is bounded on the east by the **Loei River. Charoen Rat Road** runs the length of the river, but the water is largely hidden from view by the buildings. The **post office** is on the south end of Charoen Rat Rd., and heading north, there is the Savita Bakery, several banks, the **day** and **night markets,** the Thai Udom Hotel, and the Phu Luang Hotel. Just past the markets (on the side closer to the river) going north, is the intersection with **Ruamjai Road,** which has several pharmacies, the Muang Loei Guest House, and the **main bus terminal** at the west end of the road. **Ararree Road,** south of Ruamjai Rd., connects Charoen Rat Rd. and **Ruamjit Road** (the road parallel to Charoen Rat Rd.). One block farther south is **Chuensai Road** (to the east of the traffic circle) and **Nok Kaew Road** (to the west).

PRACTICAL INFORMATION

Currency Exchange: Siam Commercial Bank, 3/8 Ruamjai Rd. (tel. 812 001). Open Mon.-Fri. 8:30am-3:30pm. **24-hr. ATM** accepts all major cards.

Post Office: GPO, (tel. 811 713) on Charoen Rat Rd., south past the footbridge; cross the river to the fitness park and it's on the left. Telegrams 8am-6pm. Open Mon.-Fri. 8:30am-4:30pm, Sat.-Sun. 9am-noon. **Postal code:** 42000.

Telephones: Overseas telephone office (tel. 811 253) is next to the post office. Open 7am-10pm. **Telephone code:** 042.

Airport: Closed for repair, but should re-open sometime in 1996. Check with **Thai Airways,** 22/15 Chumsai Rd. (tel. 812 344). Open 9am-5pm.

Buses: Small green buses to **Nong Khai** via **Pak Chom, Sangkhom,** and **Tha Bo** (every hr., 5:40-11:40am, 9 and 10:20pm, 60฿) leave from the bus terminal off Ruamjai Rd. If you miss the last bus, go to **Udon Thani** (every 25min., 5am-5:30pm, 68฿), and then catch a Nong Khai bus. Buses to **Chiang Mai** (9hr., 136฿) and **Chiang Rai** via **Phitsanulok** and **Lampang** leave *across* from the bus terminal (8 daily, 10am-10:30pm). A private bus company operates from the King Hotel, 11/9 Chumsai Rd. (tel. 811 225). A/C buses to **Bangkok** (11 daily, 241฿). Buy your tickets in advance from the hotel. **999 Government Bus Co.** (tel. 811 706), on Ruamjai Rd., has fan buses to **Bangkok** (every hr., 5-10am; every 30min., 4-11pm). Exit the Muang Loei Guest House, turn left and walk about 1 block; it's on the left. Some pass through **Khon Kaen** (express 188฿, ordinary buses 138฿).

Local Public Transportation: The usual samlors and tuk-tuks (10-20฿).

Bike/Moped Rental: Bicycles (40฿ per day) and motorbikes (150-200฿ per day) at Muang Loei Guest House 1.

Market: The **day** and **night markets** are at the same location at the north end of Charoen Rat Rd. The night market gets going at around 6pm but closes at 9-10pm.

Swimming Pool: Muang Loei Land Pool, 73 Soi 5, Loei-Chiang Khan Rd. (Hwy. 201) (tel. 812 452 or 812 544), several km north of town. Pool/recreation park is popular because of its nice mountain scenery. Admission 30฿ adults, 20฿ children. Sauna available (158฿ per hour). 40฿ round-trip tuk-tuk ride.

Pharmacy: Bun Jung Pesat Pharmacy, 83 Charoen Rat Rd. (tel. 812 138), on the corner of Ruamjai Rd. Open daily 6am-9pm.

Hospital: Loei Provincial Hospital (tel. 811 679), where Loei-Chiang Khan Rd. (Hwy. 201) meets Nok Kaew Rd., across from provincial offices. English spoken.

Emergency: tel. 191.

Police: Loei Police Station (tel. 811 245), at the north end of Charoen Rat Rd.

ACCOMMODATIONS

Thai Udom Hotel, 122/1 Charoen Rat Rd. (tel./fax 811 763 or 811 789), on the corner of Ararree Rd. A friendly hotel close to the markets, the Savita Bakery, and the night restaurants. Grand winding staircase hints at more than the run-down rooms offer. Still, you can chat on the phone, flip on the TV, and slurp bottled water. Singles 200฿, with A/C 250฿. Doubles 300฿, with A/C 400฿. VIP room 600฿. Laundry service 5฿ per piece. Hot water during the cold season.

PR House, 22/16 Chumsai Rd. (tel. 811 416) on the soi past the Thai Airways office. New condo-style building offers phone, balconies (perfect for hanging laundry), and hot water. Double 160฿. Twin with A/C, fridge, and TV 350฿.

Muang Loei Guest House 1, 103/72 Soi A. D. Ruamjai Rd., near the bus station. Walk out to the main road, turn left and walk about 2 blocks until you see the sign on the left directing you to the guest house. Hostess speaks moderate English, French, and Chinese. Adorable dust bunnies. Small, expensive menu. Not much to recommend the place except its price and proximity to the bus station. Laundry service and bikes/motorbikes for rent. Rooms 50-90฿.

FOOD

Some of the best (and cheapest) places to break bread are the **open-air restaurants** in front of the movie theater just off Ararree Rd., across from the Thai Farmers Bank. Open past midnight. The cooks occasionally put on a show, creating bursts of flames that go as high as the ceiling. Pyromaniacs can order *pakboong fai daeng* (flaming morning glory vine) and stare intensely at the ensuing fireworks display.

Savita Bakery, 137-139 Charoen Rat Rd. (tel. 811 526 or 812 499), a bit south of the markets, just past Ararree Rd. Ice cream and pastries, including tiny little banana bread cupcakes (1฿). Staff speaks hesitant English with a smile. A few western dishes (hamburger 20฿, and extensive cholesterol-laden breakfast selection). Open 6am-10:30pm.

Sor Aahaan Thai, 32/106 Nok Kaew Rd. (tel. 813 436), west of the traffic circle, on the right side of the road when walking toward the highway. English sign. A wagon wheel bonanza. Owner managed to use 27 when he built the fence and tables of this garden restaurant, and has piled the rest in a corner while he awaits further inspiration. Extensive English menu, dishes 50฿ and up. Open 8am-11pm.

Chinatown, 10/5 Araree Rd. (tel. 812 287). Don't let the name fool you. Thai and (what they call) American dishes as well as Chinese. Relax with some wonton soup (25฿) or "fried entrails" (demonstrating the problem with dictionary translations, 40฿). Open 9am-11pm.

ENTERTAINMENT

For a provincial capital of fewer than 25,000 people, this town has a surprisingly substantial nightlife, representing Isaan's three varieties of nightly entertainment: the country/western-style pub, the karaoke bar, and the swanky lounge-style nightclub where women take turns crooning off-key. Pick your poison.

Tom's Cabin, 35/10 Ruamjai Rd. Actually off Ruamjai Rd. From Muang Loei Guest House 1, walk to Ruamjai Rd., turn right, take the 1st left and walk halfway down the road; Tom's Cabin is on the left with an English sign. Fabulous pub with live Thai and western folk favorites. The crowd grows as night wears on, hooting and singing along. *The* place to be seen in Loei. Pool table and dart board in back. Open 6pm-6am. You pay for the entertainment in the food (chicken with veggies 60฿) and drinks (Singha 85฿), but it's well worth it.

■ AROUND LOEI

THA LI AND BAN PAK HUAY

Moving westward along the river from Chiang Khan district, the Mekong River splits. The northward branch goes into Laos, meeting the Thai border again up near the Golden Triangle. The Heuang River forms the division between Thailand and Laos where the Mekong leaves off. Around the Heuang River border is the rural **Tha Li** district. Songthaews to Tha Li only leave from Loei, and the highway from Chiang Khan to Tha Li district (via Bang Nong Phu), although incredibly scenic, is rarely traveled. Tha Li is best approached from Loei town.

Tha Li's isolation from the rest of the world is its selling point—the region is an area of covert trade across the Lao border. Iron-livered locals knock back **lao khao,**

the fierce, rum-like brew that makes Mekong Whiskey seem like root beer. Several nearby villages are on the river.

For those interested in spending some time in this remote area, **Ban Pak Huay** claims the sole accommodation here, the **O.T.S. Guest Home.** Bungalows go for 60-80฿, and there is a commendable menu. Oy, the helpful proprietress, rents out bicycles (20฿ ½-day, 35฿ full-day). Warning: riding on the unpaved and hilly roads can be tough on the tush. Scenic routes pass through isolated villages such as Ban Ahii and Ban Na Kazeng, and the Lao-style *chedi* called **Wat Phra Tadsadja** can also be visited by bicycle. The Heuang River running past Ban Pak Huay is easily forded—one could easily enter Laos (not a good idea). During the cool season, when the water is clear, a section of the river called Gaeng Thun is a popular place to swim and enjoy a beer.

In Tha Li district, there are frequent Thai-Lao market days at the riverside villages, including Ban Pak Huay. These start early—often at 4am—and finish quickly, doing a brisk trade in Laotian contraband, while Lao villagers scoop up Thai goods. Be careful, though: because of Tha Li's reputation, the police make guest appearances, and there are highway checkpoints.

The town of Tha Li is 50km northwest of Loei. To get there, catch a songthaew from Loei's main bus terminal (every 30min., 7:20am-5:30pm, 1hr., 15฿). To go to Ban Pak Huay, you'll be dropped off at Tha Li; wait for a songthaew that continues down the same road for about 8km to Ban Pak Huay. In Ban Pak Huay, the bus stop is at the road leading to O.T.S. Guest Home; turn left. Hourly songthaews run back and forth to Tha Li (7am-4pm, 5฿).

PHU RUA NATIONAL PARK

A 1375m-high mountain is the majestic centerpiece of this park. Rev up your engines and zip along the road to the peak. At the top, a large Buddha image surveys the scene below and a cliff shaped like the bow of a Chinese junk. For the vehicularly challenged who do not fancy 5km of asphalt, there are alternatives. One route involves a 2km trek to a waterfall, before continuing the 5.5km to the peak. On the way, you must cross a small stream; a sign on the opposite bank directs you 1.6km to the falls. The precipitous cascade is deafening after a good storm, and the spray-laden gusts make a refreshing pit stop. There you'll see a sign in Thai, the bottom of a set of three, directing you to the mountain summit.

Pick up a map and consult park rangers before starting your trip; trail conditions vary throughout the year. It's possible to complete the circuit in one day, but an overnight stay is recommended. Tent rentals for two (50฿); larger group accommodations for 5-8 people, with bath, are 250-500฿. Food is available on weekends until 6pm, and all week during the busy season. Large parties should make arrangements with the National Parks Division in Bangkok (tel. (02) 579 0529 or 579 4842).

To get to Phu Rua, catch an hourly bus going to Lom Sak (5am-5pm, 1hr.); hop off at Phu Rua (15฿). Watch for the large wooden English sign next to the highway on the right side. Disembark across from the market, where you can buy snacks. From here, songthaews make the 3.5km trip to park headquarters regularly during the tourist season. Otherwise, pickings are slim. Visitors sometimes hoof it uphill, hire private transport, or catch a ride with one of the guitar-wielding motorcyclists roaming the park. To return to Loei, wait for a bus across from the market (last bus 6pm).

PHU KRADUNG NATIONAL PARK

Its bell-shaped mountain inspired the name of this sanctuary (*"kradung"* means "bell"), the second national park established by the Thai government. Today it is one of the most popular reserves in the country. The summit is a 60 sq. km plateau criss-crossed with trails and is a great platform for viewing solar activity. Resident beasties include wild pig, Asian wild dog, black giant squirrel, yellow-throated martin, white-handed gibbon, langur, and macaque. The 9km hike from the mountain base to park headquarters is facilitated slightly by bamboo stairways; porters can tote you and your gear. Mountain-top board and lodging available.

The park is packed on weekends, holidays, and the peak tourist season. If you plan to visit during these periods, you'll have reservations for a piece of hard ground unless you plan in advance. Contact the National Park Division of the Forestry Department in Bangkok (tel. (02) 579 0529 or 579 4842). The park is closed during the rainy season (June-Oct.). To get to Phu Kradung, catch a bus from Loei bound for Khon Kaen, or vice versa (25฿). The bus will drop you off at the Amphoe Phu Kradung administrative office; from there, you can catch a minibus to the National Park Office where the trail begins.

ERAWAN CAVE

Just off the Udon Thani-Loei Hwy. (Hwy. 210), Erawan Cave is just slightly closer to Udon Thani. Coming from Loei, the gaping crevice in the distant cliffs which shelters the large Buddha is clearly visible on the left side of the highway as the terrain becomes mountainous. From the highway, it's another 2km to the cave, and if you've just hopped off the Udon-Loei bus, tuk-tuk drivers waiting at the turnoff will take you there (10-15฿). For those using their own wheels, no English sign indicates the turn-off for the cave; from Loei, keep an eye out for the tuk-tuks clustering on the left side of the road, just after you actually see the cave from the highway. From Udon, they're going to be on the right side, but the cave is not visible before coming upon them. A wat at the cliff base marks the end of the road. To the left, a huge flight of stairs ascends the mountain (marked by a statue of a three-headed elephant). Eventually the steps branch off; take the flight to the left and keep going. It's a long, awkward climb, but the smiling Buddha sitting amidst the echoes of bats will be waiting for you at the top. Once you reach the top, buy a drink, flop down in Buddha's shadow, and revel in his precept of non-action. When your legs recover, say bye-bye to the Buddha and start spelunking.

The cave boasts Dodger Stadium capacity—it could easily host a baseball game, complete with pop flies, though Tommy Lasorda (pre-Slim Fast) would be a tight squeeze. To the right, sunbeams filter through natural skylights. As you creep forward, the darkness deepens and the squeaking of bats becomes an ear-piercing shriek. The winged rodents stay put, mostly. Cryptic signs point out Thai interpretations of the various stalagmites here: "stone tree," "rock *chedi,*" etc. The next cavern leads to the "elephant rock" and the "cold room." You are directly under the mountain now, but don't fear—there's light at the end of the tunnel. Through the next cavern and up a wooden staircase, you emerge at the opposite side of the mountain, with a lovely panorama of cultivated fields and the surrounding peaks.

■■■ UDON THANI

Sheltering a six-digit population, Udon teems with air-conditioned hotels, restaurants, and coffee shops—a welcome relief after the humble simplicity of small-town, northeast Thailand. Site of a United States Air Force base during the Vietnam War, the American presence is still evident in Udon's western restaurants, its strong expat community, and an inconsequential U.S. consulate, soon to be closed thanks to Republican U.S. Congress budget cuts.

After satiating your appetite for amenities, there are several worthwhile daytrips around the province, notably the UNESCO World Heritage archaeological sites at Ban Chiang, whose discovery practically re-wrote the prehistory of Southeast Asia. A helpful branch of the TAT provides a city and provincial map and can give you more insight into Udon Thani.

ORIENTATION

Nong Khai province is immediately to the north, denying Udon Thani province access to the Mekong River. Khon Kaen province is to the south, Loei to the west, and Kalasin and Sakhon Nakhon are to the east.

Udon Thani is readily accessible by train, bus, or air. The **train station** is on the eastern fringe of town, and the **TAT office** is on the western fringe, while the hotels are in central Udon Thani. Three **traffic circles** direct vehicles along the length of **Udon-Dusadee Road.** From south to north, at the **Srisuk intersection** is the circle with a statue of the city's founder, Prince Prachak Silpakhom. At the **Phosi Road** intersection, there is a fountain (usually dry); and at **Prachak Road** is the clock tower traffic circle. **Bus stations** are on both the northern and eastern fringe of town, while the **airport** is about 3km outside the city limit, southwest on the **Udon-Loei Highway.** The city bus system is virtually non-existent—bargain viciously with the tuk-tuk and samlor jockeys for feasible fares.

The northwest part of town has a reservoir surrounded by a peaceful park. Many government offices are in this tranquil part of town, including the GPO and the doomed U.S. consulate. The rest of town buzzes with shopping districts, department stores, and traffic galore. Maps available at the TAT office and hotels, such as the Chai Porn, make finding your way around a distinct possibility.

PRACTICAL INFORMATION

Tourist Office: Udon Thani TAT Office (tel./fax 241 968), located on Thesa Rd. opposite the reservoir. Check out the brand new digs housing a fanTATstic young staff brimming with helpful information on Udon Thai, Loei, and Nong Khai provinces. Pick up a free map of the city (you'll need it!). Open daily 8:30am-4:30pm.

Consulates: United States, 35/6 Supphakitchanya Rd. (tel 244 270-72; fax 244 273), along the northern end of Nong Prachak Reservoir, close to Northeastern Wattana Hospital. Issues passport replacements (allow 10 days for processing). For friendly, knowledgeable, English-speaking people go back to the TAT. Open Mon.-Fri. 7:30am-noon and 1-4:30pm. Closed for Thai and American holidays. Soon to be closed for good.

Currency Exchange: Khrung Thai Bank, 216 Makkhaeng Rd. (tel. 247 755). **Thai Farmers Bank,** 236 Phosi Rd. (tel. 241 122). Both open Mon.-Fri. 8:30am-3:30pm. **Bangkok Bank,** 154 Prachak Rd. (tel. 221 505 or 221 556). Open Mon.-Fri. 8:30am-3pm, with extended hours for currency exchange (8am-8pm).

Post Office: GPO, Wattana Rd. (tel. 222 304). Open Mon.-Fri. 8:30am-4:30pm, Sat.-Sun. 9am-noon. Telegram office open daily 7am-11pm. **Postal code:** 41000.

Telephones: Telecommunications Ministry of Thailand, 108/2 Udon-Dusadee Rd. (tel. 244 762). North of the clock tower traffic circle but before the intersection with Wattana Rd.; look for the antennae and satellite dish. Open daily 7am-11pm.

Airport: Udon Thani Airport, Udon-Loei Rd. (tel. 246 567 or 246 644), 3km southwest of town. 2 flights daily between Udon Thani and Bangkok, 1 additional flight on Fri. and Sat. afternoons (1260฿). **THAI Airways** is at 60 Makkhaeng Rd. (tel. 243 222). Open Mon.-Fri. 7am-5pm.

Train Station: (tel. 222 061), at the eastern end of Prachak Rd. Udon lies on the railway branch originating in Bangkok (3rd-class 145฿), passing through Khorat (3rd-class, 45฿), and Khon Kaen, and ending at Nong Khai (12฿). 5 daily to and from Bangkok, and 4 daily to and from Nong Khai. Book 3-5 days in advance.

Buses: Udon Thani's bus system is refreshingly straightforward in comparison to those of other Isaan metropoli; there are only 2 main terminals and 2 smaller stations. To: **Chiang Mai** (4 daily, 13hr., 170฿); **Loei** (every 40min., 2-½hr., 38฿); **Bangkok** (every hr., 8-½hr., 134฿); and **Nong Khai** (every 30min., 1hr., 15฿) leave from the new terminal (tel. 245 715) northwest of the city along the perimeter road. To get there, snag any #6 songthaew heading north (3฿). Buses to **Khorat** (every 45min., 5hr., 75฿); **Nakhon Phanom** (every 45min., 7hr., 91฿); **Ubon Ratchathani** (9 daily, 97฿); and **Bangkok** (134฿) leave from the terminal (tel. 222 916) on Sai Lithit Rd. near Charoen Si Plaza mall. Air-conditioned buses to Bangkok (hourly, 5am-11pm, 4hr., 241฿) leave from the **407 bus company** terminal (tel. 221 121) at 125/3 Prachak Rd. The TAT has a helpful English listing of bus departure times and fares.

Local Public Transportation: A **city bus** (3฿) runs rings around the city—rather useless if you're in the center of town. The TAT has a list of **songthaew** routes and numbers (3฿). Plenty of **samlors** (10-15฿) and **tuk-tuks** (15-20฿) in town.

Rentals: Parada Car Rent, 80 Makkhaeng Rd. (tel. 248 680). Suzuki, Mitsubishi, Toyota, Mazda, and Honda autos and motorcycles for rent. Fees range from 1200-

1500฿ per day depending on the model. Open daily 7am-5pm. **Meechai Car Rent,** 546/3 Phosi Rd. (tel. 245 491). Heading south, on the right, just before the intersection with Sai-Uthit Rd. Motorcycles 300฿ per day. Open daily 5am-8pm.

Markets: Rangsina Market near the Nong Khai bus terminal, **Ban Huay Market** in the northern part of town, and **Rot Fai Market** near the train station. Largest market in town is between Mukmontri and Makkhaeng Rd., just south of Phosi Rd. **Night market** near Makkhaeng and Sri Suk Rd.

Pharmacy: 305/1 Makkhaeng Rd. (tel. 221 492 or 242 561), directly across from the market. Open daily 6am-9pm. Visa, MC. **Contact Lens Supplies: Udon Optical,** 426-428 Phosi Rd. (tel. 223 068), near the Thailand Hotel and across from Siam City Bank. Bausch and Lomb products. Open daily 8am-8pm.

Hospital: Northeastern Wattana Hospital, 70/7-8 Supphakitchanya Rd. (tel. 241 031, -33), at the north end of the Nong Prachak Reservoir.

Emergency: Tourist Police (tel. 1699). **Police: Udon Thani Police Station,** Sri Suk Rd. (tel. 222 285).

ACCOMMODATIONS

Thailand Hotel, 4/1-6 Surakan Rd. (tel. 221 95; fax 223 453). Heading south on Udon-Dusadee Rd., take a left onto Surakan Rd. at the be-statued traffic circle; the hotel is on the right, equidistant from the circle and the intersection with Phosi Rd. Doubles have bathtubs. Clean, with friendly staff. Upper floors sport nice views. Singles 200฿, with A/C 300฿. Doubles with A/C 350฿. Laundry 10฿.

Prachapakdee Hotel, 156/7-9 Prachak Rd. (tel. 221 804). Heading north on Udon-Dusadee Rd. turn left onto Prachak Rd. The hotel is on the left between the Siam Commercial and Bangkok Banks. Peaceful location; the owner raises orchids in the rear courtyard. Ignore the *farang*-hating poodle in the lobby—everyone else does. Passport required for entry. Singles 150฿, with A/C 270฿. Doubles 170฿, with A/C 320฿. Laundry 10฿. Check-out noon.

Chai Porn Hotel, 209-211 Makkhaeng Rd. (tel. 222 144 or 221 913). Heading northwest on Phosi Rd., take a right onto Makkhaeng Rd. The hotel is on the right next to the Mandarin Restaurant. First-rate staff and tidy rooms belie this old veteran's age. Doubles boast bathtubs large enough for practicing your synchronized swimming routine. Inside the lobby above the elevator, an old Vietnam War propaganda photo of US air bombers flying above the clouds has the caption "Bad News for Uncle Ho." Singles 180฿, with A/C 270฿. Doubles 270฿, with A/C350฿. Snappy laundry service 4-10฿. Check-out noon.

FOOD

Excellent western, Thai, and Isaan restaurants are scattered throughout town. Mediocre coffee shops abound; often, air-conditioning is the best thing on the menu—you'll definitely pay for the privilege.

Yawt Kai Yaang, 7/40-41 Mukmontri Rd. (tel. 241 721), on the corner of Phosi Rd. Popular Isaan restaurant, particularly crowded at lunch time (and for good reason) despite the mingling of diesel fumes with grill smoke. Rice comes in traditional woven stay-warm baskets; modernity intrudes in the form of mechanized fly dispersers which shoo pests away from the food. A very full meal of *som tam, gai yang, khao niaw,* and water costs 50฿. Open 6am-10pm.

Udon Osha, 170 Prachak Rd. (tel. 243 794), across from Prachapakdee Hotel and 3 stores to the left. If you cross the tiny alley, back up 2 shops. This restaurant lists "cooked pig face" among its specialties, but what it really does best is a northern Isaan favorite, *kai dow ga-ta* (2 fried eggs with a minced pork/scallion topping and a few oh-so-delicately arranged slices of the local sweet sausage). All for just 10฿. Add 2 wee toasted French breadlets with sausage sticks (4฿) and a cup of hot Ovaltine or coffee (7฿), all for a grand total of 30฿. Open 5am-1pm.

SP Steak and Pizza House, 63/2 Naresuan Rd. (tel 241 058), two long blocks off Phosi Rd., opposite the southwest corner of the provincial jail on the left. The Thai owner was a cook for war-time soldiers stationed here; certificates of training and achievement from the US Armed Forces line the walls. Portions large enough to placate the hungriest G.I. while you wallow in A/C-induced ecstasy.

Variety of sandwiches (30-55฿), 'slaw (35฿). Nine versions of microwave style pizza (60-245฿). Juicy T-bones (260฿). Also has a glitzy outlet on the 2nd floor of Charoen Si Plaza. Open daily 8am-10pm.

SIGHTS AND ENTERTAINMENT

There are several places to visit around the province, but the best you'll do in town is to wander around the edge of **Nong Prachak Reservoir** in the northeast section. The peaceful surrounding area has park benches and open-air pavilions. The landscaping job here is pleasant, albeit imperfect. The work is obvious: the meandering path lacks necessary enclosure and the element of discovery is zippo. A statue of a reclining woman doing leg lifts scandalizes adults and sends teenagers into hysterical laughter. Join mothers with small children and young sweethearts on the footbridge to feed the Jaws-sized catfish, that are truly a spectacle (bag of fish chow 5฿).

Another sure-fire cultural experience is packaged as Isaan's largest consumer wat, **Charoen Si Plaza,** two blocks before the train station, off Prachak Rd. Wear sturdy shoes and pack enough plastic to pacify the voracious shopping deities.

Get toasted at the **Western Pub,** 420 Pracharaksa Rd. (tel. 243 508). When you walk through the door, waitresses looking a tad bewildered underneath the wide brims of their Western hats greet you with a smile and a *wai*. Watch your nose—swinging saloon doors are installed at every possible opportunity. The cheapest whiskey lists for 1500฿. The lily-livered can guzzle Singha, Kloster (80฿), or Corona beer (120฿) in addition to 20 varieties of mixed drinks (90฿). Cokes are a whopping 60฿, but the bartender will gladly add a splash of rum for only 10฿ more. Thai and *farang* food available (40฿ and up). The five-piece band starts pounding out Thai and American country favorites at 8pm. Drunken Thais enthusiastically toast each song, thumping fists on tables piled high with unholstered portable telephones. Free popcorn. Open 5pm-1am. Visa, MC.

■ AROUND UDON THANI

Ban Chiang, 64km east of Udon, is the site of one of the most significant archaeological discoveries in Southeast Asia, which earned it recognition as a UNESCO World Heritage site in 1992. It is world-renowned for the refined, curvilinear designs of the red buff pottery found here, and its discovery has completely rewritten the prehistory of Southeast Asia, previously dismissed as a cultural black hole.

The story of the site's discovery, scandalous looting, and eventual proper excavation begins in 1966, when Stephen Young, a Harvard student doing archaeological research, tripped over a large root. Just before he kissed *terra firma*, he caught himself, only to find the round rim of a partially unearthed pot staring him in the face. Upon closer scrutiny, he found that the entire 15x50 ft. area was littered with half-buried pots. The official excavation by the Fine Arts Department of Thailand and the University of Pennsylvania did not begin in earnest until the mid-70s. In the meantime, valuable artifacts were sold to collectors in shady trading centers around the world. Since then, many objects have been recovered, but without an exact record of their provenance, they have little archaeological significance.

Despite rampant plundering, much has been learned about the people who have lived here continuously for nearly 4000 years. Cord-marked vessels and the burial of infants inside jars represent the period from 3600-1000 BC. The latter practice may indicate unusually high infant mortality rates due to environmental stresses or the widespread practice of infanticide as a population control. Carinated vessels with incised patterns and red painting are characteristic of pottery made from 1000-300 BC, while the famous red-on-buff pottery with its complex red curvilinear designs is most commonly associated with burial rites of the later periods.

Archaeologists have also found 112 skeletons which outline the story of the city's original inhabitants. Apparently, the Ban Chiang civilization possessed a knowledge of bronze metallurgy much earlier than previously estimated. (The discovery has changed previously held notions that metallurgy came to Thailand from China; it was probably just the opposite.) Some artifacts also indicate a fairly extensive trade network.

An excellent village museum documents the discovery, excavation, and history of the findings unearthed over the past several decades. Second-floor exhibits with comprehensive English captions are most impressive. Open Wed.-Sun. 9am-4pm; admission 10฿. At the other end of the village, Wat Phosi Nai's "open-air exhibit" is the first of its kind in Thailand, displaying a burial site excavation as it was initially found, with artifacts intact. Exit left from the museum grounds and walk for about 500m. The excavation will be on the right side, just before the road curves.

Orange and blue **songthaews** from Udon Thani to Ban Chiang (every 30min., 1-½hr., 18฿) leave from just beyond the gas station on the left side of Phosi Rd., south of the be-statued traffic circle. After crossing the tracks, the road becomes Nityo Rd., or Hwy. 22, the Udon Thani-Sakhon Nakhon Hwy. If the bus drops you off on Hwy. 22 at the road to Ban Chiang, take a tuk-tuk the remaining 6km to the museum (15-20฿). The last bus directly from the museum gate back to Udon leaves at noon. Otherwise, hire a tuk-tuk (15-20฿) to drive you back to the highway. From there, catch any of the numerous buses heading into Udon.

Another worthwhile stop is **Erawan Cave,** 90km out of town on Hwy. 210 (Udon-Loei Hwy.). Stalagmites and stalactites stud the interior, and the mouth has a lovely view of the countryside. To get there, leap on a Loei-bound bus at the new terminal on the perimeter road in Udon Thani (30฿). From the highway drop-off, it's a 2km walk or a 10-20฿ round-trip tuk-tuk ride to the cave. See Around Loei for details.

■■■ KHON KAEN

The second-largest city in Isaan, Khon Kaen is the approximate geographic center of the northeast. Tourists often snub this cradle of commerce, but the metropolis deserves credit for its comprehensive museum, exciting night market, decent restaurants, and thriving nightlife. Khon Kaen University, the largest in the Northeast, supplies an energetic young crowd that contributes to the evening *élan.* In addition, there's a helpful branch of the TAT worth visiting for information on Khon Kaen city and province, as well as rarely visited northeast regions such as Mahasarakham and Kalasin. In the rest of the province, several sights reward the adventuresome. The pride and joy of Khon Kaen province are both the discovery of several dinosaur fossils at Phu Wiang National Park, and the silk factories at Chonabot city.

ORIENTATION

The city is an important transportation, communication, and education center for the Isaan region. Because of its size and significance, Khon Kaen is easily reached by plane, bus, or train. The train line that goes from Bangkok to Nong Khai services Khon Kaen. The **train station** is on the west side of town along **Darunsamran Road** and directly at the end of **Ruenrom Road,** which leads into the city and intersects some of the main streets. In the evening, the **night market** closes down the part of Ruenrom Rd. between Na Muang Rd. and Klang Muang Rd. The **ordinary bus terminal** is on Prachasamosorn Rd., and the **A/C bus terminal** is off Klang Muang Rd.

The city layout is an imperfect grid, bound on the west by the railroad tracks and Highway 2. In the central district, three main parallel roads, **Na Muang Road, Klang Muang Road,** and **Lang Muang Road,** run north-south. These streets are intersected by **Prachasamosorn Road.** to the north and **Srichan Road** to the south. Most of the banks, restaurants, and accommodations, as well as night life haunts, lie between these two roads. In between these two big avenues are smaller intersecting east-west roads such as **Pimpasut** and **Ammart Roads.** A free map of Khon Kaen is available from the TAT.

PRACTICAL INFORMATION

Tourist Office: TAT, 15/5 Prachasamosorn Rd. (tel. 244 498; fax 244 497). A brown and white building on the right, close to the Lang Muang intersection, several blocks east of the ordinary bus terminal. New and very helpful, the center for information on Khon Kaen, Roi Et, Mahasarakham, and Kalasin provinces. Some staff members speak excellent English. Free maps and public transportation info (within and outside of Khon Kaen). Open daily 8:30am-4:30pm.

Tourist Police: 15/5 Prachasamosorn Rd. (tel. 236 937/8), to the left of TAT office. Also responsible for Nong Khai, Udon Thani, Loei, Sakhon Nakhon, Nakhon Phanom, Nong Bua Lamphu, and Mukdahan provinces. Before contacting the Thai police in any of these provinces, call the Khon Kaen tourist police.

Currency Exchange: Banks all over the city exchange money. **Bangkok Bank,** 254 Srichan Rd. (tel. 225 142, -6), just east of Fairy Plaza and Parrot Restaurant, offers after-hours exchange. Mon.-Fri. 8:30am-8pm, Sat.-Sun. 9am-5pm.

Post/Telephone Office: (tel 237 185) on Thaparak Rd., just north of the regular bus terminal opposite the provincial hall. Open Mon.-Fri. 8:30am-4:30pm, Sat.-Sun. 9am-noon. **Overseas telephone** and **telegram** open daily 8am-8pm. **Postal code:** 40000. **Telephone code:** 043.

Airport: Khon Kaen Airport, Airport Rd. (tel. 236 515 or 239 922), off Maliwan Rd., which is the name of Prachasamosorn Rd. west of the train tracks. To **Bangkok** (3 daily, 4 on Fri.-Sat., 1020฿). Check with **THAI Airways** for current schedule. Office located at 183/6 Maliwan Rd. (tel. 243 037, 236 523, 239 011, or 238 835; airport office 238 803). Open Mon.-Fri. 8:30am-4:30pm.

Trains: Khon Kaen Railway Station (tel. 221 112), on Ruenrom Rd. To: **Bangkok** (6 daily, 8hr., rapid 105฿, express 125฿) and **Nong Khai** (5 daily, 3hr., 35฿).

Buses: Ordinary bus terminal (tel. 237 300), on Prachasamosorn Rd. To: **Bangkok** (#20, every 30min., 6:30am-11pm, 7-9hr., 108฿); **Chiang Mai** (#175 or #633, 9 daily, 5am-6:30pm, 11-13hr., 192฿); **Udon Thani** (#211 or #262, every 30min., 5:30am-5:30pm, 2hr., 32฿); and **Ubon Ratchathani** (every hour, 5:40am-1:40pm, 70฿). **A/C bus terminal** (tel. 239 910), is on Klang Muang Rd. To: **Bangkok** (#20, every 45min., 7hr., 295฿); **Nong Khai** (#23, 1:30 and 3pm, 5hr., 79฿); **Chiang Mai** (#633, 8 and 9pm, 11hr., 307฿), **Loei** (#217, 6:30, 11:30am, and 4:30pm, 3-4 hr., 95฿); **Mukdahan** (#278, 7am, 1:30, and 3:30pm, 4hr., 84฿); **Ubon** (#268, every 2hr., 9am-3pm, 125฿); **Nakhon Phanom** (#586, 7:30am and 4pm, 5hr., 129฿); and **Chiang Rai** (#637, 6pm, 14hr., 339฿). Check with TAT office for more details.

Local Public Transportation: Samlors (10-30฿) and **tuk-tuks** (20-30฿). Many small minibuses/**songthaews** (3฿) ply the roads of Khon Kaen, but the 13 different routes are confusing. The TAT has an English pamphlet listing them; most travelers in town for just a few days simply lace up the Keds and pound the pavement, as most everything worth seeing in Khon Kaen is within walking distance.

Markets: The **day market,** between Na Muang and Klang Muang Rd. (behind all the buildings on either street; entrances on either road), takes up almost 3 city blocks just south of Srichan Rd. Open daily 5am-7pm. **Vendors** set up on Ruenrom Rd. between Na Muang and Klang Muang Rd. from 6pm-midnight are far more exciting than the **night market** near the A/C bus terminal.

Laundry: Sirirat King Center, 41/13 Langmuang Rd. "Washy mashy" sign in window. Pants/shirt set 20฿, jeans 20฿. Next-day service. Open daily 7:30am-8:30pm.

Pharmacy: Wattana Pah Sadt, 31/33 Ammart Rd. (tel. 244 468), near Langmuang intersection. Basic first-aid supplies and analgesics. Open daily 7am-10pm.

Hospitals: Sri Nakharin Hospital (tel. 237 902), north of the city on Route 2. On the green city bus route. **Khon Kaen Public Hospital** (tel. 236 005, 237 137), on east side of town on Srichan Rd. Thai sign with small green cross.

Emergency: tel. 1699.

Police: Khon Kaen Police Station (tel. 221 162), on Klang Muang Rd.

ACCOMMODATIONS

Co-Co Parrot's Guest, 58/1 Pimpasut Rd. (tel. 241 283), between Na Muang and Klang Muang Rd. Set back in an arcade of shops and bars behind First Choice Restaurant (where you check in). Ask to be dropped off at First Choice. Comfortable, well-maintained wooden complex of rooms. Downstairs baths and A/C rooms sport some unusual architecture (whiskey-bottle windows, woven ceilings, and

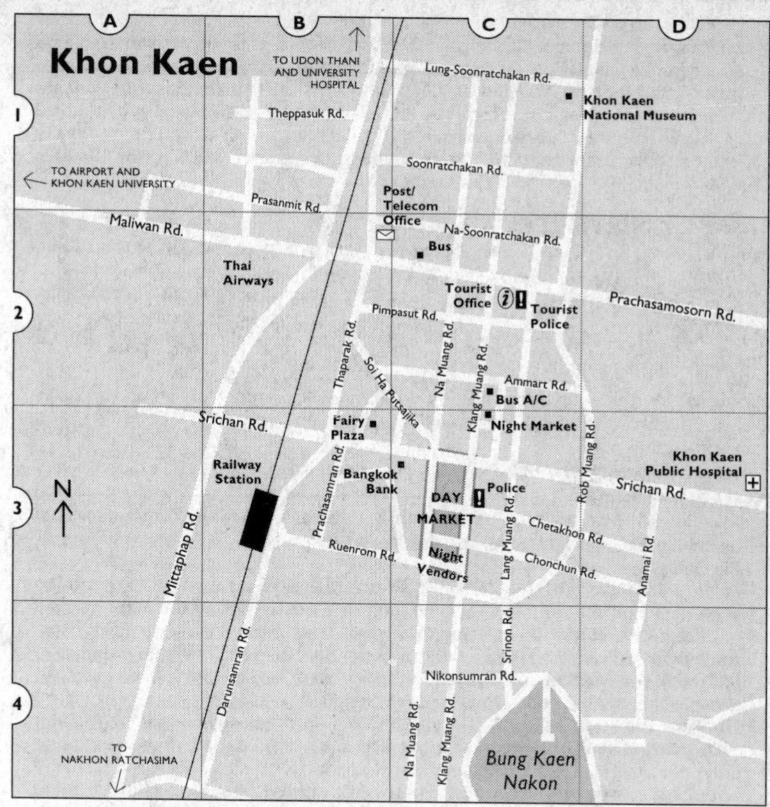

lacquered brick walls) and noisy non-avian wildlife. A hotel in guest house clothing. Fills up quickly. Singles 100฿, doubles 150฿, with A/C 300฿. Laundry service.

Sansumran Hotel, 55-59 Klang Muang Rd. (tel./fax 239 611). Cheap, clean rooms at this hotel make it the miser's choice in Khon Kaen. A basic hotel with a decent reputation. Look at the pride of wooden lions in the lobby and sympathize with the lone wood antelope. Rooms on the newly renovated 2nd floor are spacious and sparkling, but more expensive. Singles 200฿. Mammoth doubles 250฿. Singles downstairs are cheaper and shabbier, though clean 160฿. Laundry service.

Roma Hotel, 50/2 Klang Muang Rd. (tel. 237 177, 236 276, or 236 490; fax 242 458). Cavernous marble-floored lobby could double as an ice rink, if the average temperature outside weren't 86°F. The huge oil painting of a pseudo-American landscape is a classy, if incongruous touch. Higher standards translate into higher prices. A/C rooms have hot water. Singles 200฿, with A/C and TV 500฿. Doubles 250฿, with A/C 300฿, with A/C and TV 800฿. Skip the in-house Romani coffee shop (40-60฿). Laundry. Visa, MC, AmEx.

FOOD

Kai Yang Ra-Biab, 252/5 Thepalak Rd. (tel. 243 413), at the end of Lung-soonratchakan Rd. near the train tracks. No-frills authenticity, yet wildly popular at lunch-time with well-heeled Thais otherwise too cool for the street market scene (the number of cellular phones on the tables almost equals the number of sticky rice baskets). Isaan classics such as *gai yang* (served with head, neck, and feet of course), *som tam,* and *khao niaw.* Not exactly classical prices: 50฿ for a whole meal. Open daily 9am-3pm.

The Parrot, 175 Srichan Rd. (tel. 244 692), east of Fairy Plaza on the corner of a soi and next to a gas station. Polly wanna' good, inexpensive western meal? Breakfast menu 7:30-11am, fish and chips (90฿), sandwiches (35฿), pizza (55-140฿), and an entire page of vegetarian selections. Fresh-baked white and whole wheat bread (35฿). Wines and other spirits (beer 40฿) . Staff actually gives you time to order without hovering. Peruse an English language newspaper while you wait. Open daily 7:30am-10:30pm. All major credit cards.

SIGHTS AND ENTERTAINMENT

Khon Kaen city's only noteworthy sight is the **Khon Kaen National Museum** (tel. 246 170), facing Lung-soonratchakan Rd. at the far north end of town. You can get there by local public transport or hike to the north end of Klang Muang Rd., passing by many government offices. This museum documents the history of Thailand's central northeast region. An exhibit on prehistoric artifacts includes pottery from Ban Chiang Archaeological Site in Udon Thani province. Other exhibits focus on different periods following the arrival of Buddhism. Also features folk art and archaeological finds from nearby Kalasin and Mahasarakam provinces. Open Wed.-Sun. 9am-4pm; admission 20฿.

As the Northeast's premier university city, Khon Kaen majors in hard-core nightlife. For party-hearty dilettantes, the arcade near Co-Co Parrot's Guest House and First Choice is the premier option for bar-hopping, since the complex is jam-packed with karaoke bars, beer gardens, and other types of pubs.

Funan, 3/1 Srichan Rd. (tel. 239 628), several blocks past Fairy Plaza close to the train tracks on the right side of the road. MTV holds sway in the early evening until the band takes over, playing exclusively Thai music. As the night rolls on, the pub fills quickly and the crowd drinks fast. By midnight, the band switches to folk/rock standards, as the audience dances at (or on) the tables and sings (or screams) along. Beer 80฿. Open well past midnight.

Witchery Pub (tel. 241 687–90; fax 236 220), in the basement garage of Fairy Plaza. Barnum and Bailey meets the Parthenon. Colorful mosaic floors swirl up to a looming white statue of a Greek god toting a beer mug in his left hand. Very popular with young trend-setters, but the live music is as erratic as the decor is zany. Beer 120฿, soft drinks 60฿. Dinner served in the early evening. Music starts around 9pm. Open daily 7pm-2am.

Top West Pub and Restaurant, 6/2 Srichan Rd. (tel. 226 310). Heading west along Srichan Rd. from the Fairy Plaza, it's several blocks down on the left, before Funan and the train tracks. A cavernous country-western bar replete with American flags, animal pelts, and Native American trinkets. A musical showcase of live bands on Saturday nights: some groups play enjoyable rock—Eagles, Dire Straits, and the obligatory CCR ditty; others should be opening for Wayne and Garth…not! Jolly, upbeat crowd. Soda 50฿, no alcohol. Open daily 6pm-3am.

Phoebus Music Hall (tel. 332 853), located in the arcade of karaoke bars and movie theaters off Phimpasut Rd. just west of the Co-Co Parrot Guest House and across the intersection. Discophile heaven, or teenage hilarity. The bubble gum crowd averages about 16 years of age (no alcohol served, soda 50฿); they boogie on the split-level dance floor while M.C. Hammer and Paula Abdul wannabes cavort on stage. Don't be surprised if the roving video camera displays your *farang* mug on the screen above the stage. Open 8pm-4am.

■ NEAR KHON KAEN: CHONABOT

Although Khon Kaen province has plenty of sights, the scant number of tourist facilities (transportation, lodging, etc.) makes exploring the area a healthy challenge. The tiny town of **Chonabot** stocks enough hand-woven silk to outfit Zsa Zsa Gabor and her assorted wedding parties for six lifetimes.

Tour companies often advertise trips to this area, but demand up to a 25% commission from factory owners for every purchase (resulting in higher mark-ups)—it's better to go on your own. Most factories open Mon.-Sat. 8am-5pm; no formal showrooms, but they will gladly bring out wares if you give them an idea of what interests you. Often traditional tie-dyed *mut-mee* silk is sold as a two-*lah* set (one *lah* is 90cm—enough material for one skirt). *Pah puen* is plain, solid-color silk, more frequently bought by the meter. Prices vary depending on thickness and weight, ranging from the ultra-light one-ply to the thick four-ply material used for jackets. *Mut-mee* silk starts at 250-300฿ per *lah*, and *pah puen* runs 135-200฿ per *lah*.

To get to Chonabot, catch the bus to Nakhon Sawan from Khon Kaen's main bus terminal (hourly, last bus 1:30pm, 1hr., 15฿) and ask to be let off at Chonabot. The bus will deposit you along the highway. After you disembark, turn around to face the wagon-wheel fence and police station. Walk right to the first intersection, then turn left. The first factory is on the right side of the street before the post office.

To return to Khon Kaen, walk back down Phosri Sahat Rd. until it meets the highway. Wait in front of the police station; the last bus back departs at 5pm.

Southern Thailand

Southern Thailand is graced with some of the finest shorelines and islands in Southeast Asia. The warm translucent waters of the Gulf of Thailand to the east and the Andaman Sea to the west are at the center of southern life in coastal towns that are financially dependent on the ebb and flow of tourists or the daily shrimp and fish catch. Monstrous luxury hotels have conquered some coastal acreage, but most beaches remain untrammeled and ready for low-impact exploration. Down the bumpier dirt roads, at places yet undiscovered by bulldozer-toting Bangkok developers and tourist guide book writers, Shangri-La is still pristine. You just have to work harder to find it.

Heading down the coast with the Urban Bangkok empire at your back, you pass through a chain of seaside paradise-purgatories and small villages. After squeezing through the narrowest point in Thailand, the road snakes among inland swamps and coastal wetlands, through durian plantations, and along the pale sandstone cliffs that rim glowing white sand beaches. Offshore the resort islands of Ko Samui, Ko Phangan, and Ko Tao gear themselves to please the tens of thousands of foreigners who catalyze the evolution of "paradise on earth."

The ethnic mixture of the deep south slowly appears after Surat Thani, as mosques replace wats and women begin to don veils. Spicy seafoods and local fruits tend to dominate Southern diets. Specialties include *khanom jiin jam yaa* (thin white noodles with fish curry), sweet and sour fish, fish curry paste cooked in banana-leaf cups, and oyster omelettes. Mangosteen, rambutan, *langsads,* and pungent durians are the culinary cooling tools, especially for wimpy *farang* tongues.

In pint-size provinces like those south of Krabi, traveler-oriented services are few, as are the numbers who speak English. Foreigners are something of an anomaly here; don't be surprised if you find yourself under heavy scrutiny. Women may opt to wear long pants in areas with large Muslim populations.

South of Phuket, the west coast's main draw is Ko Tarutao, a group of over 50 islands comprising a national park, thus far protected from the development strangling Ko Phi Phi and Ko Samet. That coast is also home to Trang, the city where the south's feeding frenzy is at a fever pitch. The east coast from Pattani down to Malaysia is lined with blithely beautiful beaches, frequented by locals on the weekends and in the evenings. The deep, deep south from Pattani to Malaysia is rich in lovely countryside as well, plush with vegetation, unlike the area up near Surat Thani, which is stripped and paved for large gas stations and suburban housing projects.

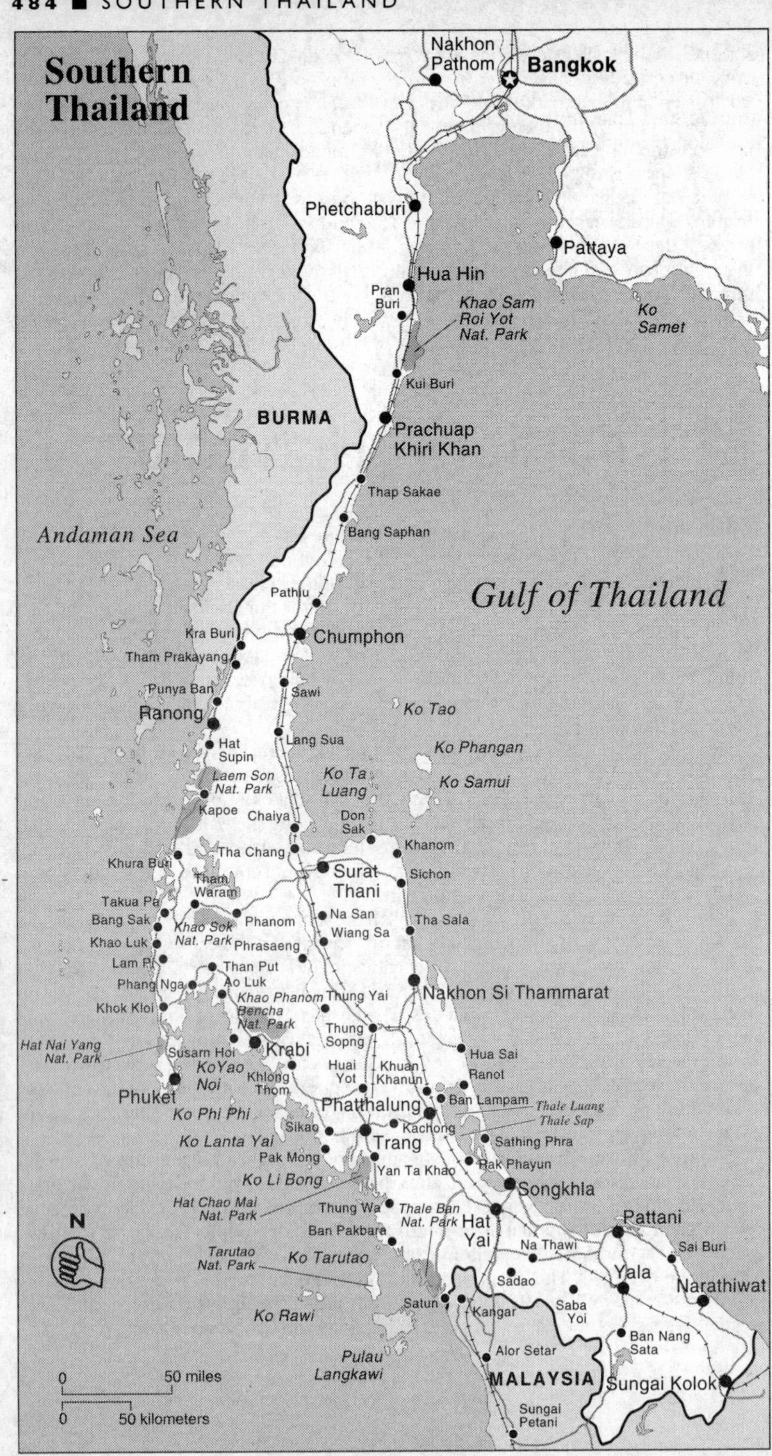
Southern Thailand
Nakhon Pathom
Bangkok
Phetchaburi
Pattaya
Hua Hin
Pran Buri
Khao Sam Roi Yot Nat. Park
Ko Samet
Kui Buri
BURMA
Prachuap Khiri Khan
Thap Sakae
Andaman Sea
Bang Saphan
Gulf of Thailand
Pathiu
Kra Buri
Chumphon
Tham Prakayang
Punya Ban
Sawi
Ranong
Ko Tao
Lang Sua
Hat Supin
Ko Phangan
Laem Son Nat. Park
Ko Ta Luang
Ko Samui
Kapoe
Chaiya
Don Sak
Khanom
Tha Chang
Khura Buri
Surat Thani
Sichon
Tham Waram
Takua Pa
Bang Sak
Phanom
Na San
Tha Sala
Khao Sok Nat. Park
Wiang Sa
Khao Luk
Phrasaeng
Lam Pi
Than Put
Phang Nga
Ao Luk
Nakhon Si Thammarat
Khao Phanom Bencha Nat. Park
Thung Yai
Khok Kloi
Thung Sopng
Hat Nai Yang Nat. Park
Susarn Hoi
Krabi
Hua Sai
KoYao Noi
Huai Yot
Khuan Khanun
Ranot
Khlong Thom
Phuket
Ban Lampam
Thale Luang
Phatthalung
Ko Phi Phi
Thale Sap
Sikao
Kachong
Ko Lanta Yai
Trang
Sathing Phra
Pak Mong
Yan Ta Khao
Rak Phayun
Ko Li Bong
Songkhla
Hat Chao Mai Nat. Park
Thung Wa
Thale Ban Nat. Park
Hat Yai
Pattani
N
Ban Pakbara
Na Thawi
Sai Buri
Tarutao Nat. Park
Ko Tarutao
Yala
Sadao
Narathiwat
Satun
Saba Yoi
Kangar
Ko Rawi
Ban Nang Sata
Alor Setar
Pulau Langkawi
0
50 miles
MALAYSIA
Sungai Kolok
0
50 kilometers
Sungai Petani

■■■ CHUMPHON

All signs point to Chumphon as Thailand's next tourist boom town. It has already usurped Surat Thani as the jumping-off point for that famous tropical trinity: Ko Tao, Ko Phangan, and Ko Samui. The town and its surrounding area are none-too-shabby themselves: 222km of white beaches, fantastic offshore islands, long coral reefs, stunning caves, and waterfalls. Consider breezing through the city for a night's stay at nearby Hat Thung Wua Laen. Chumphon city is chock a block full of tour companies and information centers, all scrambling for backpacker patronage, making travel here easy and pleasant. Things will only get easier, as an airport is currently under construction and due to be completed sometime in 1996.

Almost 500km from Bangkok, this gateway marks the convergence of the asphalt arteries connecting Phuket, Bangkok, and the tail of Thailand, as well as transition in dialect and food. *Pak tai* refers to the fast, high-toned southern dialect, and to the southern vegetable-laden culinary style which employs some of the country's most merciless spices. *Pak tai* also denotes the region farther south, where Islam is a major influence. Pursuers of trivia will be tickled to know that the town's name was abbreviated from Chumnumphon ("the gathering of blessings"), so named because ancient military troops hosted pep rallies here to raise morale before battles.

ORIENTATION

Chumphon basically follows a simple grid, with a few surprises. **Krom Luang Chumphon Road** runs east from the train station and forms the northern border of the town. **Pobaminthra Manka Road** sprawls east-west as the town's southern limit and is where you'll find the hospital, post office, and buses to Hat Sai Ree. The bus station and several tourist information centers lie on **Tha Thapao Road,** running north-south in the western part of the city. Parallel and one block to the east is hotel-and-eatery-studded **Saladaeng Road.** This is where the city grid begins to break down. Through some quirk of city planning, the last street to the right before the Saladaeng-Krom Luang Chumpon intersection as one walks north has been annexed by Saladaeng Rd. This side-street contains locally famous **Ocean Shopping Mall** as well as numerous restaurants and the Chumphon Information Center. Boomerang-inspired **Pracha Uthit Road.** straddles the city center; here you'll find the market and transport to boats to **Ko Tao** and **Hat Thung Wua Laen (Cabana Beach).**

PRACTICAL INFORMATION

Tourist Office: Chumphon Information Center (CIC), 188/141 Saladaeng Rd. (tel. & fax 503 857). Turn onto the side-street annexed by Saladaeng Rd. and walk to the end. Turn right. The CIC is a few stores down, opposite the Jansom Hotel Beer Garden sign. Acts as an information distribution center and tourist liaison. Peppy, Mickey Mouse-shod staff speaks English. Open 8:30am-9pm. The staff at **Infinity Travel Services,** 68/2 Tha Thapao Rd. (tel. 501 937) greets travelers at the train station in snazzy company jackets. Open daily 7am-11pm. Mr. O can be found at **Tiw's Restaurant,** 174 Saladaeng Rd. (tel. 502 448), at the 5-way intersection across from the cinema. Look for the English signs advertising tourist information. Open daily 2am-8pm. O is extremely knowledgeable and well worth meeting. Both he and Infinity Tours would be ecstatic to arrange tours, transportation, boats to Ko Tao, accommodations, and rental equipment for your pleasure. New kids on the block, **Chumphon Cabana Resort Co. and S.M.C. Travel,** 69/20 Tha Thapao Rd. (tel. 570 395; fax 504 442) have formed a partnership and recently opened an office across the street and 20m north of Infinity. Similar services are offered, but they can also directly arrange scuba instruction/tours with certified instructors. Open 8am-5pm.

Currency Exchange: Branches of **Thai Farmers Bank** and **Bangkok Bank** on Saladaeng Rd. Bangkok Bank 111/1-2 Saladaeng Rd. (tel. 511 446). Thai Farmer's Bank 134 Saladaeng Rd. (tel. 511 380). Open Mon.-Fri. 8:30am-3:30pm. Closed holidays.

Post Office: GPO (tel. 511 041), on Pobaminthra Manka Rd., past the market and the city shrine in the southeastern corner of town. Open Mon.-Fri. 8:30am-4:30pm, Sat.-Sun. 9am-noon. **Postal code:** 86000.

Telecommunications Office: 2nd floor of GPO building (tel. 511 885). Open daily 7am-10pm.**Telephone code:** 077. **Chumphon Cabana Resort and S.M.C. Travel Center,** 69/20 Tha Tapao Rd. (tel. 570 395; fax 504 442). Overseas service charge 30฿. Fax prices vary with destination. Open 8am-5pm.

Trains: Chumphon Railway Station (tel. 511 103), at the intersection of Rot Fai and Krom Luang Chumphon Rd. **North-bound** trains destined for **Bangkok**'s Hualamphong Station (9 daily, 7-½hr., 3rd-class 102฿, 2nd-class 192฿, sleeper cars: top bunk 292฿, bottom bunk 342฿); **Prachuap Khiri Khan** (6 daily, 3 hr., 3rd class 54฿, 2nd class 91฿); and **Phetchaburi** (5 daily, 5-½hr., 3rd class 78฿, 2nd class 142฿, sleeper cars: top bunk 242฿, bottom bunk 292฿). **South-bound** trains stop at **Surat Thani** (11 daily, 3hr., 3rd class 54฿, 2nd class 91฿). One train to **Malaysia: Padang Besar** (10:54am, 9 hr., 2nd class 229฿, sleeper car: top bunk 379฿, bottom bunk 429฿, with A/C 479฿/529฿) and **Butterworth** (13½hr., 2nd class 429฿, sleeper car: top bunk 579฿, bottom bunk 629฿, with A/C 679฿/729฿). To the border town of **Sungai Kolok** (9:36 and 10:20pm,12 hr., 2nd class 250฿, sleeper car: top bunk 400฿, bottom bunk 450฿, with A/C 500฿/550฿).

Buses: Regular buses leave from the terminal (tel. 502 725) on Tha Tapao Rd. across from the similarly named hotel. Tickets sold in the station and on the bus. To **Bangkok** (every hr., 4:25am-10pm, 8 hr., 112฿, with fan 157฿; A/C tour bus 9:30pm, 202฿; other buses pass randomly though Chumphon throughout the night but may already be full); **Prachuap Khiri Khan** (8 daily, 3-½hr., 45฿); **Phuket** (3:30, 5:30, 10:30pm, 1, 3, and 5:30am, 7 hr., 102฿); and **Surat Thani** (1:30, 2:30, 4:30, and 5:30pm, 3 hr., 57฿). **Suwanathi Tours,** 45/2 Tha Tapao Rd. (tel. 511 422 or 501 535; open 8am-10pm), located behind the bus terminal. A/C tour buses to **Bangkok** (10:00am, 2:00, and 10:00pm, 202฿). Reserve in advance. **Infinity Tourist Information Service,** 68/2 Tha Tapao Rd. (tel. 501 937; open 7am-11pm) has **mini-van** service to **Surat Thani** (every hr., 7am-5pm, 2-½hr., 90฿) while **Chumphonthansmarin** across the street (tel. 511 324) has service to **Ranong** (every hr., 7am-5pm, 2hr., 70฿).

Boats to the Islands: The **slow boat** to **Ko Tao** leaves the pier at midnight (daily, 5hr., 200฿). The last songthaew (5฿) leaves at 6pm in front of the waterworks offices on Pracha-Uthit Rd. Walk east past the market on Pracha-Uthit Rd. until it curves sharply left. The blue songthaews leave just past the covered seating on the left side of the road; look for the flock of chicken-foot vendors. The sleek, **high-speed boat** leaves from a different pier (daily, 8am, 100min., 400฿). The red songthaew for the speed boat pier also leaves from the waterworks office (5฿). CIC can arrange transportation for both you and your baggage. Infinity Tourist Information Service (50฿) or O at Tiw's Restaurant (40฿) will take you to the docks as well. To go to **Ko Maphraw** (Coconut Island) you must contact the provincial authority at least 15 days in advance for an official tour. **Ko Samet** is home to thousands of villainous Kapa vipers; most visitors stay on the boat. Contact O, Infinity travel, or CIC for info on excursions. For trips to the larger **Ko Thalu,** hire a **fishing boat** in **Hat Sai Ree,** 20km from Chumphon via Hwy. 4119 and 4098. Songthaews leave from the post office (last trip 5pm, 45min., 13฿).

Local Transportation: Deny the motorcycle taxi and *samlor* drivers—everything in the downtown area is within walking distance.

Car Rental: A/C pick-up truck or A/C car (1200฿ per day) from Tiw's Restaurant. Infinity also offers cars, pick-ups, and vans (900-1200฿) for rent; vans are insured.

Motorcycle Rental: Infinity and O at Tiw's Restaurant both rent motorcycles (200฿ with a passport deposit for 24 hr.).

Boating and Scuba Diving: Boats can be hired for daytrips to the islands. Prices range from 1500 to 2500฿ per day, depending on itinerary and boat size, so form a group to defray costs. Contact CIC, Infinity Tours, or O for details and special events. The Chumphon Cobana Resort and S.M.C. Travel Center also offers package tours (at a higher cost) and sponsors numerous **PADI** (Scuba) courses ranging from the 1-hr., 300 ฿, Discover Scuba course to the 12-day, 15,000฿, Dive Master instruction. Equipment rentals also available. Costs vary with the seasons.

March-April is cheapest, May (fishing season) is most expensive. For more information on boat trips or diving, ask O at Tiw's Restaurant.

English Bookstore: DK Book House, (not DK Bookstore) 188/142-144 Saladaeng Rd. (tel. 503 816), next to CIC. Carries *The Nation*. Open 9am-9:30pm.

Laundry: Nong Ooh 188/71-72 Saladaeng Rd. First soi on the left after Ocean Shopping Mall, as you walk toward Janson Hotel. Faded blue sign. Open 7am-9pm.

Hospital: Virajsilp Hospital (tel. 503 238), at the south end of Tha Taphao Rd. Private hospital. Open 24 hrs. English-speaking doctors.

Pharmacy: 188/105 Saladaeng Rd. (tel. 501 129), opposite Ocean Shopping Mall. Open Mon-Fri 5am-10pm, Sat-Sun. 9:30am-10pm. Green sign with orange stripe.

Emergency: tel. 191

Police: (tel. 511 300), at the north end of Saladaeng Rd., on the right past the intersection with Krom Luang Chumphon Rd. Look for the "Don't Drink and Drive" monument, a demolished motorcycle on a memorial pedestal.

ACCOMMODATIONS

Get a jump on the cheapest lodgings in Chumphon and make daytrips to the sights or pay a little extra for oceanside lodgings. The many Chinese-style hotels along cosmopolitan Saladaeng Rd. are popular with salespeople, while new bungalows are constantly appearing on Ao Thung Wua Laen, Hat Sai Ree, and the city fringes.

Suksamer Guest House, 118/4 Suksamer Rd. (tel. 502 430). Exit the train station onto Krom Luang Chumphon Rd. Follow it to the Suksamer Rd. intersection and turn right. It's at the end of the first soi on the left; there is a large sign in English at the soi's entrance. Thatched-roof house with a big coconut tree. Clean, spacious rooms with fans, or you and three friends can make like hamsters in the loft above the restaurant (50฿). Shared bathroom with showers. Open-air restaurant serves fresh baked bread (15฿) and pizza (60-130฿). All doubles 150฿.

Suriya Hotel, 125/24-5 Saladaeng Rd. (tel. 511 144). Just south of the five-way intersection, on the right side of the road with an inconspicuous red sign over the door. Or is it a nursery? Worn pink fuzzy blankets and once-bright blue walls have seen better days. Perhaps the kids moved away long ago. The nearby street intersection might keep you up at night. Singles with bath 120฿. Doubles 200฿.

FOOD

In Chumphon, find meals for chump-change in the markets (and the shopping mall food courts). The **morning market** actually hustles all day (5am-5pm) in the shade of a city-block-wide mesh of tin roofing—a fresh fruit cornucopia with "fingernail bananas" (*gluay lep meu*) and wonderfully sweet pineapples (*sapah rot*), two first-rate fruits for which Chumphon is renowned. Enter the labyrinth from Pracha-Uthit Rd. or by the row of motorcycle taxis along Pobaminthra Manka Rd. The **night market** sprawls along Saladaeng Rd. to the Ocean Shopping Mall and serves delectable dinners like *khao tom aahaan talay* (rice soup with seafood) and *khanom jiin nam ya* (vermicelli with fish curry) at prices that won't land you in debtor's prison. The **Ocean Shopping Mall,** located on the annexed side-street off Saladaeng Rd., north of the Fuji sign, is an air-conditioned oasis with a food court and typical Thai food—fried rice, noodle soup, ice cream (under 30฿). Open daily 10am-9:30pm.

Tiw's Restaurant, 174 Saladaeng Rd. (tel. 502 448), across from cinema at 5-way intersection. Decorated with great maps and pictures of the sights around Chumphon. Best place to contact O; he's even hung his own poetry about transportation on the wall. The five-star food doesn't command astronomical prices. Rice plates 15฿, fried rice 20฿. English menu. Open daily; food served 2am-1pm (yes, 2am), drinks and snacks until 8pm.

Pai Thong, 588/130 Saladaeng Rd. (tel. 501 336). On the left toward the Ocean Shopping Mall. Northeastern Thai food: roast pork, roast catfish (25-30฿), *som tam* (Thai papaya salad). Tell them '*mai sai poo,*' (nix the raw crabs), and '*mai ped,*' (cool off on the chilies). English menu. Open daily 5:30am-11:30pm.

■ AROUND CHUMPHON

To see anything interesting, a daytrip is in order. Many a gorgeous beach with white sand and gentle surf has been passed over by tourist lemmings who hightail to Cha-Am, Hua Hin, Phuket, or Ko Samui. The current hot spots for scuba diving and beach bumming, Ko Tao and Ko Nang Yuan, distance themselves from Chumphon's coast. Seldom-visited Ko Ngam Yai and Ko Ngam Noi, however, off nearby Hat Thung Wua Laen, are better locations for viewing something besides all the other divers. Renting a boat to visit the islands off Chumphon's shore will set a backpacker's budget back a couple of days; find a group, share the burden. When your tender skin tires of UV abuse and constant *coup de soleil,* Rab Ro Caves and the Ka Po waterfalls offer a soothing change of environment. Hat Thung Wua Laen, Rab Ro Caves, and Ka Po waterfalls can easily be viewed in one daytrip.

HAT THUNG WUA LAEN (CABANA BEACH)

12km north of Chumphon, this is the blockbuster beach in the area (it has no-stick sand). Thankfully, stardom has not spoiled the scene. Laws now prohibit commercial buildings on beachfront property (giving the already existing Chuan Phan complex a monopoly), ban jet skis and campfires, and maintain tough environmental standards to keep the waters clean. Fishing boats cannot enter the bay, which is naturally protected by hills flanking the gently sloping beach. The influx of bungalows and shops to the outlying area does contribute to a suburbanized sprawl, however. Offshore **Ngam Yai and Ngam Noi Islands,** prized for their swallows' nests, underwater coral reefs, and soaring cliffs and caves, are reachable by a boat from Sa Plee Pier. Check tourist information listings for group rates.

In Chumphon, yellow songthaews to Cabana Beach lurk behind the marketplace along Pracha-Uthit Rd., which begins across from the cinema at the 5-way intersection on Saladaeng Rd. by the Fuji sign. They run the length of the beach (last trip 6pm, ½hr, 20฿). If you've rented your own wheels, head north (across Krom Luang Chumphon Rd.) over the train tracks, following the signs for Chumphon Cabana Resort, which is 16km from town.

Seabeach Bungalow, 4/2 Mu 8, is at the very end of Thung Wua Laen Beach, with its brick rooms and bright blue curtains (singles with bath 250-300฿, doubles 400฿, A/C doubles 550฿). The **restaurant** has a fine selection of Thai, seafood, and *pak tai* dishes (fried rice 20฿), but the English menu offers limited selection; a little Thai might help extend your options. The only bungalows built directly on the beach can be rented from **View Restaurant and Bungalows,** 13/2 Mu 8 Thung Wua Laen Beach. The dining area has savory seafood plates (40฿) and the bohemian bungalows have steeply sloped, red-tiled roofs and great views (singles 300฿, doubles 400฿). Best of all, it's close to the main stretch. **Clean Wave Resort,** 54 Mu 8 (tel.

Gotta Love Those Swallows

For the lonely budget traveler in Southern Thailand, it's encouraging to know that the nest of the swallow is considered an aphrodisiac by herbalists in Chumphon. Although all nests work just fine, the white nests are the most powerful, and they often sell for up to 70,000฿ per kg. Harvesting nests is difficult, dangerous work, and people have shot each other just over the scraps. Not only is it a risky profession, it is a short-lived one. Harvesting is permitted for only three months during the year. This allows the swallows to make up for the many babies and eggs destroyed in the process (and it keeps the prices up). After harvesting, the nests are torn into strips. The pieces are rinsed in cold water for 24 hrs., made into a soup, and sold by the bowl. What bestows such potent powers upon these plain little strips? Perhaps it's because the swallows stay in the air *all day;* these are strong birds. Most believe, however, that it's a combination of the bird's saliva and the "love nest" itself that provides that special something for your special someone.

503 621) has a friendly staff and offers single rooms with fan (250฿, sleeps 3) as well as doubles with fan or A/C (400฿, 550฿, sleeps 4). Restaurant has a beautiful view.

■■■ SURAT THANI

Many foreign travelers know Surat Thani only as a stopover on the way to Ko Samui or other points south. Granted, there's not much to see in the downtown Ban Don area of this provincial capital, but its outlying areas are home to Thailand's most famous monks (and monkeys). Among the noteworthy sights in this area is Wat Suam Mokkha Phalaram, a respected meditation center that attracts Thais and foreigners seeking a spiritual retreat. Thai gourmands often descend upon Surat Thani to feast on the city's renowned enormous oysters. People boast of the high nutrition of this delicacy, but eat at your own risk.

ORIENTATION

If you're trying to get to Surat Thani (Ban Don) by train, you'll fall about 13km short at **Phun Phin.** (Tour companies have buses that go straight from the train station to the ferry pier, for those going to Ko Samui, Ko Phangan, or Ko Tao.) Public buses (6฿) run from Phun Phin to the Ban Don area. If you get to the pier before 11:30pm, you can catch the night boat and awake at Ko Samui.

Buses (including the one from Phun Phin) bring you to **Talaat Kaset.** The market is divided into two sections on either side of **Talaat Mai Road,** which runs straight through town and parallels the **Tapi River. Talaat Kaset 1,** on the side near the Tapi River, contains the local **bus station** with most of the connections to towns within the province, such as Phun Phin. **Talaat Kaset 2** contains the bus terminal to other provinces and has connections to Chaiya. Numbers on the over-street arches by the entrances indicate which market is which. All of the hotels and many places to eat lie within in a 200m radius of **Phanthip Tour** on Talaat Mai Rd.

Walking toward the river; you will cross **Na Muang Road,** parallel to Talaat Mai Rd. and partially running along the river. Continuing on brings you to **Talaat Laang Road** along the riverfront where the night ferry leaves for Ko Samui. **Chonkasem Road** (a block west of Phanthip Tour) intersects Talaat Mai Rd. at the GPO.

PRACTICAL INFORMATION

Tourist Office: Tourism Authority of Thailand (TAT), 5 Talaat Mai Rd. (tel. 288 818/9; fax 282 828). A 20-min. walk from Talaat Kaset, or a 5฿ tuk-tuk ride. Useful information and maps for Surat Thani, Ko Samui, Ko Phangan, and Ko Tao. Use their phone in cases of emergency. Open daily 8:30am-4:30pm.

Tourist Police: At the TAT (24-hr. tel. 281 300).

Travel Offices: Many places sell train, plane, bus, and boat tickets to *farang* who often can't discern the best or safest deals. Phanthip Tour, Songserm Travel Center, and Samui Tour are safe, convenient, and reliable. The first 2 own boats to the islands; the last arranges tickets for all modes of transport and charges no "service fee." For road travel, Songserm and Phanthip control almost all the bus/minivan routes. **Phanthip Tour,** 442/24-5 Talaat Mai Rd. (tel. 272 230 or 272 906; fax 281 223), between the 2 markets. Open 8am-5pm. **Songserm Travel Service,** 30/2 Mu 3 (tel. 285 124-7; fax 285 127), off Talaat Laang Rd., across from the night ferry pier. Open 5:30am-6:30pm. **Samui Tour,** 326/12 Talaat Mai Rd. (tel. 282 352 or 284 762), on the way to TAT office on the left. Open 5am-6:30pm.

Currency Exchange: Surat Thani has better exchange rates than the islands. Banks pile up around Na Muang Rd. in the Ban Don area. Open Mon.-Fri. 8:30am-3:30pm. **Bangkok Bank,** 195-7 Na Muang Rd. (tel. 273 927) has a booth in front. Open daily 8:30am-5:30pm. **Thai Farmers Bank,** 151 Na Muang Rd. (tel. 282 210). If your wallet needs refilling in **Phun Phin,** try one of the branches along Surat-Phun Phin Rd., just beyond the train station.

Post Office: GPO (tel. 272 013), next to the giant white building with a communications tower at the corner of Talaat Mai Rd. and Chonkasem Rd. Open Mon.-Fri. 8:30am-4:30pm, Sat.-Sun. 9am-noon. **Branch office** (tel. 273 431), at the intersection of Na Muang Rd. and Chonkasem Rd. Open Mon.-Fri. 8:30am-5:30pm, Sat. 9am-noon. **Postal code:** 84000.

Telephones: Telecom Office (tel. 281 537-9), on Donnok Rd. A 2-km hike from most of the hotels. Walking down Talaat Mai Rd. toward the TAT from the intersection with Chonkasem Rd., turn left onto Donnak Rd. The office is on the left about 20min. down the road; you can see the telecom tower from far away. Make the trip in two 5฿ tuk-tuk rides, one to the Talaat Mai-Donnak Rd. intersection and another to the office. Free Home Direct Service to US and UK. Open daily 8am-noon. **Telephone code:** 077.

Airport: THAI Air, 3/27-8 Karunarat Rd. (tel. 273 710). Flies to Bangkok (daily 12:40 and 8:40pm, 1710฿). Shuttle service to and from airport (10:45am and 6:30pm, 20km, 35฿). Phanthip Tour and Songserm Tour also book flights.

Trains: The train station (tel. 311 213) is 13km away at Phun Phin. Open daily 6am-6pm. Buses (6฿) go to the city center. Arrange tickets through Phanthip Tour, or go directly to the station. Trains tend to be pretty full going through Phun Phin, so buses offer a lot more convenience for a little more money. Plan ahead for train use. Listed fares are for 3rd-, 2nd-, and 1st-class (when available), respectively (before any surcharges). To: **Chaiya** (7 daily, 7:25am-8:42pm, 40min., 3rd-class 8฿); **Chumphon** (11 daily, 34฿, 71฿, 91฿); **Hat Yai** (7 daily, 5-6-½hr., 53฿, 114฿, 228฿); **Prachuap Khiri Khan** (6 daily, 5hr., 81฿, 147฿); **Trang** (2 daily, 4hr., 59฿, 100฿); **Sungai Kolok** (12:55am, 2nd-class upper/lower bed 320/350฿); **Butterworth** (2:07am, 2nd-class seat 378฿); and **Bangkok** (9 daily, 13hr., 3rd-class seat 127฿, 2nd-class: seat 244฿, upper bed, 314฿, lower bed 344฿, 1st-class 470฿, Sprinter 304฿; 10฿ surcharge for express).

Buses: Local bus terminal, Talaat Kaset 1, serves Surat Thani Province. To **Phun Phin** (every 5min., 6am-7:30pm, 6฿). To **Chaiya,** either catch a northbound bus that runs by Wat Suan Mok, or catch a **songthaew** (every 10min., 20฿) from Talaat Kaset 2. **Regular bus terminal,** Talaat Kaset 2 (tel. 272 341), connects to major cities and provinces around Surat Thani. To: **Bangkok** (7am and 5pm, 12hr., 158฿; A/C: 5:30pm, 10hr., 2nd-class 222฿, 1st-class 285฿; VIP: 9hr., 440฿); **Chumphon** (7am, 4hr., 58฿); **Hat Yai** (5 daily, 6hr., 85฿; A/C: 4 daily, 5hr., 120฿); and **Phuket** (2 daily, 5hr., 85฿; A/C: 139฿). Private buses also serve Bangkok. Prices vary according to quality, service, hidden commissions, and chance (200-300฿). Be wary of any offer under 200฿. Private buses to other cities are generally found at **Phanthip Tour** and **Songserm Travel Service.** Songserm costs a little more, but stops less. Phanthip's 1st-class A/C to: **Phuket** (3 daily, 112฿); **Krabi** (4 daily, 91฿); **Chumphon** (2 daily, 9:50am-1pm, 70฿).

Local Transportation: Motorcycles and **samlors** provide taxi service (10฿). **Tuk-tuks** run regular routes, but no markings that tell where they're going (5฿).

Library: The TAT has a small book nook (open Mon.-Fri. 8:30am-4:30pm) on the history of Chaiya, how monkeys are trained, and why the islands are so popular. The **Public Library** has random English books. Just beyond the park behind the TAT office along the Tapi River. Open Wed.-Sun. 8:30am-4:30pm.

Markets: Talaat Kaset 1 and 2 flood the areas around the bus stations with the usual assortment of cheap eats, blue jeans, biker t-shirts, footwear, and all timepieces known to man. The area between Na Muang Rd. and Talaat Laang Rd. by the Tapi River has adopted the **night market,** a great place to browse or stock up for the trip to Samui, since prices on the boat and island will be higher.

Hospitals: Surat Thani Provincial Hospital (tel. 284 700), 1km past the TAT on the extension of Talaat Mai Rd., known as Surat-Phih Rd. **Taksin Hospital** (tel. 273 239) is private and more expensive. Located on Talaat Mai Rd. at the opposite end of town from the TAT, 1km north of the intersection with Chonkasem Rd.

Emergency: tel. 191 or tourist police (tel. 281 300).

Police: 188 Na Muang Rd. (tel. 272 095). Try the tourist police first.

ACCOMMODATIONS

If you get stranded at the train station in Phun Phin, march regally over to the **Queen Hotel** down the road and to the right by the Singha sign (tel. 311 003; open 24 hrs.; singles 150฿, doubles 200฿, with A/C 300฿). Directly across from the sta-

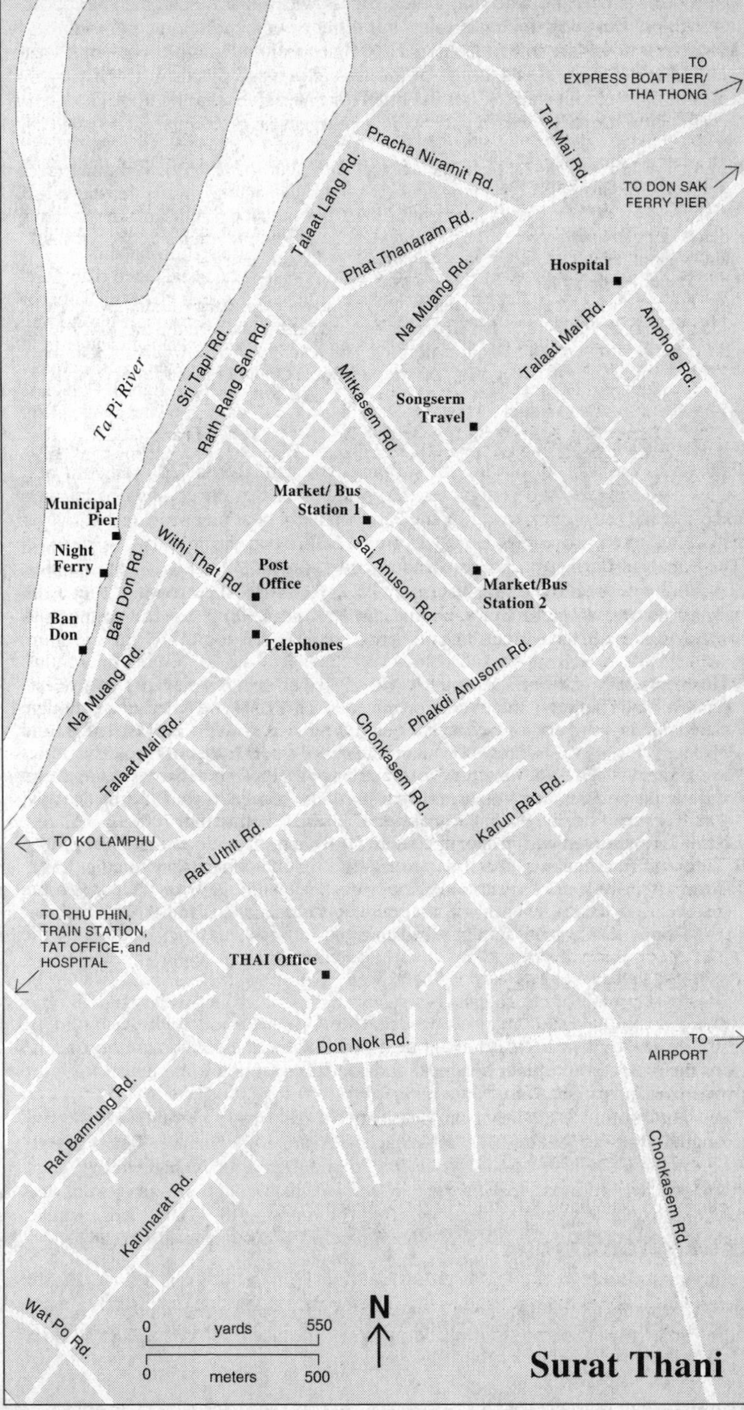
TO EXPRESS BOAT PIER/ THA THONG
Tat Mai Rd.
Pracha Niramit Rd.
Talaat Lang Rd.
TO DON SAK FERRY PIER
Phat Thanaram Rd.
Hospital
Na Muang Rd.
Talaat Mai Rd.
Amphoe Rd.
Ta Pi River
Sri Tapi Rd.
Rath Rang San Rd.
Mitkasem Rd.
Songserm Travel
Market/ Bus Station 1
Municipal Pier
Night Ferry
Withi That Rd.
Post Office
Sai Anuson Rd.
Market/Bus Station 2
Ban Don
Ban Don Rd.
Telephones
Na Muang Rd.
Phakdi Anusorn Rd.
Chonkasem Rd.
Talaat Mai Rd.
Karun Rat Rd.
TO KO LAMPHU
Rat Uthit Rd.
TO PHU PHIN, TRAIN STATION, TAT OFFICE, and HOSPITAL
THAI Office
Don Nok Rd.
TO AIRPORT
Rat Bamrung Rd.
Chonkasem Rd.
Karunarat Rd.
Wat Po Rd.
0 yards 550
0 meters 500
N
Surat Thani

tion are the **Tai Fah** and **Srithani,** where rooms with separate baths go for 100฿. These older places show their infirmity, and suffer from locomotion commotion.

All the best hotels are in Ban Don, in a 200m arc around Phanthip Tour by Talaat Kaset and the bus terminals. Some of the less expensive places in town vary in degrees of brotheldom—check out the hotel's scene before signing up for a potentially vile night. It may be worth your while to bargain for discounts.

Muang Tai Hotel, 390-2 Talaat Mai Rd. (tel. 286 390 or 272 559), at the intersection of Chonkasem Rd. The fans actually cool the spacious rooms that have the luxury of a sit-down toilet. A recent face-lift has injected youth into the sagging place. An elevator services the 5 floors. Check-out noon. Singles 200฿, with A/C 280฿. Doubles 260฿, with A/C 380฿. Open 24 hrs. Laundry service.

Thai Thani Hotel, 442/307-9 Talaat Kaset 2 (tel. 272 977 or 273 586; fax 286 129), off Talaat Mai Rd. A shy giant hidden by the market. Sanitary rooms have weathered Euro-style baths. The fan struggles to fend off humidity and heat. A/C rooms have pink bathroom sandals and phones. Singles 200฿, with A/C 280฿. Doubles 220฿, with A/C 300฿. Reception on the 3rd floor. Open 24 hrs. Laundry service.

FOOD

Surat Thani has plenty of shops where you can swipe a tasty meal for 25฿ or less. **Talaat Kaset** has stalls displaying the toppings you can have ladled over your rice (curries, eggs, meats, and vegetables). Pointing alleviates the food-word barrier. **Food stalls** and the **night market** by the Ban Don night boat pier provide great deals for stocking up on provisions, especially fruits, before boarding a ferry.

The **Sahathai Department Store's food court,** on Na Muang Rd., makes a nice air-conditioned lunch break. Dishes go for 15-25฿ (buy food coupons at the desk) and water is free at the fountain. Open daily 9:30am-9:30pm. Several restaurants along Na Muang Rd. have Thai/English menus.

J. Home Bakery, 428/5 Na Muang Rd. (tel. 273 942), near Grand City Hotel. Western fast food (burgers) and exceptionally good Thai fast food (fried rice), though baked goods—surprise!—are the specialty. White cakes with cherries 10฿, raisin cookies 3 for 5฿, raisin bread 5฿, and coffee 10฿. Open 7:30am-11pm.

Yam Bakery, 460-2 Na Muang Rd. (tel. 281 460), between Sahathai Dept. Store and the post office. Grab the hamburger-sized *khanom pia* (mung bean cake) for 10฿. They also have fresh-baked raisin loaf, breads with stringy sweet pork, and other loaves served with butter and sugar (15฿ each). Open daily 4am-8:30pm.

R. Graphic Restaurant, 522/1 Na Muang Rd. (tel. 283 098), near Sahathai Dept. store. Attentive staff can recommend picturesque dishes like *yam plaa dook foo* (fried catfish salad). Or opt for a streamlined chicken salad (30฿), fruit shake (15฿), or fried rice (25฿). Open 9am-10pm.

■ AROUND SURAT THANI

Although Ko Samui and company steal the show, the authentic culture, tradition, and art of the mainland area around Surat Thani make a fine contrast to the islands. Before heading to the opiate beaches, consider these wholesome detours. Don't worry; the islands aren't going anywhere.

The sights around Surat Thani can be planned asdaytrips from the Ban Don area, via songthaews from Talaat Kaset that service the region. The minibus system is confusing, and you may have to do some asking to find the correct vehicle in the sea of songthaews. Furthermore, leaving the Ban Don area may be agonizingly slow as designated stops chew away the time. Set off in the morning for Chaiya, since public transportation seems to dwindle as 6pm approaches; it disappears after that.

CHAIYA

The most significant mainland spot, Chaiya is the site of both an ancient city and one of the most respected meditation centers in the country, **Wat Suan Mokkha**

Phalarm, or simply "Suan Mok," a 150-acre forest temple along Hwy. 41 about 50km north of Surat Thani-Ban Don.

Suan Mok is easily recognized because of the congregation of vehicles from all over the country parked out front. Inside, the drivers and others are invoking the founder, Bhikkhu Phutthathat (or Than Phutthathat), who passed away in July 1993. He was highly respected in Buddhist circles for his "back-to-basics" approach. Masses of people sit under the wat's trees and meditate alongside the monks, following the example of Than Phutthathat. His monastic community follows the regimen of Buddha's earliest disciples, and their purist approach is reflected in the temple. Unlike other well-known wats, it is stark and barren.

Than Phutthathat described the stunning collection of paintings here as a pictorial interpretation of *dharma* (the basic principles of cosmic or individual existence). This "Spiritual Theater" is part of Phutthathat's efforts to make the Buddhist scriptures accessible to all.

Around the wat you can climb the hill to the Golden Buddha Shrine, explore the nearby forests and streams, and, of course, meditate. Anyone can attend **meditation retreats** (both Vipassana and Samatha—Insight and Tranquil forms) held by resident *farang* monks, usually on the first 10 days of the month. Contact the temple directly, and preferably in person (a minimum contribution of around 50฿ per day covers food and expenses).

At nearby **Wat Phra Borom That Chaiya** (familiarly known as Wat Phra That) the much-revered and elaborately restored 1200-year-old pagoda contains relics of Lord Buddha and is surrounded by 174 Buddha images. The structure is believed to be a remnant of the Mahayana Buddhist Srivijaya Empire which dominated before the arrival of the Theravada sect. The temple is one of the most important in the south and an excellent example of 10th-century Javanese/Malay art. Wat Phra That is also home to the **National Museum at Chaiya.** The well-maintained museum exhibits (with English translation) Thai artifacts from almost 500,000 years ago. Open Wed.-Sun 9am-4pm; donation 10฿.

To get to the wats, catch a northbound bus going to Ranong or Chumphon and get off at Wat Suan Mok first. From either Wat Suan Mok or the Chaiya bus/train station, it's a 5฿ motorcycle taxi or tuk-tuk ride to Wat Phra That.

MONKEY SCHOOL AND OYSTER FARMS

Like any New Haven university, the Surat Thani area shelters some of the world's brightest and least intelligent creatures. Some of the largest **oysters** (the dumb ones) alive are bred around the Kadaeh and Ta Tong Rivers. If you're interested in how they're raised and harvested, contact the fishing department (tel. 286 922).

Far smarter and more animated are the coconut-picking students at the **Monkey Training College.** Show is 300฿, for 3 people 400฿; check with local travel agents, who can usually give you a better deal with a larger group. To go on your own, catch a tuk-tuk or songthaew (5฿) on Talaat Mai Rd. on the Phanthip Tour side of the street. Ask to be let off at *"rong rian sawn ling."* Then take a motorcycle taxi (20฿) to the school, or face a two-km hike.

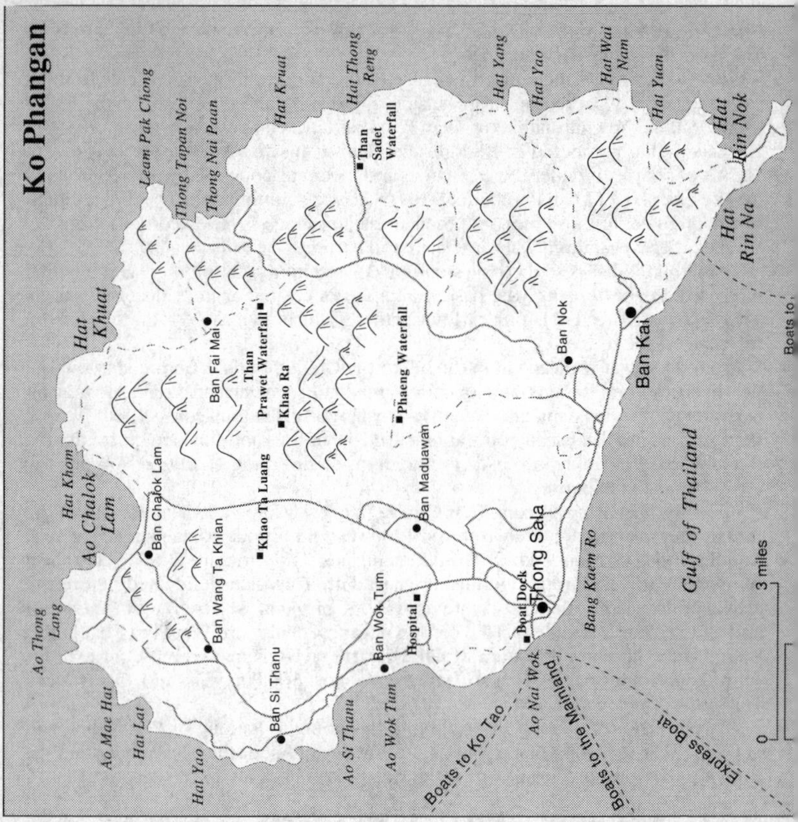

Ko Phangan

Leam Pak Chong
Thong Tapan Noi
Thong Nai Paan
Hat Kruat
Hat Thong Reng
Than Sadet Waterfall
Hat Yang
Hat Yao
Hat Wai Nam
Hat Yuan
Hat Rin Nok
Hat Rin Na
Boats to
Hat Khuat
Ban Fai Mai
Than Prawet Waterfall
Khao Ra
Phaeng Waterfall
Ban Nok
Ban Kai
Hat Khom
Ao Chalok Lam
Ban Chalok Lam
Khao Ta Luang
Ban Maduawan
Gulf of Thailand
Ao Thong Lang
Ban Wang Ta Khian
Ban Wok Tum
Hospital
Boat Dock
Thong Sala
Bang Kaem Ro
0 3 miles
Ao Mae Hat
Hat Lat
Hat Yao
Ban Si Thanu
Ao Si Thanu
Ao Wok Tum
Ao Nai Wok
Boats to Ko Tao
Boats to the Mainland
Express Boat

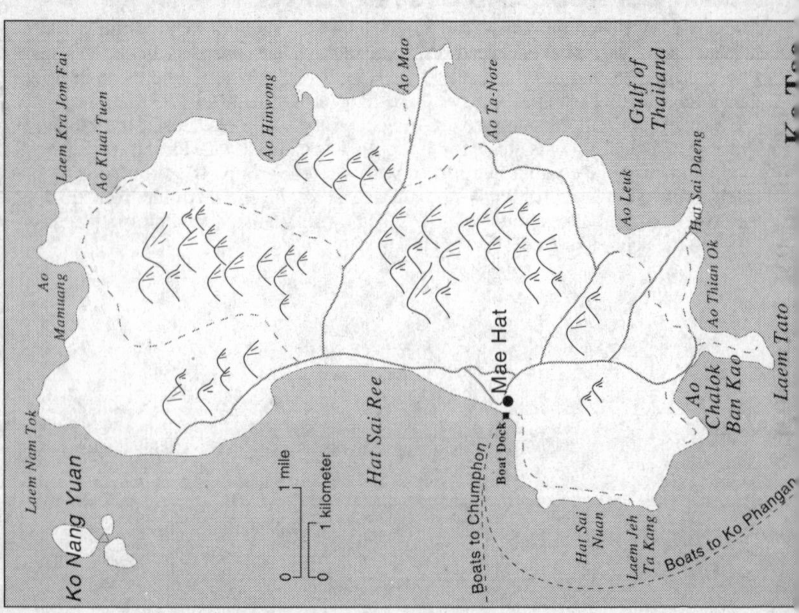

Ko Tao

Laem Kra Jom Fai
Ao Kluai Tuen
Ao Hinwong
Ao Mao
Ao Ta-Note
Gulf of Thailand
Ao Mamuang
Ao Leuk
Hat Sai Daeng
Ao Thian Ok
Laem Tato
Ao Chalok Ban Kao
Laem Nam Tok
Ko Nang Yuan
0 1 mile
0 1 kilometer
Hat Sai Ree
Mae Hat
Boat Dock
Boats to Chumphon
Hat Sai Nuan
Laem Jeh Ta Kang
Boats to Ko Phangan

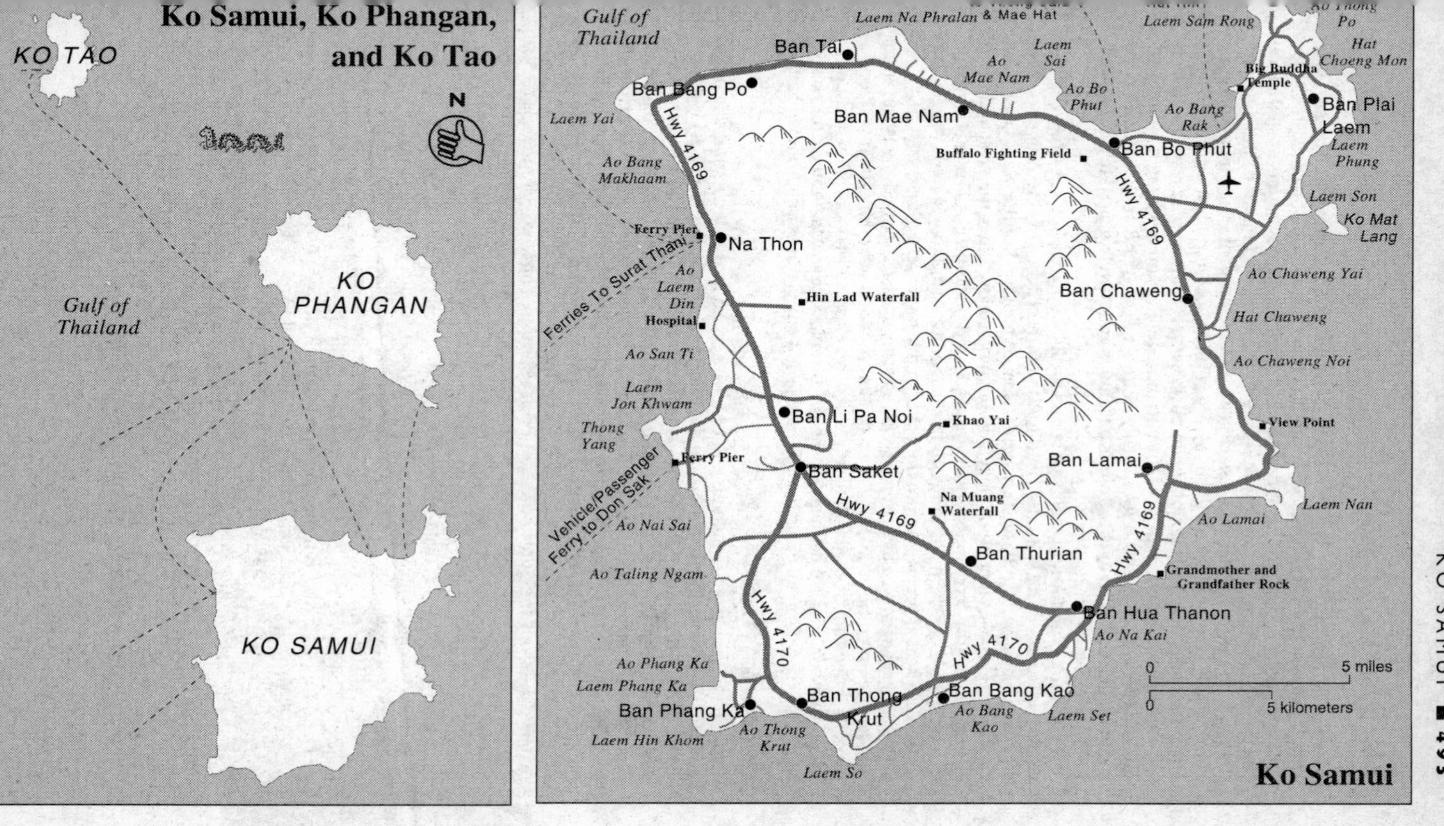
Ko Samui, Ko Phangan, and Ko Tao
KO TAO
N
KO PHANGAN
Gulf of Thailand
KO SAMUI
Gulf of Thailand
Laem Na Phralan & Mae Hat
Laem Sam Rong
Ban Tai
Ban Bang Po
Ao Mae Nam
Laem Sai
Ao Bo Phut
Ao Bang Rak
Big Buddha Temple
Hat Choeng Mon
Ban Plai Laem
Laem Phung
Laem Son
Ko Mat Lang
Ban Mae Nam
Laem Yai
Hwy 4169
Buffalo Fighting Field
Ban Bo Phut
Ao Bang Makhaam
Ferry Pier
Na Thon
Ferries To Surat Thani
Ao Laem Din
Hospital
Hin Lad Waterfall
Ao Chaweng Yai
Ban Chaweng
Hat Chaweng
Ao San Ti
Ao Chaweng Noi
Laem Jon Khwam
Ban Li Pa Noi
Khao Yai
View Point
Thong Yang
Ferry Pier
Ban Saket
Ban Lamai
Vehicle/Passenger Ferry to Don Sak
Na Muang Waterfall
Laem Nan
Ao Lamai
Ao Nai Sai
Ban Thurian
Grandmother and Grandfather Rock
Ao Taling Ngam
Ban Hua Thanon
Ao Na Kai
Hwy 4170
Ao Phang Ka
Laem Phang Ka
Ban Phang Ka
Ban Thong Krut
Ban Bang Kao
Ao Bang Kao
Laem Set
Laem Hin Khom
Ao Thong Krut
Laem So
0
5 miles
0
5 kilometers
Ko Samui

KO SAMUI

The third-largest island in Thailand sits in calm gulf waters 84km east of Surat Thani and 250km south of Bangkok. Ko Samui is a sun-worshipper's bronzing machine, equipped with enough coconut-ridden sand, cheap bungalows, and fresh seafood to keep seasoned beach aficionados happy. Samui beats Phuket in most departments, with cleaner water and less large-scale development. The air-conditioning coil is slowly conquering Samui, but plenty of rustic accommodations remain.

Tourism has not left Ko Samui untainted, however. With no water-treatment facilities and ballooning quantities of refuse to manage, Ko Samui is hanging in precarious ecological balance. Moreover, many visitors to the island are disturbed by the total absence of indigenous culture. Ko Samui is completely geared toward serving foreign tourists, at any expense.

If you want nightlife and plenty of company, kick up your heels at Chaweng and Lamai. Seek a bit more solitude? Head to the north beaches of Mae Nam, Bo Phut, and Bangrak (a.k.a. Big Buddha), where it's more mellow, but the waves and wind can be as pushy as a lunchtime bully. Although bungalows litter the west and south coasts, the nearby ferry piers, rocky coastline, and occasionally dirty gulf currents that wash up from the mainland keep this half of the island tourist-free. Magnificent sunsets are best appreciated from the coves in the southwest, off Hwy. 4170.

Peak season seems to be spilling over: last year, tourists stormed the island from August to September and November to March, when accommodations filled to capacity. Prices dip from March to July, but don't expect discounts in the most populated tourist areas. We list high season prices unless otherwise noted. In low season, prices may drop 20-50%, through established rate changes or adroit bargaining.

GETTING THERE

Surat Thani is the main launching point for trips to Ko Samui. Prices and schedules for boats and ferries fluctuate through the tourist season; double-check everything.

You have a few transport options. The first and best is the **auto ferry,** which departs from the Don Sak pier 60km east of Surat and arrives at the Thong Yang pier, 10km south of Na Thon on Ko Samui. At Thong Yang pier you may find songthaews waiting to cart you off to the major beaches, but the safest bet is to head on to Na Thon, the starting point for trips anywhere on the island. The entire trip is simplified by tour companies that sell combination bus-ferry-bus tickets. Buses depart daily from the Surat offices of both Phanthip Tour and Samui Tour (6:50, 8:30, 10:30am, 12:30, and 3:30pm, 3hr., 70฿, A/C 90฿; see Surat Thani: "Practical Information" on page 489). Samui Tour also picks up folks arriving on overnight trains to Surat, with shuttles departing Phun Phin station at 6:20 and 7:20am, in time to make the first of two daily trips to Ko Samui. If you get to Don Sak pier on your own, you can catch the auto ferryat 8, 10am, noon, 2, and 5pm (1-½hr., 40฿).

Songserm Travel Center runs the **express boat** route, though everyone seems to sell tickets. The fare to Samui is 105฿, and includes a bus ride from the Songserm Office to Tha Thong pier, 5km northeast. You can also take a 5฿ tuk-tuk ride to the pier and buy a ticket from the Songserm branch there. Buses leave the office at 7:30am and 2pm for Pak Nam boats to Na Thon (8am and 2:30pm, 2-½hr.).

The **night/sleeper boat** is especially suited for late arrivals in Surat Thani who don't want to spend the night there. Purchase tickets at the pier in Surat Thani along Talaat Laang Rd. and the Tapi River, left of the municipal pier and behind the colorful fruit stalls that set up at night. There are two fares to Na Thon: the lower deck, cargo, but no bedding 50฿, and the upper deck, mattresses 70฿ (11pm, 6hr.).

Samui Airport is between Chaweng and Bangrak beaches. Bangkok Airways makes daily flights to **Bangkok** (2080฿) and **Phuket** (1210฿).

ISLAND ORIENTATION

Once you arrive on Samui, stay with the posse: head for the songthaews that are colorfully labeled with their beach destinations. Stave off the enthusiastic touts who roam Na Thon's pier-side songthaew parking lot hoping to make your bungalow decisions for you. A new 50km paved road, **Route 4169** (Tweeratpakdee Rd.), makes a circuit around the island, giving easy access to the major beaches and **Na Thon,** the main pier town. Km markings along the road start at Na Thon (Km0) and run counter-clockwise. Most accommodations sun themselves on north and east beaches. **Route 4170** loops off the highway to cover the southwest corner of the island and accesses sights like the Butterfly Garden and some of the beaches with more picturesque sunsets. Songthaews run along Route 4169 and some beach roads; they will usually drop you off at your bungalow.

The annually revised **maps** researched by V. Hongsombud (40฿) are durable, waterproof layouts of Samui, Phangan, and Tao Islands showing every bungalow, sight, and major road along with condensed practical information.

ISLAND SIGHTS

Lounge-about lizards slither to Ko Samui for beaches, not sights. After the sand and countless coconut trees, a couple of graphic rock formations and the generically named "Big Buddha" are the most photographed attractions. The island is made for motorbike exploration (the Big Buddha, and anything along Hwy. 4169 can also be reached by songthaew until 6pm). The following is a counterclockwise outline, with km posts.

By the bend in the road by Km18 (Hwy. 4169—Southern Lamai), a sign points to **Hin Ta-Hin Yaai** (Grandfather Stone-Grandmother Stone). Supposedly, an old couple died at sea in a shipwreck and their bodies washed ashore, creating mystical rock formations. As you travel down the 400m concrete road, the postcards at the expected souvenir shops spoil the triple-X surprise. Climb the rocks to see Gramps in erect action (some 3m of solid rock!); you may have to hunt to see Granny's stone pudendum. From the tip of the rocky cape, **Hat Lamai** is in full glory below: 2km of undiluted white-sand beach backed by palms shading hundreds of bungalows.

Back on Hwy. 4169, the road heads for the hills. If you're not careful, you'll plow right through the **Lamai Cultural Hall** at Km20, where the highway takes a sharp right turn. Shift to low gear, and head up the hill. The large rocky cape and **Coral Cove** below form the south end of the longest beach on the island, **Hat Chaweng,** with its coastal reef and **Ko Matlang** in the background.

Continue on down Hwy. 4169 until Km27.5 and take a right onto Chaweng Rd. After you pass the 5km of bungalows and bars, it's open road and fresh air. Between Km8-10 on Chaweng Rd. a series of dirt roads lead to the secluded coves and rocky points on the northeast corner of the island. The **Thai Folk Music Instrument Shop** at Km9.5 is open occasionally (every 3-4 days) depending on the owner's schedule. Farther down the road check out **Big Buddha** himself. Chaweng Rd. becomes Rte. 4171 when the Huge Golden One gleams over the landscape (a good place from which to take in the views). A meditation center also occupies the grounds, and visitors are expected to dress "appropriately" (long pants) if they wish to go nearer (but it's just as impressive from afar).

After skirting Big Buddha's beach (also known as Bangrak), the road rejoins Hwy. 4169 at the town of Bo Phut. Continuing through **Bo Phut Beach,** where houses mingle with bungalows, you'll hit **Mae Nam Beach,** which has a more urban atmosphere. After this, it's a pretty quiet stretch of 10km to Na Thon along the northwest (the steep road has a superb, high-altitude view of the beach), with the **Laem Yai Lighthouse** (off Km46.5), as the only thing of note after sand, sea, and coconuts.

Power-lunch at the active port of **Na Thon;** it has the cheapest eats on the island and is a good place to take care of practical matters. Reset the km posts to zero. At Km2, you'll encounter a main intersection. Turning left, **Hin Laad Waterfalls** is a little over 1km away past the **Lizard Garden** and an abundance of durian trees. For some impressive cascades, you'll have to visit after the rainy season (around November is best) and leapfrog 1km more to **Hunam** and **Hev Khwaay Tok Waterfalls.** For more natural sights, eyeball the white waters of the **Laadwanon River** down the dirt road at Km4.5. The paved road in the other direction goes to the ferry pier at **Thong Yang** and **Laem Chon Kram** (Thief Cave).

Near Km11 (Hwy. 4169), you'll cross a river. About 500m farther, you can turn right down a surfaced road to **Na Muang Waterfall** (about 1km). It's good for swimming, having received the stamp of approval from Kings Rama VI, VII, and IX, who all left their initials on stones nearby. The most impressive waterfall on Ko Samui is probably **Na Muang II,** a solid 1-km hike away. Returning to Route 4169 before Km12, **Ban Thurian** grows plenty of Thailand's King of Fruits—durians.

Next on this action-packed tour are Ko Samui's religious sights. At Km13, **Wat Khunaram** is the permanent resting place of a mummified clairvoyant monk who predicted his death and planned to die meditating. At Km14.5, the unique **Coral Buddha image** on the left signals a right turn to access **Wat Samret,** about 500m along the dirt road, by the lake. Inside, the **Secret Coral Buddha Image Hall** conceals ancient sculptures.

A right turn onto Route 4170 brings you to the turn-off for the dirt road to the **Samui Butterfly Garden,** where butterflies foxtrot by the landscaped hill. Inspect the **Insect Museum.** A bee house and monkey show are included in admission (50฿, children 20฿; open 8am-5pm). A glass-bottom boat/snorkeling excursion visits the colorful offshore reefs. A 1-hr. stay (plus 30min. transit) costs 150฿ (children 60฿).

Heading back to Route 4170, you can turn right, meet up with Hwy. 4169, and be back in Lamai in a few minutes, but you'll miss a great sunset. If you head west on Route 4170 (km markers go down), the last official sight beckons at Km9.5. The golden **Chedi Laem Sor** and the hill-top **Khao Chedi** are home to the most-respected Buddhist monks on Ko Samui. Off Km6, a 3-km dirt road leads to **Ao Phangka,** a small bay that's perfect for making displays of Harlequin Romance affection as the sun sinks over the blue horizon.

■■■ NA THON

Na Thon is the doctor's waiting room of Ko Samui; tourists often end up here for a couple of hours anticipating the next boat. Make use of the lower prices at this communications and shopping center. The daily market on Thaweeratpakdee Rd. offers fruits for the frugal.

ORIENTATION

Walking off the pier, you'll come to **Na Thon Road** which is lined with travel agents, money changers, restaurants, a TAT branch, and the post/telecom offices. Songthaews to the beach arrive and depart in front of the pier. Parallel to Na Thon is **Ang Thong Road** where the police station is located. Beyond this is **Thaweeratpakdee Road,** better known as Km0 of **Highway 4169.** Banks, restaurants, and the daily market pepper the road.

PRACTICAL INFORMATION

Tourist Office: TAT (tel. 420 504), on Na Thon Rd. Turn left off the pier and go 200m. It's the wooden shack across from the post office. Pamphlet about Ko Samui; some info about Ko Tao and Ko Phangan. Open daily 8:30am-4:30pm.

Tourist Police: (tel. 421 281 or 421 360); stations in Lipa Yai area by Km2, south of Na Thon, 100m past the road leading to Hin Lad Temple. They usually patrol the streets by Na Thon, Chaweng, and Lamai. At night, they patrol the Green Mango, Chaweng Beach. Call the TAT and they can radio the nearest patrol.

Travel Offices: Best places to buy boat/bus/train ticket combinations to Bangkok or other major cities are near the pier in Na Thon: **Phanthip Co.,** 84/1 Na Thon Rd. (tel. 421 222); open 8am-5pm. **Songserm Travel Center,** 64/1-2 Na Thon Rd. (tel.421 316-9); open 6am-5pm. **Samui Tour** (tel. 421 092), in "Bamboo House" a few doors from Songserm on Na Thon Rd. Open 8am-5pm.

Immigration Office: 6/9 Thaweeratpakdee Rd. (tel. 421 069), 1km south of the market near the pier. Visa extensions 500฿. Open Mon.-Fri. 8:30am-3:30pm.

Currency Exchange: No problem at Na Thon, Lamai, or Chaweng. Major banks are open daily until 3:30pm and line the major roads; exchange booths open until 5pm. Other beaches' exchangers/travel agents have slightly lower rates.

Post Office: GPO (tel. 421 013), on Na Thon Rd., 150m left off the pier. Open Mon.-Fri. 8:30am-4:30pm, Sat.-Sun. 9am-noon. Private "officially licensed" **branches** exist all around the island along Hwy. 4169. Many bungalows sell stamps and deliver mail. **Postal code:** 84140.

Telephones and Telegrams: On the 2nd floor of the GPO. Open daily 7am-10pm. Other "overseas call" centers transmit through this station, and may add surcharges. Many lodgings have their own services. **Telephone code:** 077.

Boats: The ferry provides a smoother, cheaper, and occasionally faster ride than the express boat. **Ferries leave from Thong Yang, all other boats from Na Thon.** Ferry tickets can be handled at the ferry pier, while general tickets are sold at Na Thon and most travel offices, as well as on board the vessel. The schedules listed change frequently, and the boats occasionally leave late.

To the Mainland: By **auto ferry** to Don Sak (7, 8, 9, 10am, noon, 2, 4, and 5pm, 1-½hr., 40฿); with a bus-ferry-bus ticket from Na Thon through to Ban Don-Surat Thani, you can catch a bus to Thong Yang in front of either Phanthip Tour or Samui Tour 30min. before the scheduled ferry departure (3hr., 70฿, A/C 90฿). By **express boat** to Tha Thong pier in Surat (7:15am and 2:30pm, 2-½hr, 105฿, round-trip 190฿); includes transport from pier to Surat train station to catch trains to Bangkok, if you buy directly from Songserm. By **sleeper boat** to Surat Municipal pier (9pm, 6hr., lower deck 50฿, upper deck 70฿).

To Bangkok: Songserm Travel sells package tickets that include the express boat, bus transfer, and the sleeper train. Boat departs at 2:30pm for connection to trains at 5:50, 7:05, 8:42, and 10:01pm, 11-12hr., upper bunk 510฿, lower 560฿. 3rd-class seats are also available at a considerable discount.

To Ko Phangan: By **express boat** to Thong Sala (10:50am and 4:30pm, 50min., 60฿). By **tour boat** from the pier at Big Buddha Beach (Bangrak) to Hat Rin (10:30am and 3:30pm, 45min., 60฿).

To Ko Tao: By **express boat,** the 10:50am departure to Ko Phangan continues to Mae Hat (12:30pm, 2-½hr., 150฿). By **speed boat** from Bo Phut pier to Mae Hat (8:30am, 1-½hr., 400฿). Check around in Na Thon for new ways to get to Ko Tao.

Airline Office: Plane tickets booked all around Ko Samui, but the main office is **Bangkok Airways,** 72/2 Mu 3 Na Thon Rd. (tel. 420 133). Open daily 8am-5pm.

Buses/Trains: Phanthip and Songserm, both authorized State Railway agents, book bus, train, and boat combinations to the mainland. Songserm quotes: to **Bangkok** (A/C bus 280฿; minivan 450฿; night train with upper bunk 510฿) and **Kuala Lumpur,** Malaysia (Minivan and A/C bus 450฿). Phanthip generally offers lower prices and less convenience.

Local Transportation: Most songthaews (6am-6pm) have set prices posted inside. From Na Thon and Thong Yang piers to: **Ban Mae Nam** (10฿), **Ban Plai Laem** (20฿), or **Bo Phut** (15฿), **Hat Chaweng** (20฿), **Hat Lamai** (20฿). Between **Chaweng** and **Lamai** (10฿). Motorcycle taxis cost about the same.

Vehicle Rentals: Everywhere. Work out rates for ½-days or deals for rental periods for 2 or more days. Scooter 150฿ per day; motorbike 200฿ per day; jeep 400฿ per day, with A/C 800฿, with insurance 1000฿. Motorcycles are the most popular and convenient way to move around.

English Bookstores: Nathon Bookshop, 64 Mu 3, 100m down the street that runs into town left of the pier, has one of the best used book selections outside of Bangkok. Open 9am-6pm. Most popular bungalows have recent English newspapers lying around. Shops and "libraries" offer the option to buy or rent/exchange.

Hospital/Medical Services: Samui Hospital, 61 Mui, Tombon Angthong (tel. 421 230 or 421 232), located at Km2 of Hwy. 4169, near Na Thon. **Ban Don Hospital** (tel. 425 382/3), at Km32, between Chaweng and Bo Phut. For first aid, visit clinics in the areas of Na Thon, Chaweng, or Lamai. Serious accidents require emergency transport to the mainland, arranged by the tourist police.

Emergency: tel. 191. **Tourist Police:** tel. 1699.

Police: Call the tourist police first. The police station (tel. 421 095 or 621 098) is on Angthong Rd. From the pier, follow the road into town and take a right.

ACCOMMODATIONS

Sea View Guest House, 67/15 Thaweeratpakdee Rd., (tel. 420 052) opposite the Shell gas station. Immaculate establishment. Spacious hallway and sitting area. Sinks are outside clean common baths. Private showers are bright, but you still have to share the toilets. Doubles 150฿, with baths 180฿. Slightly bigger room with private flush toilet 200฿, with A/C 300฿. Open 24 hrs.

Jinta (a.k.a. Can Restaurant), 310 Mu 3, Tombon Angthong (tel. 421 323), off Hwy. 4169, south of Sanpetch Mini-Market. Wooden floors and breathing room. Hygienic Thai toilets with sinks. Titanic timbers shade marble benches. Singles 200฿, off-season 150฿. Doubles 250฿, off-season 200฿. Open daily 8am-1am.

FOOD

While waiting for a boat at the dock, keep an unruly stomach in line with *khao niaw ping* (grilled sticky rice and bananas wrapped in banana leaves, 3฿ each). On the waterfront, food carts offer fruit, meats-on-a-stick, noodles, and sandwiches.

Ruang Thong Bakery 2, 31-32 Angthong Rd. (tel. 454 241). Head into town along the street left of the pier; it's at the corner of Angthong Rd. Large selection of Thai and western dishes, plus *sukiyaki.* Dishes 30฿ and up. Open daily 7am-7pm.

Vegetarian Restaurant, 196 Angthong Rd., at the south end next to a bird shop behind Thai Farmers Bank. Say good-bye to irregularity. Thai, western, and some Japanese vegetarian dishes. Soya burger or mixed veggie with chili and rice, baked beans with mashed potatoes (50฿), *miso* soup (20฿). Open 10am-7pm.

■■■ NA THON TO HAT CHAWENG

HAT MAE NAM

The first major beach on the Km countdown runs from around Km39 to Km35 along Hwy. 4169. Tranquility zealots look no farther. The police are around Mu 1 between Km36 and 37, and bungalows are accessible by dirt roads. The rooms are fairly generic—with fan and shower for 200฿ or less (below 100฿ in low season). Near Km36, **Friendly Bungalow,** 64/2 Mu 1 Tambon Mae Nam, greets you like an old pal. Follow the signs off the highway. The kitchen serves up yummy meals; huts have baths and mosquito nets. Small wooden hut with Thai toilet and sink 60฿; concrete bungalows with sit toilets 100฿. Check-out 11am; desk open 8am-10pm. Off the same dirt road is **Rainbow Bungalow,** 44/4 Mu 1 Tambon Mae Nam. This charming, family-run pot of gold supplies a magically delicious ambience. Cubbyhole rooms have mosquito nets, barred windows, and Thai toilets. Hammocks abound. Small singles 80฿, larger singles 100฿, doubles 150฿. Check-out 11am.

HAT BO PHUT

Although it doesn't measure up length-wise to Hat Mae Nam, neighboring Bo Phut proves that good things do come in small packages. Places like **Chai Hat Water Sports** teach windsurfing (400-500฿), or rent sailboards to experienced windsurfers (150฿ per hr.). Speed boats drag people in parasails around the harbor (10min., 400฿). Jet skis rent for 250฿ per 15min. **Samui Kart Club,** 98 Mu 1 Tambon Bo Phut (tel. 425 097), opposite Ziggy Stardust Bungalow, offers a way to skitter around the island without getting wet. They have 60km/h and zippy 90km/h models (200฿ and 300฿ per 10min.; open 10am-6pm).

World Bungalow, 175/1 Mu 1 (tel. 425 355/6), near Km35 on Hwy. 4169. It may look expensive, but this is a globe-trotter's bargain-basement bunking spot. Cheap, cozy cottages buried in herbal bushes. Anything-but-mundane food. Singles are concrete-floored, bamboo-walled huts, with squat toilet, hot shower, and a small porch 200฿, low season 100฿. Doubles 500฿, low season 300฿. Doubles with A/C 800฿, low season 500฿. Open 6am-11pm. Restaurant open 11am-2am.

Peace Bungalow, 178 Mu 1 Tambon Bo Phut (tel. 425 357), Km34-35, marked by a wooden signpost. Bungalows, some on stilts, exist harmoniously with breezy, well-kept quarters where blue-pink mosquito nets drop over the beds. Doubles 300-350฿, low season 150-200฿. A/C rooms 500฿. Check-out 11am.

Ziggy Stardust, 99 Mu 1 Tambon Bo Phut (tel. 425 410). Put on your red shoes and dance at this clean, upscale inn. Enormous tiled baths; sinks and toilets sparkle, though some are missing seats. Beachfront restaurant. Laundry service. A/C rooms have hot showers, fridge, and bathtub. Fan 400฿, low season 200฿. A/C rooms 1200฿, low season 800฿. Wham bam thank you ma'am!

HAT BANGRAK (BIG BUDDHA BEACH)

Big Buddha is watching you. Buzzing bungalows swarm between Km2 and 4 of Route 4171 which branches off Hwy. 4169 at Km33, leads to Bangrak and Samui Airport, and eventually becomes the road that runs near Chaweng. These backpacker-friendly bungalows have small restaurants with a basic Thai-*farang* menu, and doze on decent beaches around the windswept emerald bay.

Kinnaree Resort, 73/2 Mu 4 Tambon Bo Phut (tel. 425 217), at Km3 of Route 4171. Narrow villa among the cooing of flower gardens and turtle doves. Neon jazzes up the basic, white-sheet rooms. Baths with sit toilets, but no sinks. Singles and doubles 100฿ all year. Open 8am-10pm.

Number One Bungalow (tel. 425 446), between Km3 and 4. Typical brown-white-coconut-strewn establishment garners high rankings. Free ride to the airport. Friendly staff. Laundry service. Open 8:30am-9pm. Check-out noon, but flexible. Rooms with bath 150฿.

LAEM THONGSON, AO THONGSAI, HAT CHOENG MON, AND AO YAI NOI

The northeast cape wraps around some of the island's best views. Beaches are down the dirt roads, off the 5km of refreshing mountain highway connecting North Chaweng to Rte. 4171. Cape Thongson can be reached by adventurous motorbikers off Km9 or 10 via 3km of occasionally treacherous dirt road. Most of the beach areas belong to Imperial Thongsai. If you persistently follow the signs for 2km, you'll reach the **Samui Thongson Resort** to the right and **Golden Pine Resort** to the left. Both alight on the tip of the promontory, overlooking white caps and a rocky cove with a small stretch of sand. Samui Thongson has singles and doubles 200฿, low season 100-150฿. Golden Pine has singles and doubles 150฿, low season 80฿.

Hat Choeng Mon, north of the small Ao Yai Noi, rims the belly of Ao Thongsai and lies just 4km north of Chaweng (between Km8 and 9). It's a world apart from Chaweng, and is worth visiting for the view, serene beaches, good swimming, and the island's grandest hotel: the **Imperial Boat House Hotel** where guests bunk in small arks. Behind the JJ Restaurant, **Choeng Mon Bungalow** (tel. 425 372) has some fan-cooled stilt houses connected to baths with hot water and sit toilet. Singles and doubles 150฿, with A/C 250฿. Check-out noon.

■■■ HAT CHAWENG

The biggest and brashest of Ko Samui's beaches, Hat Chaweng roars 5km over the eastern coast. It's the nightlife capital of the island, and the beach is the epitome of the sunbathe-eat-party-sleep-sunbathe culture. The shoreline charms some travelers so much that they stay for weeks or months; some open a bar or bungalow and never bother to leave.

ORIENTATION

Hat Chaweng's main thoroughfare is roughly 200m from and parallel to the beach. *Anything* can be found along or just off this strip: rooms, food, bars, garter belts,

TAT, tourist police, post office, golf carts, mini-marts, nightclubs, Jacuzzi tubs, souvenirs, tailors, and on and on. **Chaweng Road** connects to Hwy. 4169 via three different branches: Km28 (0.5-km access road), Km29 (1-km road where the afternoon market is located), and Km30 (3-km road). The north and south branches define **Central Chaweng.** Continuing along Chaweng Rd. up the hill at Km4, **North Chaweng** makes up the northernmost km of the beach. **Chaweng Noi** (Lesser Chaweng) makes up the southernmost km and is where all the most expensive resorts have found their niches. The other side of the rock and coral outcropping defines the south end of Chaweng proper, and is accessible from Hwy. 4169 off the slope of the mountain that hides Lamai to the south.

ACCOMMODATIONS

Central Chaweng

Scratch every accommodation over 400฿, and you're down to 40, but inexpensive rooms go quickly year-round. Prices fluctuate a good deal over the year, but bargain if a place isn't full or if you're staying a long time. The most expedient way to hunt on your own is to start with Charlie's Huts; if they're full, keep walking north.

Keep an eye on where you are in relation to the Reggae Pub, either to be close to the action or to avoid the din. The footbridge to the pub and many smaller bars is near Km2, across from the pricey Beachcomber Hotel and Chaba Samui Resort, about 200m north of Charlie's Huts.

Charlie's Hut, Viking (Charlie's Hut 2), and **Charlie's Hut 3** (tel. 422 343). This angelic trio is legendary among backpackers, and stays packed year round. If everything's full, put your name down on the waiting list. Viking is the best, but standard prices are: small hut for 1, 80฿, for 2, 100฿; with bath 140฿ and 150฿; with screens, western toilets, and fans that work all day long 200฿ and 250฿. Huts have mosquito nets and electricity only in the evening.

Suneast Bungalow, 159 Mu 2 Tambon Bo Put (tel. 422 115), just past Km3. In the middle of the thickest cluster of huts in Chaweng; a walk out to the road brings pubs, restaurants, and nightlife. At low tide, the reef appears 200m offshore, but the water's still good for swimming. Fan-cooled bungalows resplendent with fresh sheets 150฿. Solid bungalows with double beds 250฿. Open 8am-9pm.

Lotus Bungalow, 60/1 Mu 2 Tambon Bo Put, between Suneast and Lucky Mother. Singles 100฿, low season 80฿. Single with baths 150฿, low season 100฿. Double with baths 200฿, low season 150฿. **Chang Diving Center** (tel. 230 891) with PADI-certified instruction on the grounds.

North Chaweng

Rooms in the resorts nearest Chaweng proper strike four-digit baht poses, but affordable places vogue just beyond these as you ascend the hill. Ko Matlang is visible offshore, and the reef is easily reached when the waters are low. The main beach area is a leisurely beach stroll or a 5฿ songthaew ride away, during the day. At night the beach is poorly lit. Motorbikes are available through all the bungalows.

Family Bungalow, 119 Mu 2 Tambon Bo Put, next door to Oasis Restaurant. No feuding in these ultra-clean rooms with shiny tiled floor and very large, clean baths. Restaurant dishes up beauteous beach and boat views. Singles 100฿. Doubles 150฿. High season add 50฿.

Moon Bungalow (tel. 422 167), farther to the north. Funky, fanciful owner used to gaze at the moon, but now it's MTV and BBC news off the satellite dish, plus videos every night. Typical, tidy bamboo huts 100฿. Singles with baths 120฿, doubles 250฿, low season 200฿. Newer and larger rooms: singles 200฿, low season 150฿, doubles 300฿, low season 280฿. A/C rooms available.

Matlang Resort, 154/1 Mu 2 Tambon Bo Put (tel. 422 172), past the Blue Lagoon. Basic-supplies shop and good ping-pong action. Singles and doubles with fan 300฿, low season 250฿. With A/C 800฿, low season 400฿. Open 7am-10pm.

FOOD

Dining options surround **Chaweng Rd.** like a SWAT team (there's a particularly large restaurant stake-out at **Km3**), but hungry fugitives never have to leave their **bungalows** to find food reflecting the international clientele; most kitchens serve similar food and close at 10pm. Restaurants serve similar dishes for a bit more than already inflated beach prices. Explore Hwy. 4169, south by motorbike, where cliffside restaurants above **Thong Takien** offer equivalent prices and quality but a better view.

ENTERTAINMENT

The **Reggae Pub,** at the footbridge of the leech-livened lake is the most romping night spot on the island. The wildly popular pleasure palace has multiple bars, a huge atrium dance floor, high-tech equipment, and DJs who send almighty, thunderous sonic waves across the inland lake. Don't be fooled by the gigantic, wooden Bob Marley; the Pub plays anything that will induce sweaty bodies to groove. Sunday nights bring the bold to the get-bombed-at-Reggae drinking contest. If you're up to the challenge, participation is free and you may earn a place on the Wall of Fame.

Action in this Christmas-lighted partydome picks up late since the raging continues through the night. People whet their nocturnal appetites at the **Green Mango,** 21/5 Mu 3 Tambon Bo Put (tel. 422 165/6), an earlier-closing (8pm-3am, happy hour 10pm-midnight), but equally popular disco, and shuffle over to the Reggae Pub around midnight. There's no cover charge at either. Between the two, a strip of pubs tries to pick up the reveling overflow.

■■■ HAT LAMAI

The nightlife at this beach, is second only to Chaweng to the north. The best beach glides for 2km between two coral reefs that mark off North Lamai and South Lamai. South Lamai, **Ao Bang Nam Cheud,** is actually separated from Lamai proper by a small cape that's best known for its R-rated **genitalia rock formations.** A handful of bungalows are tossed down between Km17 and 21.

ORIENTATION

A small leg of Central Lamai can be reached by dirt roads leading from Km17.5 to 18.5 of Hwy. 4169. **Lamai Beach Road** is the access route that branches from Km18.5 to 21 and runs 200m away from the straightest, most beautiful part of Lamai's shore. The highway itself continues inland past the post office and takes a sharp turn at Km20 and the Lamai Cultural Hall. Near the Km21 junction, the shore veers across the stream mouth, and North Lamai actually ends up facing south. A small daily market is off the road, in Ban Hua Thanon area. Exchange booths, overseas services, and grocery stores dot the street. **Thai House Supermarket,** 126/14 Mu 3 (tel. 424 423) is open 8am to midnight. **Flamingo Bookstore,** opposite Krung Thai exchange booth, deals in books of all languages, reconfirm plane tickets, and have an overseas call booth. Open 8:30am-10pm. **Night songthaews** at the entrance to Mix Pub run to Na Thon (200฿) and parties at Chaweng (80-100฿) from 6pm and 6am. Lamai Beach Rd. is the center of booze, disco, and video action. For something a wee more sedate, North Lamai hides some of the greatest coves on the island.

ACCOMMODATIONS

North Lamai

People end up at North Lamai when there's no room at the main strip's inns. The beach here isn't as aesthetically pleasing as the south because of the reef, but it's still swell for swimming. Bungalows don't jostle for territory as much as those in Central Lamai and the area is generally more subdued. Since restaurants cluster around Central Lamai, you will probably be limited to bungalow food.

Garden Home, 138 Mu 4 (tel. 424 144), along Lamai Beach Rd. near the junction at Km23. Bunk away from the beach. Good-natured proprietor shows you to a solid bungalow he built himself. Fills quickly even in quieter months. Rooms are quite intimate, but in good condition and clean, as are the baths. Singles with bath 100฿. Doubles 200฿. Nearby restaurant serves huge portions of fried rice (20฿), oyster sauce beef and rice (20฿), American breakfast (30฿). Open 6am-midnight.

New Hut Bungalows, just off Km21.5 on Hwy. 4169 at the far north end of the beach. Bare-bones thatched roof quarters with muesli on the menu (30฿), this place draws a loyal backpacker crowd. Double mattress on the floor 60฿, with private bath 100-120฿. Food served 7am-10pm. Daily English newspapers.

No Name Bungalow (tel. 230 383), 10min. past New Hut, offers same minimalist living conditions, but will give you an electric fan for 10฿. Check-out the colorful fishing boats stranded nearby at low tide. Double mattress 80฿, low season 60฿.

Central Lamai

Between coral to the south and a stream to the north, about 50 places are suitable for backpackers. Let the lullaby of Donna Summer rock you to sleep; pubs and discos tend to run pretty late along Lamai Beach Rd. Expect everything to be occupied during the peak months. The south end of the beach hosts cheap bungalows.

Utopia Bungalow, 124/105 Mu 3 (tel. 426 151), north end of Lamai Beach Rd. High-ceilinged rooms may seem slapped together with white planks, but they're cheap with lots of windows and open up onto perfectly gorgeous beach. Concrete path connects all the bungalows; flowers blooming on the sides would send Thomas More into a tizzy. All doubles 200฿, low season 150฿. Smaller rooms are 100฿ all year. Check-out noon. Open 8am-11pm.

Marina Villa, 124 Mu 3 (tel. 424 259), in the middle of the beach. Big bungalows, tall palms, and a huge, big-screen TV in the restaurant. Weathered room with double bed, fan, and tiled bath 120฿, low season 100฿. Closer to the beach 200-300฿.

Thai House Inn, 124/16 Mu 3 (tel. 424 423), by the main intersection of Lamai, Great for the gregarious, lousy for light sleepers, but rooms are tidy and have window screens. Tiled-floor baths have sinks and sit toilets. Two chairs on the balconies face a spacious garden. Single 100฿. Doubles 150฿. Open 8am-11pm.

FOOD

Lamai's food scene is a copycat version of Chaweng's; all the bungalows serve their versions of Thai-*farang* meals until around 10pm and then let the restaurants and pubs along the main drag pick up the slack. The daily market at Ban Hua Thanon has fresh fruits and Thai munchies, but it's over before dinner time.

Nakhon Toe Rung, opposite CIOA Restaurant and has no English sign, but you'll easily notice the sizzling seafood on the grill next to a large wooden boat. Delicious and reasonably priced. Crab fried rice in curry powder 25฿, fried noodles with seafood 25฿, spaghetti in meat sauce 30฿, hot-plate beef in oyster sauce 40฿, breakfast served as well—muesli 25฿. Open 24 hrs.

Shi Bar Restaurant & Cinema. Dine and recline on Arabian pillows, while scoping English movies on big-screen TV. The bamboo hut has some low tables and cushions on the floor. No shoes allowed. Upstairs has tables set up. English and Thai food, but Israeli food is the star. Mixed plate with kebab, gyros, hummus, falafel, and salad 90฿. Shark steak during high season 70฿, Thai dishes 30-65฿. Four movies every night from 4-11pm.

ENTERTAINMENT

During daylight hours, the beach is the setting for it all. Water-skiing costs 250฿ and windsurfing 400฿, but jet-skiing, hoby-cat and parasailing require at least 500฿.

At night, some zoom over to the Green Mango and Reggae Pub on their motorbikes, but Lamai has a good share of its own hot spots, even if they don't get rolling until 11pm. The strip of bars and pubs is technically supposed to shut down at 2am, but things usually go later as owners try to stay afloat in the competitive market. **Mix**

Pub (tel. 424 200) is the most popular (and loudest) place in town. By 10pm the entrance is posted with staff in their Mix Pub T-shirts, handing out flyers on the special shows. Most drinks fetch 60-80฿, draft beer 30฿. Open 9pm-4:30am.

■■■ ANG THONG MARINE NATIONAL PARK

For some blow-you-away sea sights, take a daytrip 31km west by northwest to the "Golden Basin" archipelago. The two-hour boat ride from Na Thon (8:30am, returns at 5pm, 300฿ including lunch and breakfast) can be booked at most travel agents along the waterfront at Na Thon. Among the 40 islands are small gems like **Ko Wua Talap** (Sleeping Cow Island) where the park office is located, **Ko Saa Sao** (Tripod) with a huge rock arch and fantastic snorkeling waters, and **Ko Mae Ko** (Mother Island) with **Thale Nai** (also known as Lake Crater), the emerald saltwater lake that dazzles visitors who make the exhausting climb. Bashful rhinos and seals shy away from strangers in limestone cliffs and caves. **Ko Lak** and similar limestone formations tower 400m above the water. Make way for dolphins as you take the long-tailed boat ride around **Ko Tai Plao. Hat Chan Charat** (Moonlight Beach) does not require any legwork. The waters here are as good as Ko Tao for diving. If you want to snorkel or dive, contact the diving school on the island. They arrange diving trips and supply diving equipment. To stay overnight, make advance bed and board arrangements through **Ang Thong Marine National Park,** 145/1 Talaat Lang Rd., Muang District, Surat Thani 84000 (tel. 077 283 025), or the **National Parks Division** in Bangkok (tel. 579 0529 or 579 4842). Contact the head office at the park (tel. 286 931). Rooms for four, 400฿. Camping is allowed for a 10฿ fee. Rental tents 50฿.

KO PHANGAN

Its big sister a sunshine mecca (Ko Samui) and its little brother a scuba diving Eden (Ko Tao), Ko Phangan suffers a perpetual identity crisis. Although the increasingly famous Full Moon Parties at Hat Rin Beach have placed Ko Phangan on the traveler's circuit, the mish-mash of tourists who wander onto the island don't fund the entire local livelihood. Only 7000 people occupy the 191-sq. km island, pocked with mountainous terrain, and many still depend on fishing and farming for income. Plenty of sun-swept beaches now harvest fast-growing crops of budget bungalows, but the Ko Phangan *sans* full moon extravaganza is often overlooked.

GETTING THERE

Many boats sailing from Surat Thani make stops at Ko Samui before continuing on to Ko Phangan. Prices and schedules vary greatly through the season; check with the travel agencies for definite figures. The **ferry,** the best value for your money, leaves the mainland from Don Sak pier. Tickets, from Songserm Travel or Phanthip Tour, include transportation to the pier from Surat Thani (3-¾hr., 105฿). Buses depart from in front of Songserm Travel Service at 8am and 2:30pm; and the ferry leaves at 9:15am and 4pm. The **express boat** drops passengers off on Ko Samui before completing the trip to Phangan (3-½hr., 120฿). Transport to Pak Nam, the launching point, is included in the ticket. Buses leave from Songserm office at 7:30am and 2pm; ferries depart Pak Nam Pier 30min. later. The cheapest route to the island is the **night/sleeper boat,** which costs 70฿ for a lower deck spot (no beds) and 90฿ for the upper deck (beds). Tickets are sold at the pier in Ban Don. Boats depart Ban Don at 11pm and arrive at 6am. (For boats from Ko Samui to Thong Sala and Hat Rin see "Practical Information" on page 498 for more details).

ISLAND ORIENTATION

Ko Phangan stakes its claim approximately 100km northeast of Surat Thani and only 12km from Ko Samui at the closest point (between Hat Rin and Bo Phut). The north and west coasts of Ko Phangan have exquisite beaches along several bays created by rocky capes, and provide halcyon getaways for anyone who finds Samui a bit too touristy. The southern coast has a panoramic view of Ko Samui and an ever-increasing onslaught of bargain bungalows at the unusual **Hat Rin** which can be reached by either boat or a new paved road in mid-1996. The interior is slowly being carved away by dirt roads stretching from the main port of **Thong Sala.**

ISLAND SIGHTS

Considering the highly textured terrain, it's no surprise that waterfalls are the major tourist attractions after beaches and full moons. About 4km northeast of Thong Sala, near Ban Madeu Wan on the way to Chalok Lam, **Phaeng Waterfall** is one of the more impressive cascades on the island. Take a songthaew to Ao Chalok Lam and get off before Ban Madeu Wan, where the 1-km dirt road leads to the waterfall; alternatively, you can rent a motorbike from Thong Sala. Walk or bike the 1km down the dirt road. The most famous and probably most stupendous stretches of river on the islands of the Gulf of Thailand belong to **Than Sadet Historical Park.** Kings Rama V, VII, and IX all walked along its many waterfalls and cascades and left their initials as permanent seals of inspection. Than Sadet is best tackled as a daytrip, starting out in the morning on one of the long-tail boats that run from Hat Rin (50฿) and Thong Sala (70฿); they'll drop you at the mouth of the river. It's a refreshing 2-3km trek along the river on its parallel road just to the north.

■■■ THONG SALA

The southwestern port of Thong Sala is the lifeline for the rest of the island. This is the best place to rent a motorbike, extend your visa, stock up on beach supplies (and batteries, toiletries, and food), as well as change money. The travel agents have huddled conveniently by the pier, intercepting the herds to and from the boat. **Thong Sala Road** runs from the pier, past restaurants, travel agencies, and supermarkets. Two major roads branch off Thong Sala Rd., one to Ao Chalak Lam in the north, the other to Ban Kai (and someday Hat Rin) along the south coast. The daily market, local restaurants, clinics, and the "post office" are on this road. Only the **morning market** is at the corner of the road to Ao Chalak Lam.

PRACTICAL INFORMATION

Tourist Office: Ko Phangan does not have an official TAT office (disregard the sign by the pier). Enterprising travel agencies off the pier can field most questions.

Travel Agencies: Except for the busiest days (after a full moon), you can easily buy tickets on the pier or boat. To book in advance: **Songserm Travel Center,** 35/1 Thong Sala Rd. (tel. 377 046), straight ahead and to the left of the pier. Open daily 8am-4pm. Express boat route to Ko Samui and then Surat Thani. Authorized agent of the State Railway; the place to buy joint tickets.

Visa Extension: Sophie Silver, 2 doors from Siam City Exchange booth. 1 or 2-week extension 700฿, 1-month 800฿. 1-day processing. Open daily 8am-8pm.

Currency Exchange: Exchange booths straight off the pier. **Siam City Bank,** next to the post office. Open Mon.-Fri. 8:30am-6pm.

Post Office: GPO, 12/1 Mu 1 Tambon Ko Phangan (tel. 337 118), next to Siam City Bank. From the pier, take a right at the 1st intersection and head into town; it's on the right side 500m ahead. Open Mon.-Fri. 8:30am-noon and 1-4:30pm, Sat. 9am-noon. **Postal code:** 84280.

Telephones: Overseas calls are expensive. Expect service charges at bungalows and stores. **Café de la Poste,** 25/1 Thong Sala Rd. (tel. 377 043), across from the post office. Authorized agent with a private booth. Collect call 80฿ to Europe and North America, 50฿ to Asia. Open daily 8am-9pm. **Telephone code:** 077.

Boats: By **ferry** (6:20am and 3pm, 4-½hr., 120฿), will connect to a regular bus to the train station at **Phun Phin** or an A/C bus to **Surat Thani.** The afternoon trip is the surer bet. By **express boat** (6:15am and 12:30pm, to **Ko Samui,** 45min., 60฿, then to Surat Thani, 2-½hr., 120฿). The 12:30pm express boat will get you to Samui in time to connect you with Songserm's package deals to **Bangkok** (see Na Thon: "Practical Information" on page 498). By **night boat** to the mainland (10pm, 7hr., lower deck 70฿ or less claustrophobic upper deck 90฿. Boats to **Ko Tao** (12:30pm, 2-½hr., 150฿; get tickets at the pier). From Hat Rin to **Ko Samui,** take the Hat Rin boat to Big Buddha Beach instead of looping through Thong Sala.

Local Transportation: Go between the pier and the beaches on the labeled taxi-pickup trucks. Fares are based on distance and difficulty of the road. To: **Ban Khai** 30฿; **Ban Tai** 20฿; **Ao Chalok Lam** 30฿; **Thong Nai Paan** 60฿; **Hat Yow** 60฿. The trip to **Hat Rin** (40฿) involves both taxi and longtail boat. To get to **Thong Nai Paan,** take the taxi; the road is extremely rough for motorcycles. **Hat Khuat** (Bottle Beach) is not accessible by car (yet); take a boat from Ao Chalak Lam (30฿) or Thong Sala (80฿) after Songserm boats arrive.

Motorbike Rentals: Around the market area of Thong Sala. 150฿ per day. Larger bikes 200฿, MTX 250฿.

Market: Bovy Supermarket, 44/25 Mu 1 (tel. 377 231), straight off the pier on the right. Good prices and the largest stock. Open daily 8:30am-8:30pm. For fresh fruits, try the street parallel to the post office or go farther down Thong Sala Rd. to the **"morning" market** under the large tent on the left side.

English Book Store: Wantana Book Store, 145 Mu 1 Tambon Ko Phangan (tel. 377 024), straight off the pier and turn right at the intersection; it's on the right. Open daily 8am-8pm.

Laundromat: Phangan Laundry, down the right alley off the main road on the way to the post office. Same-day service 5฿ for t-shirts.

Hospital/Medical Services: Hospital (tel. 377 036), 3km north of Thong Sala on the way to Chalak Ban Kao. Dr. Charatpong is the only physician on the island who can speak English. His hours are Mon.-Fri. 8am-4pm and 8-9pm, Sat.-Sun. 8-9pm. Major procedures are handled on the mainland. Dr. Charatpong is at Dr. Sanae's **clinic** opposite the GPO from noon-1pm and 4-7pm, Sat.-Sun. 9am-6pm. The nurse can handle first-aid medication.Open Mon.-Fri. 10am-1pm, Sat.-Sun. 9am-6pm.

Emergency: tel. 191

Police: (tel. 377 114), at Ban Don Sai, about 2km away on the road to Al Chalak Lam. English-speaking staff.

ACCOMMODATIONS

Staying at Thong Sala means that you missed the boat or intend to catch the morning vessel. Bungalows are off the road to the right of the pier (the one headed for Ban Tai). During the low season, some of these places may be closed. Beware of dogs in this area: they roam in attack-prone packs that have to be "eliminated" occasionally. **Moon Light Bungalow,** 500m from the pier and another 400m off the highway, has rustic bungalows (60฿) that are a little longer than the mattresses inside. Clean with mosquito nets and brooms. Rooms with bamboo walls have spacious cement baths and thatched roof 100฿. Check-out 11:30am. Open 7am-2am, or until midnight in the low season. Southeast of Thong Sala (right off pier) within a one-km walk are a patch of sub-100฿ bungalows like **Petch Cottage** and **Phangan Villa.**

FOOD

Kao Kang Jae Lak, 42 Mu 1 (tel. 377 151), straight off the pier on the left, opposite Bovy supermarket. Freshly cooked curries, soups, and stir-fry every morning—fish curry and eggplant, *kai paloe* (sweet curried egg and pork), cabbage or bamboo shoot soups, stir-fried baby corn, and tomatoes. Rice with one item 15฿, 2 items 20฿. Coffee or hot cocoa 5฿. Open 7am-3pm, but most food gone by noon.

Kuai Taew Pak Tai, 145/2 Mu 1, off the southern road along the coast on the way to the market, next to Wantana Book Store. Tables are set up in front of the house. Quick hot dishes to order: rice with pepper, garlic pork, squid, or chicken; *raad naa,* rice with basil leaves, chicken, fried rice, and noodle soup—all for 20฿. English menu. Open daily 6am-10pm.

■■■ HAT RIN

Hat Rin would be just like any other stunning stretch of white Gulf of Thailand sand, if it weren't home to the world-famous **Full Moon Party.** Every month several thousand travelers converge on Hat Rin to celebrate the rising full moon at a giant beach rave, Thai style. While massive electrical generators plug away to power the pulsating beach-side speakers and spinning disco lights, body-painted revelers dance on the sand and cavort in the warm water until sunrise. The event has attracted a lunar-cycle pilgrimage of bohemian travelers from all over Southeast Asia for several years. It has also attracted increasing numbers of Thai police who aren't so entertained by Hat Rin's conspicuous hedonism.

Two beaches on opposite sides of Ko Phangan's southernmost cape make up Hat Rin. Ground zero during the full moon party is Paradise Bungalow, at the south end of Hat Rin Nok (east). During the high season (Nov.-Feb.), the revelry spans most of the rest of sleepless Hat Rin Nok, spilling onto the quieter Hat Rin Na (west) at times. Two dirt roads lined with restaurants and shops cross the cape at its north and south ends. Another dusty road runs lengthwise between the beaches (along the backdoors of Hat Rin Nok's bungalow resorts) to form an "I" street configuration. The post and telephone office, travel agents, and currency exchangers are clustered around the bottom (south) end of the "I." By mid-1996 a paved road is slated to link Hat Rin with the rest of Ko Phangan. In the meantime, long-tail boats and small ferries transport Rin-bound crowds from Thong Sala, Ban Kai, and from beaches on Ko Phangan and Ko Samui when full moon-induced demand hits.

PRACTICAL INFORMATION

Travel Agents: Phanthip Co. (tel. 01 725 0052) has set up shop on the bottom of the "I." Authorized agent of the State Railway. Joint tickets.

Currency Exchange: Branches of **Siam City,** next to Phangan Bay Resort. Open 9:30am-4pm. **Krung Thai,** 100m from the school. Open daily 9am-5pm. Both are along the "I" (follow the signs), with slightly poorer rates than Thong Sala.

Post Office/Telephones: A private, licensed branch stands on the bottom of the "I" toward Hat Rin Na. Open Mon.-Fri. 9am-5pm, Sat. 9am-noon. **Postal code:** 84280. **Overseas calls** are generally 100฿ per minute. Open daily until 9pm.

Boats: To **Thong Sala:** Long-tail boats leave from in front of Rin Beach Resort (Hat Rin Na); times depend upon when they arrive at the pier, season, and sea conditions. Boats go direct (50฿), or to **Ban Khai** where you a land taxi runs to Thong Sala (total trip 40฿). To **Thong Nai Paan** boats leave with favorable winds (around noon, 50฿), except during rainy and monsoon season (Oct.-mid-Dec.) Boats to **Big Buddha Beach, Ko Samui** (June-Oct. from Hat Rin West, and Nov.-Jan. from Hat Rin Nok; 9:30am and 2:30pm, 60฿).

Medical Services: Clinics dot the middle of the "I." The one with a green cross on a red circle has a regular nurse (tel. 723 0989). Open daily 9am-9pm.

Emergency: tel. 191

Police: Hat Rin has a police booth next to the school, but it has no phone and is open sporadically. Extra uniformed *and* undercover police officers patrol the beach during Full Moon Parties. A couple of people get busted each party during high season and (at least) have to pay a fine of 10,000฿ before leaving the island.

ACCOMMODATIONS

Hat Rin Na (West)

When the moon fills, so do all the rooms. Otherwise, it's a peaceful place to stare at Ko Samui. Beaches are best after the rainy season. For better swimming, head to Hat Rin East. Ramble along the beach or the beaten path that runs through all the bungalows until you find a decent room. The closer you are to Thong Sala, the quieter; as you approach the end of the cape, things may get full-mooned during high season.

Sooksom Bungalow, 120 Mu 6 Tambon Ban Tai (tel. 01 958 477), in the middle of That Rin Na, at the top of the "I." Bamboo huts on a small cove. On the hill 60฿, low season 50฿. On ground 80฿, low season 60฿. Restaurant entrees 30฿.

Crystal Palace (tel. 01 725 0511), about 100m before Sooksom Bungalow. Concrete bungalows, tiled patio, and flush toilets. Rooms are dazzling with light and hygiene. Singles and doubles 200฿, but rates fluctuate between 100-300฿. Check-out 11am. Open 10am-11:30pm. Two movies every night 7-11pm.

Hat Rin Nok (East)

The farther you get from the south end of the beach, where the Full Moon Parties rave, the quieter it gets. The drug culture, passing away the time until lunar fever sets in, shuffles up and down the beach. On the actual full moon, forget about sleep. Prices for rooms shoot up during this time and are higher in general than Hat Rin Na. If everything's full during Full Moon, fight for your right to party until dawn and catch a post-revelry boat to somewhere else.

Paradise Bungalow (tel. 01 725 0661), the southernmost bungalow on Hat Rin East and the first to host the Full Moon party. Quiet beach with some coral reefs. Bamboo bungalows a la Chris O'Donnell—clean, well-built, and picturesque. Bright lights, windows with screens, wholesome baths with Thai toilet, and furnished balcony. Rooms 250฿ or 150฿. Smaller huts on stilts near the rocks with no baths 80฿, 100฿ high season.

Sun Rise Bungalow, 136 Mu 6 Tambon Ban Tai (tel. 01 725 0884), in the middle of the beach. Breezy bamboo cottages replete with large beds and mosquito net. Large tiled floor bath and sit toilet make splendid writing rooms. Not many empty rooms, even in low season. Spare hand-wash laundry room. Rooms with bath 150-200฿. A handful of rooms without bath go for 80฿ all year.

Tommy's Resort (tel. 01 725 0327) at the north end of the beach. Giant beach-side speakers feed a steady flow of classic rock and acid jazz to cocktail-toting, volleyball-bouncing residents. Travel agency in back offers tours and overseas phone calls. Open 7:30am-11pm; 100฿ per min. to USA, 50฿ collect. Basic room with double bed and fan 80฿, 150฿ with the onset of full moon fever.

FOOD

Barbecued *som tam,* sticky rice, and a few sidewalk restaurants perfume the middle of the "I." Bungalows have large menus of Thai and western food (30-40฿). In the middle of the road connecting the south ends of the beaches, the **Rin Kitchen and Bakery** serves some of the best food in town. Chef Nira's curries and seafoods are well worth their bungalow prices, and her whole-wheat bread (big loaf 25฿) is fresh every morning. Open 8am-10pm. At the top of the "I," guess who runs the show at **Mama's Family Restaurant,** whipping up economical Indian and Thai meals (curry chicken 20฿, *som yam* 15฿) until the wee hours on party nights.

■■■ OTHER BEACHES

THONG NAI PAAN AND THONG TAPAN NOI

On the opposite end of the island from Thong Sala, this twin beach separated by a rocky cliff doubles the pleasure of those who endure the hour-long jeep ride along the mountains or the boat ride from Hat Rin or the north beaches. The eastern beach, **Thong Nai Paan,** is the longer and more populated of the two. At the end of the road to Thong Nai Paan's eastern point, **Nice Beach Bungalow** offers solid wooden lodgings; all rooms are singles with mosquito nets, high ceilings, and weather screens on the double doors. Rooms with no bath cost 80฿, low season 60฿, with baths 200฿, low season 100฿. Concrete rooms are larger and go for 300฿,

200฿ high season. Open 7am-11pm. In the middle of Thong Nai Paan beach is the mighty Pen's Bungalow (tel. 377 079). Thatched bungalows have clean tiled baths with sit toilets. Hammocks and benches on the beach. Rooms 100฿, low season 80฿. With bath 200฿, low season 150฿. Tile roof bungalow 300฿, low season 200฿. Check-out 10am. Open 6:30am-10pm. Owners speak English.

Thong Tapan Noi changes its size quickly with the tides. It is equally beautiful, but more rocky in certain areas near the cliff. Bungalows are off paths that run among coconut trees and high grass. In the middle of the beach, **Honey Bungalow,** 7/2 Mu 5, dribbles bed-sized bungalows on the foothill, with some leaning on enormous rocks. Thatch-roofed, tidy chambers have tiled baths and showers, but no sinks. Plank walls repel bloodsuckers. Common baths among banana trees. Bungalows 80฿, with shower 150฿, spankin' new and close to the beach 200฿. Front desk open 8am-10pm. Circling the owner's home, the concrete bungalows of **Thong Ta Paan Resort** (tel. 377 048), at the north end of Thong Nai Paan Noi on the rocky point, have plain, good-sized rooms. Most have views of the entire beach and the sound of waves on the rocks below. Some peer out to the secluded cove around the corner known as "Stoned Beach." Good water pressure and sanitary Thai toilet. Rooms 100฿. With bath, on the ground 150฿, on the hill 250฿. Open 6am-10pm.

CHALOK LAM AND HAT KHUAT (BOTTLE BEACH)

About 10km down a surfaced road from Thong Sala, taxis arrive in the belly of Chalok Lam Bay. The quiet beach is partly rocky and blackened by calamari wash from the squid boats that come ashore (April-Oct.). If you decide to stay overnight at Chalok Lam during the squid-free time, **Wantana Resort,** 17 Mu 7 Tambon Ko Phangan, is farther away from the rocky beaches and gives plenty of bang for the baht. Singles 50฿ all year, with bath 150฿. Doubles 200฿. Open 7am-11pm. Songthaews leave daily at 5, 10am, 3:30, and 7:30pm.

This is the best place to snag a boat to the quaint **Hat Khuat** (Bottle Beach), just to the east and accessible only by water or steep footpaths. The long-tail trip costs 30฿ when a group of 6-8 people show up (i.e. after a taxi arrives from Thong Sala), but you'll have to bargain if you're in a smaller group. As Bottle Beach gains popularity, there is talk of inaugurating regular boat service—ask around. The 4-km foot path from Chalok Lam is steep, ill-defined, and a lot of fun, but only worth attempting if you're armed with boots, long pants, water, and a full day of sunlight.

A handful of bungalow resorts occupy Bottle Beach's cookie-cutter sand crescent. The long-tail will probably drop you off in the middle, in front of **Bottle Beach 1.** Ship-shape mattress and mosquito net bungalows, 80, 100, and 120฿ depending on beach proximity; rates fall to 50, 60, and 80฿ in low season. White concrete rooms with baths go for 200-250฿. Electricity lights up life from 6:30-11:30pm. Stocking up on food in Thong Sala will help take the sting out of the high food prices (served 7:30am-10pm; fried rice 35฿). If the bungalows are full, **Bottle Beach 2,** next door, offers the same rooms, rates, menu, and cheerful management.

KO TAO

"Turtle Island" surfaces 74km southeast of Chumphon and 40km northwest of Ko Phangan. Like Ko Tarutao, Ko Tao was a place of exile for political prisoners; most were taken rapidly by malaria, and all eventually died on the island. Six years ago, a cold drink couldn't be found, because ice hadn't reached the island and electricity was non-existent. Five years ago, there was a building boom, opening up a steady wave of visitors. Four years ago, electricity started illuminating bungalows in the evening, and today, upstart dive shops seem to take root among the stringy palms almost as frequently as semi-luxurious bungalow resorts. All cater to scuba neophytes who come to take advantage of Ko Tao's inexpensive PADI certification course and veteran divers who want to explore the tepid Gulf waters. Getting here can be an arduous task, but growing numbers of visitors have decided that Ko Tao's pristine underwater world is worth the effort.

Ko Tao is largely underdeveloped. Not an ounce of asphalt graces the 21-sq.km island; electricity is only an evening affair, and clean water is the sole thing more valuable than scuba dollars. Beach-side accommodations are inexpensive and backpacker-friendly, and night-time scuba dives still trump the video scene. Sun-crisped coves ring the island for water-logged adventurers looking for a secluded spot to spend the day. The local divers, together with the Thai tourism officials, have firmly established most of the island and its surrounding waters as a natural reserve, thus staving off the most onerous trappings of mass tourism for the time being.

GETTING THERE

To get to Ko Tao directly from the mainland, take a bus or train to Chumphon. Catch the **sleeper boat** (midnight, 5-7hr. depending on weather, 200฿) or the **speed boat** (8am, 2hr., 400฿). From Ko Phangan take the daily **express boat** from Thong Sala (12:30pm, 2-½hr., 150฿). From Ko Samui, head to Ko Phangan and connect to the Ko Tao boat or take the **speed boat** direct from Bo Phut (8:30am, 1-½hr., 450฿). As the number of visitors to Ko Tao rises exponentially every year, so do the transportation alternatives.

ISLAND ORIENTATION

When your boat arrives at the pier at Mae Hat (Mother Beach), the center of the Ko Tao community, you'll have the option of grabbing a taxi, hopping in a long-tail boat, or walking. If you're planning to stay on the west coast near the pier (and scuba-diving schools), you can save 20฿ by following the footpath near the beach. It will bring you by several bungalows in 15-20 minutes. Otherwise, find a ride, because most everything else is an arduous hike or only accessible by boat.

Dirt roads connect **Mae Hat** (pier), **Hat Sai Ree** (2km north on the west coast), **Ao Chalok Ban Kao** (on the south coast), **Ao Thian Ok** (0.5km past Ao Chalok Ban Kao), **Hat Sai Daeng** (the southeast corner), as well as **Ao Hin Wong, Ao Leuk,** and **Ao Ta Node** (on the remote east coast). If you plan to explore the island, the *V. Hongsombud Guide Map of Ko Tao,* sold at most dive shops and some bungalows, is a worthy investment (40฿).

SCUBA DIVING

Ko Tao is touted as the best place in the Gulf of Thailand to learn to scuba dive, although the waters are not as spectacular as the world-famous diving off Phuket and the Similan Islands. The prices are standardized in Ko Tao, so a four-day Open-Water course costs 5900฿, including equipment, transportation, and snacks. The Advanced Course costs 5300฿. For those who just want a taste of the scuba experience, one-day Introduction Courses cost 1400฿ for one dive. Certified divers can go on all-inclusive trips at 500฿ for one dive, 1200฿ for two, 3000฿ for six, and 4500฿ for ten. If you tote your own equipment, a dive trip costs 450฿, or 400฿ if you plan ten or more. Snorkelers can tag along on many trips for about 150฿. For more information, stop in at any one of the dive centers that have proliferated in the pier area.

The **Samui International Diving School** (tel. 77 421 465), 20m from the pier in Mae Hat with branches on Ko Samui and Ko Phangan, was one of the first schools to set up shop on the island. **Big Blue** and **Ko Tao Divers,** next to the pier have teamed up to form one of the island's largest schools. Long-time local divers Bryan and Oi run the **Big Fish Dive Center** (tel. 77 377 196) near the middle of Hat Sai Ree; Oi was the first female Thai PADI instructor and has made over 3500 dives. At the south point of the island, **Tato Divers** at Tato Lagoon Bungalows offers stunning scenery above and below the emerald waters in a friendly, laid-back atmosphere.

In spite of its small size, Ko Tao has over 20 established dive sights within easy striking distance. **Chumphon Pinnacle** to the northwest juts up 30m from the sea floor, its peak at a depth of 16m; giant grouper, barracuda, and whale shark are often spotted here. To the southwest, the appropriately named **Shark Island** is known for its clean waters and leopard sharks. Near **Sail Rock,** midway to Ko Phangan, divers can drop into a 22m-high, sub-marine cylindrical rock chimney. Most bays around the island, such as **Ao Hin Wong** and **Ao Mamuang** contain large varieties of coral and fish in shallow waters that are suitable for snorkeling as well as scuba diving.

■■■ MAE HAT

Mae Hat ("Mother Beach") is the soul provider of this rocky island, bringing tourists, equipment, food, and fuel. Most of the island's modern facilities, including the post office, the telecommunications office, and the scuba shops, are within walking distance of the pier. Despite its metropolitan status among the island's communities, the beach is as low-key as any other and is an excellent maternal haven for travelers.

PRACTICAL INFORMATION

Tourist Information: Most dive shop staff dispense plenty of local lore. For transportation info, check with the **Nuan Yang Travel Service Center,** 10m to the right of the pier. Open daily8am-9pm.

Currency Exchange: Krung Thai Bank booth, off the pier. Changes cash and traveler's checks at mainland rates. Open daily 11am-3pm. Credit cards accepted at dive shops.

Post Office: GPO, a short right turn off the pier. Open daily 8:30am-5:30pm. **Postal code:** 84280; for Poste Restante 84820-102.

Telephones: GPO, overseas calls 360฿ for 1st 3min., plus 80฿ for additional min.; collect calls 100฿. Open daily 8:30am-5:30pm. **Nuan Yang Travel Service Center.** 280-350฿ for 3 min., plus 80฿ for additional min. Open daily 8am-9pm. Some bungalows have regular telephone lines and allow overseas calls for similar fees; others rely on radio phones and charge more exorbitant rates.

Boats: To **Chumphon,** by **night/sleeping boat** (from Mae Hat pier, 10am, 5-7hr. if the seas are choppy, 200฿) and **speedboat** (10am, 2hr., 400฿). To **Surat Thani** via **Ko Phangan** by **ferry** (9am, 7hr., 200฿); does not operate daily. To **Ko Samui: express boat** to **Ko Phangan** (9am, 2-½hr., 150฿); transfer at **Thong Sala. Speed boat** departs Mae Hat for **Thong Sala** (1pm, 1-½hr., 350฿) and **Bo Phut** on Ko Samui (2hr., 450฿); additional services are appearing quickly. To **Ko Nang Yuan** (10am; returns at 4:30pm, 15 min., round-trip 40฿). During high season, more boats to Ko Nang Yuan leave directly from the beaches.

Local Transportation: Anything beyond a 5-min. walk usually involves traversing unlit dirt roads. If you plan to walk, check the clouds and carry a flashlight; storms hit fast and hard, and some areas fall into complete darkness after dusk.

Taxis: Pick-up trucks and hell-bent motorcycles. From the pier to **Hat Sai Ree** or **So Chalok Ban Kao,** 20฿. To the back of the island, 30-50฿. At night, expect up to 100฿ for 1 person. To get to the morning boat, ask your bungalow manager (a day ahead) to arrange a taxi to the pier, but taxis usually make runs to all the bungalows around 8am. During high season, **water taxis** (generally long-tail boats) will also take you from the pier to the bays. Rough fares: **Ao Chalok Ban Kao** 20฿, **Rocky** or **Kiet Bungalows** 30฿, or to get to the other side of the island 50฿.

Motorcycle Rental: Some bungalows rent motorcycles for around 150฿ per day; be sure to point out all problems with the bike before you hand over your passport, so you don't get stuck paying for them. Some of the greatest views are only accessible by foot or a "tour boat" ride that loops around the island. This is not a place for inexperienced riders; the roads can be quite rough, sandy, and steep.

Market: The **Mae Hat pier area** is also called *talaat* (market). Everything that comes to the island arrives here: fruit, postcards, clothes, swim and snorkel gear, and basic backpacker's supplies. The **mini-mart** at Ko Tao corner to the left off the pier stocks all these goodies and sells boat tickets. Open 8:30am-9:30pm.

Weather and Peak Season: The low season (May-June and Nov.) corresponds to monsoon season, when the island is occasionally lashed by heavy rains and winds. The busiest time is Jan.-March and July-Oct., when the waters are highest, the beaches most scenic, and the snorkeling superb.

Medical Services: Public Health Center, 20m off the road to the right of the pier. Open daily 8:30am-4:30pm. A **private center** (sign is a green cross on red circle) is at the entrance to the Public Health Center. Open daily 7am-5pm, but somebody will respond 24 hrs. if you knock. Call the public phone on the island (tel. 377 196) and people will get in touch with nurses for you.

Police: 600m north of the pier, has a shiny new jail, but no phone. In case of an **emergency,** the market area is the best place to find assistance.

ACCOMMODATIONS

Dam Bungalow, only 5min. north, before the rocky hill and cape separating Hat Sai Ree. Typical bungalows with mattress and mosquito net combo. Sliding windows supply oxygen. Neon light and a balcony. Electricity 6-11pm. No baths. 80฿, low season 60฿. Closer to the beach 100฿, low season 80฿. Check-out noon. Open 8am-10:30pm.

Coral Beach Bungalow, south of the pier and over the rocks. Sky-blue bungalows dot the cape. Guests have free use of their snorkeling gear. Bungalows 80฿, larger with 2 twin beds 100฿, with bath 150฿.

■■■ HAT SAI REE

Sandy beach, peaceful coral reef, sunsets over the sea—sound familiar? They're yours for the taking. Most accommodations can be reached by following the beaten path that winds north from Mae Hat along the beach and over the hill. Take a 10-20 minute walk, or scamper into a cab for 20฿.

Ko Tao Cabana, 137/3 Mu 5 Tambon Ko Tao, a 15-min. walk past the hill. Lola and other showgirls can kick up their heels at these large, family-run bungalows on stilts 150-200฿; high season 300฿. Some of the best food on the island in the restaurant; nightly specials for under 50฿.

Sai Ree Cottage, 10/1 Mu 1, in the middle of Hat Sai Ree. Well-established, well-ventilated wooden bungalows with high ceilings front the short, narrow beach lined with coconut trees. Friendly manager. Singles 150฿, low season 80฿. With fan 200฿, low season 100฿. Larger rooms closer to beach 300฿, low season 150฿. Simple but clean huts on stilts 50฿. Open 7am-11pm.

A.C. Resort, at the south end of the beach, just over hill when walking from Mae Hat. Ah, the irony…no A/C, but all the dark-wood bungalows in a semicircle around the rustic wooden bridge have fans and screens. Rooms 200-350฿ depending on season and management's whims. Full moon parties here are a much tamer version of the Ko Phangan raves. Check-out 11am. Closed during low season.

North of Hat Sai Ree

Taxi (20฿) along the runway to these bungalows 3-4km north of the pier; otherwise walk to the end of Sai Ree beach and then continue around the island on the hillside road. Paths from the road lead to the bungalows.

C.F.T. Bungalow, 31 Mu 1, the northernmost bungalow at the end of the road. Spectacular view of the offshore island trio, and good snorkeling. It is a long walk after the songthaew drops you off—most people come by boat. During low season, some rooms are free for those traveling alone. A wooden bridge from the pier leads to simple hillside huts 50฿ (Dec.-May), free low season. Two more rooms higher on the hill are spacious and breezy, with bright, new bathrooms 250฿, low season 100฿. Check-out 2pm.

Mahana Bay Bungalow, down the path 300m beyond Golden Cape. Hike up the rocks for a different perspective on Ko Nang Yuan's famous 3-pronged beach. 12 small, basic huts scatter at the foothill, without bath 80฿, low season 40฿.

Golden Cape Bungalows, just beyond Hat Sai Ree. Bare-bones rooms (mosquito net, but no bath or fan) on the rocks 80฿, as low as 50฿ during low season.

■■■ OTHER BEACHES

AO CHALOK BAN KAO

Chalok Ban Kao Bay is carved out of the island's south end, 3km from Mae Hat. Its beach supports the densest pack of bungalows (10 at last count) on the island, but the bay's awesome beauty makes up for the population explosion. The crescent of white-sand beach has clear shallow waters that seem to form a mirror along the rocky, hill-rimmed bay. After the rainy season, the water level rises dramatically (nearly 2m), providing the most picturesque view. Before the rains, low tide turns the beach into white paste; you may think you're hallucinating when hordes of tiny crabs scuttle into holes in the beach in a coordinated disappearing act.

In the middle of the beach, **Carabao Bungalows and Diving Center** has sturdy cookie-cutter huts lined up among the palms 60-80฿; look for the "coconut diver" strung out over the entrance. **View Point Bungalows** (tel. 01 913 8224) couldn't have a more literal name. Bungalows line the point out to the right when coming from the beach and boast window screens, sit toilets, showers, and electricity when it's available (250฿, low season 150฿). Farther around the point, the completely secluded **Sunset Bungalow** has also joined the literal-name game. Widely spaced stilt huts show plenty of backpacker experience, but they're well-maintained and each one owns a commanding view of the fiery evening horizon. After that main event, the friendly, easygoing staff breaks out the guitar and guests feast on some of the best island food. Double rooms overlooking Sunset's three tiny beaches 80-100฿, in low season 50-80฿.

LAEM TATO

From the mountain viewpoint above Laem (Cape) Tato, the unique shape of Turtle Island comes into view: you're standing on the south head, with the green hills straight ahead rolling over the turtle's back and the southwest and southeast corners of the island reaching out into the gulf like two front feet. Below, the calm bay waters are translucent; dive boats seem airborne above the dark coral reefs. The **Tato Lagoon Bungalow,** on Tato Beach halfway out the cape, has simple, secluded, dreamy bungalows perched among the massive weather-beaten stones that rim the sand. Many guests are divers-in-training at the bungalow's scuba school, **Tato Divers.** Candle-lit rooms with mosquito nets 80฿, but the owner plans an upgrade soon. To make your way to Laem Tato, follow the road up the hill past the bungalows at Ao Chalok Ban Kao and turn right onto the path leading out the cape. Tato Beach is below you on the right side, 10 minutes ahead. The mountain viewpoint sits 15 sweaty minutes above and beyond the bungalows. A refreshing alternative to trudging along the road out to Laem Tato is to set out from the beach at Chalok Ban Kao and wade through the waist-deep water along the edge of the bay until you come to Tato Beach, where you can strike off onto the paths around the cape.

■ NEAR KO TAO: KO NANG YUAN

This favorite photography subject has some of the best snorkeling in the Gulf of Thailand. The three-pronged trio of beaches makes it possible to walk between its three tiny islands during low tides. Ko Nang Yuan has a viewpoint from the top of the towering rock on the southern isle—wave affectionately at sand, snorkelers, and scuba-divers. **Ko Nang Yuan Bungalow,** 10/1 Tambon Ko Tao (tel. 01 726 0085 or 726 0212; fax 726 0112) is the only game in town. The office and the restaurant are on the smallest prong, with bungalows fringing the foothill of the south isle. (300฿ for "standard" rooms—without bath, mattress under mosquito net, a simple wood shelf, neon lights that work 6-11pm, 3 sliding windows, and a balcony. 700฿ for "deluxe" rooms—modern and immaculate green-roofed bungalows along the rocks.) A daily boat comes from Mae Hat or Hat Sai Ree (10am; returns at 4:30pm; 40฿ round-trip), giving just enough time for a beautiful daytrip, and thus avoiding expensive lodgings. More frequent trips shuttle people during high season.

PHUKET ISLAND

With its ample natural resources, talcum-powdery beaches, and stunning coves and bays, Phuket Island, gleaming 885km south of Bangkok, packs the crowds into its 533 square km year-round (even during monsoon season, June-September). Phuket has always played host to visitors. When colonies, corsets, and Conrad were the fashion, European traders ambled onto this amoeba-shaped island in search of rubber, pearls, and ivory. Their influence, noticeable in the island's older architecture, is one of the ingredients floating around in Phuket's unique cultural stew. In addition to "sea gypsies," the island's first inhabitants, the population is a mix of Chinese, Malays, Indians, and Thais, most of whom arrived during the tin boom a century ago.

A rhinestone lifestyle is hard to maintain on the "Jewel of the South." Trips to the Similan Islands can be pricey, but offer excellent opportunities for scuba diving. Bargaining has withered away in Phuket; merchants scoff at attempts to "cut a deal," knowing full well that the next fat-cat tourist to enter the shop will happily pay the quoted rates. Nevertheless, there are a few bargains to be snatched up along Kamala Beach and in Phuket town, connected by songthaew (10-30฿) to all the beaches. Great food, a gorgeous coast line, and the alluring Andaman Sea conspire to keep the beach bunnies hopping in—just remember that you'll struggle to stay solvent during your sojourn.

> Phuket is known for treacherous currents during the monsoon season. There are a few casualties almost every year. Exercise caution when swimming and never swim alone. Don't panic. If you are caught in a current, float until someone comes to get you.

GETTING THERE

Phuket International Airport lies 28km outside of Phuket town on Rte. 4026. International airlines servicing Phuket include THAI Airways, Hong Kong Dragon Air, Lauda Air, Malaysia Airlines, Bangkok Airways, and China Airlines. Taxis, private mini-buses, and Holiday Charter shuttles run from the airport to Phuket town (70฿) and to the beaches (100฿). In town, the **Thai Airways International Office** is at 78 Ranong Rd. (tel. 211 195 or 212 499; open daily 8am-5pm). The most common means of transportation to Phuket is by bus. There is no train service. Most towns around and south of Bangkok have at least one daily bus line.

ISLAND ORIENTATION

No longer a meek, Clark Kent-ish escape, Phuket is now a Superman-sized resort. However, the area is a baht-sapping isle of Kryptonite to heroic budgeteers. Pioneers in search of that "off the beaten track" spot where they can experience the uniqueness of Thai culture should forge a path elsewhere.

Mangroves and prawn farms span Phuket Island's east coast, making it unsuitable for swimming. The development on the west coast's bleached beaches grows at exponential rates, and the crashing surf is drowned out by the relentless pounding of jackhammers.

For the penny-wise, Phuket town is a realistic base from which to explore the various beaches. Songthaews run from town to all the beaches (30-45min., 10-30฿) and the town still contains budget-minded bed and board. Renting a motorbike (150฿ per day) gives you the flexibility of dallying through several beaches in one day. Be aware that motorcycles have no insurance, and often no helmet, and that accidents are very common. The police are tired of careless tourists: as a "rich" *farang*, you may end up paying through the nose, even if an accident is not your fault.

The most appealing beaches for daytrips are **Nai Han, Surin,** and **Bang Tao. Nai Yang** is the only beach large enough to require an extensive stay for full exploration. **Kamala** is the only serene beach with affordable accommodations. **Patong, Karon,** and **Kata** have mini-cities built up around them, where everything costs twice as much as in Phuket town. The town itself gnaws at the southeastern tip of the island; the beaches are listed below clockwise from the town.

■■■ PHUKET TOWN

Phuket is famed in Thailand for its culinary delights; unless you are willing to make an exception and shell out the big baht, however, this may not be an obvious distinction for the budget traveler. Rather than stumbling upon cheap eats, when strolling through the city you will pass overpriced antique and gold shops, wait 10 minutes in the heat to cross traffic-ravaged streets, and meet with blank stares from other tourists searching for the "Jewel of the South" promised by travel guides. In the background, the peaceful whine of overloaded power lines will keep you wondering, how long can the city go on like this? Colonial architecture, old-fashioned cafés, and antique eateries with marble table tops allow you to retreat with a fruitshake and let somebody else worry about it.

ORIENTATION

Four main streets, two north-bound and two south-bound, radiate from the clock tower in the middle of town (the smaller one that works, in the center of the rotary, not the broken Seiko tower on the corner of Phang Nga and Thep Kasattri roads). **Thep Kasattri Road** (north) jets to the airport, intersecting Ratsada Rd., where the morning market buzzes. The market is farther down the street past the rotary, where the street becomes Ranong Rd. The songthaew station is on Ranong Rd. in front of the market; vehicles serve most destinations around the island (10-30฿). The GPO sits on **Montri Road** (north), which also originates from the clock tower, and crosses Phang Nga Rd., site of the bus station and many hotels. **Phuket Road** (south) passes the Ocean Shopping Mall and also creeps a few blocks north, to claim the TAT office (no.73-75). **Thilok Uthit I Road** (south) runs parallel to Phuket Rd. and ends in a T-intersection with Ong Sim Phai Rd. The night market sets up near here.

Although Phuket has undergone tremendous development, it is hardly an overwhelming metropolis. Nevertheless, the **central area** of Phuket town is a jumbled grid. Most accommodations are located within walking distance of the post office, as are the songthaew and inter-city bus stations, the day and night markets, and a spate of good eating spots. Your first move should be to pick up the free TAT map.

PRACTICAL INFORMATION

Tourist Office: Tourism Authority of Thailand (TAT), 73-75 Phuket Rd. (tel. 212 213 or 211 036). With the Seiko Tower at your back, go south on the right side of Phuket Rd. Cross one bridge and look left to the Honda dealership. The TAT's white facade and blue English sign are just across the street. If you reach the rotary, you've gone too far. Indispensable city and area maps, bus schedules, hotel lists, and pamphlets on entertainment, food, and shopping. Listings of official budget travel offices and agencies with bikes/jeeps for rent. Maps and info on Phang Nga and Krabi provinces. Staff speaks English, some French, Chinese, and Japanese. Open 8:30am-4:30pm.

Tourist Police: 5/39-40 Sakdidet Rd. (tel. 219 878), off the road in the St. Plaza Hotel. Emergency tel. 1699.

Budget Travel Office: Sea Tours Co. Ltd., 95-4 Phuket Rd. (tel. 218 417-8; fax 216 979), one block down from TAT on the left. Authorized representative of both **THAI Air** and **American Express.** Competitive prices for tours and flights. Books bus tickets. Open Mon.-Fri. 8:30am-5pm, Sat. 8:30am-noon. **K. International Tour,** 41/33 Montri Rd. (tel. 222 853-4), next to Downtown Tourist Shop. Affordable tours of **Similan Islands.** Reserves bus tickets. Open Mon.-Fri. 8am-6:30pm, Sat.-Sun. 8am-5pm.

Currency Exchange: Banks gather on Phang Nga Rd. in front of the On On Hotel. **Bangkok Bank,** 22 Phang Nga Rd. (tel. 211 292-5). Outside exchange booth is open daily 8:30am-5pm. Accepts Visa, AmEx at booth and ATM Machine. **Thai**

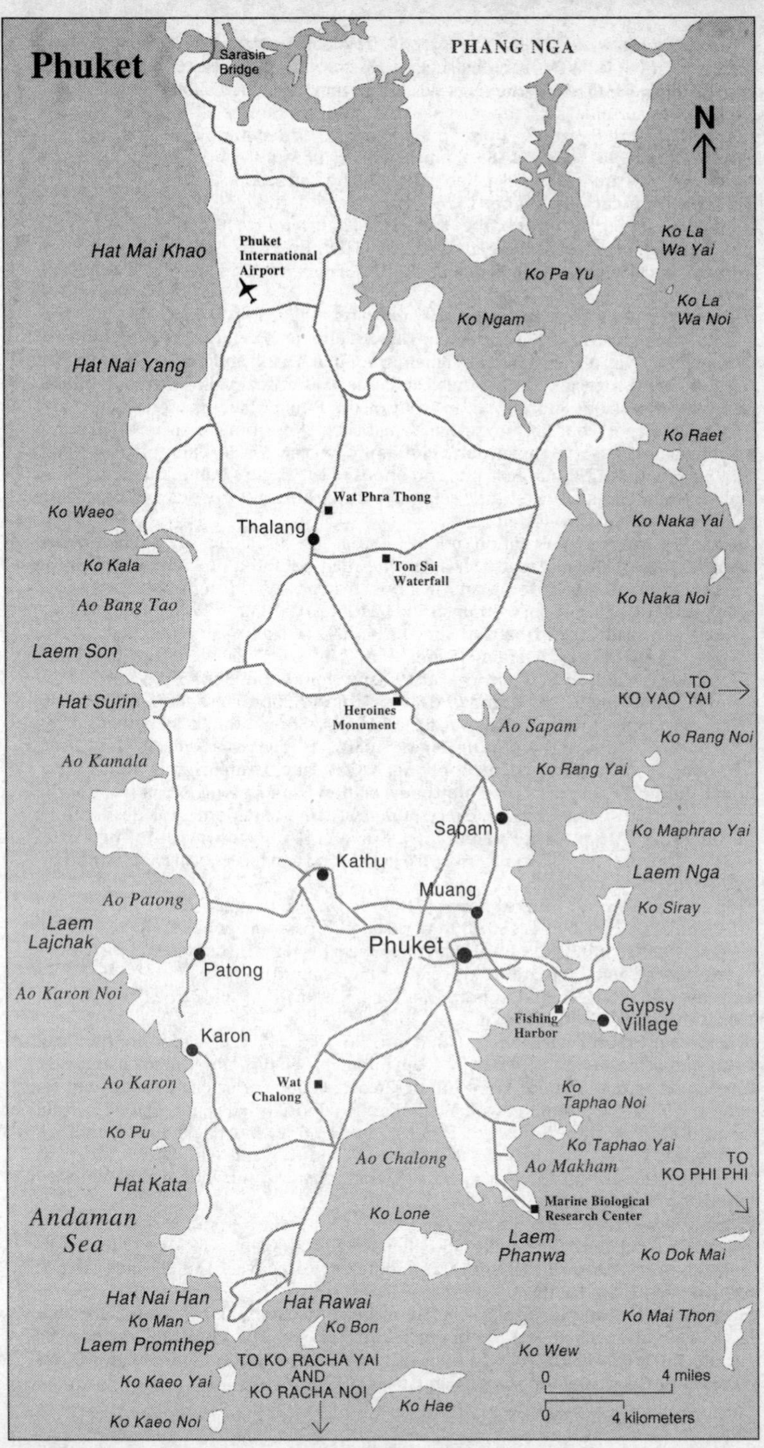
Phuket
Sarasin Bridge
PHANG NGA
N
Hat Mai Khao
Phuket International Airport
Ko La Wa Yai
Ko Pa Yu
Ko La Wa Noi
Ko Ngam
Hat Nai Yang
Ko Raet
Wat Phra Thong
Ko Waeo
Thalang
Ko Naka Yai
Ko Kala
Ton Sai Waterfall
Ao Bang Tao
Ko Naka Noi
Laem Son
TO KO YAO YAI
Hat Surin
Heroines Monument
Ao Sapam
Ko Rang Noi
Ao Kamala
Ko Rang Yai
Sapam
Ko Maphrao Yai
Kathu
Laem Nga
Muang
Ko Siray
Ao Patong
Laem Lajchak
Phuket
Patong
Ao Karon Noi
Gypsy Village
Fishing Harbor
Karon
Ko Taphao Noi
Ao Karon
Wat Chalong
Ko Pu
Ko Taphao Yai
Ao Chalong
Ao Makham
TO KO PHI PHI
Hat Kata
Marine Biological Research Center
Ko Lone
Andaman Sea
Laem Phanwa
Ko Dok Mai
Hat Nai Han
Hat Rawai
Ko Mai Thon
Ko Man
Ko Bon
Laem Promthep
Ko Wew
TO KO RACHA YAI AND KO RACHA NOI
0
4 miles
Ko Kaeo Yai
Ko Hae
0
4 kilometers
Ko Kaeo Noi

THAILAND

Farmer's Bank, 14 Phang Nga Rd. (tel. 217 125 or 211 558). Exchange booth accepts Visa, MC. ATM machine accepts Visa. Booth open daily 8:30am-6pm.

Post Office: 183/57-59 Phang Nga Rd. In the newly finished shopping plaza next to the bus terminal. A temporary location until the new post office is finished. Open Mon.-Fri. 8:30am-4:30pm., public holidays 9am-noon. Poste Restante. Also at 158 Montri Rd (tel. 211 020), on the corner of Montri and Thalang Rd.; open Mon.-Fri. 8:30am-4:30pm, Sat.-Sun. and holidays 9am-noon.

Telecommunications Office: 112/2 Phang Nga Rd. (tel. 216 861). The tall building with satellite dish east of the Phang Nga-Montri intersection on the way to the bus station. Overseas calling and fax (95-110฿ per page). Sells phone cards for domestic calls. Open daily 8am-midnight. Accepts AmEx, Visa, MC. **Telephone code:** 076.

Airport: Phuket International Airport, (tel. 327 230, through -37). On Rte. 4026, 28km north of Phuket town. Daily flights to Bangkok, weekly flights to Chiang Mai, Hat Yai, Nakhon Si Thammarat, Surat Thani, and Trang. International flights: THAI Airways, Dragon Air, Lauda Air, and China Airlines, among others. Songthaews (from Ranong Rd. in front of the Phuket daily market) run to and from the airport, but only go to Nai Yang beach 2km from the airport. Taxis and mini-buses also serve the airport. **Holiday Charter,** 74/56 Phumphon Rd. (tel. 246 088). Just off Phumphon Rd., and opposite the Eagle's Pub in the new Phumphon Night Plaza. Offers shuttle service to the airport (8-11 per day, 70฿); call for in-town pick-up at your hotel.

Buses: The inter-city bus station (tel. 211 480) is just off Phang Nga Rd. in the eastern section of the city, set back from the road behind a newly built shopping plaza. You can also ride on another bus, if it passes through your town. To: **Bangkok** (10 daily, 6am-6:30pm, 15hr., 210฿; A/C: 3:30, 5, 6pm, 14hr., 570฿); **Hat Yai** (4 daily, 6:20-10:20am, 8hr., 112฿; A/C: 6 daily, 8-11:45am, 7hr., 202฿); **Surat Thani** (8 daily, 4:45am-1:50pm, 6hr., 77฿; A/C: 7 daily, 7:30am-3pm, 5hr., 139-180฿); **Nakhon Si Thammarat** (9 daily, 4:30-11am, 8hr., 80-93฿; A/C: 7:20 and 8:20am, 7hr., 129฿; **Trang** (9 daily, 4:15am-12:20pm, 6hr., 78฿; A/C: 7 daily, 7am-5pm, 5hr., 140฿); **Krabi** (3 daily, 10:50am-2:30pm, 4hr., 47฿; A/C: 13 daily, 7am-5pm, 2-¾hr., 84฿); **Phang Nga** (5 daily, 10:10am-4:30pm, 2-½hr., 26฿); **Ranong** (3 daily, 8am-1:20pm, 6hr., 76฿; A/C: 3 daily, 10am-3:10pm, 5hr., 137฿).

Local Public Transport: The **songthaew** station is on Ranong Rd. in front of the town market; vehicles leave every 30min., (daily, 6am-6pm), for destinations around the island: **Kata Karon** (15฿), **Surin** (15฿), **Patong** (10฿), **Phromtep** (30฿), **Rawai** (10฿), **Kamala** (15฿). To get around town use local **mini-vans.** Bargain hard for a 10฿ fare.

Moped/Jeep Rental: Phuket Travel, 188 Phuket Rd. (tel. 226 175), opposite the TAT. Rents motor bikes (150-200฿ per day with passport deposit). Jeeps (700฿), trucks (800-1000฿), and cars (1200-1800฿) also for rent (insurance included, passport deposit and international drivers permit required).

Laundry: Saw Sag Reet Laundry, 34 Thep Kasattri Rd. (tel. 225 217), opposite the City Hotel. 7-15฿ per item.

Pharmacy: Pleon Pharmacy, 41/8 Montri Rd. (tel. 215 129). Opposite the Pearl Hotel, north of rotary. Open daily 10am-midnight. Fulfills minor medicinal needs.

English-Language Media: The Phuket Gazette contains articles about events on the Jewel of the South, as well as numerous editorials, ads, and general helpful info. **Radio Action,** 89 FM (tel 213 513 or 213 532) has English programming 6pm-2am. Check out the popular late show (11pm-1:30am) with DJ Marque, playing everything from King Crimson to Frank Sinatra to (no, not again!) Whitney Houston. Requests accepted.

English Bookstore: The Books, 53-55 Phuket Rd. (tel. 224 362 or 211 115), near TAT. Carries English best-sellers (Stephen King, Tom Clancy, Jackie Collins), periodicals (*SPIN, Mustang Monthly*), and some German novels. Coffee shop in back. Open daily 10am-10pm.

Hospitals: Mission Hospital at 4/1 Thepkasatri Rd. (tel. 211 173 or 212 386) has doctors who speak English. 24-hr emergency service. **The Medical Center** at 69 Krabi Rd. (tel. 212 853 or 215 666), is closest to budget accommodations. Has English-speaking doctors. Open 8am-5pm.

Emergency: tel. 1699.
Police: (tel. 212 115). Contact TAT first.

ACCOMMODATIONS

Budget lodgings in Phuket are rarer than one of Fabian Giraldo's good moods. The few digs are concentrated in the middle of town. Affordable rooms are much easier to come by during the low season (May-Sept.), when monsoons silence the touristic hullabaloo. Low-end rates remain fixed all year; middle and upscale prices fluctuate more. During the low season, specifics such as closing time are sometimes subject to unpredictable changes.

Suk Sabai Hotel, 82/9 Thep Kasattri Rd. (tel. 212 287 or 216 089). With the bus station at your back, turn right on Phang Nga Rd. Walk to 2nd intersection (Seiko Clock). The sign says Phuket Rd., it becomes Thep Kasattri Rd. Turn right and walk a few blocks until you cross a lime-green bridge. The 3-story, bright-yellow structure is visible down the next right (Suthat Rd. Soi 2). Nice and quiet, new and clean, a relaxing Calgon bath in building form. Spotless rooms with double bed and fan 140฿. Reception desk security box. Open daily 6am-midnight. Check-out noon.

Thara Hotel, 184/24 Thep Kasattri Rd. (tel. 216 208 or 213 788), 1 block north of Suk Sabai. Dim, down-trodden doubles with fans and refurbished private baths 130฿. A/C rooms, 250฿. Open at 8am; knock on the door when office is closed. Laundry service 5-7฿.

On On Hotel, 17 Phang Nga Rd. (tel. 211 154 or 225 740). With bus station at your back, turn right and walk through two intersections. Near the end of Phang Nga, across from Thai Farmer's Bank. Hotel front sports blue-green arches typical of island Sino-Portuguese style. Tidy rooms along winding wooden halls, Common shower/toilet areas sport peeling paint and interesting views. Single rooms have double beds. Rooms without baths have a sink. Singles 100฿, with bath 150฿, with A/C 250฿. Doubles with bath 220฿, with A/C 360฿. Reception desk safe 8am-9:30pm. Check-out noon.

FOOD

Chinese, western, conventional Thai, and Phuket seafood specialties mask some of Phuket's aesthetic shortcomings. The Ranong Rd. daily market snakes with aisles of finny and shelly produce and plentiful piles of tropical fruit. Eateries are mainly of the point-and-eat variety.

The **night market** at the junction of Tilok Uthit 1 and Ong Sim Phai Rd., stretches for several square blocks. With the giant broken Seiko at your back, follow Phuket Rd. south past the clock tower rotary to Metropolis Hotel. The market is on the left. Locals come to chat and flirt as much as to eat and snatch up deals on clothes, shoes, toys, and bags. Dress your fried chicken's feet in a new pair of flowered flip-flops.

Ka Jok See, 26 Takuapa Rd. (tel. 217 903). From the On On Hotel, this restaurant is 11 shops south of the Takuapa-Ratsada intersection on the right, half-hidden by a tangle of potted plants. Sit down at one of the well-worn wooden tables, amidst shelves of old china and pottery, and admire the "colored windows" that inspired the restaurant's name. Gracious dining in turn-of-the-century style. Even the food comes dressed; fried shrimp in noodle sarongs 60฿. Most dishes 50-60฿. English menu. Open Tues.-Sun. 6-11pm.

Muslim Restaurant, 1/1 Thep Kasattri Rd. (tel. 223 930) at the Thalang Rd. intersection. In the morning, there's roti, chicken curry, and of course *kow mook gai* (saffron rice with chicken, 20฿). Hot tea with sweet condensed milk soothes this vicious breakfast. Insure your tongue before opening up a flammable curry dinner. Open 7am-9pm (hours may vary).

Harry's Bar and Restaurant, 3/31 Taling Chan Lane. From the clock tower rotary look for the florescent Chinese temple. The street in front of this is Taling Chan Lane; follow this away from the rotary. Harry's is one block down, on the left. Authentic beef burgers (45฿) provide welcome relief for travelers approaching carbohydrate exhaustion. Expats often roll in for a hit of Euro (or Thai) food and English banter at breezy tables. Alert travelers can pick up the odd and useful fact about negotiating Phuket's tourist pitfalls. Open daily noon-2am.

SIGHTS

One of Phuket town's draws is its cultural melange, reflected in the Sino-Portuguese, Thai-influenced architecture. The On On Hotel and the two-story homes at the corner of Yaowarat and Thung Ka Rd. evoke images of Phuket's tin boom era.

If you're looking for an excuse to bask in the glow of A/C, the **Phuket Aquarium and Marine Biological Research Center** (tel. 391 126) fits the bill. Songthaews to the aquarium (Makahm Bay, until 5pm, 10฿) leave from Ranong Rd. The aquarium at Laem Phanwa is the last stop. The smallish aquarium is home to exotic undersea critters: electric eels, spiny lobsters, clown fish with rouged lips, and other aquatic wonders glide and slither before your eye, and peck at the divers cleaning the tanks. Whet your appetite here before going out for seafood (20฿, children 5฿).

■■■ RAWAI BEACH

Rawai can't brag about its ocean views, but it does scare up some meager budget options. During low tide, the beach becomes a swamp; its neighbor, Nai Han Beach, is more attractive and worth an overnight stay (despite the deluxe resort rooted here). Both are deserted in the low season, when monsoons menace the water.

On Rawai, **Pornmae Bungalows,** 58/1 Wisa Rd. (tel. 381 300), offers tidy bamboo bungalows with a double bed and bath for 800฿ per month, but these fill up fast year-round. If you fear Zephyrus will huff and puff and blow your bungalow down, hole up in a concrete bunker with a double bed and bath (western toilets) for 200฿, available all year. Additions to this package include refrigerator (300฿, high season 350฿) and A/C (400฿, high season 450฿). Reception is open daily 8am-10pm.

Friendship Beach, 27/1 Soi Mittrapap (tel. 381 281; fax 381 034). Two-for-one beers during happy hour (6am-7pm), excellent Thai and Euro food (ribs 100฿, lasagna 75฿), cable TV, a pool table, and occasional jazz have made this establishment the watering hole of many an expat and visiting *farang.* Beach-side bungalows come in large (sleeps 2-3 people; 300฿, high season 350฿), and *really* large (sleeps 4 people; 500฿, high season 700฿). To the left of the restaurant is the **Friendship Beach Second Hand Shop** (tel. 381 424 or 381 281; fax 381 034). The owner, Steve Brickley, stocks a modest selection of novels in English, French, and German, but the bulk of the shop is marine equipment. Sometimes Steve also has information on **yachts seeking crews for their jaunts across Southeast Asia.** Yacht owners frequently ask for money from sea-faring backpackers during high season, but will often pay for help during low season. The catch is, of course, fewer yachts pass through during the monsoons. Prior experience not necessarily requisite.

Save your appetite for Phuket Town. Otherwise **Lair Lae Thong** (tel. 381 300), next to the bungalows, has a breezy sitting area. Pricey service with a smile. Basic noodle/rice dishes 40฿ and up. Open 8:00am-11pm. Menus in English and German.

■■■ KATA BEACH

Kata Beach, a 2km banana-shaped sandy streak, is split into two sections, Kata Yai and Kata Noi, and garnished with humanely priced sleeping quarters and a splash of budget traveler flavor. At the junction between the two beach halves, Kata Center is a small town of night-owl bars, restaurants, hotels, and shops. During off-season, especially May-July, the area clears out, and prices plummet.

PRACTICAL INFORMATION

Tourist Police: tel. 212 468.

Island Travel: Kata Center Service, 114/24 Mu 4, Kata Center (tel. 330 582 or 330 135), on Patak Rd. next to Dan Kwian Restaurant, has competitive prices for trips to Phang Nga (350฿, high season 400 ฿), Coral Island (400฿ per day, high season only), and Phi Phi Island (500฿, high season 550฿). Open daily 9am-9pm.

Currency Exchange: Thai Farmers Bank, 114/6 Kata Beach (tel. 330 592) is down the street from Kata Center Service and off the main beach-side strip. Open daily 9:30am-8pm.

Post/Telephone Office: (tel. 330 937), lies on the main highway linking Phuket, Kata, and Patong. From Patak Rd. walk from the sea and turn right onto the highway. The office is one block up, on the right. Poste Restante, overseas phone, and telegram. Open Mon.-Fri. 8:30am-noon and 1-4:30pm, Sat. 9am-noon. **Postal code:** 83100. **Telephone code:** 076.

Local Transport: Songthaews from Phuket town leave from the market on Ranong Rd. daily until 5 pm (30min., 15฿). Songthaews stop near Kata Noi; you can also flag them on the main highway. **Tuk-Tuks** charge upwards of 150฿ if you miss the last songthaew back to Phuket Town. Many shops have motorbike rentals (150฿ per day).

Bookstores: Good Earth Secondhand Books, 114/52 Patak Rd., past the Kata Center office, buys and sells English books. Open Mon.-Sat. 11am-8pm. Upstairs wine bar and tea room sometimes has brownies (10฿).

Clinic: AR Clinic, 112/7 Patak Rd. (tel. 330 666), across from Thai Farmers Bank. Open Mon.-Sat. 11am-7pm. For **emergencies,** try Dr. Arin's beeper; dial 152 for an operator and then 108 650.

Police Station: Chalong Police Station (tel. 381 247) is nearby. Also a mini-station on Karon Beach.

ACCOMMODATIONS AND FOOD

Most guest houses have eateries and there are plenty of pricey seafood joints selling lobster, tiger prawns, and fish by the kilo.

Lucky Guest House sparkles at 110/44 Mu 4 Patak Rd. (tel. 330 572 or 330 334), halfway between the sea and main highway. From Pitak Rd. take the right fork at the Kata Center, go past Kata On Sea and look for the sign. Beautiful and extraordinarily clean. Singles have double beds, some rooms have balconies, and all rooms have private baths, though some are outside the rooms. Reception open daily 7am-11pm. Rooms with outside private baths (100฿, high season 250฿), with bath inside room (150฿, high season 350฿), and A/C (350฿, high season 400฿). Laundry service. Safe-deposit box open daily 10am-6pm.

Rose Inn, 110/24 Pitak Rd. Mu 4 (tel. 330 572 or 330 334), is a quiet guest house behind Kata Center Office. Quiet walkway lined with potted plants. Tidy rooms with private bath. Rooms 200฿, high season 250฿.

Dive Café, 111/15 Patak Rd., About 1 "block" toward the water from Rose Inn. Delve into that scuba diver psyche. House specialty is *Gai Manao* (lemon chicken) 45฿, coffee shakes 15-20฿. Superb. Open daily 9am-10pm.

ENTERTAINMENT

If you have the cash, this area has world-class **snorkeling** and **diving** around the Similan or Racha Islands (off the eastern and southern coasts, respectively). Otherwise, make a splash at the bar scene in Kata Center. Wince at all types of music and video.

Siam Diving Center, 121/9 Patak Rd. (tel. 330 936), at the midpoint between Kata and Karon, is a PADI five-star center with divemasters. Explore some of the world's best **diving** and **underwater coral reef formations.** Four-day diver certification courses cost 6,900฿, including transport, equipment, and food. Rentals available for 600฿ per day. Open daily 9am-6pm.

Dan Kwian, 114/21-22 Kata Center, is an old standby, a rock bar/restaurant with live music from 9pm-midnight. Liquor 40฿. Open 8am-midnight, off-season 9am-11pm. Happy hour 8-11pm.

■■■ THE NORTHWESTERN COAST

Escapees from the rat race can scurry to the quiet-as-a-mouse **Kamala Beach,** on the way to Surin from Phuket for a 20฿ bus ride (last bus to Phuket town, 3pm). There are no big hotels (yet), and the ultramarine water and snowy sand are the same as elsewhere on the island. If you want to hibernate up here, guest houses are popping up all over. Stays should be in the range of 250-300฿ in low season and about 75฿ more in high season. **Kamala Group House,** located past the police station on the left at 93/4 Mu 3 (tel. 324 426), offers miraculously spotless second floor rooms for rent (doubles with bath 300฿ year round). Downstairs, multi-lingual testaments to **Kamala Seafood's** culinary exploits graffiti the walls. Dishes average 50฿ and up. Complete the Kamala Group experience with a novel (20฿ per day) from the **Kamala Group Service Library** or rent one of their motorcycles (200-300฿ per day with passport deposit) or jeeps (700-800฿ with insurance). When not eating sleeping, or reading, mosey over to **Diver's Place.** Run by an Australian native, Diver offers 45฿ beer, Thai and foreign food, info. on lodgings, spontaneous touch football and volleyball games, all in addition to great sunset conversation (just don't bother him during Aussie Rugby games). Open 9:30am till the last beer is finished.

The deep blue waters at nearby **Surin Beach** have been spared from the voracious jaws of beachfront development; the beast is beginning to surface, however. The only lodgings here are large resorts up the road, but plans for guest houses are in the works. Small, costly seafood joints dot the beach.

Bang Tao is a long attractive beach dominated by two resort complexes that have monopolized access to the water, denying penniless pilgrims a room at the inn. Restaurants on the beach charge 60-100฿ for basic seafood meals. If you bring your own food, a towel, and some Faulkner, Bang Tao makes a nice daytrip, especially in May and July, when the heavy rains haven't hit but the crowds have skedaddled.

Nai Yang Beach, a 13km Eden of coconut and rubber trees, is part of a national park. The government recognition has kept private developers at bay, although the condo vultures anxiously circle the park boundaries. Currently, the only **accommodation** is a set of government-run bungalows. The **visitors office** (tel. 327 407) is near the entrance (open daily 8am-4:30pm). Two-person concrete bungalows with bath 250฿, 4-person set-up 400฿. Rooms away from the water (shared bath) 200฿. **Camp** on the beach (bring your own equipment) for 10฿ per night. The office has a safe and serves food from 8am to 9pm (fried rice 25฿).

THAILAND

ON THE MAINLAND

■■■ PHANG NGA

Splashing about halfway between Phuket and Krabi, Phang Nga Bay has become a popular spot for boat tours that weave between the craggy islets jutting abruptly from the water. Entrepreneurs, however, are quickly turning the beatific bay into a chaotic labyrinth. Its quiet majesty is often interrupted by the roar of out-board engines and the whir of Nikons scanning the rocky niches for neoprene-clad *Sports Illustrated* supermodels left behind from their shoot in 1988.

The steep, unique rock formations are worth a climb early in the morning or late in the afternoon, when the Phuket crowds have dwindled. For good access to the Bay, stay at the nearby Muslim fishing village of Ko Panyi, which is infinitely more satisfying than sightless Phang Nga town. The bay is not as developed as Phuket or Krabi, meaning fewer hotels and English-menu restaurants.

ORIENTATION

Emerging from the **bus station** area outside the town center, you'll be on **Phetkasem Road.** Hotels, banks, and most eating spots are several blocks off to the right.

The police station, post office, and hospital are to the left. Phang Nga town runs along Phetkasem Rd. for about 3-4km, quickly thinning out in both directions. Most facilities are within walking distance, except for the post office and hospital, which are a few km outside of the town center.

PRACTICAL INFORMATION

Tourist Information: Sayan Tour (tel. 430 348), next to the bus terminal, offers tours of Phang Nga Bay and Ko Panyi, maps, and bus schedules. Run by English-speaking Sayan Tamtopol; TAT-approved and helpful. Open daily 8am-6pm.

Currency Exchange: Bangkok Bank, 120 Phetkasem Rd. (tel. 411 362 or 411 361), across the street from the bus station, 1 block down to the right. Open Mon.-Fri. 8:30am-3:30pm. **Krung Thai Bank,** 109 Phetkasem Rd. (tel. 412 010 or 411 810) has the same hours.

Post office: (tel. 412 171). On Phetkasem Rd. about 2km to the left of the bus station. Poste Restante. Open Mon.-Fri. 8:30am-4:30pm, Sat.-Sun. 9am-noon. **Overseas calls** and telegram located upstairs. Open daily 8:30am-4:30pm. **Postal code:** 82000. **Telephone code:** 076.

Buses: Next to the Government Savings Bank on Phetkasem Rd. in the middle of town and is marked by a sign. To: **Bangkok** (Fan: 5:30pm, 14hr., 205฿; A/C: 4pm, 13hr., 346฿; VIP: 5pm, 13hr., 510฿); **Hat Yai** (Fan: 4 daily, 8:45am-12:30pm, 6hr., 94฿; A/C: 6 daily, 8:30am-1:10pm, 6hr., 163฿); **Krabi** (Fan: 13 daily, 7:30am-4:45pm, 2hr., 25฿; A/C: 5 daily, 8:30am-1:10pm, 43฿); **Phuket** (Fan: 18 daily, 6:30am-5:45pm, 2hr., 25฿; A/C: 9 daily, 11:40am-7pm, 2hr., 47฿); **Surat Thani** (4 daily, 6:30am-1:30pm, 3hr., 50฿; A/C: 3 daily, 9:30am-1:30pm, 3hr., 120฿); **Ko Samui** (9:30, 11:30am, 6-½hr., 180฿ including ferry); and **Trang** (6 daily, 7:30am-6:30pm, 4hr., 57฿; A/C: 4 daily, 9:30am-3pm, 4hr., 102฿). **A/C minivans for Malaysia** stop at Sayan Tour daily at 10am. To: **Hat Yai** (5hr. 200฿); **Penang** (9hr., 520฿); **Kuala Lumpur** (20hr., 720฿); and **Singapore** (24hr., 820฿).

Local Transportation: songthaews (5฿) run up and down Phetkasem Rd.

English Bookstore: 82 Phetkasem Rd. (tel. 412 194), near the Kodak store and the market, has *The Bangkok Post* and *The Nation.*

Pharmacy: 91 Phetkasem Rd., near the market. Open Mon.-Fri. 7-8:30am, 4:30-9pm, Sat.-Sun. 7am-9pm.

Hospital: Phang Nga Hospital, 436 Phetkasem Rd. (tel. 412 032 or 411 616), is about 2km on the left from the bus station. A busy hospital, this is where people hang out since they don't have a mall.

Police Station: 193 Phetkasem Rd. (tel. 412 073), left of the bus station about 0.5km.

ACCOMMODATIONS

Thaweesuk Hotel, 79 Phetkasem Rd. (tel. 411 686), on the bus station side of the street and several blocks to the right as you exit the station. An enthusiastic Mr. Rourke-ian manager welcomes *farang*. Rooms are basic, but the best part is the easily accessible roof-top—good for drying clothes and commanding a perfect view of the Phang Nga mountain range. Singles 100฿. Doubles 150฿. The reception desk is in the front of the grocery store next door, open 6am-11pm. Safe deposit box, tours, and laundry service are available. Check-out noon.

Muang Thong Hotel, 128 Phetkasem Rd. (tel. 412 132). Stay here if you're looking for a more indigenous flavor at your evening's lodging. The manager speaks little English, but an English sign lists the prices for a decent room, bath, and fan. The establishment is across from the bus station about 1 block down to the right. Singles with bath 120฿, and A/C 250฿. Doubles with bath 180฿, and A/C 320฿. Check-out noon. Desk open 7am-midnight.

FOOD

Phang Nga won't be over-run by galloping gourmets anytime in the near future. There are a couple of places with English menus, but translations are often accompanied by higher prices. Food quality is best gauged by crowd capacity.

The **morning market,** off Phetkasem Rd. near the Fuji shop, offers enough fruit to satisfy your RDA requirement for many moons. The late afternoon **vendors** along

Phetkasem Rd. near the hospital and post office are unobjectionable. Vendors also line up along Riverside Rim Kong Rd., showering patrons with Thai pop and affordable cuisine (30-40฿). Squat on mats around low tables and admire Phang Nga's fiery mountain sunsets. From Phet Kasem Rd., walk through the market. Exit onto the road behind the market and turn left. Walk past the Chinese Temple and turn onto the next road to the right. Handy accessories to bring are mosquito repellant and a flashlight for the trip home. Late night drinking goes on, so women alone should take precautions. Open about 4:30pm-midnight.

Duang Seafood, 122 Phetkasem Rd. (tel. 412 216), near the Muang Thong Hotel, across from the green Fuji film sign. Outclasses rivals with snazzy English menu and requisite mark-up. If you speak Thai and look like Bon Jovi the chef will blow kisses at you. Dishes above 40฿. Shrimp with corn 50฿. Open daily 10am-9pm.

■ NEAR PHANG NGA

The top-heavy calcite formations that spring from the sea have made Phang Nga Bay an increasingly popular tourist attraction. Travel offices in Phuket and Krabi book tours (at least 300฿ for a daytrip), sending squadrons of high-powered boats racing about the Bay's mangrove-lined waterway between 10am and 2pm. Big ducats are dished out for a glimpse of **Khao Ping Kan** and **Ko Tapu,** the twin nail-shaped rock-islands that preen in the bay of Khao Ping Kan island and appear in the James Bond film, *Man With the Golden Gun.* The rock's base is gradually dissolving, threatening the total collapse of the precarious formation.

Songthaews from Phang Nga town go to the pier (10฿), where long-tailed boats can be chartered for a spin around the islands (over 500฿ for a few hours). **Sayan** (tel. 430 348), whose office is located in the same lot as the Phang Nga bus terminal, offers a reputable tour service. Sayan's excursions include lesser-explored caves such as the **Naga cave,** a prehistoric site where paintings, shell middens, and burial sites can be found. Furthermore, his tour gets going before most of the tourists from Phuket and Krabi arrive. Four-hour (7:30am and 2pm, 150฿) and full-day tours (7:30am, 300฿) available daily. During low season, prices and schedule may vary based on the number of people. Try to get a group. During high season Sayan sometimes offers a tour of Phang Nga's wats and waterfalls as well. Inquire for details.

KO PANYI

Most tours dock at **Ko Panyi,** a Muslim fishing village constructed on stilts over the water. Over 250 years ago, an enterprising Indonesian fisherman agreed with two fellow seamen to search for fertile islands. Each fisherman had to raise a flag over a newly discovered island as a sign that the land was ready for habitation. Ko Panyi was settled in this way, with seafaring colonists spotting the tell-tale *panyi* (flag) and moving in. The present population is about 1500; there is a post office, health clinic, primary school, cemetery, and a mosque where almost everyone in the village prays five times a day. An overnight stay at Ko Panyi is definitely worthwhile, since the village is completely different after the daytrippers have packed up and gone back to the mainland. At the end of the day, people emerge from their homes to carry on the tasks of everyday living: cooking, cleaning, and gossiping with neighbors.

For an additional 150฿, Sayan will gladly arrange **accommodation** in his own home, a yummy Thai breakfast, and a sunrise boat trip back to Phang Nga pier the next morning. He has a notebook overflowing with multi-lingual superlatives from former house guests. Beware of imposters; many people have used Sayan's name and plagiarized his brochure to entice tourists and rip them off.

■■■ KRABI

A paradigm of Southern cities, Krabi is not a destination in and of itself, but rather a transit point for travelers who have made the *pak Thai* pilgrimage to shack up on a sassy beach nearby or set sail for a spectacular isle off the coast. The town is about 150km south of Surat Thani and attracts *farang* families and a motley bunch of backpackers in the high season. From November to March the blue waters of the Andaman Sea are calm and clear, making for smooth passage to the **Phi Phi Islands** and **Ko Lanta.** Few families remain in town during the low season, when the monsoons move in and turn the water a turbulent opaque, but young backpackers still slouch about, relishing the silence, solitude, and reduced hotel rates.

The **Phi Phi Islands** and **Ko Lanta**, along with **Ko Poda** and **Ko Hua Khwaan (Chicken Island),** offer opportunities to observe a plethora of aquatic critters. Of the nearby beaches, **Rai Lay** and **Phra Nang beaches** are the most secluded (reached only by boat) and the most beautiful. Get the goods before everyone else does.

Prices in town vacillate greatly with the seasons, as do the community's tourist services. Boats to beaches and islands halt on monsoon days; ferries to Ao Nang quiet their engines from April to September. Low-budget bungalows in Krabi as well as on Phi Phi and Ko Lanta often shut down for the low season. Remaining establishments will ransom rooms for a paltry sum.

ORIENTATION

Buses entering Krabi usually go only as far as the station, 5km out of the town. Red songthaews go from the station to town (5฿). Songthaews from the bus station drop people off on **Maharat Road.** Running parallel between Maharat Rd. and **Krabi River** is **Utarakit Road,** home to banks, the post office, tour offices, and two guest houses. Krabi's small **TAT office** is also located on Utarakit Rd., in a small, one-story building along the water. From Maharat Rd., you can walk down **Prachachoen Road** or any other cross street to access Utarakit Rd. and the river. The daily morning **market** is at the intersection of **Pruk-sa-uthit** and **Srisawat Road,** between the two roads and one block in from the river.

Boats to Phra Nang Beach, Phi Phi Island, and Ko Lanta leave from **Chao Fah Pier;** from the Grand Tower Guest House, walk down **Chao Fah Road** to the water and it will be in front of you. The **night market** is on **Kong Ka Road,** which intersects Utarakit Rd. and runs along Chao Fah Pier. That TAT office has a rather poor **map** of Krabi and the vicinity. **P.S. Tours and Guest House** sells good maps of the area for 40฿. The map is useful not only for navigating Krabi town, but also for locating the area's beaches and islands.

PRACTICAL INFORMATION

Tourist Office: TAT office (tel. 612 740), on Utarakit Rd., past the Floating Restaurant along the river, on the right as you walk toward the bus station. At least their English is better than their maps. Get better info at P.S. Tours and Guest House. Open daily 8:30am-4:30pm.

Tours: P.S. Tours and Guest House, 71/1 Utarakit Rd. (tel. 611 308). A wealth of data on Krabi's beaches as well as those on Phi Phi Island and Ko Lanta. Boat tours of Ko Poda, Ko Yung (Mosquito Island), and Ko Mai Phai (Bamboo Island). A day tour costs 250฿ (lunch, snorkeling equipment—prices will be increasing soon). To Ko Phi Phi and Ao Nang, 570฿. Good maps of Krabi and vicinity. Arranges bus service to other cities and boats to beaches. Open daily 8am-10pm. **Grand Tours,** 73/1 Utarakit Rd. (tel. 621 456 or 611 741), 1 block back toward the TAT, from the intersection of Utarakit and Chao Fah Rd. Minibus service to Hat Yai (150฿) or Phuket (180฿). Books train/bus tickets to Surat Thani, Bangkok, and Chiang Mai and reserves plane tickets. Day tours of Phi Phi and Phang Nga Bay. Open daily 6:30am-9pm. **Jungle Book Tour,** 141 Utarakit Rd. (tel. 611 148). Pamphlets and pictures of guest houses in Krabi, tours to islands in Krabi and Phang Nga, reserves guest houses and bus, train, and plane tickets to Malaysia and Singapore. Open 7am-9pm.

Currency Exchange: Bangkok Bank, 147 Utarakit Rd. (tel. 811 186 or 811 785), on the left, about 1 block from the TAT office. Open Mon.-Fri. 8:30am-3:30pm. 24-hr. ATM accepts Visa. **Siam City Bank,** 93 Utarakit Rd. (tel. 611 320), 1 block from Bangkok Bank toward P.S. Tours. Exchange booth, open daily 8:30am-4pm.

Post Office: 190 Utarakit Rd. (tel. 611 050; fax 612 914), across from P.S. Tours about ½ block up. Poste Restante. Open Mon.-Fri. 8:30am-4:30pm, Sat. 9am-noon. **Overseas calls, telegram,** and **fax service** upstairs open daily 7am-midnight. Visa/MC and AmEx accepted. **Postal code:** 81000. **Telephone code:** 075.

Buses: The **bus station** (tel. 611 804, 612 847, or 711 601) is 5km outside town. Red songthaews run between town and the bus station (every 15min., 5฿). Hail them anywhere or swing by Maharat Rd., where they often stop. To: **Bangkok** (4 daily, 3:30-5:20pm, 14hr., 161฿; A/C: 3 daily, 4-5pm, 13hr., 290฿; VIP: 5pm, 12 hr., 425฿); **Hat Yai** (4 daily, 10:30am-2:10pm, 4-5hr., 78฿; A/C: 6 daily, 12:30-5:20pm, 4hr., 127฿); **Phang Nga** (every hr., 7am-4pm, 2hr., 25฿; A/C: 5 daily, 9:30am-4pm, 2hr., 45฿); **Phuket** (3 daily, 6:30am-4:30pm, 3-4hr., 46฿; A/C: 1 daily, 2:35pm, 3hr., 84฿); and **Trang** (every hr., 6:20am-3pm, 2-3hr., 30฿; A/C: 6 daily, 9:30am-8:30pm, 2hr., 66฿). To **Surat Thani,** there is a private A/C service that leaves from Chao Fah Pier (7, 11am, and 3:30pm, 3hr., 150฿).

Boats: Long-tailed boats leave from Chao Fah Pier at the end of Chao Fah Rd. to **Phra Nang Beach** and **Rai Lay Beach** (45min., 40฿) and to **Ao Nang Beach** (1 hr., 65฿), 9am-4pm (to 6pm high season). The boat to **Ko Lanta** leaves from the pier Oct.-April daily at 1:30pm (2-½hr., 150฿). These leave as soon as they fill up, usually with 6-8 people. Boat service is irregular in the low season (May-Sept.). Convince the boatman to leave with 4 people during this time since it's usually less crowded, or charter the boat for 200฿. **Ferries** to **Ko Phi Phi** leave regularly during the high season. Regular (9:30am and 2:30pm, 2hr., 125฿); A/C express boats during high season only (10:30am and 2:30pm, 1-¼hr., 180-200฿). During the low season, ferry service may be irregular. Tour companies, including P.S. and Grand, arrange boat trips (125฿).

Local Transportation: Krabi is small enough to permit getting anywhere (except the bus station and beach areas) by foot. Local songthaews (the red ones) run to and from the bus station (5฿). Songthaews to Ao Nang Beach, Hat Noppharat Thara, and Shell Cemetery leave Utarakit Rd. near the Floating Restaurant, or from Pattana Rd., across from the New Hotel (15฿).

Motorbikes/Jeeps: Grand Tour, 73/1 Utarakit Rd. (tel. 612 948). Motorbikes 200฿ per day. Jeep with insurance 800฿ per day, with A/C 1200฿.

English Bookstore: Kong Pen, 111 Utarakit Rd., 5 stores down from Lisa Bakery toward P.S. Tour. Has English, Chinese, and German newspapers; *USA Today* (35฿). Open 7:30am-8pm. **Fai Books,** 91 Utarakit (tel. 612 178). From Tom Robbins to Tolkien in French, German, English, and Norwegian. Open 7am-7pm.

Pharmacy: 2/4 Pattana Rd. (tel. 620 545), facing Rimnam Restaurant, with the large sign advertising birth control pills. Open 6:30am-9pm.

Hospital: (tel. 611 210), 5km out of town on Utarakit Rd. From Chao Fah Pier, it's toward the TAT office. **24-hr. number:** tel. 611 227. Some doctors speak English.

Emergency: tel. 191 or call the TAT (tel. 612 740).

Police: Utarakit Rd. (tel. 611 222), on the same side of the street as the post office, about ½km down, heading out of town. Little English spoken. Bring a translator or someone from the TAT (tel. 612 740).

ACCOMMODATIONS

Jungle Book Guest House, 141 Utarakit Rd. (tel. 611 148), behind the tour office and restaurant. Just the bear necessities here. The lion sleeps tonight in box-like rooms with fans. Bright lights make up for small windows. Common showers and bathrooms. 50฿ all year. Newly assembled boxes, 80฿. Transit point for Mowglis getting on a boat.

KR Mansions and Guest House, 52/1 Chao Fah Rd. (tel. 612 761/2). From Grand Tower Guest House walk up Chao Fah Rd., away from the river. On the right about ½km up the road. Away from downtown din, with rooftop and deck chairs for enjoying breezy days. Common baths have sinks outside. Singles 120฿, with bath 150 ฿. Doubles 200฿, with bath 250฿. Prices may fluctuate with lunar cycles. Open 7am-10pm. Check-out noon. Restaurant, laundry service, tours.

Grand Tower Guest House, 73/1 Utarakit Rd. (tel. 611 741 or 621 456), on the corner of Chao Fah Rd. Lowest rates for 7th-floor digs which contain only a double mattress and flaking paint chips. No elevator. Other chambers are bright and brand new. Ceiling fan and a big window dissipate heat. Open daily 7am-10pm. Singles 80฿, with bath 180฿. Doubles with larger room 120฿, with 2 double beds 220฿. Safe-deposit and laundry services (high season).

FOOD

Krabi is a three-ring circus of big-top food. The **day** and **night markets** serve a thrilling menagerie of cuisine—it's impossible even to list the highlights. The Andaman Sea ensures a steady supply of seafood, to which the chefs of Krabi's excellent restaurants apply their exuberant imaginations.

Ruenmai Thai, 319 Utarakit Rd. (tel. 611 365), on the outskirts of town, 2km toward the hospital on the left (best to take a tuk-tuk). Fortify yourself for yet another day of frolicking with savory examples of Krabi's indigenous cuisine. Forget *pad thai*! Foreigners rave over coconut prawn soup with *pak mieng* (40฿) and spicy manila pea salad (45฿). *Nam prik* dishes (a shrimp and pepper dip) come with an assortment of 8 unique Thai herbs and vegetables. The soft-spoken owner is a local activist for sustainable development in Krabi's tourist industry. Open daily 10:30am-10pm.

Jungle Book Restaurant, 141 Utarakit Rd. (tel. 611 148), in the tour office. Your tummy will roar like Shere Kahn for their breakfasts. Muesli with fruit and yogurt 25฿, cereal 20฿, American breakfast 45฿, ham 'n cheese omelette 20฿. Excellent English menu. Open 7am-8pm.

■ AROUND KRABI

Krabi's world-renowned beaches on the mainland outside of town, as well as on neighboring islands, are some of the most popular tourist magnets in Thailand during the high season (Nov.-March). The fact certainly is not lost on the local population, which heartily embraces the arrival of transient sun-and-sand lovers and their wallets. In the high season, hotels, guest houses, and bungalows spring to life from their monsoon-drenched dormancy and fill to capacity. Recently, the local industry has shifted its target from the low-budget market to more upscale, middle-budget vacationers. There is still plenty of surf for the cash-clogged, but prices are rapidly rising, and several expensive resorts stud nearby beaches. During the low season, many beaches are inaccessible.

AO NANG

The cove is the only beach, besides Hat Noppharat Thara, that is a national park area reached by land. The sand on the long beach is not as plush as the silky silica on Phra Nang Beach or Ko Phi Phi, and rivers of traffic lend a somewhat urban atmosphere, but dry up past the Phra Nang Inn. From here, walk down a dirt road into forested areas and more secluded hideaways. Prices on Ao Nang have skyrocketed within the past year; most bungalows fold up during the low season.

Gift Bungalows (tel. 723 1128), at the center of Ao Nang Beach, screened from the road by masses of exuberant tropical vegetation, presents a decent restaurant (open during the high season) and small but well-kept bungalows. Baths are roofless—no need to turn on the faucet come rainy season. Singles 150฿ low season, 250฿ high season; doubles 200฿ low season, 300฿ high season. All rooms with bath. Open 6:30am-midnight during high season; 7:30am-5pm during low season.

Gift's Restaurant is endowed with a solid selection of western and Thai food: brown bread with jam, beans, or Nutella, Thai omelettes, and fruit pancakes. High season open 7:30am-9:30pm. At the terminus of Ao Nang Beach, where the road becomes a dusty dirt trail, there's **Last Café,** which is only open high season (drinks available in low season). Home-made brown bread rises to the occasion, and customers keep rolling in for Muesli with fruit and yogurt (35฿), Thai omelettes (30฿), or Thai noodle soup (30฿). Without electricity, the restaurant must rely on lanterns for nocturnal luminescence—the final word in romantic dining. Open 6:30am-midnight. When you're sick of the bungalow basics, the ideally situated **Phra Nang Inn**

(tel. 612 173) has surprisingly proletarian prices (40-60฿) for a *bourgeois* linen-napkined resort. Green curry soup with shrimp and rice is exceptional and rich enough to satisfy an ocean-sized appetite (60฿). Shrimp in tamarind sauce is another savory item (60฿). Open 7-10am for breakfast buffet, 10am-2pm, and 5-10pm.

Tired of arriving deafened by long-tailed boat engines at less-than-stellar tourist attractions? **Sea Canoe** was founded in 1983 with the goals of developing "sustainable business opportunities with local people that promote environmental conservation by providing high-quality recreational adventures specializing in Natural History and cross-cultural education." Sea Canoe Krabi (tel. 01 464 4403) is located opposite Phra Nang Inn and offers half-day (700฿) and full-day (1400฿) self-paddled trips along the coast, as well as rental equipment. Amex, Visa, MC accepted.

During the high season, in the center of the road that runs past the beach, where songthaews drop off and pick up, there's a small branch of **Bangkok Bank,** a **"supermarket,"** a restaurant, and two **tour offices,** but these are often closed during the low season. For **police,** the number is the same as Krabi's (tel. 611 222; **emergency** tel. 191). Songthaews from Krabi to Ao Nang (and Hat Noppharat Thara) leave from Pattana Rd. across from the New Hotel, ½-block in from the river (every 15min. or when full, 15฿). Last songthaew back to Krabi leaves at 4:30pm low season; 6pm high season.

HAT PHRA NANG AND HAT RAI LAY

Color yourself ecstatic at road-less **Phra Nang Beach,** which has whiter sand and more aqua-colored water than Ao Nang. You'll quickly descend from Cloud Nine when you find that the only beach-front lodging is a resort whose rooms command 8000-60,000฿ per night, low season 6000฿. Bungalows clump among the coconut palms on a narrow spit of land that spans east and west Hat Rai Lay. On the **East Rai Lay Beach** side, the scene is generally quieter and cheaper. **West Rai Lay Beach,** however, has a wider, whiter stretch of sand with clear water that practically washes up to you and begs for a belly-flop. Wherever you stay you will never be farther than a few minutes walk to either beach. All bungalows serve food.

Boats stop on East Rai Lay Beach. The first bungalow on the south end is **Rai Lay Bay Bungalow 2** (tel. 611 944, ext. 41), which has bamboo bungalows with small balconies and mosquito nets, Thai toilets, tin walls, and no sink (150฿, off-season 80฿). Reception open 7am-9:30pm. English movies are shown here nightly. Farther north along the beach, wooden signs posted on coconut trees advertise the **Cave Blue Bar's** famous house reggae party (April-Nov. only), a grand open-air bar, and a restaurant. Open 6pm-2am. They also have bamboo bungalows with mosquito nets, fans, showers, and Thai toilets in cement-floored bathrooms for 80-100฿, with bath 150-180฿. Closed during off-season. Check-in 6am-10pm.

An exotic new species has begun to haunt the cliffs that crowd Rai Lay's velvety beaches. Rock climbers have found the mild climate (and not so mild nightlife), as well as the verticality of Rai Lay, perfect for a winter retreat. The biggest drawback is falling coconuts. **Tex Rock Climbing School** of East Rai Lay offers beginner courses to the beach-bored—half-day (400฿), full-day (700฿), and 3-day (2000฿) courses with signed waiver of liability. Equipment rental (800฿ per day) and guides available for the experienced. Also offered are one-day treks (700฿) and pinnacle-top camping trips (1200฿).

West Rai Lay Beach can be reached by the walkway between the Sun Rise Bungalow and the **Rai Lay Bay Bungalow 1** (tel. (01) 476 4925). Passports are required to check in. Accommodations for every budget. Singles 80฿; 150฿ high season. Small and large doubles 100฿, 120฿; 300฿, 350฿ high season. Triples 200฿, 400฿ high season. Mini-chalets with tinted glass and bathtubs sleep four and are a low season bargain (200฿ low season, 500฿ high season). Singles, doubles, and triples all have concrete floors, bamboo walls, tin-walled bath with passably clean flushing toilets. Reception open 7:30am-10pm. Restaurant is pricey, but popular for its outdoor seating and gorgeous beach views. *Pad thai* 40฿, fried rice 40฿. Open 7:30am-9:30pm. Two English movies shown nightly during high season, one during low. Also has bus schedules and an overseas call booth. Next door, **Sand Sea** (tel. (01) 722 01140) has bamboo huts with mosquito nets, clean rooms, and bathrooms with tiled floors and Thai toilet. All singles 250฿, with fan 350-400฿, low-season all 100฿. Doubles that sleep 3 are newer and airy, with toilets that flush and gleam (600-650฿, 250฿ off-season). Restaurant offers fried rice with seafood 35-40฿, spaghetti 40฿. Open 7am-9:30pm. Reception open 8am-9:30pm. **Currency exchange** 9am-9pm. Next to Sand Sea is **Rai Lay Village Bungalows,** (tel. (01) 228 4366). Promenade along the coconut palm alley to your quiet single (130฿ low season, 200฿ high season; with fan: 300฿ low season, 600฿ high season) or double with fan (400฿ low season, 600฿ high season) or to the fabulous A/C room (600-1000฿ low season, 1000-1200฿ high season). Surfside **restaurant** serves ginger beef 30฿ and other Thai and American favorites. Reception open daily 7am-10pm.

Along the walkway between East and West Rai Lay Beach lounges an **English bookstore** with paperbacks for rent (10฿). Greek, French, Swedish, Greek, and Danish material also available. Two **mini-marts** have sprouted up on West Rai Lay in case you run out of 'tater chips. The **laundry service** (tel. (01) 722 22 40) lathers up at Sakuna Gift Shop (5-20฿; open 8am-midnight).

Equation for Exploitation

$$\frac{\text{Natural Beauty}}{\text{distance from mainland}} \times H_2O \text{ clarity (\% coral remaining)} = \text{tourism coefficient}$$

KO PHI PHI AND KO LANTA

Cheap deals and quiet, safe bungalows are rapidly becoming endangered species on **Ko Phi Phi,** as the island becomes an exploited paradise for increasing numbers of visitors. Phi Phi Don has the white sandy beaches, the coconuts, the lush vegetation, and blue water, but is also one of the worst examples of overdevelopment in a national park. During the high season, fresh water, food, and accommodations are precious commodities. Some hold-out bungalows still go for 100-200฿ during the high season (no fan or bath) at **Phi Phi Andaman,** (tel. (01) 723 1073, 200-400฿), **Maphrao Resort,** (180-400฿), and **Gipsy Village,** (100-250฿). Most other bungalows charge a minimum of 200-300฿ during the high season.

For getting to Phi Phi (See "Practical Information" on page 525.). Daytrips can be arranged at P.S. Tours in Krabi; they include snorkeling around **Phi Phi Don, Ao Maya** (with prehistoric cave painting), **Ko Yung (Mosquito Island), Mai Phai (Bamboo Island), Ko Poda,** and **Ko Hua Khwaan (Chicken Island).** The snorkeling is particularly good around Chicken Island and Ko Poda. Reportedly, a lonely set of bungalows with an electrical generator mopes on Ko Poda (around 550฿ with fans and baths). It costs 300฿ to hire a long-tailed boat to take you there, but if you bring your own tent you can camp for 100฿ per night. Be sure to bring food as well. Call 612 160 for more information or contact TAT. Available only during high season. Long-tailed boats for 5 people run between Phi Phi Don and Phi Phi Lay and around the islands for 300฿.

Ko Lanta, a 20-km-long giant among Lilliputian islands, is fast climbing the charts among tourists fleeing the overcrowded Ko Phi Phi. The island retires in the low season, but if you do manage to get there, most bungalows will be in the 40-50฿ range. During the high season, bungalows with bath can be found for 80฿. Your options are generally concentrated on Klong Down Beach. Singles in bamboo bungalows at **Lanta Golden Bay Cottages** (tel. (01) 723 0879) have mosquito nets and a price tag of 100฿, dipping to 50฿ during the off-season. Newer, concrete rooms with fans and potted shrubs are also available (120-150฿, 80฿ off-season). Both options have clean baths with Thai toilet. For the tenderfoot, **Lanta Sea House** (tel. (01) 722 0160) has brand-new concrete bungalows with balconies, tiled floor, and flush toilets, but no sink (500฿, 300฿ off-season). Their bamboo bungalows are older and have wooden floors. Singles 150฿, off-season 100฿. Doubles 300฿.

A good two hours by boat from Krabi, Ko Lanta is actually closer to Trang. Krabi, however, dominates the industry in these parts, and holds the cards on transport and tours to Ko Lanta for now. Boats from Krabi's pier go to Ko Lanta's **Ban Saa Laadaan Pier** daily during the high season (Oct.-May, 1pm, 2hr., 150฿) and return at 8am. During the high season, boats also leave from Ko Phi Phi for Ko Lanta (1pm, 1-½hr., 150฿). Otherwise, mini-vans depart year-round from Krabi to **Baw Muang** (10:30 and 11am, 2hr.) and then you must catch a boat to Ko Lanta, and a minibus to the bungalows (total trip 150฿).

INLAND

The **Khao Nawe Choochee Lowland Forest** is one of the last remaining forests of its kind in Thailand. Among the 290-plus species of birds that nest in the forest is the endangered *Pitta gurneyi,* a brightly colored ground-dwelling bird of which there are only about 150 living. The **Thung Tieo nature trail,** a 2.7-km path, eases you through some of Thailand's most lush and currently undisturbed slices of nature. Motorbike there from Krabi or take a songthaew out to **Khlong Thom,** the capital of that district. Contact Mr. Koyou at the Krabi Bird Club, 24 Phetkasem Rd. (tel. 699 089). TAT officials can also find him for you if you bring them cookies. Mr. Koyou will haul you around the area in his pick-up truck (300฿). A motorcycle taxi can be hired from Khlong Than (100฿ one way). Be sure to arrange return transport.

■■■ TRANG

The provincial capital stockpiles 119km worth of national park beaches and a formidable collection of small islands nearby, both of which remain miraculously undisturbed by the brazen bandits of large-scale development. Located off the well-trodden tourist circuit, Trang is an island Pepto-Bismol for travelers seeking relief from *farang*-heavy indigestion. The area is a local vacation spot, however, which keeps prices up and vacancies down. Day tours of the islands can be arranged from Trang, but they all close down in the low season.

When it comes to economic opportunity, the city has lived a charmed existence. In the 7th and 12th centuries, it was a major trading outpost for the Srivijaya Empire. At the turn of this century, rubber trees (the first in Thailand) were introduced to the area, and countless plantations sprouted. Finally, about 30 years ago, Highway Route 4 hit town and, since then, Trang has been riding another wave of prosperity.

ORIENTATION

Buses arrive at the **bus terminal** on **Ploenpitak Road;** the **train station** forms a central axis and gathering place at the city's northern tip. **Phra Ram VI Road,** a large avenue lined with hotels, originates at the train station and runs through most of Trang. **Ratchadamnoen Road** winds alongside it, and the daily **market** is between these two roads, a few blocks from the railroad. **Visetkul Road** intersects Phra Ram VI Rd. at the clock tower. **Ratsada Road** runs parallel to it. The rest of Trang's layout is an arbitrary maze of streets winding around themselves. Trang Travel has very helpful **maps** of the city with a decent province map on the back (50฿). Most of the city is within a walkable area.

PRACTICAL INFORMATION

Tourist Information: Trang Travel, on Phra Ram VI Rd. (tel. 219 598; fax 211 298), on the right side about 1 block down from the train station, facing Thumrin Hotel. Some English spoken. Decent maps (50฿), plane tickets. Open daily 8am-8:30pm, low season 8am-7pm. **Trang Tourism Business Association,** 25/2 Sathanee Rd. (tel. 211 380). Area pamphlets. Open Mon.-Sat. 8:30am-5pm.

Currency Exchange: Bangkok Bank, 2 Phra Ram VI Rd. (tel. 218 203), one block from the train station on the right. Takes 20min. to change money as carbon paper and passport circle several desks. Open Mon.-Fri. 8:30am-3:30pm.

Post/Telephones Office: GPO (tel. 218 521) on the corner of Phra Ram VI and Jermpanya Rd. From the train station, pass the clock tower, and travel about ½km until the road makes a sharp turn. You might want to take a motorcycle. Office and Poste Restante open Mon.-Fri. 8:30am-4:30pm, Sat. 9am-noon. Upstairs has **overseas phone,** fax, and telegram. Open daily 7am-10pm. More convenient branch (tel. 218 021) is near the train station on the corner of Kantang Rd. and Phra Ram VI Rd. Overseas telephone service during regular hours. Open Mon.-Fri. 8:30am-4:30pm. **Postal code:** 92000. **Telephone code:** 075.

Airport: Trang Airport on Trang-Palian Rd. (tel. 210 804), 7km south of the city. THAI Air to: **Bangkok** (Tues., Fri., and Sun., 10:40am, 2005฿); **Phuket** (Mon., Wed., Thurs., and Sat., 10:40am, Fri., Sun., 6pm, 435฿). Airport fee 30฿. Trang Travel, opposite Thumrin Hotel, runs airport vans (30฿). Tuk-tuk rides 30฿. **THAI Air** is at 199/2 Visetkul Rd. (tel. 218 066). From the train station, turn left at the clock tower and it is on the left about 5 blocks down, across from a school. Open daily 8am-5pm.

Trains: (tel. 213 082 or 218 012), located at the end of Phra Ram VI Rd. A good place to go when you don't want to be in Trang. To: **Bangkok** (1:44pm, 14-½hr., 3rd class 165฿, second class 312฿; sleeper: upper 412฿, lower 462฿; with A/C, upper 562฿, lower 682฿); **Surat Thani** (rapid: 1:40pm, 4hr., 3rd class 69฿, 2nd class 110฿; 6pm, 4hr., 3rd class 89฿, 2nd class 130฿); **Chumphon** (1:40pm, 8hr., 3rd class 94฿, 2nd class 164฿; 6pm, 8hr., 3rd class 114฿, 2nd class 184฿).

Buses: (tel. 210 455). The bus station is on Ploenpitak Rd., though some vans and buses leave from random points around the city. To: **Phuket** (A/C 6 daily, 7am-7pm, 5hr., 140฿); **Krabi** (6 daily, 6am-11pm, 2-3hr., 35฿; A/C 5 daily, 8am-7:30pm, 2hr., 66฿); **Phang Nga** (A/C 6 daily, 7:30am-7:30pm, 3-½hr., 102฿), **Hat Yai** (A/C vans every hr. or when full, 6am-4pm, 2hr., 35฿; regular local orange bus every 30min., 5:30am-4:30pm, 3hr., 30฿); **Surat Thani** (vans every hr., 8am-5pm, 3hr., 100฿; from near Sinochai Bakery); and **Satun** (buses every hr. or when full from Ratsada Rd. on the way out of town, 6am-5pm, 38฿; take a tuk-tuk to the stop). To **Bangkok** (7am and 4:30pm, 12-13hr., 203฿; A/C 4pm, 13hr., 375฿; 2 VIP at 5pm, 13hr., 565฿).

Local Transportation: Tuk-tuks (5฿) within the city. No main stop, but if there's space, try the Diamond Dept. Store and the cinema across from the Queen Hotel. Take **minivans** for points around Trang. For vans to **Kantang Pier,** from the station, turn right on Kantang Rd. They will be on the right a few hundred feet down the road. Taxis and minivans (both 10฿) leave when full (5am-7pm, 20min.). For vans to **Pakmeng Beach,** walk to the 1st stoplight on Phra Ram VI Rd. (from the train station) and take a left and walk to the large four-way intersection. Turn left here onto Tha Klang Rd. The minivans leave a few blocks down on the right (high season: 6am-6pm, 20฿; low season schedule is erratic—get there early).

Hospital: Ratchadamnoen Hospital, 25 Soi 1, Sai Ngam Rd. 2 (tel. 211 200-05), near the daily municipal market. It's a tall building with a green cross on the top, just off Ratchadamnoen Rd. More attractive than most hotels in the south. Some English. Open 24 hrs.

Pharmacy: 117/1 Phra Ram VI Rd., near Koh Teng Hotel, toward the clock tower.

Emergency: tel. 191.

Police: 6 Phattalung Rd. (tel. 218 019). From the clock tower, walk down Phra Ram VI Rd. to the next major intersection. Take a left; Phattalung Rd. is the next intersection. Some officers speak English.

ACCOMMODATIONS

Akachai Apartments, 3-11 Khao Rd. (tel. 218 751 or 210 326). From the train station, walk down Phra Ram VI Rd. to the 1st intersection. Take a left on Kantang Rd. and follow it until you reach a busy 4-way intersection. Keep heading straight; just beyond the intersection turn right onto Huay Yod Soi 2. You can see a red English sign a short way down the soi on the left. Quiet, pleasant neighborhood (except for the daily 6am temple bell nearby). Balconies and the 4th floor offer a rosy view of the world. Light snoozers should ask for back rooms. All have high-powered ceiling fans, double bed, clean bath, and four well-worn white walls (130฿). Monthly rates available. Laundry service (3-25฿). Open 6am-4am.

Koh Teng Hotel, 77-79 Phra Ram VI Rd. (tel. 218 148 or 218 622), about 5 blocks down from the train station on the left side of the main road. Notebook of *farang* travel experiences, if the manager can find it. Admire your lovely self in their antique mirrors. Large, tidy rooms, with phones, ceiling fans, keyhole locks, an enormous private bath, and so much toilet paper. Singles 160฿, doubles 250฿. Delish restaurant. Reception open 7:30am-9pm. Check-out noon.

Food on a Stick

Across the country, entire critters skewered and lashed provide hours of bone-gnawing fulfillment. In the south it's pungent satay and squidlets on skewers with curled tentacles that cringe from your very lips. In Bangkok, the sophisticated salad on a stick: demure tomatoes and lettuce leaves interspersed to ensure a well-rounded, fiber-filled treat (otherwise, you'd have to eat the stick). The best treat of all...the choco waffle dogs at Doi Suthep, Chiang Mai! A succulent hot dog veiled in its waffle shroud, dripping with chocolate syrup fresh from the can.

FOOD

Eating is unquestionably the town's greatest lure and primary social activity, especially at night. Diners congregate as late as 1 and 2am over plates of steaming rice and spicy curry, swishing their palates with cold beer or hot tea. Unlike many of southern Thailand's largely Muslim cities, Trang embraces a distinct Chinese presence, manifested in the abundance of pork. Crispy roasted honey-dipped pork with *paa tong ko* (Chinese doughnuts) and *dim sum* make a distinctly Trang breakfast. Another of Trang's unique flavors is the Chinese *goa bii,* richly brewed coffee, most often served in dark, smoky restaurants to old, somber Chinese men.

Dredge up mouth-watering meals from the **night market** mother lode. One belly-filling bazaar is next to Diamond Department Store by the train station; the other extends down Phra Ram VI Rd. near the Trang and Wattana Hotels. Amazingly succulent food includes all the standards, along with oyster omelettes (15฿), squid-on-a-stick, and batter-fried (*ka noon jam pada*) jackfruit (3 for 10฿).

Ko Lun Restaurant, 201/2 Huai Yod Rd. (tel. 219 403). Exit the bus station and cross the street. Turn left and it's on the corner of the second alley you cross. A famous coffee shop among bottomless-stomached locals who enjoy the Trang breakfast feast. Huge selection of *dim sum* dishes (3-8฿). Don't worry about not consuming all they put in front of you—they only charge for what you actually eat. Noodle soup (12฿), *goa bii* (Chinese brewed coffee served in glasses with condensed milk at the bottom, 5฿), and roast pork for 2-3 people (30฿). Open daily 5am-4pm. *Dim sum* served 5-10am.

Koh Teng Restaurant, 77-79 Phra Ram VI Rd. (tel. 218 148 or 218 622), at the Koh Teng Hotel. Park your knees under their round, antique marble tables. Thin rice noodles in Chinese sauce with pork or chicken (20฿), excellent iced coffee and tea (7฿), French toast (10฿). Most dishes run about 50฿.

Wee Rot Muslim Restaurant (tel. 219 579), on Kantang Rd. From the train station take a left at the 1st light; the restaurant is 1 block down on the left, next to Siam Commercial Bank. Sweet *rotis* (3฿, with egg 6฿), topped with either sweet condensed milk or curry base silences morning stomach snarls. Wash it down with hot tea (6฿). Good selection of curries 15-20฿. Open 6am-8pm.

SIGHTS AND ENTERTAINMENT

Violence is rampant in the mean streets of Trang. Walking along Pra Ram VI in the morning, you'll see bags of colorful **fighting-fish** for sale. Below many stilt houses are makeshift **cock-fighting** arenas. The biggest and goriest of all are the **bull-fights.** No longer as popular as they once were, they still take place one weekend a month, drawing people from neighboring provinces. Day tickets cost as much as 750฿, a trifle compared to the bets made on the blood-soaked bovines, which can exceed a million baht. When a bull enters the ring, the whole village comes to cheer. The tying of the sacred rope around the bull's horns sends the people into a frenzy. The fight itself is unpleasant, but for locals it's an art form, an exciting sport, and a legacy that spans many generations. To get to the bull-fight field, tell the tuk-tuk driver to go to Sanam Wuah Chon (5฿). Ask people in town for the schedule. Tickets for one round average 200฿. The fights starts around 10:45am.

Trang's **infamous Vegetarian Festival** is held yearly in September or October (the exact date depends on the Chinese calender). Endless ceremonies are performed, but hands-down the singular most freakish is the ritualized self-mutilation of frenzied citizens. Individuals calmly pierce their cheeks and tongues with long metal spikes, handfuls of pencils, even the intact frames of mountain bikes. Sometimes an extra long skewer will be threaded through several sets of cheeks to create a human daisy chain. The squeamish may wish to avoid Trang during this grisly time of year. Otherwise bring your camera for some unprecedented photo moments.

■ NEAR TRANG

Most visitors to Trang don't dwell on the city itself. The high season (November to May) brings locals on the run from city life to the national park beaches or to the islands off the west coast in the Andaman Sea. Low-season monsoons use the islands for target practice, and at that time there is no transport to them; re-route during these months. Though not quite idyllic, the shores are sedate, and Hat Yong Ling has wonderful rock formations. Pakmeng Beach is the busiest, leaving Yong Ling and Jao Mai relatively isolated.

HAT PAKMENG

The only mainland beach with any significant commercial presence maintains its beauty. Several food stands and restaurants line the road set back from the water and will serve you in your beach chair if you wish (pork with garlic and basil, 50฿). **Pakmeng Resort,** 60/1 Mu 4 (tel. 210 321), is at the south end of the beach, 2 km from the songthaew drop-off, toward Hat Yong Ling and Hat Jao Mai. The resort has a pleasant restaurant and bungalows in the back. Well-kept single cottages with clean bath and fan cost 200฿; doubles, 300฿. Pakmeng Resort arranges high-season day tours on long-tailed boats for groups of eight, going to Ko Mook, Ko Hai, and Ko Kradan (350฿). Motorbikes are rented at 200฿ per day. Open daily 7am-10pm.

Minivans to Pakmeng beach cost 10฿. (See "Practical Information" on page 530.) Returning from Pakmeng may take a while in the low season. Vans rendezvous at the north end of the beach near the road leading away from the water.

HAT JAO MAI AND HAT YONG LING

The national park head office (tel. 210 664; open daily 8am-4pm) is located 6km from Pak Meng Beach on **Hat Jao Mai,** keeping company with government-run concrete bungalows—two large bedrooms with simple beds that sleep two plus two floor mattresses, but no showers (100฿ for 2, 200฿ for 3, and 200-300฿ for 4 or 5). Camping is kosher and tents are 100฿. There is no restaurant, but the staff can whip up something for you on request. Bring extra food, just in case no one feels like cooking. Call ahead for reservations...if you speak Thai.

Hat Yong Ling, 16km from Hat Jao Mai, also has a national park head office (open 8am-4pm). Plain rooms (no mattress) in stilt houses with baths in the opposite shack are available for free, or you can camp out in your own tent. The beach has two coves sheltered by rocky mountains covered in wild orchids. To get to an isolated patch of sand, simply trek across a lush patch of tropical forest and through a bat cave to reach one of the best sand and sea combos in the country. Bring a light, as travel by braille is difficult in a small space filled with flying mammals. At points along the mountain base, the salty waves have carved out small coves where locals often set up camp and grill seafood. If you're lucky (and sweetly fragrant) they might ask you to join them. Vans run to Pakmeng Beach (10฿); you'll have to arrange a songthaew to Hat Jao Mai or Hat Yong Ling. Unless you can share the cost with locals, the trip can be steep (100฿) since no songthaews make it regularly. An alternative is to dart across on a rented motorbike from Pak Meng Resort.

ISLANDS NEAR TRANG

Trang's tourists are irresistibly drawn to the pheromone of island snorkeling. In addition to the cheaper Pakmeng Resort, **Trang Travel** (tel. 219 598) in Trang arranges day tours (500฿, including lunch). Equipment is an additional 30฿. Ko Hai, Mook, Kradan, Libong, and Sukorn all have a few accommodations. Boats to islands near Pakmeng, such as Ko Hai and Ko Mook, leave from Pakmeng Pier (around 100฿, depending on island). Everything is closed during the low season.

Ko Mook is the most popular island with the bottom-dollar backpacker because of its lodgings, which start as low as 75฿. The **Ko Mook Resort** has its head office at 45 Phra Ram III (tel. 212 613). Advertises rooms in a longhouse without baths at 100฿ per person (each room sleeps 2). A twin-bed bungalow with bath is 150฿, with fan 200฿. Open daily 8am-6pm. From Trang, take a minibus to Pakmeng Pier, and then board a long-tail boat for Ko Mook before noon (1hr., 60฿). Ko Mook Resort also offers a car/boat service via Pakmeng Beach for 80฿ per person.

Ko Hai has the **Ko Hai Resort** (tel. 210 317 or 211 104). Bungalows (minus bath) start at 250฿. Boats to Ko Hai from Pakmeng's northern pier are about 100฿, leaving Pakmeng at 10:30am and 2pm, and coming back from Ko Hai at 12:30pm and 4pm (45min). **Ko Hai Villa,** office at 112 Phra Ram VI (tel. 210 496) has bungalows without fans for 300฿. Their boats for Ko Chenk (Emerald Cave), Ko Kradan, and Ko Wan leave at 9am, returning at 4pm (200฿). **Ko Kradan's** bungalow options are limited to expensive resorts with villas (700-900฿). To get to **Ko Sukorn, Ko Lao Lieng,** or **Ko Petra** (the latter two have no accommodations), leap onto a boat from the ferry pier or at Hat Jao Mai.

■■■ HAT YAI

Squatting 26km away from the provincial capital, the sumo wrestler-sized city of Hat Yai maintains its considerable commercial girth, fueled by a protein-packed flow of Malaysian and Singaporean tourists. Shopping is the main event in this metropolitan arena, since commodities and food are about 35% cheaper here than they are in Singapore and Malaysia. Streets are paved with closet-like shops merchandising watches, electric razors, clothes, and gourmet cookies. Muslim women on the sidewalks sell apples, plums, and juicy grapes imported from Australia; street hawkers pace back and forth trying to convince you that you cannot function completely without a purple, fluffy ostrich on a string. Large department stores blast radio chatter into the street as tuk-tuks threaten to run over visitors bargaining for "Rolexes."

ORIENTATION

As Southern Thailand's huskiest metropolis, Hat Yai can be a bit intimidating at first as a train or bus pitches you in the midst of cars, motorcycles, trucks, and peddlers of every kind of local produce. The heart of Hat Yai pumps in a relatively small area, though, near the train station and plaza market area, where most out-of-town buses deposit passengers. The front of the train station faces **Thamnoonvithi Road,** a large cross street that runs from the train station through vendor-packed **Niphat Uthit 1, 2,** and **3 Road,** Hat Yai's busiest streets, which are laid out in a semi-grid format. **Suphasan Rangsan Road** is the top cross street and several busy streets run parallel to it (including **Pratchathipat Road, Thamnoonvithi Road**, and **Manasruedee Road**). **Phetkasem Road,** which comes into the city running by Wat Hat (site of Sorasilp Guest House), crosses the train tracks and then curves to the left going by the Plaza Cinema and market area up to the intersection with **Niphat Songkraw 1 Road** (where the GPO is located), at which point Phetkasem Rd. continues off to the right of the rotary in the direction of Songkhla.

Most inter-city buses drop people in front of the Plaza Cinema and market area near the **clock tower,** on Phetkasem Rd. The **daily municipal market** and the **night**

market extend from Phetkasem Rd. down **Montri 2 Road** to **Ratakan Road,** which runs parallel to Phetkasem Rd.

PRACTICAL INFORMATION

Tourist Office: TAT Office, 1/1 Soi 2 Niphat Uthit 3 Rd. (tel. 245 986), in the south of the city, down the last side street on the left before you reach Sri Poovanart Rd. intersection and the Florida Hotel. Next to a small branch of Hat Yai's police station. Soi 2 is clearly marked in English. English-speaking staff is responsible for Songkhla and Satun provinces. Decent maps of Hat Yai, information on Ko Tarutao, as well as hotel, restaurant, and travel agency listings. Open daily 8:30am-4:30pm.

Tourist Police: (tel. 212 213). On Sripoovanart Rd., from the TAT, walk down Niphat Uthit 3 Rd. (toward the Florida Hotel) 1 block and take a right 1 block down on Sripoovanart Rd. It's on the right, just before the next intersection. English spoken. Cordial because they are paid to be.

Budget Travel: Magic Tour, 93/1 Niphat Uthit 2 Rd. (tel. 234 535 or 236 119), below the Cathay Guest House. Budget travelers' center, with lodging upstairs. English-speaking staff organizes trips to all major cities in Thailand. Plane tickets. Bus service to Malaysia and Singapore. Open daily 7am-8pm; off-season 7am-6pm. Accepts AmEx (5% service charge), Visa and MC (3% service charge).

Immigration Office: (tel. 243 019). On Phetkasem Rd., over the bridge (from Niphat Uthit Rd.) on the left, after the police station. Can grant Visa extensions. Open Mon.-Fri. 8:30am-3:30pm.

Currency Exchange: Bangkok Bank, 39 Niphat Uthit 2 Rd. (tel. 235 330-9), near the intersection of Suphasan Rangsan Rd. Accepts Visa, MC and AmEx. ATM accepts Visa. Open daily 8:30am-5pm. **Thai Farmers Bank,** 188/1 Suphasan Rangsan Rd. (tel. 243 027), on the corner of Phetkasem Rd., near the bridge. Open Mon.-Fri. 8:30am-4:30pm.

Post Office/Telephones: GPO (tel. 243 013), at the corner of Niphat Songkraw 1 and Soi 4. Walk up Phetkasem Rd. past the Plaza Cinema to the rotary (about 0.5km). Niphat Songkraw 1 Rd. runs out of the rotary, straight ahead (Phetkasem veers off to the right). The post office is on the right a few blocks down. Open Mon.-Fri. 8:30am-4:30pm, Sat. 9am-noon. Telegram and overseas calling upstairs (tel. 245 293), open daily 8am-9pm. Another branch (tel. 244 480) is on Ratakan Rd. at the corner near the bridge. Ratakan Rd. is parallel to, and 1 block toward the train tracks from, Niphat Uthit 1 Rd. Open Mon.-Fri. 8:30am-4:30pm, Sat. 9am-noon. Overseas calling and telegram; no credit card or calling card calls possible (post office hours only). Some overseas calling services in tour offices throughout the city. **Postal code:** 90110. **Telephone code:** 074.

Airport: (tel. 251 008-12), 13km east of Hat Yai. To: **Bangkok** (3-5 daily, 2280฿); **Kuala Lumpur** (Tue. 4:40pm, Fri., Sun. 2:50pm, 2275฿); and **Singapore** (4:40pm, 2755฿). Surcharge with credit card. 300฿ airport tax for international flights. **THAI Air** has 2 offices in Hat Yai: 190-6 Niphat Uthit 2 Rd. (tel. 232 352), open Mon.-Fri. 8am-5pm; 166/4 Niphat Uthit 2 Rd., open Mon.-Sat. 8am-5pm, Sun. 9am-4pm. THAI Air runs minivans to and from the airport 1-½-2hr. before take-off (40฿). Arrange to be picked up at your hotel. Magic Tour and Sunny Tours also schedule flights. **Flight Information:** tel. 311 175.

Trains: Hat Yai Railway Station (tel. 243 705, 231 050, or 238 005), at the end of Thamnoonvithi Rd. To: **Bangkok** (rapid, 3:20pm and 4:55pm; express, 6:10pm and 6:40pm, 15-17hr.; 2nd-class, 313฿), **Surat Thani** (6:05am, 10:59am; rapid, 3:20pm and 4:55pm; express, 6:10pm and 6:40pm, 5-6hr.; 2nd-class, 144฿), **Sungai Kolok** (4 daily 11:15am-6:20pm; rapid, 5am; express, 6:56am, 4-5hr.; 2nd-class, 87฿), **Butterworth** (express, 7:20am, 4hr., 2nd-class, 75฿), **Kuala Lumpur** (express, 3:50pm, 13hr). Supplementary charges to train tickets: for rapid trains add 20฿ to the listed price; express trains add 50฿; 2nd-class top sleeper add 100฿; lower sleeper add 150฿; 2nd-class A/C upper sleeper add 200฿; lower add 250฿. For a full schedule, contact the train station or TAT office.

Buses: City bus terminal (tel. 232 789), at the south end of town on Ranchanawanit Rd. Buses stop in front of the Plaza market on Phetkasem Rd. in the center of town, arriving 10-15min. after scheduled departure time from bus terminal.

Tuk-tuk to the terminal, 10฿. For buses to Bangkok, go to the terminal. To: **Bangkok** (7:30am, 2, and 4pm, 16hr., 238฿; A/C: 7am, 3, 5, and 6pm, 14hr., 314-428฿; VIP: 7am, 3, 4, 5, and 6pm, 14hr., 500฿ or 625฿, depending on seat), **Phuket** (4 daily, 5:30-9:45am, 9hr., 122฿; A/C: 7 daily, 8am-1pm and 9:30pm, 7hr., 207฿), **Krabi** (4 daily, 5:30-9:45am, 5hr., 91฿; A/C: 7daily, 8-11:45am and 9:30pm, 4hr., 127฿), **Surat Thani** (5 daily, 5:20-11:20am, 6hr., 86฿; A/C: 4 daily, 7:10am-3pm, 5-½hr., 154฿), **Trang** (every 30min., 6am-5pm, 3hr., 40฿), **Sungai Kolok** (A/C: 5daily, 7am-3pm, 4hr., 96฿), **Padang Besar** (every 30min., 5am-6pm, 2hr., 50฿). For a complete schedule, contact TAT. Magic Tour and Sunny Tours (and most other travel agents in Hat Yai) organize minibuses from their offices to locations such as Phuket (200฿), Krabi (150฿), and Surat Thani (150฿).

Buses to Malaysia and Singapore: Government buses do not cross the Malaysian border. **Magic Tour** has daily buses to Malaysia and Singapore. The buses are Malaysian but Thai travel agents are authorized to book tickets. For most nationalities, no visa is required for Malaysia; don't be tricked into paying a "visa fee" unless you are from Bangladesh, Pakistan, India, South Africa, China, Sri Lanka, or Burma. Thai travel agents do not arrange or process visas. To: **Penang** (9:30am, 12:30, and 3:30pm, 4-½hr., 200฿); **Sungai Kolok** (every hr., 8am-noon, 4hr., 150฿); **Kuala Lumpur** (9am and noon, 9hr., 250฿; VIP 250฿; Super VIP 350฿); and **Singapore** (VIP: noon, 15hr., 400฿; Super VIP: 12:30pm, 15hr., 500฿).

Taxis: Operate more as inter-city transport and leave from the City Bus Terminal. Taxis to **Satun** (35฿) leave from Ratakan Rd. across from the post office. To **Sungai Kolok** (150฿) leave from Suphasan Rangsan Rd. From Niphat Uthit 1, 2, or 3 Rd. walk up Suphasan Rangsan to the right, a few blocks after the road curves.

Local Transport: Tuk-tuk (10฿). Motorcycle rides cost 10฿ in town.

English Bookstore: DK Book House, 2/4-5 Thamnoonvithi Rd. (tel. 230 759), in front of the train station on the left-hand side. 3rd floor is a literary grab bag. Randomly stacked selection includes both Dante and *Mr. T: An Autobiography*. Maps on the 1st floor. Open daily 9am-8pm.

Pharmacy: Thong Cun Ting, 129/11 Niphat Uthit 3 Rd. (tel. 243 411). Open 8am-10pm.

Hospital: The Prince of Songkhla University Hospital (24-hr. phone line, 212 070 or 212 074), to the east of the city off Rajyindee Rd.

Emergency: tel. 1699.

Police: Contact the tourist police first. The main Songkhla police station (tel. 243 021) is on Phetkasem Rd. just over the bridge. Coming from the train station, it's on the left side of the road.

ACCOMMODATIONS

Hat Yai is a city of illicit affairs, with a statistically significant percentage of the population reputedly engaged in them. Many of the cheapest hotels in Hat Yai offer sleazy services, often under the name of "ancient Thai massage." Men are actively courted into these establishments, while women traveling alone may be rejected at the door. To avoid sticky situations, opt for a slightly more expensive but reputable guest house suggested by the TAT hotel list.

Sorasilp Guest House, 251/7-8 Phetkasem Rd. (tel. 232 635), near the market area, on the left as you face the Plaza Cinema, just off Phetkasem Rd., with a small English sign. Breakfast service and proximity to the bus. Harley hogs can thrill to the *vroom-vroom* of nearby bikes. Clean chambers and spotless private baths with sit toilets, towels, sheets, and soap. Open 5am-2am. Check-out noon. Singles 120฿, with double bed 160฿, with A/C 220฿. Doubles 180฿, with A/C 280฿. Reservations recommended during Thai and Malaysian holidays.

Cathay Guest House, 93/1 Niphat Uthit 2 Rd. (tel. 243 815). A mecca for travelers coming from or going to Malaysia. Westerners congregate over beers in the lounge. Geriatric but large and fairly dust-free rooms. Years of backpacker bathing have worn down the baths to a smooth, clean surface. Schönberg fans will appreciate 12-tone street dissonance. Open daily 6am-2am. Dorms 70฿. Singles 140฿. Doubles 160฿. Triples 200฿. Breakfast 6:30am-noon, Muesli and yogurt 35฿; cold drinks available all day. Laundry service.

Hok-Jin Heng Hotel, 87 Niphat Uthit 1 Rd. (tel. 243 258 or 253 264). Across from Bank of Ayutthaya. 6 floors of fresh rooms are amazingly pristine. Baths with sit toilets; facilities shine like a new penny. Knock if you get there past midnight. Singles 150฿, with A/C 240฿. Doubles 240฿. Fine 1st-floor Chinese restaurant.

FOOD

Hat Yai's hustling casino of Chinese, Thais, and Malay Muslims, with a dash of international visitors, ensures a delightful gastronomic pay-off, no matter how you throw the culinary dice. The **morning market** on Niphat Uthit 3 deals mainly in fresh vegetables and seafood, including shark fin soup. Breakfast vendors' *tao huay* (soy yogurt served with sweet ginger syrup, 5฿) make a swell breakfast. The **daily market** between Montri 1 and 2 Rd., racks up a winning assortment of seasonal fruit. **Food vendors** set up day and night in the Niphat Uthit Rd. area and near the Plaza market and cinema on Phetkasem Rd. Get your crepes with shredded coconut (*khanom bueng*). In the evening, the Suphasan Rangsan Rd. stalls (away from the train tracks, after the street turns), offer a variety of freshly cooked dinner items. *Pad thai* 15฿, a good-sized bowl of Chinese noodle soup with shrimp, pork, fish balls, and vegetables 15฿. The **night market,** on Montri 1 and 2 Rd. is full of fruit, Chinese pork and noodle soup, curry, and gelatinous desserts.

Nai Yao Restaurant, 79 Niphat Uthit 3 Rd. (tel. 246 208), on the corner of Thamnoonvithi Rd., a block from the Cathay Guest House. Bring a loved one and do the *Lady and the Tramp* scenario with Chinese noodle soup mixed with roast pork, fish balls, tofu, greens, and shrimp (20฿). Set aside social niceties for the evening and point and grunt at whatever looks appealing. Open 6am-2pm and 5pm-1am.

Best Kitchen, 13-15 Juti Uthit 2 Rd. (tel. 234 479), along the Kong Toey canal, next to J.B. Hotel. Look for the pop-arty, neon duck and lobster sign. Affordable alternative to sidewalk noodle shops and impromptu tuk-tuk serenades. Professional chef prepares roast duck with special sauce that leaves you quacking with glee (25฿). Fried beef or chicken with basil leaves (25฿), fried pork ribs with garlic and pepper (45-80฿), or beef hot-plate (80฿). Vietnamese spring rolls come with a selection of fresh vegetables. English and Japanese menu. Open 10:30am-10pm.

ENTERTAINMENT

All good credit cards come to die in Hat Yai. Retire your trusty Visa before it collapses from consumer overload. Phetkasem Rd. stocks birds, fish, shoes, ethnic costumes, belts, and, of course, watches. Indian costumes and Chinese mushrooms sprout on Niphat Uthit 2 Rd. sidewalks, day and night.

Slather yourself with western pop culture at **Post Laser Disk,** 82-3 Thamnoonvithi Rd. (tel. 2323 027), about two blocks past Niphat Uthit Rd., on the right. No charge for watching the English-language movies on the second floor, but you do have to order from the pricey menu (coffee 25฿)—a small price to pay for gems like *Naked Gun, Hot Shots,* and *Ace Ventura.* Movies shown noon-midnight daily; the sign outside proclaims what's playing. Look for the colorful pinstripe tile out front.

Another equally stomach-churning Hat Yai spectator sport is **bullfighting;** bovines lock horns on the first Saturday of each month (except Buddha's Day), 10am-3pm, in the stadium up Niphat Songkraw 1 Rd. toward the Klong Wa intersection. One round has about three bullfights and admission costs 40-50฿, depending on the bull. Tuk-tuks go to the stadium for 30฿ per person.

Promote peace and harmony at the **Thai Boxing stadium** which has human fighting bouts on Saturday afternoons. Admission price varies according to the boxer, but averages around 30฿. The boxing schedule can be erratic, so contact TAT for details. Tuk-tuks go to the stadium for 40-50฿ per person.

Now you know why they call him the Big Guy. **Wat Hat Yai Nai** is known for its 35m-long and 15m-high reclining Buddha, the third-largest in the world just like the one in Georgetown. The wat is located on the way into Hat Yai (coming in on the eastern side) near Klong U. Thapao Bridge. Foreigners should wear long pants and shirts that cover the shoulders. No shoes are allowed inside, and visitors may not enter the shrine after 6pm. Tuk-tuks will go to the wat for 10฿ per person.

■■■ SATUN

Despite the gangs of motorcycles that roar through the streets at all hours, the rural province of Satun, situated on the Straits of Melaka, turns a deaf ear to the din. Tourists pass through Satun, usually headed for Ko Tarutao, the national park island off the coast. Ko Tarutao is only open from November through May, so from June to October, Satun plays solitaire. The area is a springboard point for crossing the border by boat to Pulau Langkawi.

ORIENTATION

Satun is one of Thailand's southernmost provinces, located only 20km from the Malaysian border. Buses deliver people to north-south-running **Sulakanukul Road** or **Buriwanit Road** (actually the same road, but when you cross **Samanta Pradit Road,** site of the riverside Rain Tiong Hotel, it becomes Buriwanit). The main stretch of Satun is **Satun Thani Road,** beginning at the junction with Samanta Pradit Rd. and running parallel to Buriwanit, one block away, as you travel from the river. The gold-domed **Bambang Mosque** is in the town center. Continue along Satun Thani Rd.; you'll pass the police station on the right and see the Wang Mai Hotel looming up ahead, which is the end of Satun's most urban area. The large **daily market** is along the river, to the left of the Rain Tong Hotel, as are **long-tail boats** that go to Tamalang Pier (when the water is high enough), the point where boats leave to Kuala Perlis in Malaysia.

PRACTICAL INFORMATION

Tours: Satun Travel and Ferry Service, 45/16 Satun Thani Rd. (tel. 711 453), is actually off Satun Thani Rd., on a small road next to the large Wang Mai Hotel. Representative of Kuala Perlis-Langkawi Ferry Service which operates from the Tamalang Pier. Transportation to Phuket (350฿) and Krabi (250฿; both leave at 10am) along with tours of other islands in the Andaman Sea is available. **Thanapat Tour,** 45/18 Satun Thani Rd. (tel. 711 426), two shops down from Satun Travel, sells boat tickets to Ko Tarutao (200฿) and Langkawi (300฿), and reserves bus tickets. Open 6:30am-10pm.

Currency Exchange: Thai Farmers Bank, 31 Sulakanukul Rd. (tel. 721 354-8), is down from Samanta Pradit Rd. on the left, near the police box. Open Mon.-Fri. 8:30am-3:30pm.

Post office: (tel. 711 013), on the corner of Samanta Pradit Rd. and Satun Thani Rd. Poste Restante. Open Mon.-Fri. 8:30am-4:30pm, Sat., Sun. and public holidays 9am-noon. **Overseas calling** and telegram upstairs. Open daily 8am-6pm. No credit or calling card calls accepted. **Postal code:** 91000. **Telephone code:** 074.

Immigration Office: (tel. 711 080) sits on Buriwanit Rd., next to the library, to the right if you're walking from Samanta Pradit Rd. Open daily 8:30am-4:30pm.

Buses: Leaving from Buriwanit Rd. in front of the library, on the right side of the road if you're coming from Samanta Pradit Rd. To: **Trang** (every 30min., 6am-4pm, 3hr., 38฿), **Hat Yai** (orange bus, hourly, 6am-4pm, 2hr., 28฿). **Minivans** to Hat Yai leave from the temple on Satun Thani Rd. (every 30min., 6am-5pm). **Taxis** headed that way depart when full from Buriwanit Rd., in front of the market and P. Ying store (30฿). Buses to **Bangkok** (1:30pm, 16-½hr., 234฿; A/C: 2pm, 500฿) leave from the corner of Sarit Phuminat and Hatthakam Senksa Rd. From the post office, walk up Satun Thani Rd. to the telephone office and take a right onto Sarit Phuminat Rd.; Hatthakam Senksa Rd. is the next large intersection. Buses to **Phuket** (A/C 9:30am, 7hr., 350฿) stop in **Trang** (1-½hr., 150฿), **Krabi** (5hr., 250฿), and **Phang Nga** (6hr., 300฿). They leave from Satun Travel off Satun Thani Rd. across from the Wang Mai Hotel. Satun also has buses to **Surat Thani** and **Ko Samui** (both, 5hr., 350฿). For other bus services, take a bus to Trang and transfer there.

Long-tail boats: To **Malaysia** go from the river near Rain Tong Hotel and the market to **Tamalang Pier,** about 10km south of Satun (5am-noon 30฿) during high tide. From Tamalang Pier, long-tail boats travel to **Kuala Perlis** in Malaysia as they fill up (6am-1pm, 30฿). You can also take a boat to **Langkawi Island** in Malaysia (8, 9am, 1, and 4pm., 1hr., 150฿, children 100฿). Satun Travel can arrange passage and has an A/C minivan to the pier (7:30, 8:30am, noon, 3:30pm, 20฿).

Local Transport: Go from Satun to Tamalang Pier by **songthaew** when the water is low in Bambang River. Departs from near the market in front of Chana Temple (hourly, 6am-5pm, 10฿).

English Bookstore: Ran Nang Sen Ton Mai, 45/3 Satun Thani Rd. (tel. 722 120), just past Wang Mai Hotel, has English newspapers, and some French and English fiction. Open 8am-8:30pm.

Laundry: Sai Rung Laundry, 82 Satun Thani Rd. (tel. 711 001). Look for a rainbow sign in the front. Open 6am-10pm.

Pharmacy: Pon Phaesaj, 62 Buriwanit Rd. (tel. 711 329), near the police box. Has an English sign. Open 7am-9pm.

Satun Hospital, 55/1 Hatthakam Senksa Rd. (24-hr. tel. 711 028 or 722 304), sits in the center of town. English-speaking doctors.

Emergency: tel. 191.

Police: (tel. 711 025), on corner of Yarttrasawaddee Rd. and Satun Thani Rd. about ½km up from Samanta Pradit Rd. on the right. They lock and close their huge gate at night, so don't get robbed after dark.

ACCOMMODATIONS AND FOOD

Rain Tong Hotel, 4 Samanta Pradit Rd. (tel. 711 036), is on the Bambang River, around the bend from the municipal market. The extremely kind, elderly staff will be ecstatic to assist you, but be considerate enough to not obstruct their view of the television. (It's next to the reception desk. Watch out!) Tidy but weathered bedrooms with baths and sinks. Singles 120฿, doubles 160฿. Open daily 6am-midnight. Check-out noon.

Satun's Muslim majority sets the tone of local cuisine, which consists mainly of seafood, poultry, and curry. Several breakfast *roti* places also curry favor with patrons throughout the day (one stays open all night). In addition to an extensive **daily municipal market**, there is a **night market** on Tammango Uthit Rd., which intersects Satun Thani Rd. a few blocks before the Wang Mai Hotel as you leave town (open 3pm-midnight). Duck noodle soup (20฿), chicken noodle soup—the Thai variety—15฿. **Sri Trang,** 127 Satun Thani Rd., next to a grocery store, opposite the cinema, doesn't have an English sign, but locals can point you in the direction of red massaman curry, chicken and bamboo shoot curry, and sour tamarind leaves in curried coconut milk. Rice with 1 item 10฿, with 2 items 12฿. Open 4-9pm.

■ NEAR SATUN: KO TARUTAO NATIONAL MARINE PARK

A stroll about Ko Tarutao National Marine Park is incredibly liberating for mind and body. The park is an archipelago in the Indian Ocean along the Straits of Melaka, consisting of 51 islands off the west coast of the Thai peninsula in the Andaman Sea, near the Malaysian border. **Ko Tarutao** proper is only 6km from Langkawi Island, a major point of entry into Malaysia. Covering 151 sq. km, Tarutao is the largest of the park's islands and in the 1940s was a concentration camp for political prisoners, many of whom were educated in the west. The incarcerated community adopted hobbies to pass the time, including writing a dictionary, studying Malay, and teaching law. During WWII, the government ran out of food supplies for the detainees, who turned to piracy on the high seas to support themselves. After the prisoners were pardoned, locals from the mainland moved to the island but were forced off when it became a protected area. Tarutao's best beaches sprawl on its west coast, which has a **coral reef.** The inland area seethes with waterfalls, mountains, caves, and wildlife. A two-hour **hiking trail** from Ao Phante Melaka to Ao Talo Wao, east of the island, also extends south for another three hours to Ao Talo U-Dang. From November to January, **sea-turtles** paddle ashore to deposit their ovoid offspring on **Ko Kai** (Egg Island), 15km southwest of Ko Tarutao.

The **park office** (tel. 711 383) is at Ao Phante Melaka at the north tip of Tarutao near the pier. Row housing is the cheapest government accommodation. Each room sleeps four (280฿ per room). Bungalows have two bedrooms and two baths (400฿ per room). Larger cottages also available with two bedrooms and one bath (600฿ per room). **Camping** is allowed (10฿ per night, bring your own tent). Make reservations in advance with the National Park Division of the Royal Forest Department in Bangkok (tel. (02) 579 0529), or the Pak Bara office (tel. (074) 781 285). The park is only open from November to May.

To get to Ko Tarutao from **Satun** take a local **bus** headed for Trang and get off in La Ngu about 60km from Satun (every 45min., 13฿) in front of the library on Buriwanit Rd. In La Ngu, there's a stop for **songthaews** to Pak Bara Pier, about 11km away (7฿). From Pak Bara Pier, **boats** leave daily for Ko Tarutao (Nov.-May 10:30am and 2pm, 200฿ round-trip). Boats from Tarutao to Pak Bara leave daily at 9am and 2pm. You can also charter a **long-tail boat** at the pier (500฿ and up).

From **Hat Yai** you can get a share **taxi** to La Ngu or Pak Bara in front of the post office on Ratakan Rd. near the U Thaphao Bridge (to La Ngu 50฿, Pak Bara 60฿, or 350฿ for the whole car, which holds 6). Local **buses** leave from Hat Yai for Pak Bara (7:05, 11:05am, and 2:55pm, 35฿) at the plaza market on Phetkasem Rd. near the clock tower. The regular bus from Satun to Hat Yai goes by Chalung T-intersection, from which you can take a songthaew to Pak Bara. **Air-conditioned vans** also deposit you in the midst of Pak Bara for 50฿. Vans leave from Duang Chan Rd, just off of Niphat Uthit 1 Rd., near the Krungthai Bank (every hour 6am-4pm, 2hr.).

From **Trang,** take a local **bus** to Satun which stops in La Ngu (45฿). For **taxis** from Trang to La Ngu, contact Trang Travel on Phra Ram VI Rd. across from the Thumrin Hotel near the train station (around 60฿).

■■■ NARATHIWAT

Proving that the east coast becomes increasingly photogenic the farther south you go, the beaches around Narathiwat are long, white stretches of sand, unspoiled by tourist-oriented hotels and beer bars. Narathiwat itself is relatively quiet and extremely lovely, a good place to escape the grime of urban areas and the fervent crowds of other beaches. At the north end of town, the Bang Nara River empties into the sea, and the Gulf returns the favor by washing salt water upstream with each tide. A fishing community sprawls where the two meet, and just over a small bridge, is Hat Narathat, a unique beach with several pools of water locked in by small hills of sand. A predominantly Muslim town with a beachside space-age mosque, Narathiwat echoes with early morning calls to prayer, a soothing prelude to the small barrage of fishing boat motors. While Narathiwat may seem far removed from the country's commercial economy, the closed doors hide black market trading and thriving prostitution. All traffic, the idyllic and the illicit, comes to a standstill at 6pm, however, as the national anthem is broadcast in the streets. This slightly contrived display of patriotism reminds everyone that you haven't left Thailand, yet.

ORIENTATION

Narathiwat rests on the east coast, just before the Malaysian border. From here to Pattani, the coast is lush with relatively deserted beaches. **Puphapugdee Road** runs along the river in the east and **Pichit Bamrung Road** runs parallel, one block inland, crossing the bridge at the north end of town, near the mosque, to Hat Narathat. Other roads intersect these two, forming a ladder. The most easily identified landmark is the **clock tower** on Pichit Bamrung Rd. At this intersection, take a right up **Wichit Chaibun Road** to get to Puphapugdee Rd. close to the Narathiwat Hotel, which stands on the left, a bit across the street. The **THAI Air Office** is on

Puphapugdee Rd. across from the Narathiwat Hotel. Most intercity buses stop on Pichit Bamrung Rd. a couple km south where songthaews to Ban Thom congregate.

PRACTICAL INFORMATION

Tourist Office: The TAT for the province is in Sungai Kolok.

Currency Exchange: Thai Farmers Bank, 319 Puphapugdee Rd. (tel. 511 360). A block or two up from the Narathiwat Hotel going up toward Hat Narathat. Open Mon-Fri. 8:30am-3:30pm. **Siam Commercial Bank,** 133/4 Pichit Bamrung Rd. (tel. 512 737-40) near the corner of Chamroonnara Rd. Open Mon.-Fri. 8:30am-3:30pm. If you plan on crossing the border, you must change money in Sungai Kolok; no banks here sell Malaysian ringgit. Some banks actually recommend changing your money for better rates on the black market, but it is very likely that you will be cheated. Exercise caution!

Post Office/Telephones: (tel. 511 093), on Pichit Bamrung Rd. about 2 blocks past the clock tower on the right if you're walking out of town, away from the beach. Open Mon.-Fri. 8:30am-4:30pm, Sat. 9am-noon. **Telegram** and **overseas calls** are upstairs. Telegram open daily 8am-6pm. Overseas calls (tel. 511 002) open daily 7am-10pm. **Postal code:** 96000. **Telephone code:** 073.

Airport: (tel. 511 595), 13km northwest of town. THAI Air flies to **Bangkok** via **Hat Yai** (Wed., Fri., and Sun. 3:05pm). From Hat Yai you can go to **Phuket.** THAI Air has shuttles that go to and from the airport (40฿). Check for van departure time (usually around 1:30pm). **THAI Air,** 322-4 Puphapugdee Rd. (tel. 511 161), across from the Narathiwat Hotel, near Thai Farmers Bank. Manager speaks English well and can give info on Narathiwat province. Open daily 8:30am-5pm.

Trains: The closest train station is **Tanyongmat,** 20km outside town. Take a taxi or songthaew from in front of the market on Pichit Bamrung Rd. (20฿ per person). Train to **Bangkok** (12:48pm and 3:47pm), stops in **Surat Thani.**

Buses: Transportation is quite casual. Buses to **Bangkok** (A/C, 1:30pm, 506฿) leave across from the police station on Suriyapradit Rd. Buses to Sungai Kolok stop at the end of Pichit Bamrung Rd., away from Hat Narathat.

Minivans: (tel. 511 148). Depart in front of the Yaowaraj Hotel to: **Sungai Kolok** (every hr., 6am-5pm, 1hr., 40฿); **Tak Bai** (every hr., 6am-5pm, 45min., 25฿); and **Hat Yai** (every hr., 6am-5pm, 3hr., 80฿). There are also companies on the right of Pichit Bamrung Rd., past the clock tower as you walk away from the beach.

Local Transportation: Songthaews head south to **Tak Bai** (10฿) down Puphapugdee Rd. via **Wat Khao Keng** (5฿), and from near the hospital on Rangamanka Rd. (also for **Tanyongmat**). They circulate through town all day (4-5฿ per person within 10km), but **motorcycle taxis** are more common (5฿).

Hospital: (tel. 513 480), on the right side of Rangamanka Rd., about 2km south of town if you're heading out to Tanyongmat.

Emergency: tel. 191.

Police: (tel. 511 236) on Suriyapradit Rd. From the clock tower, walk down Pichit Bamrung Rd. At the end of the road turn right. The station is 2km down on the left. Some English; probably your best bet in an **emergency.**

ACCOMMODATIONS

Cathay Hotel, 275 Puphapugdee Rd. (tel. 511 014). If you are not one of the lucky minority with a river view, ask the manager to let you onto the roof. He speaks excellent English and will enthusiastically point out landmarks across the stunning panorama. Large rooms with clean sheets, spotless private bath, and plenty of light. Singles 120฿. Double 170฿. Try bargaining. Open 6:30am-10:30pm.

Yaowaraj Hotel, 131 Pichit Bamrung Rd. (tel. 511 148), on the corner of Chamroonnara Rd. Peppy staff maintains fairly large and sterile rooms with well-kept bathrooms in this concrete Thai-style hotel. Singles with bath 120฿, and A/C 200฿. Doubles with bath 180฿, and A/C 250฿. Open 7am-10pm.

FOOD

With a little more epicurean seasoning, Narathiwat would be a perfect town. The **market,** between Puphapugdee Rd. and Pichit Bamrung Rd., almost opposite the

Narathiwat Hotel, is weaker than those in most Thai cities, with some fruit and fresh vegetables, but that's it. Unfortunately, there's no night market, besides a few portable food stands in the market area. Several **roti stands** open up in the evening along Puphapugdee Rd. and Pichit Bamrung Rd.

There's a fine Muslim restaurant, **Ruste,** on Pichit Bamrung Rd. If you walk up Chamroonnara Rd. from Puphapugdee and take a left, it's right after the Siam Commercial Bank. Noodle soups with greens and fish balls 20฿. One man speaks decent English and can order you a big plate of fried vegetables for 20฿, a good way to get the fiber riboflavin lacking in many Thai treats. (Open noon-midnight.) The **open-sided restaurant** on the corner of Puphapugdee Rd. and Chamroonnara Rd. (on the same side as the Narathiwat Hotel) has a lot of prepared meat dishes but will stir up morning glory greens with garlic (15฿), sweet and sour fish, or the nuclear-hot *sahdawe* fried shrimp (45฿ for a sloppy plateful, 20฿ for enough to flavor your rice). They're open all day through dinner. **Restaurant No. 5** at Hat Narathat gets pretty loud, but serves good food. Most restaurants tend to offer more than food for the typically male clientele, but no. 5 is a bit more respectable. They have a superb beef salad and the spicy hot shellfish on top of rice makes a pleasing accompaniment to a glass of beer. Dishes around 40-50฿. Open for lunch and dinner (until 10pm).

SIGHTS AND ENTERTAINMENT

Free your mind—sit back, relax, and enjoy the views. If you walk up Pichit Bamrung Rd. toward the water, you'll see the fishermen casting their nets where the Bang Nara River gushes into the sea. Intricately painted fishing boats bob around as naked children splash in the low tide, looking half-heartedly for shellfish. Over the small bridge, you'll arrive at **Hat Narathat,** a large, shaded area which stays back from the water, lined with coconut trees and several small restaurants (a nice place for beer *à la* sunset). The sand crawls about 100m away from the restaurant area, and stretches for kilometers, undisturbed by tourists, bungalows, or trinket peddlers. It is basically deserted until evening, when locals come for picnics to bid farewell to the departing sun. Walk to Hat Narathat or take a motorcycle taxi for 5฿.

About 10km south of town, **Wat Khao Keng** is known for the mammoth Buddha that stands its ground about 100m back from the road. The 25m-high Buddha, set in the midst of peacefull, tropical forest, is daunting even to seasoned Buddha-watchers. Remove your shoes if you walk up to the platform. Young entrepreneurs sell flowers and incense. To see the small wat, wear long pants and a shirt that covers your shoulders. Songthaews go from Puphapugdee Rd. to the Buddha for 5฿ per person. Tell them you want to go to Wat Khao Keng.

Grapefruits??

Something in the countryside around Narathiwat makes the disease *elephantiasis* —the result of that nasty little nematode, the filarial worm—quite common. This, of course, often leads to massive swelling in the testicles, so that they puff up to the size of grapefruits, and the afflicted can hardly walk. As part of a local education campaign, sufferers play guessing games with the village children, asking them how many kilos their imposing gonads weigh. Don't worry about the swelling happening to you, however; it is easily detected and just as easily cured with a potent course of antibiotics.

■■■ SUNGAI KOLOK

Sungai Kolok is a vociferous and concrete border town at the southeast tip of Thailand. Most travelers usually go straight from the border to the train station or vice-versa without staying in the primarily "short-time trade" hotels plaguing the city. If you do spend the night, almost any hotel will feature this disturbing sideline. **Ban Taba,** a small town 5km south of **Tak Bai** (on the Gulf of Thailand), is increasingly becoming the preferred border crossing point. Ferries from Ban Taba to Malaysia cost 5-10฿, and the border there is open the same hours as in Sungai Kolok.

ORIENTATION

Most of Sungai Kolok is laid out in a grid. The **border crossing** is on **Asia 18 Road,** the main thoroughfare through the city, parallel to the train tracks. If you're coming from Malaysia, the TAT and tourist police are on the right, next door to the border police. The **train station** is about 1km down from the border on the right, an easy walk. If you are entering Sungai Kolok from another point in Thailand via bus, high-jump in a rickshaw or on a motorcycle taxi to get to the border. **Charoen Khat Road** runs perpendicular to Asia 18 Rd. and the train tracks, beginning at Asia 18 Rd., directly across from the station. The **daily market** runs along Asia 18 Rd., set back on smaller streets and alleys between the train station and the border.

PRACTICAL INFORMATION

Tourist Office: TAT, Asia 18 Rd. (tel. 615 230), next to the border on the left, from the town center. You have to walk through motor vehicle customs, so don't be put off by road blocks on Asia 18 Rd. Maps of Sungai Kolok, info about the city and Narathiwat province, and transportation schedules. Open daily 8:30am-5pm.

Tourist Police: (tel. 612 008), in the building with the TAT. Open daily 8am-6pm.

Immigration Office: Narathiwat Immigration Office, 70 Charoen Khat Rd. (tel. 611 231), across from the police station, after Shern Marcar Rd., coming from the train station. Open Mon.-Fri. 8:30am-4:30pm.

Currency Exchange: Thai Farmers Bank, 1/6 Vorakamin Rd. (tel. 611 578). On the corner of Charoen Khat and Vorakamin Rd.; on the right if you're coming from the train station about 4 blocks down, just past immigration. Open Mon.-Fri. 8:30am-3:30pm. Changes your baht into ringgit (or vice versa); banks in other provinces probably won't be able to change money.

Post Office/Telephones: (tel. 611 141) on Thespathom Rd. about 3 blocks from the Thailiang Hotel and across the street, near the Plaza Hotel. Post and Poste Restante are open Mon.-Fri. 8:30am-4:30pm, Sat. 9am-noon. The **telegram** and **overseas calling** office (tel. 612 124) is around the back. Open Mon.-Fri. 8:30am-4:30pm. **Postal code:** 96120. **Telephone code:** 073.

Airline Office: THAI Airways, 31 Thespathom Rd. (tel. 612 132), across from the Plaza Hotel.

Trains: Sungai Kolok Train Station, Asia 18 Rd. (tel. 611 162). Opposite Charoen Khat Rd. To: **Bangkok** (rapid, noon, 20-½hr, 200฿, sleeper: top 468฿, bottom 498฿, plus 100฿ for A/C; express, 3pm, 19-½hr., 230฿, sleeper: top 528฿, bottom 578฿, plus 100฿ for A/C); **Surat Thani** (6:30, 11-¾hr., 86฿ and 180฿; rapid, noon, 9-¼hr., 106฿ and 200฿; express, 3pm, 8-¾hr., 126฿ and 230฿); **Hat Yai** (6:30, 9am, 12:15, and 1:25pm, 4-½hr., 42฿ and 87฿; rapid, noon, 4hr., 62฿ and 107฿; express, 3pm, 3-¾hr., 92฿ and 137฿); **Chumpon** (rapid, noon, 12-¼hr., 130฿ and 250฿; express, 3pm, 11-¾hr., 160฿ and 280฿); and **Trang** (3:15pm, 15-½hr. with layover, 79฿ and 165฿). The **advance booking ticket office** window in Sungai Kolok is open daily 7am-4pm. Advance booking can only be made for Phattalung and farther destinations.

Buses: 45/2 Worakamin Rd. (tel. 612 045). At the intersection of Wongvitee Rd. To **Bangkok** (regular (read: suicide by smoke inhalation), 9am, 21hr., 296฿; A/C, 8am, 18hr., 414฿; A/C with bathroom, 12:30pm, 18hr., 533฿); stops in: **Narathiwat** (19฿, 26฿, and 33฿); and **Surat Thani** (10hr., 143฿; 10hr., 200฿; 9hr., 256฿). Buses to **Hat Yai** leave in front of the Valentine Hotel on the corner of Waman Amoey Rd. and Thespathom Rd., across from the post office about 1 block from the Thailiang Hotel (A/C, 4 daily, 7am-3pm, 4hr., 98฿). To **Narathiwat,** from in front of the train station (every 30 min., 6:30am-4:30pm, 1hr., 16฿).

Minivans: A/C vans leave from Charoen Khat Rd. across from the train station, next to Asia hotel to **Narathiwat** (50฿) and **Hat Yai** (110฿) every hr., 7am-5pm.

Local Transportation: Motorcycle taxis are the best way around, 10฿ to the border. **Bicycle rickshaws** are 20฿ per person to the border and may cost less within the busier streets. Both run regular fares from 5am-dark. After hours costs more.

Hospital: (tel. 611 109), Saitong 2 Rd., behind the train tracks. You can see it from the TAT Office on Asia 18 Rd. Some doctors speak enough English to get by.

Emergency: tel. 1699 for tourist police.

Police Station: (tel. 611 070), on Charoen Khat Rd., near the intersection of Shern Marcar Rd., on the left if you're coming from the train station, across from the immigration office and Thai Farmers Bank. Call the tourist police instead.

ACCOMMODATIONS

Paradise Hotel, 34 Wamanumnoi Rd. (tel. 611 313). From Charoen Khat Rd. take a right down Thespathom Rd. Wamanumnoi Rd. is past the post office about 2 blocks. No noyz in this quiet 'hood. The rooms are large with windows, double beds, and bath. Newly painted an exotic shade of gray, not bad for a concrete slab. Open 6am-midnight. Rooms with bath 120฿, and A/C 190฿.

Savoy Hotel, 34 Charoen Khat Rd. (tel. 611 093), on the right from the train station, 1 or 2 blocks down. A concrete immensity, well-lit, decent-sized rooms have clean sheets, hard mattresses and pillows, fans, and bearable bathrooms. Get a room off the street—the only things stompin' around here are the motor vehicles. Open 4am-midnight. Singles with bath 100฿. Doubles with bath 150฿. Chinese restaurant downstairs open 7am-4pm.

FOOD

Sungai Kolok's **daily market** spreads out before the sun gets out of bed behind Asia 18 Rd. Agonize over a wide selection of tasty foods: deep-fried dough, pancakes rolled with shredded coconut, spicy omelets, and an assortment of sticky rice in banana leaves—all very tender on palate and wallet. At night there is a string of **food vendors** along Shern Marcar Rd., to the left if you're coming from the train tracks. The specialty is snakes (they dirty-dance in tanks at the end of the food stall chain). For those who want to sit down while they eat, try the food vendors along Vorakamin Rd., starting at the Thai Farmer's Bank. Chinese stands have glass cases full of fresh vegetables and seafood; vegetarians will be tickled pink to see such a display of green. A plate of fried vegetables with garlic and spicy sauce on rice runs 20-25฿.

Siam Restaurant, 2-4 Shern Marcar Rd. (tel. 611 360), cooks up several extravagantly garnished seafood dishes at steep prices. There is a small section on the menu (English and Thai) with 20-25฿ dishes. They have good prawn fried rice for 20฿, or sharpen your incisors on a plate of fried vegetables with baby corn, giant mushrooms, and greens on rice for 20฿. The management will recommend the 70฿ lemon "chicken;" stay away from this poultry desecration. Open 10:30am-9pm.

BORDER CROSSING

The Thailand/Malaysia border, on Asia 18 Rd. near the Sungai Kolok River, is open daily 5am-5pm Thai time (1hr. ahead of Malay time), but there is talk of extending the hours to 9pm. There may be improvised Malaysian-run tour offices in Sungai Kolok, but most companies that organize buses or book flights between Thailand and Malaysia are located in Hat Yai. Thai buses do not cross through to Malaysia, nor do trains on the eastern coast. On the Thai side a small blue English sign guides you to two booths—one for arrivals and one for departures; check out and walk across the bridge to the small town of **Rantau Panjang** in Malaysia. A short distance farther (100 ft. or so) are the taxis. Both buses and taxis run every hour from the border to Kota Bharu. Buses cost RM2.4 (Malaysian ringgit), taxis RM3.5 per person. The same schedules and fares apply from Kota Bharu to the border.

Whichever way you cross, travel early! Transportation options on both sides of the border are most abundant in the morning. Arriving during banking hours saves you from getting stuck with no appropriate currency, and possibly being forced to re-cross the border. If you are arriving from Malaysia and plan to cash traveler's checks for Thai baht, be sure to arrive between Mon. and Fri., 8:30am-3:30pm. If you are crossing in the other direction, you can go to Thai Farmer's Bank to exchange any left-over baht for Malaysian ringgit, good for taxis to Kota Bharu. Keep in mind that most banks in Kota Bharu are closed on Fridays.

VIETNAM

Prepared to be the next Asia powerhouse, Vietnam wants to prove a point to the world: this country, whose guerilla soldiers outwitted and humiliated two big-shot western powers, can once again triumph over odds. The "free world" tried to punish this nation for choosing communism over democracy and the USSR over the USA. Yet, after twenty years of struggle, neglect, and rejection, Vietnam has resuscitated itself; and the world waits avidly at its doorstep. Signs of the brutal war which was burned into the memory of a generation around the globe still linger here, and thousands of Vietnamese remain unaccounted for, but these people are ready to make peace with the past. Vietnam is no longer a war; it is a thriving country.

The passage of time has finally quelled the bitterness of defeat, as the U.S. finally extended a hand to its former enemy in July 1995, ready to put that war comfortably behind it. To the international community, the establishment of diplomatic ties is a stamp of approval, ushering in a stampede of venture capitalists ready to bless the Vietnamese with free enterprise. Massive development slated for the next few years means that all doors will soon be open and visitors will be able to travel more easily across the land. The time to see Vietnam is now. From the spectacular mists and rocky limestone crags of Halong Bay to the tangled rivers and emerald rice paddies of the Mekong Delta, Vietnam's charm and beauty still entice foreigners to its shores as it once did during a former era.

ESSENTIALS

■■■ GEOGRAPHY

Vietnam extends 1600km from China to the Gulf of Thailand, encompassing rugged mountains, flat lowlands, fertile valleys, and white sand beaches. The Hoang Lien Son Mountains circle the Red River Delta in the north; sheltered within these highlands is Vietnam's highest peak, Phan Si Phan Mountain, which rises to 3163m. To the south, the 1200km-long Annam Highlands, now called the Truong Son Mountains, stretch from Thanh Hoa Province to just north of Ho Chi Minh City (Saigon). At either end of the country are two alluvial plains, the Red River Delta in the north and the Mekong Delta in the south. The original settlement of the Viet people, the fertile soil of the Red River Delta attracted numerous people from surrounding regions. Monsoon rains often overflow the tributaries of the Red River, causing devastating floods. The Mekong Delta, although one of the richest regions in the world, was the last frontier of Vietnam until the 19th century when the French resettled Vietnamese peasants into the area. Large silt deposits often change the shoreline of Vietnam's southern tip. The central coastal strip runs along the eastern seaboard of central Vietnam, forming a narrow, low plain sometimes cut through with towering mountains that fall into the sea. The rocky land and saline soils make this region somewhat unsuitable for cultivation, but the Champa kingdom flourished here more than 1000 years ago with an abundant rice agriculture.

■■■ WHEN TO GO

Vietnam's extension over several latitudes makes for some variable climates between the three historically divided regions of the country. In north Vietnam (Bac Bo), the weather is much cooler than the south, with mild temperatures and little rainfall during the winter (November-April) and heavy rains and even violent typhoons during the summer (May-October). In the south (Nam Bo), temperatures remain constant and humid, averaging 30°C. Here, the dry season starts in November and ends in April with two months of unbearable heat just before the rain breaks, bringing in the wet season (May-October). Central Vietnam (Trung Bo), by contrast, has transitional weather. Hue, sitting in the middle of Vietnam's coastal curve, tends to be overcast throughout most of the year with constant rainfall, even in the dry season between February and April. In the interior highlands of the country, temperatures at night are pleasant and cool and can be downright freezing during the winter (October-March). The "infernal" months of March and April average a cool, pleasant 26°C.

■■■ GETTING AROUND

BY PLANE

Travel by plane is the best way to get from one end of the country to the other. You wouldn't want to be in a train or bus for a week when you can simply cover the same distance in less than 24 hours. The two hubs are, of course, Hanoi in the north and Ho Chi Minh City in the south. From each of these major cities, trains, buses, motorcycles, or cars will transport you to your destination. Haiphong, Hue, Da Nang, Nha Trang, Dalat, and Dien Bien Phu have airports of their own, but flights there are more infrequent. In addition, there is a 15,000Đ departure tax for all domestic flights. **Do not lose your baggage claim tickets because you won't be allowed to take your luggage out of the airport without them.**

BY TRAIN

Trains in Vietnam do exist, but solely for the pleasure of existing. Because the gauge of Vietnamese trains are smaller than those in the west, they move at a rather sluggish pace (maximum speed of 50km per hour), and require a lifetime's worth of patience. Furthermore, train tracks that once extended throughout the country are now in disrepair, many of them having been sabotaged by the Viet Minh or destroyed by American bombs.

BY BUS

The national bus transportation system is a dirt cheap way of traveling in Vietnam. However, it is not for the impatient, faint of heart, or those sensitive about their personal space. Buses are actually large flat-bed trucks with seats bolted in and a roof overhead. The rides are loud, dusty, and tiring. Furthermore, these "buses" are tailor-made for petite Asians, not 6-feet-tall *tay ba lo* (backpackers) who will find most seats impossibly small. For long distance trips, purchase your tickets at least one day in advance. Arrive one hour before the departure time to ensure a seat. Expect to be packed in with bikes, fruits, vegetables, and lots of sweating commuters. Hang on to your life as the driver ignores all safety precautions to speed to his destination. Hang on to your valuables, too; pickpockets can have a field day amidst the confusion.

BY BIKE AND MOTORCYCLE

Traveling by motorbike is a good alternative mode of getting from city to city without relying on the nightmarish transportation system. The laws in Vietnam allow foreigners to operate motorbikes which are 100cc and under without a motorcycle license; consequently, you can rent one anywhere. Tourists with an operator's license, however, can choose from more powerful machines. The Czech-built Jawa 350cc, dubbed the "Saigon taxi," is the motorcycle of choice among those who engage in long-distance cruising, particularly up and down the highway. The alternative to this powerful, petrol-hungry machine is the Belorussian-built Minsk 125cc. This is the workhorse driven mostly by motorcycle taxi drivers up in the mountains to the northwest of Hanoi. Both can be bought (and easily resold) by checking out the listings posted at many of the tourist cafés. In addition, these motorcycles are

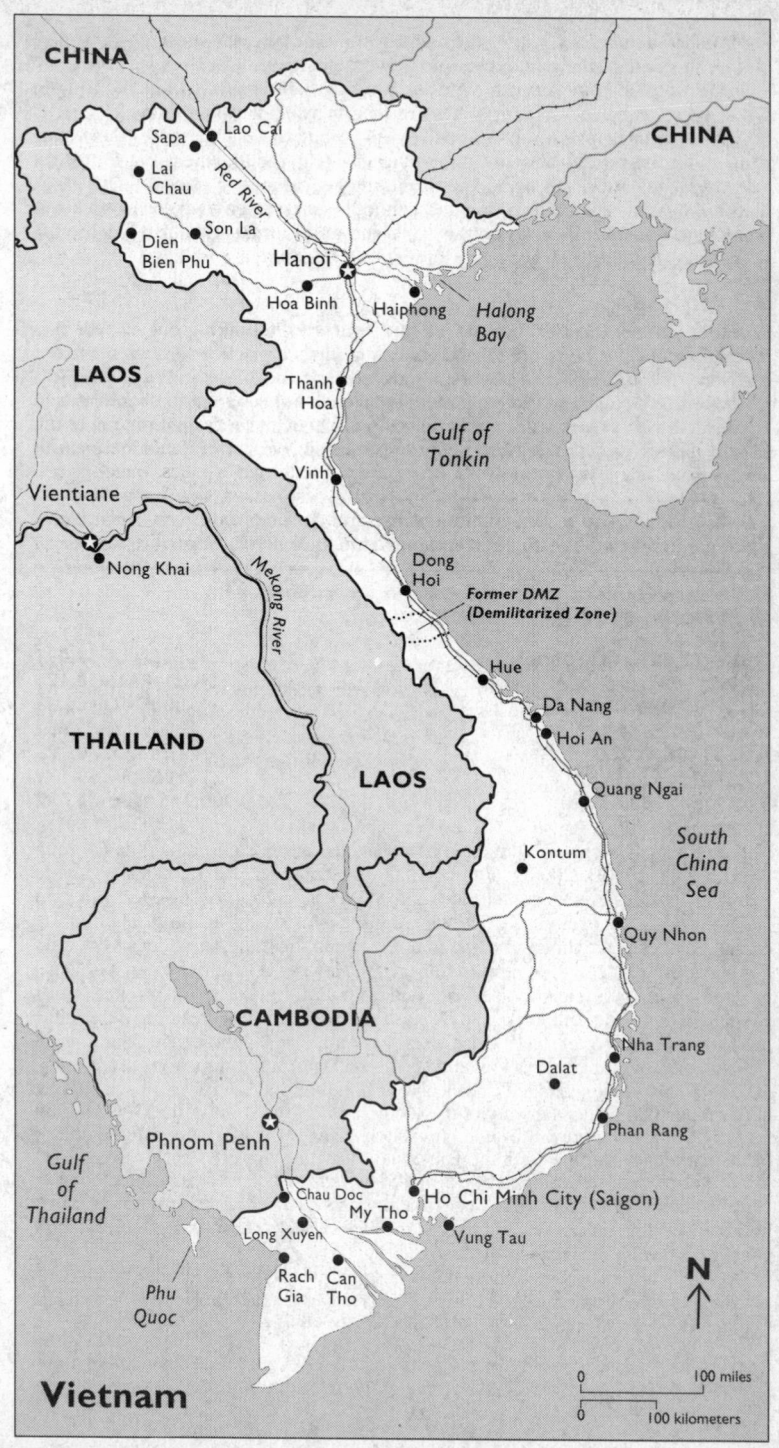

CHINA
CHINA
Sapa
Lao Cai
Lai Chau
Red River
Dien Bien Phu
Son La
Hanoi
Hoa Binh
Haiphong
Halong Bay
LAOS
Thanh Hoa
Gulf of Tonkin
Vinh
Vientiane
Nong Khai
Mekong River
Dong Hoi
Former DMZ (Demilitarized Zone)
Hue
Da Nang
Hoi An
THAILAND
LAOS
Quang Ngai
Kontum
South China Sea
Quy Nhon
CAMBODIA
Nha Trang
Dalat
Phan Rang
Phnom Penh
Gulf of Thailand
Chau Doc
Ho Chi Minh City (Saigon)
My Tho
Long Xuyen
Vung Tau
Rach Gia
Can Tho
Phu Quoc
N
0 100 miles
0 100 kilometers

Vietnam

very familiar to mechanics along the highways and can be easily serviced. If travelers choose this option, they should be sure to wear a helmet.

For those who have recently won the Tour de France, and would like to train while vacationing in Vietnam, bikes are readily available. Used bicycles cost 2-500,000Đ and will take some Trump-like deal-making to get a fair price. Many complain about the poor quality of Chinese bicycles (e.g. the Phoenix), but for tourist purposes, they are perfectly adequate and the logical budget choice. Bicycle helmets are nonexistent, so once again (it cannot be stressed enough) be careful. It is possible to transport bicycles on the buses and trains for an additional fee. Inquire specifically. Practically all guest houses rent out bikes and motorbikes.

BY THUMB

Whether you set out purposefully or find yourself hitchhiking out of necessity (breakdowns, etc.), be assured that it is a commonplace practice all along the major highways. If you flag down a bus or minibus, expect to negotiate and pay a fare. This is how many Vietnamese catch an intercity bus when the bus station is already too far afield. Private vehicles and trucks that stop to offer you a ride might or might not ask for money. It's a mixed bag. Most importantly, use your best judgment and always make safety your priority.

Let's Go urges you to use common sense and consider all the risks involved before hitchhiking. We do not recommend hitchhiking to anyone.

■■■ MONEY

US$1=11,001.10Đ (dong)	**1000Đ=US$0.091**
CDN$=8092.41Đ	**1000Đ=CDN$0.124**
UK£1=17,095.71Đ	**1000Đ=UK£0.58**
IR£1=17,425.74Đ	**1000Đ=IR£0.057**
AUS$1=8110.01Đ	**1000Đ=AUS$0.123**
NZ$1=7214.52Đ	**1000Đ=NZ$0.139**
SARand=3008.80Đ	**1000Đ=SARand0.332**

The monetary system of Vietnam is based on the **dong.** Denominations come in 200Đ, 500Đ, 1000Đ, 2000Đ, 5000Đ, 10,000Đ, 20,000Đ, and 50,000Đ. Be aware that many establishments quote prices only in US$; as a result, *Let's Go* lists prices in US$ and dong accordingly. However, **pay for everything in dong.** Fluctuating exchange rates make things cheaper in dong, and in the hinterlands, locals often do not know the rate. But more importantly, it's the law; as of October 1994, it is illegal to use US$ in transactions. Use large denomination bills (US$100) to get better exchanges for dong, but keep a small stash of US$1 and US$5 readily available for quick transportation use. *Let's Go* advises non-Americans to exchange their currencies into US$ before going to Vietnam, as this will facilitate transactions there.

US$ can also be exchanged unofficially at hotels and in jewelry shops at slightly better rates than banks. Be wary of the women who sit in front of the GPO looking for fat, US$-carrying prey; they will often shortchange you. The rates offered on the black market are hardly better and you could easily be swindled.

It's best to carry **traveler's checks** in US$ which can be exchanged for dong at certain banks—Vietcombank, Cosevina, and ANZ—for a 2% commission. Most hotels and airline offices will not accept traveler's checks. **Lost or stolen traveler's checks cannot be replaced in Vietnam.**

Tipping is not necessary, although it is customary to leave some small change. At more expensive restaurants and hotels, 10% is added to the bill. Good gifts to hand out include pens, invalid stamps, and balloons (for children).

KEEPING IN TOUCH

The **postal service** in Vietnam could use a little competition to speed it up; your friends might as well hold on to their mail and give it to you upon your return. Mail can take as long as three weeks to and from Vietnam. **Poste Restante** service is available in major cities, but cross your fingers and make a wish upon every star, fountain, and tooth you can find. Address as follows: Name of addressee, Poste Restante, city, city code, Vietnam. Packages to Vietnam will be opened and inspected.

As foreign investments pour into the country, telecommunication lines are going up tenfold. Once not too long ago, **telephones** were scarce, but today, almost all businesses have phone and fax. **Long-distance calls** placed from Vietnam can cost you a paycheck or two. Forget it! If you want to reach out and touch someone, call them and have them call you back. It is impossible to make **collect calls** from private phones; the post office will place collect calls for a 11,000Đ charge. Also try asking your hotel operator for this service. Dial 10 for long-distance calls, if you must. **Country code:** 84.

STAYING SAFE

Vietnam is quite a safe country—no rebels, insurgents, or civil wars to mar your Southeast Asian getaway. Just keep in mind some of the general rules about safety and follow your instincts. Hold on tight to all your belongings, as many pickpockets rove the streets for unsuspecting tourists, and keep your eyes out for con artists. They are especially prevalent in Ho Chi Minh City. In addition, keep in mind that the police in Vietnam are generally unfriendly and should, in most cases, be avoided. A new law prohibits the police from collecting fines directly—they can only hand out tickets—so don't be fooled into paying fines directly. **Be sure not to photograph any bridges or other military structures.**

HOURS AND HOLIDAYS

Most offices and museums open around 7 or 8am and close by 4 or 5pm with a break at midday, 11:30am-2pm. Most offices close on Sundays except museums, which close on Mondays instead. All offices close public holidays (noted below).

January 1: New Year's Day (official).
February: *Tet,* traditional new year, 1st to 7th day of new lunar month (official).

Good News For Grandma!

Although most visitors are aware that *Tet,* the Lunar New Year, is the most celebrated holiday in Vietnam, few people are aware of *Ram Thang Bay,* Vietnam's other significant celebration. Also called *Tet Trung Nguyen,* it falls on the 15th day of the seventh lunar month (around the second week of August). The festival is a time for forgiveness and centers around absolving the sins of the dead. According to legend, there once was an impoverished woman who committed one petty crime after another; her son, on the other hand, was a paradigm of virtue who equaled his mother's bad deeds with a succession of good ones. When the mother passed away she was sent to hell to suffer for her crimes. But when her son died, he instead went to heaven, where he could see all the deeds of man, on earth as well as in hell. Seeing his mother's unspeakable torments, the son approached the King of the Underworld to appeal for his mother's soul. The King weighed the deeds of the son against the sins of the mother and decided to vindicate her. He was so moved by the son's piety, in fact, that he declared a day of forgiveness in hell—a respite for those serving their penance. During the Ly (1009-1225) and Tran (1225-1400) dynasties, even prisoners were allowed to return home to visit their families.

February 3: Anniversary of the Communist Party of Vietnam (official).
March: Hai Ba Trung Day (6th day of the 2nd lunar month).
April: *Thanh Minh,* New Year of the Dead (5th day of the 3rd lunar month).
April 30: Liberation of South Vietnam and Saigon (official).
May 1: International Labor Day (official).
May 19: Ho Chi Minh's Birthday (official).
May 28: Celebration of the Buddha (official).
August: *Trung Nguyen* (15th day of the 7th lunar month). See graybox above.
September 2: National Day (official).
September 3: President Ho's Anniversary (official).
September: Mid-Autumn Festival, celebrated by children with moon cakes, lanterns, and music (15th day of the 9th lunar month).
November: Confucius' Birthday (28th day of the 9th lunar month).

■■■ POTPOURRI FOR $100, ALEX!

Streets, boulevards, roads, avenues, and lanes are all referred to in this guide as **duong,** abbreviated "D," not to be confused with "Đ" for dong. Be aware that many of the streets change names every few "blocks," in order to memorialize as many national heroes and events as possible in the city. You will notice after a while that many of the street names repeat themselves over and over and over in every city: Tran Phu, Dien Bien Phu, Quang Trung, etc.

Vietnam is seven hours ahead of Greenwich Mean Time (GMT).

LIFE AND TIMES

■■■ HISTORY

Little remains of the ancient civilizations of Vietnam, but the earliest inhabitants known to historians were the **Negritos** who vanished from the region with the arrival of peoples from the Indonesian archipelago. Not long afterward came the **Kinh,** who were forced southward from the lower Yangtze River Valley into the **Red River Delta** by the encroaching Chinese.

Located on a strategic land mass on the crossroads of trade, Vietnam was later inundated by migrating **Mon-Khmer** and **Tai-Kadai** ethnic groups, some of whom intermarried with their predecessors. These are the ancestors of the **Viet** people of today. The language of the Mon-Khmers formed the basis of the Vietnamese language while tonality was borrowed from the Thais. However, it was the later arrival of the ethnic **Chinese** who left an indelible cultural stamp on Vietnam.

In the Red River Delta, the Viet people established the kingdom of **Au Lac** which prospered peacefully until 207 BC when the Chinese began filtering into the region. A Chinese general from Guangdong subjugated the Red River Delta, which then became the southern province of the kingdom Nan Yueh, or **Nam Viet,** referring to the peoples of the south.

THE CHINESE MILLENNIUM

The **Han dynasty** fully incorporated Nam Viet into its empire in 111 BC. Thus began a millennium of brutal Chinese rule—the root of the Vietnamese people's hostility for their northern neighbors. During this long period, Chinese immigrants flooded the Red River Delta and intensified the Sinicization of the region, making Vietnam culturally distinct from the other Indianized countries of mainland Southeast Asia. The Han emperors divided Nam Viet into three administrative districts of **Annam, Tonkin,** and **Thanh Hoa.** Despite the cruelty of their oppressors, the Vietnamese people, most notably the elite, accepted aspects of Chinese culture—the classics, Confucian principles, **Mahayana Buddhism,** and Chinese characters—while thoroughly resisting Chinese rule. The culture, philosophy, politics, and technical innovations imposed by the Chinese greatly advanced Vietnamese civilization, but the more the Vietnamese people absorbed of Chinese culture, the more they craved independence. All revolts were harshly suppressed, which only intensified the hate.

The decline of the **Tang Dynasty** (618-907) marked the rise of Nam Viet. In 939, the Vietnamese, under the leadership of **Ngo Quyen,** successfully overthrew Chinese rule. Ngo declared himself king of the kingdom of **Dai Viet.**

While controlling northern Vietnam, the Chinese tried to assert itself over the **Chams** living in the south. According to early Chinese records, the Chams overthrew Chinese authority in the 1st century AD and established a kingdom near Hue. **Champa** came to be a powerful state that challenged Chinese rule outside of China proper, occasionally invading Nam Viet. A contemporary of **Funan** (see Cambodia "History" on page 63), Champa absorbed its neighbor's Indianized culture when it annexed the Funanese province of Panduranga (Phan Rang). The Chams, who belong to the Malay race and speak a language that originated from Indonesian, readily accepted the Hindu culture and its institutions. Champa outlasted Funan, but it was finally destroyed in 1471 by the expanding Vietnamese. All that remains of this matriarchal society are ruins near Phan Rang, Nha Trang, Hue, and Da Nang.

INDEPENDENT VIETNAM (939-1860)

After the downfall of the Chinese, Vietnam enjoyed nearly a thousand years of autonomy under several strong dynasties that ruled from Hanoi and Hue. Yet, the first few years of self-rule were plagued by internal disputes and incursions from the Thai kingdom of **Nanchao** and Champa. As a result, Dai Viet sought protection from China, entering an overlord-vassal relationship with its former enemy.

The rise of the **Ly Dynasty** (1009-1225) brought stability to the region over the next two hundred years. During their reign, the Lys displaced war lords and moved the capital to modern-day **Hanoi** where they created a strong centralized government based on a nine-level hierarchical bureaucracy adapted from China. Hence the new government was thoroughly Confucian in principle, and the mandarins, the undisputed intellectual leaders, promoted Confucian values throughout the kingdom. Although the Lys fiercely resisted Chinese influence, Nam Viet was already on the fast track to Sinicization.

In 1225, the **Tran Dynasty** (1225-1400) arose to overthrow the Lys. The Trans divided Dai Viet into 12 provinces in order to better administer the kingdom. A series of strong, capable rulers pursued public works projects including the building of irrigation and water control systems and embankments along the Red River. In the waning years of the Tran dynasty the Chinese once again overpowered Dai Viet. This time, their rule was even more cruel: they imposed Chinese civil service officials on the kingdom, banned the Vietnamese language, and forced all the people to carry identity cards. Those who resisted were exiled to Beijing where they were forced into service for the empire. The Vietnamese, led by **Le Loi,** rebelled against these harsh actions, and eventually drove out the hated Chinese in 1428. Le Loi then established the **Le Dynasty** (1428-1776); during this period, Vietnam became more Sinicized than it ever has been during the millennium of Chinese rule. The language, writing, religion, art, and government system of China became firmly established in Vietnamese life.

In addition to the constant threat from their northern neighbors, internal disputes broke out within the royal family. In this vulnerable state, the Le family succumbed to a despotic general who ruled Tonkin briefly until his downfall at the hands of an aristocrat named **Trinh.** Meanwhile in Hue, the prominent **Nguyen** family, once aligned with the Les, established their own sphere of influence, posing a threat to the Trinhs in the north. A struggle ensued between the two families, and a wall near the 17th parallel divided the kingdom into two territories. The Nguyen power in Annam (central Vietnam) soon spread to the south and by 1720, they had pushed out the Chams, most of whom fled to present-day Cambodia where their descendants still live. With Champa out of the way, the Nguyens were able to extend their jurisdiction into the Mekong Delta, then a part of the Khmer kingdom of Angkor, and incorporated **Saigon** into their growing kingdom.

As the Nguyens grew in strength, the Trinhs waned in authority. The **Nguyen brothers** (not to be confused with the Nguyens of Hue or the Nguyens of *Let's Go* fame) from the northern district of **Tayson** rebelled against the tyranny of the Trinh family and eventually united both kingdoms. The people of Tonkin hailed these three brothers as heroes who freed the land from the despotic and corrupt Trinhs, while those of Annam viewed them as usurpers who had taken advantage of the Nguyen king's recent death. The teenage **Prince Nguyen Anh** fled into exile, as a victorious Nguyen Hue of Tayson declared himself **Emperor Quang Trung.**

In 1787, a French missionary and supporter of Nguyen Anh returned to France on behalf of the prince. A treaty was signed in which the beleaguered King Louis XVI promised French military aid in return for a trade monopoly with Vietnam and the cession of the port of Da Nang. But the French were slow in their support. By the time a meager French army arrived in Vietnam in 1789, Nguyen Anh had already captured Saigon and was pressing on toward Hue and Hanoi.

By 1802, Nguyen Anh had installed himself at Hue as **Emperor Gia Long** of Annam, the first king of the **Nguyen Dynasty** (1802-1883), Vietnam's last royal family. Gia Long proved to be a remarkable and strong ruler who reinstituted a Chinese-based administration, Confucian principles, and a code of law. With the help of the French, the king created a navy and fortified the kingdom by constructing forts and casting weapons. The crumbling irrigation system was restored and new roads connecting the three main cities of Saigon, Hue, and Hanoi were built. Today Gia Long is regarded as the father of Vietnam and his dynasty marks the country's golden age, even though it hailed the arrival of the French.

COLONIAL RULE AND NATIONALISM (1860-1954)

The French were not the first Europeans to venture to Vietnam. In 1535, a Portuguese captain had sailed into Da Nang Bay and claimed most-favored-nation trading status for Portugal, but the Portuguese could not fully subjugate the Vietnamese. A century later came the Dutch, just in time for the territorial dispute between the Trinh and Nguyen families. Ever canny and ready to turn a profit, the Dutch set up arms factories in the north to supply the Trinhs; the Portuguese played their cards and backed the Nguyens.

A truce ended the war and a trade slump drove out the Portuguese and Dutch merchants by 1700, leaving behind them a handful of Catholic missionaries intent on "civilizing" the Vietnamese. Vietnamese officials kept missionary activity to a minimum, fearing that ideas promulgated by the Europeans would lead to a conquest of their kingdom and a breakdown of the traditional Vietnamese order. Missionary activities continued doggedly, however, until they were banned and even made punishable by death.

France, outraged at the persecution of European missionaries (not to mention the Catholicism-bashing), invaded Vietnam. Emboldened by the success of other European countries in establishing power bases in Asia, France felt obligated to get a piece of the imperialist pie. Therefore French forces attacked Da Nang in 1858 and Saigon in 1861, forcing **Emperor Tu Duc** to cede three southern provinces and pay an indemnity.

The delta was annexed and became **Cochin China.** In 1883, Vietnam was formally divided into the French territories of Tonkin (north), Annam (central), and Cochin China (south). The emperor continued to rule over Tonkin and Annam, although the French had the final say in all major decisions, while Cochin China was strictly governed by the colonialists. Over the next few years, France also expanded its influence in the region and annexed Laos and Cambodia to form **French Indochina.** French rule, often cruel and arbitrary, devastated the people through ill-conceived policies designed to drain the countries of their resources.

The early 20th century saw the rise of **nationalism** in Indochina, most notably in Vietnam. having been introduced to western ideas by elite Vietnamese who had studied in France, numerous national and anti-French societies spread rapidly, although most were clandestine and lacked well-defined political goals. Eventually, these organizations were united under the leadership of the **Indochinese Communist Party (ICP)** which was founded in 1930 by **Ho Chi Minh.** Ignored by western representatives at Versailles when he urged France to improve the administration of Vietnam, Ho turned to communist doctrine, and ultimately headed to Moscow in 1924. He spent the late 1920s organizing revolutionary groups in China, Thailand, and Hong Kong, where the ICP was founded. Meanwhile, in Vietnam, the French were ruthlessly suppressing nationalist revolts. The communists remained silent and removed while growing in numbers. After 30 years of self-exile, Ho returned to Vietnam in 1942 to lead a revolution.

The Japanese invasion of Indochina in 1941 was a welcome respite from the French, but Ho Chi Minh's forces resisted the occupation. The French remained in nominal control, but were virtual slaves to their Axis enemy. The communists, in an effort to broaden and strengthen their political and social base, willingly collaborated with non-communist groups. This united-front organization became the Vietnam Independence League, better known as the **Viet Minh.** When World War II ended, Ho Chi Minh acted quickly, expecting the French to return to reclaim Vietnam. **Emperor Bao Dai** also feared French domination, and practically handed his power over to Ho by abdicating. Already in control of much of the country, the Viet Minh declared independence for their country. Still, the French attempted to reassert control over the former colony, much to the dismay of the Vietnamese people. Negotiations failed because France was not willing to recognize Vietnam's independence; consequently a long, bitter war ensued. In May 1954, France's overwhelming defeat at the hands of the ragtag Viet Minh at **Dien Bien Phu** was a death knell for the colonialists (see Dien Bien Phu "Sights" on page 582).

THE VIETNAM CONFLICT

Dien Bien Phu marked the end of the **First Indochina War.** The **Geneva Accords** that same year divided Vietnam temporarily along the 17th parallel into two countries. Ho Chi Minh took control of North Vietnam while U.S.-backed **Ngo Dinh Diem** proclaimed himself president of South Vietnam. An all-Vietnamese election scheduled for 1956 to unify the country was never approved by either the U.S. or South Vietnam; they feared the vote would have gone to the communists. After that failed attempt at democracy, the 17th parallel became the border between the **Democratic Republic of Vietnam** (North) and the **Republic of Vietnam** (South).

With the withdrawal of the French came the arrival of the Americans, who assumed responsibility for the survival of democracy by providing financial aid and military advice to South Vietnam. Diem was extremely unpopular in South Vietnam, however. The U.S. supported Diem because of his anti-French, anti-Communist, and Christian sentiments, but unlike "Uncle Ho," he was out of touch with the Vietnamese people. Under the pressure of a continual guerilla war waged by the **Viet Cong** (a derogatory term used by Diem and Americans for the Viet Minh), Diem was so oppressive a leader that he was overthrown and assassinated in 1963 by his own troops (with U.S. approval, of course).

The civil war in Vietnam escalated with the intervention of the U.S. in August of 1964, when North Vietnamese naval crafts *supposedly* attacked the **U.S.S. Maddox** while it was engaged in espionage activities in the Gulf of Tonkin. President Lyndon Johnson, long afraid of losing the next presidential election, saw in the situation a way to salvage his image. The U.S. retaliated to the outrageous "attack" by bombing North Vietnam and sending troops to the South.

Meanwhile, South Vietnam had been in a state of anarchy since Diem's assassination. In 1965, **Nguyen Van Thieu** seized control. In an effort to control the South's dictatorial government and to escalate the war against the north, the U.S. sent 3500 Marines to Da Nang on March 7, 1965. Three years later, in the spring of 1967, over 500,000 American soldiers were stationed in South Vietnam.

The Vietnam War reached a climax with the **Tet Offensive** of February 1968 when the Viet Minh attacked more than 100 cities and military bases in the south during new year celebrations. Although a devastating military defeat for the communists, the offensive was a crucial psychological victory. Both sides suffered heavy losses and, for the first time, it was evident that the North Vietnamese were willing to make extensive sacrifices in order to win the war. Thus, the U.S. resolved to withdraw from the conflict before further embarrassing itself. Johnson decided not to seek office again and Richard Nixon was elected by promising to carry out the withdrawal of troops.

Although the U.S. began to withdraw its troops, it continued and increased saturation bombing of Vietnam, Laos, and Cambodia, culminating in an overt invasion of the latter country despite fierce protestations from Cambodian president Sihanouk (see Cambodia "History" on page 63). The **Paris Agreements of 1973** called for a cease-fire, the total withdrawal of U.S. combat forces from all three countries, and the release of American prisoners of war. Without further hesitation, the 200,000 North Vietnamese troops left in South Vietnam launched a massive offensive and were joined by comrades from across the 17th parallel. The South suffered severe losses and was unable to protect itself. Saigon fell on April 30, 1975.

The new government moved to crush all opposition. They rounded up hundreds of thousands of people and imprisoned them without trial in forced labor camps, or "reeducation camps." Rather than face the terror that came with the communist victory, thousands of South Vietnamese fled their homeland.

With the loss of much of the country's educated elite and the physical destruction wrought by the U.S., the task of rebuilding Vietnam was phenomenal. Furthermore, herbicides used by the U.S. government to destroy foliage in South Vietnam proved to have a long-term detrimental effect on rainfall, soil erosion, and consequently the productivity of the land. It is estimated that in an attempt to defoliate the rainforests which camouflaged communist guerillas, the U.S. wiped out a 30-year supply of timber that will take at least another century to replace.

Without enough outside aid, Vietnam's ambitious plans to rebuild the economic, social, and political infrastructure of the country were fruitless. The Soviet Union, Eastern European countries, and China contributed to the reconstruction effort, but the U.S.—the country that had wrought physical destruction on Vietnam in the first place—refused to give the aid that had been promised in the Paris Agreements. A campaign of repression against the country's ethnic Chinese community as well as the invasion of Cambodia at the end of 1978 prompted the Chinese to withdraw financial aid and to attack Vietnam in 1979. In addition, western nations condemned Vietnam for intervening with the situation in Cambodia in order to stop the atrocities of the Khmer Rouge regime. (See "The Vietnamese Intervention" on page 67.) Under U.S. pressure, the International Money Fund denied credit to Vietnam, and the U.S. itself led a trade embargo against the country.

■■■ VIETNAM TODAY

The end of the Cold War and the collapse of the USSR in 1991 has since forced Vietnam to seek rapprochement with the west and its capitalist Southeast Asian neighbors. Taiwan, Singapore, Thailand, and Japan are now Vietnam's largest investors. With the memories of failed hard-line communism in mind, Vietnam's new leadership is more than willing to give free enterprise a chance. As the government sees it, trade and tax treaties with the U.S. will attract and reassure international investors. The establishment of diplomatic relations with the U.S. marks the beginning of Vietnam's quest for economic success in the footsteps of Thailand, Malaysia, and, more importantly, Singapore. While willing to liberalize the market economy to a prosperous end, the not-so-hard-lined-but-still-communist leaders will not relinquish their unchallenged political authority and privilege. Amidst protestations of human rights abuses, Vietnam is seeking most-favored-nation trading status as well as investment incentives from the U.S.

■■■ THE PEOPLE OF VIETNAM

The Vietnam War dramatically shifted the demographics of Vietnam. Today, two-thirds of Vietnam's 78 million people are under the age of 25 and have few memories, if any, of the war.

VIETNAMESE

Constituting 85% of the population, the **Vietnamese** are descended from the Kinh people who migrated into the Red River Delta more that 2000 years ago. The majority of ethnic Vietnamese are Buddhist, but many continue to practice a mix of Taoism and Confucianism.

CHINESE

Today there are about one million ethnic **Chinese,** or *Hoa,* in Vietnam, most of whom live in the south. Nearly all of them have adopted Vietnamese citizenship, but most continue to follow Chinese customs and traditions. The Vietnamese government has recognized the importance of the once-persecuted Chinese in the development of Vietnam; as merchants and tradespeople who belong to highly organized ethnic enclaves in large cities, the Chinese play a leading role in the economy of the country.

CHAM

The central and southern provinces of Vietnam are home to about 100,000 **Chams.** Following the complete and final destruction of their kingdom in 1720 by the expanding Vietnamese, the Cham king and many of his people fled to Cambodia where their descendants still live to this day. Those who remained in Vietnam were dispossessed and pushed off their land, while their artistic traditions died out due to hardship and extreme poverty. Although once culturally similar, differences can be discerned among the Chams of today. Chams living in the central region still follow old Brahmanic traditions while those in the south have converted to Islam which was propagated by Indonesian merchants.

MONTAGNARD

Montagnard is a common term used to describe the numerous hill-tribes that live in the mountains of northern and central Vietnam. These ethnic minority groups vary in size, but altogether, there are 6-8 million Montagnards. The way of life of these hill-tribes is changing fast. Montagnards have found their traditions and customs undermined by alien cultural influences in their villages, and assaulted under the pressure of constant fighting with the French, Vietnamese, and even each other. Most of the hill-tribes migrate every few years and cultivate upland crops using shifting cultivation. Relatively isolated from Vietnam's mainstream society, Montagnards are often autonomous and have their own systems of government within their respective groups. Larger Montagnard tribes include: the **Tay,** who live in the northwest; the **Thai** (ethnically distinct from those in Thailand), who can be found in the river valleys of the north, as well as the slopes of the northwest mountains; the **Moung,** who make their homes in Thanh Hoa and Yen Bai provinces in the north central part of the country; the **Nung,** who inhabit northeast Vietnam near the border; the **Hmong,** who dwell in the highest altitudes, usually near the Chinese border; the **Gia Rai** (or Zria), which is the largest group in Central Vietnam; and the **Dao,** who occupy the northern frontier in Lao Cai and Ha Giang provinces.

■■■ CUSTOMS AND CULTURE

GETTING ALONG IN VIETNAM

The Vietnamese, no less than other Asian people, value manners and courtesy. It would be wise for visitors to practice moderation in all things—from conversation to compliments to drinking—and to observe the moral code of the Vietnamese people. Some of the differences between Vietnamese and western customs are small, but lapses can be extremely offensive.

Do not use typical western motions to beckon a Vietnamese, for such gestures are only used for animals in Vietnam. Do not greet a Vietnamese with a slap on the back; instead, press palms together in front of the chest and bow your head slightly. If you see an argument between some Vietnamese people, do not get involved. Above all, respect older people in Vietnam. The Vietnamese highly respect their elders, consider them fountains of knowledge, and thus accord them the highest social standing.

In addition, any public displays of emotion are considered in poor taste. It is impolite to raise your voice or gesture wildly to anyone, especially in public. While the Vietnamese disapprove of men and women walking hand in hand or embracing, it is perfectly natural to see men holding hands as a sign of friendship.

RELIGION

Vietnam has no official religion; instead, some of the major world religions are widely practiced here and have had a profound impact on the people and their culture. Animism, Buddhism, Confucianism, and Taoism have all shaped Vietnamese society. Underlying these faiths is a widespread belief in ancestor worship, and the result is a unique melange of beliefs.

Animism is the oldest religious system in Vietnam as well as in most other countries in Southeast Asia. Considered the "people's religion," animism is popular in rural areas, especially among the Montagnards. Animists believe in the spirit world and hold that each person has a spirit which exists even after death. Since all spirits are associated with people, they can possess all the traits, good and bad, known to man. As a result, believers try to placate spirits and keep them happy through elaborate ceremonies and animal sacrifices.

Believed to have been brought to Vietnam by conquering Chinese, or even by the Viet people themselves, **Taoism** pervades daily Vietnamese life. Although the religion is not formally organized in Vietnam today, its tenets and convictions continue to influence and shape Vietnamese society. The Tao is essentially a way of life by which man attains harmony with nature as well as with the mystical currents of the spiritual world. Taoism holds that whatever happens is inevitable and man must attune his thinking and actions to this end.

The Kitchen Gods

In Vietnamese homes, the kitchen is not a separate, detached room, but an integrated part of the house which is connected directly to the outside. The greater part of most food preparation occurs around a single, wood-burning hearth composed of a single brazier with three supports to accommodate cooking pots and pans. In the times before the braziers, however, the Vietnamese used three clay blocks or stones as a hearth; these three "kitchen gods," as the stones were known, symbolized spousal fidelity. The origin of this image derives from a popular folk tale about a merchant and his wife. After waiting several years for the return of her husband from the sea, the wife gave up hope and remarried. However, as luck would have it, he returned home after a harrowing journey. The wife still loved her former husband, but feared that her new husband would discover the truth, so she hid her first husband under a stack of wood. When her new husband returned home from a long day's hunting, he set the wood afire to roast his dinner, consequently killing his predecessor. The wife, distraught and guilt-ridden over her first husband's death, threw herself into the fire. The new husband, ever devoted to his wife, searched out the same fate. Consumed by the fire, these three metamorphosed into the hearth stones at the heart of all Vietnamese kitchens. A hot *menage à trois,* to say the least.

Another Chinese belief that found its way to Vietnam, **Confucianism** is an important key to understanding the Vietnamese of today. Founded by Confucius 2500 years ago as a philosophical way of being, this belief system emphasizes the need for good government and harmonious relations among men, but not the salvation of the soul. This is the golden rule of Confucianism: "Do not to others what you would not want them to do to you." Ever the humanist, Confucius also urged filial piety, which has evolved into the rites of ancestor veneration still practiced today.

In such a thoroughly Sinicized country, **Buddhism** stands out as the only great Indian influence on Vietnam. Introduced to the Vietnamese people in the 2nd century AD by Chinese and Indian monks, Buddhism stresses the "Middle Way," which can be achieved through the Four Noble Truths and the Noble Eightfold Path. But nothing is as important to Buddhism as the doctrine of karma, which states that one is responsible for one's own past, present, and future actions. The Vietnamese people follow the Mahayana Buddhist sect, unlike the rest of mainland Southeast Asia—another influence from China. Altogether, these last three religions and their concepts have been melded into a philosophy and religion known as The Three Teachings, which forms the bedrock of all traditions, customs, and manners of the Vietnamese people.

Travelers should be respectful of all religious iconography in Vietnam, where society is still defined by religion. Do not point at any Buddha figures, and dress modestly when visiting pagodas and shrines.

WOMEN IN VIETNAM

Women's liberation came to Vietnam years ago. Stepping out of their traditional roles, women were a catalyst behind the sweeping social changes blazing through Vietnam. Traditionally, Vietnamese women had been subordinate to men, but they always exercised a great deal of influence in family financial affairs. In fact, many women ran and supervised businesses, as well as households. Today, they are often willing to work long hours and as efficiently as any man. The positions held by young men before the war were filled by women who continued to perform these roles even in peace time. Although many still want happy domestic lives, Vietnamese women today are more career-oriented and desire higher levels of education.

■■■ THE ARTS

Unlike Angkor and the rest of Southeast Asia, Vietnam developed a rich literary tradition, rather than an artistic one. Although magnificent artistry and architecture can be found throughout the country (most notably the imperial palace at Hue), the art of Vietnam is a reflection of Chinese styles. The Vietnamese never created a visual art form that was strictly Vietnamese.

ART AND ARCHITECTURE

The earliest art found in Vietnam dates from 500 BC and belonged to the **Dong Son** civilization near modern-day Thanh Hoa. Little is known about this culture, but the magnificent bronzes left behind were clearly of Chinese influence.

Early architecture can be found in central Vietnam, where the Hindu kingdom of **Champa** once prospered. Between the 6th and 11th centuries, Champa produced some splendid temples and fine carvings, although most traces of them have disappeared with time and war. At the beginning of the 8th century, Cham art was strikingly similar in style and form to that of the Gupta period in India. Even this early in its development, the Cham art already showed native influences; by the end of the 9th century, it had become distinctively Cham.

The complete annihilation of Chams in the 15th century by the Vietnamese marks the end of Cham architecture. Vietnamese art and architecture progressed through several periods coinciding with the various dynasties, but since they were Chinese prototypes, they never gained their own characteristics.

DANCE AND DRAMA

Many Vietnamese enjoy a popular theater form known as **cai luong** (old music), which originated in the 1920s. Similar to American musicals, *cai luong* uses dialogue and singing to communicate with the audience. *Cai luong* is universally appealing in its simplicity, understandable to even non-Vietnamese people could understand. Today *cai luong* is written by writers who have modernized classic plots. Actors perform in traditional Vietnamese as well as western dress. **Hat boi,** once a popular dance form, originated from classical Chinese opera, in which gestures are of primary importance and singing replaces dialogue. Performances incorporate old Chinese music and traditional Chinese dress. Unfortunately, there has been no attempt to revive *hat boi,* since it nearly vanished after the division of Vietnam in 1954. In addition to these foreign-inspired theatrical forms, Vietnam has cultivated its own dramatic art form called *mua roi nuoc* or **water puppet theater.** *Mua roi nuoc* originated in northern Vietnam perhaps as early as the 1st century AD. In water puppet theater, all the water's a stage and the puppets in it are legendary heroes from historical and religious epics. Puppets are carved from a light, water resistant wood and then painted. Hanoi boasts the most famous water puppet theater tradition, but the art form has spread out through most major cities in Vietnam.

LITERATURE

Under a millennium of Chinese rule, literature flourished, forming the foundation for the development of a strong literary heritage. Examples of early Vietnamese literature recorded on mulberry bark remain a testament to the great literary tradition of Vietnam. Before the Vietnamese adopted a written script much like Chinese, folk tales, legends, songs, and proverbs were passed on orally from generation to generation. In the 13th century, a new script called **nom** was developed and used thereafter to immortalize literary works, even though this literature remained largely Chinese in style. From the 15th century on, *nom* literature took on a form of its own. Considered to be truly Vietnamese in nature, these works were simple and addressed the problems and injustices of the age. The many pieces composed during the *nom* literary movement continue to be favorites among the Vietnamese today.

The 17th and 18th centuries saw the birth of **truyen** (verse novel) which was much like Homer's epic poems. Traveling storytellers mesmerized audiences with *truyen* tales, which quickly became popular throughout the kingdom. It was not until the 19th century, however—a period fraught with social and political unrest—that Vietnamese literature attained its height. Prolific poets and writers churned out Vietnam's greatest masterpieces during this epoch, including the highly celebrated **Truyen Kieu** (Tale of Kieu).

The arrival of the French proved to be another important marker in the development of Vietnamese literature. The **quoc ngu** script created by Father Alexandre de Rhodes in the 17th century came into more widespread use and, consequently, Vietnam's dependence on Chinese traditions ceased. The new script was adopted in the 1920s and a decade later, Vietnamese literature had taken on a decidedly western tone. A new form of poetry emerged that expressed the nationalist sentiments of the Vietnamese people and the desire for liberation from foreign oppression. Unfortunately, during the past 20 years, Vietnamese literature has declined dramatically due to a government crack down on free speech and the press.

MUSIC

From ABBA to Chinese ballads to reggae, the music scene in Vietnam today is an eclectic blend of old and new and eastern and western. There are two styles of popular music that can be heard in the cities. Renditions of western pop, called **nhac ngoai,** have become the fad in the fledging music industry. Sung in the original language or in Vietnamese, these bootleg songs are immortalized on music videos across the country. The other popular music trend harkens back to another time:

slow melancholy ballads, or **nhac tru tinh,** are songs from before 1975. These songs are returning to popularity now that the times are changing.

■■■ FOOD AND DRINK

Vietnamese cuisine, considered the heart and soul of the country, can be summed up in three words: fish sauce (*nuoc mam*), mint (*hung*), and rice (*com*). Supplement them with some vegetables, eggs, and small amounts of meat and fish, and you're in business. While similar to Chinese, Vietnamese food uses less fat for frying. Fruits like bananas, mangos, oranges, coconuts, pineapple, and papayas are well-loved by the people and sometimes serve as colorful garnishes for popular dishes.

Names of most dishes are the same throughout the country, although they are spiced and presented differently in their own regions. Local specialties abound. The most renowned and celebrated of all Vietnamese dishes is *pho.* This hot, light meat stock soup has flat rice noodles, beef, beef tripe, or chicken mixed with chili sauce, *nuoc mam,* mint, bean sprouts, and lemon for a hot tangy flavor. For those humid tropical days, try *bun,* a cold salad of lettuce, cucumbers, shredded carrots, thin rice noodles, grilled meat or egg rolls topped with peanuts and a sauce made with fish sauce. Rice dishes are usually eaten by the Vietnamese with a vegetable dish, a meat dish (roast pork, broiled chicken, or caramel-stewed beef), a pickled dish (often greens), and the ubiquitous *nuoc mam*. In addition to these national dishes, Vietnam serves up some scrumptious cool drinks, including *mia da* (pressed sugarcane with ice), *che* (sweet bean drink), *nuoc chanh so da* (soda lemonade), and, of course, *bia hoi* (draft beer).

NORTH VIETNAM

■■■ HANOI

Stern and austere, Hanoi has through its long history been the intellectual, artistic, and political center of Vietnam. It has seen the effects of French colonialism, revolutionary communism, and today, the opening of its economy to the world market. Each of these historic influences are visible throughout Hanoi, from the tree-lined avenues which dress the yellow French villas, the massive no-nonsense structures of the state (the National Bank), and the latest presence of small companies which have the words "joint-venture" or "foreign investment" in their names. The city that spawned a communist revolution is now going through a revolution itself. Since 1988, when the government, taking a cue from Gorbachev's *perestroika* policies, adopted a new course of economic policy dubbed *Doi Moi* (Renovation), Hanoians have put down their Russian textbooks for English, and have forsaken Marx for Smith.

Hanoi has long seen its cousins to the South prosper. Its large collection of artists and thinkers have suffered the cliched existence of poverty, but things are changing fast. These days the name "Honda" is becoming more common than Nguyen, and the Dream II is the model of choice among the *nouveau riche* of Hanoi. The migration of business into Hanoi has already brought the Marlboro Man and the Energizer Bunny into the Old Quarter. At last word, Joe Camel and the Yes-I-Am guy were waiting for their visas.

Despite the rapid influx of Southeast Asian and western investment, Hanoians are aware of the destruction that capitalism can incur in its wake. Proud residents are keen to preserve the rich heritage of Hanoi, and its traditions can still be seen at the numerous lakes where people gather to talk, meet, and play Chinese chess. The resilient people of Hanoi didn't let the bombings of the war destroy their city, and they are not about to let the war between Pepsi and Coke do it either. While Saigon may be the pocket book, Hanoi will always be the heart and mind of Vietnam.

GETTING THERE AND AWAY

By Air

Flights into Hanoi land at **Noi Bai International Airport** (tel. 269 090), 35km north of the city center. If you have diligently filled out your customs and entry/exit cards, the wait should be no longer than one hour. Keep your baggage claim tickets secure—you will not be allowed to exit with your bags without them. **Note:** Keep your stamped, white immigration card with your passport. Accommodation establishments are required to register guests with the local police and will need your card for that purpose.

Beware of the sharks that circle in search of unsuspecting and naive tourists. They will try to take you for a ride with their initial prices, but you can work them down to 110,000Đ. An metered taxi will take you into town for 220-275,000Đ. For 44,000Đ, take the minibus shuttle (Toyota minivans) waiting outside the terminal. The shuttle departs when all seats are filled and will drop passengers off at the **Vietnam Airlines office,** 1 D. Quang Trung, just south of Hoan Kiem Lake. The only other option is renting a car. If you choose this alternative, they stamp "sucker" on your forehead and charge you 495,000Đ per day, and 3850Đ per km to boot.

Flights out of Hanoi are subject to a tariff of 15,000Đ for domestic flights and 66,000Đ for international flights. Domestic flights to **Ho Chi Minh City** (daily, throughout the day, 1,870,000Đ); **Hue** (daily, 6:30am and 2:30pm, 880,000Đ); **Da Nang** (daily, 7, 11:40am, and 2pm, 990,000Đ); and **Nha Trang** (Tues., Thurs., and Sat., 7am and 12:40pm, 1,430,000Đ). Book all tickets at Vietnam Airlines. Other international and domestic flights available.

By Train

Travelers arriving in Hanoi from Haiphong, Lao Cai, and all points south disembark at **Hanoi Railway Station** (Ga Hanoi), 126 D. Trang Tien at the west terminus of D. Tran Hung Dao, about 1km southwest of Hoan Kiem Lake. A 10-minute cyclo ride (5-8000Đ) from the station will quickly bring visitors to the heart of the city. Usually prices for foreigners are considerably higher than for native Vietnamese. Tickets for foreigners can be purchased at window #3 (open 7am-7:20pm) just beyond the fare kiosk. Buy train tickets 2-3 days in advance, as this is probably the safest and most efficient form of ground transportation, seats disappear fast.

Three classes of trains depart from Hanoi for **Ho Chi Minh City:** slow (S1, Mon., Thurs., and Sat., 7pm, 36hr.), slower (S3, daily, 10am and 7:30pm, 40hr.), and slowest (S5, daily, 10am and 7:30pm, 44hr.). Soft seats to: **Hue** (220-286,000Đ); **Da Nang** (264-330,000Đ); **Nha Trang** (473-605,000Đ); and **Ho Chi Minh City** (550-715,000Đ). For trips overnight, take hard sleepers to: **Hue** (330,000-495,000Đ); **Da Nang** (385-550,000Đ); **Nha Trang** (660-990,000Đ); and **Ho Chi Minh City** (803-1,188,000Đ). Two trains daily to: **Lao Cai** (LC3 at 5:30am, LC1 at 8:20pm, 10hr., 198,000Đ soft); **Lang Son** (DD1 at 6am, HD1 at 10pm, 7hr., 110,000Đ soft); and **Haiphong** (HP3 at 6:25, HP1 at 3pm, 3hr., 44,000Đ soft).

By Bus

Kim Ma Bus Station (to points west and northwest), on D. Nguyen Thai Hoc just after the intersection with D. Giang Vo on the left about 3km west of Hoan Kiem Lake (8-10,000Đ cyclo ride). Open 3am-5pm. To: **Son La** (4am, 12-14hr., 21,000Đ) and **Dien Bien Phu** (5am, 22-24hr., 51,000Đ; service is sometimes discontinued during the rainy season).

Southern Bus Station (to all points south), on D. Giai Phong (tel. 641 453), the south extension of D. Le Duan, 5km past the train station on the left side. A cyclo ride or motorcycle taxi (*xe om*) should run about 10-15,000Đ. Open 4am-5pm. To: **Haiphong** (3:30pm, 3hr., 13,000Đ); **Thanh Hoa** (10-12 daily, 6am-4pm, 4hr.,

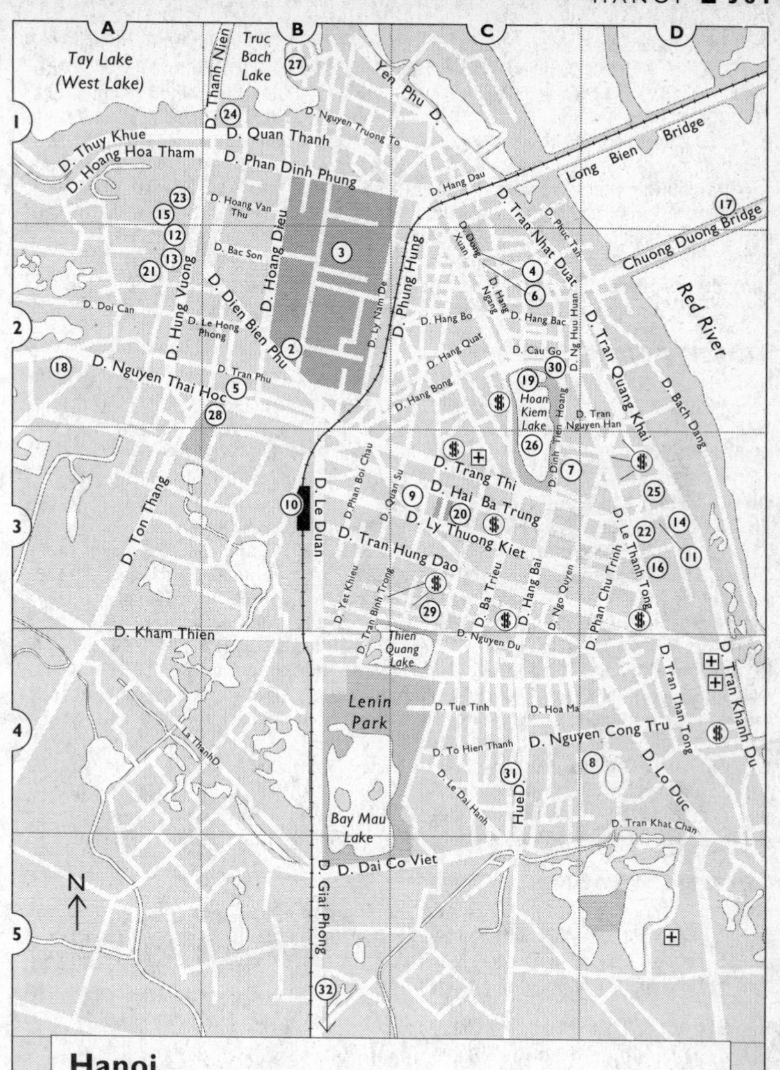

6

7

Hanoi

Quan Su Pagoda, **1**
Army Museum, **2**
The Citadel, **3**
Dong Xuan Market, **4**
Fine Arts Museum, **5**
48 D. Hang Ngang, **6**
General Post Office, **7**
Gia Lam Bus Station, **17**
Hai Ba Trung Pagoda, **8**
Hanoi Hilton Prison, **9**
Hanoi Railway Station, **10**
Hanoitourism, **11**

HCM Mausoleum, **12**
HCM Museum, **13**
History Museum, **14**
Ho Chi Minh's House, **15**
Hom Market, **31**
Hon Gai (Halong Bay) Buses, **16**
Kim Ma Bus Station, **18**
Ngoc Son Pagoda, **19**
19/12 Market, **20**
One Pillar Pagoda, **21**
Opera House, **22**

Presidential Palace, **23**
Quan Thanh Pagoda, **24**
Revolutionary Museum, **25**
Southern Bus Station, **32**
Tortoise Tower, **26**
Tran Quoc Pagoda, **27**
Van Mieu Pagoda, **28**
Vietnam Airlines, **29**
Water Puppet Theater, **30**

($) Bank
(+) Hospital

15,000Đ); **Sam Son Beach** (7:40am and 1:40pm, 4-5hr., 78,000Đ); **Vinh** (5:45, 6:30, and 7:30am, 8-10hr., 30,000Đ); **Dong Hoi** (8am, 18-20hr., 30,000Đ); **Hue** (6:30am, 24hr., 40,000Đ); **Da Nang** (5:30 and 7am, 27hr., 45,700Đ); **Quy Nhon** (8am, 42hr., 70,000Đ); **Nha Trang** (10am, 50hr., 80,000Đ); **Dalat** (6 buses, Wed.-Sun., 90,000Đ); and **Ho Chi Minh City** (8am, noon, and 3pm, 60hr., 123,000Đ). The schedule fluctuates often (that's why it's written in chalk), but these are their ordinary times and expected hours of travel. Be aware that men who operate their own buses may approach you; they do not have permits to drive their buses from the station, so they solicit there. Use your judgment in dealing with these characters.

Gia Lam Bus Station (to points north and northeast), off D. Nguyen Van Cuu, 1km after crossing Chuong Duong Bridge from the city and partially obscured on the left side. Buses do run from here, but there is no permanent schedule.

ORIENTATION

Hanoi is a city of lakes. Throughout the city, they serve as hubs of business, as well as centers of leisure. At the heart of the city is **Hoan Kiem Lake,** Hanoi's most useful and picturesque landmark. Just to the north of Hoan Kiem Lake is the **Old Quarter** of the city, a veritable backpacker's haven with its thriving market of narrow streets. To the south of the lake are five parallel, east-west boulevards from north to south: **Duong Trang Thi/Hang Khay/Trang Tien, Duong Hai Ba Trung, Duong Ly Thuong Kiet, Duong Tran Hung Dao,** and **Duong Nguyen Du**—which demarcate an area full of banks, embassies, businesses, shops, restaurants, and street merchants. These three sections form the downtown area, **Hoan Kiem District.** To the south of Hoan Kiem is **Hai Ba Trung District,** where **Lenin Park** and small specialty shops can be found. **Dong Da District,** one of the poorest sections of Hanoi, sprawls out west of Hai Ba Trung. **Ba Dinh,** Hanoi's fourth district, lies to the west of Hoan Kiem Lake and is bounded on the east by the **citadel** and on the south by **Duong Nguyen Thai Hoc.** This district has attracted a lot of foreign investment and is even now under heavy development; it is likely to become the new and future Hanoi. In the center of this section of the city sits the **Ho Chi Minh Mausoleum** with the cold solemnity of a dead communist leader. **Tay Lake** swallows up almost the entire area north of the mausoleum, and its north shore is heavily settled by expatriates. Bordering the southeast corner of West Lake is **Truc Bach Lake;** the strait separating the two lakes is a popular night hangout for the young and hip of Hanoi.

GETTING AROUND

Although Hanoi has a public bus system, don't count on it. Buses come as often as the Messiah and the routes and signs take a Ph.D. to figure out. As a result, most people get around on two-wheelers. Don't despair; four-wheeled animals are slowly making their mark and beginning to multiply.

By Bicycle and Motorbike

Most hotels and guest houses will rent motorbikes for 55-110,000Đ per day. A motorbike can be a great way to explore beyond the Hoan Kiem and Ba Dinh districts and get you to the pockets of Hanoi seldom visited by *tay ba lo* (backpackers). Be prepared to fork over 500-1000Đ each time you park your bike. Insist on a helmet when you rent. As your driver's ed teacher used to ask, "Would you rather look stupid or would you rather look dead?"

Although some feel Hanoi is a little bit too large to navigate by bicycle, for the fit and hearty it is a great alternative to the motorbike. Bicycles allow you to soak in more of the landscape and are nimbler as well as easier to handle. The best way to obtain a bicycle is through your hotel or guest house (6-10,000Đ per day).

By Cyclo and Motorcycle Taxi

Perhaps one of the most delightful and comfortable ways to get from place to place is on the three wheels of a **cyclo.** These ubiquitous vehicles can be found on almost every corner or in the streets hunting for customers. Don't let yourself get nickeled and dimed out of a fortune. Always agree on a price before you get on (5000-8000Đ should get you anywhere within a 3-4km distance). You can also hire cyclos by the hour (11,000Đ per hour). This is a great way to see the city at night. Motorcycle taxis are less common in the city than their human-powered cousins. They are faster and more useful for distant rides (like to the Southern Bus Station) and therefore have slightly higher rates of 2000-3000Đ per km. They can also be found loitering on street corners with cyclo drivers or can be hailed and/or found at signs that say *"Xe Om"* (motorcycle taxi).

By Car

Well who's Mr. Fancy? Cars are still not commonplace in the city yet but this does not mean you can't rent one. Renting a car also means getting a driver so you can cruise around and feel special. If you must, rent from **Especen** (see "Practical Information" below) for 308,000Đ per day in town and 3080Đ per km for travel outside of Hanoi.

By Taxi

Taxis line up across the street from the Vietnam Airlines office on D. Bai Trieu waiting to take passengers to the airport (165-220,000Đ, 45min.). **Hanoi Taxi** (tel. 535 252 or 533 171) and **Thang Long Taxi** (tel. 265 241) will also pick you up and deliver your to your destination for a heavy toll (22,000Đ plus 7700Đ per km).

PRACTICAL INFORMATION

Tours: Vietnamtourism, 30A D. Ly Thuong Kiet (tel. 264 154 or 264 089; fax 257 583), and **Hanoitourism,** 18 D. Ly Thuong Kiet (tel. 257 886 or 256 036; fax 254 209), offer a wide array of pricey tours, as well as a variety of visa services: extensions, changes of entry and exit points, and misplaced visas. Both are open Mon.-Sat. 7:30-11am and 1:30-5pm. **Especen,** 79 D. E. Hang Trong (tel. 251 659 or 261 071; fax 269 612). The choice of the backpacker community, this tourist conglomerate offers the same services as the other two, in addition to money exchanges and bike, car, and motorbike rentals. Come here if you want all your needs taken care of in one place. Open Mon.-Sat. 7:30-11:30am and 1:30-5pm. Visa, MC, AmEx. **Note:** don't bother going directly to the Ministry of Foreign Affairs for visa services; they will send you to one of the tourist companies.

Embassies and Consulates: Australia, 66 D.Ly Thuong Kiet (tel. 252 763; fax 269 005). **Cambodia,** 71A D. Tran Hung Dao (tel. 253 789; fax 265 300). **Canada,** 31 D. Hung Vuong (tel. 235 500; fax 235 333). **Indonesia,** 64 D. Ngo Quyen (tel. 251 785). **Laos,** 22 D. Tran Binh Trong (tel. 254 576; fax 228 414). **Malaysia,** A3 Van Phuc Quarter (tel. 253 371; fax 232 166). **Singapore,** 41-43 D. Tran Phu (tel. 233 966). **Thailand,** 63-65 D. Hoang Dien (tel. 235 042). **UK,** 16 D. Ly Thuong Kiet (tel. 252 510; fax 267 562). **US,** 7 Lang Ha (tel. 431 500 or 431 510).

Currency Exchange: Vietcombank, 47-49 D. Ly Thai To (tel. 265 501; fax 269 067). Exchanges most major currencies; no commission. 0.5% commission on traveler's checks. Traveler's checks to cash, 1.2% commission. Visa and MC advances, 4% commission. Branch offices have same services. Open Mon.-Sat. 8-11:30am and 1:30-4:30pm. **ANZ Bank,** 14 D. Le Loi To (tel. 258 190; fax 258 188). Eats 1.5% commission on exchanges and 4% on traveler's checks and Visa or MC advances. Open Mon.-Fri. 8:30am-12:30pm and 1:30-3:30pm, Sat. 8:30am-noon. **Citibank,** 17 D. Ngo Quyen (tel. 251 950; fax 243 960). At the time of this writing, Citibank had not yet moved to this address and had not set up currency exchange services. **Banque Nationale de Paris (BNP),** 8 D. Tran Hung Dao (tel. 253 175; fax 266 982). Good place to exchange money if you're in the areas south of Hoan Kiem Lake. Rates similar to those of ANZ Bank. Open Mon.-Fri. 8:15am-noon and 1:30-5:15pm.

American Express Office: 51 D. Ly Thai To. Was about to open, at the time of this writing. The leather couches were being dusted, but the doors were still closed.

Post Office: GPO, 75 D. Dinh Tien Hoang, southeast of Hoan Kiem Lake, handles all foreign and domestic mail. Packages are handled down the street at 77 D. Dinh Tien Hoang). Pick up Poste Restante here at the counter to the right. Address held letters: Henry "Evil Knievel" NGUYEN (or name of addressee), Poste Restante, GPO, Hanoi, VIETNAM. Telegram and telex services available. For express mail service overseas go to the DHL booth on the corner of D. Dinh Tien Hoang and Le Thach. The entire postal complex is open daily 7:30am-7:30pm.

Telephones: Telephone office, 75B D. Dinh Tien Hoang (tel. 259 771; fax 260 970), adjoining the GPO. Most reliable place for overseas calls. Because of exorbitant rates (44,000Đ for 1st min., 33,000Đ each additional min.), give your party the above telephone number and have him or her call back. It costs 11,000Đ to receive an overseas call. Fax. Open daily 6:30am-9:30pm. **Branch office,** 66 Luong Van Can (tel. 262 999). Domestic and overseas calls at the same rates. Open 6am-9pm. **Telephone code:** 4. **Information:** tel. 16.

Luggage Storage: No official places for luggage storage. Ask the hotel or guest house where you are staying to hold you bags and indicate when you will pick them up. Most places do this for free, but take valuables with you. Tourist cafés will do it with a smile if you take one of their tours. Otherwise, expect a small fee.

Lost Property: Handled by the police. Good luck—trying to recover lost items will be as easy as finding an officer who has never taken a bribe.

English Books and Media: Green Bamboo Café, 42 D. Nha Chung, has book exchange. The national English daily, *Vietnam News* (2000Đ), covers world, and Vietnam current events as well as major sports. Available at most news stands.

Library: The National Library, 31 D. Trang Thi. Large reading room filled with young, studious Vietnamese (often with their English readers and textbooks). To the left of the reading room building is the periodical building. 2nd floor has a hodgepodge of foreign language magazines, particularly English and French.

Convenience Store: EuroFood, 65 D. Hang Trong (tel. 257 809), just west of Hoan Kiem Lake. Dry and canned goods, cereal, soft drinks, soaps, detergent, and shampoo. Reasonable prices. Open daily 6:30am-7:30pm.

Laundry: Rumba at 15 D. Le Van Huu, around the corner from Hom Market. 1500Đ per piece. Same-day service if it's left by 9am. Open daily 7:30am-7pm.

Swimming Pool: Army Sports Club, 19 D. Hoang Dieu, the Citadel, has a gym, lap pool, and other athletic facilities, including showers and lockers. Admission 10,000Đ. Open daily 7:30am-7:30pm.

Pharmacies: Nha Thuoc Nguyen Van Luan, 3 D. Trang Thi (tel. 268 644). A good pharmacy. Open daily 8am-noon and 2-6pm. The **large pharmacy,** 2 D. Hang Khay (tel. 259 573), is down the street, across from the State General Dept. Store. Open daily 7am-7pm. Both are just south of Hoan Kiem Lake. Most western prescription drugs are available over the counter in Vietnam.

Hospitals: T Swedish Clinic (tel. 252 464), in the Van Phuc area opposite the Swedish embassy 3.5km west of the center of town. Western hospital with western prices. **Bach Mai Hospital International Department** (tel. 522 005 or 522 083), on D. Giai Phong 2.5km south of the train station. Dated but adequate Soviet-built facility. English-speaking doctors available. Open 24 hrs. **Viet Duc Hospital,** 48 D. Trang Thi (tel. 253 531), 2 blocks west of Hoan Kiem Lake. **24-hour** surgical hospital with German-, French-, and English-speaking doctors. Well-stocked pharmacy. **Dr. Raphael Kot,** Van Phuc A2, Room 101 and 102 (tel. 430 748; cellular tel. 019 041 919), is a western-trained doctor who offers vaccinations at cost and charges 550,000Đ per consultation. **Medevac** services through **AEA International,** 4 D. Tran Hung Dao, 4th Floor (tel. 213 555; fax 213 523).

Police: Central station, 2 D. Le Thi To (tel. 254 108), on the southwest corner of Hoan Kiem Lake at the intersection of Le Thi To and D. Trang Thi.

Emergency: tel. 15. **Police:** tel. 13.

ACCOMMODATIONS

You will find yourself long on budget choices in Hanoi with a large variety of prices and quality to choose from. No price is written in stone; negotiate yourself a better deal, particularly if you have a multiple-day stay. In hotels, inexpensive rooms are on the upper floors because there are no elevators and in the summer, heat rises with a vengeance. On the bright side, you get a great view and the mosquitoes won't bother you as much. Rooms are usually two-bed doubles; negotiate for singles. If you came to Vietnam to hang out with other westerners and to eat watered-down, sterile Vietnamese food, tourist cafés are the place to go. Cafés are not all bad, however, as they offer a gnarly place to hook up with other travelers, invaluable budget-travel info, beds, and decent tours of the region. Made from the same mold, they all have the same kind o' food, the same kind o' rooms, and the same kind o' info.

Hoan Kiem District

Unlike the frenetic activity of the markets in the Old Quarter, Hoan Kiem Lake serves as a quiet sanctuary from the hustle and bustle. You'll find many great deals when looking for a bed for the night. Be careful not to get too entranced by the lake and Old Quarter; you'll miss what the rest of Hanoi has to offer. Almost all accommodations have laundry services.

Tan Vinh Hotel, 1 D. Hang Phen (tel. 258 707). From the northern edge of the lake, walk up D. Luong Van Can 3 blocks and turn left on D. Hang Bo. Go 1 block and turn right on Thuoc Bac. It's on the corner with Hang Phen. The rosewood furniture in the reception room makes you feel you're getting red carpet treatment. They really roll it out in the rooms, with deliciously soft beds, seats of "real" Corinthian leather, and balconies in front. All rooms have bathrooms, A/C, and telephones. Doubles 132-165,000Đ, with TV, fridge, and balcony 275,000Đ.

My Kinh Hotel, 72-74 D. Hang Buom (tel. 255 726 or 269 159). Head north up D. Dinh Liet/Ta Hien from the lake until it ends. Turn left on Hang Buom, a few paces to the right. The reception room is often filled with foreigners from all parts of the globe swapping adventure stories over sodas and iced coffee. All rooms with A/C and shower. Doubles 110-330,000Đ. English spoken.

A Dong Hotel, 46 D. Luong Ngoc Quyen (tel. 256 948; fax 282 602). Just across the street from Guesthouse. Small, 9-room hotel offers outstanding rooms at bargain basement rates, and an open courtyard offers visitors an island of peace and quiet in the middle of it all. Friendly staff is ready to serve up some of the local cuisine. Doubles with A/C and TV 110,000Đ, with shower 132,000Đ, with balcony 165,000Đ.

Maison D'Hotel, 18 D. Dinh Liet (tel. 267 322; fax 253 584). Head straight up from the northern tip of the lake to Dinh Liet. 50m on your left (the entrance and building is unassuming and easy to miss). This small guest house has only 3 rooms with a hodgepodge of furniture. Nevertheless, you'll appreciate the homey feel and spring mattresses. All rooms have A/C and 2 have attached, well-kept baths. A small, empty café is on the 1st floor to accommodate your thirst. Doubles 77,000Đ, with shower 132,000Đ. English spoken.

Nam Phuong Hotel, 16 D. Bao Khanh (tel. 258 030; fax 258 964), is off D. Ly Thai To on the northwest side of the lake. Walk 100m up Bao Khanh and the hotel is on the right. The Nam Phuong Hotel offers up a wide array of room choices for the soft, the hardened, the miserly, and even the Croesus-like traveler. All 10 rooms have the luxury of A/C. If they're full, they'll gladly bring you over to their second hotel a block away. Singles and doubles with shower 110,000Đ. Doubles with TV, fridge, and phone 165-330,000Đ. Double suite 440,000Đ. Broken English spoken.

Viet Thang Hotel, 71 D. Hang Luoc (tel. 282 638; fax 258 044). From the lake, head north up D. Luong Van Can for 5 blocks where it turns into Hang Luoc; it's on your right. This elegant hotel is tastefully furnished and so clean that it will have you eating off the bathroom floor. In addition, you can get rooms with luxurious extras, such as carpeting, TV, fridge, bath tubs, and telephones (even in the bathroom), but you pay for what you get. Doubles with fan and bathroom 165,000Đ. Doubles with the works 275-440,000Đ. English spoken.

Hang Dao Hotel, 30 D. Hang Dao (tel. 257 193; fax 261 218). Just north of Hoan Kiem Lake up Hang Dao on your left. Well-appointed, poised, and greets travelers with huge, bright rooms, terrific tile floors, and ultra-clean baths. While it has only 6 rooms, the Hang Dao offers breakfast and a bar. Every tourist service imaginable. From basic A/C and bathroom to TV, telephone, and large refrigerators. Pay for the level of luxury you want. Doubles 165-440,000Đ. English spoken.

Nam Long Hotel, 10B D. Dinh Liet (tel. 266 054). Just up the street from Maison D'Hotel. Here you find that the proprietors are a little gentler, time passes a little slower, and the walls are a little yellower. Quiet, humble mini-hotel's prices fit any budget. Bare-bones accommodations with adequately kept baths. Singles for agoraphobes 66,000Đ. Doubles with bath 143,000Đ, with A/C 165,000Đ.

Binh Minh Hotel, 50 D. Hang Be (tel. 267 356; fax 247 183). Across the street from Bao Long. The 18 rooms have soothing blue walls with mosquito-hungry geckoes patrolling for prey (don't be alarmed—these innocuous creatures are your best ally). The center of all the action with the sounds of traditional Vietnamese music outside your window on occasional evenings. Helpful staff, down to the playful parrot, is ready to help. Doubles 77,000Đ, with shower, A/C, and TV 110,000Đ, with telephone165-275,000Đ.

Guesthouse, 55 D. Luong Ngoc Quyen (tel. 268 539). From the north tip of the lake, walk up D. Dinh Liet 3 blocks (becomes D. Ta Hien) and hang a left on Luong Ngoc Quyen. Guesthouse is several paces on the left. Though the proprietor was upset about placing 2nd in the Chamber of Commerce's original name contest, he still offers good rooms at excellent prices. Rooms, all with baths, are pretty sterile. Double with balcony, A/C, shower, and TV is light and airy. Singles with fan 66,000Đ. Doubles with fan 88,000Đ. 6 rooms total.

Guest House 73 Ma May (tel. 244 425). From the lake, go north up D. Dinh Liet 2 blocks and then take a right onto Hang Bac. Walk 1 block and take a left onto Ma May ½ block on the right. This is the place that beat Guesthouse in the original name contest. Frequented by French and Southeast Asian travelers. Despite a bar downstairs and tables set out for guests, no one seems to hang out much. Rooms are well-kept with very clean baths. All 6 rooms even have A/C and TV. Doubles 165-220,000Đ. Triples 275,000Đ.

Bao Long Hotel, 39 D. Hang Be (tel. 240 434). From the east side of Hoan Kiem Lake, walk straight up D. Dinh Tien Hoang to D. Hang Dau past the Water Puppet Theater. Hang Dau becomes Hang Be; Bao Long is 50m on your right. Long on budget, short on privacy, but does offer the cheapest place to lay your head. Dorm-style rooms have 4 beds with net, fans, and attached bath (one with a flush-it-yourself toilet!). Beds are not to be used as "liaison offices." Beds 33,000Đ, floor mattresses 22,000Đ. English and French spoken.

Green Bamboo Guest House, 42 D. Nha Chung (tel. 268 752; fax 264 949). From the south tip of Hoan Kiem Lake, go west, young man, on D. Trang Thi for 2 blocks and make a right turn up Nha Chung 70m on your left. Part of a tourist café which will take care of almost any tourist need. The 7 rooms are burrowed in the heart of the block, nicely sheltered from the street. You'll sleep like a baby. All rooms (doubles and some triples) with A/C 165,000Đ. English spoken.

Queen Café, 65 D. Hang Bac (tel. 260 860; fax 250 000). Follow the hordes of backpackers north on D. Dinh Liet and swing right on Hang Bac after 2 blocks. 8 rock-bottom rooms right above the crowded café. If you're looking for your own private Idaho, this ain't it. Rooms are a little beat up from the high traffic of *tay ba lo,* but are relatively clean. Communal bathrooms. Singles 44-55,000Đ. Doubles 66-77,000Đ. A multitude of languages understood here.

Other Districts

Lotus Guest House, 42V D. Ly Thuong Kiet (tel. 268 642). From Hoan Kiem Lake, head south on D. Ba Trieu 2 blocks and turn left on Ly Thuong Kiet. Walk 2 blocks and the guest house is on your left. Lotus is what every guest house should be—warm, friendly, and cozy. No reception desk, just a smile and hello from Dr. Nguyen, who owns this place with her doctor husband. Hang out in the small living room, order from a small menu of drinks and snacks, and swap stories. Most importantly this is the place to stay if you are sick—two doctors are at your disposal. Dr. Nguyen has been the loving mother to countless travelers. Dorm bunk 44,000Đ. Singles 66-88,000Đ. Doubles 99-132,000Đ. Additional guests 22,000Đ.

Pham Guest House, 22 D. Nguyen Thai Hoc (tel. 232 545). From the lake walk 1.5km west on D. Trang Thi; after a large intersection the road becomes Nguyen Thai Hoc. On the right at the end of a short alley. If you want to experience life with a Vietnamese family, this is the place. Mom, Pop and their two kids look after the 2 rooms and will take you in as if you were a long-lost relative and offer you meals with the fam. Doubles 132-165,000Đ with A/C and bathroom.

Khach San 30-4, 115 Tran Hung Dao (tel. 260 807; fax 252 611), across the street from the train station. Named after the date the communists captured Saigon, this hotel celebrates the victory by offering low-cost rooms to tourists disembarking from the train. The large reception room offers a bar for guests to sit and watch the parade of traffic. Interior courtyard buffers outside noise for quiet-seekers. Rooms vary from bare beds to full amenities. Singles 77,000Đ. Doubles 99,000Đ, with A/C and shower, 165,000Đ, with TV, refrigerator, and telephone 385,000Đ.

Hotel Bich An, 189 D. Son Tay (tel. 232 701; fax 234 981), up the street from Kim Ma bus station, on left heading away from town. With a bar and restaurant within, you won't have to go far to for your vittles either. Clean, bright rooms with A/C, satellite TV, telephone, and refrigerator might even cause you to not stray from your room. Doubles 220-440,000Đ (bathtubs available). Visa, MC, AmEx.

FOOD

Hanoi, as the hub of the north, offers up many of the great specialities of this region. The best place to get your hands on traditional Vietnamese dishes like *pho* or *bun* is out in the markets, from the vendors on the street, or from small stalls and one-room operations where ordering is looking and pointing. A full and delicious meal can be easily had for under 11,000Đ.To dine this way, arrive early (7-8am for breakfast, 11:30am-noon for lunch, and 5:30-6pm for dinner). All dishes are made in advance and sit out for the duration of meal time. Early arrival means fresh and hot food. After you've stuffed your face, gorge yourself on exotic fruits from street vendors at the **19/12 Market.** Cool off with refreshing drinks like *mia da* (pressed sugarcane with ice), *che* (sweet been drink), or *nuoc chanh so da* (soda lemonade). And don't forget to try Hanoi's two local brews, Halida (brewed in conjunction with Carlesberg) and Bia Hanoi, which comes in bottles and draft (*bia hoi*).

Hoan Kiem District

Chi Tam, 36 D. Bat Dan, on the corner with D. Hang Dieu. From the lake, head north up D. Luong Van Can 2 blocks and turn left on Hang Bo. Walk 200m and look to the right. Ok, ok, not a restaurant *per se,* but the best damn *bia hoi* stand and food stall this side of the 17th parallel. A consensus pick by locals, expats, and visitors alike, this is a place not to be missed. Tam, the proprietor of this humble establishment, is a sweet lady who'll stuff you full of food and beer and won't try to overcharge you. One price for locals and tourists—this is where you should be instead of a tourist café. Beers and a meal will not exceed 22,000Đ. Open 6:30am until everyone is passed out drunk.

Quang An Restaurant (Restaurant 22), 22 D. Hang Can (tel. 267 160). Go up D. Luong Van Ca until it turns into Hang Can. The restaurant is on the left up a small alleyway. Frog, pigeon, crab, fish, pork, beef, and chicken each cooked in a variety of ways. If it moves, they'll throw it in the pot. Try the *duck l'orange* or a rabbit dish for change. Many dishes go heavy on garlic, so bring mints lest your breath kills your companions. Entrees 20-50,000Đ. Open daily 11am-10:15pm.

Sofia, 6 D. Hang Bai (tel. 259 893), south from the lake down Hang Bai. A hop, skip, and jump away on your right. Newly renovated, this place is an A/C haven in a city of heat. Furnishings are exquisite and the ambiance fetching. The menu is a mixture of French, Chinese, and traditional Vietnamese fare. The crab soup is something to definitely try (8000Đ). Entrees 10-50,000Đ.

Piano Restaurant & Bar, 50 D. Hang Vai (tel. 232 423), around the corner from Quang An Restaurant. Take a left on D. Lan Ong, which becomes Hang Vai. No piano and no bar really, but plenty of restaurant. Specializing in Vietnamese and Chinese cuisine, everything from eel to *escargot* can be found on this menu. Do you have the intestinal fortitude to stomach the tortoise soup? Entrees 20-50,000Đ. Open daily 11am-midnight.

Tin Tin Pub, 32 D. Hang Bo (tel. 255 116). Head 2 blocks north on Luong Van Can and turn left on Hang Bo. Tin Tin is a tiny place on your right. Fans of Tin Tin will be happy to find their pal happy and healthy in Hanoi. In addition to the bottled and canned beers, patrons come for the Vietnamese versions of hamburgers, pizzas, and crepes. Open daily 7am-2am.

Other Districts

Banh Tom Ho Tay, 1 D. Thanh Vien (tel. 257 839), on the north tip of Truc Bach Lake. Park your motorbike and find a table outside on the water. Don't bother looking at the menu. Just order a double serving of the shrimp cakes (*banh tom*) and 2 bottles of Hanoi beer. Then sit back and enjoy the flashing neon signs on the other side of the lake. If you are a shrimp-lover and miss this place, go directly to jail—do not pass go, do not collect $200. Open daily 11am-10pm.

Restaurant 202, 202 D. Hue (tel. 259 487), 1.5km south of Hoan Kiem Lake. Tons of business cards from expats and those who have passed through. The menu may be French, but don't be surprised to hear Pearl Jam if you're there for lunch. Catch the fruit desserts. Entrees 20-40,000Đ. Open daily 11am-10pm.

Restaurant Bistrot, 34 D. Tran Hung Dao (tel. 266 136). An extremely large menu with somewhat large prices. Sit in this quaint, music-laden place while traffic roars outside. Duck is one of the many specialties. Entrees 30-60,000Đ. Open daily 11am-10pm. All major credit cards accepted.

Hanoi Café, 252 D. Hang Bong (tel. 250 216), near the amazingly chaotic intersection with D. Dien Bien Phu and Nguyen Thai Hoc. One of the few good things that the French left in Vietnam was delicious pastry, and you'll find a lot of that here. Quick to brag that it was visited by Catherine Deneuve during the filming of *Indochine,* this café offers sandwiches, in addition to fluffy sweets. Beats the pants off the other cafés for food quality and ambiance. Open daily 6:30am-11pm.

SIGHTS

Concentrated in the districts of Hoan Kiem and Ba Dinh, most of Hanoi's attractive and interesting sights can be easily reached on foot. Those preferring not to leg it can easily be a part of one of Hanoi's most hypnotic sights—the traffic—by renting a bike or motorbike.

Hoan Kiem District

Hoan Kiem Lake, or Lake of the Restored Sword, was named because of a 15th-century legend. The **Emperor Le Thai To** (1428-33 AD), having returned victorious from a confrontation with an army of invading Ming Chinese, was cruising the lake in search of quiet and relaxation, not unlike the many modern-day Hanoians who dot its shores. His day cruise was rudely interrupted, however, when an overly rambunctious giant turtle rose from the waters and snatched away his sword. Having no other explanation for his butterfingers, the emperor declared it was divine intervention—a sign from the heavens that the struggle had ceased and that the sword had been returned to its divine source—and the people believed him. The **Tortoise Tower** on a tiny island in the center of the lake commemorates this event and is one of the enduring symbols of Hanoi. Today the park serves as a meeting place, napping quarters, and exercise grounds for the city's residents.

Heading up to the northeast quadrant of the lake, you'll see a luscious green and tree-laden island on which **Ngoc Son Temple** (Jade Mountain) is situated. Dating back to the Tran dynasty (1225-1400 AD), the small shrine was successively embellished over generations. The temple was last renovated in 1865 and is dedicated primarily to **Van Xuong,** the god of literature. **Tran Hung Dao,** the 13th-century hero, and the physician **La To** are also honored and worshipped here. The entrance to the temple is through **Tam Quan** (Three Passage) gate on the northeast shore. Atop the gate are inscribed the characters *phuc* (luck) and *loc* (wealth). Flanking the center entrance are two scrolls written in the hand of **Nguyen Van Sieu,** an eminent 19th-century Confucian scholar. On the other side of the gate stand **Thap But** (Pen Tower) and **Dai Nghien** (Writing Pad). From there, a striking red bridge arches from the shore to the island. Named **The Huc** (Morning Sunbeam), the bridge is lit up like a Christmas tree during Tet. The vermilion of the bridge's posts also blends harmoniously into the fireworks of blooming flame-trees in early June, which signifies the dreaded exam periods in Hanoi's schools. Once over the bridge, the temple stands beyond a pavilion and embankment. The sanctuary to Van Xuong is behind the **Hall of the Cult** as you enter. Open daily 7:30-11am and 1-4pm; admission 10,000Đ.

North of Hoan Kiem Lake is the **Old Quarter.** Bordered on the west by the Hanoi citadel, the labyrinthine part of town stretches up to Long Bien Bridge, which was continually bombed and repaired during the war. The area was once a snake-and-alligator-infested swamp, but 2000 years ago, the Viet people built villages of stilt houses here. In the 11th century, Ly Thai To, the first emperor of independent Vietnam, built his palace here, and not long after, the Old Quarter gained a reputation for its lovely crafts. Over time, guilds began to form as the Old Quarter became a patchwork of craft communities living, working, and selling together. Because street-front real estate was valuable and merchants were taxed by the length of their storefronts, the houses were long, thin structures which extended their way deep into the middle of the block. Typical dimensions of such homes can be 3m by 50-60m long and such structures earned the fitting name **"tube houses."** These traditional homes still exist today, but are under growing threat from developers.

The **Dong Xuan Market,** Vietnam's oldest and largest market, is in the north part of the Old Quarter; it once sat at the confluence of the To Lich and Red Rivers and was one of the busiest in Southeast Asia. The French used the market to facilitate taxes and enlarged it in 1885 with five gates; each one for specific goods. The market was recently the sight of a great fire and is in the process of being rebuilt. South from Dong Xuan Market is **48 D. Hang Ngang,** where Ho Chi Minh drew up his Declaration of Independence for Vietnam in 1945. The founding father of Vietnam relied heavily on the words of Thomas Jefferson and America's own Declaration in his composition. However, he felt that his Declaration had been betrayed when the U.S. sent ground troops into Vietnam in 1965. Open daily 8-11am and 1-4pm; free.

On the west side of Hoan Kiem Lake, in a square at the intersection of D. Bao Khanh and Nha Chung stands **St. Joseph's Cathedral.** This massive, neo-Gothic church with twin square towers flanking the entrance was finished in 1886. The main gates are open 5-7am and 5-7pm for morning and evening services. You can also enter the cathedral through the gate at 40 D. Nha Chung. Ring the bell on the door to the right as you pass through the gates to call a steward of the cathedral.

Three blocks southwest of St. Joseph's is the former **"Hanoi Hilton,"** the nickname given to the prison which held American POWs during the war. Bounded by D. Hai Ba Trung, Tho Nhuom, and Hoa Lo, you won't find much here today except a massive construction project. The former **Hao Lo Prison** was torn down for the construction of a massive five-star hotel and shopping center. One can only hope guests there will receive better treatment.

A block south from the famous prison is **Quan Su (Ambassador's) Pagoda,** 73 D. Quan Su, between D. Ly Thuong Kiet and Tran Hung Dao. The official center of Buddhism in Hanoi, this site was a guest house for visiting Buddhist ambassadors. The structure as it stands today was completed in 1942. Inside are many interesting depictions of Buddha, including the Buddha as school teacher, in one of the classrooms in the back. Open Tues.-Sun. 8:30-11am and 1-4pm; free, but asks for donations at the altar. Dress respectfully, no shorts or tank tops.

Moving back east down D. Ly Thuong Kiet from Quan Su, you'll hear and smell the **19/12 Market** on the left. Five blocks farther down Ly Thuong Kiet, take a left on D. Phan Chu Trinh. Go two blocks north and look to your right. In the large open square stands the majestic, French-built **Opera House.** Looking like a little piece of Versailles in Hanoi, the off-yellow structure built in 1911, is less used as a performance center than as an advertising space out front (it was the battleground for the opening volley in the cola wars). Inside you'll find a grand theater with box and balcony seats and a two-story stage. Ask the guard at the side entrance to let you in to take a look around. Bring a flashlight if you can (sometimes the guard will provide one), because the theater is pitch-black inside.

To the north of the Opera House is the **Revolutionary Museum,** 25 D. Ton Dan. Reopened in August 1995 after renovations, the museum presents Vietnam's continual struggle for independence from outside invaders. The beloved singer Khanh Ly recounts in a popular song, the revolutionary struggle lasted 1000 years with the Chinese, 100 years with the French, and 20 years of internal feuding with the American presence. You'll see a short history of what she means here as well as some interesting artifacts like a guillotine, anti-war banners in several languages, and pictures of protests from around the world saved by the North's wartime propaganda machine. Open Tues.-Sun. 8-11:30am and 1-4pm; admission 10,000Đ.

Behind the Opera House and a short distance from the Revolutionary Museum is the **History Museum** at 1 D. Pham Ngu Lao. When you first walk in, you will be greeted by who else but Ho Chi Minh himself. Beyond this statue is the museum's collection of prehistoric and ancient Vietnamese artifacts. The objects are labeled only in Vietnamese. Although there are no official tours, it is possible to find a curator to guide you through for a small fee (around 5-10,000Đ). Even if you go it on your own, there are interesting things such as the Dong Son bronze drums and ceramics on the second floor, in addition to objects from the Khmer and Champa civilizations. Open Tues.-Sun. 8-11:45am and 1:15-4:15pm; admission 10,000Đ.

Ba Dinh District

Ba Dinh Square, the site of Ho Chi Minh's delivery of Vietnam's Declaration of Independence from Japanese and French authority on September 1, 1945 and the Ho Chi Minh Mausoleum overlooking the square are the principle sights west of Hoan Kiem Lake. The most convenient and interesting way to head out to this area is via D. Dien Bien Phu. Along the way, you'll see a small park where there is a **statue of Lenin,** one of the few still left standing. The 20-ft. high statue stares out at children playing soccer and badminton on the greenery, and depicts Lenin in motion—perhaps trying to escape the fate he has suffered throughout the former USSR.

Across the street from Lenin's statue is the large Hanoi **Citadel,** comprising a 12 city-block area to the north. Inside its gates is the **Army Museum** at 28A D. Dien Bien Phu. Built in 1859, the museum presents the checkered history of Vietnamese military and might. Out front you'll see a symbolic image of communist superiority over the west as a propped up MiG-21 jet "flies" over the wreckage of a U.S. plane. Inside are relics from the battle at Dien Bien Phu and the tank that crashed through the gates of the Presidential Palace in Saigon. On the grounds of the museum the **Hanoi Flag Staff** stands 31m tall. Built in 1872, it proudly carries the yellow star of Vietnam. Open Tues.-Sun. 8-11:20am and 1:30-4pm; admission 10,000Đ.

From the gates of the Army Museum, turn right and head northwest up D. Dien Bien Phu toward the **Ho Chi Minh Mausoleum.** After 200m, turn left on the D. Le Hong Phong and proceed 500m to the intersection of D. Ngoi Hai. One of the things you cannot fail to do, as Hanoians will tell you, before leaving Hanoi is pay your respects to, or rather, stare at Bac Ho (Uncle Ho) in the mausoleum. With the communist propensity to preserve their great leaders, Ho Chi Minh could not escape his present fate despite his wishes to be humbly cremated. Completed in 1975, the raised, granite structure strikes an imposing figure. Used as a receiving stand for high officials and party leaders during parades and state ceremonies, the complex keeps the well-preserved Ho Chi Minh in the middle of all the action *sans* pulse.

When visiting Uncle Ho, be certain to wear respectable attire: no shorts, short skirts, or tank tops, and, if possible, something better than a T-shirt. Be polite and refrain from talking. If you have never before visited a dead and pickled communist leader, then you are in for a treat. In a room at the top of the flight of stairs lies Ho Chi Minh in a glass case covered up to his stomach with a wool blanket (probably because of the A/C), and his hands folded together on his chest. Open Tues.-Thurs. and Sat., 8-11am, Sun. 7:30-11:15am. It is closed for one month (usually September) when Ho Chi Minh takes a vacation to Russia, to visit Lenin and join him in relaxing formaldehyde baths.

The exit of the mausoleum will place you in the garden behind it. Heading north will lead to the **Presidential Palace.** The former residence of the Governor's General of French Indochina, the palace has served as a state guest house since 1954, when the French were unceremoniously cleared by the Viet Minh. Ho Chi Minh shunned the palace as a residence, believing the building belonged to the people. Instead, he chose an electrician's house on the palace grounds.

South of the palace and park, past the mausoleum stands **One Pillar Pagoda,** one of the few structures remaining from the original city. Although one of the most-revered monuments in Hanoi, it is a little disappointing at first sight; it's just one pillar. The architecture is elegant, but not astounding (the pillar is pretty big). Built in 1049, the pagoda is dedicated to Quan An, the goddess of mercy. The heirless Emperor Ly Thang Tong built the pagoda after he dreamed that he saw the goddess, sitting on a lotus flower, hand a boy to him; soon afterwards he was gifted with the birth of a son. Open daily 8am-5pm.

A short way from the One Pillar Pagoda on the shores of a carp pond is one of **Ho Chi Minh's residences.** The hut is an austere structure which has a meeting room on the first floor. His personal area upstairs, like most Vietnamese residences, is modest and has been attentively "preserved" right down to his slippers and personal book collection. Open daily 8am-5pm.

On the Trail with Ho Chi Minh: 30 Years of Budget Travel

The Vietnamese have a saying that goes, "A day on the road is a day of wisdom gained." Although most are not aware of it, Ho Chi Minh spent thirty years traveling across the globe in search of adventure, wisdom, and a path to deliver his country from French colonialism, before returning to Vietnam at age 55. Behind the mask of this charismatic revolutionary leader lies a mysterious figure with a penchant for pseudonyms, who remains to this day a conundrum to historians. As is often the case, it is difficult to separate the man and his personal history from the image and the idealism.

In 1912 at age 22, Ho Chi Minh left his homeland after being turned down for admissions at a prestigious colonial school in Vietnam. Assuming the name of Nguyen Va Ba (his fourth alias), he spent some time tracing the shores of North Africa and the Iberian Peninsula. Eventually, he found his way to the "melting pots" of New York and Boston. Two years later, he skipped across the pond to London where he spent a few years doing odd jobs and even had a stint as an apprentice to a renowned pastry chef. He hung out with Irish nationalists, Fabian socialists, and migrant workers from China and India, then British subjects. Following World War I, Minh, now known as Nguyen Ai Quoc, the "patriot," hopped the Channel to the Paris of Picasso and Hemingway and engaged himself in politics, joining the anticolonial crowd of Vietnamese expatriates. During these years, he wrote voluminous political tracts, numerous letters of petition, pamphlets, and newspaper articles.

Despite his absorption with French sophism, he grew weary of the French (as many do) and headed for Moscow in 1924 under the new name, Ly Thuy. There he was recruited by the Comintern and founded the Revolutionary Youth League to train Vietnamese activists. While in Moscow, the Chinese national struggle was under way, and Minh hoped Southeast Asia would soon follow. The next year, he made his way to China, changing his name to Wang, but the splintered Vietnamese struggle and the adverse political climate slowed his plans. From China he went to Hong Kong where he was able to consolidate the various leaders of other independence movements under the aegis of the newly formed Indochinese Communist Party (ICP) in 1930. But an informer tipped off the French and Minh was thrown in jail for two years before he was diagnosed with tuberculosis. A series of medical transfers found him back in Moscow, but he returned to China after the Japanese invasion of Manchuria. In the spring of 1941, he and his tattered group of revolutionaries made their way along a jungle trail into Vietnam where he made his last name change to Ho Chi Minh, "He who enlightens." He bided his time until the expulsion of the Japanese when he delivered his historic Vietnamese Declaration of Independence in Ba Dinh Square, Hanoi on September 2, 1945. And he did it all without an internal frame pack!

On the way through the gates of the mausoleum area, the huge granite mass of the **Ho Chi Minh Museum** soars out of the Hanoi landscape. The three stories of the museum chronicle Ho Chi Minh's life and times. The third-floor's ultra-stylized presentation is a paradigmatic example of communist kitsch. Among the highlights is a 1958 Edsel crashing through a wall a la Hard Rock Café, a symbol of American commercial and capitalist failure. Many captions are translated into English. Nevertheless, the major themes of the museum are fun to decipher and no big mystery. Open 8-11:30am, 1:30-4pm. Free.

Three blocks south of the mausoleum and Ba Dinh Square is the **Vietnam Museum of Fine Arts,** 66 Nguyen Thai Hoc St. Despite its diverse collection of silk paintings and ancient sculptures from dynastic Vietnam, the museum is an undiscovered treasure. You can get a good flavor of the history and tradition of Vietnamese art by working your way from the right side of the third floor toward the first floor. This tour will take you chronologically through Vietnamese art from the relics of Vietnam's aboriginal peoples, Siva and Buddha sculptures, objects of the imperial dynasties, and finally silk paintings from 1954. The outdoor balconies of the French colonial building lead you from one exhibition room to another. A sale room even offers the opportunity to take the same art home with you (all major credit cards accepted). Open Tues.-Sun. 8am-noon and 1-4pm. Admission 10,000Đ.

To the north of the art museum, across the street is the **Temple of Literature.** To gain access to the walled complex, head to the south side of the temple to the bonsai-tree laden entrance of the **Four Pillars.** Built in 1070, during the reign of Emperor Ly Thang Tong, the Temple of Literature and National University are two of the oldest vestiges of the history of ancient Hanoi. Once an important Confucian center for the imperial court and the children of mandarins, the complex today takes up the area of two city blocks and has quiet courtyards. The succession of open courts is established by a series of gates, in analogy to the academic experience, passing through each gate as one attains more experience, wisdom, and education. The first set of gates are the **Gates of Talent and Virtue.** The next set heading north are those of letters, which lead to the **Well of Heavenly Clarity,** and to one of the most interesting artifacts in the temple, the **82 Tortoise Stelae** on which the names of the 1306 doctoral laureates from the years 1484 to 1780 are inscribed. Proceed farther into the temple means passing through the **Gate of Synthesis** and into the sanctuary, which houses a colorful statue of Confucius and his four greatest disciples. The Temple of Literature often hosts small rituals and performances of traditional Vietnamese music and dance, and sometimes even water puppet performances. Open Tues.-Sun. 8-11:30am and 1:30-5pm. Admission 12,000Đ.

To the north of the Ho Chi Minh Mausoleum and Ba Dinh Square lies **Ho Tay,** or West Lake. The location of choice for foreign investors and developers, this area is the front-runner for the site of New Hanoi. The largest lake in the city, West Lake covers 5 square km. The shore of the lake bordering Truc Bach Lake is a popular hangout spot for Hanoi's young lovers.

Trekking out from the city center will let you see the face of Hanoi with the mask of tourism off. Half the fun is getting there. Spend a relaxing day at **Lenin Park,** the largest in Hanoi, lying 1km south of the train station. The large lake and serene atmosphere of the park make for an enjoyable afternoon of reading. Another 1km south down Hwy. 1 (D. Le Duan) from Lenin Park, right on D. Trung Chinh, and another 1km on the left is the **Air Force Museum.** Hardly anyone visits this museum, but it has an interesting collection of planes, including a MiG in which you can climb and ham it up for the cameras. Open Tues.-Sun. 8-11am and 1-4pm. Free.

ENTERTAINMENT

Travelers to Hanoi will find a dearth of entertainment options in this quaint capital city. There are, however, the **water puppets**—a definite don't-miss—at Kim Dong Theater, 57B D. Dinh Tien Hoang (tel. 255 450; fax 245 117), up the street two blocks north of the GPO. Named after the king who was a great patron of the art, the Thang Long Water Puppet Troupe has performed its art in festivals all over the world. Dating back as far as the 1st century AD, this form of puppetry originated in the rice paddies where peasants directed their creative energy. The puppets perform incredible movements and feats, but you'll see no strings on these animals and characters. The manipulating apparatus to each is hidden under water. More delightful than the physical movements of the puppets themselves are the individual skits and stories presented. Each has some sort of aquatic theme (surprise, surprise) attached and funky special effects. Shows are nightly at 8pm and last 1½-2hr. Tickets are 22-55,000Đ depending on your location and souvenir desires. (See "Dance and Drama" on page 558.)

Of course, for plain, simple, mindless entertainment, catch the latest (in Vietnam, that is) movie at **Fansland Theater,** 84 D. Ly Thuong Kiet, next to Saigon Hotel. Operated by a man who loves American films, the small screen here is adequate for viewing movies, but you'll have to bring your own popcorn. Tickets 5-8000Đ. Show times usually 5:30 and 8pm, sometimes with a matinee at 3pm. Check theater or back pages of *Vietnam Investment Review* for schedule.

NIGHTLIFE

Full-blown communism has left a nightlife scene that is still nascent. However, you won't be starved for fun in Hanoi. When the *bia hoi* (beer) runs out, most travelers and expats take shelter in the bars. The more lively head to one of the few clubs.

The Royal Palace, 20 D. Hang Tre (tel. 244 233), inside the Royal Hotel to the northwest of Hoan Kiem Lake. This dance joint is hopping every night with a live Filipino band. The Asian crowd shows up early while the expats join the party after 10pm. Giulio, the manager, is a good source of info on Hanoi and all that is happening and hip. Cover 55,000Đ. Drinks 44,000Đ. Open daily 8pm-2am.

Centropell Club and Café, 46 D. Hang Cot (tel. 257 773), in the north half of the Old Quarter. A terrific venue to hear live music, it turns into a romping discotheque with a flick of a switch. Gourmet coffee and tea is served, but the place is by no means dry—Chivas Regal and Martell make sure of that. The ethic here is the appreciation of music and the arts, and the occasional art movies here cater to the sensitive and sophisticated. Karaoke available for the less sensitive and sophisticated. Cover varies. Drinks 44,000Đ. Open daily 11am-2am.

Gold Cock, 5 D. Bao Khanh (tel. 250 499). From Le Thai To on the west side of Hoan Kiem Lake, turn onto Bao Khanh. Walk 20m up and turn right on the small street (still Bao Khanh) heading north. The bar will be on the right. The eminent gay bar in Hanoi, this place is popular among expats and tourists alike. Clientele munches on burgers, hot dogs, pizzas, and salads while slurping their beers. 44-66,000Đ. Open daily 4pm-midnight.

The Emerald, 53 D. Hang Luoc (tel. 259 285), up Luong Van Can until it becomes Hang Luoc. It's on your right. A bit o' Dublin in Hanoi. The ale house's luscious wood bar and a couple of pints of Bass will make you forget you're in Vietnam. There's whiskey to last you through all of happy hour (11am-7pm). Pool, darts, and other pub games will keep you busy. Pints 44-66,000Đ (no one said bringing Ireland to Vietnam was cheap). Open daily 11am-midnight.

Sunset Pub (tel. 351 382), on top of the Dong Ho Hotel on D. Giang Vo. Its slogan, "The place where foreigners meet," and its claim to be Hanoi's largest bar are not far off the mark. Jazz on Thurs. and Sat. nights has become one of its mainstays, and its pizza is said to be the best in town. Open daily 5pm-1am.

Nugget Bar, 36 D. Hang Trong (tel. 268 480), just west of Hoan Kiem Lake. Missing American sports or European football? Traveling during the Olympics? Catch all the sports at the Nugget. Open 24 hrs.—or so the owner says—to accommodate live telecasts from the other side of the globe. So trek on down, grab a brew, and join the other fanatics. Drinks 33-55,000Đ.

SHOPPING

Virtually all of Hanoi could be characterized as a public market—street vendors and shops abound. The **State General Department Store,** at the intersection of D. Hang Bai and Trang Tien at the southeast corner of Hoan Kiem Lake, is the largest and offers a variety of consumer goods of inconsistent quality. Open daily 7am-6pm. **Dong Xuan Market,** on D. Hang Giay, is Hanoi's oldest market, sprawling in the north section of the Old Quarter. It is now in the midst of being rebuilt after a fire ravaged it last year. When operating, it is large and lively, peddling traditional medicines, birds, and exotic plants. **Hom Market,** on D. Hue, burgeons six blocks south of Hoan Kiem Lake. Hom is a concrete market like Dong Xuan but only smaller. Open daily 6:30am-7pm. **19/12 Market** comprises a city block between D. Hai Ba Trung and Ly Thuong Kiet just to the west of D. Quang Trung. A frenetic produce market that gets an injection of adrenaline thrice daily just before mealtime. Live chickens and ducks look on as buyers and merchants perform the haggling tango. The produce right at the entrance tend to be more expensive (and of poorer quality) than at the stands deeper within. Open daily 6am-6pm.

In addition to these markets, Hanoi's Old Quarter, also known as the **"36 Street" area,** is a gold mine of shops with specialized services and products. The names of the streets are believed to have been derived from the original number of guilds in ancient times, when the streets were named after their product, service, or location. A majority of the streets (especially those representing the original guilds) start off with the word *hang,* which means "merchandise" or shop. Though most of the streets have been transformed from their original name and function, merchants offering similar products and services still cluster together, and some of the more celebrated streets of today include the following: **Hang Gai** sells ready-made and tailored silk clothing, embroidery, and silver products; **Hang Quat,** originally sold feather fans and silk, and now peddles brightly colored funeral flags and religious objects; **Hang Ma** sells paper products including votives burned for ancestors; **Lang Ong** emanates the sweet scent of herbal and medicinal products; **Hang Bac** specializes in silver (formerly in metal currency exchange) and has several jewelrysmiths; **Hang Dao,** formerly the central silk-dying and silk products street, now sells ready-made clothing; and **Hang Thiec** was and is the street of tinsmiths—you can still hear and watch the smiths pounding out the sheet metal.

■■■ HAIPHONG

Haiphong tourist literature never fails to boast that Haiphong is Vietnam's 3rd largest city. Anyone who sees the city during an afternoon siesta will find this hard to believe, however, as the city does an impressive disappearing act for the post-lunch nap. There is good reason why the people in Haiphong rush home—the food in Haiphong is some of the best in Vietnam. The pervasive small-town atmosphere is deceptive, nonetheless; as the gateway to the Red River, lifeline of the North, and Hanoi's seaside vassal, Haiphong is Vietnam's largest port city. Because of its importance, Haiphong got a lion's share of bombing during the war. The U.S. lost over 300 planes trying to destroy the port and ground oil tanks. The port has since been rebuilt, and the town has been invigorated by the influx of foreign trade. Today the city is a thriving market town with renewed economic optimism.

ORIENTATION

Located 103km east of Hanoi at the mouth of the Red River delta Haiphong has a compact population center with its heavy industry and ports radiating out from there. The road in from Hanoi crosses the **Tam Bac River** over the **Lac Long Bridge** and once it enters town becomes **Duong Dien Bien Phu,** the main east-west road in the city. D. Dien Bien Phu parallels the **Cua Cam River,** one of the delta branches of the Red River which runs into the **Gulf of Tonkin,** 10km to the east. The central part of the city resembles an "L" lying on its back. The twin, parallel roads which determine this shape run 20m apart and form the city's central park as well as an artificial reservoir, **Tam Bac Lake,** which many locals use as a canal. **Duong Tran Hung Dao** and **Duong Tran Phu** run north-south from the Cua Cam River which forms the north border of Haiphong, for 1km before it starts to make a dog-leg turn westward where the names of the roads change to **Duong Quang Trung** and **Duong Nguyen Duc Canh.**

PRACTICAL INFORMATION

Tourist Offices: Vietnam Tourism in Haiphong, 15 D. Le Dai Hanh (tel. 429 89; fax 426 74). Friendly staff greets you with useful info about the city and trips to Do Sen Beach and Halong Bay. Detailed city maps. **Branch office,** 57 D. Dien Bien Phu. Open Mon.-Sat. 7:30am-11:30am and 1:30-4:30pm. **Transport rentals.**

Post Office: GPO, 5 D. Nguyen Tri Phuong (tel. 425 63), at the intersection with D. Hoang Van Thu. DHL International overnight service. **Telegram. Telex.** Open daily 7am-8pm.

Telephones: (tel. 120 01; fax 425 21), inside the GPO. Standard overseas rates. Can receive calls and faxes. Open daily 7am-8pm. **Telephone code:** 31.

Currency Exchange: Vietcombank, 11 D. Hoang Dien (tel. 426 58; fax 411 17), Exchanges currencies and traveler's checks, no fee. Visa, MC, AmEx advances, 4% commission. Open Mon.-Sat.7-11:30am and 1:30-5pm. **JP Bank,** 39 D. Dien Bien Phu (tel. 417 92; fax 417 93). Open Mon.-Sat. 7-11:30am and 1:30-5pm.

Airport: Cat Bi Airport, 7km southwest of the center of town.To: **Ho Chi Minh City** (daily 11:30); **Da Nang** (Mon., Wed., and Sat. 2:20pm); and **Nha Trang** (Thurs. and Sun. 11:30). **Vietnam Airlines Office,** 30 D. Tran Phu (tel. 424 14). Open Mon.-Sat. 8-11:30am and 1:30-4:20pm. Get to the airport by taxi (40-50,000Đ) or motorcycle taxi or cyclo (15-20,000Đ).

Trains: Haiphong Railway Station, 75 D. Luong Khanh Thien (tel. 464 33), at the end of Pham Ngu Lao St. To **Hanoi** (daily, 3hr.).

Buses: Niem Nghia Bus Station, the intercity terminal, on D. Tran Nguyen Han, 3km south of Cho Sat, on the left. To: **Hanoi** (6, 7am, 1pm, 12,500Đ); **Thanh Hoa** (6:10, 7:40am, 24,000Đ); **Hoa Binh** (7am, 21,000Đ); **Thai Nguyen** (7am, 21,000Đ); and **Nam Dinh** and **Thai Binh** (every hr., 6am-4pm, 13,000Đ).

Ferries: The dock is north of town on the Cua Cam River, close to the Tam Bac River branch. At the end of D. Cu Chinh Lan, head toward the Lac Long Bridge and north up Cu Chinh Lan from the Industrial and Commercial Bank of Hang Bong. To and from **Cat Ba Island and National Park** (1:30pm, returning 6am, 55,000Đ); **Halong Bay** (6:30am, round-trip 110,000Đ); and **Halong City** via **Halong Bay** (6, 11am, and 4pm, 44,00Đ). Purchase tickets at the dock from Vietnam Tourist one day in advance. To really see the bay, glide through in a **junk.**

Local Transportation: Cyclos are the main transport. 5-10,000Đ should get you anywhere in the city. However, the city is small enough for energetic walkers.

Taxis: Haiphong Taxi (tel. 419 99).

Markets: Haiphong is a city of active and flourishing markets, **Cho Sat** (Steel Market), at the intersection of the Cua Cam River and Tam Bac River. A large modern market where foreign and domestic ships drop their goods. **Open air market,** near the train station. One of the most active markets. Produce stalls line D. Nguyen Khuyen and D. Tran Nhat Duat, just west of the station.

Pharmacy: Hong Bang Haiphong Pharmacy, 63 D. Dien Bien Phu (tel. 429 26). Well-stocked with necessities. Open Mon.-Sat. 8am-7pm, Sun. 8am-2pm.

Hospital: Vietnam-Czechoslovakia Friendship Hospital, 1 D. Nha Thuong (tel. 462 36), on the corner of D. Sinh Tien Hoang and D. Tran Quang Khai.

Emergency: Police: tel. 13. **Ambulance:** tel. 15.

ACCOMMODATIONS

If you're in a sleepy town that takes its rest seriously, then you better find a good place to lay your head as well. There isn't a lack of options, but since Haiphong is host to many shipping moguls and small-time businessman, the prices at most hotels cater to a more upscale crowd.

Hoa Binh Hotel, 104 D. Luong Khanh Tien (tel./fax 469 07), one block west. Across the street from the train station, this hotel sucks up backpackers like a Hoover Deluxe. Friendly and energetic atmosphere. Guests gather to watch TV as well as to shoot pool. Doubles with bath 88,000Đ, and A/C110-385,000Đ.

Nha Khach Hai Quan (Nauy Guest House), 27C D. Dien Bien Phu (tel. 428 56), across the street from the Haiphong Naval Station. Ever wonder what it would be like to be in the Vietnamese Navy? Mattress-free beds with mosquito nets, for full barrack experience. With bath and A/C: doubles 88-165,000Đ, triples 99-220,000Đ. Blue and white navy uniforms not included.

Bach Dang Hotel, 42 D. Dien Bien Phu (tel. 424 44; fax 416 25). Rooms in all price ranges. Recently renovated, they cornered the market on tacky furniture—fake leather and plastic. Surprisingly, the ensemble works. Restaurant and bar downstairs. Doubles with bath and A/C 132-220,000Đ. Suites 275-605,000Đ.

Mini Hotel, 20B D. Minh Khai (tel. 424 43), the cheapest place in town. Split in two complexes, rooms at 20B are better. If these are gone, you're exiled across the street. Mounting the stairs feels like entering a factory. Modest rooms with mosquito net and fan. Doubles and triples 44,000Đ, with A/C and bath 110,000Đ.

Artex Hotel, 56 D. Dien Bien Phu (tel. 429 45; fax 425 10). This place is a clone of so many other modern minihotels in Vietnam that it will make you think the Central Planning Committee has a hand in hotel design. All rooms have A/C, bath, TV, and phone. Doubles 165-220,000Đ.

Ben Binh Hotel, 6 D. Ben Binh (tel. 422 60), 100m east of the ferry dock. Stumble out of bed to the pier. This pumped-up B&B makes you feel like a VIP. Gated complex—quiet, comfortable nights. Double with bath and A/C 220-550,000Đ.

Duyen Hai Hotel, 5 D. Nguyen Tri Phuong (tel. 421 57; fax 411 40), east of the GPO across the street. Hosts a cross-section of visitors from foreign businessmen to penny-pinching backpackers. Budget rooms, few and far-between, are worth it if available. Doubles 132,000Đ, with bath 132-165,000Đ, with A/C, TV, and phone 242,000Đ.

FOOD AND ENTERTAINMENT

Haiphong is one of the great culinary centers in Vietnam benefitting from the expertise of Hanoi and the abundance of the sea. The **food stalls** on the corner of D. Dien Bien Phu and D. Minh Khai have a good selection of indigenous plates, but food disappears quickly so get there early. There are also a number of great stalls on D. Tran Hung Dao. Got a hankering for some pastry? Head over to **Bao Ngoc,** 11 D. Tran Phu (tel. 544 23) for some cream horns. Open daily 8am-10pm.

You would think a port city like Haiphong, running rampant with sailors and ship captains, would have a plethora of entertainment options. Well, think again. Although there is no lack of sidewalk cafés and small bars, you'll be hard pressed to find a rollicking time. If dancing is your thing, head to **Trivoli,** 107 D. Dien Bien Phu (tel. 417 48). The small club pumps out disco music most nights and occasionally has live music. The all black interior will make you wonder if Trent Reznor has made a recent visit. Cover 33,000Đ. Open daily 7:30pm-midnight.

SIGHTS

An enduring symbol of Haiphong, the **Municipal Theater,** often called the "Great Theater," dominates the center of the city, situated along the main drag of D. Quang Trung and D. Tran Hung Dao. Built in 1904 by the French, this stately cousin of the Opera House in Hanoi relied on construction materials imported all the way from the Continent. In spite of its French origins, the square in front of the theater was the site of a bloody 4-day standoff between French colonial forces and Viet Minh revolutionaries on November 20, 1946. These days the square, now a popular hangout for city residents, hosts state and municipal ceremonies.

Nearby on D. Quang Trung, the fine, pagoda-like, four-post **Flower Stalls,** built in 1944, dot the city landscape with vibrant mosaic colors straight from Monet's palette. Heading farther west on the same street will lead to one of the busiest **trading and merchant areas** in the city. Here, hawker shops flank D. Quang Trung and its side-streets, overflowing with cloth, blankets, clothes, durable goods, shoes, hats, and crafts. At the far east end of D Quang Trung on the site of one of the city's most ancient rice markets, the modernistic behemoth known as **Cho Sat** (steel market) rises six-stories above the rest of Haiphong. Built in 1992 as a joint venture with

China, Cho Sat is a bustling conglomeration of restaurants, clubs, and offices on the upper floors and a center of trade on the lower levels.

Heading back east on D. Nguyen Sue Canh, you'll pass **Tam Bac Lake** on your left with numerous *sampans* and rafts scattered across on the placid surface. After about 1km turn right on the D. Linh and then an immediate left on D. Le Chan. Keep walking until you hit **Nghe Temple.** The colorful temple, renowned for its exquisite carvings and structured balance, commemorates Le Chan, who led the Two Tung Sisters insurrection against the Chinese and then founded An Bien Village, Haiphong's predecessor. Inside the sanctuary, a statue of the petite yet proudly defiant Le Chan guards the temple. Open daily 8am-4:30pm. **Le Chan's birth** and **death** are celebrated on the eighth day of the second lunar month and the 25th day of the 12th lunar month respectively. On the eve of the Lunar New Year, throngs pay homage to Le Chan by laying little red sacks of salt on her altar.

Move on south down D. Me Linh and turn left on D. To Hien. Walk 500m down and then make a right onto D. Hang Khen. Go south for another km until you reach the **Hang Khen Communal House.** This 140-year-old L-shaped structure demonstrates architectural styles from the Le and Nguyen dynasties. Wood carvings, statuettes, and icons of worship clutter the rooms of the house. Dragons, gongs, drums, bronze flamingos, elephants, and horses festoon all objects and surfaces imaginable within the walled compound. At its center stands a statue of Ngo Quyen, the legendary liberator and king of Dai Viet (for more details, see "The Chinese Millennium" on page 550).

From D. Hang Khen head back up to D. To Hien, go east for 1.5km, and then turn left on D. Chua Hang. On your left 500m down stands the grand **Du Hang Pagoda** with a well-kept garden and a large bell tower. Built between 980 and 1308 during the Tran dynasty, the pagoda was restored earlier this century. The J-shaped pagoda houses various artifacts, including bronzes, such as bells, gongs, and cauldrons, and an ornate altar.

■ AROUND HAIPHONG

With Vietnam's mist-shrouded and phenomenal Halong Bay a hop, a skip, and a jump away from Haiphong, many people forget that other natural wonders exist nearby. **Cat Ba Island National Park,** a popular destination among backpackers, lies some 50km east of Haiphong, covering over 200sq km. This pristine island and its elements, including artifacts dating back 6000 years, have remained untouched and well-preserved by the forces of the industrialization. The park covers most of the island, but a small town and beautiful fine sand beaches grace the south side, the most popular spot being **Cat Co Beach.** Tunnel through or hike over hills to reach most beaches—the greater the effort, the greater the rewards. The slopes of Cat Ba are rife with grottoes, stalactites, and other attractive geological formations while the clear waters offer fantastic views of coral and sea floor life. Although the park widely advertises its wildlife, actually seeing any of the François monkeys or other animals is harder than finding a polite Frenchman. Nevertheless Cat Ba promises mountains rising up to above 300m and primeval forests blanketing the rugged terrain. To get to Cat Ba, take the ferry from Haiphong daily at 1:30pm and return at 6am (55,000Đ each way). From the drop-off on Cat Ba, a bus will transport you into Cat Ba town (2000Đ).

■■■ HALONG BAY

In the 1993 film *Indochine,* a French lieutenant and his Vietnamese lover needed the mystical powers of Halong Bay as cover while fleeing the French tribunal and police. Lucky for you, you'll probably have time to enjoy the wonders of the bay without feeling like a fugitive. Declared a World Heritage Sight in 1993, Halong Bay has attracted a flood of tourists, foreign and domestic, to its cache of wondrous islands. Instead of running from French police, you'll be fleeing French tourists.

Just northeast of Haiphong and covering over 1500sq km, Halong Bay contains over 1500 islands and islets of limestone rising from the sea. Meaning the "Descending Dragon," Halong Bay has long been an area of legend and mystery. One explanation of its name tells of a dragon who helped the Vietnamese defeat an invading Chinese fleet. The divine dragon descended from heaven and spit out divine pearls which linked themselves into a defensive barrier against the invaders. Once the enemy had been turned back, the dragon descended and settled in the bay, rent-free. The scales of the dragon's back form the maze of rocks that has since been the object of Vietnamese imagination. Natives and tourists alike have identified features of many of the shapely rocks. There are two roosters fighting, a tortoise, bird, a monkey, and a tower, and all are named accordingly. The French even took to calling one the Mitterrand Rock, and are now looking for a large-nosed Chirac Rock.

ORIENTATION

Halong Bay is 165km east of Hanoi and can be reached by road from Hanoi or Haiphong or by ferry from Haiphong. Halong Bay proper is thousands of limestone outcrops in the sea. The launching points for most ships are actually **Bai Chay** and **Hon Gai,** collectively referred to as **Halong City.** Bai Chay and Hon Gai are in the northeast corner of the bay and are separated by the strait that connects Halong Bay to **Cua Loc Bay** in the north. In both Bai Chay and Hon Gai, the main road runs parallel to the shore. In Bai Chay, it is a reverse L and has no name. In Hon Gai, the larger of the two cities, the main drag is **Duong Le Thanh Tong.**

PRACTICAL INFORMATION

Tourist Offices: Halong Tourist Company (tel. 464 05; fax 462 84), Bai Chay, just south of the ferry to Hon Gai. **Vietnam Tourism in Haiphong (Halong Branch),** 2 D. Le Thanh Tong (tel. 272 50). Both can help you arrange tours of the bay, and are open Mon.-Sat. 7:30-11am and 1:30-5pm.

Post Office: Hong Gai GPO, at the end of D. Le Thanh Tong, in the center of town, 2km from Bai Chay ferry. Open daily 6:30am-8pm. **Halong City Post Office** (tel. 464 17), near the ferry to Hon Gai. Open daily 7am-7pm.

Telephones: (tel. 255 39; fax 255 44), international office in the GPO. Receives calls and faxes. **Telephone code:** 33.

Currency Exchange: Commercial Bank of Quang Vinh (tel. 252 97), 1.5km south of the ferry to Hon Gai. All major currencies and traveler's checks exchanged. Open Mon.-Sat. 8-11am and 1-4pm.

Buses: Bai Chay Bus Station, 1km south of the ferry. Daily routes to **Hanoi** (every hr., 5am-2pm, 20,000Đ); **Hue-Da Nang** (Sun-Mon., Wed.-Sat., 6:30am, 65,000Đ); and **Ho Chi Minh City** (Sun.-Mon. 7am, 110,000Đ).

Ferry: From Bai Chay to Hon Gai (6am-midnight, 1000Đ per person).

Library: Hon Gai Public Library, 174 D. Le Than Tong, just down from Hon Gai GPO, on the shores of the bay.

Hospital: Quang Minh Provincial Hospital, 651 D. Le Thanh Tong, 1km east of Hon Gai GPO (tel. 254 90).

Emergency: tel. 254 86.

ACCOMMODATIONS

It is hard to escape the rising prices of a popular tourist destination. Grand hotels are springing up everywhere, and when the construction dust settles, budget travelers are left with relatively few choices. Bai Chay houses the more expensive choices and bargain-basement steals. Good mid-range rooms are in Hon Gai, closer to downtown, but a ferry ride away from the modest Bai Chay beach and the docks.

Bai Chay

Nha Nghi Xuan Huong (tel. 464 18), 1km south of the ferry. Centrally located and close to the water. It ain't the Ritz-Carlton, but you'll spend more time in it asleep than not. Doubles with fans 77-110,000Đ, with A/C 132-165,000Đ.

Nha Nghi Binh Dan, just under 2km south of the ferry. Welcome to summer camp, Vietnamese-style. The hard beds and cold shower outside your room might have you writing home about homesickness, but at least it's cheaper than Camp Minnehaha. Doubles with fan 55-66,000Đ. Dorm 22,000Đ.

Hoang Tong Hotel (tel. 461 32), near Bai Chay. Take the long climb up the daunting hill in which the hotel hides away with a million dollar view. Large and well-groomed with a relaxed environment. Doubles with A/C, TV 220,000Đ. Visa, MC.

Hon Gai

Nha Nghi Son Ha, 63 D. Le Thanh Tong (tel. 265 53). Down the street from the ferry, easy to reach from anywhere in Halong City. This small, family-run guesthouse is charming and cheap. Doubles, a few with A/C 88-132,000Đ.

Nha Nghi Huong Giang, 39 D. Le Thanh Tong (tel. 274 97). Extremely well-kept and friendly, this 3-room guesthouse actually makes you feel like a guest in somebody's house. Double with fan 110,000Đ. double with A/C, TV 132,000Đ. Double suite 165,000Đ. All with bath.

Viet Anh Hotel, 113 D. Le Thanh Tong (tel. 262 43). Sterile and boring mini-hotel, but if the price fits, wear it. Doubles with fan 110-132,000Đ, with A/C 165-220,00Đ. All with bath.

Nu Hoang Hotel, 159 D. Le Thanh Tong (tel. 256 84). Far south from the ferry, if you wanted greater access to the metropolis of Hon Gai, you've got it at this upscale mini-hotel. Doubles with A/C, phone, bath, and TV 132-275,000Đ.

FOOD AND ENTERTAINMENT

Although Halong City lies on the rich waters of the bay, its food is disappointing compared to what you'll find elsewhere in Vietnam. Avoid the pricey restaurants near the beach at Bai Chay and cross the ferry into Hon Gai. Just south of the ferry dock are several **food and bia hoi stalls** where you can get a good bowl of *pho* and a glass of beer for less than 5000Đ. Farther south on D. Le Thanh Tong as it veers east is the **large market.** For the brave, there is a variety of exotic seafood to sample. At night, most visitors sit out on the beach snacking on dried squid and beer. Others shake their booty down at the **Top Disco Club,** near Bai Chay Beach.

SIGHTS

Halong Bay may be the prime tourist destination in the north outside of Hanoi, but other small diversions await to amuse the landlocked. Those with an itch for sun and sand should head out to **Bai Chay Beach,** but don't expect any killer waves. The limestone islands that so majestically rise out of the water also serve to neutralize it.

If you are not seeing the bay via a tour from Hanoi, go check out your boat options at the Travel Wharf (1km south of the ferry on the Bai Chai side). The most pain-free way is to purchase a ticket from the small travel booth at the wharf. A four-hr. tour will run you 55,000Đ per person, but you have to wait until it reaches critical mass before it shoves off. Groups can charter their own boat: a wooden ship for 25 people will set you back 220,000Đ, steel ships 330,000Đ. The most enjoyable cruise, try to find a **junk,** although they are hard to come by and are at the whim of Mother Nature. Tourist cafés in Hanoi offer excursions to the bay for those who'd rather sit back and enjoy Vietnam without having to worry about finding a boat.

Among the principal sites that most tours hit is the cavernous **Dango Grotto.** Carved by thousands of years of sea erosion, the grotto includes three caverns whose entrance is close to 200m above sea level. The monstrous outer cavern can easily hold several thousand people while the central cavern houses stalagmite standing up from the ground like miniature Cham towers. The last cavern is narrow but replete with fresh water year-round. Legend has it that the Vietnamese hid wood here for shipbuilding during their conflicts with the Chinese around the turn of the millennium, hence the name Dango ("hiding wood"). Another site is the **Virgin Grotto,** named for a stalagmite figure that resembles a young maiden (she sure looks like a Cham tower). This amazing hole winds more than 2km into the island with a showcase of natural limestone sculptures along the way.

NORTHWEST VIETNAM

Heading west and northwest from Hanoi into the Hoang Lien Son Mountains toward Laos and China is a trying and tiring experience, particularly if you elect to do it by bus like the locals. The roads in this section of the county are by far the worst in Vietnam thanks to the torrential rainy season (May-Oct.) and the lack of funds to invest in infrastructure. Snail-like climbs up mountain passes and impossibly narrow stretches of road will scare the wits out of you as they skirt the rim of the Grand Canyon-esque abyss. Rest assured that accidents are fairly rare, but there is nevertheless an element of risk in travelling these roads. Needless to say, bus schedules are not always reliable; make sure a bus will leave when you expect it to. Hours of travel on these roads will often make you wonder if these French-built "highways" have ever been re-paved since they were constructed over 50 years ago. You'll have plenty of time to ponder this, particularly when your vehicle gets stuck in mud-holes on unpaved sections of the highway.

Saint-like patience in transit pays large dividends in dramatic scenery, places, and people that remain relatively untouched by the forces of the industrial world. The smoke from brickworks, the pastel garments of hill-tribe women, and the rows of corn growing on steep mountainsides become common images. The Vietnamese, the majority of whom were forcibly resettled in this area by the state, pass their time playing pool or gambling. On the whole, they harbor great prejudice against the Montagnard hill-tribes who inhabit this rural and mountainous region. Opposed to social and economic integration, the hill-tribes continue on with subsistence farming and remain unfazed by the traffic of tourism.

In northwest Vietnam, it is difficult, and sometimes impossible, to get certain goods and services. Exchange all the currency you anticipate on needing for this portion of the trip. Gold and jewelry shops may exchange U.S. dollars, but traveler's checks will prove worthless here.

■■■ SON LA

This town once played host to exiles, misfits, and dissidents, who were shipped here by the French for having (gasp!) anticolonial thoughts. Although today it is the capital and the largest city in the eponymous province, not much has changed. There is still an oppressive air about the city although Son La is by no means economically depressed; it just seems more emotionally so. To most tourists, it is nothing more than a stopover point on the arduous mountain journey to Dien Bien Phu. Those who take this view miss a great deal of its subtle charm, its great beer, and its horrific penal history.

Orientation and Practical Information Son La rests between two high hills 310km west of Hanoi and two-thirds of the way between the capital and Dien Bien Phu on **Route 6.** It's basically a one-intersection town. **Duong Cau Trang,** which runs west toward Dien Bien Phu, and **Duong Truong Chinh,** which runs south to Hanoi, meet to form the center of Son La. Running parallel to D. Truong Chinh to the west is **Duong To Hien.** Between these two main boulevards is a **giant rice paddy** smack in the middle of the city. The **GPO,** on D. To Hien, lies 500km from the intersection with D. Cau Trang on the right; an **international telephone office** (tel. 524 21; fax 521 97) can be found in the lobby. Open daily 6:30am-8pm. **Telephone code:** 22. The **bus station** (Ben Xe Khact Thi Xa Son La) is on the left of D. Truong Chinh, 100m north of the intersection with D. Cau Trang. To: **Hanoi** (daily 3am, 12-16hr., 35,000Đ) and **Dien Bien Phu** (daily—but erratic, depending on the season—5am, 6-8hr., 25,000Đ). If trying to get to Dien Bien Phu and there is no direct bus, take one to Tuan Giao (halfway to Dien Bien Phu) and find connecting service there. A **medical clinic** is located just up the street from the bus station heading north on the left. Open Mon.-Sat. 8-11am and 1-4pm. A **phar-**

macy, Nha Thuoc Ming An, sits at the intersection of D. Truong Chinh and Cau Trang (open daily 7am-7pm).

Accommodation and Food The accommodations in Son La are what you might expect from a socialist nation—little variety, limited choices. But the situation isn't all too grave. Your best option is **Cho Song Da Hotel,** also off Rte. 6 coming from Dien Bien Phu. Though located on the slope of a steep hill, this hotel offers rooms at level, fair prices. Doubles with bath, TV, and fan 132,000Đ. Quads with bath, TV, and fan 165,000Đ. **Khach San Son La** (tel. 527 02), east of the intersection with D. Truong Chinh on D. Cau Trang, is a large, rather quiet hotel. With touch-up renovations continually going on, this old but decently maintained hotel offers tidy rooms at a reasonable cost. Doubles with bath 132-165,000Đ, some available with A/C and/or TV. **Khach San Cong Duan** (tel. 572 44) is a popular choice with Vietnamese travelers. Off Rte. 6 on the way into town from Dien Bien Phu (look for the directional sign), the hotel can also be reached from the GPO by heading north and turning left after about 500m at the sign. Doubles 110,000Đ, with bath 165-220,000Đ.

Getting food in Son La is a mixed-bag affair, but you can't go wrong if you follow the locals. Make tracks for the **food stalls** and go quackers over the roast duck (*vit quay*). For that restaurant atmosphere, join other denizens at the popular **Khach Hang La Thuong De** (tel. 521 12), just north of the GPO on D. To Hien. Before leaving Son La, indulge in beer heaven with Son Duong Beer, a definite don't-miss.

Sights The principle sight in Son La is a gruesome vestige of its past—the old **French prison.** Built in 1908, this prison held the leaders and supporters of the anti-colonial revolts after the French seized the city from the Black Thai hill-tribe. Inmates were subjected to forced labor, held for long periods in solitary confinement, and incarcerated in groups in dungeon chambers beneath the main level of the prison. The most horrifying record of group incarceration comes from a period in the 1930s when 156 prisoners were held for 16 days in a dungeon where each man had barely enough room to sit. The prison was liberated in 1954 with the departure of French colonial forces.

To get to the old prison, head toward Dien Bien Phu from the center of town for about 1km. Along the way, you will see **To Hien Monument** on your left, dedicated to the "favorite son" of Son La. Just 100m beyond the monument, take a right at D. Khau Ca and head another 200m to the top of the hill. The entrance to the prison is on the path to the right of the set of buildings that the city uses for official meetings and functions. Once inside the walls of the prison, you will quickly see that it is in ruins except for the walls themselves and the guard towers which rise menacingly from their corners, although the remnants of the interior cells are still discernible. The dungeon, on the other hand, sits under the kitchen in close to the original condition. A peach blossom tree, whose roots are beginning to displace the stones in the walls around it, serves as the prison's only memorial to those prisoners who died during their incarceration. The museum on the grounds details the history of the prison through photographs, paintings (some by the renowned Van Tho), and artifacts. Although little is written in English, the visual testimony speaks for itself. Open daily 7-11:30am and 1:30-4pm.

■■■ DIEN BIEN PHU

Large construction trucks race up and down Dien Bien Phu's main drag competing over which can kick up the most dust. Having recently been named the new capital of Lai Chau province, Dien Bien Phu is in the midst of a boom as state buildings are being raised all over town to accommodate the physical and administrative relocation. As the site of the disastrous French defeat in 1954 at the hands of Ho Chi Minh's Viet Minh forces, Dien Bien Phu is advertised in cities all around Vietnam as a popular street name for main boulevards and large thoroughfares. Despite all this advance billing and storied history, most will find there's really not much to the budding city. It's a larger-than-average, one-street town adjoining a large flood plain. It just so happens that it's here that French military strategy suffered a humiliating defeat. Maybe that's reason enough to visit.

Orientation and Practical Information Over 450km northwest of Hanoi and just 34km from the Laotian border, Dien Bien Phu is situated in the Muong Thanh Valley. Afternoon rains wash **Duong Be Van Dan,** the main street of the city, which runs north-south parallel to the **Nam Yum River.** To the west of the Nam Yum is the large **battlefield** which is connected to D. Be Van Dan by a bridge over the river. **Highway 12** connects Dien Bien Phu to Lai Chau and runs north on the west side of the river. The **GPO** is located on D. Be Van Dan 500m south of the bridge on the west side of the street. Has Poste Restante and an **international telephone office** (tel. 258 32; fax 258 36). **Telephone code:** 23. The **airport** at the time of this writing was undergoing renovation and expansion. When it reopens in the middle of 1996, twice-weekly service to Hanoi is expected to continue and perhaps expand. The **bus station** (Ben Xe Dien Bien Phu) lies west over the bridge to the battlefield, on the corner of Hwy. 12 heading north to Lai Chau. To: **Hanoi** (Wed. 5am, 18-24hr., 51,000Đ); **Son La** (every 4th day, 5am, 5-8hr., 25,000Đ); and **Lai Chau** (daily 11am, 10-16 hr., 15,000Đ). The largest **hospital** is located off D. Be Van Dan. Head south from the GPO for about 500m and turn left on the street before the **War Memorial and Cemetery.** Walk 200m and take the right fork. The stone white building is on your right. A **pharmacy** is located on the east side of D. Be Van Dan at the intersection with the bridge. Open daily 7am-7pm.

Accommodation and Food The hot, dusty afternoons of the summer will make you want to find shelter in a comfortable A/C room. At press time, only one hotel was open and operating. The old hotels such as the People's Committee Guest House have been shut down with new structures being built to replace them. Large hotels are being constructed on D. Be Van Dan, and a couple of minihotels are being built on the street which crosses the Nam Yum River. But as it is, your only option is the **Dien Bien Phu Mini Hotel** (tel. 243 19), about 200m north of the bridge on the west side of the street. Doubles with A/C, bath, and fridge 220,000Đ. In the lobby of the hotel, there is a **restaurant** that serves decent Vietnamese and French dishes at a reasonable price. For a wider, cheaper selection of food, hit **D. Be Van Dan** in the area of the GPO. Tiny little shanties and bamboo huts line the east side of the street where the protocol is point-and-eat. A large **market** lies 500m south of the GPO and filled with hawkers selling local fruits and produce.

Sights The only sights in Dien Bien Phu pertain to the battle itself, and for good reason. To the Vietnamese, the battle was the triumph of self-determination over colonialism, will over might. It was the decisive moment that they sent the French packing, and so, the Viet Minh thought, won autonomy for a united Vietnam. In the early morning of May 6, 1954, the day before the Geneva Conference on Indochina was to convene, the Vietnamese detonated a charge behind French lines in a tunnel that had been dug by Hon Gai coal miners from over 1km away. The explosion signaled the beginning of the Viet Minh's final assault of the two-month siege that forced the French to pull out their second national flag, the white one. In the resulting negotiations in Switzerland, the Geneva Accords of 1954 were hammered out, granting Vietnam independence but dividing the country at the 17th parallel.

To tour the remnants of the battle, start at the **Dien Bien Phu Museum,** which has a collection of artillery pieces scattered around its grounds. (Many of the displays just look like junk yard scrap metal heaps.) Inside, pictures and displays give a decidedly Vietnamese slant on the history of the battle. Approach the curator about arranging a guide to take you around the battlefield sights. Open Mon.-Sat. 8-11am and 2-4pm; admission 5000Đ. From the museum, cross the street to the **War Memorial and Cemetery.** The seemingly random times the gates are open is a little frustrating, but you can still catch a glimpse of the graveyard where the tombstones of those killed in the battle rest gently under the shade of scattered trees. Just north of the cemetery is **Hill A1** (Eliane2 to the French), the scene of some of the fiercest fighting. In front of the hill, a map shows the locations of a hollowed-out tank, an old bunker, and a war memorial. Around back, on the east side of the hill, is the **entrance to the tunnel** the Viet Minh dug to get behind enemy lines.

From the hill, cut across the street and through the market to a small bridge across the river to the battlefield. On the battlefield you will find a mishmash of artillery pieces including hollowed out French tanks propped up on concrete blocks and even U.S. guns. In the middle of the field lies **Colonel Christian de Castries' command bunker** which has been restored recently by the Vietnamese government. Open daily 8-11am and 2-4pm; admission 2000Đ. Crawl in and experience what it must have felt like to get the tar kicked out of you by a force of guerilla fighters.

■■■ LAI CHAU

Not many come through Lai Chau by choice, and when you arrive it will be obvious why. It's hard to describe Lai Chau as a one-street town because the one main street is about as long as a football field and barely wide enough to fit two vehicles. The street has shops hawking jewelry, consumer products, and some food and drink stands. At night, Lai Chau is about as fun as kissing your sister (unless of course you're from West Virginia).

Orientation and Practical Information Buses run frequently to other towns in the region and less to major cities. To: **Hanoi** (on the 4th, 10th, 20th, and 26th day of the lunar calendar, 5am, 24-30hr., 75,000Đ); **Dien Bien Phu** (daily 11:30am, 5-7hr., 15,000Đ); and **Lao Cai** (daily 5am, 35,000Đ). To get to **Sapa,** take the Lao Cai bus and indicate to the driver that you want to be let out in Sapa. From the bus station turn left and walk 50m until the road intersects with the main boulevard. A bridge leads to Doi Cau, a small town where the **regional hospital** is located. To the left is the main stretch of Lai Chau. It runs for about 100m before it ends at the intersection of the "highway." The main street, Lai Chan, spreads out to the left. The road to the right will take you to Sapa and Lao Cai. Turning left at this intersection will lead to another intersection with **Route 6.** Here, the **GPO** (open daily 7am-8pm) guards over the corner.

Accommodations and Food The **bus station** has four rooms with four beds a piece (22,000Đ per hard wooden bed) for those who have to stay overnight to catch the morning bus out. **Hawker stalls** at the back of the station offer light meals, snacks, and beverages.

Sights The most interesting sight in Lai Chau can be seen, fittingly, on the road out of town heading toward Lao Cai and Sapa. Just 1km out of Lai Chau, the road crosses the Da River via a steel suspension bridge anchored on the mountain slopes of each side. The French-built bridge is one of the infrastructural monuments of the colonial period. This and Hwy. 12, which runs from Lai Chau to Dien Bien Phu, were built by provincial governor Auguste Pavie to provide greater ease of transport and troop movements for the military and were instrumental for soldiers fleeing to Dien Bien Phu from the Viet Minh advance. Today these highways, carved out of the side of the mountains, offer some of the most gorgeous road scenery in Vietnam. Suspension foot bridges span river valleys and waterfalls crash down mountain faces alongside the bus. The waterfall at Binh Lu, halfway between Sapa and Lai Chau, is one of the largest in Vietnam. Minority hill tribes, particularly the Hmong and Thai, can also be seen working the corn fields outside their villages on the hills and valleys near the road.

■■■ SAPA

Meaning "town of sand," the name Sapa suggests a hot coastal beach town, although it is actually the opposite. Often called the Dalat of the North, this delightfully cool town is nestled 1650m above sea level on the side of a hill in the Hoang Lien Son Mountains. Discovered by a Jesuit missionary in 1918, the area was rapidly settled and developed by the French, who built a hill station in 1922 as an outpost near the Chinese border. Because of its fresh air and cool climate, the French soon expanded it into a health and vacation resort, building a hydroelectric plant and over 200 villas. A multitude of conflicts, including the struggle between the French and Viet Minh in the 1950s and the border skirmishes between Vietnam and China in 1979, have destroyed virtually all of these original structures. However, in their place, small hotels and guest houses have popped up like weeds since 1993 when tourists were officially allowed to visit. A perfect base for trekking to the minority villages of the Giay, Hmong, and Dao, this small town has attracted an exponentially growing number of visitors in the past couple of years. It is a great escape from the noise and fumes of Hondas and motorscooters, as well as a great place to kick back and enjoy the silence.

ORIENTATION

Sapa is over 350km northwest from and 1500m higher than Hanoi. It's located off **Highway 4,** 30km west of Lao Cai and 120km from Lai Chau. Unfortunately, none of the streets in town have a name, but fret not; it's pretty much impossible to get lost. The **market** is the principal landmark. Up the market stairs is the main street of Sapa, which runs north-south. The majority of hotels and restaurants line this strip, which is no more than 300m long. In the center of town sits a **ruined church,** another prominent landmark for guiding yourself around the small town.

PRACTICAL INFORMATION

Tourist Information: Pick up the informative guide *Sapa,* edited by Leigh Stubblefield, at the Auberge Restaurant and Guest House (30,000Đ). This rare gem details all aspects of the town and surrounding area, including the minority hill-tribes.

Currency Exchange: Almost all guest houses exchange U.S. dollars for you, but at a rate considerably lower than in Hanoi (almost 10% less). Traveler's checks can be exchanged at the Auberge Restaurant and Guest House.

Post Office: GPO, east of the church on the road leading back to Lao Cai, on the right. Poste Restante. Open daily 7am-8pm.

Telephones: International Phone Office (tel. 712 92; fax 712 82), located in the GPO. **Telephone code:** 20.

Bus: Sapa bus station, 2km from the center of town on Hwy. 4 toward Lao Cai. Bus service is extremely irregular and there is no permanent schedule. Your best bet if you want to take a bus to Lao Cai or Lai Chau is to flag down one on Hwy. 4 and negotiate a price: **Lao Cai** (10,000Đ), **Lai Chau** (30,000Đ).

Pharmacy: Two, across from each other next to GPO. Both open daily 6am-9pm.

ACCOMMODATIONS

All the accommodations in Sapa fit the mini-hotel mold. These small, family-run establishments usually have less than 10 rooms and are meticulously attentive to the needs of visiting tourists. A/C is not needed; in fact, blankets are a must year-round. Some hotels raise the rates of their rooms by 11-22,000Đ during the weekend.

Thanh Binh Hotel (tel. 712 50). From the market, go up the stairs and turn left. Go to the end of the street and head to the top of another set of stairs. Turn left and follow the road for 200m; it banks right and heads to the hotel. Newly built place, this hotel sits on one of the highest points in Sapa. Consequently, its 2nd-floor rooms and balconies afford glorious views of Phan Si Pan Mountain and river valley. It's a million-dollar view, and you get it for the price of a bright, airy room. Doubles with bath 99-132,000Đ. Guides 55,000Đ per day.

Viet Hung Hotel (tel. 712 74), across the street from the GPO. Rooms are clean and comfortable and extensive services compensate for the lack of spectacular views. Information about out-of-the way places like Binh Lu Caves, transportation booking, and rental services (motorscooters 88,000Đ per day). Guides to hill-tribes and Phan Si Pan Mountain. Doubles with bath 55-77,000Đ.

Guest House Rose (tel. 712 63), on the main street intersecting the market. Turn right from the market stairs and it's 75m on the left. This nondescript hotel has clean, well-kept rooms. Conveniently, it sells tickets for minibuses back to Lao Cai which depart from out front (daily 2pm, 15,000Đ). Also sells tickets to Lai Chau by car (88,000Đ). Singles 44,000Đ. Doubles with bath 88,000Đ.

Waterfall Guest House (tel. 712 18), so close to the market you could roll out of bed and down the market steps. The reception on the 1st floor doubles as a drug-store selling batteries, film, and toiletries. Doubles with bath 77,000Đ.

Phuong Nam Hotel (tel. 712 86), at the opposite end of the market street from the stairs. Situated on a ledge over the valley below, many rooms have incredible views of the surrounding landscape. The terrace at the back of the hotel is an unbeatable hangout. Who brought the beer? Doubles with bath 66-132,00Đ, depending on the view.

FOOD

Food in Sapa is hardly spectacular. Because of the high density of tourists, many of the restaurants serve watered-down Vietnamese food and standard tourist fare like French fries. However, on account of Sapas temperate climate, fruits such as plums and apricots grow in abundance. They can be bought in handy straw containers for less than 3000Đ. **Stalls** at the market also serve breakfast, lunch, and dinner at lower rates than in the restaurants.

Auberge Restaurant and Guest House (tel. 712 443), far down the main street past the Student Guest House on the left. Backpackers galore! Tourists come in droves to the 2nd-floor restaurant for the vegetarian plate which serves more food than one person can eat (12,000Đ). Hang out on the balcony or eat inside—food's all the same. Good source of tourist info. Open daily 7am-11pm.

Nha Hang Minh Huu, near the market in the opposite direction from the stairs. Come here for a bowl of *pho* or an order of fried spring rolls. Entrees 11-22,000Đ. Smoke from the wood-burning stoves will get in your eyes. But don't worry; perk up by having an iced coffee with milk. Open daily 6:30am-10pm.

Nha Hang Thu-Dong (tel. 712 38), down main street toward the Student Guest House on your right. What is this I see? Oh, yes, that is French fries on the menu. Sweeeet! Well, at least the food is good and "laughing and talking are still free." Hey, no one told me that the socialist government had been toppled. Open daily 7am-11pm.

SIGHTS

It's not hard to see the sights of Sapa—they're all around you. **Phan Si Pan Mountain** is right in your face across the valley. Rising over 3000m, these mountains, the highest in Vietnam, were called the "Tonkinese Alps" by the French. It's possible to hike to the top of the highest peak via a hard three-day expedition (see Viet Hung Hotel). A little closer to home is the **ruined church** which lies in the middle of town. Built in 1930, the now-roofless structure has seen better days, but the bell still rings out the hours, and a sad, headless statue of Notre Dame de Lourdes still stands. The church looks as it does today thanks to French shells which were launched into Viet Minh-occupied Sapa in 1952. The largest and most renowned attraction of Sapa is the **Saturday Market.** Hordes of the montagnards descend upon the town in addition to the swell of tourists from Hanoi. It is a colorful and frenetic affair, but you can skip the massive influx of backpackers by going there during the week.

■ TREKKING AROUND SAPA

The principal attraction in Sapa is **trekking** across the hills to the scores of **hill-tribe villages** sprinkled around the town. Unlike places like Chiang Mai, Thailand, where hill-tribes have learned to put on a show for tourists trekking through their villages, the people around Sapa remain generally uncorrupted by outside forces. You don't have to go far to interact with the Montagnards. Without a doubt, they will approach you hawking some of their handicrafts and wares,. From silver bangles to patterned beanies, they will try to sell you everything. Bargaining is done with the fingers and their knowledge of western language is limited to the exhortation *"Jolie!"*

Day hikes from Sapa offer less commercial interaction with the hill tribes (for tour guides, see Viet Hung Hotel). Itineraries range from strenuous all-day hikes to short three-hour excursions. Remember to treat the hill-tribe peoples with respect. Don't go into any home or snap a picture of someone without permission.

LAO CHAI, TA VAN RAY, AND CHAI MAN VILLAGES

The round trip to all three villages will take anywhere from four to eight hours, depending on if you are wired on caffeine or stopping to smell the roses, and can be appended at any point by backtracking to Sapa. From Sapa, head out of town past the Auberge Restaurant. Along this road many of the hill-tribe people enter and leave town sporting backpacks or straw baskets. Stalls along the road keep your fuel gauge near full with tea, fruit, and snacks. About 1½hr. into your hike (about 8km) you will pass a small waterfall. A little past it is a path to the right which crosses a foot bridge to the Hmong village of **Lao Chai.** Backtrack to the road and continue heading away from Sapa for another 3km past a second waterfall. Another path and bridge that veer off the road to the right lead to the Giay village of **Ta Van Ray,** to the left after the bridge. Here you can cut back to Lao Chai village via a single track connection between the two villages or you can backtrack to the road and head 3km farther out toward the Dao village of **Chai Man.** Notice the prehistoric etchings on rocks along the road. Again, a path to the right crosses a foot bridge. Take the left fork and cross the waterfall over the stepping stone to the village.

SIN CHAI AND CAT CAT VILLAGES

From the market, head away from the stairs and follow the path that leads northwest along the valley. Shortly on you will pass one of the old, destroyed French villas built in the 30s. About 10 minutes into your journey, a small path splits off on the main track to your left. After 5km, the main path leads to the Hmong village of **Sin Chai.** But if you decide to turn left, you will reach **Cat Cat,** another Hmong village, less than 1km away. Head past the village deeper into the valley and the old **hydroelectric power station** will come into view. Continue along the path over the bridge and stop to dip your feet before reaching the power station. West from the power station are fruit trees and grazing fields for water buffalo. Meander here for a while and go back the way you came when you've had your fill of fresh air.

■■■ LAO CAI

The northern terminus of Highway 1, Lao Cai is a border town full of mud. Rapid construction runs rampant in town as earth is pushed around to make room for imposing administrative buildings which provide the requisite layer of bureaucracy and red tape for a burgeoning border and trade town. Despite rapid growth of trade between China and Vietnam (of the legal and illegal variety), the town moves at a slow pace that bores visitors passing through. Perhaps this explains Lao Cai's unofficial motto, "We're more fun than a root canal."

Orientation and Practical Information Over 300km northwest of Hanoi, Lao Cai is situated on the Red River on the border of south China. It is where both **Highway 1** and the **rail line** from Hanoi terminates. Tourists traveling from China to Vietnam or vice versa use Lao Cai as a border crossing. The bulk of the city runs along two parallel north-south streets on opposite sides of the Red River; a large bridge connects the two. On the east side is **Duong Pho Moi Lao Cai** on which the **border checkpoint** is located in the north end; the **train station** is over 2km south of it. (If you are entering Vietnam and Lao Cai is not on your visa as an entry point, you will be charged an outrageous 440,000Đ to change it. However, you can extend your visa at a bargain rate of 55,000Đ.) Most hotels are on this street near the border station. On the west side of the river is **Duong Hoang Lien** which intersects Hwy. 1 at its southern tip across a narrow steel bridge.

Currency (U.S. dollars only) can be exchanged at **Nhan Hang Nong Nghiep Lao Cai** (tel. 300 13), on the right just around the bend from the border crossing on D. Pho Moi Lao Cai if heading north toward the border. Open daily 7-11:30am and 1-5pm. The **GPO,** 200 D. Hoang Lien, has an **international telephone office** and **fax** service. Mail, phone, and fax can also be obtained at the **branch office,** 13 D. Pho Moi Lao Cai (tel. 220 03; fax 300 20). Open daily 7am-8pm. **Telephone code:** 20.

Ground transportation to and from Lao Cai stops at the **bus station** (Ben Xe Khach Lao Cai) just over the bridge on the west side of the river. To: **Sapa** (daily, 6 and 6:20am, 2hr., 5500Đ); **Lai Chau** (daily, 6:30am, 10-14hr., 35,000Đ); and **Hanoi-Haiphong** (every 4th day, 14-20hr., 60,000Đ). If you are heading to Sapa, your other options include renting a **taxi** (220,000Đ) or hiring a **motorcycle taxi** (55,000Đ per person). Most taxis wait in and around the bus station. The **train station** is on D. Pho Moi Lao Cai about 2km south of the bridge. The **LC2** and **LC4** depart daily to **Hanoi** at 6:30pm and 9:40am, respectively (1-hr., 210,000Đ soft seat). To get to town from the train station, hire a motorcycle taxi (10,000Đ).

A **pharmacy, Quay Ban Thuoc** (tel. 301 87), lies on the west side of the bridge near the rotary circle. Open daily 7am-9pm. The large provincial **hospital** is on the edge of town off D. Hoang Lien. When coming into town from Hwy. 1, turn right at the first turn after the city road divides. It is a 3-story white building on the right.

Accommodations and Food Hotels in Lao Cai are located on D. Pho Moi Lao Cai, where you can see gaggles of Chinese wearing floppy yellow hats walking around menacingly in groups. The **Post Office Guest House,** 13 D. Pho Moi Lao Cai (tel. 300 33), has a variety of accommodations to suit the budget of most travelers. Dorm beds with fans 55,000Đ. Doubles with A/C, TV, and bath 165,000Đ. Triples with fans 110,000Đ. Across the street is **Khach San Hong Ha** (tel. 300 07). Balconies here give you great views of the metropolis of Lao Cai. Doubles with A/C, TV, bath, and fridge 88-110,000Đ. Triples with fan and bath 110,000Đ. Just south of the Post Office Guest House is **Nha Khach Cong Ty Xuat Nghiep Khan Lao Cai,** 39 D. Pho Moi Lao Cai (tel. 300 85). Big name, big hotel, big rooms. Doubles with A/C, TV, bath, and fridge 165,000Đ. For food, you can scour the streets like a stray dog or hit some of the **food stalls** near the hotel. Most serve *pho* or simple plates of chicken or pork with rice. The **market** south down the street from the bus station is the place to pick up fruit, snacks, and sweeter delights.

CENTRAL VIETNAM

■■■ FROM HANOI TO HUE

THANH HOA

Thanh Hoa is the definition of one-street town: shops, food stalls, and hotels line the highway and execute the town's seemingly only function—being an oversized pit stop for motorscooters, cars, trucks, and buses. Despite its mundane existence, Thanh Hoa and surrounding provincial areas were once a great center of civilization for the Kinh, the ancestors of the Viets. If only they were alive to see Thanh Hoa today, they wouldn't have to spend all that time rolling over in their graves.

The town lies on both sides of **Highway 1,** 150km south of Hanoi and 300km north of Dong Hoi. Getting oriented is as easy as *pho.* The highway assumes the alias **Duong Quang Trung** and rips through town like a gaping wound, with small alleys and dirt roads radiating from it. **Duong Le Hoan,** the road to **Sam Son Beach,** spurs off to the east, marking an approximate halfway point. North of the intersection is the **bus station.** Buses head north or south from the station, but it's easier to flag one down at the side of the road. When one stops, state your destination and quickly negotiate a price (a good price is about 10,000Đ per 100km). Nearby is the **Thanh Hoa Train Station.** The S3 and S5 from Hanoi head south to **Ho Chi Minh City** and points in between (arriving at 11:07pm and 2:26pm, respectively and departing 3 minutes later). The S4 and S6 stop at 7:19am and 1:44pm, respectively, and head for **Hanoi** 3 minutes later. Reserve ahead. From either station, it's a comfortable (but long) walk to town. A **motorcycle taxi** to a hotel shouldn't cost over 8000Đ. The **GPO** is south of D. Le Hoan on the east side of the highway, beside the **international telephone office. Telephone code:** 37. Farther south and across the street is the **Thanh Hoa Tourism Office,** 25A D. Quang Trung (tel. 522 17).

A few model Motel-6 hotels on the highway welcome weary travelers. The large **Thanh Hoa Hotel,** 25A D. Quang Trung (tel. 525 17), home to the tourist office, has rooms in all price ranges. Doubles with fans 55,000Đ, with hot water 88-110,000Đ, with A/C 165,000Đ. On the opposite side of the road to the south is **Nha Khach Thanh Hoa.** Doubles with fan 66,000Đ, with bath 88,000Đ. For a highway town, Thanh Hoa offers an unusually high number of **food stalls** and hawkers selling specialty items like rice cakes, sweet bean gelatins, and ice cream. As at most rest stops, prices are higher but not unreasonable. Many buses stop at the food stall on steroids known as **Restaurant Phuong Nam** (tel. 533 75).

The Dong Son civilization had many of its principal settlements along the Ma River. Remnants of this fascinating, mysterious culture include bronze drums now seen in museums across Vietnam. The only theory as yet put forth about the people's disappearance suggests that they spontaneously combusted during a rendition of Spinal Tap's "Stonehenge." Spanning the Ma River on the south entrance to the city is **Ham Rong Bridge** (Dragon's Jaw Bridge), one of Thanh Hoa's most interesting sights. A source of frustration for American fighter pilots, the divinely protected steel-beam structure cost the U.S. more than 70 downed planes in eight years before it was finally wiped out in 1972. Two other notable bridges nearby date from Thanh Hoa's golden age during the late 14th and 15th centuries, when the city was the capital of Vietnam. In 1397 the **Ho Citadel** and a large, ornate **city gate** were constructed to safeguard the city, but to no avail—the Chinese overran the capital several years later. (The natives eventually managed to expel the Chinese forces in the Lam Son uprising.) To visit the gates, now being excavated and restored, consult a guide from the tourism office.

SAM SON BEACH

Sixteen km southeast of Thanh Hoa, Sam Son Beach offers 3km of fine sand and a heavy dose of beach cheeze, including plastic lobsters and strange sea sculptures of shellfish. Summer rates for rooms are double what they are in other seasons, usually 220-440,000Đ for foreigners. Motorcycle taxis are the quickest, most convenient way to get from Thanh Hoa to Sam Son (15-20,000Đ). Buses also run regularly from Hwy. 1; stand on D. Le Hoan in Thanh Hoa and flag down any bus headed for the surf (5000Đ). The road from Thanh Hoa makes a beeline for the shore and intersects with a road running parallel to the water along the beach. The **bus station** is near this intersection. Turn right and head south for 1km to reach the beach **hospital.** The **post and telephone office** is back toward Thanh Hoa from the beach; turn right after 200m. It is another 100m down the road. **Telephone code:** 37.

Some good hotels are on the beach just north of the intersection with the road to Thanh Hoa. The **Hoa Hong II Hotel** (tel. 215 05) and **Huong Bien Hotel** (tel. 213

17) have large doubles with A/C and TV (220-330,000Đ). Less expensive is **Nha Nghi Cong Ty Cap Noai Thanh Hoa** (tel. 213 12), 50m north of the Huong Bien. Doubles, triples, and quads with fan run 77-176,000Đ. Get a massage on the beach or rent an inner tube to ride the meager waves.

DONG HOI

The first major town above the 17th parallel, Dong Hoi received the lion's share of American bombs throughout the war. Although the town has since been rebuilt, some areas remain bare and dotted with crater scars. Situated on the banks of the Nhat Le River several km inland from the South China Sea, Dong Hoi is primarily a fishing town. Tourism is still in its infancy, but the wide, empty avenues are waiting to embrace an anticipated boom.

Dong Hoi is on **Highway 1,** 500km south of Hanoi and 170km north of Hue. The town's one major intersection is marked by the massive white **civic center.** On the opposite corner is the **GPO,** with the **international phone office** (tel. 225 78; fax 220 77) in its lobby. Open 6:30am-8pm. **Telephone code:** 52. North of the intersection Hwy. 1 becomes **Duong Ly Thuong Kiet;** south of the intersection it is **Duong Quang Trung,** parallel to the **Nhat Le River.** The crossing street, **Duong Xuan Ky** (which may change names soon), runs 1km west away from the river to the bus station. To: **Hue** (daily, 6, 8:30am, and noon, 5-7hr., 18,000Đ); **Da Nang** (daily, 6 and 9am, 8-10hr., 22,000Đ); and **Thanh Hoa** (daily, 6am, 12-14hr., 30,000Đ). One km west is the **train station.** Cross the bridge over the tracks to the terminal. The S3 and S5 to **Ho Chi Minh City** stop at 7:22am and 11:57pm and depart 3 min. later. The S4 and S6 stop at 11:02pm and 4:30pm, respectively, and leave for **Hanoi** 3 min. later.

A plethora of **pharmacies** lines D. Ly Thuong Kiet. Most close by 7pm. The **Vietnam-Cuba Hospital,** a gift from Señor Castro, is 1km north of town (go left on Hwy. 1). At 50 D. Quang Trung, in a small office around back, is **Tour and Guide Office** (tel. 220 84). Mr. Truong can make arrangements for visiting **surrounding sights.** Open Mon.-Sat. 8-11am and 1-4:30pm. Next door at #48, **Vang Ba Cong Ty** may be able to **exchange** U.S. dollars. Open Mon.-Sat. 8-11am and 1-4pm.

Accommodations along Hwy. 1 are less expensive than those along the river. The **Hoa Binh Hotel,** 52 D. Ly Thuong Kiet (tel. 22 347), is one of the largest and oldest in town, with useful and friendly **tour information.** Doubles with fan 88-110,000Đ, with A/C 165,000Đ. **Ngu Nghi Du Lich Hai Thanh,** 102 D. Ly Thuong Kiet, supplies the minimum for sleep, but the price is right. Doubles with fan 66,000Đ. The **Nhat Le** (tel. 221 80), on the river just south of the main intersection, offers a righteous view. Doubles with fan 110,000Đ, with A/C 220-440,000Đ. Famous for its seafood, Dong hoi's streets are lined with **food stalls** serving fish cooked every which way. Go for the sour fish stew, with a serving of rice and greens.

Phong Nha Caves

Queued up behind Halong Bay, **Phong Nha Caves** are perhaps Vietnam's second greatest natural landmark. Vietnam is trying hard to attract more people to this wondrous monument forged by the lithe hands of time and water. A good bet for reliable transportation is to go through the Dong Hoi tourist office, but the dates are erratic and require individual chartering and free-lance negotiating. Transportation arranged by Tour and Guide Service 66-110,000Đ per person round-trip; admission and 2-hr. boat trip through the caves 66,000Đ per person. Be prepared to wait; the boat will not push off until it reaches critical mass. An even better option for touring is offered through the Hue tourist office (275,000Đ one day, 385,000Đ two day).

■■■ HUE

If you could transplant the heart of a small city into a large one, Hue is what you would get. Excessively gracious and accommodating denizens (who speak with a drawn-out mellow tone somewhat analogous to the American southern drawl) welcome visitors to the ancient imperial capital with open arms and a friendly curiosity not found in many other parts of Vietnam. As the spiritual, artistic, and cultural center of Vietnam, Hue has a rich, storied past and an incredible concentration of impressive sights and ruins.

In the 19th century, under the capable rule of the Nguyen Dynasty (1802-1945), Hue reached preeminence—and for the first time in its long history, Vietnam, stretching from Chinese Yunnan to the Gulf of Siam, was united under a single court. In Hue, the dynasty established a city that was admired by all who visited, foreigners and Vietnamese alike. It was not long, however, before the death knell sounded for this brilliant golden age. French ships blockaded and prepared to attack the city in 1833; the Emperor, realizing the technological might of the French, sued for peace instead, making Vietnam a French protectorate. The colonial administration did much to protect the treasures of Hue and preserve its historic integrity, but the preservation was to no avail. Hue became a combat zone during the Vietnam War, particularly during the 1968 Tet Offensive, in which the citadel was constantly taken and retaken by both sides as fighting raged even on the sacred grounds of the Imperial City.

Today, the streets of Hue are literally engulfed with the aroma of some of the finest food in Vietnam and the resonant melodies of the city's traditional music and folk songs. Quiet discoveries await around each corner; just meander down the tree-lined streets and soak in the almost tangible atmosphere of this royal city.

ORIENTATION

A little over 100km south of the 17th parallel and 16km inland from the South China Sea, Hue is bisected by the **Perfume River** (Song Huong). On the northwest side of the river is the ancient, square-shaped **Citadel of Hue,** within which is the protected **Royal Palace** and **Imperial City** of the Nguyen Dynasty. On the southwest side is **new Hue,** where the lion's share of hotels, restaurants, and tourist services flourish. **Highway 1** cuts through Hue from the northwest corner of the Citadel, following along its walls until it crosses the Perfume River. The highway then knifes south through the middle of new Hue toward Da Nang and Ho Chi Minh City.

On the Citadel side, **Duong Le Duan/Tran Hung Dao** runs between the river and the Citadel wall. At the center of this side of the wall, just inside the Citadel, is the **Flag Staff of Hue,** which marks the front gate of the Royal Palace and the Imperial City. **Duong Nguyen Trai** and **Duong Dinh Tien Hoang** intersect with D. Le Duan/Tran Hung Dao and run northwest through the gates of the Citadel flanking the Imperial City on either side. On the southeast bank of the Perfume River, **Duong Le Loi,** the main tourist strip on this side, runs parallel to the water. **Duong Hung Vuong,** which 500m from the river becomes Hwy. 1, intersects with D. Le Loi and runs southeast and south away from Hue. Two bridges connect the two halves of Hue. **Cau Trang Tien,** a visual string mass of repeated steel arches, carries most city traffic. **Cau Phu Xuan,** a little farther upriver, is where Hwy. 1 crosses the river and begins to run away from Hue.

PRACTICAL INFORMATION

Tourist Offices: Thua Thien Hue Tourism, 15 D. Le Loi (tel. 223 69; fax 248 06), offers a variety of services including one-day tours of the DMZ (165,000Đ) and Phong Nha Caves (275,000Đ). Open Mon.-Sat. 7:30am-9pm. **DMZ Tour,** 26 D. Le Loi (tel. 252 42). The definitive place for tours of the DMZ. Book the tour from your hotel or directly from the office. Open daily 5:30am-9:30pm. **Art Tourist Services Center (ATC),** 44 D. Le Loi (tel. 245 00), will book plane and train tickets and arrange for car rentals. Open daily 7am-8pm.

Currency Exchange: Vietcombank, D. Hoang Hoa Tham (tel. 246 29; fax 246 31), next door to the GPO. Exchanges all major currencies and traveler's checks. Cash advance on Visa, MC. AmEx moneygram. Open Mon.-Sat. 7-11:30am and 1:30-4:30pm (summer) or 1-4pm (winter).

Post Office: GPO, 8 D. Hoang Hoa Tham, south of D. Le Loi. The post office has satellite TV for music videos or international sports events while you wait. **Poste**

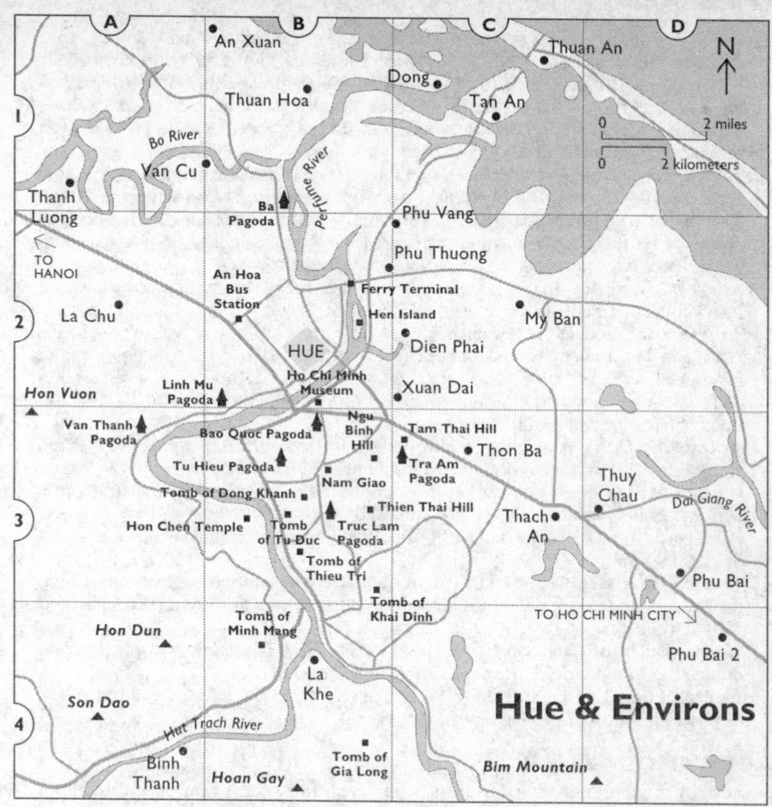

Restante. U.S. dollar currency exchange. Open daily 6:30am-9pm. **Train station post office** (tel. 231 09; fax 250 56). Open daily 6:30am-8:30pm.

Telephones: International Phone Office (tel. 220 00; fax 238 58), in the GPO lobby. Receives and sends faxes. Open daily 6:30am-9pm. **Telephone code:** 54.

Airport: Phu Bai Airport, 10km south of the city off Hwy. 1. Expect to pay 88-110,000Đ for a taxi to the airport (no meters). **Vietnam Airlines Office,** 7 D. Nguyen Tri Phuong St. (tel. 247 09; fax 224 70), in the lobby of Thuan An Hotel, will reserve and book your tickets. Open Mon.-Sat. 8-11:30am and 1:30-4:30pm. To: **Dalat** (Tues., Thurs., and Sun. 1:30pm); **Hanoi** (daily 9am and (except Tues. and Thurs.) 12:30pm); and **Ho Chi Minh City** (daily (except Sat.) 8:30am and (except Tues. and Thurs.) 4:30pm; Tues., Thurs., and Sun. 1:30pm); both 990,000Đ. International to: **Bangkok** (daily (except Sat.) 8:30 and 9am; Sat. 12:30pm); **Hong Kong** (Mon. and Thurs. 8:30am, Sat. 9am, and Sat.-Sun. 12:30pm); **Kuala Lumpur** (Mon. and Fri. 8:30am); **Phnom Penh** (daily (except Sat.) 8:30am); and **Singapore** (Tues., Thurs., and Sun. 8:30am).

Trains: Hue Railway Station, on D. Le Loi, at the southwest end over the bridge. To: **Ho Chi Minh City** (daily S1, S3, and S5 at 8:58, 11:29am, and 4:01am) and **Hanoi** (daily S2, S4, and S6 at 4:55, 7:46, and 12:48pm). Special LH1 runs from Hue to **Ho Chi Minh City** and all points in between (Tues., Thurs., and Sat. 9:30am). Cyclos to the station (5-10,000Đ).

Buses: An Hoa Bus Station, outside the walls of the Citadel at its northwest corner off of Hwy. 1, runs north to: **Dong Ha** (daily every 30min. 6am-2pm, 15,000Đ); **Khe Sanh** (daily 5am, 6hr., 30,000Đ); **Dong Hoi** (daily 6am, 7hr., 25,000Đ); **Thanh Hoa** (daily 5am, 16-18hr., 45,000Đ); and **Hanoi** (daily 5am, 24-28hr., 100,000Đ). **An Cuu Bus Station,** 1km south of the Perfume River on D.

Hung Vuong, primarily serves points south. To: **Da Nang** (daily 8am, 3-4hr., 25,000Đ); **Dalat** (daily 5:30am, 20-24hr., 150,000Đ); **Ho Chi Minh City** (daily 5:30am, 36hr., 190,000Đ); and **Hanoi** (daily 5:30am, 24-28hr., 100,000Đ). Purchase tickets for long trips 1 day in advance. The **local bus station** (*Ben Xe Dong Ba*) is on D. Tran Hung Dao, on the Citadel side of the Perfume River. Transport to **Thuan An Beach** all day (5000Đ).

Boats: Tourist Boat Pier, 5 D. Le Loi, next to the Floating Restaurant. Hire a boat for a one-day tour up the Perfume River to **Thien Mu Pagoda** and the **Royal Tombs** or to **Thuan An Beach** (132-165,000Đ for 8-person boat). The **folk songs of Hue** boat tour and performance leaves every night at 7pm and returns 2-3 hr. later with rave reviews (352,000Đ for 8-person boat).

Taxi: ATC Taxi (tel. 333 33). Unmetered rides to anywhere within reason. Call 1 hr. in advance to ensure a ride.

Motorscooter and Bicycle Rental: Best done through hotels. Next best bet is **Madame Ti** (or as she writes on her card), who runs a cigarette concession stand in front of 46 D. Le Loi, across from the Century Riverside Hotel. She rents bikes (7-10,000Đ per day) and motorscooters (88-110,000Đ per day for 100cc), and also books boat, car, and minibus transport.

Market: Cho Dong Ba, on the Perfume River at the northeast terminus of D. Tran Hung Dao. The largest market in Hue, and one of the most celebrated in Vietnam. Large crowds frequent the market throughout the day. Open daily 6:30am-7pm.

Laundry: Hai Quang, 44 D. Le Loi (tel. 220 64), in a souvenir and crafts store. Hand-wash service 5000Đ per outfit or 2500Đ per piece. Same-day service. Open daily 6am-9pm.

Library: Thu Vien Hue, 20 D. Le Loi, frequented by a stampede of students during the June exam season, when it is closed to visitors. Open Mon.-Sat. 7-11:15am and 1:30-4:30pm.

Pharmacy: Thuoc Tay, 1 Nguyen Huy Tu (tel. 286 02), around the corner from the front entrance to the hospital. Open daily 7am-7pm.

Hospital: Hue City Hospital, 16 D. Le Loi (tel. 223 25). Some western-trained physicians. A little bit of English spoken by some staff.

ACCOMMODATIONS

Because of the high density of tourists, there is a hotel, guest house, or mini-hotel every 50m on the southeast side of the Perfume River—and more are on the way. The fierce competition between hotels and their touts creates a buyer's market.

Guest House Thanh Thuy, 46/4 D. Le Loi (tel. 245 85). A total family operation. Brother, sister, mom, and dad work hard to make sure their fledgling hotel offers all the creature comforts. Balconies off the front rooms are great for hanging out and soaking in Hue's night air. Excessively clean bathrooms. Ask for a discount for long stays. Singles with A/C and bath. Doubles with A/C, bath, and balcony.

Ben Nghe Guest House, 4 D. Ben Nghe (tel. 236 87), head south from the Century Riverside Hotel down D. Han Ngu Lao to the skewed intersection and veer right down D. Ben Nghe. Guest house is on your right. Chock full of budget travelers, the guest house provides info about activities in Hue. Doubles 66-77,000Đ, with bath and A/C 132,000Đ. Triples 77-99,000Đ.

Hue City Tourism Guest Villas, 5, 6, 18 D. Ly Thuong Kiet. Spacious French villa-type structures converted into budget guest rooms. The 3 different locations offer similar rooms for similar rates. Although the rooms are old, the accommodations are very comfortable and quiet. Singles 66-88,000Đ. Doubles 110,000Đ.

Dong Phuong Mini Hotel, 26 D. Nguyen Tri Phuong (tel. 253 33). From Trang Tien Bridge, head south on D. Hung Vuong and turn left on D. Nguyen Tri Phuong after 2 blocks. Modern facilities. A large restaurant offers Vietnamese and Euro nosh. Doubles with bath 110,000Đ, and A/C 165,000Đ.

Mimosa Mini Hotel, 46/6 D. Le Loi (tel. 280 68; fax 238 58), down a little alley across from the Century Riverside Hotel. Quiet and clean. It is one of many small new hotels along this passage and will often accept an offer lower than the declared rate to keep you from going next door. All rooms with A/C and bath. Singles 77-110,000Đ. Doubles 110-165,000Đ.

Thanh Loi Hotel, 7 D. Dinh Tien Hoang (tel. 248 03; fax 253 44), just outside Thuong Tu Gate to the Citadel. Has been around for years; popular with Vietnamese visitors. Has tours of the Citadel and Royal Tombs and car rentals. Doubles 66,000Đ, with bath and A/C 132,000Đ. Triples 88,000Đ.

FOOD

The food in Hue is some of the best cuisine in Vietnam. What sets Hue apart is not necessarily better preparation or fresher ingredients, but rather its large assortment of regional specialties, which, though imitated throughout the country, never taste as good as they do in Hue.

Quan 169, 169 D. Chi Lang. From Citadel side of the river, head northeast on D. Tran Hung Dao and across a small bridge. Go straight through the rotary onto D. Chi Lang and proceed about 0.75km to the restaurant on your left. The griddles out front radiate the sweet smell and sounds of the *banh khoai* sizzling over the red embers. The taco-like dishes are served with a sweet plum sauce and a healthy serving of lettuce and fresh greens (4000Đ each). Yum.

Quan Ba Do, 9 D. Nguyen Ninh Kniem. Just up the intersection 50m from Quan 169 on the left. Local fishermen bring in baskets of fresh shrimp before sunrise and the women here start right in boiling the shrimp with rice flour. They have to start early to satisfy the throngs who pour in all day long craving *banh beo, banh loc,* and *banh nam.* 4000Đ per serving. Open daily 10am-7pm.

Quan An Chay, 44 D. Hung Vuong (tel. 241 34). Regarded as the best vegetarian restaurant in Hue. A large selection of dishes available, from rice to soups to small appetizers. Most entrees around 10,000Đ. Open daily 7am-10pm.

Café Familial, 3 D. Le Loi (tel. 245 14). Just over the bridge from the train station. As the name suggests, this is a family-run business, operated by the Nguyen clan. Offering great beef and shrimp choices as well as Vietnamese-style *guacamole* dip, this establishment attracts a large number of tourists who come not only for the food and hospitality, but also for the variety of tour services. Entrees 10-20,000Đ. Open dawn to midnight.

Restaurant Huong Sen, 42 D. Nguyen Trai (tel. 23 201), inside the city Citadel. Cross Phu Xuan Bridge and turn left on D. Le Duan; enter the last gate on the southeast side by turning right on D. Nguyen Tra. Go 2 blocks until you see a 16-sided structure in the middle of a lotus pond. Delicious food, prompt service, inviting atmosphere. What more could you ask for? Give the blood curd with crab a try; you won't regret it. Entrees 22-55,000Đ. Open daily 7am-11pm.

Sinh Coffee, 20 D. Le Loi (tel. 25 726), in the Hue public library complex. Stop for a pit stop and get a delicious fruit shake. Hook up with other travelers and swap stories over flan or ice cream. Mr. Trung Toan, the proprietor, is an amiable and

Hue-Cool Cuisine

Warning: this copy of *Let's Go: Southeast Asia* will self-destruct if you visit Hue without sampling the superexcellent regional dishes. Great local favorites include *banh khoai,* a crispy, fried flour-batter folded in half, stuffed with pork, shrimp, bean sprouts, onions, and other fresh, minty greens, and *banh xeo,* a common derivative, resembling an omelette. Two simple ingredients—rice flour and fresh shrimp—comprise the basis of three other tasty delights: *banh beo, banh loc,* and *banh nam.* Cooking *banh beo* involves pouring water and rice flour into circular molds, steaming until the consistency becomes gelatinous, and then sprinkling dried shrimp and fried onions or rinds on top. In *banh nam,* long rectangular pieces of gelatinized rice flour are sprinkled with dried shrimp and wrapped inside a banana leaf. *Banh loc* uses a whole shrimp, encased in the gelatinized rice flour and wrapped inside a banana leaf. Fish sauce accompanies all of the above dishes. A popular breakfast in Hue—definitely *not* for the squeamish—is *com hen.* This spicy rice chowder, mixed with miniature clams, will ignite if left unattended. Put out the fire and wash down all of Hue's food with Huda, the local brew touted on its bottle as "brewed by Danish technology."

knowledgeable soccer fanatic. He offers some of the best deals in town for motor-scooter or boat rental. Open daily 7am-11pm.

SIGHTS

The ancient Citadel and Imperial City and Royal Tombs dominate the tourist landscape of Hue. The fascination with royalty and their exclusive private lives draws thousands of tourists to the ancient imperial capital year after year. The grandeur of the ancient palaces and tombs captures the undivided attention of all who come upon them and lights an imaginative fire in those trying to comprehend and reconstruct the imperial Hue of the past. Trying to see all that Hue has to offer can be overwhelming at first, but renting a bike and using the divide-and-conquer method—splitting up the sights over at least two days—will allow you to attack the city's great monuments and find some hidden gems along the way.

The Citadel and Imperial City

Emperor Gia Long, founder of the Nguyen Dynasty, began constructing the Citadel in 1805 with rampart walls made of piled-up dirt from excavations of the surrounding moat. Emperor Minh Mang completed the fortification by bricking the 6m-high, 20m-wide wall and expanding the moat to its current size (4m deep, 23m wide). Today, the massive square-shaped citadel is 10km in circumference, with four gates on its front side along the Perfume River and two on each of the other three sides.

Just inside the Citadel, between the central front gates, the 47-m high **Flag Pole of Hue** is one of the city's enduring landmarks. The tallest in Vietnam (the actual pole stands 30m but sits upon three terraces that rise 17m), it has been rebuilt several times since its construction in 1807. Opposite the flag pole and outside the citadel, just off Hwy. 1, lies the **Pavilion of Edicts.** Built in 1810, the large square was used by Gia Long to announce successful candidates of the national exam and declare important edicts. The Emperor Minh Mang is said to have enjoyed watching duels between tigers and elephants staged here.

Across from the flagpole inside the citadel is the **Noon Gate** (Ngo Mon). Admission 55,000Đ. Open daily 6am-6pm. This is the grand entrance to the Imperial City, a square within the square of the Citadel. Built in 1833, the gate served as both an entrance and a ceremonial enclave called the **Five-Phoenix Pavilion,** which sits atop the gate from where the emperor and his court would watch the ceremonial proceedings below. The middle of the three arched entrances to the Imperial City was reserved exclusively for the emperor and even today remains closed to the public, who enter through flanking entrances (foreigners to the left). Just inside the Noon Gate, the **Trun Gao Bridge** leads to the **Hall of Salutation** where the emperor greeted official guests. Just behind this, the **Palace of Supreme Harmony**—the spiritual center of the imperial grounds—once housed the emperor's throne. Emperor Gia Long built it in the center of the Imperial City in 1803, but Minh Mang moved the ornate red and gold structure to its present location. The different levels of the courts in front of the throne correlated to the standing of the mandarins (the court's intellectual elite); they were further differentiated with military leaders on the right and the civil leaders on the left.

North of the throne, the Imperial City has suffered both the trials of time and nature and the ravishes of the Viet Minh, who used it as a base during the war. These open fields once housed the grand residences of the emperor and empress. Called the **Forbidden Purple City,** the formerly walled residence area lies on the same vertical axis as the Imperial City and Citadel. The **Royal Library,** on the right when facing north, is one of the few structures still intact inside the Purple City. West of the Purple City are the residences of the Queen Mother and Great Queen Mother. These structures are undergoing extensive renovations with funds from UNESCO, which has declared Hue a World Heritage Site. In the southwest corner of the Imperial City is **Thien Mieu Temple,** dedicated to Gia Long and his successors. Offerings were made to the small thrones on the altars. In front of the temple squat the **Nine Dynastic Urns,** representing members of the dynasty. Ornate reliefs concerning nature and man are cast into the potbelly sides of each giant bronze vessel.

About 3km west of the Citadel is **Thien Mu Pagoda.** Head west out D. Le Duan and continue across the train tracks to D. Kim Long. Situated on a high hill overlooking the Perfume River, the pagoda is dedicated to a legendary 16th-century woman who declared that a time of great prosperity would come if a Buddhist pagoda were built on the site. Lord Nguyen Hoang heard her decree and built the pagoda in 1601. The seven-level tower at the top of the stairs is one of the many representative icons of Hue. The first monk to publicly immolate himself in Saigon during Ngo Dinh Diem's presidency came from this pagoda, and his car is on display as a memorial.

Royal Tombs

In addition to the magnificent Citadel and Imperial City, Hue is home to the tombs of seven emperors of the Nguyen Dynasty. Located a few km outside the city center, predominantly to the southwest, the tombs are accessible by motorscooter or bike. These tombs provided not just noble burials, but also comfortable afterlives. Many of the tombs were the crowning life pursuits of the emperors; each designed his individually. In this way, each tomb represents the expressive spirit of an emperor as well as the architecture of the time, Vietnamese with French influences.

Although the tombs are visually and structurally different, they share certain formal elements. Each encloses a large open court guarded by statues of mandarins, a stele inscribed with the eulogy, and a temple dedicated to the worship of the emperor. The entrance fee to many of the tombs is expensive (22-55,000Đ). All are open daily 6am-6pm (or until sunset).

Starting from D. Le Loi, head west toward the train station. After crossing the small bridge, turn right on D. Bui Thi Xuan. Follow this street along the river for just under 3km and turn left. About 100m on your right is the **Royal Arena,** built in 1830. Similar in size and function to a Roman arena, Hue's version primarily hosted duels between elephants and tigers; the emperors used the elephant crushing the wild tiger as a handy metaphor for their imperial authority. Head south from the arena another 2km, and turn left to the **tomb of Tu Duc** (take care not to turn at the first left after 1.5km). Ruling from 1848 to 1883, Tu Duc had the longest—and perhaps most challenging—reign of any Nguyen emperor. The scholarly and literary leader had to face the challenges that European influences, particularly the French, posed to Vietnam's future. Although he had many children, Tu Duc never sired an heir; he often found solace from this misfortune in the fairy-tale construction of his tomb, particularly the island in the middle of the lake. Admission 55,000Đ.

Down the street, 500m from the tomb of Tu Du, is the **tomb of Dong Khanh.** In contrast to his uncle Tu Duc, Danh Khanh ruled only three short years, 1886-89, and was never involved in the planning of his tomb; the absence of an outer wall to tie together the tombs of his mother, wife, and himself reflects the incompleteness of his reign. Relatively few visitors of Tu Duc's tomb walk over to this one. Admission 25,000Đ. From here, backtrack out to the street that led into the two tombs. Then head south down the road for 1km and turn onto the gravel access road to the entrance of **the tomb of Thieu Tri.** (Taking the left fork just before the tomb will take you toward the **tomb of Khai Dinh.**) Basically abandoned except for the ticket taker, this tomb has a mode of design similar to that of Dong Khanh's tomb. The caretaker may lavish you with a personal tour and allow you to poke your head into its hidden spaces. Admission 22,000Đ.

Back on the road, head south 2km until you see the boats that ferry passengers over to the **tomb of Minh Mang;** built from 1841 to 1843, it is considered by many to have the greatest architectural balance and poise. From the three porticoes of the Hong Mon Gate in front, you'll enter the largest greeting court of all the tombs, filled with stone elephants and mandarins guarding and paying homage to the emperor. Next, three sets of stairs lead to the stele pavilion that bears Minh Mang's eulogy, composed by Thieu Tri. Descending from the pavilion, you'll reach three large courtyards dedicated to Minh Mang and his wife. Opposite these stands the Minh

Lau Temple, which houses an altar to the king's eternal prosperity and longevity. Over a stone bridge, you'll approach the tomb proper; look for the large mound of dirt. The bronze circular door (the main entrance) represents the sun.

The **tomb of Gia Long** (ruled 1802-20) lies several km from Minh Mang's, so it is best bike there. Follow the road southeast, passing through Minh Mang Village until you reach a tributary of the Perfume River. Cross over on a ferry (1000Đ) and take the dirt path there, which will lead to the tomb. Due to its distance from the other tombs, Gia Long receives few visitors. This mausoleum, built between 1814 and 1820, boasts a courtyard surrounded by a lotus pond and guarded with horses, elephants, and mandarins. A set of steps will take you to the burial chamber where Gia Long and his wife lay in eternal slumber. The wild mango, cassava trees, and unruly bush camouflage a fitting resting place for the father of united Vietnam.

Head back through the gauntlet of youngsters selling hats and fans on the road from the tomb to the ferry dock and go back across the Perfume River. From there, turn left up the road and, after 200m, turn right toward the **tomb of Khai Dinh.** Constructed on the side of a hill over a span of 11 years, it was completed in 1931, six years after Khai Dinh's nine-year reign. The last of the tombs to be built, this one has a style strikingly different from the others—it shows great deference to European styles, and many visitors comment on the similarity of its ornamentation to that of France's Palace of Versailles. The organization of the tomb follows the basic pattern, but here you have to climb a long flight of stairs to reach each successive pavilion and court. At the top of the tomb, a large altar houses a guilded statue of Khai Dinh; this is the only tomb that contains a visual representation of the emperor.

From Khai Dinh's tomb, head north up the road until it terminates near the **Nam Giao Altar,** a giant open-air monument reminiscent of three-tiered wedding cakes. It was here that the emperor made sacrifices to God in supplication and thanksgiving. The three levels, a circle over two rectangles, represent the concepts of Heaven, Earth, and Man. A large and bright royal procession went to the altar at least once a year, usually in autumn, to give thanks for the bountiful harvest. To get back to the city center, just head north up D. Phan Boi Chau. Before returning to the city, however, stop at the **Bao Quoc Pagoda;** take a left down D. Dien Bien Phu and then a right just after the train tracks. Built in 1670, this pagoda sits at the top of the stairs in a quiet sanctuary among the trees. The altar is flanked by classrooms, where monks have been teaching their students for over 50 years. A draw for many visitors is the **talking parrot.** The parrot knows a variety of phrases, but its most practical occupation is being the monks' doorbell.

■ NEAR HUE

THUAN AN BEACH

The perfect place to kick back between long days of sight-seeing is the beach in nearby Thuan An. Head northeast on D. Le Loi. for about 13km; about halfway there you'll pass the **Huda beer factory.** Eventually you'll cross the bridge over a lagoon, with several shrimp and fish farms. The trip takes one hour by bicycle, but can also be made by boat from the pier or bus from the intracity bus station in **Dong Ha,** near the large market by the southeast corner of the citadel. The beach is pretty empty on weekdays, but receives a flood of visitors from the city on weekends.

THE DEMILITARIZED ZONE (DMZ)

According to the guidelines of the Geneva Accord following the First Indochinese War with France in 1954, Vietnam was divided at the 17th parallel. It was stipulated that a buffer area above and below the dividing line would be established as a zone where no military presence or buildup would be permitted. Ironically, the area known as the **Demilitarized Zone (DMZ)** became home to some of Vietnam's bloodiest fighting. It was also the location of the extensive networks of the Ho Chi Minh Trail, which the U.S. military tried with great effort to detect and destroy in order to cut off the supply and intelligence lines of the Viet Minh. Nonetheless, the McNamara Wall, the military line against the communists, did little to stem the tide.

Touring the area is next to impossible without a guide and proper vehicle, as most of the prominent military sites are spread far apart and there are still **live mines and undetonated shells. Use extreme caution.** Although you can find a guide in Dong Hoi and even in Dong Ha (halfway between Dong Hoi and Hue), the easiest and most reliable way to tour is from Hue, where tour services leave daily and come a dime a dozen. For the war history enthusiast, hiring a guide is a more edifying and interesting experience, yet not too much more expensive than the packaged tours (165,000Đ for guide without transportation versus 165,000Đ for a full tour). Renting a motorscooter is adequate transportation to cover this ground.

The **Ben Hai River** delineates the 17th parallel political division. The **Hien Luong Bridge,** 59km north of Hue, crosses the river and was one of the first transfluminal targets destroyed by American fighter jets. On the north side of the rebuilt bridge is a large concrete spire with the requisite communist star and commemorative date, dedicated to the struggle of war and the reunification. North of the river, a set of winding roads leads to perhaps the most interesting sight in the DMZ, the **Vinh Moc Tunnels.** "Tunnels" is somewhat of a misnomer; Vinh Moc was more of an underground city, which, unlike the Cu Chi Tunnels in the south, had less of a direct military purpose. Started in 1966 and finished less than two years later, Vinh Moc was built as the U.S. bombings became increasingly threatening to the area around the village. The 2.8km of tunnels burrow for 25m underground and were dug by hand using a clever system of pulleys to carry the earth out of the excavation. The underground city has walkways high enough for people up to 1.5m tall and 1.2m wide, a maternity ward (where tours are quick to mention that 17 babies were born), and a deep freshwater spring. Small arched chambers line the sides of the passageways that served as family residences and utility areas. During the war, Vinh Moc was a vital supply link to Con Co Island, a strategic Viet Minh stronghold.

Twenty km south of the 17th parallel and Ben Hai River is **Dong Ha.** On Hwy. 1, here called Duong Le Duan, **Khach Trung Tau Bus Station** runs buses daily 6am-2pm, every 30min. to both Hue (20,000Đ) and Da Nang (30,000Đ). 100m south, **Dong Ha Hotel,** 15 D. Le Duan (tel. 522 92), has an adjoining tour office that works with tour services in Hue (guide 132,000Đ). Guides are also available (110,000Đ per day) at the **Quang Tri Tourism Company,** 135 D. Le Duan (tel. 529 27; fax 529 37).

From Dong Ha, Rte. 9 runs 60km west to Laos. This road was one of the principal highways the Americans used for artillery and troop transport in holding the line against further Viet Minh ingressions south. About 15km west on the highway is **Cam Lo,** where a road heads north to both **Con Thien Firebase,** the site of a fierce battle in 1968 that served as a diversion for the general offensive and uprising of Tet, and **Ruong Son National Cemetery,** a memorial to the tens of thousands of soldiers who died in the Annamite Mountains along the Ho Chi Minh Trail. Five km west of Cam Lo, an unpaved road turns left off Rte. 9 to **Camp Carroll.** Now overseen by a state agricultural enterprise, the overgrown camp was once a strategic headquarters for the U.S. military. Another 7km west on Rte. 9 from Camp Carroll stands the **Rockpile.** This large rock outcropping rises from the landscape and was an unassailable (or so the Marines thought, until it was stormed by Viet Minh commandos) helicopter landing pad where essential military supplies like Budweiser were dropped. Another 20km west toward Khe Sanh is **Dakrong Bridge,** built from 1975 to 1976 with the assistance of the Cubans. Finally, 10km from the bridge on the climb toward Khe Sanh is the **Khe Sanh Combat Base** of Bruce Springsteen fame. Site of perhaps the bloodiest battle of the war, this is the base where Marines were airlifted to safety when the U.S. abandoned the outpost; now it is just a barren field of mud.

■■■ DA NANG

In Da Nang, tourists are not the same point-stare-and-wave-at-the-*tay ba lo* spectacle that they are in other Vietnamese cities. The town overall seems indifferent to their presence and proceeds at its own pace. Perhaps this is because the city has played host to foreigners for so long. In more ancient times, Da Nang saw the presence of the Chinese, Cham, and Khmer. Then the French came and renamed the city Tourane. Recognizing Da Nang as an important port, the colonial administration urged its settlement in the early 1900s. A decade after the expulsion of the French, an amphibious operation by the U.S. military washed up on Da Nang's shores to secure the nearby airfield. For the next 10 years, the city was a principal base of American military operation as well as the gateway to China Beach, the celebrated R&R spot for men fighting near the 17th parallel. Today, an assortment of foreigners are back in Da Nang doing business or just visiting. But as usual, it doesn't matter to the locals.

ORIENTATION

Almost at the dead center of Vietnam, some 750km south of Hanoi and 990km north of Ho Chi Minh City, Da Nang lies on the **Han River,** protected from the South China Sea by **Da Nang Bay.** The main thoroughfares of the city generally run north-south along the river. **Duong Bach Dang** runs one way north along the east bank of the river while one block inland, **Duong Tran Phu** runs south. Another three blocks east is **Duong Phan Chu/Le Loi,** a two-way street parallel to D. Bach Dang and D. Tran Phu. These three main streets are intersected by **Duong Dien Bien Phu/Ly Thai To/Hung Vuong,** the east-west boulevard which spurs off from Hwy. 1 and dissects the city into northern and southern halves. Although these streets effectively provide a grid in which to easily navigate the city, pick up a tourist map from newsstands along the river; the irregular networks of tributary streets can be confusing.

PRACTICAL INFORMATION

Tourist Office: Vietnamtourism, 158 D. Phan Chu Trinh (tel. 244 12; fax 213 02). The large conglomerate offers car rentals and visa services. **Danang Tourist,** 68 D. Bach Dang (tel. 221 12; fax 215 60). Provides good information about local sights like Marble Mountains, China Beach, and Hai Van Pass/Lang Co Beach.

Currency Exchange: Vietcombank, 104 D. Le Loi (tel. 221 10), exchanges major foreign currency and traveler's checks. Visa, MC, AmEx Moneygram. Open Mon.-Sat. 7:30-11am and 1-4pm.

Post Office/Telephones: GPO, 60 D. Bach Dang (tel. 238 81; fax 212 79), just north of the intersection with D. Hung Vuong. **Poste Restante.** Open daily 6am-10pm. **International phone office** inside. Fax available. Closes 30min. before the post office. **Telephone code:** 51.

Airport: Da Nang International Airport (tel. 263 94; fax 233 93), 3km from the city center. **Vietnam Airlines,** 35 D. Tran Phu (tel. 211 50), has flights to major cities in Vietnam. Open daily 7:30-11am and 1:30-4:30pm. To: **Hanoi** (daily 9:30am, 2, and 4:10pm, 990,000Đ); **Ho Chi Minh City** (daily 9am, 1:50, and 4:20pm, 990,000Đ); and **Nha Trang** (Tues. and Thurs. 10:45am). International to: **Bangkok** (daily 9, 9:30am, and 1:50pm); **Hong Kong** (Mon. and Sat. 9 and 10am, Thurs. 9 and 10:45am, Sat and Sun. 9:30am and 2pm); **Kuala Lumpur** (Mon. 9 and 10am, Fri. 9am); **Phnom Penh** (daily 9am); and **Singapore** (Tues. and Thurs. 10:45 am and 1:50pm, Sun. 1:50pm).

Trains: Da Nang Railway Station, 2km west of city center on D. Tran Cao Van. To: **Ho Chi Minh City** (daily S1, S3, and S5 arrive at 11:41am, 2:47pm, and 7:30am, and leave 20min. later); and **Hanoi** (S2, S4, and S6 arrive at 1:36, 4:05pm, and 8:44am, and leave 30min. later). Cyclos to the train station cost 10-15,000Đ.

Buses: Ben Xe Lien Tinh, 33 D. Dien Bien Phu (tel. 212 65), 2km west of the city toward Hwy. 1 just past 29/3 Park. To: **Hue** (daily every hour, 6am-2pm, 4hr., 9500Đ); **Dong Hoi** (daily 7am, 8-10hr., 15,000Đ); **Thanh Hoa** (daily 5am, 20hr., 48,000Đ); **Hanoi** (daily 5am, 24hr., 56,000Đ); **Haiphong** (daily 5am, 28hr., 57,000Đ); **Quy Nhon** (daily 6am, 10hr., 11,000Đ); **Nha Trang** (daily 5am, 14hr., 38,500Đ); **Dalat** (daily 5am, 18-20hr., 55,000Đ); and **Ho Chi Minh City** (daily 4, 4:30, 5, 5:30, 6, and 7am, 36hr., 79,500Đ). Buy tickets to Hanoi and Ho Chi Minh City a day in advance. **Minibus** travel in Toyota minivans is more comfortable, but more expensive. A private minibus chartering service, 111 D. Le Loi (tel. 282 05)

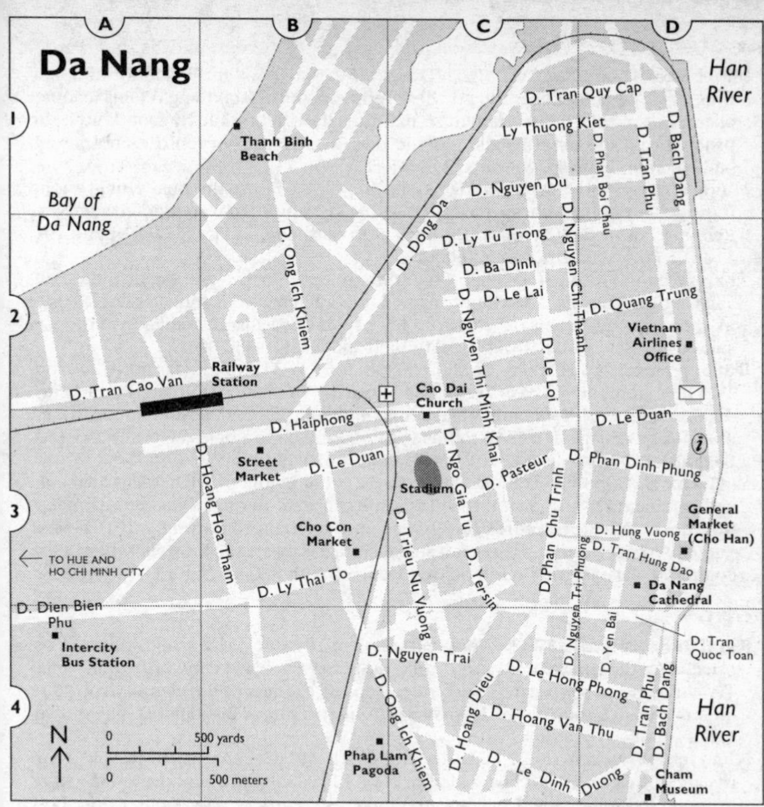

will accommodate your needs. Vehicles run to all the destinations listed above. All leave at 5am from in front of the ticket office. Purchase tickets (176-352,000Đ) as far in advance as possible.

Ferry: Ben Pha Da Nang, 9C D. Bach Dang (tel. 215 28), just south of the D. Hung Vuong intersection. Regular ferries take you across the Han River (500Đ) to the shanties and fishing villages of Da Nang. Open daily 4:30am-9pm.

Local Transportation: Cyclos offer rides all over town, and some motorcycle taxis compete for fares. Getting anywhere around town should never exceed 10,000Đ. **Taxis** are easiest to obtain by booking through hotels. Bike and motorbike rentals available at most accommodations.

Car and Motorscooter Rental: Tram Du Lich, 69 D. Le Loi (tel. 244 51), rents 4-seat (242,000Đ per day) and 12-seat (297,000Đ per day) **vehicles** with driver to take you to places nearby: China Beach, Marble Mountains, Hoi An, and My Son. Also sells tickets to Hue for 66,000Đ (daily departure). **Motorscooters** can be rented at the Danang Hotel (see Accommodations below).

Markets: Cho Han, at the intersection of D. Hung Vuong and D. Tran Phu, is a general market; open 6:30am-7pm. A large outdoor **produce market** is just south of Cho Han on D. Bach Dang. **Cho Con,** at the corner of D. Hung Vuong and D. Ong Ich Kiem, is a behemoth general market in one of the busiest parts of town. Open daily 7am-7pm.

Pharmacy: Pharmacy Nghia An, 16 D. Phan Chu Trinh (tel. 256 60). Open daily 7am-9pm.

Hospital: Da Nang Hospital, 74-76 D. Haiphong (tel. 221 16). An old American-built hospital serving the province.

Emergency: tel. 14.

ACCOMMODATIONS

Mini Hotel Thuan An, 14 D. Bach Dang (tel. 205 27), is a small, family-run operation. This cozy hotel near the northern terminus of D. Bach Dang retains its quiet charm but remains close enough so that the city is accessible by foot. Watch the fishing boats and sampans glide on the Han River from your room. Doubles with bath and fan 77,000Đ, with A/C 143,000Đ.

Hung Vuong Hotel, 95 D. Hung Vuong (tel. 239 67), on the busy Hung Vuong thoroughfare, offers cheap rooms close to Da Nang's busy commercial activity. Reminiscent of French villas. Doubles with bath and fan 55-77,000Đ, with A/C 110-165,00Đ, with bathtub 220,000Đ.

Thanh Thanh Hotel, 50 D. Phan Chu Trinh (tel. 212 30; fax 298 86), near the Danang Cultural Theater. This doubly-named hotel will make visitors do doubles over its sheer size: 53 rooms of wondrous joy play host to a large audience of tourists and businessmen alike. Doubles with bath and fan 110-132,000Đ.

Danang Hotel, 3-5 D. Dong Da (tel. 232 58; fax 234 31), on the far north section. This relic from the war years is today a haven for Vietnamese tourists. Rooms cluster together, with four individual rooms radiating off a shared common room, much like a college dorm. All rooms with A/C and bath. Singles 66,000Đ. Doubles 88,000Đ; larger rooms 132-165,000Đ. Triples 110,000Đ.

Vina Pha Hotel, 80 D. Tran Phu (tel. 250 72). Run by the provincial pharmaceutical manufacturer and distributor. Large pharmacy downstairs doubles as reception desk. Rents cars, hires out guides, and exchanges currency. If that isn't enough service, you can also get a steam bath and massage. But wait, where's the complimentary aspirin on the pillow? Doubles with A/C and bath 176-198,000Đ.

FOOD

Kim Do Restaurant, 176 D. Tran Phu (tel. 246 10), one of Da Nang's finest. A bit pricey, but the *canard roté* and shrimp paste toast will make it worth your while. Try the *canh,* a soup eaten with rice. Top off the meal with flan or fruit. The menu reads like the *Oxford English Dictionary.* Entrees 20-60,000Đ. Open daily 11am-11pm.

Nha Hang Vietnam, 25-27 D. Ly Tu Trong (tel. 238 45). Throngs of people, tourists and locals alike. Offers a wide selection of basic Vietnamese dishes. If you're in the mood for steamed rice and traditional side orders, this is one of the best economical bets in the city. Large crowds at night. Valet parking for your motorscooter. Entrees 11-33,000Đ. Open daily 7am-11pm.

Nha Hang Mai Trang, 40 D. Bach Dang (tel. 209 45). Spreads the sweet scents of Vietnamese cuisine along the banks of the Han. Guests crowd here during lunchtime for good, cheap eats. The fried spring rolls come straight from Ma's oil cooker, and the seafood is fresh from the river. Good vegetarian choices. Entrees under 22,000Đ. Open daily 5am-11pm.

Hana Kim Dinh Restaurant, 7 D. Bach Dang (tel. 300 24). A gorgeous, newly built restaurant on the river. If A/C is too cold, then head outside to the terrace where enticing dishes on display make ordering simple. The best appetizer is the view. Well-stocked bar. Sat. and Sun. buffet. Vietnamese and western dishes, including burgers and pasta. Entrees 33-77,000Đ. Open daily 11am-2pm and 5-10pm.

Song Xanh, 179 D. Tran Phu (tel. 200 51). This ice cream shop/café serves Vietnamese versions of universal delights. Its special selection of yogurts (or, as the Vietnamese say, *yaourt*) is a great sampler of local flavor. If that's not enough, tell them to crank up the karaoke. Oh yessss… Open daily 6:30am-10pm.

SIGHTS

There is little in the way of sights in Da Nang, but it does boast Vietnam's premier museum of Cham artifacts collected form the 7th to 15th century. Built in the style of Cham architecture, the **Cham Museum,** 1 D. Tieu La (walk southward down D. Tran Phu or D. Bach Dang), is, for good reason, the most visited tourist attraction in Da Nang. Founded in 1915 by the French School of the Orient, the small museum houses a wide collection of Cham sandstone carvings, from altars to sculptures and images of Siva and Brahma. Cham art, throughout its evolution, reflects elements and style from all over Southeast Asia; Indonesian art figured prominently in its early phases while Khmer are influenced its latter phase. The museum offers guides who can take you through the Cham relics in great detail; making this service is particularly worthwhile if you have an interest in Cham civilization. An informative guidebook, *Museum of Cham Sculpture—Danang,* can also be purchased (10,000Đ) when you pay for admission (10,000Đ). Open daily 6am-6pm.

A block west of the museum, you will encounter an elegant yellow-orange pagoda known as **Tam Bao Pagoda,** 253 D. Phan Chu Trinh. Built in 1953, this towering combination of French, Chinese, and Cham architectural styles has five tiers, which represent the steps in the ascension to heaven. North from here, six blocks over on D. Tran Phu, is the **Danang Cathedral,** which was built in 1923 to serve the French Catholic community. More commonly referred to as the rooster cathedral by locals due to the weathercock atop the cross on the steeple, this massive, unbuttressed white church is well-preserved and cuts an imposing figure against the sky. Masses are still held daily at 5am and 5pm, Sunday Mass 6am and 4:30pm.

Cut back over to D. Phan Chu Trinh and head north to get to the **Danang Cultural Theater,** where large concerts and special performances are often held (check the theater's box office for events). Out front is a small amusement park and haven for kids. Three blocks farther north up this street (Phan Chu Trinh changes its name to D. Le Loi along the way), turn left at D. Haiphong. On your right after two blocks and across the street from Da Nang Hospital is the **Cao Dai Temple.** Built in 1955, this is the largest Cao Dai structure outside of its site of origin. The two gates for entering the complex are reserved for either sex—the left one for women, the right for men. The entrance to the temple is organized in a similar way with a center door reserved for priests of the church. Inside the temple, prayer services are conducted daily at 6am, noon, 6pm, and midnight. Above the altar, Muhammed, Lao-tze, Jesus, Buddha, and Confucius, depicted on a picture, watch silently over those in prayer. A simple sentence epitomizes this seemingly odd combination of deities: "All religions have the same source."

ENTERTAINMENT

Christie's Harbourside, 9 D. Bach Dang (tel. 266 45), on the river south of the D. Hung Vuong intersection. Bob Christie, the New Zealand proprietor, just wants his visitors to be comfortable, well-fed, and laden with a full pint of beer. Along with beers (33,000Đ) and cocktails (55,000Đ), this bar and grill also serves up burgers, pasta, and steak imported from Australia. If that isn't enough, there's a satellite TV. Don't miss the pictures of Mohammed Ali above the bar. This place moves like a butterfly and stings like a bee. Open daily 11am-11pm.

The Orient, 80 D. Tran Phu (tel. 250 92), on the second floor. Patrons here can guzzle up and boogie down. For those who prefer not to shake their thang in public, there is also that insidious entertainment and pastime, karaoke. Happening some nights and dead calm others, but there seems no rhyme and reason for this. Live band and dancing keeps the place romping until the wee hours on certain nights. Cover 22,000Đ. Open 7pm-whenever.

VIP Club, 11C D. Quang Trung (tel. 232 95), part of the chain of VIP club chain. Home of the rich, famous, and cool of Da Nang. Ever hip, ever bad, and always stylish. If you've brought along your clubbing gear, live it up. Otherwise suffer the stares, you poorly dressed backpacker. Cover 33,000Đ. Open daily 8pm-2am.

■ NEAR DA NANG

CHINA BEACH

China Beach is famous for two reasons: U.S. troops landed here during the Vietnam War, and the TV series of the same name was a post-M.A.S.H. hit. Today the beach makes a great daytrip from either Da Nang or Hoi An, but don't expect to run into any Dana Delaney look-alikes. You'll find few foreigners here and even fewer Vietnamese, though the new Non Nuoc resort hotel complex (tel. 362 16; fax 363 35) has been constructed in the hopes of luring another wave of invaders to the area. The hotel offers everything a good resort should: taxi service, lockers on the beach, tennis courts, dance hall, and souvenir shops, to name a few. Rooms start around 330,000Đ, and services are priced for a foreign clientele (i.e. high). There should be no need to stay here overnight, however, since the beach is so close to the larger cities. Rent a motorbike and drive yourself. The clean, wide, quiet beach is perfect for an afternoon's repose and a dip in the ocean; stone benches and tables shaded by small thatch roofs will shield you from the sun. You will be required to pay an access fee for the beach as well as some nominal charges for your vehicle (should be less than 11,000Đ total).

MARBLE MOUNTAIN (NGU HANH SON)

Marble Mountain, 17km north of Hoi An and 12km south of Da Nang, has a setting straight out of an Indiana Jones movie. The huge, naturally hollowed caves, winding paths punctuated with carved icons, and breathtaking views combine to form a dazzling daytrip from either of the two bigger cities. Originally, Cham people lived here; much later, in the 19th century, Emperor Minh Mang made this place one of his retreats. Even more recently, the mountain served as a base for the Viet Minh; when U.S. troops found out, they bombed the site heavily. A gaping hole in one of the mountain chambers remains as testimony to the attacks.

The mountain gets its name from—you guessed it!—the marble and limestone quarries that cluster at the base. Sculptures, figurines, jewelry, and tiles reportedly made of mountain's marble will be offered to you again and again on your journey to the top. There are also packs of persistent children who speak assorted garbled versions of English; they will follow you through the mountain, fill the air with chatter about the sights, and then attempt to charge you a fee. Ignore them studiously unless you want to pay them; 11,000Đ will do.

Head up 123 steps after you begin your journey up the mountain to get to the **Linh Ung Pagoda,** decorated with mosaics of bottle and ceramic pieces that give the Pagoda an uncharacteristically blue and green tinge. The Linh Ung Buddha brings luck and talent, but people also come here to pray for their child to be a certain sex. On this level of the path there is also a square stone platform which legend claims the fairies and gods use for playing checkers. Wanna-be divinities can play a quick game before continuing up.

The path continues up through natural rock arches, and niches along the way reveal Buddha statues—sometimes carved directly out of the living rock and still a part of the mountain. Sixty steps up from the Linh Ung Pagoda is the Vong Hai Dai (Simply Stunning Sea View). Squeeze past the photo-happy Vietnamese tourists on a clear day to catch a glimpse of the ocean.

A mere 58 steps later you will reach the **main cave.** The four rather cartoonish warrior statues guarding the entrance of the cave date from Emperor Minh Mang's time, and are intended to protect the cave from evil spirits. The ceiling in this cathedral-like cavern is 15m high. In front of you will be two bridges, Cau Duyen (Happiness Bridge) and Cau Lok (Luck Bridge). Cau Duyen, the one on the right of the entrance, is thought to bring happiness to married couples; watch newlyweds cling to each other as their families snap photos. Behind the bridge is a small cave where childless couples go to pray for fertility. Just before you get to Cau Lok is a small hole in the stone; reach in to where you can hit a drum, and then see if you can figure out what makes the noise. People come to pray at the red altar next to the bridge for luck and prosperity. Behind both of the bridges are the Marble Mountain Rorschach Tests: locals claim that you can see an ostrich and an elephant carved into the cave's wall by running water. If you fail that test, you can't miss the 5m Buddha carved high into the wall at the far end of the cave. One of the chambers here has stairs leading to a lookout perch known as Dong Van Thong (The Way to the Clouds), but *Let's Go* does not recommend trying to ascend to heaven from here. Admission to Marble Mountain 10,000Đ. Open 6am-6pm.

■■■ HOI AN

This tranquil, ancient town, only 30km south of Da Nang and 5km from the sea, is a favorite of foreign visitors: the slow, syrupy pace of life is sure to calm any Saigon-pumped, hell-bent tourist. The pace wasn't always this slow, however; Hoi An (then called Faifo) was once an important trading town during the 18th century and home to many Chinese merchants who left a legacy of beautiful houses and pagodas, while the Japanese, not to be outdone, constructed a covered bridge over the Bach Dang River. The town's 100,000 inhabitants continue to practice the ancient handicrafts, line the streets with their wares, and keep the city picture-perfect.

ORIENTATION AND PRACTICAL INFORMATION

This small, ancient town unfurls on the north banks of the **Thu Bon River,** which then divides into smaller tributaries just west of Hoi An. One main street curves along the river; it starts out from the west as **Duong Nguyen Thi Minh Khai,** then morphs into **Duong Bach Dang** between two bridges, and finally a third time into **Duong Phan Boi Chau. Duong Tran Phu,** the next major street over, is lined with pagodas and ancient Chinese houses. Two main thoroughfares cut through these streets: **Duong Le Loi/Nguyen Truong To** and **Duong Hoang Dieu,** the latter of which extends into a bridge over Thu Bon.

The Hoi An **tourist office** waits for you in the Hoi An Hotel complex at 6 D. Tran Hung Dao (tel. 613 62 or 613 73; fax 616 36). The staff rents cars, bicycles (5,000Đ per day), and motorbikes (60,000Đ per day); plans tours and boat trips; and offers other typical tourist services. **Exchange currency** at any hotel, the post office, or the bank across the street from the **post office** at 4 D. Hoang Dieu (tel. 613 40; open daily 7-11am and 1:30-5pm). A **telephone office** is at 4B D. Tran Hung Dao (tel. 612 64), to the right of the Hoi An Hotel (open 6am-10pm). **Telephone code:** 51. Trains stop in Da Nang, not here, but the **bus station** keeps travelers happy on the west edge of town on D. Phan Chu Trinh (tel. 612 84; open 5am-6pm). Check with the Vinh Hung Hotel, below, for information on **minibuses.** Slightly cheaper **motorbike and car rentals** are across the street from the Hoi An Hotel with Six Brothers Transportations Service, 15 D. Tran Hung Dao (tel. 615 18). Proprietor Hieu leads tours in English. The **market** is at the intersection of D. Nguyen Hue and D. Bach Dang.

ACCOMMODATIONS

Hoi An Hotel, 6 D. Tran Hung Dao (tel. 613 62 or 613 73; fax 616 36). Several renovated buildings make up this gigantic complex. Owned by the Hoi An Tourist Service Company, the Hoi An Hotel's tourist monopoly is slowly being challenged by smaller hotels. Features immaculate, modern rooms, attentive service, and all the amenities of a 4-star hotel. Attractive courtyard is a great place to relax. Doubles with fan 66-132,000Đ, with A/C, 275-550,000Đ. Breakfast included.

Vinh Hung Hotel, 143 D. Tran Phu (tel. 616 21). This hotel can't brag about its size, but it should be proud of everything else. Chinese furniture and decor fit in perfectly with ancient Hoi An. Amiable staff knows how to please guests. Rooms have fridge and phone; there's also a beautiful rooftop terrace. Doubles with fan 165,000Đ, with A/C 220-330,000Đ. Includes breakfast.

Thien Trung Hotel, 63 D. Phan Dinh Phung (tel. 617 20 or 617 79). Gorgeous new whitewashed villa has 2 stories of clean rooms. Open interior courtyard with fountain that exposes guests to lots of noise. Travelers often gather at the small restaurant/café to socialize and exchange travel tips. Doubles and triples with fan 110-165,000Đ, with A/C 220-385,000Đ.

Thanh Binh Hotel, 1 D. Le Loi (tel. 612 97). The tiny lobby holds its own against continuous foot traffic. Modern interior with tile floors and fresh paint can get a bit noisy, but the price leaves little room for complaint. Immaculate doubles with fan 110-132,000Đ, with A/C 187,000Đ.

FOOD

The specialty of Hoi An is *cao lau,* a soup containing rice noodles made with special water found only in a local well; the well's location is a town secret, sort of. Most establishments are open daily 6am-10pm.

Han Huyen Floating Restaurant, D. Bach Dang (tel. 614 62), just before the covered Japanese Bridge. Sit inside or outside this wooden hut on Bach Dang River, while enjoying a gorgeous view of the river and daily Vietnamese life. Tourists rave about the food and you'll see why: excellent service, rock-bottom prices, a huge selection, and meals all run less than 20,000Đ. Honest owners will even chase after you to return your pocket change.

Faifo Restaurant, 5 D. Nguyen Hue (tel. 617 82), not the same as the Faifo on D. Tran Phu. This small restaurant with good food, friendly service, and reasonable prices has yet to be discovered by foreigners. The cheery owner-waitress dishes out travel advice and excellent *cao lau.* A meal including appetizer and drink rarely exceeds 15,000Đ per person.

Huong Xuan Restaurant, 8 D. Le Loi (tel. 614 98). Their location opposite Hoi An Pagoda and two hotels assures a foreign clientele. Clean and spacious interior. Average Euro and Asian dishes for average prices.

Restaurant Cao Lau, 42 D. Tran Phu. Guess what their main dish is? This is your typical restaurant with cheap food and courteous service, so sit down and eat up.

Café Can, 74 D. Bach Dang (tel. 615 25). The riverside location has potential for a much more romantic ambiance, but the café is anything but charming. The menu is obviously geared towards foreigners, and offers western-style drinks and vegetarian dishes. Try the set seafood menu for 35,000Đ.

SIGHTS

Above all else, let yourself wander through Hoi An. The centuries-old buildings here lend a tranquil aura to this well-preserved city. One of the first things you'll see in town is the **Japanese Covered Bridge/Pagoda,** at the west end of D. Tran Phu. The bridge is believed to have been built by the Japanese in the 16th century, although no documentation exists to support this. It leads across a small canal to D. Nguyen Thi Minh Khai.

The **Phung Hung Home,** 4 D. Nguyen Thi Minh Khai, was built over 200 years ago and has housed eight generations of the Vietnamese Phung Hung family. Inside you'll find a mixture of Chinese, Vietnamese, and Japanese architectural styles, along with 80 ironwood columns, yin-yang tiles on the ceiling, and a stunning assortment of Vietnamese furniture. Test the beds at your own risk. The square opening in the ceiling was originally for storing trade goods in case of floods. Chinese lanterns and red panels with Chinese characters lead the way to the ancestral family altar. Bow respectfully three times, or you risk offending powerful ancestral spirits. Open daily 7:30am-6pm. A little farther down this street is the **Diep Dong Nguyen House,** 80 D. Nguyen Thai Hoc, the former home of a Vietnamese trader. Look for a small blue sign out front. This dark brown, two-story, Chinese-style house showcases Chinese porcelain, antiques, and wooden carvings. The pictures on the altar represent six generations of the family. Open daily 7-11am and 2-4pm.

The most well-known historical home in Hoi An is unquestionably **Tan Ky Old House,** 101 D. Nguyen Thai Hoc (tel. 614 74); it also holds the distinction of being the first private house to be recognized by Ministry of Culture for its historical and cultural value. Tan Ky was built nearly 200 years ago and has seen seven generations of happy Chinese, along with many commercial transactions in the 15th to 17th centuries. Wooden columns with marble bases support the interior, while the exterior bricks and tiles keep the house cool in summer and warm in winter. The house is also famous for its curved "crabshell" ceiling design (they claim the wood ceiling beams look like a crabshell; you make the call). Family members will eagerly show you family heirlooms with family sayings in inlaid mother-of-pearl from great-grandfather's time. Open daily 8am-12pm and 2-5pm. Admission 2000Đ.

Moving onto D. Tran Phu will lead to **Phuoc Kien Pagoda,** at number 46, the 300-year-old temple built by the Fukien *kongsi,* one of Hoi An's four prominent "clans." It's the biggest pagoda in Hoi An. Pass through the ornate pink and green gate in the courtyard to get to the pagoda, but admire the fountain and accompanying fish and dragon statues while you're there. In a glass box on the altar sits fat lady Thien Hau Thanh Mau, goddess of the sea and protector of sailors. She's very popular in Hoi An; a mural to the right of the entrance depicts her largeness rescuing a sinking vessel. As you tour the Pagoda, look out for annoying vendors, beggars, and photographers. Open daily 7am-5pm. Admission 5000Đ.

Continue to lumber down this lane of pagodas until you come to **Guangdong Assembly Hall/Pagoda,** 176 D. Tran Phu, (tel. 617 36), which will effectively satisfy any urges you have for the color red. This spate of ruddiness is typical of pagodas in Guangdong, China, even up to the happy, red-faced Buddha inside. Dragons on the rooftops peer at their larger scaly cousin splashing the courtyard's pool. The pagoda was built in the early 18th century, and has undergone four name changes since. Like the Phuoc Kien Pagoda, it is dedicated to the worship of our large lady Thien Hau, and once specialized in helping sick and unfortunate sailors. Open daily 7:30am-5pm. Admission 4000Đ. **Hai Nam Pagoda,** 178 D. Tran Phu, commemorates the 108 merchant-sailors from Hai Nam Island who were mistakenly executed by the king in 1851; he thought they were traitors. Doh! Open 6am-12pm and 1-8pm. Free. **Ngu Bang Pagoda,** at number 64, is another typical Chinese pagoda built in the 16th century. You can guess who the fat lady of the house is, but walk past the green iron gates if you're still not sure. Open daily 7am-5pm. Free.

Quan Cong Mieu or **Ong Pagoda,** 24 D. Tran Phu, is actually two pagodas built back-to-back. The Quan Cong and Quan Am pagodas, both constructed in 1653, are dedicated to the two heroes Cong and Am. Chinese architecture, red columns, the fish pond in courtyard, and bonsai trees will reassure the tourist with their regularity. The pagoda is right on the street and fits in like a house; look for the red doors with dragons on them. The **museum** in back displays millennia-old relics; the three periods represented are pre-Champa, Champa, and Greater Viet. Open daily 7-11:30am and 1:30-5pm. Admission 5000Đ to the museum and pagoda.

■ NEAR HOI AN

When the Chinese architecture in Hoi An finally loses its picture-perfect pulchritude, rent a motorcycle and putter to **Cau Dai Beach.** This somewhat crowded and small beach lies 5km east on D. Tran Hung Dao from Hoi An. In the daytime, locals pack the sand; at night the families of fishermen fry their food. The water is clear 24 hours a day, though.

Boat rentals to reach the following places on the banks of the river run about 80,000Đ round-trip to both and last roughly two hours. Hire a boat (usually marked Tourist and consequently hard to miss) at the Hoi An dock on D. Bach Dang next to the market. Tours leave from 6:30am to 5pm. Hoi An Tourist Service Company also runs boat trips to these sites, but they're more expensive. The **Ceramics Village (Lang Gom)** is the first stop from Hoi An. Brick kilns fire the products that hard-laboring locals create by hand. Their dexterity is astounding; artisans kick the clay-shaping wheel with their feet while working the clay with their hands. Admission 2000Đ. Don't be misled by the name of the **Carpenter's Village (Lang Moc):** only one family here does any carpentry, so don't expect Santa's Village. The family does produce beautiful artwork and furniture, however, and have passed the tradition through the generations. An ancient tree trunk in their front yard is all the advertisement they need. Many people come here to custom-order their dream piece of furniture, and the carpenters will ship it anywhere in the world. The village itself is beautiful, and the 10-minute walk to the carpenter's house is a good chance to enjoy the serene setting.

MY SON

The **My Son Cham ruins,** the largest group of Cham ruins in Vietnam, are 37km from Hoi An. Be aware that if you don't hook up with a tour group leaving from Da Nang or Hoi An, you are guaranteed to lose about 110,000Đ per person in the numerous "admission" fees charged by the provincial police. Remember that April to July is the dry season here; from October to November, the locals claim that it rains "until the dirt rots." July to April is the high season of tourist traffic.

From Hoi An, Hwy. 1 leads south for 7km to Tam Ky town. At the town, drivers turn right (east) and continue down a rough road for 20km until a wooden bridge comes into view. Cross the bridge and continue on (if the bridge is closed, vehicles must go around; take a little road behind some houses farther down the road). A few km later but still some distance from the site you will have to pay for a tour guide and motorcycle, if you don't have one already (they make you leave your vehicle at this point; this is where the random charges begin, so be prepared to be charged for even the air you breathe on). Admission 10,000Đ; each photo you take will cost 5000Đ; a permit to make video recordings runs 20,000Đ.

The winding, occasionally steep dirt path to the ruins sometimes require you to get off the motorcycle and walk, but in the meantime the greenery of the local mountains will please the eye and soothe the soul. There are no facilities once you've left the towns, and guides charge exorbitant rates for bottled water. The ruins themselves are an impressive collection of five "groups" of temples, even if the statues that once adorned the temples now reside in museums around the world (like Paris's Louvre). The first two groups of temples should satisfy the most Cham-starved tourist, but you can also take the whole day and visit all five.

The complex was built as a pilgrimage site for the Cham people in the third century AD, and 70 towers flowered at the site when it was the center of the Cham kingdom. The Vietnamese kicked the Cham out in the 13th century, but are currently trying to atone for their insensitivity by restoring the towers. Many of the ruins would be in better condition if U.S. forces had not bombed the area in the late 60s and early 70s—this was one of the head locations of the Viet Minh. In 1990, a generous German woman donated money towards the restoration of the towers' interiors; unfortunately, they were still closed in the summer of 1995.

QUANG NGAI

Pass through Quang Ngai, 98km south of Hoi An, on your way to Nha Trang, or as a stopover point to see the village of Son My (the site of the My Lai Massacre). Do your best to arrive early and catch a bus or minibus to somewhere else as soon as possible. There are no maps for the town, but don't worry: **Highway 1** (also referred to as **Duong Quang Trung**) leads into town and serves as a main street; the other main street is **Duong Hung Vuong** (formerly Duong Phan Boi Chau). **Buses** (tel. 228 95) to more interesting locales leave from Hwy. 1 (as you're going south, turn left at the first intersection and the bus station will be on your right; open 4am-4:30pm). Buses to: **Hoi An** (10-11am, 4hr.); **Da Nang** (15 per day, 4hr., 11,000Đ); **Ho Chi Minh City** (some mornings of the week, 20hr., 45,000Đ); **Hanoi** (30hr., 50,000Đ); **Nha Trang** (13-15hr., 41,100Đ); and **Dalat** (4am, 20hr., 35,000Đ). You can also try to catch an air-conditioned **minibus** at the intersection of Hwy. 1 and D. Hung Vuong: flag it down, since the government doesn't technically allow minibuses to stop here. To **Hoi An** (30,000Đ). **Exchange money** at **Cong Thuong,** 46-48 D. Hung Vuong, or at any jewelry store. You can make calls from the **post office** (tel. 492 31) at the end of D. Hung Vuong; just ask the locals for directions to the *buu dien.* Open daily 6am-9pm. **Telephone Code:** 55. If you are forced to stay here for whatever reason, head to the **Kim Thanh Hotel,** 19 D. Hung Vuong (tel. 234 71). Cars can park right inside the "lobby." It's clean, and that's enough. They may forget to give you your own personal set of threadbare towels, so remind them; be aware that the shower blasts on unexpectedly if you turn the water on past a few drops. Singles with fan 66,000Đ. Doubles 88,000Đ, with A/C 110,000Đ. Quads 165,000Đ. After this, it's a sharp step down in quality to the **Vietnam Hotel,** 41 D. Hung Vuong (tel. 236 10), where you shouldn't expect too warm a welcome. Singles 55,000Đ. Doubles 66-88,000Đ, with A/C 110,000Đ. Food in this rest stop is decent. There are few restaurants, but if you have to eat, mosey on over **Restaurant 26,** 27 D. Phan Dinh Phung. Cheap plastic tables and chairs contrast with the pricey food: 44,000Đ per person for a meal.

SON MY (MY LAI)

Rent a motorcycle or car in Quang Ngai (motorcycle about 60,000Đ) and head east to one of Vietnam's most beautiful and saddening villages. On March 16, 1968, Son My (also referred to as Tinh Khe) went from being a collection of quiet farming villages to a somber testimony of war time atrocities. U.S. soldiers came in and opened fire on four of the hamlets that make up Son My; almost all of the inhabitants of My Lai were killed: 504 died, mostly women, children, and elderly people. The officers responsible went on trial the following year. Twenty-seven years later, relations have finally been "formalized" between the U.S. and Vietnam, and the museum that now rests at the former site of My Lai enshrines the memory of the My Lai tragedy.

From Quang Ngai, the ride begins 1km north on Hwy. 1 (D. Quang Trung) over the grayish cement bridge near the Song Tra Hotel; a huge memorial sign directs drivers down the dirt road to the right. (Veterans and nonprofit organizations are sponsoring renovations in 1995 that will pave the road.) Bamboo thickets, thatch houses, rice paddies, corn fields, and water buffalo line the serene 13-km road; this is one of the few truly rural places left in Vietnam.

Along the way lies the **My Lai Health Center,** funded by the U.S. Hope Organization. At the end of the road stands a huge cement gate reading *Khu Chung Tich Son My* (Son My Memorial Park) and *Khong Co Gi Quy Hon Doc Lap Tu Do* (There is Nothing More Precious than Independence and Liberty). Leave your vehicle here and proceed through the red iron gates up the stone path. On the left, just past the red gates, is a small untended **mass grave** containing the remains of a certain Mrs. Thong, her five children, and two relatives. Visitors must first stop at the museum office, the first building on the left after the gate; here you can secure a photo permit. Truong Thiem Huong heads the office; she lives in the village and leads tours of the museum in English. The well-manicured **gardens** to the right are dotted with statues commemorating the people killed in the massacre. At the end of the stone path stands a much larger commemorative statue. The blooming flowers, trimmed hedges, and chirping birds are a strange contrast to the bloody history of this site.

The center of the former town is the **Memorial Museum.** Its façade reads: *Mai Mai Khac Sau Long Cam Thu Giac My Xam Luoc* (We Will Never Forgive the Evil Acts of the American Imperialist Forces). To the right of the entrance is an altar with the world-famous picture of crying My Lai residents before their deaths; above the altar is a black stone engraved with the names of all the My Lai victims. Pictures on the walls of the Museum feature those considered responsible for the tragedy and U.S. involvement in Vietnam in general: President Diem, President Eisenhower, various U.S. cabinet officials, Colonel Henderson (the leader of the 11th brigade), and Captain Medina (the leader of the platoon that razed the village) in front of the U.S. Court Marshall. There are also sobering before and after pictures of the village itself. Open Tues.-Sun. 7:30-11am and 11:30am-4pm. Admission 10,000Đ.

SOUTH VIETNAM

■■■ NHA TRANG

Nha Trang is the "City of the Blue Sea": azure waters meet white beaches, coconut palms, and rolling mountains. Before Nha Trang became a playground for beach bums, it was a small fishing village, and in spite of Nha Trang's current incarnation, fishery remains the town's biggest industry. Local seafood is exported internationally, but ironically, this means that the best seafood is unavailable for local consumption. The resort has been compared favorably to the French Riviera, Caribbean islands, and Hawaii. For better or for worse, development projects will soon put this Vietnamese paradise on par with her rivals. Water sports exist here in every variety, so tourists can engage in fishing, diving, snorkeling, parasailing, jet-skiing, or boating. The town itself is a commercial mecca, and gives the vacationer no reason to leave the beach except to forage for food.

ORIENTATION

The 6-km long **Duong Tran Phu** runs along the beach from north to south. Everything else (meaning the rest of town) spreads off to the west of D. Tran Phu. Just outside of the train station lurks the town's only six-street intersection; take **Duong Ly Tu Trong** from here to get to the beach. If you're on the beach, walk north (with the beach on the right) along D. Tran Phu until the post office; turn left onto **Duong Le Loi** to get to the market and restaurants in town.

PRACTICAL INFORMATION

Tourist Office: Khanh Hoa Tourism, 1 D. Tran Hung Dao (tel. 222 57 or 227 53; fax 242 06). **Tour booking office** on D. Tran Phu across from the Grand Hotel. Open 7-11am and 1:30-9pm. They do everything: book train and air tickets, extend visas, book tours and hotels, rent boats and cars, and sell maps (5000Đ). Smaller, similar offices at **Vinagen Travel Agency,** across from the Grand Hotel (tel. 235 91), and **Nha Trang Travel Agency,** 75 D. Hoang Van Thu (tel. 224 66).

Currency Exchange: Vietcombank, 17 D. Quang Trung (tel. 210 54), or most hotels.

Post Office: 4 D. Le Loi (tel. 212 50), at the northern end of D. Tran Phu, on the first block of D. Le Loi. Take a left from D. Tran Phu on to D. Le Loi. Fax, mail and telephone services. Open daily 6:30am-8pm.

Telephones: 50 D. Le Thanh Ton (tel. 238 66; fax 219 07), across the street from the Vien Dong Hotel. Open 6:30am-9:30pm. **Telephone code:** 58.

Airport: Nha Trang Airport (tel. 237 98). A few km south. The yellow Vietnam Airlines Airport Bus (tel. 235 89) will drop you at any hotel (22,000 per person). Motorcycles (with drivers) and cars may try to take you into town for much more. The **Vietnam Airlines Booking Office** waits at 12B D. Hoang Hoa Tham (tel. 237 97). To: **Da Nang** (Tues. and Thurs. 8:40am); **Hanoi** (Tues. and Thurs. 8:40am, plus Sat. 4pm); **Ho Chi Minh City** (daily 8:35am, 12:30, and 4:30pm); **Bangkok** (daily, except Tues. and Thurs., 8:35am; Thurs. 12:30pm); **Hong Kong** (Mon. and Sat. 8:35am; Thurs. 12:30pm); **Kuala Lumpur** (Mon., Wed., and Fri. 8:35am); **Phnom Penh** (daily 8:35am, except Tues. and Thurs. 12:30pm); and **Singapore** (daily 8:35am, except Tues. and Thurs. 12:30pm).

Trains: The **train station,** on D. Thai Nguyen past the 6-street intersection and before the intercity bus station. Book **tickets** at 17 D. Thai Nguyen (tel. 221 13) 8am-2pm, or at any hotel. Buses run to all major cities. Prices depend on which train you take, but average 132,000Đ per hard seat to Ho Chi Minh City, 154,000Đ to Da Nang, 187,000Đ to Hue, and 407,000Đ to Hanoi.

Buses: Local bus station (Ben Xe Noi Tinh), to the west of the market on D. 2/4. The **intercity bus station** (Ben Xe Lien Tinh), next to Long Son Pagoda on D. 23/10 heading towards Ho Chi Minh City (tel. 223 97). Open daily 5am-4pm. Regular connections with major cities (from 22-33,000Đ). Private **minibuses** organized by travel agencies are cheaper and more comfortable than regular buses or trains. Book one at any hotel or travel agency; they'll pick you up at your hotel. Minibuses usually leave in the early mornings and late afternoons. To: **Hoi An** or **Ho Chi Minh City** 110,000Đ per person; **Dalat** 88,000Đ per person.

Local Transport: Car rentals available at any hotel or travel agency, like **Hung Dao Garage,** 22B D. Tran Hung Dao (tel. 230 08), and **Hung Vu Travel Service,** 64 D. Thong Nhat (tel. 231 06). Prices average 220,000Đ per day in the city and 440,000Đ per day outside of the city for a 4-seat sedan. 12-seat vans cost a bit

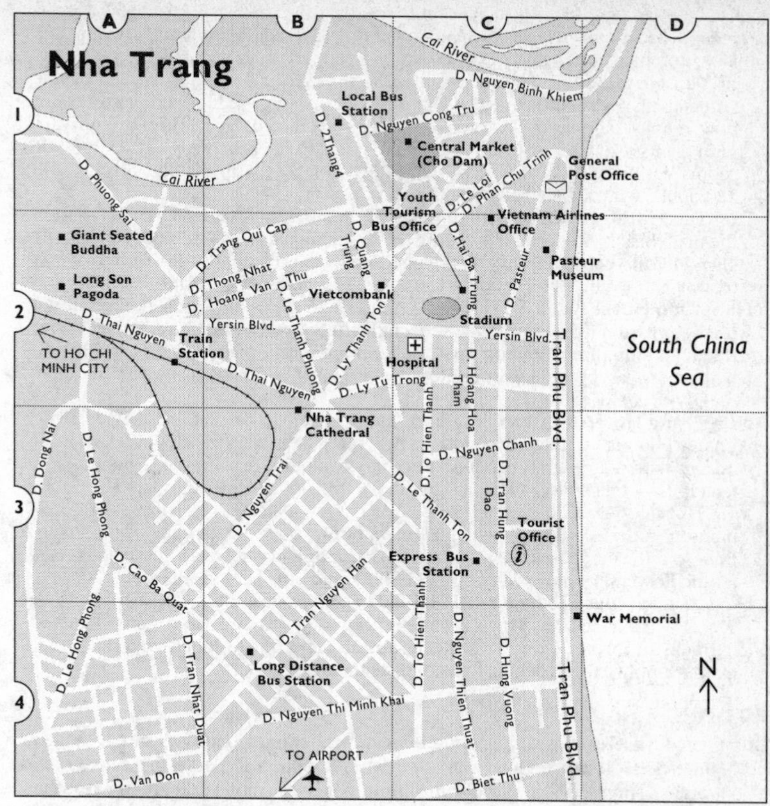

more. **Bike rentals** also at any hotel for 10,000Đ per day. **Motorbike rentals** across from Grand Hotel: 11,000Đ per hour or 66,000Đ per day.

Market: Dam Market is to the north of the city west of the post office near D. Phan Boi Chau. A typical market, with an emphasis on electronic equipment.

Police: tel. 210 79.

Hospital: 19 d. Yersin (tel. 221 75).

Directory Information: tel. 108.

Emergency: tel. 221 75 (hospital number).

ACCOMMODATIONS

Nha Trang has one of the best selections of hotels and budget accommodations around. Most congregate around the beachfront on D. Tran Phu. It may be possible to bargain prices down during the low-season (April-July). Budget travelers stick to the rooms with fans to save money, even in the summer months; Nha Trang's seaside location makes it bearable without the A/C.

Grand Hotel (or Hotel 44), 44 D. Tran Phu (tel. 224 45 or 226 65). Grand colonial building with a slightly institutional feel in central beach location. Some rooms with French windows and breathtaking views of the sea; ceilings high enough for Michael Jordan. Basic, clean, and airy rooms. Singles with fan and phone, 99-121,000Đ. Doubles and triples 121-154,000Đ. A/C, hot water, phone, and fridge run 242-319,000Đ. With extra bed, bathtub, TV, and ocean view 451,000Đ. Breakfast included for all rooms.

Guest House 78, 78 D. Tran Phu (tel. 263 42 or 263 47). 3-min. walk from the main beach, and a favorite of budget travelers. No extra perks but immaculate indeed. Bathrooms where bare feet do not fear to tread. Friendly and attentive service. Rooms with fan 88-132,000Đ (up to 4 people), with A/C 154-176,000Đ.

Hai Yen Hotel, 40 D. Tran Phu (tel. 228 28 or 229 74), opposite main beach. Offers it all: restaurant, dance hall, hairdresser, massage parlor, badminton court, boat rentals...and so on. Attractive, newly restored resort features a courtyard with plants. Uninspiring decor, but you're going to the beach anyway. Dorm-style rooms with shared bathroom 55-220,000Đ. Doubles with fan and private bath 220,000Đ, with A/C 440-1,100,000Đ.

Duy Tan Hotel, 24 D. Tran Phu (tel. 226 71 or 228 92). 4-star facilities across from the main beach. Modern architecture (read: rectangular cement block) and all the glitz: elegant, carpeted, slightly cramped bedrooms. A good value for red-carpet treatment. Singles 198-550,000Đ. Doubles 242-605,000Đ. Breakfast included.

Hung Dao Hotel, 3 D. Tran Hung Dao (tel. 222 46 or 270 05). 1 block from beach to the left of Vien Dong Hotel (through the gates behind Nha Trang Travel Agency). Communist decor: basic accommodations with cracking walls. The bathrooms can be intimidating. Rooms with fan 77-110,000Đ (up to three people), with A/C 132,000Đ.

Nha Trang Hotels has three locations: 129 D. Thong Nhat (tel. 222 24); 21 D. Le Thanh Phuong (tel. 229 56); and 22 D. Tran Hung Dao (tel. 239 33). A bit far inland, with nondescript rooms. Bathrooms could use renovations. Doubles with fan (and not much else) 110,000Đ, with A/C 132,000Đ, with hot water 165,000Đ.

Vina Hotel, 66 D. Tran Phu (tel. 230 09 or 273 44). Nude Greek babes, Greek columns, and Greek fountains will make you think you're vacationing in the Peloponese rather than Southeast Asia. Gray carpeting clashes with the fluorescent, plastic flowers. Doubles with A/C 385,000Đ, add 30% per extra person.

Navy Guest House (Nha Khach Hai Quan), 58 D. Tran Phu (tel. 263 03 or 229 97). Down a wide alley. The Navy might have used this three-story compound for barracks in former glory days. Reception may be out to lunch anytime. Price makes supply exceed demand. Doubles with fan 132,000Đ.

FOOD

Don't leave Nha Trang without trying *nem nuong,* the regional specialty of grilled pork and vegetables rolled into rice paper and dipped in a special fish sauce mix. You'll be hard-pressed to find *nem nuong* in any other city, and certainly not the way they make it in Nha Trang (kinda like cheese steaks in Philly). Restaurants specializing only in *nem nuong* abound in the Dam Market area, around the west end of D. Le Loi (Head north up D. Tran Phu, and turn left at the post office). Cheap restaurants with Vietnamese food also congregate in this area. The few restaurants on the beach front may provide better ambiance, but will also serve less tasty food and vacuum your wallet. As always, don't limit yourself to the listings below.

Nem Ninh Hoa, 16 D. Lan Ong (tel. 267 37). Large servings of delicious *nem nuong* for 6000Đ per person. The service is indifferent, but the food is great.

Nem #9, 9 D. Le Loi. One of the *nem* specialty shops the locals recommend. Often crowded. Average prices.

Dong Hai Restaurant, 17 D. Le Loi (tel. 253 22) Serves *nem* and other Vietnamese dishes. *Nem* 6000Đ per person. Open 6am-midnight.

Vietnam Restaurant, 7 D. Hoang Van Thu (tel. 265 88 or 244 54). Aggressive owners wave you down from blocks away, guaranteeing "good food, or no pay." Highly-acclaimed by locals, but pricier than most joints. Open 7am-11pm.

Saiga, 18 D. Tran Phu (tel. 245 79). One of the best restaurants on the beach. Watch the sun descend into the sea from the rooftop terrace as Madonna and other pop stars pump out background music. Dim, yellow Christmas lights add that certain special something. Obliging, attentive service. Average prices for the beachfront, which means a bit costlier than town restaurants.

SIGHTS

The **Ponagar Cham Temples** or **Thap Ba (Temple of the Lady)** are just north of the city on D. 2/4, immediately past the Xom Bong Bridge. Walk or bike the 2km from town, or take a cyclo ride for about 10,000Đ. Once there, a flight of stone steps leads past hordes and vendors to the temples at the top of the hill. The main tower, measuring 22.5m, was dedicated to the Goddess Ponagar (Mother of the Land). This matriarch-Creator was, like most big mamma goddesses, responsible for birth, agriculture, and household tasks; note the wrinkles on her belly, symbols of multiple births, and the glittering, eye-glaring yellow garb, a symbol of poor fashion sense. Incense darkens the air of the main tower; remember to remove your footgear before entering. The local importance of agriculture is evident in the worshipping of a stone fruit in one of the towers.

Compare the rounded, intricate design of the main tower to the more elongated, steep structure of the other towers. This results from the different periods of construction, which span from the 7th to the 12th centuries. The main tower was constructed in the year 817 AD, and part of it was still under renovation in 1995. The hexagonal monument of 10 columns on the side of the hill offers a photo-worthy view of the fishing dock and estuary below. Visit in the early morning or late afternoon to avoid the heat. Open daily 6am-6pm. Contributions to help the preservation effort appreciated. Admission 5000Đ.

The **Long Son Pagoda,** Nha Trang's postcard pagoda, waits at the end of D. Yersin on Duong 23/10. The pagoda was built in 1963 and is dedicated to the memory of the Buddhists who gave their lives protesting the American-supported Diem regime. Long Son is most renowned for its 9m-high white hilltop statue of Buddha sitting in the lotus position. Ascend the staircase above the pagoda to the statue and enjoy the great view of town. Open daily 6am-6pm.

Cau Da Villa is another former vacation residence of King Bao Dai, Vietnam's last monarch. The yellow colonial villa perches on a hilltop at the south end of D. Tran Phu, between the Linh Son pagoda and the Cau Da Pier. The villa has been converted to a hotel, so budget travelers should content themselves with joining the photo-taking tourist herds outside. Contact Khanh Hoa Tourism for information and reservations if you want a night's stay (roughly 440,000Đ per night).

Boat tours will take you to the **islands** off the coast of Nha Trang. You'll pass Han Mun (Ebony Island) on your way out; **Hon Mieu** contains the Tri Nguyen "Aquarium," which is actually two rather large ponds with fish and some turtles. **Hon Yen** (Salangane Island) features the bird's nests (complete with eggs) that Nha Trang inhabitants harvest and send as delicacies to wealthy Asian gourmands. Another island featured on the boat tours is **Hon Tre** (Bamboo Island), uninteresting except for the snorkeling opportunities offshore. Look out for the blobs of oil in the water and the sharp coral underfoot, but paddle away. Book tours at any hotel or travel agency, or directly with Mama Linh (tel. 266 93) in front of the Hai Yen Hotel. All tours cost 77,000Đ per person, leave at 8am, and return around 5pm. Price includes transportation from the hotel to Cau Da Dock, snorkeling equipment, and lunch.

On the highway to Nha Trang rest the **Poklong Garai Towers** (also known as the Cham Towers) on Trau Hill, 7km northwest of Phan Rang town. These towers were built at the end of the 13th century to honor the generous King Poklong Garai (1151-1205). Known for his good deeds towards the Cham people, he constructed the local irrigation system. It's an easy climb up an untended path to the three redbrick towers; the sign nearby tells you about the site in English. Carved gods and dragons and the ornate, cursive Cham script adorn the exteriors of the towers, while graffiti defaces the dimly illuminated interiors. Inside the main tower is the statue of a kneeling calf that doubles as an altar; incense slowly burns in front of the bent bovine. A bust of the thin, bearded King Poklong Garai reposes underneath the red wood lattice ceiling. The hill itself features a great view of the rather dry and cactus-friendly surrounding area. Open daily 7am-5pm, but you can basically head up anytime. Admission 5000Đ, whenever there's someone there to charge it.

■■■ DALAT

Nestled away in the bounteously floric, green hills of the Langbian Mountains, Dalat is one of the few places in Vietnam where a jacket is useful year-round. This former French hill resort (altitude 1500m) produces an abundance of fruits, vegetables, and flowers. Ride a horse through the valleys and listen to the trickling of the many lakes and waterfalls surrounding Dalat, or stroll the streets and admire the elegant old European villas that remain as testimony to the city's colonial heritage. In addition to the vivid flowers and well-preserved villas, the hill-tribes in the region and the crush of tourists year-round add a splash of color to this emerald sea.

ORIENTATION

Dalat awaits the romantic traveler 300km north of Saigon via Bien Hoa Highway. Planes from Saigon land in the **Lien Khuong Airport,** with connecting flights to other destinations. Dalat's streets follow the contours of the hills rather than the plan of any organized city designer, so the city remains a tangle of winding boulevards and tree-lined avenues. At the center of the spider's web unfurls **Dalat Market** (*Cho Dalat*) and the serene **Xuan Huong Lake.**

PRACTICAL INFORMATION

Tourist Office: Lamdong Tourist Company, 4 D. Tran Quoc Toan (tel. 221 25 or 225 20; fax 226 61). This is your primo tourist info stop; the English-fluent staff is helpful and does everything a tourist office should: rents bikes and cars and runs tours to the Lat villages and hikes into the beautiful Langbian Mountains. **Dalat Tourist,** 9 D. Le Dai Hanh (tel. 224 79). A smaller, less patronized office.

Currency Exchange: Industrial and Commercial Bank, 46 D. Hoa Binh (tel. 224 95), or any major hotel in town.

Post Office: 14-16 D. Tran Phu (tel. 223 47). **Telephone Code:** 63

Airport: Lien Khuong Airport (tel. 433 79), 30km south of the city. Airport to city transport 33,000Đ. **Vietnam Airlines Booking Office:** 5 D. Truong Cong Dinh (tel. 228 95). To: **Ho Chi Minh City** (Tues., Thurs., and Sat. 3:30pm) and **Hue** (Tues., Thurs., and Sat. 11:30am).

Train: Dalat has no train connections with other cities due to the mountainous terrain. There is a **railroad station** to the north of Dalat, but trains only run twice daily, making a slow and painful 7-km trek to the village of **Trai Mat.**

Bus: Two private bus stations: on D. Nguyen Thi Minh Khai south of Dalat Market and behind the 3/4 Cinema directly north of Dalat Market. Similar services with express buses to major cities. Leaves early mornings and late afternoons, as soon as they fill up. To: **Nha Trang** (5hr., 33,000Đ); **Da Nang** (55,000Đ); **Hanoi** (88,000Đ); and **Hue** (77,000Đ).

Car Rental: Car rental in Dalat is more expensive than in Saigon. Expect to pay 165-220,000Đ per day within the city, and 330-550,000Đ per day for intercity trips in a 4-seat car with driver. Foreigners cannot rent a car without a driver. Twelve-seat vans cost marginally more. If you're still interested, ask at any hotel reception desk or try **Lien Hiep Tourist Service,** 147 D. Phan Dinh Phung (tel. 225 56) or **Tourist Transportation Enterprise,** 9 D. Le Dai Hanh (tel. 224 79).

Motorcycle Rental: Ask at any hotel or at the bus stations in town or around the Dalat Market area. 110,000Đ per day, with driver 9900Đ per hour.

Market: Dalat Central Market, in the center of town. Crowded and colorful with floors for clothing and crafts, ready-to-eat food, groceries, and souvenirs. In a country of market cultures, Dalat's really stands out.

Hospital: Lamdong General Hospital, 4 D. Pham Ngoc Thach (tel. 221 55).

Police: 2 D. Hai Thuong (tel. 220 98).

ACCOMMODATIONS

It may seem like there are more hotels than houses in Dalat, but be aware that most of them cannot take in foreigners (they are reserved for Vietnamese tourists). Hotels open to foreigners tend to be more costly here than in other cities in Vietnam. Most establishments do not have air-conditioning; it's not needed.

Mimosa II Hotel, 118 D. Phan Dinh Phung (tel. 221 80). Impeccable service coupled with decent living space keep this place popular and full. Clean bathrooms have hot water and bathtub (a rare treat). Spacious doubles 110-220,000Đ. Some rooms accommodate 6-person groups at 44,000Đ per person. Mimosa I is at 170 D. Hong Hoa.

Hai Son Hotel, 1 D. Nguyen Thi Minh Khai (tel. 223 79 or 226 22; fax 226 23), in the central square across from the market. Best-known hotel in Dalat. Open and airy structure. Three-dimensional wooden wall murals differ from the traditional Vietnamese decor. Professional and obliging staff. Doubles 88-330,000Đ. Restaurant, dancing, and—yes!—karaoke.

Thanh Binh Hotel, 41 D. Nguyen Thi Minh Khai (tel. 229 09; fax 226 61), across from Hai Son Hotel next to Dalat Market. Temporary home for many foreigners; helpful staff. Clean and comfortable, and usually full. Reserve ahead. Singles 77-198,000Đ; doubles 132-286,000Đ.

Peace Hotel, 64 D. Truong Cong Dinh (tel. 227 87). Minimalist rooms but low-priced. Enthusiastic staff claims to speak 6 different languages. 55-77,000Đ for a bed in a single, double, or quad. Peace Hotel 2 is across the street at 67 D. Truong Cong Dinh.

Hong Phuoc Hotel, 26B D. Hai Ba Trung (tel. 252 56 or 254 22). Loud lovers beware: we can hear EVERYTHING, and the paper walls may come down if you breathe too hard. Don't let the enterprising staff charge you for your driver's room. Doubles 220,000Đ, quads 275,000Đ.

Duy Tan Hotel, 83 D. 3/2 (tel. 222 16). Recently renovated, impressive villa-style architecture will wow any weary wanderer. Not surprisingly, offers luxurious services and amenities. Imposing gates and private courtyard lend a quiet and exclusive atmosphere. Singles 363-418,000Đ. Doubles 429-572,000Đ.

Anh Dao Hotel, 50-52 Hoa Binh Square. Convenient central location. This place may be mistaken for a warehouse or a YMCA with its cheap glass exterior, but the interior is much more inviting: rooms feature TV, fridge, and hot water. A tourist shop, Thai massage parlor, and karaoke all eagerly await your post-boob tube needs. Doubles 330-396,000Đ. Another location, formerly called Thuy Tien Hotel, at 7 D. 3/2 (tel. 217 31; fax 226 61).

FOOD

Dalat's natural setting supplies a cornucopia of fruits and vegetables, as well as a dazzling array of wild meats like boar, rabbit, bird, eel, and frog. Freshness, variety, and herds of hungry tourists mean that Dalat's food will keep you happy and scurvy-free; try to shop in the inexpensive markets or your wallet could become money-free. Markets and restaurants tend to be open daily 6:30am-10pm.

Hai Son Restaurant, 1 D. Nguyen Thi Minh Khai (tel. 229 49). The owners will welcome you into their eatery with a large menu and friendly, polite, English-speaking servers. American pop and light rock music fill the air, while plants complement the decor. Average entree 22-33,000Đ. Breakfast (fried eggs or Vietnamese noodle soup) averages 7150Đ per person.

Lien Hiep Restaurant, 147 D. Phan Dinh Phung (tel. 225 56). Popular with the Vietnamese crowd. 16,500Đ will fill your tummy with yummy Vietnamese and Chinese food, but the noise level may fill your sensitive ears.

Thuy Ta Restaurant (tel. 222 68). One of many lovely lakeside establishments. Heartwarming coffee served up in the evenings by waiters who will listen to your traveling woes.

Thanh Thuy Restaurant, 2 D. Nguyen Thai Hoc (tel. 222 62). Another romantic lakeside locale, perfect for a late-night lover's tryst, or a cup of expat coffee.

Kim Linh Restaurant, 58 D. Phan Dinh Phung (tel. 254 06). This Chinese restaurant also serves Vietnamese and Euro dishes. (Aw heck, we're all friends, right?) The food leaves little room for criticism but the prices are less commendable.

Giac Duc Vegetarian Restaurant, 15 D. Phan Dinh Phung (tel. 250 54). Exclusive home to strict herbivores. Menu includes Vietnamese soups, pancakes, rice dishes, and amazingly, vegetables. Oh wait—this is a vegetarian restaurant. "Advantage given to monks, nuns, and Buddhists." Dishes run 4-15,000Đ.

SIGHTS

Lake Xuan Huong ripples gently at the center of town. While somewhat less impressive than its national reputation for beauty would indicate, it is still appealing for its tranquil setting and the beautiful houses that line its banks.

The creative Buddha, Thich Ca, awaits your visit in **Linh Son Pagoda,** a short walk from the market. Head north up D. Nguyen Van Troi (you'll pass the uninspiring town cathedral on you right) to the red brick staircase with two cement dragons along the banisters and columns topped by pink lotuses. The standard Buddhist bell and drum sit in front, and just inside to the left reposes the God of Talent, with eyes on his stomach (a sign of his all-seeing powers; talent and skill are thought to reside in the stomach). In case you're wondering, the square design on the straw mats all over the pagoda say "Happy Family." The pagoda's interior courtyard features thigh-high bonsai plants that horticulturists will eye jealously. Pagoda open 6am-8pm. Knock if the door is closed; monks will allow visitors in upon request.

The former **Governor General's Residence** or Palace II sits southeast of the lake at 12 D. Tran Hung Dao. While the pretty yellow building itself is closed to tourists, the view from the parking lot in front is worth the trek. An enclosed garden to the right features a neoclassical rotunda with a burbling fountain.

Two km southwest of Lake Xuan Huong is the slightly more impressive **Palace of King Bao Dai** or Palace III, D. Trieu Viet Vuong (tel. 220 93 or 224 11), at the end of D. Le Hong Phong. King Bao Dai (extremely French-influenced) was the last king of the Nguyen Dynasty and of Vietnam. He reigned as King from 1926-1945, but kept his hold on power when he became Chief of State under the Republic in 1949 and chose Dalat as capital city. Bao Dai left the country in 1954 to live in France. King Bao Dai, Queen Nam Phuong, and their five children lived here during vacations and holidays. The Palace, based on the design of a French-Vietnamese architect team, was begun in 1933 and completed five years later; the first floor was for greeting guests, while the second floor was the private space of the royal family. Even though you're required to take off your shoes when you enter, enthusiastic Vietnamese tourists have a tendency to jump on all the furniture when posing for pictures. Patient museum employees follow behind to straighten things up. Open 7am-12pm and 1pm-5pm. Admission 10,000Đ.

■ NEAR DALAT

Dalat's train only goes to **Trai Mat Village.** There's not much to see in the village, but the beautiful **Linh Phuoc Pagoda,** 120 D. Tu Phuoc (tel. 254 10), features a massive colorful cement dragon around the fountain in the courtyard. Strangely, some young enterprising monk has listed all the names of contributors on a wall of the pagoda—along with the precise amounts they donated. Well-wishers come from around the world, and though the pagoda is still being built, you can always go inside. Open 6am-7pm.

Camly Falls is a touristy nightmare 2km from Dalat's city center. Hardly a waterfall despite its name, Camly's brown water flows into a pond with cement shores. A colorful gazebo awaits the photo-addicted, and the staff there provide you with bright, plastic, "ethnic" costumes and makeup. No, Vietnamese people don't really dress like this. 2000Đ per costume. Admission 5000Đ. Open 7am-6pm.

Vendors await the unwary 10km south of Dalat at **Prenn Falls** (Prenn Pass). After your driver drops you off, walk over a little wooden bridge, turn right down a steep, windy, and rocky path, pass a statue of horse and rider to your left, and you'll arrive at Dalat's premiere waterfall. A huge bamboo bridge allows you to walk under the waterfall; cool off in the waters, but be careful—it can be very slippery. Some of the most interesting sights here are the women dressed in long, tight, traditional evening dresses and high heels. They're here to take their dream photos, but try not to dwell on how they got down the steep path into the valley dressed like that. Open 7am-5pm. Admission 10,000Đ.

Datanla Falls, 5km from the city next to Lake Tuyen Lam, is a beautiful 1-km hike from the road. The red clay road winds uphill through forest, and can be wet and slippery during the rainy season; listen for the falls as you get closer. While not as pulchritudinous as Prenn, the falls are louder and wider, and in a slightly more natural setting (though still bedecked with tourists). Open 6am-5pm. Admission 3000Đ.

The **Langbian Mountains** are a rural retreat 12km north of Dalat, with peaks as high as 2163m. Here you can go mountain climbing, para-gliding and trekking. At the foot of the mountains lies the **Lat Village,** home to the Lat and Chill ethnic groups. The climb up features breathtaking views, but all tourists must secure a **visitor's license** before heading up. Grab one at the tourist office (55,000Đ), or take the easy way up and go with a tour. Lamdong Tourist Company organizes 3-hr. treks into the Langbian Mountains for 165,000Đ per person, and they'll take care of the paperwork and tell you about the sights. Tours leave in the morning around 8am.

VALLEY OF LOVE

Honeymooners and hikers should hire a motorcycle and driver (10,000Đ per hour) and putter over to the **Valley of Love** (Thung Lung Tinh Yeu). This verdant paradise lies 6km north of Dalat's city center, and features forests, trails, rolling hills, lakes, views of the Langbian Mountains, and swarms of foreign and Vietnamese tourists (tel. 214 48 for information; open 7am-5pm; admission 4000Đ). On the other side of the crowds and souvenir stands, horses and guides chomp at the bit to take you through the valley for 66,000Đ per hour—the horses will trot no matter what you do. Fascinating views give way to lakes where you can rent boats. Overall, the valley is great place to fall in love, if you can find your own spot; people are all over the place, and all over each other. Vendors will follow you everywhere and are in league with the guides, so try to avoid purchasing drinks from them. The romantic nature of this valley is rooted in history: the **Lake of Sighs** (Ho Than Tho) gets it name from the story of the Vietnamese Romeo and Juliet. Two star-crossed lovers came here to bemoan their separated fates, and eventually committed suicide rather than remain apart. (Of course, no one seems to know how they did it—but that's not the important part.) Their graves are next to the lake. Follow the tourist hordes and the vendors to the lake.

■■■ HO CHI MINH CITY (SAIGON)

From as far back as any living Vietnamese can remember, this former "Pearl of the Orient" has been the center of wealth for Vietnam. Saigon is the place where Vietnamese can dress *comme* "the westerners," own more motorbikes than bicycles, and go dancing without attracting neighborhood rumors. At the same time, this metropolis is home to more beggars, thieves, and prostitutes than any other city in the country. Starry-eyed country girls and enterprising young lads who come to seek fame and the big bucks often find themselves at the end of a disappointed dream. As Hollywood and Paris well know, some do make it, most don't.

Most foreign visitors share a love-hate relationship with Saigon. They delight in the astounding array of bars and nightclubs while frowning at side-effects of modernity, like pollution, overcrowding, and fast living. Love or hate, no picture of Vietnam the country is complete without including Saigon, "the City." Saigon may not represent the typical image of Vietnam, but it has played a major role in the country's recent history, and records of a few too many wars are there to prove it.

After the reunification of 1975, the new Communist government changed Saigon's official name to Ho Chi Minh City, after Vietnam's foremost hero. The new name hasn't quite caught on, however, and foreigners will be forgiven for calling this capital of the south what the locals do—Saigon.

GETTING THERE AND AWAY

By Air

Saigon's hub for welcoming foreigners is **Tan Son Nhat International Airport** (tel. 446 513 or 443 250 for airport operator). The airport shuttle will transport you from your plane to the terminal, where long lines await at the passport counter and customs. Fill out the immigration documents on the plane before arrival to avoid any hassles. Overseas Vietnamese should expect airport personnel to ask for "tips" with several euphemisms. Ignore these pleas; they are illegal and dishonest. Watch your bags as you make your way through the crowds of awaiting families and taxi drivers. The lease insane and most secure way to leave the airport is to hop into a taxi. All fares are metered; the 20-minute ride into town costs 55-77,000Đ. Big groups can rent a van for about 165,000Đ (call tel. 441 704).

Domestic flights to: **Da Nang** (daily 7:20, 11:50am, and 1:50pm); **Hanoi** (daily, every 15-30min., 6:45am-6pm); **Haiphong** (daily, 8:30am; Mon., Wed., and Sat. 9am); **Hue** (daily 6:30 (except Sat.) and 10am); **Nha Trang** (daily 7:05am; Thurs. and Sun. 2:40pm, 990,000Đ); and **Rach Gia** (Tues. and Sat. 11:30am). International flights to: **Bangkok** (Tues., Thurs., and Sat. 11:30am; the other 4 days 12:40pm; Thurs. and Sun. 4:15); **Kuala Lumpur** (Wed. 10:30am; Mon. and Fri. 1:30pm); **Phnom Penh** (daily 7am and 2:45pm); **Singapore** (daily 10:20am; Tues., Thurs., and Sun. 4:20pm); and **Vientiane** (1-3 per day, every 15min., 6:45-7:30am).

By Train

Trains from all over Vietnam stop at the **Saigon Railway Station,** 1 D. Nguyen Thong (tel. 443 952). Open daily 6am-6pm. Currency exchange is available. To get to downtown Saigon, take a taxi for a short, 22,000Đ, air-conditioned ride.

Trains move at a turtle's pace (on average 30km per hour) to major cities in Vietnam. The ride to Hanoi takes three days, but the hard seats become unbearable after the first hour. Your best bet is to buy a soft seat. Long-distance trains usually leave early in the morning and evening; fares vary with train and seat types. Call ahead for fare and schedule information; rates tend to vary wildly depending on the day, the type of seat, and the destination. Most hotels also have a fare and schedule timetable. Better yet, let your hotel purchase the ticket for you.

By Bus

Three major stations: **Van Thanh Bus Station** (tel. 997 576 or 994 839), on D. Dien Bien Phu. Vans and small buses to the immediate north: **Dalat** (7hr., 27,500Đ). A/C available for chartered vehicles. **Mien Dong Bus Station,** #13 Highway 13 (tel. 994 056), near Binh Trieu Bridge. Service to all major cities to the north: **Hanoi** (10am and 3:30pm, 132,000Đ) and **Hue** (6:30am, 77,000Đ). Buses to **Nha Trang** (5-8am, 33,000Đ) and **Dalat** (5-10am, 77,000Đ) depart as soon as they fill up. No A/C. Open 5am-4pm. **Ben Xe Mien Tay** (tel. 755 955/6) serves destinations to the south. Open 5am-4pm. Buses and vans to the **Mekong Delta** (Vinh Long, Can Tho, Rach Gia, Ha Tien, Chau Doc; 6, 10am, and 2pm, 27,500Đ). For 41,000Đ you can be packed in with 15 other people in a 12-seat van instead. Tickets can also be bought at 1B D. Huynh Tran Cong Chua (tel. 244 097) 6am-8pm.

ORIENTATION

The **Saigon River** curves to the east, forming that border of Ho Chi Minh City, while a series of canals and channels runs through the southern part of Saigon. **Districts 1** and **5** are major centers of tourism and commercial activity; they form a quarter-moon sickle along the bend of the river, traversing almost the entire length of the metropolis, from northeast to southwest. The **Ben Nghe Canal** flows southwest from the river. **Duong Tran Hung Dao** runs parallel to the canal and connects District 1 to **Cho Lon,** the Chinatown of Saigon. Tourist traffic radiates from **Ben Thanh Market,** sprawled out near the traffic circle closest to the river and canal. Here, D. Tran Hung Dao divides the circle and continues on the other side, changing into

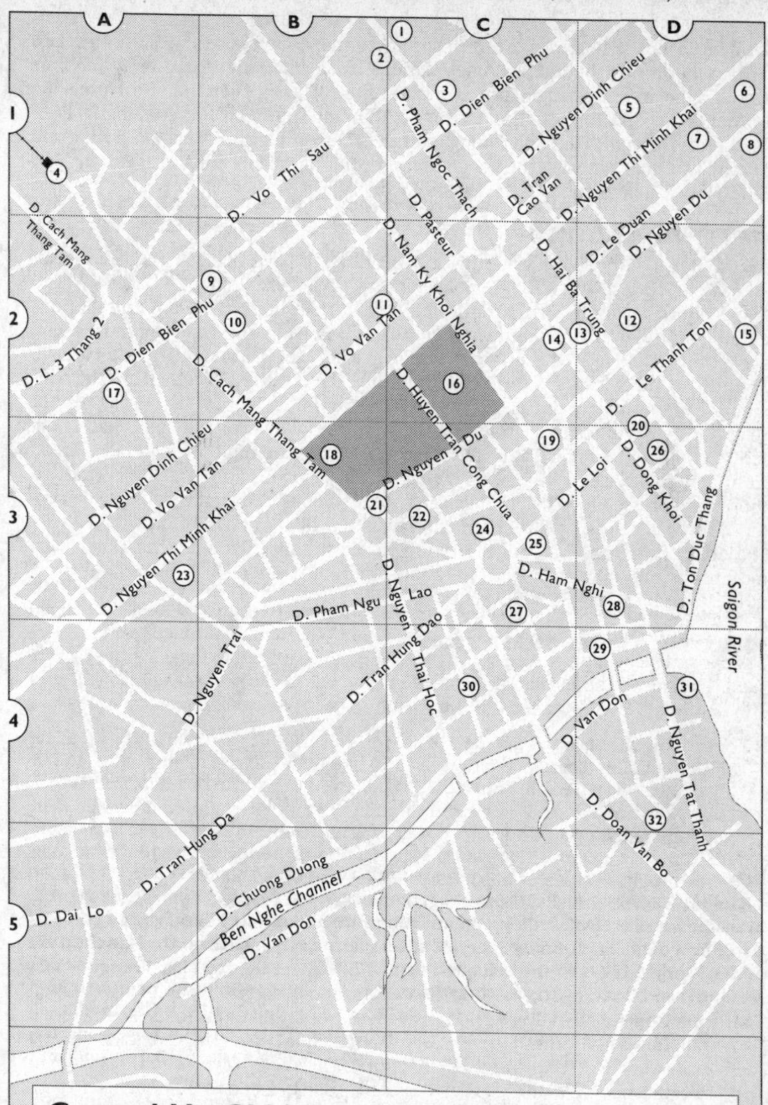

Central Ho Chi Minh City (Saigon)

Art Museum, **27**
Bac Ton Museum, **15**
Ben Thanh Market, **24**
Binh Dan Hospital, **17**
Central Saigon Mosque, **26**
Culture Park, **18**
Dien Bien Phu Hospital, **9**
Foreign Exchange Bank, **29**
Historical Museum, **6**
Ho Chi Minh Museum, **31**
Immigration Police Office, **21**
Le Van Tham Park, **3**
Main Post Office, **13**
Mariamman Hindu Temple, **22**
Mililtary Museum, **7**
Nhi Dong II Hospital, **12**
Notre Dame Cathedral, **14**
Opera Theatre, **20**
Phung Son Tu Pagoda, **30**
Reunification Hall, **16**
Revolutionary Museum, **19**
Saigon Hospital, **25**
Saigon Station, **4**
Stadium, **5**
Tan Dinh Church, **2**
Tan Dinh Market, **1**
Vietnam Bank, **28**
War Crimes Museum, **11**
Women's Hospital, **23**
Xa Loi Pagoda, **10**
Xom Chieu Market, **32**
Zoo/ Botanical Garden, **8**

VIETNAM

Duong Le Loi. The area west of this traffic circle comprises the **Pham Ngu Lao area,** where most budget accommodations cluster. **Duong Pham Ngu Lao** cuts through the area at an angle from the traffic circle. **Duong Dien Bien Phu** forms the border of Saigon proper to the northwest. Running southeast and crossing D. Dien Bien Phu, **Duong Phan Dinh Phung** intersects **Duong Nguyen Thai Minh Khai** and **Duong Le Duan** almost at the geographical center of the city, ending at **Duong Ton Duc Thang,** which parallels the Saigon River.

GETTING AROUND

Traffic flows surprisingly smoothly in Ho Chi Minh City, because regulations are strictly enforced by the watchful police on street corners and in traffic circles. Try to avoid contributing to street traffic during the rush hours (7-10am and 4-6pm), although it is hardly the nightmare here that it is in Bangkok. **Taxis** are most useful for getting to and from the airport; if you're in a big group, a taxi might be a bargain. Four taxi companies service Ho Chi Minh City, the cheapest of which are the reassuringly yellow **Vinataxis** (tel. 422 888; 7500Đ for the 1st km, 1500Đ per 200m after that). Or try the efficient, purple (*not* the green and white Saigon Taxis; that's a different company) **Saigon Taxis** (tel. 424 242). **Cyclos** are omnipresent, but banned from certain streets; transport anywhere in the city runs about 10,000Đ (though those hard-pressed for small change can try bargaining). Seeing the sights in the center of town is easiest by foot; touring on **bike** may be more of a burden than a convenience. In general, if you're looking to see the city overall, rent a bike or a motorcycle; if you're staying on the tourist path, just **walk.** Many hotels and guest houses rent bikes (55-88,000Đ per day).

PRACTICAL INFORMATION

Before taking on the city, pick up a **map** (4400Đ) from a street vendor, bookstore, major hotel, or general post office.

Tours: Saigontourist, 49 D. Le Thanh Ton (tel. 298 914 or 298 129), is a mammoth operation that encompasses over 50 hotels and 40 restaurants. Efficient but impersonal. **Ben Thanh Tourist,** 121 D. Nguyen Hue (tel. 224 148 or 222 506) is Saigon's other big name in tourism. Competitive prices and better service than Saigontourist. **Saigon Tours,** 95 D. Hai Ba Trung (tel. 294 253), is best for personalized tours. Organizes tours to Laos and Cambodia, and bike trips to the Mekong Delta. Brochure contains impeccable English and useful advice.

Budget Travel: SINH Office, 179 D. Pham Ngu Lao (tel. 355 601), sends express **minibuses** to **Dalat** (7:30am and 2pm, 77,000Đ) and **Nha Trang** (7:30am, 165,000Đ) daily. Daytrips to **Cu Chi Tunnels** and **Cao Dai Cathedral** (66,000Đ). Tours to the delta and up north. Also rents cars and bikes, extends visas, and books flights and train tickets. Pay for and confirm trips before 10pm.

Embassies and Consulates: Australia, 76 D. Le Lai (tel. 299 387). **Cambodia,** 41 D. Phung Khac Khoan (tel. 292 751). **Indonesia,** 18 D. Phung Khac Khoan (tel. 223 799). **Laos,** 181 D. Hai Ba Trung (tel. 297 667). **Malaysia,** 53 D. Nguyen Dinh Chieu (tel. 299 023). **New Zealand,** 455 D. Nguyen Dinh Chieu (tel. 396 227). **Singapore,** 5 D. Phung Khac Khoan (tel. 225 173). **Thailand,** 77 D. Tran Quoc Thao (tel. 222 637). **UK,** 261 D. Dien Bien Phu (tel. 298 433).

Currency Exchange: At most hotels, gold stores, and the GPO. **Vietcombank,** 29 D. Ben Chuong Duong (tel. 252 831). Cash advances on Visa and MC. **Credit Lyonnaise,** 17 D. Ton Duc Thang (tel. 299 226). Credit card advances and money transfer. **Nam Do Bank,** 175 D. Ham Nghi, across from Ben Thanh market. Open 7am-7pm. **Eden Tourist,** 104-106 D. Nguyen Hue (tel. 298 839). Cash for Visa. Western Union to the rescue! Open 8-11:30am and 1:30-5:30pm.

Post Office: GPO, 2 Cong Xa Paris (tel. 299 615), on left side of Notre Dame Cathedral. Info desk to the left of entrance. Sells stationery. Post Restante. DHL and FedEx. **Photocopy, fax, telex,** and telegram. Domestic calling cards. Open daily 6am-10pm.

Telephones: Domestic and international calls can be made at hotels, post offices, and the telephones-for-hire (look for square blue signs with a red phone). Hotels have a surcharge; private telephones double the price. The post office is cheapest. Public telephone booths only place domestic calls. Purchase a calling card from any post office or major bookstore. Dial 108 for directory assistance in any city in Vietnam. **Telephone code:** 8.

Markets: Saigon is one gigantic market. For serious shopping, consider the streets and markets famous for certain products. Electronic products ride the waves in the market stalls on **D. Huynh Thuc Khanh** in District 1 and **D. Tran Hung Dao** in Cho Lon. D. Huynh Thuc Khanh also overflows with bootlegged CDs, videos, and video games smuggled in from China. 27,000Đ will get you the Beatles, Madonna, Nirvana, or any other artist. **D. Nguyen Dinh Chieu** is famous for quality, foreign products. **D. Pham Hong Thai,** near Thai Binh Market, displays a dizzying array of bicycles. Fabrics and clothing are best at **An Dong** and **Binh Tay** markets in Cho Lon and **Tan Dinh Market** on D. Hai Ba Trung in District 1. **Ben Thanh Market** is a big rip-off for the most part.

Hospitals: Saigon Hospital, 125 D. Le Loi (tel. 297 709 or 291 711) is the emergency center of the city. **Cho Ray Hospital,** 201 D. Nguyen Chi Thanh (tel. 554 137 or 550 874) and the **Australian AEA International Emergency Service and 24-Hr. Clinic,** 65 D. Nguyen Du (tel. 298 520) are more popular with foreigners.

ACCOMMODATIONS

Since most sights and other tourist-friendly services congregate in District 1, budget travelers usually stay there rather than venture to Cho Lon for accommodations. The low quality of the handful of budget hotels in Cho Lon is not particularly inviting anyway. Be aware that prostitution abounds in this area. It's best to stay in District 1 and take the 20-minute cyclo ride (5500Đ) to this commercial center. Nevertheless, for the Cho Lon addict, some good abodes are available.

Pham Ngu Lao Area

Le Le Hotel, 269 D. De Tham (tel. 322 110). Across the street from Kim Cafeteria. One of the best deals in the neighborhood. New tile floors and pristine walls complement elegant decor. Small but modern bathrooms give even more value for your money. Singles 66,000Đ, with A/C 275,000Đ. Doubles 132,000Đ, with A/C 330,000Đ. Another location at 171 D. Pham Ngu Lao (tel. 323 124).

Guest House 70, 70 D. Bui Vien (tel. 330 569). Friendly family knows how to welcome guests (with great English and shining smiles) in this homey, comfortable nest. Spotless bathrooms delight the bare feet. Shared bathroom. Doubles 88,000Đ, with A/C 198,000Đ. Continental breakfast included.

Xuan Vinh Hotel, 40-42 D. Thach Thi Thanh (tel. 200 519 or 200 521). Near Le Van Tam Park, a 25-min. walk to city center; if the heat gets you down, take a cyclo (4400Đ). The extra distance is no pain to gain dirt-cheap luxury. A brand-new hotel with 3-star quality at a fraction of the price. Obliging family will help with almost anything. The daughter of the house makes some of the best food in Saigon. Doubles with A/C, fridge, phone, TV 220,000Đ. Triples and larger rooms 330-385,000Đ.

Vien Dong Hotel, 275A D. Pham Ngu Lao (tel. 393 001 or 353 010). A head above the rest in value. No, you didn't get lost. The polite doorman, modern elevator, fancy lobby, and rich façade comes with budget prices. Quiet interior. Clean and functional bathrooms. Check out the mermaid in the courtyard. Doubles with fan 132,000Đ. A/C rooms are not for the budget traveler but 352-770,000Đ.

Sinh Hotel, 1 D. Le Loi (tel. 324 877), on the street behind Sinh Café. The same comfort as Sinh Guest House at a much sweeter deal. Dormitory beds squeeze seven to a room. Shared baths cater to massive crowds, but the price makes almost anything bearable at 22,000Đ per bed.

Guest House 72, 72 D. Bui Vien (tel. 330 321). Six rooms on top of a tailor shop. A bargain if you don't mind passing sewing machines and fabric all the time. Light and airy architecture contrasts with the gloom of most hotels on Pham Ngu Lao. Shared bathroom. Doubles only 77-88,000Đ, with A/C 110-132,000Đ.

Tao Dan Guest House, 35A D. Nguyen Trung Truc (tel. 230 299 or 291 977). Foreigners are no stranger to this happy den. Attentive staff, spacious rooms, and safe location. Bathrooms are clean and functional. Doubles with fan 132,000Đ, with A/C 242-286,000Đ.

My Man Mini Hotel, 373/20 D. Pham Ngu Lao (396 544). Inconvenient location in an alley behind Thai Binh Market. Hurdles of vendors and produce conceal the discreet and tranquil lodgings. Scenic wallpaper offers countryside serenity amidst metropolitan chaos. Narrow bathrooms. Spic 'n' span floors. Doubles with fan 110,000Đ, with A/C 154,000Đ.

Thai Binh Hotel, 325 D. Pham Ngu Lao (tel. 399 544). This Saigontourist joint always filled to the max. The attractive price is their claim to fame. Vietnamese-style bathrooms match nondescript rooms. All rooms with fan: singles 55,000Đ, doubles 77,000Đ, triples 88,000Đ.

Hoan Vu Hotel, 265 D. Pham Ngu Lao (tel. 396 522). Cheerful service makes up for the less-than-proficient English. Brave the ancient elevator to spacious rooms. Worn-out bathrooms. Singles with fan 88,000Đ. Doubles 110,000Đ. Triples 132,000Đ. With A/C 154,000Đ, 187,000Đ, 220,000Đ respectively.

Hotel 269, 269 D. Pham Ngu Lao (tel. 322 345). A new kid on the block. Low on the amenities (no phone or hot water in fan rooms) but sweet-smelling. The flowers and tea spell hospitality. Cartoon characters on towels bring out the kid in you. Top floors only for the physically fit—no elevator! Doubles with fan 110-132,000Đ, with A/C 187,000Đ.

Prince Hotel, 187 D. Pham Ngu Lao (tel. 322 657). In the center of the backpacker district. Make way through the crowd of cyclo drivers in front. Ascend the narrow staircase to the rooms. Antique telephones and threadbare bedding. Average value for the area. Singles 77-88,000Đ. Doubles 99-110,000Đ. Fans only, no A/C.

Sinh Guest House, 185/4 D. Pham Ngu Lao (tel. 324 877). Across the street from Sinh Café, in an alley behind the Prince Hotel. Little comfort for the price. Closet-size rooms open to narrow hallways blocked with sleeping staff. Singles with fan 88,000Đ, with A/C 132,000Đ. Doubles with fan 110,000Đ, with A/C 165,000Đ.

Cho Lon Area

Thien Thien, 177 D. Tran Binh Trong (tel. 350 936 or 394 189). Service is serious business at this new mini-hotel. Affable family makes tea and conversation readily available to guests. The place to stay in Cho Lon. Doubles with A/C 220,000Đ.

Hoa Binh Hotel, 1115 D. Tran Hung Dao (tel. 355 113 or 353 941). A 10-story building on a busy street corner. Fresh and inviting, inside and out. Bathe with a bucket; showers haven't made it here yet. Doubles 88,000Đ, with A/C 165,000Đ.

Phoenix Hotel (Phuong Hoang Hotel), 411 D. Tran Hung Dao (tel. 551 888 or 551 199). At a major intersection with D. Chau Van Liem. Enter from Tran Hung Dao. Look for the big red sign. Even Mr. Clean would be proud of this "home." Watch Saigon wheeze by from the balcony. Great view from top floors. Doubles with fan 77-165,000Đ, with A/C 275,000Đ.

FOOD

A listing of all the great places to eat in Saigon would rival the New York City phone book in size, but since the best budget eateries here are mom-and-pop establishments, tuck your *Let's Go* into your backpack and strike out on your own. Explore the market food stalls, the sidewalk stands, and the steamy, hole-in-the-wall greasy spoons. These places may not care much for ambiance, but they cook it up like the best. **Family restaurants** (*com binh dan*) are universally equipped with plastic and metal furniture; the typical food features rice with any number of toppings. Check out the cart in front for the "menu"—dishes or rice with mouth-watering sauces of salted chicken, vegetable stir-fry, boiled greens, tofu, roast meats, and fish. In general, look for deals in the Pham Ngu Lao area and keep your eyes open for where the locals eat. You'll see the businessmen and foreign investors populating the overpriced, English-menu restaurants, but avoid their company and head for the authentic, inexpensive food all over town.

Restaurant 13, 13 D. Ngo Duc Ke (tel. 291 417). Highly acclaimed by the expat community. Customers swarm like bees to hover under the sidewalk canopy and the yellow light bulbs. Excellent food and service, but a bit pricey. Average meal costs 44,000 per person.

Ngoc Huong, 9 D. Dong Du. A reasonably priced family restaurant with excellent food. Check out the cart in front for your eating options. The convivial, elderly Vietnamese proprietress will feed you well. Dinner for one 5000Đ.

Pho Hoa, 260C D. Pasteur (tel. 297 943). Absolutely the best *pho* in town—ask any Saigonese. The 10,000Đ bowl makes an entire meal.

Vietnam House Restaurant, 93 D. Dong Khoi (tel. 291 623). Authentic Vietnamese food served up for foreigners. Traditional music fills the air. Piano bar downstairs provides the *apéritif,* upstairs is where you chow. Entrees average 40,000Đ.

Sinh Café, 6 D. Pham Ngu Lao (tel. 355 601 or 357 722). A "foreigners only" sign couldn't have done a better job of keeping out the locals. Busy tourist-bus-stop atmosphere provide adequate setting for exchanging travel tips. Besides budget food, Sinh sells budget tours, budget accommodations, and budget bike rentals. Very helpful and courteous staff.

Kim Cafeteria, 270 D. De Tham (tel. 398 177). The other big backpacker hangout. The only thing foreign to this cafeteria is ambiance. Lengthy menu makes up for the lack of decor. Tasty food, friendly prices. Also runs tour office next door.

Bambou, 158C D. Dong Khoi (tel. 299 459 or 291 261). You can't sit in the bamboo carriage, but try the bamboo tables and chairs. Delightful ambiance with good service to boot. Expensive Vietnamese and Euro nosh (55-88,000Đ). Happy hour 5-7pm. Live music starts at 8:30pm. Open 8am-midnight.

Tram Phan Tram! (Bottoms up!)

Vietnamese take beer-drinking seriously—so seriously that you might think you're in Germany when it comes to quaffing *lager* with the locals. Although most *bia hoi* (draft beer) stands on the sidewalks and side roads fall short of a Munich *biergarten,* the enthusiasm and passion with which the Vietnamese drink their beer rivals malt-drinkers anywhere in the world, and for good reason: the beer in Vietnam is fresh and delicious. Every morning, beer is delivered fresh in mini-kegs (known affectionately as "beer bombs"), which means that there are no preservatives and less of a chance of getting a hangover should you imbibe too liberally. But be warned: while Vietnamese beer may not have as much body as many international beers, it certainly has a kick.

Almost every city or region has its own local brews: in Hanoi, try Bia Hanoi and Halida; in Hue, drink Huda; in Saigon, don't miss 333 and Bia Saigon. Regardless of where you go, locals will insist that their city's beer is the best in Vietnam—and you know that the only way to know for sure is to do careful, empirical research. To locate a good beer stall, look for peanut shells on the floor or a crowd of people. You'll find that a good *bia hoi* is the great social equalizer: doctors and lawyers share the camaraderie of good beer elbow-to-elbow with cyclo drivers and shoe-shine boys. Get to your favorite stall early, since kegs are often kicked by mid-afternoon, and grab a handful of peanuts in the shell (*lac*) or dried squid (*muc*) to help it go down right. Sorry, no beer nuts, Norm.

SIGHTS

You need to leave District 1 only to see the famous markets and pagodas of Cho Lon. The most efficient way to cover all the sights downtown is to follow a horseshoe path starting with the Historical Museum and City Zoo in the northeast and ending with the Ho Chi Minh Museum in the southeast. Divide the horseshoe up and take two or three days to see everything, otherwise you (and your feet) will curse every museum and monument in Saigon. Do your sight-seeing in the mornings and late afternoons to avoid the scorching midday sun.

Begin your tour with a comprehensive history lesson of Vietnam at the **Historical Museum,** 2 D. Nguyen Binh Khiem, inside the Botanical Garden/Zoo complex (a 5000Đ cyclo ride from Ben Thanh Market). Entrance to the museum is only through the main gates of the zoo on D. Nguyen Binh Khiem, open 6am-6pm. You must pay a 11,000Đ admission to enter the zoo. Once inside, pay another 11,000Đ at the entrance of the museum. Don't fret; the zoo and botanical garden are worth the extra dong. The Historical Museum is the grand orange structure to the left of the zoo entrance. Inside, the first-floor display highlights a segment of Vietnamese society that is not often seen; clothing, tools, handicrafts, and artwork from many of Vietnam's ethnic cultures impress viewers with color, creativity, and craftsmanship. The next room pays tribute to the ancient Champa Kingdom that existed in southern Vietnam before the Kinh people (the majority of Vietnamese) overran them in the 15th century. Examine the distinctive Champa art form in the cement statues and other relics from the 10th and 11th centuries. All Hindu statues are manifestations of the gods that the Chams worshipped. Catch a glimpse of the clay model of the Poklong Garai Towers before you mount the real things in Phan Rang. The room with the big, black bust of Uncle Ho (what Vietnamese museum could do without one?) contains a 3000-year-old Dong Son bronze drum discovered in 1902. An array of bronze Chinese incense burners hints at the large role the Chinese played in Vietnamese history. The adjoining chamber houses Buddha statues from Vietnam, China, Thailand, Cambodia, and Japan. Compare the distinctive regional conceptions of the Buddha, who wears almost as many faces as Jesus does in the Louvre! Follow the arrows to more historical treasures or take a break in the Venetian courtyard. The trickling fountain and blooming plants know how to refresh a weary soul. Open Mon.-Sat. 8-11:30am and 1:30-4:30pm, Sun. 8:30am-4:30pm.

From the exit of the Historical Museum, there is a pagoda on the opposite side of the zoo entrance. Visitors come here to worship at the **altar of Emperor Hung**. The revered first emperor is highly regarded as the father of ancient Vietnam. The pagoda carries displays of some of the emperor's tools and armor and the altar, draped entirely in red, highlights the importance of ancestor worship. Open 8-11:30am and 1:30-4:30pm, except Mon.

Although it is Vietnam's largest, the **zoo and botanical garden** has only a modest collection of traditional animals; but the landscape is nothing to scoff at. Lovers will enjoy the stroll along the lily pond. For 5500Đ, ask the itinerant palm reader if you'll get lucky tonight. Jurassic Park is a big sell for zoo photographers (there really is a big plastic dinosaur!). Say good-bye to the waving orangutan before you go.

Straight down D. Le Duan are the French and British consulates and the former U.S. embassy. Men in green uniforms now guard these compounds, but you may request a look-see if passive, lifeless architecture appeals to you. The **former U.S. embassy** building is particularly disappointing with its 60s bomb shelter look. The plaque in front commemorates the 1975 evacuation of American forces.

Near the intersection of D. Le Duan and D. Dong Khoi lurks the **Notre Dame Cathedral** (turn left from Le Duan onto Dong Khoi). The red cathedral, built around 1880, is a miniature of its more grand and more famous sibling in Paris, twin spires and all. Three stained-glass windows barely shed enough light on the interior. A mix of Romanesque and pagoda-esque altar styles adorn prayer cubicles along the sides of the cathedral. In front, a white statue of Mother Mary blesses passersby from atop her pedestal. Open 5-11am and 2:30-5:30pm. Wednesday masses at 5:30am and 5pm. Sunday masses at 5:30, 6:30, 7:30, 9:30am, 4:30, and 6:30pm.

To the left of the cathedral, in the same square, stands one of the most beautiful post offices in the world. The **General Post Office** was constructed in the 1880s and is one of Saigon's colonial architectural treasures. After Notre Dame and the post office, continue down Le Duan to the **Army Museum** (Bao Tang Quan Doi), 2 Le Duan. You can't miss the awkward plane and tank in front. Inside, a few war photographs recall what is already in the distant past for most Vietnamese.

Steps away from the Army Museum on D. Nam Ky Khoi Nghia, is the **Reunification (Thong Nhat) Palace.** This 60s-style building is actually the second of two palaces built on this site. The original Norodom Palace was constructed in 1868 by the French to house their Governor General. After the French left the country in 1954, South Vietnam's President Ngo Dinh Diem took over the colonial mansion and changed its name to Independence Palace. On February 27, 1962 two Saigon Air Force pilots attempted to assassinate Diem by bombing the palace. The president survived, but his humble abode had to be razed to the ground and replaced by the present structure. Not long after, on April 30, 1975, a communist tank plowed through the gates of the palace to set up the current regime. Independence Palace then became Reunification Palace, undergoing a new political era and another name change. Visitors see the palace as it was in 1975. Guided tours begin in the red-carpeted Conference Hall, easily recognized by the bust of Bac Ho (Uncle Ho) against the far wall, and proceed through all four floors to the rooftop terrace. Among the highlights of the tour are the President's International Reception Room, which resembles a hunter's den with the giant tusks of some poor ancient mammoth; the Credentials Presentation Room with an impressive 40-piece, wall-size lacquer painting; the private living space of the president and his family, the most serene and least ostentatious part of the palace; and the helicopter on the rooftop terrace. For 11,000Đ, tourists can pose for a picture in the helicopter, with panoramic Saigon in the background. Open 7:30-10:30am and 1-4pm. Admission 44,000Đ, includes brochure and guide, though the guide's English may be worse than the brochure's.

The **War Crimes Museum,** 28 D. Vo Van Tan, lies one block north of the palace. The Museum is about as cheery as you'd expect, and filled with an assemblage of war mementos, not to mention an ironically eclectic mix of architecture (a French-style villa is part of the complex). Weapons, defused bombs, strategic diagrams, an F-5A plane, fetuses damaged by side-effects of Agent Orange, and the requisite tank in the courtyard are supplemented by brochures in Chinese, French, and English. Most of the displays consist of unadorned photographs; some captions include an English translation. An exception to this rule is the extensive coverage of the My Lai (Son My) Massacre. Perhaps more frightening than the museum itself is the presence of a souvenir shop hawking ethnic clothing, costume jewelry, and small plastic weapons. Take refuge from history in the airy courtyard; a goldfish pond with a fountain and a small bridge provide relief to disaster-fatigued eyes. One of the simplest and most eloquent exhibits in the museum is a beautiful statue of a mother, made from bomb fragments. Open 7:30-11:45am, 1:30-4:45pm. Admission 7000Đ.

Past the municipal library is the **Revolutionary Museum,** 65 D. Ly Tu Trong (tel. 299 741 for information). Traditionally dressed Vietnamese women lead tours in doubtful English through this white, colonial-style building. Exhibits sing to the unsurprising "our patrie, our homeland" tune, and inspiring socialist statues of heroes, mothers, and soldiers wait for you around every corner. While the museum staff is polite and the rough English of the brochures entertaining, the dearth of Vietnamese visitors may lead one to question just how appreciative the Vietnamese are of their revolutionary history. Chocolate-brown chairs from a more vinyl era are available for resting tour-tired feet.

Near the museum at 45 D. Trung Dinh stands the **Mariamman Hindu Temple.** This aqua and pink house of worship is distinguished from the more common red ones by lions, multi-headed icons, and other figurines gracing the façade. The interior features the standard raised prayer platform; remove your shoes before ascending. Although consecrated to Hinduism, Buddhists also come here to worship. Open 7am-7pm.

From the temple, head to the intersection containing the Rex Hotel, City Hall, and the Municipal Theater. The **Rex Hotel** is a holdover from French glory days; it was once the place for late-night carousing amongst the French elite. You can enjoy a panoramic view of the city and a cup of coffee on the rooftop terrace a the relatively exorbitant 20,000Đ. Christmas lights and manicured trees add that certain *je ne sais quoi.* Pass the **Municipal Theater** on your way to City Hall; this slightly dilapidated white colonial building occasionally houses propaganda rallies and traditional concerts. Those still craving pictures with Uncle Ho have a perfect opportunity in front of **City Hall** (also referred to as Independence Hall). The beautiful, massive, and well-preserved pastel yellow colonial building features a statue in the mini-park out front of Bac Ho consoling a child.

One block south of the quadrangle at 66 D. Dong Du is the blue **Saigon Central Mosque.** Built in 1935 by Indian Muslims living in Saigon, the building still conducts services for a practicing Muslim community of roughly 200 Cham, Vietnamese, and Indian faithful. As with all mosques, no shorts, open shoes, or sleeveless shirts are allowed inside. Those accustomed to densely decorated temple interiors will be surprised by the relatively austere interior (no iconography allowed). A shallow, tranquil pool surrounded by cool, clean tiles waits peacefully to the right of the entrance. Unlike traditional mosques, visitors are allowed into the main prayer room. The large niche in the wall marks the main altar; in front of is a prayer rug pointing towards Mecca. Open 7am-8pm.

Head away from the mosque to the east, and turn right down D. Hai Ba Trung towards the water. In the square at the water's edge sits a **statue of Tran Hung Dao,** the well-loved Vietnamese hero who successfully defended the kingdom from a Chinese incursion in 1228. **Floating restaurants** lurk in large numbers along the river; these are restaurants on boats that tour the river starting around 8pm. Many feature dancing on board. Organize a watery dinner yourself or inquire with Saigontourist (dinner run around 220,000Đ).

Those who want to know more about Ho Chi Minh, Vietnam's premiere hero and revolutionary leader, should cross the river and turn left for the **Ho Chi Minh Museum,** D. Nguyen Tat Thanh (the building was formerly known as the Dragon House Wharf). While many Vietnamese might not agree with everything he did, most everyone admires him. Student groups come here for the requisite history field trips, and your Vietnam tour would never be complete without one more picture with Uncle Ho. Open Tues.-Thurs. and Sat-Sun. 8-11:30am and 2-6pm.

More adventurous visitors should head 35km outside of the city to the reconstituted and expanded **Cu Chi Viet Cong Tunnels.** Enterprising Vietnamese have widened the former tunnel networks to accommodate larger European tourists, but claustrophobes should stay away. Inquire at the Sinh Café or Kim Cafeteria. A tour including a visit to one of the local temples leaves at 9am and costs 66,000Đ.

NIGHTLIFE AND ENTERTAINMENT

Nightlife is the biggest form of entertainment in Saigon, and not surprisingly, the most developed sector of Saigon's economy. Best get your own fill of boogie-ing and boozing here. Once you leave Saigon, the flood of bars and clubs instantly disappears to a drop in the bucket that dries out by 10pm. Every night is fun night in Saigon, but save your best threads for Friday and Saturday. As the weekend rolls around, rich locals jam the streets heading for the hippest discos, karaoke parlors, or cafés. The action never stops on D. Nguyen Hue and D. Dong Khoi near the Rex Hotel; they're packed 24 hrs. with the hip, the hep, and the slap-happy.

Bars and Cafés

Buffalo Blues, 72A D. Nguyen Du (tel. 222 874; fax 230 464). Watch a cute Vietnamese lady pump out "New York, New York" and other jazz favorites with a Harlem accent and a no-nonsense attitude. Tuyet Loan has been singing the blues for over 20 years. The Brothers Jazz Band also play here. Barbecue food and plenty of boozin' blues.

Long Phi Café, 163 D. Pham Ngu Lao (tel. 314 819). Acid jazz, blues, and reggae move the furniture in this cavernous joint. Orange spray paint on black makes the ceiling glow. Serves food, cocktails, and beer. Best ambiance in the Pham Ngu Lao area. Open 11am-2am.

Apocalypse Now, 2C D. Thi Sach (tel. 241 463). New location. Casual hangout for budget travelers and expats alike. Black walls, helicopters on ceilings, blaring rock music, and pool table; London hit Saigon. Free popcorn with the beer. Witty menu has a wisecrack for every drink. Open 6pm-when the guests call it a night.

Saxo Club, 91 D. Hai Ba Trung (tel. 228 305). Modern art is the theme in this recent addition. Curvy black metal tables and chairs complement Picasso-inspired paintings perfectly. Groovy spiral staircase leads to a billiards table upstairs. Live jazz Tues., Thurs., and Sat. Open 5pm-2am.

Hard Rock Café, 24 D. Mac Thi Buoi. No, *that* Hard Rock chain hasn't hit Saigon yet. The same name, but definitely not the same thing. No superstar paraphernalia to overwhelm your senses, but loud rock music does lend credit to the moniker. A dark and dim place with a halo of light over the pool table. Open 4pm-2am.

The Gecko, 74/1A D. Hai Ba Trung (tel. 242 754). Small, cozy café/bar. Dark, wooden interior, pint-size tables, and soft music makes it easy to relax and be intimate with that special someone. Get a little closer! Open 9am-1am.

Nightclubs and Discos

Nightclubs and discos in Saigon resemble their western counterparts: loud, ear-popping music, flashing lights, video screens, and the occasional live band. The music here is what it is anywhere—European and American pop rock and techno. Unfortunately, most clubs cater to foreigners and therefore house "hostesses" (often prostitutes), who get paid to provide conversation and company to the lone male. Good luck trying to find a joint without them. No shorts and sandals in these nightspots.

Down Under, 1A Me Linh Square (tel. 290 783). Down under the Floating Hotel, a very popular place with expats. The most casual dance joint around. Jeans and shorts are acceptable even though the sign says no. Cover 66,000Đ, one drink. Open 8pm-2am.

Starlight, 68A D. Nguyen Hue (tel. 231 818), in Century Saigon Hotel. They're not kidding about the starlight. Vietnamese singers crank out Phil Collins and Madonna live amidst falling stars and whirling planets. More for the older crowd and business community. Thursday night is expat night. No cover charge, but you'll pay for it in the drinks. Open 6pm-2am.

Rosy Nightclub, 119 D. Nguyen Hue (tel. 224 378), to the left of Kim Do Hotel and opposite Century Saigon Hotel. Who needs a dance floor when boogie-ing on speakers is the fad? The semiformal dress (no shorts, no open shoes) doesn't stop anyone from getting wild. Cover 44,000Đ. Open 8pm-2am.

My Man, 27 D. Ngo Duc Ke (tel. 225 753). Claustrophobes shouldn't go past the entrance of this popular disco. Dance skin to skin with wealthy young Saigonese doing the MC Hammer in hardly a square foot of space. No roving hostesses. Cover 33,000Đ.

■■■ VUNG TAU

Two hours south of Saigon lies one of Vietnam's largest beach resorts. Although the beaches here can't boast fine white sand or crystal-clear waters, their location guarantees Vung Tau a booming tourist population year-round. Hang out on the beach and spend money; friendly locals are always ready to help a visitor dispose of cash. Massage parlors, prostitutes, and pickpockets lurk only a few steps away, and lucripetous costermongers specialize in parting partiers from their payola. In spite of these drawbacks, Vung Tau may still be your favorite fun-spot if you ignore the extra and unwanted "services" and seek out the town's halcyon hideaways.

ORIENTATION

Four beaches run the length of Vung Tau's peninsula: **Bai Dau** lies in a small alcove to the northwest of town; **Bai Truoc** (Front Beach) guards the shore in front of the town but is too rocky for swimming; **Bai Dua** lies on the coast south of Nui Nho; and **Bai Sau** (Back Beach) runs up the east coast. **Duong Tran Phu** traverses the coast from Bai Dau to the town, where it becomes **Duong Quang Trung.** Once past Bai Truoc, D. Quang Trung becomes **Duong Ha Long,** which extends to the point of the cape, curves northeast along Bai Sau, and mutates once again into **Duong Thuy Van. Duong Hoang Hoa Tham** connects Bai Truoc to Bai Sau.

PRACTICAL INFORMATION

Vung Tau's **tourist office** recently moved to 18 D. Thuy Van on Bai Sau. **Currency exchange** is available at **Vietcombank,** 27 D. Tran Hung Dao. Another bank waits down the street at 59 D. Tran Hung Dao; major hotels also exchange currency. The **post office** is at 4 D. Le Hong Phong. Place your **international phone calls** here, too (**telephone code:** 64). Buses to Saigon leave sporadically from a small **bus station** on D. Tran Hung Dao (roughly 10,000Đ). The town is so small that walking is the most viable option, but for those who'd prefer not to haul themselves to the beach most hotels and guest houses rent **bicycles** (average 5000Đ per day). The **airport** is 8km north of town on Hwy. 51A.

ACCOMMODATIONS AND CAMPING

Accommodations in Vung Tau are expensive, while the ones that fit the budget traveler's pocket are often former Russian compounds. Most of these cluster around the more popular beach areas of Bai Truoc and Bai Sau. Bai Truoc's conveniently located accommodations in town are more costly, but it's a long hike to the more pleasant beach at Bai Sau. Bai Dau and Bai Dua are tucked away from the hustle and bustle but lack decent accommodations and favorable swimming conditions.

Bai Truoc Nice accommodations here will be out of the budget traveler's reach; the establishments listed below are all former Russian compounds and equally institutional. **Hai Son,** 27 D. Le Loi (tel. 329 55), has good service and doubles with fan for 66,000Đ, with A/C 88-110,000Đ. **Thang Long,** 45 D. Thong Nhat (tel. 521 75) is a dapper place currently under renovation, so expect prices to increase in 1996. Singles and doubles with fan 110,000Đ. **Rang Dong,** 5 D. Duy Tan (tel. 521 33), is yet another former Russian compound. Sense a theme yet? Hold-it-yourself shower heads. Professional staff. All rooms have A/C and range in price from 121-220,000Đ. **Song Hong Hotel,** 12 D. Hoang Dieu (tel. 521 37; fax 524 52), is just around the corner from the Rang Dong, so don't blink. Looks like a Russian compound but offers great services and comfy living. All rooms have A/C, fridge, and TV. Singles 297,000Đ. Doubles 330,000Đ.

Bai Sau If your wallet is fast thinning out, there is a **campground** on D. Thuy Van to the right of #46. Reception is open 8am-4pm, and the price is only 3000Đ per person. Bring your own equipment. Or try one of the many budget bungalow-compounds along D. Thuy Van. **29 Thuy Van** (tel. 534 87) is located where you would imagine. Extremely polite and convivial family speaks great English. Popular with backpackers. Has a refreshing side yard. Less expensive rooms share toilet. Doubles 44-88,000Đ. **Bimexco** (tel. 599 16; fax 534 70), on D. Thuy Van, awaits you on the northern end of the beach. It's a tree-filled, quiet camp environment, but minimize contact with the indolent staff. Bathrooms are tiny and toilets sometimes leak, but it's still nicer than the other compounds. Rooms with fan 110-176,000Đ, with A/C 198-275,000Đ. Surcharge for weekend stays. **Hoa Hong Hotel** (tel. 536 75 or 526 33; fax 592 62) sits on Ngoc Tuoc Hill near the north end of D. Thuy Van. The cheapest room costs 330,000Đ. If you want to treat yourself for a night and be king of the hill, go to this secluded new villa.

Bai Dua **Bai Dua Villas,** 22 D. Ha Long (tel. 562 85), features incredible views of the sea from the terrace. Deluxe rooms with A/C and huge bathrooms with bath-tub 220-385,000Đ. **Nha Khach Nhgiep House o' Red** (tel. L-E-N-I-N), overlooking the sea. Tucked away from the din of Vung Tau's decadent capitalism. A few hour's hike with backpack in tow will lead to this haven for the masses. Each room, decorated in shades o' red, is named: Ho, Mao, Lenin. A reading room has all the essentials you'll need, from *Mao's Little Red Book* to *Das Kapital* to the *Marx-Engels Reader*. An enjoyable stay for all, even the staunchest Bob Dole. All singles with A/C a bargain at proletarian prices 25,000Đ. Early morning *tai chi* will quell those conservative yearnings.

FOOD

Hue Anh Restaurant, 446 D. Truong Cong Dinh, Bai Truoc. Seafood soaked in delicate sauces and aromatic herbs. You can't come here without savoring their excellent fish. Pleasant outdoor café under the trees. 30,000Đ per person.

Bai Dua Restaurant, 22 D. Ha Long, (tel. 562 81, ext.444), Bai Dua, at the tip of the peninsula. Much nicer than the Seaside Restaurant next door. This new structure, with its elegant Doric columns and red-tiled roof, sits on a terrace above the sea; so enjoy the cool breezes. Relax on the wicker furniture and live your colonial fantasies. Entrees 30,000Đ.

SIGHTS

There isn't much to do in Vung Tau aside from rolling in the sand and macerating in the water; this is a town for city denizens to loll about and escape their clangorous urban environment. With that in mind, those who'd like a break from the beaches should head to **Lang Ca Ong Pagoda** on D. Dinh Thang Tam. This three-building complex sits amidst verdant plants and surrounds a simple courtyard. The Pagoda was built in 1911 to honor the whale (not Moby Dick but his older, more friendly, Vietnamese cousin Ca Ong, Vung Tau's patron god) for protecting and rescuing men at sea. Open 7am-4pm.

Across the street is **Linh Son Co Tu Pagoda,** 61 D. Hoang Hoa Tham, more of a pastel-colored storybook cottage with scattered red lotuses than a 100-year-old pagoda. Twinkling Christmas lights adorn the rather embarrassed, velvet-clad Buddha. The courteous monks open the doors when you knock, usually 5am-10pm.

Move on up to the **Thich Ca Phat Dai Pagoda,** one of Vietnam's more famous sights. Built in 1961, this huge complex is dedicated to the Thich Ca Buddha, the god of creativity. The Buddha worship seems to have created a miraculous number of souvenir shops in the area around the pagoda, featuring paraphernalia of every type (purists will love the ever-popular Mary and Jesus souvenirs). Follow the winding, untended path through the complex; you'll see people making their way up the steep path to their plumbing-free huts. Statues of Buddhas, elephants, and monkeys adorn the road. The first pagoda, where the tangy smell of incense overwhelms you, houses the typical gold-clad Buddha and bell, but remains humble in its other furnishings. The top of the hill features a stunning view of the ocean. Open 6am-6pm.

Vung Tau has its share of large statues; the **Thich Ca Phat Dai,** a giant white statue of Buddha in the lotus position, meditates atop the hill at Bai Dau north of the U.S. Airforce Base. Christianity, not to be outdone, provides the graying **Statue of Saint Jacques**—*not* Jesus, as is often thought—atop Nui Nho at the top of the cape.

MEKONG DELTA

Although the Delta lacks officially organized services for tourists, as well as historical sights, backpack-laden adventurers will be greeted with up-close daily life of Vietnam. The pace of life plods on here as it always had for years, and the people remain largely unfazed by the encroachment of tourists. This is the agricultural region, the rice bowl of the country—with a good mix of fruits thrown in for color. Traversing the flat landscape of the Delta is a sight in itself; the land stretches out for miles in all directions, an endless horizon of pristine green cut through occasionally by rod-straight tributaries of the Mekong River. Can Tho is the largest city in the Delta, connected by Hwy. 1 to everywhere else. Roads tend to be smooth except in the deeper south near Rach Gia.

GETTING THERE AND AROUND

Buses to the Delta navigate ferry crossings with agility, loading themselves directly onto any requisite water transport. (Catch them in Saigon at the Ho Chi Minh City Mien Tay bus station.) More romantically inclined (but tougher) travelers should

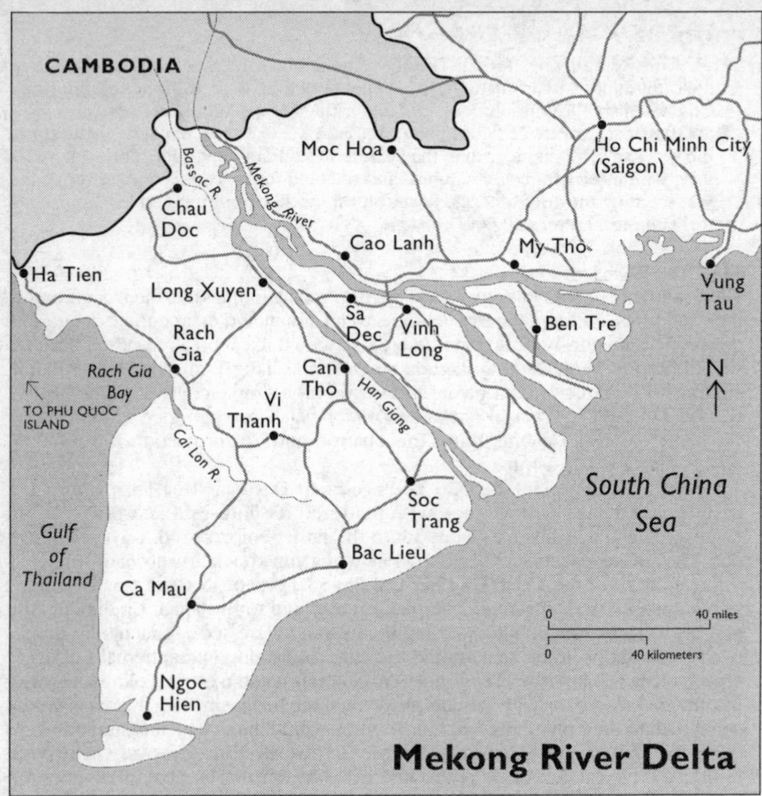

consider the slow, uncomfortable **ferries** from Saigon; boats are equipped with hammocks, but also tend to be wooden trading vessels powered by engines more noisy than a busload of pubescent schoolchildren. (About 30,000Đ.)

Once in the Delta, rent a **motorbike** or **bicycle** to get around within cities. Between cities, take buses or drive a motorcycle (the latter only if you're coordinated and fearless; bikers don't wear helmets in Vietnam). Roads are well cared for, so it'll be smooth sailing, er, driving, until Chau Doc. Because there is a lot of trading between Delta cities, **buses** are frequent and inexpensive. **Cyclos** in this region are slightly different from elsewhere in Vietnam: the driver sits in front and drives a motorcycle or bike while the passenger sits in a carriage in back. **Ferries** within the Delta region are mind-bogglingly slow; take food onto the boat if you go.

■■■ CAN THO

Can Tho is a good base for exploration into the Delta region. More than that, this wealthy, modern city offers a slice of Vietnamese life a la Saigon—but without the hectic pace. In fact, this Saigon-by-the-Rice-Paddies was a sleepy Delta town until foreign investors decided they needed an industrial center outside of Saigon; the development doesn't seem to have had any detrimental effects on the splendid scenery, while a relaxed pace adds to the city's overall charm. Wide boulevards make transit more convenient for the city's 400,000 inhabitants, and accommodate the rapidly growing industry and port.

ORIENTATION AND PRACTICAL INFORMATION

Even though Can Tho is one of the biggest Delta towns, that's not saying much. It would take some effort to get lost here. The city straddles the banks of the **Bassac (or Can Tho) River.** Its main thoroughfare is **Duong Hai Ba Trung,** which runs parallel to the river.

Tourist Office: Can Tho Tourism, 20 D. Hai Ba Trung (tel. 218 52 or 218 04; fax 227 19). Organizes tours to destinations throughout the Delta, and will welcome you with open arms and wide smiles. Open daily 7:10-11am and 1-5pm.

Currency Exchange: Vietcombank, 7 D. Hoa Binh (tel. 204 45; fax 206 94); **Exchange Bureau,** 27 D. Phan Dinh Phung (tel. 201 92), or hotels.

Post Office: 2 D. Hoa Binh (tel. 221 05). Open 6:30am-8pm. EMS and DHL service in the EMS building to the left of the post office (tel. 205 84 or 205 48). Open 6:30am-8pm.

Telephone Code: 71.

Ferries: Dock is 2.5km northwest of town on the corner of D. Hai Ba Trung and D. Ngo Quyen near the market. To **Ho Chi Minh City** (24hr., 20,000Đ). The local ferry is used by locals to visit relatives in more remote Delta destinations.

Tourist Boat Station: (tel. 218 52) at D. Hai Ba Trung on the quay before Ninh Kieu Hotel. A Gilligan-free, 3-hr. tour of the floating market and garden costs 30,000Đ per person. Boats usually take 5 people, even though they can accommodate many more. Trips run from 6am-3pm. Average rate 10,000Đ per person per hour.

Airline Office: Vietnam Airlines Booking Office, 20 D. Hai Ba Trung (tel. 218 53 or 218 04), is run by Can Tho Tourism (above).

Buses: The **bus station** (tel. 214 75 for info) is northwest of town on D. Nguyen Trai, near the intersection with D. Hung Vuong and Rte. 4. Frequent buses to Delta destinations (average 10,000Đ). Daily departures to: **Ho Chi Minh City** (3hr., 15,600Đ); **Dalat** (10hr., 38,600Đ); and **Nha Trang** (12hr., 48,800Đ). Open 3:30am-4:30pm.

Market: On D. Hai Ba Trung between D. Ngo Quyen and D. Chau Van Liem. Here you'll find food, vegetables, clothing, and the usual crush of locals.

Hospital: On the corner of D. Chau Van Liem and D. Hoa Binh.

ACCOMMODATIONS

Khai Hoan Hotel, 83 D. Chau Van Liem (tel. 244 19), offers clean, standard rooms for low prices. Shared toilets, but private showers. Squishy brown sofas await your weary body. Doubles with fan 40,000Đ.

Phong Nha Hotel, 75 D. Chau Van Liem (tel. 216 15). Popular with foreigners; amiable owner speaks decent English. Colorful neon lights attract backpackers at night like a bug zapper. Rooms are clean and comfortable. Doubles with fan 66-88,000Đ, with A/C 110,000Đ.

Can Bo 30 Guest House, 3 D. Hoa Binh (tel. 221 76), on a major street in the heart of the city; a little rough around the edges, but the place works hard to make guests happy. Manager Hung speaks great English and gives tours of Can Tho. Shared bathrooms. Doubles with fan 55-88,000Đ, with A/C 165,000Đ, hot water and a tub add 55,000Đ.

Hau Giang Hotel, 34 D. Nam Ky Khoi Nghia (tel. 218 51; fax 218 06), owned by Can Tho Tourist Company. Narrow lobby gives way to clean, basic rooms. Bathrooms shiny and new. A/C works too well. Doubles with fan 88,000Đ, with A/C 132,000Đ. Another location at 27 D. Chau Van Liem (tel. 216 36 or 219 50).

Can Tho Hotel, 14-16 D. Hai Ba Trung (tel. 222 18), on the riverfront. The dorm atmosphere and spartan, functional furnishings may not remind you of home, but the spaciousness and clean bathroom will serve well. Some rooms with river view. Doubles with fan 110,000Đ, with A/C 154,000Đ.

International Hotel, 12 D. Hai Ba Trung (tel. 220 79 or 220 80), offers a front-row view of daily trading life: noise, dust, friendly flies, and the pungent aroma of fish add a touch of authenticity. Out front are car and boat rentals, should you decide to roam. Doubles with fan 132,000Đ, with A/C 330-605,000Đ. Breakfast included.

Ninh Kieu Hotel, 2 D. Hai Ba Trung (tel. 245 83 or 252 85), at the end of the wharf. Helpful staff makes your stay more enjoyable and action-packed; the sign reads "We have all kinds of means to satisfy the Guests." Rooms are quiet, new, and many feature river views. There is also a restaurant to keep you vitamin-packed. All rooms have A/C 275-396,000Đ.

FOOD

Restaurants in Can Tho tend towards the functional rather than the fru-fru, but the food will definitely fill you. There is not a large selection of restaurants, but they all offer the same types of food. Specialties of the area include *lau* (seafood soup with vegetables), and *canh chua* (sour fish soup). Seafood is generally good and fresh.

Vinh Loi Restaurant, 42 D. Hai Ba Trung (tel. 211 24). If you wake up in the middle of the night with your tummy rumblin' for attention, stumble over to Vinh Loi. This greasy spoon features good food, average prices, friendly staff, and chirping locusts to make it go down just right. Rice with chicken or spareribs, or breakfast 6000Đ. Open all day, every day.

Thien Hoa Restaurant, 26 D. Hai Ba Trung (tel. 219 42). Friendly servers offer a comprehensive and mouth-watering menu of seafood dishes. Chinese stewed shrimp is the specialty. All entrees less that 15,000Đ. Open 9:30am-midnight.

Ninh Kieu Restaurant, 2 D. Hai Ba Trung (tel. 211 04 or 211 71), in Ninh Kieu Hotel. The high ceilings, water view, open-air terrace, and exclusive ambience are almost as good for the soul as the food. Your dishes are made to order, with any mixtures of yummy morsels like veal, beefsteak, and roast chicken. Full bar. Entrees run 20,000-30,000Đ.Open 6:30am-10pm.

A Chau Restaurant, 91 D. Chau Van Liem (tel. 221 30). A huge restaurant with two floors; they give you map at the door so you don't get lost. A/C will keep you cool if you do. Grilled snake for three only 50,000Đ, grilled shrimp 30,000Đ, and the rather incongruous beef and fries at 10,000Đ. Open daily 7am-9pm.

California Ice Cream, 18 D. Hoa Binh. Not quite Ben and Jerry's, but enough to remind you of home. They claim the ice cream is imported from America, but the only thing that might have arrived from those foreign shores is the machine. Teeny tiny dish 3000Đ. Open 8am-10pm.

SIGHTS

You're probably not in the Delta to see more pagodas, but if you want to wander through Can Tho, head to the **Munirangsyaram Pagoda,** 36 D. Hoa Binh. This gaudy Khmer Hinayana Buddhist Sanctuary was built by Cambodian Khmers; it has distinctive detail carvings and a slender design. Steep steps up to the temple entrance may make you dizzy, by the Thich Ca Buddha inside will calm your seasick soul. Uncrowded. Open 6am-5pm. The **Vang Pagoda,** also on D. Hoa Binh is an unexceptional town pagoda.

Ho Chi Minh Museum, on D. Hoa Binh to the left of post office, awaits anyone still not saturated with socialist sights, but may not satisfy the seeker; the museum remains in a state of disrepair, with random construction materials scattered amongst the displays. Supposedly open 7am-4pm, but the sleeping guard may ignore your knocks if they come during his 4-hr. midday nap; free. The brand new **Weapons Museum** behind the Ho Chi Minh Museum features canons, surface-to-air missile launchers, and a hollowed-out Huey helicopter. As if anyone needed any more reminders of war around here.

Can Tho Park at the intersection of D. Chau Van Liem and D. Hoa Binh has a friendly ferris wheel and an appealing patch of greenery. It's a welcome break from the concrete of the city; come here to watch the submarine races.

Other waterside activities include hopping a boat to the **Floating Market** at Phung Hiep. Browse through the stall and look for Delta souvenirs; just be careful that you don't fall into the water—when you see it you'll know why. The town's regulation issue 7-m high **statue of Bac Ho** (Uncle Ho) stands in a salute on the quay and is soooo much bigger than you.

■ NEAR CAN THO: LONG XUYEN

Long Xuyen is yet another transit town in the Mekong Delta; you'll pass through here with 54km to travel before reaching Chau Doc. In spite of the town's lack of tourist appeal, it is the capital of An Giang Province and for some strange reason, home to the tourist office for Chau Doc. The **bus station** i sits across the street from 96 D. Tran Hung Dao. If you need a change of venue, hop the **ferry** at 86 D. Tran Hung Dao. Look for the red sign with an arrow pointing down a side street, and walk down the street for about 20m. Ferries to Chau Doc leave at 4am (11hr., 60,000Đ). That regional **tourist office** we mentioned eagerly awaits you at 83-85 D. Nguyen Hue (tel. 520 36). Get all the information you can for Chau Doc, because there isn't a tourist office there. They also organize tours to destinations throughout Delta. Open 8am-4pm.

■■■ CHAU DOC

Chau Doc is 117km away from Can Tho, and arguably the most popular destination in the Delta. This beautiful town on the Cambodian border offers cool breezes, green parks, and an open invitation to stroll; the pace here is even slower than in Hoi An. A small Chinese population lives here, and the Khmer women of the area wear scarves on their heads rather than the usual straw hats. While Chau Doc's proximity to the border raises questions about smuggling organizations, a more important tourist activity involves making the pilgrimage to the Buddhist Pagoda of Lady Xu on Nui Sam Mountain.

ORIENTATION

Chau Doc, like Can Tho, requires no map to get around; the city, lying on the southern bank of the **Hau River,** is an organized grid of streets, and so small that all distances are easily navigated on foot. **Duong Gia Long/Le Loi** runs the length of the shore. The grassy area in the center of town is actually a garden where you can admire the Christmas tree lights on the pagoda; the town **market** is a little north of here, sandwiched between **Duong Bach Dang** and **Duong Chi Lang.**

PRACTICAL INFORMATION

Currency Exchange: Chau Doc Bank, on the corner of D. Nguyen Huu Canh and D. Phan Van Vang. Open Mon.-Fri. 7-11am and 1-4pm.

Post Office/Telephone: GPO, 73 D. Le Loi (tel. 661 91 or 661 93). Make those calls inside. **Telephone code** is 76.

Buses: The **bus terminal** lies south east of town at the intersection of Hwy. 91 and D. Le Loi, but you can inquire at hotels for **minibus** services (see below).

Ferry: The **ferry terminal** is a little closer to town at 427 D. Le Loi; a crossing to the other side of the river runs 500Đ. Open 5am-7pm. Also leaves from the **wharf** on D. Ton Duc Thang. To **Ho Chi Minh City** (15,000Đ).

ACCOMMODATIONS

Thanh Tra Hotel, 77 D. Thu Khoa Nghia (tel. 667 88 or 668 45). Quiet with a peaceful enclosed courtyard and a huge, brightly lit lobby. Rooms are basic but clean, and the bathrooms will please with their shininess. Ask the savvy maid where to eat in town. Doubles with fan 60,000Đ, with A/C 100,000Đ.

Tai Thanh Hotel, at 86 D. Bach Dang (tel. 661 47), may look a little dilapidated and have somewhat cramped rooms (just enough room for the bed), but the spotless bathrooms will make up for it all. Doubles with fan 50,000-60,000Đ. Quads 70-80,000Đ. No A/C.

Chau Doc Hotel, 17 D. Doc Phu Thu (tel. 664 84), has humongous rooms and spotless hallways that almost allow you to forgive the seatless toilets and leaky plumbing. Doubles with shared bathroom 50,000Đ, with fan and private bathroom 60,000Đ, with A/C 100-130,000Đ.

Hoa Lan Hotel, 60 D. Nguyen Huu Canh (tel. 664 82), offers big rooms with shared, Turkish-style toilets. Sterile shower stalls complete the less-than-satisfying bath experience. Doubles with fans only 30-60,000Đ.

FOOD

Intense competition between restaurants in Chau Doc means that prices are similar between restaurants; in general, food in Chau Doc is cheap and averages 15,000Đ per entree for two. Most of the good joints concentrate on D. Chi Lang, so head on down and watch them fight over you. All open from around 9am-9pm.

Lam Hung Ky, 71 D. Chi Lang (tel. 667 45), the cleanest and best looking restaurant on the block. Excellent food here.

Hong Phat, 77 D. Chi Lang (tel. 669 50), where chatty servers will eventually bring you your tasty food.

Restaurant 88, 88 D. Doc Phu Thu (tel. 668 43), has a great location in Chau Doc Square opposite the public gardens. Polite service, good-size portions, excellent food, and rare delicacies like snake, turtle, and bird (order one hr. ahead) make this a great place to chow down.

Truong Van Restaurant, 15 D. Quang Trung (tel. 665 67 or 674 32) also has a good reputation with the locals.

SIGHTS

The "Famed Beauty Spot" and primo pilgrimage point of **Nui Sam Mountain** lies 5km from town. The Lady Xu Temple was built here in early 19th century when Lady Xu's holy statue was found atop the mountain. (The truly dedicated can look for Lady Xu's original pedestal; it's still there.) The people of the nearby Vinh Te Village moved her to her current abode, but had to rebuild it in 1972 because of structural problems. (You would think the goddess of longevity could take care of herself, but those jungle termites are vicious.) Curved roofs covered with glazed tiles currently shelter the red statue and her monstrously large headdress from the elements. The Lady even gets bathed by the faithful in the Tam Ba (Bathing the Lady) Ceremony. The 23-25th days of the fourth lunar month are the Lady's official pilgrimage days. These days the Lady presides over theater performances in the compound, and visitors may run across the odd honorary graduation ceremony.

■ RACH GIA AND PHU QUOC ISLAND

Think about the port town of **Rach Gia** as a transit point to the more idyllic, relaxing beach resort on Phu Quoc Island. The dusty town has nurtured some new hotels due to tourist traffic; this is the only point from which foreigners can get to Phu Quoc Island. The **Kein Giang tourist office,** 12 D. Ly Tu Trong (tel. 620 81; fax 621 11), can help plan your stay in Phu Quoc. Open Mon.-Sat. 7-11am and 1-5pm. If you must stay here overnight, crash at the **Chau Hotel,** 4F D. Le Loi (tel. 673 18). The standard rooms will tide you over until you can move on. Doubles with fan 77-121,000Đ; with A/C, TV, and hot water 154-275,000Đ. If you just can't curb your appetite, grab a bite at the **Tai Tam Restaurant,** 12 D. Tran Phu, across from Lao Dong Cultural House. The staff are a little reticent, but the food will be all you need.

Phu Quoc Island is an island resort where no street names or addresses are necessary; just let your feet do the navigating and you'll be fine. Why stress? You're here on vacation, after all. While the island's nationality is contested by Cambodia and Thailand, and real-estate developers chortle lasciviously with hotel plans in mind, your personal trial will be deciding where to lay your towel. The only town prepared for tourists is the tiny **Duong Dong Town,** so make sure your boat goes to this destination: if you debark at another part of the island you could be faced with a 2-hr. commute to Duong Dong. The **tourist office** in town is also a guest house, **Huong Bien Guest House** (tel. 460 50). Rooms run 132-187,000Đ. If you really must escape from or get back to reality, **Vietnam Airlines** flies from Ho Chi Minh City to Duong Dong every Wednesday and Saturday (715,000Đ one way).

WESTERN INDONESIA

Indonesia's national motto, the Old Javanese phrase *"bhinneka tunggal ika,"* translates to "unity in diversity." The country's diversity is readily apparent; over 350 ethnic groups have absorbed centuries of peaceful and imperialistic influences from at home and abroad. The unity of Southeast Asia's largest nation rests upon a common heritage of subjugation by and nationalist resistance against the Dutch. Having celebrated 50 years of independence in 1995, a younger generation with no memory of this heritage knows a nation held together by its "benevolent dictator," President Soeharto and his military New Order government. While Indonesia's diversity is a source of pride for nearly all its people, its tenuous unity is maintained through political repression and unspoken threats of violence by the New Order since its rise to power in 1965-66. The resulting stability has brought increased prosperity: foreign investments keep rolling in as per capita income rises and growth rates run at a yearly clip of 6-7% or higher. The New Order gains respect and legitimacy from the people for its dedicated improvements in education and public health.

Visitors to Western Indonesia (Sumatra, Java, and Bali) are justly rewarded for their perseverance in a country where little English is spoken and independent travel can be confusing and frustrating. Having even a few words of Bahasa Indonesia under your belt will help you make a genuine connection with the people. An Indonesian friend will reveal the sides of Indonesian life that tourists rarely see. A personal tour through the Jakarta morass, a visit to a Balinese village, or a late-night chat over *jagung bakar* (grilled corn) at a streetside eatery in Yogyakarta will stand prominently beside memories of clamoring over the colossal Borobudur, surfing those killer waves of Bali and Nias, or hiking the moonscape craters of Mt. Bromo. The observant traveler to Indonesia will not only be captured by a kaleidoscope collection of adaptable cultures, stunning landscapes, and historical legacies, but also be touched by the spirited laughter, deep tolerance, and muted sorrows of a people moving through everyday life in this vast, provocative nation.

ESSENTIALS

■■■ GEOGRAPHY

Measuring 5150km from east to west, Indonesia constitutes the world's largest archipelago. Stretching between the Australian and Asian mainlands, these islands divide the Pacific and Indian Oceans at the Equator. The country comprises an estimated 17,508 islands, though only about 6000 are inhabited. Many of the islands have volcanoes—active, extinct, or dormant—and large regions of dense jungles.

■■■ WHEN TO GO

When you come to Indonesia should depend on whether you like it dry or wet. Though areas near the equator receive fairly consistent amounts of rain year-round, other regions have pronounced wet and dry seasons. Dry weather comes with the East Monsoon from June to Aug/September; the West Monsoon from Nov/December to Feb/March brings rain (varying amounts in different regions). The humidity (75-100%) and the temperature (21-32°C or 70-90°F) remain fairly stable year round (higher altitudes can get much colder). You may also want to plan your trip around festivals and holidays.

■■■ GETTING AROUND

Any entry and exit without a special visa must be made through specific gateways: by air at Jakarta, Bali, Medan, Manado, Biak, Ambon, Surabaya, and Batam; by sea at Semarang, Jakarta, Bali, Pontianak, Balikpapan, Tajung Pinang, and Kupang.

BY PLANE

Air travel is the easiest, most comfortable way to get around Indonesia. National carriers **Garuda** and **Merpati** run to all provincial district capitals. Garuda's Visit Indonesia Air Passes give special fares on domestic flights; buy a pass from a Garuda office in USA, Europe, Australia, or Japan. Other domestic airlines include **Sempati, Bouraq,** and **Mandala.** Airport tax for international flights is Rp21,000; for domestic travel tax varies but averages about Rp8000.

BY SEA

Government-owned PELNI ships serve all main points in Indonesia (bi-weekly) with A/C but spartan accommodations, basic food, slow journeys, and mediocre prices. Reserve ahead (office on Jl. Angkasa, Jakarta). To smaller ports, PELNI operates less comfortable Pelayran Perintis, with deck class only. Ferries also run between islands. Alternatively, with a letter of permission from your embassy and a willing schooner, you may sometimes be able to hop on a boat for free.

BY TRAIN OR BUS

Trains run only in Java and parts of Sumatra, and are often slow and delayed, but are sometimes your best bet for long trips. Reserve in advance. Most locals get around by bus; though often slow, overcrowded, and unpredictable, buses are cheap. Overnight buses (*bis malam*) are usually faster but arrive at inconvenient hours.

BY CAR, TAXI, OR MOTORBIKE

You can hire a car with or without a driver; the former (mostly available in major cities) are Rp75-120,000 per day, and the latter are about Rp8-10,000 per hr. (more for out-of-town). Catch taxis, metered in large cities, around busy public places. On major routes, share-taxis carry 5 passengers. Registered taxis, minibuses, and hired cars have yellow license plates (private vehicles have black plates, government vehicles have red). Motorbikes and motorcycles run Rp12-25,000 per day.

OTHER LOCAL TRANSPORTATION

Other forms of transport include the **becak** (bicycle rickshaw), **bajaj** (orange motorized three-wheeler), **bemo** (minibus), **oplet** (a larger form of bemo, a.k.a. **daihatsu, angkutan, angkot, microlet, sudako,** or **colt**), **ojeks** (motorcycle taxis), and **andong** (horse-drawn carts).

■■■ MONEY

US$1=2237.14rupiah (Rp)	**Rp100=US$0.045**
CDN$=Rp1645.64	**Rp100=CDN$0.061**
UK£1=Rp3476.51	**Rp100=UK£0.029**
IR£1=Rp3543.62	**Rp100=IR£0.028**
AUS$1=Rp1649.22	**Rp100=AUS$0.061**
NZ$1=Rp1467.11	**Rp100=NZ$0.068**
SARand=Rp611.86	**Rp100=SARand0.163**

The Indonesian unit of currency is the **rupiah.** Coin denominations are Rp25, Rp50, Rp100, and Rp500; notes come in Rp100, Rp500, Rp1000, Rp5000, Rp10,000, Rp20,000, and Rp50,000. The US$ is the most readily accepted currency (both cash and traveler's checks). You can change traveler's checks at banks (particularly main branches), money changers (often better rates than banks), and some hotels (variable rates). Only major hotels, restaurants, and travel agencies accept credit cards.

Bills at major hotels usually include a 10% **service charge. Gratuity** is not expected, but a 5-10% tip is always appreciated. Tips for taxi and hire-car drivers are not necessary, but for satisfactory service Rp1000 is appropriate for a taxi, and a bit more for a hire-car. At the airport, give porters Rp2000 for a small bag, Rp3000 for one that weighs more than 20kg.

■■■ KEEPING IN TOUCH

Indonesia's postal service is not terribly reliable—**register important mail.** Check in Practical Information listings of any city to see if its post office holds Poste Restante. For **telephone calls,** medium to large towns have Perumtel or Wartel offices, which often also send faxes. Major cities and several hotels in Bali and Jakarta have IDD. For an overseas operator: British Telecom, 001-801-44. Canada Direct: 001-801-16. New Zealand Telecom, 62-178-6400. Telecom Australia, 008-0161. US, AT&T: 001-801-10; MCI: 001-801-11; Sprint: 001-801-15. Long-distance calls within Indonesia can be direct-dialed (0 + city code + destination number). *Let's Go* lists telephone codes in the Practical Information sections.

THE MEDIA

The national radio network, Radio Republik Indonesia, has stations throughout Indonesia and broadcasts about one hour of English-language news and commentary per day; there are also about 900 private stations. In addition, most areas in Indonesia receive some TV. State-controlled TVRI, based in Jakarta, broadcasts to stations in nine cities; each of these also shows local events and news. Another network, though subject to state censors, is private and runs its own programming. Many hotels receive programs from the Philippines, Singapore, Thailand, and Malaysia; some large hotels also have CNN news. Tourists may freely use private video cameras, except in certain areas where restrictions apply. An annual quota limits the importation of foreign movies and helps encourage domestic film production; in 1993, more than 450 national feature films were produced. About seven million newspapers and magazines circulate daily through Indonesia. Jakarta's English-language dailies are the *Jakarta Post, Indonesia Times,* and *Indonesia Observer/Sunday Observer.* International publications available in major cities include the *International Herald Tribune,* the *Economist, Time,* and *Newsweek.*

■■■ STAYING SAFE

On all the islands, you can call **emergency police** at 110 and an **ambulance** at 118. Although Indonesia is generally safe and violence is rare, young single women should be cautious; western women in particular are often seen as easy targets for harassment. Beware of pickpockets, particularly on public transportation; carry all valuables in a moneybelt and avoid toting large amounts of cash. Also watch out for the scams prevalent in tourist areas—be skeptical of limited-time-only "bargains."

BISEXUAL, GAY, LESBIAN TRAVELERS

Although a certain degree of homophobia has taken root in the western-oriented middle class, homosexual acts are legal, and some men maintain sexual relationships with other men. However, public displays of affection are not advisable for *any* couples, straight or gay. Defying categories assigned by the west, Indonesia has its own alternate gender, known as *waria,* and defined as a man with the soul of a woman. While not wholly accepted by Indonesian society, *waria* participate in a subculture of their own, and common knowledge about *waria* among the Indonesian population at large is growing (see "Waria" on page 717). Though no laws deal specifically with AIDS or HIV, affected persons may be denied entry or even quarantined under certain other restrictions. For more information on Indonesia's fledgling gay and lesbian scene, *waria* communities, and AIDS activism in Indonesia, pick up a copy of *GAYa Nusantara,* a 'zine published in Surabaya. Check the Practical Information listings of Jakarta, Bandung, Yogyakarta, Surabaya, Malang, and Denpasar for locales where this publication is sold.

■■■ HOURS AND HOLIDAYS

Generally, businesses are open 8am-4pm or 9am-5pm, breaking for lunch between noon and 1pm; many are closed on Saturday. Government offices are open Mon.-Thurs. 8am-3pm, Fri. 8-11am, Sat. 8am-2pm. Though normal banking hours are Mon.-Fri. 8am-2:30pm and Sat. 8am-noon, some branches in hotels have longer hours. Department stores and supermarkets in the large cities are typically open 9am-9pm, with shorter hours on Sun. Shops in smaller cities may close 1-5pm.

When planning a trip, you may want to keep in mind public holidays and festivals. Approximate dates for 1996 events are listed when possible; keep in mind that associated celebrations may occur on different dates in different countries.

January 1: New Year's. Celebrated with the most fervor in Christian areas.
Jan/Feb: Al Miraj. The archangel leads Muhammad through the 7 heavens.
February 19: Imlek, Chinese New Year. Many businesses close for 2 days or more.
March 1: Idul Fitri. The end of Ramadan (month-long Muslim fast).
March/April (spring equinox): Nyepi, Balinese Saka New Year, a day of total silence and stillness. The day before, sacrifices are made and priests chant mantras; at night families bang cymbals and parade with torches.
March/April: Wafat Isa Al-Masih (Good Friday).
April 21: Kartini Day. Birthday of Raden Ajeng Kartini, pioneer of the fledgling women's rights movement in Indonesia. Women dress in national dress; husbands and kids are supposed to pamper them.
May: Waisak Day (Buddha's birth/death date). Monks carry flowers, candles, fire, and images of the Buddha from Candi Mendut (outside Yogyakarta) to Borobudur.
May: Kenaikan Isa Al-Masih (ascension of Christ).
May 20: Tahun Baru Hijriyah (Islamic New Year).
May-June: Idul Adha. A Muslim day of sacrifice, commemorated with mass prayers. Animals are sacrificed and the meat given to the needy.
August 22: Maulid Nabi Muhammad (birthday of Muhammad).
August 17: Indonesia Independence Day. The most important national holiday, marked by dancing, processions, and other festivities.
October 1: Hari Pancasila. Celebrates Soekarno's five principles (see page 640).
October 5: Armed Forces Day. Anniversary of the founding of the Indonesian Armed Forces. Celebrated with military parades and demonstrations.
December: Isra Mi'raj Nabi Muhammad SAW (Ascension of Muhammad).
December 25: Hari Raya Natal (Christmas Day).

■■■ POTPOURRI FOR $100, ALEX!

DATE AND TIME

Indonesia extends over 3 time zones. Eastern Indonesia Standard Time (Maluku and Irian Jaya) is 9hrs. ahead of GMT; Central Standard Time (East and South Kalimantan, Sulawesi, Bali, and Nusa Tenggara) is 8hrs. ahead of GMT; Western Standard Time (Sumatra, Java, Madura, and West and Central Kalimantan) is 7hrs. ahead of GMT.

A STREET BY ANY OTHER NAME

Most streets in Indonesia are labeled as **jalan** (as in Jalan A. Yani), usually abbreviated as **Jl.** Small walkways and alleys off a street are usually called **gang,** abbreviated as **Gg.** Gang addresses are often labeled first by the jalan it is attached to, followed by the name of the gang and the house number.

Let's Go regularly uses a few other words in Bahasa Indonesia. Instead of bathrooms (Indonesia has none) one uses a **mandi,** which has either a sit-down or a squat toilet, and a tub of water; scoop water from the tub with a hand-held bucket, and pour it over yourself. The word **gunung** means mountain, and there are many worth climbing on the **pulau** (islands) of Indonesia. **Danau** means lake and **pantai** means beach. An **alun-alun** is a town square, **wartel** is a telephone office, and **pasar** is a market; there are several in every major town. Hang out and memorize these words over a snack at a **warung** (a makeshift street-side restaurant) or at your **losmen** (cheap hotels).

LIFE AND TIMES

■■■ HISTORY

PREHISTORY

Fossils discovered at Trinil, Mojokerto, and Sangiran in the past century have distinguished the region of Central Java as one of the earliest sites of hominid occupation outside of Africa. Discoveries of similar fossils in East Asia and Africa confirmed that **"Java Man"**—with a characteristic low-vaulted, thick-walled skullcap and large browridges—is within the species *Homo erectus.* While it is generally agreed that *Homo erectus* is an evolutionary predecessor of modern humans, it is not true that Java Man evolved into the various Malay peoples that exist today in Indonesia. Rather, *Homo erectus* probably died out in Java about 350,000 years ago, while modern humans evolved from hominid populations in Africa and migrated in waves to repopulate Java Man's former home.

EARLY HINDU-BUDDHIST KINGDOMS

The earliest and perhaps most significant polity of pre-colonial history was the maritime kingdom of **Srivijaya.** Little physical evidence remains of its former glory, but most scholars agree that the seat of Srivijaya's power was in and around Palembang in Southern Sumatra from the 7th to 14th centuries, reaching its peak around the turn of the millennia. Manuscripts from China, the Middle East, and India all mention this prosperous maritime empire, which comprised all of Sumatra, the Kra peninsula, West Java, and parts of Borneo. Srivijaya's enigmatic lack of physical remains may be partly explained by its religion, an early form of **Buddhism,** which did not require monumental stone temples honoring a pantheon of deities; another major factor may have been the swampy geography of the southeast coast of Sumatra. Despite the lack of evidence on Srivijaya, there is little dispute over the kingdom's lasting impact on the western Indonesian archipelago. Its language and courtly culture spread out over the islands roughly at this time, bringing Sumatra, Malaya, the Riau archipelago, and the coastal regions of Indonesia's other islands into the same linguistic and cultural sphere. Srivijaya began to decline following an attack led by a bitter prince from south India, who felt that the kingdom's trade regulations were exploiting the trading interests of his merchants.

Outside Srivijaya's control, a succession of neighboring kingdoms in Central Java gained prosperity not through trade but through intensive agrarian production. From the 8th through 10th centuries, the Mahayana Buddhist kingdom of **Sailendra** ruled in Central Java. This dynasty—descended from Funanese migrants who fled south Vietnam and Cambodia at the rise of the Chenla kingdom—is responsible for the magnificent **Borobudur,** the world's largest Buddhist stupa. At its height, the Sailendra kingdom reconquered parts of Indochina, ending the Chenla dynasty there (dynastic revenge! Better than *Dallas*!). Sailendra maintained cordial relations with Srivijaya through marriage alliances.

Contemporaneous with Sailendra, the **Hindu** kingdom of **Sanjaya** also ruled in Central Java. Known for its own gargantuan monuments of a Shaivite Hindu variety (such as the temples of **Prambanan**), Sanjaya attained its wealth through control of international trade routes throughout the archipelago as far east as the Moluccas (Maluku). Perhaps it was Sanjaya's maritime nature that allowed for peaceful coexistence with the agrarian-based Sailendra kingdom. Disputes over control of the Straits of Melaka brought Sanjaya into conflict with Srivijaya, who attacked Sanjaya's capital in 1006 and brought an end to Sanjaya's majesty.

Central Javanese dominance and its prodigious architecture came to an abrupt halt at the beginning of the 10th century, and the focus of Javanese power suddenly shifted to the east (most likely due to a violent eruption of Mt. Merapi). Sanjaya degenerated into a series of short-lived and divided dynasties: **Kediri and Janggala** (1050-1222) and **Singasari** (1222-1292). Indonesia's last great Hindu-Buddhist kingdom was the **Majapahit** empire, centered at Trowulan in East Java. It reigned from 1292 until 1478 and spanned most of the archipelago—including the Malay peninsula—with contacts throughout mainland Southeast Asia. Majapahit is pragmatically remembered and honored by modern Indonesia as the kingdom that unified the archipelago under one rule, thus justifying an Indonesian entity even before the arrival of the Dutch. Majapahit's greatest rulers, **Hayam Wuruk** (the king) and **Gajah Mada** (his Prime Minister) are memorialized for fostering Java's "Golden Age," the height of Indonesian arts and power. Majapahit's glory was ultimately usurped by the Sultan of Melaka, and the weakened kingdom fell to the Sultan of Demak. The royal court fled to **Bali,** which today remains the last surviving outpost of Indonesia's great Hindu-Buddhist traditions.

THE RISE OF ISLAMIC SULTANATES

As early as the 7th century, the Indonesian archipelago was introduced to **Islam** through contact with Arab and Indian Muslim traders. However, the first Muslim communities did not appear until the 13th century, when records show the existence of sultanates along the north coasts of Sumatra facing the Straits of Melaka. These small trading communities soon became centralized beneath the state of **Aceh,** a staunchly independent sultanate whose capital city of **Banda Aceh** rose to prominence in the 17th century as an international trading port and learning center.

From Northern Sumatra, Islam spread through the entire island, and eventually to Java and as far east as Maluku and the southern Philippine islands. Sultanate states arose along major trade routes throughout the archipelago in those areas that weren't dominated by Hindu-Buddhist traditions. The spread of Islam on Java is associated with the legendary **wali songo** (nine saints) who brought Mohammed's teachings to the island. A series of sultanates arose along the north coast of Java during the 15th and 16th centuries. In inland areas, where diluted Hindu-Buddhist traditions still prevailed, Islam spread more slowly.

Islam successfully penetrated inland Java with the rise of the **Mataram Kingdom,** ruled by **Sultan Agung** (1613-1645) and located between Surakarta and Yogyakarta. The last of the Java's great kingdoms, Sultan Agung united nearly all of Java except the prosperous trading port of Batavia (Jakarta) where the Dutch had begun to establish themselves. While Sultan Agung cultivated the growth of Islam, the religion became a curious syncretism of preexisting Hindu-Buddhist and Javanese traditions with a Muslim veneer. For example, although Sultan Agung was not a god-king of former Hindu-Buddhist empires, he was considered to be endowed with divine qualities; in addition, the courtly arrangements greatly reflected Hindu-Buddhist cosmology, which places the king, his palace, and his city in the center of the universe.

THE COLONIAL ERA

In 1511, the **Portuguese** arrived in Indonesia searching for lucrative spices and spreading the good news of **Catholicism.** They were primarily interested in trade, and today the Portuguese legacy consists merely a few fort ruins in the eastern islands of Maluku, the incorporation of some vocabulary into the Malay language, and a few pockets of Catholic communities such as those in Flores and Timor.

The first **Dutch** ships arrived in 1596 in search of trade prospects. In 1692, private investors organized **Vereenigde Oost-Indische Compagnie (VOC)** to monitor and regulate Dutch trade interests in the archipelago. Within 10 years, through military force and exploitative diplomacy, the VOC had gained a monopoly on all trade in the region. As powerful outsiders, the Dutch were brought in to settle disputes between local dynasties, creating power imbalances; the local aristocracy became increasingly dependent on Dutch "favors." Whenever they saw a chance to solidify the VOC hegemony, the Dutch employed "divide and subjugate" tactics.

In 1799, the corrupt VOC went bankrupt and the government stepped in to pursue an official colonization of the **Dutch East Indies.** Soon Dutch interest in the East Indies far exceeded trade control; production was now in the hands of the Dutch with over 2000 estates set up across the islands. A whole bureaucracy and administration was set up, along with a caste system which kept the "natives" effectively separated from the Dutch ruling elite. Local rulers willing to comply with Dutch policies served as middlemen between colonial officials and the masses slaving away on plantations. Colonial rule was centralized on Java; complete control over the outer islands took longer, especially in rebellious areas such as Aceh and Bali.

At the dawn of the 20th century, collective Dutch guilt over the massive wealth extracted from the islands and the living conditions suffered by the Indonesian people led to the creation of the **Ethical Policy,** a new colonial policy that took into account the welfare of the native population. No longer content to exploit the Indonesians for cheap labor alone, the Dutch implemented educational and public health reforms to create a smarter, healthier populace that would be able to afford Dutch imports. The early 20th century was also a time of intensive investment in the outer islands and greater inter-connectedness between the islands. Java, increasingly overtaxed and overpopulated, became dependent on the wealth of the outer islands.

The Ethical Policy did bring some Indonesians closer to European ideas. Educated Indonesians, particularly among the Javanese and Minangkabau of West Sumatra, started organizing amongst themselves on the basis of religious or ethnic identity and political ideology. Trade cooperatives, communist parties, and various other organizations—some Islamic, some ethnic, and some elite—became vehicles for political action, and often presented grievances to the Dutch. Yet their special interests frequently conflicted with each other, and no united nationalist movement emerged at this time.

REVOLUTION AND INDEPENDENCE

The stage was set for the rise of the **Partai Nasional Indonesia (PNI),** the Indonesian Nationalist Party, founded in 1927 and headed by the virile **Soekarno.** Ever charismatic, Soekarno espoused a nationalist ideology that subordinated all other ideologies to the cause of a united and independent Indonesia. On this point most people could agree, and the PNI drew support from the educated elite, villages, Marxists, Christians, minority groups, and Muslims. In 1929, Soekarno was arrested for his fiery anticolonial rhetoric and sentenced to four years in prison in Bandung. During the worldwide Great Depression, the Dutch were no longer willing to keep the terms of their Ethical Policy, and oppression became their renewed pastime. Around this time, nationalists systematically employed the Malay language and renamed it **Bahasa Indonesia** (Indonesian Language) in an effort to create greater unity among the islands. Soekarno was released early in December of 1931 but was arrested again two years later and exiled to the island of Flores without trial. He was later transferred to Bengkulu, where he lived under house arrest from 1938 until the **Japanese invasion** during World War II.

On March 8, 1942, the Dutch surrendered to Japan in the East Indies, bringing an end to 350 years of Dutch rule over the islands. Most Indonesians welcomed the Japanese for liberating them from the European oppressors, but everyone soon discovered that Indonesia's incorporation into the **Greater East Asia Co-Prosperity Sphere** was a fate far worse than Dutch rule had ever been. After three and a half years of the most brutal colonial regime to occupy Indonesia, the Japanese surrendered to the Allies on August 15, 1945, leaving behind a highly politicized nation unwilling to tolerate the demands of colonialism any longer.

Soekarno had collaborated with the Japanese in order to ensure the survival of Indonesian nationalism. Anxious to take charge before the return of the Europeans, he declared independence on August 17. The Dutch returned hoping to restore their former colonial empire, and were surprised to confront a mobilized and chaotic population willing to go to war for the independence of their newly declared **Republik Indonesia.**

The **Indonesian Revolution** lasted from 1945 until 1950 and unified the nation against the Dutch, but did little else. The fledgling republican government was plagued with internal disputes, especially between the **Indonesian Communist Party (PKI),** the **Nationalists** and their ragtag military, and a variety of **Islamic parties.** Ideological disputes were barely set aside for the sake of fighting the Dutch. By the fifth anniversary of Soekarno's declaration of independence, the Dutch—embarrassed by the continued conflict in which the international community sympathized with the Indonesians—officially transferred sovereignty to the young republic.

Soekarno wrote the **Pancasila,** or "five principles," which has been the ideological basis of the Indonesian constitution since independence. The five principles are: **belief in God, nationalism, humanitarianism, social justice, and democracy.** The definition of these terms was ambiguous enough that the various governments over which Soekarno presided could basically carry out whatever policies he called for. From 1950 to 1957, Soekarno tried to form a government based on **representative democracy.** Those years were the most politically free period in Indonesia's history, but in a nation that was largely poor and illiterate, the result was corruption and stagnation; political differences within the fractious government led nowhere.

By 1957, after several regional rebellions and the onset of a failing economy, Soekarno announced his new concept of **"Guided Democracy,"** which gave the president more dictatorial powers. Guided Democracy accomplished nothing, but it did keep Soekarno in the center spotlight, making flamboyant speeches invoking the spirit of the Revolution (*Revolusi! Merdeka!*). In the early 60s, the masses were riled up for the "liberation" of **West Irian** from the Dutch. Without an honest vote of self-determination, sovereignty over the west half of New Guinea was transferred to Indonesia on May 1, 1963 and the province was renamed **Irian Jaya.** In January of 1963, Soekarno launched his **konfrontasi** campaign against Malaysia because of the country's supposedly neocolonialist arrangements with the British. All for Soekarno's Revolution, troops were deployed in the Malay territories of Borneo and senseless skirmishes were waged against the British and Malaysian armies. Soekarno was a master at manipulating symbols, persons, and groups to keep them within his vacuous orbit; in reality, after independence he had nothing left to offer his people because he never articulated anything beneath his nationalist rhetoric. By the 1960s, the aging Soekarno had become a decadent caricature of himself, a master *dalang* (puppeteer) precariously balancing the characters of a *wayang* theater the size of an entire island nation.

THE NEW ORDER

Soekarno's balancing act collapsed tragically on the night of September 30, 1965, when a **failed coup,** supposedly perpetrated by the PKI and involving the murder of 6 high-ranking generals, resulted in a **right-wing military backlash** throughout the nation; more than half a million Communists and suspected sympathizers were brutally massacred. Soekarno was implicated in the events of that night because of his alleged sympathies with the PKI, and thus his leadership was effectively delegitimized for betraying the nationalist military forces. In the aftermath of these events, **Major General Soeharto** emerged as the military commander in charge of the situation. Over the next year and a half, Soeharto systematically dismantled Soekarno's presidential powers and replaced the failed Guided Democracy with his **New Order** government, retaining only the *Pancasila* from Soekarno's original ideological basis for the Indonesian state. After Soeharto assumed the presidency, a broken Soekarno lived under house arrest in Bogor until his death in 1970.

Soeharto's New Order was born upon Indonesia's most violent historical event, a massacre of Communist Indonesians by other Indonesians. This indelible event brought **an end to political activism,** leaving a fear-inducing military in unquestioned control over the affairs of the state. Indonesia's subsequent stability has been achieved by keeping alive the memory of the Communist coup and its consequences. Soeharto's first measures were banning the PKI, ending the *konfrontasi* campaign and making peace with Malaysia, and encouraging relations with and investment from the west, which Soekarno had repeatedly rejected and spurned.

The past thirty years under the New Order have brought stability to the government, impressive economic growth, and major improvements in infrastructure, public health, and education—at the expense of free speech, individual human rights, and regional autonomy in the outer islands. In 1975 **East Timor,** newly independent from the Portuguese, was on the verge of forming its own government when civil war broke out. Claiming that the Timorese posed a Communist threat to the region, the Indonesian army invaded on December 7, 1975 and made East Timor the 27th province of Indonesia, thus rounding out the national borders of Indonesia to include the entire archipelago (see "East Timor: Jakarta's Failure" on page 659).

Bung Karno/Pak Harto

Indonesianists in academia have noted the radical difference between Indonesia's first and second presidents, but it doesn't take a linguistic anthropologist to see that the characters of Soekarno and Soeharto are easily distinguished in the terms commonly used by the Indonesian people. The moniker "bung" is a shortened form of the word *abang* which means "older brother" or "dear friend," while the term "pak" is a shortened form of *bapak* which means "father." While Soeharto might prefer to be called *"Bapak Presiden Soeharto,"* a title that reinforces concepts of hierarchy and power, Bung Karno relished the brotherly relationship he cultivated with his nation's people. Known also as *Penyambung Lidah Rakyat Indonesia* (Voice of the Indonesian People), Soekarno is remembered for his powerful oratory, a skill he often used to inspire Indonesians to carry out his Revolution. In contrast, Pak Harto speaks through his ministers as it is Javanese custom for the *bapak* to remain a silent figure of respected authority.

■■■ INDONESIA TODAY

Observers of the New Order discern two characteristic trends. **Stability and rapid development** have resulted in successful social welfare programs which win praise from the international community. On the other hand, Indonesia's military government has perpetrated some of the worst **human rights violations** over the past three decades. Today, an oppressive military induces a climate of violence and fear in areas of civil unrest such as East Timor, Irian Jaya, and Aceh.

In addition to the crisis in East Timor (see page 659), there are a host of other domestic issues in Indonesia that are rarely mentioned in the international press but which contribute to a sense of uncertainty as the military tries to maintain an outdated status quo. Indonesia attracts much foreign investment due to the availability of cheap wage labor; of central concern lately is the **Indonesian labor movement,** which the government has tried to regulate by allowing only one nationally sanctioned labor organization. In the summer of 1994, a factory worker named **Marsinah,** who tried to organize her co-workers to demand higher wages, was brutally murdered and her corpse left in a shack outside a Javanese village. The subsequent trial suggested military involvement. On May Day, 1995, over 1000 marchers launching a **national campaign to raise the minimum wage** from $3 to $4.50 per day were beaten and arrested on the street, sparking student protests in Jakarta, Semarang, Yogya, and Solo. **Student protesters** in Medan on April 20, 1995 demanded greater openness and democracy and were arrested for insulting Soeharto. With more educated Indonesians and an emerging middle class, there is a sense that the time has come to develop a more open political system that allows dialogue for change. In early 1994, President Soeharto announced that open dialogue in the form of a freer press would actually become a reality. By mid-1994, however, the nation's leading news magazines *Tempo*, *Editor*, and the tabloid *Detik* had their publishing licenses abruptly revoked for covering stories that came dangerously close to exposing opposed factions within the government. Information Minister Harmoko justified the press crackdown by claiming that such openness of the press is counterproductive to national unity. Ironically, the protests that resulted from the press bannings were more threatening to national stability than the stories that were published.

A 74-year-old Soeharto with reported kidney trouble adds to the perception that Indonesia seems on the brink of disorder. This brings up the issue of **presidential succession.** Memories of the last succession stir fears of what may happen in the next few years. Pragmatic observers predict a relatively smooth succession, claiming that the bureaucratic and military conglomerate of the New Order have too much invested in the status quo to rock the boat after Soeharto retires or passes away (this is in stark contrast to the fall of Soekarno, when Indonesia was an economic mess and had nothing to lose). Nevertheless, Soeharto has not named a successor, and as his legitimacy and influence wanes with his health, anxiety over Indonesia's future becomes no small concern—especially as major players from the military and presidential cabinet jockey for power in anticipation of Soeharto's imminent passing.

Ask any Indonesian who will succeed Soeharto, and you will get a smiling "I don't know..." replete with feigned ignorance about the pervasive intrigue. It is not a comfortable topic of conversation. Warm up to your Indonesian friends and they will eventually give you their personal scenario: both **Vice President Try Sutrisno** (formerly the commander of the military) and **Minister of Technology Habibie** are pragmatic choices, but Habibie's recent announcement of imminent retirement from public service leaves people wondering. Though highly disliked for his endless boring speeches on television, **Minister of Information Harmoko** is begrudgingly mentioned as another possibility. Though a long shot at best, an inspiring figure on the sidelines is **Megawati,** Soekarno's daughter, who heads the **Indonesia Democratic Party (PDI).** While the PDI doesn't stand a chance of usurping the hegemonic power of the New Order's party, **GOLKAR,** the government fears a rebirth of a fiery Soekarnoism among Megawati's supporters. Rather than inspire the reactionary and xenophobic nationalism that her father espoused, Megawati has gained support by broadening the PDI's scope beyond its usual Christian base to include Muslims and various army factions. "We are a young party, with young leaders," she says. "People want change. Globally, democracy is an idea whose time has come."

■■■ THE PEOPLE OF INDONESIA

With a population surging past 190 million, Indonesia ranks as the fourth most populated nation in the world and one of the more diverse, with over 350 ethnic groups and over 250 spoken languages throughout the archipelago. Over 60% of the people live on the islands of Java and Bali, which account for only about 8% of Indonesia's total land mass. Population pressures on these inner islands have been a focus of domestic policy since the Dutch era, when transmigration schemes to the outer islands were begun. Today, **transmigrasi** remains an optional program for Java and Bali's poverty stricken, landless inhabitants. However, the number of people who participate in the program hardly makes a dent in the population density of the inner islands. The program has also led to ethnic conflicts in the outer islands in areas where Javanese settlements are beginning to outnumber local communities.

Accusations in the outer islands of ethnic genocide and neocolonialism by the Javanese bring into question the lasting benefit of such large-scale migration projects.

A more effective program introduced by the government has been the **national family planning,** or **Keluarga Berencana (KB)** program. In contrast to Soekarno—who encouraged families to have many children (at least 5) who could continue the Revolution—the New Order has heavily emphasized a two-child family through billboards, television, radio, and even national currency. Initially introduced in the 70s, KB has been intensified dramatically and integrated into social welfare programs for women and children. The hallmark of the KB effort has been the use of community influence and pressure at the village level instead of coercive methods upon individuals to meet national demographic targets. The program has succeeded in lowering the nation's total fertility rate (number of children per woman) from 6 in 1965 to 3.3 in 1985. Indonesia's family planning efforts have received international recognition and have served as a model for other nations facing similar population pressures.

The following descriptions cover the major ethnic groups represented on the islands covered by *Let's Go*:

BALINESE

Tolerant hosts to Indonesia's largest tourist destination, the Balinese have withstood innumerable characterizations by publications like this one. Bali is the most concentrated outpost of Hinduism outside India, and 90% of its inhabitants are adherents of Balinese-Hinduism; the remaining 10% are Buddhist, Muslim, or Christian. Outside the cities and backpacker ghettos, Balinese community life centers around the *banjar* system, a democratic council comprised of the male heads of every household in the village. The Indonesian government has found Bali's stable local *banjars* to be the perfect vehicle for introducing and implementing national programs such as family planning. The Balinese are known for their flourishing arts, which have been subject to the best and worst influences of the consumerist tourism glut. Outside of the tourist corridors and with a little bit of Bahasa Indonesia (or better yet, Bahasa Bali), visitors discover that the Balinese can be the warmest people in Indonesia, revealing Bali's lasting appeal despite its perpetual influx of tourists.

BATAK

Living in the mountain valleys of north-central Sumatra, the Batak have been misrepresented by coastal Malays and colonial administrators alike. The term "Batak" has a negative stigma, evoking images of cannibals, thieves, and ferocious warriors. Truth be known, the Batak stopped eating human flesh less than a century ago, though the practice was reserved for ceremonial occasions, and specific ethical boundaries were attached to it. The various Batak tribes descend from wandering Karen tribes of Thailand and Burma who were forced to migrate south 1500 years ago because of expanding tribes from the north. These people mingled with Indians trading in Sumatra and adopted several aspects of early Hindu civilization. Today, the Batak are roughly divided into 6 tribes: the Karo, Pak Pak, Simelungun, Toba, Angkola, and Mandailing. Some tribes are Islamic, others are Christian, but many are only nominally affiliated with a major religion and still adhere to various animist traditions.

CHINESE

Records show contact between China and the Indonesian archipelago as far back as the 5th century, but Chinese migrants didn't settle *en masse* in Indonesia until the Dutch brought them in as laborers early in the colonial era. Eventually they were utilized as middlemen between the Dutch and the Indonesian populations, and thus became the merchant class in colonial society. Today, the Chinese comprise only about 2% of the population of Indonesia, but they own more than half of all businesses. Chinese-Indonesians have been scapegoated by ethnic Indonesians for centuries. As many as 200,000 Chinese-Indonesians were slaughtered following the failed coup in 1965. Urban unrest in all major cities almost invariably degenerates into violence directed at the Chinese community. Because of the stigma attached to the 1965 coup and Soekarno's close ties with Beijing back in the PKI heydays, all publications in Chinese characters are banned, Chinese languages are not spoken in public, and all Chinese-Indonesians must take indigenous Indonesian surnames.

JAVANESE

Walk into a Javanese household asking humble pardons, "*Nuwun sewu...*," and you will be greeted with a warm welcome, "*Monggo...*" The Javanese penchant for being polite, respectful, and accommodating to others borders on a parody of itself at times, and has become the butt of many jokes by other ethnic groups in Indonesia. Even simple conversations are formalized to express humility and respect for one's position in society. The Javanese language has multiple levels of formality built into it; one picks and chooses words based on who is being spoken to. Javanese people live throughout Central and East Java, though the heart of Javanese culture lies in the royal courts of Yogyakarta and Surakarta in Central Java, where Javanese manners are at their most refined. The culture, customs, and language of the Javanese—the largest and dominant ethnic group in Indonesian society—pervade all the other islands, if not through the Javanese-dominated central bureaucracy, then through the Javanese transmigrants being moved throughout the archipelago. Under-the-breath remarks from other Indonesians about Javanese imperialism across Indonesia suggest that their jokes are not entirely in jest.

MINANGKABAU

Matrilineal and staunchly Muslim, West Sumatra's Minangkabau people manage to combine their two seemingly irreconcilable traits without conflict. The Minang are the fourth-largest ethnic group in Indonesia and have contributed much to Indonesia's national character, not the least of which is *Nasi Padang,* the spicy Minang cuisine found all over Indonesia. While women control family households, inheritance rights, and marriage proposals, young men are expected to leave the house, make a living for themselves, and return home a desirable bachelor. This explains the preponderance of *Nasi Padang* restaurants all over Indonesia, the huge representation of Minang people in Jakarta, and the high educational standards the Minang set for themselves. Minang figures were instrumental in the nationalist movement and continue to rank among the leading intellectuals and authors of Indonesia.

SUNDANESE

The Sundanese are the dominant ethnic group of West Java outside Jakarta. They speak their language with a lilting, singsong intonation that contrasts with the Jakartan dialect. In general, the Sundanese are more dedicated Muslims than the Javanese, but otherwise they have much in common with their neighbors.

■■■ CUSTOMS AND CULTURE

GETTING ALONG IN INDONESIA

Basic elements of Southeast Asian etiquette apply throughout Indonesia. By observing basic cultural norms, you will have more meaningful connections with Indonesians, receive less hassling from hawkers, and help counter stereotypes of westerners as abrasive and self-centered. Looking neat and clean is a priority. In Muslim parts of the country such as West Sumatra and Aceh, keep your shoulders and legs covered. Women may wear long skirts, but should always wear a bra. Those in beach-wear on the street (especially women) will probably be hassled. The following guidelines are particularly important in Java and Bali.

Never give or receive anything with your left hand, point with your feet or forefingers (use your thumb instead), or touch others on the head. Crossed arms, arms on hips, and prolonged eye contact are aggressive postures. When you speak to older people or those to whom you wish to show extra respect (such as Balinese priests), your arms should hang in front of you, left fingers around right wrist. To receive something from an older person, an official, or another respected person, hold out your right arm and touch your right elbow with your left fingers. Keep your head no higher than a respected person's head—when walking in front of a seated older or respected person (generally not strangers), bend down, hunch your back and neck, and extend your arm in front of you as you pass. Indonesians tend to be affectionate with same-sex friends, but PDA between sexes is rare and frowned upon.

Javanese and Balinese tend to be very polite and, as a courtesy bias, may be too embarrassed to answer no if you are, say, asking directions. If it seems that people are not giving you accurate information, try rephrasing your requests so you are not asking yes or no questions. If you are offered food or a drink, wait until your host/ess invites you to eat *"silahkan,"* (please). Conversely, if you offer a person food, they may not begin until you say "please" or *"silahkan."* Eating is generally not a social activity and many eat quickly, without speaking. In general, avoid talking politics.

Before disposing of bandages, tampons, or other items with blood on them, wrap them in paper and/or plastic. After washing clothes, try to hang underwear below waist level. Many homestays have laundry lines with lower rungs for this purpose.

ADAT AND ITS (AB)USE

With such a multitude of ethnic groups, Indonesia naturally has a wide diversity of customs and cultures. For centuries the peoples of Indonesia have understood and respected the differences between themselves, summed up in the common cliche "*lain desa, lain adat*," meaning "other villages, other customs," which reflects a resigned acceptance of regional diversity. Since independence, Soekarno and Soeharto have wisely understood that Indonesia's unity rests upon recognition of the vast nation's diversity. Discussion of *adat*s (customs) has since become an officialized discourse, as each recognized ethnic group's *adat* has been formalized for village-level justice procedures. The downside of *adat* being a part of the government's rhetoric is that each ethnic group's traditions are now written into timeless, static "always-has-been-and-always-will-be" tomes by the Ministry of Culture, preventing the creative adaptability that marks the continued survival of any culture. Furthermore, there remain several groups of Indonesian people whose *adat* have yet to be officially recognized by the government because they are still "uncivilized" and not ready to settle and embrace *Pancasila*, the nation's state ideology. It is a telling irony that selective recognition of diversity and *adat* has become a tool for control and subordination of Indonesia's people, customs, and culture.

RELIGION

Pancasila guarantees freedom for five of the world's major religions: Islam, Protestantism, Catholicism, Buddhism, and Hinduism. Every citizen is required by law to believe in one supreme being as described by one of the above faiths (anyone who doesn't believe in God is obviously a Communist), and every citizen's ID card has his or her religion printed on it. This makes for creative interpretations of local religious traditions. The Karo Batak of North Sumatra, for example, have obtained recognition of their indigenous faith by claiming that it is related to Hinduism.

Over 90% of the population claims adherence to Islam, making Indonesia the largest Muslim nation in the world. The most devout Muslims are in West Sumatra, Aceh, and certain coastal areas. Many Javanese are only nominally Muslim and follow indigenous Javanese spiritual beliefs more fervently. Since the dawn of nationalism earlier this century, various Islamic organizations have tried to integrate their religion with state law (as in Malaysia), but the government has astutely recognized that Christians and Hindus, while among the religious minority, would not accept religious hegemony of any sort; thus, the government has remained secular.

WOMEN IN INDONESIAN SOCIETY

Women in Indonesia have a great deal of autonomy in agriculture and commerce, but the state doesn't recognize the variety of roles women hold throughout society. Instead, through organizations such as the Family Welfare Association, the New

Order encourages five aspects of the ideal wife: faithful companion, manager of the household, caretaker of the nation's next generation, educating mother, and loyal citizen. These aspects, however, ignore the reality of lower class women as economic providers for the family. Women achieve much more in the society than the state is willing to admit. Today, every civil servant's wife must join the *Dharma Wanita,* the official national women's organization which promotes blind acceptance of the status quo and other issues "relevant" to women, like tupperware.

■■■ THE ARTS

ARCHITECTURE

The ancient monuments of Central and East Java (known as *candi*, translated as 'sepulchral monument' or 'ancient shrine') testify to Indonesia's legacy of architectural grandeur. Using a mixture of Indian and local styles, the Central Javanese Period (730-929 AD) produced the great monuments of Candi Borobudur, Candi Prambanan, and a host of other temples in the region. The East Javanese Period (929-1527) continued and developed the traditions begun in Central Java, but on a smaller scale. *Candi* of note in East Java include Candi Kidal and Candi Singasari. By the time of the Majapahit Kingdom, Javanese *candi* were being built as a series of courtyards and shrines, a tradition that most characterizes the temples of Bali, known as *pura.* Bali has over 20,000 *pura*; families often have one of their own in their yard, but the largest one of all is Pura Besakih, Bali's mother temple, built on Mount Agung.

The arrival of Islam on Java saw the construction of mosques instead of temples, though the influence of Hindu-Buddhist traditions was hardly abandoned. The *kraton* palace complexes of Yogyakarta and Surakarta are authentic examples of this confluence of architectural styles. A common Javanese structure used in the *kraton* as well as in Javanese households is the *pendopo*, an open-sided pavilion with a raised floor and wooden pillars supporting a roof of wooden beams that slope upward to meet in a point at the center. Soekarno-Hatta International Airport utilizes this architectural style to excess, while a more classic example of a *pendopo* is at the grand mosque of Yogyakarta in front of the *kraton*.

Every region of Indonesia has its own *rumah adat* (customary house), such as the Minang wooden houses, whose roofs slope up at the ends like buffalo horns, or Batak longhouses, built on piles with spaces reserved for storing ancestors' bones.

BATIK

The world-renowned textile art of producing intricate patterns through a series of waxing and dyeing has been most developed on Java, though batik has become a common technique throughout Indonesia and the rest of Southeast Asia. Originally done by hand, *batik tulis* is made with a *canting,* a tool that holds a small amount of liquid wax. The wax pours from a spout and is used like a pencil to create designs on fabric. The cheaper *Batik cap* is made with pre-patterned metal stamps dipped in wax and then pressed repeatedly onto fabric. Batik shirts are the common dress for men on formal occasions, and women often wear batik *sarung* instead of skirts. In the past 20 years or so, batik paintings have become a popular art form. The best and cheapest batik paintings are found around the tourist areas of Yogyakarta; many of these galleries also give tourists the chance to make their own paintings.

DANCE

Particularly in Java and Bali, Indonesian dance traditions are quite highly developed. Javanese dance—meditative, deliberate, meticulous, and extremely challenging—is difficult for foreigners to follow, and many westerners find it slow and boring. The Javaense, however, can appreciate the muscle-cramping postures, limber movements, contemplative pauses, and distant stares that mark a good dancer. Balinese dancing shares the meticulous and detailed maneuvers of Javanese dance, but is differentiated by quick and jerky movements accompanied by the explosive Balinese *gamelan.* Traditionally, Balinese dancers keep all limbs and joints in constant motion, right down to darting eye glances and fluttering fingers. Dances may take place on almost any occasion, and usually narrate stories from ancient Indian epics or everyday life. The most popular dances are the *Barong,* depicting a battle between good and evil, and the *Kecak* (a.k.a. monkey dance), which reenacts a scene of the *Ramayana* around flame torches while 100 or more men sit in concentric circles shouting and chanting in rhythm. In the much simpler Sumatran dances, only single women are allowed to dance. Each village has its own variation of handkerchief dances (handkerchief held between a man and a woman) and candle dances (*tari lilin*).

DRAMA

Modern drama was never developed to any extent outside Java, and even there it was influenced heavily by the rapid-fire succession of state ideologies during the past century. *Ludruk* is an all-male performance medium in which the roles of women are humorously, though somewhat derogatorily, rendered on stage. *Kethoprak* is grounded in the classic epic stories and myths of India and Java, but usually with a contemporary twist. For example, in a typical *kethoprak* depiction of an episode of the *Ramayana* epic, it would not be surprising to see Sita and Rama discussing and extolling the virtues of KB, the national family planning program. *Ludruk* and *kethoprak* are very popular throughout Java in both rural and urban communities, and the government sponsors traveling troupes and televised performances as a means to disseminate various aspects of state ideology.

LITERATURE

Classic literature throughout western Indonesia is largely based on epics, poems, and courtly histories, each with their own cycles. Most Indonesians are familiar with the *Ramayana* and *Mahabharata* epics transmitted from India over a millennia ago, which have since been considerably Javanized, Balinized, etc. Equally popular are stories from the indigenous cycle of *Panji* stories, which tell about the military victories and mythical adventures of the hero Panji. These classic stories are sources of inspiration for modern drama, *wayang* performances, and dance performances.

MUSIC

Gongs and other metallic instruments are found all over Southeast Asia, but the *gamelan* orchestra—a sophisticated ensemble of tuned gongs, metallophones, and drums, with a few vocalists and string and wind instruments—is unique to Java and Bali. Sundanese, Javanese, and Balinese each have their own variations of *gamelan* and each is quite different from the other. Javanese *gamelan* is trance-like and difficult for western ears to follow. Balinese-style *gamelan* is fast-paced, dramatic, and grabs attention. The discernible melodies of the Sundanese variety are the most tuneful for western ears. *Gamelan* accompanies dance, *wayang*, other performing arts, and special ceremonies, so visitors to Java and Bali are almost certain to hear a sample. While *gamelan* may seem amorphous to the first-time listener, patient learners will find that it gradually becomes more accessible.

Indonesia's popular music traditions are diverse and dynamic, drawing upon outside influences over the past millennia and on the rich body of musical traditions across the islands. The lilting *kroncong* music, with its characteristic ukuleles, guitars, and violins, gained popularity in the 30s and draws influence from Portuguese music. Today, an older generation listens nostalgically to the sounds of a bygone era whenever a cheezy Sinatra-esque *kroncong* artist croons over late-night television. *Dangdut* music draws upon an Indian and Arabic rhythm for its hip-grinding popularity among the urban poor of Indonesia. Originally a vehicle for the dissemination of Islamic morals in the 70s, this musical medium has now become a multi-billion-rupiah industry, replete with sexually suggestive lyrics and a slick new *techno-dangdut* sound for the 90s. The Batak of North Sumatra are famed for their beautiful voices and their melancholy tunes, which frequently involve unabashed sobbing by the vocalists; the uninitiated find it hilarious. Unknown to most lay people, Jakarta hosts a yearly jazz festival, *Jakjazz*, which draws international acts. Indonesia has a fledgling fusion jazz scene; the premier jazz group in the country, *Krakatau*, has quite a following largely due to the talented lead singer, Tri Utami. Their latest work incorporates the sounds and scales of the *gamelan* into their work.

Finally, there is quite a dynamic rock and top 40 scene, whose sounds are borrowed straight from Euro-American pop music. Top 40 acts turn into sensations overnight as soon as their videos are aired on the national television. It's the same old dribble: inoffensive love songs with a catchy refrain with which the whole nation can sing along. A few rock musicians with a message are out there, but they are carefully monitored by the censor board. Iwan Fals sings about government corruption and environmental issues with a Lou Reed/Bruce Springsteen attitude. Gombloh, a folk-rock legend, sang humorous yet stirring Dylan-esque tunes about his people and country before he died of cancer in the mid-80s.

WAYANG

The ancient Javanese art of shadow puppetry and its permutations probably have their roots in ancestor worship prior to the Indianization of the archipelago. Two-dimensional puppets carved from animal hides were held in front of a flame, casting shadows through a cloth screen, in order to call down ancestors from the spirit world. As a conduit of spirits, the *dalang* (puppeteer) had a shamanistic quality about him. Today the *dalang* is still highly respected for his ability to manipulate several puppets at once, speak their lines in different voices, conduct the *gamelan* orchestra behind him (a trick managed through vocal signals and foot taps), know an entire pantheon of characters and their historical context, entertain, amuse, and provide lessons for his audience, and keep it all going from 9pm to 5am without intermission. The stories are drawn from episodes of the *Ramayana* and *Mahabharata* Indian epics, as well as from a number of indigenous stories such as the *Panji* cycle. Like the *kethoprak* dramas, *wayang* puppet theater is a common medium utilized by the government to disseminate state ideology in popular format. On the other hand, *wayang* performances are also forums where state ideology is subtly mocked for hilarious and critical effect.

Wayang kulit is the original shadow puppet art form, but it has been built upon by a number of subsequent traditions throughout Java and Bali. *Wayang golek* shows, more common in West Java, are similar, but their puppets are wooden three-dimensional figures and no screen separates the puppets from the audience. *Wayang topeng* and *wayang wong* both employ human actors who dress up as and mimic the typical movements of the two-dimensional puppets; in *wayang topeng* the actors cover their faces with masks and the *dalang* still does the voices for the actors and directs them on and off stage.

■■■ FOOD AND DRINK

One look at all the varieties of bananas (*pisang*) found in Indonesia makes it clear that describing the nation's vast array of cuisines is quite a feat. With the nation's size and multiplicity of cultures, Indonesia has the largest menu in all of Southeast Asia. Below are a few of the national dishes that are found throughout the archipelago; regional specialties are listed in the towns where they are most famous.

Indonesian cooking is distinct from most anything else: the cuisines employ spices most people have never tasted before, and coconut cream is present in almost every dish and sauce. *Nasi goreng,* fried rice, is readily available everywhere and is generally spicier than the fried rice served in other Asian countries. *Nasi goreng* typically employs red hot chili peppers, fried egg, fresh tomato and cucumber (sometimes pickled), and shrimp or chicken. *Gado-gado* is Indonesia's most famous vegetarian dish, a vegetable salad topped with peanut sauce. Vegetarians will also delight in the fact that *tahu* (tofu) and *tempeh* (tempe) are virtually staple sources of protein in the Indonesian diet, served everywhere and cooked in almost everything. *Mie goreng*, fried noodles with vegetables, shrimp paste, meat, chilies, and eggs, is as common as *nasi goreng*. *Soto,* a meat soup commonly found with chicken (*soto ayam*), is not like the chicken soup your Jewish grandmother used to make—unless she used coconut cream in the broth. *Sate* consists of small pieces of meat grilled on skewers, served with peanut sauce and steamed rice. Try these dishes from place to place throughout Indonesia to see how each region elaborates on the basic recipes. Lovers of pork (*babi*) will have to ask for it nicely in Chinese restaurants or wait until arriving in Bali, where it is a local favorite; the vast majority of Indonesians are Muslim and avoid this non-*halal* meat. Common snack foods or side-dishes are crisply cooked *kerupuk* "chips." They are most often made from shrimp (*kerupuk udang*), but other varieties include *kerupuk kerbau* (from buffalo meat) and the uniquely delicious *emping* (made from the "We've-never-heard-of-it-either" mellingo nut).

Fun drinks unique to Indonesia, aside from *Teh Sosro*, almost invariably contain shredded coconut or coconut milk. *Es kelapa muda* is young coconut shaved into sweetened coconut milk and served with ice and sometimes a rose-colored syrup. Sold on the street and served in restaurants, *es kelapa muda* refreshes and invigorates the road-weary backpacker. *Es kopyor* is the same as *es kelapa muda* except that the coconut is aged and "rotten"; it's found only in a few restaurants and is significantly more expensive, but is worth trying—it is a drink of ecstasy surpassed only by the orgasmic *bubur cha-cha* of Peninsular Malaysia. Other common sweet coconut-milk-based drinks are *es dawet* and *es cendol*, both of which have rice-flour gummy things in them to prevent boredom while you sip.

One regional cuisine found all over Indonesia is *Nasi Padang,* made by the Minangkabau from West Sumatra. Generally more expensive than other restaurants, Padang-style eateries bring out all the dishes, from which customers pick and choose and only get charged for what they take. Minang cuisine uses an abundance of curries and coconut and is renowned as the spiciest food from a nation where hot, eye-watering food is *de rigeur*. Most common is the *rendang,* a beef-coconut curry stewed until dry. The list of items on a Padang menu gets long and unusual: after the fried chicken, vegetables, goat, liver, eggs, and prawns, don't be surprised to be presented with fried lung, simmering hearts, brains, and tripe. After you finish eating with trepidation and cool off your mouth, look up at your waiter, smile (to let him know how much you enjoyed it), and say "*sedap...*"

After trying over 40 varieties of banana, each with its own taste, look for the fruits you've never seen at home. Hairy *rambutan* just needs to be peeled before you sink your teeth into this lychee-esque (only better!) fruit. *Salak* is sometimes referred to as "snake fruit" in English because of its distinctly scaly and eminently peelable skin. The fruit inside tastes both sweet and tart, and leaves the tongue dry and the lips smacking for more. *Belimbing*, star fruit, is juicy and sweet, best eaten cold. Mangosteens (*manggis*) are rarely in season, but when they are they fall in full force. Eat the refreshing white fruit inside the thick, purple, "touch-me-and-I'll-stain-you" skin before it gets rotten with the yellow gunk that quickly infests mangosteens. The gargantuan *durian* is the mother-lode of all Southeast Asian fruits and tends to be the savior and/or downfall of foreigners who try it. The scent alone evokes the sewage system of Phnom Penh, but many claim the taste is like a caramel heaven. Be careful, though: eating too much *durian* causes a serious fever.

Eating establishments in Indonesia are similar to others all over Southeast Asia. Unique to Indonesia, though, are *warungs*, makeshift streetside establishments that set up for part of each day. They often consist of just a few tables, stools, and tent-like walls to protect diners from heat and street pollution. While the cleanliness of these places may vary (a quick glance should clue you in), you'll find the cheapest and most delicious food here, since most *warungs* specialize on one particular food or drink—whether it be a *mie goreng,* a regional specialty, or warm milk. To play the *warung* scene particularly safe, order your dish without meat and your drink without ice (not all ice is made from boiled or bottled water).

Java

One cannot ignore the centuries-old importance that Java has held over the rest of the archipelago. From the monumental Sanjaya and Sailendra dynasties responsible for Indonesia's largest ancient temples, to the classical Majapahit Empire which united the archipelago before the arrival of the Dutch, to the sophisticated court cultures of the Yogyakarta and Surakarta sultanates, and finally to the powerful military government centered in Jakarta, Java has almost always played center stage across island Southeast Asia.

Java's vast rice fields and innumerable mosques provide nutritional and spiritual sustenance for more than 100 million inhabitants. Rich volcanic soils have provided well, but swelling urban centers filled with increasing numbers of landless poor, and huge numbers of transmigrants pouring out to other Indonesian islands reflect the precarious balance in which the Javanese live with the environment. Outside the cities, many still live as they always have, with woven cane houses and tile roofs only slowly being replaced by brick and sheets of tin. The market is still the focus of the town, even after supermarkets appear. Women hold hands crossing the streets, and men walk along with an arm around one another at the end of a day's work.

After your first ride in the front seat of an intercity bus, you will probably realize that cliches about Javanese being gentle, passive people are shallow. In fact, Javanese seem to take out their aggressions behind the wheel. Time spent on these buses is of course an excellent way to get a deeper feel for the island. Landscapes can be as lush and mountainous as the Puncak or Dieng Plateau, quilted with tidy grass stairs and dotted with small towns and villages, while lowland cities such as Jakarta and Surabaya ramble with reckless, maze-like urbanity. Throughout the changes in landscape, there are constants: penny sized candy wrappers trail locals like breadcrumbs. Legions of ancient *candi* and modern-day phallic monuments dedicated to the egos of Indonesian leadership rival each other for vertical height. Mosques compete with food vendors' calls for air time.

Life inside Javanese vehicles can be just as stimulating, if a little crowded, hot, and hectic. Throughout the overland process, visitors to Java are in a prickly, schizophrenic position: in order to survive the traveling sport, visitors must be willing to put their faith, potential arrival, and perhaps valuables in the hands of strangers, while also being wary of the ubiquitous slack-spined pickpockets. As the bus pulls into the next stop, it becomes apparent that the Javanese landscape is almost as crowded outside the bus as it was inside. The sheer numbers of people on Java alone are its signature feature. Packing 60% of the nation's population on 8% of Indonesia's land mass, it is hardly surprising that no other Indonesian island claims such high density; it is the cumulative centripetal effect from being the central linchpin of the archipelago for centuries.

■■■ JAKARTA

The capital city of the fourth-most-populous country in the world is inseparable from its traffic. The city exists and expands because it is the magic portal for people who want to get somewhere, and although most of them do not get beyond Jakarta to the rest of the world, they spend a great deal of time trying to get anywhere, locked in traffic jams around the capital province. Sputtering orange *bajajs,* pastel taxis, *microlets,* scooters, and soot-begrimed buses roar and honk like Jurassic beasts. It isn't pretty at first sight, but there is a grace and art at work here.

Construction is continual, from back alleys to office blocks. On smaller buildings, bamboo and plank scaffolding looks like an engineer's drunk fantasy, and even seven stories up, men are working barefoot. The colored mirrored glass of new skyscrapers reflects surly tropical skies and looks out over a maze of *kampungs* where

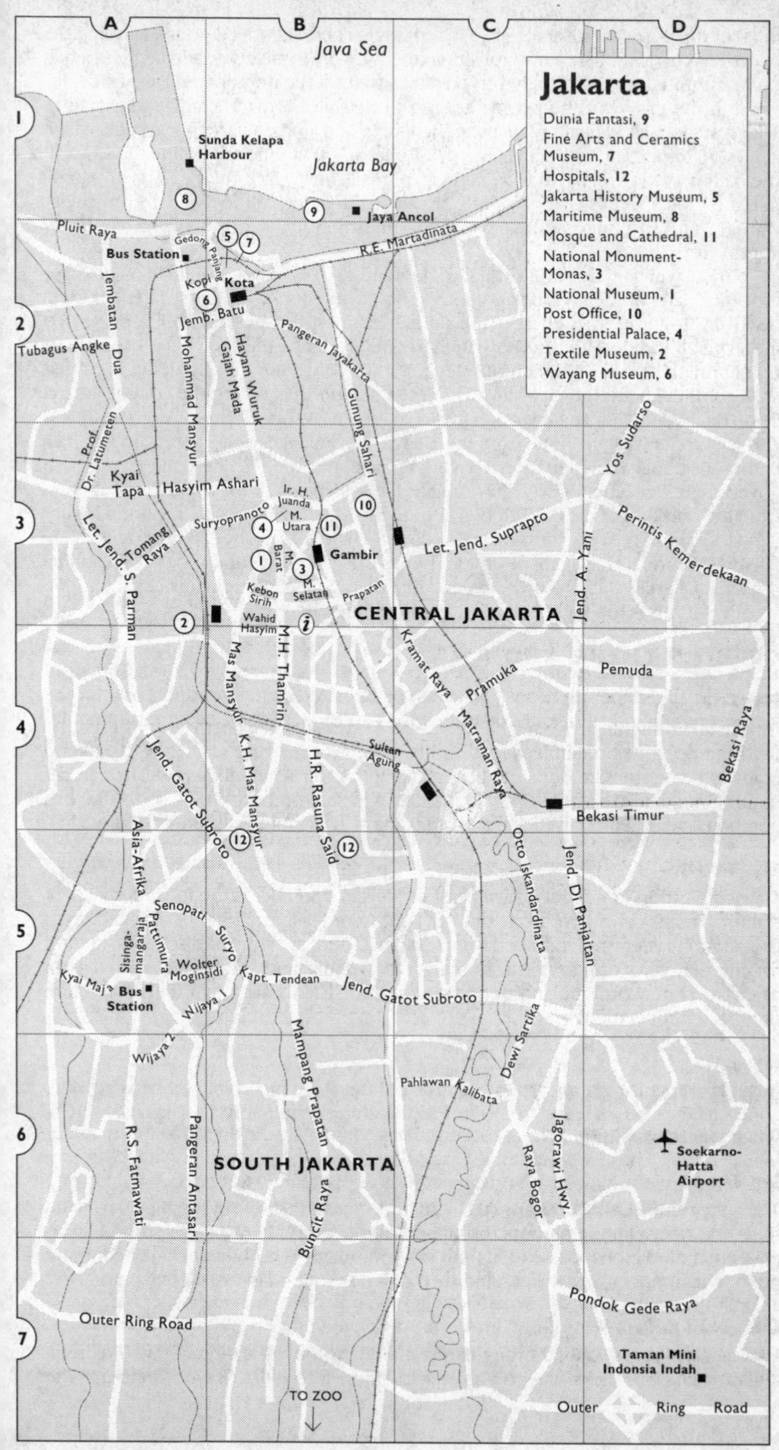
Jakarta
Dunia Fantasi, 9
Fine Arts and Ceramics Museum, 7
Hospitals, 12
Jakarta History Museum, 5
Maritime Museum, 8
Mosque and Cathedral, 11
National Monument-Monas, 3
National Museum, 1
Post Office, 10
Presidential Palace, 4
Textile Museum, 2
Wayang Museum, 6
Java Sea
Jakarta Bay
Sunda Kelapa Harbour
Jaya Ancol
Pluit Raya
Bus Station
R.E. Martadinata
Kota
Pangeran Jayakarta
Gunung Sahari
Tubagus Angke
Hayam Wuruk
Gajah Mada
Mohammad Mansyur
Hasyim Ashari
Kyai Tapa
Suryopranoto
Gambir
Let. Jend. Suprapto
Yos Sudarso
Perintis Kemerdekaan
CENTRAL JAKARTA
Jend. A. Yani
Kramat Raya
Pramuka
Pemuda
M.H. Thamrin
Sultan Agung
Matraman Raya
Bekasi Raya
Bekasi Timur
Jend. Gatot Subroto
K.H. Mas Mansyur
H.R. Rasuna Said
Otto Iskandardinata
Jend. Di Panjaitan
Asia-Afrika
Senopati
Suryo
Kapt. Tendean
Wolter Moginsidi
Kyai Maja
Wijaya I
Wijaya 2
Mampang Prapatan
Pahlawan Kalibata
Dewi Sartika
Jagorawi Hwy.
Raya Bogor
Soekarno-Hatta Airport
SOUTH JAKARTA
R.S. Fatmawati
Pangeran Antasari
Buncit Raya
Pondok Gede Raya
Outer Ring Road
Taman Mini Indonsia Indah
TO ZOO

most of the population scrapes by. When it rains here, it indeed pours, keeping the occasional patch of green lush, pushing open sewers to capacity, and sending a barrage of umbrella-toting boys to busy districts to ferry the unprepared for a price.

Life is not easy, but the people are most often pleasant and exchange greetings with a smile. Talking, eating, playing, hawking, and smoking are five aspects of life at least as important as the five tenets of *Pancasila* that officially define the spirit of the nation. A *warung* with food and cigarettes is never far, and they are still dominated by local rather than western products. McDonald's does a brisk business, though, and in concession to a predominantly Muslim population, has *halal* approval.

Tourists typically detest Jakarta, arriving and then leaving as quickly as possible for other parts of the archipelago. The visitor who chooses to linger in Jakarta will discover, however, that every major ethnic group of Indonesia is well represented in the neighborhood *kampungs* which frequently define themselves on the basis of ethnic origin. It can be difficult to decipher all the various cultural influences that shape and decorate the city but it is in these *kampungs* where the soul of Jakarta lies. The myriad uniformed workers who run the basic operations of every business and government office come from there each day and take to the streets on Jakarta's enormous public transportation network while expatriates, Chinese merchants, and government bureaucrats who have made the system work for them come and go from the outskirts of the city, hidden behind the tinted windows of imported luxury vehicles. These movers and shakers finding their way to work each day will shape Jakarta's future, just as it shapes them, but as the city grows and groans beneath its millions, Jakarta's dichotomy between affluent and destitute remains constant; one wonders if this is too high a cost for "getting somewhere."

GETTING THERE AND AWAY

By Air

International flights arrive at the **Soekarno-Hatta Airport** northwest of the city. Outbound flights are subject to a highly variable departure tax. Have Rp20,000 ready to be on the safe side. The best way into Jakarta is by public bus. They are air conditioned and cost only Rp3000. (A taxi will set you back Rp25,000.) The bus goes to Gambir Station in the center of Jakarta, a 10-minute walk from Jl. Jaksa.

By Train

Gambir Station in central Jakarta, east of Merdeka Square, is the most convenient station. Trains arrive here from all over Java. In order to arrange for a ticket, go to the station master, preferably a day in advance. There are student discounts, but not for the deluxe overnight express trains (the "Bima" and "Mutiara" to Surabaya). Trains are rarely on time and poorly announced. The locals might help you figure out the announcements.

By Bus

Buses are great for getting around Jakarta, but trains are preferable for trips beyond. Long distance buses leave from the **Pulo Gadung** terminal in East Jakarta; check when you book your ticket.

By Boat

The state-run **PELNI Company** (tel. 421 19 21) has a fleet of seven ships that wind their way between big harbors throughout the country. PELNI ships provide spartan accommodations, basic food, and slow journeys, with bi-weekly schedules at not-so-cheap prices. For ticket sales, their office is on Jl. Angkasa, Kemayoran.

ORIENTATION

Jakarta has many types of thoroughfares, and if you know the direction you're heading, the *gangs*, or alleys, can be a quieter and more interesting way to get there. The focus of Jakarta is **Merdeka Square.** In the center of it is the **Monas,** the phallic national monument. To its east is **Gambir Station;** to the north is the **Istiqlal Mosque** and **Istana Merdeka, the Presidential Palace;** to the west is the **National Museum;** to the south is **Jalan Jaksa.** North toward the harbor is **Glodok,** or Chinatown, and farther north, around **Kota Station,** is the **old Dutch area. Sunda Kelapa,** near the Dutch area, is where the big, wooden schooners dock. **Jaya Ancol** is east, along the harbor of **Tanjung Priok.** The **Ragunan Zoo** and **Taman Mini** are south of the city center.

GETTING AROUND

There is no easy, quick way to get around Jakarta. For short distances, let your feet do the walking or hire a **bajaj** (orange motorized three-wheelers). **Taxis,** with an initial charge of Rp900, and then Rp450 per km, offer air-conditioned comfort, but **buses** do their job well as little gets in their way. City buses for around Jakarta can be caught outside McDonald's on Jl. MH Thamrin—on the same side if you are going south, or take the overpass if you are going north. (Rp250 and 550, A/C buses Rp1300. Buses run daily 6am-8pm.) To make sure you get off at the right stop, ask everyone "*Ada juah ke*...?" (Is it far to...?"). Small minivans called **microlets** have set routes and charge according to the distance (Rp300-500). Knock with a coin against the roof or a pole of buses and microlets to alert the driver that you want to get off. **Cars** charge by the hour within the city (Rp8000-10,000 per hour, with a minimum charge), and by distance beyond Jakarta. There are several desks at the airport, or in the city see **Avis,** Jl. Diponegoro No. 25 (tel. 331 974), **Blue Bird,** Jl. HOS Cokroaminoto No. 107 (tel. 325 607), or **National** at Kartika Plaza Hotel, Jl. MH Thamrin No. 10 (tel. 333 423). Travel offices also often book cars (see Practical Information below).

PRACTICAL INFORMATION

Tourist Office: Jl. Thamrin No. 9 (tel. 314 20 67). On corner of Jl. Thamrin and Jl. Wahid Hasyim. From Jl. Jaksa walk south (away from Monas), and then turn right on Jl. Wahid Hasyim. Entrance is along inside hall of Djakarta Theater building. A/C office, helpful staff offers free maps and information missing from the brochures. Open Mon.-Fri. 8:30am-4:30pm, Sat. 8:30am-1pm.

Budget Travel: Many Jl. Jaksa hostels can book bus tours and transportation, but **Jl. Jaksa** and **KH Wahid Sahim** budget travel and holiday offices cover the travel spectrum.

Embassies and Consulates: Australia, Jl. Rasuna Said Kav. C15-16 (tel. 522 71 11). Take bus #P11 to Kunigan Plaza. Open Mon.-Thurs. 8:30am-1:30pm, Fri. 8:30am-noon. **Canada,** Wisma Metropolitan I, 5th fl., Jl. Jend. Sudirman Kav. 29 (tel. 525 07 90). Take bus #P12, 10, or 1 to the Metropolitan I. Open Mon.-Thurs. 7:30am-4:15pm, Fri. 7:30am-1pm. **Laos,** Jl. Kintamani Raya C-15 No. 33 (tel. 520 26 73). Bus #11 to Mulia Centre. **Malaysia,** Jl. HR Rasuna Said Kav. X/6 No. 1-3. Bus #P11 to Jl. Prof. Dr. Satriol. Open Mon.-Thurs. 8am-1pm and 2-4pm. **Singapore,** 2 Jl. HR Saruna Said Blok X/4 (tel. 520 14 89). Open Mon-Fri 8:30am-12:30pm, and 1:30-5pm. **Thailand,** 74 Jl. Imam Bonjol (tel. 390 42 25). Walk southwest from the Jl. Thamrin/Kebon/Kacang Raya traffic circle on Jl. Bonjol. Open Mon.-Fri. 8:30am-3:30pm (until 4:30pm for embassies affairs). **UK,** 74 Jl. MH Thamrin (tel. 330 904), a short walk from Jl. Jaksa. Open Mon.-Thurs. 7:45am-4pm, Fri. 7:45am-12:45pm. **US,** 5 Jl. Merdeka Selatan (tel. 360 360), between Gambir Station and Jl. Jaksa. Open Mon.-Fri. 7:30am-4pm. **Vietnam,** 25 Jl. Teuku Umar (tel. 310 03 58). A short walk southeast of Jl. Jaksa. Open Mon.-Sat. 9-11:30am and 1:30-4pm.

Currency Exchange: At the airport, various bank desks are open when flights arrive. There should not be a commission. In the city, there are a slew of banks offering slightly better rates, along Jl. Thamrin, including **Daiwa Perdania Bank, Bali Bank,** and **Bank Surya.** Their hours are generally 8:30am-3pm on weekdays and 8:30-11am on Sat. In a pinch, there's always Jl. Jaksa; some hostels and many travel offices change money. **Sarinah Department Store** also has an exchange desk, open 8am-7:30pm.

American Express Office: Jl. Rasuna Said Block X/1 Kav., 03 Exchange House (tel. 521 61 06)

Post Office: General Post Office, Jl. Pos No. 2, Pasar Baru (tel. 344 69 88). Open Mon.-Sat. 9am-8pm, Sun. 9am-4pm. Use bus #P12. **Poste Restante** is at counter 55 (tel. 361 561 ext. 232) Address Poste Restante as follows: Andrew WILLIAMS, AE wonder boy, or name of addressee, GPO Jakarta, Poste Restante, Jl. Lapangan Banteng Ugara, Jakarta 10000. Stamps at counter 47. **Warpostel,** Jl. Jaksa No. 2 (tel. 390 45 01), open daily 8am-midnight. May not be as reasonable for airmail prices. **Postal code**: 10000.

Telephones: There is no shortage of phones along the streets, though many of them are phonecard only (gray phones). Blue coin phones can be found in shopping centers and public buildings. Indosat has **"Home Country Direct"** service from special phones, which put you directly in touch with the operator of your choice. These can be found at the **airport** and at the **Public Phone Office** (Pelayanan Telekomunikasi Untak Umum), Jl. MH Thamrin No. 9 across from the Tourist Office. They have dozens of carpeted booths and a Jakarta **yellow pages** in English. Open 24 hrs.

Luggage Storage: Left Luggage Office, at the airport. Charges Rp3000 per day. Open 24 hrs.

Lost and Found: At the airport, on the left past Immigration. Open noon-3pm.

English Language Visual Media: The *Times* and *Jakarta Post* are English dailies. News stands also have English weekly magazines, including *Time* and *Newsweek*. Old American series show up on TV each night.

English Bookstores: Times, is on the lower level of the **Plaza Indonesia Shopping Center,** beneath the Grand Hyatt on Jl. MH Thamrin. Open daily 10am-9pm. Also look near Jl. Jaksa, in hostels and near major hotels.

Library: National Library, Jl. Ampera Raya III (tel. 780 58 51). Open 8am-4pm.

Religious Centers: Istiqlal Mosque on Jl. Medan Merdeka Utara. The Catholic **Kathedral** on Banteng Square, opposite the Mosque, with masses daily 4-6pm.

Convenience Stores: Golden Truly Supermarket, Jl. MH Thamrin No. 9 (tel. 359 232). Get a guitar with your groceries. **Ramayana Department Store,** Jl. H. Agus Salim No. 22A (tel. 337 713). **Sarinah Department Store,** Jl. MH Thamrin No. 11 (tel. 327 425). Sarinah's is a fascinating place with 2 floors of Indonesian crafts, and a **Hero** supermarket (tel. 390 35 59) in the basement.

Pharmacies: Apotik Melawai, Jl. Salemba Raya No. 59 (tel. 315 09 53). By RS St. Cardus. Open 24 hrs. **Gambir Apotik,** Jl. Kebon Sirih 77A (tel. 331 089), is very close to Jl. Jaksa. Open Mon.-Sat. 9am-9pm. *Warung* on the streets have some basic remedies; supermarkets have good selections as well.

Hospitals: MMC Kuningan, Jl. Rasuna Said Kav. C21 (tel. 522 52 01), is a general hospital, as is **RS Jakarta,** Jl. Jend. Sudirman Kav. 49 (tel. 573 22 41). **Ufar Madica Clinic** (tel. 331 389), is next to the Gambir Apotik on Jl. Kebon Sirih. Open Mon.-Sat. 9am-9pm.

Gay and Lebian Resources: IPOOS/Gaya Betawi, c/o Alfa Salon, Jl. Dr Muwardi IV/21, Grogol, Jakarta Barat (tel. 566 05 89). *GAYa Nusantara* available here.

Emergency: Police, tel. 110. **Fire,** tel. 113. **Ambulance,** tel. 118. **City Health Service,** tel. 119.

Police: Jl. Jend Sudirman No. 45 (tel. 570 41 89). Open 8am-midnight.

ACCOMMODATIONS

Budget accommodations are primarily located around Jl. Jaksa. There is enough demand to keep seedier places in business, as well as to generate the opening of some hotels (at markedly higher rates). Ask about the number of beds in a double. Make sure the room has a fan and good screens to keep out mosquitoes. Most places have a lounge and TV, which makes up for the cramped rooms, but nothing makes up for a sweltering night in the company of winged-blood suckers. Front doors close at midnight. The following listings are organized by street; Jalan Kebon Sirih Barat and Timur I are just off of Jalan Jaksa and easy to find as there are guest house signs pointing the way.

Jalan Jaksa

Norbek Hostel, Jl. Jaksa No. 14 (tel. 330 392). The woman in charge is determined to keep a good reputation, so security from outsiders is tight. There are dividers in the dorm to make quasi-singles with A/C. Singles Rp9000. Dorm Rp10-13,000. Doubles Rp16,000. Triples Rp21,000. To reserve a room you must pay in advance. Shared *mandis* (Indonesian-style bathroom).

Jusran Hostel, Jl. Jaksa No. 9 (tel. 314 03 73), a faded sign points you to the end of the alley. Friendly management and a distance from the street are in its favor, even though the clean rooms are small and lack amenities. Singles Rp8-10,000. Doubles Rp14-15,000. Triples, Rp21,000. Shared *mandis.*

Hotel Tator, Jl. Jaksa No. 37 (tel. 323 940). Out of place on Jl. Jaksa, Hotel Tator's sleek black and white tile makes it as shiny and manicured as a Marriott, and only a little more cramped. You pay for the luxury of a private bath: singles Rp22,500. doubles Rp45,000, with hot water Rp50,000. Breakfast included.

Wisma Delima, Jl. Jaksa No. 5 (tel. 337 026). The first one you encounter coming from Gambir Station, with its old AYH sign out front. Facilities are all right, but nothing special. AYH discount of Rp500 for dorms. Used books for sale. Dorms Rp6500. Singles Rp7500. Doubles: bunk Rp14,000; room Rp15,000.

Nick's Corner Hostel, Jl. Jaksa No. 16 (tel. 336 754). An incubator if you can't deal with Jakarta full on. The A/C is the justification for high prices. Clean and secure. Open 24 hrs. Dorm Rp8000. Doubles: with fan Rp20,000; with A/C Rp37-65,000. Half the rooms have private bathrooms.

Djody Hostel, Jl. Jaksa No. 27-29 (tel. 314 17 32) and **Djody Hotel,** Jl. Jaksa No. 33-35 (tel. 390 59 76). A motel-like setup with plenty of pricey, white, boxy, but well-kept rooms. The hostel has rooms with fans, the hotel has A/C. Rooms are not thoroughly screened, so you may have to close window slats at night. At the hostel: singles Rp16,000, doubles Rp27,000, triples Rp35,000. All shared *mandis.* At the hotel: Doubles with shared *mandi* Rp35,000, with private bath Rp45,000. Breakfast included. Open 24 hrs. Visa/MC.

Jalan Kebon Sirih Timur I

Bloem Steen Hostel, Jl. Kebon Sirih Timur I No. 174 (tel. 323 002). Set in a rambling, older building, the highlight here is the comfy lounge furniture. Doubles Rp12,000 to Rp14,000 in peak season. Shared *mandis.*

Kresna Hostel, Jl. Kebon Sirih Timur I No. 175 (tel. 325 403). This building rambles vertically. Watch out for the stairs, no handrails, slippery tiles, and steep incline. The management is generally friendly and will hold your mail for you. Books for sale. All doubles: Rp12,000, Rp16,000 for private *mandi.*

Jalan Kebon Sirih Barat

Bintang Kejora Hostel, Jl KS Barat Palam No. 52 (tel. 323 878). The laid-back, friendly management will do whatever they can for you and keep clean rooms for your dusty bones. Travel office on premises. Singles Rp15,000. Doubles Rp20,000. Triples Rp25,000. Shared *mandis.* Breakfast included. Check-out 1pm.

Borneo Hostel, Jl. KS Barat Dalam No. 35 (tel. 320 095). Large, clean, and efficient with spacious lounges and an attached cafe (**Borneo Cafe**). Dorms Rp7000. Singles and doubles Rp30,000 with bathroom.

FOOD

In Jakarta, you are never more than a block away from a *warung* (a food cart with seating along a bench or sidewalk stools) any hour of the day. Food will also come to you, balanced in baskets across shoulders of hawkers or in bicycle-driven carts. Nice restaurants are not exorbitant and offer precious air conditioning

Jalan Jaksa offers convenient food at backpacker prices, but it is worth walking to Jalan H. Agus Salim. You'd have to stay in Jakarta almost as long as Stevie Wonder recorded funky music to try everything available here. *Sate* and *Padang* food are specialties of the *warung*, or you can pretend you're not in Jakarta and lurk into a western fast-food joint a block further down. The corner of Jl. W. Hasyim and Jl. Thamrin is all lights and neon with the Green Pub, Chili's, and the Hard Rock Cafe.

Not even hard-core, go-native trampers can pass up a Rp500 McDonald's ice cream cone. Then again, maybe they can.

If you're hankering for some subcontinental cuisine, take Bus 12 to Jl. Veteran I, just west of Istiqlal Mosque. Amid a series of travel offices, are two reasonable Indian restaurants: **Queen's Tandoor** at Jl. Veteran I No. 6 (tel. 344 72 45, entrees Rp8-10,000), and **Sahara Restaurant** at Jl. Veteran I No.23 (tel. 360 452, entrees Rp9-12,000).

There are also concentrations of restaurants around the shopping areas of Pasar Baru and Blok M, and in Glodok, (Chinatown). For **market** food, meander through Pasar Jaya (the traditional market) behind Gondagia Station on Jl. Srikaya, about two blocks east of Jl. Jaksa, where all the *bajajs* are parked.

Jalan Jaksa

Borneo Cafe, Jl.KS Barat Dalam No. 35 (tel. 320 095) You guessed it, another backpacker hangout. Very good Indonesian food, including a spicy rendition of *gado-gado* which will leave you howling for extra *kerupuk* and water. While you're eating, the owners will continue with their evening business—feeding their pets and talking with family around the tables.

Angie's Cafe, Jl. Jaksa No. 15 (tel. 326 224). Caters to the backpacking crowd with a wide variety of foods at good prices. Convenient if your hostel doesn't include breakfast. Try the icy banana juice for a cool treat.

Senayan Satay House, Jl. Kebon Sirih 31A (tel. 326 238), at the head of Jl. Jaksa. The lung and gizzard dishes will make you glad for the translations on the menu. Seafood and Indonesian entrees, Rp3-6000.

Memories Cafe, Jl. Jaksa No. 17. Across from Norbek Hostel, Offers good food, American tunes, and an almost certain visit from hawkers of English newspapers.

Jalan H Agus Salim

Ignore the glut of fast food places which have spread across the area like kitchen grease. If none of the restaurants on the main road are what your looking for, Salim has plenty of *warung*, with excellent options as well as the adjacent alleys which have food opportunities every ten feet.

Paradiso 2001, Jl. H Agus Salim 30 (tel. 321 739). A cheery place to watch TV while you eat, this vegetarian restaurant offers a wide variety of excellent dishes, from Rp3-6000. Esther will cheerfully serve you. Quiet and relaxed; set back from the street.

Happy Day Family Restaurant, Jl. H Agus Salim No. 59 (tel. 314 30 03). A chain which offers big portions of *halal* food including juicy steaks. Not cheap (Rp6000, up to Rp30,000 for the steaks), but a full sensory experience with music, videos, and shiny surfaces everywhere.

Hot Pot Garden, Jl. H Agus Salim No. 16A (tel. 334 438). There is no menu; go pick up your seafood from the refrigerated racks in the back and have it cooked up for you. Prices are reasonable. You always know what you're getting, and it beats going to Pasar Ikan (the fish market) at 3am!

Restoran Sabang, Jl H Agus Salim No. 51A (tel. 324 873). Wedged between the fast-food atrocities of international corporatism, Sabang's pastry display, Chinese food (Rp4-7000), Indonesian food (Rp2-8000), and steaks (Rp14,000) offer plenty of chances to escape.

SIGHTS

The important points in Jakarta are nicely placed around the city, almost in enclaves of related sights. The city center, at Medan Merdeka (Merdeka Square), presents the memorialization of the nation and its religions. Northeast in Fatahillah Square are many museums, celebrating the art, culture, and history of Jakarta and Indonesia. The Dutch trading post, Sunda Kelapa, is wrapped with Dutch history and reminders of its influence on the city. Farther east is the realm of recreation, with resort facilities and the amusement park. To the south the zoo and Taman Mini encapsulate the reality of Indonesia in caged theme parks for your one-day viewing pleasure.

Medan Merdeka

Relatively easy to get around, there is a lot to see here that helps put Indonesia in a cultural and historic context. On the west side of the square is the **National Museum.** The classical building houses sculptures, artifacts, ceramics, textiles, and school children from all over the archipelago. *Ganeshas,* replicas of Java man, bronze drums, as well as some recently discovered gold treasure provide ample opportunity to stroll among numerous, though not exhaustive descriptions. Tours: English Tues.-Thurs. 9:30am; German Thurs. 10am; French Wed. 9:30am; Japanese Tues. 10am. Open Tues.-Thurs. and Sat. 8:30-2:30pm, Fri.8:30-11am, Sun 8:30-1:30pm. Admission Rp200, students and children Rp100; cameras charge Rp100. If you've taken a particular cotton to textiles, go to the **Textile Museum** a few blocks southwest of Jl. Jaksa at Jl. KS Tubun No. 4, with examples of over 300 types of fabric. Open Tues.-Thurs. 9am-2pm, Fri. 9-11am, Sat. 9am-1pm.

In the center of Medan Merdeka is **Monas,** the **National Monument** (tel. 340 453). Also known as Soekarno's Last Erection, this intentionally phallic monument represents the fertility of the nation. The base represents a *yoni,* and the obelisk, a *lingga,* a union which symbolizes said fertility. Standing 137m high, the torch is coated with 35kg of gold. Enter behind the statue of **Diponegoro,** north of the monument. Beneath Monas is an enormous room with dioramas on all four walls representing important moments in official Indonesian history with English explanations. Open daily 8am-5pm. Admission for museum Rp500, students Rp250. Admission to go to the top Rp2000, students Rp1000.

At the top of the square is **Istana Merdeka**, the presidential palace. You can look at it from the sidewalk across the street only, as the guards take their job seriously, and although it looks like an immaculate, scaled down version of the White House, they are not planning any reenactments of "1600 Pennsylvania Avenue: The Year in Review" any time soon. Surrounded by some magnificent old trees, it is only used for formal functions by President Soeharto.

Northeast of the square is the enormous dome of **Istiqlal Mosque,** the largest mosque in Southeast Asia. Visitors are welcome, though women should bring a sarong or dress appropriately. Avoid noon prayer call; enter from the north, on Jl. Veteran. A *bapak* takes you through and makes sure to point out the dome (45m across), the number of pillars (some relation to *Pancasila*), and the big drum from Kalimantan. Your *Bahasa Indonesia* needs to be pretty good to get much beyond the facts and figures, but they're very friendly toward visitors.

With characteristic in-your-face recognition and respect for religious diversity by the government, the Catholic Cathedral, **Kathedral,** is just east of the mosque. With spires of metal banding, like mini Eiffel Towers, it casts an unusual silhouette. Open for evening mass daily, there is an open-air shrine to the Virgin Mary outside with prayer benches and candles.

Fatahillah Square

Lying just northeast of Kota Station is Fatahillah Square. The Dutch buildings give this area an old feeling that the nearby history museums confirm. The former Batavia Town Hall with its teal shutters is now the **Jakarta History Museum,** *Museum Sejarah Jakarta* (tel. 679 101). If you're interested in colonial furniture, they have some massive pieces. Downstairs there are scattered old maps, a few stone carvings from the classical period, and some weaponry. Its a fairly disorganized museum in need of a curator and a little light. Bring a flashlight if the shutters are still closed. Open Tues.-Thurs. and Sun. 9am-3pm, Fri. 9am-2:30pm, Sat. 9am-12:30pm. Admission Rp150, children Rp50; Rp100 on Sunday.

The **Wayang Museum** (tel. 678 560), on the west side of the square houses an extensive collection of *wayang kulit* (leather) and *wayang golek* (wooden) puppets from across Indonesia and a few other countries. The diversity of the collection makes room for the unconventional, such as Adam, Eve, and Christ *wayangs*. Modern-image puppets include a collection of bureaucrats (you always knew someone was pulling their strings). Visually satisfying displays, but more descriptions would be helpful. Open Tues.-Thurs., Sun. 9am-3pm, Fri. 9am-2:30pm, Sat. 9am-12:30pm. Admission Rp150, children Rp50; Sun. Rp100.

The **Fine Arts and Ceramics Museum** *(Museum Seni Rupa dan Keramik),* (tel. 676 090) is in a big classical building on the east side of the square. With no descriptions for guidance, you can merrily interpret the preponderance of war and family paintings as a reflection of the national psyche. The ceramics are mostly modern "kreatif" pieces, but there are interesting, eerily carved tree-trunk totems in the south courtyard. As with the other museums, it could use a curator with inspiration. Displays of fragile ceramics in department store cases and unlit, knee-high cabinets distract from the pieces themselves. Open Tues.-Thurs., Sun. 9am-3pm, Fri. 9am-2:30pm, Sat. 9am-12:30pm. Admission Rp150, children Rp50; Rp100 on Sunday.

On the north side of the square are **Si Jagur,** a Portuguese cannon reputed to help childless women, and **Cafe Batavia,** a late-night hangout with live music.

Sunda Kelapa

This old harbor is a few blocks north of Fatahillah Square. The neighborhoods take on a maritime feel, with sails being sewn and ropes and chains sitting in big heaps. Head past the old **watchtower** and down Jl. Pasar Ikan to get to the oldest part of the city. The **Maritime Museum** (*Museum Bahari;* tel. 669 05 18), is located in the old storehouses of the Dutch East Indies Company. The displays are currently being upgraded with the help of the Dutch Historical Society. There are many models and a few full-size boats from different regions, navigational devices, and a display of photos from the heyday of sea travel. Gives a good sense of old Batavia, and some good views of the area today. Open Tues.-Thurs., Sun. 9am-4pm, Fri. 9am-3pm, Sat. 9am-1pm. Admission Rp150, children Rp100. Tours in Dutch and English.

Meander through the alleys toward the big, long tile roof building to reach **Pasar Ikan**, the fish market. It runs from 10pm to 2am, but there may still be some fish on ice in plastic containers for tomorrow's market. Cross a wood plank bridge (Rp100) to get to the **oldest part of Jakarta.** It's possible to hire a small boat and tour the harbor amid a maze of wooden schooners, or you can walk along the docks for Rp100.

Jaya Ancol Dreamland/Dunia Fantasi

You can take bus #64 or 65 from Kota, or Microlet 15 from Sunda Kelapa to **Jaya Ancol** (tel. 682 417) for an escape from Jakarta. Jaya Ancol is the name of the whole complex, encompassing resort facilities, the **Pasar Seni** art market, and the **Dunia Fantasi** amusement park (tel. 682 000). The immaculate modern park has a roller coaster, water rides, and technology palaces (Robocop 21st Century Theater, Puppet Castle, *Ramashita*—A Legend of the Future!). It's mindless predigested bliss far from the traffic and grime of the city at a bargain price. (Jaya Ancol open 24 hrs. Admission Rp1500, Sat.-Sun. Rp2000; children Rp1000, Sat.-Sun Rp1500. Park admission Rp8000, with rides Rp16000; Sat. Rp2000 extra, Sun. Rp4000 extra.)

South Jakarta

South of the city, you can see some of Indonesia's unique fauna, including Komodo dragons, tapirs, orangutans, and Sumatran tigers and elephants at **Ragunan Zoo,** (tel. 782 975; take the #P19 bus.) Open daily 9am-6pm. Admission Rp500. In the southeast corner of Jakarta "you can see all of Indonesia in a day" at **Taman Mini Indonesia Indah** (Beautiful Indonesia in Miniature, tel. 840 92 29). There are 27 pavilions with several full-scale houses from each Indonesian province. The houses are beautiful, but the history and function of the designs are lost on the tourist. The interiors have native dress on display, but most buildings merely serve as a shaded resting place for families. There are also museums, gardens, an IMAX theater, and a small waterpark, each with a separate charge. On Sunday mornings there are free dance performances in the pavilions. (Open 8am-5pm. Admission Rp2000, children Rp1000. Take bus #P10 or 11 from Sarinah, or bus #15 from Blok M, then either take a microlet or walk the last 500m.)

ENTERTAINMENT

For cheap beer, nothing beats Jl. Jaksa. The weekend crowd puts away Bintang and Heineken like there's no tomorrow. For something a little more upscale, restaurants with live music include **The Blue Note,** Standard Chartered Bldg., Jl. Jend. Sudirman Kav 33A Lt. Desar (tel. 573 28 83), **Planet Hollywood,** Hotel Kartika Chandra, Jl. Jend. Gatot Subroto Kav. 16, (tel. 562 7827), and the previously mentioned **Green Pub, Hard Rock Cafe,** and **Cafe Batavia.**

There are two nightclubs at Jaya Ancol: The **Hailai International Executive Club** (tel. 689 868) and **Samrocks** (tel. 683 969). The **Music Room** at Borobudur Inter-Continental Hotel (tel. 380 55 55) is a highly rated discotheque, as is the **Tanamur** (tel. 353 947) at Jl. Tanah Abang Timur 14.

The **Djakarta Theater** is at Jl. MH Thamrin No. 9. Mostly American action/adventure/intrigue flicks. Several evening showings; "*Hari Ini*" means today. Rp10,500.

SHOPPING

Shopping is always an experience in Jakarta. In department stores you often must take your purchase to a salesperson who will write you a receipt and take your items to the *kassa* (teller), where you pay and then can collect your package. In markets and with street vendors, bartering is the rule (except with food items), and a sense of humor and patience are paramount. If you think a price is ridiculous, walk away—if you were right, they'll stop you. Different streets have different characters. Jl. Surabaya is particularly famous for its antique stalls. Be aware that some expertise may be necessary to get a good deal. The definition of an antique is apparently not universal, or even consistent from stall to stall.

For a general selection of goods, there are a number of options along Jl. H Agus Salim. One that stands out is the **Sarinah Department Store** (Jl. MH Thamrin No. 11), like a Macy's or Harrods with an overwhelming variety of Indonesian handicrafts at reasonable prices on the third and fourth floors. While local handicrafts are cheaper when bought in the regions where they were made, the quality here is guaranteed. Open 8am-8pm daily. Beneath the Grand Hyatt, farther south on Jl. Thamrin, is the **Plaza Indonesia. Pasar Baru** (Jl. Pasar Baru), **Blok M Mall** (Jl. Sultan Hasanuddin), **Glodok Plaza** (Jl. Pinangsia Raya), and **Gajah Mada Plaza** (Jl. Gajah Madah 19-26), are all the focal shopping centers of the areas they serve.Jl. Pasar Baru is a great place to have a *batik* shirt made. *Batik* and *ikat* fabrics are available by the meter or in 3m lengths at Sarinah. Shirts should take one day

Kepulauan Seribu, the "thousand islands" northeast of Jakarta's coast are a popular ocean destination. Book boats through a travel office. Different islands cater to different price ranges, but none are cheap. Boats depart from Jaya Ancol marina.

East Timor: Jakarta's Failure

In the past decade, the New Order has come under increasing international pressure over the issue of **East Timor,** a former Portuguese colony occupied by Indonesia since 1976. The United Nations has never recognized Indonesia's sovereignty over the area, and since the end of the Cold War the "Communist threat" of an independent East Timor no longer justifies the occupation of the tiny destitute province. In 1991, the Indonesian military opened fire on hundreds of peaceful protesters in **Dili,** causing international uproar that persists to this day. In July of 1995 **General Herman Mantiri,** the nominee for ambassador to Australia, was asked to step down because of the Australian public's outrage over his support of the Dili massacre. Although events such as the "Mantiri affair" underscore the importance the western world has placed on the rights of East Timorese, the front lines are not at the U.N. or in the province itself. The real war seems to be happening among power brokers in Jakarta unwilling to admit that their policies in East Timor have failed. And until the New Order begins to work in the best interests of the East Timorese, international diplomacy and activity within East Timor are likely to go nowhere.

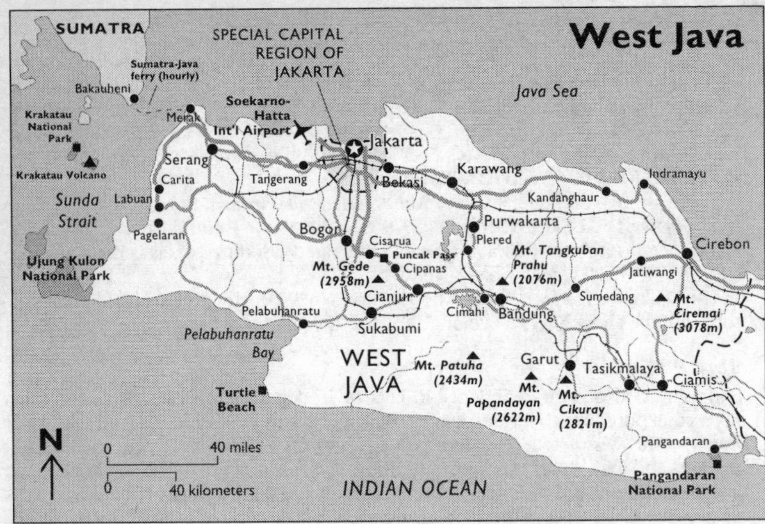

■■■ LABUAN AND CARITA

Labuan's bustling scene is disappointing after the long journey here; it's very tempting to dash for Carita and put this town's seediness behind. However, Labuan makes the best base for individual treks to Ujung Kulon reserve. And though strangers here become the focus of attention (and of stopped traffic and cheering rallies), when given a chance the locals are great resources and Labuan's most redeeming feature. Labuan's beach, beyond the goat-picked garbage piles, has a wealth of beautiful shells. Carita Beach is better for recreation and spectacular sunsets, but several miles of beachfront are about to become the Carita Bay Resort, and the town may never be the same.

ORIENTATION

There's one road in, one road out. The big bus and minibus **terminals** are right next to one another and just up from the market, where the road turns right. The terminals are all in **Labuan; Carita** is 10km farther up the road.

PRACTICAL INFORMATION

Tourist Offices: PPA Office, Jl. Permtis Kemerdekaan 51, Labuan (tel. 817 31). Tickets and insurance to Ujung Kulon and Krakatau, as well as helpful maps and information. Open Mon.-Thurs. 7:30am-3:30pm, Fri. 7:30-1pm.

Tours: Tourist Information "Mega Indonesia", Jl. Perintis Kemerdekaan 290, Labuan (tel. 810 41) and **Tourist Information Black Rhino,** Jl. Raya Carita Km10 (tel. 810 72), next to the Sunset View Losmen, run tours to Ujong Kulon and Krakatau. Expensive tours to Ujung Kulon (4 days, US$125). Boats to Krakatau (Rp50,000 for a slow boat, Rp100,000 for a fast one) are reasonable if you go with 8 other people. You can reserve directly with boat captains in Labuan, but the journey is rough, so it's important to a seaworthy boat and trustworthy crew.

Currency Exchange: BRI in Labuan, the big white building before the bus terminals, exchanges US dollars, but **traveler's checks** will take you a 30min. bus ride north to **Cilegon,** where there are many banks.

Post Office: GPO (tel. 813 91) is in Labuan, 1km beyond the terminals, around the corner and beyond the bridge. Open Mon.-Sat. 8am-2pm. **Postal code:** 42264.

Telephones: Wartel is across from the Hotel Caringin, a little farther up. International phones and fax service. Open 24 hrs. **Telephone code:** 0253.

Buses: Buses and minibuses run all day long—though at staggered intervals—to **Jakarta, Bogor, Bandung, Merak, Cirebon, Garut,** and **Rangkes.**

Local Public Transport: The usual swarm of **becaks** tool around Labuan, but to get to Carita take a **colt** (Rp500) or **ojek** (motorcycle taxi, Rp2000).

Rentals: Aci Dive Shop, at Km10, next to the Black Rhino, rents scuba/snorkeling equipment, bikes (Rp5000 per day), tents, and sleeping bags (Rp10,000 per day).

Market: The **market** at the corner of the road just past the squalid bus station is not glamorous, and after a rain the mud is awful. The nearby **Super Bazaar Supermarket,** Jl. Jend. Sudirman 21 (tel. 813 18), is essential for food and water supplies for Ujung Kulon treks. Open 9am-9pm.

Pharmacy: Apotik, Jl. Jend. Sudirman 145 (tel. 817 28). Across from the bank. Open Mon-Sat. 7am-10pm.

24-hr. Clinic: Jl. Jend. Sudirman 8 (tel. 810 09). By the green cross sign at Puskemas Labuan, between the police station and the bank.

Police: Jl. Jend. Sudirman 176 (tel. 811 10), next to the bus terminal and across from a big dirt road. Helpful staff. Open 24 hrs.

ACCOMMODATIONS

Labuan

Hotel Rawayana, Jl. Raya Carita 41 (tel. 813 86), across from the PPA office. A relative gem, set away from the road, where a clean double with *mandi* and fan is Rp25,000 (Rp30,000 on weekends), with A/C Rp50,000. Free tea and coffee.

Citra Ayu Hotel, Jl. Printis Kemerdekaan 27 (tel. 812 29), past the market toward Carita. With clean rooms, Indonesian breakfast, and tea and coffee. Singles Rp15,000. Doubles Rp20,000. A mosque-for-the-hard-of-hearing across the street provides free 4am wake-up broadcasts. *Mandi* in room. Fans Rp2500 extra.

Hotel Caringin, Jl. Printis Kemerdekaan 20 (tel. 813 88), farther along, across from the post office. Spartan rooms. Doubles Rp15,000. Triples Rp20,000. Private *mandis,* but no fans.

Carita

Wira Carita (tel. 813 38), at Km9. Rather aseptic rooms with *mandi* and fan sleep up to 4 people (Rp45,000, weekends Rp60,000), plus 10% tax. Extensive facilities include 2 restaurants, a pool, and game areas, close to a bit of free beach.

Filand Memories Guest House (tel. 810 72), at Km10. Shared *mandis.* Small fans. Free tea and coffee, and memories of Filand. Singles Rp10,000. Double Rp15,000.

Sunset View Losmen (tel. 810 75). Next door to Filand Memories, Sunset is a very social place with ping-pong tables, 10-years accumulation of interesting things (paperbacks, *gamelan* instruments, petrified wood), and a kitchen for guest use. Doubles Rp20,000. Triples Rp30,000. Private *mandi*, but no fans. A paid-entry beach area across the street, some decent restaurants and *warung* nearby.

FOOD

There are no restaurants in Labuan, but the **market** serves some very good food, and there's plenty of seafood. Carita is also primarily fed by **warungs,** though new resort hotels will add new dimensions (in both cuisine and price) to the menu.

SIGHTS

From Carita Beach, **sunsets** are pulchritudinous and women sell sarongs until it's too dark to see. In the hills behind Carita, there is a **waterfall at Curug Gendang.** Buy tickets (Rp1500) from the Pondok Wisata booth by Filand Memories and Sunset View. It is about a one-hour walk, and you can jump from the falls to the pool.

■ UJUNG KULON NATIONAL PARK

Visiting Ujung Kulon is the best reason to pass through Labuan/Carita, where you can get tickets to the park and info and advice from locals who have worked there. The park is home to about 60 seldom-seen Javan rhinos, along with lots of squirrels, bats, snakes, lizards, monkeys, wild buffalo, and estuarine crocodiles. This is what Java would be like, minus 100 million people—and admirably, there is no intention of making access easier: as a UNESCO World Heritage site, the park is to remain as preserved and protected as possible. Permits allow one-week access to the park.

Near the coast and on the beaches some effects of the 1883 Krakatau explosion and ensuing 40m *tsunami* can still be seen, with younger trees here than inland, and old coral platforms raised high and dry. The beaches of the south coast are untamed, with waves coming straight from Antarctica without interruption. Trash washes ashore to make man's presence known, but there are few of the species to be seen. In this researcher's esteemed opinion, it's a great place to run around naked. Ujung Kulon is a well-kept secret among nature and wildlife enthusiasts and it requires some effort and planning, but like childbirth, it is a unique experience that can be very rewarding.

The park is about four hours south of Labuan. Load up on food and water and leave your bags at your hostel; take a minibus to **Summer** (Rp3500, about 3hr.), then an ojek to **Tamanjaya** (30min., Rp5000). A **PPA office** at Tamanjaya sells tickets (Rp2000, plus Rp2500 insurance) and helps arrange for **guides,** required on any trip (Rp10,000 per day, plus food) and porters. Choose your guide carefully and request an English speaker. Porters are helpful for three-day outings—trails and dodgy bridges are difficult with a large water supply strapped to your back. You can see beautiful beaches and stretches of jungle without a boat, but unfortunately, the best wildlife hangs out in the least accessible areas, around **Handeleum Island** and **Peucang Island** (Rp100,000 and Rp200,000 for a boat from Tamanjaya). For overnights in Tamanjaya, there are **bungalows** with electricity and *mandi* ($30) and limited space at **homestays** (Rp10-15,000). No electricity. Shared *mandi*. Meals available. Some **rooms** are available at guideposts within the park, and some nicer accommodations (at steep prices) on the islands, but camping with a mosquito net and waterproof groundpad is feasible. There is no need to wear boots to trek; rugged sport sandals may be best for those who enjoy walking through muddy ooze. Other essential items to bring (in a plastic bag): insect repellent, tweezers, and disinfectant.

■■■ BOGOR

Virtually a suburb of Jakarta, Bogor is cosmopolitan enough to satisfy any traveler's longings for the creature comforts of home—from American movies, to pirated Japanese video games, to a surplus of donuts (with and without cheese). Still, Bogor's true heart and soul are the world-renowned Botanical Gardens, nourished by the highest average rainfall in West Java. Though Bogor is easily navigated (neon-green angkots are everywhere), try to get an early start since rainy afternoons are frequent here. It may preferable to stay in Bogor and explore Jakarta rather than vice-versa, but beyond the Botanical Gardens, Istana Bogor, and the Gong Factory, there's more here for the umbrella-toting anthropologist than the tourist.

ORIENTATION

Bogor is built around the **Botanical Gardens,** which also contain **Istana Bogor** and the **zoo.** The gardens are bounded by **Jalan Ir. H. Juanda** on the west (where the **post office** is located), **Jalan Otista** to the south (with the entrances to the zoo and gardens), and **Jalan Raya Pajajaran** on the east; followed south, Jl. Raya Pajajaran continues to the Puncak and Bandung, with a toll-road turnoff to Jakarta as well. Leading away from Jl. Ir. H. Juanda is **Jalan Capten Muslihat,** which leads to **Jalan Dewi Sartika** (a right-hand turn), home to the day and night market area. Following Jl. Capten Muslihat past the train track, the next major intersection is with **Jalan Mayor Oking** turning to the right and **Jalan Palendang** to the left. Most of the backpacker joints sit along the Jl. Mayor Oking/Jl. Paledang stretch.

PRACTICAL INFORMATION

Tourist Office: Jl. Ir. H. Juanda 10 (tel. 338 052), right of *Balai Kota* (town hall). Supersaturated map and Bogor and Indonesia info. Open Mon.-Fri. 8am-4pm.

Travel Agencies: Travel Bureau Wisata, Jl. Mayor Oking 18-20 (tel. 324 150) books bus, plane, and PELNI tickets. Open daily 7am-6pm. **Kantor Cabang Tours and Travel,** on Jl. Capten Muslihat, in the beige and brown hat-shaped building at Taman Topi, below the railway station. Offers similar services. Open Mon.-Fri. 8am-7pm, Sat. 8am-4pm, Sun. 9am-1pm. **Garuda Indonesia** (tel. 338 436). Open Mon.-Fri. 7:30am-5pm, Sat.-Sun. and holidays 9am-1pm. **24-hr. reservations:** tel. (021) 251 22 29.

Currency Exchange: Bali Bank, Jl. Capt. Muslihat 17A (tel. 312 990), near the railway station. Open Mon.-Fri. 8am-3pm. Has an **ATM. Bank BNI,** Jl. Ir. H. Juanda 52 (tel. 311 46), just south of the GPO. Open Mon.-Fri. 8am-4pm.

Post Office: GPO, Jl. Ir. H. Juanda 5, across from where Jl. Paledang intersects the road around the gardens. The orange overhang is the giveaway. Open Mon.-Fri. 8am-6pm. Poste Restante. **Postal code:** 16124.

Telephones: Jl. Pengadilan Blk. 14 (tel. 312 487). A big blue building with international phones, fax, telegrams, and phonecards. At Taman Topi, **"Wartel Exotica"** has international phones, fax, and telegrams. Open 24 hrs. At the entrance to the Botanical Gardens is another **24-hr. Wartel,** with Home Country Direct phones and telegram services. **Telephone code:** 0251.

Trains: The train station (tel. 324 529) is just northwest of the Botanical Gardens, on Jl Permas. To: **Jakarta** (every 30min., 1-1½ hr.) and **Sukabumi.** Economy trains to **Surabaya** (Rp1000); make a reservation.

Buses: The bus terminal is southeast of the gardens, off Jl. Raya Pajajaran. To: **Jakarta** (40min., Rp1000); **Bandung** (4hr., Rp2-3000—via **Puncak Pass** on weekdays, via **Sukabumi** on weekends); and **Pangandaran** (10hr., via **Banjar**). Buses leave from the terminal when full. For a more comfortable (more expensive) ride, contact a tour company.

Local Transport: Green **angkots** are everywhere (fixed Rp300). There are various routes, and they can be hailed from almost any street. There are also **delman** (pony carts) on the south and east sides of the gardens.

English Bookstores: Gunung Agung (tel. 326 876), at the Bogor Internusa Shopping Center, 2nd floor, on Jl. Raya Pajajaran.

Market: Pasar Kebon Kembang on Jl. Dewi Sartika has the usual fruit and maze of little stalls. **Pasar Baru,** Jl. Suryakencana 3, near the gate to the Botanical Gardens behind the Bogor Plaza Shopping Center, with more of the same, and the meat-market floor slippery with…something.

Public Toilets: In shopping centers.

Swimming Pool: Villa Duta on Jl. Pakuan (Rp4000). Angkot #303 to "Villa Duta."

Hospitals: RS Salak, Jl. Jend. Sudirman 8 (tel. 324 678). Has a pharmacy and a doctor available 24 hrs. **Apotik RB Dr. R. Soekojo,** Jl. Paledang 29 (tel. 324 209). 24-hr. clinic and **pharmacy.**

Emergency: Police: tel. 110. **Fire:** tel. 113. **Ambulance:** tel. 118.

Police: Jl. Capten Muslinat #16 (tel. 322 463), near where the tracks cross the road. Open 24 hrs.

ACCOMMODATIONS

Abu Pensione, Jl. Mayor Oking 15 (tel. 322 893). The happening place in Bogor, covering all services and price ranges. Good, but overpriced, restaurant overlooks the river. English spoken. Travel agency for flights, overland tours, Istana Bogor tours, and intercity share taxis. The more you pay, the nicer the room you get; beware the 10% tax. Dorms Rp5500. Singles Rp10,000. Twins Rp15,000. Doubles Rp25-45,000; may include breakfast, A/C, and hot water. Tea and water included.

Amour Pensione, Jl. Mayor Oking 11/4 (tel. 326 261). Next to Abu's, it has fewer facilities but its comfortable rooms aren't a bad value. Dorms with shared *mandi* Rp5000. Singles in a twin room with private *mandi* Rp10,000; for 2 it's Rp15,000. Extra bed Rp2500. Laundry and breakfast available.

Puri Bali, Jl. Paledang 50 (tel. 317 498), southeast of the gardens. Run by the venerable octogenarian I. Made Tawan, an unstoppable fountain of information who speaks English much better than he can hear or see. The huge, quiet rooms are dim but colorful. Singles around Rp6-13,000, doubles about Rp16,000.

Firman Pensione, Jl. Paledang 48 (tel. 323 426). Next door to Puri Bali, with more of a backpacker's atmosphere. Firman's friendly family will take you on some of their outings (including fruit-picking) if you behave. Front rooms are noisy. Restaurant has good prices. Dorm Rp6000. Singles Rp8000. Doubles Rp14-17,000, with private *mandi* Rp20-30,000. Triples Rp25,000. All have fan and include breakfast, tea, coffee, and water. Laundry service.

Wisma Mirah I, Jl. Martadinata 17 (tel. 333 520), a long walk from the town center (or a short ride on angkot 12 from the train station). Fair prices, decent rooms, and spring mattresses may be worth the pseudo-trek. Economy doubles with fan and shared *mandi* Rp25-30,000, plus 15% tax. For Rp36,500-45,500 you can have your own *mandi*, and hot water too. Extra bed Rp12,000.

Wisma Permata, Jl. Raya Pajajaran 35 (tel. 318 007). Alone on the east side of the gardens, they clearly want you to feel at home—but leaving clean, old shirts for guests' use may be a bit too reminiscent of older brother's hand-me-downs. Economy doubles with fan and *mandi* Rp35,000. Moderate rooms with TV and A/C Rp55,000. All prices 15% more on weekends and holidays. Credit cards accepted. Restaurant open 6:30am-midnight with steak-centered menu. Live music at night.

FOOD

At night, **warungs** line up all along Jl. Dewi Sartika. Those planted by the railway station are seedier, but they make many great varieties of *martabaks.* Try a *martabak manis*—like a cake, with a layer of chocolate, peanuts, and sugar, just as yummy as it sounds. Plenty of **fast food** lurks between the curious concrete hats. **Bakeries** are part of almost every supermarket, but particularly noteworthy is Singapore Bakery at the corner of Jl. Capt. Muslihat and Jl. Mayor Oking. For Sundanese food, **Mirah Sari,** Jl. Merdeka 9 (tel. 314 727), has good, inexpensive options, even for vegetarians. You'll also find many small restaurants at Taman Topi. **Rumah Makan 88** has cheap Sundanese and Indonesian food, and wide selections of Chinese and seafood.

SIGHTS

That's right, 87 hectacres of **Botanical Garden,** or *Kebun Raya.* Enter on the south side of town, at Jl. Suryakencana; within the gates stands a memorial to Sir Stamford Raffles' wife. Only with a hired guide can you visit the vast array of tropical plants. Even if you go solo, a stroll through the daisies and tumbled stone paths can be very rewarding—indulge in views of frangipani trees, waterlilies, a cactus garden, an orchid house, Istana Bogor (the Presidential Palace), and the replica of "The Little Mermaid" statue standing out back). Best of all are the jumbo vines, stirring up latent Tarzan-envy, and the massive engulfing tree roots; you'll want to snuggle up and tell them all your problems—or at least pose there for a photo. The gardens are havens for birds, but also for bugs, so put on plenty of bugspray before entering this domesticated jungle. Admission Rp2100 on weekdays and Saturdays, Rp1100 on Sundays and holidays. Open 8am-4pm.

For nature of a more enclosed, nonliving variety, check out the stuffed animals and skeletons at the **Zoological Museum** (tel. 322 177), left of the garden entrance. Open Sat.-Thurs. 8am-4pm, Fri. 8am-3pm. Admission Rp600. A little farther, close to the GPO, is the **Ethnobotany Museum,** Jl. Ir. H. Juanda 5 (tel 322 035). Dedicated to the interaction of the people and plants of Indonesia, the fledgling museum bestows on its visitors a renewed appreciation of those glorious growing greens. Admission Rp500. Open Mon.-Wed. 8am-4pm, Thurs. 8am-3:30pm, Fri. 8-11am.

Getting admitted to **Istana Bogor,** the **Presidential Palace,** is a bit tricky. You can arrange a group tour through the tourist office, but unless you have formal wear stashed in your pack, the "no t-shirt" rule will require you to don loaner duds, sure to make for fashion atrocities. Abu Pensione also arranges tours (1hr., Rp10,000). Despite the skimpiness of the guide's descriptions, Indonesian history buffs will easily detect Soekarno's influence in the inordinate number of statues and paintings of nude women. These women, along with his four wives, surely helped to brighten up Soekarno's house arrest here from 1967 to 1970.

Like so many Indonesian military exhibits, the **Bogor Army Museum,** Jl. Merdeka 56 (tel. 326 377), has guns. Lots of them. Its displays progress through the country's battle for independence. Open Mon.-Thurs. 9am-2pm. Admission Rp300.

The **Gong Home Factory,** at Jl. Pancasan 17, is like a visit to Thor's workshop, with men sweating away and hammering in sequence as they pound out the shape of a gong. Embers glow and sparks dance in the small, very flammable-looking room. Visitors are cheerfully welcomed to take pictures and then burst into flames. Open Sat.-Thurs. 8am-noon and 1-4pm.

Zigzag back to the adjacent alley to visit another cottage industry—a **kerupuk factory.** The dough is kneaded, spun into cakes, dried, and dropped into hot oil (kerplunk), 6am-3pm. To get there, take angkot 02 to catch a Ciapus-Rancamaya angkot by Pasar Baru, which will take you right there. Angkot 02 will also take you to a nearby *batutulis* (**inscribed stone**) on Jl. Batutulis, dating from the reign of the second Hindu kingdom here in the 16th century. It records the rule of King Surzawisesa, and was erected by one of his sons. Open daily 8am-4pm. Donations requested.

The Life of Sir Stamford Raffles: Part the Fourth

Perhaps realizing that Indonesia would one day be the 4th most populous nation in the world, Sir Stamford Raffles, eventual founder of Singapore, had the perspicacity to plot the conquest of Java from the Dutch and served as Lieutenant-Governor from 1812 to 1816. His wife Olivia died during this tenure, but she, like Raffles, was so loved by the locals that her spirit lives on through her statue in the Botanical Gardens in Bogor. On his return to England, Raffles, the most popular man in the commonwealth, married a second wife, Sophia, and published the definitive two-volume *History of Java*. One wonders when this illustrious hero slept. (To read more about Sir Stamford's adventures, see page 771.)

■ NEAR BOGOR

Most places are more than a day's outing from Bogor. **Pelabuhanratu**, a coastal town to the southwest, takes four hours to reach by share taxi (talk to Abu's) or an indeterminate time by colt (which only move from Sukabumi when full). The beach is quite nice, but currents render it unsafe for swimming. Though it gets crowded on weekends, there are plenty of accommodations. The **Cibodas** extension of the Botanical Gardens, about an hour away by bus or colt, makes a good daytrip; climbs farther into the park should be based from Cibodas itself. See The Puncak for info.

■■■ THE PUNCAK

The impressive mountain pass that draws Jakartans like flies lends its name to the entire region, called the Puncak. Route 2, known as Jalan Raya, runs through the Puncak from Bogor to Bandung. On the Bogor side of the pass, the road runs by miles of tea plantations as it carves its way up the mountain. On both sides, the main drag has seen unchecked development, but a short walk off the road offers a return to terraced hills and valleys. Along with the mountain scenery, the cool climate and fresh breezes are a trump card for this elevated region. Just a few hours from Jakarta, Bogor, and Bandung, the pass is lined by several small towns. Cisarua, on the Bogor side, offers a mediocre view of the Puncak, but is convenient for touring the tea plantations. Cibodas, a few km off Jl. Raya in Cipanas, has accommodations serving the Botanical Gardens and Gede Pangrango National Park, and offers fine views.

GETTING THERE AND AWAY

Public buses have trouble navigating Route 2 on weekends, when traffic is snarled, gnarled, and generally unpleasant. Otherwise, public buses run almost every 30 minutes from Jakarta, Bogor, and Bandung. On weekends it is possible to come from Bandung to Cianjur by bus, then by angkot the rest of the way. You can catch minibuses from the Bogor side, but Jl. Raya swarms with Jakartans on Sunday night.

ORIENTATION AND PRACTICAL INFORMATION

Cisarua

The **post office** is at Jl. Raya 525. Open Mon.-Thurs. 8am-4pm, Fri. 8-11am and 1-4pm, Sat. 8am-3pm. **Postal code:** 16750. The **phone office** up the street has coin and card phones. **Phone code:** 0251. The **pharmacy,** Apotik Cisarua, at Jl. Raya 617 (tel. 255 075), is open Mon.-Sat. 8am-10pm, Sun. 8am-4pm.

Cibodas

The post office, *wartel,* bank, and minimarkets are located a few km toward Bandung in Cipanas. The **post office** is at Jl. Raya Cipanas 109 (tel. 513 466), open Mon.-Thurs. 8am-2pm, Fri. 8-11am, Sat. 8am-1pm. **Postal code:** 43253. Right next door is the **24-hr. wartel,** which handles international calls, telegrams, and faxes. **Phone code:** 0255. **Bank BNI,** Jl. Raya Cipanas 167 (tel. 512 022), a couple hundred meters up the road toward the Pass, will cash up to $300 in traveler's checks per day. Open Mon.-Fri. 8am-3pm. The Cipanas **angkot station** is up the street, next to the post office and past the **market.** There are a couple of pharmacies in town, but a **24-hour emergency clinic** (tel. 512 665) lies just toward Bandung at the intersection of Jl. Cibodas and Jl. Raya, at #17; the clinic has a **lab** and **pharmacy** on the premises.

ACCOMMODATIONS AND FOOD

Cisarua

The only option is the **Kopo International Youth Hostel,** Jl. Raya Puncak 557 (tel. 254 296), next to the gas station. English and Bahasa Indonesia signs extol the virtues of considerate social behavior and separate-sex dorms. The small, clean rooms are well set back from the road, and come with a blanket, bright light bulbs, and breakfast. Dorms Rp7000, members (with IYH card) Rp6000. Doubles Rp16,000, members Rp14,000. Shared bathroom and no hot water. Doubles with bathroom and hot water Rp27,000, members Rp22,000. Their local map details recommended daytrips, and the game facilities include volleyball and ping-pong. Closes at 11pm.

Kopo also has a pretty good café, but countless stalls sell fruits and veggies on the main street. Watch out for banana peels! The specialty here is sweet corn roasted *sate*-style. Next to Kopo is the **Puncak Raya** hotel/restaurant/supermarket/theater (tel. 255 120). The restaurant has a wide menu of various meats (Rp4-12,000). Open 10am-10pm. A km or so toward the Pass is the **Ibu Cirebon,** across from the pharmacy, serving Indonesian food and Cirebon specialties like *nasi lengko* at Jl. Raya Puncak 654 (tel. 255 573). Most dishes Rp2-6000, some specials Rp13-15,000.

Cibodas

There are a few more choices in Cibodas than in Cisarua, and all overlook the beautiful cultivated valley, graced with birds and butterflies. To reach the following lodgings, take a bemo several km up Jl. Cibodas from the junction at Jl. Raya (Rp300).

Freddy's Homestay (tel. 515 473) is the first you'll come to, 100m short of the tall (non-functioning) admission gate to the Botanical Gardens. It's on the right, between some houses and across from the haphazardly numbered 133. Small, clean doubles Rp10-20,000. Breakfast and tea included. Shared *mandis*. Run by a Dutch woman, this place caters to western crowds and serves them well. Birdwatchers will want to see Freddy's logbook. Packs are available for trekking into the park.

Just beyond the admission gate to the right is the **Pondok Pemuda** hostel (tel. 512 807), for the hardy, the hard-pressed, or the hard-up. The beautiful wood buildings with tent-like roofs stand among well-kept shrubs and flowers. Though the 12-person "dormitories" (3 side-by-side mattresses on 4 platforms) could use a little more attention, they come with a blanket for a bargain Rp5000. If you come during the week you may well have it to yourself. Next door is the **Wisma Jamur** (tel. 512 413), behind an unusually shaped whitewashed main building. Cane-woven walls make for dark rooms with little to justify the price of a triple (Rp22,500) or a quad (Rp30,000), but there are plenty of common areas for hanging around. Shared *mandis*; omelette or *nasi goreng* breakfast included.

There are numerous *warung* around the front gates of the park, and Freddy's has a small restaurant. Pondok Pemuda's restaurant closes unpredictably. For a nice setting (but limited choice), try the **Valley View Restaurant** (tel. 512 051), on Jl. Cibodas a couple km down from the Botanical Gardens. Come during daylight hours for the best view. Open 9am-9pm. Drinks and snacks Rp2500, entrees Rp8-11,000. You can take a break and eat out in style at **Puncak Cafe,** Jl. Sindanglaya Raya 180 (tel. 511 335), the restaurant at the 5-star Summit Panhegar Hotel. Take an angkot toward Cipanas. The prices aren't too bad (Rp3500-24,000, desserts Rp2500-8500)—but beware the 21% tax! Credit cards accepted. Open 24 hours.

SIGHTS

Cisarua

An hour's walk from the Kopo hostel lie the seven **Air Terjun Cilember** (Cilember Waterfalls). After paying Rp250, then Rp550, you have some steep climbing ahead of you. A guide will join you at one of the gates (though he may speak only limited English). The red clay trails are tough going, but the falls are worth the effort. Many Indonesians camp here on holiday, but your guide will help prevent you from coming upon a bathing group. Back in town, catch an angkot or bus to the **Gunung Mas Tea Factory** (Gunung Mas Pabrik Teh) sign, from which a 15-minute walk takes you to the tea factory. If you drive up to the pass early in the day, you'll see women in big umbrella-like hats picking the young tea leaves. There is also a safari park, **Taman Safari,** with roaming wildlife, swimming pool, and assorted entertainment. Either walk or take an angkot to the Safari junction, then take a bemo to the park gates (Rp750). Rp5000 admission includes a lift back to the junction.

Cibodas

The **Kebon Raya Cibodas,** an extension of the Bogor Botanical Gardens, rests just 1km beyond the Jl. Cibodas accommodations. Home to thousands of high-altitude species, the area is a bird-watcher's paradise—even a walk to the gardens along Jl. Cibodas, in the company of bopping butterflies, is incredible. Residents participate in the nursery business, and bonsai and flowering plants line the whole 4km stretch. The **gardens** spread out on the lower fringe of the **Gede Pangrango National Park,** a large, protected area with substantial wildlife. Gardens open Mon.-Thurs. 8am-3:30pm, Fri. 8am-3pm, and Sat.-Sun. 8am-2pm, though the ticket booth takes a lunch break. Admission Rp2000, but groups of students may get in for Rp1000 each. To walk the trails to the hot springs (2 hrs.), waterfalls (1 hr.), summit, and caldera of the Gunung Gede (2958m tall, 5 hrs.), or the Gunung Pangrango summit (3019m tall, 3 hrs.), you must get a permit and pay nominal insurance. Obtain permits at the **Wisma Cinta Alam Visitors Center,** an official set of buildings to the right of the gardens' entrance. English-speaking guides can be hired. Officials will check that those planning overnight treks have sleeping bags, warm clothing, and basic gear. Come prepared with plenty of food and water.

■■■ BANDUNG

Once "the Paris of the East Indies," Bandung has aged, but is still a surprisingly attractive and friendly city. Westerners will experience a little visual *déjà vu*, with the art deco architectural heritage that still influences building. Bandung is a manufacturing center; clothes, especially jeans, can be purchased all over the city for low prices. Traffic (and the accompanying noise and pollution) are a challenge for those looking to relax, but Bandung makes a good hub for exploring volcanoes and hot springs, and many of the museums here are free.

As the capital of the province of West Java, Bandung is something of an intellectual capital as well, with its numerous universities. The great numbers of students, no doubt keep the manufacturers on top of current western fashion. The traffic aside, there is a laid-back attitude among the people, and some will gladly spend a few hours helping you out and showing you around, so they can practice their English. (If this appeals, drop by the English Club at UNPAD). Bandung still caters to an international clientele, as its first-rate hotels like the Savoy Homann will attest, but its easygoing feel and cool climate make it a pleasant transition between Jakarta and the smaller cities and country towns to the east.

ORIENTATION

A sense of location is more important than a sense of direction for Bandung's highly angular layout. Things generally do run north-south or east-west on a large scale, however. **Jalan Asia-Afrika** runs west through the center of town, by the **alun-alun** (town square), **BRI building,** and the **Hotel Savoy Homann. Jalan Otto Iskandardinata** ends at the north of the **Governor's Mansion,** and crosses **Jalan Kebonjati/ Jalan Suniraja.** This street runs parallel to Jl. Asia-Afrika, and changes names in front of the **railway station. Jalan Braga,** once the Dutch and art deco heart of town, runs north-south next to the **Museum Asia-Afrika** at Jl. Asia-Afrika 65. The north suburbs sport tree-lined boulevards, and volcanic peaks rise around Bandung on all sides.

PRACTICAL INFORMATION

Tourist Office: Tourist Information Center, (tel. 420 66 44). Northeast corner of the *alun-alun.* Dr. Aryan Suripatty is in charge, and will share his knowledge happily. A rather useless map is available, as well as a more dated but thorough information book. Tours in and around Bandung can be booked here. Open Mon.-Sat. 8am-4pm. There is also a branch at the railway station.

Post Office: GPO, Jl. Asia-Afrika 49 (tel. 161). International phones and telegrams available. Poste Restante. Open 8am-8pm.

Telephones: International phones available at the **GPO** and the **Wartel,** Jl. Suniaraja 119 (tel. 420 79 58). Jl. Suniraja is the east arm of Jl. Kebonjati. Open 8am-11pm. They also do telegrams, faxes, and collect calls. **Telephone code:** 022.

Travel Agencies: Pacto Tours and Travel (tel. 420 47 39) in the Savoy Hotel, Jl. Asia-Afrika 112. **American Express** agent as well. Open Sun.-Fri. 8am-5pm, Sat. 8am-2pm. **Sari Holiday** (tel. 420 77 37), north of Jl. Asia-Afrika on Jl. Tamblok. Open Mon.-Fri. 8am-8pm, Sat. 8am-1pm. Most hostels book tours around Bandung, as well as express buses to Pagandaran, Yogya, Surabaya, and Denpasar.

Currency Exchange: Bank Nusantara Patahyangan, Jl. Jend. Sudirman 30-32 (tel. 420 20 88). Says **Devisa** on the doors. Exchange on second floor. Open Mon.-Fri. 8am-4pm, Sat. 8:30am-2pm. **Golden Moneychanger,** Jl. Lembong 36 (tel. 420 55 34), next to the Army Museum. Also Jl. Otto Iskandardinata 180 (tel. 438 438). Open Mon.-Fri. 8:30am-4:30pm, Sat. 8:30am-2pm.

Airport: Husen Sastra Airport (tel. 615 871), is west of the city center, only a short trip by minibus to the gate. Daily flights are available throughout the archipelago. **Garuda/Merpati Airlines,** Jl. Asia-Afrika 73 (tel. 441 226), across from the Savoy Hotel. **Sempati Airlines,** Jl. Merdeka 2 (tel. 420 16 12). **Bouraq,** Jl. Ciampelas 27 (tel. 437 896).

Trains: The railway station is behind the *angkutan kota* station (*terminal setasion*) off of Jl. Kebonjati, on Jl. Setasion Barat. The station master's office (tel. 420 69 17) is open 24 hrs. Reservations for weekend trains can be made 1 week in advance. To: **Jakarta** (5, 6:15, 9:10, and 10:45am, 2:50 and 4:10pm; 3hr.; 2nd class Rp7500, 1st class Rp10,000); **Yogya** (5:30, 7:40am, and 5:30pm; 9hr.; 3rd class Rp3800, 2nd class Rp5000, 1st class Rp8500).

Buses: Long-distance buses leave from **Kebon Kelapa Terminal** on Jl. Dewi Sartika for destinations to the west. Buses to the east and north leave from **Terminal Cicaheum** on Jl. Jendirman A. Yani. Get to either station by taking the Ciberu-

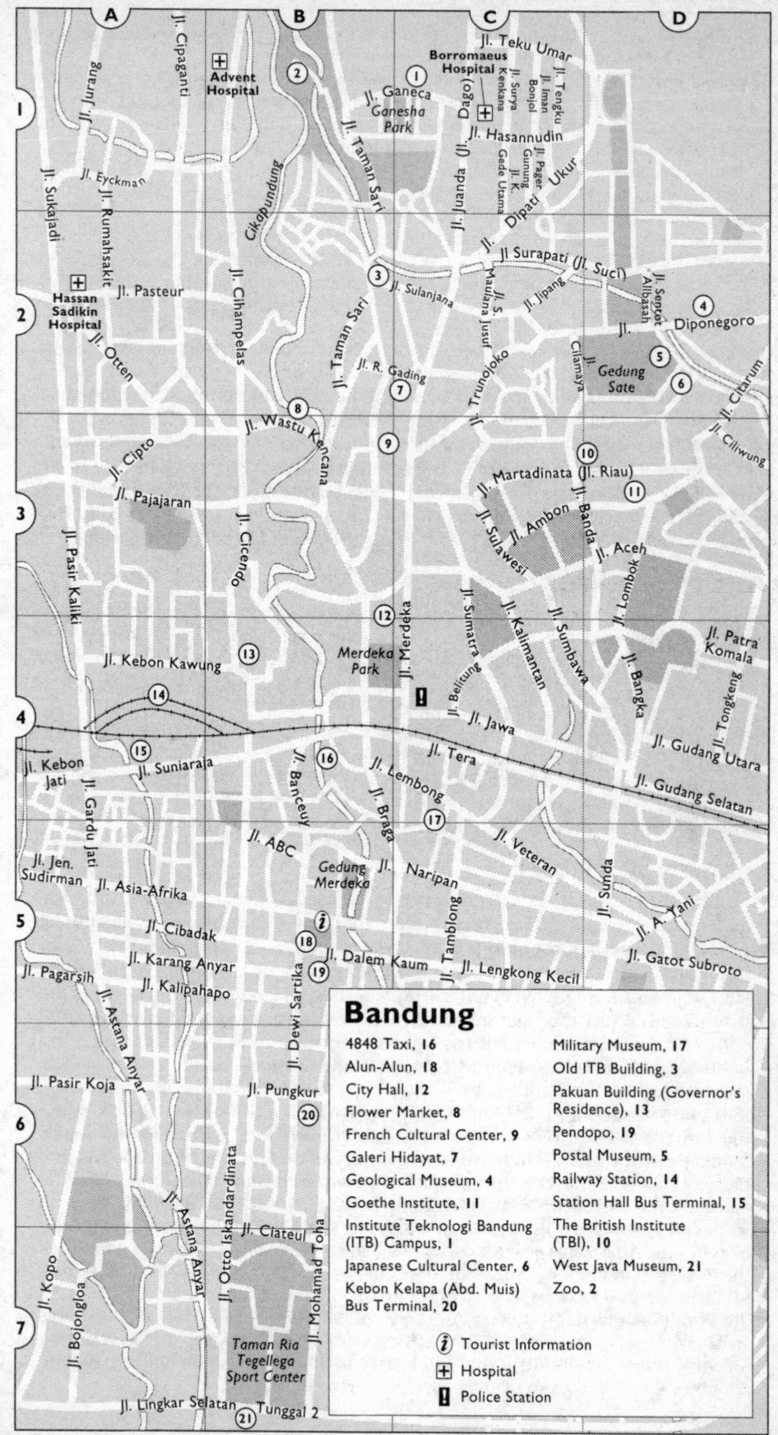
Bandung
4848 Taxi, 16
Alun-Alun, 18
City Hall, 12
Flower Market, 8
French Cultural Center, 9
Galeri Hidayat, 7
Geological Museum, 4
Goethe Institute, 11
Institute Teknologi Bandung (ITB) Campus, 1
Japanese Cultural Center, 6
Kebon Kelapa (Abd. Muis) Bus Terminal, 20
Military Museum, 17
Old ITB Building, 3
Pakuan Building (Governor's Residence), 13
Pendopo, 19
Postal Museum, 5
Railway Station, 14
Station Hall Bus Terminal, 15
The British Institute (TBI), 10
West Java Museum, 21
Zoo, 2
Tourist Information
Hospital
Police Station
Borromaeus Hospital
Advent Hospital
Hassan Sadikin Hospital
Ganesha Park
Gedung Sate
Merdeka Park
Gedung Merdeka
Taman Ria Tegellega Sport Center
A
B
C
D
1
2
3
4
5
6
7

Kebon Kelapa or Cicaheum-Kebon Kelapa city buses (Rp300). Book tickets through hostel tour agents or at the station.

Local Public Transport: City buses (Rp200) have north-south and east-west routes, so you can reach your destination by going across and then up or down along the main roads. This is complicated a little by the many one-way roads in the city center: Jl. Asia-Afrika is westbound; Jl. Kebonjati is eastbound; Jl. Otto Iskandardinata is southbound; and Jl. Astanaanyar is northbound. **Angkutan kotas** (angkots) ply the city for Rp300 and surrounding regions at prices that vary according to distance. In front of the railway station is a major terminal. **Becaks** also are scattered about, but probably best left until evening, when traffic dies down. **"4848 Taxis"** (tel. 434 48 48) are available throughout the city, and can be chartered as well, which is probably easier than renting a car.

Car rentals: Media Wisata, Jl. Cassa 2 Terusan Pasteur (tel. 217 024). Rentals for 6-, 12-, and 24-hr. periods.

Luggage Storage: Locker Office, at the railway station. Rp750 for less than 24 hrs. Rp1500 per day. Open 5am-6pm.

Cultural Organization: British Council, Jl. Lembong 4/16 (tel. 420 37 88), near the Hotel Panhegar.

Public Markets: Manufactured goods line the sidewalks downtown all day long. **Pasar Baru** offers textiles and clothing within and fruit outside on Jl. Otto Iskandardinata, near Jl. ABC. **Pasar Malam** (night market) is mostly *warungs*, off the northeast corner of the *alun-alun.*

Supermarkets: Hero Supermarket, in the shopping center on the east side of the *alun-alun.* **Super-Ekonomi** is on the third floor.

Swimming Pools: Centrum, behind the jeans stores on Jl. Cihampelas and the **Karangsetra** pool in Northern Bandung off of Jl. Sukajadi. Both are public.

Library: The main **government library** is behind Gedung Asia Afrika. The Universities of ITB, UNPAD, and Catholic also have libraries.

Bookstores: Gramedia, Jl. Merdeka 43 (tel. 433 287), has the best selection of English books. Open Mon.-Sat. 8:30am-9pm, Sun. 8:30am-10pm. Bookstores on Jl. Braga have a smattering of English books.

Pharmacy: Kimia Farma 12, Jl. Ir. H. Juanda 1 (tel. 420 07 11). Open 24 hours.

Hospital: RS Kebonjati, Jl. Kebonjati 152 (tel. 614 058).

Gay Men's Resources: GAYa PRIAngan, c/o Salon Wyl's, Jl. Pelesiran 5, Taman Sari (tel. 250 43 25). *GAYa Nusantara* available here.

Emergency: Police: (tel. 110). **Fire:** (tel. 113). **Ambulance:** (tel. 118).

ACCOMMODATIONS

A bustling backpacker scene has given rise to the usual street of cheap accommodations. You have to look farther and pay more for hot water, however, and Bandung can be chilly. The **Jl. Kebonjati** accommodations have simple restaurants where there is usually a TV going on all day, and are good places to talk to the young Indonesians who semi-cooperatively run the hostels and local tours. They're perhaps the best source of information on mundane matters, and seem to keep an eye on the street to take care of their patrons. Unless otherwise indicated, each hotel has shared *mandis* but no fans. Laundry is available everywhere.

The Old Sakadarna, Jl. Kebonjati 50 (tel. 439 897). A little ways back from the busy street. It has a very friendly feel (thanks to Yeddi), and wonderful smells emanate from the kitchen. Some locals come during the holidays, but it's designed to give tourists some respite. An upstairs terrace compensates for the small rooms. Singles Rp7000. Doubles Rp10,000. Triples Rp20,000.

Le Yossie Homestay, Jl. Kebonjati 53 (tel. 420 54 53). Behind pastel green shutters lies the American-owned Yossie. Has a small, lively restaurant. Nice tapestries provide a bit of culture. Dorms Rp5000. Singles Rp9000. Doubles Rp13,500 (trundle bed leaves no extra space). Triples Rp16,500. Free tea and coffee.

The New Sakadarna, Jl. Kebonjati 34 (tel. 420 28 11). Pleasantly spacious rooms with windows and lumpy pillows. Kick back and chat away at the hopping evening scene downstairs. Daily *Jakarta Post.* Singles with two beds Rp10,000. Doubles Rp20,000. Extra mattress Rp2500. Free tea and coffee.

Hotel Hegar, Jl. Setasiun Selatan 1-3 (tel. 420 33 02), next to the angkot station; things quiet down even later than on Kebonjati. Decently sized, darkly paneled rooms are a bit cave-like. More of a local scene than a backpacking scene. Singles Rp10,000. Doubles Rp15,000; with *mandis* Rp20,000. Triples Rp22,500. All prices subject to 10% tax. Free tea and coffee.

Hotel Surabaya, Jl. Setasiun Selatan 1-3 (tel. 436 791). A very impressive building where history lingers in the pictures and posters, colored-glass window, and the furniture of the deluxe rooms. Economy class rooms: Singles Rp11,500. Doubles Rp20,000. Triples Rp30,000. Quads Rp35,000. Standard class rooms include towels and blankets for about Rp2000. All rooms have wardrobes and tables. Free tea.

By Moritz, Jl. Luxor Permai 17 (tel. 439 024). South off Jl. Kebonjati, about 20m. Follow the By Moritz sign with the big heart. Small rooms, but Sundanese cane weavings cover the walls. Distance from Kebonjati brings welcome quiet. A second Moritz, with a pool, should open down the street by the end of 1995. Dorms Rp6000. Singles Rp12,000. Doubles Rp16,000; with *mandi* Rp17,500.

Hotel Sahara, Jl. Otto Iskandardinata 3 (tel. 420 46 84), northeast of the train station, just below the Governor's Mansion. Sahara is at the north terminus of the street, across the overpass. An old building with dim, but furnished rooms set back from the street. Singles Rp14,000. Doubles Rp21,000; with *mandi*, TV, and fan Rp35,000. Breakfast included.

Dewi Sartika Hotel, Jl. Dewi Sartika 18 (tel. 431 190). Two blocks south of Jl. Asia-Afrika. Functional rooms no quieter than Jl. Kebonjati. Standard *mandi*. Singles Rp24,000; with fan and shower Rp31,200. Doubles Rp31,200; with fan and TV Rp38,400. Triples Rp35,000. Breakfast included.

Hotel Ace Abode, Jl. H. Sarip 2. Off Jl. Alkateri, west of the GPO; upstairs in a semi-art-deco building. Well-kept and quiet. Clean rooms have colored glass windows and nice wood. Private *mandi*, A/C, hot water, and bathtubs with a double bed for a "discount" rate of Rp33,000. Ignore the stated Rp50,000; persist gently.

FOOD

An awful lot of travelers seem to fall ill in Bandung, so it's best to stick to well-frequented **warung** that look clean, if not cafes, restaurants, or food courts. *Bakso,* a noodle soup with balls of meat, and *tahu* (tofu), are available everywhere, and the area around Pasar Baru offers a fabulous array of fruit. *Bandrek,* made of ginger, and *bajigur,* made of coconut milk and brown sugar, are local specialty drinks. There are a number of **bakeries** with tasty-looking treats as well.

Sidang Reret, Jl. Naripan 9 (tel. 420 34 40), at the corner of Bragat Naripan. Traditional Sundanese food in a clean setting at good prices (Rp3-6000), though you may feel a bit lonely in such a large dining room. On Saturday night (7-9pm) it fills up for *wayang golek* performances, free with dinner.

Queen Restaurant, Jl. Dalem Kaum 79 (tel. 420 45 61), a block east of the southeast corner of *alun-alun.* A popular, rather pricey Chinese/Cantonese restaurant (Rp10-17,000) with a large menu. Kids run amok between tables. Entertaining decor, slithering ceiling mouldings, and a half-crocheted rainbow rug on the wall.

Braga Permai Bakery, Jl. Branga 58 (tel. 433 778). Eat in style at this restaurant/cafe, and then select from several shelves of chocolate for dessert. Menu items Rp5-15,000. Open 10am-10pm.

Pondok Kapau, Jl. Asia-Afrika 43 (tel. 436 116). A well-lit, but smoky, place to get Padang food. There's no menu, so you can point and try to make your requests understood.

French Bakery, Jl. Braga 35 (tel. 439 282). Eat-in or take-out. A large selection of breads and sweets. The tortes look too decorative to eat. Open daily 7am-9pm.

SIGHTS

Bandung's architecture can be difficult to appreciate when you're weaving between the parked cars and those rushing headlong down the street, or when you're trying not to step on sidewalk displays without tumbling off curbs taller than small children. However, an **Art Deco** movement swept through here in the '30s, courtesy of the architects Wolf Shoemacher, A.F Aalbers, and F.W. Brinkman. Some funky buildings still remain, and many newer buildings have also received streamlined touches, to keep the atmosphere alive. Curious visitors can take one-hour tours (Rp15,000; book through the tourist office) or contact the **Bandung Society for Heritage Conservation** at their office in the Art Deco **Hotel Savoy Homann,** Jl. Asia-Afrika 112 (open Mon.-Sat. 9am-5pm). This smooth, radioesque building faces the less dramatic, but also Deco, **Gedung Merdeka,** which houses the **Museum Asia-Afrika** (tel. 438 032). The museum has a display of pictures, headlines, and memorabilia from the 1955 Non-Aligned Movement Conference in Bandung, where 29 African and Asian nations identified themselves as a collective power, and agreed to pursue noninterference policies during the Cold War. As one wall display shows, the meeting thrust Indonesia into the international spotlight. Open Mon.-Fri. 8am-4pm. Free. The **Army Museum,** Jl. Jembang 38, (tel. 420 33 93) is above Jl. Braga, entered from an interior courtyard of a clearly military building. You will be escorted through—don't hope to rush. The explanations lay out the many glories of the Siliwangi division with an interesting "Blame it on the Communists" theme. Open Mon.-Thurs., Sat. 9am-1pm, Fri. 8-10:30am. Free, but a donation is requested.

A block south, off Jl. Pangarang, is **A. Ruchiyat's wayang golek factory** (tel. 420 13 35), actually a cottage industry on Jl. Pangarang Bawah IV. Follow the alley as it turns right, then left, and you're there. Tourists are welcome to take photos and be suitably impressed by the craftsmanship. Look beyond the painting, since it is the intricacy of carving that sets the price. The factory sells puppets at fixed prices (Rp15-18,000). Open Mon.-Fri. 8am-7pm, Sat. 8am-2pm. About 2km south is the **Museum of West Java,** (*Museum Jawa Barat,*) Jl. Otto Iskandardinata 638 (tel. 510 976). It's Rp200 for a look at Sundanese history and artifacts.

By taking a minibus from Kebon Kelapa toward Kopo you can get to a **kerupuk factory** at Jl. Kopo Gang Pak Sahdi 27, across from the Immanuel Hospital. Made from flavored and colored tapioca dough, kerupuk is deep fried for crispy eating. Open Mon.-Sat. 8am-4pm.

West of the city are three other cottage industries promoted by the city. **Lilian Candle Factory,** Jl. Aksan 18 (tel. 612 200), crafts many red candles, primarily for Chinese temples. Open Mon.-Sat. 8am-6pm. Near Lilian's on Jl. Jend Sudirman, **Yun Sen Tofu Factory** make tofu and tempeh more appealing, once you see that they don't come from outer space, but can be made in a day. Open Mon.-Fri. 1pm-3pm. To reach both places, take a bus out Jl. Jend Sudirman to Jl. Suriani.

North of the city is the **Kebun Binatang,** or **zoo,** (tel. 250 73 02) on Jl. Taman Sari. A komodo dragon and various other animals all inhabit rather dismal cages. The butt-smoking orangutan could definitely use a trip to Bukit Lawang's rehab center. Open 7am-5pm daily. Admission Rp1750, Sun. and holidays Rp2000. Cultural performances here Sun. 9am-1pm. Across the street is the **ITB** complex (Bandung Institute of Technology), another art deco building. Take an angkot to Kebun Kelapa, then take one headed in the Dago direction and get off at ITB. Also in the north suburbs is the **Geology Museum,** Jl. Cilaki 37 (tel. 774 705), which has lots of mundane rocks, but some fantastic fossils—including an enormous tortoise and **Java Man's skull.** Open Mon.-Thurs., Sat. 9am-2pm, Fri. 9-11am. Free. Just up the street is **Gedung Sate,** so named for the inverted *sate* skewer that tops this huge building. Hidden in one of its wings the **Post and Philately Museum** (tel. 439 950). Take the St. Hall-Sadangsebang angkot from the railway station to Jl. Diponegoro.

ENTERTAINMENT AND NIGHTLIFE

There is plenty of nightlife in Bandung, if you know where to look. The cafes and backpackers quiet down by 11pm, but there are late-night movies, karaoke clubs, and discotheques to turn to. The **North Sea,** Jl. Braga 82 (tel. 420 89 04), "Bandung's only real bar," is set like a ship, complete with water running between panes of glass; the view of the street from inside is just a blur. It's Dutch owned, with Dutch and English papers available, weekend afternoon movies, free pool table, live music on Fri. and Sat. night, and sturdy Dutch food. A great place to while away a few hours with locals and expats. Open Mon.-Fri. 5pm-1am, Sat. noon-2am, Sun. noon.-1am. Just a block farther is the decadent **Caesar's Palace,** Jl. Braga 129 (tel. 433 291). Be prepared to part with Rp20,000 up front. Open nightly 10pm-3am.

In the *alun-alun* area, there are several **theaters.** The Matahari Shopping Plaza, east of the square, has six screens; just south of the square are four more, with films as current as censorship allows.

Just north stands the big BRI building at Jl. Asia-Afrika 57-59. On the 15th floor is the **Polo Room Discotheque** (tel. 420 53 25), where you can dance the night away every night, 10pm to 2 or 3am (cover Rp10,000). Next door, sink into leather sofas in the dark **Canopy Karaoke Lounge** (tel. 420 55 17). Min. Rp15,000. Open 2pm-2am. Farther down, where Jl. Asia-Afrika becomes Jl. Jend Sudirman, is **O'Hara's Tavern,** on the ground floor of the Hotel Perdana Wisata at No.66 (tel. 438 238 ext 181). The wood paneling here seems more reminiscent of a Wild West tavern than a pub from the Isles. There's live music nightly, generally rock 'n' roll. Min. 1 drink.

Slightly more cultured entertainment is available, though broken into bite-size pieces, instead of all-night dramas, for the tourist. Saturday dinner at **Sindang Reret** guarantees a *wayang golek* performance. **Pak Udjo's workshop,** Jl. Padasuka 118 (tel. 717 14) puts on *angklung* (hand-held bamboo chimes) performances when at least 20 people come. Take an angkot toward Cicaheum, then walk up Jl. Padasuka. Shows 3:30pm; Rp5000. **The Institute of Fine Arts (ASTI)** puts on performances as well; ask about the current offerings at the tourist office.

SHOPPING

Shopping in Bandung almost qualifies as entertainment unto itself. As Yogyakarta is to handmade goods, so Bandung is to manufactured ones. The sidewalks of the old **Chinatown** area around Pasar Baru are like a feeding frenzy of shirts, shoes, socks, shorts, snapshots of stars, and vegetable peelers. **Pasar Baru** itself is an immense maze of textile and shoe shops. Should you decide you need a mosquito net, your best bet is to get the fabric here and make one. Behind Pasar Baru on Jl. Pasar Selatan and nearby streets, you can get a taste of the frivolity that makes the jean shop store-fronts on **"Jeans Street" (Jl. Cihampelas)** so amusing. Neon colors and enormous pop-culture heroes (James Bond, Superman, Batman, the Power Rangers) are worth a look and maybe a picture. Get there by angkot to Jl. Pasir Kaliki, then walk west to Jl Cihampelas. The nicest mall in town is **Plaza Bandung Indah,** Jl. Merdeka 56 (tel. 407 10), across from the Gramedia Bookstore. It has big-name western stores, a discotheque, a playland (with bumper cars), and a six-screen theater. Open daily 9am-9pm. Southwest of *alun-alun* on **Jl. Dalem Kaum** are many shopping centers. Take precautions here: your personal space and belongings may be invaded.

■ NEAR BANDUNG

The town of **Lembang,** a 30-minute, Rp1000 angkot ride from the railway station, is the first stop on what can easily be a half-day trek to **Tangkuban Prahu,** the "cap-sized boat" **crater.** If you have the time, you can get off at Jl. Jayagiri in Lembang and head straight up, paying Rp650 to climb through first a pine, then a tropical forest. It's slick when rainy, and a solid 8km hike. If you want, get an angkot to the front gate, or (even better) to the upper or lower parking lots. At the lower carpark and gate, the forest trail emerges and everyone must pay Rp1250. There are *warungs* at the lower lot, and minivan *bemos* to the top, which is only steps from the upper lot. The big grey caldera of **Ratu** sits impressively and bubbles a sulphur and steam. The view of Bandung can be impressive if there are no clouds, so go early. A path leads to the smaller **Domas Caldera** from the lower lot (get a guide for this route). At 1830m, Ratu is pretty, and you can get away from all the tourists and hawkers to appreciate it better. To enjoy the power of the volcano, head back down to the main gate and take an angkot toward Subang. After winding through tea plantations, get off a few km away at the top of the road to the "Air Panas Crater," the **hot springs** at **Sari Ater Resort,** Jl. Taman Sari 72 (tel. 200 319), open 24 hrs. At Rp1500 per person, it's not a bad deal for a hot shower. Skip the sanitized swimming pools, which cost extra, and head for the natural pools and waterfall. The water is quite hot, and passing rains make a great counterpoint. As the resort gets a lot of business from families, it caters to them with a somewhat haphazard playland atmosphere.

Dating from the 8th century AD, **Candi Cangkuang** is the oldest Hindu temple in West Java. Located on an island in a lake, the temple lies on the way to Garut, 48km from Bandung. To get there, take a bus from the Cicaheum terminal toward Tasikmalaya and Banjar. Get off in Leles, and walk from there. The boat ride over should cost about Rp4000. Some of the guest houses on Jl. Kebonjati offer tours to the temple plus **Papandayan Volcano** and **Tarogong hot springs,** which is more than one can do alone by public transport in a day.

■■■ CIREBON

On the north coast of Java, at the Sundanese/Javanese cultural crossroads where West and Central Java meet, Cirebon offers a look into Indonesia's attic with its *kratons* and museums. With wide uncongested streets and an unbelievable number of *becaks*, Cirebon presents a leisurely and stately appearance whose calm is enforced by a large military presence; you can see soldiers doing their workouts in the park when they are not at the many barracks and posts across town. Cirebon is a center for both *kerupuk* (shrimp crackers) and Daihatsu production, in an odd cultural collision that seems somehow fitting for a small Indonesian city.

ORIENTATION

By train you arrive at the north end of Cirebon, set back from the major street, **Jl. Siliwangi.** By bus or plane, it is necessary to take an angkot (colt or minibus) to your destination. The station and town hall are at the north end, the hotels cluster around Jl. Siliwangi between **Jl. Kartini** and **Jl. Kalibaru** (the middle of town), and the *kratons*, harbor, and GPO are at the south end, a few km away. Angkots G5 and G6 run up and down Siliwangi. From Kartini south, you can catch G8.

PRACTICAL INFORMATION

Currency Exchange: Djasa Valasamas Artha, Jl. Yos Sudarso 56. (tel. 205 082). Banks line Jl. Siliwangi: **BCA Bank** (tel. 813 90) and **Bumi Daya** (tel. 202 125).

Post Office: GPO, Jl. Yos Sudarso 7 (tel. 161 234). Open 8am-8pm; coin and card phone. No official Poste Restante, but they hold packages in back.

Telephones: Wartel, not far from town hall, Jl. Kartini 7. Open 6:30am-2am; Home Country Direct and fax service. **Telephone code:** 0231.

Airport: (tel. 270 85). Domestic flights. Take angkots GC or GG05.

Trains: Take angkots G5 and G6. Frequent trains to Jakarta, Yogya, and Semarang.

Buses: Stations for local minibuses and long distance, are south on Jl. Bypass, reached by angkot G8.

Local Transportation: Angkots, the nickname for *angkutan kota* (city transport), set rates Rp300. Take a more leisurely ride on a **becak**—be sure to bargain.

English Bookstore: Gunug Agung Bookstore (tel. 512 15). Take angkot G6 then GM, at the Cirebon Mall, by the harbor.

Public markets: Pasar Kanoman, in front of the Kraton Kanoman. **Pasar Pagi,** behind the Mandala Cinemba Bldg. on Jl. Siliwangi.

Laundry: **Bandung Binatu,** Jl. Pasuketan 5 (tel. 203 320).

Public Bathrooms: The old and new Yogya shopping centers on Jl. Siliwangi and Jl. Karanggetas respectively.

24-hr. Pharmacy: Kimia Farma Apotek, Jl. Parujakan 12 (tel. 208 954).

Hospital: RS Gunung Jati (tel. 202 444), on Jl. Kesambi. Take angkot 300.

Emergency: Ambulance: tel. 188. **Police:** tel. 110. **Fire:** tel. 113.

ACCOMMODATIONS

Cirebon seems empty most of the time, but in November devout Muslims pour in and fill its many hotels to celebrate the anniversary of the birth of Sultan Gunung Jati, one of the first Islamic missionaries to Java.

Losmen Famili (tel. 279 35) at Jl. Siliwangi 66, next to the train station, has well-worn, but adequate rooms (and a loud TV). Singles Rp6000. Doubles Rp10,000. Triple Rp20,000. **Losmen Semarang** at Jl. Siliwangi 124 is airy and pleasant with big strong doors and tall ceilings. Singles Rp8500. Doubles Rp16,000. Triples Rp22,500. Both have shared *mandis* and no fans.

Langensari (tel. 201 818) at Jl. Siliwangi 127 is a very good value, with *mandis* in the room, painted walls, and breakfast included. Double with fan Rp20,000; with A/C Rp 30,000. Triple with A/C Rp40,000. **Hotel Priangan** (tel. 202 929) at Jl. Siliwangi 108 has a pleasant interior courtyard with fish in a Chinese-garden pool, and clean rooms with too much furniture in them. Doubles with fan and *mandi* are Rp22-24,000. Triples with A/C Rp33-58,000 (with satellite TV and minibar at the high end). Prices listed are without the 10% tax and 10% service charge. **The New Grand Land** (tel. 208 867) at Jl. Siliwangi 98 has rooms with a 70s feel to get you in the mood for their discotheque. Doubles go for Rp38-58,000 with varying degrees of amenities, but A/C and *mandi* are standard.

Hotel Nooraeni (tel. 204 906) is just beside the bus station if you can't be bothered to go into town. Clean rooms. Double with *mandi* Rp16,500; with fan Rp17,500; with A/C Rp29,000. Extra bed Rp4000. Probably never quiet because of the bus noise, but it is set apart from the street by a fence and near some *warungs*.

FOOD

Cirebon has always been a fishing town known as Kota Udang, or "City of Shrimp." Many seafood dishes are available, although not necessarily cheap. **The Marina Seafood Restaurant** (tel. 100 33) at Jl. Karanggetas 64 has fantastic views over Cirebon and the sea from the 4th floor of the new Yogya Dept. Store. Dishes from Rp6-18,000, Sun. *dim sum* frin 7:30-10:30am. **Jumbo Seafood** (tel. 203 606) at Jl. Siliwangi 191 has dishes from Rp5-20,000. You can listen to local lite-rock, and watch the blinking LED toilet sign. The new **Grand Land** and **Silodadi Hotel** on Jl. Siliwangi have restaurants with Indonesian and Chinese goods for Rp3-5000. The **food court** in the old Yogya Department Store has *warung* prices in a more relaxed setting. **Warungs** around the train station or Pasar Pagi serve Padang food as well as Cirebon specialties like *nasi lengko* (rice with bean sprouts, onion, cucumber, and tempe) and *nasi jamblang* (rice in dried teak leaves). McDonald's has just reared its ugly head, opening while at the time of research, but we won't tell you where.

SIGHTS

The *kratons* and their museums offer a glimpse into the long history of Cirebon. **Kraton Kasepuhan,** at Jl. Dalam Kraton Kasepuhan, (tel. 40 01), was built in 1677 (though much renovated since then) and has a brick split-gate entrance with Chinese, Portuguese, and Dutch tiles set into it. Within the cool, quiet rooms of the main building there are more inset tiles and china, as well as French chandeliers. The museum has a lot of 1500s "stuff": gamelans, cannons, chests, armor, and knick-knacks from faraway places. There is also a stable with several carriages, and the Singa Barong Carriage (part elephant, part *naga,* part *garuda*) should not be missed. When pulled, the wings would flap! Open 8am-4pm; admission Rp1000.

Kraton Kanoman at Jl. Dalam Kraton Cirebon, (tel. 26 65), is a variation on the same theme, with split gates, inset tiles, a worldly collection of pieces, and a *paksi-naga-limen* (elephant-serpent-bird) carriage. The proprietor speaks fairly good English, however, and the objects become much more interesting with descriptions. Open 8am-4pm; admission Rp1000. It lies beyond the **Pasar Kanoman,** where fruit, dried fish, goldfish, and textiles are sold.

There are many old mosques and churches in town, and the **Mesjid Agung** dating back to 1480, across from the Kraton Kasepuhan, is a favorite. Its architecture was influenced by contemporary Hindu-Buddhist buildings.

Not far from the train station, the **Balai Kota** (town hall), with its art-deco design and giant shrimp on the front bays looks transported in from a Batman movie set, minus the dramatic spotlights. Taking angkot G6 or a *becak* to the harbor, a **Chinese Buddhist temple** from 1629 rests nearby. The **Sunyaragi Gardens** from the 1700s are now mostly a series of caves where locals hang out on weekends. Take angkot G2 to the Jl. Bypass, and walk to the right.

The **Tomb of Sultan Gunung Jati,** the pilgrimage sight that keeps Cirebon's hotels in business, is reached by taking angkot GG or G6 to Makam Gunung Jati. If you want to see Cirebon-style *batik* being made at workshops, head to **Trusmi** by taking angkot GP or G4 to Pelred and then turning right and following the signs. Cirebon has a distinctive, Chinese-influenced *batik* design which incorporates clouds, rocks, gardens, and royal animals.

■■■ PANGANDARAN

The increasingly popular coastal beach resort, Pangandaran dangles from the south coast of Java like a mango, milking its status for all its worth. With beaches, dense forests, and decent surf all nearby, it is a favorite destination of Jakartans as well as Europeans. There's late-night entertainment, kitschy shell sculptures, and gorgeous stargazing to be had. Someone with savvy put up front gates on the main roads where tourists are charged admission (Rp1000) every time they enter. Since the main market is just outside the gates, a little bit of daily life is kept hidden from those too proud to pay the toll over and over again.

ORIENTATION

A palm-lined well-lit boulevard leads down from the main entrance to the west beach, where **Jl. Pamugaran** runs north and south. **Jl. Kidang Pananjung** is the other north-south road, running down the center of the peninsula. After a bend toward the **East Beach,** its end is the entrance to **Penanjung,** the national park. The **West Beach** is the main swimming beach.

PRACTICAL INFORMATION

Tourist Office/Tours: Luta's Tour Co., Jl. Kidang Pananjung 107, (tel. 639 294). Brilliant service by Willy, a multi-lingual Dutch woman who explains options well and honestly. Also rents motor bikes, has a fax, and reconfirms flights. All over town there are "tourist offices" which sell standard package tours approved by a central office in Pangandaran. Many have rough maps of town, with important landmarks. Open 8am-10pm. Jungle treks to the forests of the park (4-5 hr., Rp9000). Green Canyon tours (an all day trek, Rp30,000). They also book buses to Yogya (Rp12,500), Wonsobo (Rp12,500), Jakarta (Rp17,500; with A/C Rp30,000), Bogor (Rp17,500), and Bandung (Rp10,500; with A/C Rp14,500).

Currency Exchange: Bank Rakyat Indonesia, on Jl. Kidang Pananjung by the intersection with Jl. E. Jaga Lautan. Open Mon.-Thurs. 8am-3:30pm, Fri. 8am-1pm. Another branch outside the main gate. Most tourist offices also change money at the standard rates.

Post Office: Jl. Kidang Pananjung III (tel. 639 284). Open Mon.-Thurs., Sat. 8am-2pm, Fri. 8-11am, Sun. 9-11am. Poste Restante. **Postal code:** 49396.

Telephones: Telecom Office, Jl. Kidang Pananjung 5, (tel. 639 333). Open 24 hrs. Home Country Direct, fax, telex, phone cards. **Telephone code:** 0265. Coin and card phones abound on the streets and at accommodations.

Buses: The bus terminal is about a Rp1000 *becak* ride from town. Express buses run direct to: **Jakarta** (9hr.); **Bandung** (5-6hr.); **Banjar** (1-2hr); and **Bogor** (8hr.). Morning and evening departures.

Trains: Trains run from Banjar for Yogya (7hr.).

Local Transport: *Becaks* and bicycles rule the roads.

Bike Rental: Many places along the north-south roads rent bicycles (Rp5000 per day; tandems Rp10,000—but barter!)

Motorcycle Rental: Luta's Tour Co., Jl. Kidang Pananjung 107. Rp12,000 per day.

Public Markets: The **main market** is next to the bus station, outside the main gates. The **art market** burned down and is now haphazard stalls on the West Beach, south of Jl. Pramuka. **Fish market** is reached via *gang* (alleys). Head toward the East Beach on Jl. Pramuka, then turn north a little before the beach.

Public Toilets: Little signs everywhere point to "*WC umum*"; may cost Rp200.

Swimming Pool: Bimasakti Hotel, Jl. Bulak Laut 45, has a pool "for friends of guests." Rp5000 for 4 hr.

English Bookstores: The Magic Mushroom, Jl. E. Jaga Lautan and **Adam's Cafe** on Jl. Pantai Barat (near the entrance boulevard).

Pharmacy: There is an *apotek* (pharmacy) on the back side of the main market (tel. 639 574). Open 7am-8pm.

Hospital: Jl. Parapat 1, (tel. 639 118). A small hospital with an ambulance. Open 24 hours for emergencies.

Emergency: Police (tel. 110).

Police: (tel. 639 075). Located outside the main gate.

ACCOMMODATIONS

Pangandaran's many accommodations are aimed at beach-bound tour groups and families, not backpackers, and tend to lack both character and phones. Rooms are generally quite clean when presented, but follow local custom and remove your shoes at the door to keep the sand out. Rooms are also usually spacious and a single will have a double bed. Prices go up in high season for Indonesian holidays: mid-June to mid-July, after Ramadan, Christmas, and New Year.

Delta Gecko, several km up the west beach at Sindang Laut Rt. 01/02. It is necessarily a village unto itself, well removed from the tourist scene with no phones or electricity. If you need to pull your head together as well as get a tan, this is the place. Take the bus past the Pangandaran terminal to Jl. Pamugaran, Cikembulan (Rp500 extra), and then take an *ojek* (motorcycle taxi, Rp1000). Vegetarian restaurant, arts and crafts, special tours, library of informative literature, and free bikes. Eco-groovy Aussie, Kristina, and her unusual animal friends make great company. With breakfast and attached *mandi*. Dorms Rp 6000. Singles Rp8000. Doubles Rp12,500 or 15,000. Family houses Rp25-60,000.

Holiday Beach, Jl. Buka Laut 50 (tel. 639 285). At the upper end of the beach. Older bungalow-style rooms are fun but don't keep critters out; keep your candy safely hidden. Screens do keep out mosquitoes. New modern section at higher prices. Popular with backpackers. Fan and *mandi* standard, 2 night min. Singles Rp7500. Doubles Rp10-20,000. Restaurant, travel service, and safe deposit box.

Hotel Mini, Jl. Kidang Pananjung (tel. 639 296). The rooms even *smell* clean, and include screen, fan, and breakfast. Sit along the horseshoe-shaped courtyard. Singles Rp8000; with *mandi* Rp10,000. Doubles Rp12,500; with *mandi* Rp15,000.

Setia Famili Losmen, Jl. Kidang Pananjung 199. Inland from the swimming beach, but inland a little way. At the dirt-cheap end of the spectrum. Not a home away from home, but Ibu is nice. No screens, but this is common. Singles with no fan and shared *mandis* Rp5000. Double with fan (some with *mandi*) Rp10,000.

Aquarium, near the south end of Jl. Pamugaran, has squishy mattresses, fans, and clean rooms, and an unimpressive dirt courtyard. Still very local, so not much of a backpacker scene. Doubles with *mandi* Rp20,000. Triples with *mandi* Rp30,000. 2 triples with outside *mandi* and nice beach views Rp20,000.

Atang G-H, Jl. Kidang Pananjung 152 (tel. 639 082). Across from Indra Jaya Tour Co., at south end of Jl. K.P. There is no sign, but this quiet group/family-oriented hotel is pleasant. Some rooms have a fan, two rooms share a *mandi* off of a common "family room." Singles Rp15,000. Doubles Rp20,000. Triples Rp30,000.

FOOD

Tons of restaurants are tucked away in Pangandaran, and often well-tucked, since signs are old, faded, and not prominently displayed. Most are quite cheap (Rp3-8,000 an item), and most are open form 9am-10pm. Those attached to accommodations usually have longer hours.

Cilicap "Chez Mama" and **Sympathy Cafe** at the southern end of Jl. Kidang Pananjung are popular drinking hangouts offering standard Indonesian and Chinese food. **Holiday,** at the Holiday Beach on Jl. Bulak Laut has good western food, as well as Chinese and Indonesian food. Fresh Indonesian victuals are served up at **Bunga Laut,** two doors closer to the Western Beach. Across the street, **Relax Coffee Shop** has decadent ice cream, homemade breads and relaxing coffee *(?!).* **Padang Jaya,** a little north of Jl. Hanjatan on Jl. Kidang Pananjung serves good Padang food. **Adam's Cafe** (at Adam's Homestay) at the top of Jl. Pamugaran will satisfy your coffee and cappuccino addiction. **Delta Gecko Village** has vegetarian food miraculously palatable to all, and just next door **Francisco Brillo** puts Italian genius into his varied cuisine. (It is some distance out there, so ask him about a **room for the night.**)

SIGHTS

Visitors may find themselves uncomfortably targeted by touts for tour offices as they pass by. They are a fair source of information and a necessary evil in order to get to the two major sights: Penanjung Park and Green Canyon. The first bit of **Penanjung Park** includes white sand beaches with great snorkeling. (Open 8am-4pm; admission Rp1250). To see the rest of the park, including limestone caves, the enormous but rare Rafflesia flower, deer, bats, monitor lizards, monkeys, and porcupines (depending on your luck), you must book a guided tour in town, about Rp9000 for a six-hr trek. **Green Canyon** is about 30km away, reached by minibus then boat. Stops along the way include *kerupuk,* tempeh, and *tahu* (tofu) factories, as well as a *wayang golek* carver. The river's lovely jade color gives the sight its name, and the boats dock below a pool and water falls under a rainbow-arched rock. The swimming is zesty, just warm enough that you don't feel hot. Lunch and another swim are at **Batu Karas,** on the coast. It's a small fishing village with a gentle surfbreak, and a few *losmen* right on the beach (Pusaka Indah, Alana's, and Teratai Cottages). Batu Karas is best reached from Cijulang, along the main road from Pangandaran.

ENTERTAINMENT

Bring your friends and make your own party, or perhaps go to the **disco** just beyond the Art Market on Jl. Pamugaran. Open nightly 9pm-2am. There is also a **cinema** on Jl. Kidang Pananjung, just south of the intersection with Jl. Bulak Laut Shows at 2, 4, 7, and 9pm; Sat. midnight double feature. Admission Rp1500; double feature Rp5000. **The Delta Gecko** has a Saturday night fish-fry, cultural show, and bonfire, starting around 7pm.

SHOPPING

There's a lot of *batik* available at roadside stalls and stores. At **Isson Art Gallery,** Jl. Kudang Pananjung 71, just north of the cinema, you will find Isson making *batik* paintings by day, and practicing his *wayang kulit* by night. He learned the art from his father in Yogya, but has moved to the more peaceful surroundings to avoid the big city *batik*-hustling scene. He is happy to have an audience, and starts around 7pm. Shell sculptures and stuffed turtles are for sale by the beach if you want to have fun at customs. The main local products are culinary—*kerupuk, tempe, tahu,* coconuts, and fish. They make them all by hand, so enjoy them while you're here.

■■■ YOGYAKARTA

In 1755, Prince Mangkubumi built Yoygakarta's royal *kraton* and named himself Sultan Hamengkubuwono, meaning literally "the universe on the lap of the king."

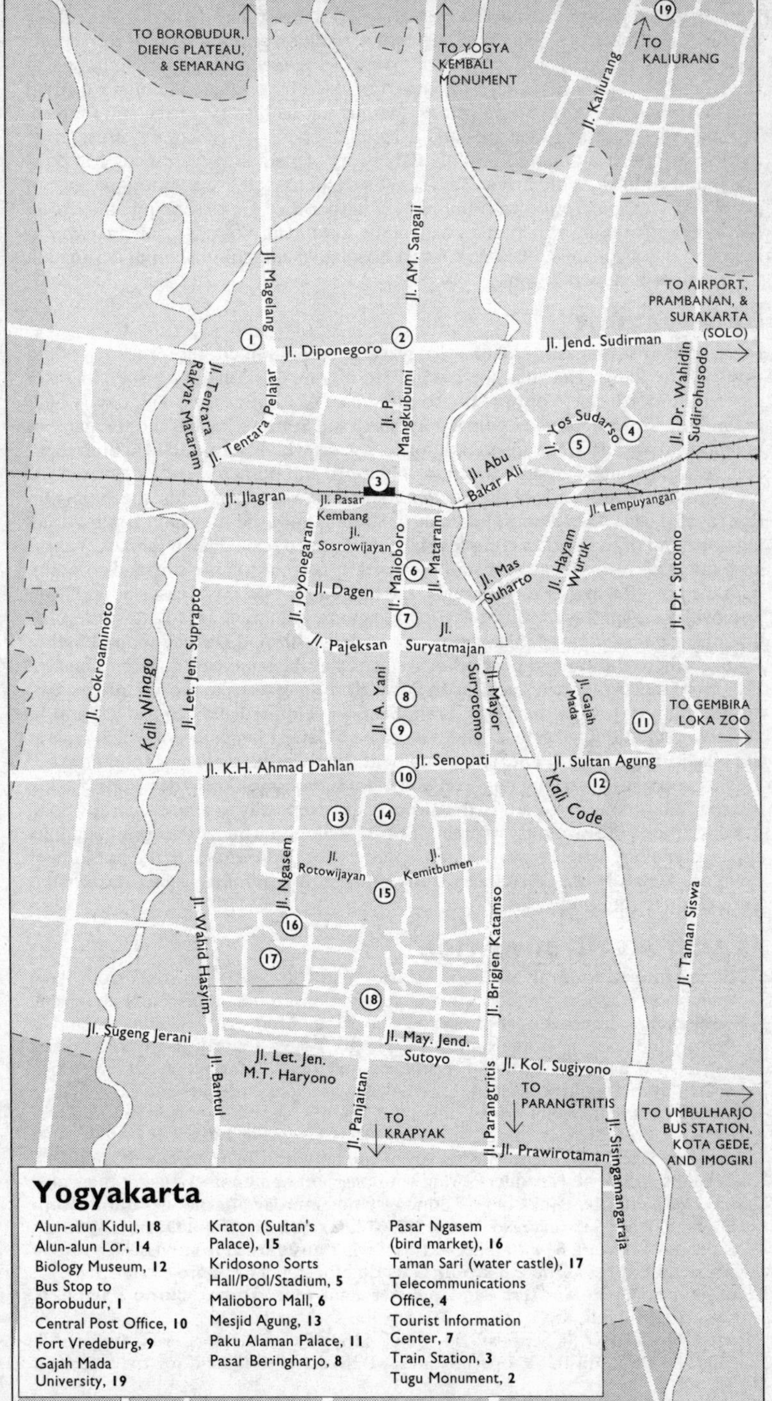
TO BOROBUDUR, DIENG PLATEAU, & SEMARANG
TO YOGYA KEMBALI MONUMENT
TO KALIURANG
TO AIRPORT, PRAMBANAN, & SURAKARTA (SOLO)
TO GEMBIRA LOKA ZOO
TO UMBULHARJO BUS STATION, KOTA GEDE, AND IMOGIRI
TO PARANGTRITIS
TO KRAPYAK
Jl. Kaliurang
Jl. Magelang
Jl. AM. Sangaji
Jl. Diponegoro
Jl. Jend. Sudirman
Jl. Dr. Wahidin Sudirohusodo
Jl. Tentara Rakyat Mataram
Jl. Tentara Pelajar
Jl. P. Mangkubumi
Jl. Yos Sudarso
Jl. Abu Bakar Ali
Jl. Jlagran
Jl. Pasar Kembang
Jl. Sosrowijayan
Jl. Lempuyangan
Jl. Joyonegaran
Jl. Malioboro
Jl. Mataram
Jl. Mas Suharto
Jl. Hayam Wuruk
Jl. Dr. Sutomo
Jl. Dagen
Jl. Pajeksan
Jl. Suryatmajan
Jl. Cokroaminoto
Kali Winago
Jl. Let. Jen. Suprapto
Jl. A. Yani
Suryotomo
Jl. Mayor
Jl. Gajah Mada
Jl. K.H. Ahmad Dahlan
Jl. Senopati
Jl. Sultan Agung
Kali Code
Jl. Ngasem
Jl. Rotowijayan
Jl. Kemitbumen
Jl. Wahid Hasyim
Jl. Brigjen Katamso
Jl. Taman Siswa
Jl. Sugeng Jerani
Jl. Let. Jen. M.T. Haryono
Jl. May. Jend. Sutoyo
Jl. Kol. Sugiyono
Jl. Bantul
Jl. Panjaitan
Jl. Parangtritis
Jl. Prawirotaman
Jl. Sisingamangaraja
Yogyakarta
Alun-alun Kidul, 18
Alun-alun Lor, 14
Biology Museum, 12
Bus Stop to Borobudur, 1
Central Post Office, 10
Fort Vredeburg, 9
Gajah Mada University, 19
Kraton (Sultan's Palace), 15
Kridosono Sorts Hall/Pool/Stadium, 5
Malioboro Mall, 6
Mesjid Agung, 13
Paku Alaman Palace, 11
Pasar Beringharjo, 8
Pasar Ngasem (bird market), 16
Taman Sari (water castle), 17
Telecommunications Office, 4
Tourist Information Center, 7
Train Station, 3
Tugu Monument, 2

Despite the name's pomp, his lineage has survived until today, ten sultans later, due in part to Yogyakarta's combined respect for tradition and tradition of respect. As well as being the geographical hub of "Yogya," the *kraton* complex (comprising the sultan's palace and its surroundings, enclosed by a square-kilometer fortress wall) encapsulates what Yogya is most famous for: its history, crafts, and tourism. Through museums, classical arts, and daily interactions, Yogyakartans effuse pride in their city's semi-autonomous status and history of resistance against colonial powers. But in contrast to the first sultan, Yogya's residents achieve a curious balance of character, wrapping pride with humility. Whether they are describing an intricate *batik* design, offering transport, or bargaining for durian, Yogya's locals are eager to help and quick to smile, making Yogya a hospitable and culturally rich destination for travelers of all persuasions.

ORIENTATION

Lying 603km southeast of Jakarta, Yogyakarta (pronounced Jōg-ja-karta) is 30km north of the Indian Ocean at the base of Mt. Merapi (2911m). With Solo, its sister city to the northeast, Yogya is the tourist heart of Central Java. The city is built around the **kraton complex** which consists of the **Sultan's Palace** and the maze of neighborhoods inside the square km fortress walls which surround it. Within these walls can be found **Taman Sari, Pasar Ngasem,** and numerous *batik* galleries. At the north and south ends of the *kraton,* there are two square fields, the **Alun-alun Lor** (north), and **Alun-alun Kidul** (south). Starting from the Alun-alun Lor and leading north out of the *kraton* complex, **Jalan Malioboro** (called **Jalan Jend. A. Yani** at its south end) forms Yogya's main boulevard. It is an inevitable stop-and-go point, with the huge **Beringharjo Market** and the **Malioboro Mall** on its east side and **Jalan Sosrowijayan,** lined with tourist accommodations, branching off to the west. At its first major intersection, Jl. Malioboro crosses **Jalan Ahmad Dalan/Senopati/Sultan Agung,** where the **central post office** is located at the southeast corner. Where Jl. Malioboro meets the train tracks **Jalan Pasar Kembang** turns to the left. After crossing the railway tracks, the **Tugu Train Station** is immediately to the left and Jl. Malioboro, continuing north, changes its name to **Jalan Mangkubumi** which ends at the phallic **Tugu Monument.** The monument stands in the middle of another major intersection with **Jalan Diponegoro/Sudirman/Sumoharjo/Solo/Adisucipto.** Taking this road all the way east leads to the **airport,** and eventually to Prambanan and Solo.

Aside from the Sosrowijayan area off of Jl. Malioboro, budget accommodations also cluster along **Jalan Prawirotaman,** southeast of the *kraton*. On the outskirts of town are **Gajah Mada University** to the north and **Umbulharjo bus station** and **Kota Gede** to the southeast.

PRACTICAL INFORMATION

Tourist Information: Jl. Malioboro 16 (tel. 566 000). A 10-min. walk from Tugu train station. Offers brochures, maps, reservations, tours, information about cultural events. International phone service. Open Mon.-Fri. 7:30am-noon and 1-8pm, Sat. 8am-4pm. Hours subject to change. **Yogya Rental,** Jl. Pasar Kembang 85 (tel. 587 648), is a smaller, privately owned tourist information center a block or two from Tugu train station. Excellent English spoken. Tours and car rental.

Tourist Police: Jl. Malioboro 14 (tel. 377 777).

Immigration Office: Jl. Laksda Adisucipto Km10 (tel. 586 130)

Currency Exchange: In the Sosrowijayan and Prawirotaman areas there are plenty of banks and money changers. Bring your passport or a photocopy of it to change traveler's checks. Banks closed Sundays and Saturday afternoons. **Bank Bumi Daya,** Jl. Jend. Sudirman No. 7 (tel. 587 672; fax 622 56). **Bank Duta,** Jl. Achmad Dahlan No. 14 (tel. 514 701; fax 621 54), will transfer cash from Visa/MC.

American Express Office: Natour Garuda Hotel, Jl. Malioboro 89 (tel. 565 345; fax same). Open Mon.-Fri. 8am-7pm, Sat. 8am-4pm. **Ambarrukmo Palace,** Jl. Laksda Adisucipto Km5, PO Box 10 (tel. 566 488; fax 563 283).

Post Office: GPO, Jl. Senopati No. 1 (tel. 515 800). At the southeast corner of Jl. Jend. A. Yani and Jl. Senopati. General Delivery mail is held for two weeks if addressed to: Holly Kretschmar *yang cantik* (or name of addressee), Poste Restante, Kantor Pos, Jl. Senopati #2, Yogyakarta, 55121. Money changer and tourist info service inside. Open Mon.-Fri. 8am-8pm, Sat. 8am-12pm.

Telephones: Look for **wartels** throughout the city which have international calling service. International (credit card and collect) calls can also be made at: **Natour Garuda Hotel,** Jl. Malioboro 89; **Tourist Information Center,** Jl. Malioboro 16; **the airport;** and **Airlangga Guest House,** Jl. Prawirotaman 6-8 (tel. 378 044). Some public phones take coins and others take phone cards, which can be purchased at many locations throughout the city, including post offices and bookstores. **Telephone code:** 0274.

Airport: Jl. Adisucipto (tel. 565 840). 8km from the center of Yogya, take a taxi or catch a bus from Umbulharjo Station. Several Indonesian carriers, including: **Garuda Indonesia,** Jl. Mangkubumi 56 (tel. 561 440); **Sempati,** Century Yogya International Hotel, Jl. Adisucipto (tel. 560 706); and **Merpati Air,** Jl. Panglima Sudirman 63 (tel. 514 272). On Garuda fly from Yogya to **Jakarta** for Rp129,200.

Trains: Tugu train station, Jl. Mangkubumi 3 (tel. 512 612) on Jl. Pasar Kembang and Jl. Malioboro. Frequent trains to Jakarta, Bandung, Surabaya, and other locations. The 7-hr. train to **Jakarta,** costs Rp18,000 economy class.

Bus: Umbulharjo Station, Jl. Veteran (tel. 377 834) can be reached by city buses **#1** and **14** from the Malioboro and Prawirotaman areas. Buses travel all over Java, as well as to Sumatra and Bali. You can find schedules and fares at ticket agencies on Jl. P. Mangkubumi, Jl. Sosrowijayan, and Jl. Prawirotaman.

Local transportation: City buses run north to south between Umbulharjo station and Gajah Mada University along Yogya's main streets. Flag down buses at any point along their route. Route maps are hard to find; ask bus drivers if they pass by your destination. Buses are less frequent after 5pm. (City bus fare: Rp300) Metered **taxis** (Rp800 and approximately Rp500 per km) can be hailed (or phoned at tel. 29 76 or 20 27). **Becaks** can be slow (the drivers may have to walk and push the cab uphill), but provide a comfortable vantage point for touring the city. Negotiate a price before boarding. If you'd rather solicit the sweat of an animal as opposed to a human, hire an **andong,** a horse-drawn carriage. *Becak* and *andong* wait on street corners and outside the bus and train stations.

Rentals: Cars, bikes, and **motorbikes** can be rented from many locations on Jl. Pasar Kembang, Jl. Malioboro, Jl. Prawirotaman, and Jl. Sosrowijayan. **Fortuna Rental,** Jl. Jlagran 20-21 (tel. 564 680) is beside and west of Tugu train station. Bikes approximately Rp5000 per day, motorbikes Rp15,000, and cars Rp75,000. No age restrictions for car rental, just bring a license, a passport, and moxie.

Luggage Storage: The **Tourist Information Center** will store baggage for one day, until closing time. **Tugu station** stores baggage at Rp1000 for 6 hours.

English Language Media: Sari Ilmu, Jl. Malioboro 117-119 (tel. 516 031) has good maps, travel guides, and some English language books, including English newspapers, magazines, and children's books. **Gramedia** (tel. 560 641), in the lower level of the Malioboro Mall. Open 9:30am-9:30pm.

Markets: Yogya has several **public markets** (*pasars*) that warrant a visit for their spectacular value alone. **Beringharjo Market,** at Jl. A. Yani (the southern end of Jl. Malioboro) and Jl. Pabringan, is an indoor, multi-story flurry of public and private selling (the complex includes a budget department store). Open 5am-4pm, but activity slows down mid-afternoon.

Laundry: Gita Benara, Jl. Kemitbumen 1 (tel. 379 390) and at most hotels.

Public toilets: On Jl. Malioboro, near the Tourist Information Center and the police station.

Pharmacy: Kimia Farma, Jl. Malioboro 123 (tel. 514 980). Open 24 hrs.

Hospitals: Rumah Sakit Bethesda, Jl. Jend Sudirman 70 (tel. 566 300 or 588 876). **Rumah Sakit Panti Rapih,** Jl. Kolombo 10 (tel. 587 129 or 562 233).

24-hr. Clinic: Ludira Husada Tama Hospital, Jl. Wiratama No. 4, Tegalrejo (tel. 513 651) will make hotel/guest house calls.

Medical Assistance: Lentera, Jl. Tentara Rakyat Mataram, Gang Kapas (tel. 586 767). Northwest of and a *becak* ride from Jl. Malioboro, Lentera organizes educational programs and outreach about HIV. Provides STD testing (Rp5-10,000) and anonymous HIV testing (Rp7500). Stop by the office for information on dramas,

awareness walks, and other Lentera-sponsored events. Also distributes *GAYa Nusantara,* Indonesia's 'zine for gay, lesbian, and *waria* awareness.
Local information: tel. 108. **Inter-local information:** tel. 106.
Emergency: Ambulance: tel. 118, **fire:** tel. 113, **police:** tel. 110.
Police: Kapolresta, (tel. 512 940) on Jl. Reksobayan.

ACCOMMODATIONS

The nicest bargain accommodations are in the Jl. Sosrowijayan and Jl. Prawirotaman areas, where restaurants, bars, and shops line the streets. Hotels near the airport and bus station are available but are not up to par with the accommodations in town. They are generally populated by Indonesians in Yogya for business.

Sartika Home Stay, Jl. Prawirotaman 44 (tel. 372 669). Bus #2 or #15 from Umbulharjo station. 3 floors of tastefully decorated hallways that circle an attractive garden. Dark rooms contrast to cool, floral balcony. Fish tank television and electric piano in the lobby make the atmosphere complete. Singles Rp12,500. Doubles Rp15,000. Includes breakfast. Motorbike rental Rp12,000 per day.

Vagabond Youth Hostel, Jl. Prawirotaman MG III/589 (Jl. Sisingamangaraja No. 28B) (tel. 371 207; fax 371 207). Take public bus #2 or #15 from Umbulharjo bus station. Gray leather couches and faded paisley wall paper. Not aesthetically pleasing, but management is friendly and eager to please. A good place to meet other travelers. Guests pick nightly movies ranging from *The Rocky Horror Picture Show* to *The Piano*. Prices for HI members and students: dorm bed Rp.4500, singles Rp8000, doubles Rp10,500. Non-members welcome. Price includes breakfast. Free nearby swimming pool. Safety box if you bring your own mini-padlock. Café. Library with maps and phrasebooks. *Wartel* nearby. Fax service. Reception open 24 hr. Check-out noon.

Bladok Losmen, Jl. Sosrowijayan 76 (tel. 604 52), turn right out of the Tourist Information Center, then take your 3rd left onto Jl. Sosrowijayan and walk for a few min. Rooms are airy and furnished, including a fan, towel, and soap. Most rooms face a courtyard (complete with waterfall) or a breezy balcony overlooking it and the surrounding rooftops. Double Rp18,500 includes washroom (with elephant foot) and breakfast. Check-out 2pm. Restaurant. Bike rental.

Wisma Djoglo, Jl. Laksda Adisucipto Km6 (tel. 871 09; fax 648 53). On the same road as the airport, the hotel's most celebrated asset is the stretch of rice fields before it. If you want a peaceful view, the attractive fields will compensate for the plain rooms. Occasionally mismatched bedspreads, traditional Javanese-style architecture. Towels provided. Singles with A/C Rp35,000. Doubles with A/C and hot water Rp50,000. Price includes continental breakfast, not the 21% service charge and government tax. Restaurant with karaoke. 24-hr. room service. Laundry service. Safety deposit box. Car rental. AmEx, V, MC.

Ghandi Losmen and Art Gallery, Jl. Sosrowijayan Wetan Gang II/75 (tel. 28 41). From Tugu train station, exit onto Jl. Pasar Kembang, walk left and then turn right at the telephone *wartel,* onto an alley running between Jl. Pasar Kembang and Jl. Sosrowijayan. Ghandi Losmen is at the end of the alley, a 5-min. walk from Tugu; 10-min. from the Tourist Information Center on Jl. Malioboro. The "Art Gallery" is not the main attraction. Small, decent rooms (most have fans, some have windows). Singles Rp4500, doubles Rp6000. Price includes a glass of tea or coffee.

Loka Nendra, Jl. Veteran 161 (tel. 711 12). Neighbors with the Umbulharjo bus terminal, this Motel-6-type hostel's best asset is its convenience. Smog from the main road seems to have seeped into the place, killing large life forms in the stagnant pond and (dis)coloring the once-white walls. Good for an emergency one-night stand. Singles Rp12,000. Doubles Rp15,000. Snack bar.

FOOD

Inexpensive restaurants cluster around guest houses in the Sosrowijayan and Prawirotaman areas. Check out the enormous **Beringharjo market** on Jl. Malioboro. Jl. Malioboro's **sidewalk restaurants,** after 9pm, and the *pasar* at the western end of Jl. Prawirotaman. Also find **food stalls** in the northeast corner of the Alun-alun Utara and on the east side of Jl. Mangkubumi. In the *pasar* bargain for fruits you've never seen before (especially delicious *salak*). In a **warung,** counter curious stares with broad smiles and ask for standard Indonesian fare such as *nasi goreng* (fried rice), *bakmi goreng ayam* (fried noodles with chicken), or *gado-gado* (vegetables in peanut sauce) as not all *warungs* have menus. Most dishes here usually cost Rp1000. If you want to Yogya's culinary specialty is **gudeg,** a sweet jackfruit and coconut based dish with chicken, boiled egg, cow hide, and chili peppers for condiments. Look for restaurants, *warungs,* and market stalls which specialize in it. If you're desperate for packaged—and familiar—products, visit the **Matahari Supermarket,** Jl. Malioboro 11A. If you're too cheap to buy any of the overpriced pickings, just get relief from Matahari's intense A/C campaign. **Fast food restaurants** are found by the Tugu Monument and along Jl. Malioboro.

Lotus Breeze (tel. 377 649), on Jl. Prawirotaman 300m from Jl. Parangtritis. Has 3 levels, a view, and an excellent, lotus-breezy atmosphere. Frequented by famous Indonesian models and soap opera stars who want to cheer up their friends. Pepper steak Rp5600.

Gado-Gado Bu Hadi, second level of the Beringharjo market on Jl. Malioboro. Reputed to be the most delicious *gado-gado* in town, Bu Hadi's *warung* is a cool respite from the chaos of the market, with a view and unbeatable prices (Rp900) to boot. Bu Hadi doesn't speak English, but conveniently the menu is limited: *"gado-gado"* is all you need to know.

Ayam Goreng Nyonya Suharti, Jl. Laksda Adisucipto Km7 (tel. 515 522). Just outside of Yogya, you can't miss the huge sign and Nyonya Suharti's portrait looming on the left side of the highway on the way toward the airport. Come here for some of the best gourmet Indonesian fried chicken (½ chicken Rp6500, large chicken Rp12,000) available anywhere. Ibu Suharti's special blend of herbs and spices catapulted her from mobile street seller to owner of this huge, primarily Indonesian-populated restaurant. Her success has been so great that chain restaurants have been opened in Jakarta, Semarang, and Denpasar.

New Superman Restaurant, Sosrowijayan Wetan GT I/71 (tel. 513 472). Uniquely housed within a Javanese *pendopo,* the spacious room, high ceiling, and tables bordered by bird cages and potted plants make for pleasant surroundings right in the heart of Sosrowijayan's backpacker slum. Known for the exchange students who come and hang with the owners. Various Indonesian and western entrees Rp3000. Open 7am-11pm.

Jagung Bakar, Jl. Tentara Pelajar No. 4B. From Jl. Malioboro, turn left onto Jl. Pasar Kembang and walk past Tugu train station for ¾km until you can hang a right onto Jl. Tentara Pelajar. Have dinner or a late night snack at this local hotspot. The specialty is roasted corn on the cob with salty, sweet, or spicy flavored butters (Rp800). *Roti bakar* (toasted bread) and *pisang bakar* (cooked bananas) are also served with strawberry, chocolate, pineapple, or cheese toppings. The menu and clientele are Indonesian, but the traveler should not be intimidated. Take off your shoes before sitting on the mats; this is the place to let Yogya's subtle magic put you at ease. Open daily 6-11pm.

Lotus Garden, Jl. Prawirotaman MG III/93A (tel. 377 649) offers vegetarian fare, seafood, steak (entrees Rp4000), and nightly dance performances in its romantic, arbored courtyard. Open 8am-11pm.

Samirono, Jl. Colombo 105/38 (tel. 880 645). A carnivore's paradise, this family-style local hangout lets you watch the goat and chicken *sate* (Rp3000) chunks get speared before they're fanned over hot coals. Lime-green interior, large tables, and expired calendars on the walls, but do you always expect *Let's Go's* secret finds to have fabulous decor?

Colombo, Jl. Malioboro 25 (tel. 512 589). Though it's billed as Chinese food, the non-discerning tongue will find meat-oriented Indonesian food on the menu of this Chinese-owned, local favorite. *Bakmi goreng* Rp4500.

Bu Tptro, Jl. Adisucipto Km9 (tel. 587 662) 200m outside the airport. Local clientele, dozens of tables and benches, attached gift shop. Choose from a mouth-watering selection of fried cow lungs (Rp2000), fried chicken intestines, and the mysterious cow's soft skin parts. The less adventurous can have fried chicken (Rp9000) or shrimp cakes (Rp800).

Heru Jaya, Sosrowijayan Wetan GT I/79 GG II (tel. 515 055). In plastic furniture, eat for bargain prices in a casual, no-risk environment. Open 6am-9pm.

SIGHTS

Many of Yogya's historical and cultural sights are found within the square kilometer fortress walls of the *kraton* complex. The **Sultan's Palace** makes up the locus of the complex, and it is open in selected areas for visitors. With multi-lingual guides, guests can tour the grounds, pavilions, and museums owned by Yogya's past 10 sultans. Though additions have been made over the years, the ornate, richly symbolic, original palace buildings were built in 1755; they stand today as impressive examples of classic Javanese architecture. The museum housing the collection of gifts given to the sultans (chandeliers, vases, decorative bowls) is enjoyable, if for the irony of the gifts' immediate display behind glass. The current sultan, Hamengkubuwono X, age 48, is active in the Indonesian government and lives in the *kraton* with his wife (unlike many of his predecessors, he has only one) and his five daughters. Most Javanese accept that his role is largely ceremonial but still hold him in very high esteem; they are not fazed by the near-certainty that the sultan's brother (and his sons) will usurp the sultan's seat when he dies. To reach the main entrance of the *kraton*, walk down the west side of the Alun-alun Lor to Jl. Rotowijayan, continue south for another block and then turn left. Admission Rp1500, with camera Rp2000. Open Sun.-Thurs. 8:30am-2pm and Fri.-Sat. 8:30am-1pm.

Upon exiting the *kraton,* it is a short walk west down Jl. Rotowijayan, and then a left turn on Jl. Ngasem to get to **Pasar Ngasem,** the bird market. Exotic birds from all over the archipelago are bought and sold here, though there are more doves, pigeons, chickens and roosters for sale than anything else. The occasional bat, monkey, and other small mammals are sold here as well. A flurry of market activity, Pasar Ngasem fascinates both the naturalist and the anthropology-minded visitor.

If you're standing in front of Pasar Ngasem, the crumbling ruins of **Taman Sari** are visible behind it. Taman Sari means "fragrant garden," though the Dutch referred to this complex as the "water castle." Built shortly after the *kraton* was built, Taman Sari was used only for a brief duration as a pleasure garden for the sultan and his family before it fell into disrepair. There is a network of **underground tunnels** to explore, ruins to climb which afford **views of the city** (best seen early in the morning, when Mt. Merapi is still visible), and a deteriorated **underground mosque** where children play hide and seek. Local legend holds that the tunnels reached all the way to Parangtritis Beach 27km south of the *kraton.* Visitors can see where these tunnels have been blockaded so as to prevent people from getting lost or trapped. Parts of Taman Sari have been restored, and for Rp300 tourists can see the pools that were used by the sultan and his wives and children.

Back at the southwest corner of the Alun-alun Utara, check out **Masjid Agung,** the grand mosque of the *kraton.* It is a beautiful example of Javanese architecture, built in a *pendopo* supported by intricately painted columns and cool tiled floors.

For over two centuries, the yearly **sekaten** festival has been celebrated in honor of the birth of the prophet Mohammed. *Sekaten* lasts roughly a month, during which time the Alun-alun Lor is filled with amusement-park-style fun and games, exhibitions, and hordes of hawkers selling sweet snacks. During this time, an old set of *gamelan* instruments are brought out and played several times a week at Masjid Agung. *Sekaten's* schedule changes each year, as the time of celebration is dictated by an incomprehensible combination of the Islamic and Javanese calendars, but it is usually held sometime between June and September. You'll know it is *sekaten* time when you see circus tents and general disarray covering the Alun-alun Lor.

Every year during June and July, Yogya also hosts an arts festival. Location and exact dates change every year; contact the Tourist Information Office for details regarding *wayang*, dance, and music performances, open studios and galleries.

ENTERTAINMENT

Wayang Kulit, shadow puppet theater, is an original Javanese art form. Ornate, two-dimensional puppets are played by a *dalang* (puppeteer) in front of a lit screen. The puppet's shadows and the *dalang's* voice enact Javanese myths and fables. The Tourist Information Center has a list of performances throughout the city. Also check the center for a list of *Ramayana* **ballet shows** at hotels and theaters in Yogya, and also at Prambanan during the full moons of summer.

Cultural performances are held daily in the *kraton's* Golden Pavilion: Sunday, classical Javanese dance performance, 11am-noon; Monday, Javanese *gamelan*, 10:30am-noon; Tuesday, *gamelan*, 10:30am-noon; Wednesday, *wayang golek* (wooden puppet show), 9am-noon; Thursday, *gamelan,* 10:30am-noon; Friday, poetry reading, 10:30am-noon; and Saturday, *wayang kulit* (leather puppet show), 9am-1pm. Admission to the performances is free save for the *kraton* entrance fee.

If you're tooling about Jl. Malioboro after dark, you may run into a troupe of fire-eaters at the south end of Jl. Malioboro (called Jl. A. Yani) who put even the Lesbian Avengers to shame with their flame-in-mouth feats and other death-defying stunts (e.g. glass-eating) while in a trance. Otherwise, stroll or *becak* it ¾km to **Alun-alun Kidul,** south of the *kraton*. A popular hangout for young Indonesians, the attraction here is as fun as it is cheap: bring a bandana (or rent a blind fold for Rp250), wear it, and try to walk 100m in a straight line from the road to the passage between two enormous trees in the center of the yard. Success, which is reputed to bring good luck, is surprisingly difficult, particularly if you begin walking off the well-trodden path and on to the grass. Most blindwalkers invariably veer to the left of the trees; experts walk through the opening blindfolded and backwards.

If the street scene at Jl. Malioboro and the alun-aluns grows tiresome, stop by a **cinema** and enjoy mostly western Bruce Willis-type movies with Indonesian subtitles. **Ratih** is at Jl. Mangkubumi 26. **Indra** is at Jl. Jend. A. Yani 13A. **Empire 21** and **Regent** are together on Jl. Urip Sumoharjo. The following clubs also rate highly.

Borobudur Sate House and Bar. Jl. Pasar Kembang 17. Friendly, laid-back atmosphere. Wooden walls and tables, small dance floor. Crowd is diverse by gender, nationality, and sexual orientation. Although known as a gay hangout, the substantial straight crowd blends in happily. All-you-can-eat breakfast buffet 6-11am, Rp4000 per person.

Mix Club, Yogya Century Hotel, Jl. Laksa Adisucipto 38 (tel. 564 272). Just opened. Techno-pop beat, dance floor with music-syncopated colored lights, and a timid, primarily local crowd. Open Sun.-Fri. 10pm-2am, Sat. 10pm-3am. Rp15,000 cover charge per person (includes a free drink).

SHOPPING

The most rupiah-friendly way to spend an afternoon in Yogya is, ironically, to go shopping. Without buying anything, a traveler can have an educational, entertaining, and cultural experience rolled into one. **Pasar Beringharjo,** on the south end of Jl. Malioboro, is the largest and most convenient market in Yogya. A kaleidoscope of activity, the multi-story indoor *pasar* sells everything from pork fat chips to parkas, just like Grandma's general store in Mississippi. Smell the enormous baskets of beans, seeds, and flower petals. Wonder at the dozens of kinds of bananas. Indulge in Bu Hadi's *gado-gado*. Open early morning until 4p; best early in the morning.

The west side of Jl. Malioboro is lined with stalls that sell Yogya's handicraft claims to fame: **batik,** hand-waxed or stamped fabric (**Lucy Batik** on Jl. Sosrowijayan Gang 1 gives *batik* lessons); **leather,** made into *wayang kulit* puppets, bags, lampshades, and souvenirs; and **silver** (also available in Kota Gede). While the goods sold along Jl. Malioboro are certainly cheap and function well as souvenirs, those who are looking for higher quality craftwork should visit specialized workshops and their sales rooms, many of which are found within the walls of the *kraton.* Ask at the tourist office for recommended shops. Javanese handicrafts can also be purchased through **Yakkum Craft,** Jl. Kaliurang Km13.5, Desa Besi (tel. 953 86) where bags, toys, carvings, decorations, and housewares are made by physically disabled adults. Open Mon.-Fri. 8am-4pm, Sat. 8am-12:30pm.

Kota Gede, to the southeast of Yogya, is worth visiting if you're in the market for silver. Jl. Kemasan is lined with shops, many of which will take orders for brass, copper, and silver work.

■ NEAR YOGYA

BOROBUDUR

Touted as one of the world's seven wonders, **Borobudur** is the largest Buddhist monument in the world. Built between 778 AD and 856 AD during the Sailendra dynasty, the magnificent monument reflects extraordinary dedication to the Mahayana Buddhist philosophy. In accordance with the Buddha's Way, temper your desire to see the monument straight away and go first to the Audio-Visual Center, which shows a 35min. video (in English and other languages) describing the symbolic value of Borobudur's terraces and reliefs. At the monument, walk the concentric circles, comply with locals who may want to have their picture taken with you, and improve your luck by reaching into the stupas to touch the stone Buddhas' hands and navels. Beset with thousands of tourists every year, Borobudur's magnitude can be hard to appreciate if you're dodging between high schoolers' group photos. Make the pilgrimage early and during the week if possible. Ticket office opens daily 6am-5pm; park/monument open 6am-5:30pm (tel. 029 382 682 17). Rp5000 for non-Indonesians; Rp2000 for non-Indonesian students with ID. Admission includes entrance to the **Archaeological Museum,** which exhibits test tubes of the fungi that suck on Borobudur's volcanic rocks as well as photos of the monument's impressive reconstructions.

PRAMBANAN

Seventeen km to the northeast of Yogya are the **Prambanan temples.** From Yogyakarta, ride a bus from Umbulharjo station or take an intercity bus heading toward Solo (approximately 30min.). Get off the bus and see Mt. Merapi and the main Prambanan temple from the road. But go first to the **tourist information service** (open 7am-5pm), across the street from the intercity bus drop off at the far east (left if your back is to the temple) side of the *pasar.* If you plan to see more than just the main Prambanan *candi* (temple), rent a bike and lock and get a map at the tourist office for Rp2000 per day and head off to the *candi*. Built in the 9th century by the Hindu Sanjaya dynasty, the Prambanan complex consists of a series of inspiring temples surrounded by gardens. The enormous, tiered stone offerings to the gods Siva, Vishnu, Brahma, and their mounts are humbling (at least until you climb the stairs to peek inside the temples and realize that some visitors have mistaken the holy place for a *kamar kecil*). The rubble surrounding the temples are the remains of the temples destroyed by Mt. Merapi's eruption in 1006. If the kids get bored, usher them to the playground and check out the archaeological museum. Admission to Prambanan complex of Rp5000 (Rp2000 for students with ID) includes a camera pass, English-speaking guide, free access to toilet, playground, and intercom (for paging lost friends). Beware of pick pockets. The Prambanan complex shows **Ramayana ballet performances** in an outside theater (May-Oct. during the full moon, 7-9pm; tickets Rp4000-35,000) and in an indoor theater (Tues.-Thurs. 7:30-9:30pm; tickets Rp7500-15,000).

If you're temple happy, visit **Candi Lumbung, Candi Bubrah, Candi Sewu,** and **Candi Sojiwan,** all within walking distance of the main Prambanan temples. **Candi Plaosan,** to the north, is best visited by bike or *becak* from Prambanan, as are **Candis Banyunibo, Sari, Kalasan,** and **Sambisari. Kraton Ratu Boko,** 2km south of Prambanan, is worth visiting for its panoramic view. It you've rented a bike, ride south along the road to the west of the market (the side closest to Yogya). Follow signs to Kraton Boko, park your bike (Rp200) and hike uphill. At a bend in the road, turn right and walk up a steep, rocky hill to the *kraton,* bypassing the entrance fee.

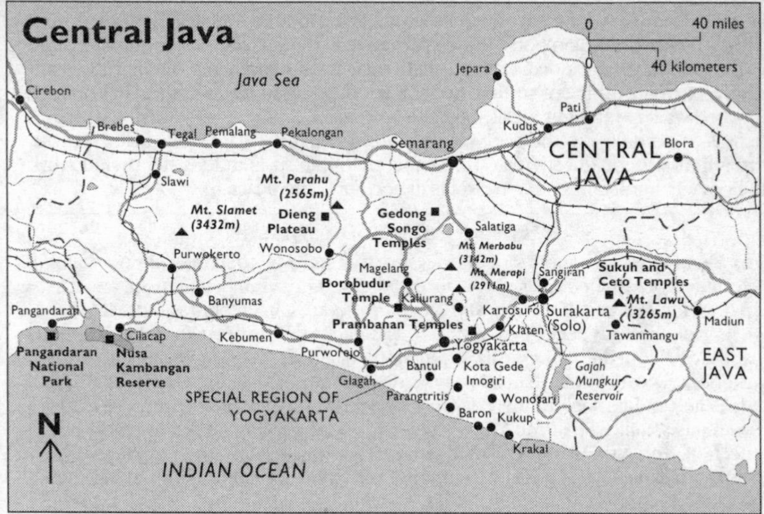

If you miss the turn (approximately 250m before the main entrance), you may get a map and pay Rp250 at the main gate. The mysterious palace consists of a series of stone foundations built on plateaus overlooking trees and valleys below. Be sure to see the gorgeous view of the Prambanan plain from the northern side of the *kraton*. For **accommodations** near Prambanan, **Ny. Murti Guest House** (tel. 961 03), is opposite the entrance to Prambanan temple. Singles with bath Rp15,000. Doubles with bath Rp17,500.

IMOGIRI

Rumor has it that no one can count them exactly, but there are roughly 345 steps to the top of **Imogiri Royal Cemetery.** Seventeen km south of Yogya, Imogiri can be reached by bus from Umbulharjo bus station. The cemetery was built in 1645 by Sultan Agung and houses royal tombs from the Islamic Mataram, Yogyakartan, and Surakartan kingdoms. When you're all hot and sweaty at the top of the cemetery, pay Rp1000 to get wrapped into Javanese formal wear to enter the tombs. Men wear a sarong, long-sleeved shirt, and hat (with a fake egg in the back); women keep their shoulders bare and wear a sarong and batik boob tube (or halter). The tombs are best visited with a guide, but if you're on your own, use a *peta* (map handed out at the dressing station), and humility to navigate through the burial chambers. In each room, enter quietly, make a donation (Rp100 will do) and kneel by the cool marble. After paying your respects to the more recent royalty, be sure to visit the sacred burial chambers of Sultan Agung and Hamengkubuwono I, near the top of the hill. Cool off after the hot and sometimes crowded burial chambers by climbing up to the view from the hill behind the tombs. The graves are open Mon. 10am-1pm and Fri. 1:30-4pm.

PARANGTRITIS

Parangtritis beach is 27km south of Yogya and can be reached by public bus from Yogya's Umbulharjo bus station, or by bus or colts leaving from Jl. Parangtritis at the southeast corner of the *kraton* walls. The desert-like landscape of this beach is hardly ideal for swimming—the undertow of the Indian Ocean is deadly. Locals claim that the yearly victims are abducted by Nyai Loro Kidul, goddess and Queen of the South Seas. Local custom dictates that no one should wear green clothing, as that is her favorite color. Dramatic cliffs to the east shelter secluded coves and there are caves worth exploring. For a daytrip, visitors enjoy the smell of the ocean, drink *es kelapa muda* (young coconut milk) from its freshly axed shell, and canter up and down the black sand on horse drawn carriages. Romantic couples, meanwhile, find a spot among the secluded coves to share their private moments. Parangtritis is not a beach for sunbathing or surfing, rather it is a site of significant mystical importance for the Javanese; at night locals meditate before the crashing surf. Spending a night here is recommended (there are plenty of *losmen* in the village), especially beneath the full moon; the ghostly pale landscape, rhythmic surf, and insistent wind work their magic upon contemplative souls in need of some peace.

It's Not Easy Being Green

At Parangkusumo, about one km west of Parangtritis, there is a shrine which commemorates the mythical romance and consummation between Sultan Senopati of the Mataram kingdom, and Nyai Loro Kidul, Queen of the South Sea. Forever jealous of his decision to return to Mataram, she has been known to kidnap and drown anyone who wears green along her beaches. Rumor has it that the tunnels beneath Taman Sari in Yogyakarta once reached all the way to Parangtritis Beach. While such tunnels may have served strategic defense purposes, they were also built so that the Yogya Sultanate could perpetuate the mythical connection with Nyai Loro Kidul after Mataram was divided into the Yogyakarta and Surakarta Sultanates. Locals at Parangtritis offer prayers and offerings to her each week, and to this day the old clothes, hair and fingernail clippings, and assorted other offerings from the Sultan himself are sent out on a raft to appease this testy goddess. You too would be wise to leave something for her at the shrine and leave your green clothes at home.

GUNUNG MERAPI AND KALIURANG

The occasionally active **Mt. Merapi** rises 2920m above sea level and is 30km north of Yogya. The best view of Merapi is from the observatory of **Plawanga,** an hour's hike from Kaliurang. From Selo, north of Merapi, the brave can hike up the volcano (with or without a guide) and reach the top in four hours. From Yogya, ride a bus to Kartosuro, then to Boyolali, then to Selo; or, from Kaliurang, walk to Selo in one hour. Start at 1am to reach the summit in time for sunrise. Dress warmly, but be prepared to shed protective clothing after daybreak. Sunrise is surreal from above a blanket of clouds, sitting on warm rocks along the moonscape crater.

For a tamer (and lava-less) adventure, stick around **Kaliurang,** 28km north of Yogya on the slopes of Merapi. From Yogya, take the bus from Umbulharjo or the Terban station on Jl. Simanjuntak. Kaliurang is cool and tourist-friendly, with several cheap hotels, a campground, and a youth hostel. The hostel, **Vogels Homestay,** is at Jl. Astamulya 76 (tel. 952 08), off the main road. It's in a rather run-down area, but it's cheap: small doubles Rp5000 for members/students and even cheaper dorm-style accommodations. Vogels also has a restaurant. The Kaliurang **market** is dominated by a million varieties of bananas, but look out for Kaliurang's specialty: sweet, brown-red *tempe* or *tahu bacem* and the mild *jadah,* made from glutinous rice. A piece of *tempe* or *tahu* is eaten with a *jadah* patty; it makes a tasty, filling snack.

To explore the town's hiking paths, head to **Telaga Putri,** a walkable but significant distance away from the youth hostel. Hike on bricked paths under gigantic trees and cool off by clambering up to the observatory for a view of the valley. Listen for loudspeakers announcing the park's closing; the gates shut at 4pm. If you get shut in, don't panic—it's easy to climb over the gate.

Mt. Merapi erupted in November 1994, killing thousands. It is now closed, though guides still offer (pester) to take visitors up, assuring that it is safe. While hiking up Merapi to within 2km of the top and seeing live lava can be exciting, this is risky. Travelers do it, and guides are available, but be forewarned: **hiking an active volcano is dangerous!**

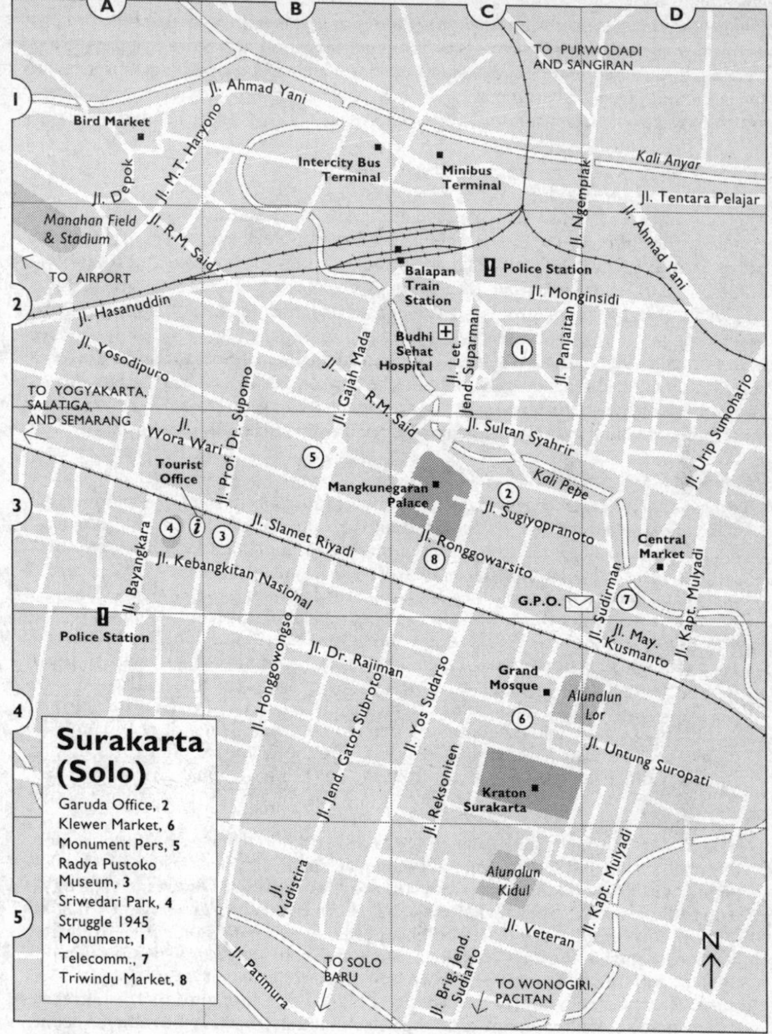

■■■ SURAKARTA (SOLO)

Ask the Solonese what's special about their city and they'll probably knee jerk with something along the lines of "Solo is the cultural heart of Java." Solonese seem to be fed on this kind of city pride even before they're weaned onto *nasi goreng*. And with good reason, too: Solo boasts two *kratons,* a host of classical art to support them, the second oldest museum in Indonesia, and an exponentially successful *batik* industry. As a result, Solonese, like their sibling Yogyakartans, tend to be proud of their city and its history, which began when Sunan Pakubuwono moved his Mataran kingdom to the city in 1745. Solo's comparatively mild interest in glitzy multi-story mall complexes and other facets of the McDonald-ization occurring elsewhere in Java is perhaps another product—or even the cause—of this civic pride. Even if Solo does join the flock of quickly developing Javanese cities grazing on commercialism, its main streets will still be linked by crooked, often hidden *gangs* (alleys) that give it a community atmosphere. All this is not to say that Solo is a city without transactions; it has two shopping centers, perhaps more eyeglass stores than anywhere else in the world, and a hectic, Wall Street-esque flurry of activity at the *batik* market outside the central *kraton*. A clean, friendly city with artsy energy and plenty of cheap accommodations, Solo makes a hospitable and popular stopover for budget travelers.

ORIENTATION

The city's most frequently mentioned landmark is **Jalan Slamet Riyadi,** which cuts east-west through town and is traveled by Solo's double-decker buses. The **tourist office** is on the west side of Jl. Slamet Riyadi, with the **post office** and **telephone office** on **Jalan Jend. Sudirman,** off the street's east side. Many of Solo's restaurants and *warungs* cluster on streets off the center of Jl. Slamet Riyadi, with the **Puro Mangkunegaran** *kraton* at their north edge. Homestays can be found off both sides of Jl. Slamet Riyadi, particularly to the south, off **Jalan Gatot Subroto,** near **Singosaren Plaza.** Other significant bases include the **Kraton Surakarta** and the **batik market** in the southwest, the **airport** in the northwest (8km from the town center), and the **Tirtonadi/Gilingan bus station** and **Balapan train station** to the north.

PRACTICAL INFORMATION

Tourist Office: Dinas Pariwisata, Jl. Slamet Riyadi 275 (tel. 711 435). From Balapan railway station, hire a *becak* (about Rp1000) for the 5-min. ride down Jl. Gajah Mada to Jl. Slamet Riyadi. Free map with important locations, city brochures, and a calendar of events. Open Mon.-Fri. 9am-5pm.

Tours: Rosalia Indah Tour and Travel, Jl. Slamet Riyadi 121 (tel. 713 172).

Currency Exchange: Bank BNI, Jl. Arifin 2 (tel. 459 09), accepts some traveler's checks. Open Mon.-Fri. 7:30am-noon and 1-3pm, Sat. 7:30-11am. **Bank Central Asia (BCA),** Jl. Slamet Riydai 7 (tel. 461 16), accepts traveler's checks and will transfer money from Visa and MC. Open Mon.-Fri. 8am-2pm, Sat. 8-11am.

Post Office: GPO, Jl. Jendral Sudirman 8 (tel. 472 39 or 472 23). General delivery and Poste Restante held indefinitely. Open Mon.-Fri. 8am-7pm, Sat. 9am-1pm.

Telephone: Jl. Mayor Kusmanto 1 (tel. 486 00). The major telephone, telegraph, and telex office is across the street from the GPO. International service available 24 hrs. There are *wartels* all over town. Ask for the nearest one at your hotel. **Telephone code:** 0271.

Airport: Adi Sumarmo Airport (tel. 324 88), 10km northwest of the city. One terminal. Carriers: Garuda, Sempati, Bouraq, Merpati, Mandala. Garuda has several flights per day to: **Jakarta** (one way, 1hr., Rp130,300); and **Denpasar** via **Yogyakarta** (one way, 2-½hr., Rp121,500). Taxis from the airport to downtown Solo (10km) cost about Rp10,000. The cheapest ride to town is on buses from the main road outside the airport. Take a blue minibus to Kartosuro station (10min., Rp300), and then a double-decker (Rp200) down to Jl. Slamet Riyadi.

Trains: Balapan railway station (tel. 632 228), on Jl. Monginsidi. To: **Jakarta,** Pasar Senen station (economy class, Rp5000, children Rp3000); **Surabaya** (economy class, night trains, 4-½hr., Rp7500, children Rp5000; business, daily, Rp15,000; executive, daily, Rp36,000); **Semarang** (economy, 3-½hr., Rp1300, children Rp1000); and **Yogyakarta** (business, all trains through Solo stop in Yogya, 1hr., Rp2000).

Buses: Tirtonadi (tel. 717 759 or 717 297), the main intercity bus station, on the north side of town on Jl. Ahmad Yani. Double-decker buses circle between terminals **Gilingan** (at the same location as Tirtonadi) and **Palur,** east of Solo. The double-decker buses run along Jl. Slamet Riyadi and Jl. Veteran only (every 10min., 5am-8pm, Rp200). Seats on intercity buses, which may have toilets, A/C, and movies, can be booked through **Raya,** Jl. Sutan Syahrir 13 (tel. 635 838) and **Bali Cepat,** Jl. Kolonel Suharto 21 (tel. 635 068). **Minibuses** leave from several locations on the outskirts of town, including Gilingan and Palur, and weave in and out of town (Rp200), petering out after 9 or 10pm.

Local transportation: Becaks are best, and can be hailed at most street corners.

Taxis: P.T. Solo Central Taxi, Jl. Adisucipto 41 (tel. 715 678).

Car rental: Hayuningrat Tours and Travel Service (tel. 485 60), in front of the Kasunanan Keraton, is available at most large hotels. Usually includes a chauffeur.

Bike rental: Relax Homestay, Rp1500 per day. **"Westerners" Homestay,** Kemlayan Kidul #2 (tel. 331 06), Rp2500 per day.

English Bookstores: Sekawan Bookstore, Jl. Kartini 4 (tel. 373 77) has some English-language books, as well as maps. **Budhi Laksana Bookstore,** Jl. Diponegoro 52 (tel. 633 932), usually stocks English-language paperbacks. Open 9:30am-2pm and 5:30-9pm.

Markets: Solo's main food market is **Pasar Gede,** at the intersection of Jl. Mgr. Sugiopranoto and Jl. Kapten Mulyadi, on the east side of town, near the main telephone office. Open around 8am until between 3 and 4pm.

Laundry: Many homestays will do laundry for a fee. For professionals, go to **Hong Kong Laundry and Dry Cleaners,** Jl. Slamet Riyadi 88 (tel. 489 62). Pants and blouses, Rp1000; jeans, Rp1500 in 1-2 days. Open Mon.-Sat. 8am-8pm and 4:30-9pm. Many homestays and hotels have buckets, brushes, and drying racks available. Small packets of "Rinso" brand detergent are Rp100-200.

Swimming Pool: Swimming allowed for non-guests at the palatial **Kusuma Sahid Prince Hotel** (tel. 463 56) on Jl. Sugiyopranoto. Tickets are Rp3500 per person. Open 8am-7pm.

Pharmacy: Apotek Wijaya, Jl. Slamet Riyadi 202 (tel. 633 885). Open Mon.-Sat. 8am-8pm. Some English spoken. **24-hr. pharmacy** at **Rumah Sakit Kasih Ibu Hospital,** Jl. Slamet Riyadi 404 (tel. 714 422).

Hospitals: In addition to the Rumah Sakit Kasih Ibu (listed above), other hospitals include **Kustadi Hospital,** Jl. Kapten Mulyadi 249 (tel. 430 13); **PKU Muhammadiyah Hospital,** Jl. Ronggowarsito 130 (tel. 714 578); and **Panti Kosala Hospital,** Jl. Brigjen Katamso 55 (tel. 431 39).

Police: Main station (tel. 714 500) on Jl. Adisucipto Manahan and another on Jl. Monginisidi 76 (tel. 569 69).

ACCOMMODATIONS

Paradise Homestay and Guest House, Kemlayan Kidul 1/3 (tel. 541 11; fax 529 60), one *gang* past the Relax Homestay. From Balapan train station, a *becak* costs about Rp1500. From Jl. Gatot Subroto, on the left side of the street, pass the Singer shop and turn left at the 4th *gang* (look for a yellow ADA textile sign overhead). It's at the end of the *gang* on the left. From Jl. Yos Sudarso, Paradise is on the right at the beginning of the 3rd *gang;* turn just before the Batik Keris store. Gleaming rooms, attractive sitting area, spanking new bar, fish pond, and quiet flowering garden. The cheaper rooms are a bargain seeker's Eden. Doubles with fan Rp9500, with netting Rp10,500, with fan and net Rp13,500. Large, furnished rooms Rp15,500. Doubles with A/C, bathtubs, and carved modern decorations Rp30,000. Laundry service, taxi service, restaurant, and coffee shop.

Happy Homestay, Jl. Honggowongso Gg. Karagan #12 (tel. 712 449). From outside the airport or railway station, find an orange minibus (or the double-decker bus) that drives along Jl. Veteran. Get off at Jl. Honggowongso; there's a sign about 100m along the *gang* on the left. Slightly removed from Solo's central activity, Happy is very much a homestay; all the rooms are under one roof, which is shared with the owner's family. Not incredibly private, and you're encouraged to make yourself at home, but it's colorful, well-kept, and one of the most wad-friendly places in town. Singles Rp6000. Doubles Rp8000. Breakfast, tea, and coffee included. Laundry service, bike rentals, and guided bike tours of Solo (9am-3pm, Rp7500). Discounts for long-term guests.

Remaja Homestay, Jl. Cockro 1 Kauman (tel. 477 58), on Jl. Yos Sudarso. Remaja's *gang* is opposite the Batik Keris store and the *gang* leading to the westerners and the Paradise. An undiscovered bargain offered by an exuberantly friendly family who stuffs you with yummy nosh. Basic singles with fan Rp6000.

Relax Homestay, Empu Sedah 28, Kemlayan (tel. 464 17). From Jl. Slamet Riyadi, turn south onto either Jl. Gatot Subroto or Jl. Yos Sudarso. On a small *gang* that links the 2 streets. Walking down Jl. Gatot Subroto on the left (or east) side of the street, pass two *gangs* and turn left onto the 3rd, opposite the Singer sewing machine shop. Relax is a short distance on the left. Variable rooms and prices;

most are homey, with a multi-colored paint splatter motif, facing a garden and fishpond. Singles with fan and large bed Rp8500. Doubles Rp11,000. Breakfast (toast, fruit salad, banana pancake) Rp1000. Manggus, the friendly manager who owns the Relax and the Ramayana Restaurant, works at the tourist office, and is fluent in English. He is an invaluable source of info about Solo and Indonesia in general. Camping allowed (bring your tents) for Rp2000. Check-out 2pm.

Joyokusuman/Nendra Guest House, Gajahan Rt. 2/3 #7 (tel. 548 42). One of Solo's oldest homestays, this guest house is behind the Surakarta Kraton's south yard (Alun-alun Kidul). It's hard to find (take a *becak* from Jl. Veteran) and removed from Solo's most concentrated activity, but once you're insulated in it's brick, moss, and carved wood, you won't miss anything. Rooms vary in price, privacy, and luxury. Some have patchwork quilts and ornate furniture. Those by the garden face an enormous tree and its base, used for meditation and dance classes. The place has a hushed, *Secret Garden* feel, and is home to several long-term visitors studying meditation, dance, and Javanese culture. Prices start at Rp15,000.

"Westerners"/Pak Mawardi Homestay, Kemlayan Kidul #2 (tel. 331 06). From Jl. Gatot Suboto, just before and opposite the Paradise. One of the oldest and most heavily trafficked homestays, the "Westerners" is "for Westerners/foreigners only." Frequently full, it ends up supplying business for neighboring homestays. Basic rooms in *kampung* family-style environment. Dorms Rp6000. Singles Rp7000. Doubles Rp7000. Breakfast Rp2000. Free tea and cold water. Bike rentals and tour arrangements.

Homestay Solo, Jl. Ahmad Dahlan, Gg. Panda 2, Keprabon. From Balapan train station, take a 5-min. *becak* ride, or get off a double-decker or minibus at Jl. Ahmad Dahlan and walk to the first *gang* on the right. In the heart of tourist-oriented facilities (across from "Warung Baru" restaurant), with budget digs around a dim courtyard and porch seating. With fan: singles Rp6000, doubles Rp8000. For larger, brighter rooms: singles Rp10,000, doubles Rp12,000. Breakfast, tea, and coffee included. *Batik* classes (make a t-shirt, Rp7500).

Hotel Jayakarta, Jl. Monginsidi #106 (tel. 460 13). Outside the Balapan train station. Oriented toward families, Hotel Jayakarta has large, plain rooms that border a garden. Singles Rp10,000. Doubles with fan Rp15,000.

FOOD

The cheap and informal way to eat is to buy food from roadside *warungs,* stalls, and mobile carts, particularly dense at night along Jl. Gatot Subroto and Jl. Teuku Umar. **Ibu Mari's,** an outdoor squat-around-the-campfire set-up across from Ligna Furniture at the top of Jl. Gatot Subroto, specializes in *nasi gudeg* and *nasi liwet,* Yogya and Solonese specialties. One plate costs about Rp1000. Ibu Mari cooks from 4pm 'til she runs out of customers. Another local favorite is **Bu Wongso Lemu's** place, marked by a white sheet stretched from her impromptu kitchen to the sidewalk in the middle of Jl. Diponegoro. Bu Wongso Lemu serves Solonese fare—generally sauces on pre-cooked rice with combinations of vegetables or chicken—in banana leaves. She sits in front of a large porch-like area with low tables, floor mats, and men talking politics in the corners.

If the roadside sellers are too intimidating, too informal, or too unpredictable, try some of the more traditional, though cheap, restaurant-style Indonesian hangouts. Start with the **food bazaar** at the Matahari Department Store, Singosaran Plaza's 3rd floor, at Jl. Rajiman. Open daily 9am-9pm. If you're itching to satisfy that sweet tooth, go look over the mounds of doughnuts, danishes, cookies, and snacks at either the **American Bakery** at Jl. Slamet Riyadi 90 (tel. 326 07; open 8:30am-8:45pm) or the **Holland Modern Bakery,** Jl. Slamet Riyadi 135 (tel. 324 52). **Vegetarians** in Solo should have no problem, even though menus are not ordinarily geared toward them. Just ask for your dish *"tanpa daging"* (without meat), and with a *tempe* or *tahu* substitute.

Yonisya, Jl. Gajah Mada #4 (tel. 525 04). Just off Jl. Slamet Riyadi on the right. Locals recommend the seafood hot plate (Rp6000) and the special *nasi goreng* (Rp4000). Open 6am-2:30pm and 4:30-10pm.

Restaurant Rindu, Jl. Honggowongso #112 (tel. 377 53), a short walk from the tourist office off Jl. Slamet Riyadi. Extensive menu of Indonesian food around Rp1500, served on plastic covered tables by waitresses in purple uniforms who hum along to the piped Indo-pop. Open 10am-midnight.

Warung Hijam, Jl. Diponegoro 47, on the left side of the street. Relaxed environment where you can sit and watch your meal be prepared in the tiny kitchen, or gaze at family photos of the owners and their kids. Basic Indonesian dishes Rp1000-2000. Open 10am (or whenever the owners wake up) to 10pm.

Ayam Bakar Goreng, Jl. Diponegoro 14 (tel. 359 14). Off Jl. Slamet Riyadi. Amidst mirrored walls and potted plants, this place specializes in fried chicken. Roast chicken thigh Rp1700.

Ramayana Restaurant, Jl. Imam Bonjoi 49 (tel. 466 43), racks up orders for its *sate ayam* (chicken on a stick, Rp2000), *burung dara goreng* (fried pigeon, Rp7000), and *ikan bakar* (grilled fish, Rp8000).

Monggo Pinarak, Jl. Ahmad Dahlan 58. Scrumptious Indonesian, vegetarian, and Indian food. Mixed vegetable *masala* (a creamy orange and tomato sauce), Rp1500. Fantastic homemade *chapati* (Rp400). Open 7am-11pm.

Gamelan Restaurant, Jl. A. Dahlan 28 (tel. 416 40), up the street from Monggo Pinarak. Bamboo tables, roof, and walls in a traditional Javanese weave. Highlights are on the international menu, and include *pecel lele* (fish with vegetables, Rp3000). Open 8am-11pm.

Warung Baru, Jl. A. Dahlan 23 (tel. 563 69). The infamous Warung Baru is an international hub where travelers alternatively eye each other suspiciously and swap advice on where the most authentic (i.e., non-touristy) culture is to be had. This sanctuary is orchestrated by friendly management who serve lickety-split (and quite tasty) food. Homemade bread with jam (Rp1000) and Indonesian basics (some vegetarian) such as fried vegetables with tempeh (Rp1000). The menu lists sights, tours, and *batik* classes.

The Kantin Bahagia, Jl. Gatot Subroto 91, just before the Matahari Mall Complex. Serves beer and some basic western and Indonesian dishes, including vegetarian spaghetti (Rp3000) and french fries. The western food is not without Indonesian touches, such as the *katsup*-flavored spaghetti "sauce." Open 10am-10pm.

SIGHTS

For visitors restricted to the few rooms open to the public, Solo's two *kratons* pale in comparison with Yogya's smaller palace. Nevertheless, the *kratons'* presence focuses and perpetuates Solo's classical arts and symbolizes important historical and architectural components of Solonese culture. The Kraton Surakarta, or **Kasunanan Palace,** is in the southeast part of Solo, bordered by the large north and south yards *(alun-alun)* and the *batik* market, and is partially open to tours. The *kraton* was founded in 1745 by Pakubuwono II, who had his royal palace moved from the ransacked Kartasura (about 12km west of Solo). The palace is home to the present sunan, Pakubuwono XII, 72 years old with six wives and 38 children. Besides the main hall where the sunan receives guests, visitors can wander through the impressive museum, which displays a random assortment of objects connected to the palace: *topeng* dance masks, ancient weapons, royal games, and statues. Admission Rp1000. Guides available. The *kraton* is open daily except Fri., 8:30am-1:30pm; 8:30am-3pm in June and July, during school vacation. Children perform **traditional Javanese dances** at the *kraton,* Sun. 9-11am; adult traditional dance Sun. 2pm.

The less impressive **Puro Mangkunegaran,** at the center of town, is the home of Prince Mankunegoro. The main attraction is the central pavillion and its roof, which is decorated with symbols of the Javanese zodiac, and a museum. Open Mon.-Sat. 9am-2pm, Sun. 9am-1pm. Admission Rp1500 (includes a guide). The **Museum Radyapustaka,** beside the tourist office on Jl. Slamet Riyadi, is the second oldest museum in Indonesia and exhibits Mataram Kingdom artifacts, including a collection of *wayang* puppets, *keris* knives, statues, and ancient Javanese philosophical texts. Open Tues., Thurs. 8am-noon, Fri.-Sun. 8-11am.

One of the most entertaining activities in Solo is perusing the markets. Outside of the main Surakarta Kraton, behind the Alun-Alun Lor, or front yard, is the **Pasar**

Klewer, the *batik* market. The two floors of the indoor market are a crowded, chaotic maze of stalls, many selling exactly the same merchandise: thousands of reels of fabric (both modern and traditional), bedspreads, buttons, clothes, and more, all for at least half the price of the stores in town. Bathrooms on the second floor. Inside open 8am-4pm; outside fruit market and *warungs* stay open past dark. **Pasar Bladek,** the bird market, is on the outskirts of town (a Rp2-3000 becak ride from Jl. Slamet Riyadi), west of the Gilingam bus station. Watch your head as you walk under and between hundreds of cages of parrots, cockatoos, pigeons, finches, chickens, bats, and even a monkey or two; this place looks like a zoo (and smells like one too). The market is open 8am-4pm. Solo's main **fruit market** (Pasar Gede) is down the street and diagonally across from the post office, behind the central telephone office on Jl. Urip and Jl. Mgr. Sugropranoto. Open 8am-3pm. Solo's unique **Pasar Triwindu** is one of Central Java's only flea markets. Use hard bargaining to get what you want: Dutch-imported china and tea sets, painted Buddhas and Hindu figurines, puppets, beads, candelabras, toys, bones and other oddly indecipherable bric-a-brac. The Triwindu antique market borders an extensive, museum-like market specializing in auto and bike parts. Open at 8am, and winds down around 3 or 4pm.

ENTERTAINMENT

Performances of traditional *wayang orang* dance can be viewed from 8 to 11pm every night except Sunday at the **Sriwedari Park,** beside the tourist office on Jl. Slamet Riyadi. **Gamelan Performances** are held nightly in the lobby of the Kusuma Sahid hotel, 5 to 8pm. *Keroncong* music is performed Thursday 8 to 9pm. Let loose at **Freedom Discoteque,** Jl. A. Yani, Taman Balekambang (tel. 459 64). For **Indonesian film,** head to Jl. Slamet Riyadi 134, at the intersection of Jl. Gatot Sabroto. Class I tickets Rp1750. Class II tickets Rp1500. **Atrium theater,** at the intersection of Jl. Dahlan and Jl. Slamet Riyadi (tel. 471 18), shows some American movies.

■ NEAR SOLO

Targeting sights around Solo is a good excuse to get off your *losmen*'s cushy lawn furniture. Plus, it gives you something definitive to say to the ubiquitous "where you going, mister?" from every *becak* driver. Working your way through the sights demands a sort of zen; to enjoy yourself, you have to be willing to absorb as much out of getting to the sight as from the sight itself. Travelers can test their patience at Solo's two most highly hyped excursions: Sangiran museum and Sukuh temple. Fifteen km north of Solo, **Sangiran** is where the fossil skull of *Pithecanthropus erectus* (aka 'Java Man') was discovered by a Dutch paleontologist in 1936. The discovery of *Pithecanthropus erectus,* now considered a subspecies of *Homo erectus,* revamped theories about early humans' possible migration from Africa to Java. Excavations are still proceeding at Sangiran, and a small museum there showcases some pig and hippopotamus teeth, a glassed-in diorama of home on the prehistoric range, and some staggering mammoth bones. To get to Sangiran (remember to enjoy the ride, since it may last eight times as long as your stay in the museum), catch a double-decker or a minibus to Gilingam Station, then take a minibus toward Purwodadi or Kalijambe, and ask to get off near Sangiran, where *ojeks* will ride you up the hill (Rp1000 one way, or walk the 4km) to the museum. Open Mon.-Sat. 7am-5pm; admission Rp1000. To return to Solo from the *ojek* stand, hop on a large bus with BERSERI printed on its front; it's Rp400 to Jl. Slamet Riyadi.

Touted as "the most erotic temple in the world," **Sukuh temple**, 34km northeast of Solo, is believed to have been carved with the intent of providing sex education to the 15th century's offspring. The carvings around the temple are hardly X-rated, but they are better preserved and more detailed than many other temples' in Central Java. However, the exact function and builders of Sukuh temple remain a mystery, and its Maya-reminiscent structure, unusual for Javanese architecture, has confused archaeologists for decades. Resting on the slopes of Mt. Lawu, Sukuh is not easy to reach, it's but worth it for the views from the temple's "roof" and from its environs.

To get there, catch a double-decker bus from Jl. Slamet Riyadi (Rp200) and ride until Palur. From Palur, ride a big bus heading for Karang Pandan (30min., Rp500). Then ride a minibus to Sukuh (20min., Rp300). Unless you travel on a market day, the minibus will dump you off at the bottom of a hill; you can either pay Rp1500 for an eagerly waiting *ojek* ride to the temple, or you can walk up the steep hill (about 30min.). Admission Rp300. The most popular stop after Sukuh is **Tawangmangu,** a 2-½-hour, clearly marked trek that ends at a 100m waterfall. With the "journey-is-as-important-as-goal" maxim in mind, you won't be disappointed by the skimpy waterfall. The last bus from the waterfall to Karang Pandan leaves at 4:30pm.

Candi Ceto is 7km north of Sukuh, from where *ojeks* can whisk you (for Rp9000). Or you could walk the steep path (3-4 hrs.). Built in 1470, Ceto, also Maya-like, is higher than Sukuh and offers better views, but less stone carving decoration.

■■■ SEMARANG

Unlike Yogya or Solo, Semarang does not direct its energy toward international visitors. Instead, the city seems intent on turning its youth into mall rats, with glitzy, multi-story shopping complexes sprouting up at major intersections. The effect of Semarang's virginity to tourist hordes is two-fold. On the one hand, the city can be refreshingly tuned out to foreigners' tastes, thereby revealing the workings of a true Javanese city. On the other hand, always being the object of attention and curiosity can be draining. Some travelers, particularly women on their own, may be taken under the wing of generally harmless chaperones who are eager to practice their English and show you the sights, but who do not consider independent travel to be a desirable or virtuous activity.

ORIENTATION

The capital city of Central Java province, Semarang is on its north coast, accessible by air, bus, and train from most points in Java. Semarang's airport, harbor, and train tracks, including the **Tawang Railway Station,** border the north edge of the city. **Jalan Haryono,** running north-south on the east side of the city, and **Jalan Pandanaran/Yani,** running northeast-southwest through the city center, insulate the busiest commercial areas from the more residential and hilly southside. At the heart of activity are three roundabouts, at **Simpang Lima** (the main square), **Tugu Muda** (the monument commemorating Indonesian youths' battle against the Japanese), and the north end of **Jalan Pemuda,** near the giant **Metro Grand Park Hotel** called the **"Johar Complex."** The streets linking these points form a triangle and offer exhaustive shopping and eating opportunities. Other areas that may interest tourists—particularly architecture buffs—are **Chinatown,** to the south of **Jalan H. Agus Salim,** and the ritzy colonial-style hills of **Kintelan** district, southwest of downtown.

PRACTICAL INFORMATION

Tourist Information: Semarang Regency Tourist Office (tel. 921 424), Matahari Dept. Store, Jl. Jend. A. Yani. At Simpang Lima Square. Open Mon.-Fri. 8am-3pm. **Central Java Provincial Tourist Office,** Jl. Madukoro Blok BB/PRPP complex (tel. 607 184; fax 607 182). From Tugu Muda, ride a city bus away from town (west) on Jl. Sugiopranoto and ask to get off at PRPP or Jl. Amjasmoro. From the bus stop, cross the street and find a *becak* to take you to the "Kantor Pariwisata" (about Rp1000). Though in an inconvenient location, this office deals with tourism in all of Central Java and is an excellent source of info and advice. Pak Djatmiko is quite knowledgeable and speaks good English. Open Mon.-Fri. 8am-3pm. **Semarang Municipal Tourist Office,** Jl. Srivijaya 29 (tel. 311 220), can be reached by orange colt or *becak*. Ask to get off at the old zoo, the *kebun binatang*. The office is just inside the zoo's gates. Open Mon.-Fri. 8am-3pm.

Post Office: Jl. Pemuda 4 (tel. 161 for postal information). No general delivery. No Poste Restante. No. No. No. Open Mon.-Sat. 6:30am-8pm, Sun. 8am-8pm.

Telephones: International *wartels* are all over Semarang. Ask at your *losmen* for the closest one. **Wartel II,** Jl. Alun-Alun Timur #2. Behind the post office. Fax service. Open 7am-8:30pm. **Local phone info:** tel. 108. **Inter-local phone info:** tel. 106. **Telephone code:** 024.

Currency Exchange: BDNI, Jl. Pemuda 175A (tel. 553 920), at Tugu Muda, will exchange traveler's checks and advance cash (minimum US$200) from AmEx card. **P.T. Supit Money Changer,** Jl. Pemuda #39C (tel. 542 461).

Airport: A. Yani Airport (tel. 544 735) on Jl. Siliwangi, 5km west of town. One terminal. Carriers: Merpati, Sempati, Bouraq, Mandala. Merpati Airlines flies to **Jakarta** (7 daily, last flight at 6pm, Rp117,900), and **Surabaya** (Rp72,800). Go to and from the airport by taxi (approx. Rp5000).

Trains: The Tawang Railway Station, off Jl. Merak, has trains leaving daily for Solo, Surabaya, Tegal, and Jakarta.

Buses: Terboyo, Jl. Kaligawe (tel. 581 921), is the main terminal, with buses running to Yogya, Solo, Surabaya, Jakarta, Sumatra, and Denpasar, among others. Private intercity bus services include **Bus Patasnusantara,** Jl. Dr. Cipto 108C (tel. 545 417), with buses between Semarang, Wonosobo, and Solo, among others. Buses have A/C, TV, and toilet.

Local Transportation: Semarang's **small orange buses,** alternately called "colts," "minibuses," or "Daihatsus," and its large **biskota** (city buses) have overlapping, inefficient routes. Minibuses generally cost Rp200—pay this until you are asked for more, or ask a local (other than the driver) what the "*harga biasa*" (usual price) is. Stand expectantly by the road and shout out the name of your destination when bus workers (assistants) lean out of the doors. Minibuses become scarce after 9pm. Large, intercity buses cost Rp250 (for all distances) and stop running after 9 or 10pm. **Becaks, ojeks,** and **andongs** can be hailed throughout the city, day or night.

Taxi: Puri Kencana Taxi, Jl. Imam Bonjol 144 (tel. 511 761). **Indra Kelanan Taxi,** Jl. Pemuda 83 (tel. 542 570).

Car Rentals: Metro Hotel, Jl. Salim #2 (tel. 547 371; fax 510 863), rents Panthers (12 hrs., Rp120,000).

Markets: Pasar Johar is the main public market on the side streets between Jl. Haryono and the north end of Jl. Pemuda, opposite the Metro Grand Park Hotel. Tools, squash rackets, clothes, mounds of cucumbers, and everything in between. Shops inside open early morning and close in the evening; some stalls outside stay open all night.

Laundromat: Binatu Semarang, Jl. Gajah Mada 18 (tel. 546 848), does dry cleaning and laundry. Laundry takes 4 days (or twice the price for 1 day return). Pants Rp1800, shirts Rp1500. Some *losmen* or hotels will do laundry for a price.

English Language Bookstore: Gramedia, Jl. Pandanaran 122 (tel. 318 495), has some English-language maps, guides, and novels. Open 9am-9pm.

24-hr. Pharmacy: Kimia Farma, Jl. Pemuda 135 (tel. 542 646 or 541 510).

Hospital: Tlogorejo Hospital (tel. 413 305) on a small road north of Jl. Panjaitan that runs parallel to the river. **Dr. Kariadi Hospital** (tel. 413 476) on Jl. Kariadi.

Police: Main office, Jl. Dr. Sutomo 19 (tel. 311 390). **Provincial Police,** Jl. Pahlawan #1 (tel. 311 382 or 412 280).

Emergency: Fire: tel. 113. **Police:** tel. 110. **Ambulance:** tel. 118. **Red Cross:** tel. 311 891 or 541 237.

ACCOMMODATIONS

In comparison to Yogya and Solo, tourism has not hit Semarang; hence, prices stay high while daily standards wane. Many of the budget accommodations in Semarang are not nice places to visit, much less spend the night. The landscape is bleak, and you may find yourself forking over more than what you're getting in return. Interestingly, domestic travelers tend to flock to the more inhospitable joints, apparently without effective complaints. But don't be discouraged. Cheap, decent rooms are to be had; they just require some extra patience for their humble reward.

Hotel Rahagu, Jl. Imam Bonjol 35 (tel. 542 532). Halfway between the main post office and the Poncol Railway Station. Most Semarang natives know Rahagu by name; it is also across from the well-known Surya hotel. Rooms are not spotless and can be quite loud if near the street or the common TVs in the hall, but compared to budget hotels near the city center, Rahagu is a furnished, spacious oasis. Doubles Rp15,000. Tea or coffee included. Attached restaurant. Check-out 1pm.

Hotel Singapore, Jl. Imam Bonjol 12 (tel. 543 757). A 5- to 10-min. walk from the Metro Hotel and post office area, or take a short *becak* ride to the top of Imam Bonjol; Hotel Singapore is on the left. The tiled floors and beds are spotless. Plush, red, throne-like chairs in the lobby and psychedelic, brown tiles on the walls of the "standard" rooms (Rp11,000), which are otherwise not much different from the "economy" rooms (Rp9000). Check-out 1pm.

Hotel Candi Indah, Jl. Dr. Wahidin 112 (tel. 312 912; fax 312 515). On the south side of town, just past the intersection of Jl. Sultan Agung and Jl. Wahidin, on the right if walking downhill near the Candi Gold Course. Removed location, but Candi Indah has excellent, spic 'n' span rooms with modern furnishings, a radio, and gleaming floors. Single bed Rp25,000, with A/C Rp45,000. Double bed with A/C Rp50,000. For Rp10,000 per person, you can sleep the night away in "driver rooms," dorm-style accommodations in tight bunk-bedded closets. Restaurant with Rp3000 entrees. AmEx, MC.

Hotel Candi Baru, Jl. Rinjani 21 (tel. 315 272; fax 314 738). Take an intercity bus heading to the Kintelan area and get off at the Grasia Hotel on Jl. Parman. With your back to Grasia, cross the main road and walk straight for 200m. A 1-star hotel, Candi Baru is on a hill overlooking the town and harbor. Cheapest rooms are small, basic, and fairly clean. Economy rooms for two with attractive view go for a steep Rp29,040. Breakfast and an afternoon snack with tea included. Restaurant serves entrees for Rp3000. AmEx, MC.

Nendra Yakti, Gang Pinggir 68 (tel. 544 593; fax 550 593). From Jl. Agus Salim, walk or *becak* 500m; Nendra Yakti is on the left. A multi-story hotel in Chinatown with a variety of rooms. The large, furnished "economy" rooms have a view of the less-than-attractive green river below. Singles Rp18,000. Doubles Rp19,000. Both have *mandi* and fan; for A/C Rp35,000. Check-out 2pm. AmEx, MC, and DC.

Hotel Telomoyo, Jl. Gajah Mada 138 (tel. 545 436; fax 547 037). Central location in Chinatown across from the Bali department store. Very small, decent rooms in a village-like atmosphere with a maze of rooms around a construction area strewn with bikes, lawn furniture, and a ping-pong table. Large, comfy A/C lobby with leather sofa chairs and TV. Economy rooms with 2 beds and outside *mandi* Rp22,500. Standard rooms with A/C, phone, TV, bath and shower, and hot water Rp60,000. Breakfast included. Check-out 1pm. AmEx, MC, and DC.

FOOD

Semarang is teeming with **restaurants, outdoor stalls,** and **mobile carts,** particularly along the south end of Jl. Gajah Mada and the north end of Jl. Pahlawan by the Citraland Mall and Simpang Lima. Vegetarians may find themselves eating *gado-gado* and *nasi goreng* (sometimes available with *tempe* or *tahu*) time and again; try Pringgading for some variation. For carnivores who have a hankering for grease, there's a certain fast food joint on Jl. Pandanaran.

Nusantara, Jl. Pandanaran No. 6 Ruko 11 & 12 (tel. 411 801). Just past the Tugu Muda intersection on the left. Meaty dishes galore, all displayed in bowls in the window. Fried chicken (Rp1300); fried shrimp (Rp6000). Open 24 hrs.

Danish, Jl. Pandanaran 43 (tel. 313 088), across from Nusantara. Bakery, ice cream, and pizza parlor. Pick up a tray and tongs by the door and choose your own treats to eat in or *dibungkus*—wrapped to go. Chocolate sprinkled donuts (Rp1000). Open daily 7:30am-9:30pm.

Nasi Uduk, Jl. Gaja Mada 172 (tel. 317 360). Exit the Citra Land Mall and walk right; it's on your right. Outdoor seating by the noisy street, where you can pick out, watch, and hear your meal being fried in *woks* and mobile carts behind the tables. Cheap, good-quality Indonesian food in an efficient, busy environment. Look for sweet, thirst-quenching ice drinks (try *es siwalan*, from coconut) served with a spoon in a bowl. Open nightly 5-10:30pm.

Toko Oen, Jl. Pemuda 52 (tel. 541 683). Large, colonial-style restaurant with doors opened to the busy street. Checkered floor and stained-glass windows falling out of panes. Indonesian, Chinese, European, and ice cream. Entrees Rp3000-7000.

Pringgading, Jl. Pringgading 54 (tel. 516 991). Extensive menu focusing on Chinese-style seafood, served with fancy folded napkins by hovering, pink-uniformed waitresses. Good vegetarian options and A/C to the max. Specialties include *babi goreng kering* (fried pork, Rp9000 for 4 people), *mie sup* (noodle soup, Rp7000), and *ayam mente* (chicken with cashew nuts, Rp10,000 for 4 people). Open daily 9am-2:30pm and 5-9:30pm.

ENTERTAINMENT

After dark, the most common activity—especially for the Semarang youth—is mall hopping. The **Citraland Mall,** at Simpang Lima, has more shoe stores than anything else, as well as a pricey supermarket and a food court. The mall is open daily 10am-10pm, and has a movie theater (tel. 415 971) on the 3rd floor that generally shows American movies with Indonesian subtitles (tickets Rp4500).

■ AROUND SEMARANG

GEDONG SONGO

The **Gedong Songo Temples** are at least a day's trip from Semarang, but are well worth the long and sometimes crowded voyage. Buses from Semarang's Terboyo station for Bandungan leave regularly and cost Rp1000 (you may have to pay extra if your bag is large). With stops, the ride takes roughly 90 minutes winding along terraced valleys, rivers, and ravines. Just the ride is worth the trip. Ask to get off at Bandungan's Pasar Joho. Walk up the hill with the *pasar* at your left—several *losmen* summon travelers, including **Losmen Muria,** Jl. Gintungan; the rooms are far from luxurious, but they're fine for a night, and the price is right: all rooms Rp8000. Don't go to Bangdugan in need of a *mandi*; unless you wash in the hot springs by the temples, the water in Bangdugan is frigid. **Wisma Gaya** is up the hill from Muria, with their cheapest rooms at Rp40,000 (MC). The best way to get from Bangdungan to Gedong Songo is by *ojek,* hired motorcycle, for Rp3000 (15 min.). Drivers may try to talk you into traveling to the *candis* by car, but the ride can run you Rp20,000. Once inside the Gedong Songo area, hike on your own (4 hrs.) or ride on horseback (Rp7000) around the temples. A guide will walk behind the horse and wait while you examine the hot spring and the nine fairly basic, square temples that squat amidst a fantastic view. With the breezy, gorgeous landscape, the serene temples, and the horse, this excursion is downright romantic. Five times the normal crowds come on weekends. It's a popular getaway for Indonesian tourists. Tons of kids and students jostle around tenting, smoking, playing guitars, and feeling very cool. Admission Rp350. Camping allowed. Open daily 6am-8pm.

DIENG

Dieng Plateau, via **Wonosobo,** is accessible from Semarang (119km northeast), Yogya (107km southeast), or Bandungan/Gedong Songo. From Bandungan, buses leave regularly for Ambarawa market (20 min., Rp300), where buses can be caught to Secang (30 min., Rp500). From Secang, bus it toward Wonosobo (buses may stop at Parakan) for about two hours (Rp1100). Several *losmen* await travelers from Wonosobo bus station, as does a **tourist office,** which will store (until it closes) luggage while you hike to the temples at Dieng. Open Mon.-Fri. 7am-3pm. From Wonosobo's bus station, walk 1km or ride a horsecart (Rp500-1000) to the Dieng bus station. From there, ride the beautiful, last leg of the journey (26km, 45 min., Rp800) to Dieng Plateau. At Dieng, stop by the tourist office to buy a ticket (Rp2000 for foreign travelers, Rp1000 for domestic) and pick up a map of the plateau. Open Mon.-Fri. 7am-3pm. The map and the paths and signs leading to the temples are straightforward, but guides can be hired (Rp10,000) to provide history and running commentary. A two-hour circuitous walk leads through and around sulfuric hot springs, a lime-green lake, a museum of ancient, broken stone figures, and several of the oldest temples on Java. Trippers to Dieng are strongly recommended to spend the night in the Wonosobo/Dieng area or arrive very early in the morning to avoid the fog and see the best views.

From the Wonosobo bus station, find connections to **Magelang** (every 10 min., last bus at 4pm), then switch for a bus to **Yogya, Semarang** (every hr., last bus at 6:15pm), and **Solo** (last bus at 12:55pm).

■■■ SURABAYA

Surabaya has skyscrapers, homeless people, parking garages, gyms, ATMs, and public markets the size of small towns. On the heels of Jakarta, it is the second-largest city in Indonesia, and lives up to it, boasting a population over 3 million, a six-lane "street" through the center of town, and at least five major indoor shopping complexes. Surabaya is wholeheartedly a commercial center, and travelers seeking "authentic" Java may be disillusioned by the city's modern pace and restlessness after Surabaya's few "sights" have been checked off. The Stairmaster demonstrations in the malls and the video game-ish horror of trying to cross Surabaya's streets may leave travelers wondering what the exotic allure of East Java is all about. But don't be fooled into thinking that true Java is better sought elsewhere; a quick ride in the Tunjungan Plaza elevator is enough to remind you that you are indeed among Javanese, who enthusiastically undertake every challenge to cram four times capacity into phone-booth-sized spaces.

Surabaya is hot and smoggy (*becak* drivers wear cloths over their noses and mouths), with noticeable economic disparity among its residents, who do not all share in the city's general wealth as a manufacturing center and major seaport. Surabaya may not have the typical attributes of a tourist destination, but it gives an interesting glimpse at the potential future of other quickly developing Indonesian cities.

ORIENTATION

Surabaya is a sprawling harborside city with a river that snakes between and under its more popular spots, and it can be a challenge to navigate. Key areas include the **Joyoboyo bus terminal** and the **Surabaya Zoo** at the south end of town, the Simpang Hotel/Tunjungan Plaza area, where **Jalan Tunjugan** and **Jalan Pemuda** run into each other, and **Siola,** the crossroads north of Tunjungan, named after the Siola Department store on the corner of Jl. Genteng Kali. **Jalan Genteng Kali** heads toward the river and hosts a daily fruit market and food stores at night. **Gubeng train station** is at the end of Jl. Pemuda after the **Delta Plaza** and the **tourist office** and on the other side of the river from **Jalan Kayum,** which is lined with restaurants and the morning flower market. Farther south, at the end of **Jalan Raya Darmo,** is the Surabaya Zoo. Following the river north is **Jalan Peneleh,** where travelers can find a cluster of reasonably priced accommodations. Still upriver is the **General Post Office** and the **Kota train station,** as well as the **Arab Quarter** and **Chinatown. Jalan Tanjung Perak** and the river eventually head to sea, to the **Madura ferry terminal,** and to Surabaya's harbor.

PRACTICAL INFORMATION

Tourist Office: Jl. Pemuda 118 (tel. 524 499). Across the street from the Delta Plaza. From Gubeng train station, walk left on Jl. Gubeng Pojok, and then right heading across the river on Jl. Pemuda. The office is on the left, opposite the enormous shopping plaza. English spoken. Open Mon.-Sat. 8am-7pm. Other tourist offices at **Surabaya Airport** and on **Jl. Basuki Rakhmad** (opposite the Hyatt Hotel). Open Mon.-Sat. 8am-7pm.

Travel Agencies: Linda Jaya, Jl. Ngagel Jaya 30 (tel. 604 78) and Jl. Yos Sudarso 18 (tel. 510 038). **Natour,** Jl. Pemuda 1 (tel. 510 149). **Pacto,** Jl. Tunjungan 65 (tel. 433 51).

Embassies and Consulates: Australia, Mr. Heath McMichael, d/a World Trade Center, Jl. Pemuda 27-31 (tel. 602 75). **UK,** Mr. Charles Moncrieff, d/a Hong Kong Bank, Jl. Basuki Rakhmad 33. **US,** Jl. Dr. Soetomo 33 (tel. 582 288) or Jl. Untung Suropati 56 (tel. 577 530).

Currency Exchange: Bank Duta, Jl. Pemuda 12 (tel. 510 449). AmEx traveler's checks only. Visa, MC. Open Mon.-Thurs. 8am-3pm, Fri. 8-11am and 1-3pm. **Bank Bumi Daya,** Tunjungan Plaza. Visa, MC. **Pasopati Tour and Travel Agency,** Jl. Raya Darmo 1A (tel. 574 000). AmEx traveler's checks only. Open Mon.-Sat. 8am-11pm, Sun. 9am-noon. **24-hr. ATM: Bank Bali,** Jl. Tunjungan 52 (tel. 515 500 or 511 342). Visa, MC, Cirrus, AmEx. Banking hours Mon.-Fri. 8am-2pm. Accepts traveler's checks Mon.-Fri. 10am-2pm.

American Express Office: (tel. 571 403), at Bank Panin on 1st floor.

Post Office: GPO (*Kantor Pos Besar*), Jl. Kebonrojo 10. Poste Restante 24 hrs. Mail counters (tel. 342 200) open 7:30am-10pm. **General postal information:** tel. 101. Unless you're expecting Poste Restante mail, use more convenient post office locations, including the **branch** at Jl. Pemuda, just past the General Soerjo Statue on the left. Open Mon.-Sat. 8am-2pm, Fri. 8-11am. **Postal code:** 60175.

Telephones: 24-hr. Wartels: G.D. Gapura Surya, Jl. Jambrut Ntara 1 (at Tunjungan Plaza). International, collect (Rp1000 charge), telex, fax. **Juanda,** Surabaya Airport. International, collect, telegram, telex, fax. **Indosat** (tel. 512 003), Jl. Kayun. Credit card calls. Other international *wartels:* **Surabaya Mall,** Jl. Kunsuma Bangsa 116. **Komplex Darmo Park,** Jl. Mayjen Sungkono. Most *wartels* do not accept credit card calls. **Telephone code:** 031.

Airport: Juanda Airport. General info (tel. 831 831). Many flights per day to **Denpasar** (Rp92,900). One way to **Yogya** (Rp65,400). The easiest transport from the airport to town is via taxi (Rp15,000) or the Damri airport bus (Rp2500), which shuttles 5-6 times per day between the airport and the north harbor. If you tire of waiting for the Damri, consider taking a taxi (or walking) 3km to the public *bemo* stop, where you can ride a *bemo* (Rp350) into town. Ask drivers if they will go on to your destination. **Garuda Airlines,** Jl. Basuki Rahmat 124 (tel. 511 234).

Trains: Surabaya's 3 main train stations are: **Gubeng,** Jl. Gubeng Pojok (tel. 400 80; for ticket reservations 535 3993); **Kota/Semut,** Jl. Setasiun Kota; and **Pasar Turi** (tel. 450 14), Jl. Semarang. Trains traveling through Gubeng stop at Kota/Semut and vice versa. Trains to Kota/Semut—usually to or from north Java—are a separate line. From Gubeng to: **Malang** (7 daily, 7:25am-5pm, 2-5hr., economy Rp2000); **Banyuwangi** (3 daily, 7hr., economy Rp3500, business Rp7000); **Gambir Station, Jakarta** (12:15pm, economy Rp10,000; 3pm, business Rp26,000; Bima (night train): 4pm, 15-16hr., executive B Rp44,000, executive A Rp58,000, khusus Rp61,000, special Rp94,000); **Yogya** and **Solo** (5 daily including deluxe Bima and Mutiara night trains, early morning-5pm, economy Rp7500, business Rp14-18,000). You can order Tickets 7 days in advance. Ordinarily, the reservation charge is Rp1500 for executive and business class (Rp1000 for economy, but reserving is unnecessary). From Pasar Turi, trains go to **Pasar Senen, Jakarta** (5 and 6:30pm, economy Rp10,000; Mutiara, 4:30pm, 11hr., Rp36-58,000). Both trains go to **Semarang** (economy Rp7500, business Rp27,500, special Rp52,000). Ticket office open daily 8am-1pm. The executive ticket office is on the left side of the Pasar Turi station if you are facing the platform; business and economy tickets are sold on the right side, from a separate office, open 8am-2pm.

Buses: City Buses: The main terminals are **Joyoboyo,** on Jl. Joyoboyo by the Surabaya Zoo, and **Bungurasih/Purabaya,** 10km south of town. Two useful **city bus** routes to know are those of buses marked C or P-1. From Bungurasih bus terminal in the south, city buses C and P-1 pass the zoo, stop at the bus stop by KFC on Jl. Basuki Rakhmad and at "Toko Nam" on Jl. Embong Malang, and continue north past Pasar Turi train station, the PELNI ferry office, the GPO, and from PELNI harbor to Kalimas harbor and the ferry station to Madura Island. The C or P-1 buses from the north begin at **Perak bus terminal** (by the harbor) and swing past the GPO, the PELNI office, the bus stop in front of Tunjungan Plaza, the bus stop on Jl. Sudirman (between Jl. Kenongo and Jl. Tanjung), and go on to the zoo and Bungurasih bus terminal. City buses marked C ("Damri" buses) are Rp200; P-1 "Patas" buses (less crowded and make fewer stops) cost Rp400. Buses begin running at

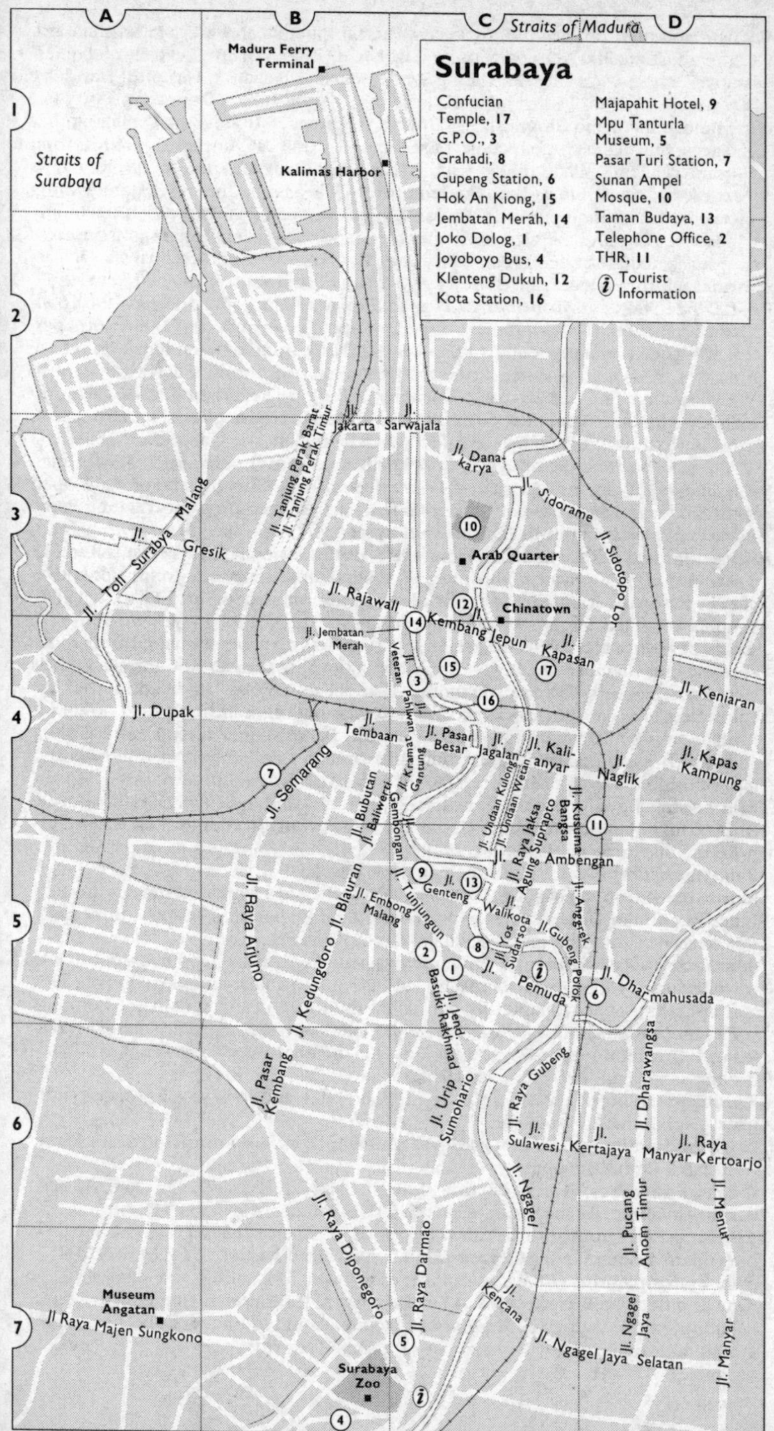
A
B
C
D
Straits of Madura
Surabaya
Confucian Temple, 17
G.P.O., 3
Grahadi, 8
Gupeng Station, 6
Hok An Kiong, 15
Jembatan Merah, 14
Joko Dolog, 1
Joyoboyo Bus, 4
Klenteng Dukuh, 12
Kota Station, 16
Majapahit Hotel, 9
Mpu Tanturla Museum, 5
Pasar Turi Station, 7
Sunan Ampel Mosque, 10
Taman Budaya, 13
Telephone Office, 2
THR, 11
Tourist Information
Madura Ferry Terminal
Kalimas Harbor
Straits of Surabaya
1
2
3
4
5
6
7
Jl. Jakarta
Jl. Sarwajala
Jl. Tanjung Perak Barat
Jl. Tanjung Perak Timur
Jl. Dana-karya
Jl. Sidorame
Jl. Sidotopo Lor
Arab Quarter
Chinatown
Jl. Toll Surabya Malang
Jl. Gresik
Jl. Rajawali
Jl. Kembang Jepun
Jl. Jembatan Merah
Jl. Kapasan
Jl. Veteran
Jl. Keniaran
Jl. Dupak
Jl. Pahlawan
Jl. Tembaan
Jl. Pasar Besar
Jl. Jagalan
Jl. Kali-anyar
Jl. Kramat Gantung
Jl. Naglik
Jl. Kapas Kampung
Jl. Semarang
Jl. Bubutan
Jl. Baliwerti
Jl. Gemblongan
Jl. Undaan Kulon
Jl. Undaan Wetan
Jl. Raya Jaksa Agung Suprapto
Jl. Kusuma Bangsa
Jl. Ambengan
Jl. Raya Arjuno
Jl. Kedungdoro
Jl. Blauran
Jl. Embong Malang
Jl. Tunjungun
Jl. Genteng
Jl. Walikota
Jl. Yos Sudarso
Jl. Gubeng Pojok
Jl. Anggrek
Jl. Pemuda
Jl. Dharmahusada
Jl. Jend. Basuki Rakhmad
Jl. Pasar Kembang
Jl. Urip Sumohario
Jl. Raya Gubeng
Jl. Dharawangsa
Jl. Sulawesi
Jl. Kertajaya
Jl. Raya Manyar Kertoarjo
Jl. Ngagel
Jl. Raya Diponegoro
Jl. Raya Darmao
Jl. Pucang Anom Timur
Jl. Menur
Museum Angatan
Jl Raya Majen Sungkono
Jl. Kencana
Jl. Ngagel Jaya
Jl. Ngagel Jaya Selatan
Jl. Manyar
Surabaya Zoo

6am and peter off at 9pm. **Intercity Buses:** Bungurasih/Purabaya terminal services buses to and from parts of Java, Bali, and Lombok. Travelers can catch executive/deluxe (AC, video, reclining seat, toilet, meal, snacks) buses to: **Bandung** (every hr., 4-8pm, 13hr.); **Jakarta** (every hr., 3-8pm, 16hr.); **Denpasar** (every hr., 4-8pm, 12hr.); and **Singaraja** via **Lovina** (every hr., 5-8pm, 11hr.); among other places. Buy tickets for executive buses at least 1 or 2 days ahead (from the station or travel agents). Patas buses (with A/C and significant leg room) to: **Solo/Yogya** (every hr., 6am-3pm, 6-7hr.); **Malang** (every hr., 6-8pm, 2hr.); and **Banyuwangi** (every 2hr., 6am-8pm, 6hr.). Pay on the bus; no reservation needed. Economy buses are cheaper, slower, more crowded, and leave when full. **Night buses** to Javanese cities can be purchased through travel agencies and companies such as: **Kalisari,** Jl. Jend. A. Yani 258 (tel. 819 282); **Cakrawala,** Jl. Makam Peneleh 77 (tel. 522 984); and **Continental Megah Express,** Jl. Argopuro 51 (tel. 406 18).

Ferries: PELNI, the government-owned shipping company, has 1000-15,000 person capacity passenger ships in 4 classes leaving from Tanjung Perak. Purchase tickets 15 days in advance at the ferry terminal or from the PELNI office on Jl. Pahlawahan 112 (tel. 210 42). **Surabaya** (Tanjung Perak) to **Kamal** (Madura) (every 30min., 30min., Rp350); **Kalianget** (Madura) to **Jangkar** (East Java) (7am, 3-4hr., Rp2500). Economy class tickets can be bought the day of travel, but class 1, 2, and 3 should be bought 3 days in advance. PELNI office open Mon.-Thurs. 8:30am-3pm, Fri. 8:30-11am and 1-3pm. If ships leave Sunday, the office is open the preceding Saturday 8:30am-noon. The port is 100m from the Tanjung Perak bus terminal. Economy class fares to elsewhere in Indonesia: **Jakarta** (Rp29,000), **Medan** (Rp82,000), and **Bali** (Rp26,000). **Kalla Lines PT,** Jl. Perak Timur 158 (tel. 341 203), a private company, sells tickets from Surabaya to **Johor, Malaysia.**

Taxis: Base fare of Rp900 for the first km and approximately Rp450 for each additional km. **Taxi Super,** Jl. Ngemplak 20 (tel. 420 96).

Local transportation: There are 37 different **bemo** routes weaving through the city; almost half use Joyoboyo terminal on Jl. Joyoboyo, near the Surabaya Zoo, as a base. The best way to ride *bemos* is to ask locals or *bemo* attendants if they are heading to your destination. Yellow **anguna** wagons can be flagged down off main streets; they are taxis with no meter. Bargain on a price before getting inside. **Becaks** are available in some areas but are limited to one-way roads and are prohibited from main streets, so they tend to take circuitous routes.

Car rental: Toyota Rent-a-Car, Jl. Jend. A. Yani 210 (tel. 819 999). First day, self-drive Rp90,000, each additional day Rp80,000. Must have International Drivers Permit or hire a chauffeur.

Luggage storage: at Pasar Gubeng. Rp1000 per day.

Bookstore: Gunung Agung stocks English dictionaries, children's books, and several shelves of Dickens, Shakespeare, and the like. Located on floor 2 (actually level 4) of Tunjungan Plaza. Open 9:30am-9:30pm.

Markets: Pasar Kayun on Jl. Kayun is a daily flower market lined with restaurants from 9am to 10pm. **Pasar Genteng,** on Jl. Gentang Kali, is an indoor and outdoor fruit and miscellany market by day, and a food market by night. The enormous **Pasar Pabean** off Jl. Rajawali is a traditional meat and vegetable market. Runs from early morning until 4 or 5pm. **Pasar Baluran,** the gold market, is on Jl. Baluran, at the end of Jl. Embong Malang.

Laundry: Undagi Karya, Jl. Dupak 81 (tel. 469 02), and **Wijaya Chemical Laundry,** Jl. Pucang Anom 52 (tel. 578 959).

Swimming: Allowed for non-guests at Simpang Hotel, opposite Tunjungan Plaza, Rp2500. Open 9am-9pm.

24-hr. Pharmacy: Kimia Farma, Jl. Raya Darmo 2 (tel. 577 777) and **Apotik Pusura Clinic,** Jl. Yos Sudarso 9A (tel. 507 334).

Hospitals: Dr. Soetomo General Hospital, Jl. Dharmahusada 6 (tel. 400 61-6). **William Booth General Hospital,** Jl. Diponegoro 54 (tel. 576 133 or 578 917-8). **St. Vencentius (RKZ),** Jl. Diponegoro 51 (tel. 577 562).

Gay and Lesbian Resources: GAYa Nusantara, Jl. Mulyosari Timur 46, Surabaya Timur (tel. 593 49 24; fax 593 90 70). The publication source of the *GAYa Nusantara* magazine.

Information lines: Local telephone info (tel. 108); **inter-local telephone info** (tel. 106); and **international phone info** (tel. 102).

Emergency: tel. 110. **Fire:** tel. 113. **Ambulance:** tel. 118, 119, or 334 030.

Police: 3 offices on Jl. Raden Saleh 1 (tel. 420 94), Jl. Dukuh Kupang Barat XV 1/6-8 (tel. 579 040), and Jl. Jend. A. Yani (tel. 838 258 or 838 359).

ACCOMMODATIONS

It's slim pickings if you're looking for cheap, good quality accommodations in Surabaya. If catching your ZZZ's dorm-style appeals, head for the Bamboe Denn. Otherwise, unless you're up for an out-of-town location, peruse the singles and doubles in the Peneleh area (several homestays are close together, making it easy for travelers to shop around).

Bamboe Denn Hostel, Jl. Ketabang Kali 6A (tel. 403 33). From Gubeng railway station, walk right along the river on Jl. Gubeng Pojok, turn left onto Ketabang Kali, and cross the intersection with Jl. Yos Sudarso. Follow the second right (away from the river) past the tennis courts. Bamboe Denn is near the end of the street next to the Governor's House (about 20min.). With the cheapest dorm beds in Surabaya, the hostel is so well-frequented that *becak* drivers all over town offer shouts of "Bamboe Denn! Bamboe Denn?!" to foreign wanderers. On a quiet street about 15min. from Tunjungan Plaza, communal facilities (two large rooms bursting with bunk beds) require socialization with other westerners. Bruno, the de facto manager, is a fountain of useful info and advice that's more than worth the price of staying here. He's even compiling a guidebook to Surabaya and environs that rivals *Let's Go.* Bring mosquito repellant and a lock and key for the lockers. Dorms Rp5000. 2 single rooms Rp6000. 2 doubles (bunk beds) Rp12,000. Restaurant and sitting area with television.

Hotel Paviljoen, Jl. Genteng Besar 94 (tel. 434 49). From Gubeng railway station, hop in a *becak* (about 30min., Rp1000) or walk down Jl. Pemuda past Tunjungan Plaza. Stay straight and to the right where Jl. Pemuda becomes Jl. Tunjungan, then hang a right onto Jl. Genteng Besar at the large Honda sign. You can see the hotel (on the left) from the turn. Enter into a long hallway with a high ceiling and padded bamboo chairs. Fresh rooms come complete with accessories—soap, towels, furniture. Doubles with fan Rp22,700-27,500. Breakfast included.

Roleen Homestay, Jl. Ngagel Jaya Utara 117 (tel. 574 063). Owned by RObert and kathLEEN Augustin, Roleen is on the south side of town, near Ubaya University and between Jiwa Menur and Air Force Hospitals. From the *bemo* stop outside the airport, take a green H4 *bemo* toward Joyoboyo station and ask to get off at Pentelon. From there, ride a big bus with "YKP" on the front heading toward Pasar Turi. Ask to get off at Jl. Ngagel Jaya Utara. Not a bargain or in a great location, this is a true homestay (with only 5 rooms) in a very nice house located in a quiet residential neighborhood. Rooms come with furniture and doodads to help you feel at home. Friendly family of fluent English speakers. Rp33,000 for 2 beds with 2 fans and bath. Rp44,000 for a double with A/C. Breakfast included.

Hotel Bali, Jl. Makam Peneleh 77 (tel. 545 01 55). From Kota train station, walk along the river for approx. 10min. on Jl. Semut Kali, which becomes Jl. Peneleh. The outside of the hotel bears a likeness to coffee-stained styrofoam. Rooms are variable: some are decent, some have primitive life forms on the walls. Popular with domestic tourists. Singles Rp10,000, with fan and bath Rp15,000. Doubles with fan and bath Rp17,000; with A/C, TV, and bath Rp32,500. Price includes tea and coffee. Visa, MC. Check-out 2pm.

Losmen Puri, Jl. Makam Peneleh 92 (tel. 535 19 39), is 100m past Hotel Bali (turn away from the river) on the left. All rooms have 1 large double bed and 1 twin, bath, and fan Rp15,000. Knock loudly after midnight, when the office closes.

Losmen Sari, Jl. Makam Peneleh 51. Across the street from Losmen Puri. Shoebox rooms, some with bunk beds and screened-in spaces between wall tops and ceilings. Less than spotless communal bathrooms, but this *losmen's* good location and price make it a bargain.

Hotel Singaraja, Jl. Peneleh 60 (tel. 535 47 52). The hotel's hallway is lined with orange plastic subway seats anchored to the ground, so you can sit and admire your reflection on the freshly mopped floors. Attractive rooms. Singles with double beds Rp12,500; with fan and bath Rp17,500; with fan, bath, and TV Rp25,000.

Ganefo Hotel, Jl. Kapasan 169 (tel. 311 169). A *becak* ride or a 15-min. walk up Jl. Bunguran along the river, until the intersection with Jl. Kapasan. Turn right; Ganefo is back from the main street on the right. A large, Colonial-style hotel with tiled floors and high ceilings; not in a particularly good location. Basic, well-kept rooms. Doubles Rp24,000, with fan Rp25,000, with A/C and bath Rp45,000.

FOOD

Some of the best places to find good, cheap food are in the **riverside restaurants** along Jl. Kayun, and in **warungs** and **night stalls** lining Jl. Genteng Besar. To reach Jl. Kayun from the Tunjungan Plaza area, walk 15 minutes down Jl. Basuki Rakhmad, past the Hyatt Regency, until the road merges with Jl. Sudirman/Sumoharjo. Walk left on Jl. Sudirman, then take any right-hand alley toward the river and Jl. Kayun. Alternatively, hop on a bus that will let you off at Hotel Brantas and then walk along the river. Flower market by day, **Kayun Park** is bordered by a long string of small, cheap eateries that serve excellent Indonesian, Chinese, seafood, and more. Specialties include fried snake (*ular*). Look out for **Depot Sari Laut Karisma,** Taman Rekreasi (Taman Park) #95, with bamboo nooks, friendly management, and Rp1500 entrees. Open 10am-11pm. The *pasar* and night stalls on **Jalan Genteng Besar** are within walking distance of Tunjungan Plaza, Bamboe Denn, and Jl. Peneleh. With Tunjungan Plaza at your heels, walk left, use the blue stairs to cross the harrowing six-lane "street," and follow Jl. Tunjungan (it's the right limb of the fork with Jl. Embong Malang) until the first major right-hand intersection with Jl. Genteng Besar.

Several Indonesian restaurants cluster in the **Siola** (the name of a department store) area, one street farther along Jl. Tunjungan after the turnoff to the night stalls (Jl. Genteng Besar). You can indulge in western food at various bakeries in Surabaya, including **Borobudur Bakery,** Jl. Ambengan IV (tel. 455 00). Open 6:30am-8:30pm. Most malls in Surabaya have a fast food chain or two.

Mie Tunjungan, Jl. Genteng Kali 121, just past the intersection and the Siola department store. Specializes in *mie pangsit* (chicken noodle with wonton) for Rp2250. Open Mon.-Sat. 9am-9pm.

Sri Reejeki Ayam Goreng, Jl. Genteng Kali #158 (tel. 516 20), across the street and down from Siola; they serve fried chicken and the unique *pempek Palembang* (Rp2500), a hard-boiled egg inside a condensed rice and batter-fried exterior. Open Mon.-Sat. 8am-4pm and 5-11pm, Sun. 8am-midnight.

Café Venezia, Jl. Ambengan 16 (tel. 430 91 or 433 35), one street parallel north and across the river from the Siola area. Specializing in steak (sirloin Rp9900) and ice cream, the restaurant also has Indonesian and Japanese food, omelettes, hot dogs, and a favorite—Venezia tomato soup (Rp4200). Inside, look for fake red flowers on the tables, upholstered chairs and benches, and a painting of Venezia on the wall. Outside seating in bamboo alcoves by an artificial waterfall disguises the fact that the café is beside a loud, busy street. Open 10am-11pm.

Pengampon, Jl. Kusuma Bangsa 128, is on the same side of the street and close to Surabaya Mall and THR complex. The enormous restaurant has a hefty menu of Indonesian and Chinese food, including pig's bowels soup (Rp7500) as well as vegetarian dishes with noodles and bean curd. Mixed vegetables with rice go for Rp4500. Tables all face a stage, used for a live band and karaoke. Open 10am-2pm (lunch, karaoke) and 5-10pm (dinner, band). Visa, MC, DC.

Metro Café, Jl. Tunjungan 101 (tel. 443 51), opposite Tunjungan Plaza at the base of the stairs arching over the street. Booths, lace curtains with windows, and Indonesian food with tempeh and tofu on request. *Nasi pecel* (rice with veggies in peanut sauce) Rp2250. Open 9:30am-9pm.

Benny's Gelati, Ice Cream and Donut/Istana Buah Restaurant, Jl. Tunjungan 88 (tel. 511 172). Down the street from the plaza, look for the big red apple. Brand new face on the block, with an Australian owner and a hip, glossy café interior. Serves beer. Open 9am-9:30pm.

SIGHTS AND ENTERTAINMENT

Surabaya's main attraction is not its sights, but its commercial activity, which is nearly impossible to avoid. Even if you don't usually find yourself in malls, Surabaya's are worth strolling through, if only to enjoy some soft ice cream and a refreshing A/C-pick-me-up. **Tunjungan Plaza** (open 9am-9pm), in two interconnected sections, is particularly impressive, and is reputed to be the largest mall in Indonesia. If you wander past the high fashion boutiques, countless shoe stores, and Esprit, you'll arrive at a collection of restaurants on the top floor. The somewhat spooky **THR (People's Amusement Park)** behind the THR Mall, is past its heyday, though traditional dance and music performances still go on (schedules available in the tourist office). The THR is attached to the **Golden Theatre 21,** Jl. Kusuma Bangsa 116 (tel. 457 73), showing current U.S. flicks. **Mitra Movie Theatre,** Jl. Pemuda 15 (tel. 442 67), shows five movies, usually around 2, 5, 7, and 9pm (Rp7000).

Visitors to the **Surabaya Zoo** (*Kebun Binatang*), in the south of town at the end of Jl. Raya Darmo, should be prepared to feel not just sympathy but empathy for the animals; there is debate as to whether the animals or the tourists are the real attraction (even the giraffes stare). To reach the zoo from the Tunjungan area, catch a Damri or Patas bus from the bus stop by the Simpang Hotel; tell the attendant you're heading to the *Kebun Binatang*. Bus rides take about 15 minutes. Heading back from the zoo, ask to get off at "Toko Nam" (just beyond the intersection of Jl. Embong Malang and Jl. Tunjungan) to end up near the Tunjungan area. Aside from the fact that the zoo is badly in need of trash cans, it is quite extensive and worth an afternoon, with collections of birds, reptiles, restless elephants, white tigers, some chubby jaguars, an adorable long-nailed sloth bear, and a Komodo Dragon. Open daily 7am-6pm. Admission Rp1500.

The **Arab quarter** of town and the **Sunan Ampel Mosque,** the oldest mosque in East Java, are worth an afternoon's wander. The mosque was built by Sunan Ampel, one of the *wali songo,* nine Muslim holy men, who initiated the spread of Islam in Java. To get there, take any *bemo* (*bemo* 10 is ideal; it passes along Jl. Walikota Mustajab, the east end of Jl. Genteng Besar) to Jembatan Merah terminal and take a *becak* (Rp1000) or walk 15 minutes northeast to Sunan Ampel. To head from the mosque back to the Simpang Hotel bus stop, take city bus P-1 (Rp400) or C (Rp200) and ask for Simpang. Travelers venturing to the Arab quarter might be wise to opt against wearing short-shorts or skirts. Also worth a stroll is the **Tanjung Perak/Harbor area,** which can easily be reached by Damri or Patas city buses.

NIGHTLIFE

Tequila Willies, Jl. Kayon 62 (tel. 527 138). Across the street from the restaurants lining the river. This Mexican restaurant and pub serves hearty fare, such as burritos (Rp6500) and crab and asparagus soup (Rp4000). Has live music from 10pm-2am, a stripper at midnight, and canned disco until 3am. Two men on guard to throw the doors back when you enter. Marilyn and Madonna grace the walls of a room with darts, pinball, and classy wooden bar stools. No cover. Draft beer Rp5000. Restaurant open 7-10pm. Club open until 3am.

Club Deluxe, Jl. Tunjungan 3, Tunjungan Center 4th Floor (tel. 519 572). Karaoke, restaurant, and self-described "luxury disco." Open Mon.-Fri. 10pm-2am, Sat. 10pm-3am.

■ AROUND SURABAYA

Madura Island lies three km from the East Java coast. On the bright side, Madura's rock and sand landscape is beautiful and the island is remarkably untouristed. On the downside, Madura is not yet especially hospitable to tourists. It has limited accommodations, comparatively poor and unexciting sights (by Javanese standards), and aggressive locals. 160km long by 30km wide, the island is probably not any traveler's primary reason for coming to East Java. That is, unless travelers are voyaging between August and October, when the island's famed **bull races** (*kerapan sapi*) are held. The races, which last only a few seconds, are held over the months in stadiums around the island until the grand finale, held in the capital, Pamekasan. The final race accompanies a festival of *gamelan,* dancing, and parades. Before the race, the bulls are led about town wearing bejeweled headdresses, yokes, flowers, ribbons, and parasols, followed by an entourage of handlers and musicians. For details about the times and places of the races, contact the tourist offices in Surabaya or the **Madura Tourist Information Office,** Baparda Sumenep, Jl. Dr. Cipto 33, Sumenep (tel. 216 10). Madura has three main cities, between which colt minibuses run and offer a low-budget way to tour the low, shallow side of the island near the port to Surabaya. A 2 to 3 hour colt ride east of **Bangkalan** is **Pamekasan,** the capital, in the south-central part of Madura. South and slightly west of the capital is **Camplong,** a swimming beach. The best beaches can be found near **Sumenep,** the most popular destination on the east side of the island. Siring Kemuning, in **Tanjungbumi,** competes with Salopeng at **Ambunten,** on the north shore, for being the most beautiful beach. Accommodations can be found in Bangkalan, Kamal, Sampang, Camplong beach (bungalows), Pamekasan, Sumenep, Kalianget, and Pasongsongan. The **Losmen Bahagia** (Bapak Taufik Rahman), Jl. Trunjoyo in Pasongsongan, has singles for Rp8000 and doubles for Rp10,000. In Sumenep, **Losmen Wijaya I** and **II,** near the bus terminal, have singles for Rp5000 and doubles for Rp8000. Prices island-wide go up during bull racing season.

Madura is easily reached from Surabaya. Ferries from Surabaya's port, Tanjung Perak, leave every 30 minutes between 4am and midnight for Kamal Port on Madura. At Kamal, take colt minibuses to see the island or ride *becaks,* which are available in the three main cities.

■■■ MALANG

Foreigners who live in Malang joke that "it's a nice place to live, but I wouldn't wanna visit." Malang *is* smaller than most Javanese towns with comparable tourist populations and its charms may be simple—cool air, a view of the mountains from downtown, conscientious cooking—but the expats have it wrong. Malang is definitely worth a few days, particularly if you're en route from Java's larger and sweatier cities and could use a few days to cool off, take walks, and read. It's an ideal transition to the stark landscape of Bromo and other nature-oriented sights in East Java. Malang has tree-lined streets, steeples that rise up off street corners, and a small-town, somewhat European feel to it. Playing host to some of East Java's best schools, Malang has a reputation for being a student town. Malang is also well-known for its apples, which are sold by the bunches to those same students, eager to impress their teachers.

ORIENTATION

Malang lies 90km south of Surabaya, bordered on three sides by volcanoes: **Mt. Butak** (2868m) to the west, **Mt. Arjuna** (3339m) to the north, and **Mt. Semeru** (3676m) and **Mt. Bromo** (2329m) to the east. Malang's three bus terminals are all on the outskirts of town; **Arjosari,** frequented by most visitors, is in the northeast. The main **train station,** just east of the **Tugu Monument,** is slightly northeast of the center of town. In town, the points of interest are all within walking distance of each other: the **alun-alun** (the main town square) borders banks, restaurants, and the city's busiest shopping area. **Jalan Agus Salim,** shooting east off the *alun-alun,* is lively day and night, with restaurants, shopping centers, and accommodations. Parallel to and south of this street is **Jalan Pasar Besar,** home to the **general market.**

PRACTICAL INFORMATION

Tourist Office: Jl. Semeru 4 (tel. 662 16). With your back to the train station, walk straight on Jl. Kerta Negara until you hit the roundabout at the Tugu Monument. Walk halfway around the rotary and take Jl. Kahjuripan. It's over the river, at the Jl. Basuki Rakhmat intersection, behind the Dunkin' Donuts. English spoken.

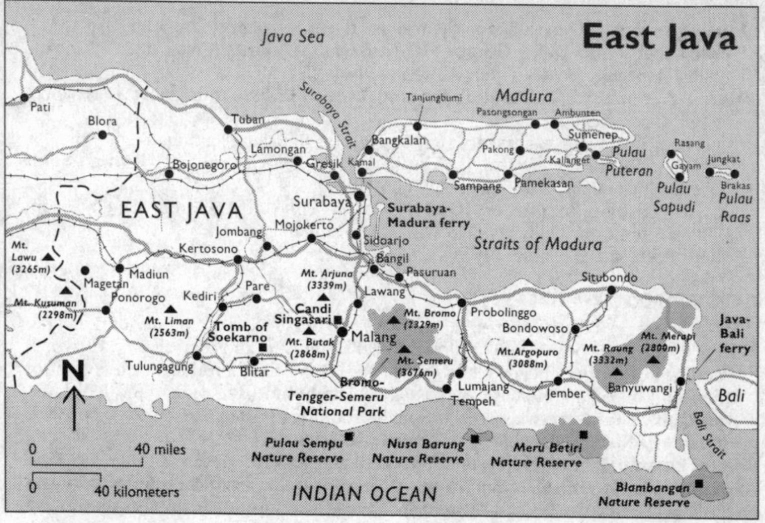

Good Mt. Bromo information. Open Mon.-Sat. 8am-5pm, Sun. 8am-1pm. **Branch office:** Jl. Tugu 1 (tel. 276 61). Open Mon.-Thurs. 8am-2pm, Fri. 8-11:30am.

Currency Exchange: Bali Bank, on Jl. Basuki Rakhmat, back from the street, opposite Toko Oen and behind Sarina Department Store. Open Mon.-Fri. 8:30am-7pm, Sat. 8:30am-1pm.

Post Office: Kantor Pos dan Giro, Jl. Merdeka Selatan 5 (tel. 622 54). Open Mon.-Thurs. 8am-noon and 1-8pm, Fri. 8-11:30am and 1-8pm, Sat.-Sun. 8am-8pm.

Telephone Office: on Jl. Basuki Rakhmat, next to Toko Oen. Open 24 hrs. **Telephone code:** 0341

Airport: Abdul Rakhman Saleh Airport, 6km east of Malang center. Daily flights to **Jakarta** (one way Rp173,500). To get to town from the airport, hop an airport bemo to Blimbing (Rp500), then change to a bemo heading toward town (Rp350). **Merpati Airlines,** Hotel Kartika Prince, Jl. Jaksa Agung Suprapto 41, (tel. 694 94). **Garuda Airlines,** Lippo Bank (tel. 659 14), on Jl. Merdeka Timor.

Trains: (tel. 622 08), on Jl. Trunojoyo, east of the Tugu Monument. Trains to: **Surabaya** (7 daily, 3rd class, Rp1400); **Banyuwangi** (10:43am); **Jakarta** (2 daily, executive class, Rp58-70,000); and **Solo, Yogya,** and **Jakarta** (3:15pm, economy and business class, Rp18,000 to Jakarta). Purchase tickets at the station 8am-6pm.

Buses: Arjosari bus terminal is northeast of town. **Private companies** vie for your ticket to **Jakarta** (approx. Rp37,000) or **Denpasar** (A/C night buses, Rp21,000). Buy tickets through the tourist office or at **ANS,** Jl. Basuki Rakhmat (tel. 236 67); **Pahala Kencana,** Jl. Ade Irma Suryani 70/34 (tel. 264 23); **Kramet Jati,** Jl. Sutoyo 17 (tel. 427 03). **Public buses** to **Surabaya** (every hr., 2-½hr.), **Banyuwangi,** and **Denpasar** also leave from Arjosari. **Landung Sari bus terminal,** in northwest Malang, has intercity buses to **Batu, Kediri,** and **Jombang. Gadang station** south of town, has intercity buses to **Lumajang, Dampit,** and **Blitar.** To enter the bus terminals, riders and visitors must pay Rp100.

Local Transport: Becaks available in town. **Bemos** (Rp300) have routes between terminals labelled on the bemo as follows: **A-D,** Arjosari to Dinoyo. **A-G,** Arjosari to Gadang. **D-G,** Dinoyo to Gadang. **D,** Gadang to Dinoyo. **E, F, or G,** Dinoyo to Arjosari. **F,** Dinoyo to Arjosari.

Taxis: Rp800 flag fare, plus Rp300 per km. **Citra Taxi** (tel. 451 01, 514 12, or 456 47); **Argo Mandala** (tel. 474 747); **Argo Perdana** (tel. 404 44).

Car Rental: Tourist officials can call up their friends and rent their cars to you.

Public Market: Pasar Besar (Big Market), on Jl. Pasar Besar, is open 8am-5pm. **Pasar Bunga** (Flower Market), off Jl. Kahuripan, at the river, is open 24 hrs. The **bird and fish market,** behind Pasar Bunga, is open daily 8am-5pm.

Luggage storage: Next door to the train station. Open daily 4am-9pm.

Bookstore: Toko Buku Gramedia, Jl. Basuki Rakhmat 3 (tel. 662 77). Some English language books. Open daily 9am-9pm. Visa, MC.

Ticket Agencies: P.T. Tanjung Permai Travel, Jl. Basuki Rakhmat 41 (tel. 271 41) for plane tickets.

Pharmacy: Apotik Kabupaten, (tel. 647 09) on Jl. Basuki Rakhmat.

Hospitals: General Hospital, Jl. Ikhwan Ridwan Rais (tel. 662 12). **Rumah Sakit Kristen Indonesia,** Jl. Kawi 11 (tel. 645 59).

Gay and Lesbian Resources: IGAMA, c/o Yoseph Bridal Salon & Dance Group, Jl. Raya Sumbersari 254C. *GAYa Nusantara* available here.

Police: Polresta, Jl. Slamet Riyadi (tel. 664 44).

ACCOMMODATIONS

Bamboe Denn Youth Hostel, Jl. Arjuno 2 (tel. 662 56), at the corner of Jl. Arjuno and Jl. Kawi, opposite Bank Rakyat. Recently moved and may again, but worth seeking out for the cheapest beds in Malang. Run by the brother of the owner of the Denn owner in Surabaya, this hostel is family style; the owner and his generous family shuttle between beds to make room for guests. Dorms Rp3000; with student ID Rp2500. Double (only one available) Rp10,000.

Hotel Pelangi, Jl. Merdeka Selatan 3 (tel. 651 56). On the street with the GPO, bordering the *alun-alun*. Excellent bang for your buck, even the cheapest rooms have a TV, hot water, and a thermos of tea. Restaurant and gift store. Singles Rp16,500. Doubles Rp22,000. Visa, MC, AmEx. Check-out 1pm.

Hotel Tosari, Jl. Akhmad Dahlan 23 (tel. 269 45; fax 670 98), about 15min. from the train station. With your back to the station, turn left and walk to the "T" intersection with Jl. Gatot Subroto. At the second main intersection, turn right on Jl. A. Dahlan. Tosari will be on your right. Two rows of adequate rooms, divided by a strip of potted plants. The hotel motto could be: "No perks, no dirt." Economy doubles Rp16,000, with bath Rp24,000. Additional 10% tax.

Hotel Malang, Jl. Zainul Arifin 85 (tel. 251 03) From the *alun-alun,* walk along the southernmost street, away from the mountains with the post office on your right. Walk for 1 block and turn right on Jl. Zainul Arifin; the hotel is on the left. Small, low-key hotel with a *losmen* feel. Nice rooms have ceilings that would dwarf Shaquille O'Neal—and you could eat off the communal *mandi* floors. Doubles Rp12,500, with bath Rp22,500

FOOD

Malang has excellent food, reasonable variety, and tame prices. The best place to sample Indonesian fare (or California Fried Chicken) is at the **food center** on Jl. Agus Salim, beside Mitra Mall. **Mitra Drinks,** has all the iced drinks you've been wanting to try, and next door, **Muncul Chinese Food** serves a mean *nasi goreng* for Rp2200. The food center is open daily 10am-9:30pm. **Pasar Besar,** the main market on Jl. Pasar Besar, has **foodstalls** and **warung.**

Ikan Segar, Jl. Agus Salim 36 (tel. 246 81). First-class Indonesian food and drinks. *Nasi kare ayam* (chicken curry with rice) is popular (Rp1750). English menu. Vegetarian food available; ask to substitute tempeh or tofu. Open 7am-10pm.

Toko Oen, Jl. Basuki Rakhmat 5 (tel. 640 52). Just as colonial and pricey as its sibling in Semarang; a favorite with westerners. Dutch and Indonesian food, fruit juices, and ice cream. Reminisce about the good ol' days of occupation as you sip on your watermelon juice (Rp2250) or lick a corn-flavored ice cream cone (Rp4000). Open daily 8am-9pm. Tourist office with tours to Bromo attached.

Melati Pavillion, Jl. Tugu 3, attached to the Tugu Park Hotel facing the Tugu Monument. Head straight here if you're in the mood for ambience. Carved wood galore, nice bathrooms, and smells like flowers. Copious offerings of Euro, Indonesian, and Dutch fare; beef burger and fries (Rp7500); spaghetti with shrimp (Rp11,000). Open 24 hrs. Attached to Melati is **Und Corner,** a casual, bar with magazines, tourist info, baked goods, coffee, and chicken sandwiches (Rp4000).

Jack's Cafe, Jl. Kahuripan 11A (tel. 206 23). The only place in town that serves espresso (Rp1500). With a decidedly western bent, Jack's has matching pink tables, a Debbie Gibson poster on the wall, and live music Wed. 10pm-midnight and Sat. 10pm-2am. Indonesian and western food from a Javanese manuscript.

SIGHTS

As the well-trafficked terminal of travelers en route to the majestic Mt. Bromo, Malang offers few true sights of its own. The **Eng An Kong Chinese Pagoda,** at the intersection of Jl. Gatot Subroto and Jl. Zainul Zakse, is a colorful, powerful dose of Chinese Buddhist culture in the midst of a bustling Indonesian city. No guides, but the intricate carvings, enormous archways, candles, incense, and shrines add to the quiet mystery of the place. Open 6am-8pm. Free.

Malang's other highly hyped sight, **Brawijaya Museum,** at Jl. Besar Ljen 25A, consists of two main halls with photographs, weapons, portraits, battle plans, and other memorabilia associated with the 5th Brawijaya Division, the third of Java's KODAM, or military area commands. Good for a military paraphernalia fans, but Indonesian labeling and a lack of English-speaking guides make the displays difficult to appreciate. Open 7am-3pm; donation requested.

Malang is a convenient base from which to visit several nearby temples, including Jago and Kidal temples to the east, and Singosari, 12km to the north. From Arjosari bus station, **Candi Singosari** can be reached by public bus to Lawang or Singosari town (20min., Rp300). Ask to get off at the *candi*. The temple was built between 1268 and 1292 by the last king of Singosari, Kertanagara, and according to local tales, his ashes are buried here. Two heads of Kala hang over the entrance to the temple, but only one of them has the intricate detail typical of Javanese carving. The stone figures that once guarded the six chambers around the *candi* are mostly gone—to museums in Holland. The figure of Agastya, a student of the god Siva, remains, peering over his distended belly that is said to contain the sea water he devoured in a fit of rage. During school holiday, English-language students loiter near the temple and offer to give tours. Open 7am-5pm. Donations accepted.

■■■ MOUNT BROMO

The vista from Java's active volcano, Mt. Bromo (2329m; located within the Bromo-Tengger-Semeru National Park) is one of the few sights in the country that is as satisfying as it is touristy. Named for the Hindu god "Brahma," (pronounced "Bromo" in Javanese), the locals in the area are Tenggerese, descendants of the Majapahit Kingdom, and the last group of Hindus left on Java. Despite the hundreds of visitors that hike to the volcano every day and elbow for room at the summit during sunrise, the scenery remains gorgeous. The throng of spectators, most of whom walk or ride horseback for the several-km trip to Bromo, turns the journey into a sort of pilgrimage through a misty "sea of sand" and up a long steep flight of stairs to the precarious edge of the crater. The trek can be made at any point during the day, but travelers who do not spend the night in the Bromo area will miss the unforgettable journey to watch the sunrise.

GETTING THERE AND AWAY

Bromo can be reached via several routes. The most popular is from Probolinggo, on the northeast coast of Java, through Sukapura, and Ngadisari (6km northeast of Bromo) where guest houses are available and then on to Cemoro Lawang, the village closest to the crater. From Probolinggo, minibuses leave every 45 minutes for Cemoro Lawang (2hr., last bus 6pm, Rp2500) via Ngadisari. The entrance to the National Park is at the Ngadisari; all visitors passing through must pay the Rp2100 entrance fee.

Bromo can also be approached via Pasuruan, on the coast between Probolinggo and Surabaya, and Tosari, 31km south of Pasuruan, on the north slopes of Bromo. From Pasuruan, take a minibus to Tosari, then walk or hire a jeep to the crater. Alternatively, you can reach Bromo from Malang; catch a bemo from Malang to Blimbing (30min., Rp600), then a bus to Tumpang (1hr., Rp1000), and then to Gubugklakah

(Rp600), to Ngadas, and finally to Jemplang, 14km from Bromo's crater. If you arrive in Gubugklakah too late to find a public bus, hire a jeep (Rp5000 per person) to Jemplang, where guest houses await weary, travel-fried troops. If you're stuck in Ngadas, you can walk (about 1hr.) to Jemplang.

To leave the Bromo environs, go back the way you came, to one of the north coast towns, Pasuruan or Probolinggo. Frequent buses leave Probolinggo from 6am to 5pm for Surabaya, Malang (Rp1700), and Ketapang (Rp3500, 5-7hr.), the ferry station at Banyuwangi. Patas buses, which are more expensive than public buses, leave from Probolinggo and travel direct to Denpasar, Bali (8am, noon, and 7pm, 13hr.; times subject to change).

Probolinggo bus station is conveniently located between Surabaya and Banyuwangi; Probolinggo doesn't merit a stop on the itinerary, but guest houses are available to shelter stranded travelers. Upon arrival, you will undoubtedly be grabbed by extremely aggressive "tourist office" pushers. They will pretend to make arrangements for express, A/C buses, but actually just take your money and hustle you into one of the frequent regular public buses. Avoid these touts and head to orange uniformed station workers for guidance. If you can not communicate with the station employees, consider asking for info at the "tourist office," but be extremely wary of their offers and don't give them any money.

ACCOMMODATIONS AND FOOD

The best place to spend the night is in the strip of homestays closest to the crater, in Cemoro Lawang. The **Lava View Hostel** (tel. 234 58), is a good source of information about the volcano and environs, and has singles for Rp6000 (Rp5000 with student ID), doubles for Rp8000 (Rp7000 with student ID). The Lava View and others in Cemoro Lawang have restaurants, but the *warungs* outside serve the same food for a fifth of the price. Lava View also has a money changer, but it gives crummy rates; exchange money before coming to Bromo.

DOIN' THE MOUNTAIN

Particularly if you're staying in Cemoro Lawang, try to get in gear early enough for a sunrise Bromo experience, and watch the thick volcanic mud drape down the bowls. Ask the hotel manager to wake you at 3:30am (the sun rises at 5am), wear all of the clothes you've brought to Indonesia, pack a camera, some biscuits, a flashlight (although not essential), and a water bottle, and join the midnight masses en route to the mythic mountain. The walk—on a cobbled stone path until the turnoff to the "sea of sand" (which stretches for 3.5km before the Bromo crater)—takes approximately 45 minutes. You can rent a horse (Rp6-10,000) for either leg of the journey. Alternatively, guest house employees may offer to take you by jeep (for a fee, of course) to see the fabulous sunrise over Bromo from the "viewpoint" at Mt. Penanjakan. Afterwards, they can drive you down into the valley below Bromo (10km), where you can hike up to see the crater. A guide to the crater is not necessary, since the trail through the black sand is marked with white, gravestone-like rocks. Once at the top of Bromo, after the crowds begin to disperse at daybreak, consider hiking around the crater. Though precarious, the walk is not strenuous.

Bali

Guidebooks, brochures, and word of mouth have settled on a handful of clichés to gloss the most heavily visited island in Indonesia: Bali—Magical Isle of Paradise;

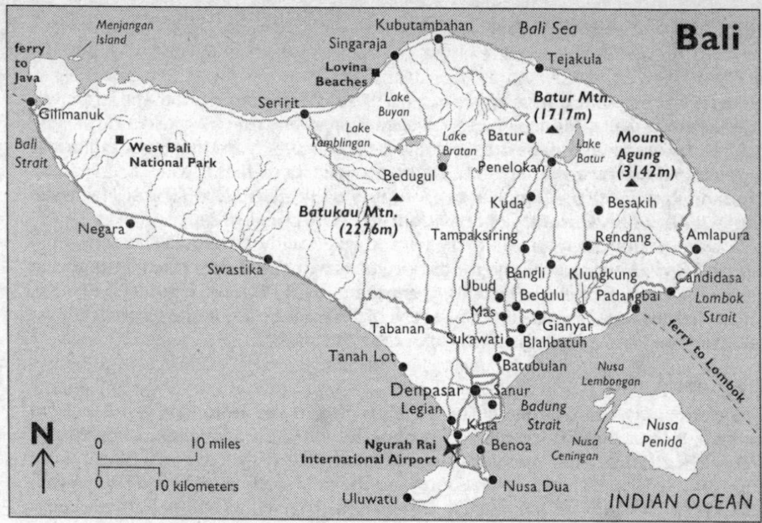

Bali—Island of the Gods; Bali—Morning of the World; Bali—Land of 10,000 Temples; Bali—Where Everyone is an Artist; and Bali—Destroyed by Tourism.

Visitors in search of the Bali promised by postcard photos, however, miss the real Bali right before their eyes. Stopping to notice the details gives the island more depth: intricately carved temples; *barong* demon shirts; in-your-face sarong/watch/massage hawkers; plane-size kites; gardenia and incense; jam-packed bemos; crispy frog road kill; "transport! transport!"; hairless dogs; the song of food vendors; and palm and petal offerings on street corners, bemo dashboards, and surfboard racks.

Bali, an island of 3 million people on 5700sq km, plays host to over 1 million tourists each year. Despite travelers' favorite complaint—that Bali is being destroyed by travelers—tourism has been relatively contained to the south, several areas in the island's center, and along the coast. Panoramic landscapes, attractive beaches, watersports, and consistently good weather (in the dry season, April-October) aside, locals realize that these typical lures aren't what attracts the majority of Bali's visitors. The hottest commodity is Bali's culture, and in general, the Balinese enjoy showcasing what have become the signature features of their society. In Sanur, Kuta, Ubud, Lovina, Candi Dasa, and other hot spots, visitors can buy tickets to see Balinese dance, *gamelan* orchestras, cremations, tooth fillings, temples, and more. Though these shows are worth an evenings' entertainment, one of the fastest ways to get to the heart of Bali is through public markets, *warung,* and family homestays—a low budget way to be spoon-fed Bali without the canned aftertaste.

Leaving the postcard images of Bali for the racks and noticing the less advertised details of Bali is good medicine for the "Bali is spoiled" plague that is common to visitors who are disturbed by their own impact. Certainly tourism has left its unmistakable imprint on the island, but Bali's relationship with the industry may not be as precarious as it seems. Bali's population, 95% Hindu in a predominantly Muslim nation, seems to be resilient to foreign (and domestic) persuasion. Like many Indonesians, the Balinese are remarkably unaggressive, seeking harmony and continuity over progressive change. Unlike many westerners who visit here, the Balinese tend to be neat and restrained and to value refined, respectful behavior. The people of Bali smile patiently through tension, wait calmly through discomfort, and feel sorry for people who are alone. In addition to vibrant dancers, dramatically placed temples and island breezes, Bali is where belief, etiquette and social relationships inform daily life; one of the worst insults is to call a Balinese person "not well brought up."

GETTING THERE AND AWAY

By Air

Ngurah Rai International Airport (tel. 751 011, 24-hr. information 164), immediately south of Kuta. Money changer, baggage storage, and ATM (takes Cirrus and AmEx). **International departure tax:** Rp20,000 per person (including children). **Domestic departure tax:** Rp7700. Flights to: **Jakarta** (7 flights daily, Rp222,000), **Medan** (Rp457,000); **Yogyakarta** (3 flights daily, Rp122,000); and **Mataram** (Rp55,000). **24-hr. Garuda Confirmation:** tel. 751 011 ext.1124.

Beware of porters who will carry your luggage without being asked and then demand Rp500 per piece. From the airport, taxis with fixed rates take passengers to **Kuta** (Rp6500), **Sanur** (Rp15,000), **Denpasar** (Rp11,000), or **Ubud** (Rp40,000). Public **bemos** and **chartered transport** vehicles linger outside the airport area on the main road and are invariably cheaper than the taxis.

By Ferry

Ferries run between **Gilimanuk** (on west tip of Bali) and **Ketapang** (on East Java) every half hour, Rp650. Ferries to **Lombok** leave from **Padangbai,** on Bali's east coast. **PELNI,** the state-owned shipping company, has daily ferries (8, 10am, noon, and 2pm, Rp5000). Tickets can be bought at the PELNI offices at Benoa Harbor (tel. 228 962 or 771 483) or Denpasar (Jl. Diponegoro 165; tel. 234 680). **Express boats** to **Lembar port** in Lombok leave from **Benoa Harbor** in south Bali (2hr., economy class US$12.50). Tickets can be bought at the **Mabua Express** office at Benoa (tel. 261 212). Bemos to Benoa leave from Suci terminal in Denpasar. To get to Padangbai on public transport, catch a bemo from Batubulan. Alternatively, explore one of the "shuttle bus" services, such as Perama, or others offered through tour agencies.

By Bus

Overnight buses leave regularly for Java from Bali and vice versa. Tickets can be bought through tour agencies such as **Bali Buana Artha,** Jl. Diponegoro 131A, Denpasar (tel. 227 370) or Jl. Hasanudin 97, Denpasar (tel. 222 663).

GETTING AROUND IN BALI

Metered taxis have recently made their appearance on Bali. Make sure the fixed rate meters are set to Rp800 at the beginning of the ride and insist on metered rates, since bargaining will always be more expensive. Taxis cannot usually stop where bemos or local drivers are parked, so flag one elsewhere. **Ojeks** are motorcycle taxis that congregate at key intersections where bemos do not run.

Public **bemos,** minivans identified by their yellow license plates, are best caught in the early morning and generally stop running after sundown. Bemos can be privately **chartered**—cheaper than taxis and more efficient than public bemos. Denpasar is the hub of bemo activity for the south part of Bali. The five terminals that service other parts of the island as well as Denpasar's own terminals are as follows:

Batubulan, 6km northeast of Denpasar. Bemos east to Padangbai, Candi Dasa, Amlapura, and Tirtagangga, and north to Ubud, Penelokan, and Kintamani.

Kereneng, on the east end of Denpasar off Jl. Hayam Wuruk. Has connecting bemos to the other terminals.

Suci, near the corner of Jl. Hasanudin and Jl. Diponegoro. Serves Benoa Harbor.

Tegal, on the west end, near the intersection of Jl. G. Willis and Jl. Imam Bonjol. South to Kuta, Legian, Ngurah Rai Airport, Sanur, Nusa Dua, and Uluwatu.

Ubung, north of Denpasar on Jl. Cokroaminoto. Trips north and west, including Singaraja, Bedugul, Tanah Lot, Gilimanuk, and points in Java.

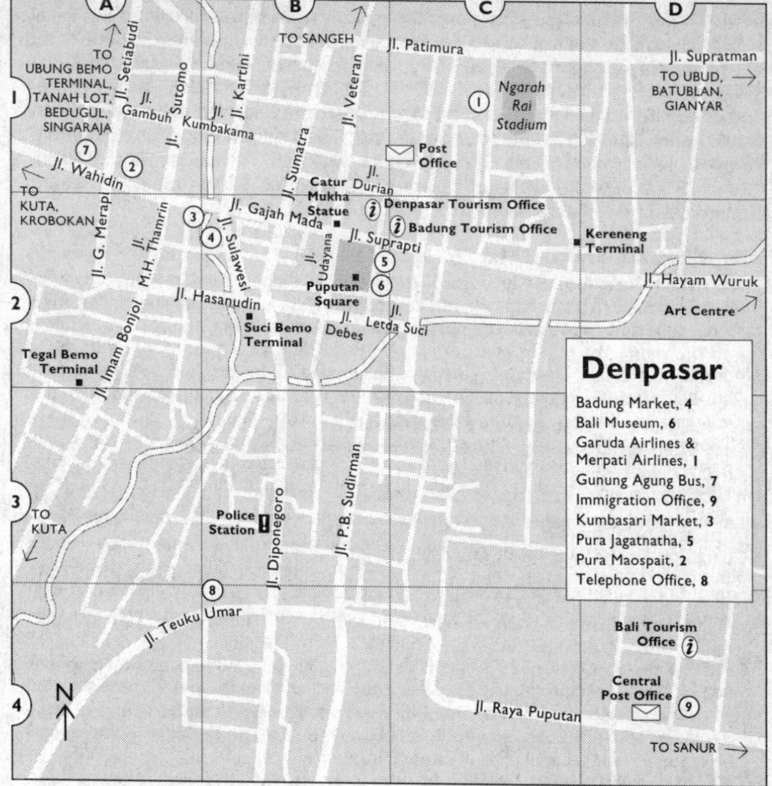

■■■ DENPASAR

Denpasar, Bali's provincial capital, is in the island's south corner. Theoretically, it incorporates both Kuta, its south neck, and Sanur, the east coast area, but these popular tourist destinations have taken on status (and reputations) of their own. Thus, "Denpasar" usually refers to the central, most congested part of town. Though it used to be the primary tourist destination, Denpasar now gets a bad rap in comparison to Sanur, Kuta, and its neighbor, Ubud. It isn't on the water, it doesn't have many sights, and its accommodations are expensive and poor in quality relative to those in outlying areas. However, if you can snatch up decent lodgings, or if you're in the mood for a daytrip from a nearby city, Denpasar has its pluses. It's the most convenient jumping-off point for south or east Bali. In addition, the museum here provides an introduction to Balinese culture that will make further exploration of the island more rewarding, and hunting through the Denpasar market scene may result in bargains not easily found elsewhere on Bali.

ORIENTATION

In the north of Denpasar, the dense market area lies between the parallel, east-west **Jalan Hasanudin** and **Jalan Gajah Mada,** which are connected by **Jalan Sulawesi.** East of the markets, between the same streets, is **Puputan Square;** the Badung Government Tourist Office is across the street. In the south of town are the Central Post Office and the Bali Government Tourist Office, both near **Jalan Raya Puputan,** the road leading east to Sanur. Also on the south side are **Udayan University** and the massive **Matahari Department Store;** they border **Jalan Diponegoro,** which heads north toward the market *(pasar)* area. Denpasar's **main bemo terminals** are **Tegal,** on **Jalan Imam Bonjol** just south of its intersection with Jl. Hasanudin; **Ubung** to the north; and **Kereneng,** to the east of Puputan Square off **Jalan Suropati.** (Jl. Gajah Mada becomes Jl. Suprapati to the east, which then changes to **Jalan Hayam Wuruk** farther on.) To walk to the market area from Tegal terminal, turn right onto Jl. Imam Bonjol and walk to Jl. Hasanudin; then turn right, pass the river, and turn left onto Jl. Sulawesi. To get there from Kereneng Station, walk straight along Jl. Hayam Wuruk (about 25 minutes). Alternatively, from Jl. Hayam Wuruk, turn right and catch a bemo heading to Tegal terminal, then walk from there.

PRACTICAL INFORMATION

Tourist Offices: Dinas Pariwisata, Jl. Suropati 7 (tel. 222 387). From Kereneng bemo station, exit through the thickest market area and walk to the closest main road, Jl. Hayam Wuruk. Turn right and walk about 2 blocks (10min.). The office is on the right, just before and opposite Puputan Square. Open Mon.-Thurs. 8am-2pm, Fri. 8-11am. **Dept. of Tourism Regional Office** (tel. 256 49), on Jl. Raya Puputan. **Bali Government Tourism Office** (tel. 222 387), on Jl. S. Parman.

Tickets and Tours: Gapura Jaya Tours, Jl. Hayam Wuruk 74 (tel. 228 460). There are oodles of other tour/transport options. **Ayung River Rafting Company,** Jl. Diponegoro 150 B-29 (tel. 224 236). Rafting trips north of Denpasar $63.

Embassies and Consulates: Australia, Jl. Moh. Yamin 1, Renon (tel. 235 002; fax 31 990).

Immigration Office: Jl. Niti Mandala, Renon, Denpasar (tel. 227 828).

Currency Exchange: Bank Duta, Jl. Hayam Wuruk 165 (tel. 226 578). Accepts Visa, MC. Open Mon.-Fri. 8am-noon, Sat. 8-11am. **Bank Central Asia (BCA),** Jl. Hasanudin 58 (tel. 431 012). Visa, MC. Open Mon.-Fri 8am-2pm, Sat. 8am-noon. **ATM: Bank Bali,** on Jl. Diponegoro where it hits Jl. Teuku Umar, near the telephone office. Visa, MC, Cirrus.

Post Office: GPO (tel. 223 565 or 223 568), Jl. Raya Puputan, Renon, Denpasar, 80235. Poste Restante. Open daily 8am-9pm. Other **branches:** Jl. Kamboja 6, outside Kereneng bemo station. Open Mon.-Thurs. 8am-noon and 1-9pm, Fri. 8am-noon and 1:30-9pm, Sat. 8am-8pm, Sun. 8am-9pm. Also on Jl. Teuku Umar, across from the phone office. Open daily 8am-9pm.

Telephones: at Jl. Teuku Umar 6, near the intersection with Jl. Diponegoro. International, collect, or calling card calls from booths outside the office. Calls can also be made from hotels. **Telephone code:** 0361.

Airlines: Garuda Indonesia, Jl. Melati 61 (tel. 225 245). **Merpati Nusantara,** Jl. Melati 57 (tel. 222 864 or 225 841). **Bouraq Indonesian,** Jl. Sudirman 19A (tel. 224 656 or 223 564).

Public Transport: See "Getting Around in Bali" on page 712.

Car Rental: Surya Agung Dewata Rent-a-car, Jl. Diponegoro 69 (tel. 233 448).

Bookstore: Gramedia (tel. 221 026), in the basement of the Duta Plaza, Jl. Dewi Sartika. English-language paperbacks, coffee table books, magazines (limited selection), guide books, and maps. Open daily 9:30am-10pm.

Pharmacy: Kimia Farma 34, Jl. Diponegoro 125 (tel. 227 812), where Diponegoro meets Jl. Teuku Umar. Open 24 hrs.

Emergency: Police: tel. 110. **Ambulance:** tel. 118 or 27 911.

Hospitals: Sanglah Public Hospital, Jl. Kesehatan Selatan 1 (tel. 235 456). **24-hour clinic: Manuaba Clinic,** Jl. Cokroaminoto 28 (tel. 426 393).

Gay and Lesbian Resources: Gaya Dewata, c/o Yayasan Citra Usadha Indonesia, Jl. Belimbing Gg. Y No.4 (tel. 222 620; fax 229 487). Also an AIDS education center. Sells *GAYa Nusantara.*

Police: (tel. 234 928) on Jl. Gunung Agung or (tel. 225 456) on Jl. A. Yani.

ACCOMMODATIONS

Few tourists stay for more than a few hours in Denpasar; this is probably both the cause and the effect of the few quality budget accommodations. Many cheaper hotels and *losmen* in Denpasar will turn away western wanderers by explaining that their suspiciously quiet rooms are "full." This could mean that the managers don't dole out rooms to foreign travelers, since they want to avoid the hassle of filing a police report—mandatory for all foreign visitors. If you find a particularly good deal and will be staying in Denpasar for a few days, offer to make the report in person; the hotel may allow you to stay. The procedure is simple: bring your passport, dress preppy, and explain that you wish to file a report on behalf of your accommodation.

Adi Yasa, Jl. Nakula 23B (tel. 222 679), on a fairly quiet street, 5-10min. from Denpasar's main action. From the Kumbasari market on Jl. Gajah Mada, walk up Jl. Kartini until about the third right, Jl. Nakula; Adi Yasa is on the left. Popular with westerners and domestic tourists. Singles (Rp15,000) and doubles (Rp20,000) with bath are nice by Denpasar standards, with shower, fan, and full-length mirror. Rooms without bath (Rp12,500) are spartan but compensated for by the pleasant porch and constant supply of tea. Semi-satisfying breakfast included.

Nakula Familiar Inn, Jl. Nakula 4 (tel. 226 446), across the street and 50 yards west (toward Jl. Kartini) from Adi Yasa. Gorgeous, fresh rooms, some with balcony, curtains, and jumbo bathrooms, all crowded around a small outside dining area and courtyard. Beware of the seemingly amicable dog. Doubles Rp16,000.

Hotel Jaya, Jl. Hasanudin 26 (tel. 222 911). Central, at the intersection of Jl. Hasanudin and Jl. Diponegoro, 2 of Denpasar's busiest streets. The rooms have fake wood paneling and framed posters of dew-dropped rose buds on the walls. Those near the street can be quite noisy. Doubles with bath Rp35,000.

Hotel Nusah Indah Raya, Jl. Beliton 10 (tel. 269 51), behind Hotel Jaya. Take the first right off Jl. Diponegoro after it intersects Jl. Hasanudin. Below average rooms but a great price that foreign visitors may be able to get if they offer to report their own arrival to the police. Singles with bath Rp7500. Doubles Rp10,000.

FOOD

The cheapest place to grab dinner is the **night market** (6pm-midnight) behind the Badung Market, off Jl. Gajah Mada. Another night market comes to life on Jl. Diponegoro near the Kertha Wijaya Shopping Center, and there are **warung** set up throughout the day at Kereneng bemo terminal. Don't expect to see other tourists eating at these markets, but do expect to be a spectacle; just the way you hold your fork is enough to arouse curiosity. Denpasar's **supermarkets** and **fast food** joints (Balinese and western) can be found in shopping centers: **Dewata Ayu Supermarket** (open 8am-midnight) is at Jl. Teuku Umar and Jl. Sudirman, the **Tiara Dewata Supermarket** and shopping center are at the north end of Jl. Sudirman, and the Kertha Wijaya Complex with a **Matahari Supermarket** is on Jl. Diponegoro 98, within walking distance of Jl. Hasanudin and Denpasar's market area. If you're in the mood for a **restaurant,** hit the south end of Jl. Diponegoro and the west end of Jl. Teuku Umar.

Pondok Indah, Jl. Diponegoro 134 (tel. 327 85). A mostly Balinese menu with English translations of various fish, frog, and steak entrees, most Rp3-7000. Tables are set up outside on the concrete, barely sheltered from the multi-laned Jl. Diponegoro; a good place to go if intimate conversations are not your goal. Also a choice spot for trying the Balinese food you've curiously eyed in less tourist-friendly hangouts. Fried carp with sweet and sour sauce (Rp7500). Divine *es teler* (sweet iced coconut and avocado drink/dessert, Rp1250).

Rumah Makan Siang Malam, Jl. Diponegoro 124A (tel. 223 534), on the Jl. Teuku Umar side of the Kertha Wijaya Shopping Center. Dishes of Balinese food are stacked in the window. Atmosphere dominated by street noise, the TV, and the Arabic inscriptions on the wall. Formica tables. Popular with locals. Open 24 hrs.

Ha..Ha..AA Coffee House and Restaurant, Jl. Gajah Mada 111 (tel. 434 79 39). western fare in the Denpasar market area. Attractive tables, padded chairs, and *batik* napkins under low lights in a laid-back atmosphere. BLT (Rp3500). Spaghetti (Rp4000). Open daily 8am-9:30pm.

Rumah Makan Betty, Jl. Sumatra 56, 1 block east of Jl. Sulawesi. One of several small, low-budget eateries on Jl. Sumatra that cater to Indonesians. Betty is a large, glassed-in, cafeteria-like joint specializing in East Javanese food. Popular *sop buntut* (soup) with pork (Rp3000). Some vegetarian options. Open daily 7am-9pm.

Warung Nasi Bali, Jl. Hayam Wuruk 69A (tel. 223 889). Walk east (left) from the Kereneng bemo station, on Jl. Hayam Wuruk. Warung Nasi Bali is on the left, 350m before Jl. Nusa Indah (the locale of several other small, relaxed Balinese restaurants). The *warung* has no menu, but offers Balinese delicacies like *lawar* and *babi guling* (braised suckling pig) at Rp 2200 per portion. Open 7:30am-6pm.

SIGHTS

East of Puputan Square on Jl. Wisnu stands Denpasar's essential attraction, the **Bali Museum.** Arranged around airy courtyards, each building houses artifacts that provide newcomers with an introduction to Balinese society. Unfortunately, the museum does not have English-speaking tour guides or detailed labels, but wandering through green courtyards and rooms filled with masks, puppets, costumes, dioramas of cremation and tooth-filling ceremonies, bells and religious symbols used by Hindu priests, an ancient Balinese calendar, textiles, and equipment used to drive away *bhuta-kala* (demons), informs and educates nonetheless. Open Tues.-Thurs. and Sat.-Sun. 7:30am-2:30pm, Fri. 7-11:30am. Admission Rp200, children Rp100.

Beside the museum is the unusual **Pura Jaganatha.** Bring a sash or borrow one (Rp1000). A tall, intricately carved steeple headed by a gold Hindu figurine is surrounded by two square levels and a lime-green moat. Tourists can walk around the exterior of the moat only. If you're feeling less-than-holy, ask a temple attendant to sprinkle sanctified water on you and press some rice grains onto your temples and forehead, Balinese style. The temple is crowded on the evenings of *purnama* (full moon) and *tilem* (dark moon), when Balinese bring offerings, incense and prayers to the moon. Visitors are welcome if they dress in sarong and sash. *Wayang kulit* (shadow puppet theatre) begins on *purnama* or *tilem* at approximately 9pm.

Puputan Square, outside the museum and Pura Jaganatha, is a large, grassy field with a monument, fountain, and benches at its north side. The monument depicts a family prepared to enter battle, commemorating the solemn *puputan* of 1906, when the last king of Badung—with his family, court, and followers—marched into the bullets of Dutch soldiers.

Every June and July, Bali holds an **art festival** with dances, music, and exhibits at the **Werdi Budaya Art Center** (tel. 227 176), at the corner of Jl. Hayam Wuruk and Jl. Nusa Indah. The tourist information office provides a schedule of events. The Art Center also holds a nightly *kecak* performance, unique to Bali, from 6:30-7:30pm (admission Rp6000). *Kecak* is a dance and musical event characterized by the percussive, monkey-like chattering and "chak-chak-chak"-ing of the male chorus.

SHOPPING

Perhaps the most interesting part of the city is the market area on Jl. Sulawesi, where food, wares, fabric, and art markets clump together. **Pasar Badung,** the largest and oldest market in Bali, is a multi-story jumble. Meat, fish, fruit, and vegetables pile up beside offerings and burning incense on the first floor. The second floor sells baskets of shiny red chilis, hunks of palm sugar, spices, and ginger. The third floor has everything else—including jewelry, sarongs, kids' clothes, and fake hair pieces. Outside, locals buy multi-colored flower petals for offerings.

Alongside these markets is Jl. Sulawesi, the heart of Denpasar's **fabric district.** If you have designs on having clothes made in Bali, Jl. Sulawesi is the best place to shop, as it's lined with stall after stall selling a wide variety of fabrics. Shop around and bargain for reasonable prices. Denpasar has tailors in the fabric district, though prices may be more expensive in the city than in outer areas.

■ AROUND DENPASAR

PURA ULUWATU

Uluwatu Temple overlooks cliffs on the southwest tip of Bukit Peninsula, the mushroom shaped area south of Denpasar and Kuta. Uluwatu is one of the *Sadkahyangan,* the six most important temples in Bali. The temple's erection, thought to date from the 11th century, is associated with the Hindu Saint Danhyang Nirartha, who explored Bali in 1500 BC. Legend has it that he meditated in various picturesque spots and then suggested that villages build temples to salute the spirits that inhabit those serene locations. Nirartha is reputed to have achieved *moksa,* or unity with God, at Uluwatu. It's not hard to imagine why Nirartha was moved to meditate in such a dramatic landscape. The temple itself is relatively modest but perches at the very edge of dark, vertical cliffs that fall 70m into waves crashing at the rocks below. The "Good Sunset View This Way" signs attest to Uluwatu's popularity with visitors, but the temple is nevertheless a tranquil place, save for the monkeys who could use some help from Jenny Craig. Visitors who wish to pray (to any god) may enter the temple's inner court. Paths wander along the edges of the cliffs on either side of the main temple, leading to quiet, windy outlooks over the ocean. Uluwatu is also popular with **surfing** enthusiasts; the Kuta Tourist Office has info on board rentals.

Reaching Uluwatu can be a challenge for the car- or motorbike-less. Bemos leave for Uluwatu from Denpasar's Tegal station in the morning only; after noon you'll be hard pressed to find public transport that runs far enough south. From Kuta, you can pick up the bemo from Tegal by waiting on the road heading away from the Duty Free Shop, near the gas pump on Jl. Raya Kuta. Bemos may run all the way to Uluwatu or they may drop you at Pecatu (Peh-CHA-Too) on the Bukit Peninsula, from where you can hire an *ojek* (about Rp1000) to the temple. Private transport can be hired from Kuta for Rp20,000. The distance from Kuta to Uluwatu is bikeable (20km), but the roads near the temple are excruciatingly steep.

Entrance to Uluwatu Temple is Rp1000, children Rp500. Bring a sarong and sash or borrow one (Rp500) from the office at the entrance gate. As at other temples, shorts and sleeveless shirts are not considered respectful garb. Uluwatu is open from 5am until the last visitors have left, and is most crowded at sunset.

TANAH LOT

If Tanah Lot weren't the most photographed temple in Bali, it might be a more enjoyable place to visit. But postcards advertising Tanah Lot at various stages of sun-

Waria

Fitra is anatomically male but she insists that she and her boyfriend, a Javanese policeman who visits her on his lunch breaks, are not gay. "He doesn't like men," Fitra insists as she brushes her long, black hair. As a teenager, she began to wear dresses and makeup full time. Though no one has ever explained it to her, she believes what most *waria,* members of Indonesia's alternate gender, believe: God gave her a female soul inside her male body. When Fitra was 13, she dressed in a female's tunic and veil, went to mosque with her family, and confronted this belief. In the mosque, she sat for a few moments on the female side of the room, since she would stand out in the male section dressed as she was. The women next to her began to shift uneasily away, making it clear that they were uncomfortable in Fitra's "cross-dressed" presence. As Fitra explained it, they felt she was polluting the purity of their prayer.

Fitra doesn't go to mosque anymore. She prays alone, on the red prayer mat that hangs over the door to her room, which is a concrete cell in a compound filled with other Javanese immigrants who are hoping to strike it rich in the tourist-fed economy of Bali's capital city. The intricacies of Fitra's belief distinguish her from the western categories of transvestite, hermaphrodite, homosexual, and transsexual. According to Fitra, she is neither "cross" dressing nor wearing the clothes of another gender. She has a masculine body, but she believes that her female soul distinguishes her from homosexual men attracted to other men. She has not had, nor does she wish to have, genital surgery; she is who she is. Fitra has recently updated her National Identity Card, an identification card carried by all Indonesians. The card describes her status—once printed as male beneath her long-haired photograph—as *waria.*

set have the effect of summoning masses of tourists who inevitably find that, for most of the day, the real thing is without sunset or serenity. If you have a hankering to be in other people's home movies, don't miss Tanah Lot. Concrete stairs and a path lead past a zoo of souvenir, sarong, and strawberry Fanta hawkers to a black sand beach. Unless you have come in *pakaian adat*—formal Balinese threads—and intend to pray at the temple, you are not permitted to enter Tanah Lot, which sits on a cliff above the beach. Paths weaving around the main temple to smaller shrines make for pleasant walking along the coast and away from the hordes. Open 7am-8pm; admission Rp1050. The Tanah Lot complex has almost as many WCs as sarongs for sale, as well as a money changer, restaurants, and some *losmen*. The **Tanah Lot Losmen** is at the entrance opposite the police booth. Rooms Rp10,000.

To get to Tanah Lot from Denpasar's Tegal Station, take a bemo to Ubung (Rp500), then a colt minibus to Kediri (about 20min., Rp500). If you have a moment at Kediri, walk outside to the crossroads, where you can see gorgeous *sawah* rice terraces stretching one block west. From the Kediri terminal, hop a bemo to Tanah Lot (Rp500). Bemos slow down in late afternoon, so visitors aiming at Tanah Lot for sunset may have to find alternate transport. The last bemo back to Kediri leaves around 5pm, though it may be possible to hire an *ojek* (Rp3000) to Kediri, from where you can catch a bemo back to Denpasar. Alternatively, ambitious travelers can walk the gorgeous and untrammeled coast from Kuta to Tanah Lot (15km).

■■■ SANUR

Home to a large population of Hindu priests from *Brahmana* (high caste) families, Sanur also hosts a large number of high-rise hotels, which loom over the sea for tourist pleasure. The priests are concerned with placating and managing the powerful spirits that inhabit the ocean. Some Balinese say that the tourists who flock to Sanur's seashore are symbols of the combined forces that the ocean spirits possess. On the one hand, there's the expanding economy, increased jobs, and the tourist shops that line Sanur's main drag, most of which brandish the American Express decal on prominent bamboo pillars. On the other hand, Sanur's tourism has decreased local commitment to religious ceremony. Since many of Sanur's natives are essential to hotel operations, they forego rituals that would interrupt the timing of, say, Texas Night at the ten story Bali Beach Hotel. If Texas Night (a Javanese banjo quartet whose number one hit is *Hava Nagila*) sounds enticing, or if you just want to compare social security benefits, then Sanur is for you!

Most travelers to Sanur have medium to high budgets; budgeteers will find that the cost of living here seriously curbs that rupiah supply unless they eat meals at the market and refrain from the overpriced beach equipment. Sanur is well known for its talented *gamelan* orchestras, dancers, *pendanda* (high priests), and kite festivals, all of which add to a community spirit that makes Sanur a laid-back place to visit.

ORIENTATION

Sanur is the district on the southeast coast of Denpasar. The most commercial and touristed area stretches in a long and narrow band between the shore, the main drag that runs beside it, and the **Ngurah Rai Bypass,** which runs the length of Sanur approximately one km from the ocean. The north part of Sanur is dominated by the multi-story **Bali Beach Hotel** and its golf course, pools, cottages, and complex of banks, airline offices, and tour agents. **Jalan Sanur/Jalan Hang Tuah** runs west from Denpasar to the shore, crossing the Ngurah Rai Bypass and marking the north perimeter of the Bali Beach Hotel sprawl. Parallel to Jl. Hang Tuah on the Hotel's south side is **Jalan Danau Buyan** (on the Denpasar side of the Bypass; called **Jalan Segara Ayu** on the beach side). Also parallel to these two roads and slightly farther south is **Jalan Sindhu.** The main drag, **Jalan Danau Tamblingan,** runs north-south along the shore; from Jl. Segara Ayu it runs past Jl. Sindhu, turns right at the night/

fruit market, continues through the area called **Batujimbar,** and terminates at the far south end of Sanur, known as **Semawang.**

PRACTICAL INFORMATION

Tourist Office: The nearest office is in Kuta, but hotels and tour operators provide info and copious offers to take you (and your money) where you want to go. A private tourist and tour information office (tel. 288 056) is at the south end of Jl. Tamblingan 107, past the Hyatt. Open Mon.-Fri 8am-8pm, Sat.-Sun. 8am-4pm.

Embassies and Consulates: US, Jl. Segara Ayu 5 (tel. 288 478).

Currency Exchange: Money changers on Jl. Danau Tamblingan and in the larger hotels like the Bali Beach Hotel. **P.T. Artha money changer** (tel. 288 965), beside the pool at the Bali Beach Hotel. Open 8am-9pm.

American Express: Mail can be addressed to AmEx card members or check holders at: Holly Friendless (or name of addressee), c/o PACTO, Hotel Bali Beach, Sanur (tel. 288 449). Keeps letters 1 month, then returns to sender. Only card holders can buy checks here. Does not receive packages. Open Mon.-Fri. 8:30am-4:30pm, Sat. 8:30am-12:30pm.

Post Office: GPO, Jl. Danau Buyan, Banjar Taman, Sanur, Denpasar. Poste Restante. Open Mon.-Thurs. 8am-noon and 1-5pm, Fri. 8am-noon and 1:30-5pm, Sat. 9-11am,Sun. 8am-noon. **Postal code:** 80228.

Telephones: Make local, collect, and cash international calls at the *wartel* at the corner of Jl. Segara, beside Hey Cafe. The Bali Beach Hotel has 24-hr. Home Country Direct. Phones are behind the first main porch on the right.

Airlines: All the following offices are at the Grand Bali Beach Hotel Arcade: **Garuda Indonesia** (tel. 287 920). Open Mon.-Fri 8am-5pm; weekends and holidays 9am-1pm. **Sempati Air** (tel. 288 823). **Singapore Airlines** (tel. 287 940 ext. 1587). Open Mon.-Fri. 8:30am-1pm and 2-4:30pm, Sat. 8:30am-1pm. **Ansett Australian Airlines** (tel. 289 635-7).

Bemos: Can be flagged down on Jl. Danau Tamblingan. Short distances within Sanur cost Rp300. The **Sanur terminal** is at the south end of town, at the end of Jl. Danau Tamblingan, in Semawang. To **Denpasar:** blue and green bemos head for Kereneng Station Rp600.

Taxi: Praja Taxi (tel. 289 090 or 289 191).

Rental: Wirasana, Jl. Danau Tamblingan 126 (tel. 288 706) and Jl. Ngurah Rai Bypass 545x (tel. 286 066), opposite the police station. Cheapest cars Rp35,000 per day. Motorbikes Rp15,000 per day. MC/Visa.

Tickets and Tours: Santa Bali Tours, at Hotel Grand Bali Beach (tel. 263 009), and plenty of others.

Laundromat: Sharm Laundry Shop, Jl. Tanjung Sari 12 (tel. 756 814), next to the night market.

Swimming Pools: Puri Kelapa Hotel (tel. 286 135), on the corner of Jl. Segara and Jl. Danau Tamblingan. Rp5000, from 6am to 8pm. **Bali Beach Hotel,** Rp15,000 includes a hamburger, drink, towel, and borrowable lawn chair.

Medical Assistance: Bali Beach Hotel has a **clinic** (tel. 288 511, ask for the clinic). Open Mon.-Fri. 7am-9pm, Sat. 7am-8pm, Sun. and holidays 10am-6pm. Doctor on hand Mon.-Sat. 8am-noon.

Emergency: Police: tel. 110. **Ambulance:** tel. 118 or 279 11.

Police: (tel. 288 597) on the Ngurah Rai Bypass, at the edge of the golf course.

ACCOMMODATIONS

Sanur has fairly slim pickings. But for around Rp15,000, you can hit the hay near the beach and feel smug; your neighbors paying ten times the price can't be having *that* much more fun. If you're arriving in Sanur at night or don't want to bother traipsing around the beachside accommodations seeking bang for your buck, check out the hotels on Jl. Danau Buyan, approximately 400m from the beach. Bemos from Denpasar pass them on the left before crossing the Ngurah Rai Bypass. **Hotel Rani,** Jl. Danau Buyan 33 (tel. 288 578), has a restaurant, laundry service, and the nicest rooms of the three. Rooms from Rp17,000 (with fan) to Rp45,000 (with A/C).

Yulia Homestay, Jl. Danau Tamblingan 38, opposite the Subec Discoteque. From the Sanur market, walk straight, and hug the corner by the Red Center Cafe. The Yulia is 75m from the corner on the right, with an art shop in front. Owners are fastidious, amiable, and open to teaching interested guests about daily Balinese life. Eight rooms are positioned around a well-kept garden and the owners' living quarters. Billy, the family dog, wags his tail at guests who stay more than 48 hours. New and old rooms with porches, baths, fans, and woven blankets that make you feel snug as a banana in its peel. Lending library. Rooms are Rp25-30,000, with breakfast and discounts for long-term guests.

Ananda Beach Hotel, Jl. Hang Tuah 43 (tel 288 327). North of the Bali Beach Hotel, on the beach. If you're coming from Denpasar on a bemo, tell the driver you want to go to the *pantai* or the Bali Beach Hotel. With the Bali Beach Hotel's grounds on your right, walk to the end of Jl. Hang Tuah, toward the beach. Turn left when you hit sand; Ananda is on the left. Rooms are a fantastic beachside value. Most singles Rp20,000. Doubles Rp25,000 and up. The two Rp15,000 rooms get snatched up fast; those aiming for this price range should call ahead.

The Watering Hole, Jl. Hang Tuah 35 (tel. 288 289), before Ananda and opposite the north entrance to the Bali Beach Hotel. Not extravagant but popular, with nice rooms, some upstairs with a balcony. Just 100m from the beach. Restaurant in front. Rooms with fan Rp21-26,000, with AC Rp35,000.

FOOD

Most restaurants, like everything else in Sanur, are overpriced. If you're contemplating going hog wild, spend your few thousand extra at one of the suave-looking spots on Jl. Danau Tamblingan; many have Balinese dance performances during dinner.

The **public market** *(pasar)* is at the corner of Jl. Danau Tamblingan where it bends south to east after crossing Jl. Sindhu. **Pasar Sindu** is a flurry of bananas, pineapples, mangoes, *salak,* jackfruit, papaya, and coconuts changing hands. Open 5-11am. The **night market** is open from 4pm until midnight, and contains stalls (some with benches, all with take-out) offering Indonesian rice dishes for Rp1000 per plate. The **terang bulan** (literally, bright moon) seller makes a scrumptious sugar and nut covered pancake-like dessert for a few hundred rupiah per slice. The **roasted corn** seller coats ears with spiced butter and roasts them over an open flame on his cart (Rp300), keeping you coming back on a daily basis. Another night market sets up at dusk in the dusty lot on Jl. Buyan, before the post office.

Sanur's **supermarket** is **Galael Dewata** (tel. 288 199), on Ngurah Rai Bypass. From the intersection with Jl. Segara, turn right at the Splash Bakery and walk about 200m; it's on the left. Expensive, but useful for packaged necessities.

Cafetaria Sanur, to the left after the entrance to the Sindu market. One of the least expensive places for a sit-down dinner, the large Cafetaria Sanur generally caters to westerners who like the idea of being in the market but are shy about participating in it. Bright lights and not much ambiance, but the large glass windows let you take in the hustle and bustle of the *pasar* as you sit safely behind a menu. *Nasi campur* (Rp2000). Open 7am-10pm.

Warung Lesse'an, Jl. Danau Toba 10B (tel. 286 343). Caddy-corner from the *wartel* on the corner of Jl. Segara. Lesse'an has a few tables where visitors can sit on the floor or in chairs. Artwork on the walls, calming music, and attractive lighting. Small but artfully served gourmet portions at prices that tempt you to get two.

Hey Café, Jl. Danau Tamblingan 1A. Across the street from Warung Lesse'an and beside the *wartel.* Outdoor seating and relaxed atmosphere. Get an earful of the live music (almost every night) before you decide whether or not to stay. European and particularly good Indonesian food. Chicken curry with rice (Rp7000). Fabulous *tempe manis* (sweet fried tempeh) Rp2500. Open 7:30am-midnight.

Cumi-cumi, Jl. Danau Tamblingan 86 (288 807) on the mainland side of the street past the art market. Look for the pluorescent green tables and furfle fainted wicker chairs. Indonesian dishes, fizza and spaghetti (Rp5000), plaming *sate* (Rp6000). Pree farmesan and cheese and no extra charge if you preely exchange F's and P's, like the menu and staff. Open 7am-11pm.

Hotel Santai's Vegetarian Restaurant, at the south end of Jl. Danau Tamblingan in the Batujimbar area, on the mainland side of the street. On the 2nd floor above the hotel lobby. Tables are set up in a large, breezy room overlooking a balcony. Santai serves excellent food and if you're lucky, the manager of the restaurant will chat you up and tell you more than you thought you could know about the eco-friendly, semi-self-sufficient commune he's started. Entrees Rp2-3000.

Choice Bakery and Coffee Shop, Jl. Danau Tamblingan 150 (tel. 288 401), next to the Santai Restaurant. Excellent, health-conscious-oriented food. Homemade granola. 2 slices of brown bread (Rp1000). Dip into Thai *tom yam gai* (chicken, mushrooms, vegetables, chili, and coconut milk Rp4000). Open 7:30am-9:30pm.

Café Batujimbar, Jl. Danau Tamblingan 152 (tel. 287 374). One door down from the Choice Bakery. Peaceful, pleasant atmosphere. Steeper prices, but intensely satisfying fare. Spicy Manado fish curry (Rp6400). Burritos (Rp6900). Salads, desserts, and freshly baked bread. Open Mon.-Sat. 7am-11pm, Sun. 8am-4pm.

SIGHTS

Sheltered by a reef and overlooked by the majestic volcano Gunung Agung, Sanur's **beach** is wide, clean, and, unlike other beaches on Bali, safe. The water is too shallow for swimming in the true sense but is perfect for wading, lounging, and shallow-water fishing, practiced patiently by locals in the afternoons. North of the Bali Beach Hotel, where the sand turns black, locals come to *mandi,* play, and paddle on rented boards in the early evenings. Sundays can be crowded; many Balinese travel to wade in Sanur's warm, benign waters. Stroll down this stretch of beach and take in the lively scene of squatting grandmothers, screeching kids, secretive couples, and splash wars.

In contrast, walking down the white and tan beach south of the Bali Beach Hotel can be equally amusing to peruse the quickly reddening foreigners in various stages of undress. Unscrupulous travelers staying at the roadside hotel across the street often sneak into the Bali Hyatt grounds for a dip in the private swimming pool. The hotel personnel regards such "guests" with suspicion when travelers do anything other than stand or swim laps, but the situation may be calmed with a quick "I'm with my grandparents."

ENTERTAINMENT

Check local restaurants for traditional Balinese dance and *gamelan* performances. The **Sanur Beach Hotel** (tel. 288 011), at the far south end of the main drag, has a Frog (or Prog) Dance performance on Sundays, Legong dance on Mondays, and *Ramayana* ballet on Wednesdays. Admission is Rp47,000 with buffet dinner, Rp10,000 without. Performances run 7:30-11:30pm. **Swastika Restaurant** (in Bali swastikas are a symbol of auspiciousness), Jl. Danau Tamblingan 124, near the art market, has Frog Dance performances on Thursdays and Legong dances on Sundays, both at 8:30pm.

For do-it-yourself dancing, head to **Subec Disco,** on the beach side of Jl. Danau Tamblingan where it bends along the coast past the night market. Cover Rp10,000. Ladies' night Mondays. Opens at 10pm. On the opposite side of the same road you'll find **#1 Club;** it's situated in the Batujimbar area past Jl. Pantai Karang, the small road that leads to the beach. Cover Rp10,000.

The **Kantor Jelati Willis** booth on Sanur Beach where Jl. Segara runs into the sand, offers most of the water sports visitors could want, including traditional sailing boat with driver (1hr., $10); water scooter (15min., $15); windsurfing (1hr., $15); motorboat (15min., $15); paddle surfboard (15min., $15); surfboard (1hr., $8); snorkel equipment (1hr., $3); glass bottom boat ride (1hr., $10); waterskiing (15min., $15); parasailing (once around, $10); and scuba diving (see instructors).

■■■ KUTA

Long and thin, Kuta links the Bukit Peninsula with mainland Bali and Denpasar. Like Sanur, Kuta lies technically within Denpasar, but largely due to the tourist explosion it has essentially become a separate district. Of all the popular tourist destinations in Bali, Kuta has the most infamous reputation. In other parts of the island, the very mention of Kuta spurs controversy, rolled eyes, exasperated sighs of disgust, and kindled longing to join the party. The Kuta scene is not for the faint of heart or those with a discerning taste for stubbornly elusive "authentic Bali." Kuta is a hectic bumbling-gatherum of restaurants, accommodations, shops, and aggressive hawkers—all oriented toward YOU, dear *Let's Go* reader! Those sensitive to traditional Balinese etiquette will no doubt be alarmed or at best amused; many fellow and sister travelers strut teeny bikinis, thongs, or even less into restaurants (one popular joint is called the Pink Pussy), public transport vehicles, and government offices. Perhaps because of this abundant display of flesh and other behaviors that confirm local perceptions that all foreigners are 90210 stunt doubles, the per-km number of "Hi Honeys" and more creative greetings are dramatically higher than in other areas.

Kuta's sand, surf, and spectacular sunsets continually lure foreigners to its beach strip. Experienced wave runners usually head elsewhere, but beginners and intermediate amateurs can still get stoked. Swimmers should take precautions with the ocean's untrustworthy undercurrents; the Kuta lifesaving club saves a few swimmers every year a la *Baywatch*.

ORIENTATION

The most prominent landmark is the **Ngurah Rai International Airport,** north of **Jimbaran Beach** and immediately south of Kuta. The **Ngurah Rai Bypass** runs the length of south Kuta, continues east of the airport, and eventually heads east to Sanur. North of the airport are three beaches: **Tuban** to the south, **Legian** in the north, and **Kuta** in between. Most activity is concentrated in the Kuta area—on **Jalan Pantai Kuta** (one-way west, beachward) and **Jalan Legian** (one-way south) which meet at **Bemo Corner.** From Bemo Corner, it's a short walk to the **night market** (north, on Jl. Tanjung Sari), to the beach (south), and to **Poppies Lanes I** and **II,** which intersect Jl. Legian to the north. Parallel to Jl. Legian, **Jalan Raya Pantai Kuta** runs one-way north along the coast; the two roads are joined by Jl. Pantai Kuta, Poppies Lanes I and II, and **Jalan Melasti.** North of Jl. Melasti, the Legian district begins and Jl. Legian is linked to four generally parallel roads: **Jalan Padma, Jalan Pura Bagus Teruna, Jalan Double Six,** and **Jalan Dyana Pura.**

PRACTICAL INFORMATION

Tourist Office: Bali Government Tourism Information Center, Jl. Bakung Sari 1 (tel. 756 176). From Bemo Corner, with your back to Jl. Legian, walk down Jl. Buni Sari to its termination at Jl. Bakung Sari. Turn left; the office is on the left. Extremely helpful and used to assisting bewildered westerners. Free copies of the monthly *Tourist Indonesia* newspaper. Open Mon.-Thurs. 7am-6pm. **Branch office** (tel. 510 11), at Ngurah Rai International Airport. Open 8am-6pm.

Tickets and Tours: Bali Baris Ceria, Jl. Raya Kuta 106C (tel. 755 633). As elsewhere in Denpasar, there are also numerous other options.

Immigration: Jl. I Gusti Ngurah Rai, Tuban, Kuta (tel. 751 038).

Currency Exchange: Money changers and banks galore line Jl. Legian and Jl. Pantai Kuta. Most banks close 2-4pm on weekdays and open on Sat. in the mornings only. Money changers often stay open until 9 or 10pm, but most close on Sun. **Bank Duta,** Jl. Raya Kuta 57 (tel. 753 134), has a **24-hour ATM** and accepts MC and Visa. Rp100,000 minimum withdrawal. Open Mon.-Fri. 8am-3pm. **P.T. Krishna Money Changer** (tel. 510 53), on Jl. Legian near Bank Danamon and the entrance to Poppies Lane II. Open 9am-9pm.

Post Office: GPO (tel. 754 012), on Jl. Raya Tuban, at the end of the driveway that's opposite the elementary school. Poste Restante address: Holly WOOD, or name of addressee, Jl. Raya Tuban, Kuta, Denpasar, 80361. Open Mon.-Fri. 8am-

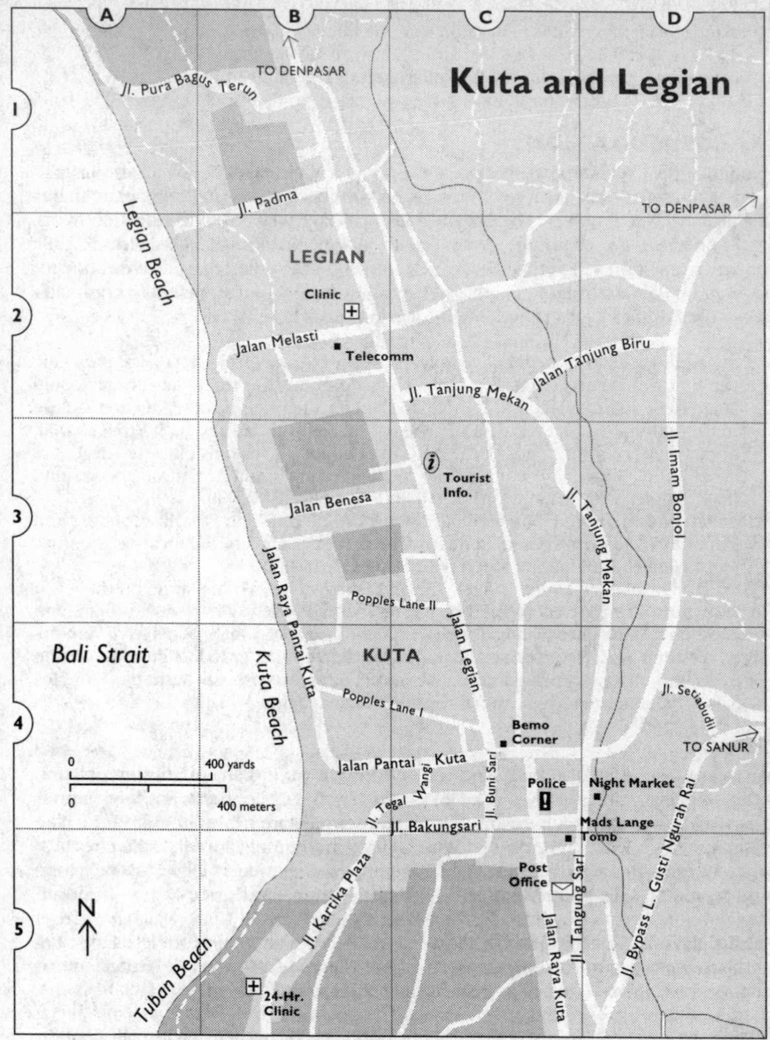

4pm, Sat. 9am-2pm, Sun. 9-11am. **Ida's Postal Agent** (tel. 751 574), Jl. Legian, Kuta, Bali 80361. At the intersection of Jl. Legian and Poppies Lane II. Poste Restante. Open Mon.-Sat. 8am-8pm.

Telephones: at the airport, and on Jl. Legian next to Peanuts Disco and near the intersection with Jl. Melasti. **Home Country Direct** with calling card. Open 24 hrs. **Telephone code:** 0361.

Airlines: Garuda Indonesia, Natour Kuta Beach Hotel, Jl. Pantai Kuta 1 (tel. 751 179). **Singapore Airlines,** Ngurah Rai Airport (tel. 751 011, ext. 2119). **Sir New Zealand,** Kartika Plaza Beach Hotel, Jl. Kartika Plaza (tel. 753 593; fax 753 592).

Bemos: Run from **Bemo Corner** along Jl. Pantai (toward the beach) to Legian. Bemos also run from east of Bemo Corner, by Jl. Tanjung Sari, to Tegal Station in Denpasar. Private bemos can be hired at Bemo Corner as well.

Car Rental: CV Bali Wisata Motor Co. (tel. 751 474), on Jl. Imam Bonjol. **Bali Car Rental Service** (tel. 288 539), on Jl. Ngurah Rai Bypass.

Laundromat: try your accommodation or hit **Windana Tailor,** Jl. Tamblingan 717X (tel. 288 717), before the Sanur Beach Hotel. Pants and shirts Rp 2000.
Emergency: Police: tel. 110. **Ambulance:** tel. 118 or 279 11.
Police: (tel. 751 598), on Jl. Raya Tuban, across from Bank Duta.

ACCOMMODATIONS

Finding a relatively inexpensive place to stay in Kuta is easy-cheesy; all you have to do is stand on a street corner with a pack on your back and wait for someone to holler "Room?! Need room!?" The cheapest *losmen* have western-style toilets, showers, and sometimes even bathtubs. Prices usually include breakfast: fruit salad and a jaffle or pancake with tea. If you've got your sights set on the quieter Legian area, look for *losmen* on Jl. Melasti and Jl. Padma. In central Kuta, low-budget places to crash cluster in the Poppies Lanes I and II area. Bargain everywhere.

Puri Agung, on Gang Bedugul. Turn onto Poppies Lane I from Jl. Legian, then take the first right. Puri Agung is a short ways down on the right. The rooms could stand to be reincarnated but they're not bad for the price and the location—close to the action, but generally out of earshot. Singles with fan and bath Rp15-20,000.

Taman Ayu, opposite Puri Agung on Gang Bedugul. 15 rooms clustered around a compound. Rooms are comparable to Puri Agung's, but are all on the ground floor. Singles with fan and bath Rp10,000. Doubles Rp15,000.

Komala Indah, on the right side of Poppies Lane I, opposite Poppies Cottages and just before the turn to Gang Bedugul. The price is right and the location is convenient. Singles and doubles Rp10,000. Triples Rp15,000.

Suci Bungalows, Jl. Pantai 25 (tel. 753 761), halfway down the street on the left if your back's to the beach. Each room has its own little porch, overhead fan, and bamboo lounge chair facing a well-manicured garden. Some rooms have reminders of their age, but they are generally attractive. Suci couldn't be more in the heart of things, which makes it convenient, but not necessarily desirable. Doubles Rp15,000, but rates are seasonal. Light breakfast included.

FOOD

All menus are in English, and Kuta's a good place to find spaghetti, burgers, and other western staples. Above the McDonald's on Jl. Legian, there is a **food emporium** with Swensen's ice cream, and Japanese, Italian, and Indonesian fare. The main streets in Kuta are crowded with tourist-oriented restaurants. The cheapest place to eat is the **night market** (on Jl. Tanjung Sari), but don't expect to be a lone visitor; many stalls and *warung* have English menus and prices a few hundred rupiah higher than elsewhere on the island. From Jl. Pantai Kuta, walk away from the beach and take your third right; the market is 100m down on your left. Low-budget *warung* are hard to come by in Kuta, but there are a few on Jl. Legian's north end, near the intersection of Jl. Pura Bagus Teruna and Jl. Legian.

Warung Kopi, Jl. Legian Tengah 427 (tel. 753 602). This place is a small nook of yummy nosh prepared under the guidance of friendly owners who studied cooking in India. South Indian pumpkin curry Rp6500. Indian buffet Wed. evening after 7pm, Rp16,000 per person with a reservation. Open 8am-11:30pm.

Kedin's Inn, on Poppies Lane I. Look for the giant yin-yang rock mosaic on the back wall. Come here for fantastic, traveler-oriented food that won't leave you with a gaping billfold. Individual cone lamps over each table, and movies in the evenings. Menu boasts vegetarian, pasta, Indian, Thai, Indonesian, and Euro food. Chicken in ginger sauce Rp6500. Free anchovies on pizza. Open 7:30am-10pm.

Café Excelso, on Jl. Legian, near Poppies Lane II. Unfriendly prices, but with avocado coffee (Rp4000), how can you resist? Egg and mushroom sandwiches Rp4700. Tinted glass tables and ice cream; popular with Europeans.

Warung Murah, Jl. Legian Kaja 85A/Basangkasa 87A, on the beach side of Jl. Legian past Jl. Bagus Teruna. Warung Murah (*murah* means cheap) serves up seafood, soups, and some Chinese and Indonesian entrees, all Rp2-5000. Long tables face the street. Super-convivial management. Open 8:30am-midnight.

Made's Warung (tel. 751 923), on Jl. Pantai Kuta just beachward of Bemo Corner. Taking great liberties with the term *warung,* guests sit at small, round tables, some on a balcony, and graze to piped jazz and the klinking of silver against china. Made's turns tables non-stop, which may explain the staff, whose wistful expressions tell the tale of the travelers' stampede through Kuta. Made's has a tome-like menu, with entrees from Rp3000 (*gado-gado*) to Rp30,000 (tuna in blue cheese). Tofu burgers (Rp5000). Open 8:30am-midnight.

ENTERTAINMENT

Kuta's nightlife turns on hours after visitors to Bali's other hot spots are dreaming of tomorrow's pried frawn. Two of the most popular clubs in Kuta are owned by the same person and alternate nights. Unless you have Solid Gold technique, you may not want to start shaking you booty until after 2am, when the crowd faucet turns on full force. In addition to being primarily pre-dawn hangouts, both **Gado-Gado** (tel. 730 955), off Jl. Dhyana Pura in Legian, and **Double Six,** slightly south (on the Kuta side) of its sibling, are popular clubs with a spectrum of nationalities, sexes, orientations, and nightly services. Gado-Gado is open Tues., Wed., and Thurs. 11:30pm-4:30am; Double Six is open Mon., Fri., and Sat., at the same time. Both have a Rp10,000 cover charge which includes a beer or soft drink. Other clubs in the central Kuta area are easy to find; just listen for the sound of velcro (popular attire with Australians, who stagger down runways and fling themselves on velcroed walls).

Peanuts Disco (tel. 754 149), on Jl. Legian. A short walk from Jl. Pantai, on the right side of the street before the BCA bank. Live band and a disco dancing area. From 8 to 10pm, beer costs Rp1250; otherwise, it's Rp2500. Open 8pm-4am.

The Bounty Club (tel. 754 040), on Jl. Legian, 300m Legian-ward of McDonald's, across from the Sol Inn. A pirate ship-cum-restaurant/bar/disco, with no cover. Small beer Rp4000. From 6 to 8pm, buy a beer and get one free. Open 8pm-3am.

Waterbom Park, Jl. Kartika Plaza, Tuban, Kuta (tel. 755 676). 5-min. walk from Bemo Corner toward the airport. Waterpark has a waterslide, tubing and a poolside restaurant. Standard ticket Rp15,000. Visa, MC. Open 9am-6pm.

Bali Bungy Co., Jl. Pura Puseh, Legian Kelod, Kuta (tel./fax 752 658). From Jl. Pantai Kuta, turn left on Jl. Legian, then right on the mainland extension of Jl. Melasti. Bali Bungy Co. is 2 blocks down, where the road bends right. Take the plunge (from a 45m tower) or watch from the Bungy Bar and Restaurant. Free pick-up service from Kuta and Sanur, videos available, and the reassurance of knowing that Bali Bungy has jumped 500,000 clients without an accident. Open 9am-late.

■■■ UBUD

Most travelers to Ubud end up staying days, months, or years longer than they'd planned. In addition to the quality budget food and accommodations and the relaxed atmosphere here, there are enough activities to tire Sophia Scott. Your options include art galleries, beautiful walks through *sawah,* dance performances, *gamelan* lessons, temples, royal bathing pools, and make-your-own *batik*...not to mention shopping. Ubud's main streets are corridors of textile, silver, handicraft, painting, and woodcarving shops, and the majority of travelers walk the town laden with bulging shopping bags. Touted as Bali's cultural center, the city has become home to a growing number of artists' communities and foreigners studying dance, music, and painting. Although the number of tourist-oriented facilities has multiplied exponentially in recent years, development seems to be under control—Ubud is still a far cry from Kuta. Instead of discos and McDonald's, this city offers its visitors Inner Power courses and vegetarian-friendly restaurants. There are a few busy roads, but smaller streets to the north, east, and west, particularly along the Ayung River, wander through quiet villages and beautiful green stretches of *sawah.*

ORIENTATION

Ubud's main drag, **Jalan Raya Ubud,** runs north-south to the town's most touristed area, where it turns and continues east-west; most other major roads are perpendicular to it. South of Jl. Raya Ubud on the west side of town, **Jalan Monkey Forest** (also traveler-oriented) runs alongside the **pasar** (market) to Ubud's **monkey forest.** There it U-turns and becomes **Jalan Hanoman,** which leads back onto Jl. Raya Ubud, east of the market. Farther east, parallel to Jl. Monkey Forest and Jl. Hanoman, are **Jalan Sugriwa, Jalan Jembawan** (the **post office road**), **Jalan Tebe/Saya/Sukma,** and, at the top of the hill, **Jalan Raya Peliatan,** which heads south and then east, where it intersects the road to Denpasar. North of Jl. Raya Ubud, Jl. Raya Peliatan becomes **Jalan Raya Andong/Tegalalang,** which runs past the **police station** and the **telecom office** toward Kintamani. North of Jl. Raya Ubud, from west to east, are **Jalan Kajang** (bordering the **Museum Puri Lukisan**), **Jalan Suweta** (opposite Jl. Monkey Forest), **Jalan Sri Wedari** (opposite Jl. Hanoman), **Jalan Sandat** (opposite Jl. Sugriwa), **Jalan Tirta Tawar, Jalan Jerogandung,** and Jl. Raya Andong/Tegalalang.

Ubud's Mangy Worm-eaten Hellhounds

In addition to being a magnet for tourists, Ubud is also the **Hairless, Lame, and Crusty Dog Capital of the World.** Particularly at night on poorly lit roads, dogs will howl, bark, and trot after you until you pass the house they are attached to. Do not pet unpredictable dogs (even ones with fur) and avoid capricious bitches with rabid pups. You will find that most of the aggressive barkers are actually pathetically wimpy. If a dog barks at your heels, bend down as if to pick up a rock, fake a throw, or, if this doesn't make them scram, really throw a rock. Of course, 0.1% of the time this will send the unreasonable muts into a mindless rage that can only be quenched with blood and scabby gore. Shining a light into the dog's snot-filled eyes may be enough to shut them up. In general, walk assertively, carry a rock if it makes you feel better, and don't let them smell your fear.

PRACTICAL INFORMATION

Tourist Information Centers: Ubud does not have an official office (the closest one is in Gianyar), but private info centers offer shuttles, car and bike rentals, dance performance tickets, tours, and Balinese boyfriends. **Ubud Tourist Information** (tel. 962 85), on Ubud's main drag, has a message board, performance schedule, trekking, and meditation class info. Open daily 8am-9pm. Some agencies sell tickets for public events such as cremations. Don't pay for a public event (like a temple ceremony) that, with a little research, you can get to on your own.

Police Station: (tel. 975 316) opposite the telecom center on Jl. Raya Andong.

Currency/Exchange: Most **money changers** open daily 8:30am-8pm.

Post Office: With the market on your right, walk until your 4th right; it's 30m from the main road. Check for Poste Restante under the first letter of your last and first names. Large envelopes and packages are filed separately from the regular Poste Restante. Newly arrived Poste Restante sits unfiled for 24 hours. Send letters to Scabby DOG (or name of addressee), Poste Restante, Jl. Jembawan 1, Ubud 80571. Open Mon.-Thurs. 8am-noon and 1-4pm, Fri. 8-11:30am and 1-4pm.

Telephones: 24-hr. Home Country Direct booths at the post office, the main Ubud market, and the telecom center opposite the police station. **Nomad Telecommunication Service,** Jl. Raya Ubud 33x (tel. 975 520; fax 975 115), next door to Nomad Restaurant on the 2nd floor, is quieter but more expensive. Local and collect calls for a charge. Fax service. Open daily 8am-11pm. **Telephone code:** 0361. **Information:** tel. 118.

Public Transport: Bemos hang in front of the market from before dawn until dusk. Brown bemos head toward **Batubulan** terminal (Rp1000). The last bemo from Batubulan to Ubud leaves between 4 and 5pm. Orange bemos head to **Gianyar** (Rp800), and blue bemos head to **Sukawati** and **Payangan;** check the names on the front and sides for bemo routes. Bemos coming from Batubulan turn off before the market onto Jl. Hanoman, and then turn right at the soccer field, looping back toward the *pasar* on Jl. Monkey Forest.

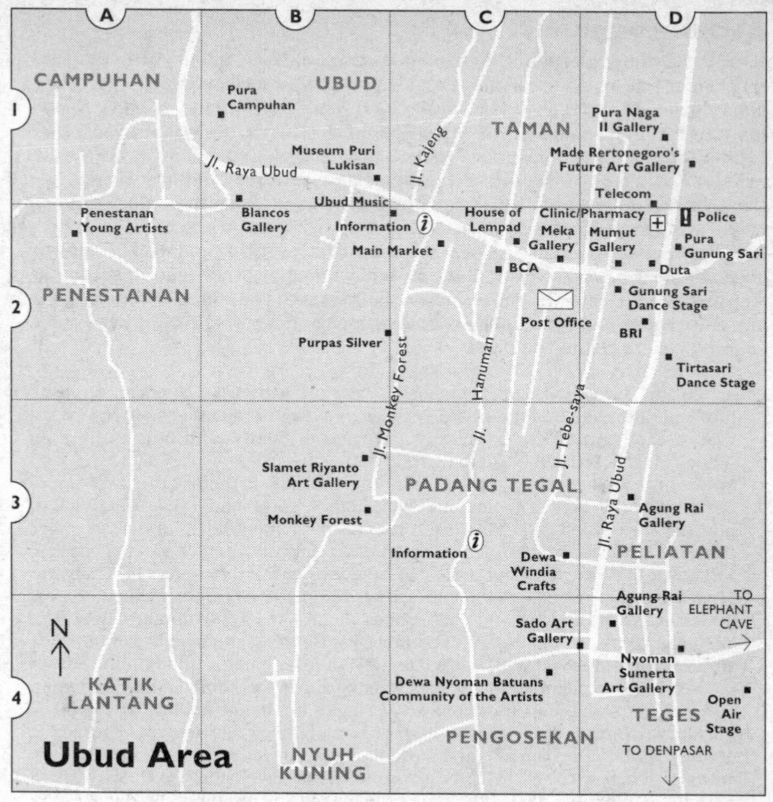

Private Transport: Hire vehicles from the corner of Jl. Raya Ubud and Jl. Monkey Forest; bargain to the bone and use the walking-away tactic. "Shuttle bus" services are offered by tourist info centers, travel agencies, and some homestays. Many stores advertise times and fares to destinations such as the airport/Sanur/Kuta (Rp5000), Kintamani/Lovina (Rp6-11,000), Candi Dasa/Padangbai (Rp6000).

Rental: Most tourist info offices rent cars, bikes, and motorbikes. Prices are negotiable. **Sinta,** Jl. Raya Ubud 14 (tel. 962 85), near the market. Open daily 9am-9pm. Sedans Rp40,000 per day, with insurance Rp50,000; motorbikes Rp10,000, with insurance Rp15,000; push bikes Rp3-5000. (All prices for 12 hrs.)

Bookstores: Ganesha, new and used books, Indonesian language books, new age trinkets, jewelry and musical instruments (*gamelan* lessons available). Open daily 9am-6pm. **The Ubud Bookshop,** Jl. Raya Ubud 7X (near Ganesha). Coffee table books on Indonesia. *Newsweek, Time, The Herald Tribune, USA Today,* and other daily papers. Open daily 8:30am-8:30pm.

Library: At Pondok Pekak, behind the football field. Excellent, privately run resource center. Useful for travelers curious about Balinese and Indonesian culture. Message board, low-cost book borrowing, 60-80% buy-back rates, and an ingenious water refill service.

Market: At the corner of Jl. Raya Ubud and Jl. Monkey Forest. Sales of fruits and vegetables begin before dawn. Livestock sold every 3 days. Clothes, hardware, offerings, handicrafts, and more. Stalls open 7am until evening, some until 11pm.

Pharmacy: Ubud Farma (tel. 974 214), on Jl. Raya Ubud, opposite the post office. Open daily 8am-10pm. Clinic open Mon.-Sat. 5-7pm.

ACCOMMODATIONS

Ubud has the best selection of accommodations on the island. Prices have risen over the last few years, but are bargainable and generally an excellent value—particularly in the "quiet season" (Jan.-Feb., April-May, and Sept.-Nov.), when prices fall. Ubud's mid-range accommodations tend to have pools, woodwork, hot water, and views of *sawah (*rice paddies). Low-priced rooms are similar, with private baths, showers, twin beds, and fans. Most prices include breakfast. Beware of hustlers who bargain for a price, and then add a Rp1000 per night tax. Some "homestays" do not have a family living in them, but are managed by employees and overseen by an owner who lives elsewhere. These *losmen* lack the chickens, small children, and early-to-bed-early-to-rise characteristics of a true family homestay; they tend to accommodate more guests. Families may be more willing to teach you about ceremonial offerings and expose you to the family craftwork. Many homestays have the head of the family's profession listed on them.

Rice Paddy Bungalows, Jl. Hanoman 55, near the end of Jl. Hanoman, opposite the Three Brothers Restaurant. Rooms have one large bed and hot water, making this an excellent value. Owned by a gregarious family with one son in high school. Singles Rp10,000. Doubles Rp20,000.

Taman Indah Homestay, on Jl. Sandat, the second left (before the post office) from the market. Three rooms sit behind homes, cows, and 5-year-olds trying to ride 10-speed bikes. Follow the signs that claim "Taman Indah, in ricefield, very peaceful." Indeed, Taman Indah is quiet and removed from Ubud's main hustle and bustle. The owner is not usually in, so guests check themselves in. Prices are posted and the owner's absence forecloses the possibility of bargaining. Rooms have fans, mosquito nets, and double beds. Singles Rp10,000, doubles Rp15,000, including breakfast, but not 10% tax. Bikes, motorbikes, and laundry service.

Taman Bunga Homestay, Jl. Sri Wedari, 250m from Jl. Raya Ubud on the left up the hill. Don't be alarmed by the cats walking above the bamboo ceilings. Quiet, near rice fields and few other homestays. Singles Rp10,000; doubles Rp15,000.

Ngurah Homestay, Jl. Sri Wedari 20, past Taman Bunga on the right. 3 attractive rooms with *batik* bedspreads and mosquito nets. Singles and doubles Rp15,000.

Taman Cottages (tel. 964 77). Past Ngurah Homestay farther up Jl. Sri Wedari. After the bend in the road at the top of the hill, it's the 3rd house on the left, bordering a rice field. Four bungalows facing a pond with lily pads. The river runs behind the houses. Bungalows Rp20-30,000. Discount for long stays.

Warsa's II, Jl. Jembangan 70, at the far corner where it makes a 90° turn toward Jl. Hanoman. Warsa's has some of the nicest rooms in its vicinity. Large, new rooms with porch areas that face a garden. Showers but no sinks. Good breakfasts and tour, rental, and shuttle service. Managed by two hard-working young chaps. Singles Rp15,000; doubles Rp20,000. In the quieter months, singles Rp8000; doubles Rp12,000. Prices do not include 10% tax.

Sulendra, next door to Warsa's. The home of a painter. Rooms are snug and bamboo-lined, some with balconies. Same prices as Warsa's.

Wang Bang, Jl. Tebe Saya/Sukma 61, at the far end of the road on the left. Two simple guest rooms with white brick walls and low beds. Owned by a sweet family. Singles Rp8000. Doubles Rp12,000.

Pande Permai Bungalows (tel. 975 436), on Jl. Monkey Forest, at the end of the road on the right, before the Monkey Forest on the hill. Rooms are spotless, have hot water, and some have a view of *sawah.* A pool is in the works, so prices may rise. Singles Rp25,000. Doubles 30,000.

FOOD

When Ubud's night market closed two years ago, low-cost *warung* scattered to the streets off the main drags, where owners are happy to see a foreign mug. Jl. Raya Ubud and Jl. Monkey Forest have mid-range restaurants and several classy, atmospheric eateries. Ubud's most popular **supermarket** is **Tino,** on Jl. Raya Ubud. From Jl. Monkey Forest, turn left onto Jl. Raya Ubud; Tino is on the left. Open 8am-10pm.

Dewi Mas Market is a cleaner version (tel. 975 300) on the right at the end of Jl. Hanoman, just before the fork with Jl. Monkey Forest. Open 7:30am-8pm.

Dewa Warung, on Jl. Sugriwa. From the market on your right, turn right off Jl. Raya Ubud onto Jl. Hanoman and walk until your first left turn onto the end of Jl. Jembarawa, the post office road (not the narrow alley). After about 100m, turn left onto Jl. Sugriwa, which is parallel to Jl. Hanoman. Dewa Warung is on the right, with long tables where westerners and locals rub elbows. Excellent, dirt-cheap food in a casual, fun atmosphere; eaters may play chess or the resident guitar. Indonesian entrees Rp1-1300. Try the coconut pie (Rp1000).

Shadana Vegetarian Restaurant (tel. 975 630) on Jl. Raya Ubud, opposite its intersection with Jl. Hanoman. A few dimly lit tables under sarongs and handicrafts for sale. Prices to tempt even carnivores: vegetable curry, tempeh, and tofu entrees (Rp2-3000). Passion fruit milkshake (Rp1500). Open daily 8am-9pm.

Warung Padang, on Jl. Hanoman, a few doors before the intersection with Jl. Raya Ubud, on the left. Come here if you're tired of small portions. Choose from the various dishes on display in the window (chicken, pork, vegetables, tempeh, fried potatoes) and mush it up with white rice. Wash your fingers in the bowl of water provided and eat with your right hand—it tastes better that way. Or, get your treats wrapped to go. Pay per item; a full plate is usually Rp1-2500.

The Dirty Duck (tel. 975 489), at the end of Jl. Hanoman, just before the fork with Jl. Monkey Forest. A uniformed waitstaff, glossy darkwood tables, a lily pond, and a gourmet menu. Mushroom cashew pâté (Rp4500). Gourmet vegetarian sandwich with brie cheese, eggplant, peppers, and tomatoes Rp7500. Entrees (including pasta and bratwurst) generally Rp7-10,000. Open daily 10am-10:30pm.

Three Brothers (tel. 975 525), toward the end of Jl. Hanoman, past where it intersects the skewed end of the post office road, on the left. More atmosphere than other dives with similar prices: woven bamboo walls, high A-frame ceiling with hanging palmleaf decorations, and tables on three levels. Japanese-style floor seating, soft music, and food served in baskets. *Pepes Bali* (grilled chicken with rice and coconut wrapped in a banana leaf (Rp2000). Open 7:30am-11pm daily.

Casa Luna (tel. 962 83), at the end of Jl. Raya Ubud, past the market on the left. Excellent food, and movies every night. Offers cooking classes. The cashier sits behind a counter of freshly baked bread and cakes, cheese, walnuts and other imported treats. Pumpkin and sweet potato soup (Rp2500). Open 9am-11pm

Diang's Cafe, at the end of Jl. Tebe Saya (parallel to the post office road), on the right. Indonesian basics for Rp2000. Don't miss the black rice pudding (Rp800). Menu advertises that all fruit and veggies are washed in boiled water.

Kubuku Vegetarian Restaurant, on the bend of Jl. Monkey Forest after it forks off Jl. Hanoman. On the left side of the Monkey Forest; the entrance is slightly hidden by greenery. Cushions surrounding wide, 2-foot high tables that face *sawah* create a soothing, romantic atmosphere. Entrees Rp5000. Open 9am-10pm.

SIGHTS

Lush green rice paddies, grazing cows, clucks of ducks, the Ayung River rapids, and small village life are all within km of Ubud's most crowded streets. Explore the area by push bike, which can be rented in town. The ride west on Jl. Raya Ubud and north to the **Sayang Ridge** and the **Ayung River** leads to popular views of rice paddies. Heading south of Jl. Raya Ubud toward Denpasar leads to **Mas,** a village famous for its wood carvings. Farther south, the road passes through **Sukawati's crafts market** to **Celuk,** the hub of gold and silversmithing for southern Bali, and then to **Batubulan** (literally, "moon rocks"), a center for carving statuary from stone. The brown bemos from Ubud to Batubulan travel through these villages.

The number-one sight on most travelers' "to do" list is usually Ubud's **Monkey Forest,** at the south end of Jl. Monkey Forest. The dense forest has an attractive path leading through the woods to Ubud's *pura dalem* (temple of the dead), but the entire place is overrun by an agressive horde of obese monkeys. The monkeys have been known to bite and steal loose clothing or purses out of visitors' hands. A sign at the entrance to the forest reads "For your safety it is forbidden to touch and feeding the monkey as they may spoilt either react with unpredictable manners"—keep this in mind. Admission Rp1050, kids Rp550; video camera Rp1000; camera Rp500.

Museum Puri Lukisan (tel. 975 136) is off Jl. Raya Ubud on the right, past the info center, heading toward the bridge. Several buildings in a gorgeous garden house both a permanent and a rotating collection of artwork. Drop by to see past and future trends in Balinese art. Open daily 8am-4pm. Admission Rp2000.

Goa Gajah (Elephant Cave), is one of Ubud's best-known sights. On the outside, the cave is carved into the face of a demon; the entrance is through the demon's mouth. Inside the large, dark meditation cave, visitors can peer at a stone carving of the Hindu deity Ganesha and three *linga,* or stone phalluses, representing the three gods, Brahma, Vishnu, and Siva. A large bathing pool sits outside the caves, filled from the stone jugs of carved, heavy-breasted ladies. Paths lead behind the pool and the cave to the **Petanu River.** Wear long pants and bring or rent a sash. Menstruating women are requested not to enter. It's a short ride from Ubud; take a brown bemo heading to Batubulan or bike from Jl. Raya Ubud right onto the main Peliatan Road. Follow it along the 90° turn east past the turn-off to Denpasar and Tengkulak. The cave is on the right, 4km outside of Ubud. Admission Rp1050, children Rp550; video camera Rp1000; camera Rp500. Open 7:30am-6pm.

Gunung Kawi, in Tampaksiring, is a strange and mysterious complex of tombs and a temple, built from rock in the 11th century. Visitors walk past people selling crochet and intricate coconut shell carvings down a long stone flight of stairs to an impressive rock doorway. The queens' tombs loom to the left of the stone archway and are thought to be the burial site of King Anak Wungsu's four concubines. Opposite these tombs across the river are royal tombs of the king and his four wives. On the far side of the river beside the royal tombs is a courtyard and a series of caves and rock passages, presumably cut for Buddhist priests living at Gunung Kawi. A sign by the caves requests visitors to be silent, tread lightly on the fragile stone, and remove their shoes. The rock is spattered with green, white, pink, and rust-colored moss, and pocked with dark hollows scattered with flower petals and offerings. Even better than the caves is the walk behind them through *sawah* and into jungle-like vegetation to a waterfall, a popular bathing spot. The caves are prettiest in the afternoon (4pm) or early morning light. From Ubud to Gunung Kawi, hop an orange bemo to Gianyar (Rp300), get off at the intersection where the bemo turns right, south toward Bedulu. Then take a second bemo up the hill to Gunung Kawi (Rp400). Alternatively, ride a bike to the temple. The ride is almost entirely uphill and takes about one hour. Admission Rp1050, kids Rp550; video Rp1000; camera Rp500. Dress: sarong and sash (can be rented).

ENTERTAINMENT

Gamelan, dance, and other performances are held nightly at temples and stages throughout Ubud. The Ubud Tourist Information Center (tel. 962 85), on Jl. Raya Ubud, has a comprehensive list of performances. Tickets cost Rp5000 and are sold via the info center, tour agencies, or on the street. Shows start at 7 or 7:30pm; if you walk the streets, particularly at dusk, you will invariably be asked if you want to see a show. Legong dance, *wayang kulit,* and the *kecak* (kay-CHAK) performance, where men's repeated "chak-chak-chak-ing" composes the percussive background music for a Rama and Sita dance, are particularly worth seeing. The Ganesha Bookstore (tel. 963 59) on Jl. Raya Ubud has **gamelan lessons** on Tuesdays from 6-7:30pm for Rp15,000. **Balinese dance courses** are offered at Dewi Sekar Ayu 26, on Jl. Hanoman. With your back to Jl. Dewi Sita, where it intersects Jl. Hanoman, turn right and walk about 100m; Dewi Sekar Ayu is on the left. **Batik courses** and materials can be explored through the Crackpot, on Jl. Monkey Forest. With the football field on your left, the Crackpot is 100m beyond the field on the left. Design your own t-shirt or cushion cover for Rp25,000. Open 9am-8pm. The Meditation Shop, on Jl. Monkey Forest, 400m from the Monkey Forest, on the right if you're walking from the football field, offers **free meditation workshops.** Stop by for details or join the evening meditation 6-7pm. Open daily 5-9:30pm. **Sukadana,** in the middle of Jl.

Jembawan on the left if walking from the post office, offers Balinese and Indonesian language courses. **Bali Adventure Tours** (tel. 751 292 or 262 316; fax 754 334), Jl. Tunjung Mekar, Legian Kelod, leads rafting trips on Ubud's Ayung River for US$56.

■ NEAR UBUD

BESAKIH

Gunung Agung, called Bali's navel, is the most imposing volcano and most revered mountain on the island. Besakih, a dark and holy spot on the navel, is thought of as Bali's mother temple—it's an enormous complex of at least 22 smaller temples, each representing a Hindu god and a district in Bali. From the entrance to the temple, visitors walk up a hill past sarongs, fruit, handicrafts, and sashes (Rp2000) toward a long flight of stairs and the giant, black, split-entry gate to the main temple. Although you can wander around the temples, you may not be allowed to enter unless you intend to pray. But don't be scared away—"praying" is loosely interpreted and mostly has to do with form and the showing of respect.

The best time to visit Besakih is during one of its *odalan,* or birthdays. Ask at the tourist information office for the exact date, as they correspond to the unique Balinese calendar. If you are not visiting Besakih during a holiday, or if you are not interested in Balinese religion and symbolism, you may be disappointed by the temple complex. On a regular day, when Besakih is crowded with tourists, cameras, and clouds that obscure the view of Mt. Agung, it may be hard to appreciate the temple's enormous importance to Balinese people. No matter when you visit, be very wary of "tour guides"—announced or not—who attach themselves to you and ask to be paid Rp30,000 or more after a five-minute "tour" of the complex. Be firm

Temple Etiquette in Bali

Participating in rituals is a great way to get a feel for Balinese life. Most Balinese enjoy teaching westerners about their religion; they realize that prayer in a *pura* can be educational rather than religious. When you enter the temple, kneel or sit cross-legged before the covered tables and colored parasols. A *pemanku* (lay priest) will bring you incense and a *canang sari* (offering), a palm leaf box filled with flowers. Close your eyes and raise your pressed palms to your forehead twice. Repeat this three more times, but with flower petals between your fingertips. Notice which color petals others in the temple choose; each color symbolizes a god. Then hold out your open palms as the *pemanku* sprinkles you with *tirtha* (holy water). Next, cup your hands (right over left) and slurp three times from the *tirtha* that he or she pours in. The fourth time the *pemanku* pours *tirtha* in your hands, splash it on your head; the fifth time on your face. (*Tirtha*—fresh spring water sanctified by a high priest and mixed with flower petals—is extremely important to Balinese Hinduism; sipping and washing with it is a symbol of prayer's effect on the spirit. Do not ask whether it has been boiled.) The *pemanku* will give you wet rice grains to press onto your forehead and throat, or may press them for you. Finally, he or she will hand you a flower. Break it in two and place each half behind an ear by crossing your arms before you; the flower in your right hand goes behind the left ear, and vice-versa.

In all Balinese temples, dress modestly (no shorts or bare shoulders) and wear a sash. If possible, wear a sarong and have a Balinese person help you tie it (men and women wear them differently). Never walk in front of a person who is praying or take flash photos at a ceremony. Balinese Hindus in mourning are not allowed to enter temples for several days; the loss of a loved one is seen as a distraction that hinders the ability to be open and empty—a state necessary to be receptive to god. People bleeding or menstruating are also seen as distracted and requested to not enter temples. As one priest explained, "If a western woman is brave enough to enter a temple while she is bleeding, how will I know? I can't sniff her out; I'm only human. But if it were me, I wouldn't be brave enough."

and up front about the fact that you will not be handing out rupiah. The entrance ticket to Besakih is Rp1000; you are then requested to make a donation and sign a guest book. Open 6:30am-6pm. To get to Besakih on public transport, take an early morning bemo from Ubud or Batubulan station to Gianyar (Rp800), then to Klunkung (Rp1000), then to Besakih, sometimes with a stop/change at Rendang. Tour groups also go daily but may cost as much as Rp20,000 or more.

■■■ MOUNT BATUR

Present-day Mt. Batur (Gunung Batur), in northeast Bali, is only the stub of the original Batur volcano, which erupted centuries ago, leaving the mountain (1717m) and its companion crater lake, Lake Batur. Inside the giant crater was the village of Batur. A tremendous eruption in 1917 killed over 1000 people, and destroyed 65,000 homes and 2000 temples, but the lava halted at the foot of Batur village's temple—a seemingly good omen. The village remained until another disastrous eruption in 1926 destroyed everything but the highest temple shrine. Partly thanks to the Dutch administration's foresight and evacuation of the village, few lives were lost in the second eruption, and the villagers agreed to relocate to the outer west rim. Second only to Gunung Agung in importance, Gunung Batur, the clear crater lake, and the gorgeous landscape around this area are well-touristed and accommodate a steady flow of visitors, most of whom stay for only a day or two.

GETTING THERE AND AWAY

To reach the Batur area, take a public bemo to Kintamani, on the west side of the crater. From there, take bemos if you're traveling before late afternoon. Alternatively, hire a motorcycle taxi. *Ojek* drivers are bound to spot you if you're walking dazedly with a pack on your back. If public transport is not your cup of Kopi Bali, consider private shuttle bus service to Penelokan (or Kintamani) and stay there—otherwise, bemo-it or hop (or charter) an *ojek* toward the lake and the nicest scenery and accommodations. The privately run tourist info office on Tirta's main street has "shuttle" buses to Lovina (10:30am, Rp12,500), Ubud (10:30am and noon, Rp8000), Candi Dasa (10:30am and noon, Rp12,500), and Sanur/Kuta (10:30am and noon, Rp17,500). Inquire about the bus routes; most are indirect. To get public bemos to those locations from Tirta, stand facing the mountain and take a bemo to Penelokan (Rp500-1000). From Penelokan, large buses leave for Singaraja (Rp1500), Amlapura, and Denpasar. Public transport is more frequent in the morning.

ACCOMMODATIONS AND FOOD

Accommodations—along with hot springs, and hikes leading up Gunung Batur—can be found in several villages around the crater, including Kedisan, at the south tip of the lake, and Tirta on the west side. **Tirta** (also called Toyabungkah) is an easy location to start the pre-dawn hike up Batur for sunrise, and its public, hot spring bathing areas (for Rp1000) are near a variety of accommodations and the cool lake.

Low and middle range accommodations line Tirta's main drag and Lake Batur. Places near the lake have better views of the clean, clear water and cost more. **Darma Putra Homestay,** on the left side of the road just after Tirta village begins, has singles with bath for Rp7500, and doubles for Rp12,000. Breakfast included. **Awangga Bungalows,** farther along the road on the lake, has slightly less well-kept rooms but it faces the water. Singles with bath Rp7500. Doubles Rp10,000. Singles with bath and hot water, Rp15,000. Doubles Rp25,000. Breakfast included.

Tirta's restaurants all serve the local specialty—grilled fish—for comparable prices. **Arlina's** (tel. (3066) 511 65), next to Darma Putra on the main drag, has a mean grilled fish with garlic and lemon for Rp2000.

DOIN' THE MOUNTAIN

Most people climb Batur before dawn, so the sweaty are rewarded with sunrise breaking over the crater. Trekking up lava for 2 hrs. in the dark can be frustrating, however, and though the sunrise *looks* warm and fuzzy, it won't necessarily make you and your scratched knees feel that way. If you have a flashlight and the desire to rise at 4am, hike pre-dawn. If not, you will miss one of many sunrises but will gain a better appreciation for Batur's unique terrain. At any time of day, you will get endless demands to "guide" you (i.e., show you the way) up the mountain. If you don't want to go alone, consider hiring a guide for no more than Rp5000. But even in the dark, if your torch is strong, the path is not hard to find. If in doubt, pause for a bit and wait for a guided group to head your way. Guides get annoyed at freeloaders, so make your "waterbreaks" (that just happen to be at forks in the path) discreet.

To begin hiking from where the lake laps Tirta's main drag, face the mountain and walk left to the yellow sign for Kawasan Toyobungkah on the side of the road. Opposite this sign is one for Tampurhyang. If you're alone, the sure-fire path is by these road signs at the entrance to Tirta. If it forks, disregard Frost and take the most trodden branch, through gardens and corn crops, until you hit the woods, where a temple sits on the right. One hundred meters farther (hard to see if it's dark), the path crosses a smaller one; turn left, off the wide path. (If you miss the turn, you'll emerge from the woods and pass another, smaller temple on your right. You may be able to reach the top on this path, but hikers report that the route is less clear.) After turning left, stick with the path for about 45 minutes until the trees stop and the terrain turns to volcanic rock, sand, and ash. From here, there are no real "paths," so don't worry too much about following other groups. The way to go is up. At the peak, repose on benches in ramshackle *warung* set up to tempt you with hot drinks (Rp2000). The top can be chilly in the mornings, especially if you're sweaty; bring a pack with water, snacks, and extra clothes. Also, wear your sturdiest shoes. Barring any mishaps Teva-style sandals will do, but it's nice to have socks to keep your feet warm and prevent volcanic ash from lodging beneath your toenails.

Be sure not to miss Batur's most recent earthworks. Great gusts of villainous steam pour through vents in the newer, more active areas at the top where the ground is cankered with crusts of yellow sulfur. Incredible photo-ops—real Gates of Hell material! Just be careful not to get too close to foul, stinging vapors or slide down the fine volcanic soil and into the gaping craters. If arriving after 8-9am, you'll have the whole place to yourself to explore.

■■■ SINGARAJA

Singaraja, on the north coast of Bali, is not a tourist hot spot, but it is the closest major town and bus connection to the popular Lovina beaches. During the Dutch occupation, Singaraja was the capital of Bali and a prominent shipping port. The city is no longer an important trading post, but it is the capital of the Buleleng regency. Though Singaraja is clean, well-organized, and hospitable, most tourists head to the more tempting resorts southwest of Singaraja. Minutes away by public bemo, Singaraja is where visitors can find those big city necessities. The over-beached can explore the Gedong Kertya Historical Library, one of Singaraja's few claims to fame.

ORIENTATION

The commercial district centers around **Jalan A. Yani,** which runs southwest-northeast. Intersecting Jl. A. Yani and running northwest-southeast through town are **Jalan Ngurah Rai/Jalan Pramuka** and **Jalan Gajah Mada,** both of which begin at the Singaraja Harbor. On the south side of the city, both Jl. A. Yani and Jl. Gajah Mada cross **Jalan Veteran,** home to the library, the tourist office, and the market.

PRACTICAL INFORMATION

Tourist Office: Dinas Pariwisata, Jl. Veteran 23 (tel. 251 41), where the road crosses Jl. A. Yani on the city's south side. From Banyuasri station, take a yellow bemo. Free map of Singaraja and Lovina and a brochure about the Buleleng regency. Open Mon.-Fri. 7am-3pm.

Currency Exchange: BCA Bank (tel. 237 61), on the south side of Jl. A. Yani (on the right from the Banyuasri terminal). Cash from Visa and MC, Rp5000 charge. Open Mon.-Fri. 8am-2pm, Sat. 8am-noon.

Post office: Jl. Gajah Mada 156, at the intersection with Jl. A. Yani. Poste Restante address: Holly HOBBY (or name of addressee) Kantor Pos, Poste Restante, Jl. Gajah Mada 156, Singaraja 81113. Open Mon.-Thurs. 8am-noon and 1-4pm, Fri. 8am-noon and 1:30-4pm, Sat. 9am-noon.

Telephones: Wartel Kopegtel, Jl. Gajah Mada 154, near the post office. Collect or cash international calls. Open 24 hrs. **Telephone code:** 0362.

Flights: Garuda Airlines, on the north side of Jl. A. Yani, just west of the river.

Public Transportation: Banyuasri terminal, on Jalan A. Yani on the west edge of town. **Bemos** shuttle between Singaraja's terminals. To: **Lovina** (Rp500). **Regular minibuses** leave Banyuasri for **Gilimanuk** (Rp2500) and **Denpasar. Sangket terminal** (also known as **Sukasada**), at the south end of Singaraja, has buses to: **Denpasar** (Rp3000); **Bedugul/Lake Bratan** (Rp1500); and **Gigit Waterfall** (Rp1000). **Penarukan terminal,** on Jl. Surapati on the east side of town, has buses to: **Amlapura** (Rp3000); **Kintamani** (Rp3000); **Klungkung** (Rp3000); and **Sanih Beach** (Rp1500). City bemos cost Rp500: Banyuasri to Sangket is yellow, Sangket to Banyuasri is red, Penarukan to Sangket is blue, Penarukan to Banyuasri is green or brown. Buses and bemos die out after 6pm.

Market: Buleleng market, at the corner of Jl. Veteran/Jl. Semeru and Jl. Gajah Mada/Jl. Mayor Metra.

English Bookstore: Indra Jaya Bookstore, Jl. Diponegoro 30 (tel. 223 31), has a smattering of English-language books.

24-hour pharmacy: Wijaya Kusuma Apotik, Jl. Ngurah Rai 23 (tel. 228 90).

Hospital: Kertha Usada, Jl. A. Yani 108 (tel. 223 96).

Emergency: Police: tel. 110. **Ambulance:** tel. 118.

Police: on Jl. Pramuka (the north end of Jl. Ngurah Rai), just south of Jl. A. Yani.

ACCOMMODATIONS AND FOOD

Most travelers stay in Lovina, where the competition between hotels is steeper, raising the quality of accommodations. **Losmen Duta Karya,** Jl. A. Yani 59 (tel. 214 67), is down the street from Hotel Gelar Sari, 10 minutes from Banyuasri. Basic rooms face a garden of sorts and would be relaxing if street sounds didn't travel. Singles Rp10,000. Doubles with bath and fan Rp15,000. Breakfast included. Singaraja's food options are limited, but try **Pasar Senggol,** Singaraja's night market, on the small road opposite the police station on Jl. Pramuka/Ngurah Rai (open 7-11pm).

SIGHTS

Singaraja's pura dalem (temple of the dead), on Jl. Gajah Mada, is at street level, below the crematory (where bodies are kept until they can be cremated) with a wall of fantastic reliefs depicting Balinese heaven *(sorga)* and hell *(nraka)* and the consequences of earthly behavior. The scenes of *nraka* are graphic and gross: people having their arms sawed off and tongues pulled out, or being boiled, beaten, and pitted against each other just as the Balinese set their game cocks against each other.

The **Gedong Kertya,** Jl. Veteran 20 (tel. 226 45), next door to the tourist office, keeps the world's largest collection of palm leaf manuscripts on its crowded and dusty shelves. Hindu priests, scholars, and students come to the library to consult its volumes of ancient Balinese literature and drawings. Visitors can examine the stylus tools used to inscribe the *lontar,* books made of strips of palm tied between two ruler-like pieces of wood. Donation requested.

■■■ LOVINA

Compared to south Bali's beach resorts, Lovina is quiet and relaxed, closer perhaps to the imagined holidays of Bali's vacationers: calm blue waters, dolphins, and fabulous, technicolor sunsets. The sand, however, is lava black, making romantic midday barefoot strolls a challenge. And though the beach-patrolling youths in Lovina are a distant relation to the in-your-face hawkers of Kuta, attaching yourself to a walkman will not stop them from lifting an earphone to ask if you want to see Lovina's dolphins. The city's short dark beaches and shallow waters may, in the end, protect the area from developing into the next Kuta or Sanur.

ORIENTATION

The Lovina beaches are a short bemo ride southwest of Singaraja, facing the Bali Sea. The area is 8km of sand, divided into three regions: **Temukus, Kalibukbuk,** and **Anturan.** The main **Seririt-Singaraja Road** runs close to the shore in the Temukus and Kalibukbuk areas, and forks off in the Anturan area, so that most accommodations in the east section are along small roads that run north-south from the shore, and are not visible from the main road.

PRACTICAL INFORMATION

Tourist and Police Office: On the beach side of the main Seririt-Singaraja Rd. in Kalibukbuk. Well-organized with helpful employees. Open Mon.-Sat. 8am-8pm.

Postal Agent: (tel. 413 92) On the main drag. Open 8am-6pm.

Telephones: (tel. 411 01), beachside, on the main road in the Temukus area. Open 9am-11pm. **Telephone code:** 0362.

Currency Exchange: Several money changers, some of which offer better rates than the banks in Singaraja. The money changer at the *wartel* is open 9am-5pm.

Transportation: In addition to the bemos and buses available to and from Singaraja, tour agencies along Lovina's main drag offer "shuttle bus" service to popular tourist destinations around Bali. To: **Denpasar/Kuta** (Rp12,000); **Ubud** (Rp15,000); and **Candi Dasa** (Rp15,000).

Rental: Various tour agencies and accommodations rent at the following seasonally variable rates: **car rental** Rp60,000-190,000 per day, **motorbike rental** Rp10,000 for 12 hrs., **bicycle rental** Rp5000 for 12 hrs.

ACCOMMODATIONS

Lovina is chock-full of backpacker-friendly and mid-range accommodations. All are near the beach. Lovina has almost as many mosquitoes as it has restless, long-haired gigolos. Think mosquito nets and coils when deliberating over where to park your pack. Most places in the Lovina area jack up prices during high season (June-August), so think of the prices below as a guide instead of as set in stone.

Manggala Holiday Inn (tel. 413 71), a few doors west of Purnama. The oldest *losmen* in town, run by a charming Balinese couple. The more expensive rooms have individual Balinese names. Room prices Rp10,000-20,000. Restaurant (the popular fish in ginger and oyster sauce is Rp3000). Check-out 1pm.

Purnama, on the beach side of the main road at the Kalibukbuk/Temukus border, 100m from the beach. Rooms sit behind the masters' quarters, have contact-paper-covered concrete floors, and could use a paint job. But the partially outdoor *mandis* are pleasant, and if you're around in the afternoon, you can join the owners in a round of radio-stimulated living room aerobics. Rooms with fan and bath Rp10,000, Rp9000 in the quiet months, but bargainable. Breakfast included.

Janur's Dive Inn (tel. 410 56), in Kalibukbuk. From the main road, heading toward Singaraja, turn left after the RRI tower and KJ Siwa Bungalows onto the small street leading to the beach. The Dive Inn is at the beach end of the road on the right. The *mandis* are extravagantly "landscaped" with rock and carved clay walls. Restaurant with a cheap menu; entrees Rp2000. Doubles with bath and fan Rp10,000; off-season Rp8000. Breakfast included.

Mas Bungalows and Restaurant (tel. 417 73), on the same street as Janur's, toward the road. Simple rooms. Enormous bathrooms. Doubles Rp15,000.

FOOD

Mid-range restaurants crowd the main drag and beach-side streets in the central Kalibukbuk area. Dirt-cheap prices are harder to find; keep an eye out for the few *warung* in the area or make an excursion to the **night market** (Pasar Senggol), in Singaraja. **Puri Taman Lovina,** Jl. Pantai Binaria Rte. IV, Kalibukbuk (tel. 411 91) has friendly owners, tables set up on concrete, and good food. Entrees Rp2-4000.

SIGHTS AND ENTERTAINMENT

Lovina has reasonable **snorkeling** opportunities. Equipment and a guide for the afternoon can be hired at the beach or your *losmen* for Rp15,000. On the beach, you can rent a **sailboat** (with sailor) for Rp15,000 per person. **Morning dolphin sighting** trips are two to three hours and cost Rp10,000 per person. If no dolphins are seen, the disappointed pay half price. **Scuba diving** lessons are available through the **Permai Diving School** (tel. 414 71).

Malibu Club (tel. 416 71), on the main road in Kalibukbuk. Has a bored-looking reggae band that plays the same music every night. See the incongruous decor: disco ball, pool table, Bob Marley paraphernalia, and visitors of all shades who can't dance. The owner struts around the place in skin-tight trousers. The Malibu Restaurant has Chinese food, baked goodies, pizza, and vegetarian entrees for Rp4-8000. Open 8am-noon and 7pm-2am.

■■■ CANDI DASA

Only a few years back, Candi Dasa was a well-kept secret of ex-pats and long-time travelers in the know, but now its main drag is wall-to-wall hotels, restaurants, money changers and tour agencies, most of which are younger than the average life span of Balinese flip-flops. Such turbo-development has left Candi Dasa with some kinks to iron out. Many of Candi Dasa's staff members seem as though they're in a permanent bad mood. In a place where the good ol' days were only last year, locals have a right to be disgruntled, or at least bewildered. Candi Dasa's second shortcoming is its beach, which is not really a beach at all, but a wall of black stone that shelters the hotels from the lapping tides. At low tide, you can stroll reasonably well along the shore, though not without getting your feet wet.

ORIENTATION

Candi Dasa is on the east coast of Bali in the Karangasem Regency. The touristed area consists of one main road, which stretches for 1km toward Amlapura. The south side of the road is dotted with accommodations; the north side is strung with restaurants. The village is bordered on the south by the crescent-shaped **Amuk Bay,** and on the north by hilly green rice terraces. The slime-covered **Candi Dasa Lagoon** is on the sea side of main road at its east end.

PRACTICAL INFORMATION

Tourist Office: No official office, but you'll pass dozens of "tourist information" signs on the main road.

Currency Exchange: Money changer at the west end of the main road, on the ocean side, next door to the Calypso Diving School. Open 8am-7pm.

Postal Agent: At the west end of the road on the mainland side. Open Mon.-Fri. 8am-9pm. Nearest official post office is in Amplapura.

Telephones: (tel. 413 32). The *wartel* is a few doors east of the postal agent. Home Country Direct, Rp2500. Open 8am-11pm. **Telephone code:** 0363.

Local Transport: Bemos head toward Amlapura, where you can catch buses to other major cities. "Shuttle" bus companies abound, of which **Perama** is the king. The Perama central office is on the mainland side at the west end. Perama buses leave daily for the Denpasar/Kuta/Sanur/airport area (Rp10,000), Ubud (Rp7500), Lovina/Singaraja (Rp15,000), Padangbai, and Kintamani (Rp15,000). For certain routes you can buy an open ticket that allows you to stop off in a city on the buses' journey for as long as you like before resuming your trip.

Rental: Many accommodations and tour agents rent bikes and beach equipment. **Dewa Bharata Bungalow's** tourist info service (tel. 410 90) rents push bikes for Rp5000, motorbikes for Rp15,000, and snorkel equipment for Rp10,000.

Books: Several used book traders and sellers line the main street. **Gandhi Ashram** (tel. 411 08) has a reading room by the slime-infested lagoon. Most are in English: history, children's fiction, and Mahatma Gandhi's own works. Open 8am-4pm.

Swimming: The Park Resort Candi Dasa Hotel (tel. 413 73), at the far east end of the beach (Rp4000; 1 drink included).

Police: tel. 110. At the west end of the main road, on the north side.

ACCOMMODATIONS

Dewi Bungalows, on the Amlapura side of the slime-covered lagoon. Despite slightly ominous "silence is the best time for our brain" signs posted around the grounds, Dewi Bungalows is attractive, light, and managed by friendly employees who may offer to practice yoga with you. Individual bungalows with their own porch and *mandi.* The light comes through tiny holes in the woven bamboo walls in the mornings, and each bungalow faces a yard/garden area. Singles Rp7000. Doubles Rp10,000. Breakfast included.

Geringsing Homestay (tel. 410 84), near the police station and the Perama Bus service. Romantic, bamboo-lined rooms joined to partially outdoor *mandis,* some with views of the mountain rising in the background. Traditional *ikat*-woven curtains, a garden linking the rooms, and an antique shop in front. Singles Rp8-9000. Doubles Rp12,000. All have mosquito nets and baths. Breakfast included.

Pondok Bamboo Cottages (tel. 355 34), A few hundred meters west of the disease-ridden lagoon. Attractive bamboo rooms with porches and rock landscaped *mandis.* Overpriced compared to others in the area, but Pondok offers little perks, like the daily newspaper for borrowing and mosquito nets upon request. All rooms with bath. Singles Rp20,000. Doubles Rp25,000. Breakfast included.

Puri Bali Homestay (tel. 410 63), A few doors lagoon-ward of Segara Wangi (still on the west side of the skanky lagoon). Two strips of decent rooms facing one another and a poorly lit walkway. More expensive rooms closer to the beach have fancy, carved doors. All with bath and mosquito net. Singles Rp10,000. Doubles Rp20-25,000 plus 10% tax. Breakfast included.

Barong Beach Inn, From the main road, turn right where it makes a 90° turn toward Amlapura. Follow signs; Barong is off the side street to the right, on the water. White brick rooms are isolated from the main Candi Dasa action, but tend to be dark. Singles with bath Rp10-15,000. Doubles with bath Rp 15-25,000.

Lilaberata, a few hundred meters before the raunchy lagoon (on the west side). Some of the cheapest rooms in Candi Dasa are here, but they're worth investigating closely before you dive under the itchy, scratchy covers. Rooms are large and close to the beach (you can hear the waves from bed). If you are modest (or a female alone), don't change in front of the flimsy curtains. Doubles Rp6000.

FOOD

Warung Rasmini, on the mainland side of the street just before the gooey lagoon on the west side. The *nasi campur* is to die for, and only Rp1000. Warung Rasmini might possibly be the best *warung* in all of Bali.

Warung Srijati, across from the Gandhi Reading Room by the mucky lagoon. Balinese dishes Rp1500-3000. Try the Balinese vegetable *urap* (vegetables in coconut sauce) Rp2000.

Murni's Cafe, near the *wartel* on the west side of town. Offers a spark of originality: sweet and sour fried shrimp (Rp4000), Balinese chicken curry (Rp5000), onion rings (Rp1500). Open 9am-10pm.

Candi Dasa Restaurant (tel. 411 07). Opposite the Geringsing Accommodations on the west side of the road. Come here for the prices. Seafood, basic Balinese dishes, soups, and fish with garlic butter sauce (Rp4000). Most entrees Rp2-4000.

Astawa, on the ocean side of the street on the Amlapura side of the lagoon. Taking a stab at character, Astawa is set back from the road with evening candles on each table and piped New Age music. *Nasi goreng* (Rp3000); *sate* (Rp5000); grilled fish (Rp5000). Open 8am-10pm.

■ NEAR CANDI DASA

Seven km northwest of Amlapura, **Tirtagangga** is easily accessible by public transport from Candi Dasa. Catch a bemo heading toward Amlapura and get off at the terminal there (Rp500). From the terminal, get a red bemo heading up the hill toward Tirtagangga (Rp300). Tirtagangga's royal bathing pools, built by the last king of Amlapura in 1947, are in a beautiful spot carved into a hill of rice fields. Visitors enter through a stone archway, and can wander around two large and several smaller pools, filled by stone beasts spewing fresh spring water. The lily pads, the fountains, the gorgeous *sawah* stretching to the horizon, and the constant sound of falling water will soothe your soul. Tirtagangga is serene and restful, with a Secret Garden-like mystery; its a perfect place to lunch (at the pricey restaurant overlooking the pools, check out their rice pudding with coconut milk) or have a picnic. Bring a swimsuit if you wish to *mandi* in the cool, mountain-stream-fed pools. The upper pool costs Rp2000; the lower pool costs Rp1000. Changing rooms are available. **Tirtagangga Homestay,** run by two descendents of the king who built the place, has singles for Rp25,000, and doubles for Rp30,000. Admission to Tirtagangga Rp550, children Rp300. Open 7am-5:30pm.

Sumatra

A steamy omnium-gatherum straddling the equator, the enormous island of Sumatra baffles visitors with its bustling cities, isolated islands, and remote villages. Notorious for its long distances, poor roads, and fickle climate, travel through Sumatra takes time, although it is possible to explore the northern highlights, coming and going via Medan, without missing much in the way of "easy" sights or spending too much time in a bus.

Loud, chaotic, and incorrigibly unfriendly, Medan is an unfortunate place for travelers to begin their tour of Sumatra and the rest of Indonesia, but it remains the most convenient gateway to the region. Those with a little more time may consider the transit island, Pulau Bintan, and enjoy island hopping their way there.

As the western flank of Indonesia, and one of the largest islands of the nation, Sumatra plays second fiddle only to Java in politics and economics. The Malay communities of the island, such as the Minangkabau of West Sumatra and *orang Melayu* of the east coast, have donated their native languages to the rest of Indonesia, and have thus helped mold the archipelago into a unified nation under Bahasa Indonesia. Sumatra also contributes more than its fair share of revenue to the Indonesian government as the vast oil fields off the east coast will readily attest. In return, Sumatra receives a healthy percentage of transmigrants from Java and Bali, who add even more incongruity to the island's ethnic rumble-bumble.

Sumatra is decidedly top-heavy in terms of sights. After suffering Medan, the adventurous might head north to the staunchly Islamic province of Aceh, but most make their way south to the mountains around Berastagi and the refreshing crater lake, Danau Toba, by way of the Bukit Lawang orangutan rehabilitation center. Nature-loving hikers head to Bukittinggi in West Sumatra province, the heart of Minang culture. Continuing south requires perseverance and a penchant for exploration, though a stop in the backwater provincial seat of Bengkulu is warranted for

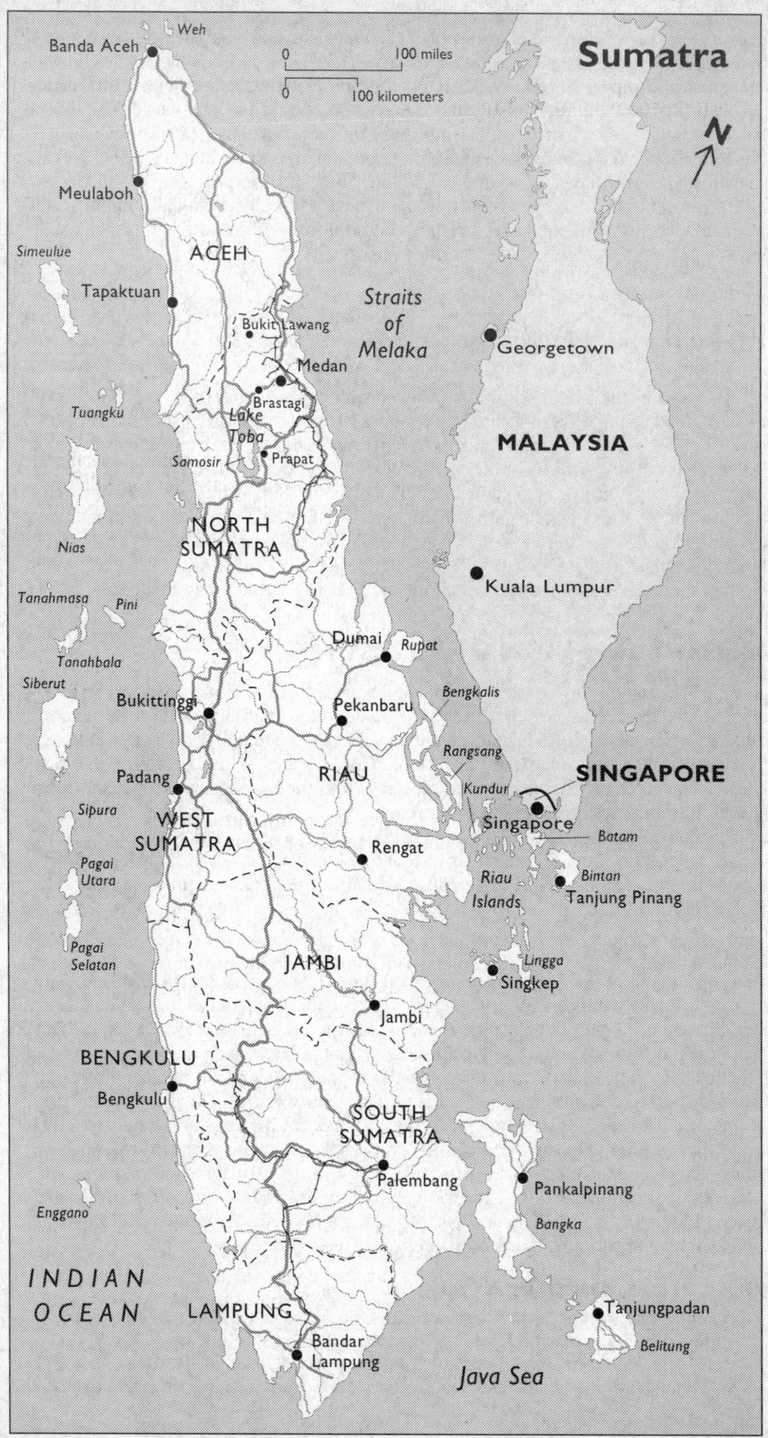
Sumatra
0 100 miles
0 100 kilometers
N
Weh
Banda Aceh
Meulaboh
Simeulue
ACEH
Tapaktuan
Straits of Melaka
Bukit Lawang
Georgetown
Medan
Brastagi
Lake Toba
Tuangku
Samosir
Prapat
MALAYSIA
NORTH SUMATRA
Nias
Kuala Lumpur
Tanahmasa
Pini
Dumai
Rupat
Tanahbala
Siberut
Bengkalis
Bukittinggi
Pekanbaru
Rangsang
Padang
RIAU
SINGAPORE
Kundur
Singapore
Sipura
WEST SUMATRA
Batam
Rengat
Pagai Utara
Riau Islands
Bintan
Tanjung Pinang
Pagai Selatan
JAMBI
Lingga
Singkep
Jambi
BENGKULU
Bengkulu
SOUTH SUMATRA
Palembang
Pankalpinang
Enggano
Bangka
INDIAN OCEAN
LAMPUNG
Tanjungpadan
Belitung
Bandar Lampung
Java Sea

even the most amateur Soekarno-philes. Bandar Lampung, at the southern tip of Sumatra, welcomes travelers en route to Java.

Dubbed *"Suma Tera"* (Black Earth) by the first Europeans to colonize the island, Sumatra is one of the few Indonesian islands to retain its colonial name. The island has changed much in spite of its lingering moniker, but Sumatra still poses many challenges to foreigners who visit. Many regions prove to be inaccessible for even the most determined, and women traveling alone may experience acute harassment. But aside from the uncomfortable journeys and bellicose locals, Sumatra still offers exciting destinations and a variety of traditions. For the intrepid traveler willing to explore, this "black earth" frontier-land awaits.

PULAU BINTAN

A tiny island in the middle of the 3000 even tinier islands that form the Riau Archipelago, unassuming Bintan Island has become a major transportation hub for points south to Java, west to Sumatra, north to Singapore, and even east to Kalimantan. A stay here is common on most itineraries (Marco Polo even paid a visit in 1202), but most wanderlust travelers make it as brief as possible. Still, if trapped for a few days waiting for the next boat to adventure, discover Bintan's oft-overlooked charms. Urban trekkers lose themselves along the colorful wharves and alleys of Tanjung Pinang and the antique coasts of Pulau Penyenget just off-shore. Other travelers cloister themselves along the quiet shores of Trikora beach on the east coast.

■■■ TANJUNG PINANG

Bintan, depressingly, is coming under increasing influence from Singapore. Travelers arriving from Java or Sumatra will find accommodations and food here more expensive; the good news is that it is still cheaper than Singapore. In fact, weekends find Tanjung Pinang crowded with visitors from the city-state, determined to purchase as many cheap staples as they can cram into their designer backpacks. Upon arrival, travelers are besieged by touts trying to make a quick commission off their transportation and accommodation needs. Be calm, and have a plan of action. Many are students who signed up in order to practice English and are friendly if you *don't* go with them. Tanjung Pinang also has its share of pickpockets so keep your valuables secure as well.

ORIENTATION

Tanjung Pinang is the largest city on Pulau Bintan, and much of the city's activity focuses on the wharves. Most travelers arrive at the **main pier** on the east end. Straight down the pier and past the dock offices the first road is **Jalan Merdeka.** This is the main drag and runs roughly east-west, from the large arch near the pier to the fruit market, police box, and taxis to Kijang and the airport. Walking straight through the Merdeka intersection leads to **Jalan Yusuf Kahar.** Roughly parallel and to the east is **Jalan Bintan** where Sempati and Merpati Air roost. The next parallel street east is **Jalan Teuku Umar,** home to the excellent **night market. Jalan Pos** winds from Jl. Merdeka at the post office toward the other smaller piers and wharves of the north shores. The police station and PELNI office are outside of town. PELNI port is in **Kijang** at the south tip of Bintan. **Pulau Penyenget,** that dollop of archaeological joy, floats off-shore to the west of the city.

PRACTICAL INFORMATION

Currency Exchange: Bank Negara Indonesia, #630 Jl. Teuku Umar (tel. 214 32), opposite the taxi stand. Changes Singapore dollars at the best rates. Cashes traveler's checks. Open Mon.-Fri. 8am-5pm. **Lippobank,** #11, Jl. Merdeka (tel. 279 47). Changes S$ and cashes AmEx traveler's checks but requires original purchase

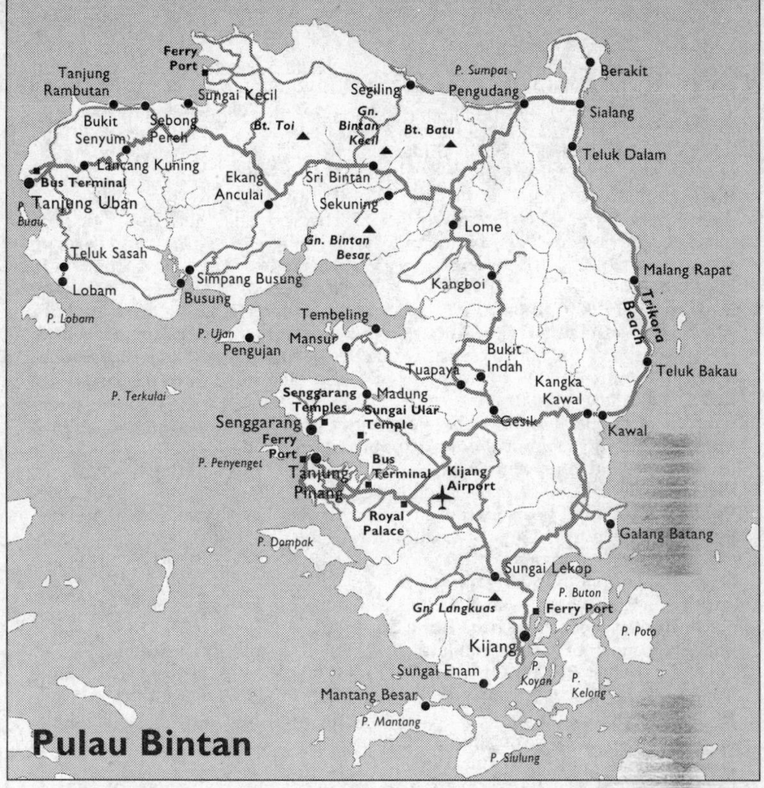

receipt. Accepts Visa and MC with a 4% surcharge. Exchange counter open Mon.-Fri. 8am-2pm. There are also **money changers** near the Jl. Pos and Jl. Merdeka intersection, but rates are not great.

Post Office: At the corner of Jl. Pos and Jl. Merdeka. About 100m through the west arch and on the left. Open Mon.-Sat. 8am-8pm, Sun. 8am-1pm. **Main branch,** on Jl. Katamso, about 3km out of town. Poste Restante. Open Mon.-Thurs., Sat. 8am-2pm, Fri. 8am-11pm. **Postal code:** 29111.

Telephones: Telekom Office (tel. 217 77 or 231 83), on Jl. Hang Tuah, the road to your right from the main pier, near a large waterfront statue of a seashell. Long distance available 24 hrs. **Telephone code:** 07111.

Airport: 20km east of the city. **P.T. Pinang Jaya,** #44 Jl. Bintan (tel. 212 67 or 220 02; fax 220 46), in a big, yellow building. Cash only for Merpati flights to **Jakarta** (Tues., Fri, and Sun. 3:20pm, Rp220,500) and **Pekanbaru** (Mon., Thurs., Sat. 9:30am, Rp113,800). **P.T. Agesti Jayasakti,** #9 Jl. Bintan (tel. 213 77; fax 221 16), 100m toward Jl. Merdeka. Cash only, one way Sempati flights to: **Pekanbaru** (Tues., Thurs., and Sat. 3:20pm; Wed. and Sun. 11am; Fri., 9:15am; Rp113,800); **Padang** (Tues., Thurs., and Sat. 3:20pm; Wed., Sun. 11am; Fri., 9:15; Rp131,400); and **Jakarta** via **Pekanbaru.** For more options, try Batam Airport, Pulau Batam.

Buses: Local station, 7km outside of town. Reached by a Rp500 minibus ride. From here buses circle the island every 2hr. till 3pm, chugging past the beaches to the east (Rp2000) and heading north to the alternate port of **Tanjung Uban.**

Local Transport: Honking **minibuses** startle travelers on corners. Within the city Rp300, past the Km5 mark Rp500. **Motorcycles** take to the streets for Rp300.

Taxis: Bargain hard at the fruit stand on Jl. Merdeka for fares to: the **airport** (Rp10,000 per car); **Kijang** (Rp2500 or Rp12,500 per car); and **Trikora Beach** (Rp5000 or Rp25,000 per car).

Ferries: New Oriental sells tickets for ferries from the main pier to: **Singapore** (9am and 1pm, Rp50,000; 10am and 2pm, Rp54,000; 2hr.); **Dabo** (noon, 3-½hr., Rp20,000); **Tanjung Balai** (1pm, 2-½hr., Rp16,500; via **Sekupang,** noon, Rp21,000); and Malaysia: **Pasir Gudang** (1pm, 2hr., Rp48,500) and **Belungkor** (noon, 3hr., Rp50,000). Others points: **Daik** (Mon., Wed., Sat., 2-½hr., Rp12,500); **Dabo** (daily, noon, 3hr., Rp30,000); **Dumai** (Mon., Wed., Fri., 7:30am, 9hr., Rp52,000); **Pekanbaru** (Wed.-Thurs., 10am, 35hr., Rp31,500 with meals, mattress Rp2000; and **Jakarta** (Thurs., 5pm, 38hr., Rp80,000); **Tanjung Batu** (daily, Rp22,000); **Moro** (daily, 15,000); **Lingga** (Tues., Sat., Rp10,500); and **Penuba** (Tues., Sat., Rp10,500). Mon., Wed., and Fri. ferries to: **Belakang Padang** (Rp13,000), **Balai** (Rp22,500), **Selat Panjang** (Rp37,000), **Bengkalis** (Rp47,000), and **Dumai** (Rp52,000). PELNI runs ferries from Kijang to: **Dumai** (Fri., 9pm, 9hr., Rp25,000, 1st-class Rp86,000) and **Jakarta** (Sun., 10am, 40hr., Rp41,5000 plus Rp2000 for mattress, 4th-class Rp75,000, 3rd Rp95,000, 2nd Rp112,000, 1st Rp157,000).

Boats: Small wooden motorboats to **Penyenget Island** depart from half-way down the main pier throughout the day (Rp500). It's a good idea to keep two crisp Rp500 bills hand to prevent disputes. Oar-driven *sampans* to **Senggarang** across the harbor depart two piers over Rp500 per person; motorized transport Rp1000. **Pulau Batam** speedboats leave from the main pier (every 30min. until 4:30pm, Rp9-10,000) and from Tanjung Uban, north of the city (Rp6-8000). From Batam, catch taxis to **Sekupang** (Rp3000 per person, Rp15,000 per taxi) for boats and buses (about Rp500) to **Singapore.**

Motorcycle Rental: Mr. Johanes at P.T. Maduratna can arrange something.

English Bookstores: The Lotus Book Shop, #28 Jl. Merdeka (tel. 218 26). Dated but detailed map of Batam and Bintan Rp12,5000. Open daily 8am-8pm.

Travel Agencies: PELNI Office (tel. 215 13; fax 219 33), at Km5 (Batu Lima, Rp500). Open Mon.-Fri. 8am-4pm, Sat. 8am-noon. **P.T. Maduratna** (tel. 295 66), left onto Jl. Merdeka from the pier. Through the Arch and on the left, the middle of three. Mr. Johanes Tayun speaks excellent English, gives travel advice, and sells boat tickets. **P.T. New Oriental** (tel. 216 14; fax 241 45), farther down Jl. Merdeka opposite Jl. Teuku Umar. Extensive ticketing, including points in Malaysia.

Market: The expansive daily market is sandwiched between Jl. Gambir and the waterfront. Turn right, through the alley-ways, as you walk toward the jetty.

Hospital: Along Jl. Sudirman, in the south of the city. **Malaria is supposedly prevalent. Start medication before you arrive.**

Police: (tel. 211 10), at Km5. **Police box,** on Jl. Merdeka opposite the fruit market.

ACCOMMODATIONS

Bong's Homestay, #20 Jl. Lorong Bintan II (tel. 226 05). From the pier walk through the Jl. Merdeka intersection and up the road as it curves left. Turn left down the 1st alley, just before the Sempurna Jaya Hotel. Walk down the alley and turn again at the 1st left. Bong's is the 2nd-to-last house. Dorms Rp5000, private room Rp10,000. Light breakfast included. Guests gather with Mr. Bong over beers in the living room to exchange tales and admire the Mona Lisa, Def Leppard, and Depeche Mode posters. Those feeling lucky can challenge Mrs. Bong to a game of Scrabble or Wheel of Fortune. Doors locked at midnight. Cheap laundry and good travel tips.The homestay next door will pick-up the overflow.

Hotel Surya (tel. 218 11), on Jl. Bintan. From the jetty, turn left on Jl. Merdeka. After the arch, take the 1st right; it's near the end of the street on the left just before the Merpati office. Rooms form a horseshoe around a court with a small fountain. Most have a mini-porch in front, each with its *very own* potted plant. Doubles Rp18,000, with bath Rp20,500. Triples Rp20,500, with bath Rp23,000.

FOOD

The windows of Tanjung Pinang are overflowing with edible options. Try exploring the **wharves' nooks** and crannies for extraordinary morning coffee, spiced with a dash of chaos. Every afternoon locals take turns buying each other lunch at **outdoor stalls** huddled around the stadium on Jl. Bintan. In the evenings scoop the loop at the extensive **night market** near the taxi stand, off Jl. Teuku Umar. The following listings are intended as culinary first-aid hints for transit travelers in crisis.

Lucky Fried Chicken, #50 Jl. Pos. Across from the Sanno Hotel. Fortunately, Carpenters' singles mix favorably with the drone of A/C at Lucky Fried Chicken! Fresh from Singapore? Feeling overwhelmed by the island's sensory onslaught? Cringing from the anarchy of the streets? Join other cel-phone-clad tourists for a chicken burger (Rp2500) and "Mesjid Raya Sultan Riau" cucumber juice with yellow straw in this haven of order. English menu. Waitstaff will even ask if you want it "to go?" NO, I'm eatin' at Lucky Fried Chicken! Open daily 10am-9pm.

The Nameless Curry Shack, just before the Merdeka intersection on the left, across from the souvenir shop. A typical curry stall with wares precariously stacked in the window. More importantly, it's 4 walls provide refuge for the tout-besieged. Duck in and grab an iced tea (Rp500) in the cool, dim rooms while planning your next move. Open daily 8am-8pm.

■ AROUND THE ISLAND

PULAU PENYENGET

Diminutive Pulau Penyenget (2-½sq. km), just off Tanjung Pinang was the regal seat of the Riau Raja's far-flung Kingdom for hundreds of years. History has tattooed its slopes and shores with a complex collection of crumbling forts, palaces, and royal tombs. The last remnant of a culture considered to be the seed of Malay civilization, pure Bahasa Melayu is still spoken here. To get to the island catch one of the motorboats moored half-way down the main pier (10min., Rp500). The boat deposits you at Penyenget jetty where you must pay an additional Rp500 entrance fee.

Just beyond the jetty shines **Mesjid Raya Sultan Riau,** a refreshing 178-year-old mosque. Locals say it is held together with egg-white mortar, but its tangy yellow and green walls, domes, and minarets look like they were painted with Hi-C Citrus Cooler. Its library houses a rare collection of antique tomes and manuscripts including five hand-written copies of the Koran. Not usually open to the public. No bare shoulders or shorts. Avoid visiting on Fridays.

To tour the other historic sites, exit the mosque and pass through the arch to the left, turning left down the small concrete path. The **tomb of Raja Abdurrachman,** a small **munitions store,** and the **ruins of the island fort** are about 100m down on the right. The path then winds through the quietly moldering shell of **Raja Ali's palace,** abandoned this century. Farther along are the ruins of an old house and the **tombs of Raja Jaafar and Raja Ali Ibni.** At the end of the road, turn right and walk five minutes to see a **modern Riau palace,** or circle back to the jetty via more tombs.

Pilgrims travel here to venerate the **royal interments** along these paths including those of Raja Ali Jajai, writer of the 1st Malay grammar and Engku Puteri Permaisuri, who received the isle as her dowry. She ruled until her death in 1844, and members of the royal scion still live along the south shores. You will also pass the remains of the **Rusydiah Club,** in name a cultural and literary club, founded by the final ruling Sultan Abdurrachman Muazan Syah (1883-1911). Actually it was an underground para-military group, organized by the canny young man who realized direct action against the Dutch who controlled the island was imprudent. In time the organization's efforts were to be of great aid in achieving Indonesian Independence.

TRIKORA

Beach bunnies can find powdery bliss along Trikora's secluded east coast beaches. After a good storm, lucky beach combers will find the shores freckled with 400-year-old shards of Ming Dynasty porcelain, washed from sunken Chinese junks. Local fishermen have built structures in the shallow waters off-shore to raise fish for the market, and at night their camplights form glittering chains across the horizon. The only time to avoid Trikora is monsoon season (November-March).

Yasin's Guest House is a collection of 14 beach huts strewn around Mr. Yasin's own concrete abode. Ask to see your options. Some cots are fanciful creations with lofts tucked here and there, broad porches, and attached baths; one tiny hut is even perched over the ocean's waves, accessible via a small bridge. Other rooms are mere thatch boxes without bathroom. All are Rp17,500 per night including 3 square meals. Yasin can also arrange **snorkeling** and **island tours,** about Rp30,000 per boat. Prices for **camping** (with your own equipment) can be negotiated. To get to Yasin's, take a local minibus to the bus station 7km out of town (Rp500). Buses run to the east coast until 3pm (every 2hr., Rp2000). Tell the driver you want to get off at Yasin's. Share taxis leave when full from Jl. Teuku Umar until noon (Rp3000 per person, 5 people per taxi). To rent a private taxi after noon costs Rp13-30,000 per car.

MAINLAND SUMATRA

■■■ MEDAN

Poor Medan. Few Southeast Asian cities are as maligned by travelers, many of whom look forward to three days in Medan as they might to a 72-hour root canal. The city's choking pollution, perpetually snarled traffic, lack of sights and activities, and the reputation of the Medanites are all strikes against her. Nevertheless, as north Sumatra's gateway city and chief transportation hub, Medan is usually a stop on the backpacker's itinerary.

But take heart; this metropolis of 2 million souls is anything but dull. Under the Dutch, Medan, strategically situated on the Straits of Melaka, grew from a backwater town to an industrial center. Immigrants from across the archipelago and beyond flocked to Medan to share in its prosperity. Today the population is a vibrant mix of coastal Malay, Batak, Indian, and Chinese, making it one of the country's most cosmopolitan cities. Its accordingly rich religious heritage accounts for many of Medan's most intriguing sights, from the fanciful Mesjid Raya (Grand Mosque) to the colorful Candi Hindu (Hindu Temple). Much to the delight of budget *gourmands,* this ethnic diversity ensures that cheap, delicious, and varied cuisine abounds.

Caught up in the frenetic crush of daily life, many Medanites reserve little patience for the foreigners in their midst. As a general rule, the neater you dress and the more Bahasa Indonesian you learn, the better you will be treated. And remember, within a few hours you can be swimming in Lake Toba's blue water, or hiking the rainforested volcanoes of Brastagi, to name but a few of North Sumatra's many delights. Medan, like dental work, may be a necessity, but it need not be prolonged.

ORIENTATION

Medan rambles with little rhyme or reason. Like many Indonesian cities, the streets shed monikers quicker than Zsa Zsa sheds hubbies. The main north-south thoroughfare changes names more than six times. It starts out as **Jalan Balai Kota.** After passing **Merdeka Square** it becomes **Jalan A. Yani.** South of the intersection with **Jalan Palang Merah,** it briefly becomes **Jalan Pemuda,** before changing to **Jalan Brigjen. Katamso,** passing the **Istana Maimun** and several travel agencies. Jl. Palang Merah, which leads west from Jl. A. Yani (and quickly becomes **Jalan H.Z. Arifin**), passes through the Chinese and Indian area of the city. A number of cheap *warung* and delicious bakeries line Jl. H.Z. Arifin. The other important road for travelers to learn is **Jalan Sisingamangaraja,** which roughly parallels Jl. Pemuda/Jl. Brigjen. Katamso, passing the **Mesjid Raya** and **Bukit Barisan Hero's Cemetery.** A number of hotels and guest houses catering to every budget can be found in the vicinity of the Mesjid

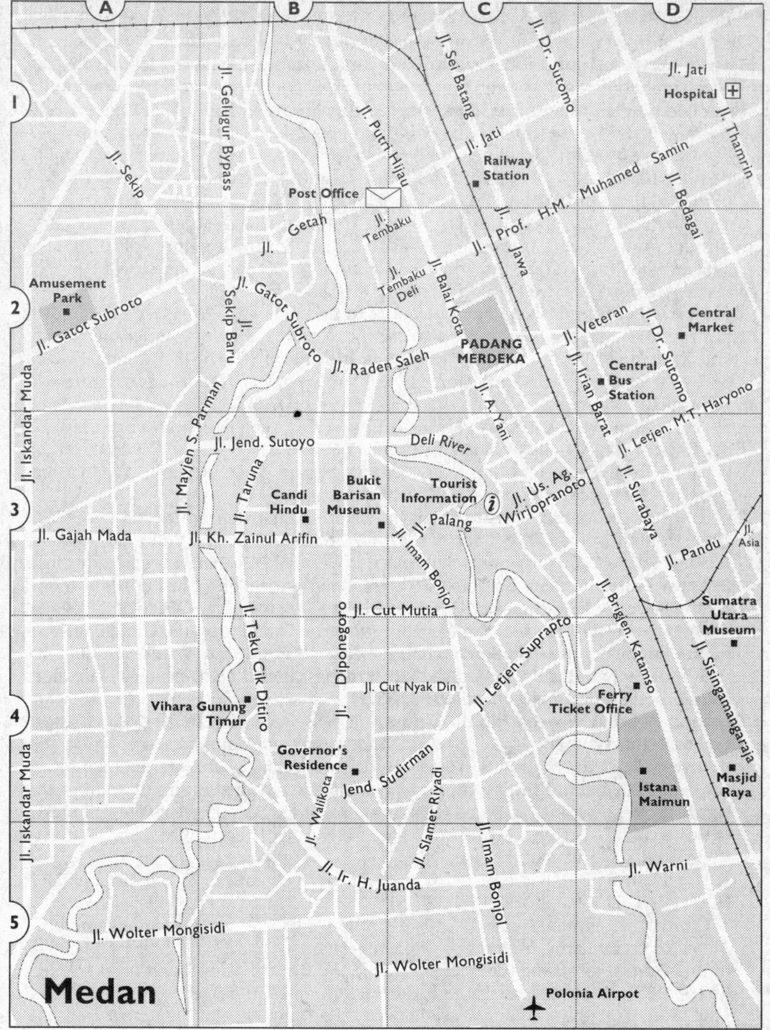

Raya. Sadly, Medan's two bus terminals, **Stasiun Pinang Baris** and **Stasiun Amplas,** are inconveniently located on the north and south edges of the city, respectively.

PRACTICAL INFORMATION

Tourist Office: Provincial Tourism Office of North Sumatra, 4 Jl. A. Yani 107 (tel. 538 101; fax 538 643). Just north of Jl. Palang Merah on the right. Eager staff has useful maps of Medan. Beware: map is not to scale. Leave packs here for a day of sight-seeing. Open Mon.-Thurs. 7:30am-4:15pm, Fri. 7:30-11:30am.

Travel and Tour Agencies: Most agents are on Jl. Brigjen. Katamso south of Jl. Letjen. Suprapto. **Trophy Travel and Tour,** Jl. Brigjen. Katamso 33DE (tel. 555 666 or 555 777; fax 510 340 or 511 243). Medan's largest travel agency. Open Mon.-Sat. 8am-6pm, Sun. 8am-noon. All major credit cards. **Pacto Tours and Travel,** Jl. Brigjen. Katamso 35G (tel. 510 081 or 516 827; fax 513 669). Arranges treks through Gunung Leuser National Park (6 days, US$20, all expenses included) and Alas River rafting (6 days, US$685 per person, min. 6 people). Trips leave on fixed dates; will organize special trips for groups. Open Mon.-Fri. 8am-4pm, Sat. 8am-1pm. **Indo Prima Tour and Travel,** Jl. Palang Merah 15D (tel. 538 845; fax 555 804). Open Mon.-Fri. 9am-5pm, Sat. 9am-3pm, Sun. 9am-noon.

Embassies and Consulates: Malaysia, Jl. Diponegoro 43 (tel. 531 342 or 535 271; fax 534 681). Open Mon.-Thurs. 8am-1pm and 2-4pm, Fri. 8-11:30am and 1:30-4pm. **Singapore,** Jl. Tengku Daud 3 (tel. 513 366; fax 513 134). Open Mon.-Fri. 8am-12:30pm and 1:30-4:30pm. **UK,** Jl. J. Ahmid Vani 2 (tel. 519 992; fax 518 699), 3rd floor. Open Mon.-Fri. 7:30am-12:30pm. **US,** Jl. Imam Bonjol 13 (tel. 552 200; fax 518 711). Open Mon.-Fri. 7:30am-4pm; but will close soon.

Immigration Office: Jl. Binjei 268A (tel. 852 112). Several km north of town; take a *damri* bus from Jl. A. Yani and ask to get out at "Kantor Imigrasi." One-month visa extension Rp86,000. Open Mon.-Fri. 8:30am-4:15pm.

Currency Exchange: Exchange rates tend to be lower than in Jakarta, but Sumatran rates outside Medan are even worse. Most banks are along Jl. Palang Merah, and Jl. Pemuda/Jl. A. Yani. **Bank Negara Indonesia (BNI),** Jl. Pemuda 12 (tel. 538 166; fax 513 281). Open Mon.-Fri. 8:30am-2pm. **P.T. Delimagan Valutindo Money Changer,** Jl. A. Yani 94 (tel. 513 535 or 512 342). Open Mon.-Fri. 9am-5pm, Sat. 9am-3pm. Cirrus **ATMs** at Deli Plaza shopping center and most hotels.

Post Office: GPO, Jl. Bukit Barisan 1 (tel. 517 828 or 513 001; fax 515 633), on the corner with Jl. Balai Kota, opposite Merdeka Square. Poste Restante. Open Mon.-Sat. 8am-7pm. **Postal code:** 2011.

Telephones: Indosat central office, Jl. Perintis Kemerdekaan 39 (tel. 524 972). IDD, Home Country Direct service. Open 24 hrs. All major credit cards. Many *wartels* around the city. Some will place collect calls, others accept only cash. **Wartel Tiara,** Jl. Imam Bonjol 15 (tel. 550 386; fax 550 385), just north of the Jl. Palang Merah intersection near the Irama Hotel. Open 24 hrs. **Office** at Jl. Sisingamangaraja 45 (tel. 745 384; fax 745 386), near the Grand Mosque. Open 7am-midnight. No collect calls. **Telkom,** central office, Jl. Putri Hijau 1 (tel. 524 800; fax 537 530), north of the GPO on the left, just past BNI. 1 HCD phone. No collect calls. Open 24 hrs. **Telephone code:** 061.

Airport: Polania International Airport (tel. 538 444), 3km south of town at the end of Jl. Imam Bonjol. Info on: Garuda Indonesia (international, ext. 140; domestic ext. 127), Sempati (ext. 210), and Merpati (ext. 259). The international terminal is directly behind the main gate, the domestic terminal is about 300m to the right. From town take a *becak* (Rp2000) or metered taxi (Rp5000). **Garuda Indonesia,** Jl. Letjen. Suprapto 2 (tel. 322 600) flies to: **Jakarta** (5 daily, Rp337,000); **Denpasar** (Fri.-Sat., Rp455,400); **Singapore** (1 daily, US$127); and **Kuala Lumpur,** Malaysia (1 daily, US$77). **Branch office,** in the Dharma Deli Hotel, Jl. Balai Kota 2 (tel. 515 277, 515 722, or 514 877; fax 538 502), next to THAI Airways. Open Mon.-Fri. 7:30am-4:30pm, Sat. 7:30am-1pm, Sun. 9am-noon. All major credit cards. **Merpati,** Jl. Brigjen. Katamso 72/122 (tel. 514 102; fax 514 057). Flights to: **Padang** (daily, Rp151,200) and **Batam** (Mon.,Wed., and Fri.-Sat., Rp193,000). Book tickets through Garuda. Open Mon.-Fri. 8am-5pm, Sat. 8am-3pm, Sun. 9am-3pm. All major credit cards. **Sempati,** Jl. Cut Meutiah 1 (tel. 551 612 or 516 000; fax 538 477), on the ground floor of the Tiara Convention Center. Services major cities. Open Mon.-Sat. 8am-9pm, Sun. 9am-5pm. All major credit cards. **SMAC,** Jl. Imam Bonjol 59 (tel. 537 760 or 538 643), to **Nias** (daily, Rp117,100). Open Mon.-Fri. 8am-5pm, Sat.-Sun. 8am-1pm. All major credit cards. **Bouraq Airlines,** Jl. Brigjen. Katamso 43 (tel. 552 333). Cheaper flights to: **Jakarta** (daily, Rp215,000); **Denpasar** (Rp456,000); and **Batam** (Rp193,000). Open Mon.-Fri. 7am-6pm, Sat.-Sun. 7am-noon. All major credit cards. **Malaysia Airlines (MAS),** Jl. Imam Bonjol 17 (tel. 514 300; fax 547 400), ground floor of the Danua Toba Hotel. Flies to **Kuala Lumpur** (2 daily, US$77 credit, US$60 cash) and **Penang** (1 daily, US$74 credit, US$55 cash). Open Mon.-Fri. 8:30am-4:30pm, Sat. 8:30am-2pm, Sun. 9am-1pm. All major credit cards. **Silk Air/Singapore Airlines,** Jl. Jend. Sudirman 14 (tel. 537 744; fax 537 798), ground floor of the Polonia Hotel. Daily to **Singapore** (US$127). Open Mon.-Sat. 8am-5pm, Sat. 8am-1pm, Sun. 8am-noon. All major credit cards.

Buses: Medan has two main bus terminals. Ticket prices depend on the degree of comfort; fares are approximate as they vary between companies. Cheapest are rattle-trap "public buses" with no A/C and no guarantees. Avoid the mob of touts, who will literally drag you to their buses, and head for the tourist info booths in both terminals. Helpful, English-speaking representatives can direct you to the next appropriate bus. **Pinang Baris terminal,** 8km north on Jl. Pinang Baris, services points north of Medan. Hop on any northbound *damri* on Jl. A. Yani/Jl. Balai Kota. Check to ensure it's going to Pinang Baris (Rp200). To: **Bukit Lawang** (every hr., 7am-6pm, 2-½hr., Rp1500); **Brastagi** (every hr., 7am-5pm, 2hr., Rp1500); and **Banda Aceh** (every hr. 9am-7pm, 12hr., Rp13,000, A/C Rp27,000). Bus info open Mon.-Sat. 7am-4pm. **Amplas terminal,** 3km south on Jl. Medan Tenggara, off Jl. Sisingamangaraja, services the south. To: **Prapat** (every 10-15min., 6:30am-8pm, 4hr., Rp3500, A/C Rp8-12,000); **Bukittinggi** (every hr., 10am-4pm, 12hr., Rp18,000, A/C Rp22-35,000); **Jakarta** (8am-7pm, 48hr., Rp55,000, A/C Rp60,000-125,000 with karaoke); **Denpasar** (2 daily, A/C only); and **Bandung** (8am-5pm, 72hr., Rp60,000, A/C Rp80-125,000). Tourist info booth open Mon.-Sat. 8am-4pm (tel. 714 101 or 716 499). For those who wish to avoid Medan's bus terminals, **Antar Lintas Sumatera (ALS),** the island's largest bus company, has its office at Jl. Amaluin 2A (tel. 719 459 or 718 499). Take a *sudako* down Jl. Sisingamangaraja to the Mesjid Raya (Rp200); Jl. Amaluin is on the left before the mosque. A/C buses to: **Jakarta** (4 daily, Rp50,000, with toilet Rp75,000, Super VIP (with karaoke!) Rp120,000); **Padang** (3 daily, Rp18,000, Rp23,000, and Rp35,000); **Bukittinggi** (3 daily, Rp17,000, Rp20,000, and Rp35,000).

Ferries: Leave from Belawan, 26km north of Medan. **Penang Ekspress Bahagia,** Jl. Sisingamangaraja 92A (tel. 720 421 or 720 964; fax 717 522). Open Mon.-Sat. 8:30am-5pm. To **Georgetown,** Malaysia (Tues., Thurs., and Sat., 10am, 5hr., Rp90,000). Visa. Cash only for same-day purchase. **Perdana/Langkawi,** Jl. Brigjen. Katamso 35D (tel. 545 306 or 545 803) runs a catamaran to **Georgetown** (Fri. and Sun., 10am, 5hr., Rp90,000). Open daily 7am-6pm. Both offer free transport to Belawan at 7am. To **Perdana/Langkawi**, (Wed., 10am, 6hr., Rp90,000). **PELNI Lines,** Jl. Kol. Sugiono 5 (tel. 518 899; fax 517 474). To **Jakarta** (Mon., 36hr., economy Rp63,500). Tickets go on sale the Tues. before. Cash only. Open Mon.-Fri. 8am-3pm, Sat. 8-11am.

Local Transportation: Yellow and blue **sudakos** (minibuses) careen along set routes; major destinations are usually written on the windshield but check with the driver first. *Sudakos* leave from the Central Market for **Amplas** (Rp300). To **Belawan,** take a *sudako* marked "Morina" from Jl. A. Yani (Rp500). To **Pinang Baris** take government **bis damris** which run along Jl. A. Yani/Jl. Balai Kota (Rp200). **Becaks** and **becak misin** (motorized) prowl the streets. Fare within downtown should not exceed Rp2000. Metered **taxis** start at Rp700 and Rp100 per km. From airport to downtown Rp4000, from Amplas Rp7000.

Car Rental: National Car Rental, Jl. Balai Kota 2 (tel. 327 641 or 327 991, ext. 102-109; fax 327 153). Rates begin at US$55 per day for a Toyota Kijang, $288 weekly; unlimited mileage. Insurance $5 per day, $60 flat-rate insurance (12 days or more). Must be 17 years old with an International Driver's Permit. Open Mon.-Fri. 8:30am-4:30pm, Sat. 8:30am-12:30pm. All major credit cards accepted.

Luggage Storage: Polania Airport, domestic terminal. Rp3500 per day, per item.

Laundry: Several shops on Jl. H.Z. Arifin near Candi Hindu. **Serba Baru,** Jl. H.Z. Arifin 83/69 (tel. 512 641). Open daily 8am-9pm.

Swimming Pool: Dharma Deli Hotel, Jl. Balai Kota 2 (tel. 557 744). Large and clean with snack bar. Rp5000 per person. Open daily 6-10am, 3-6pm.

Library: Perpustakaan Daerati Sumatera Utara, Jl. Brigjen. Katamso 45K (tel. 512 746). 2nd floor has large English language collection on Indonesia. Open Mon.-Thurs. 8am-3:15pm, Fri. 8am-11:30am, Sat. 8am-noon.

English Bookstore: Gama Utama Book Center, Jl. Sisingamangaraja 12 (tel. 741 125 or 712 642). Small English section, with guide books and maps of Indonesia and Sumatra, including Medan and Lake Toba (Rp8000). Phrasebooks and Bahasa Indonesia textbooks. Open daily 8am-10pm. Visa, MC accepted.

Pharmacy: Apotik Sudirman, Jl. Letjen. Suprato 2PQ (tel. 510 903 or 518 197). Everything you need for a romantic evening in Sumatra: Listerine, condoms, and anti-malarial pills. Open daily 8am-10pm. **Contact Lens Supplies: Optik Lichin,** Jl. A. Yani 102 (tel. 556 266). Open Mon.-Sat. 9am-8pm, Sun. 11am-4pm. Visa, MC.

Hospital: St. Elizabeth Hospital, Jl. Haji Misbah 7 (tel. 544 737 or 544 164; fax 543 168), near the Polonia Hotel. English-speaking doctors. **Klinic Specialis Banda,** Jl. Sisingamangaraja 17 (tel. 715 772 or 711 45; fax 714 411), closer to downtown. Private clinic with English speaking doctors. Open 24 hr. Visa, MC.

Emergency: Police tel. 110. **Ambulance** tel. 118.

Police: Jl. H.Z. Arifin 7 (tel. 538 077). **City headquarters** (tel. 522 948 or 520 971), on Jl. Durian.

ACCOMMODATIONS

There is no shortage of cheap beds in Medan. Several cheap *losmen* act as backpacker clearing houses, where travelers shack up for a night before heading to the country. The more popular ones fill up quickly, so arrive early. Most medium- to high-end hotels are clustered along Jl. Sisingamangaraja near the Grand Mosque.

Shahiba Guest House, Jl. Armada 1A/3 (tel. 718 528). Head south on Jl. Sisingamangaraja; at the far end of Bukit Barisan Hero's Cemetery turn right onto Jl. Armada. Shahiba is 20m down on the right. Run by an affable Toba Batak family; the distinctive red, black, and white stenciling on the walls is a dead giveaway. Rooms from Rp12-25,000. Doubles with private bath Rp25,000. Probably the finest dorm in Medan. 7 beds with 2 ceiling fans (Rp6000). All prices include breakfast and fan. Laundry service. Check-out noon.

Losmen Irama, Jl. Palang Merah 112S (tel. 326 46). From the Jl. Palang Merah/Jl. Pemuda intersection, head west and cross a small river to a traffic triangle with a sculpture of a violinist. It's on the next small street to the right. Perhaps the most popular backpacker dive, Irama fills up fast when the afternoon boats from Penang get in. Helpful staff; some speak excellent English. Dorm Rp4000, doubles Rp8000, triples Rp12,000. Fan Rp2500. Windows in front rooms. Shared *mandi*. Laundry facility. HCD phones. Door is locked at midnight. No alcohol.

Sarah's Guest House, Jl. Pertama 10/4 (tel. 719 460). From the Grand Mosque, head south on Jl. Sisingamangaraja. Take a right before the large Toyota dealership, a left 20m later, and then a right onto Jl. Pertama about 200m down. Sarah's, on the right of this quiet side-street, is the best cure for the Medan blues. Call if lost. The manager will make Medan as painless as possible. Doubles with fan Rp10,000, and bath Rp15,000. Good, inexpensive Asian and western food (Rp1-3000). Books ferry, bus, and plane tickets; no extra charge. Free transport to the airport or ferry. Laundry service.

Wisma Yuli, Jl. Sisingamangaraja, Gg. Pagaruyung No. 79B (tel. 719 704). Gg. Pagaruyung is directly opposite the Grand Mosque; look for the sign near the end of the alley on the right. Light sleepers beware: the Grand Mosque's massive speakers are an effective "spiritual" alarm clock—at 4:45am. Still a pleasant place to stay, near the Belawan shuttle bus stop. Doubles with fan, writing desk, and shared *mandi* Rp10,000. Dorm on the 4th floor has swell views of the mosque's onion domes. Swish rooms with fan and bath Rp20,000. Prices include breakfast. HCD phone. Check-out 1pm.

Zakia Hotel, Jl. Sipsopiso 10/12 (tel. 722 413). Directly behind the Grand Mosque off Jl. Sisingamangaraja. Near the center of town but removed from the busy thoroughfares. Scope out Medan's skyline of corrugated aluminum roofs, TV antennae, and graceful minarets. Less than 2 years old; certainly a step above the rest. Spacious dorm rooms Rp6000. Doubles with fan and private bath Rp20,000 on 2nd floor, Rp15,000 (slightly smaller) on the 3rd floor. Triples Rp25,000 on 2nd floor, Rp21,000 on the 3rd. Large TV. Breakfast. Laundry service.

Tapian Nabaru Hotel, Jl. Hang Tuah 6/20 (tel. 512 155). Head south on Jl. Cik Ditiro from Jl. H.Z. Arifin. Jl. Hang Tuah is the 1st right past the Methodist church. Tapian is beyond a Chinese pagoda in a quiet, residential neighborhood. The hotel (actually a *losmen* in disguise) offers a respite from the crush of central

Medan. Few amenities, save a Home Country Direct phone. Dorm Rp3000, single bunk Rp6000, double Rp6500. Two not-so-clean *mandis* and western toilets.

FOOD

The traffic may be abominable, the touts relentless, and the dust choking, but at least you can feast on cheap, delicious food. *Warung* and tiny hole-in-the-wall restaurants abound. Medan's chief culinary specialty is Padang food, West Sumatra's spicy regional specialty. The city's large South Asian population brings delicious Indian food, particularly North Indian. One of the best places for cheap Padang and Indian food is the **warung** on Jl. Pagaruyung, a sidestreet north of Jl. H.Z. Arifin past the Candi Hindu temple. Open 6-11pm.

Surya Food Center, Jl. Imam Bonjol 6, next to the Dirga Surya Hotel, supports over 30 stalls selling Indonesian, Indian, and Chinese favorites (Rp1-2500 per dish). Open 6:30pm-2am (4am on Saturdays). The **Seri Deli Recreation Garden,** on Jl. Mesjid Raya, opposite the Grand Mosque, has a large number of stalls surrounding a small man-made pond where fishermen pay to cast a line into the putrid water in hopes of snagging an Edsel. Open 4:30-11pm. Proving yet again that Southeast Asia is **where bad fast-food joints go to die,** the Deli Plaza "boasts" three, count 'em, **three fried chicken outlets!**

G's Koh-I-Noor Meal House, Jl. Mesjid Raya 21 (tel. 513 953). Turn left onto Jl. Perdana from Jl. A. Yani, then a right onto Jl. Mesjid Raya. G's is on the right. A favorite of Medan veterans. The scrumptious North Indian food reduces experienced travelers to orgasmic blubbering. The cheerful owners, Mr. and Mrs. Singh, are full of candid travel advice. Large portions: mutton curry (Rp4000), vegetable curry (Rp2000), sweet fruit *lassi* (Rp2000). Pre-order for *tandoor* chicken. Open daily 8:30am-10pm.

Rumah Makan Famili, Jl. Sisingamangaraja 33 (tel. 321 285 or 718 787). From the Grand Mosque head north on Jl. Sisingamangaraja. It's about 2 blocks up on the right, next to the Ibunda Hotel. Very popular Padang food, heavy on the chili and coconut milk. Filled to the gills at lunchtime: signature dishes include goat curry and...stuff cooked in coconut (choose from brains, viscera, bowels, or fish). Dishes Rp1-3000, but most forego the menu and order "Padang food"—6 or 7 different dishes including chicken, mutton, veggies, and seafood. You'll be charged for what you eat. Great for groups, but a bit expensive for loners (Rp15-20,000).

Tip Top Restaurant and Ice Cream Palace, Jl. A. Yani 92 (tel. 532 042). North of the Jl. Sukamulia-Palang intersection, on the left before Merdeka Square. Tip Top opened when Sumatra was Dutch; the covered street-side patio still has well-worn wicker furniture and a dark, columned interior. A hangout for travelers and expats alike; most just come for a beer on the patio but there is a large menu of Chinese, European, and Indonesian food. Most dishes (Rp3-8000). Chicken curry (Rp1450). Beer (Rp2-5500). Ice cream (Rp1250). Open daily 9am-11pm.

Tahiti Bakery and Cake Shop, Jl. Taruma 70-72 (tel. 519 692 or 514 457; fax 324 817). Just north of Jl. H.Z. Arifin near the Jl. Cik Ditiro intersection. As you enter and the wonderful, intoxicating smells emanating from the kitchen hit your nostrils, ask yourself this question: why are the world's best Boston Creme donuts in Medan? (Rp700). Indonesian sweets (Rp3-400). Ice cream, fresh bread, and pudding. Open daily 7:30am-9:30pm.

SIGHTS

The city's chief crowd-pleaser is undoubtedly its impressive architectural legacy. The majestic black domes, brilliant turquoise tiles, and towering minaret of the **Mesjid Raya,** or Grand Mosque, seem lifted straight from an Arabian tale. Built by Sultan Mahkmun Al-Rasyid, it was actually designed by a Dutch architect and constructed in 1908, with materials from all over the globe (marble from Italy, a chandelier from Holland, and stained glass from China). Inside, on the right is the solid marble *mar-mar,* a platform where the *imam* stands to lead the faithful in prayer. The smaller building to the left of the mosque is used by worshippers for ritual cleansing. Several past sultans and their families are buried in the surrounding garden. The mosque is at the corner of Jl. Sisingamangaraja and Jl. Mesjid Raya, open daily 7am-6pm. Visitors are expected to dress respectfully and must cover their legs. Women must keep their heads covered. Donations requested.

Not far from Mesjid Raya on Jl. Brigjen. Katamso is the **Istana Maimun.** The large, low palace, an eclectic mix of Asian and western styles, has been the home of the Deli sultans since its construction in 1888 by Sultan Mahkmun Al-Rasyid with money gleaned from the lucrative tobacco trade. The current sultan (the 12th in the Deli line) and his family still live in the palace, though the big guy spends most of his time in Jakarta, dabbling in politics. Only the large throne room is open to the public, and although some of the luster has faded from the gold leaf, it is not hard to picture how opulent it must have been during Sultan Al-Rasyid's days. Open daily 8am-5:30pm. Donation requested.

The **Vihara Gunung Timur,** a Buddhist temple sacred to Medan's influential, yet low-profile, Chinese community, is on Jl. Hang Tuah off Jl. Cik Ditiro. The ceiling of the tranquil sanctuary is covered with red prayer lanterns, and a large glass case contains many Buddha images of various styles and sizes. The smell of incense permeates the chamber. Open during daylight hours. Photography prohibited. Not far from the Vihara Gunung Timur, on Jl. H.Z. Arifin, is the **Candi Hindu,** a Hindu temple decorated with hundreds of brilliantly colored and life-like statues of gods, heroes, and mythical creatures. The temple was recently refurbished, and placards identify some of the scenes. Open during daylight hours.

Medan has two museums. By far the more interesting is the **Museum Sumatera Utara,** Jl. H.M. Jon 51 (tel. 716 792) whose large collection documents the geological, natural, and cultural history of the province, beginning with exhibits explaining the island's volcanic inception and model bone fragments from "Java Man," our 600,000-year-old ancestor. The undisputed highlight of the museum is its extensive collection of Batak artifacts and handicrafts from the six main Batak groups in North Sumatra: the Toba, Pak Pak, Karo, Simalungun, Mandailing, and Angkola. Open Mon.-Sat. 9am-5pm. Admission Rp200 (Rp250 extra for camera). To get to the museum take a *sudako* down Jl. Sisingamangaraja. From the south end of the Bukit Barisan Hero's Cemetery, Jl. H.M. Joni is on the left, and the museum is 300m down the street on the right. A second museum, **Museum Bukit Barisan,** Jl. H.Z. Arifin 7 (tel. 326 927), lies opposite the police station. The entrance is flanked by cannons, indicating that it is Medan's military museum; it mainly documents North Sumatra's role in the struggle against Dutch colonial forces. The collection consists of a single room crammed with weapons of every size and description. A few paintings depict major battles in gory detail. Traditional Batak houses stand in the rear courtyard surrounded by jeeps and motor scooters. Open Mon.-Fri. 8am-1pm. Donations requested.

■■■ BUKIT LAWANG

Technically, Bukit Lawang is not really a town at all, but a traveler's colony carved out of the rubber and cocoa plantations northwest of Medan. In terms of sights, Bukit Lawang is largely a one-horse—or rather, one-ape—town. Its *raison d'être* is the Bohorok Orangutan Station where the gentle primates, illegally kidnapped from the Sumatran rainforest and sold as pets all over the world, have been reintroduced to their natural habitat. No matter how touristy Bukit Lawang may be, the sight of a mother orangutan, child on her back, swinging out of the high jungle canopy to share a meal of bananas a few meters from your camera lens is a truly unique and exhilarating experience, and not one to be missed (or slighted).

Beyond attending a few orangutan feedings, however, there is little to detain you in Bukit Lawang, and most travel south to Brastagi or Lake Toba or north to Banda Aceh after a night or two. As to be expected, resourceful guest house operators have done all they can to make Bukit Lawang a sort of mini-Club Med with great apes. Tubing down the Bohorok River, hiking through the park, or more ambitious rafting trips on the nearby Wampu River are popular diversions.

ORIENTATION

The Visitor's Center, PHPA office, and tourist information center cluster near an **empty dirt lot bus "station."** The path leading upriver from the bus stop is sometimes referred to as **"Jalan Orang-utan."** About 500m upriver is an elaborate gate marking the entrance to a **public campground;** many of the most popular guest houses are beyond the campground along the river. The **Bohorok Orangutan Center** is about 1km upriver from the Visitor's Center on the opposite bank. The **Visitor's Center** puts out a helpful **map** of the guest houses and major attractions.

PRACTICAL INFORMATION

Tourist Office: Bukit Lawang Visitor's Center (tel. 544 491), on Jl. Orang-utan opposite the bus station. Organizes treks and rafting trips. Documentary on Bukit Lawang's famous red apes (Mon., Wed., and Fri., 8pm). Donations requested. Open daily 8am-3pm. **PHPA Ranger Station** (tel. 542 574), next door to the Visitor's Center. Organizes treks and nature walks with a ranger or local biologist. Direct questions about safety or permits here. Tickets to see the orangutans should be purchased here (but if you arrive late they can be bought at the feeding station). Rp4500 per person, good for 7 days (4 feedings). Open daily 7am-3pm. A **tourist information center** is down a path, left of the Visitor's Center. More for tours than for info. Organizes treks, rafting, and float tube trips downriver to Bohorok. Leave a message on their board if you are trying to put together a trek. Open daily 7am-6pm.

Currency Exchange: In a pinch, traveler's checks can be cashed at the *wartel* kiosk, Brastagi Tours and Travel, and some guest houses at awful rates.

Post Office: No post office. There are letter collection boxes. **Postal code:** 20774.

Telephones: Telephone kiosk on the left, off the path to the Bukit Lawang cottages behind the tourist information center. Rp2000 service fee for international collect calls, or pay with a credit card (5% fee). Open daily 8am-7pm.

Buses: The bus "station"— a small dirt parking lot—is near the Visitor's Center. To **Medan** (every hr., 5:30am-5pm, 3hr., Rp1300). Tourist buses leave daily at 7:30am to: **Brastagi** (5hr., Rp13,000); **Prapat** (10hr., Rp21,000); and **Bukittinggi** (with a change in Prapat, Rp45,000). Book at least one day in advance. Purchase tickets at tourist information, the Visitor's Center, or a guest house.

Medical Services: There is a tiny polyclinic next to the PHPA office.

Police: The nearest station is a few km down the road in Bohorok.

ACCOMMODATIONS

When the orangutan rehabilitation center was established in 1973, Bukit Lawang boasted a single grubby *losmen.* Today there are over 15, with more on the way. Room quality varies greatly, so ask to see a room and the *mandi.* The popular places fill up quickly, so come early for the best selection. There is a small **campground** about 500m upriver from the PHPA office just beyond a tall entrance gate. It's used almost exclusively by Indonesian students. With bamboo tent frameworks and little else. For info contact the PHPA office. No reservations needed. Rp200 flat rate to cover clean-up costs.

Ariko Inn (formerly the "Beverly Hills Resort"), about 800m beyond the orangutan rehab center. The path is long and at times a bit treacherous. Set amidst a bamboo grove surrounded by forest (with the nearest neighbors almost 1 km away), Ariko's as close to a tropical Shangri-La as Bukit Lawang gets. Excellent swimming hole, and the jungle teems with wildlife. Charming, simple bungalows—all constructed with local materials—along the river for Rp4000 (shared *mandi*). Smaller rooms above the central lodge and restaurant Rp3000. Attentive staff organizes treks. Laundry service.

Eden Inn, right before the campground entrance gate on the left, a short walk from the center of "town." Amiable place with clean, cheap, if slightly worn rooms offers excellent, well-established treks and rafting trips. They only employ HPI-licensed guides and post a list of those who can work in the Bukit Lawang area. Doubles with private balcony overlooking the rapids and shared *mandi* Rp3000.

Concrete bungalows on the river Rp5000 with private *mandi.* Inexpensive restaurant. Laundry service. Check-out 12:30pm.

Jungle Inn, about 400m beyond the campground entrance gate, conveniently located near the orangutan center. Bills itself as "simple but sweet." This Bukit Lawang institution has a 2-story restaurant decorated in true jungle style, complete with bamboo chairs and gnarled, twisting vines. Cheapest doubles are scurvy but clean with mosquito netting (Rp5000). Slightly larger rooms with *mandi* Rp8000. Rooms built over the river are some of the nicest in town—one of them has a large tree growing through the middle of the private *mandi* Rp10-12,000. Well-established trekking/rafting service. Laundry service.

Farina 53 Guest House, just past the campground entrance on the right. Hip and friendly. Chill at the bar with the upbeat staff and count the number of times "Hotel California" comes on the stereo. Built on a steep hillside, rooms have fabulous views of the jungle. All rooms have private shower and toilet. Basic double Rp5000 up to Rp6-8000 for more elbow room and better views. Deluxe rooms with porch, shower, western toilet, and jungle vistas befitting a Tarzan flick Rp12,500. Cheap restaurant. Laundry service.

Wisma Bukit Lawang Cottages (tel. 545 061), downstream from the bus station and across the river. Look for the Bintang Beer sign and follow the arrows. Popular with package tours. The grounds look like a tropical botanical garden. Simple, large doubles with private *mandi* (Rp7500) set back from the river; rooftop porch with trap-door entrance is way cool—an ideal spot to watch those cheeky monkeys. Traditional bungalows on the river are some of the nicest for the price (Rp10,000 with private *mandi*). Hotel-quality rooms with shower Rp20-25,000. Restaurant. Visa, MC.

Yusman Guest House, near the bus station. Look for their large sign and private bridge. A break from the stuffy rattan rooms of cheaper guest houses. Light, clean doubles with riverfront balcony, mosquito netting, writing desk, private shower, and fan Rp6000. Simpler wooden rooms minus shower and view Rp3000. Laundry service. Trekking and rafting trips available.

FOOD

There are **cheap warung and Padang joints** along the river near the bus station.

Goa Restaurant, just beyond the PHPA office. One wall of this fabulous restaurant is formed by a large river-weathered rock. Postcards sent to Goa's congenial owner from all over the world testify to its popularity. Curries are the name of the game, cooked to order and served in mammoth bowls. Vegetable curry with rice is a don't-miss (Rp2000). Chicken curry (Rp3500). *Gado-gado* and rice (Rp2000). A number of fruit juices. Open daily 7am-midnight.

Jungle Inn Restaurant, part of the Jungle Inn Guest House, near the river crossing to the orangutan rehab center. Even travelers staying elsewhere come to this renowned restaurant. A large menu of "jungle cuisine": *gado-gado* (Rp2500), *chapati* (Rp2000), and the mysterious "jungle food" (Rp2000). But this place's reputation was built on their titanic fruit salad of passion fruit, papaya, bananas, watermelon, and half a pineapple. Gasp at the size, laugh at the price (Rp1700). Fruitshakes (Rp1600), "exotic herbal tea" (Rp1200). Open daily 7:30am-midnight.

SIGHTS

Bukit Lawang's most famous guests are not backpackers but *pongo pygmaeus abelli,* the orangutans who live in the town's best known guest house—the **Bohorok Orangutan Station.** The station was founded in 1973, with grants from the World Wildlife Fund and the Frankfurt Zoological Society, to reintroduce orangutans who had been illegally captured back into their natural habitat. The entire process from the time they are brought to the station to the time they are released takes about three years. During this time the orangutans must be taught how to be orangutans again, from tree-climbing to nest-building and food-foraging. Initially, the orangutans are kept in pens which can be seen at the center. Later on, they are released into the forest around the station but are still fed by PHPA rangers twice a day. Finally, when the staff pronounces them to be sufficiently "street smart," the orangutans are taken deep into the park and left to fend for themselves. Since 1973, the orangutan rehabilitation project has successfully returned more than 140 animals to the Sumatran rainforest. For more information on the orangutans and the rehab project, the Bukit Lawang Visitor's Center shows an informative film on the subject every Mon., Wed., and Fri. at 8pm.

The station is about 1 km upriver from the Visitor's Center on the opposite bank. Visitors are allowed to observe the two daily feedings (8am and 3pm), which occur at a raised platform about 500m into the forest from the station. Rangers, armed with plenty of bananas and a tubful of enriched powdered milk, mount the platform and ring the dinner bell (by banging a stick against the floor).Within minutes, the awkward-looking but surprisingly agile creatures swing into view, patiently awaiting their turn on the platform. The primates are not camera shy, so bring plenty of film; a flash may be necessary during morning feedings or when skies are overcast. Permits good for two days (four feedings) can be purchased at the PHPA office or at the station (Rp4500).

Demonstrating once again the Southeast Asian tourism industry's love of subterranean attractions, there is a series of caves that can be explored south of town (downstream). Holy Hiking Trip! The best **"Bat Cave"** is about 2km south of Wisma Bukit Lawang Cottages, a 20-minute walk. Take the trail that begins behind the Wisma's main lodge; the path winds through a rubber plantation before turning right to the cave (there are signs). The cave itself is quite dramatic. To reach the entrance, which is partially obscured by hanging vines, you must first clamor up a series of rickety wooden ladders. The dark, dark (a flashlight is essential) cavern is filled with...bats. It's just like the cave in the beginning of *Raiders of the Lost Ark* where Indy takes the golden idol, minus the poison darts, rats, and giant boulder. A narrow corridor leads from the back of the cavern some 600m into the hillside. Guides can be hired at the entrance gate for Rp3000. Admission Rp500. About 1km beyond the Bat Cave is the **"Swallow Cave,"** named for its chief inhabitants.

■■■ BRASTAGI

On the surface, this former Dutch hill station is nothing but a dusty drag on the tourist bus route south to Lake Toba. But more active folks will find Brastagi, set against the ethereal beauty of North Sumatra's mountainous hinterland, a veritable garden of outdoor delights. Founded in the early 1900s as a retreat for plantation owners and colonial officials, Brastagi may well be the fruit capital of Southeast Asia. Its dark, fertile volcanic soil yields a cornucopia of exotic, succulent fruits, including the luscious *marquisa* passion fruit, famed around the world for its tastebud-titillating flavor.

The area around Brastagi is sometimes known as the "Karo Highlands," as it is the homeland of the Karo Batak people and a number of traditional villages. Climbers of all ages can tackle steaming Mt. Sibayak, which dominates the northern approaches to town and appears to be perpetually on the verge of another eruption. For diehards, there's regal Mt. Sinabung, 30km south of town, whose lower slopes are cloaked in damp, verdant jungle.

ORIENTATION

Downtown Brastagi consists of a single divided thoroughfare, **Jalan Veteran.** At the north end of Jl. Veteran stands a tall columnar **war memorial.** Here Jl. Veteran divides with **Jalan Gundaling,** to the left, leading up the hill past the fruit market toward **Mt. Sibayak** while Jl. Veteran, to the right, leads downhill out of town, eventually becoming the **Brastagi-Medan Highway.** The tourist info center, post office, and *wartel* offices are all clustered near the memorial. Heading south (downhill from the memorial), Jl. Veteran passes the bus station and **central market,** before dividing. The left-hand road continues 12km to **Kabanjahe** while the right-hand road, **Jalan Udara,** leads to **Mt. Sinabung** and the Karo village of **Lingga.**

PRACTICAL INFORMATION

Tourist Office: Tourist Information Center, Jl. Gundaling 1 (tel. 910 84). At the north end of town just to the left of the war memorial. Friendly, with excellent info on transport. Check here for upcoming Karo ceremonies. Guides to climb Mt. Sinabung and Mt. Sibayak. Will organize rafting and/or trekking trips in Gunung Leuser National Park. Open daily 8am-7pm. **Sibayak Guest House Losmen,** Jl. Veteran 199, is also an excellent source; they hire guides for treks and rafting and organize trips to Karo celebrations. Blackboard lists travelers assembling groups for ascents of the volcanoes or trekking/rafting.

Currency Exchange: Bank Rakyat Indonesia, Jl. Veteran 84 (tel. 912 32). Open Mon.-Fri. 8am-3pm. **P.T. Pura Buana,** Jl. Veteran 55 (tel. 911 50 or 915 14; fax 915 13). Visa, MC advance, 10% commission. Open daily 7am-noon. Also a *wartel.*

Post Office: Jl. Veteran 4. Next to the tourist office. Open Mon.-Thurs. 8am-2pm, Fri. 8-11am, Sat. 8am-2pm. **Postal code:** 22156.

Telephone/Telegram office: Telkom, Jl. Perwira 1 (tel. 914 06; fax 914 14). Next to the post office. HCD phone. Open 24 hrs. **Telephone code:** 0628.

Buses: Station is in front of the central market on Jl. Veteran. To cities other than those below, transfer from Prapat or Medan. To: **Medan** (every 10min., 4:30-8pm, 1-½hr., Rp1200; most stop at the war memorial also); **Pangururan** (every hr., 9am-3pm, 4-½hr., Rp4000); and **Kotacane** (every 30min., 9am-4pm, 5-6hr., Rp5500). No scheduled stop in Brastagi; ask at the tourist office or guest house to help you flag it down. Take a *sudako* from the market to **Kabanjahe** (Rp300). **Tourist buses,** in Prapat provide the only direct service to Bukit Lawang, passing through Brastagi at about noon, but there is no guarantee you'll get a seat. To: **Prapat,** with a stop at Sipisopiso falls (4hr., Rp12,000); **Bukit Lawang,** with a stop at Asam Kumang crocodile farm (6hr., Rp13,000). Book at least 1 day in advance. Purchase tickets at tourist office and most guest houses.

Pharmacy: Apotik Dharma Bakti, Jl. Veteran 49A (tel. 913 21). Open daily 8am-8pm.

Hospital: Public Health Center, Jl. Veteran 36 (tel. 910 28).

Police: Brastagi sector, Jl. Perwira 161 (tel. 911 10). Convivial cops!

ACCOMMODATIONS

Brastagi boasts some of the best and most professional guest houses in North Sumatra, with delicious kitchens and excellent information services. Many will also organize trekking and rafting expeditions in Gunung Leuser National park. Most of the *losmen* and cheap hotels are concentrated along the north end of Jl. Veteran near the war memorial.

Sibayak Guest House Losmen, Jl. Veteran 119 (tel. 911 22 or 910 95). From the war memorial head downhill; the guest house is about 200m on the left. One of the most popular guest houses in North Sumatra; the "tourist information" sign is no joke: the walls are plastered with helpful posters explaining Karo culture and rituals and documenting the area's many attractions. A great place to check if you want to organize a rafting, climbing, or trekking group. Warm staff keeps the rooms spic 'n' span. Dorms Rp3000. Singles Rp3500. Doubles Rp6000, with bath Rp7500. Triples with bath Rp9000. Excellent restaurant. Laundry service. Small bookshop on ground floor.

Wisma Ikut Guest House, Jl. Gundaling 24 (tel. 911 71). From the tourist office head north on the left branch of Jl. Veteran, passing the fruit market. Turn right just before the GKPS church. This rambling old wooden hillside mill once served as a restaurant and dance hall for colonial *soirees.* The towering ceilings and creaky floorboards remain, not to mention stunning views of Mt. Sibayak. Dorms Rp2000. Singles Rp4000. Smaller doubles Rp7000. Large doubles with private porch Rp10,000. All bathrooms outside. Restaurant. Laundry service.

Wisma Sibayak Guest House, Jl. Udara 1 (tel. 916 83 or 911 04). From the bus station, head south on Jl. Veteran. The guest house is set back from the road where Jl. Udara branches to the left. The same unparalleled info and maps as the Sibayak Losmen, but quieter and slightly more relaxed. Dorms Rp3000. 1 single Rp3500. Doubles Rp6000. Triples Rp9000. Outside bathrooms. Laundry service.

Ginsata Hotel and Guest House, Jl. Veteran 27 (tel. 914 41; fax 915 13). Across the street from the tourist office; lobby is behind the Irfan Padang Restaurant. Basic hotel (singles Rp7500, doubles Rp10,000) but the jewel is the guest house in an old villa around the corner from the hotel, removed from the hubbub of Jl. Veteran. Singles Rp4000; doubles Rp6000; large, airy doubles Rp7500. Endearing, homey atmosphere. Manager speaks fluent English and organizes excellent rafting and trekking expeditions in Gunung Leuser National Park. Laundry Service.

Crispo Inn (tel. 910 23), on Jl. Veteran. On the right of the road to Medan, a few meters beyond the spot where Jl Veteran forks. The swish lobby is lavish with antique furniture and carvings, but rooms are strictly proletarian. Cramped, if clean doubles with outside *mandi* Rp10,000. Rooms on the north side have windows. Plants in the halls break the monotony. Includes breakfast on the roof, which affords excellent views of Mt. Sibayak. Laundry service. Check-out 1pm.

FOOD

Save the luscious fruit, the eating in Brastagi isn't stellar. The best and most competitively priced food can probably be found in your guest house's kitchen. The Sibayak Guest House Losmen, in particular, has a lengthy menu of local and western favorites and mammoth portions. **Rumah Makan Irfan,** at Jl. Veteran 79 (tel. 914 41), on the ground floor of the Ginsata Hotel, opposite the tourist office, serves Padang food. The display case bulges with spicy curries, fried chicken, and Padang-style fried potatoes. English menu is helpful for neophytes. *Ayam gulai* Rp1700. *Kari kambing* (mutton curry) Rp3000. A number of fruit juices including Brastagi's finest: chilled *marquisa* passion fruit juice Rp1500. Open daily 9am-11pm.

SIGHTS

Brastagi boasts two bustling markets, both of which are worth visits as you wait for your aching leg muscles to recover from climbing the volcanoes. The massive, muddy, and aromatic **Pasar Sentral** (central market) is on Jl. Veteran behind the bus station. Hundreds of stalls selling everything from *sate* to CD players, though very few offer "souvenirs." Toothache? A tooth-puller will be happy to pop the offending molar out for a few thousand rupiah. Market open daily 6am-6pm (except Wed.). A vast **produce market** sets up in a field next to the central market, recognizable by the sea of umbrellas the farmers use to shield their goods from the elements. Flat-footed foreigners must keep on their toes to avoid being run over by careening handcarts loaded with several hundred kilos of veggies. Most produce is sold in wholesale quantities. A better place to sample Brastagi's famous fruit is, sensibly enough, the **fruit market** on Jl. Gundaling behind the tourist info center. Most fruit mongers speak some English and will sell fruit in 0.5kg quantities or more. Let your taste buds run wild. Choose from succulent mandarin oranges, divine mangosteens, the curious Brastagiapple (a hybrid of an apple, a peach, and a tomato), or the queen of them all, the heavenly *marquisa* passion fruit, an ecstasy rivaling the *bubur cha-cha* of Pulau Penang. The fruit market has become a regular stop for tourist buses en route to Lake Toba or Bukit Lawang. For the best deals come before the coaches arrive. The market opens at 8am, and some stands stay open until around 9pm.

HIKING THOSE SPEWING MOUNTS

Brastagi has been a tourist town since its founding in the early 1900s when even colonial officials from British Malaya would take time off from the exhaustive job of making others work for them to golf, ride horses, and attend lavish dinner parties. Today, most visitors come to Brastagi for more invigorating pursuits, chiefly hiking the volcanoes that make the landscape so spectacular. Most popular is the 2370m **Mt. Sibayak,** whose lopsided summit appears to be smoking, an illusion created by the very active sulphur steam jets on top. An exceptionally well-maintained trail (in better condition than sections of the Trans-Sumatran highway), complete with concrete steps, winds up the west slope of the volcano. The trail first descends down into a small valley, then climbs up through lovely tropical foliage en route to the large sandy-bottomed crater on top. The summit is truly martian, with nary a bush or shrub in sight, and dotted with shrieking sulphur jets injecting noxious-smelling steam into the air. The actual summit is fenced off and cannot be reached, as it contains a number of meteorological instruments, but the view of the valley below—a patchwork of fields and orchards—is breathtaking, provided the top isn't shrouded in low-lying clouds, as is often the case. An alternate route down the east slope of Sibayak to the Semangat Gunung Hot Springs slants away to the right from the lip of the crater. Despite being inlaid with steps, the trail is quite steep and during the wet season can be slick and treacherous. If you wish to climb this way, it is wise to begin from Semangat Gunung, and hike up, saving the easier western route for the way down. Bemos run between the central market and Semangat Gunung (Rp600). To reach the trail head for the west route, head north on Jl. Veteran, bearing left at the war memorial onto Jl. Gundaling. Turn right at the end of a soccer field just before the large Sibayak Multinational Hotel. Follow the road uphill for 30 minutes or so, passing the "Karo Hill Bungalows." Admission Rp500.

Mt. Sibayak can be climbed in 2-½hr; the descent will take 2hr. For the best chance of having an unobscured view from the top, start early as clouds tend to set in during the early afternoon. No matter what the guest house owners tell you, a guide is certainly not necessary to climb Mt. Sibayak. It is unwise to climb alone, but single travelers should have no problem attaching themselves to a group since the climb is one of the most popular activities in Brastagi. Remember that the weather can change dramatically in a matter of minutes; pack a rucksack with water, fruit, and a sweater, as it can be surprisingly chilly on top.

There are two sets of hot springs (*air panas*) northeast of Brastagi near the foot of Mt. Sibayak: the **Lau Debuk-debuk hot springs,** 14km from Brastagi, and the **Semangat Gunung hot springs,** 2km farther down the road toward the volcano. The Lau Debuk-debuk falls are the larger of the two, with several bathing pools allowing you to macerate comfortably in the sulphurous waters. Admission varies depending on the depth and poshness of the pool (Rp500-2500). Get there by minibus from the central market; ask for "Semangat Gunung" (Rp600) or hike down from Mt. Sibayak. The springs are open during daylight hours.

Sadly, Mt. Sibayak's slopes are now littered with refuse dropped by careless hikers. Serious hikers who wish to climb a more pristine, more challenging peak can hike **Mt. Sinabung** (2450m), a majestic, cone-shaped volcano, about 27km south of Brastagi. In addition to being higher than Mt. Sibayak and more remote, Mt. Sinabung should only be attempted by experienced climbers in good physical condition. Unlike Mt. Sibayak, the trails on Mt. Sinabung are crude and completely devoid of markings. There have been several fatalities on Sinabung over the last few years, most recently in August 1995, when a Danish hiker, climbing alone, plummeted 30m to his death. For all these reasons, it is highly advisable that travelers who wish to climb Mt. Sinabung heed the advice of the tourist office and guest houses and **hire a guide** for around Rp80,000 per day. The Sibayak Guest House Losmen has plenty of information about the volcano and several guides; make sure your guide is licensed by the HPI. Most hikers begin at the village of Sigaranggarang and end at Lake Kawar for a post-climb swim. Much of the hike is spent in beautiful virgin jungle. Although most Karo Batak are now Christian, they continue to believe that the forest is home to powerful spirits which must not be upset. Thus a Karo will often leave a small offering, such as a burning cigarette, at the foot of a tree when entering the forest. When hiking, do not yell loudly or curse and risk upsetting the powers that be. The final few hundred meters to the summit is over loose volcanic rock. The climb should take 3hr. on the assent, and 2-½hr. on the descent. The earlier in the morning you begin, the better your chances of having something to look at from the top will be; on a clear day it is possible to see shimmering Lake Toba 30km to the south. Chartering a bemo from your guest house is the best way to ensure getting an early start (Rp10,000 each way).

VISITING KARO VILLAGES

The highland region around Brastagi is the heart of Karo Batak country, and there are a number of Karo villages that can be reached in a day. Obviously, the farther from town you venture, the less heavily touristed the village will be, though these days you can count on paying an entrance fee (usually Rp300) and being pestered to buy things wherever you go.

Closest to town is the small village of **Peceren,** on the road to Medan, about 1.5km past the war memorial, just beyond the Rose Garden Hotel on the right. Karo dwellings complete with buffalo horns on the gables and thatched roofs sit side-by-side with modern, concrete houses topped with satellite dishes. Though guest house operators decry it as "impure," Peceren is a much more realistic look at Karo life than other artificially "traditional" settlements. The best time to visit is in the evening when the souvenir sellers have packed up. A not-so-stringently enforced Rp300 admission fee is required.

There are several other **Karo villages** a bit farther away including Barusjahe, with houses more than 200 years old (16km from Kabanjahe), Serdang (20km from Kabanjahe), and Dokan (23km from Kabanjahe). All can be reached by minibus from Kabanjahe. Check with the tourist info center for details. The Sibayak Guest House Losmen has mapped out a 3-hr. walking tour from Brastagi through several smaller villages, then to the larger, tourist-oriented village of **Lingga.** Check at their office for details.

LAKE TOBA (DANAU TOBA)

Few changes can be as dramatic (or as welcome) as the ones that occur during the short 180km drive south from Medan to Lake Toba. Gone is the muggy, oppressive heat of the Sumatran coastal plain, which is replaced by the cool, invigorating air of the Lake Toba highlands—a light sweater may be a necessary addition to your evening wardrobe. Physically, the shift from pancake-flat rubber and palm oil plantations to soaring volcanic cliffs is just as swift, and startling enough for first-time visitors to question whether they can possibly be on the same island.

Southeast Asia's largest body of fresh water, Lake Toba is widely regarded as one of the region's most beautiful and unique areas. The steep, craggy slopes that ring Toba form the rim of an ancient volcano, whose cataclysmic eruption some 80,000 years ago created the lake and may even have triggered the last Ice Age. In addition to being the largest crater lake in the world, the 590-m Lake Toba is also one of the deepest. In good weather, the water gleams a deep blue, contrasting brilliantly with the lush evergreen forests which ring the shore. When the skies are overcast and clouds spill over the surrounding cliffs, Lake Toba's beauty becomes almost surreal, as if you have reached the mythical "roof of the world" where earth and sky meet.

Not seen by western eyes until the 1850s, Lake Toba was then, as now, the home of the Toba Bataks, largest of the five principal Batak groups who inhabit the interior of North Sumatra. Despite the influx of tourists and the accompanying development boom, the Toba Bataks have stubbornly clung to traditional ways of life (minus the cannibalism). The towering, crescent-moon-shaped roofs of brightly painted *rumah adat,* or customary houses, are frequent sights in many lakeside villages, still governed by traditional laws. For travelers, Lake Toba offers something for everybody and every energy level—from swimming, trekking, or biking for the active, to simply lounging about with a gratifying book, and wallowing in the natural splendor.

■■■ PRAPAT

Nestled at the foot of a series of high, rolling hills on the eastern shore of Lake Toba opposite Samosir Island, Prapat enjoys the sort of picture-book location tourism developers salivate over...which is precisely what they did, largely spoiling the village in a prolonged frenzy of hotel construction. These days finding a square meter of undeveloped land is difficult. Even the picturesque hills that rise *alla Roma* in the middle of town, once topped only by quaint Batak churches, are now encrusted with boxy concrete hotels and hokey faux-Batak bungalows.

Visit Prapat on a weekday, when 90% of the rooms are empty, and you'll wonder how anyone, even rapacious tourism promoters, could justify such an orgy of construction. On weekends and holidays, caravans of buses from Medan roll into town, unleashing hundreds of weary urbanites escaping the insolubilities of their home city. Most backpackers feel as comfortable in Prapat and her grossly overpriced hotel rooms as Exxon execs at a Greenpeace picnic, and stay in town only long enough to leap on a ferry bound for Samosir Island. Still, a night in Prapat beats a night in Medan and—for the moment anyway—the excesses of tourism have not managed to eliminate the truly spectacular natural setting.

ORIENTATION

Jalan Sisingamangaraja is the main road, swinging roughly west-to-east through town, passing the police, *wartel,* and post office, as well as the bus station before heading toward Bukittinggi. **Jalan Kol. T.P.R. Sinagara** (formerly Jl. Pulau Samosir) branches off Jl. Sisingamangaraja at a large "Welcome Gate" along the lake, and follows the shore before crossing a small ridge and becoming **Jalan Haranggaol,** which leads downhill to the Samosir **ferry pier.** Countless souvenir stalls are along Jl. Haranggaol near the ferry launch.

PRACTICAL INFORMATION

Tourist Office: Jl. Kol. T.P.R. Sinagara 1 (tel. 411 11). Beneath the Welcome Gate. Will likely direct transportation inquiries to a travel agency. Open daily 8am-9pm.

Tour Companies: There have been reports of travelers paying large amounts of money for a meaningless slip of paper. Safest is to buy from established travel companies. **Andilo Nancy Travel Service,** the largest, has 3 offices: the bus station (tel. 412 76). Open daily 8am-10pm; Jl. Sisingamangaraja 76; and Tingaraja pier (tel. 415 34). Open daily 7am-6pm. **Raja Tour and Travel,** Jl. Sisingamangaraja 30 (tel. 412 46; fax 411 77). Booking for ANS buses. Open daily 7am-11pm.

Currency Exchange: Rates in Prapat are atrocious. Plan ahead. **Sejahtera Bank Unum (Bank SBU),** Jl. Kol. T.P.R. Sinagara 8 (tel. 417 03 or 414 93; fax 415 70). On the grounds of the Toba Hotel. Open Mon.-Fri. 8am-4pm. There are several **money changers** along Jl. Haranggaol, but rates are still poor.

Post Office: Jl. Sisingamangaraja 75 (tel. 414 88). Open Mon.-Thurs. 8am-2pm, Fri. 8-11am, Sat. 8am-2pm. **Postal code:** 21174.

Telephones/Telegram: Wartel Office, Jl. Sisingamangaraja 72 (tel. 411 58; fax 411 77). Collect call service, must pay for 1st min. Open daily 7:30am-midnight. **Telephone code:** 0625.

Buses: Purchase tickets at the station or through a travel agency for the safest, most comfortable alternative. Book in advance, particularly for far-off locales like Jakarta. Public buses and most private coaches leave from the station on Jl. Sisingamangaraja, about 1km east of the police station. The following fares are for non-A/C public buses. A/C fares are those quoted by ALS Bus company. To: **Medan** (5, 6, 9, 10am, noon, and 2pm, 4hr., Rp3500); **Brastagi,** take a bus to **Pemangtangsiantar** (a.k.a. Siantar) (every hr., 1hr., Rp1800), then switch to **Kabanjahe** (last bus 5pm), go the rest of the way by minibus (Rp300); **Bukittinggi** (noon, 18hr., Rp18,000; A/C noon, 2, and 4:30pm, Rp24,000); **Padang** (noon, 24hr., Rp24,000; A/C noon, Rp35,000); and **Jakarta** (noon and 1pm, 48hr., Rp52,000; A/C noon and 2pm, Rp75,000).

Ferries: Passenger ferries to **Samosir Island** leave from the Tingaraja Pier. Separate boats go to the main tourist destinations—Tomok, Tuk-Tuk, and Ambarita—on the eastern shore. Boats drop passengers at the accommodation of their choice. Touts on the boat will try to convince you to disembark at their accommodation. To: **Tuk-Tuk** (every hr., 9:30am-4:30pm, 40min., Rp800); **Tomok** (every hr., 8am-7pm, 40min., Rp800); **Ambarita** (every hr., 10am-5pm, 40min.,

Rp800). A rusting car ferry shuttles back and forth between the Ajibata pier (south of Tingaraja) and Tomok, following roughly the same timetable.

Local Transportation: Bemos shuttle continuously from Tingaraja to the center of town and the bus station. Should not cost more than Rp200.

Sports Equipment Rental: An array of watercraft, from inner tubes to speedboats, can be rented per hr., along the beach behind the ritzy Nataur Prapat Hotel, Jl. Marihat 1 (tel. 410 12 or 410 19; fax 410 19). Paddle boats Rp5000. Water scooters Rp25,000. Speed boats with driver Rp 65,000. Open daily 7am-6pm.

Market: There is a small Batak market every Tues. and Thurs. at the Tingaraja pier (6am-1pm), and a larger market on Sat. (6am-6pm); the best deals tend to be had in the mornings when sellers offer the ubiquitous "morning price."

Hospital: Parapat Public Hospital (tel. 413 32), on Jl. Rumah Sakit, which is on the left on a steep hill, about 800m past the bus station of Jl. Sisingamangaraja.

Police: (tel. 415 71), on Jl. Sisingamangaraja next to the large Welcome Gate.

ACCOMMODATIONS

Despite the mind-boggling number of hotels in tiny Prapat, there are surprisingly few decent budget accommodations. Still, the glut of pricier hotels means that, particularly during mid-week, it may be possible to extract bargains. There is a free public **campground** overlooking Prapat and Lake Toba. From the post office, head uphill (toward the bus terminal) on Jl. Sisingamangaraja; take a left onto Jl. Ranggur Sinaga about 20m past the first Pertamina gas station. Walk straight along this road about 30min. (it gets quite steep as it winds its way up the mountain). The campground is past a Protestant church on the right, behind a small radio station.

Pago Pago Inn, Jl. Haranggaol 50 (tel. 413 13). From the Natour Hotel, about halfway down Haranggaol, toward the pier, on the right. "Laid back" does not do the atmosphere justice, yet rooms are kept clean. Pleasant, hardwood-floor rooms upstairs, with a lounge and a balcony overlooking the lake and Samosir. Singles Rp7000. Doubles Rp10,000. Triples Rp12,000. Sparkling shared *mandis.*

Singgalang Hotel, Jl. Sisingamangaraja 52 (tel. 412 60; fax 413 32). About 50m past the police station on the right. Conveniently located near the bus terminal and inexpensive restaurants, but a bit removed from the tourist "strip" at Tingaraja. Large and slightly worn, but very clean rooms, each with 3 or 4 beds. Rates increase with the number of bodies—Rp7500 for 1, Rp15,000 for 2, Rp25,000 for 3, Rp30,000 for 4. The friendly English-speaking manager is eager to establish his place as a traveler's hangout and willing to cut deals. Shared *mandis* are squeaky clean. Check-out 1pm. Laundry service. Chinese restaurant downstairs.

Wisma Purnama, Jl. Haranggaol 85 (tel. 416 63). Heading down Jl Haranggaol, toward the ferry, it's on the left just before the Torgadero Restaurant. Rooms are clean, if dark. Paper thin, plywood walls don't give much privacy. Communal *mandis* are fairly clean. Owners don't allow for much English, but are eager to please. Singles Rp5000. Doubles Rp10,000.

FOOD

A number of restaurants line Jl. Sisingamangaraja, including a cluster of overpriced Chinese spots near the water; prices drop farther uphill, where cheap Padang dives abound. A **small fruit market** sets up daily near the Tingaraja pier where cheerful young women make a killing off the tourist bus crowd, who often forget to bargain.

Rumah Makan Yose, on Jl. Haranggaol, adjacent to the Pago Pago Inn on the uphill end of Jl. Haranggaol. R.M. Yose packs in more locals than a Balinese bemo. A wide range of curries (*kari*), like mutton, chicken, or veggie, and *soto* (soups). For a delicious meal for less than the cost of a New York cup of coffee, try the veggie curry and rice. For the more extravagant, there's shrimp in chili paste or fried lake fish. Most dishes Rp800-2500. No English menu, so learn the names of a few dishes or let your fingers do the talking. Open daily 9am-9pm.

Hong Kong Restaurant, Jl. Haranggaol 9/11 (tel. 413 95). Near the crest of the hill opposite a string of souvenir stalls. Large and popular with travelers, though more expensive than the smaller Padang shops (average Rp3-5000). *Gado-gado* like Soekarno's Mom used to make (Rp2500). Prawn hot plate (Rp6000). Choose from a number of fruit and vegetable juices (Rp1750-2000). Open daily 8am-10pm.

Hidangan Khas Minang, Jl. Sisingamangaraja 108 (tel. 414 61). About 100m past the Singgalang Hotel on the right. One of a gaggle of cheap Padang joints on Jl. Sisingamangaraja. The cleanliness and English menu set it apart from the crowd. All your Padang favorites including *ayam gulai* (chicken curry soup; Rp2250), *rendang* (Rp1500), and octopus chili (Rp3500). Fried fish straight from Lake Toba (Rp3500). *Nasi goreng* (Rp1750). Open daily 6am-1am.

SIGHTS

Unless you have an abiding interest in the usage of **concrete** in late 20th century **hotel construction,** there is not much to see in Prapat. There are several beaches along the narrow peninsula separating Tingaraja from the rest of Prapat (west of the Natar Prapat Hotel) which are popular on weekends and holidays, but the swimming is better on Samosir. Thankfully, no amount of "development" has been able to mar Lake Toba's truly spectacular natural setting. There are wonderful panoramic views of the lake and Samosir Island from the public campground, on a hill above Prapat; vistas are best in the early morning and at sunset. On Saturdays many Batak craftsmen flock to the Tingaraja market to hawk their wares.

■■■ SAMOSIR ISLAND

Samosir Island is, in fact, not really an island at all but a large mushroom-shaped peninsula jutting into Lake Toba; it officially became an "island" when the Dutch dug a canal across the peninsula's narrow neck at the town of Pangururan. Whatever its geographical circumstance, Samosir is an inevitable stop on most traveler's itineraries. There can be no denying the island's physical beauty, particularly along the eastern shore, where steep cliffs tower above coastal villages and rice fields, occasionally cut by narrow waterfalls which from a distance look like long strands of silvery saliva from Paul Bunyan's stony face. On Sundays, Batak hymns drift over the rolling fields, adding an almost ethereal soundtrack to the natural beauty of the setting. Oh, the hills *are* alive with the sound of music.

Sadly, Samosir is no longer the little-known backpacker's retreat of ten years ago. Tuk-Tuk peninsula has grown thick with guest houses, souvenir stalls, and restaurants. Furthermore, many locals, even those who make their livings off the tourist trade, have grown tired of the hordes of foreign visitors and make little effort to conceal their dislike. Nevertheless, Samosir remains an ideal spot to take a respite from the grind of travel in rural Sumatra: take advantage of the unparalleled swimming, trek through the unspoiled hinterland, or simply swap traveler's tales with your comrades-in-Tevas over cool banana *lassis* in one of the lakeside cafes.

ORIENTATION

Roughly 40km long and 20km wide, Samosir covers approximately 650sq km. The largest town on the island is **Pangururan,** the seat of local government, on the western shore. A single perimeter road circles the oval-shaped island, connecting Pangururan with **Tomok** on the eastern shore, where many of the ferries from Prapat land. At the northern tip of the island is the pleasant village of **Simanindo.** Most visitors stay on the **Tuk-Tuk peninsula** about 4km north of Tomok. The **Tuk-Tuk Ring Road** branches off the main road to the right about 3km north of Tomok at a small benzine station. The narrow strip of pavement, scarcely wider than a broad sidewalk, passes Tuk-Tuk's gold coast of guest houses and *warung* and continues along the shore to the small village of **Ambarita,** 3km up the coast. About 8km inland from Ambarita is the tiny hamlet of **Partokoan,** a popular stopover point for hikers on the Ambarita-Pangururan traverse. A second inland village, **Roongurni Huta,** on the trail from Tomok to Pangururan, is reachable by *sudako* from Pangururan.

PRACTICAL INFORMATION

Tourist Office: There is no official tourist office on Samosir Island but a number of restaurants in Tomok and Tuk-Tuk bill themselves as "Tourist Information Centers." But you'll probably get better info and advice from your guest house.

Currency Exchange: There is a tiny branch of the **Bank Rakyat Indonesia** on the main road in Ambarita. Rates are abysmal, as are those in the guest houses which provide exchange services. Change your money in Medan.

Post Office: Ambarita, Jl. Raya 39 (the main road). Open Mon.-Thurs. 8am-2pm, Fri. 8am-11am, Sat. 8am-2pm. **Postal code:** 22395.

Telephones/Telegraph: Overseas collect calls can be made from the **Abadi Guest House** in Tuk-Tuk and **Timbul Bungalows** in Ambarita. **Telephone code for Ambarita:** 0625. There is a new **Indosat office** in Pangururan, on the west side of the island, Jl. Dr. Fl. Tobing (tel. 201 24; fax 203 00), about 800m past the intersection with Jl. Sisingamangaraja, on the road headed along the south section of the island. Open 24 hrs. **Telephone code for Pangururan:** 0626.

Travel Office: A few tiny travel agencies on Tuk-Tuk sell tourist bus tickets, ferry tickets from Medan to Penang, and even airline tickets (though without phones, they cannot confirm flights). Most guest houses also sell tourist bus tickets. Beware of frauds; make your travel plans at a reputable travel agency in Prapat. **DWI Lucky Tour Service,** on Tuk-Tuk, near the Carolina Cottages Resort. Sells tickets for the tourist coach to Bukittinggi, Brastagi, and Bukit Lawang.

Buses: Pangururan has the only bus station on Samosir. **Pribumi Co.,** Jl. Sisingamangaraja 18. To: **Medan** via **Brastagi** (4 daily, 8am-3pm; Brastagi, 3-½hr., Rp4500; Medan, 6hr., Rp5000); **Medan** via **Prapat,** crossing at **Tomok** (6 daily, 7am-7pm, 6hr., Rp5000); and **Tarutung,** for **Bukittinggi** (8am, 3hr., Rp4500).

Ferries: To **Prapat** (7am-4pm, Rp800), leave from Tomok's public landing. Tuk-Tuk and Ambarita ferries leave from along the shoreline, passing all of the guest houses en route. Wave from your accommodation's pier. Everyone has a different opinion about when the last boat leaves. Tomok to **Ajibata** car ferry (every 3hr., 7am-7pm). Simanindo to **Tigaras,** north of Prapat (every hr.).

Local Transportation: Buses shuttle between Pangururan and Tomok (8am-4pm, Rp1500), tracing the north shore. Buses are quite small; when one arrives, it may be too full to fit you. To **Simanindo** (Rp600). Two *sudakos* per day run between **Pangururan** and **Roongurni Huta** (5am and 5pm, Rp600).

Rentals: DWI Lucky Tour Service, Tuk-Tuk. Bikes (Rp8000), motorscooters (Rp20,000), motorcycles (Rp25,000), and minibuses (Rp125,000; self-drive). All prices per day. Open daily 9am-8pm. Nearly every guest house will rent bikes and motorbikes for about the same rates.

English Language Bookstore: Gokhon Library, Tuk-Tuk. Owned by a Batak-Australian couple. Paperback thrillers, no guidebooks. Rents Rp2500-3000 flat rate or swap (Rp1500 transaction fee). Open daily 8am-7pm.

Medical Services: There is a tiny health center in Tuk-Tuk near the Mafin Guest House and a slightly larger one in Ambarita about 200m beyond the bank. Not recommended; in an emergency, return to Prapat or Medan.

Police: A tiny police box is on Tuk-Tuk near the "Carolina Cottages." Larger station in Ambarita is behind the Bank Rakyat Indonesia office opposite a soccer field.

ACCOMMODATIONS

As the premier backpacker destination in North Sumatra, there is no shortage of cheap guest houses in Tuk-Tuk and Ambarita, and because of this competition, the services are among the best and most complete. Not too long ago, Ambarita was considered an escape from the thick guest house concentration of Tuk-Tuk; these days, however, guest houses crowd the shore all the way to Ambarita and beyond. Still, the density does decrease away from Tuk-Tuk and it is possible to feel, if not exactly isolated, then at least not claustrophobic. Any accommodation worth its **Batak Bungalow** offers bike and motorcycle rental, laundry service, and food. With the exception of the best-known guest houses, there are no fixed room rates; prices depend on the proprieter's whim and your bargaining acumen. Prices tend to be lowest in the late afternoon when owners are faced with the unhappy prospect of an empty room; it is widely held that any foreigner with a large pack must be on the verge of physical collapse and therefore willing to pay more, so come *sans* pack.

Tuk-Tuk

Samosir Cottages, on the northeast shore of the peninsula, about 50m off the perimeter road. May provide the best combination of value and quality on Tuk-Tuk. Freshly scrubbed rooms boast a fab view, privacy, and tranquility. Simple motel-style rooms with large picture windows, terraces, and private baths: Rp8000 for 1, Rp12,000 for 2. Larger doubles with hot shower Rp20,000. Typical faux-Batak bungalows a stone's throw from the water Rp10,000. Catch a big-ass fish in the large freshwater pond; the kitchen will cook it up Batak-style (Rp3000). Satellite TV, VCR. Cross-island treks and rafting expeditions.

Bagus Bay Stayhouse, on the south "neck," at the beginning of the string of guest houses. A large, popular guest house, run by a Batak man and his Australian wife. On a placid inlet great for swimming; guests are free to use the canoes and wind-surfer. Simple, if impersonal, singles and doubles, with shared *mandis,* Rp4000 and Rp5000. Bungalows in split-level Batak-style cottages with private bath Rp10,000. Economical Indonesian and western food at the central lodge. Batak music every Wed. and Sat. night. Laundry service.

Abadi Guest House (tel. 415 17), on the north shore of the neck of the peninsula, 50m past Reggae. One of Tuk-Tuk's original guest houses, with gracious professional management. All rooms face the steep, dramatic cliffs that separate the peninsula from the rest of Samosir. Cramped, spartan doubles Rp3000 for 1, Rp4000 for 2. More spacious doubles Rp5000-7500. Hot water doubles Rp10-15,000. Restaurant dishes Indonesian, Chinese, and Euro nosh. International collect call service. Laundry service. Check-out 11:30pm.

Mafir Guest House (tel. 414 62), at the crest of a small hill on the south shore of the peninsula between the Bagus Bay and the Carolina Cottage. In a place where stunning vistas are de rigeur, Mafir's southern exposure is one of the best. Large, clean, pastel rooms with large picture windows. Attached shower and Asian toilet. Singles Rp5000. Doubles Rp8000. Triples Rp12,000. Large souvenir shop and restaurant with homemade yogurt. Laundry service.

Tony's Guest House (tel. 412 09). On the north shore of the peninsula, near Abadi and Reggae Guest Houses. Simple, clean rooms have private verandas, bathroom, and writing desk, across the road from the lake: Rp4000 for 1, Rp5000 for 2. Larger rooms with hot water Rp6-10,000. Batak cottages on the lake Rp3-5000. Intimate restaurant with superb views of the hills and waterfall serves cheap Indonesian and Chinese fare (Rp1500-3000). Check-out 10am.

Reggae Guest House, on the extreme north tip of the peninsula before it begins to narrow again. Nary a Marley banner in sight and Indonesian pop dominates the stereo. Pleasant all-wood rooms would have Bob wailin'; all rooms have private bath but forgo the *mandi,* get up, and take a morning dip in the water, 4 feet away. The open-sided "Nelson Vugo Restaurant" is a great spot for sunset gazing (Rp500-3000). Laundry service.

Ambarita

MAS Accommodation. Squeezed onto a narrow strip of land between the lake and a steep hill; you're never more than a hop, skip, and jump from the water. It's as isolated as Ambarita gets these days. Large rooms with picture windows, verandas, and western bathroom Rp4000 for 1, Rp7000 for 2. Upstairs Rp500 more for the view. Swanky new rooms with hot water Rp15-20,000. Batak houses Rp4-7000. Waves lap the walls of the glassed-in restaurant, a spectacular spot to watch incoming rain squalls. Kitchen prepares traditional Batak feasts (Rp30,000 for 2). Laundry service. Check-out 11am.

Timbul Bungalows (tel. 413 73). About 300m north of MAS. Built on a mini-peninsula with lake views in 3 directions. Most rooms are individual cottages which afford privacy. Basic bungalows Rp5000. Larger rooms with western toilet and shower Rp6-10,000. 2 Batak houses built on hills take first place for view and privacy (Rp5000). International collect call service from restaurant. Laundry service.

Barbara's Guest House (tel. 412 30). About 3km north of Ambarita village on the road to Simanindo, the Ambarita ferry stops here. On the grassy, windswept coast with stunning views of the lake and the Samosir highlands. Jovial staff and an array of services including overseas collect calls. Excellent swimming spot. Dorm Rp2000. Rooms Rp5000 for 1, Rp7500 for 2. Spacious doubles with private bath (western toilet, shower) Rp10,000, Rp7500 for 1 person. Laundry service.

FOOD

Most travelers eat at their guest houses, whose kitchens offer a wide range of food at rock-bottom prices. There are throngs of *warung* and small restaurants in Tomok and Tuk-Tuk, many proudly offering "Magic Mushroom" omelettes. Beware: hallucinogens might sound like fun, but visitors have reported getting sick. *Let's Go* does not condone this activity.

Tabo Vegetarian Restaurant and Bakery, Tuk-Tuk. On the south neck of the peninsula, 40m east of the Bagus Bay Stayhouse. Tabo offers a funky atmosphere and great vegetarian food. Run by a German-Indonesian couple; guests sit in wicker chairs at tables hewn from tree trunks or on cushions at low tables. Sandwiches made with freshly baked bread. Tofu, tempeh, and veggie burgers (Rp3000). For the decadent, rice soufflé and crepes. Most dishes Rp2-3500. Open daily 8am-11pm.

No Name Pizzeria and Bookshop, Ambarita. Located about 4km north of town on the road to Simanindo, past Barbara's and Sibala guest houses. Bizarre interior: ceiling covered with fishing nets gives it a cobwebbed Halloween feel, while Christmas signs decorate the stone walls. Although owned by a Neopolitan, it is the Balinese chef who dishes up mouth-watering pizzas using mozzarella, oregano, and ham imported from Italy. Offers 7 kinds of pizza (Rp5000-65,000) from vegetarian to the "Diablo." *Buonissima.* Pasta dishes (Rp5-6000), and salads (mixed greens Rp3000). Shakes and *lassis* for dessert. Free transport back to your guest house if you're staying in Tuk-Tuk or Ambarita. Open daily 10am-11pm.

SIGHTS

Most travelers come to Samosir Island for the chance to spend a few lazy days splashing in the lake, to mix with their fellow wanderers, and to take advantage of the rock-bottom prices. Nevertheless, for slightly more active and cultural pursuits, the island boasts worthwhile attractions, mostly along the east shore, within 20km of Tomok. Motorcycles and bicycles are far and away the best way to get around Samosir, saving you from the infamously unreliable bus system.

There are several **megalithic tomb complexes** in Tomok near the public landing. The refrigerator-sized coffins, adorned with highly stylized and enigmatic faces, were built to house the remains of a line of local Batak kings, the Sidobutars (whose descendants still live in Tomok). From the pier, head west across the main road. The first complex is on the right a few meters up, surrounded by a stand of bamboo trees. In addition to several tombs (Sidobutar *Rajahs* #7, 8, and 9), there are a number of stone chairs and statues of humans and animals, all hewn from single blocks of stone and now overgrown with moss and lichen.

Continuing down the path past the first set of tombs brings you to the **Museum of King Sidobutar,** in a small, traditional Batak house. The collection consists of a random assortment of Batak artifacts, including musical instruments, swords, and a bewildering series of black and white photographs, presumably of the king's family (there are no captions). Farther uphill is the **tomb of Rajah Ompu Soribuntu Sidobutar** himself, which lies beneath the bows of a majestic *bariam* tree. Don't expect to be awed by the silent grandeur of the sights, or to feel as if you had suddenly been transported to Batak's golden age; the king's tomb is now encrusted with souvenir shops, hawking everything from "Batak calendars" and "Batak medicine bottles" to the tie-dyed shirts and baggy fisherman's pants that are all the rage among Tuk-Tuk's tourist populace. For the best deals, come early. Admission to museum and tombs is by donation. Open during daylight hours.

A more interesting, and slightly less commercialized megalithic site, **Siageller village,** is 8km up the road in Ambarita, behind the post office and near the town harbor; the Tuk-Tuk road leads right to it. Hidden behind a row of well-preserved Batak houses is a collection of stone chairs, a stone table, and what appears to be a stone sofa (it's only missing the stone TV set to make the perfect Flintstone living room). It was here that village honchos would arbitrate quarrels; if the offense was grievous enough, the loser would be led to the second set of stone furnishings, where he or she would be cooked and eaten. The Toba Batak were known to practice cannibalism, albeit sparingly, into the 20th century.

North of Ambarita, the island perimeter road passes through peaceful farmland, and the dramatic cliffs behind Tomok and Tuk-Tuk gradually recede into rolling hills, occasionally dotted with Batak shrines. Some 20km later it reaches the village of **Simanindo,** on the northern tip of the island. Simanindo is home to the **Hut Bolon Museum,** famed for its performances of **traditional Toba Batak dance,** pictures of which figure prominently in postcards sold throughout the archipelago. The show takes place in "Huta Bolon Village" a small well-preserved Batak Village (now strictly a museum show piece) surrounded by a meter-high stone wall. Most interesting of the traditional buildings is the large *rumah rajah,* or king's house whose ornate, red, white, and black gables are stenciled in the distinctive Toba Batak style. Helpful sheets explaining the village and each dance routine are provided as part of the Rp3000 admission. At the end of the performance members of the audience are invited to don sashes and join the Batak dancers. The actual museum consists of a single *rumah adat,* but the collection of Batak tools and handicrafts, including some fine carvings, is well-explained and presented. Open daily 9am-4pm. Dance performances are held Mon.-Sat. at 10:30am and 11:45am, Sun. at 11:45am; each lasting about 45 minutes.

If you find yourself stuck in Simanindo without transport back to your guest house on the east coast, spend the night at the **Bintang Restaurant,** which has several basic rooms for Rp3000 per night (outside *mandi*). Off Simanindo is the small resort island of **Pulau Tao,** where very nice private bungalows can be had for about Rp50,000 per night. To get there, hire a boat from the public pier, at the end of the dirt road that passes Huta Bolen Museum.

Gray, uninspiring **Pangururan,** on the west coast, is Samosir's largest town. Come here for scenic forays into the hills on the mainland, such as the **Mt. Belirang hot springs** or **Mt. Tele.** Easily reached as a daytrip from the east coast, trapped visitors can stay at the friendly **Barat Accommodation,** Jl. Sisingamangaraja 66, (tel. 200 53), in the center of town. Basic rooms with communal *mandi* Rp4000, doubles Rp7000. The restaurant downstairs serves basic backpacker fare. Mr. Barat, the friendly Batak owner speaks good English and is an excellent source of info on Batak culture, history, and lore. Also has helpful maps of town, the hot springs, and cross-island hiking trails.

Kurt Stüttecker and his wife run **rafting and trekking trips on the Sahan River,** 30km south of Prapat, in Parhitoon. Mr. Stüttecker, who has 10 years' experience leading trips all over the world, gears for budget travelers (US$35 for 2 days, US$15 per additional day), with a "European" level of safety. Trips offered for all skill levels; Stüttecker estimates their most challenging float, the "most extreme whitewater trip in Asia" to be class VI rapids. They also organize treks, staying in highland villages, or combined trekking/rafting trips. Inquire at the Bagus Bay Guest House or the Tabo Vegetarian Restaurant in Tuk-Tuk, or at the Andilo Nancy travel company in Prapat.

HEY, I'M HIKING ACROSS SAMOSIR ISLAND

The cure for claustrophobic blues is an invigorating hike across the breadth of the island for a glimpse of modern Batak life that is less tarnished by tourism. There are two basic routes, from either Ambarita or Tomok, west to Pangururan, or, conversely, from Pangururan east to Ambarita or Tomok. Either way, it is possible to complete the traverse in a single day if you start early and hike fast; hiking from west to east is generally regarded as the faster route, as you miss the very steep section along the east coast. Well-marked trails wind around isolated Batak villages, which have not been prettied up for the tourist trade, and numerous coffee, clove, and tapioca plantations; at certain times of the year, the air is heavy with the rich aroma of roasting coffee beans.

A better way to fully appreciate the interior is to stay the night in one of several villages with homestays. Hikers setting out from Ambarita (the preferred route) will pass tiny **Partokoan,** home of two guest houses, **John's** and **Jennie's.** John, who speaks some English, puts travelers up in his traditional Batak house with his family. Near Partokoan is **Sidihoni Lake,** with good swimming. Past Partokoan, where the trails from Ambarita and Tomok merge lies the larger village of **Roongurni Huta** where there are several more homestays.

From Ambarita (38km from Pangururan), the path begins opposite the Bank Rakyat Indonesia office; look for the large sign advertising John's Guest House in Partokoan. From Tomok (51km from Pangururan), the trail begins behind the tomb of King Sidobutar. From Pangururan, the dirt road to Roonguri Huta branches off to the left off Jl. Dr. Tobing, opposite a Catholic Church. Less ambitious hikers may choose to hike only part of the way up from Ambarita, where you can catch lovely views and colorful sunsets. Another trail leads to the narrow waterfall that cascades down the jungle-covered cliffs opposite Tuk-Tuk. The trail begins next to the small benzine petrol station at the intersection of the main road and the Tuk-Tuk perimeter road (2km). A pleasant alternative route from Tuk-Tuk to Ambarita begins here as well. Follow the waterfall path for about 200m and then take a right. The narrow dirt road leads through several small villages, past churches and across rice fields before rejoining the main road near Ambarita.

SOUTH OF LAKE TOBA

■■■ BUKITTINGGI

Perched amid the mountains at 1000m, Bukittinggi is a large town with a small backpacker heart. The full cafés in the evening give the impression that the town is overrun by tourists, and it is, but Bukittinggi has so many sights that during the day you'll only see a few foreigners at a time. Where tourists go, all aspects of the tourist industry follow: there are more travel agents offering culture and adventure tours than there are brilliant accommodations listings below. Minangkabau culture predominates, most notably in food and architecture. Traditional arts and crafts (woodcarving, silver, and *songket* weaving) can be bought in the market and in nearby villages.

ORIENTATION

The hills in the center of town lead to winding roads and tricky navigation; let an angkot drop you at your destination. **Jalan A. Yani** is the heart of the backpacker scene. The stylized miniature **Minang house,** which stands over the lower end of the street, supports a footbridge connecting the **zoo** and the site of the old Dutch **Fort de Kock** on the hills on either side. Walking uphill, you shortly reach **Jam Gadang** and the **upper market** (Pasar Atas). Heading west brings you to **Jalan Yos Sudarso,** and **Jalan Teuku Umar,** which heads to Panorama Park, the Ngarai Canyon, and villages such as Kota Gadang.

PRACTICAL INFORMATION

Tourist Office: (tel. 224 03), on the left of Jam Gadang, with a good view of the town below. Friendly and organized, with information on local sights and events; can help find qualified guides. Open Mon.-Thurs. 8am-noon, Fri. 8-11:30am.

Travel Agencies/Tours: Everywhere on Jl. A. Yani. They arrange air, bus, and taxi travel; rent motorbikes and safeboxes; change money; and offer a variety of tours.

P.T. Randy, by Hotel Gangga. Open daily, 8am-8pm. 6- and 10-day tours to Siberut Island are best arranged here. Talk to travelers to find good guide.

Currency Exchange: Bank BNI, Jl. A. Yani 126 (tel. 225 78), offers competitive rates. Open Mon.-Fri. 8am-4pm. Travel agents exchange at slightly better rates.

Post Office: GPO, Jl. Jend Sudirman 75, a bit south of town. Open Mon.-Sat. 8am-5pm, Sat. 8am-noon. Branch office, by the tourist office. **Postal code:** 26116.

Telephone: Central wartel (tel. 343 96), on Jl. A. Yani. No collect calls; cash only. Open daily 7:30am-8:30pm. P.T. Randy, and other travel agents will sometimes handle collect calls. **Telephone code:** 0752.

Local Transportation: Angkots run around town for Rp200.

Buses: Long-distance journeys are best arranged via travel agent. **City bus terminal,** at Amur Kuning 3km out. Buses to **Padang** (2-3hr., Rp1500).

English Language Bookstores: Along Jl. A. Yani: **Tilas** near the footbridge and **Setia** near the top of the hill. Exchanges welcome.

Market: Pasar Atas (upper market) and **Pasar Bawah** (lower market) merge twice a week (Wed. and Sat.) as small stalls line the distance between the two. Open daily on a smaller scale.

Pharmacy: Apotik Al-kautsar, Jl. Kesehatan 17, just past the bottom of Jl. A. Yani and to the left. Open 24 hrs.

Police: (tel. 110), on Jl. Jend Sudirman, south of town.

Emergency: Ambulance: (tel. 118 or 210 13). **Fire:** (tel. 113).

ACCOMMODATIONS

Accommodations roughly cluster in price range in the same manner that they cluster along Jl. A. Yani—most places are at the lower end.

Hotel Gangga, Jl. A. Yani No. 40 (tel. 229 67). As busy as those fraggles and doozers. Has singles for Rp3500 and Rp5000, doubles Rp6000 and Rp8000, triples Rp1500; all with *mandi* Rp10,000-20,000. They make most of their money from the drinks sold at night, however.

Hotel Yany, Jl. A. Yani No. 101 (tel. 227 40), has rather minute, bottom-end room that Kermit and Miss Piggy could use for their honeymoon for Rp3000, 5000, and 7000. Better rooms Rp6000, 10,000, and 15,000. Tag on hot showers for Rp1750.

Tigo Balai, Jl. A. Yani No. 100 (tel. 218 24). Has decently lit rooms and clean beds, like the one you had when you kept Star Wars actions figures beneath your pillow, dressed like a Jawa, and only spoke in chirps. Singles Rp5000 and 7000. Doubles Rp7000 and 9000. Triples Rp10,500. Quads Rp14,000.

Hotel Grand, Jl. A. Yani No. 111 (tel. 211 33). Upstairs rooms are in high demand. Fight like one of the Masters of the Universe for them, and then calm down with one of the morals taught at the end of *He-Man* episodes. Singles Rp5000, doubles Rp7000, triples Rp10,000. With *mandi* Rp15,000 and Rp20,000 respectively.

Rajawali Homestay, Jl. A. Yani No. 52 (tel. 319 05). At the bottom of the hill, a geographical technique also followed by David the gnome. Dorm beds Rp3000, singles Rp6000, doubles Rp7000. All with private *mandi.*

Bamboo House 27, Jl. A. Yani No. 132 (tel. 233 88). Whatever happened to the first 26? Nice dorms for Rp4000. Singles and doubles with *mandi* Rp8000 and Rp10,000 respectively.

Singgalang Inn, Jl. A. Yani No. 130 (tel. 215 76). Insulated from pedestrian traffic but has standard rooms where Sylvester could chase Tweety all day long. Singles and doubles with shared *mandi* Rp8000.

Hotel Nirwana, Jl. A. Yani No. 113 (tel. 212 92). Depending on your length of stay, room rates can be as "flexible" as Gumby and Pokey. Average rates: singles Rp7000, doubles Rp8000; with *mandi* for 2-4 people Rp20,000-25,000.

Just Tropical Homestay, Jl. Yos Sudarso 19 (tel. 349 46), up Jl. A. Yani and off to the right. Rooms are almost as cheerful as Malibu Barbie's Beach Condo. Singles Rp8000, with *mandi* Rp12,500. Doubles Rp10,000, with *mandi* Rp15,000.

Mountain View, Jl. Yos Sudarso 31 (tel. 216 21), has average rooms in a prime, relaxing location, with, of all things, a mountain view. Singles Rp12,000. Doubles Rp16,000. Triples Rp20,000. All with *mandi.*

Hotel Marmy, Jl. Kesehatan 30 (tel. 233 42). Downhill from Hotel Sr Kandi to the right, the road becomes Jl. Kesehatan. Marmy is fairly spacious and nice, kinda like Sesame Street. Singles and doubles Rp15,000, both with *mandi* Rp20,000.

FOOD AND ENTERTAINMENT

Tasty Minang food dominates the culinary spectrum at backpacker cafés and *warungs*. Cheapest meals can be had on big market days, amid the maze of stalls in **Pasar Bawah.** *Warung* hawk their treats around **Pasar Atas** and on Jl. A. Yani at almost any hour. Backpacker cafés cluster at the bottom of Jl. A. Yani. The most happenin' places include **Rendezvous Café, Under the Bridge** (a little more expensive), **Three Tables, Harow Cliff, Cosy Cave Café, The Coffee Shop** (for light meals and drinks), and the **Jazz and Blues Café** with its groovy, break-beat atmosphere. All serve Indonesian, Minang, and western food at inexpensive prices. The hangouts tout tours as well as disseminate info about the Indonesian travel circuit.

Bukittinggi hosts nightly **dance performances** as well. The Saliguri troupe does traditional Minangkabau dances on Tuesday and Friday (8:30-10:30pm) at a small theater down the hill behind the tourist office. It is a lively cultural introduction well worth the Rp7500. Bring all your recording devices. For those with time, they even offer dance instruction on a personal basis.

SIGHTS

Bukittinggi's market bustles on Wednesdays and Saturdays making for daring adventures and bargaining galore as you stock up on souvenirs for those left behind. Towering above the marketplace, the charming face of **Jam Gadang,** a big Dutch-built clock with Minang roof, oversees the din and activity. On the hillside to the east, above Jl. A. Yani, the city **zoo,** another disharmonious Dutch innovation, houses a small collection of stuffed animals and whole skeletons. The live animals in the zoo, from gibbons and orangutans to alligators and elephants, meander rather abjectly in 1930s-era Dutch cages. The park surrounding the zoo connects by the footbridge above Jl. A. Yani to the site of the Dutch **Fort de Kock.** Admission to these is Rp1100. Open daily 7am-6pm. Also in the park, in the Minang *rumah adat* is a **museum** chock-full of interesting psychological and religious commentary on Minang culture. Admission Rp300. Open Sat.-Thurs. 8am-5pm, Fri. 8-11am and 2-5pm. From Jl. Panorama, southwest of Jam Gadang, you can reach **Panorama Park,** which has, well, panoramic views of **Ngarai Canyon,** as well as entrances to the **Japanese tunnel system,** where many Indonesians died from enforced labor by the Japanese during the WWII occupation. Admission Rp300. Across from Jl. Panorama is an **Army Museum** with military relics and disturbing photos. Donations requested; open Sat.-Thurs. 8am-5pm, Fri. 8-11am and 1-5pm.

If you crave meandering through the Ngarai canyons, skip Panorama Park and hike to **Kota Gadang,** a silver-working town across the canyon. Follow Jl. Teuku Umar, head left at the fork in the road, and take the trail behind a coffee shop at the first big switchback. Stop at the coffee shop to inquire after Rev—his knowledge of flora and fauna makes him an invaluable guide for the curious.

Farther afield is **Kota Baru,** renowned for its Tuesday and Saturday evening buffalo fights. To get there, hop on a bus from Aur Kuning terminal—no need for a tour. **Pandai Sikat** is a handicraft town, specializing in carvings and *songket* weavings. Take a bus to Kota Baru, then catch an angkot, or walk the last 2km. Buses also run to **Batang Palupuh,** a nature reserve for the Rafflesia flower named after who else, but Sir Stamford Raffles! (For more info, see page 771.) To the northeast is the beautiful nature reserve, **Harau Canyon.** Buses run from Aur Kuning to Lamaksari (44km); from there, your feet will have to finish the 3-km to the entrance. For those who like to be on top of things, a climb up **Mt. Singgalang,** just southwest of Bukittinggi, is invigorating but not too difficult. The trail starts from Pandai Sikat, and the top is at 2878m. Many people climb at night and come down after sunrise. **Mt. Merapi** last erupted in 1979, but is still considered dangerous and is officially closed to climbers. Barely taller than Singgalang at 2891m, it has a broad flat top and looks a bit more menacing. The climb is arduous, so think twice before thrill-seeking.

Lake Maninjau fills an extinct volcanic crater, 36km from Bukittinggi. Still rather untouristed, small-scale plantations and jungle claim most of the caldera walls. The road to Maninjau village probably qualifies as one of the most tortured strips of asphalt built for transportation purposes. The descent to the lake involves 44 hairpin bends, but the weaving and careening is balanced by the soporific sound of the engine. There is a jungle path down from the top—take a bus to Matur or Lawang (Rp700), climb the last couple km, then descend (Rp200) in a couple of hours (watch out for the ground-dwelling leeches in wet areas!). Or take a bus all the way to Maninjau from Aur Kuning (Rp800). There are accommodations in Maninjau, and some secluded, cheap "beachfront" bungalows in **Bayur,** like the small **Rizal Beach Homestay** (tel. 614 04); singles Rp4000 and doubles Rp 6000.

■■■ PADANG

Whether you approach by ground or air, arrival in the seat of West Sumatra's provincial capital involves a dramatic descent from Bukit Barisan to the coastal lowlands. Welcome signs are topped with miniature Minangkabau roofs which curve up to impossible points, like the horns of the tiny buffalo that toppled its Goliath-buffalo adversary centuries ago, and from which the Minangkabau ("buffalo-winner") take their name. Local beaches are fair, but offshore islands are excellent. Padang's catch-22 weather, however, complicates your travels: when the sun is out it's too hot to wander for long; when it rains (which it often does) it may dampen your day and deprive the vistas of their colors. Logically enough, the city is *the* place for Padang food; if it gets too spicy, reach for a bowl of bananas.

ORIENTATION

The coast runs from north to south along Padang's west edge. The **bus terminal** is on **Jalan Pemuda,** one block over (called **Jalan Diponegoro** south of the terminal and **Jalan Veteran** farther north). The main street is **Jalan M. Yamin,** which runs east to west and intersects at the south corner of the bus terminal. Moving east, Jl. M. Yamin runs past the **oplet** station, the **market,** and the unmistakable **Matahari Plaza.** The next main intersection is **Jalan Aziz Chan/Jalan Sudirman.**

PRACTICAL INFORMATION

Tourist Office: Dinas Pariwisata (Regional Office), Jl. Sudirman 43 (tel. 342 31). Helpful brochures with maps of W. Sumatra, some info on the rest of Indonesia. English spoken. Walkable distance, or catch a colt or bus kota (14A) headed up Jl. Sudirman. Open Mon.-Thurs. 7:30am-4pm, Fri. 7:30am-3pm.

Tours: Hotel Candrawasih, Jl. Pemuda 27 (tel. 228 94), across from the bus terminal, organizes 7-10 day jungle treks and daytrips to offshore islands.

Travel Agencies: Katanam Tours and Travel, Jl. Pemuda 17C (tel. 254 44), across from the bus station. Mostly for airline tickets and currency exchange. Open Mon.-Fri. 8am-3:30pm, Sat. 8am-noon.

Currency Exchange: Bank Bumi Daya, Jl. Sudirman 2A (tel. 338 40), central and friendly. Open Mon.-Fri. 7:30am-3pm. There are **money changers** along Jl. Pemuda, but banks give better rates.

Post Office: Pos Besar Padang, Jl. Aziz Chan 7 (tel. 278 15). Poste Restante. Open Mon.-Fri. 6am-8:30pm, Sat.-Sun. 8am-6pm. **Postal code:** 25000.

Telephones: Wartel CV Ria, Jl. Belakang Tangsi 3 (tel. 376 90), just off Jl. Yamin. Open 24 hrs. Fax, telex, and international and collect calls. **Central office,** Jl. A Dahlan 17 (tel. 250 09), north of town. **Telephone code:** 0751.

Airport: Bandara Tabing Airport, about 10km up Jl. Pemuda. Buses and *oplets* will take you there; a taxi will cost Rp5-6000 to the airport, but more coming into town. **Mandala Airlines,** Jl. Pemuda 29A (tel. 327 73) runs daily to **Jakarta** and to other points from there. **Merpati and Garuda,** Jl. Sudirman 2 (tel. 318 50), fly 3 times per week to **Singapore** and daily to **Jakarta, Medan,** and **Palembang.**

Sempati, Jl. Ir. Juanda 79 (tel. 516 21) flies daily to **Jakarta,** twice per week to **Kuala Lumpur,** and 4 times per week to **Pekanbaru. Pelangi,** Jl. Diponegoro 13 (tel. 342 64) flies 4 times per week to **Kuala Lumpur.**

Local Transportation: Bemos will have officially disappeared at the end of 1995. There are plenty of **angkots**, whose rates range Rp200-400. Their terminal is by the market. **City buses,** with their throbbing bass systems and deafening airhorns, also vary in price. **Dokars,** called **bendis,** have some almost horse-sized ponies here. **Taxis** are easily hailed.

Ferries: Teluk Bayur harbor is the way out of Padang by sea. **Pelni,** Jl. Tanjung Priok (tel. 336 24), at the harbor, has boats to the islands of **Sikakap** and **Sioban** and to **Jakarta.** There are also boats to other **Mentawi Islands** for good surf.

Car rental: Pt. Natrabu, Jl. Pemuda 29 (tel. 330 08), a travel agent across from the bus terminal, rents cars and minibuses. Open daily 8am-5pm.

Market: You could spend several days in the **Pasar Raya,** a few blocks of throbbing buildings. Lots of *batik* tablecloths and bedsheets.

Public Toilets: Matahari Plaza Building

Swimming Pool: Pangeran Beach Hotel, Jl. Juanda 79. Admission Rp5000.

Pharmacy: Apotik Wirasakti, Jl. Kani 106 (tel. 271 81). Centrally located. Open Mon.-Sat. 8am-2pm.

Hospital: RS Dr. M. Jamil, (tel. 223 55) on Jl. Kemerdekaan.

Emergency: Police: tel. 110. **Ambulance:** tel. 118 or 323 72.

Police: (tel. 239 66), on Jl. Yamin.

ACCOMMODATIONS

Padang is as hot as its food, but keeping cool will cost you. Just to avoid lugging their bags too far, many forego slightly nicer places for the sake of convenience.

Hotel Benyamina, Jl. Aziz Chan 19 (tel. 223 24), down an alley behind Femina. Well worth braving the heat, if you're willing to venture beyond the bus station. Upstairs rooms get a nice breeze, and it's clean and pleasant. Tea and morning snack are included. 10% tax is extra. Singles Rp13,500. Doubles with fan and *mandi* Rp21,500. Triple suite with TV Rp32,500, with A/C Rp40,000.

Sriwijaya, Jl. Alang Lawas I/1 (tel. 235 77), follow the signs to the right off Jl. Yamin/ Jl. Proklamasi. Another nice spot for a good value. Economy rooms have fans, but share *mandis* Rp 8-, 12-, 16-, and 20,000, single to quad. With *mandi:* single 12,500, double Rp15,000. With A/C, rooms range Rp17-26,000. Small restaurant and juice available.

Hotel Minang, Jl. Diponegoro 17 (tel. 333 83), a few blocks south of Candrawasih, where Jl. Pemuda changes names. Expensive rooms, but also a frequently empty dorm room with 4 bunkbeds, shared *mandi*, and no fan for Rp6000.

Hotel Tiga Tiga, Jl. Pemuda 31 (tel. 226 33). Across from the bus terminal, Tiga Tiga has many rooms of decent cleanliness and mosquito-proofing, but not soundproofing. High volume turnover of backpackers. A minuscule restaurant, but good common areas. Economy rooms, with no fan and shared *mandi* are Rp10-, 15-, and 20,000 for 1, 2, or 3 people. Standard rooms with fan and *mandi* are Rp20-, 26-, and 32,000. With A/C Rp25-, 33-, and 41,000.

New Tiga Tiga, Jl. Veteran 33 (tel. 221 73). About 1km directly north of the terminal. Rooms are a little nicer, catering to a less transient crowd, but more expensive. Singles, doubles, and triples with fan, Rp20-, 25-, and 30,000. With A/C Rp25,000, 32,500, and 40,000. All rooms have *mandi*, price includes breakfast.

Hotel Candrawasih, Jl. Pemuda 27 (tel. 228 94), also across from the terminal. The rooms are dark and uninviting, but jungle treks and day trips to offshore islands are organized here. No fan, shared *mandi* Rp 8-, 14-, and 18,000 from single to triple. With fan and grimy *mandi*, rooms are Rp18-, 22-, and 28,000.

Hotel Machudum's, Jl. Hiligoo 45 (tel. 322 83), to the right of Jl. Yamin, across from the market. Nothing special in the budget range. A haven for businesspeople who love to lurk, talk, and hand out their cards. Economy rooms with fan Rp10,000; with *mandi* Rp15,000; with A/C and hot water Rp22,500.

FOOD

For the less daring Padang restaurants have more than Padang food. The **Simpang Raya** chain does brisk business, so what you eat probably hasn't been sitting in a window all week. **Fruit** can be had behind the Matahari building for breakfast; **lunch warungs** are at the bus terminal; at **night, Jalan Yamin** is alive with culinary activity, and there are also warungs set up along the **beach,** where Jl. Yamin ends. There is an A/C food bazaar on the second floor of **Matahari** with lots of variety.

SIGHTS

Most "culture" in this city is pre-digested to some extent. The **Taman Budaya** (Cultural Center), Jl. Diponegoro 19, stages traditional dances most evenings, so go by to check the schedule. Across the street at Jl. Diponegoro 10, the **Museum Negeri** is easy to find, in a traditional Minang house with two rice barns out front. The gate is at the far end on Jl. Gereja. The upstairs cultural exhibits aren't bad, while the downstairs display exhibits some untranslated propaganda (unlikely to convert the English-only reader) and some equally untranslated textiles. Open Tues.-Sun. 9am-4pm. Admission Rp250.

Padang's beach is dangerous to swim in, but locals go there to exercise in the mornings, running back and forth between rock pylons. The beach at **Air Manis** is long and tame, and it's possible to walk out to a small, forested island during the low tide. Get there by walking south along the beach until you hit the river—narrow boats ferry across for Rp200 per person. On the other side, the path leads past **Japanese fortifications,** through a **Chinese cemetery,** and eventually to the beach (about 4km; admission to the path Rp300, same for the beach). From the far end of the beach it's about 1km more until the road, where angkots shuttle in the shadow of the immense cement plant. In the more distant waters there are **coral-ringed islands** for snorkelling; excursions run from the Candrawasih Hotel.

■■■ BENGKULU

A friendly, backwater provincial capital, Bengkulu will remind weary travelers of why they love Indonesia. The city is a pleasant surprise on the southwest coast of Sumatra, just west of the Barisan mountains. It is one of the pilgrimage hot spots for Soekarno fanatics, with Bung Karno's former house and cell. It's also a good place for Rafflesia hunting—the flower was "discovered" here by Sir Stamford Raffles in 1818 when he decided Sumatra was too difficult to govern and turned his attention to the surrounding wilderness. There's not a lot to *do* in Bengkulu, but that's part of the charm. Uncrowded, unspoiled, convenient beaches are hard to come by, and with a full range of accommodations nearby, Bengkulu can't be beat.

ORIENTATION

The main road into town runs southeast to northwest and changes names from **Jalan Parman** to **Jalan Suprapto** at the BNI Bank boat sculpture; from Jl. Suprapto to **Jalan Jend. Sudirman** at the tall red-roofed Jamic Mosque; and continues sinuously to the left as **Jalan Jend. A. Yani.** The **beach** is on the southwest coast.

PRACTICAL INFORMATION

Tourist Office: (tel. 212 72), on Jl. Pembangunan. Take a yellow colt headed out of town. More convenient **travel agents** have the same brochures. Don't put much faith in local maps.

Currency Exchange: BCA, Jl. Suprapto 150A (tel. 217 04), downtown and willing to trade. Open Mon.-Fri. 8am-2pm. Be aware that a lot of banks along Jl. Parman does not mean a lot of exchange options.

Post Office: GPO, on Jl. Parman III, far, far away. Take a yellow colt headed out of town. A **closer branch** is at Jl. A. Yani 38 near Ft. Marlboro. Open Mon.-Thurs., Sat., 8am-2pm, Fri. 8-11am. **Postal code:** 38223.

Telephones: Telkom office, Jl. Suprapto 132 (tel. 200 00). Open 24 hrs. International and collect calls. **Telephone code:** 0736.

Airport: 14km south. **Merpati Airways,** Samudera Dwinka Hotel, Jl. Jend. Sudirman 246 (tel. 633 37), has daily flights to **Jakarta** and **Palembang.** Open Mon.-Fri. 8am-5pm, Sat. 8am-2pm, Sun. and holidays 8am-1pm.

Buses: Citra Rafflesia (tel. 203 13; open 24 hrs.) and **San Travel** (tel. 218 11; open daily 6am-6pm). Both are a sharp right from the Jamic Mosque on Jl. Haryono and provide trans-Sumatran and Javan transport.

Local Transport: Becak, dokar (pony carts), or freshly painted, dust-free **microlets** (Rp250).

Market: Pasar Minggu, just north of Jl. Suprapto off Jl. Abidin. A few supermarkets on Jl. Suprapto, including **Puncak Dept. Store,** Jl. Suprapto #28.

Hospital: RS Jiwa (tel. 229 88), on Jl. Bakti Husada.

Emergency: Ambulance: tel. 211 18.

Police: (tel. 210 41), by the BNI Bank boat.

ACCOMMODATIONS

Bengkulu has dirt-cheap *losmen* with friendly, laid-back atmospheres. It's worthwhile to invest in a fan and some mosquito coils (Rp500 for 10). Even odd-hour arrivals can be handled; just knock persistently.

Bumi Endah Guest House, Jl. Fatmawati 21 (tel. 216 65), left of the mosque at the BNI Bank boat. Clean, pleasant rooms with white sheets and light walls, on a quiet street close to town. Singles Rp13,200. Doubles Rp19,800. With A/C all are Rp27,500. Prices include tax and a small breakfast.

Nala Seaside Cottages (tel. 218 55), on Jl. Pantai Nala down a walk-way behind a white gate just past the Horison Hotel. Pink cottages are snug, with standard A/C. Singles Rp30,000. Doubles Rp33,000. Extra bed Rp7500 including tax and breakfast. 1 restaurant, 2 monkeys, and many great views.

Hotel Vista, Jl. Haryono #67 (tel. 208 20). Prime location if you want to be near the bus area. Lovely, quiet rooms in back, a restaurant up front, and friendly management in between. Singles (at their most basic) Rp6500. Doubles range from Rp7500-Rp15,000 according to location and amenities. The Rp12,500 rooms with fan and *mandi* are a solid choice.

Losmen Damai, Jl. Abidin #18 (tel. 229 12). In the heart of town, north of Jl. Suprato on the way to Pasar Minggu. A bit dark in the small rooms, but cheap, cheap, cheap. Singles Rp3000, with *mandi* Rp6000. Doubles Rp4000, with *mandi* Rp7500. Fan is Rp1000.

Losmen Surya, Jl. Abidin #26 (tel. 213 41). Across from Damai, Losmen Surya has great rooms up front on the 3rd floor, with a great view and a cool breeze; other rooms are fair. All share *mandi*. Singles Rp6000. Doubles Rp8000. Fan Rp1000.

Losmen Samudera, Jl. Benteng 203, next to Fort Marlboro. A lot of rooms with nice windows for lighting, but the airport-style lineup of W/C and *mandi* stalls in the back is a bit seedy. Singles Rp3500. Doubles Rp7000. Triples Rp10,500.

FOOD

There are no particularly special restaurants in Bengkulu, but you can find many Padang eateries. A collection of **warung** lies on Jl. Jend. Sudirman, near the theaters, and another is behind the market. **Bakeries** on Jl. Suprapto serve the bread-starved, but Wall's ice cream hasn't made it here yet. Try a *pokat coklat* to satisfy your sweet-tooth (avocado puree with chocolate swirls and sweetened condensed milk).

SIGHTS

Easy to find (thanks to the blue streetsigns) is the **Rumah Bung Karno** (Brother Karno's Home) down to the right of the mosque by the BNI ship on (what else?) Jl. Soekarno-Hatta. The house where Soekarno served in internal exile from the Dutch is small, but it has pictures, Bung Karno's bicycle and wardrobe, a collection of his (all Dutch) books, and a small case filled with books about him. Open daily 8am-5pm. Admission Rp200. Farther into town, at the end of Jl. A. Yani, is **Benteng Mar-**

lboro (Ft. Marlboro) overlooking the sea. Reconstructed a few years ago, it's in good shape now, has a small caisson with historical pictures of the fort, and good views of the sea and town. The cell where Soekarno was imprisoned is no longer marked, so make your own best guess. Open Sun.-Thurs. 8am-2pm, Fri. 9-11am, Sat. 8am-noon. Admission Rp100. To get there you pass by the **Proklamasi Monument,** which is in front of the **Balai Kota** (Governor's House). **Chinatown**, such as it is, is located behind the Pasar Bengkulu building, by the sea to the left of the fort. If you make it to the tourist office, the **Bengkulu Museum** in its impressive building, is nearby on Jl. Pembangunan. They have ancient artifacts as well as good examples of Bengkulu's distinct *batik*, *kain besurek,* which is based on Arabic script motifs.

Bengkulu's beaches, accessible on foot by waltzing through the Nala Seaside Cottages or continuing down their road and paying Rp200, are clean and wide. Surf breaks on a rocky reef offshore by the cottages at **Pantai Panjang.** Farther south is the white beach of **Pasir Putih,** by the **Pulau Baai harbor,** about 19km away. The harbor is the departure point for Pelnis weekly service to **Enggano Island,** home to a few villages that rarely see visitors. To stay on Enggano contact the *kepala desa,* the village head, upon arrival. Enjoy the beaches, but beware the poisonous snakes in the jungle. The Samudera Dwinka Hotel, Jl. Sudirman 246, arranges boats to **Pulau Tikus** (Rat Island) visible from the beach. It has a lighthouse and is a popular day-trip fishing spot.

There is a dried **Rafflesia** flower at the university campus, and the motif is found in many designs, but those hoping for the real thing should go first to the PHPA office at Jl. Mahoni 11. The PHPA office should have hints about where to look, on the outskirts of Tabapenanjung and Kepahiang. Rafflesias typically bloom during July and August for a couple of weeks. The yearly 10-day **Tabot Festival** in early July commemorates the martyrdom of two Islamic heroes, Hussin and Hassan, with colorful props and parades.

The Life of Sir Stamford Raffles: Part the Fifth

With fame and fortune secure in England, after his highly important stint in Bogor, the Colonialist Wonder, Sir Stamford Raffles, relentlessly devoted to oriental exotica, returned to the archipelago as the administrative advisor in Bencoolen (present day Bengkulu) in southwest Sumatra. Finding the Sumatrans too unruly even for him, Raffles (and some botanist named Arnold), discovered the world's largest flower, which he fittingly named after himself, *Rafflesia arnoldy.* (To uncover one of Sir Stamford's greatest achievements, see page 271.)

■■■ PALEMBANG

As the capital of South Sumatra province, Palembang's wealth flows from the ground; Pertamina oil refineries provide much of the city's infrastructure. The Srivijaya empire reigned here for about five centuries, though very little remains to show for it. There are some statues at the museums, and a few graves scattered about. Reigning much later, the Dutch left their mark with the bakeries across the city, but the influence has been distorted away from hearty bread to chocolate sprinkles.

ORIENTATION

All the facilities are on the northern **Ilir** side of the river. **Jalan Jend. Sudirman** runs northwest from the **Ampera Bridge** and is the noisy and dusty main drag. **Jalan Iskandar** runs east from the intersection at the **International Plaza,** and runs past **Jalan Kol. Atmo** which parallels Jl. Sudirman. Farther up, **Jalan Sudirman** crosses **Jalan Kapt. Rivai.**

PRACTICAL INFORMATION

Tourist Office: Dinas Parawisata, on the ground floor of the Museum Budaya, behind the MONPERA monument. Brochures for Palembang and South Sumatra.

Open Mon.-Thurs. 8am-4pm. The head of the office can give a full history lesson, and will negotiate for a day of guide services.

Currency Exchange: Bank BNI, Jl. Sudirman 142 (tel. 313 502). Open Mon.-Fri. 8am-4pm, Sat. 8am-1pm.

Post Office: GPO, Jl. Merdeka 3 (tel. 352 626), next to the MONPERA. Open Mon.-Fri. 7am-8pm, Sat.-Sun. 7am-6pm. **Postal code:** 30132

Telephones: Jl. Merdeka 5 (tel. 360 056). Right of the GPO. Fax, telegrams, telex, and international and collect calls. Open 24 hrs. **Telephone code:** 0711

Airport: Sultan Mochmud Badarddin II Airport, 12km north of town. Taxis run there; buses are caught 2km away on the main road. Merpati, Garuda, and Mandala serve **Palembang.** Bouraq and Sempati serve **Bangka** and **Belitung Islands.**

Trains: The station is south of the river and west about 4km. Morning and evening trains to **Bandar Lampung** and **Lubuklinggau.** Buses and minibuses to town.

Buses: The best way to leave town is by bus. A rash of bus companies on Jl. Kol. Atmo, north of Jl. Iskandar by Gramedia Book Store, go every which way in A/C comfort. **ANS** (tel. 364 814), **PO Putra Remaja** (tel. 356 185), and **CSH 88** (tel. 357 107) are open daily until early evening and run to: Padang and Bukittinggi (15hr.); Malang (24hr.); Jakarta (17hr.); Bandung (20hr.); Yogya and Surabaya (22hr.); Denpasar (30hr.); Medan (34hr.); Aceh (45hr.); and Bengkulu (10hr.).

Ferries: Ferries to **Bangka** and **Belitung Islands** can be arranged through most travel agents such as **Lukuta Ltd.,** Jl. Kol. Atmo 609 (tel. 364 029)

Local Transportation: Oplets and **buses** of all colors zoom around, and have more legroom than usual (Rp200). There's a terminal by the train station and one near the GPO. **Becaks** help slow down traffic, unrestricted from anywhere.

Taxis: They're around, or call **Trans Ampera Taxi** (tel. 811 520).

Market: The **Pasar 16 Ilir** really has no clear boundaries and extends some distance just across the bridge, northeast of Jl. Jend. Sudirman. A few km up Jl. Jend. Sudirman is **Pasar Cinde,** north of the intersection with Jl. L. Jalmas.

Public toilets: On every floor of International Plaza on Jl. Sudirman; other shopping centers as well, and at Pasar 16 Ilir.

Swimming Pool: Lumban Tirta, on Jl. POM IX Kampus. Open daily 8am-7:30pm. Admission Rp1500; check for student discounts.

Pharmacy: Apotik Rora (tel. 350 086), opposite International Plaza. Open 24 hrs.

Hospital: RS Caritas, Jl. Sudirman 809 (tel. 353 375).

Emergency: Police: tel. 110. **Ambulance:** tel. 118 or 354 088.

Police: Jl. Iskandar 35 (tel. 354 350). Open 24 hrs.

ACCOMMODATIONS

Palembang offers nothing budget-oriented and nothing spectacular. Stay somewhere convenient, then move on. There are plenty of expensive hotels, but *losmen* seem to have slipped out of existence here. Wherever you stay, you'll want a fan.

Hotel Sintra, Jl. Jend. Sudirman 38 (tel. 354 618). Enter from the "Seman Baturaja" overpass and head up the stairs. Rooms that face the street (but are far enough from the street to be nice) and rooms that don't, with big corridors in-between. Basic, with fan, singles Rp20,000, doubles Rp25,000. With TV, singles Rp27,500, doubles Rp33,000. Pleasant A/C rooms Rp38,500-Rp44,000. Anything above basic has a spring mattress. Coffeshop downstairs. Price includes breakfast.

Hotel Sari, 1301 Jl. Kapt. A. Rivai (tel. 313 320), at the intersection with Jl. Jend. Sudirman. All rooms have A/C, TV, bathtubs, and hot water. Singles Rp30,250. Doubles Rp37,500. Includes breakfast. Restaurant next door.

Hotel Sriwidjaya, Jl. Iskandar 31 (tel. 355 555) is down an alley on the south side of the street. Rooms are pretty clean and come with towels. With *mandi* and fan: Singles Rp17,875-20,350. Doubles Rp18,700-24,750. With A/C and TV: Singles Rp 29,425. Doubles Rp32,450. Includes breakfast.

FOOD

The best place for a variety of options is the **International Plaza** food court. From bland fast food to classic Indonesian fare to spicy local specialties like **pempek** (soft dough around chilis, veggies, and more). It's all here, even carrot juice for the health food crowd! Small restaurants and bakeries run the length of **Jl. Sudirman,** with low prices but no menus. Fish, fruit, and veggies for sale at **Pasar 16 Ilir.**

SIGHTS

The **Ampera Bridge** is a good place to view life on the Musi River. As you stroll across it and out of the city, the architecture shifts from urban concrete behemoths to the traditional wooden *rumah limas* homes, raised above the swampy land on stilts. If you want to cruise the Musi, bargain with a captain at the **Boom Baru dock** and expect to pay Rp25,000 for four hours. To the immediate left on the north side of the river is **MONPERA,** standing like a concrete origami experiment, or a very well-folded napkin. It's actually a military monument with Rp250 admission. Across the street is **Mesjid Agung,** a mosque built in 1738 but since restored. Behind MONPERA is the **Museum Budaya** in an old, restored Dutch building, upstairs from the tourist office. Open Tues.-Sat. 9am-2pm, Sun. 8am-2pm. Interesting Srivijayan artifacts lie about the grounds in varying states of decay. The **Museum Negeri Propinsi Sumatra Selatan** (tel. 411 382), 5.5km north of the city, has well-organized (but not translated) collections. The textiles and traditional outfits are interesting, as are the traditional *rumah limas* and the statues out back. Some of the more curious sculptures, including a larger-than-life cow pitcher, are inspired by museum pieces. Open Tues.-Thurs. and Sun. 8am-2pm, Fri. 8-11am, Sat. 8am-12:30pm. Take a bus heading for Km12 and get off at the museum turnoff. From there it's about 0.5km to the left.

There is a public garden, **Hutan Wisata Puntikayu,** on the way to Km12. The gardens are popular with couples, but not as nice as the one in Bogor. Palembang is also a departure point for **Bangka** and **Belitung Islands** in the waters to the east, toward Kalimantan. They are both fully equipped tourist spots with accommodations and transport available to pristine white-sand beaches and fine diving spots; contact the tourist office for info and equipment.

■■■ BANDAR LAMPUNG

The port city Telukbetung and its hillside neighbor Tanjungkarang comprise the urban region of Bandar Lampung. The capital of Lampung province, the city is a natural rest-stop for the weary backpacker in Sumatra and an excellent source of "ship cloth" tapestries and *tapi* sarongs, distinct with their gold and silver embroidery. Backpackers are likely to end up in this transportation hub anyway; air, train, and bus routes pass through the city, and *becak* drivers may throw themselves at you to convince you that you need a ride. Nevertheless, most of Bandar Lampung is necessarily laid-back due to the equatorial heat. Surrounded by beaches and islands, its most famous neighbor is the infamously not-laid-back Krakatau, the island-volcano that demolished Telukbetung in 1883. Every July the people of Bandar Lampung commemorate this mass destruction with traditional Lampung dances and music, along with parades, races, car rallies, and a foot and boat biathalon around Krakatau.

ORIENTATION

Ferries from Merak, Java arrive in Bakauheni, 90km southeast of Bandar Lampung. **Merak** is served by buses from almost everywhere in West Java; the most frequent are from Jakarta's Kalideres station (3-½hr). There are also trains from Tanah Abang Station. **Bakauheni** is a crowded Rp1700 bus ride to the Rajabasa bus terminal, 10km north of Bandar Lampung (1-½hr, plus a few minutes to the city itself).

The **Rajabasa bus terminal** and **airport** are both well north of the city; the **train terminal** is just down the road from most of the cheap accommodations on **Jalan Kotaraja,** which intersects with **Jalan Kartini.** Jl. Kartini runs N-S, changing names a few times along the way, but the Kartini area is the center of administrative functions, and most buildings cluster around it.

PRACTICAL INFORMATION

Tourist Office: Department of Tourism, Post, and Telecommunications, Jl. Kotaraja 12 (tel. 650 84). While it doesn't seem to be officially set up as a tourist info center, the office has Lampung and Bengkulu brochures for tourists. Open Mon.-Thurs. 8am-3:30pm, Fri. 8am-2:30pm.

Travel Agency: Femmy Tours and Travel, Jl. Monginsidi 143 (tel. 446 90), far south on the corner where Jl. Kartini is Jl. Monginsidi. Sells Merpati flight connections to **Jakarta.** Also charters **minibuses** for up to 8 people for Rp200,000 per day. Open daily 8am-4pm.

Currency Exchange: BCA Bank, Jl. Bukittinggi 18D (tel. 665 65). Bring a purchase agreement and passport. Max. on AmEx US$300 per day. Open Mon.-Fri. 8am-12:30pm. **Bank BNI,** Jl. Kartini 51 (tel. 55 202). Max. US$100 per day. Open Mon.-Fri. 8am-4pm.

Post Office: Jl. Kotaraja 12, next door to the tourist office. Open Mon.-Thurs. 8am-1pm, Fri. 8-11am, Sat. 8am-noon, Sun. 9am-5pm. **Postal code:** 35111.

Telephones: Telecom, Jl. Majapahit 14 (tel. 674 31). Open 24 hr. Catch a green colt. Home Country Direct and collect calls. There are also **Wartels** at the Telcom Building on Jl. Bukittinggi, just past the police station, which do international calls, fax, and telex. **Telephone code:** 0721.

Airport: 24km north of the city. **Merpati Office,** Jl. Kartini 90 (tel. 632 26), also sells Garuda tickets, flights daily to **Palembang** and **Jakarta**. Open Mon.-Thurs. 7:30am-noon and 1-4:45pm, Fri. 7:30-11:20am and 1:45-4:45pm, Sat., Sun., and holidays 9am-1pm. Visa, MC, DC accepted.

Buses and Colts: Damri public buses and multicolored **colts** loop around the city. Leaving the central Tanjungkarang area will involve several changes. Trips between each terminal cost Rp200-300. Many destinations will involve stopping at more than one terminal, and you will have to pay each time.

Ferry Crossings: The 27km ferry crossing from Merak to Bakauheni is included in bus and share-taxi fares, but deprives you of the option of the **small fast boat,** which offers A/C, TV, and comfy seats (4 daily, under 1hr., Rp3000). The big proletarian boats serve cars and buses as well (every hr., 2hr., 3rd class Rp1300, 2nd class Rp1900, 1st class Rp2400).

Taxis: All over town. **Dynasty Taxi,** Jl. KH A Dahlan 53 (tel. 456 74). For destinations outside the city, **Po Ratu Intan,** Jl. Kartini 102 (tel. 513 35) runs **share-taxis** to: **Jambi** (12hr.); **Palembang** (7hr.); **Pekanbaru** (20hr.); **Pulau Batam** (20hr.);and **Jakarta** (5hr.) For the comfort of A/C and snacks, prices aren't bad. Also charters **minivans.** Open daily 10am-10pm.

Car Rental: The ostentatious **Sheraton Inn Lampung,** Jl. Monginsidi 175, (tel. 486 666) can arrange a car with Indonesian-speaking driver for Rp175,000 per day. English speaker on request.

Market: Bambu Kuning Plaza, between Jl. Bukittinggi and Jl. Imam Bonjol, is a textile/clothing/shoe market with fruit and veggie vendors outside. **Pasar Seni,** by the Telcom office, has a variety of wares and some great *batiks.* Open daily. **Tanjung Karang Plaza,** has a **supermarket** on the 3rd fl., about a 15-min. walk down Jl. Kartini. Open daily 9am-9pm.

Swimming Pool: The Sheraton Inn has a pool with an Rp8000 "cover charge"; unclear if uninvited guests can swim, but if you dress nicely and eat a light lunch at their restaurant (watch the 21% tax!), they'll probably allow it.

Pharmacy: There's one on almost every block. **Apotik Tanjung Korang,** Jl. Bukittinggi 112 (tel. 523 07). Open daily 8am-9pm.

Hospital: RS Dr. H. Abdul Moeloek, Jl. Sriwijaya 15 (tel. 523 73).

Emergency: Police: tel. 55 110. **Ambulance:** tel. 118.

Police: (tel. 532 83). On the intersection of Jl. Kartini and Jl. Imam Bonjol, by the pedestrian overpass. Open 24 hrs.

ACCOMMODATIONS

Affordable accommodations are smack in the center of Tanjungkarang. From the bus station, take the Damri bus to where it turns onto Jl. Kotaraja, and the road it leaves becomes Jl. Kartini. Most things come in threes: there are 3 sleazy *losmen* on Jl. Kotaraja, and 3 low-price hotels on Jl. Kartini. **Hotel Berke** at Kotaraja 19 offers rooms for Rp5000. Next door at #21 the **Hotel Gunungsari** (tel. 520 72) has doubles for Rp7500 and triples for Rp9000. **Hotel Renny** is down the *gang* at #23, with rooms for Rp10,000. All have shared *mandis*, dark, dubious rooms, and no fans.

For those with only a little more money but fewer self-destructive tendencies, **Hotel Ria,** Jl. Kartini 79 (tel. 539 74), offers a range of options from unexciting rooms with fan and shared *mandi* for Rp17,500 and rooms with fan and *mandi* for Rp24,500 up to the Rp34,500 room with A/C, TV, blankets, room breakfast, and little extras (shampoo, towels, house phone, etc.). Every room "class" is grouped around a sitting area. Extra bed Rp9500. Coffee-shop downstairs. The **Garden Hotel,** Jl. Kartini 72 (tel. 555 12) is a good value. Rooms have *mandi*, but no fan, for Rp10,000 and Rp12,500. Rooms with fan run Rp15,000 and Rp18,500. With A/C, doubles run Rp20-33,000, triples Rp38,500. Prices depend on a room's size and what floor it's on. Lots of those little pluses here: showerheads, nice patios on each floor, towels with racks, house phones, breakfast, and clean rooms.

FOOD

Jalan Kartini and the streets south of Jl. Kotaraja are booming with **bakeries,** but the Indonesian and Padang **warungs** hang out around the Garden Hotel and Hotel Mini. The same food is served at the **Garuda Restaurant,** Jl. Kartini 31 (tel. 521 09), by Tanjung Karang Plaza. Run by Mulsim men, the juice bar serves 'em up deliciously un-spiked. The A/C room is for Padang food, the non-A/C for Indonesian. Dishes run about Rp2-5000. Open daily 7am-11pm. Across the street a *warung* incongruously serves **spaghetti. Food carts** selling **martabak** food carts come out along Jl. Kartini at night; keep an eye out for the **steamed corn on the cob.**

AROUND BANDAR LAMPUNG

Out in Lampung Bay are **Sebesi and Sebuku Islands.** Sebesi is closest to Krakatau and is served by a morning and afternoon ferry (Rp3000). There is accommodation available, and local boats can be chartered for the 3-½hr. trip to Krakatau. Just southeast of Bandar Lampung is **Pasir Putih,** a small, pleasant beach looking out to **Condong Island.** If you're interested in agronomy, labor conditions, or just seeing where your food comes from, ask at the tourist office about the pineapple, sugarcane, clove, pepper, rubber, and coffee **plantations** to the north and east. A popular destination, best reached by private vehicle, is **Way Kambas National Park and Elephant Training Center,** a 2-hr. drive east of the city. The small Sumatran elephants undergo training to entertain visitors. The park's sanctuary zone is home to Sumatran tigers and rhinos, along with plenty of smaller fauna. Sorry, no camping. The nearby **Way Kanan River** is a popular bird-watching spot, and you can charter boats. Bukit Barisan (the Marching Hills) form a spine on Sumatra's west coast; the **Bukit Barisan National Park** begins at the southmost tip at Tampang, and stretches up the coast. You can take a boat from Kota Agung to Tampang to explore the **Lake Menjukut Natural Area.** There is a camping area near **Wonsobo,** farther north, at Sukaraja. Near the border with Bengkulu Province, **Krui** is close to some surfing beaches, and **Liwa** is a base for **Ranau Lake** explorations. On the way to Liwa and Krui is Sumbur Jaya, where a road leads to the **Purawiwitan Archaeological site.** Closer to Bandar Lampung, the popular **Pugang Raharjo**—with megaliths from a Buddhist period in the 12th-17th centuries—can be reached from Talang Padian.

INDEX

L

M

Don't forget to call home!

While LET'S GO sets you on the road to adventure, AT&T connects you to your loved ones back home.

When traveling abroad you can rely on AT&T USADirect Service to make calling home easy and affordable. From over 130 countries, you'll get connected directly to an English-speaking AT&T Operator, so there are no language barriers to overcome. You'll know how to use the phone from practically anywhere you travel! And, it won't blow your budget either. You can access USADirect Service with your AT&T Calling Card, local phone company calling card, by calling collect or with an AT&T Global PrePaid Card™.

Now, AT&T and LET'S GO are offering you a $5 AT&T Global Prepaid Card which will connect you to AT&T USADirect Service, so you can see for yourself just how great it is. For FREE! Here's the deal:

To receive your $5 AT&T Global Prepaid Card™

1. Fill out the survey on the other side of this page.
2. Clip and include the "proof-of-purchase corner" from the upper left hand corner of the back of this book.
3. Enclose in a stamped envelope and mail it to us at the address indicated on the survey **ON OR BEFORE 5/31/96.**
4. Allow 4 weeks for delivery.

Name

Address

City State

Zip Telephone #

AT&T Calling card (exclude pin #)

Please circle your answers - pick one response per question:

1. Have you ever heard of AT&T USADirect Service?
   1. Yes 2. No

2. How do you plan on paying for your phone calls while you are abroad?
   1. Calling card 2. Call collect 3. Coins 4. Other

3. Where would you like to get information on how to call home from abroad?
   1. Newspaper/magazine 2. TV 3. Direct mail 4. Travel agent
   5. Hotel 6. Study abroad orientation program

4. How old are you?
   1. Under 17 2. 17-23 3. 24-30 4. 31-40 5. 41-55
   6. over 55

5. Where did you purchase the guide?
   1. Superstore 2. Chain store 3. University store
   4. Independent book store 5. Other

6. Why did you buy LET'S GO?
   1. I used it before 2. The AT&T offer
   3. Friend/Fellow traveler recommended it 4. Store clerk recommended it
   5. Saw it in bookstore display 6. Other

Fill out this survey, clip and include the "proof of purchase corner" from the upper left hand corner of the back of this book. Enclose in a stamped envelope and mail it to us, at the address below **on or before 5/31/96**. Limit one per customer. No photocopies will be accepted.

Address: LET'S GO / AT&T Promotion
P.O. Box 15680
Mascoutah, IL 62224

Thank you.

Sponsor not responsible for lost, late, mutilated, postage due or misdirected mail.
Void where taxed, prohibited or restricted by law.

ALSO AVAILABLE FROM ST. MARTIN'S PRESS

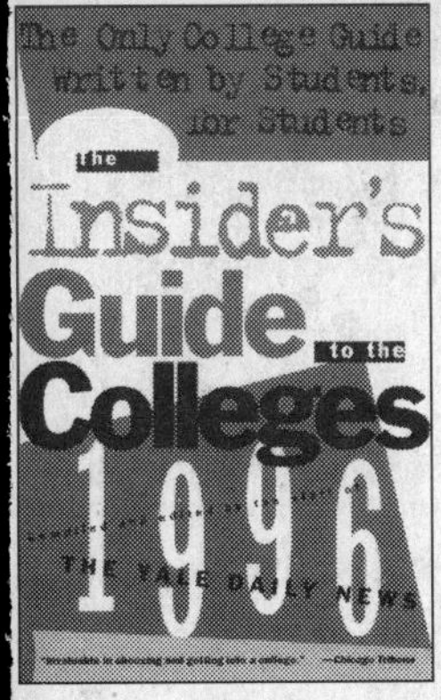

FEATURES INCLUDE:

- Profiles of more than 300 schools in the U.S. and Canada, focusing on academics, housing and food, social life, student activities, and the campus and vicinity
- Insider tips on the application and admissions process
- Up-to-date statistics on tuition, acceptance rates, average test scores and more
- Plus: a College Finder, which picks the right schools in dozens of categories

Please send me___copies of **THE INSIDER'S GUIDE TO THE COLLEGES** (0-312-13522-X) at $14.99 each.
I have enclosed $3.00 for postage and handling for the first book, and $1.00 for each additional copy.

Name ______________________

Address ______________________

City __________ State __________ Zip __________

Send check or money order with this coupon to:
St. Martin's Press • 175 Fifth Avenue • New York, NY 10010 • Att: Nancy/Promotion

"A crash course that could lead to a summer job—or a terrific party." —*Boston Globe*

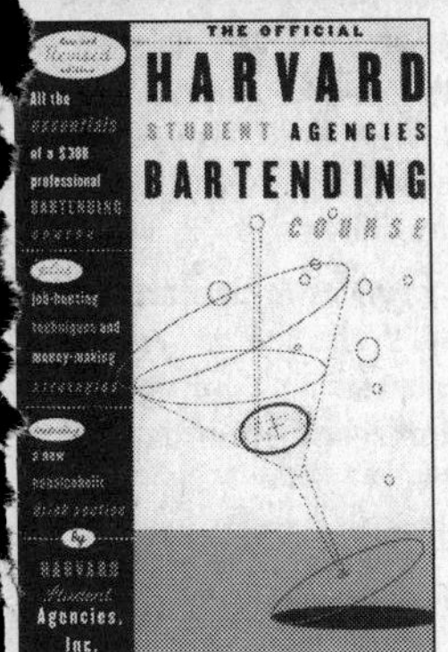

With **THE OFFICIAL HARVARD STUDENT AGENCIES BARTENDING COURSE**, you could find yourself mixing drinks professionally and earning great money, or at least, giving fabulous cocktail parties!

- Over 300 recipes for the most asked-for drinks—including a section on popular nonalcoholic beverages
- Tips on finding top-paying bartending jobs
- How to remember hundreds of recipes
- How to serve drinks and handle customers with aplomb

Please send me___copies of **THE OFFICIAL HARVARD STUDENT AGENCIES BARTENDING COURSE** (0-312-11370-6) at $9.95 each. I have enclosed $3.00 for postage and handling for the first book, and $1.00 for each additional copy.

Name ______________________

Address ______________________

City __________ State __________ Zip __________

Send check or money order with this coupon to:
St. Martin's Press • 175 Fifth Avenue • New York, NY 10010 • Att: Nancy/Promotion

AVAILABLE MARCH 1996

LET'S GO®
MAP GUIDE
NEW YORK CITY
KNOW IT LIKE A NATIVE

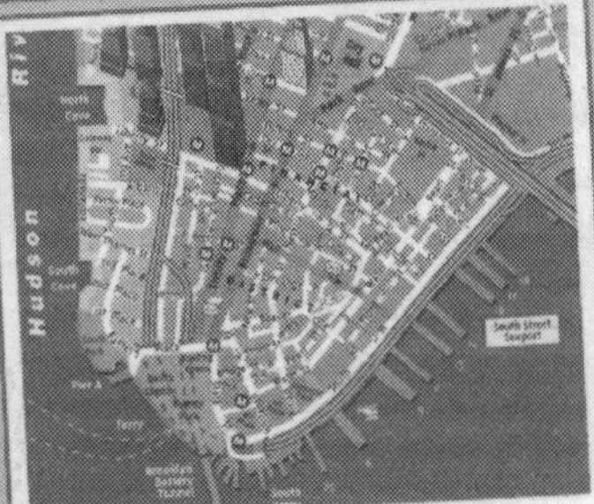

COMPLETE STREET FINDER AND CITY GUIDE

SUBWAY, BUS, AND CAR ROUTES

ENTERTAINMENT • NIGHTLIFE
MUSEUMS • PARKS • SIGHTS

BEST BUYS IN RESTAURANTS AND HOTELS

ESSENTIAL PHONE NUMBERS AND ADDRESSES

LET'S GO,

the world's bestselling budget travel guides, introduces its new

MAP GUIDE SERIES

- New York City
- Washington, D.C.
- Boston
- San Francisco
- London
- Paris

This unique combination of pocket guide and street finder will be an essential tool for tourists, new residents, and natives alike.

- Detailed maps of the downtown area, neighborhoods, city overview, and transportation routes
- Complete street index and grid coordinates
- Symbols locating airports, train and subway stations, points of interest, visitor centers, post offices, police stations, and hospitals
- Easy-to-fold, weather-resistant, laminated map
- Complete descriptions, addresses, phone numbers, and prices for restaurants, entertainment, sights, museums, and hotels
- Practical information on everything from renting bicycles to tipping to emergency numbers

Please send me the following copies in THE LET'S GO MAP GUIDE SERIES at $7.95 each. I have enclosed $3.00 for postage and handling for the first book, and $1.00 for each additional copy.

Name______________________

Address______________________

____

City__________ State_____ Zip__________

No. of copies

_____ **New York City (0-312-13764-8)**
_____ **Boston (0-312-13765-6)**
_____ **London (0-312-13766-4)**
_____ **Paris (0-312-13767-2)**
_____ **San Francisco (0-312-13768-0)**
_____ **Washington, D.C. (0-312-13769-9)**

Send check or money order with this coupon to:
St. Martin's Press • 175 Fifth Avenue • New York, NY 10010 • Att: Nancy/Promotion